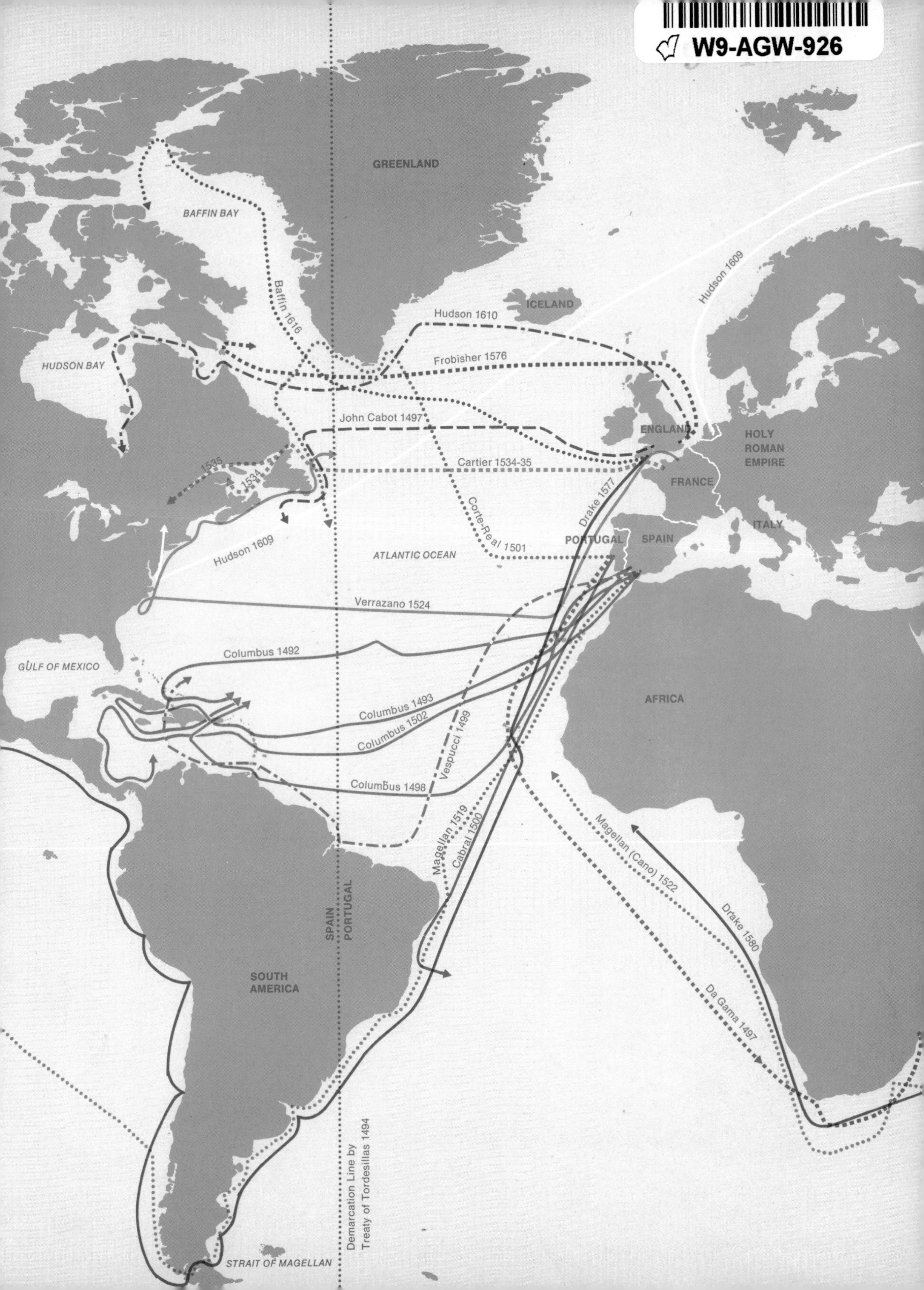

W9-AGW-926
GREENLAND
BAFFIN BAY
ICELAND
HUDSON BAY
Baffin 1616
Hudson 1610
Hudson 1609
Frobisher 1576
John Cabot 1497
ENGLAND
HOLY ROMAN EMPIRE
1535
1534
Cartier 1534-35
FRANCE
Corte-Real 1501
Drake 1577
ITALY
PORTUGAL
SPAIN
Hudson 1609
ATLANTIC OCEAN
Verrazano 1524
Columbus 1492
GULF OF MEXICO
AFRICA
Columbus 1493
Columbus 1502
Vespucci 1499
Columbus 1498
Magellan 1519
Cabral 1500
Magellan (Cano) 1522
Drake 1580
SPAIN
PORTUGAL
SOUTH AMERICA
Da Gama 1497
Demarcation Line by
Treaty of Tordesillas 1494
STRAIT OF MAGELLAN

A History of the United States

THE AMERICAN NATION

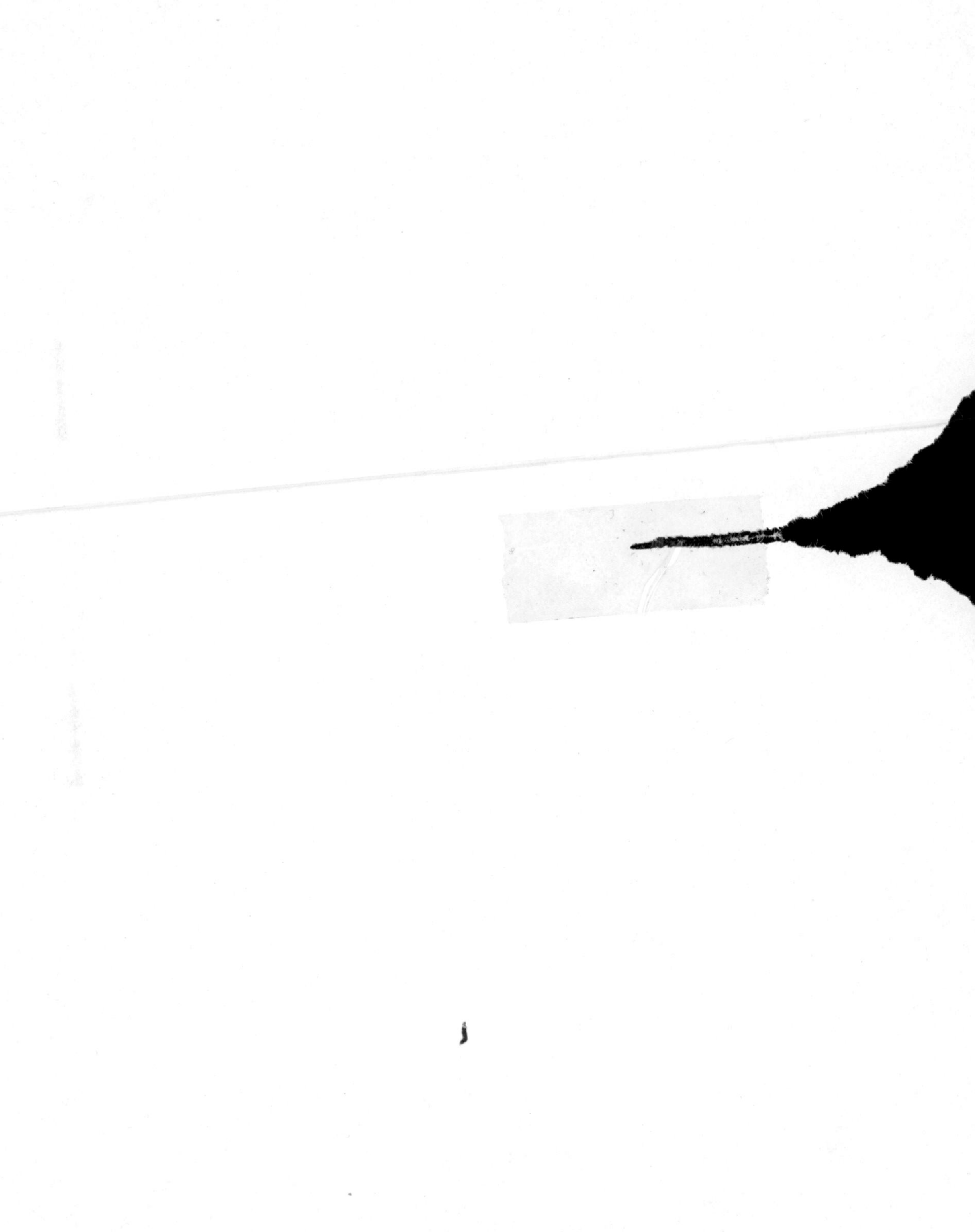

A History of the United States THE AMERICAN NATION

SECOND EDITION

John A. Garraty

COLUMBIA UNIVERSITY

A Harper-American Heritage Textbook

Harper & Row, Publishers New York, Evanston, San Francisco, London

American Heritage Publishing Co., Inc. New York

The American Nation

SECOND EDITION

Library of Congress Catalog Card Number: 72-141176
ISBN: 8281-0168-X

FOR KATHY, JACK, AND SARAH

Editorial Direction
Stephen W. Sears, American Heritage
John G. Ryden and Mary Lou Mosher, Harper & Row
Art Direction
Janet Czarnetzki and Barbara Asch,
assisted by Terrence J. Gaughan
Assistant Editors
Harriet Robbins, John Terry Chase, and Denis A. Dinan
Picture Editors
Margaretta Barton and Lucia Scala
Production Supervision
Francis X. Giordano
Maps and Graphs
Francis & Shaw, Inc.

The author makes grateful acknowledgment to:

Professor George W. Pierson, Yale University, for permission to quote from *Tocqueville and Beaumont in America*, Oxford University Press, 1938. Copyright 1938 by George W. Pierson.

New Directions, New York; Faber & Faber, London; and A. V. Moore, Knebworth, Herts, England, for permission to quote from "Hugh Selwyn Mauberley" by Ezra Pound. From *Personae* by Ezra Pound. Copyright 1926, 1954 by Ezra Pound. Reprinted by permission of the publisher, New Directions Publishing Corp.

New Directions, New York, for permission to quote "The Great Figure" by William Carlos Williams, from *Collected Earlier Poems*. Copyright 1938 by William Carlos Williams. Reprinted by permission of New Directions Publishing Corp.

Harcourt Brace Jovanovich, Inc., New York, and MacGibbon & Kee Ltd., London, for permission to quote E.E. Cummings, "the first president to be loved by his." Copyright 1931, 1959 by E.E. Cummings. Reprinted from his volume *Poems 1923–1954* by permission of Harcourt Brace Jovanovich, Inc., and MacGibbon & Kee Ltd.

Alfred A. Knopf, Inc., New York, for permission to quote from "The Man with the Blue Guitar" by Wallace Stevens. Copyright 1935, 1936 by Wallace Stevens. From *The Collected Poems of Wallace Stevens*, Knopf, 1957.

Preface

While history is certainly worth studying for its own sake, as a record of men's struggles and achievements divorced from present affairs, it can also serve as a tool for those who wish to understand how things have come to be as they are. From decade to decade, sometimes almost from day to day, the objects of this curiosity change; every generation, reacting to current events, asks new questions about the past. For example, Americans have always wanted to "know all about" the American Revolution, but modern Americans are especially fascinated by aspects of it that did not deeply concern their parents and grandparents. Present-day interest in the Negro makes us look anew at the Revolution; so do matters as unrelated as the recent Supreme Court decisions establishing the principle of "one man, one vote" in apportioning seats in state legislatures, and the efforts of the people of Asia, Africa, and South America to free themselves from the restrictive influence of foreign powers.

It is the job of the historian to supply answers to the historical questions that contemporary events bring to mind. At the same time, books and articles about the Revolution and about countless other events constantly appear which amplify and refine our knowledge of American history without regard for the particular problems of the present. And of course the mere passage of time makes new history every day. Ours—as we are often reminded—is a dynamic age. Periodically, historians have to assess this new information and relate it to what earlier students have written about the subject.

Thus, in addition to carrying the story down to the mid-1960's and dealing with the whole span of the past as comprehensively and as authoritatively as possible within the limits of a single volume, this new survey of American history focuses especially on those historical events and trends that seem most important for understanding our own time.

No one can read, much less master, all the literature of American history, but ignorance is not the major difficulty that the writer of a history of the United States has to overcome. Anyone who tries to trace the course of our evolution from the time of the first explorers to the present in one narrative faces organizational problems of immense proportions. Indeed, the more he learns, the more complicated this organizational task becomes. Besides considering the fundamental framework of political developments, he has to assimilate masses of information about how Americans made their living, what social patterns they created, what ideas influenced their lives, how they interacted with the people of other countries, what works of art and literature they produced, and a variety of other matters. He must relate these political, economic, social, and cultural facts to one another too, else he will end with several different histories rather than one. The historian surrounds himself with mountains of facts, considers dozens of alternative methods of ordering his data, but remains acutely aware that he cannot record all he has learned and that by adopting any scheme of organization he automatically sacrifices the advantages of many other possible schemes. His problem is like that of a chef intent on creating a new dish. If he employs the wealth of spices and sauces in his kitchen cleverly, he may achieve a gastronomic triumph, but if he blunders, his concoction may turn out to be an indigestible disaster. This risk must be taken. The historian must strive for profundity and completeness; he cannot safely take refuge in shallow oversimplifications lest, like a cook who confines himself to frying ham and eggs, he quickly dulls his readers' taste for his verse and drives them to more daring and knowledgeable sources of information.

I hope this book records the story of the American past clearly and intelligibly, but also with adequate attention to the complexities and subtleties of its immense subject. Of course, it is not the final word—that will never be written. It is, however, up-to-date and as accurate and thoughtful and wide-ranging as I could make it. Aside from the picture portfolios, which provide a wealth of graphic material dealing with subjects that are difficult to explain with words alone, its special features are products of a personal point of view. Being a biographer, I am very interested in historical personalities. I reject the theory that a few great men, cut from larger cloth than the general run of human beings, have shaped the destiny of mankind; but I do think that history becomes more vivid and comprehensible when attention is paid to how the major figures on the historical stage have reacted to events and to one another. I have attempted to portray the leading actors in my account as distinct individuals and to explain how their personal qualities influenced the course of history. I also believe that generalizations require concrete illustration if they are to be grasped fully. Readers will find many anecdotes and quotations in the following pages along with the facts and dates and statistics that every good history must contain. I am confident that most of this illustrative material is interesting, but I think that it is instructive too. Above all I have sought to keep in mind the grandeur of my subject. One need not be an uncritical admirer of the American nation and its people to recognize that the history of the United States from its colonial foundations to its present position of world influence is a great epic. I have tried to treat this history with the dignity and respect that it deserves, believing, however, that a subject of such magnitude is not well served by foolish praise or by slighting or excusing its many dark and even discreditable aspects.

What follows is my own work, for better or worse, but I want to acknowledge here my indebtedness to the many persons who have contributed to whatever virtues it possesses. None, of course, should be held accountable for its weaknesses. First of all, I am obligated to the hundreds of historians whose works I have consulted. I have referred to many of these in the course of my narrative, for a sound knowledge of American history should include some familiarity with the works of the scholars whose researches make the writing of that history possible. Though the large majority are not specifically mentioned, my debt to them is immense. Secondly, I wish to thank the many experts who have read the manuscript in whole or in part and allowed me to profit from their criticisms and insights. These include Herman Ausubel, Rowland Bertoff, David Brody, Bruce Catton, E. David Cronon, George Dangerfield, Alexander De Conde, Sigmund Diamond, Robert A. Divine, Clement Eaton, Norman A. Graebner, Jack P. Greene, Bray Hammond, John Higham, Brooke Hindle, Philip S. Klein, Madison Kuhn, William E. Leuchtenburg, Arthur Mann, Richard B. Morris, Roy F. Nichols, Bradford Perkins, John Roche, Bell I. Wiley, Charles M. Wiltse, and Louis B. Wright.

I am also grateful to Edwin Barber of Harper & Row and Stephen W. Sears of American Heritage, and to those members of their staffs who have worked to make this book as accurate and useful as possible. Finally, I wish to thank Dr. Ralph Tyler and his colleagues at the Center for Advanced Study in the Behavioral Sciences at Stanford, California. A year spent as a Fellow at the center enabled me to formulate many of the ideas developed in the following pages.

John A. Garraty, COLUMBIA UNIVERSITY

Preface to the Second Edition

In preparing this new edition of *The American Nation,* I have kept in mind the same objectives that motivated me when I originally wrote the book: up-to-dateness, relevance, a personal point of view. My intention has been to create a truly new book, a history of the United States as I see it in the summer of 1970, not merely the earlier version with errors corrected and a few pages on recent events added. The passage of five years has produced not merely five more years of events, but also a great deal of important historical research on past events, and it has raised many new questions about the character and significance of American history. I have attempted to take these various developments and changes into account in my writing.

My method has been to look at each chapter freshly in the light of the literature published since 1965, of the new perspectives thrown on the material by this literature, and of the changes—some subtle, some relatively drastic—that have occurred in my own thinking in recent years. Minor errors, many pointed out to me by teachers and students who have used the first edition, have, of course, also been corrected.

To generalize about the changes resulting from my re-examination of American history is very difficult because so many of them are in themselves discrete and relatively minor. Beyond question, however, the most significant relate to the history of American Negroes, which is neither a discrete nor a minor matter. This subject illustrates all the reasons why histories have to be revised repeatedly. An enormous amount of important work has been done on black history since the mid-sixties; recent events have sent scores of historians burrowing into the records of the past, the better to understand such "modern" issues as black nationalism, American race prejudice, the problem of the ghetto, and the like. Thus, this new edition contains a picture portfolio on African culture and society, a subject ignored in its predecessor, and also a great deal of new material on early European attitudes toward Africans, on the treatment of blacks in the American colonies, on the impact of the Revolution on slavery, on the abolition movement, on white attitudes toward slavery and race before, during, and after the Civil War, on the history of militancy among Negroes, and many other subjects treated, I now realize, too superficially in the first edition. All these matters have required changes in most of the sections dealing with the nature of democracy in America, with generalizations about the American character and about American prosperity, and many other topics. Other general shifts in my approach relate to the degree of uniformity in American social attitudes at various times in history, to the role of ethnic groups, and to the importance of urbanization, not merely in the recent past but throughout the 19th century. I have made extensive alterations in my treatment of New England puritanism, of the causes of the Revolution, of the nullification crisis, of Jackson's "Bank War," and literally dozens of other subjects. Finally, of course, I have rewritten large parts of the material dealing with the period since World War II and have brought the general narrative down to mid-1970.

Once again I wish to thank (in addition to the historians whose works I have consulted) the many persons who have generously aided me by pointing out errors and by reading sections of the revised manuscript. These include James B. Allen, Elliott R. Barkan, John H. Bracey, Jr., James T. Doyle, John Duff, Lawrence O. Ealy, Herbert Ershkowitz, David H. Flaherty, Kenneth T. Jackson, Charles W. Johnson, James C. King, Herbert Klein, Alexander W. Knott, Peter M. Mitchell, Daniel E. Peterson, Harold Seymour, and Alden T. Vaughan. Stephen W. Sears and his staff at American Heritage have again employed their editorial skills with great effectiveness and drawn upon the incomparable pictorial resources of their organization in illustrating this new edition. John Ryden and Mary Lou Mosher of Harper & Row have given me every conceivable assistance at each stage of the revision. My wife, Gail, has listened patiently and (she claims) with interest to my many attempts to understand controversial and difficult points better by "explaining" them to her. None of these persons, of course, bears responsibility for any errors or inadequacies in what follows.

J.A.G.
July 14, 1970

Table of Contents

Maps and Graphs

1

The Age of Discovery and Settlement

History sometimes chooses its heroes strangely. Leif Ericson ventured before the day of the compass into the void of the North Atlantic and, around the year 1000, reached the shores of Labrador, the first European to set foot in the New World. Yet Ericson's remarkable discovery passed practically unnoticed for centuries, and to most modern inhabitants of the New World he lives only in legend.

Amerigo Vespucci, a clever Italian with an eye for publicity, visited the coast of what is now the Guianas in South America as a supercargo in 1499 and wrote an account of his experiences that was widely circulated. In 1507, after reading a somewhat distorted copy of Vespucci's tale, a German geographer, Martin Waldseemüller, concluded that the author was the discoverer of the New World and suggested that it be named "America" in his honor. Today hundreds of millions of people call themselves Americans, but few of them know much about Amerigo Vespucci.

Another Italian mariner, Cristoforo Colombo, brave, persistent, an inspired sailor but a fumbling administrator, an impractical dreamer, and (fortunately) a poor judge of distances, spent a decade cruising in the Caribbean Sea under the mistaken impression that he was next door to China. He killed some natives, established a few rickety settlements, ventured no nearer to North America than Cuba, and died poor, embittered, and frustrated, hotly denying that he had found anything more than a new route to the Orient. Today, whether he be known as Colombo, Colón, or Columbus, he is revered by the masses of the Old World and the New as the discoverer of the Western Hemisphere.

Why Columbus rather than Ericson, the real pioneer, or Vespucci, whose name has become immortal? The answer is that Ericson came upon the scene several centuries too soon and Vespucci a few years too late. Europe in the year 1000 was not yet ready to find the New World, and by 1499 it had already found it. Amerigo Vespucci gave his name to the region, but Christopher Columbus was the man whose actions inspired the development of the whole vast area between Hudson Bay and the Strait of Magellan.

Columbus and the Discovery of America

About two o'clock on the morning of October 12, 1492, a Spanish sailor named Roderigo de Triana, clinging in a gale to the mast of the ship *Pinta*, saw a gleam of white on the moonlit horizon and shouted: "*Tierra! Tierra!*" The land he had spied was an island in the Bahamas, distinguished neither for beauty nor size. Nevertheless, when Triana's master, Christopher Columbus, went ashore bearing the flag of Castile, he named it San Salvador, or Holy Saviour. Columbus selected this imposing name for the island out of gratitude and wonder at having found it—he had sailed with three frail vessels across more than 3,000 miles for 33 days without sight of land. The name was appropriate, too, from history's far larger viewpoint. Neither Columbus nor any of his men suspected it, but the discovery of San Salvador was probably the most important event in the history of western civilization since the birth of Christ. Besides unleashing a series of events that improved man's material prospects, the discovery also advanced man's spiritual prospects enormously.

San Salvador was the gateway to two continents. Columbus did not know it, and he refused to learn the truth, but his voyage threw open to the crowded peoples of western Europe a new and largely uninhabited region of more than 16 million square miles, an area lushly endowed with every imaginable resource. Thus he made possible a mass movement from Europe (and later from Africa and to a lesser extent from other regions) into the New World. Gathering force rapidly, this movement did not slacken until the present century, and still has not ceased entirely. What this has meant in material prosperity and in opportunity for self-development and self-expression, both for those who came to the Americas and for those who remained at home, is the epic of modern times. The history of the United States is a major element in the story.

Columbus was an intelligent as well as a dedicated and skillful mariner; his failure to grasp the significance of his accomplishment can only be explained by his commitment in advance to a different explanation of what he observed. He was seeking not a new world but an old one: China and Japan and the Indies, the amazing countries described by the Venetian Marco Polo in the late 13th century. Having read carefully Marco Polo's account of his adventures in the service of Kublai Khan, Columbus had decided that these rich lands could be reached by sailing directly west from Europe. His idea was not original, but he pursued it with brilliant persistence while others merely talked about it. Some authorities (and Columbus, being no mere adventurer, had mastered the geographical data available in his day) claimed that Asia lay only about 2,500 miles west of Europe. If one could sail there directly, the trading possibilities and the resulting profits would be limitless. Oriental products were highly valued all over Europe. Spices such as pepper, cinnamon, ginger, nutmeg, and cloves were of first importance, their role being not so much to titillate the palate as to disguise the taste of spoiled meats in regions that had little ice. Europeans also prized tropical foods like rice, figs, and oranges, as well as perfumes—often used as a substitute for soap—raw silk and cotton, rugs, textiles such as muslin and damask, dyestuffs, fine steel products, precious stones, and various drugs.

These products flowed into western Europe by way of the Italian city-states. By the 11th century Venice had established a thriving trade with Constantinople, shipping the great metropolis on the Bosporus large quantities of European foodstuffs. The Venetians also supplied large numbers of young Slavs, captured or purchased along the nearby Dalmatian coast, to the harems of Egypt and Syria. (The word *slave*, it will be noted, originally meant merely a "Slav.")

When the Venetians began to bring oriental products into western and northern Europe, the effect was like that of tossing a stone into a pond. Europeans began to bestir themselves, searching for something to offer in exchange. They possessed surpluses of grain and foodstuffs, but such bulky products were expensive to transport over long distances. However, in Flanders, in the Low Countries, woolen cloth of high quality was being manufactured. Other areas were producing furs and lumber. Demand led to increased output; thus the flow of commerce stimulated manufacturing, which in turn spurred the growth of towns. As towns became larger and more numerous, the market for food expanded and local trade quickened. For example, the increased demand for Flemish cloth stimulated the expansion of towns like Bruges, Ghent, and Lille. This led surrounding rural areas to increase their agricultural activity.

It also created a demand for more clothmakers. The resulting labor shortage in both town and country produced important changes in the structure of medieval society. The manorial system, based on serfdom, soon began to change radically. As their labor became more valuable, serfs won the right to pay off their traditional obligations in money rather than in service and to leave the manors and move to the towns or to newly opened farmland. The lords themselves often instituted this change, for they wished to increase agricultural output by draining swamps and clearing forests and willingly granted freedom to serfs who would move to the new lands. Also, they needed money rather than the services of serfs to buy the expensive oriental luxuries being dangled before their eyes by traders.

The Crusades further accelerated the tempo of this new activity. Genuine religious motives seem to have inspired these mighty efforts, protracted

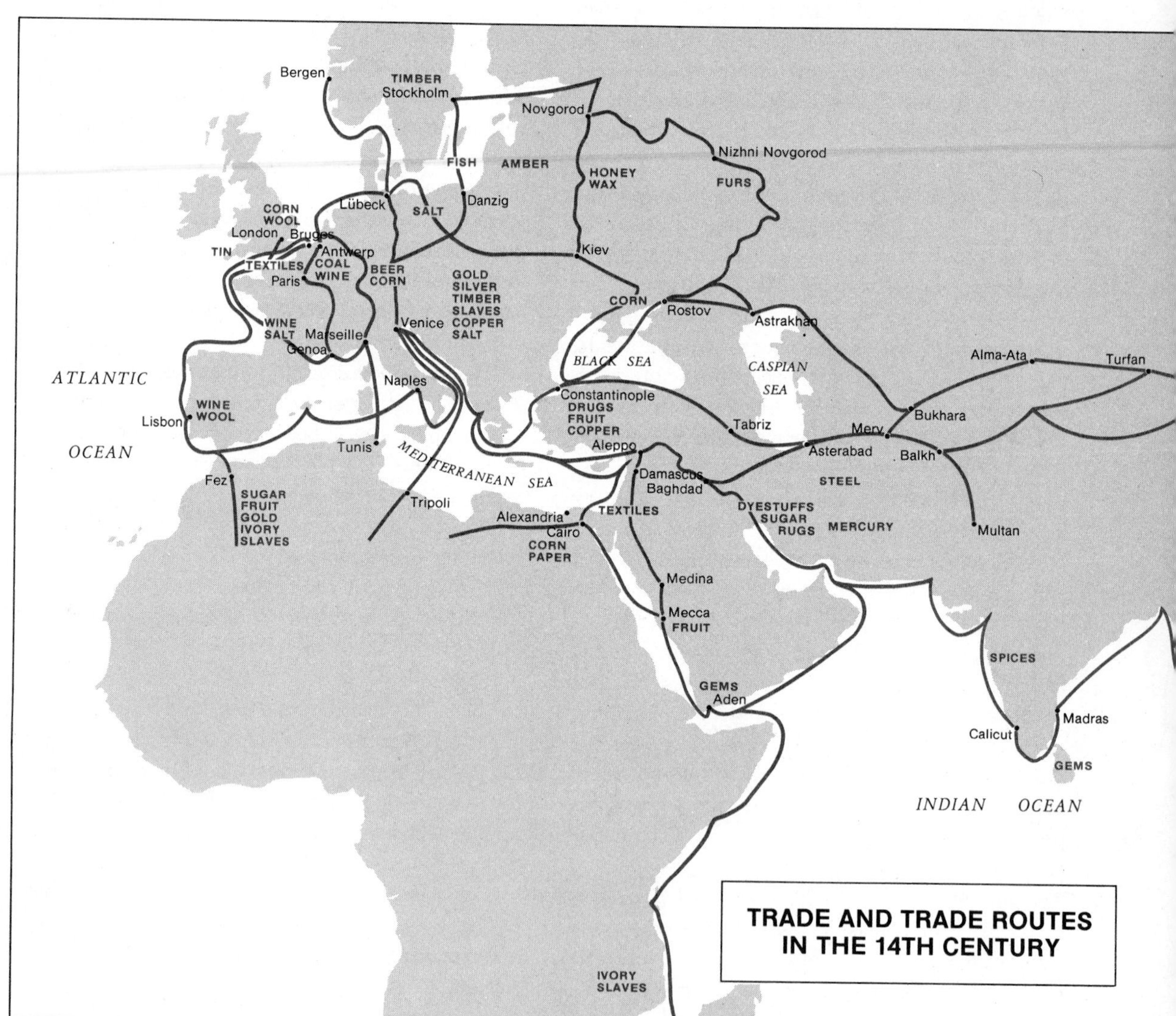

over two centuries from 1095 to about 1290, to drive the Moslems from the Holy Land. Once the crusading armies had won a foothold in Asia Minor, the commerce of Venice and of other Italian cities increased still more, and their merchant fleets expanded. The business of transporting and supplying the European armies was itself extremely profitable. Furthermore, when the waves of Crusaders returned home, they brought with them more oriental products and a taste for these things that persisted after the goods themselves had been consumed.

The volume of this trade cannot be exactly determined. It was large enough to keep the fleets of the thriving Italian cities busy, and it tended to grow with the years. Yet it was not impressive by modern standards; the great Belgian historian Henri Pirenne estimated that the whole tonnage of the 13th-century Venetian fleet would scarcely fill a large 20th-century freighter. Nor did the increase in trade cause universal prosperity or even a steady economic expansion in western Europe. Actually, the period of the 14th and early 15th centuries seems to have been marked by depression and economic decline in the west.

This decline resulted principally from the terrible losses occasioned by the plague known as the Black Death, which ravaged Europe in the mid-14th century. Part of the difficulty, however, stemmed from the steady drain of precious metals to the Orient because of the unfavorable balance of east-west trade, and from the high cost of oriental goods. It was easy to blame this on the greed of the Italians, who monopolized east-west trade. Certainly the Venetians have never possessed a reputation for altruism nor the Pisans for being poor businessmen. However, even if the Italians had labored only for the joy of serving their fellow men, or if other merchants had been able to break the Italian monopoly, the cost of eastern products would have remained high. To transport spices from the Indies, silk from China, or rugs, cloth, and fine steel from the Middle East was extremely costly. The combined sea-land routes were long and complicated—across strange seas, through deserts, over high mountain passes—with pirates or highwaymen a constant threat. Every petty tyrant through whose domain the caravans passed levied taxes, a quasi-legal form of robbery. Few merchants actually operated on a continental scale; typically, goods passed from hand to hand many times between eastern producer and western consumer, with each middleman exacting as large a profit as he could. In the end, the western European con-

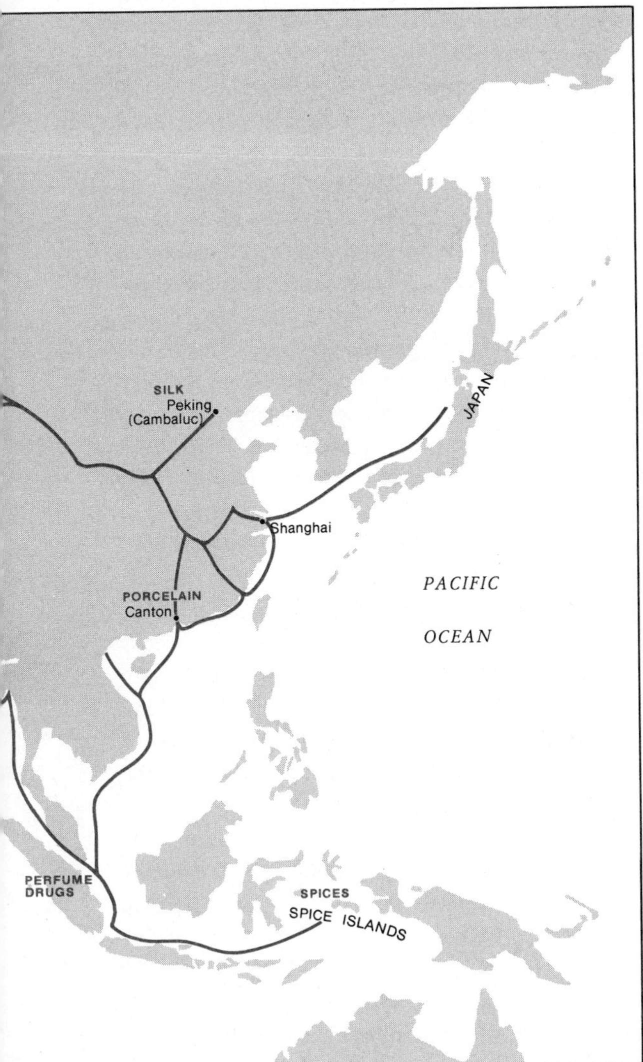

The chief products of trade in the late Middle Ages are labeled here at their points of origin. By 1350 there was little direct contact between western Europeans and the East: the Arabs who dominated the oriental trade sold their goods to Venetian and Genoese merchants in eastern Mediterranean ports.

BIBLIOTHEQUE NATIONALE

Henry of Portugal, "Henry the Navigator," one of two known contemporaneous portraits. It was painted by Nuno Gonçalves for a chronicle of exploration.

sumer had to pay for all this. As time went on, merchants in the west began to cast about for a cheaper way of obtaining oriental products, and by the 15th century thought was beginning to be transformed into action.

The great figure in this transformation was Prince Henry the Navigator, third son of John I, king of Portugal. After distinguishing himself in 1415 in the capture of Ceuta, on the African side of the Strait of Gibraltar, he became interested in navigation and exploration. Sailing a vessel out of sight of land was still, in Henry's day, more an art than a science and extremely hazardous. Ships were small and clumsy. Primitive compasses and instruments for reckoning latitude existed, but under shipboard conditions they were very inaccurate. Navigators could determine longitude only by keeping track of direction and estimating speed; even the most skilled could place little faith in their estimates.

Henry attempted to improve and codify navigational knowledge. To his court at Sagres, hard by Cape St. Vincent, the extreme southwestern point of Europe, he brought geographers, astronomers, and mapmakers, along with Arab and Jewish mathematicians. He built an observatory and supervised the preparation of tables measuring the declination of the sun and other navigational data. Henry's captains explored the Azores, the Madeiras, and the Canaries, then gradually pushed south along the coast of Africa. In 1445 Dinis Dias reached Cape Verde, site of present-day Dakar.

Henry was interested in trade, but he also cared for the advancement of knowledge, for national glory, and for spreading Christianity. When his explorers developed a profitable business in slaves, he tried to stop it. Nevertheless, the movement he began had, like the Crusades, important commercial overtones. Probably half of the Portuguese voyages were undertaken by private merchants. Without the gold, ivory, and other African goods, which brought great prosperity to Portugal, the explorers would probably not have been so bold and persistent. Yet, like Henry, they were also idealists, by and large. The Age of Discovery was, in a sense, the last Crusade; its leaders all displayed mixed religious and material motives along with a love of adventure. (Perhaps this is always the case with explorers. We probe into space today not merely for prestige, for commercial gain, nor even for national defense, but because it has come within our ken; we must know its secrets no matter what the cost.) In any case, the Portuguese realized that if they could find a way around Africa, they might well sail directly to India and the Spice Islands.* The profits from such a voyage would surely be spectacular.

For 20 years after Henry's death in 1460, the Portuguese concentrated on exploiting his discoveries. But in the 1480's King John II undertook systematic new explorations focused on reaching India. Gradually, his caravels probed southward along the sweltering coast—to the equator, to the region of Angola, and beyond.

Into this bustling, prosperous, expectant little country in the corner of Europe came Christopher

*The Moluccas, west of New Guinea. In the geography of the 15th century the Spice Islands were part of the Indies, a vague term that encompassed the southeast rim of Asia from India to what is now Indonesia.

Columbus in 1476. Columbus was a weaver's son from Genoa, born in 1451. He had taken to the sea early, ranging widely in the Mediterranean. But his arrival in Portugal was unplanned, since it resulted from the loss of his ship in a battle off the coast. For a time he became a chartmaker in Lisbon. He married a local girl. Then he was again at sea. He cruised northward, perhaps as far as Iceland, south to the equator, westward in the Atlantic to the Azores. Had his interest lain in that direction, he might well have been the first man to reach Asia by way of Africa, for in 1488, while he was in Lisbon, Bartholomeu Dias returned from his voyage around the southern tip of Africa, bringing the sensational news that the way lay clear for a voyage to the Indies. But by this time Columbus had committed himself to the westward route. When King John II refused to finance him, he turned to the Spanish court, where interest in commercial exploration was as great as in Portugal. After many disappointments, he finally persuaded Queen Isabella to equip his expedition, and in August 1492 he set out from the port of Palos with his tiny fleet, the *Santa María*, the *Pinta*, and the *Niña*. A little more than two months later, after a stopover in the Canary Islands to repair the *Pinta*'s rudder, his lookout sighted land.

Columbus' success was due in large part to his single-minded conviction that the Indies could be reached by sailing westward for a relatively short distance and that a profitable trade would develop over this route. He had persuaded Isabella to grant him, in addition to the title "Admiral of the Ocean Sea," political control over all the lands he might discover and ten per cent of the profits of the trade that would follow in the wake of his expedition. Now his conviction cost him dearly. He refused to accept the plain evidence, which everywhere confronted him, that this was an entirely new world. All about were strange plants, known neither to Europe nor Asia. The copper-colored natives who paddled out to inspect his fleet could no more follow the Arabic widely understood in the East than they could Spanish. Yet Columbus, consulting his charts, convinced himself that he had reached the Indies. That is why he called the natives "Indians." Searching for treasure, he

PALAZZO COMUNALE, GENOA; BROGI

A portrait attributed to the Florentine painter Ridolfo Ghirlandaio shows a disillusioned Columbus, his hair turned white after "years of great anxiety."

pushed on to Cuba. When he heard the native word *Cubanocan*, meaning "middle of Cuba," he mistook it for *El Gran Can* (Marco Polo's "Grand Khan") and sent emissaries on a fruitless search through the tropical jungle for the khan's palace. He finally returned to Spain relatively empty-handed but still certain that he had explored the edge of Asia. Three later voyages failed to shake his conviction. (Columbus' voyages and those of other major explorers noted in this chapter are shown on the front endsheet map.)

Columbus died in 1506, but by this time other captains had taken up the work, most of them more willing than he to accept the New World on its own terms. As early as 1493 Pope Alexander VI had divided the non-Christian world between Spain and Portugal. The next year, in the Treaty of Tordesillas, these powers negotiated an agreement about exploiting the new discoveries. In effect, Portugal continued to concentrate on Africa, leaving the New World, except for what eventually became Brazil, to the Spanish. Thereafter, from their base on Hispaniola (Santo Domingo), founded by Columbus, the Spaniards

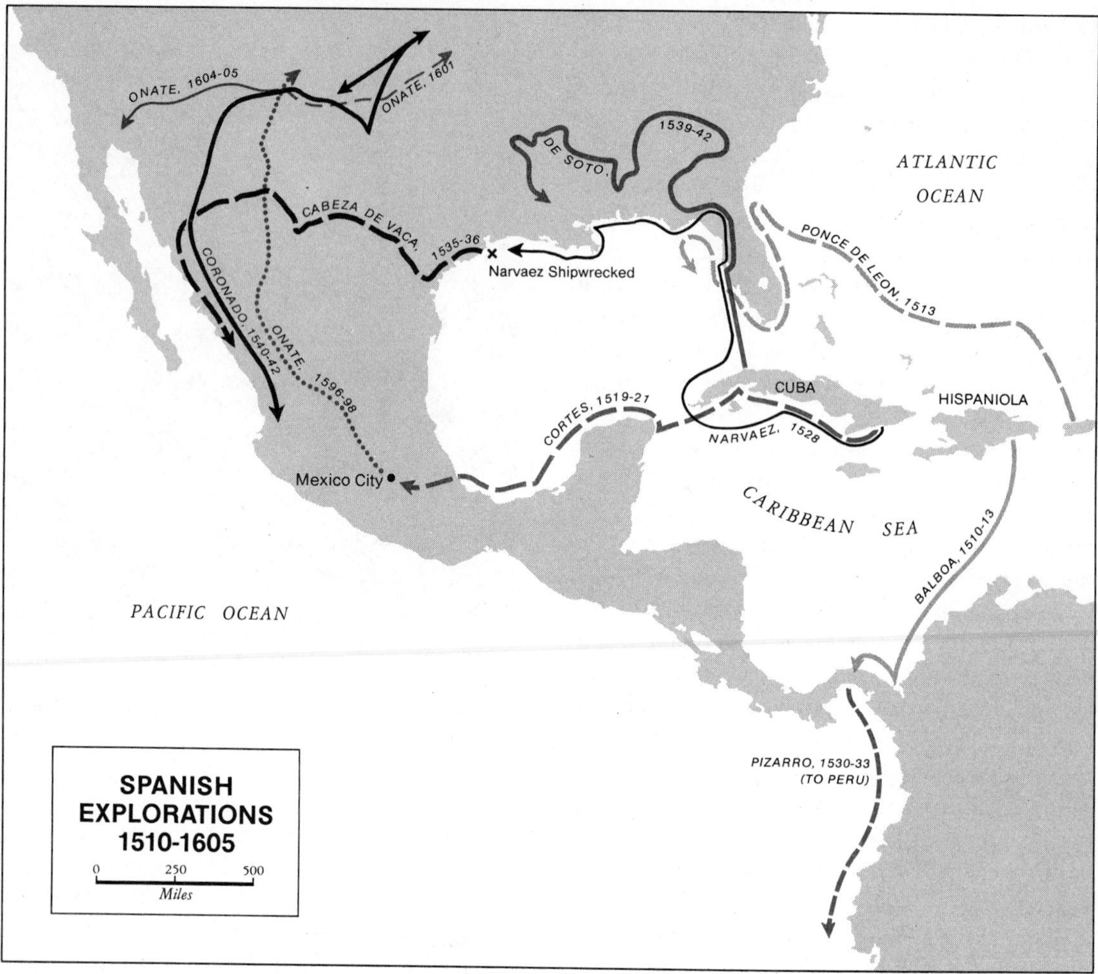

quickly fanned out all over the Caribbean and then over large parts of the two great continents that bordered it.

The Caribbean islands were easily conquered. In 1513 Juan Ponce de León made the first Spanish landing on the mainland of North America, exploring the east coast of Florida. In the same year Vasco Nuñez de Balboa crossed the Isthmus of Panama and discovered the Pacific Ocean. In 1519 Hernán Cortés landed an army in Mexico and overran the empire of the Aztecs, rich in gold and silver. That same year Ferdinand Magellan set out on his epic three-year voyage around the world. By discovering the strait that bears his name, at the southern tip of South America, he gave the Spanish a clear idea of the size of the continent. In the 1530's Francisco Pizarro subdued the Inca empire in Peru, providing the Spaniards with still more treasure, drawn chiefly from the silver mines of Potosí. In 1536 Buenos Aires was founded by Pedro de Mendoza. Within another decade Francisco Vásquez de Coronado had marched as far north as Kansas and west to the Grand Canyon, and Hernando de Soto had discovered the Mississippi River. Fifty years after Columbus' first landfall, Spain was master of a huge American empire.

What explains this mighty surge of exploration and conquest? Greed for gold and power, a sense of adventure, the desire to Christianize the Indians —mixed motives propelled the *conquistadores* onward. Most saw the New World as a reincarnation of the Garden of Eden, a kind of fairyland of infinite promise. Ponce de León and many others actually expected to find the Fountain of Youth in America. As one 18th-century Spanish historian put it, the explorers bathed hopefully in every river, brook, lake, and puddle they encountered on their adventures. Their vision, at once so selfish and so exalted, reflects something more than the often-mentioned "coexistence of contradictory tendencies" in the celebrated paradoxical Spanish character. It reflects also the central paradox of New World history. This immense land brought out both the best and the worst in human beings. Virgin America—like all virgins—inspired conflicting feelings in men's hearts. They worshiped it for its purity and promise, yet they could not resist the opportunity to take advantage of its innocence.

The Indian and the European

The *conquistadores* were brave and imaginative men, well worthy of their fame. It must not, however, be forgotten that they wrenched their empire from innocent hands; in an important sense, the settlement of America ranks among the worst examples of naked aggression in human history. Of the Lucayans, the native inhabitants of San Salvador, Columbus wrote: "The people of this island . . . are artless and generous with what they have, to such a degree as no one would believe. . . . If it be asked for, they never say no, but rather invite the person to accept it, and show as much lovingness as though they would give their hearts." The Indians behaved this way because the Spaniards seemed the very gods. The products of Europe fascinated them. For a bit of sheet copper an inch square, they would part with a bushel of corn, while iron tools and weapons were beyond price to tribesmen whose own technology was still in the Stone Age.

But the Spaniards would not settle for the better of the bargain. Columbus also remarked of the Lucayans: "These people are very unskilled in arms . . . with fifty men they could all be subjected and made to do all that one wished." He and his compatriots tricked and cheated the Indians at every turn. Before entering a new area, Spanish generals customarily read a *Requerimiento* (requirement) to the inhabitants. This long-winded document recited the history of mankind from the Creation to the division of the non-Christian world by Pope Alexander VI and then called upon the Indians to recognize the sovereignty of the reigning Spanish monarch. ("If you do so . . . we shall receive you in all love and charity.") If this demand was rejected, "we shall powerfully enter into your country, and . . . shall take you, your wives, and your children, and shall make slaves of them. . . . The death and losses which shall accrue from this are your fault." This arrogant harangue was read *in Spanish* and often out of earshot of the Indians. When they responded by fighting, the Spaniards decimated them, drove them from their lands, and held the broken survivors in contempt. As a priest among them said, the *conquistadores* behaved "like the most cruel Tygres, Wolves, and Lions, enrag'd with a sharp and tedious hunger."

Not only the Spanish, but all the colonizing powers mistreated the natives. When the Portuguese reached Africa, they carried off thousands into slavery. When they reached India, one historian writes, "Cities were devastated, ships burned at their docks, prisoners butchered and their dismembered hands, noses, and ears sent back as derisive trophies; one Brahmin, mutilated in this way, was left alive to bear them to his people." The Dutch behaved no differently in the East Indies, nor did the French in their colonial possessions—although in North America at least, the French record was better than most.

English settlers described the Indians as being "of a tractable, free, and loving nature, without guile or treachery," yet in most instances they exploited and all but exterminated them. "Why should you take by force from us that which you can obtain by love?" one puzzled chieftain asked an early Virginia colonist, according to the latter's own account. The first settlers of New England dealt fairly with the local inhabitants, whom some considered descendants of the lost tribes of Israel. They made honest, if somewhat misguided efforts to Christianize and educate them, and to respect their rights. But within a few years their relations with the Indians deteriorated and in the bloody King Philip's War (1675–76) they destroyed the tribes as independent powers.

Of course the victims of white cruelty were not always innocent "noble savages." American Indians, being men, suffered from all the human failings in one form or another. Cruelty and war existed in the New World long before Columbus. Moreover, the terrible decimation that was everywhere their fate resulted more from European diseases like smallpox and measles, against which they had no natural immunity, than from warfare or mistreatment. The fact remains, however, that in conflicts between red men and white, the whites were in nearly every case the aggressors.

Narrow cultural nationalism, not greed or callousness, best explains the settlers' behavior. The relativity of cultural values escaped all but a handful of the conquerors. Many came with high motives; their difficulty was that they considered the Indians subhuman, or, at best, childlike. If the American Indians were naive in thinking that the invaders, with their huge ships and their potent

BOTTOM RIGHT: RARE BOOK ROOM, NEW YORK PUBLIC LIBRARY; OTHERS: WILLIAM L. CLEMENTS LIBRARY, UNIVERSITY OF MICHIGAN

Spanish mistreatment of the Indians was condemned by the crusading priest Bartolomé de Las Casas, who won partial reforms. He often exaggerated for effect, however, resulting in a "Black Legend" widely exploited by Spain's enemies. These water colors, purporting to show Spanish atrocities, were done for a 1582 French edition of his Very Brief Account of the Destruction of the Indies. *Although not used, they were the basis for later depictions of the Black Legend, such as the engraving (lower right) in a 1598 Latin edition.*

firesticks, were gods, these "gods" were equally naive in their thinking. "[Indians] do but run over the grass, as do also the foxes and wild beasts," an Englishman wrote in 1622, "so it is lawful now to take a land, which none useth, and make use of it." Despite much elevated talk about spreading Christianity, laboriously spelled out in charters and grants, many Europeans thought the native populations incapable of becoming true believers. It took a papal bull to establish the Indians' right to be converted, and when Spain introduced the Inquisition into its colonies in 1569, the natives were exempted from its control on the ground that they were incapable of rational judgment and thus not responsible for their heretical beliefs.

Other troubles came from misunderstandings based on this same ethnocentricity. English colonists assumed that Indian chieftains ruled with the same authority as their own kings; when tribesmen sometimes failed to honor commitments made by their leaders, the English accused them of treachery. Alien concepts of family relationships and inheritance seemed incomprehensible and sometimes foolish to Europeans, who did not realize that such conceptions as the Salic law, through which some of their own rulers traced their descent, and primogeniture, the principle that all of a man's property must go to his oldest legitimate son if he died intestate, were equally arbitrary. The European inability to grasp the communal nature of land tenure among Indians also led to innumerable quarrels.

All in all, the European assumed that differences meant inferiority. This was his fatal error, his fundamental sin. Because of it, deception became cleverness, kidnaping and slavery simply efficient means of obtaining and organizing a labor force. And because of it, there is a "Negro problem" in the United States today.

The Spanish Decline

While Spain waxed fat on the wealth of the Americas, the other nations of western Europe did little. In 1497 and 1498 King Henry VII of England sent John Cabot to the New World, where he explored Newfoundland and the northeastern coast of the continent. Cabot's explorations formed the basis for later British claims in North America, but they were not followed up for many decades. In 1524 Giovanni da Verrazano made a similar voyage for France, coasting the continent from Carolina to Nova Scotia. Some ten years later the Frenchman Jacques Cartier explored the St. Lawrence River as far inland as present-day Montreal. However, like the British, the French made no permanent settlements until the next century.

There were many reasons for this delay, the most important probably being the fact that Spain had achieved a large measure of internal tranquillity by the 16th century, while France and England were still torn by serious religious and political conflicts. The Spanish also profited from having seized upon those areas in America best suited to producing quick returns. Furthermore, in the first half of the 16th century Spain, under Charles V, dominated Europe as well as America. Charles controlled the Low Countries, most of central Europe, and part of Italy. Reinforced by the treasure of the Aztecs and the Incas, Spain seemed far too mighty to be challenged openly in either the New World or the Old.

Under Philip II, who succeeded Charles in 1556, Spanish strength seemed at its peak, especially after Philip added Portugal to his domain in 1580. But beneath the pomp and splendor, so well captured by painters like Velázquez and El Greco, the great empire was in trouble. The corruption and vacuity of the Spanish court had much to do with this. So did the ever-increasing dependence of Spain upon the gold and silver of its colonies, which tended to undermine the local Spanish economy. Even more important was the disruption of the Catholic Church throughout Europe by the Protestant Reformation.

The drive to reform and "purify" Christianity, begun by Martin Luther and carried on by men like John Calvin, had taken on important political overtones. In 1534 King Henry VIII threw off papal control and established himself as head of an *English* church. In the Low Countries resentment at Philip's attempt to suppress religious dissent was buttressed by a nationalistic desire for political independence. Philip was a religious zealot; the Spanish Inquisition crushed every glimmering of heresy at home and sought to do the same throughout the empire. At the same time Philip allowed religious issues to dominate his relations with foreign powers. Thus he supported the claims of Mary Queen of Scots to the throne of England against Queen Elizabeth I primarily because Mary was a Catholic and Elizabeth a Protestant. Elizabeth perforce became anti-Spanish, aiding the Dutch rebels, encouraging her sailors to attack Spanish shipping, and challenging Spain's monopoly in the New World.

This growing political and religious conflict also had economic overtones. Modern students have exploded the theory that the merchant classes were attracted to Protestantism because the Catholic Church, preaching outdated concepts like "just price" and frowning on the accumulation of wealth as an end in itself, stifled their acquisitiveness. Few merchants were more devoted to the quests for riches than the Italians, for example, yet they remained loyal Catholics. So did the wool merchants of Flanders, among the most important in all Europe. As a matter of fact, the Catholic Church began making its own adjustments to the new commercial capitalism well before the time of Luther. Nonetheless, in some lands the business classes tended to support Protestant leaders, in part because the new sects, stressing simplicity, made fewer financial demands upon the faithful than the Catholics did. Merchants generally supported Elizabeth against the Catholic Mary in England, and the friends of independence against Philip in the Low Countries.

As the commercial classes rose to positions of influence, England and the newly free United Provinces of the Netherlands experienced a flowering of trade and industry. The Dutch merchant marine became for a time the largest in the world, with Dutch traders capturing most of the Far Eastern business once monopolized by the Portuguese and infiltrating even into Spain's Caribbean stronghold. A number of English merchant companies, soon to play a vital role as colonizers, sprang up in the last half of the 16th century. These organizations, known as joint-stock companies, were the ancestors of the modern corporation. They enabled groups of investors to pool their capital and limit their individual responsibilities to the sums actually invested, a very important protection in such risky enterprises. The Muscovy Company, the Levant Company, and the East India Company were the most important of these joint-stock companies. "The merchants took on a new importance," writes the historian Wallace Notestein in summarizing this trend. "To the public they became almost heroes."

English Beginnings in America

English merchants took part in many kinds of international activity. The Muscovy Company spent large sums searching for a northeast passage to China around Scandinavia and dispatched six overland expeditions in an effort to reach the Orient by way of Russia and Persia. In the 1570's Martin Frobisher made three voyages across the Atlantic, hoping to discover a northwest passage to the Orient or new gold-bearing lands.

Such projects, particularly in the area of America, received strong but concealed support from the Crown. Queen Elizabeth invested heavily in Frobisher's expeditions. She knew that England was still too weak to challenge Philip openly but hoped to break his overseas monopoly just the same. Elizabeth also encouraged her boldest sea dogs to plunder Spanish merchantmen on the high seas. When Captain Francis Drake was about to set sail on his fabulous round-the-world voyage in 1577, the queen said to him: "Drake! . . . I would gladly be revenged on the King of Spain for divers injuries that I have received"; Drake, who hated the Spaniards because of a treacherous attack they had once made on the fleet of his kinsman and former chief, Sir John Hawkins, took her at her word. He sailed through the Strait of Magellan and terrorized the west coast of South America, capturing the Spanish treasure ship *Cacafuego*, heavily laden with Peruvian silver. After exploring the coast of California, which he claimed for the Crown, Drake crossed the Pacific and went on to circumnavigate the globe, returning in triumph to England in 1580. Although Elizabeth took pains to deny it to the Spanish ambassador, Drake's voyage was officially sponsored. Elizabeth being the principal shareholder in the venture, most of the

NATIONAL PORTRAIT GALLERY, LONDON

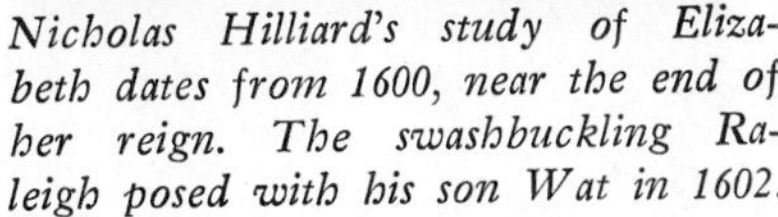

Nicholas Hilliard's study of Elizabeth dates from 1600, near the end of her reign. The swashbuckling Raleigh posed with his son Wat in 1602.

ill-gotten Spanish bullion went into the Royal Treasury rather than Drake's pocket.

When schemes to place settlers in the New World began to mature at about this time, the queen again became involved. The first Englishman to try to establish a colony in America was Sir Humphrey Gilbert, an Oxford-educated soldier and courtier with a lifelong interest in far-off places. Gilbert owned a share of the Muscovy Company; as early as 1566 he was trying to get a royal grant for an expedition in search of a northeast passage to the Orient. But soon his interests concentrated on the northwest route. He read widely in navigational and geographical lore and in 1576 wrote a persuasive *Discourse . . . to prove a passage by the north west to Cathaia.* Two years later the queen authorized him to explore and colonize "heathen lands not actually possessed by any Christian prince." We know almost nothing about his first attempt except that it occurred in 1578–79, but in 1583 he set sail again with five ships and over two hundred settlers. He landed them on Newfoundland, then evidently decided to seek a more congenial site farther south. However, no colony was established, and on his way back to England his ship went down in a storm off the Azores.

Next, Gilbert's half brother Sir Walter Raleigh took up the work. Handsome, ambitious, and impulsive, Raleigh was a great favorite of Elizabeth's. He sent a number of expeditions to explore the east coast of North America, a land he named "Virginia" in honor of his unmarried sovereign. In 1585 he settled about a hundred men on Roanoke Island, off the North Carolina coast, but these settlers returned home the next year. In 1587 Raleigh sent another group to Roanoke, including a number of women and children. Unfortunately, the supply ships sent to the colony in 1588 failed to arrive, and when help did get there in 1590, not a single soul could be found. The fate of these pioneers has never been determined.

One reason for the delay in getting aid to the Roanoke colonists was the attack of the Spanish Armada on England in 1588. Angered by English raids on his shipping and by the assistance Elizabeth was giving to the rebels in the Netherlands, Philip had decided to invade England. His motives were religious as well as political and economic, for England was now seemingly committed to Protestantism. Philip's great fleet of some 130 ships bore huge crosses on the sails as if on another crusade. The Armada carried 30,000 men and 2,400 guns, the largest naval force ever assembled up to that time. However, the English fleet badly mauled Philip's ships, and a series of storms completed their destruction. Thereafter, although the war continued and Spanish sea power remained formidable, Spain could no longer block English penetration of the New World.

Experience had shown that the cost of planting settlements in a wilderness 3,000 miles from England was more than any individual purse could bear. Raleigh, for example, lost some £40,000 in his various overseas ventures; early in the game he began to advocate government support of colonization. Indeed, as early as 1584 Richard Hakluyt, England's foremost authority on the Americas, made a convincing case for royal aid. In his *Discourse on Western Planting*, Hakluyt stressed the military advantages of "the plantinge of two or three strong fortes" along the Atlantic coast of North America. Ships operating from such bases would make life uncomfortable for "king Phillipe" by intercepting his treasure fleets—a matter, Hakluyt added coolly, "that toucheth him indeede to the quicke." Colonies in America would also provide a market for English woolens, bring in valuable tax revenues, and perhaps offer employment for the swarms of "lustie youthes that be turned to no provitable use" at home. From the great American forests would come the timber and naval stores needed to build a bigger navy and merchant marine.

Queen Elizabeth read Hakluyt's essay, but she was too cautious and too devious to act boldly on his suggestions. Only after her death in 1603 did full-scale efforts to found English colonies in America begin, and even then the organizing

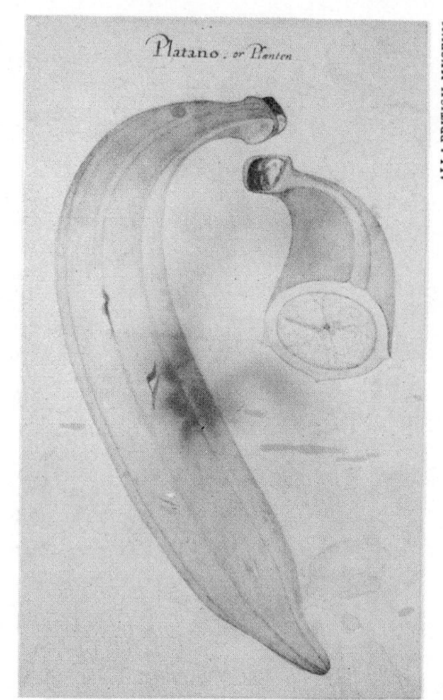

ALL: BRITISH MUSEUM

This sampling of the first authentic views of New World flora and fauna is the work of John White, an English water colorist who was with Raleigh's Roanoke colonists in 1585 and who later served as governor of the ill-fated colony. White sketched the box tortoise above at Roanoke. The banana-like horn plantain (upper left), "Allagatto," pineapple, and flamingo were done in the Caribbean, where the Raleigh colonists stopped on their voyage to Roanoke.

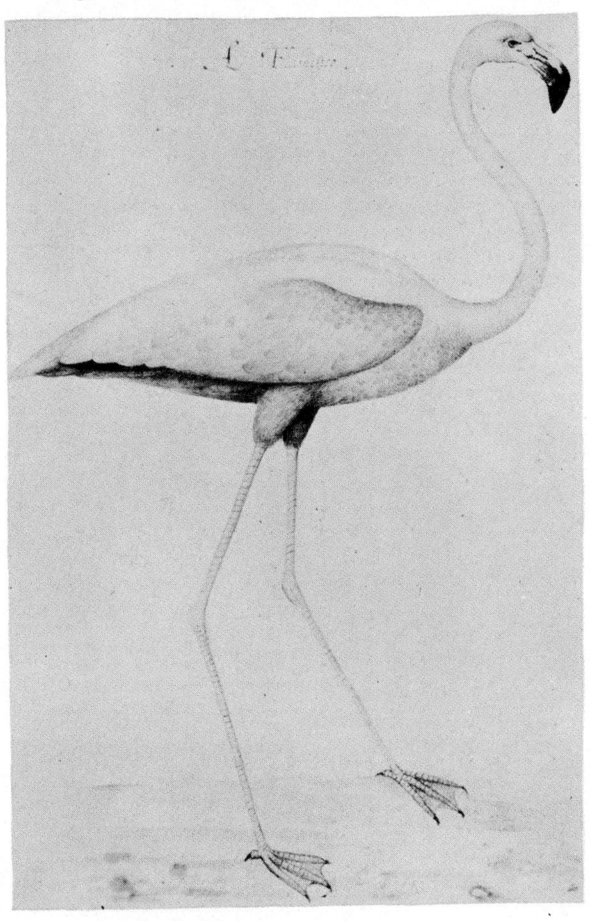

force came from merchant capitalists, not from the Crown. This was unfortunate, because the search for material rewards, and especially for quick profits, dominated the thinking of these enterprisers. Larger national ends (while not neglected, because the Crown was always involved) were subordinated. On the other hand, if private investors had not taken the lead, no colony would have been established at this time.

The Settlement of Virginia

Sometime in September 1605 two groups of English merchants petitioned the new king, James I, for a license to colonize Virginia, as the whole area claimed by England was then named. This was granted the following April, and two joint-stock companies were organized, one controlled by London merchants, the other by a group from the area around Plymouth and Bristol.* Both were under the control of a Royal Council for Virginia, but James appointed prominent stockholders to the council, which meant that the companies had considerable independence.

This first charter revealed the commercial motivation of both king and company in the plainest terms. Although it spoke of spreading Christianity and bringing "the Infidels and Savages, living in those Parts, to human Civility," it stressed the right "to dig, mine, and search for all Manner of Mines of Gold, Silver, and Copper." The London Company acted first under this grant. On December 20, 1606, it dispatched a group of about a hundred settlers aboard the *Susan Constant*, *Discovery*, and *Godspeed*. This little fleet reached the Chesapeake Bay area without serious mishap and in May 1607 founded Jamestown, the first permanent English colony in the New World.

From the start, everything seemed to go wrong. The immigrants established themselves in what was practically a malarial swamp simply because it appeared easily defensible against Indian attack.

*The London Company was to colonize south Virginia, while the Plymouth Company, the Plymouth-Bristol group of merchants, was granted northern Virginia.

They failed to get a crop in the ground because of the lateness of the season and were soon almost without food. Their leaders, mere deputies of the London merchants, did not respond to the challenges of the wilderness, and the main body of settlers, lacking the skills that pioneers need, fell to bickering among themselves. Too many, in the words of one modern British historian, were "ne'er-do-wells and misfits." During the first winter more than half of them died.

The trouble resulted from lack of experience and the company's commercial orientation. All the land belonged to the company and most of the settlers were only hired laborers who had contracted to work for it for seven years. This was unwise, for many able-bodied Englishmen of good character were eager to migrate if offered a decent opportunity to make a new life for themselves. In England times were bad. The growth of the textile industry had led to an increased demand for wool, and great landowners were dismissing laborers and tenants and enclosing their fields in order to convert to sheep-raising. Inflation, caused by a shortage of goods to supply the needs of a growing population and by the influx of large amounts of American silver into Europe, worsened the plight of the dispossessed. Instead of seeking out these landless farmers, the company satisfied itself too often with "unruly gallants," criminals, and loafers.

Still more important, the merchant directors of the London Company, knowing little or nothing about Virginia, failed to provide the colony with effective guidance. They set up a council of settlers, but kept all real power in their own hands. Although they continued to pour capital into the venture and to recruit thousands of additional settlers, they made poor use of their assets. Instead of stressing farming and public improvements, they directed the energies of the colonists into such futile labors as searching for gold (the first supply ship devoted precious space to two goldsmiths and two "refiners"), glass-blowing, silk-raising, wine-making, and exploring the local rivers in hopes of finding a water route to the Pacific and the riches of China.

One colonist, Captain John Smith, tried to stop some of this foolishness. Smith had come to

Engravings from Captain John Smith's General Historie of Virginia . . . *(1624) depict Smith captured by Indians (left) and being rescued by Pocahontas (right). The engraver was indebted for his settings and figures to Theodor de Bry's* America, *a 1590 volume of engravings based in large part on John White's water colors. In the scene at left, for example, Smith has been inserted into a composite of no less than four de Bry engravings.*

Virginia after a fantastic career as a soldier of fortune in eastern Europe, where he had fought many battles, been enslaved by a Turkish pasha, and triumphed in a variety of adventures, military and amorous. Quickly realizing that finding food was the job of first importance, he developed into an expert forager and Indian trader. "A plaine soldier that can use a pickaxe and a spade is better than five knights," Smith said. Whether he was actually rescued from death at the hands of the Indians by the fair princess Pocahontas is not certain, but there is little doubt that without him the colony would have perished in the early days. However, he only stayed in Virginia for two years. As a result, lacking intelligent direction and faced with appalling hardships, the colonists failed to develop a sufficient sense of common purpose during the first years. Some were lazy and refused to work and others profited by selling weapons to the Indians, a shortsighted if not actually treasonable activity.

Thus each year settlers died in wholesale lots. The nominal causes of death were disease, starvation (there was even a case of cannibalism among the desperate survivors), and Indian attack, but the real causes were ignorance and folly. During the period between 1606 and 1622, the London Company invested more than £160,000 in Virginia and sent over about 6,000 colonists. Yet no dividends were ever earned for the stockholders and of the 6,000, fewer than 2,000 were still alive in 1622. The only profits were those taken by certain shrewd investors who had organized a joint-stock company to transport women to Virginia "to be made wives" by the colonists.

One major problem—the mishandling of the local Indians—was largely the colonists' own doing. It is quite likely that the settlement would not have survived if the Powhatan Indians had not given the colonists food in the first hard winters, taught them the ways of the forest, introduced them to valuable new crops like corn and yams, and showed them how to clear dense timber by girdling the trees and burning them down after they were dead. The settlers accepted Indian aid, then took whatever else they wanted by force. "[They] conciliated the Powhatan people while they were of use," one historian has written, "and pressed them remorselessly, facelessly, mechanically, as innocent of conscious ill will as a turning wheel, when they became of less value than their land." The Indians did not meekly submit to such treatment. They proved brave, skillful, and ferocious fighters, once they understood that their very existence was at stake. The burden of Indian fighting might easily have been more than the frail settlement could bear.

What saved Virginia was not the brushing aside of the Indians but the cultivation of tobacco, which flourished there and could be sold profitably in England. Once the settlers discovered tobacco, no amount of company pressure could keep them at wasteful tasks like looking for gold. The "restraint of plantinge Tobacco," one company official commented, "is a thinge so distastefull to them that they will wth no patience indure to heare of it." John Rolfe, who is also famous for marrying Pocahontas, introduced West Indian tobacco—much milder than the local "weed" and thus more valuable—in 1612. With money earned in England from the sale of tobacco, the colonists could buy the manufactured articles they could not produce in a raw new country; this freed them from dependence on outside subsidies and led to rapid expansion. It did not mean profit for the London Company, however, for by the time tobacco caught on, the original colonists had served their seven years and were no longer hired hands. To attract more settlers, the company had permitted first tenancy and then outright ownership of farms. Thus the profits of tobacco went largely to the planters, not to the "adventurers" who had organized the colony.

Important administrative reforms also helped Virginia to forge ahead. A revised charter in 1612 extended the London Company's control over its own affairs in Virginia. Despite serious intracompany rivalry between groups headed by Sir Thomas Smythe and Sir Edwin Sandys, a somewhat more intelligent direction of Virginia's affairs resulted. First the merchants appointed a single resident governor and gave him sufficient authority to control the settlers. Then they made it much easier for settlers to obtain land of their own. In 1619 a rudimentary form of self-government was instituted: a House of Burgesses, consisting of delegates chosen in each district, met at Jamestown to advise the governor on local problems. The company was not bound by the actions of the Burgesses, but from this small seed sprang the system of representative government that became the American pattern.

These reforms, however, came too late to save the fortunes of the London Company. In 1619 the Sandys faction had won control and started an extensive development program, but an Indian uprising in 1622 was a discouraging setback. James I, who disliked Sandys personally, easily convinced himself that the colony was being badly managed. In 1624 he caused the charter to be revoked and Virginia became a royal colony. As a financial proposition the company was a fiasco; the shareholders lost every penny they had invested. Nonetheless, by 1624 Virginia was firmly established and beginning to prosper.

Sociologist Sigmund Diamond has offered an interesting theoretical explanation of how and why the Virginia colony changed from a mere commercial organization to a real society. In the beginning, he asserts, there was no cement binding the colonists into a community; either employees or bosses, they were all oriented toward company headquarters in London. In order to attract more settlers and motivate them to work, the company had to grant them special privileges and status, such as political power and the right to own land, which had the effect of making them more dependent upon one another. By thus destroying the reliance of the colonists on the company, these actions undermined company control over the colonists. "The new relationships in which [the Virginians] were now involved," Diamond explains, "were of greater importance than the company relationship. . . . It was the company's fate to have created a country and to have destroyed itself in the process."

The Pilgrims of Plymouth Plantation

While the Virginia colony limped along under merchant control, a community of Englishmen living in Holland approached Sir Edwin Sandys, seeking permission to establish a settlement near the mouth of the Hudson River, which was within the London Company's grant. This group of religious dissenters, called Pilgrims, had fled England in 1608 to escape persecution and had settled in Leyden. Now, a decade later, unable to earn a living in Holland and distressed by the fact that their children were losing contact with their English traditions, they had decided to seek a place to live and worship as they pleased in the emptiness of the New World—another example of the hope that America inspired in the hearts of Europeans. Sandys, while not sympathetic to their religious views, appreciated their inherent worth and saw to it that their wish was granted. Since the Pilgrims lacked financial resources, they formed a joint-stock company with other prospective emigrants and some optimistic investors who paid their expenses in return for half the profits of their labor. In September 1620, about a hundred strong—only 35 of them Pilgrims from Leyden—the group set out from Plymouth, England, on the ship *Mayflower*.

These were the first settlers to leave the mother country primarily for religious reasons. In England the Protestant Reformation, while based on real differences of religious principle, never escaped completely from the political motives that had led Henry VIII to break with Rome. Henry had revolted chiefly in order to rid himself of a barren wife and to strengthen his control of the realm. Nor did his daughter Elizabeth adhere to the new order primarily for reasons of conscience; power politics—particularly the enmity of Catholic Spain and the strategic importance of the Protestant rebels in the Low Countries—dictated her stand on religious questions.

However, most Englishmen were not so callous about philosophical and spiritual issues. Many remained steadfastly Catholic. Others considered the state-sponsored Anglican Church too "popish" and hoped to push the Reformation further. While professing to be good Anglicans, they wanted to "purify" their church by ridding it of Roman Catholic vestiges. Services should be simpler, they believed, all the higher clergy should be eliminated, and each parish should have more to say about local church affairs.

Unlike these "Puritans," "Separatists" thought the Anglican Church too corrupt for salvage;

A 1641 English cartoon comments on the religious turmoil of the period. The Roman Catholic at right is joined in a game of "abusing" the Bible by three Protestant sects opposed to the Church of England.

each congregation ought to run its own affairs without any hierarchy controlling it. The Separatists also believed that every man must decide his religious beliefs for himself. In the England of James I, Puritans could satisfy both Crown and conscience, but Separatists like the Pilgrims, who refused to acknowledge the authority of the Anglican Church, had to go underground or flee. Having tried both these alternatives without finding peace, the Pilgrims were now seeking a third way out in America. King James, possibly feeling that the American wilderness would either kill them off or cure them of their heretical beliefs, authorized their departure and promised not to bother them if they made no trouble.

Had the *Mayflower* reached its intended destination, the Pilgrims might well have been soon forgotten. Instead the ship touched America slightly to the north, on Cape Cod Bay. Unwilling to remain longer at the mercy of storm-tossed December seas, the settlers decided to remain. Since they were outside the jurisdiction of the London Company, some members of the group claimed to be free of all governmental control. Therefore, before going ashore, the Pilgrims drew up the Mayflower Compact. "We whose names are underwritten," the Compact ran, "do by these Presents, solemnly and mutually in the presence of God and one another covenant and combine ourselves under into a civil Body Politick . . . and by Virtue hereof do enact . . . such just and equal Laws . . . as shall be thought most meet and convenient for the general Good of the Colony."

In this simple manner, ordinary men created a government. The Compact, prototype of many similar covenants, some explicit, others existing by tacit agreement, illustrates the impact of the immense emptiness of the New World on pioneers. Alone in the wilderness, men recognized their interdependence and came to see the need for social and political organizations. This realization had much to do with the development of American republican government and democracy.

Arriving on the bleak Massachusetts shore in December, at a place called Plymouth, the settlers had to endure a winter of desperate hunger. About half of them died. But in the spring the local Indians provided food and advice. After a bountiful harvest the following November, they celebrated the first Thanksgiving feast, thus establishing another tradition. Thereafter, although they grew neither rich nor numerous on the thin New England soil, the Pilgrims' place in history was assured. They won their battles not with sword and gunpowder like Cortés nor with bulldozers and dynamite like modern pioneers, but with simple courage and practical piety. They are our American symbol of the honest strivings of all people for a better life. The story of their trials and eventual triumphs has been preserved in *History of Plimmoth Plantation,* the first American history, written by the wise William Bradford, who served 30 terms as governor.

Massachusetts Bay Puritans

Actually, the Pilgrims were not the first Englishmen to inhabit the northern regions. The Plymouth Company settled a group on the Kennebec River in 1607. These colonists gave up after a few months, but fishermen and traders continued to visit the area, which was christened "New England" by Captain John Smith after an expedition there in 1614. Several more or less permanent trading posts were founded. Then, in 1620, the Plymouth Company was reorganized as the Council for New England. More interested in real-estate deals than in colonizing, the council disposed of a number of tracts in the area north of Cape Cod, including a large grant in 1622 to its most influential member, Sir Ferdinando Gorges, and his friend John Mason, former governor of an English settlement on Newfoundland. Their domain included a considerable part of what is now Maine and New Hampshire. The most significant of the council's grants, however, was a very small one made to a group of Puritans from Dorchester, who established a settlement at Salem. In 1629 these "Dorchester Adventurers" organized the Massachusetts Bay Company and obtained a royal grant to the area between the Charles and Merrimack rivers.

The Massachusetts Bay Company was conceived of as another commercial venture, but England had become a very difficult place for Puritans by this time. Charles I was now king and much influenced in religious matters by William Laud, the staunch Anglican cleric. Laud strengthened the elaborate ritual and tight central control that Puritans found so distasteful in the Anglican Church. With the king's support, he attempted to force all churchmen to conform to his views, summarily removing from their pulpits ministers with Puritan leanings. Since it was no longer possible for conscientious Puritans to remain within the fold, the leaders of the Massachusetts Bay Company decided to migrate to America in force. Taking their charter with them, a crucial step which meant that their colony became practically self-governing, they set out in the summer of 1630 with almost a thousand settlers. By fall they had founded Boston and a number of other towns, and the Puritan commonwealth was under way.

The settlers suffered fewer hardships in the early years than had the early Jamestown and Plymouth colonists and were immensely aided by a constant influx of new recruits, for continuing bad times and the persecution of Puritans at home led to the "Great Migration" of the 1630's. Only a minority came to Massachusetts (many thousands poured into the new English colonies in the West Indies), but by 1640 well over 10,000 had arrived. This concentrated group of industrious and fairly prosperous colonists made for the early development of a complex civilization. Agriculture, while essential, was not particularly profitable; therefore many settlers turned to fishing, the fur trade, and shipbuilding.

The directors of the Massachusetts Bay Company believed they were engaged in a divinely inspired enterprise and saw themselves as governing the settlement as God's agents. That religion and politics were interrelated they regarded as axiomatic. As Perry Miller, the great modern historian of Puritanism, wrote, the original government of Massachusetts was "a dictatorship . . . of the holy and regenerate."

Before leaving England, the stockholders had elected John Winthrop governor of the colony. Winthrop, a wise and practical man who preferred to achieve his ends by negotiation and persuasion, realized that the handful of men who held power under the charter could not govern effectively without popular support. A broader-based authority was essential to growth and social harmony. He and the other leaders soon decided to make about a hundred of the adult male settlers "freemen" of the commonwealth, thus permitting them to participate in political affairs. Apparently, some of these men were not church members, but thereafter nonmembers were specifically barred from freemanship. The freemen quickly won the right to choose the governor and to elect representatives to a local legislature called the General Court. The system was not democratic in the modern sense, but in the early days, while the community retained a high degree of cohesiveness and commitment to Puritan beliefs, it worked well.

While ministers were prestigious figures in the Puritan commonwealth, they were ultimately subject to the control of their parishioners; questions of church policy were decided by the majority vote of members of the congregation.

Charles I, prejudiced against Puritans to begin with, frowned upon such examples of colonial self-rule. Unwilling to stop the migration to New

England, he sought to bring the colony under royal control by having his Privy Council issue an order recalling the Massachusetts Bay charter. Fortunately for the colonists, the outbreak of revolt in Scotland in 1639 prevented the government from enforcing this order.

Other New England Colonies

From the successful Massachusetts Bay colony, settlement radiated outward to other areas of New England, in part because of population growth and in part because of Puritan intolerance. In 1629 Sir Ferdinando Gorges and John Mason had divided their holdings, Gorges taking the Maine section (enlarged in 1639) and Mason New Hampshire, but neither succeeded in making much of his claim. Massachusetts gradually took over these areas. The heirs of Gorges and Mason managed to regain legal possession briefly in the 1670's, but Massachusetts bought title to Maine for a pittance (£1,250) in 1677. New Hampshire, however, became a royal colony in 1680.

Meanwhile, beginning in 1635, a number of Massachusetts congregations had pushed southwestward into the fertile valley of the Connecticut River. The most important of these, a group headed by the Reverend Thomas Hooker, founded Hartford in 1636. Hooker was influential in the drafting of the Fundamental Orders, a sort of constitution creating a government for the valley towns, in 1639. The Fundamental Orders were patterned after the Massachusetts system, except that they did not limit the right to vote to church members. Other groups of Puritans came directly from England to settle towns in and around New Haven in the 1630's. These were incorporated into Connecticut shortly after the Hooker colony obtained a royal charter in 1662.

Hooker and some of the other Connecticut pioneers had quarreled with the Massachusetts leaders about religious questions, but they did not differ over basic principles. This was not true, however, in the case of all early settlers, and when real dissenters spoke up, the dominant majority harshly repressed them. Roger Williams, a Salem minister, was a religious zealot even by Puritan standards. His belief in the freedom of each individual to practice his own faith led him to object to the alliance between the church and the civil government in Massachusetts Bay. Since "forced religion stinks in God's nostrils," magistrates should have no authority in religious affairs, he insisted. He also advanced the radical idea that the colonists (and for that matter the king) had no right to American land until they had bought it from the Indians. When he persisted in advocating these heresies, he was banished. He took refuge in the Narragansett Bay area with a group of his followers, founding Providence in 1636. Anne Hutchinson, wife of a prominent Boston settler, also got into trouble with the dominant clique in Massachusetts. Mrs. Hutchinson, a headstrong, rather opinionated woman, presumed to discuss and sometimes to disagree with the sermons of her minister. Her own mystical brand of Puritanism, a variety of Antinomianism, denied any necessary relation between moral conduct and salvation. Possession of God's grace, not mere good behavior, was the key to the gates of heaven. Even the authority of the Bible, she argued, let alone that of the ministry, must yield to insights directly inspired by God in the individual. This rather loose and intellectually imprecise interpretation of "salvation by grace" attracted many followers but clashed with the official theology. She too was banished. Her group settled near Providence, and soon other dissidents collected in the area.

In 1643, despite the Civil War, Williams went to England and the next year managed to obtain a charter for these settlements. The colony was called the Rhode Island and Providence Plantation. Its government was relatively democratic, with complete religious freedom allowed to all men and a rigid separation of church and state maintained. After the restoration of Charles II in 1660, a new charter substantially confirmed Rhode Island's liberal system.

French and Dutch Settlements

While the English were settling Virginia and New England, other European powers were also challenging Spain's monopoly in the New World. French explorers had pushed up the St. Lawrence as far as the site of Montreal in the 1530's, although they failed to establish a permanent colony. Another French expedition under Jean Ribaut set up a post in Florida in 1562, but the Spanish quickly destroyed this group. Beginning in 1603, Samuel de Champlain made several voyages to the St. Lawrence region. In 1608 he founded Quebec, and he had penetrated as far inland as the Georgian Bay area of Lake Huron before the Pilgrims left Leyden. The French also planted colonies in the West Indian islands of St. Christopher, Guadeloupe, Martinique, and others of the Lesser Antilles after 1625.

Through their West India Company, the Dutch also established themselves in the Lesser Antilles. On the mainland they founded New Netherland in the Hudson Valley, basing their claim to the region on the explorations of Henry Hudson in 1609. As early as 1624 there was a Dutch outpost, Fort Orange, on the site of present-day Albany. Two years later New Amsterdam was located at the mouth of the river, and Manhattan Island was purchased from the Indians by Peter Minuit, the director-general of the West India Company, for trading goods worth about 60 guilders.

The Dutch traded with the Indians for furs and plundered Spanish colonial commerce enthusiastically. Through the Charter of Privileges of Patroons, which authorized large grants of land to individuals who would bring over 50 settlers, they also tried to encourage large-scale agriculture. Only one such estate, Rensselaerswyck, on the Hudson south of Fort Orange, owned by the rich Amsterdam merchant Kiliaen

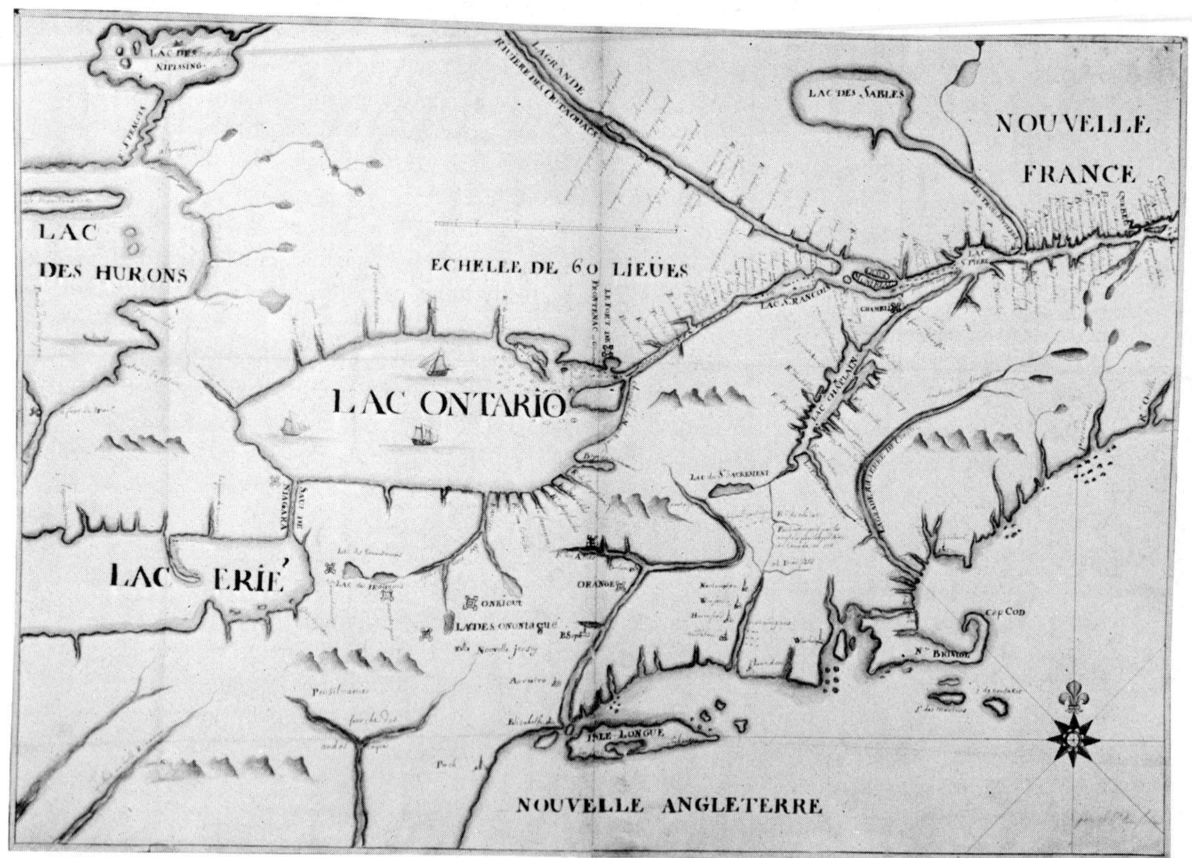

SERVICE HYDROGRAPHIQUE DE LA MARINE, PARIS, ATLAS 4044B

A French cartographer's view of New France and New England, c. 1700. The placement of geographic features is reasonably accurate, but their sizes and shapes are often more imagined than real. Quebec, capital of New France, is at the upper right. The wide-ranging explorations of French trappers are reflected in the vessels on Lake Ontario and the detailed labeling of settlements, portages, and streams emptying into the major rivers.

Van Rensselaer, was successful. It is interesting to note that Peter Minuit, who was removed from his post in New Amsterdam in 1631, organized a group of Swedish settlers several years later and founded the colony of New Sweden on the lower reaches of the Delaware River. New Sweden was in constant conflict with the Dutch, who finally overran it in 1655. But the Dutch were never deeply committed to colonizing America; their chief activity came in the Far East, where they took over the role formerly played by the Portuguese.

Maryland and the Carolinas

The Virginia and New England colonies were essentially corporate ventures, but most of the other English colonies in America were organized by individuals or by a handful of partners who obtained charters from the ruling sovereign. Commercial companies had failed to pay dividends; furthermore, it was becoming easier to organize and establish new settlements in America, for experience had taught Englishmen a great deal about the colonization process. New settlers knew better what to bring with them and what to do after they arrived. Moreover, the psychological barrier was much less formidable. Like a modern athlete seeking to run a mile in less than four minutes, after about 1630 colonizers knew that what they were attempting *could* be accomplished. Also, mid-17th-century conditions in Europe encouraged thousands to migrate. Both in England and on the Continent the economic future seemed unpromising, while political and religious persecution constantly erupted in one country or another, each time supplying America with new waves of refugees.

Numbers of influential Englishmen were eager to try their luck as colonizers. The grants they received made them "proprietors" of great estates which were, at least in theory, their personal property, to be exploited almost entirely as they saw fit. Proprietors generally did not invest large sums in their colonies. By granting land to settlers in return for a small annual rent, they hoped to obtain a steadily increasing income while holding a valuable speculative interest in all undeveloped land. At the same time their political power, guaranteed by charter, would become increasingly important as their colonies expanded. In practice, however, the realities of life in America limited their freedom of action and their profits.

One of the first of these proprietary colonies was Maryland, granted by Charles I to George Calvert, Lord Baltimore. Calvert had a deep interest in America, being a member both of the London Company and of the Council for New England and owner of a colony called Avalon in Newfoundland. He hoped to profit financially from Maryland but, since he was a Catholic, he also intended the colony to be a haven for his co-religionists.

Calvert died shortly before Charles approved his charter, so the grant actually went to his son Cecilius. The first settlers arrived in 1634, founding St. Mary's just north of the Potomac. The presence of the now well-established Virginia colony nearby greatly aided the Marylanders; they had little difficulty in getting started and in developing an economy based, like Virginia's, on tobacco. However, an acrimonious dispute raged for some years between the two colonies over their common boundary. Despite the emptiness of the American wilderness, settlers quickly proved that they could squabble over a few acres as bitterly as any European peasants.

The Maryland charter was based on that of the wild, isolated county palatine of Durham in the north of England whose bishop-overlords had almost regal authority. Although Lord Baltimore had the right to establish feudal manors in Maryland, hold men in serfdom, make laws, and set up his own courts, he soon discovered that to attract settlers he had to allow them to own their farms and that to maintain any political influence at all in such a remote region he had to give these settlers considerable say in local affairs. Other wise concessions marked his handling of the religious question. He would have preferred an exclusively Catholic colony, but while Catholics did go to Maryland, there existed from the beginning a large Protestant majority. Lord Baltimore solved this problem by "accepting" a Toleration Act (1649) that guaranteed freedom of religion to anyone "professing to believe in Jesus Christ."

Because the Calverts adjusted their pretensions to American realities, they made a fortune out of Maryland and maintained an influence in the colony until the Revolution.

During the period of the English Civil War and Oliver Cromwell's Protectorate, no important new colonial enterprises were undertaken. With the restoration of Charles II in 1660, however, came a new wave of settlement, for the government wished to expand and strengthen its hold on North America. To do so, it granted generous terms to settlers–easy access to land, religious toleration, and political rights–all far more extensive than those available in England.

Most of the earlier colonies were organized by groups of merchants; those of the Restoration period reflected the concerns of great English landowners. The first new venture involved a huge grant south of Virginia to eight powerful proprietors with large interests in colonial affairs, including the Earl of Clarendon, Sir Anthony Ashley Cooper, and Sir William Berkeley, a former governor of Virginia. The region was called Carolina in honor of Charles I. The Carolina charter, like that of Maryland, accorded the proprietors wide authority. These men did not intend to recruit large numbers of European settlers, depending instead upon the "excess" population of New England, Virginia, and the West Indies. They (and the Crown) hoped for a diversified economy, the charter granting tax concessions to exporters of wine, silk, oil, olives, and other exotic products.

With the help of the political philosopher John Locke, the proprietors drafted a grandiose plan of government called the Fundamental Constitutions, which created a hereditary nobility and provided for huge paper land grants to a hierarchy headed by the lords proprietors and lesser "landgraves" and "caciques." The manpower to support this feudal society was to be supplied by peasants called "leet-men." Of course this pretentious system proved unworkable in America. A number of landgraves and caciques were given grants, but none could find leet-men willing to toil on their domains. Probably the purpose of all this elaborate feudal nonsense was promotional; the proprietors hoped to convince men with capital

This print of Charleston dates from the late 1730's. Like most 18th-century views of American cities, it stresses the busy harbor and substantial buildings on the waterfront. Colonial promoters used such "commercial" prints to attract capital and settlers.

that they could make fortunes in Carolina rivaling those of English lords, and in this they were not greatly stretching the truth. Life followed the pattern established in Virginia and Maryland, with nearly all white colonists owning their own property and possessing a good deal of political power.

The first settlers arrived in 1670, chiefly Englishmen from the sugar plantations of Barbados, where slave labor was driving out small independent farmers. Charles Town (now Charleston), located where the Ashley and Cooper rivers flow into the Atlantic, was founded in 1680. Another center of population sprang up in the Albermarle district, just south of Virginia, settled largely by individuals from that colony. Two quite different societies grew up in these areas. The Charleston colony, with an economy based on a thriving trade in furs and on the export of foodstuffs to the West Indies, was prosperous and cosmopolitan. The Albemarle settlement was poorer and far more "backwoodsy." Eventually, in 1712, the two

STOKES COLLECTION, NEW YORK PUBLIC LIBRARY

were formally separated into the colonies of North and South Carolina.

The Middle Colonies

Gradually, it was becoming clear that the English would dominate the whole stretch of coast between the St. Lawrence Valley and Florida. After 1660 only the Dutch challenged their monopoly. The two nations, once allies against Spain, had fallen out because of the fierce competition of their textile manufacturers and merchants. England's efforts to bar Dutch merchant vessels from its colonial trade also brought them into conflict in America. Charles II precipitated a showdown by granting his brother James, Duke of York, the entire area between Connecticut and Maryland. This was tantamount to declaring war. In 1664 English forces captured New Amsterdam without a fight—there were only 1,500 people in the town—and soon the rest of the Dutch settlements capitulated. New Amsterdam became New York. The duke did not interfere much with the way of life of the Dutch settlers, and they were quickly reconciled to the new dispensations. New York had no local assembly until the 1680's, but this had been equally true under the Dutch.

In 1664, even before the capture of New Amsterdam, the Duke of York gave New Jersey, the region between the Hudson and the Delaware, to two friends, John, Lord Berkeley and Sir George Carteret. To attract settlers, these properietors offered land on easy terms and established freedom of religion and a democratic system of local government. A considerable number of Puritans from New England and Long Island moved to the new province.

In 1674 Berkeley sold his interest in New Jersey to two Quakers. The Quakers were extreme left-wing Separatists who believed that men could communicate directly with their Maker; their religion required neither ritual nor even ministers. Originally a sect emotional to the point of fanaticism, by the 1670's the Quakers had come to stress the doctrine of the Inner Light—the direct, mystical experience of religious truth—which they believed possible for all men. They were at once humble and fiercely proud, pacifistic and avoiding all show, yet unwilling to bow before any man or to surrender their right to worship as they pleased. They distrusted the intellect in religious matters and, while ardent proselytizers of their own beliefs, they tolerated those of others cheer-

HISTORICAL SOCIETY OF PENNSYLVANIA

The only known authentic likeness of William Penn is this charcoal study by Englishman Francis Place.

fully. When faced with opposition, they resorted to passive resistance, a tactic that embroiled them in grave difficulties both in England and in most of the American colonies. In Massachusetts Bay, for example, six Quakers were executed when they refused either to conform to Puritan ideas or leave the colony. The acquisition of New Jersey (when Sir George Carteret died in 1680, they purchased the rest of the colony) gave the Quakers a place where they could practice their religion in peace. The proprietors, in keeping with their principles, drafted an extremely liberal constitution for the colony, the Concessions and Agreements of 1677, which created an autonomous legislature and guaranteed settlers freedom of conscience, the right of trial by jury, and other civil rights.

The main Quaker effort at colonization, however, came in the region immediately west of New Jersey, a fertile area belonging to William Penn. Son of a wealthy admiral, Penn had early rejected a life of ease and had become a Quaker missionary. As a result, he was twice jailed. Yet he possessed qualities that enabled him to hold the respect and friendship of men who found his ideas abhorrent. From his father, Penn had inherited a claim to £16,000 that the admiral had once lent Charles II. The king, reluctant to part with that much cash, agreed to pay off this debt in American land; in 1681 he gave Penn the region north of Maryland and west of the Delaware River, insisting only that it be named Pennsylvania, in honor of the admiral. The Duke of York then added Delaware, the region between Maryland and Delaware Bay, to Penn's holdings.

William Penn considered his colony a "Holy Experiment," and he applied himself to its development with high idealism. He treated the Indians fairly, buying title to their lands and trying to protect them in their dealings with settlers and traders. Anyone who believed in "one Almighty and Eternal God" was entitled to freedom of worship. His political ideas were paternalistic rather than democratic—the assembly he established could only approve or reject laws proposed by the governor and council—but individual rights were as well protected in Pennsylvania as in New Jersey.

Penn's altruism, however, did not prevent him from taking excellent care of his own interests. He sold land to settlers large and small on easy terms but reserved huge tracts for himself and attached quitrents* to that which he disposed of. He also promoted Pennsylvania tirelessly and shrewdly, writing a series of glowing, although perfectly honest, descriptions of the colony which were circulated widely in England and, in translation, on the Continent. These attracted many settlers, including large numbers of Germans—the Pennsylvania "Dutch" (a corruption of *Deutsch*, meaning "German").

Penn was neither a doctrinaire nor a closet philosopher. He came himself to Pennsylvania and agreed to adjustments in his first Frame of Government when local conditions demonstrated the need for change. Although not a believer in democracy in the modern sense, his combination of wisdom, liberality, and good salesmanship helped the colony to prosper and grow rapidly from the start. Of course the presence of well-settled colonies on all sides and the richness of the soil had much to do with this happy state of affairs. By 1685 there were almost 9,000 settlers in Pennsylvania, and by 1700 twice that number. This provided a heartening contrast to the early history of Vir-

*See below, p. 69.

ginia and Plymouth. Pennsylvania produced wheat, corn, rye, and other crops in abundance and found a ready market for its surpluses on the sugar plantations of the West Indies.

The Settlement of Georgia

The settlement of the Pennsylvania area all but completed the foundation of the English colonies in America. Nearly 50 years later, however, a final colony was established. This was Georgia, and the circumstances of its founding were most unusual. A group of London philanthropists concerned over the plight of honest men imprisoned for debt conceived of settling these unfortunates in the New World where they might make a fresh start in life. (Once again, here is striking proof that Europeans, even in the 18th century, were beguiled by the prospect of regenerating their society in the New World.) They petitioned for a grant south of the Carolinas, and the government, eager to create a buffer between South Carolina and the hostile Spanish in Florida, readily granted a charter (1732) to a group of "trustees" who

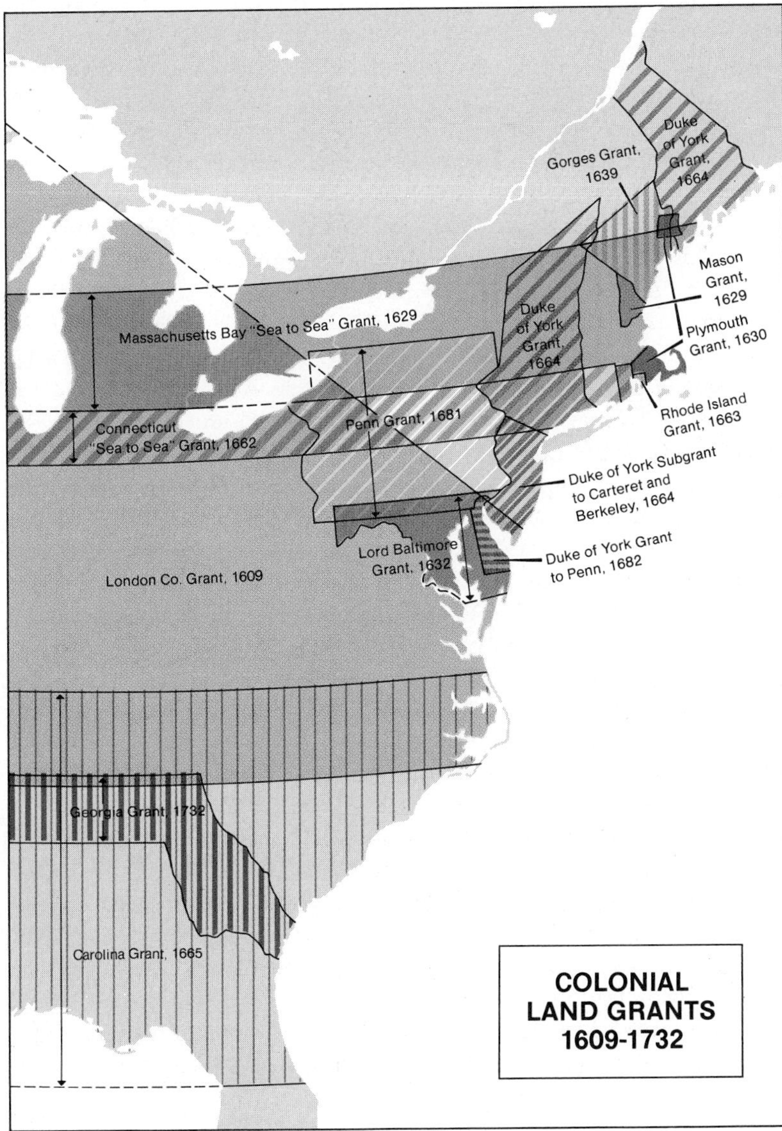

A welter of conflicting and overlapping colonial grants (only the more important are shown here) caused boundary disputes that dragged on well into the 19th century.

were to manage the colony without profit to themselves for a period of 21 years.

This plan called for settling the debtors on 50-acre, nontransferable farms. To insure sobriety and industriousness, liquor and slaves were banned. In practice, however, this idealistic system worked no better than the aristocratic schemes of the Carolina proprietors. James Oglethorpe, leader of the trustees, founded Savannah in 1733, but only a handful of his hundred-odd colonists were poor debtors. While willing enough to battle Spaniards and Indians, the settlers refused to live the kind of Spartan existence envisioned by the founders. They soon discovered ways of extending their holdings beyond 50 acres. Within a short time, rum flowed, slaves were imported, and Georgia had developed an economy much like South Carolina's. In 1752 the trustees, much disillusioned, abandoned their responsibilities, and Georgia became a royal colony.

SUPPLEMENTARY READING There are interesting accounts of the early explorers in Paul Horgan, *Conquistadors in North American History** (1963), J.B. Brebner, *The Explorers of North America** (1933), and H.I. Priestley, *The Coming of the White Man* (1929). S.E. Morison's biography of Columbus, *Admiral of the Ocean Sea* (1942), is a model of sound scholarship and good writing.

The European background of colonization is discussed in E.P. Cheyney's *Dawn of a New Era** (1936) and W.C. Abbott's *Expansion of Europe* (1938). Fuller accounts of the English background can be found in Wallace Notestein, *The English People on the Eve of Colonization** (1954), A.L. Rowse, *The Elizabethans and America** (1959), and Carl Bridenbaugh, *Vexed and Troubled Englishmen* (1968).

Full discussions of the culture and history of the American Indians are provided by Clark Wissler, *Indians of the United States** (1940), by A.M. Josephy, Jr., *The Indian Heritage of America** (1968), and by William Brandon, *The American Heritage Book of Indians** (1961), the latter profusely illustrated and covering the tribes of the entire hemisphere. A.T. Vaughan, *New England Frontier** (1965), argues persuasively that New Englanders treated the Indians fairly. On the African background of Negro slaves, see B. Davison and K. Buah, *History of West Africa to the 19th Century* (1967); on the slave trade, P.D. Curtin, *The Atlantic Slave Trade* (1970).

The finest general account of the history of English colonization is C.M. Andrews' *The Colonial Period of American History** (1934–38). T.J. Wertenbaker's *The First Americans* (1927) is a brief summary, and W.F. Craven's *The Colonies in Transition** (1968) is a first-rate study of late 17th- and early 18th-century developments. On the southern colonies, W.F. Craven's *The Southern Colonies in the Seventeenth Century* (1949) is excellent, while G.F. Willison's *Behold Virginia* (1951) is popular history at its best. Willison's *Saints and Strangers** (1945) is an equally good study of the Pilgrims, but see also G.D. Langdon, Jr., *Pilgrim Colony: A History of New Plymouth** (1966).

Historians have always been of two minds about the Puritan colonies. S.E. Morison, in *Builders of the Bay Colony** (1930), presents a favorable account; J.T. Adams presents an anti-Puritan interpretation in *The Founding of New England** (1921). For the middle colonies, see T.J. Wertenbaker, *The Founding of American Civilization: The Middle Colonies* (1398), part of a trilogy, the other two volumes of which are *The Old South* (1942) and *The Puritan Oligarchy** (1947). No student should miss at least dipping into the great works of Francis Parkman on the history of the French in America. His *Pioneers of France in the New World* (1855) covers the early period. On the Spanish in America, see Charles Gibson, *Spain in America** (1966).

Biographies worth noting, in addition to Morison's life of Columbus, include P.L. Barbour, *The Three Worlds of Captain John Smith* (1964); Bradford Smith, *Captain John Smith: His Life and Legend* (1953); E.S. Morgan, *The Puritan Dilemma: The Story of John Winthrop** (1958) and Morgan's *Roger Williams: The Church and the States** (1967); and C.O. Peare, *William Penn: A Biography** (1957).

*Available in paperback.

TRUSTEES OF THE BRITISH MUSEUM

PORTFOLIO

I *The Heritage of Africa*

Although the Portuguese who began inching their way down the west coast of Africa in the 15th century were searching for a new route to the Indies, they were willing to be distracted by whatever trade prospects appeared on the horizon—including 29 black men kidnaped near Arguin in 1443 and sold in the markets of Lisbon. For centuries the trans-Saharan trade had enriched such inland empires as Ghana and Kanem; now, as trade with Europe increased, new states emerged nearer the coast. The reshaping of these societies under the warping pressures of the slave trade, examined in the following pages, contributed to the demise of some, the growth of others.

A few early European merchants recognized the African gift for sculpture and commissioned works in ivory, such as this ceremonial saltcellar (with a ship on the lid), an African view of the fierce white strangers who came from the sea. Such secular items were rare in Africa, where most art served religious or political purposes. By coincidence, the slave trade was concentrated on those peoples most productive of art; this artistic talent, examples of which illustrate this portfolio, was one more victim of the institution of human bondage.

From the Senegal to the Gambia

Among the emerging coastal societies were the peoples of Senegambia (the area between the Senegal and Gambia rivers), heirs to the ancient western Sudanic empires. For example, a group of Fulani, in alliance with some of the Malinke, conquered the area along the south bank of the Senegal in 1559. Previously nomadic herdsmen, the Fulani now settled in neat, well-ordered towns like the one shown below.

Senegambia was the first sub-Saharan area to experience contact with the Europeans. By 1500 gold, ivory, pepper, gum arabic—and some slaves—were being exported in exchange for horses, fabrics, and metalware. All this changed when the Spanish Caribbean islands began to raise sugar on a large scale in the mid-17th century; to meet the insatiable demand for labor, slaves became Africa's most important export. Senegambia was profoundly affected. Bondage had existed there only as a semifeudal relationship, and slaves were rarely sold. But once slavery became commercially profitable, Senegambians built up an "inventory" by making enslavement the legal punishment for most crimes and by earmarking for export captives taken in warfare with their neighbors.

F. SHOBERL, *The World in Miniature*, 1817–2

NATIONAL MUSEET, COPENHAGEN; ELIOT ELISOFON

DR. & MRS. ERNST ANSPACH COLLECTION; WERNER FORMAN

The antelope headdresses of the Bambara people, above and below, were worn by masked young men in agricultural rites. They always appeared in pairs, representing male and female, in leaping dances on the newly sown fields. They memorialized Chi Wara, half man and half animal, who in myth had taught man how to cultivate. Bambara empire-building wars in the 1730's resulted in the export of many war captives, often by Malinke merchants. Figures such as the one at left were given to Malinke girls to carry in dances celebrating their coming of age. This one is decorated on the arms and head with precious cowry shells from the Indian Ocean, a form of currency used in many parts of Africa.

P. VERITE COLLECTION; ANDRE HELD

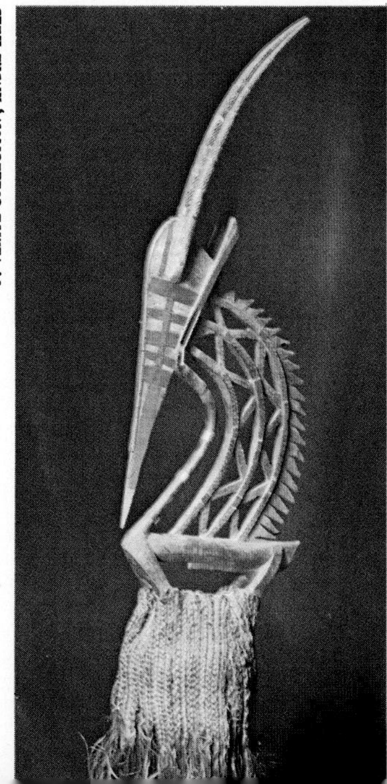

MR. & MRS. PAUL TISHMAN COLLECTION; MARC & EVELYNE BERNHEIM—RAPHO GUILLUMETTE

The helmet mask above belonged to the women's secret society of the Mende people, the only known instance in Africa of female masking. The crested hairdo and exaggerated high forehead were marks of beauty.

MUSEUM OF PRIMITIVE ART

MUSEUM OF PRIMITIVE ART; WERNER FORMAN

The tall Baga serpent spirit of the waters at left presided over initiation rituals. The streamlined mask above may have represented a water spirit of the coastal Grebo or Kru peoples, who were expert boatmen.

The Windward Coast

Religion was an all-pervasive force among the peoples of Africa, affecting, as the examples at left of sculpture from the societies of the Windward Coast reveal, all aspects of social, economic, and cultural life. Most Africans believed in a creator god who was worshiped directly by the individual, but who could be influenced only through the intercession of a pantheon of lesser, specialized deities. The goals of religious practices were increase and fertility. All material things, animate and inaminate, were believed to be imbued with spirits, and death or destruction did not extinguish their vital forces. Thus ancestors, recent or remote, remained influential in the affairs of the living through the activities of cults.

The role of ancestor cults varied. In monarchies they became virtually a state religion glorifying the legendary, heroic, semidivine origins of the ruling dynasty. Among the smaller societies, such as those of the Windward Coast, where life was regulated by men's secret societies, these cults stressed the continuance, unity, and order of the clan.

African art embodied all these ideas. The creator god was never portrayed, and only rarely were the lesser deities depicted, for the gods were considered too abstract for visualization. Rather, sculptures such as those shown here were expressionistic images of nature or ancestor spirits.

MR. & MRS. PAUL TISHMAN COLLECTION; MARC & EVELYNE BERNHEIM—RAPHO GUILLUMETTE

MUSEUM OF PRIMITIVE ART; LISA LITTLE

The Senufo "fire-spitter" mask above is a dynamic composite of animal features. Its visual complexity reflects its symbolic character; in ritual use it incarnated a spirit force capable of protecting the people from a variety of evils. The many-beaked Bobo bird mask at right was worn in ritual dances to promote agricultural fertility. Both these inland peoples were probably enslaved and exported by the Kru or the Ashanti.

The Gold Coast

The Ashanti people probably migrated in the 17th century to the area of present-day Ghana where they quickly subdued and organized the numerous small states of the area into a loose confederation. About 1700 Osei Tutu, who reigned in the principal state of Kumasi, summoned a council of all the rulers. The assembled throng witnessed the appearance of a Golden Stool, or throne, the repository of the nation's soul and symbolic of Osei Tutu's supreme authority as Asantehene, king of kings. At the same time, a civil and moral code of 77 laws was sanctified.

The Ashanti nation flourished, principally because of its valuable gold resources and its strong, well-organized military caste. All the gold, which symbolized royalty and the sun, belonged to the Asantehene, although it circulated as currency in the form of dust and nuggets. The provinces paid tribute, and the Asantehene also collected duties on trade. All the gold of deceased or disgraced persons reverted to his coffers, as did any dust or nuggets dropped during trading in the marketplace.

Gold had drawn merchants across the Sahara for centuries and it was of course the first attraction for European traders. Later a slave trade developed, supplied by tribute from vassal states and by prisoners of war. The Ashanti were generally content to allow the coastal Fanti people to act as their middlemen in the sale of these captives to the Europeans. T. E. Bowdich, an 1817 visitor, observed that the Ashanti did not engage in commerce "lest their genius for war . . . be enervated." They did trade for guns, however, which they were careful to prohibit being traded further so as to retain their military ascendancy over neighboring states.

Bowdich, among the first group of Europeans to visit Kumasi, witnessed the great annual festival celebrating the yam harvest. All the provincial rulers gathered for several days of religious ceremonies, festivities, and the promulgation of new laws. Above right is a detail from Bowdich's portrayal of the festival. The Asantehene (under the red umbrella) and his captains watch the dancing, served by attendants carrying gold regalia and elephant-tail fly whisks.

T.E. BOWDICH, *A Mission from Cape Coast Castle to Ashantee*, 1819

NELSON GALLERY—ATKINS MUSEUM

The stools crafted by the Ashanti were thought to be the habitations of their spirits, and those belonging to clan founders and kings were cherished as altars for ancestor cults. The royal Golden Stool was (and still is) kept in a sacred secret place and rarely seen. The example above, decorated in silver, belonged to the Asantehene Kofi Karikari, and the gold mask on the opposite page is from his treasury. It may be a depiction of the ruler of a conquered people.

ALL: TRUSTEES OF THE BRITISH MUSEUM EXCEPT AS SPECIFIED

Gold weights, made of brass, were used to measure the Ashanti gold-dust currency. The majority were probably cast in symbolic geometric shapes, but many others were figurative compositions, often illustrating proverbs. These weights, one to four inches tall, give a unique picture of daily life. Above left is a bent old man In the family group above right, the wife (right) grinds together cassava and yams.

MARGARET W. PLASS COLLECTION

Here (left to right) a man climbs a palm tree seeking its gourd, a source of palm wine; a successful hunter smoking a pipe returns from the bush with his prey slung over his shoulder (tobacco was introduced into Africa from the New World in the 16th century, that grown in Brazil being a particularly popular trade item); and a priest plays one of the tall Ashanti drums with bent drumsticks.

MARGARET W. PLASS COLLECTION

Below, a mounted warrior smokes his long pipe. Above left, a man sacrifices a cock to the sky god. A mother (center) carries both her child and a bowl. The lion (right) was a symbol of kingship. Literally as well as proverbially, "the weights of the king are heavier than those of a common man." The king paid expenses with weights heavier than standard, allowing his retainers to keep the change.

H. STORRER COLLECTION; WERNER FORMAN

MR. & MRS. PAUL TISHMAN COLLECTION; MARC & EVELYNE BERNHEIM—RAPHO GUILLUMETTE

The Fon of Dahomey

The Fon peoples of Dahomey began moving inland to the Abomey plateau around 1600, probably seeking to escape the instability brought on by the Dutch presence on the coast. By 1645 the Fon had founded a strong monarchy based on a concept of government, unique in Africa, that stressed the individual's responsibility to his king. This idea, open to all peoples, ran counter to traditional African theories of a feudal monarchy which considered the king as the "father" of his subjects and vassal states. Dahomey was a military state, and when it entered the slave trade, its war captives formed a ready source of supply. Guns traded for slaves further strengthened the might of its standing army. As the Fon kingdom expanded, rebellions broke out among its subject peoples, fomented by devotees of the indigenous gods. The revolts failed and whole cult groups were sold into slavery, the exiles carrying their gods with them to the West Indies, Brazil, and Louisiana.

Meanwhile, the nearby coastal kingdoms were being reshaped by the competition for European trade and by the Europeans' meddling in their political affairs. The kingdom of Ouidah tried unsuccessfully to monopolize the trade by building a free port, with separate mud-walled compounds for each foreign company engaged in trade. Ouidah's port, opposite, was drawn in 1725 by the captain of a French slaver.

By this time Dahomey was encroaching upon these coastal states. In the 1720's, King Agaja took advantage of their dynastic and internal squabbling and made them his vassals. There is evidence that Agaja sought to end the slave trade; certainly the business declined in these years. If this was his intention, it was not to be realized. Outraged by Agaja's repudiation of its traditional feudal relations to these states and threatened by his limitations on access to the sea trade, the powerful neighboring Oyo nation swept down on Dahomey. By 1730 Agaja, chastened by four years of devastating campaigns, was back in the slave trade.

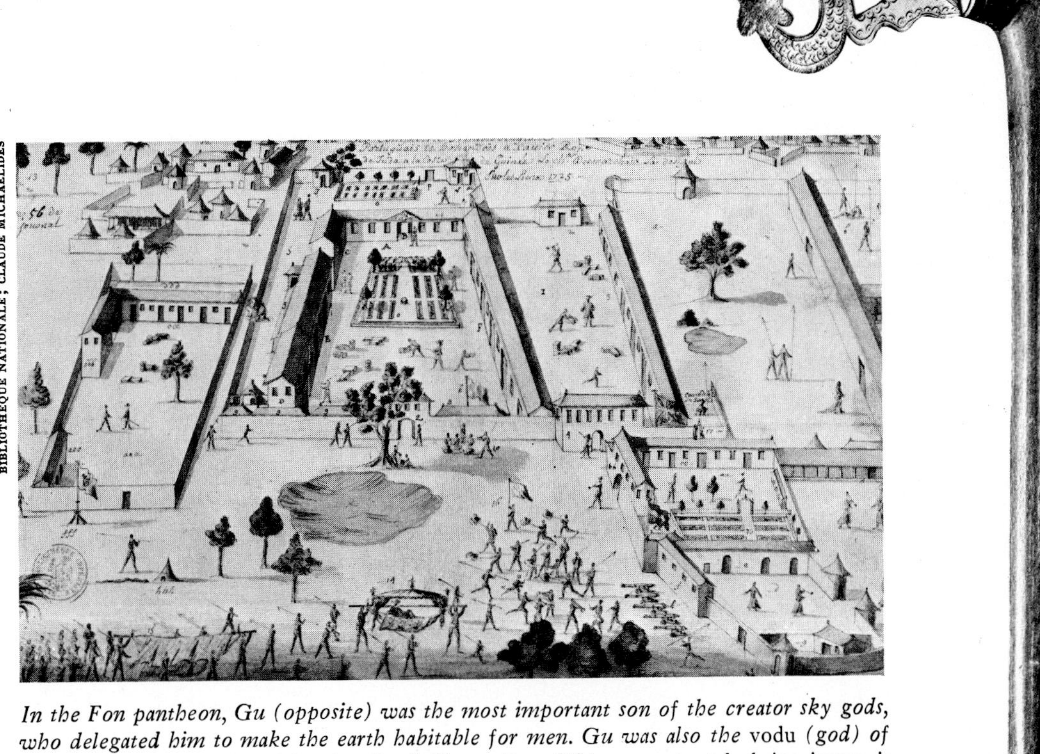

BIBLIOTHEQUE NATIONALE; CLAUDE MICHAELIDES

MUSEE DE L'HOMME

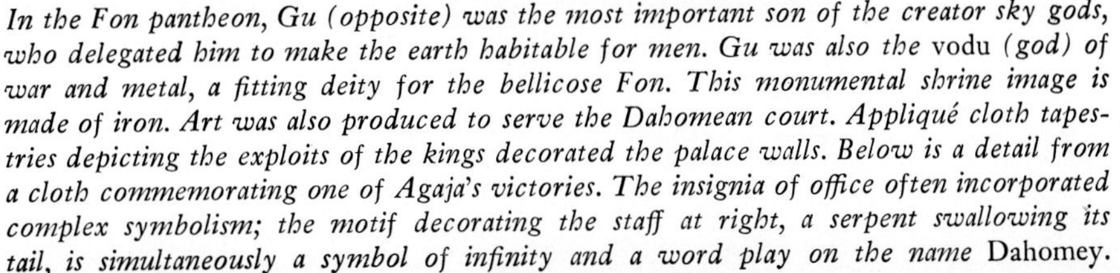

In the Fon pantheon, Gu (opposite) was the most important son of the creator sky gods, who delegated him to make the earth habitable for men. Gu was also the vodu *(god) of war and metal, a fitting deity for the bellicose Fon. This monumental shrine image is made of iron. Art was also produced to serve the Dahomean court. Appliqué cloth tapestries depicting the exploits of the kings decorated the palace walls. Below is a detail from a cloth commemorating one of Agaja's victories. The insignia of office often incorporated complex symbolism; the motif decorating the staff at right, a serpent swallowing its tail, is simultaneously a symbol of infinity and a word play on the name* Dahomey.

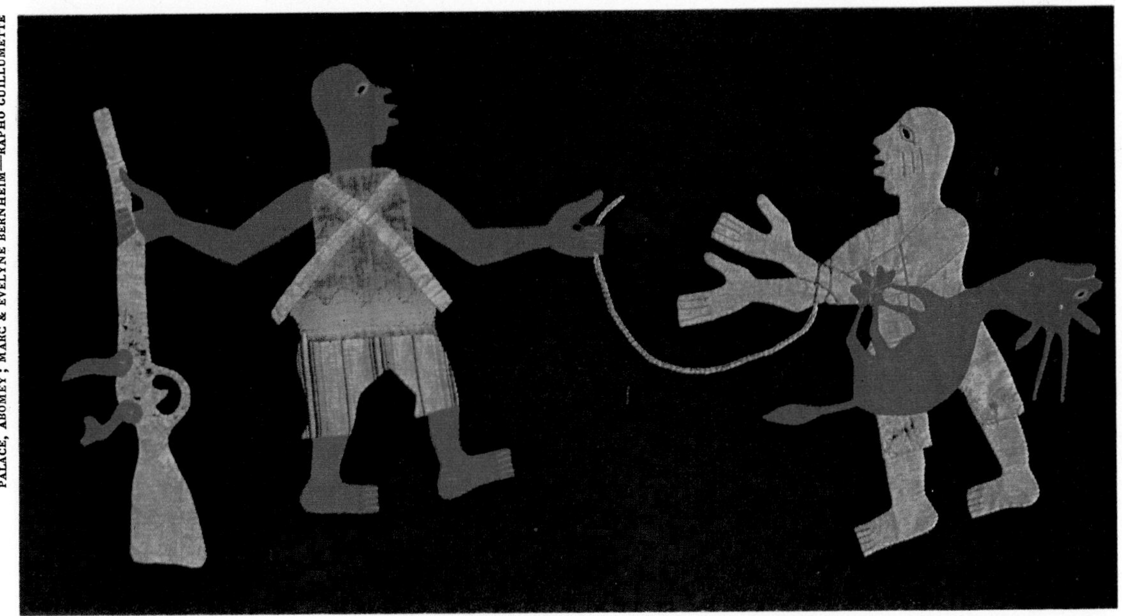

PALACE, ABOMEY; MARC & EVELYNE BERNHEIM—RAPHO GUILLUMETTE

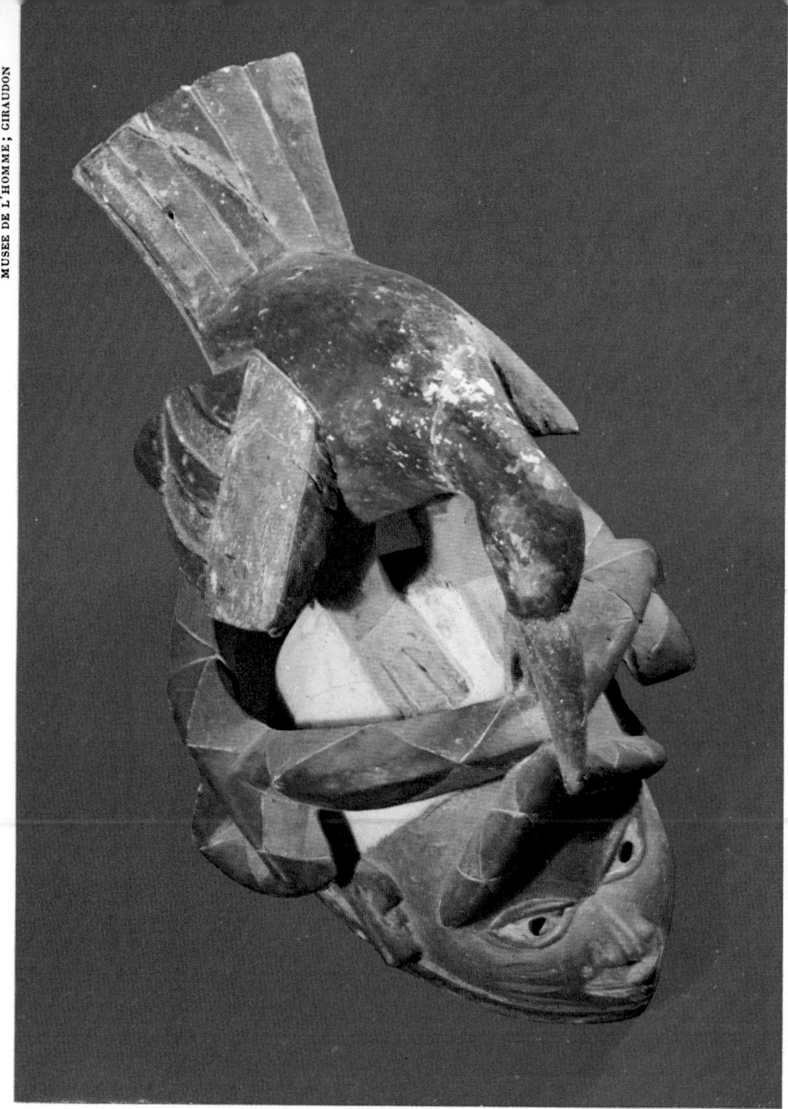

The Yoruba gelede *society was devoted to counteracting the evil work of witches. Some of its masks were used in sacred rituals held at night. Others, like the painted, figured one at left, were used the following day in secular plays, often humorous tales of human foibles.*

The Yoruba of Oyo

In legend, Oranmiyan, Prince of Ife, founded Oyo and its ruling line around 1200 after establishing a dynasty in Benin. In his person Oranmiyan symbolized the familial relationship of the Yoruba kings and the peoples of over 20 separate states. Although very junior in this "family," Oyo by 1700 dominated the lands from Dahomey to Benin. The Yoruba were markedly urban, and in their towns, trades and crafts—notably sculpture—flourished. Oyo's strengths were its stable, limited monarchy and its favorable position to trade for horses raised on the northern grasslands. The powerful Oyo cavalry was feared throughout the region. By the late 1600's Oyo was exporting many slaves through its vassels, Allada and Ouidah. When King Agaja of Dahomey menaced this trade, the Oyo cavalry overran Dahomey and made it tributary. Although Oyo was at its zenith for the rest of the 18th century, state policy was the subject of bitter debate between the leading commercial and military families. The commercial interests won out: the army was allowed to decline while trade, particularly in slaves, increased. (Oyo never imported firearms in quantity and seemed not to have grasped their significance.) In the slave trade were the seeds of ruin, and Oyo's collapse was swift. It was beset simultaneously by slave rebellions, revolts of subject territories, and attacks by neighboring states armed with guns. With the Oyo cavalry no longer a match for any enemy, the nation disintegrated; by 1850 even the once-thriving capital lay deserted.

DR. & MRS. ERNST ANSPACH COLLECTION; WERNER FORMAN

Oyo was the center of the cult of the legendary king Shango, a major deity in the Yoruba pantheon. He ruled thunder, lightning, and rain—and, consequently, fertility. The shrine figure of a mother and child at left represented Shango's power to cure barrenness. His devotees wore a headdress shaped like a double ax, symbolizing his thunderbolts. The mounted warrior above decorated an oshe shango, *a staff carried by worshipers when Shango "rode their heads." Below, a warrior in padded armor is carried on the shoulders of a retainer.*

DEPARTMENT OF ANTIQUITIES, NIGERIA; WERNER FORMAN

MUSEUM OF PRIMITIVE ART; LISA LITTLE

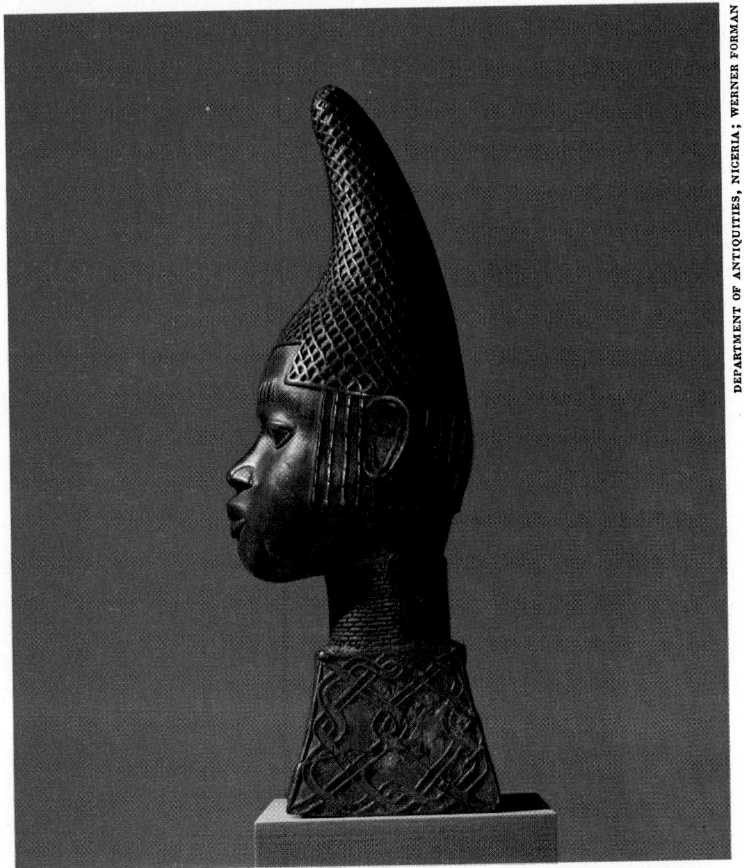

DEPARTMENT OF ANTIQUITIES, NIGERIA; WERNER FORMAN

Benin's artists were in the service of its semidivine rulers. Leopards, symbol of the oba, were kept at court and immortalized in bronze (left). Above is a queen mother wearing a headdress of precious coral beads.

The Empire of Benin

According to Benin's oral traditions, the Bini people asked the ruler of Ife to send one of his sons to them. About 1200 Prince Oranmiyan founded Benin's ruling line of obas, or kings. Six generations later the oba sent to Ife again for a smith to teach the use of brass to Benin's sculptors, so that they could cast memorial heads like the one above for the oba's ancestor altars. The semidivine oba devoted much of his time to ceremonies honoring his ancestors, and an analogous ancestor worship was observed in families and craft guilds.

Benin's history is one of steady expansion and the development of a strongly centralized government. Rulers of villages and provinces had to be initiated into the Palace Society before assuming power. Benin City had some 40 craft guilds, each with its highest-ranking members in the Palace Society.

Benin's most glorious era was the 15th and 16th centuries. It was known as "a time of much brass"—used in sculpture—obtained through trade. The Portuguese arrived in 1485 to offer diplomatic and trade relations as well as Christianity. The oba's response was measured; he placed strict controls on the European trade and very early decreed that no male Bini could be sold for export (although, as elsewhere, criminals and prisoners of war were "commercial items"). This measure limited commerce for a time, but many of Benin's provinces, seeing the chance for both profit and independence, entered the slave trade readily, exchanging captives for firearms. Thereafter, Benin's decline was inevitable.

MUSEUM FUR VOLKERKUNDE, BERLIN; WERNER FORMAN

The walls of the oba's palace—a city within a city—were of red clay, polished so that it shone like marble. The brass box above, representing a part of the palace, bears copper birds and a python that ornamented its wooden roof. The men may represent Portuguese musketeers who aided Benin's army on several campaigns.

THREE PLAQUES; TRUSTEES OF THE BRITISH MUSEUM; ANDRE HELD

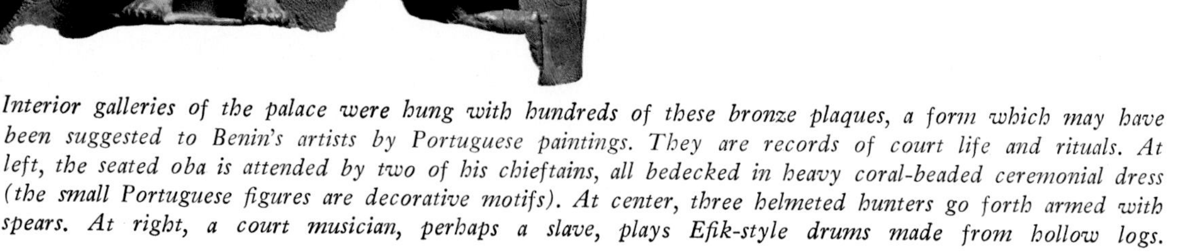

Interior galleries of the palace were hung with hundreds of these bronze plaques, a form which may have been suggested to Benin's artists by Portuguese paintings. They are records of court life and rituals. At left, the seated oba is attended by two of his chieftains, all bedecked in heavy coral-beaded ceremonial dress (the small Portuguese figures are decorative motifs). At center, three helmeted hunters go forth armed with spears. At right, a court musician, perhaps a slave, plays Efik-style drums made from hollow logs.

All ivory belonged to the oba; this pectoral mask was probably part of his regalia. The crest alternates Portuguese faces and mudfish, both associated with the god of the sea and wealth.

MUSEUM OF PRIMITIVE ART; LEE BOLTIN

AMERICAN MUSEUM OF NATURAL HISTORY

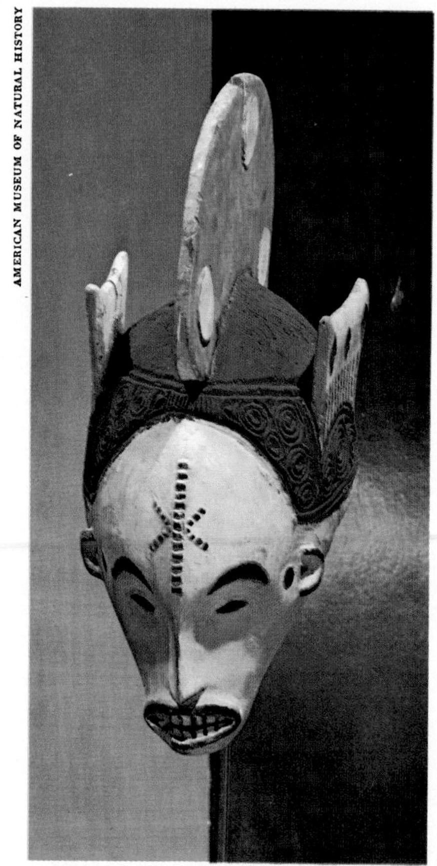

KATHERINE WHITE RESWICK COLLECTION; WERNER FORMAN

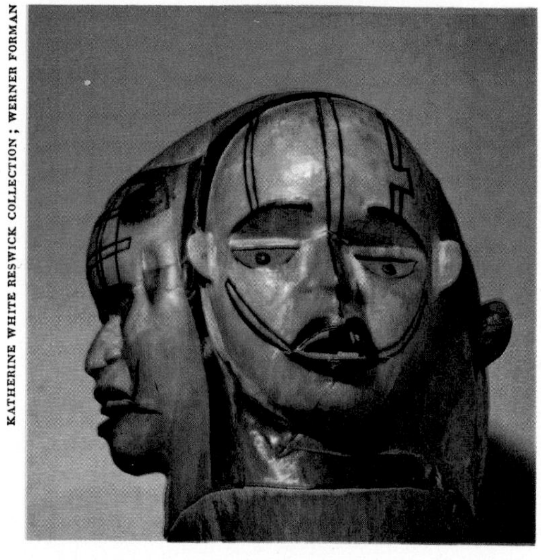

DEPARTMENT OF ANTIQUITIES, NIGERIA; WERNER FORMAN

The Ibo family group above is part of a terra-cotta altar dedicated to the spirit of the yam—the staple of life. The most important force among these peoples was the men's secret societies, such as the Ibo mmwo *and the Ekoi* ekpe. *Deriving their authority from ancestor spirits, they used their power to keep peace. The mask at upper left represented a female spirit in the* mmwo *ritual (white symbolized death). The Ekoi mask at left portrayed deceased society members.*

Bonny and Old Calabar

In contrast to the great kingdoms which rose nearby, the peoples of the Niger Delta formed small political groups. This reflected the fragmented character of the land itself, heavily forested and crisscrossed by river tributaries and lagoons. Traditionally linked to Benin, they were interrelated economically by the river trade and socially by their similar institutions.

The coastal city-states, particularly Old Calabar and Bonny, prospered in the slave trade. The Efik clan, whose name derived from the Ibibio word *oppress*, monopolized Old Calabar's trade, usually supplying upcountry peoples, bought or kidnaped, to the slavers. On one occasion, however, when trade rivalries were acute, one section of the town conspired to sell its neighbors.

The inland Ibo of Aro capitalized on their famous oracle of the god Chukwu. Aro's emissaries acted both as the oracle's spokesmen and as merchants, manipulating the power of the oracle to exact fines and payments in slaves to be "eaten by Chukwu." In reality, of course, these unfortunates filled the slave ships at Bonny.

These efficient river ports became a major center of the slave trade in its later years. So important was the trade to the local economy that the king of Bonny vigorously protested its abolition. "We think that this trade must go on," he insisted. "That also is the verdict of our oracle and the priests. They say that your country [Great Britain] however great, can never stop a trade ordained by God himself."

TRUSTEES OF THE BRITISH MUSEUM; HAMLYN PUBLISHING CO.

MR. & MRS. PAUL TISHMAN COLLECTION; MARC & EVELYNE BERNHEIM—RAPHO GUILLUMETTE

Two Ibibio clans, the Efik and Oron, lived in the Cross River area. The Efik of Old Calabar kept order among freemen and slaves through the ekpe *society; at left is a ritual skin-covered headdress. The Oron people made dignified bearded figures, like that above, for their ancestors' graves.*

The Kingdom of Kongo

The first Portuguese mission to Kongo, in 1485, found a well-established state. Its ruler, the Mani Kongo, welcomed their missionaries, diplomats, and merchants, and his successor, Mvemba Nzinga, was converted to Christianity and baptized Affonso I. Affonso was a believer in the benefits to be derived from European ways. He corresponded with his "royal brother," the king of Portugal, requesting priests, teachers, and doctors. Paid in slaves, they quickly became traders. By 1526 Affonso was writing to his royal brother: ". . . we cannot reckon how great the damage is, since the . . . merchants are taking every day our natives, sons of the land. . . . So great, Sir, is the corruption and licentiousness that our country is being completely depopulated. . . . It is *our will that in these kingdoms there should not be any trade of slaves nor outlet for them.*"

But the trade did not stop; it was too profitable. By the 1530's most slaves were drawn from beyond the Kongo kingdom—Teke from the north, Mbundu from the south. This led to border tensions and raids, and these, combined with Portuguese intrigues, so weakened Kongo that it could offer little resistance when, in 1568, the warlike Yaka swept through the country. The Portuguese, alarmed by the chaos they themselves had engendered and attracted by rumors of silver mines, turned their attention to the south.

RIJKSMUSEUM VOOR VOLKENKUNDE, LEIDEN; ANDRE HELD

DR. & MRS. ERNST ANSPACH COLLECTION

Stone grave guardians like the one at left commemorated Kongo kings and chiefs and symbolized the continuity of government. They were said to be "thinking of the welfare of the people." The Kongo-made cast brass crucifix above dates from the Portuguese era. Even after their meaning had been forgotten, such crosses were carried by chiefs as power emblems.

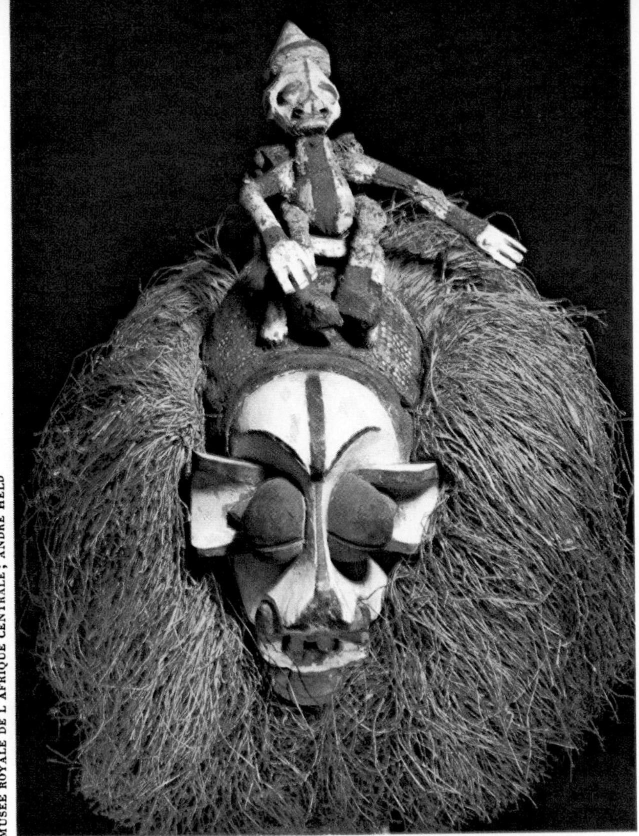

MUSEE ROYALE DE L'AFRIQUE CENTRALE; ANDRE HELD

The fierce aspect of the Yaka mask at left suggests the terror they inspired. Such masks, surmounted by legendary characters, were worn by young men during celebrations of their initiation into status as adults.

CHARLES RATTON COLLECTION; ANDRE HELD

MUSEE DE L'HOMME; CLAUDE MICHAELIDES

The Kota effigy above is a mbulungulu, *which guarded ancestral relics and protected their vital force. The Kota people lived north of the Teke and may have obtained the copper and brass used to plate these images through the network of Kongo trade routes—in exchange for bondsmen.*

The Teke worshiped nature spirits and the shades of the recently dead. The mysterious, highly abstract face mask at left is a rare Teke spirit mask; its meaning and use are not known. The Teke furnished the Kongo with copper and ivory for trade with the Portuguese before slaves surpassed these items in value.

ISBRANDTSEN COLLECTION, ON LOAN TO THE SOUTH STREET MUSEUM

"Traffick in Men"

I must own . . . that I was first kidnaped and betrayed by [those of] my own complexion, who were the first cause of my exile and slavery," wrote an ex-slave in 1787. "But if there were no buyers, there would be no sellers." The earliest buyers were the Portuguese, but by 1600 the Dutch, French, and English also realized the profits in "man-stealing." They were soon followed by the Prussians, Danes, Swedes, and Genoese. Never was there more than a handful of Europeans in the trading stations. Business was conducted directly at the major ports or through the "trust trade"—giving local merchants goods to barter inland for slaves. For the Europeans it was a killing business; only one out of two survived the climate and local diseases. Living arrangements were ramshackle: a warehouse on a malarial river island, as above, or a rotting ship anchored in an estuary. Only on the Gold Coast did the kings lease land for a few of the traders' "castles" which, in European imaginations, rimmed the African shores. The local king dictated the rules of trade and filled a slave ship in his own good time. The Europeans' power lay in the insidious luxuries which became necessities: liquor and firearms. In 1723 New England merchants, lately come to the trade, introduced rum to Africa; soon it was more popular than French brandy or English gin. "The kings of Africa," commented a Swedish observer, "incited by the merchandise shown them, which consists principally of strong liquors, give orders to . . . attack their own villages at night."

MR. & MRS. JOHN FRIEDE COLLECTION; WERNER FORMAN

The pig-tailed European trader above right, an 18th-century ivory from Kongo, proffers a "dash" of liquor. Below is a slave coffle en route to a coastal slave market. The captives were beset by terrors of the unknown. "I was . . . persuaded," one said, "that I had got into a world of bad spirits . . . I asked the others if we were not to be eaten by those white men with horrible looks, red faces, and long hair. . . ."

BUELL, *Heroes of the Dark Continent*, 1890

MUSEE DES BEAUX ARTS, NANTES

The slave brig Marie Séraphique *rides at anchor off Haiti in 1773, as planters inspect her cargo. This delicate rococo painting commemorated a successful passage from Angola. Its mood is sharply at variance with the grimmer realities evident in the deck-packing plan opposite, which illustrated a 1792 report on the slave trade.*

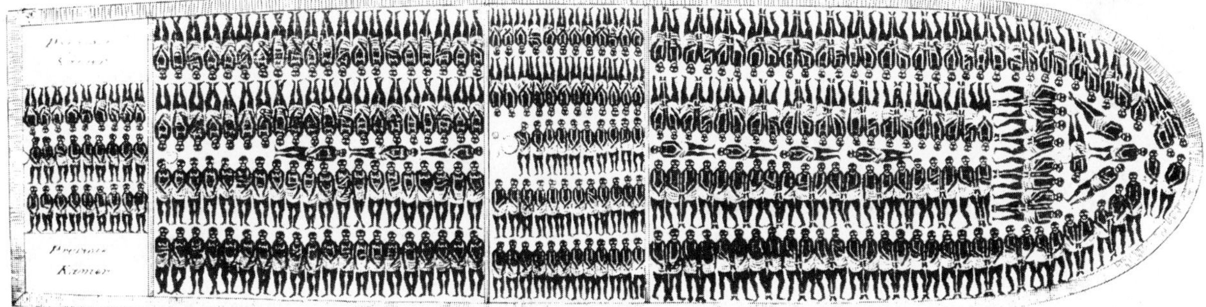

Abstract of Evidence on . . . Slave Trade, 1792

"*These Valuable People*"

There is no buying slaves here [the Gold Coast] without you give two ounces of gold on each . . . and you may think yourself happy to get [them] even at that rate," wrote a trader in 1772. The going price in another port for "these valuable people" was 115 gallons of rum for a healthy man, 95 for a woman. Market preferences varied; some peoples were esteemed as house servants, others as field workers. The Ibo were considered melancholy and suicidal in slavery, the Ashanti rebellious. The French favored Dahomeans; the Spanish, Yoruba; the English, the Gold Coast peoples. The Portuguese concentrated on the peoples farther south. The Portuguese at least did not deny that Africans had souls; their unique rationalization for slavery was "redemption" in a Christian land, and the ports of the Congo and Angola witnessed mass baptisms of human cargoes before shipment.

The terror and dehumanization of the Middle Passage exceeded even that of the slave markets. This second leg of the triangular trade generally took two or three months—longer of course from East Africa. In the West Indies, the cargoes were either sold or disembarked for "seasoning"—acclimatization—before being sent on to North or South America. Statistics on the slave trade before 1700 are scanty at best, and incomplete for the 18th century. Conservative estimates on the number of Africans sold range from 10 to 20 million; the mortality on the Middle Passage may have averaged 20 to 30 per cent. This varied considerably depending on the length of the voyage, and was aggravated by the fact that the cargoes tended to rebel or commit suicide if allowed topside. The obvious solution was to confine them below, on decks about five feet high, layered "in two rows, one above the other like books on a shelf" and packed, one trader said, as close as spoons fitting together.

"The stench of the hold while we were on the coast was intolerably loathsome," an ex-slave recalled. "But now that the whole ship's cargo were confined there together it became absolutely pestilential. The closeness of the place and the heat of the climate, added to the number in the ship, was . . . aggravated by the galling of the chains . . . and the filth of the necessary tubs, into which the children often fell. . . ." "They had not so much room as a man in his coffin," according to testimony taken from a ship's surgeon. "He has known them to go down apparently in good health at night and be found dead in the morning . . . and therefore concludes [they] died of suffocation." Another surgeon complained of the difficulty of treating the captives below decks because of air so foul and heat "so excessive . . . that a candle would not burn."

"The sights I witnessed may I never look on such again," wrote the captain of a slaver after his first voyage. "This is a dreadful trade." Yet such were the profits to be earned on the Middle Passage that he remained in the trade for more than 20 years.

2

The Colonial World

Great Britain's American colonies were settled chiefly by Englishmen at first, with a leavening of Germans, Scots, Scotch-Irish, Dutch, French, Swedes, Finns, Portuguese, and a scattering of other nationalities. These people brought with them cultures that varied somewhat according to the nationality, social status, intelligence, and taste of the individual, but which were all easily identifiable as European. Of course they never lost this heritage entirely, but they—and certainly their descendants—became something quite different from their brothers who remained in the Old World. They became what we call "Americans."

An American Civilization

The subtle but profound alteration that occurred when Europeans moved to the New World was hardly self-willed. Most of the settlers came, it is true, hoping for circumstances different from those they left behind—for a more bountiful existence, but sometimes also for nonmaterialistic reasons, such as the opportunity to practice a religion barred to them at home. But even the poorest and the most rebellious seldom intended to develop a new civilization; rather they wished to reconstruct the old on terms more favorable to themselves. Nor did the "American" type result from the selection of particular kinds of Europeans as colonizers. The typical settler was young and unmarried, but persons from every walk of life entered the emigrating stream and probably in rough proportion to their numbers in Europe if we exclude the highest social strata. Certainly there was no selection of the finest grain to provide seed for cultivating the wilderness.

When then did America become something more than another Europe? Why, for example, was New England not merely a new England? The chief reason is that their physical surroundings transformed the people. America was isolated from Europe by 3,000 miles of ocean. The Atlantic served as an umbilical cord but also as a barrier; it was practically closed to commerce during the wild winter months and dangerous enough in any season. Men did not undertake an ocean voyage lightly in colonial times, and few who made the westward crossing ever thought seriously of returning. Indeed, the modern mind can scarcely grasp the awful isolation that enveloped the settler, the sense of being alone, of having cut all ties with home and past. One had to face forward (westward) and construct a new life, or perish—if not of hunger, then of loneliness. One may see in these circumstances the roots of the Americans' celebrated self-reliance and individualism, but they serve equally well to explain some of the less attractive elements of the national character. Throughout the early years, men habitually carried weapons during every waking hour. They became inured to violence, to settling disagreements directly and by force, to seizing the main chance, to thrusting aside anything and anyone who stood in their way.

The emptiness of the continent also changed the colonists. In Europe land was scarce and labor plentiful. In America conditions were exactly the opposite; if every settler—or rather, every *white* settler—did not own land, he had at least a reasonable expectation of owning some. This could not help affecting his point of view: the mentality of the peasant and of the sturdy beggar were equally out of place. The settlers managed their own affairs because they were on their own. They were free in the sense of being uninhibited; no effective power fettered them. They were largely self-governing not because they were too proud to submit to dictation but because the mother country was too far away to govern them. Each colonist, at least in the early days, was his own landlord, businessman, artisan, and explorer, not because of any inherent versatility but because his primitive world did not permit much specialization. By the time a more complicated society had evolved, the new pattern of thinking—an American pattern—was well established.

The rich resources of America, its fertile soil and the abundance of fish and game, supplied settlers, after a brief period of "seasoning," with unlimited amounts of food. Men might be poor, but few ever went hungry. Children were easy to support and, in a land always short of labor, seldom unwanted. Within a few generations keen observers were noticing that Americans were generally bigger than their European cousins, and there can be little doubt that the plenitude of calories and proteins affected the colonists not only physically but psychologically as well.

Even the shape of the New World affected the colonists' lives; geography wielded a considerable influence, largely negative, on early American history. In a civilized land men overcome physical obstacles. They bridge streams, irrigate deserts, drain swamps, carve roads through forests and over mountains. Eventually, Americans did all these things on a scale undreamed of in Europe, but in the formative years such tasks were beyond their resources. They had to adjust to the contours of their new home before they could grow strong enough to alter them.

Geography made itself felt both in the general shape of the continent and in its impact on local regions. The Appalachian range is not particularly impressive as mountains go, but it affected formidably the life that evolved along its eastern slopes. Its grandest manifestation can be seen in the difference between French and English colonists in America. The French funneled through the St. Lawrence Valley behind the mountains and into the heart of the continent. While some became farmers, many others followed the rich fur trade over thousands of miles, became creatures of the woods, lived (and thought) more like Indians than Europeans. The English were blocked off from easy penetration inland in most areas and had to settle down to farming.

Within British America the effect of the Appalachians varied according to the region. In Virginia the mountains are set well back from the sea; the rivers flow gently to the Atlantic. Navigable far inland, they became the roads of the tobacco colonies. Farms sprang up in Maryland and Virginia along the banks of rivers. Merchant vessels from Europe delivered European products to the individual farmer at his own wharf and took away his produce in exchange. There were few seaports because seaports were not needed as depots and centers of commerce. Civilization fanned out thinly along every navigable tributary; life was rural. "Southern hospitality," the slowness of the region to develop a school system, the scarcity of artisans—factors as disparate as these can be explained in large part in geographical terms.

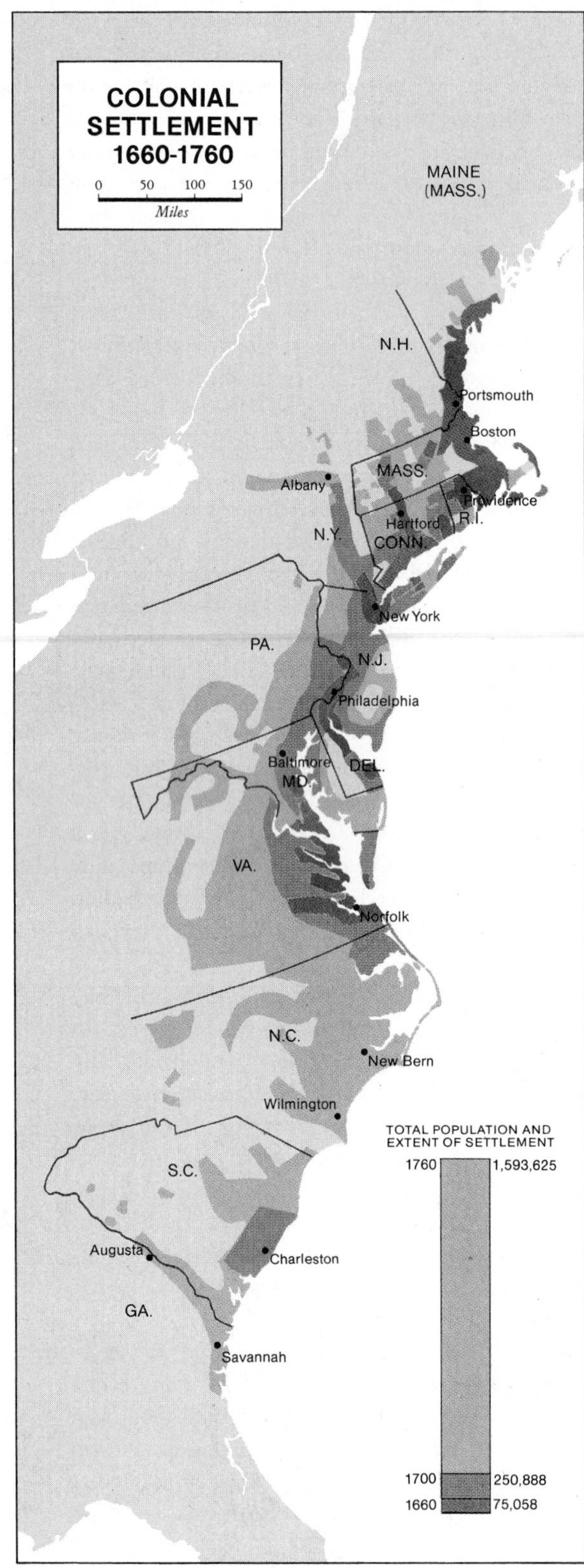

In the northern regions no such network of navigable streams existed. Seacoast towns grew up where sheltered harbors provided space for the loading and unloading of ships. To reach them the inland settlers had to build roads, and since roads were expensive, settlement tended to be compact. Village centers quickly dotted the farmlands, and village life differed profoundly from life in the south. That southerners had no inherent dislike of urban ways was proved as soon as settlement spread upstream beyond the limits of navigation. Towns like Richmond (on the James), Fredericksburg (on the Rappahannock), and Wilmington (on the Cape Fear, in North Carolina) all mark points where ocean-going ships must stop or run aground. They were founded to serve as centers of trade for farmers farther inland.

Local situations best understood in geographical terms are numberless. The sand bars and flats that block so much of the North Carolina coast explain the poverty of the region and its dependence upon Virginia. The Hudson-Mohawk Valley, allowing easy access to the interior, made possible the extensive fur trade of New York. Everywhere rapids and waterfalls accounted for the location of grist and lumber mills. Of course religious differences, the quirks of individual leaders, pure chance, and many other factors influenced regional patterns; but geography was very important, especially in the vital early years.

Southern Land and Labor

Two basic patterns of life sprang up in British America, and again the division between them was geographic. Maryland, Virginia, the Carolinas, and Georgia followed one path. Pennsylvania and those colonies to the north followed another. Let us look first at the southern group.

Agriculture was the bulwark of southern life; the tragic experiences of the Jamestown settlers revealed this quickly enough. Jamestown also suggested that a colony could not succeed unless its inhabitants were allowed to own their own land. The first colonists, it will be recalled, were employees of the London Company who had agreed to work for seven years in return for a share of the profits. Of course when their contracts expired there were no profits. To satisfy these settlers and attract new capital, the company declared a "dividend" of land, its only asset. The 350 surviving colonists each received 50 acres. Thereafter, as prospects continued poor, the company relied more and more on grants of land to attract both capital and labor. A number of wealthy Englishmen were given immense tracts, some running to several hundred thousand acres. Lesser men willing to settle in Virginia received more modest grants. Whether dangled before a great tycoon, a country squire, or a poor farmer displaced by the enclosure movement, the offer of land had the effect of encouraging migration to the colony. This was a much-desired end, for without the labor to develop it the land was worthless.

Soon what was known as the "headright" system became firmly entrenched in Virginia, and when the Crown took over in 1624 the system was not disturbed. Behind it lay the eminently sound principle that land should be parceled out according to the availability of labor to cultivate it. For each "head" entering the colony a grant of land, usually 50 acres, was to be made. The headright was not a deed but rather a license authorizing the holder to take any 50 acres not yet occupied by another. To "seat" his claim and receive title to the property, he had to mark out its boundaries, plant a crop, and construct some sort of habitation upon it. This system was effective, and it was adopted in all the southern colonies and in Pennsylvania and New Jersey as well.

The first headrights were issued with no strings attached, but generally the grantor demanded a small annual payment called a quitrent. A quitrent was not a rent at all, for the man who paid it was not a tenant. It was a tax, perhaps a shilling for 50 acres, which provided a means by which great proprietors could derive incomes from their colonies. By the middle of the 18th century the Calvert family, for example, was collecting over £4,000 a year in Maryland from this source. A quitrent differed from a modern tax in that it bore little relation to the value of the property and was not assessed to pay for public services. Manorial in origin, it was a tribute paid in recognition of the "sovereignty" of the grantor, a commutation of feudal obligations that had never really existed in America. Qutirents were therefore much resented in the colonies and always hard to collect.

The headright system encouraged landless Europeans to migrate to America. More often than not, however, those most eager to come could not afford passage across the Atlantic. In order to bring together those with money who sought land and labor and those without funds who wanted to go to America, the indentured servant system was developed. An indentured servant resembled an apprentice. In return for his passage he agreed to work for a stated period, usually about five years. During that time he was subject to strict control by his master and received no compensation beyond his keep. Although legally he contracted with his employer as an equal, his actual position was not unlike that of a child: he lacked full political and civil rights, and his master could administer physical punishment and control his movements much as a father manages a son.

After the servant completed his years of labor, he became a free man. Usually he was entitled to an "outfit" (a suit of clothes, some farm tools, seed, and perhaps a gun) that would enable him to take up farming on his own. Custom varied from colony to colony and according to the bargain struck by the two parties when the indenture was signed. In the Carolinas and in Pennsylvania, for example, servants received small grants of land from the colony when their service was completed.

Headrights issued when indentured servants entered the colonies went to whoever paid their passage, not to the servants. Thus the system gave a double reward to the man with capital—land and labor for the price of the labor alone. Nevertheless, most servants became landowners before many years had passed. Either they continued to work for wages until they had saved enough to buy land, or they became "squatters" on land along the fringes of settlement that no one had yet claimed. Squatting often made for trouble, because eventually someone was sure to ı up with a legal title to the squatter's prop-. Squatters then demanded what they called atters' rights," the privilege of buying the from the legal owner without paying for mprovements they had made upon it. This to arguments, lawsuits, and sometimes to olence. Whatever the outcome, even the most owly were almost always able to scratch a livelihood from some patch of ground. A dispossessed squatter could push a little farther west and begin the whole process again.

About the time that the earliest indentured servants appeared, African Negroes were also brought into America. The first blacks arrived on a Dutch ship and were sold at Jamestown in 1619. Early records are vague and incomplete, so it is not possible to say whether these men were treated as chattel slaves or freed after a period of years like indentured servants. What is certain is that by about 1640 *some* Virginia Negroes were slaves (a few, with equal certainty, were freemen), and that by the 1660's local statutes had firmly established the institution in Virginia.

Whether slavery produced race prejudice in America or prejudice slavery is a hotly debated, important, and difficult-to-answer question. Most 17th-century Englishmen were prejudiced against Africans; the usual reasons that led Europeans to look down on "heathens" with customs other than their own were in the case of Negroes greatly reinforced by their blackness, which the English equated with dirt, the Devil, danger, and death. "Black is the Colour of Night, Frightful, Dark and Horrid," a popular disquisition of 1704 proclaimed. That Africa was also the habitat of the great apes suggested, furthermore, that black men were somehow related to these human-appearing creatures, and thus inherently bestial and inferior. Yet Englishmen also knew that the Portuguese and Spaniards had enslaved blacks—*negro* is a Spanish word, identical in meaning with "black"; that Englishmen adopted it as a name for Africans suggests that their treatment of Africans in the New World may also have derived from the Spanish.

Probably the Africans' blackness lay at the root of the tragedy, but Winthrop D. Jordan,

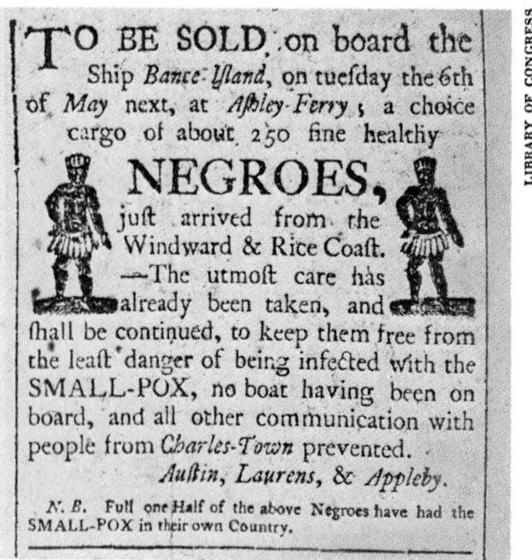

TO BE SOLD, on board the Ship *Bance-Yland*, on tuesday the 6th of *May* next, at *Ashley-Ferry*; a choice cargo of about 250 fine healthy

NEGROES,

just arrived from the Windward & Rice Coast. —The utmost care has already been taken, and shall be continued, to keep them free from the least danger of being infected with the SMALL-POX, no boat having been on board, and all other communication with people from *Charles-Town* prevented.

Austin, Laurens, & Appleby.

N. B. Full one Half of the above Negroes have had the SMALL-POX in their own Country.

This notice of an impending slave auction appeared in a Charleston newspaper in 1763. The danger of smallpox infection was very real; slavers such as this from the West Indies often carried the disease.

whose researches have added enormously to our understanding of the question, properly stresses the process by which prejudice and existing enslavement interacted with each other as both cause and effect, leading to the total debasement of the African.

> The concept of Negro slavery [in the tobacco colonies] . . . was neither borrowed from foreigners, nor extracted from books, nor invented out of whole cloth, nor extrapolated from servitude, nor generated by English reaction to Negroes as such, nor necessitated by the exigencies of the New World. Not any one of these made the Negro a slave, *but all.*

In any case, Negro slavery took root throughout English America, even in Massachusetts Bay where there was no economic need for it. The Massachusetts Body of Liberties of 1641—strange title—provided that "there shall never be any bond-slavery . . . amongst us; unlesse it be lawful captives taken in just warrs [*i.e.,* Indians] and such strangers as willingly sell themselves, or *are solde* to us." However, relatively few Negroes were imported until late in the 17th century, even in the southern colonies. White servants were much more highly prized. The African, after all, was utterly alien to both the European and the American way of life. In a country starved for capital, the cost of slaves—roughly five times that of servants—was another disadvantage. So long as white servants could be had in sufficient numbers there were few slaves in British America.

Agriculture in the South

Land and labor made agriculture possible, but it was also necessary to find a market for American crops in the Old World if the colonists were to enjoy anything but the crudest sort of existence. They could not begin to manufacture all the articles they required; to obtain from England such items as plows and muskets and books and chinaware, they had to have something to offer in exchange. Fortune favored the southern colonies in this search for a cash crop.

The founders of Virginia tried to produce all sorts of things that were needed in the old country: grapes and silk in particular, but also indigo, cotton, oranges, olives, sugar, and many other plants. But it was tobacco, unwanted, even strongly opposed at first, that became Virginia's great staple.

Tobacco was unknown in Europe until Spanish explorers brought it back from the West Indies, nor was it widely smoked in England until the time of Sir Walter Raleigh, when it quickly proved irresistible to thousands of devotees. However, since it clearly contained some habit-forming drug, many people were opposed to its use. At first the London Company discouraged the colonists from growing it, and King James I wrote a pamphlet attacking the weed in which, among other things, he anticipated modern cancer researchers by saying that smoking was a "vile and stinking" habit "dangerous to the Lungs." When English smokers and partakers of snuff ignored their king, the Virginia colonists ignored their company. In 1617 a pound of tobacco was worth more than five shillings in London. Company and Crown then changed their tune, granting the colonists a monopoly and encouraging them in every way. Little wonder that production in America leaped from 2,500 pounds in 1616 to 500,000 in 1627, and to nearly 30 million a year in the late 17th century. By the 1770's it exceeded 100 million pounds.

Of course such a tremendous expansion of the supply caused the price to plummet. By the middle of the 17th century the English market was glutted, and the colonists were seeking desperately to curb production. Their efforts failed because of intercolonial rivalry. For example, when Virginia limited the number of plants a farmer could set out, Maryland producers would not go along. This was perhaps the first illustration of a paradox of American politics. Despite wide belief in states' rights, local regulation of the economy in a free national market has always been very difficult.

The low price of tobacco in the last decades of the 17th century did not stop the growth of the tobacco colonies, but it did alter the structure of their society. Small farmers found it more difficult to make a decent living. At the same time a number of favored individuals were accumulating large tracts of land by grant and purchase. If well managed, a big plantation gave its owner important competitive advantages over the small farmer. For example, tobacco was notorious for the speed with which it destroyed the fertility of the soil—the man with large holdings could shift frequently to new fields and thus maintain a high yield. Nevertheless, while no exact statistics exist, it is probably true that throughout the 17th and 18th centuries small farmers controlling no more than four or five slaves or servants raised well over half the tobacco crop of Virginia and Maryland.

In South Carolina, after a few decades in which furs and cereals were the chief products, Madagascar rice was introduced into the low-lying coastal areas in 1696 and quickly proved its worth as a cash crop. By 1700 almost 100,000 pounds were being exported annually; by the eve of the Revolution rice exports from South Carolina and Georgia exceeded 65 million pounds a year. Rice culture required great supplies of water for flooding of fields. At first freshwater swamps were adapted to the crop, but by the middle of the 18th century the chief rice fields lay along the tidal rivers and inlets. A series of dikes and floodgates allowed fresh water to pour across the fields with the rising tide; when the tide fell, the gates closed automatically to keep

the water in. The process was reversed when it was necessary to drain the land. Then the water ran out as the tide ebbed, and the pressure of the next flood pushed the gates shut.

In the 1740's a second successful cash crop, indigo, was introduced in South Carolina. Indigo was especially welcomed in the region because it did not compete either for land or labor with rice. It prospered on high ground and needed care in seasons when the slaves were not busy in the rice paddies. The British, too, were delighted with indigo, because the blue dye was important in their woolens industry. Parliament quickly placed a bounty on it to stimulate production.

The production of tobacco, rice, and indigo, along with furs and forest products like tar and resin, meant that the southern colonies had no difficulty in obtaining manufactured articles from abroad. Since their goods were highly prized in Europe, merchants eagerly sought them out. The early tobacco planter, for example, could count on English ships coming right to his riverside wharf to pick up his crop and to deliver farm tools, fine cloth, indentured servants, or whatever else he needed. Later, as the economy expanded, the planters dealt with agents in England, called factors, who managed the sale of their crops, filled their orders for manufactures, and supplied them with credit.

This was a great convenience but not necessarily an advantage, for it made the colonists dependent upon European middlemen, who naturally exacted a price for their services. It also tended to prevent the development of a diversified economy. Throughout the colonial era, while small-scale manufacturing was flourishing in the north, it was stillborn in the south. Crude craft work was done on the plantations by slave carpenters, blacksmiths, and the like, but almost nothing was produced for sale, and little high-quality craftsmanship could be found. It was too easy to rely on England for fine goods. Even in the decade before the Revolution it was not unheard of for a Virginia planter to send a fine piece of silk—itself an import of course—all the way to London to be dyed because it had become soiled. There were some local businesses such as iron-mining, flour-milling, lumbering, and barrelmaking (the largest southern craft). But according to Carl Bridenbaugh's study, *The Colonial Craftsman,* even Charleston, a thriving community of 12,000, "did not nourish an outstanding craft or produce a single eminent

These scenes decorated colonial maps made in the 1770's. At left is a South Carolina indigo plantation, showing the method of extracting the dye. At the right, a lordly tobacco planter ships his crop.

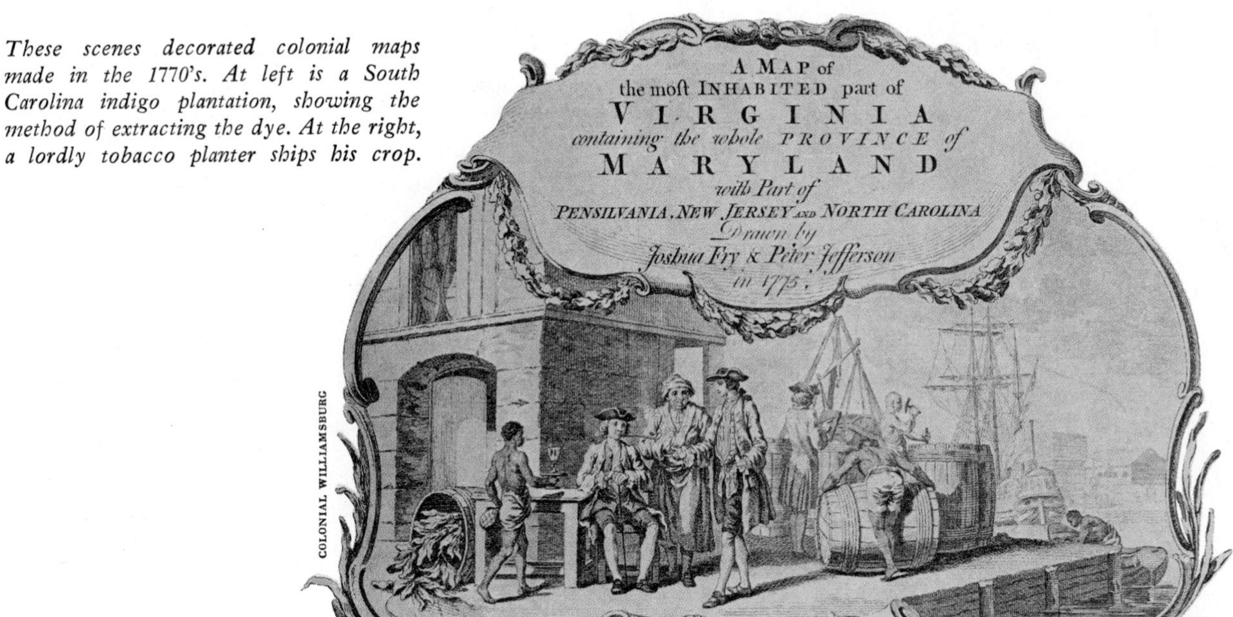

COLONIAL WILLIAMSBURG

workman before the Revolution." Despite its rich export trade, its fine harbor, and the easy availability of excellent lumber, Charleston's shipbuilding industry never remotely rivaled that of northern ports. The city was typical of the whole south in this respect.

Southern society was agricultural and therefore rural; Charleston was the only city of importance in the region, and even in Charleston the dominant elements were rice planters who maintained town houses in order to escape the unhealthy conditions of their swampy domains in summer. Still, there were widely varying patterns of existence in the south. The gap between the North Carolina tobacco farmer struggling to make a living on a few sandy acres and the South Carolina master of a great rice plantation along the Cooper or the Edisto was formidable. Small farmers made up the majority, especially along the westward-moving edge of settlement. But the planters, with their slaves, Georgian mansions, and broad acres, set the tone of society and provided political leadership.

By 1700 slavery had become firmly established in the south. Declining prices in the tobacco colonies combined with the opening up of rich lands in Pennsylvania to reduce the attractiveness of the region to indentured servants. Yet tobacco cultivation required a great deal of labor. Its tiny seeds—10,000 in a teaspoonful—were sown in special beds, and after sprouting, each little plant was moved to the fields. Constant weeding was essential. During the growing period, shoots ("suckers") had to be removed and the top bud clipped off at the critical moment or the plant would become a tall and spindly "Frenchman" instead of a rich, broad-leaved specimen. When the supply of servants dwindled, the planters turned to Negro slaves, more readily available after the formation of the Royal African Company in 1672, and this accelerated the trend toward large-scale agriculture.

On the South Carolina rice plantations slave labor predominated from the beginning, for free men would not submit to its backbreaking and unhealthy regimen. Thus, the first quarter of the 18th century saw an enormous influx of Africans. By 1730 about 30 per cent of the population south of Pennsylvania was black, and in some districts the concentration was far higher.

Given the existing race prejudice and the degrading impact of slavery, this demographic change had an enormous effect on southern life, all the more drastic because it occurred without plan and with little understanding of its significance on the part of the whites. In each colony regulations governing the behavior of Negroes both slave and free were gradually worked out. These increased in severity as one moved southward, that is, as the density of the black population increased. Negroes, of course, had no civil rights under these codes, and punishments for violating them were sickeningly severe. Whipping—the Biblical 39 stripes—was common for minor offenses, death by hanging or even by being burned alive for serious crimes. Negroes were sometimes castrated for sexual offenses—even for lewd talk about white women—or for repeated attempts to escape.

That the blacks resented slavery goes without saying. Organized slave rebellions were very rare, and while individual assaults by blacks on members of the master race were common enough, it must be remembered that personal violence was also common among whites all through American history. But the masters had sound reasons for fearing their slaves; the particular viciousness of the system lay in the fact that oppression bred resentment, which in turn produced still greater oppression.

What is superficially astonishing is that white men—absolute masters of their human property—grossly exaggerated the danger of slave revolts. They pictured the Negro as a kind of malevolent ogre, powerful, bestial, and lascivious, a caldron of animal emotions that had to be restrained at any cost. Probably the characteristics they attributed to the blacks were really projections of their own passions. The most striking illustration of this process was the universal white fear of the "mongrelization" of the race: if Negroes were free, they would interbreed with whites. Yet in practice, the interbreeding, which indeed took place, was almost exclusively the result of white men using their power as masters to seduce female slaves.

Thus the "peculiar institution" was fastened upon America with economic, social, and psychic barbs. Ignorance and self-interest, lust for gold and for the flesh, primitive prejudices and complex social and legal ties all combined to convince the colonists of the early 18th century that Negro slavery was not so much good as a fact of life. With the passage of time a barely perceptible trend toward ameliorating the harshness of bondage emerged, but talk of abolishing slavery was

HENRY FRANCIS DU PONT WINTERTHUR MUSEUM

A Charleston dinner party held about 1754, candidly sketched by George Roupell, one of the guests. The host, Peter Manigault (second from left, holding a decanter), was one of the city's elite. As toasts are made and a guest (foreground) playfully waves a wig, a young servant dozes off (far right).

almost nonexistent until the eve of the Revolution. A few isolated reformers, mostly Quakers, attacked the institution on the religious ground that all men are equal before God: "*Christ* dyed for all, both *Turks, Barbarians, Tartarians,* and *Ethyopians.*" But a few Quakers owned slaves, and even the majority who did not usually succumbed to color prejudice. The Negro's blackness was a defect, but no justification for enslavement, they argued. And they attracted little attention anywhere—none in areas where slavery was important.

PRIVATE COLLECTION

William Byrd II, the very model of the Virginia aristocrat, was painted in London by Sir Godfrey Kneller between 1715 and 1719. Byrd's secret diary, kept in shorthand, is one of the more informative—and entertaining—documents of the colonial period.

Southern Intellectual and Religious Trends

The disruptions in England caused by the Civil War and the great interest that the English gentry took in America after the restoration of Charles II brought many wealthy and educated men to the southern colonies, and they unquestionably impressed many of their values on the region. Southern society, however, was less formal and more flexible than English society. The crudeness of life in a land so recently wild acted as a leveling force, and the opportunity for advancement tended to prevent class lines from hardening.

Prosperity and the social implications of a system that allowed a fortunate few to exploit the labor of great numbers of slaves encouraged some large planters to "indulge their propensity to consume" rather than to plow back profits and increase their efficiency; but at least until late in the colonial period most of them led busy, fruitful, and interesting lives. For example, the great landowner William Byrd II (1674–1744), whose father migrated to Virginia about 1670 to manage his family's holdings, often rose from his bed at three in the morning in order to catch up on his reading before beginning his daily round. Besides his tobacco fields, Byrd operated a sawmill and a gristmill, engaged in the Indian trade, planted orchards, and prospected for iron, coal, and copper. He was also deeply engaged in colonial politics, and he carried on an extensive correspondence with a number of important Englishmen.

"New" men were constantly on the rise; by their industry and ambition they gave society a tone of bustle and drive. Daniel Dulany of Maryland offers a good example of the type. He arrived in Maryland in 1703 as an indentured servant. Ten years later he was a lawyer and landowner. He married well and prospered. Soon he was reaping further rewards in land speculation. His descendants, one historian writes, "made up a dynasty of social significance in the colony." For these reasons the large planters could be said to *predominate* in the southern colonies but not to dominate them. Gradations of wealth and status did not in themselves produce basic conflicts of interest. As Aubrey C. Land, an authority on the social structure of the colonial south, has put it, "probably never since . . . have the favored few enjoyed such harmony with the less fortunate." *Class* harmony did not, however (as we shall see), mean the absence of social conflict.

Slavery, of course, was not an equalizing or

JOHN WALKER,

LATELY arriv'd in *Williamſburg* from *London*, and who for ten Years paſt has been engag'd in the Education of Youth, undertakes to inſtruct young Gentlemen in Reading, Writing, Arithmetick, the moſt material Branches of Claſſical Learning, and ancient and modern Geography and Hiſtory; but, as the nobleſt End of Erudition and Human Attainments, he will exert his principal Endeavours to improve their Morals, in Proportion to their Progreſs in Learning, that no Parent may repent his Choice in truſting him with the Education of his Children.

Mrs. *Walker*, likewiſe, teaches young Ladies all Kinds of Needle Work; makes Capuchins, Shades, Hats, and Bonnets; and will endeavour to give Satisfaction to thoſe who ſhall honour her with their Cuſtom.

The above-mentioned *John Walker*, and his Wife, live at Mr. *Cobb*'s new Houſe, next to Mr. *Coke*'s, near the Road going down to the Capitol Landing; where there is alſo to be ſold, Mens Shoes and Pumps, *Turkey* Coffee, Edging and Lace for Ladies Caps, and ſome Gold Rings.

A tutor's advertisement printed in a Williamsburg newspaper in 1752 suggests the kind of education that was made available to the children of wealthy southern planters.

harmonizing force, for it increased the psychological barrier between rich and poor by degrading all labor and accustoming men to draw invidious comparisons between one type of human being and another. Slave labor never drove the small farmer out of business, however. The widespread use of slaves was the *result*, not the cause, of falling tobacco prices. Slaves were cheap enough in the colonial era to be widely owned by men of only middling wealth, and the great plantation employing 50 or more Negroes was always the exception.

Colonists north and south continued to look to the mother country for intellectual and cultural leadership, but this was especially true of southerners because of their close economic ties with the homeland. Wealthy planters wore imported clothes, drove about the countryside in English coaches, used fine imported china and furniture, and built up first-rate libraries of English and continental books. Many sent their children abroad to be educated. William Byrd II studied law in London, and a fellow Virginian, the great slaveowner Robert "King" Carter, sent five children to English schools. So many South Carolinians studied in England that Charleston became a kind of cultural replica of 18th-century London. Scions of the leading Catholic families of Maryland often studied on the Continent. Charles Carroll, a signer of the Declaration of Independence, was educated at the Collège de St. Omer and studied law in Paris.

In matters of education, however, there was a tremendous gap in the south, not only between rich and poor, but also between the rich and the moderately successful majority. It is true that the College of William and Mary was established at Williamsburg, Virginia, in 1693, but almost no effective primary or secondary system existed in the southern colonies. The rural nature of society, with the population scattered along countless rivers and bays, helps account for this unfortunate fact. Well-to-do planters could afford private tutors for their children, and occasionally two or three families combined to hire a teacher. This solution, of course, was only for the rich. A good many of the small farmers (and all of the slaves) remained unlettered.

By the middle of the 18th century the Anglican Church had been established in all the southern colonies, which meant that ministers of that faith were supported by public funds. The Virginia assembly had made attendance at Anglican services compulsory in 1619, and in later years deprived dissenters of the right to vote. Many non-Anglicans were driven from the colony. In Maryland, Lord Baltimore, although intolerant of non-Christians, had sought to persuade the Protestant majority to adopt a live-and-let-live attitude toward Catholics by imposing stiff fines on individuals who used terms like "heretick" and "papist" in what his Toleration Act defined as "a reproachful manner." This law did not survive the invasion of that colony by militant Puritans. It was repealed in 1654 during the Cromwellian period, re-enacted in 1657, and then repealed again in 1692 when the Anglican Church was established. Catholics, who made up less than ten per cent of Maryland's population, were repeatedly discriminated against: in 1704 priests were forbidden to say mass and in 1718 Catholics lost the right to vote. In the Carolinas the proprietors' original desire to encourage the immigration of men of all faiths—including Jews and Quakers—could not be carried out in practice. The Anglican Church was established in 1706. In Georgia, where no state religion existed at the start, Anglicanism was established in 1758.

However, the Anglican Church was not a very powerful force in the south. The scattering of population militated against any organized religion just as it did against schools, and the English hierarchy made matters worse by neglecting their American parishes. When someone suggested that the Crown provide funds to buttress the faith in America, Sir Edward Seymour, Lord of the Treasury, is alleged to have said, "Souls? Damn your souls! Make tobacco!" Since there was no Anglican bishop in the colonies, novices had to sail to England to be ordained, something few colonists were willing to do. Those English pastors who migrated to America were mostly second-rate men unable to obtain a decent living at home; they and their American flocks were in almost constant conflict.

In Virginia Anglican ministers were usually paid in tobacco vouchers annually worth the market value of 17,280 pounds of the crop. But in 1758, after a drought drove up the price of tobacco, the House of Burgesses passed a law providing that "tobacco debts" for the year 1759 be honored at a rate of two pence per pound. Since tobacco was selling at more than twice that price in 1759, this Two-Penny Act deprived the ministers of a much-desired windfall.

Indignant clergymen appealed to the Privy Council in London, which voided the law. Thereupon several ministers went to court to sue for back pay. One test case, involving the claim of the Reverend James Maury, attracted immense interest throughout Virginia, revealing how thoroughly the Anglican clergy had failed to win the respect of the populace. The judge ruled in Maury's favor, but a young frontier lawyer, Patrick Henry, so beclouded the issue with oratorical pyrotechnics, attacking the clergy as unpatriotic, money-grubbing "enemies of the community," that the jury awarded Maury only one penny in damages. "The ready road to popularity here," Maury grumbled after the trial, "is to trample under foot the interests of religion, the rights of the church, and the prerogative of the Crown." This "Parson's Cause," settled in 1763, has long been regarded as one of the earliest portents of the Revolution, for it demonstrated that in a clash of royal and local authority, most Americans would stand by their local leaders. Much of Henry's success in swaying the jury—he knew little law and did not try to justify the Two-Penny Act on legal grounds—resulted from his denunciation of the Privy Council's decision as a highhanded assault on the liberties of the colonists.

Among dissenters in the south, religion remained a more powerful influence, despite the problems posed by the rural nature of society. The pious Presbyterians and Baptists who poured into the southern back country in the 18th century made great sacrifices to build churches and willingly traveled long distances to attend services. Members of these sects, however, were in the minority in the south throughout the colonial period, except possibly in North Carolina.

Agriculture in the North

North of Maryland the vast majority of people were also farmers in the colonial era, but the society that grew up there was quite different. (The distinction commonly drawn between New England and the middle colonies—New York, New Jersey, Pennsylvania, and Delaware—has little significance for any discussion of their economic development.) In these colder regions tropical and semitropical plants like sugar, rice, and indigo would not grow. Except in a few limited areas, most notably in the Connecticut River valley, tobacco did not flourish either. The northern colonies raised the standard cereal crops, produce not readily salable in Europe. In the 17th and 18th centuries even England normally harvested more than it needed of such grains as wheat and barley and oats. Aside from furs, forest products, and a few minor items, there was little demand in Europe for the products of the northern colonies.

Nevertheless, the facts of colonial life made it inevitable that most northern settlers become farmers. Indian corn was their principal crop for many decades, for its yield per acre under rough frontier conditions was far higher than that of other grains. The Indians taught the first settlers to plant corn in drills spaced between the stumps on freshly cleared forest land. Since this method postponed the backbreaking work of rooting out stumps and stones and plowing the fields, the pioneers, who had little labor to spare and needed to get a crop in the ground quickly, adopted it eagerly. Once planted, corn required almost no attention beyond an occasional hoeing, and the growing crop was both resistant to disease and untroubled by hungry birds and other animal pests. It was also a versatile product, nutritious and tasty when prepared in a variety of ways for human consumption and an excellent fodder for livestock. In the form of corn liquor it was easy to store and to transport. In all the colonies, south as well as north, corn became the basic food of the early settlers.

However, once land was cleared and fenced, other grains could also be produced in quantity. Wheat was the most important, especially in Pennsylvania. In New England, however, wheat suffered greatly from a disease called the blast, so rye, oats, barley, and other grains were widely cultivated, as were other European vegetables and native plants like pumpkins and potatoes. The northern colonists, particularly the New Englanders, also engaged extensively in fishing, for the offshore reaches from below Cape Cod to Newfoundland constituted one of the finest fishing grounds in the world. Yet there was no better market for colonial fish in northern Europe than for grain, since the British, Dutch, and other maritime powers were already oversupplied.

Thus, while the northern colonists could feed themselves without difficulty, they had no direct way of turning their surpluses into the European-manufactured products they desired. English ships did not flock to northern waters as they did to the tidal streams of the south and to the West Indian sugar ports.

Northern Manufacturing and Commerce

Nevertheless, the northerners found ways to surmount this problem. During the long winter months farm families manufactured all kinds of objects, from bone buttons to leather breeches and hemp-string bags. Nearly everyone raised a few sheep, and spinning wheels were almost as ubiquitous in northern farmhouses as tables, chairs, and beds. The weaving of linen from local flax was also widespread. Indeed, as late as 1750, 90 per cent of the farmers of Pennsylvania made most of their own clothing.

This view of the Hudson Valley farmstead of one Martin van Bergen was painted on the paneling above the van Bergen fireplace by an unknown itinerant artist in the mid-1700's. The owner and his wife stand with obvious pride in front of their sturdy Dutch-style farmhouse, surrounded by members of their family, several black servants, and a variety of livestock. A milkcart is at right center. In the background are the Catskills.

Inevitably under such conditions, families began to specialize, for no one could master all the manufacturing skills. And specialization meant producing goods for sale and exchange, not merely for use within the family. Speaking of a slightly later period, the early American economist Tench Coxe commented on "the great convenience and advantage to the neighborhood" that resulted from the local manufacture of farm carriages, tools, hats, shoes, furniture, and many other items. Both specialization and producing for a market tended to increase the quality as well as the quantity of such manufactures. The thriving state of northern manufacturing and the general colonial manpower shortage redounded to the advantage of the workingman. Richard B. Morris, the leading authority on early American labor, estimates that real wages in the colonies averaged between 30 and 100 per cent higher than in England.

Local manufacturing could not possibly supply all the goods that the colonists needed, however, and there remained the problem of disposing of surplus farm products in an overwhelmingly rural society. The solution was to seek out markets in far corners of the earth. This necessitated, first of all, the building of a merchant fleet. Fortunately, the colonists had at hand huge supplies of some of the finest timber in the world; from early in their histories, Boston, Salem, Newport, Portsmouth, Philadelphia, and other northern ports became centers of shipbuilding. American vessels were soon ranging the Atlantic. A Boston skipper, for example, might take a cargo of dried fish, lumber, and various cereals to the West Indies, where the one-crop sugar economy made the planters dependent upon the outside world for their needs. In the Indies he could fill his hold with sugar and make sail for England, there to exchange the sugar for the manufactured goods that the northern colonists craved.

This "triangular," or better, "multiangular" trade took many forms. Its impact on the colonies was complicated and almost entirely beneficial. For example, the West Indian planters produced large quantities of molasses, a by-product of sugar refining. Merchants soon dis-

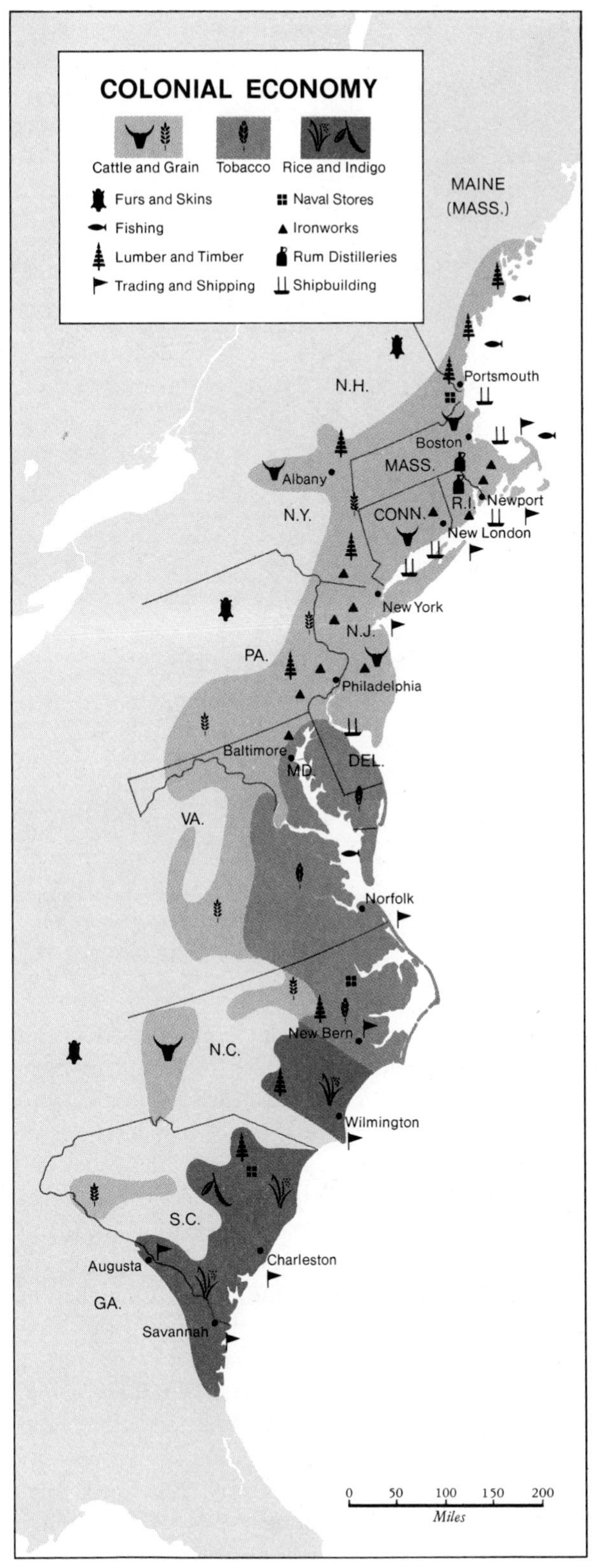

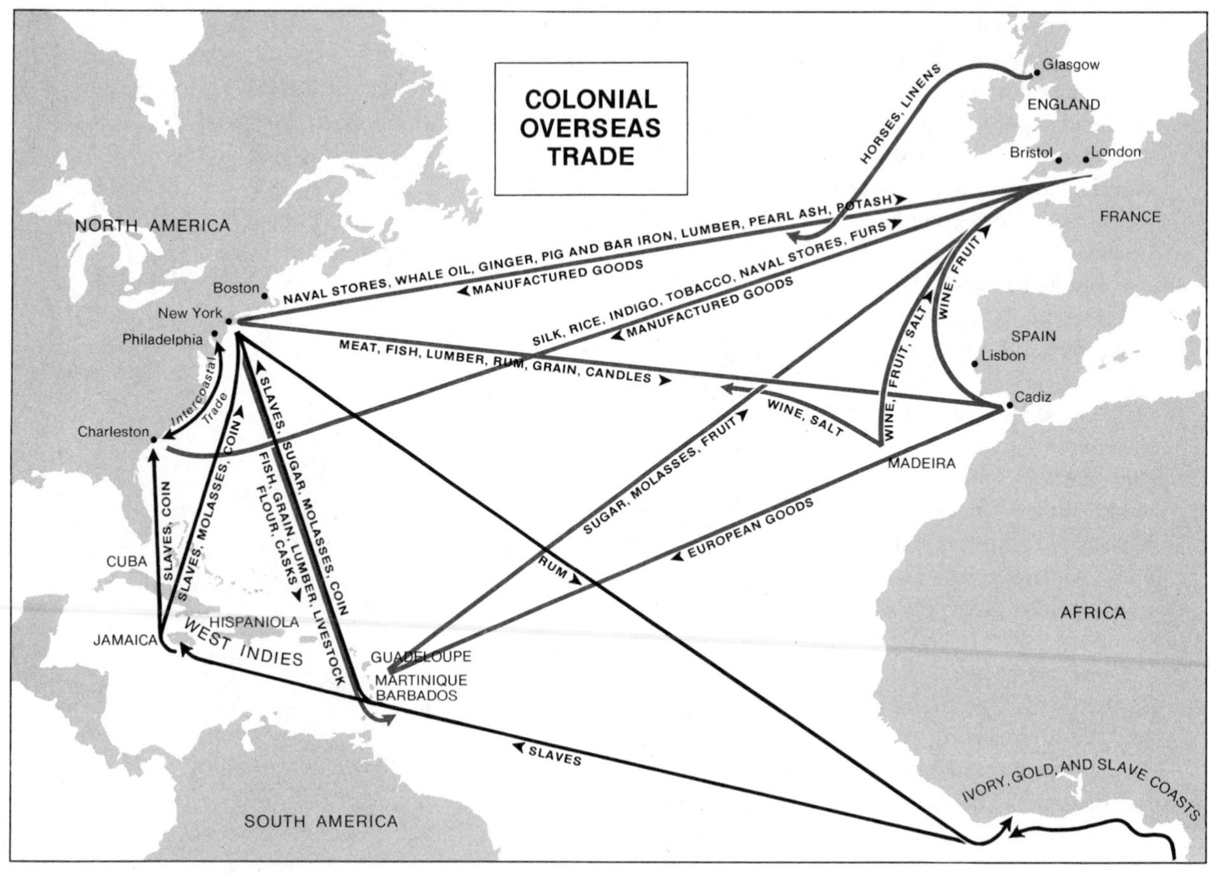

This map summarizes the chief routes and products of colonial foreign trade in the 1700's. The triangular slave trade is in black for clarity. Most southern exports went to England, but a lack of English markets led the northern and middle colonies to seek outlets for their products in the West Indies and southern Europe.

covered that they could exchange American products for molasses, which they sold to New England distillers who turned the molasses into rum, creating still another local industry. Not all of this rum was consumed in America—although mighty efforts were made in that direction. The surplus was shipped to Africa and exchanged for slaves, who were carried to the Indies, thus completing the cycle. A number of Yankees made fortunes by engaging in this noxious but profitable commerce.

Foreign trade led to increased local trade too. English manufactured goods sometimes found their way to the tobacco colonies by way of northern ports, while northern fishermen, kept from the stormy Atlantic in winter, frequently went off on coasting voyages in that season laden with mixed cargoes of local products to exchange for tobacco and rice. Colonial merchants, skippers, and ordinary seamen also had an important impact on Europe. They were almost the only Americans who returned frequently to the homeland. Inevitably they made contacts, and their tales (sailors have never been noted for understatement) did much to advertise the wonders of the colonies. No one knows how many English artisans decided to migrate after hearing stories about high wages, countless opportunities, and respect for the place of the laborer in society from the lips of Yankee seamen in London taverns.*

*Undoubtedly, the letters of satisfied colonists to friends and relatives in the old country were an even more effective means of recruiting immigrants.

So trade became the key to prosperity in the northern colonies, important all out of proportion to its immediate value and to the number of persons engaged in it, a condition reflected in the social importance of northern merchants. They were the leaders and trend-makers of that region, just as a relative handful of great planters set the tone for society in the south.

Foreign commerce also stimulated the growth of cities in the northern colonies. In 1690 Boston had about 7,000 inhabitants, Philadelphia and New York some 4,000 each. Fifty years later these towns had become thriving, dynamic urban centers: Boston's population had jumped to 16,000, Philadelphia's to 13,000, New York's to 11,000.* Into these communities flowed the manufactured goods and luxury products of Europe, and the grain, fur, and lumber of America. The resulting interchanges supported a host of profitable enterprises. Besides the merchants and sailors and the many employers and artisans engaged in the building of ships, a variety of wholesalers and retailers flourished, together with carpenters, silversmiths, tailors, and many other craftsmen, even dancing masters.

Most colonial cities were crowded and dirty. Being seaports, they were always full of sailors on leave and other transients bent on having a good time. Crime and vice vexed civic-minded citizens; even Puritan Boston had at least a dozen prostitutes as early as the 1670's, and every town had a well-populated, if not always very secure, jail. Many aspects of the modern "problem of the cities" existed in minuscule in these towns.

But by the middle of the 18th century every large colonial community also had a weekly newspaper, and in some, books were published. Taverns served as meeting places for serious clubs and as centers for intellectual and political discussion, as well as for drinking, gambling, and other forms of dalliance. All towns had schools

*After 1740 Boston stopped expanding until after the Revolution, but in 1775 Philadelphia had 40,000 inhabitants and New York 25,000. The only important southern city, Charleston, grew from 6,800 to 12,000 between 1740 and 1775. On the eve of the Revolution at least eight other towns, including Baltimore, Newport, and New Haven, had populations of over 5,000.

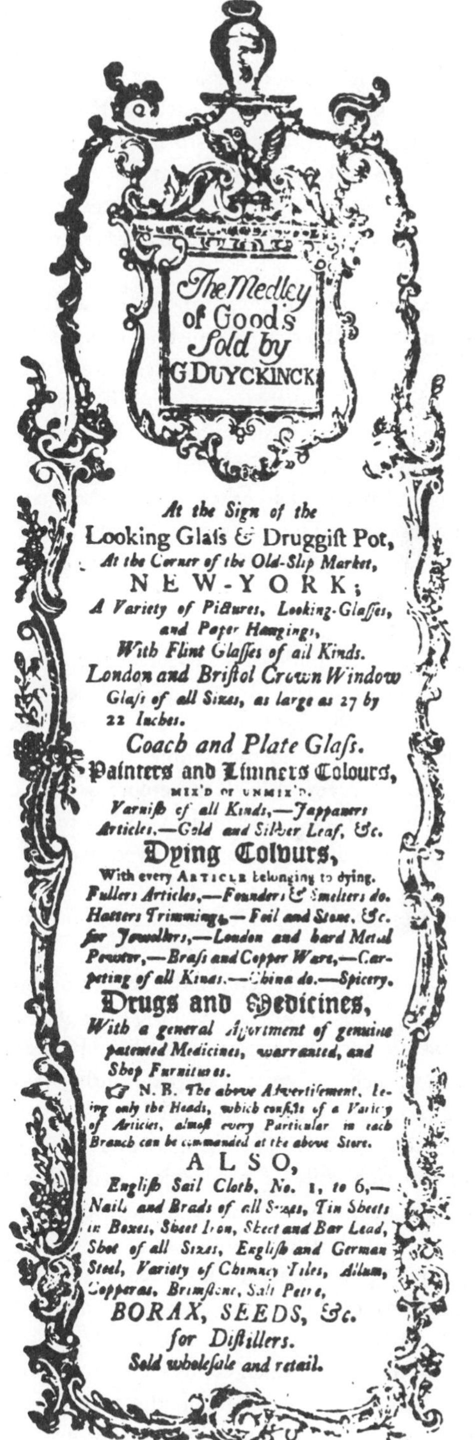

NEW-YORK HISTORICAL SOCIETY

The variety of articles brought into the colonies from overseas can be glimpsed in this "Medley of Goods" advertised by a New York merchant in 1769.

as well. Traveling limners painted likenesses of the urban rich; philanthropy and other indications of social consciousness were well developed; New York had a theater as early as 1732. According to Carl Bridenbaugh, historian of early American urban life, a comparison of the colonial towns with any in Great Britain except London "would not have resulted in discredit to the former."

The cities, in short, were the intellectual centers of colonial America. English books and ideas from all over Europe literally entered America through the seaport towns, and it was in the towns that the most ambitious and intelligent colonials–Benjaman Franklin is only the most famous of many–made their fortunes and thought their thoughts. The cities were places where men from different regions met one another, exchanged ideas, reached, no doubt, the first vague awareness of their common *American* interests. Certainly in the mid-18th century, the magnetic attraction of urban life, which became so powerful in the 19th and 20th centuries, was already exerting its force on the people. It must be kept in mind, however, that all the colonies were overwhelmingly rural. As late as 1775 no more than five per cent of the population lived in the towns.

Land and Labor in the North

Despite the importance of commerce in the northern colonies, the independent farmer was the backbone of the region. In many areas he obtained his land in much the same way that southerners did. The headright system flourished in Pennsylvania and New Jersey. The proprietor's easy terms and the rich soils of the region made Pennsylvania particularly attractive to 18th-century immigrants, both those who paid their own way and those who arrived as indentured servants. Thousands of Germans came into that colony quite early in its history. Scotch-Irish settlers (Presbyterian Scotsmen whose ancestors had migrated to northern Ireland in the 17th century), discouraged by deteriorating conditions in the Irish woolens industry, flocked to Pennsylvania in great numbers beginning about 1700. These rugged Scotch-Irish pioneers pushed west to the valleys of the Appalachian range and then funneled southward into the back country of Virginia and the Carolinas. Often they became squatters, for difficult conditions did not dismay them, and they felt perfectly capable of fighting for their "rights" when challenged.

In New York a few great families like the Van Rensselaers had engrossed huge areas; tenant farming was common there as nowhere else in British America, but since decent freeholds were not easy to obtain, the colony grew slowly.

The New England colonies adopted a different method of land disposal, one that both reflected the community-mindedness of the settlers, and, in turn, had a very important impact on the local way of life. Instead of encouraging individual pioneers, the New England colonial governments, which held legal title to all wilderness property within their boundaries, granted land in 36-square-mile blocks called townships to *groups* of settlers. When the grant had been made, these town "proprietors" chose a suitable location for a village. Around a town common, each family selected a plot of land large enough for a house and a good-sized vegetable garden. Beyond this village center the settlers cleared fields for general farming. These they divided into many strips so that no one individual would get all the best soil, each family receiving enough land to provide for its needs. Usually the leading families and the local minister were awarded extra-large allotments, but no one could engross large tracts, and no one had to pay for his property. The rest of the township belonged to the community as a whole. All residents had the right to pasture livestock and to use the timber and other forest products on the common land.

This system made for compact expansion, since the legislatures assigned townships in an orderly manner along the edge of the settlement. It also insured the quick establishment of community life. Each village soon boasted at least a church activities could grow.
and a school, and around these centers other

Although township life appears to have been idyllically simple from the viewpoint of modern society, it was far more complex and stimulating for the average citizen than life in the rural south.

Every kind of craftsman could be found in these towns: carpenters, tailors, glaziers, masons, weavers, blacksmiths, and many others. Towns vied with one another to attract skilled men. It was not unusual, for instance, for the citizenry to build a house for a trained workman in return for his promise to practice his craft in the community for a period of years.

As trades prospered they inspired local specialization. As early as the 1760's, Lynn, Massachusetts, was turning out 80,000 pairs of shoes a year. Specialization also fostered new trades; the development of shoemaking, for example, led to a demand for tanners. Life was dynamic in the New England village; all residents profited from the presence of so many individuals of different training and interests.

The township system also made for orderly expansion within the community. Newly arrived settlers could be admitted to citizenship in the town only by vote in town meeting. Then they received house plots and land for cultivation, carved from the common holdings. From the start the new man was acutely conscious of becoming a part of a going social organization and of sharing the privileges and responsibilities that this entailed. Beyond question, the tone of society was influenced by the institutional framework within which settlement took place.

The towns were never very large by modern standards; the largest seldom held more than 2,500 persons in the colonial period. But as they grew, the communal character of life began to break down. Compact and relatively isolated family farms sprang up around the periphery of the villages. As population expanded, the remaining commons shrank and tended to rise in value. To protect their privileged positions, older residents sometimes tried to deny political rights to newcomers. Such actions created social as well as economic distinctions in town life. As expansion went on, the colonial governments started to treat the wilderness lands somewhat differently too. Beginning in the 1720's they began to sell townships to speculators, a complete reversal of the original policy of making land available without charge to men of good character who could use it. In the single year 1761 Governor Benning Wentworth of New Hampshire disposed of nearly 80 townships on such terms. Men of wealth and political influence could obtain whole towns or shares in several towns. Ezra Stiles—minister, scholar, and later president of Yale College—owned shares in perhaps a dozen townships in several colonies, and he bought and sold these holdings much as a modern investor trades in stocks.

Nevertheless, the township way of life was essentially democratic. Local issues were settled by majority vote in town meeting, while the towns, in turn, sent representatives to the colonial legislature, thus insuring a roughly equal distribution of political power in the larger community. If the grandsons of original proprietors tended to scorn newcomers and to use their control of the machinery of local government to withhold economic and political privileges, they were seldom able to do so for very long. The logic of the system was all against them to begin with, and in a Puritan *commonwealth* the force of logic generated considerable moral pressures. Probably more important, the law of supply and demand was against them. As in other parts of America, labor was needed more than land. Although gradations of wealth and personal influence existed in every community and men were acutely conscious of the difference, say, between a "gentleman" and a "goodman" and between the latter and a mere servant, the beckoning frontier precluded the growth of an underprivileged *class*. Towns that held too tightly to their commons and denied newcomers a voice at meeting simply ceased to grow.

Although slavery existed in every northern colony, it was nowhere as important as in the south. Of the 150,000 blacks in the colonies in 1740, only about 18,000 lived north of Maryland. The absence of staple crops that could be cultivated by gang labor and the long winters when the need for farm labor was minimal militated against the importation of Africans in large numbers. Most northern Negroes, slave and free, worked as household servants or held menial jobs in the towns. New York City's population in the 18th century was about 15 per cent black, Boston's about 8 per cent.

Life for northern slaves was on the average easier than in the plantation colonies, but not because masters were more humane. The governing factor everywhere was the ratio of black to white. Nor did the somewhat more relaxed attitude of northerners toward Negroes reflect a different evaluation of the Negro race; northern prejudices and misconceptions were just as irrational, passions just as easily stirred. Free Negroes were not usually denied the right to vote by law, but if property qualifications did not disfranchise them, local "custom" did. And when northern blacks caused trouble, or when northern whites *thought* they were causing trouble, they were subjected to punishments as severe and cruel as any devised by southerners. After subduing a genuine uprising of New York City slaves in 1712 in which 9 whites were killed, the authorities hanged 13 slaves, burned 4 alive—one over a slow fire—broke one on the wheel, and left one to starve to death in chains. Another Negro "plot" in New York in 1741, possibly a figment of overheated white imaginations, led to the execution of 31 blacks, 13 by fire.

The Impact of Puritanism

Conditions of soil and climate affected the economy of New England, and the township system shaped the social and political history of the region, but Puritanism, both as a religion and as a way of thinking, permeated every aspect of New England life.

The Puritans had come to America for religious reasons; to establish a "purer" church than existed anywhere in Christendom was their main objective. They believed man to be essentially sinful; he could be regenerated or "saved" only by the grace of God. Since the Deity did not dispense this grace lightly, the majority of the human race was doomed to roast forever in Hell. Each man's fate, according to Puritan logic, was foreordained, for an omniscient God must know in advance the future of every soul. Yet life was not without hope; men must never give up seeking salvation.

God's blessings being material as well as spiritual, success in the accumulation of worldly goods was a likely, although not a necessary, indication of salvation. Thus hard work, thrift, and strict attention to business were qualities to be cultivated by those who hoped to enter heaven. The Puritans, in other words, were pre-eminently behavioralists; they wanted to create a "visible" kingdom of God on earth.

Nevertheless, they believed that good behavior, like material success, was an indication, not a guarantee, of salvation. The essential proof of grace was to have had some extraordinary emotional experience, some mystical sign of intimate contact with God. Pious men prayed for years to be worthy of such an experience; many were never rewarded despite long hours of soul-searching. Those who were proclaimed that fact in church, and if they convinced the congregation that the experience had been genuine, they were elected to church membership. Their combination of elitism and zeal meant that the Puritans had little interest in converting sinners. Since few could achieve salvation in any case, there was no point in being concerned with the rest except to punish their transgressions. These miserable souls might—indeed they must—attend church, but only the elect of God had a say in the affairs of His house.

Although church and state were not separated in the modern sense in most of the colonies, in Massachusetts Bay and, except for Rhode Island, in the rest of New England, the tie between the churches and the civil government was extremely close, going far beyond the mere use of public funds to support a particular religion. In early Massachusetts, for example, church attendance was compulsory, and magistrates enforced moral law as well as civil. When anyone was guilty of blasphemy, the "venting [of] corrupt & pernicious opinions," or "schismaticall" activities, the magistrate was expected "to put forth his coercive powr" and punish the offender. On the other hand, although clergymen could not hold office, they played a large role in nonreligious affairs, advising the magistrates, supervising the social activities of the people, and pontificating on everything from the harvesting of crops to the meaning of such natural phenomena as storms and droughts. While clergymen in other regions

MASSACHUSETTS HISTORICAL SOCIETY

Increase Mather was a statesman and the rector of Harvard as well as a celebrated Puritan theologian. His portrait was painted in 1688 by Jan Vanderspriet.

also tried to influence the everyday life of their parishioners, they had much less success.

Religious toleration being inconceivable to most 17th-century Christians, all the colonies refused to tolerate unbelievers, but since they were driven by such a tremendous sense of their own mission, the Puritans were especially hard on dissenters. They enforced their own moral standards on others not so much to lead them to the light as to prove that they themselves were moral. That they had themselves been victims of persecution did not make them any less inclined to persecute others. This was particularly unfortunate because many settlers could not in conscience subscribe to all the Puritan tenets. By the 1670's at least half—estimates run as high as four-fifths—of the residents of Massachusetts Bay were unregenerate, which meant not only that they were not church members, but also that they could not vote in civil elections. Cotton Mather's story of the tough-minded citizen who rose in church after his minister had said that religion was "the main end" of colonization to point out that *his* "main end" in coming to America had been to catch fish has become hackneyed because it is so apt. Even for true believers, Puritanism was often too intense, too inhibiting, too smug. It bred in some of its devotees a narrow, almost psychopathic harshness and rigidity, an overconcern with sin that approached relish. For those who dissented—zealots like Anne Hutchinson, pious men of independent mind like Roger Williams, or characters like the roistering Thomas Morton, who danced with his followers around a maypole—the Puritan response was jail, banishment, and even, for a few stubborn Quakers, death.

But there was more to Puritanism than bigotry and repression. Puritans opposed not enjoyment but frivolity—not wine, for example, but drunkenness. ("Drink," said one early Puritan divine, "is in itself a good creature of God . . . but the abuse of drink is from Satan.") While intolerant of other religions, Puritans were deeply committed to examining every nook and cranny of their own beliefs, testing them always against reason as well as Scripture, never content with oversimplified answers to hard philosophical questions. As Perry Miller put it, "they made no concessions to the forest." They detested the "ignorant sinner" almost as much because of his ignorance as because of his sin. Despite the rigors of life in the wilderness, they insisted upon educating their children, for how could the next generation achieve salvation if it could not read the Bible? They considered a learned ministry vital, for the ordinary citizen needed expert guidance if he hoped to understand the complexities of his faith; thus within six years of the founding of Boston, the Puritans had created a college (Harvard), certainly one of the most remarkable achievements in the history of colonization.

In the 18th and 19th centuries optimists tended to deride Puritan talk about the weakness and sinfulness of human beings; but our own century, enlightened by the bright beams that Freud projected into the dark corners of the mind and chastened by the failure of reason and science to make a universal Eden of the globe, has viewed the Puritan evaluation of human nature more respectfully. If to be saved by God's grace is translated to mean the achievement of peace of mind through self-understanding, then real salvation is as rare in the 20th century as the Puritans thought it was in the 17th. Looking about in their wilderness Zion, the Puritans saw that man was weak and a sinner, that nature was capricious, that fate was blind. Their glory was twofold: they accepted this sad reality without self-delusion and then struggled to rise above personal limitations, subdue savage surroundings, and be worthy of whatever fortune came their way.

The Puritan faith was another reason why New England village life was so stimulating and dynamic. The town was the battlefield on which the struggle for eternal salvation was fought. Its inhabitants were alert, assertive, self-conscious citizens, not the simple peasants of European village communities. Thus, while philosophically undemocratic, Puritanism contributed enormously to the development of American political institutions, particularly by its stress on *limited* government (since men are sinful by nature, they cannot be trusted with much power over their fellows), on *self*-government (the basic principle of congregationalism), on individualism (every man must read and interpret the Bible for himself), and on the right of the community to control its members in the common interest. The contradictions inherent in these concepts, of course, have never been resolved; probably they never can be. The tensions they produced in colonial New England have persisted through all American history. Are individuals morally bound to obey laws they consider evil? Which shall take precedence, the will of the majority or the liberties of an individual? Such questions were asked during the American Revolution, during the Civil War . . . and they are being asked today.

However, the actual heydey of New England Puritanism was short. Economic prosperity, while not shaking men's faith, worked in subtle ways to undermine the church-centered community. The most devout merchant often found his business interests in conflict with such Puritan concepts as just price, community solidarity, and intolerance of dissent. Religious intolerance, for example, discouraged immigration, thus restricting the growth of domestic markets, and gave New England merchants a bad reputation in other regions. More generally, the success of the merchants inevitably brought them prestige and power, destroying the pre-eminence of the clergy. Gradually, class antagonisms and westward expansion broke down social unity.

It was not, despite the thundering jeremiads of the old guard, that the Puritan communities became riddled with vice and greed, although the clergy, assembled at Boston in 1679, produced a long and circumstantial catalogue of such transgressions, ranging from the "great and visible decay of the power of Godliness" through Sabbath-breaking and extravagance of dress to "the sinn of whoredom." The majority of the settlers remained hard working, clean living, and pious. But these Puritan virtues led to the amassing of wealth, to expansion, and to diversity—all changes that undermined the Puritan commonwealth.

Religion itself was affected. Orthodox Puritan theology taught that children of the elect could be baptized, but that they could not become full church members and partake of communion until they personally had experienced God's grace. Many, as they became adults, had not. Therefore, in 1662, this strict rule was modified by the Half-Way Covenant, which permitted these persons to submit their own children for baptizing, and to remain themselves as "half-way" members of the church. From the point of view of the elect, this compromise was both humane and politically essential. They were unprepared to see their own grandchildren grow up under the stigma of Adam's sin; as Cotton Mather explained: "The good old generation could not, without uncomfortable apprehensions, behold their offspring excluded from the baptism of Christianity." At the same time the elect made sure that the church would not simply die of old age, and (incidentally) that the half-way members, being still "members," could continue to vote in civil elections.

Even this compromise could not, however, long preserve the monopoly of the original "visible saints." By the early 18th century, in congregations professing to be Puritan, it was possible for anyone to be received without a public confession of faith.

The conflict between the idea of a powerful clergy and the belief that men must personally understand the meaning of Holy Writ was bound to weaken the church. So did the confusion between the intellectual and the emotional sides of Puritanism. The Puritan must *understand* his religion, yet he must also *feel* it to be saved. Which was the more important? Men walked down different paths in search of the answer. Some, in the end, became Unitarians, embracing a religion so highly intellectualized as to seem to some not a religion at all. Others took the less taxing path that led to the evangelical faiths, with their stress on hymn singing, camp meetings, and perfervid preaching.

By the time of the restoration of Charles II in 1660, orthodox Puritans were bemoaning the decay of religious standards in New England. Thereafter, the resurgent royal authority added to their woes. In 1661 the Crown granted a small measure of relief to Quakers in the region by transferring the trials of Quakers to England. Other edicts providing for greater toleration followed, although they were often difficult to enforce. In 1684 the Massachusetts Bay charter was annulled, and soon all the colonies north and east of Pennsylvania were brought into the Dominion of New England under one powerful governor, Sir Edmund Andros. Although Puritan Congregationalism remained the established religion, the loss of the charter seriously weakened the political influence of the clergy. Church membership ceased to be a requirement for voting, and Andros even forced the congregation of the Old South Meeting House in Boston to permit its use for Anglican services. Fearing that Andros intended to establish the Anglican church in Massachusetts, the Puritan hierarchy thereafter adopted a more tolerant attitude.

When news of the Glorious Revolution and the accession of William and Mary to the English throne reached the colonies, Andros was overthrown and the Dominion dissolved, but Massachusetts never recovered its original charter. The former "Bible commonwealth" became a Crown colony in 1691. The Puritan clergy continued to fight religious laxity and the secularization of life with a zealous "counterreformation" which may have inadvertently contributed to the Salem witchcraft mania of 1692, in which 20 miserable "witches" were put to death. When this hysteria had spent itself, the shamefaced general public blamed the trouble on the orthodox clergy, especially on the Reverend Cotton Mather, who had published a book on witchcraft a few years earlier. This was unfair, for nearly everyone believed in witches in the 17th century. In the 18th century, as settlement spread westward, and as strip farming around a village center gave way to consolidated farms scattered through the townships, both church attendance and the quality of the clergy tended to decline. The average man's intensity of interest and conviction in religious matters slackened.

The Great Awakening

In all the colonies, religious fervor had declined somewhat in the early 18th century, but the right of local communities to provide public support for the predominant faith was beginning to be accepted. Immigration produced a proliferation of religions (Quakers, Mennonites, Lutherans, and Presbyterians in Pennsylvania, Dutch Reformed in New York, Baptists in Rhode Island, pockets of Jews and Catholics in the seaboard cities, and so on), and this, together with the developing worship of reason that characterized the 18th-century Enlightenment, seems to have fostered skepticism in many quarters. Many Puritan churches were invaded by Arminianism, a creed that played down hellfire and predestination, placed more emphasis on the free will of the individual, and argued that a life of good works and quiet respectability was enough to assure salvation. On the other hand, the multiplication of religions did not make for harmonious relations between groups. The stress on local self-determination produced sects—churches that believed that they alone knew all the answers, that all others were professing false creeds.

This state of affairs was modified in the 1740's by a mass movement known as the Great Awakening. Sporadic revivals of intense religious feel-

"The last and greatest of the royal line of Puritan mystics," was how Vernon L. Parrington described Jonathan Edwards, portrayed here by Joseph Badger.

ing had been common in the colonies before that time. As early as 1733 a brilliant theologian named Jonathan Edwards had deeply stirred his congregation in Northampton, Massachusetts. A tall, slender figure, with piercing eyes and a thin but arresting voice, Edwards preached the power of God and the depravity of man. Although he was not characteristically a hellfire-and-brimstone preacher, he could picture the tortures of eternal damnation vividly when necessary. His parishioners, even little children, were soon trembling over the fate of their eternal souls and experiencing repentance and "conversion" in wholesale lots.

Emotional appeals of this sort tended to divide congregations; often what today would be called a "generation gap" appeared. The older people wished to preserve past forms, the younger ones espoused the new emotional approach to salvation. The explosion of the Great Awakening, which tipped the balance in favor of the new, was set off by a young English minister, George Whitefield, who was already famous in the mother country as an inspired preacher. Beginning in November 1739, Whitefield toured America, releasing everywhere an epidemic of religious emotionalism. Although not nearly Edwards' equal as a thinker—Whitefield's theology, one authority wrote, was "scaled down to the comprehension of twelve-year-olds"—he had few peers as an orator and actor. David Garrick, king of the London stage, is supposed to have said that he would give a hundred guineas to be able to say "Oh" as Whitefield did. Whitefield had his greatest impact in the south and in frontier regions, but even in New England he caused a storm. In Boston 19,000 people thronged to hear him during a three-day visit. His oratorical brilliance aside, Whitefield succeeded because his message was well-suited to American ears. He attacked the narrowness of the sects, calling for unity among believers. "God help us to forget party names and become Christians in deed and truth," he prayed. While not denying the truth of predestination, he hinted that God could be persuaded to open the gates of heaven to all good and faithful Christians.

Whitefield attracted dozens of disciples and imitators among the clergy, including some who were plainly mentally unbalanced. "Popular response increased beyond ministerial dream," historian Ola Winslow writes. "Scores of parishes became centers of religious frenzy. Sermons were preached every night in the week, and there were private gatherings at all hours of the day. Meetinghouses were packed; conversion was the theme of the hour."

The Awakening flared sporadically for nearly a decade. A typical high point occurred when Edwards delivered his famous sermon "Sinners in the Hands of an Angry God" at Enfield, Connecticut, on July 8, 1741. When Edwards warned, "O sinner! Consider the fearful danger you are in: it is a great furnace of wrath, a wide and bottomless pit, full of the fire of wrath, that you are held over," a great moaning reverberated through the church. People cried out: "What shall I do to be saved?" and "O I am going to Hell." As one witness later recorded, "the shrieks & crys were piercing & Amazing."

Such emotional intensity could not be long maintained; the excesses of the Great Awakening disgusted many people, and this led to factional disputes in many congregations. Conservatives began by questioning the emotionalism of "New Light" preachers like Whitefield and ended by challenging the very idea of predestination on the ground that it was unreasonable to believe that a benevolent God would not be swayed by the actual behavior of his creatures. In a general atmosphere of hysteria, basic religious values were unlikely to flourish. Edwards, for example, broke with his church and became first a missionary among the Indians and then president of the College of New Jersey, now Princeton.

But while it caused divisions, the Awakening also weakened sectarianism. Whitefield and his followers preached wherever they could find an audience. Their efforts caused the idea of denominationalism to flourish among Protestants, each group claiming its right to its own forms and ideas, but granting to other Protestant churches equal freedom to practice the common faith as they wished. The Awakening also led Protestants to move away from reliance upon state support on the theory that politics was a divisive and corrupting influence in religion. The founding of church-financed colleges (Brown, Dartmouth, and Rutgers, for example) followed, along with many other institutions aimed at improving mankind, such as orphanages and Indian missions.

The Impact of the Enlightenment

The Great Awakening was one of the first truly national events in colonial history; every district from New England to Georgia, from the seaport towns to the scattered cabins of the far frontiers, felt its impact. In a sense it casts light on the growing interrelationships that would eventually make America a nation; 13 isolated settlements, expanding north and south as well as westward, were becoming one. Powerful bonds were being forged. Intercolonial trade had always existed, but as time went on it became more and more important. Increasingly, the British tried to centralize the administration and regulation of this trade. As early as 1691, there was a rudimentary colonial postal system. In 1754, not long after the Great Awakening, the farsighted Benjamin Franklin advanced his Albany Plan for a colonial union to deal with common problems like defense against the Indians.

These stirrings of national self-consciousness did not mean that Americans were escaping from European influences: their culture was heavily derivative throughout the colonial period and for decades thereafter. Howard Mumford Jones has pointed out the degree to which the Renaissance image of the well-rounded man of culture (*uomo universale*) was reflected in early American life. While few settlers could be said to have achieved the level of sophistication attributed to the great figures of the Renaissance, many, from Captain John Smith through William Byrd to Thomas Jefferson, had an astounding variety of intellectual interests, together with the typical Renaissance fondness for amorous adventure, chivalry, and all the social graces.

A more significant influence on culture was the 18th-century Enlightenment in Europe. The founders of the colonies were contemporaries of the astronomer Galileo (1564–1642), the philosopher-mathematician René Descartes (1596–1650), and Sir Isaac Newton (1642–1727), the genius who revealed to the world the workings of gravity and the other laws of motion. American society matured amid the excitement generated by these great discoverers, who provided both a new understanding of the natural world and a new mode of thought. Instead of seeing a universe responding to the caprice of an omnipotent and sometimes wrathful Deity, men began to envisage a universe based on impersonal, scientific laws that governed the behavior of all matter, animate and inanimate. Earth and the heavens, man and the lower animals—all seemed parts of an immense, intricate, but logically designed machine; God was the master technician (the divine watchmaker) who had conceived and created the marvelous structure and who now watched over it, but who never interfered with its immutable operation.

Furthermore, the nature of this universe and the laws controlling its behavior had been discovered not by abstract philosophizing (deduction), but by the patient collection and study of facts (induction). It therefore appeared that human reasoning power rather than God's revelations was the key to knowledge; it followed that knowledge of the laws of nature, by enabling man to understand the workings of the universe, would enable him to master his surroundings and thus to improve himself infinitely. "It is possible to attain knowledge that is very useful in life," Descartes wrote in his *Discourse on Method* (1637). "Instead of that speculative philosophy that is taught in the schools, we may find a practical philosophy by means of which, knowing the force and the action of fire, water, the stars, heavens and all other bodies that environ us . . . we can . . . employ them in all those uses to which they are adapted, and thus render ourselves the masters and possessors of nature."

Most of the creative thinkers of the Enlightenment realized that men were not entirely rational and that complete understanding of the physical world was impossible, but readers of their works tended to ignore the qualifying phrases. By the 18th century European and American intellectuals were responding eagerly to the new view of man and the world. They scanned stellar space and scoured the earth, collecting and cataloguing masses of data, sure that no mystery could long elude their search for truth. Their faith produced the so-called Age of Reason, and while their confidence in man's rationality seems to us naive and the "laws" they formulated no longer appear so mechanically perfect (the universe is far less orderly than they imagined), they added immensely to human knowledge.

Americans accepted the underlying assumptions of the Age of Reason wholeheartedly. The inevitability of progress seemed self-evident to a people so successfully transforming a wilderness into a rich and civilized society, and the immensity of the task only strengthened their belief that the task could be accomplished. That human beings were capable of self-improvement appeared axiomatic to men living in the flexible and dynamic colonial environment. Deism, a faith that revered God for the marvels of His universe rather than for His power over mankind, was especially popular in America, attracting thousands of converts among the educated minority.

Colonial America produced no Galileo or Newton, but it contributed significantly to the collection of scientific knowledge. The unexplored continent provided a great laboratory for those concerned with the study of natural phenomena. John Bartram, a Philadelphia Quaker who flourished in the middle years of the 18th century, ranged over America from Florida to the Great Lakes, gathering and classifying hundreds of American plants. Bartram also studied the Indians closely, speculating about their origins and collecting information about their way of life. Cadwallader Colden, lieutenant governor of New

The pioneering work of the naturalist John Bartram was carried on, after his death, by his son William. These drawings by William show (from left) a Florida bobolink and speckled snake; Florida alligators; a study of snails; and the ruellia, a Georgia flower.

York from 1761 to 1776, also made important contributions to the systematic study of American flora and fauna, conducting an extensive correspondence with the great Swedish botanist Linnaeus and other noted European scientists.

Equally significant work was done in other fields. Professor John Winthrop (1714–79) of Harvard, descendant of the first governor of the Massachusetts Bay colony, measured the earth's distance from the sun with an accuracy of over 98 per cent. David Rittenhouse constructed the first orrery (a mechanical model of the solar system) in America in 1767. Even the Puritan divine Cotton Mather was an avid scientist. He helped introduce smallpox inoculation in America, having no patience with the belief of many religious persons that it was sacrilegious to interfere with the unfathomable workings of God's will. Science strengthened religion, he insisted. "Gravity," he wrote, "leads us to God, and brings us very near to Him."*

The accomplishments of Benjamin Franklin, the greatest figure of the Enlightenment in America, are detailed in Portfolio II. The breadth of his interests, so staggering to our own highly specialized age, was characteristic of 18th-century intellectual life. A busy planter like William Byrd dabbled in medicine, amassed a library of over 3,600 volumes, and collected botanical specimens for British scientists in the Royal Society, of which he was an active member. Cotton Mather wrote about subjects as diverse as rattlesnakes, magnetism, and church history; his massive *Magnalia Christi Americana* (1702) is a veritable attic of miscellaneous information. Cadwallader Colden, in addition to his botanical interests and his political career, was a physician, astronomer, mathematician, surveyor, Latinist, and student of Indian lore. Thomas Jefferson, although he made no single contribution to the advancement of knowledge equal to some of Franklin's, represents the culmination of the American Enlightenment: linguist, bibliophile, political scientist, architect, inventor, scientific farmer, and—above all—apostle of reason. "Fix reason firmly in her seat," he wrote, "and call to her tribunal every fact, every opinion."

Of course the ordinary settler was not a scientist, a philosopher, or even much of a reader; few colonial homes contained many books other than

*In general, the "worship" of reason did not lead to attacks on religion. Even Newton believed in the possibility of miracles, which he saw as temporary suspensions of the laws of nature by their Creator.

ALL: BRITISH MUSEUM

the Bible. Most Americans were practical rather than speculative men, tinkerers rather than constructors of grand designs, little concerned with intellectual questions of any kind. As one 18th-century observer noted, they were easily diverted "by Business or Inclination from profound Study, and prying into the Depth of Things." They took their world as it was and for what they could make of it, having neither time nor patience for searching out large generalizations. Nevertheless, by the mid-18th century the intellectual climate in the colonies was one of eager curiosity, flexibility of outlook, and confidence in the ability of men to solve the manifold problem of existence.

Social Mobility

Important social and economic lines of demarcation clearly existed in the colonial world. Black men, even those who were not slaves, were discriminated against both legally and socially. Men of wealth had status denied the common run of colonists, most of whom deferred automatically to those they considered their betters, as their ancestors in Europe had done for centuries past. If few Americans were poor and if the richest of them lived quite modestly compared with a peer of the realm or a great merchant prince in England, this fact did not alter drastically the views of most about the proper order of society—although American conditions undoubtedly modified their attitudes in the long run. Moreover, most settlers, again in line with the beliefs of their forebears, took it for granted that only persons with some material stake in the country could be counted upon to preserve the social order. For this reason, all the colonial governments established modest property qualifications for voting and somewhat higher ones for office-holding.

Nevertheless, in all the colonies property was so widely held that large numbers of ordinary citizens could vote. The charter of Massachusetts Bay provided that only men owning a "40 shilling freehold" (land that would rent for 40 shillings a year) or other property valued at £50 could vote in provincial elections. However, as Robert E. Brown's exhaustive researches in Massachusetts town records have shown, most settlers could meet one or the other of these requirements. "Cheap land, high wages, and economic opportunity promoted almost universal property ownership, while the amount of property needed for voting was extremely modest," Brown concluded. "There were doubtless a few men who could not vote, but they must have been few indeed." In Virginia the situation was similar; few white men failed to fulfill the voting requirements: owning 25 acres of improved land, 100 acres of unoccupied land, or a house and lot in a town. Even in colonies like South Carolina and New York, where property qualifications were stiffer, a much larger percentage of the people could vote than in England.

However, it is incorrect to think of colonial society as being democratic in the modern sense. Practical democracy was far in advance of popular thinking about democracy throughout America. The plain farmer or artisan did not consider himself the equal, socially or politically, of the great planter or merchant. In Virginia, for example, the political leaders of the colony were nearly all what we would call aristocrats, typified by men like Washington and Jefferson. At any time the mass of ordinary farmers in the colony could have voted these men out of office; instead they freely chose their "betters" to represent them. As Charles S. Sydnor has explained in his important study, *Gentlemen Freeholders,* "the small farmer . . . accepted [planter] leadership as natural and proper."

Social distinctions, however, were far less rigid than in Europe and more directly related to material wealth, since there was no native nobility, no *permanently* privileged class. The undeveloped, expanding country offered almost unlimited opportunities for ambitious men to grow rich, and with wealth, as in any society, came social status. Colonial politics were characteristically chaotic for this reason. The elite might rule, but new elites emerged at every turn—great "new" planters in Virginia in the mid-17th century, merchant princes in booming Baltimore a hundred years later. Thus, while still prisoners of European social and political ideas, while aping, as provincials nearly always do, the standards of the homeland, the Americans were actually establishing a way of life more flexible and more democratic than any in the world. Men were respected for what they were and for what they had done, not for the achievements of some forgotten ancestor. The insatiable needs of the empty continent compelled the settlers to reward ability and to value talent highly whenever and wherever it appeared.

Sectional Conflicts

In part because of the rich opportunities available and the lack of social rigidity, sharp conflicts often broke out between different sections. America was a huge land, and travel between distant regions was slow, uncomfortable, and expensive. Relatively few persons had firsthand knowledge of districts other than their own. The residents of one colony found it difficult to believe they had much in common with strangers hundreds of miles away in another British settlement. The historical accident that led to the establishment on the continent of 13 separate political units bound together only indirectly through the Crown and the royal bureaucracy acted to prevent the colonists from thinking of themselves in national terms. In their own eyes they were Virginians or New Yorkers or, at most, New Englanders. Beyond that they saw themselves as subjects of the king. "American" was not a term with much political significance, even in the mid-18th century, although recent studies suggest that the people, by that time, were beginning to feel a sense of community, a kind of latent nationalism.

Local conditions varied greatly and the people with them, as we have seen. However, perhaps because the settlers were not yet accustomed to thinking in continental terms, few really important intercolonial conflicts disrupted Britain's American empire. A certain amount of suspicion based on ignorance existed, to be sure, and a measure of friendly rivalry, but no irreconcilable troubles. Occasionally, nasty quarrels over boundaries arose, but these rarely became critical. The conflicting claims of Massachusetts, Connecticut, New York, Pennsylvania, and Virginia to the Ohio Valley were only beginning to assume serious proportions in the mid-18th century, being overshadowed by the common threat to these claims posed by the French. Slavery, the great disruptive force of the next century, did not arouse much controversy in the colonial era. Isolated reformers like the Quaker mystic John Woolman spoke out against the institution, but Negroes were held in bondage in every colony.

Between different regions of individual colonies, relations were not always so serene. Sectionalism, a national disease in the 19th century, was a local scourge in the 18th. To some extent regional conflicts were inevitable, being based on fundamental clashes of economic interests. Principally these flared up between eastern and western sections, between the older, settled areas and the frontier. Westerners, for example, wanted land policies that encouraged rapid exploitation. Easterners tended to disagree, fearing that the opening up of new land would depress the value of their own holdings. Westerners also wished to spend public money on the construction of roads and what later came to be called "internal improvements," whereas in the already developed areas most people objected to such expenditures. Westerners were *always* anti-Indian. A state of almost perpetual warfare existed along the frontier, where the jagged teeth of settlement chewed inexorably into the Indians' hunting grounds. Even in times superficially calm the threat of Indian attack never vanished in the western districts. Yet eastern colonists, far removed from danger, urged restraint upon the frontiersman because warfare was a costly drain upon the whole community. When the easterner sanctimoniously advised his western cousin to live at peace with the Indians or offered Indians firearms and liquor in order to obtain furs on the best terms, the frontiersman became as hostile toward the easterner as he was toward the red man.

These geographical conflicts were both balanced and complicated by counterforces within each region. For example, eastern land speculators favored the rapid growth of the west as much as western farmers, while eastern fur traders, eager to preserve the western wilderness as a hunting ground, had enthusiastic allies in the frontier districts. Eastern merchants joined their western customers in demanding better roads. Descriptions of colonial conflicts phrased only in terms of east *versus* west are usually oversimplifications. The headstrong, on-the-make attitude of both fron-

BURGERBIBLIOTHEK, BERN

The "Indian menace" was always uppermost in the minds of those living on the frontier. A drawing made in 1711 by Christopher von Graffenried, the founder of a Swiss-German colony in North Carolina, shows Graffenried, his surveyor, and their black servant held captive by the Tuscarora. A tribal dance (right) was followed by the torture of the bound prisoners. Graffenried and his companions were later ransomed.

tiersmen and members of the eastern establishments had a great deal to do with most of the clashes of the colonial era. With a rich and thinly settled land, an expanding economy, and few institutional fetters on the ingenuity of free men, there need have been no serious communal strife.

When trouble occurred, however, the fact that the newer western counties were denied equal representation in the provincial legislatures was usually involved. Beginning with the first meeting of the Virginia House of Burgesses in 1619, colonials apportioned seats in legislative bodies on a geographical basis. Whether the unit was the county, the borough, or the township, each lawmaker represented an area of land, not a specific number of people. So long as the districts were of roughly equal size and the population spread evenly over the whole area, the system worked well. But as civilization moved westward, some colonial legislatures discriminated against settlers in the newer regions by giving them far less representation than their numbers warranted. This was easily done, since the older areas controlled the machinery by which new districts were established. In North Carolina at the time of the Revolution, the seaboard counties still elected two-thirds of the members of the legislature. In Pennsylvania the area around Philadelphia exercised an even more striking control over political affairs.

Western settlers were therefore unable to back their views with appropriate political force. When conflicts of interest sprang up over such things as Indian policy, they were overwhelmingly outvoted. In a democratic system the loser may grumble, but he respects the right of the majority to prevail. When a minority makes the decision, however, he is righteously wrathful. Further, when one element easily predominates it tends to become contemptuous of other interests. The give-and-take of democratic debate, which settles conflicts by compromise, does not take place. This unfortunate state of affairs aggravated colonial social and economic conflicts; tempers flared; sometimes it even led to armed revolt.

Troubles rising out of eastern disregard for western interests can be spotted all through colonial history. In Virginia, for example, a major explosion led by an impetuous and ambitious young planter named Nathaniel Bacon took place in 1676. Despite western growth, there had been no election in Virginia since 1662, and a clique in the entourage of the royal governor, Sir William Berkeley, held most of the government jobs in the colony. A poll tax, much resented by small western farmers, had been imposed. When Indians ravaged the frontier early in 1676, Berkeley, who was sympathetic toward the red man, insisted that reprisals be confined to those tribes that had caused the trouble. Bacon, although himself wealthy and a member of the Virginia upper crust, was with regard to Indians a typical frontiersman. He did not relish such fine distinctions. He raised an extralegal army, killed some peaceful local tribesmen, and then turned on the colonial government at Jamestown. After a spectacular series of ups and downs in which Jamestown was burned and a number of the rebels executed, some important reforms were enacted. Right and justice were by no means entirely on the side of Bacon and his followers, either before or during the troubles. The conflict was as much between rival groups of large landowners as between small farmers and the eastern establishment. The rebels were neither democrats nor opposed to English rule. But the uprising might never have occurred if the colonial government had been more truly representative of the opinions of all sections and interests.

The 1763 uprising of the "Paxton Boys" in Pennsylvania, though less complicated, was also triggered by eastern indifference to Indian attacks on the frontier, indifference made possible by the fact that the east outnumbered the west in the assembly by 26 to 10. Fuming because they could obtain no help from Philadelphia against the Indians, the Boys, a group of Scotch-Irishmen from Lancaster county, fell upon a village of peaceful Conestoga Indians and murdered them in cold blood. Then they marched on the capital, several hundred strong. Fortunately a delegation of burghers, headed by Benjamin Franklin, talked them out of attacking the town, partly by promising to vote a bounty on Indian scalps!* In 1771 a similar uprising of a band of North Carolina frontiersmen known as the "Regulators" had a more unfortunate outcome. A pitched battle was fought in the western part of the colony between Regulators and government troops. The Regulators were crushed and their leaders executed.

The New England frontier, by contrast, did not suffer from eastern domination. Since each township was represented in the legislature, and since all townships were the same size, no great disproportion could arise. If anything, western communities, being less densely settled, were overrepresented; the seaport towns of the Massachusetts Bay colony, for example, had only 14 representatives in a legislature of nearly 200. In all New England, although conflicts of interest between east and west arose from time to time, no Bacons, no Paxton Boys, no Regulators appeared to take up arms against the constituted government.

But while colonial history is full of broils and tumults, in a significant sense social relations were remarkably harmonious. Men competed fiercely for wealth and status, yet save for the shameful subordination of the Negro populace (admittedly a most important exception), the rules of the competition were reasonably fair and the prizes so abundant that few losers retired empty-handed from the contest. Although the fluidity of society, the uncertainty of life in the New World, was no doubt psychologically disturbing to many persons, colonial Americans were a happy people, taken all in all. Though still few in number and legally subordinate to Great Britain, they were growing steadily more prosperous and more powerful. Staggering tasks faced them as they labored to make a garden of their continental wilderness, but the future was clear to all but the most obtuse, and it was a pleasing prospect indeed.

*However, fairer representation did not come to Pennsylvania until the Revolution.

SUPPLEMENTARY READING Among recent general interpretations of colonial life, D.J. Boorstin's *The Americans: The Colonial Experience** (1958) and H.M. Jones's *O Strange New World** (1964) are stimulating and provocative. David Hawke, *The Colonial Experience* (1966) is a general survey of colonial history containing many new perspectives on the period. The writings of F.J. Turner on the influence of the frontier on American history, conveniently collected in R.A. Billington (ed.), *Frontier and Section** (1961), are particularly applicable to the colonial era. D.M. Potter's *People of Plenty** (1954) is another general interpretation of American civilization that is especially convincing when tested against the facts of colonial life. Carl Bridenbaugh's *Myths and Realities: Societies of the Colonial South** (1952) is excellent, while two volumes in the History of American Life series, T.J. Wertenbaker's *The First Americans* (1927) and J.T. Adams' *Provincial Society* (1927), are very useful.

On economic conditions, three older works provide a mass of detail: L.C. Gray, *History of Agriculture in the Southern United States* (1933), P.W. Bidwell and J.I. Falconer, *History of Agriculture in the Northern United States* (1925), and E.R. Johnson *et al., History of the Domestic and Foreign Commerce of the United States* (1922). On colonial land disposal, see Marshall Harris, *Origin of the Land Tenure System in the United States* (1953). R.B. Morris, *Government and Labor in Early America** (1946), is a standard work, while A.E. Smith, *Colonists in Bondage* (1947), is a good study of indentured servitude; although covering only the last years of the colonial period, *The Journal of John Harrower* (1964), edited by E.M. Riley, provides interesting glimpses of the life of an indentured servant in Virginia. On slavery, see U.B. Phillips, *American Negro Slavery** (1918), D.B. Davis, *The Problem of Slavery in Western Culture** (1966), W.D. Jordan, *White Over Black: American Attitudes Toward the Negro** (1968), and Lorenzo Greene, *The Negro in Colonial New England* (1942). On the New England township system, R.H. Akagi, *Town Proprietors of the New England Colonies* (1924). See also D.R. Rutman, *Winthrop's Boston** (1965), K.A. Lockridge, *A New England Town: The First Hundred Years** (1970), and S.C. Powell, *Puritan Village: The Formation of a New England Town** (1963). Stuart Bruchey, *The Roots of American Economic Growth** (1965), attempts to explore the dynamics of American economic development.

Bernard Bailyn, *The New England Merchants in the 17th Century** (1955) is an excellent study, as are F.B. Tolles, *Meeting House and Counting House: The Quaker Merchants of Colonial Philadelphia** (1948), and L.B. Wright, *The First Gentlemen of Virginia** (1940). R.M. Tryon, *Household Manufactures in the United States* (1917), is still the best survey of the subject, while Carl Bridenbaugh, *The Colonial Craftsman** (1950), is full of interesting information. Bridenbaugh's *Cities in the Wilderness** (1938) is the best source of information on colonial urban life up to about 1740, while his *Cities in Revolt** (1955) deals with the immediate pre-Revolutionary years.

On social and cultural history, see L.B. Wright, *The Cultural Life of the American Colonies** (1957). V.L. Parrington, *The Colonial Mind** (1927), the first volume of his monumental *Main Currents in American Thought,** is extremely stimulating, although most modern historians consider his stress on the difference between aristocratic and democratic modes of thought something of a distortion.

A standard study of colonial religion is W.W. Sweet, *Religion in Colonial America* (1942). Of the many books on the Puritans, Alan Simpson, *Puritanism in Old and New England** (1955), is a good introduction. On the New England Puritans, the works of Perry Miller are outstanding. See especially his *Errand into the Wilderness** (1956), *Orthodoxy in Massachusetts* (1933), *The New England Mind: The 17th Century** (1939), and *The New England Mind: From Colony to Province** (1953). S.E. Morison, *The Intellectual Life of Colonial New England** (1956), K.B. Murdock, *Literature and Theology in Colonial New England** (1949), E.S. Morgan, *The Puritan Family** (1965), and *Visible Saints** (1963) are also valuable. On the Anne Hutchinson controversy, see Emery Battis, *Saints and Sectaries* (1962). For the Great Awakening, consult E.S. Gaustad, *The Great Awakening in New England** (1957), and W.M. Gewehr, *The Great Awakening in Virginia* (1930). Perry Miller analyzes the thinking of the greatest of colonial theologians in *Jonathan Edwards** (1949), while the best biography of

Edwards is O.E. Winslow, *Jonathan Edwards** (1940). Bernhard Knollenberg provides an excellent brief discussion of the Parson's Cause in *Origin of the American Revolution** (1960). Other important studies of colonial religion and its relation to broader developments are Allan Heimert, *Religion and the American Mind from the Great Awakening to the Revolution* (1966), and Carl Bridenbaugh, *Mitre and Sceptre: Transatlantic Faiths, Ideas, Personalities, and Politics** (1962).

Colonial education is treated in Bernard Bailyn, *Education in the Forming of American Society** (1960). S.E. Morison, *Tercentennial History of Harvard College and University* (1935–36), and his briefer *Three Centuries of Harvard* (1936) are model volumes of their type.

On the Enlightenment in America, see Max Savelle, *Seeds of Liberty** (1948), and Brooke Hindle, *The Pursuit of Science in Revolutionary America** (1956). The definitive biography of Franklin is Carl Van Doren, *Benjamin Franklin** (1938), but V.W. Crane's brief *Benjamin Franklin and a Rising People** (1954) is also first-rate. E.T. Martin, *Thomas Jefferson: Scientist** (1952), is a useful summary.

Voting in colonial America and its relation to social structure has been subject to intensive examination. R.E. Brown has made the most important contribution with his *Middle-Class Democracy and the Revolution in Massachusetts** (1955) and, with B.K. Brown, has also produced *Virginia: Democracy or Aristocracy?* (1964). J.T. Main, *The Social Structure of Revolutionary America** (1965), sees colonial society as prosperous and highly mobile. Other studies of the suffrage in particular colonies include C.S. Sydnor, *Gentlemen Freeholders* (1952) (available in paperback as *American Revolutionaries in the Making*), on Virginia, R.P. McCormick, *The History of Voting in New Jersey* (1953), and Theodore Thayer, *Pennsylvania Politics and the Growth of Democracy* (1953). A more general treatment is Chilton Williamson, *American Suffrage: From Property to Democracy** (1960). The writings of F.J. Turner, already mentioned, are full of material for the study of sectionalism in the colonies. On Bacon's Rebellion, see Wilcomb Washburn, *The Governor and the Rebel** (1957).

*Available in paperback.

3

America and the British Empire

Since the colonies were founded piecemeal over more than a century by persons with varying motives and backgrounds, common traditions and loyalties developed very slowly. For the same reason, the British government was slow to think of its American possessions as a unit or to deal with them in any centralized way. From the time in 1497 when Henry VII authorized John Cabot and his sons to search out new lands, the "rule, title, and jurisdiction" over these lands had resided in the Crown. These were the *king's* possessions. As a good sovereign he was obligated to use them in a manner consonant with the national interest, but it was left to him and his advisers to decide what that interest was. No authority challenged his right to dispose of one section of his American domain to this group of merchants under such-and-such terms and another to that personal friend or creditor under some different arrangement. Thus, the particular circumstances that led to its founding determined the specific form of each colony's government and the degree of local independence permitted it.

The British Colonial System

Nevertheless, there was a pattern basic to all colonial governments and a general framework to the system of imperial control for all the king's overseas plantations. Whether imposed on the new lands by the mother country or established locally by the settlers, English political and legal institutions (the common law, private property, more or less representative legislative assemblies, systems of local administration) were sure to take hold in British America. While the colonists and the home authorities often had different motives in establishing new settlements, these were seldom conflicting motives. Colonists might leave home with grievances, bent on securing certain rights denied them in England, but prosperity, political and economic expansion, and the reproduction of Old World civilization in a new environment were aims common to ruler and the ruled, to Englishman and to American.

In the earliest days of any settlement, the need to rely upon home authorities was so obvious that few questioned England's political sovereignty. Thereafter, as the fledglings grew strong enough to think of using their own wings, distance and British political inefficiency combined to allow them a great deal of freedom. Although royal representatives in America tried to direct policy, England generally yielded the initiative in local matters to the colonies while reserving the right to veto any action it considered against the national interest. External affairs were controlled entirely in London.

Each colony had a governor. By the 18th century he was an appointed official, except in Rhode Island and Connecticut. Governors were chosen by the king in the case of the royal colonies and by the proprietors of Maryland, Delaware, and Pennsylvania. They had powers in the colonies much like those of the king in Great Britain. They executed the local laws, appointed many minor officials, summoned and dismissed the colonial assemblies, and proposed legislation to them. They also possessed the right to veto colonial laws, but, again like the king, they were financially dependent on their "subjects" in most colonies.

Each colony also had a legislature. Except in Pennsylvania, these colonial assemblies consisted of two houses. The lower houses, chosen by qualified voters, had general legislative powers, including control of the purse. In all the royal colonies except Massachusetts, members of the upper house, or council, were appointed by the king and functioned primarily as advisory groups, although they did possess some judicial and legislative powers. Judges were also appointed by the king and served at his pleasure. Yet both councilors and judges were normally selected from among the leaders of the local communities; London had neither the time nor the will to investigate their political beliefs. The system, therefore, tended to cement the local power of already entrenched colonials without significantly strengthening the influence of the mother country in America.

Although the power of the lower houses of the legislatures was severely restricted in theory, these assemblies tended to dominate the government in nearly every colony. Financial power, including the right to set the governor's salary, gave them some importance, but the fact that the assemblies usually had the backing of public opinion was also significant. As Jack P. Greene has demonstrated in his important study *The Quest for Power*, colonial legislators were, in the main, pragmatists: knowing their own interests, they pursued them steadily, without much regard either for political theories or the desires of the royal authorities. In the words of one Virginia governor, they were "Expedient Mongers in the highest Degree." They extended their influence by slow accretion. Governors came and went but the lawmakers remained, accumulating experience, building upon precedent, widening decade by decade their control over colonial affairs.

Moreover, the official representatives of the Crown, whatever their powers, whatever their intentions, were prisoners of their surroundings. A royal governor lived thousands of miles from London, alone in a *colonial* world. To defend the British position at every turn when one had to make one's life amid a vigorous and strong-willed people, who usually had strong practical arguments to buttress their side if it clashed with the Crown's, was no easy task. Governors had no security of tenure, serving at the whim of the powers in London. In their dealings with the assemblies they were often bound by rigid and impractical royal instructions which restricted their ability to maneuver, and they had relatively little in the way of jobs and favors to offer in their efforts to influence the actions of legislators. Judges might perforce interpret the law according to English precedents, but in local matters, colonial juries had the final say, and they were seldom overawed by precedents when these clashed with their own conceptions of justice.

Since the colonies were the property of the Crown, within the British government the king's Privy Council had the responsibility for establishing colonial policy. But it did so on an *ad hoc* basis, treating each situation as it arose and seldom generalizing. Everything was decentralized: the Treasury had charge of financial matters, the army of military affairs, and so on. The Privy Council could and did "disallow" (annul) specific colonial laws, but it did not proclaim constitutional principles to which all colonial legislatures must conform. It acted as a court of last appeal in colonial disputes but handled each case as it came up. One day the council might issue a set of instructions to the governor of Virginia, the next a different set to the governor of South Carolina. No one office directed colonial affairs; no one man or committee thought broadly about the administration of the overseas empire. On the other hand, parliamentary legislation did apply to the colonies generally—but again, there was little distinctively *American* legislation. For example, Parliament passed laws regulating the trade of the entire British empire and until late in the colonial period directed its attention specifically to North American conditions only on rare occasions.

At various times the British authorities, uneasy about their lack of control over the colonies, attempted to create a more effective and centralized system of administration for the empire. Whenever possible the original, broadly worded charters were revoked. To transform proprietary and corporate colonies into royal colonies (whose chief officials were appointed by the king) seems to have been London's official policy by the late 17th century. The Privy Council appointed a number of subcommittees to advise it on colonial affairs at this time, the most important being the Lords of Trade, which had its own staff and archives and wielded great influence. In the 1680's when James II attempted to unify all of New England, New York, and New Jersey under one administration, the Dominion of New England, the move was deeply resented by the colonists; when James was deposed in the Glorious Revolution, the Dominion collapsed. Thereafter, there were no large-scale efforts at unification; indeed, the tendency was in the other direction. Delaware was at least partially separated from Pennsylvania in 1704, and the two Carolinas were formally split in 1712.

In 1696 a new supervisory body, the Board of Trade, took over the functions of the Lords of Trade and expanded them considerably. It nominated colonial governors and other high officials and reviewed all the laws passed by the colonial legislatures, recommending the disallowance of those which seemed to conflict with imperial policy. The efficiency, assiduousness, and wisdom of the Board of Trade fluctuated over the years, but the Privy Council and the Crown nearly always accepted its recommendations. Colonists naturally disliked having their laws disallowed, but London exercised this power with considerable restraint; only about five per cent of the laws reviewed were actually rejected. Furthermore, the board served as an important intermediary for colonists seeking to influence king and Parliament. All the colonies in the 18th century maintained agents in London to present the colonial point of view before board members. The most famous colonial agent was Benjamin Franklin, who represented Pennsylvania, Georgia, New Jersey, and Massachusetts at various times during his long career.

At no time did the British develop an effective, centralized government for the American colonies. Probably this fact more than any other explains our present federal system and the wide areas in which the state governments are sovereign and independent. Local and colony-wide government in America evolved from English models, but if a rational central authority had been superimposed in the early days, the colonies would almost certainly have accepted it. Then, even in revolt, they would probably have followed a different path.

The Theory of Mercantilism

The Board of Trade, like the Lords of Trade before it, was concerned with commerce as well as colonial administration. According to prevailing opinion all over western Europe, colonies were important chiefly for economic reasons. In the 16th, 17th, and 18th centuries economic thinkers believed that the possession of gold and silver was the best barometer of national prosperity. This theory, called mercantilism, led the powers to value colonies highly, for gold and silver could not be mined in significant amounts in western Europe. Every early explorer set out dreaming of finding *El Dorado*—and usually with a royal contract describing how the hoped-for loot was to be divided. Spain was the initial winner in this competition, and from the mines of Mexico and South America, a rich treasure in gold and silver poured into the Iberian Peninsula. The mightiness of 16th-century Spain—actually more the result of dynastic politics and shrewd royal marriages than of any economic development—seemed to contemporaries to prove the importance of bullion in achieving national power. Failing to control the precious metals at the source, the other powers tried to obtain them by guile and warfare, as witness the exploits of Sir Francis Drake.

In the mid-17th century another method, less hazardous and in the long run far more profitable, called itself to the attention of the statesmen of western Europe. If a country could make itself as nearly self-sufficient as possible and at the same time produce surpluses of items marketable in other lands, it could sell more abroad than it imported. This state of affairs was known as "having a favorable balance of trade," but that term is misleading. In reality, trade, which means exchange, always balances unless one party simply gives its goods away, a practice never recommended by the mercantilists. A country with a "favorable" balance is merely importing gold or silver instead of other commodities. Nevertheless, in the overall scheme of things, mercantilism came to mean concentrating on producing for export and limiting imports of ordinary goods and services in every way possible. In such a system even colonies that did not contain deposits of precious metals were valuable if they yielded raw materials that would otherwise have to be purchased from foreign sources, or if they provided markets for the manufactured products of the mother country.

If the possession of gold and silver signified wealth to a mercantilist, then trade was the path that led to riches, and merchants were the guides who would pilot the ship of state to prosperity and power. "Trade is the Wealth of the World," Daniel Defoe wrote in 1728. "Trade makes the difference as to Rich and Poor, between one Nation and another; Trade nourishes Industry . . . and Trade raises new Species of Wealth, which Nature knew nothing of. . . ." One must, of course, have something to sell, so internal production must be stimulated. The British Parliament, for example, placed heavy duties on foreign foodstuffs and enacted all kinds of tariffs and subsidies to encourage the manufacture of textiles, iron, and other products. But the nurture of commerce was fundamental. Toward this end a whole series of laws was passed known as the Navigation Acts. These laws, enacted over a period of half a century and more, were designed to develop the imperial merchant fleet, to channel the flow of colonial raw materials into England, and to keep foreign goods and vessels out of colonial ports (since the employment of foreign ships in the carrying trade was as much an import as the consumption of foreign wheat or wool). Together with other acts aimed at steering the colonial economy in certain directions, these regulations made up what the historian George Louis Beer called "The Old Colonial System."

The Navigation Acts

The system had its origins in the 1650's during the Cromwell period and was initially a response to the stiff commercial competition offered by the Dutch. Having won their independence from Spain, the Dutch had constructed a magnificent merchant fleet of more than 10,000 ships. Their sailors roamed the world's oceans in search of business. They dominated the coastal trade of France, threatened to do the same with that of England, and practically monopolized the whale fisheries of the North Atlantic. They established themselves in South America, in India, and in both the East and West Indies. Before 1650 a large share of the produce of the English colonies in America was reaching Europe in Dutch vessels; the first slaves in Virginia, it will be recalled, arrived on a Dutch ship and were doubtless paid for in tobacco that went finally into the clay pipes of the burghers of Amsterdam and Rotterdam.

Dismayed by this trend, Parliament in 1650 and 1651 barred foreign ships from the British colonies except when specially licensed and prohibited the importation of goods into England except in English ships or those of the country where the goods had been originally produced. All foreign vessels were also excluded from the English coasting trade. Although phrased in general terms, this legislation struck primarily at the Dutch, and in 1652 the English provoked the first of three wars with the Dutch Republic that were only extensions of the policy laid down in these first Navigation Acts.

But the laws of 1650–51 could not be rigidly

enforced, for England simply did not have the shipping to supply her overseas possessions. The colonies protested vigorously and then blandly ignored the regulations. Nevertheless, the English persisted. New laws were passed after the restoration of Charles II in 1660, and as the British merchant marine expanded (tonnage doubled between 1660 and 1688) and the Royal Navy gradually reduced Dutch power in the New World, enforcement became fairly effective.

The Navigation Act of 1660 reserved the whole trade of the colonies to English ships and required that the captain and three-quarters of his crew be English. (Colonists, of course, were Englishmen, and their ships were treated on the same terms as those sailing out of London or Liverpool.) This act also provided that certain colonial "enumerated articles"–sugar, tobacco, cotton, ginger, and dyes like indigo and fustic–could not be "shipped, carried, conveyed or transported" outside the empire. Three years later, Parliament required that with trifling exceptions all European products destined for the colonies be brought to England before being shipped across the Atlantic. Since trade between England and the colonies was reserved to English vessels, this meant that the goods would have to be unloaded and reloaded in England. Later legislation in 1673 and 1696 was concerned with enforcing these laws: it dealt with the posting of bonds, the registration of vessels, the appointment of customs officials, and the like. Early in the 18th century the list of enumerated articles was expanded to include rice, molasses, naval stores, furs, and copper.

English mercantilists looked upon the empire broadly; they envisioned the colonies as part of a great economic unit, not as servile dependencies to be exploited for England's selfish benefit. A planned economy, with England specializing in manufacturing and the colonies in the production of raw materials–this was the grand design. Thus the growing of tobacco on English soil was prohibited, and valuable bounties were paid to colonial producers of indigo and naval stores. By and large the system suited well the realities of life in an underdeveloped country rich in raw materials and suffering from a chronic shortage of labor.

Much has been made by some historians of the mercantilistic restrictions placed on colonial manufacturing. The Wool Act of 1699 prohibited the *export* (but not the manufacturing for local sale) of colonial woolen cloth. A similar law regarding hats was passed in 1732, and in 1750 an Iron Act outlawed the construction of new rolling and slitting mills in America. No other restric-
Iron Act outlawed the construction of new rolling
century of mercantilistic regulation. At most, the Wool Act stifled a potential American industry; the law was directed chiefly at Irish woolens rather than American. The hat industry cannot be considered a major one. Iron, however, was important; by the middle of the 18th century the industry was thriving in Virginia, Maryland, New Jersey, and Pennsylvania, and one historian estimates that in 1775 America was turning out one-seventh of the entire world's supply. Yet the Iron Act was designed to steer the American iron industry in a certain direction, not to destroy it. Eager for iron to feed English mills, Parliament eliminated all duties on colonial pig and bar iron entering England, a great stimulus to the basic industry. As Andrew Carnegie proved a little over a century later, one could carry on a very profitable iron business without undertaking to manufacture finished products.

The Effects of Mercantilism

In the colonial period mercantilism reflected more than it molded the economic system. The laws encouraged England to be the colonies' main customer and chief supplier of manufactures, but this would have been true in any case, and it remained true after the Revolution when the Navigation Acts no longer applied to America. The chronic colonial shortage of hard money was superficially caused by the flow of specie to England to meet the "unfavorable" balance that resulted from this trade, but this, too, reflected natural conditions. The rapidly developing colonial economy consumed far more manufactured products than it could pay for out of current production. To be "in debt" to England really meant that Englishmen were investing capital in America, a state of affairs that continued until World War I.

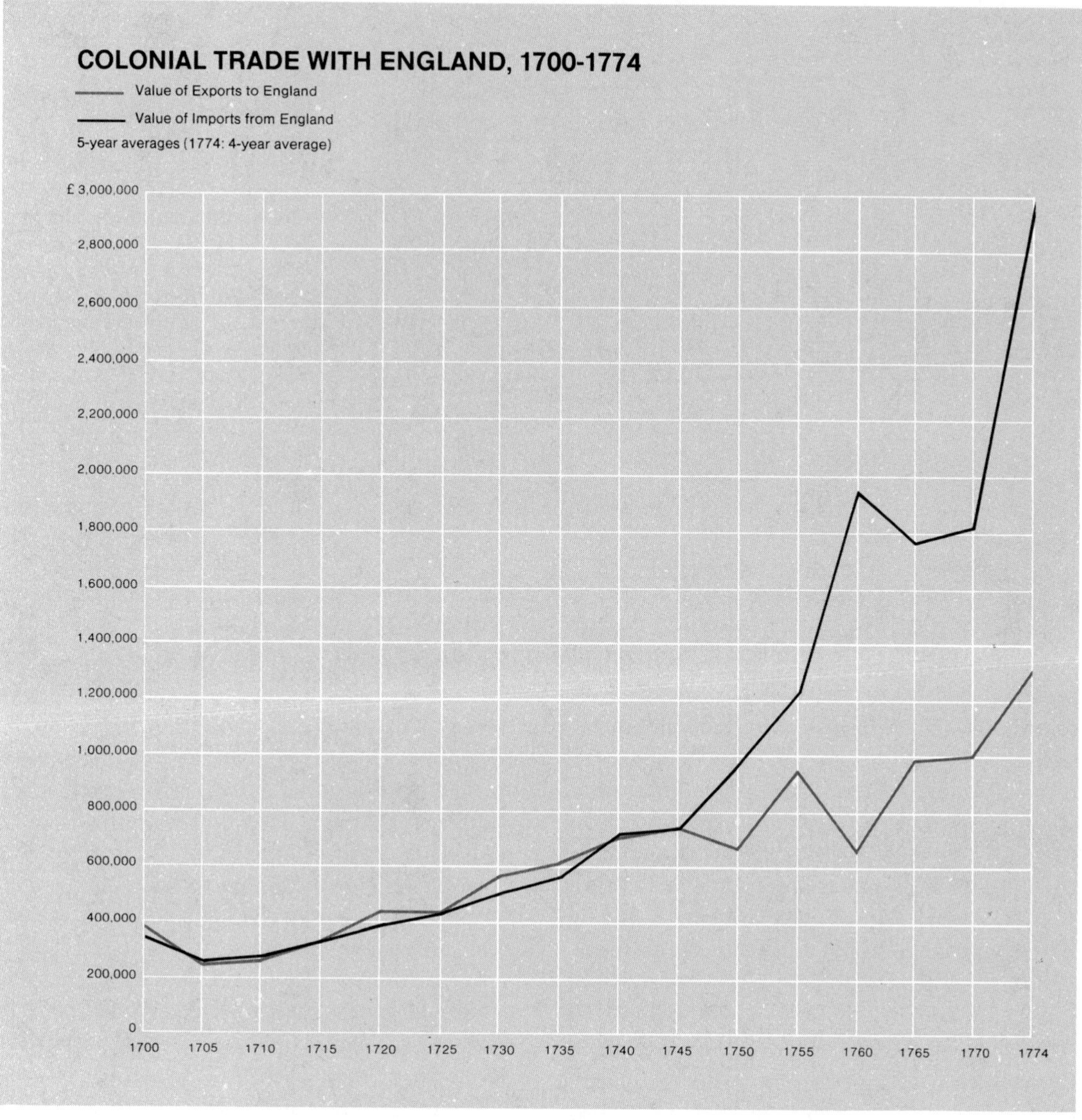

Furthermore, important colonial products for which no market existed in England, such as fish, wheat, and corn, were never enumerated and moved freely and directly to foreign ports. Most colonial manufacturing was untouched by English law. Shipbuilding, for example, was actually stimulated by the Navigation Acts, since many English merchants bought vessels built in the colonies. Between 1769 and 1771 Massachusetts, New Hampshire, and Rhode Island yards constructed perhaps 250 "topsail ships" of 100 to 400 tons for transatlantic commerce and twice that many sloops and schooners for fishermen and coastal traders. The manufacture of rum both for local consumption and for the slave trade was also significant, and so were barrelmaking, flour-milling, shoemaking, and literally dozens of other crafts, all operating without restrictions.

Two forces that worked in opposite directions must be considered before arriving at any judgment about English mercantilism. While the theory presupposed a general imperial interest above that of both colony and mother country, in practice the latter nearly always predominated when conflicts of interests arose. The Hat Act may have been good mercantilism, but Parliament passed it because English feltmakers were concerned over the news that Massachusetts and New

BOTH: H. DUNSCOMBE COLT COLLECTION

"Ye Flourishing City of New York" was how William Burgis titled his panoramic drawing, done about 1717. These two details are from a copperplate engraving of the Burgis view. At left is the boat basin at the Battery, near the tip of Manhattan Island, with New Jersey in the background. The buildings are distinctly Dutch in style. The detail at right also looks across the East River from Brooklyn. Several ships under construction can be seen on the Manhattan waterfront. The ships in the river are thought to be firing salutes to honor George I's birthday.

York were turning out 10,000 hats a year. The requirement that foreign goods entering the colonies must first be unloaded in England simply increased the cost of certain goods to Americans for the benefit of English merchants and dockworkers. The enumeration of tobacco and other colonial products meant that English merchants could profit by re-exporting surpluses to the Continent; by 1700 this re-export trade amounted to 30 per cent of the value of all England's exports. Whenever Parliament or the Board of Trade resolved an Anglo-American disagreement, the colonists tended to lose out. "It cannot be expected," the Board of Trade announced in 1706, "that encouragement should be given by law to the making of any manufactures made by England in the plantations, it being against the advantage of England." Complementary interests conspired to keep conflicts at a minimum, but in the long run, as the American economy became more complex, the colonies would have been seriously hampered and much more trouble would have occurred had the system continued to operate.

On the other hand, the restrictions of English mercantilism were greatly lessened by inefficiency. The English government in the 17th and 18th centuries was, by modern standards, incredibly cumbersome and corrupt. The king and his ministers handed out government posts to win political favor or to repay political debts, regardless of the recipient's ability to perform the duties of his office. Transported to remote America, this bumbling and cynical system scarcely functioned at all when local opinion resisted it. Smuggling became a respected profession in the colonies, the bribery of English officials standard practice. New rolling mills were openly constructed in Pennsylvania after the passage of the Iron Act, and the finished-metal trades took a great spurt after 1750. Despite a supposedly prohibitive duty of sixpence a gallon imposed by the Molasses Act of 1733, French molasses continued to be imported, for the duty was seldom collected. A customs officer in Salem offered to pass French molasses for ten per cent of the legal tax, and in New Jersey the collectors "entered into a composition with the Merchants and took a Dollar a Hogshead or some such small matter.'"

Unquestionably mercantilism hurt certain colonial interests (the tobacco planters were the most important of these), but it helped others, and most people proved adept at getting around those aspects of the system that threatened them. In any case, the colonies enjoyed almost continuous prosperity in the years between 1650 and the Revolution, as even so dedicated a foe of mercantilism as Adam Smith admitted.

By the same token, England profited greatly from her overseas possessions. With all its inefficiencies, mercantilism worked. Sir Robert Walpole's famous policy of "salutary neglect," which involved looking the other way when Americans violated the Navigation Acts, was partly a bowing to the inevitable, but it was also

the result of complacency. English manufactures were, in general, better and cheaper than those of other nations. This fact, together with ties of language and a common heritage, predisposed the Americans toward doing business in England. All else followed naturally; the mercantilistic laws merely steered the American economy in a direction it had already taken. At least this was the case until the end of the French and Indian War.

Thus, as the colonies matured, their relations with Crown and Parliament remained reasonably harmonious. The great majority of the settlers were of British descent and their interests generally coincided with those of their cousins in the mother country. It was fortunate that this was the case, however, because the British authorities were poorly equipped to deal with trouble in America. As one leading authority on 18th-century English politics has said, there was "immense ignorance and even vaster indifference" in the government with regard to all American questions. When trouble did come, intelligence and diligence would be called for—and found lacking.

Early Colonial Wars

The British colonies were part of a great empire, but that empire was part of a still larger world. Seemingly isolated in their remote communities, scattered like a broken string of beads between the wide Atlantic and the trackless Appalachian forests, the Americans were constantly being affected by outside events both in the Old World and in the New. Under the spell of mercantilistic logic, the western European nations competed fiercely for markets and colonial raw materials. War—hot and cold, declared and undeclared—was almost a permanent condition of 17th- and 18th-century life, and when the powers clashed they fought wherever they could get at one another, in America and elsewhere as well as in Europe. All the maritime nations considered the Spanish treasure ships fair game. England's capture of New Amsterdam was part of a larger Anglo-Dutch war.

Although in a sense the American colonies were minor pieces in the game, sometimes casually exchanged or sacrificed by the masterminds in London, Paris, and Madrid in pursuit of some supposedly more important objective, the colonists quickly generated their own international animosities. North America, a huge and almost empty stage, evidently did not provide enough room for French, Dutch, Spanish, and English companies to perform. Frenchmen and Spaniards clashed savagely in Florida in the 16th century. Before the landing of the Pilgrims, Samuel Argall of Virginia was sacking French settlements in Maine and carrying off Jesuit priests into captivity at Jamestown. Instead of fostering tranquillity and generosity, the abundance of America's resources seemed to make the settlers belligerent and greedy.

The North Atlantic fisheries quickly became a source of trouble between Canadian and New

England colonists, despite the fact that the waters of the Grand Banks teemed with limitless supplies of cod and other valuable fish. To dry and salt their catch the fishermen needed land bases, and French and English Americans struggled almost constantly to possess the harbors of Maine, Nova Scotia, and Newfoundland.

Even more troublesome was the fur trade. Unlike that of the sea, the yield of the forest was easily exhausted by indiscriminate slaughter, and traders contended bitterly to control valuable hunting grounds. The French in Canada conducted their fur trading through tribes like the Algonquins and the Hurons. This brought them into conflict with the "Five Nations," the powerful Iroquois Confederation centered in what is now New York State. As early as 1609 the Five Nations were at war with the French and their Indian allies. For decades this struggle flared sporadically, with the Iroquois more than holding their own both as fighters and as businessmen. They combined, according to one contemporary French account, the stealth and craftiness of the fox, the ferocity and courage of the lion, and the speed of a bird in flight. They brought quantities of beaver pelts to the Dutch and later the English at Albany. They preyed on pro-French tribes north of Lake Ontario and dickered with Indian trappers in far-off Michigan, "to carry," as one indignant French official complained, "the furs of our land to the Dutch." When the English took over the New Amsterdam colony they eagerly adopted the Iroquois as allies, buying their furs and supplying them with guns. By sending their *coureurs de bois* into the Illinois country and even beyond the Mississippi in search of skins, the French managed to bypass the Iroquois, but they never conquered or neutralized them. In the final showdown for control of North America the friendship of the Iroquois was vitally important to the English.

By the last decade of the 17th century it had become clear that the Netherlands lacked the strength to maintain a big empire and that Spain was fast declining. The future, especially in North America, belonged to England and France. In the wars of the next 125 years European alliances shifted dramatically, but the English and what John Adams called "the turbulent Gallicks" were always on opposite sides.

In the first three of these conflicts French and English colonists in America played only minor parts. They disliked one another cordially, but each lacked the resources to get at the other effectively. Fighting consisted chiefly of sneak attacks on isolated outposts. In King William's War (1689–1697), the American phase of the War of the League of Augsburg, French forces raided Schenectady, in New York, and a number of frontier settlements in New England. The English colonists retaliated by capturing Port Royal, Nova Scotia, only to lose that outpost in a counterattack in 1691. The Peace of Ryswick in 1697 ended the war and restored all captured territory in America to the original owners.

The next struggle was the War of the Spanish Succession, fought to prevent the union of Spain and France under the Bourbons. The Americans named this conflict, which lasted from 1702 to 1713, Queen Anne's War—actually a misnomer, since the anti-Bourbon coalition was organized by Anne's predecessor, William III, though he died before hostilities began. In America it was much like the previous Anglo-French war. French-inspired Abenaki Indians razed Deerfield, Massachusetts. A party of Carolinians burned St. Augustine in Spanish Florida. The New Englanders retook Port Royal. However, in Europe the forces of England, Holland, and Austria, led by the brilliant Duke of Marlborough, won a series of decisive victories. As a result, by the Treaty of Utrecht in 1713, France yielded Nova Scotia, Newfoundland, and the Hudson Bay region to Great Britain.

The American phase of the third Anglo-French conflict, the War of the Austrian Succession (1740–1748), was called King George's War. There was no fighting before 1744 in America; then the usual Indian raids were launched in both directions across the lonely forests that separated the St. Lawrence settlements from the New York and New England frontier. A New England force managed to capture the strategic fortress of Louisbourg on Cape Breton Island, guarding the entrance to the Gulf of St. Lawrence. The Treaty of Aix-la-Chapelle in 1748, however, required the return of Louisbourg to the French, much to the chagrin of the New Englanders.

While these conflicts did not directly involve any considerable portion of the colonial populace, they served to increase the bad feelings between settlers north and south of the St. Lawrence. Already suspicious of the French because of their religion, the English colonists now associated them with devilish treachery and the most wanton cruelty. Every Indian raid was attributed to French *provocateurs*, although more often than not the English themselves were responsible for the Indian troubles. Conflicting land claims further aggravated the situation. Massachusetts, Connecticut, and Virginia possessed overlapping claims to the Ohio Valley, and Pennsylvania and New York also had pretensions in the region. Yet the French, ranging broadly across the midcontinent, insisted that the Ohio country was exclusively theirs.

The Great War for the Empire

In this beautiful, almost untouched land, a handful of men determined the future of the continent. Over the years the French had established a chain of forts and trading posts throughout the northwest: from Mackinac Island in northern Michigan to Kaskaskia on the Mississippi and Vincennes on the Wabash, and from Niagara in the east to the Bourbon River, near Lake Winnipeg, in the west. By the 1740's, however, Pennsylvania fur traders, led by George Croghan, a rugged Irishman, were setting up posts north of the Ohio River and dickering with Miami and Huron tribesmen who ordinarily sold their furs to the French. In 1748 Croghan built a fort at Pickawillany, deep in the Miami country, in what is now western Ohio. That same year agents of a group of Virginia land speculators who had recently organized what they called the Ohio Company reached this area. A rival Virginia group, the Loyal Land Company, was also making ready to send settlers beyond the mountains.

With trifling exceptions, an insulating area of wilderness had always separated the French and English in America. Now the two powers came into actual contact. The immediate result was war—not a mere local reflection of a European dynastic quarrel but a showdown battle for control of North America. Thoroughly alarmed by the presence of Englishmen on land they had long considered their own, the French struck hard. Attacking suddenly in 1752, they wiped out Croghan's post at Pickawillany and drove his traders back into Pennsylvania. Then they built a string of barrier forts south from Lake Erie along the Pennsylvania line: Fort Presque Isle, Fort Le Boeuf, Fort Venango. The Pennsylvania authorities chose to ignore this action, but Lieutenant Governor Robert Dinwiddie of Virginia, who in addition to his official position was also an investor in the Ohio Company, dispatched

RARE BOOK ROOM, NEW YORK PUBLIC LIBRARY

The French-Indian attack on Deerfield during Queen Anne's War typified the savagery of frontier warfare. The raiders killed 53 and carried off 111 captives to Canada. This scene is from a 19th-century edition of an eyewitness account.

a 21-year-old surveyor named George Washington to warn the French that they were trespassing on Virginia property. (That Pennsylvania and Connecticut also claimed this particular land was later to cause still further trouble.)

Washington, a gangling, inarticulate, but courageous and intensely ambitious young planter, made his way northwest in the fall of 1753 and delivered Dinwiddie's message to the *commandant* at Fort Le Boeuf. It made no impression. "[The French] told me," Washington reported, "That it was their absolute Design to take Possession of the *Ohio*, and by G-- they would do it." Governor Dinwiddie thereupon promoted Washington to lieutenant colonel and sent him back in the spring of 1754 with 150 men to seize a strategic junction south of the new French forts, where the Allegheny and Monongahela rivers join to form the Ohio.

Eager but inexperienced in battle, young Washington botched his assignment. As his force labored painfully through the tangled mountain country southeast of the forks of the Ohio, he received word that the French had already occupied the position and were constructing a powerful post, Fort Duquesne. Outnumbered by perhaps four to one, Washington foolishly pushed on. He surprised and routed a French reconnaissance party, but this brought upon him the main body of enemy troops. Hastily he threw up a defensive position, aptly named Fort Necessity, but the ground was ill chosen; the French easily surrounded the fort and Washington had to surrender. After tricking the young officer, who could not read French, into signing an admission that he had "assassinated" the leader of the reconnaissance party, his captors, with the gateway to the Ohio country firmly in their hands, permitted him and his men to march off.

Nevertheless, Washington returned to Virginia a hero, for although still undeclared, this was war, and he had struck the first blow against the hated French. In the resulting conflict—the French and Indian War—the English colonists had a huge numerical advantage over the French, outnumbering them by about 1,500,000 to 90,000. But they were divided and disorganized, the French disciplined and united. The French already controlled the disputed territory, and most of the Indians took their side. With an ignorance and arrogance typical of 18th-century colonial administration, the British mismanaged the war and failed to make effective use of local resources. For several years they stumbled from one defeat to another.

General Edward Braddock, a competent but unimaginative soldier, was dispatched to Virginia to take command. In June 1755 he marched against Fort Duquesne with 1,400 Redcoats and a smaller number of colonials, only to be ambushed and decisively defeated by a much smaller force of French and Indians. Braddock died bravely in battle and only 500 of his men, led by Colonel Washington, who was serving as his aide-de-camp, made their way back to Virginia.

Elsewhere Anglo-American arms fared little better in the early years of the war. Fort Beauséjour in Nova Scotia was taken, but this was of small strategic import. Expeditions against Fort Niagara, key to all French defenses in the west, and Crown Point, gateway to Montreal, bogged down. Meanwhile the Indians, armed by the French, bathed the frontier in blood. Venting the frustrations caused by 150 years of white advance, they attacked defenseless outposts with unbelievable brutality. Crazed with hatred, they poured molten lead into their victims' wounds, ripped off the fingernails of captives, raped, kidnaped—even drank the blood of the brave who endured their tortures stoically. The most feared of the "French" Indians were the Delawares, a once-peaceful Pennsylvania tribe that had been harried from their homelands by Englishmen and Iroquois. General Braddock paid his own Indian allies only £5 each for French scalps, but offered £200 for the hair of Shinngass, the Delaware chieftain.

In 1756 the conflict spread to Europe to become the Seven Years' War, or what Lawrence Henry Gipson more accurately calls the Great War for the Empire. Prussia sided with Great Britain, Austria with the French. On the world stage, too, things went badly for the British. Finally, in 1757, as defeat succeeded defeat, King George II was forced to allow William Pitt, whom he personally detested, to take over leadership of the war effort. Pitt, grandson of "Diamond" Pitt, a *nouveau riche* East India merchant, was an unstable man who spent much of his life on the verge of madness, but he was an imaginative planner and a passionate orator, capable of inspiring the entire nation in its hour of trial.

Pitt recognized, as few contemporaries did, the potential value of North America. Instead of relying upon the tightfisted and shortsighted colonial assemblies for men and money, he poured regiment after regiment of British regulars and the full resources of the British Treasury into the contest, mortgaging the future recklessly to secure the prize. Grasping the importance of sea power in fighting a war on the other side of a great ocean, he used the British navy to bottle up the enemy fleet and hamper French communications with Canada. He possessed a keen eye for military genius, and when he discovered it, he ignored seniority and the outraged feelings of mediocre generals, promoting talented young officers to top commands. His greatest find was James Wolfe, whom he made a brigadier at 31. Wolfe and Major General Jeffrey Amherst, only ten years his senior and another of Pitt's discoveries, recaptured the Louisbourg fortress in July 1758.

NATIONAL PORTRAIT GALLERY, LONDON

William Pitt, Earl of Chatham, was painted c. 1766 by a follower of the portraitist Richard Brompton. The water color below, of Amherst's seizure of the French fortress of Louisbourg in 1758, is the work of Thomas Davies, an English artillery officer. Louisbourg is at center, under attack from Amherst's siege lines at right and Admiral Boscawen's British fleet lying offshore. French ships are aflame in the harbor.

ROYAL ARTILLERY INSTITUTE, LONDON

That winter, as Pitt's grand strategy matured, Fort Duquesne fell and was appropriately renamed Fort Pitt. The following summer Fort Niagara was overrun. Amherst took Crown Point, and Wolfe sailed up the St. Lawrence to Quebec. There the French General Montcalm had prepared a most formidable defense, but after months of probing and planning Wolfe found and exploited a chink in the city's armor, and on the Plains of Abraham defeated the French, although both he and Montcalm died in the battle. In 1760 Montreal fell, and the French abandoned all Canada to the British. Spain attempted to stem the British advance but failed utterly. A Far Eastern fleet captured Manila in 1762, and another British force took Cuba. The French sugar islands in the West Indies also fell, while in India British troops reduced the French posts one by one.

Peace was restored in 1763 by the Treaty of Paris. Its terms were very moderate considering the extent of the British triumph. France abandoned all claim to North America except two small islands in the St. Lawrence; Great Britain took over Canada and the eastern half of the Mississippi Valley, Spain (in a separate treaty) the area west of the great river and New Orleans. But Guadeloupe and Martinique, the rich French sugar islands, were returned by the British, as were some of the captured French possessions in India and Africa. Spain got back both the Philippine Islands and Cuba but in exchange the Spanish ceded East and West Florida to Great Britain. France and Spain thus remained important colonial powers.

From the point of view of the English colonists in America, the victory was overwhelming. "Half

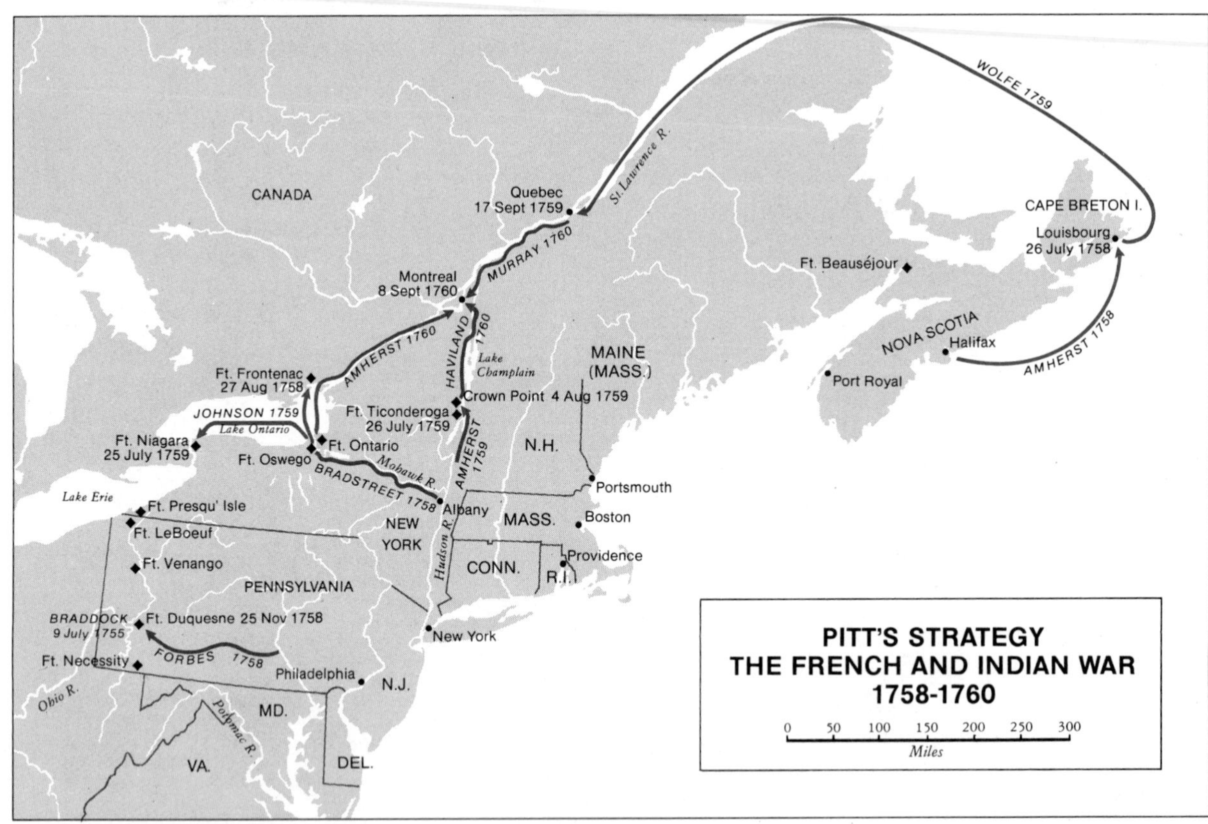

A key phase of Pitt's American strategy involved the reduction of French strongpoints guarding the approaches to Canada: Louisbourg, protecting the St. Lawrence; Ticonderoga and Crown Point, on Lake Champlain; and Fort Duquesne, in the Ohio Country. Colonial forces played a significant role in this strategy, John Forbes seizing Fort Duquesne, John Bradstreet winning control of Lake Ontario, and William Johnson taking Fort Niagara.

the continent," as the great historian Francis Parkman so aptly put it, "had changed hands at the scratch of a pen." With this stroke all threat to their frontiers seemed to have been swept away. Surely, they believed in these first happy moments of victory, their peaceful and prosperous expansion for countless generations was now assured.

And no honest man could deny that the victory had been chiefly won by British troops and with British gold. Colonial militiamen fought well in defense of their homes or when some highly prized objective seemed ripe for the plucking, but they usually lacked discipline and determination when required to fight far from home and under the command of men they did not know. As one American official frankly admitted to the British conmmander in chief, it was difficult to get New Englanders to enlist "unless assurances can be given that they shall not march to the southward of certain limits." General Wolfe had only contempt for colonial troops, and another English officer compared the ordinary run to "broken innkeepers, horse jockeys and Indian traders." Although colonials naturally did not accept this evaluation, they were happy enough to see the scarlet-clad British regulars bear the brunt of the fighting and happier still when the Crown shouldered most of the financial burden of the long struggle. The local assemblies contributed to the cost, but except for Massachusetts and Virginia their outlays were trivial compared with the £82 million poured into the worldwide conflict by the British.

Little wonder that the great victory produced a burst of praise for king and mother country all over America. Parades, cannonading, fireworks, banquets, the pealing of churchbells–these were the order of the day in every colonial town. "Let us fear God and honor the King, and be peaceable subjects of an easy and happy government," one New England minister declared. Ezra Stiles, later president of Yale, extolled "the illustrious House of Hanover," whose new head, the young George III, had inherited the throne in 1760. "Nothing," said Thomas Pownall, wartime governor of Massachusetts and a student of colonial administration, "can eradicate from [the colonists'] hearts their natural, almost mechanical affection to Great Britain."

Postwar Problems

In London peace proved a time for reassessment; that the empire of 1763 was not the same as the empire of 1754 was obvious. The new, far larger dominion would be much more expensive to maintain. Pitt had spent a huge sum winning and securing it, much of it borrowed money. Great Britain's national debt doubled between 1754 and 1763. Now this debt must be serviced and repaid, and the strain that this would place upon the economy was clear to all. Furthermore, the day-to-day cost of administering an empire that extended from Hudson Bay to India was far larger than that which the already burdened British taxpayer could be expected to bear. For example, before the Great War for the Empire, Britain's North American possessions were administered for about £70,000 a year, but after 1763 the cost was five times as much.

This American empire had also grown far more complex. A system of administration that treated it as a string of separate plantations struggling to exist on the edge of the forest would no longer suffice, for growth had produced clashes of interest that demanded cooperation and compromise, the weighing and balancing of complex forces. The old system was not properly equipped for such tasks.

The war had been fought for control of the Ohio Valley but had not settled the questions of exactly who would govern the region or what was to be done with it. Seven years of Indian terror had dammed up the westward movement. Now pressures were mounting for renewed expansion. Yet conflicting colonial claims, based on charters drafted by men who thought the Pacific lay over the next hill, threatened to make the great valley a battleground once more. The Indians remained unpacified, urged to fight on by Spaniards in the area around New Orleans who sought to check and throw back the American advance. Rival land companies contested for charters, while fur traders, eager to absorb the riches formerly controlled by France, strove to hold back the wave of settlement that must inevitably destroy the world of the beaver and the deer. One Englishman who traveled through America at this time predicted that if the colonists were left to their own devices "there would soon be civil war from one end of the continent to the other."

Apparently only Great Britain could deal with these problems and rivalries, for when a far-sighted man like Franklin had proposed a rudimentary form of colonial union—the Albany Plan of 1754—it was almost universally rejected by the Americans themselves. Unfortunately, however, the British government did not rise to the challenge that the new empire posed. Perhaps this was to be expected, given the singularly ineffective, sordid, and corrupt nature of 18th-century British politics. The government, according to the modern English authority J. H. Plumb, was "an extremely complex system of political bargaining and blackmail." Increasingly the British public was coming to look upon Parliament as "debased and rotten." A handful of aristocrats (there were fewer than 150 peers active in government affairs) dominated every phase of mid-18th-century political activity, and they were far more concerned with local offices and personal advantage than with large questions of policy. An American who spent some time in London in 1764 trying to obtain approval for a plan for the development of the west reported: "The people hear Spend thire time in Nothing but abuseing one Another and Striveing who shall be in power with a view to Serve themselves and Thire friends." As for the 18th-century Hanoverian kings, George I and George II were not indifferent to national affairs and George III was not a tyrant, as once was commonly believed, but the first two were stupid and the third at best an inept politician.

Furthermore, even the best-educated Englishmen were nearly all monumentally ignorant of American conditions. The British imperial system lacked effective channels of communication. Most of the knowledge about American attitudes available to the government came from royal officials in the colonies and others with special interests to protect or advance, or from the colonial agents and merchants in London, whose information was often out of date. Serene in their ignorance, most English leaders insisted that colonials were uncouth and generally inferior beings. During the French and Indian War, officers possessed of royal commissions outranked all officers of the colonial militia, regardless of title. Young Colonel Washington, for example, was irritated and frustrated by what one of his biographers called his "ambiguous and anomalous" position. On one occasion he was forced to travel all the way from Virginia to the headquarters of the commander in chief in Boston to establish his precedence over one Captain John Dagworthy, a Maryland officer who had *formerly* held a royal commission and who did not propose to let a mere colonial colonel outrank him.

Many Englishmen also resented the colonists, partly because they made poor soldiers and were stingy about contributing to the cost of the fighting during the wars with France, and partly because the colonies were rapidly becoming rich and powerful. Shortly after the war, John Adams predicted that within a century America would be wealthier and more populous than Great Britain.* If Englishmen did not say much about this possibility, they too considered it from time to time, and naturally without Adams' relish. The willingness of many American merchants to continue trading with the French West Indies during the wars especially irritated patriots in the mother country. Such activity was both disloyal and illegal, but the French sugar planters needed American food, lumber, and other products desperately and would pay well for them; for many merchants this fact outweighed patriotism, law—and morality.

Tightening Imperial Controls

The attempt of the inefficient, ignorant, envious, and indignant British government to deal with the intricate colonial problems that resulted from the Great War for the Empire led to the American Revolution—a rebellion that was costly and unnecessary, but

*As early as 1751, Franklin predicted that in a century "the greatest number of Englishmen will be on this Side of the Water."

which produced excellent results for the colonists, for Great Britain, for the rest of the empire, and eventually for the entire world. The trouble resulted from the decision of British authorities after the war to intervene more actively in American affairs. Theoretically, the colonies were entirely subordinate to Crown and Parliament, yet the practice of more than a century had been to allow them a remarkable degree of freedom to manage their own affairs. Of course they had come to expect this as their right.

Parliament had never attempted to raise a revenue in America. "Compelling the colonies to pay money without their consent would be rather like raising contributions in an enemy's country than taxing Englishmen for their own benefit," Benjamin Franklin wrote. That shrewd judge of men Sir Robert Walpole, initiator of the policy of salutary neglect, recognized the colonial viewpoint. He responded to a suggestion that Parliament tax the colonies by saying: "I will leave that for some of my successors, who may have more courage than I have." Nevertheless, the *legality* of parliamentary taxation, or of other parliamentary intervention in colonial affairs, had not been seriously contested. For instance, during King George's War and again during the French and Indian War many British officials in America suggested that Parliament tax the colonies.

However, nothing was done until 1759, when British victories had made ultimate triumph sure. Then a general tightening of imperial regulations began: important Virginia and South Carolina laws were disallowed, and royal control over the colonial courts was tightened. In Massachusetts the use of general search warrants (writs of assistance) was authorized in 1761. These writs, enabling customs men searching for smuggled goods to invade homes and warehouses without evidence or specific court orders, had been employed without opposition in wartime when trading with the enemy was tantamount to treason. Once the emergency was over, however, their use seemed to violate basic civil liberties. James Otis, futilely arguing the case of some Boston merchants, claimed that writs of assistance were "against the Constitution" and therefore "void," thus suggesting that Parliament's authority over the colonies was not absolute.

After the signing of the peace treaty in 1763, events pushed the British authorities to still more vigorous activity in America. Freed of the restraint imposed by French competition, Englishman and colonist increased their pressure on the Indians. Cynical fur traders now cheated them outrageously, while callous military men hoped to exterminate them like vermin. The British commander in the west, Lord Jeffrey Amherst, suggested infecting the Indians with smallpox, and another officer expressed the wish that they could be hunted down with dogs. Led by an Ottawa chief named Pontiac, the desperate tribes made one last effort to drive the white men back across the mountains. Pontiac's Rebellion caused much havoc, but it failed. By 1764 most of the western tribes had accepted the peace terms offered by a royal commissioner, Sir William Johnson, one of the few white men who understood and sympathized with the Indians. Meanwhile, with the frontier in flames and rival groups of land speculators clamoring for trans-Appalachian grants, the British government had proclaimed a new policy: no settlers were to cross the Appalachian divide. Only licensed traders might do business with the Indians in this prohibited zone. The purchase of Indian land was outlawed. In compensation, three new colonies—Quebec, East Florida, and West Florida—were created, but these were not permitted to set up local assemblies.

This Proclamation of 1763 excited much indignation in America. Some settlers had already pushed into what is now Kentucky; these were abandoned to the vengeance of the red men. The frustration of dozens of schemes for land development in the Ohio Valley angered many influential colonists. Colonel Washington, for example, referred to the proclamation contemptuously as "a temporary expedient to quiet the minds of Indians," and he continued to stake out claims to western lands. The licensing of fur traders aroused opposition, especially when the British mishandled the task of regulating the trade.

Originally, the British had intended the proclamation to be temporary. With the passage of time, however, sentiment for maintaining it in-

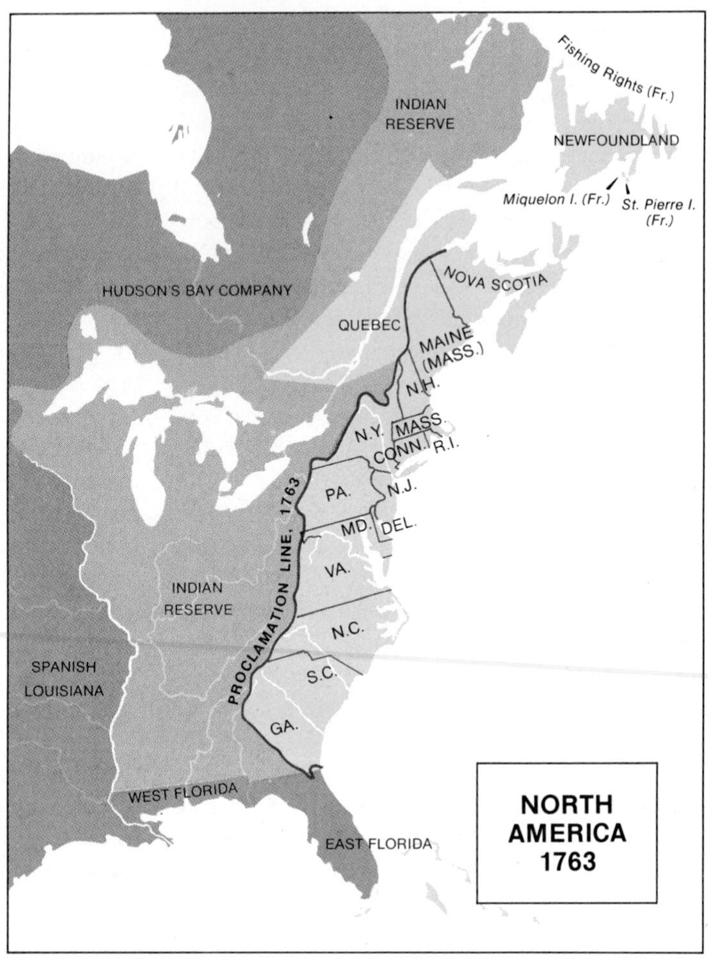

George III's Proclamation of 1763 in effect reserved for the Indians the vast area of trans-Appalachia (except for the new royal colonies of Quebec, East Florida, and West Florida) as far west as Spanish Louisiana and as far north as the Hudson's Bay Company preserve.

creased. To some officials, checking the westward expansion of the colonies seemed a good way of keeping them tied closely to the mother country. The proclamation line, the Board of Trade declared, was "necessary for the preservation of the colonies in due subordination."* Naturally, this attitude caused bitter resentment in America. To close off the west temporarily in order to pacify the Indians made some sense; to keep it closed, as Great Britain apparently wished to do, was almost like trying to contain a tidal wave.

*The British were particularly concerned about preserving the colonies as markets for their manufactures. They feared that the spread of population beyond the mountains would stimulate local manufacturing because the high cost of land transportation would make British goods prohibitively expensive.

Beginnings of the Great Debate

Americans disliked the new western policy, but since sensible men realized that the western problems were knotty and that no simple solution for them existed, colonial protests were somewhat muted. Great Britain's effort to raise money in America to help support the increased cost of colonial administration caused far more vehement complaints. George Grenville, who became prime minister in 1763, was a fairly able man, although long-winded and rather narrow in outlook, with a reputation as a financial expert based chiefly on his eagerness to reduce government spending. His program for meeting the postwar financial crisis, though logical, was not particularly imaginative; it was also unrealistic and ineptly executed.

Under his leadership Parliament passed, in April 1764, the so-called Sugar Act. This law placed tariffs on sugar, coffee, wines, and many other products imported directly into America in substantial amounts. Taxes on European products imported by way of Great Britain were doubled, and the enumerated articles list was extended to include iron, raw silk, potash, and several other items. The sixpence-per-gallon tax on foreign molasses, first imposed in 1733 and designed to be prohibitively high, was reduced to threepence, at which level the foreign product could compete with that of the British West Indies. At the same time, new measures aimed at enforcing all the trade laws were put into effect—a threepenny molasses duty would not produce much revenue if it were as easy to avoid as the old levy had been. Those accused of violating the Sugar Act were to be tried before British naval officers in vice-admiralty courts. Grenville was determined to end both smuggling and the corruption and inefficiency that had plagued the customs service for decades.

These measures and also the decision of the government in London to restrict the printing of paper money in the colonies disturbed Americans deeply. Throughout the 18th century local assemblies had issued paper currency in anticipation of tax payments to finance emergencies such as wars. To meet more general needs, some had experimented with land banks, institutions which issued paper money backed by mortgages on land. Although in a few instances these issues of paper money had been allowed to get out of hand, thus causing inflation, in most cases the colonial governments had managed the issues responsibly and the money had held its value well. The act of 1764 merely imposed restrictions on colonial paper; it did not prevent its use. But coming at a time when Americans had large debts outstanding and when business was poor after a long wartime boom, the combination of possibly deflationary legislation and new taxes seemed most alarming.

Far more alarming, however, was the nature of the Sugar Act and the manner of its passage. Even if the legality of the act had been beyond question, it would have been natural for the colonists to feel threatened, since Parliament had never before tried to exercise the tax power in America. The Navigation Acts had imposed duties of many kinds, but these had been intended to regulate commerce and the sums actually collected had been trivial. Indeed, the Navigation Acts might well be considered an instrument of imperial foreign policy, an area of government that everyone willingly conceded to London. Few Americans, however, were willing to concede that Parliament had the right to tax them. As *Englishmen* (and as readers of John Locke) they believed that no one should be deprived arbitrarily of his property, and that, as James Otis put it in his stirring pamphlet *The Rights of the British Colonies Asserted and Proved*, every man should be "free from all taxes but what he consents to in person, or by his representative." Property, as Locke had made clear in his *Second Treatise of Government* (1690), ought never be taken from a man without his consent, not because material values transcend all others but because human liberty can never be secure when arbitrary power of any kind exists. "If our Trade may be taxed why not our Lands?" the Boston town meeting asked when news of the Sugar Act reached America. "Why not the produce of our Lands and every Thing we possess or make use of?" And the New York assembly asked: "Who can call that his own which can be taken away at the Pleasure of another?"

To most people in Great Britain the colonial protest against taxation without representation seemed a hypocritical quibble. The distinction between tax laws and other types of legislation was artificial, they reasoned. Either Parliament was sovereign in America or it was not, and only a fool or a traitor would argue that it was not. If the colonists were loyal subjects to George III, as they claimed, they should bear cheerfully their fair share of the cost of governing his widespread dominions. As to representation, the colonies *were* represented in Parliament; every member of that body stood for the interests of the entire empire. If Americans had no say in the election of members of Commons, neither did most Englishmen.

This concept, known as "virtual" representation, accurately described the British system, but it made no sense in America, where from the time of the first settlements members of the colonial assemblies had represented the people of the districts in which they stood for office. Thus, the confusion between virtual and "direct" representation revealed the extent to which colonial and British political practices had diverged over the years. Yet the British were partly correct in concluding that selfish motives influenced colonial objections to the Sugar Act. The colonists denounced taxation without representation, but would have rejected the offer of a reasonable number of seats in Parliament if it had been made, and would probably have complained about paying taxes to support imperial administration even if imposed by their own assemblies. American abundance and the simplicity of colonial life had enabled them to prosper without assuming any considerable tax burden. Now their maturing society was beginning to require communal rather than merely individual solutions to the problems of existence, and not many of them were prepared to face up to this hard truth.

Over the whole course of colonial history Americans had taken a singularly narrow view of imperial concerns. They had avoided complying with the Navigation Acts whenever they could profit by doing so. During the wars with France merchants had continued to trade with the French West Indies. Colonial militiamen compiled a sorry record when asked to fight for Britain or even for the inhabitants of colonies other than their own, and colonial legislatures had been extremely reluctant to spend money to help the general cause in time of war. Most Americans professed loyalty to the Crown, it is true, but not many would voluntarily open their purses except to benefit themselves. In short, they were provincials, in attitude as well as in fact. Many of the difficulties they faced after they won their independence resulted from this narrowness of outlook.

Nevertheless, the colonies were genuinely concerned about the principle of taxation without representation. In every section men denounced it vigorously. However, they were unable to agree upon a common plan of resistance. Many of the assemblies drafted protests, but these varied in force as well as in form. A number of merchant groups tried to organize boycotts of products subject to the new taxes. They met with only indifferent success. Then in 1765 Parliament provided the flux necessary for welding colonial opinion by passing the Stamp Act.

The Stamp Act Crisis

The Stamp Act placed stiff excises on colonial newspapers, legal documents, licenses, and virtually all other kinds of printed matter, including playing cards. Stamp duties were supposed to be relatively painless and cheap to collect; in England, similar taxes brought in about £100,000 annually. Grenville hoped the Stamp Act would produce £60,000 a year in America, and the law provided that all this revenue should be applied to "defraying the necessary expenses of defending, protecting, and securing, the . . . colonies."

Hardly a farthing was actually collected, for the colonists rose almost as one man to resist the new law. The Sugar Act had been at least related to Parliament's uncontested power to control colonial trade, but the Stamp Act was a direct tax. When Parliament ignored the politely phrased petitions of the colonial assemblies, more vigorous protests quickly followed. Virginia took the lead. In late May of 1765 Patrick Henry, fresh from his triumph in the Parson's Cause controversy, introduced resolutions in the colonial assembly redundantly asserting that the House of Burgesses possessed "the only and sole and exclusive right and power to lay taxes" on Virginians and suggesting that Parliament had no legal authority to tax the colonies at all. Henry spoke for what the royal governor called the "Young, hot and Giddy Members" of the legislature, and the more extreme of his resolutions failed of enactment, but the debate they occasioned attracted wide and favorable attention in many quarters. On June 6 the Massachusetts assembly proposed an intercolonial Stamp Act Congress which, when it met in October, passed another series of resolutions of protest. During the summer an irregular organization known as the Sons of Liberty began to agitate against the act. Although led by men of character and position, the "Liberty Boys" frequently resorted to violence to achieve their aims. In Boston they staged a vicious riot, looting the houses of the stamp master and the lieutenant governor and destroying important government records. The Maryland stamp master was burned in effigy when he refused to resign. He fled to New York and went into hiding, but the local Sons of Liberty rooted him out, and in the end he also resigned. The fate of most of the other stamp masters was little different.

The stamps themselves were printed in England and shipped to stamp masters (all Americans) in the colonies well in advance of November 1, 1765, the date the law was to go into effect. When the stamps reached New York harbor, all vessels in the port lowered their colors in protest. At Portsmouth, New Hampshire, "patriots" ceremoniously buried a copy of the law. Some of the stamps were quickly snatched up by mobs and put to the torch amid rejoicing. Others were locked up in secret by British officials or held on shipboard. For a time after November 1, no business requiring stamped paper was transacted; then, gradually, people began to defy the law by issuing and accepting unstamped documents. Threatened by mob action should they resist, British officials stood by helplessly. The law was a dead letter.

That Americans would dislike the Stamp Act was a foregone conclusion. Nevertheless, Parliament had not anticipated that they would react so violently and so unanimously. They did so for many reasons. Business continued poor in 1765, and the stamp taxes (20 shillings for a liquor license, 5 for a will, 2 for an advertisement in a newspaper) represented a heavy additional burden. The taxes affected every colony and a variety of important interests: lawyers, merchants, newspaper editors, tavernkeepers, and even clergymen dealt with papers requiring stamps. These were articulate and influential men; their combined protests had an immediate and powerful impact on public opinion. But the greatest cause of alarm to the colonists was Great Britain's clear violation of the principle of no taxation without representation. To buy a stamp was to surrender all claim to self-government, or so the colonists believed. Almost no colonist in 1765 wished to be independent of Great Britain, but all valued highly their local autonomy and what they called "the rights of Englishmen." They saw the Stamp Act as only the worst of a series of invasions of these rights. Already Parliament had passed still another measure, the Quartering Act, requiring the colonists to house and feed new British troops sent to the colonies. Reluctantly, many Americans were beginning to fear that the British authorities had organized a conspiracy to deprive them of their liberties, indeed, to subvert the liberties of all Englishmen.

In the 18th century, Englishmen on both sides of the Atlantic considered themselves, with justice, the freest people in the world. They attributed their freedom to what they called their "balanced" government. In England, power appeared to be shared by the Crown, the House

PRINT DEPARTMENT, METROPOLITAN MUSEUM OF ART

A woodcut reveals the unsubtle methods used by New Hampshirites to intimidate a stamp master. As his effigy is stoned and jeered, a mock funeral procession (at left) begins.

of Lords (representing the aristocracy), and the House of Commons (representing the rest of the realm). The governors, councils, and assemblies seemed to play analogous roles in the colonies. In reality, this balance of separate forces never existed, either in Britain or America. The apparent harmony of society and the resultant freedom was in both instances product of a lack of seriously divisive issues, not of dynamic tension between rival forces. But the new laws seemed to Americans to threaten the balance, and this idea was reinforced by their observations of the corruption of English elections and the cynical way in which the ministry controlled Parliament by the use of patronage. A clique, seeking unlimited power, was trying to destroy balanced government in Britain and in America, they thought.

There was no such conspiracy, that is clear, but to the question: "Were American rights actually in danger?" no certain answer can be made. Grenville and his successors were English politicians, not tyrants. They looked down on bumptious colonials but surely had no wish to destroy either them or their prosperity. The British attitude was like that of a parent making a recalcitrant youngster swallow a bitter-tasting medicine: protests were understandable, but in the patient's own interest they must be ignored. On the other hand, British leaders did feel that the time had come to assert royal authority and centralize imperial power at the expense of colonial autonomy. And they were psychologically unready to deal with Americans as equals or to consider American interests on a par with their own. Above all, they knew little about America and were uninterested in learning more. In the long run, American liberty would be destroyed if this attitude were not changed.

Beside refusing to use stamps, Americans responded to the Stamp Act by boycotting British goods. Nearly a thousand merchants signed nonimportation agreements. These struck British merchants hard in their pocketbooks, and they in turn began to bring pressure on Parliament for repeal. After a hot debate—Grenville, whose ministry had fallen over another issue, advocated using the army to enforce the act—the hated law

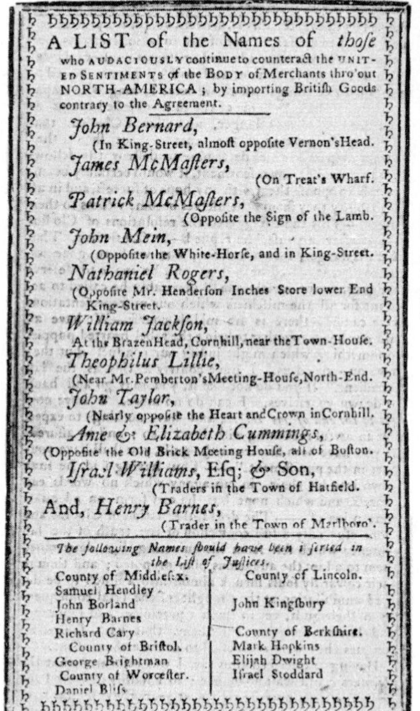

A LIST of the Names of *those* who AUDACIOUSLY continue to counteract the UNITED SENTIMENTS of the BODY of Merchants thro'out NORTH-AMERICA; by importing British Goods contrary to the Agreement.

John Bernard,
(In King-Street, almost opposite Vernon's Head.

James McMasters,
(On Treat's Wharf.

Patrick McMasters,
(Opposite the Sign of the Lamb.

John Mein,
(Opposite the White-Horse, and in King-Street.

Nathaniel Rogers,
(Opposite Mr. Henderson Inches Store lower End King-Street.

William Jackson,
At the Brazen Head, Cornhill, near the Town-House.

Theophilus Lillie,
(Near Mr. Pemberton's Meeting-House, North-End.

John Taylor,
(Nearly opposite the Heart and Crown in Cornhill.

Ame & Elizabeth Cummings,
(Opposite the Old Brick Meeting House, all of Boston.

Israel Williams, Esq; & Son,
(Traders in the Town of Hatfield.

And, *Henry Barnes,*
(Trader in the Town of Marlboro'.

The following Names should have been inserted in the List of Justices.

County of Middlesex.
Samuel Hendley
John Borland
Henry Barnes
Richard Cary

County of Bristol.
George Brightman

County of Worcester.
Daniel Bliss

County of Lincoln.
John Kingsbury

County of Berkshire.
Mark Hopkins
Elijah Dwight
Israel Stoddard

RARE BOOK ROOM, NEW YORK PUBLIC LIBRARY

The "blacklist" above, from the North-American Almanack, *was intended to put pressure on merchants in and around Boston who refused to sign nonimportation agreements. Whether they signed or not, merchants such as Boston's John Amory, painted below by John Singleton Copley, suffered economic losses.*

MUSEUM OF FINE ARTS, BOSTON

was repealed in March 1766. The influence of William Pitt and of the young George III was decisive. In America there was jubilation at the news, and the ban on British goods was lifted at once. Colonists congratulated themselves on having stood fast in defense of a principle and having won their point.

However, the great controversy over the constitutional relationship of colony to mother country, an attempt, as Edmund S. Morgan has said, to put into words "the dimensions of an authority hitherto unmeasured," was only beginning. The same day that it repealed the Stamp Act, Parliament passed a Declaratory Act stating that the colonies were "subordinate" and that Parliament could enact any law it wished "to bind the colonies and people of *America*."

To most Americans this bald statement of Parliamentary authority seemed unconstitutional—a flagrant violation of their conception of how the British imperial system worked. Actually, the Declaratory Act highlighted the degree to which British and American views of the system had drifted apart. Englishmen and colonials were using the same words, but giving them different meanings. Their conflicting definitions of the word *representation* was a case in point. Another involved the word *constitution*. To Englishmen, the constitution meant the totality of laws, customs, and institutions that had developed over time and under which the nation functioned. In America, however, partly because their governments were based upon specific charters, men used the word to mean a written document or contract spelling out, and thus limiting, the powers of government. If in England, Parliament passed an "unconstitutional" law, the result might be rebellion, but that the law existed none would deny. "If the parliament will positively enact a thing to be done which is unreasonable," the great 18th-century English legal authority Sir William Blackstone wrote, "I know of no power that can control it." In America, the colonists were beginning to think that an unconstitutional law simply had no force.

Even more basic were the differing meanings that Englishmen and Americans were giving to the word *sovereignty*. As Professor Bernard Bailyn has explained in *The Ideological Origins of the American Revolution*, 18th-century English political thinkers believed that sovereignty (ultimate political power) could not be divided. Government and law being based ultimately on force, some "final, unqualified, indivisible" authority had to exist if social order was to be preserved. The Glorious Revolution in England had settled the question of where sovereignty resided—in Parliament. The Declaratory Act, so obnoxious to Americans, seemed to Englishmen the mere explication of the obvious. That colonial governments had passed local laws Englishmen did not deny, but they had done so at the sufferance of the sovereign legislative power—Parliament.

Given these ideas and the long tradition out of which they had sprung, one can sympathize with the British failure to follow the colonists' reasoning, which, furthermore, had not yet evolved into a specific proposal for constitutional reform. But the fact remains that most responsible British officials refused even to listen to the American argument.

The Townshend Acts

Nor, despite the repeal of the Stamp Act, did the British abandon the idea of taxing the colonies. Perhaps direct taxes were inexpedient, but indirect ones like the Sugar Act certainly were not. To persuade Parliament to repeal the Stamp Act, some Americans, most notably Benjamin Franklin, had claimed that the colonists objected only to direct taxes. To draw such a distinction as a matter of principle was absurd, and in fact few colonists had done so. British leaders quickly saw the absurdity, but easily convinced themselves that Americans were actually making the distinction. The government was hard pressed for funds to cover an annual budget of over £8.5 million. Therefore, in June 1767, the chancellor of the exchequer, Charles Townshend, introduced a series of new levies on glass, lead, paints, paper, and tea imported into the colonies. Townshend was a charming and witty man, experienced in colonial administration, but he was something of a playboy (his nickname was "Champagne Charlie"), and he lacked both integrity and common sense. He liked to think of Americans as ungrateful brats; he once said he would rather see the colonies turned into "Primitive Desarts" than treat them as equals. Townshend thought it "perfect nonsense" to draw a distinction between direct and indirect taxation, but in his arrogance he believed the colonists were stupid enough to do so.

By this time the colonists were thoroughly on guard, and they responded quickly to the Townshend levies with a new boycott of British goods. In addition they made elaborate efforts to stimulate colonial manufacturing, and by the end of 1769 imports from the mother country had been almost halved. Meanwhile, administrative measures enacted along with the Townshend duties were creating more ill will. A Board of Customs Commissioners, with headquarters in Boston, took charge of enforcing the trade laws, and new vice-admiralty courts were set up at Halifax, Boston, Philadelphia, and Charleston to handle violations. These courts operated without juries, and the new commissioners proved to be a gang of rapacious racketeers, who systematically attempted to obtain judgments against honest merchants in order to collect the huge forfeitures–one-third of the value of ship and cargo–that were their share of all seizures.

The struggle forced Americans to do some deep thinking about both American and imperial political affairs. Some kind of union was probably inevitable considering the colonies' common interests and growing economic and social interrelationships; trouble with England naturally pushed them toward cooperation more rapidly. In 1765 the Stamp Act Congress had brought the delegates of nine colonies to New York. Now, in 1768, the Massachusetts General Court took the next step by sending a "Circular Letter" to the legislatures of the other colonies summarizing Massachusetts' feelings about the Townshend Acts and soliciting suggestions as to what should be done. The question of the limits of British power in America was also much debated, and this too was no doubt inevitable, again because of change and growth. As the colonies matured, the balance of Anglo-American power *had* to shift or the system would become tyrannical. Even in the 17th century the attitude of mind that led Parliament to pass the Declaratory Act would have been both insupportable and unrealistic. By 1766 it would have been vicious were it not absurd. Once intelligent men examined the political system closely, they found themselves challenging Britain's view of imperial relations.

After the passage of the Townshend Acts, a lawyer named John Dickinson wrote a series of *Letters from a Farmer in Pennsylvania to the Inhabitants of the British Colonies.* Dickinson was no revolutionary; he considered himself a loyal British subject trying to find a solution to colonial troubles. "Let us behave like dutiful children, who have received unmerited blows from a beloved parent," he wrote. Nevertheless, he also stated plainly that while Parliament was sovereign, it had no right to tax the colonies, although it might collect incidental revenues in the process of regulating commerce.

STOKES COLLECTION, NEW YORK PUBLIC LIBRARY

Paul Revere's engraved view of the landing of two regiments of Redcoats on Boston's Long Wharf in 1768 bears Revere's sarcastic comment that the British ships anchored with "Cannon loaded, a Spring on their Cables, as for a regular Siege."

Many Americans were much more radical than Dickinson. Samuel Adams of Boston, for example, a genuine revolutionary agitator, organizer of the nonimportation agreements and something of a rabble-rouser, believed by 1768 that Parliament had no right to legislate at all for the colonies. Few were ready to go so far, but fewer still would accept the reasoning behind the Declaratory Act. The British, however, ignored American thinking. The Massachusetts Circular Letter had been framed in moderate language and clearly reflected the convictions of most of the people in the Bay Colony, yet when news of it reached England, the secretary of state for the colonies, Lord Hillsborough, ordered the governor to dissolve the legislature, and two regiments of British troops were shipped to Boston.

Such vindictiveness, hardly calculated to win support in any case, convinced still more Americans that the British were conspiring to destroy their liberties. The citizens of Boston found it galling that companies of Redcoats should patrol their streets with the country at peace and no enemy in sight. A series of petty incidents between soldiers and townspeople, culminating in the Boston Massacre (March 1770) in which Redcoats fired upon an angry crowd, killing five, exacerbated public feeling. Such tragic and useless violence played into the hands of radicals like Samuel Adams, who, for complicated motives involving ambition, conviction, and personal insecurity, was now bent upon driving a permanent wedge between Great Britain and the colonies.

However, the British authorities finally gave up trying to raise revenue in the colonies, and in April 1770 repealed all the Townshend duties except the threepenny tax on tea. They maintained the tea tax as a matter of principle. "A peppercorn in acknowledgment of the right was of more value

MUSEUM OF FINE ARTS, BOSTON

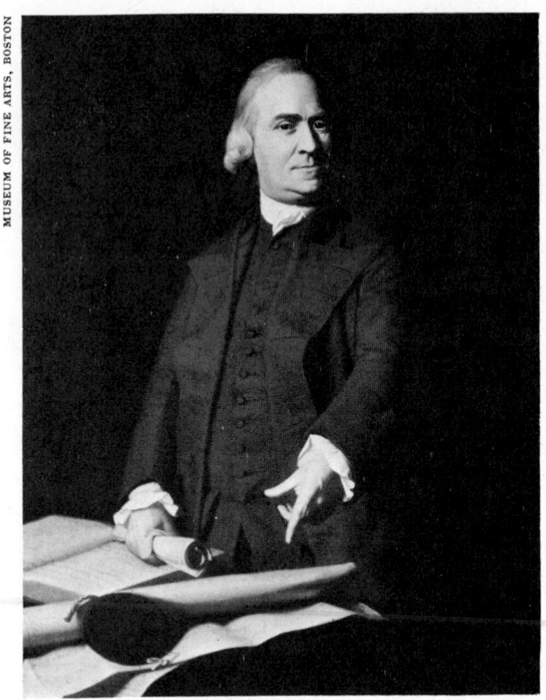

In Copley's flattering portrait, painted in 1771, Samuel Adams points to the Massachusetts charter as if reminding Great Britain of the colonists' rights.

than millions without it," one British peer declared smugly—a glib fallacy. At this point the nonimportation movement collapsed; although the boycott on tea was continued, many merchants imported British tea and paid the tax too. "Drank green tea," one patriot wrote in describing an afternoon at the merchant John Hancock's. "From Holland, I hope, but don't know." For the next two years no serious crisis developed. Good times returned. So long as the British continued to be conciliatory, the colonists seemed satisfied with their place in the empire.

Then, in 1772, new troubles broke out. The first was plainly the fault of the colonists involved. Early in June the British patrol boat *Gaspee* ran aground in Narragansett Bay, south of Providence, while pursuing a suspected smuggler. The *Gaspee*'s commander, Lieutenant Dudingston, had antagonized everyone in the area by his officiousness and zeal; that night a gang of local people boarded the helpless *Gaspee*; Dudingston was wounded and the ship put to the torch. This action was clearly criminal, but when the British attempted to bring the culprits to justice no one would testify against them. The British, frustrated and angry, were strengthened in their conviction that the colonists were utterly lawless. Meanwhile, Governor Thomas Hutchinson of Massachusetts suddenly announced that he would receive his salary henceforth from the Crown rather than from the local legislature. Since control over the salaries of royal officials gave the legislature a powerful hold on them, this development was most disturbing. Colonial suspicions of British motives mounted once again, especially when it was revealed that henceforth judges would also be paid by the London government. Groups of radicals in the various colonies, forming into "committees of correspondence," stepped up communications with one another, planning joint action in case of trouble.

The Tea Act Crisis

Then, in the spring of 1773, an entirely new event precipitated the final crisis. Throughout the colonial period the British East India Company held a monopoly of all trade between India and the rest of the empire. For example, no American ship could enter an Indian port. Over the years this monopoly had produced fantastic returns, but decades of corruption and inefficiency together with heavy military expenses in recent years had weakened the company until it stood in grave danger of bankruptcy.

Among the assets of this venerable company were some 17 million pounds of tea, stored in English warehouses. The decline of the American market, a result first of the boycott and then of the smuggling of cheaper Dutch tea, partly accounted for this glut. Normally, East India Company tea was sold to English wholesalers. They in turn sold it to American wholesalers, who distributed it to local merchants for sale to the consumer. In addition, a substantial British tax was levied on the tea as well as the threepenny Townshend duty. Now Lord North, the new prime minister, decided to remit the British tax and to allow the company to sell directly in America through its own agents, thus eliminating both British and American wholesalers. The sav-

PRINT DEPARTMENT, METROPOLITAN MUSEUM OF ART

Revere's famous engraving of the Boston Massacre was potent propaganda fully exploited by the Boston radicals. His view of a deliberately ordered, concerted volley fired into a goup of innocent citizens bore slight resemblance to fact. At the trial of the British soldiers, the jury was warned against "the prints exhibited in our houses" that added "wings to fancy." Two soldiers were punished mildly, the rest acquitted.

ings would permit a sharp reduction of the retail price and at the same time yield a nice profit to the company. The Townshend tax was retained, however, to preserve (as Lord North said when the East India Company directors suggested its repeal) the principle of Parliament's right to tax the colonies.

Selecting a group of American merchants to act as its agents, the company then consigned 1,700 chests of tea to various colonial ports. Many Americans were tempted by this high-quality tea offered at bargain prices, but after a little thought nearly everyone appreciated the grave danger involved in buying it. If Parliament could grant the East India Company a monopoly of the tea trade, it could parcel out all or any part of American commerce to whomever it pleased. More important in colonial eyes, the act seemed utterly diabolical, a dastardly trick designed to trap them into paying the tea tax. The plot seemed obvious: the real price of Lord North's tea was American submission to parliamentary taxation.

Once this was realized, opposition was almost unanimous. In London American captains refused to carry the tea across the Atlantic; in America the unfortunate tea consignees suffered the fate of the stamp masters of 1765. Public indignation was so great in New York and Philadelphia that when the tea ships arrived, the authorities wisely ordered them back to England without attempting to unload. The tea could only be landed "under the Protection of the Point of the Bayonet and Muzzle of the Cannon," the governor of New York reported. "Even then," he added, "I do not see how the Sales or Consumption could be effected."

The situation in Boston was different. The tea ship *Dartmouth* arrived on November 27. The people of the region, marshaled by Sam Adams, were determined to prevent it from landing its cargo, but Governor Hutchinson was equally determined to collect the tax and enforce the law. For days the town seethed. Thousands of people milled in the streets to be harangued by Adams and his friends, while the *Dartmouth* and two later arrivals lay at their moorings. Then, on the

CULVER PICTURES

BOSTON, *December* 2, 1773.

WHEREAS it has been reported that a Permit will be given by the Cuſtom-Houſe for Landing the Tea now on Board a Veſſel laying in this Harbour, commanded by Capt. HALL: THIS is to Remind the Publick, That it was ſolemnly voted by the Body of the People of this and the neighbouring Towns aſſembled at the Old-South Meeting-Houſe on Tueſday the 30th Day of *November*, that the ſaid Tea never ſhould be landed in this Province, or pay one Farthing of Duty: And as the aiding or aſſiſting in procuring or granting any ſuch Permit for landing the ſaid Tea or any other Tea ſo circumſtanced, or in offering any Permit when obtained to the Maſter or Commander of the ſaid Ship, or any other Ship in the ſame Situation, muſt betray an inhuman Thirſt for Blood, and will alſo in a great Meaſure accelerate Confuſion and Civil War: This is to aſſure ſuch public Enemies of this Country, that they will be conſidered and treated as Wretches unworthy to live, and will be made the firſt Victims of our juſt Reſentment.

The PEOPLE.

N. B. Captain *Bruce* is arrived laden with the ſame deteſtable Commodity; and 'tis peremptorily demanded of him, and all concerned, that they comply with the ſame Requiſitions.

The inflammatory handbill at left, attributing to the "Enemies of this Country" an "inhuman Thirst for Blood," typified the propaganda that flooded Boston from the presses of the Sons of Liberty during the tea crisis. The city was virtually under mob rule; two weeks later the Tea Party (right) took place. This sketch is by German artist Johann Ramberg.

night of December 16, as Hutchinson was preparing to seize the tea for nonpayment of the duty, a band of colonists disguised as Indians boarded the ships and dumped the hated tea chests in the harbor. A huge crowd gathered at wharfside cheered them on.

The destruction of the tea was a serious crime for which many persons, aside from the painted "Patriots" who actually jettisoned the chests, were responsible. Of course the British burned with indignation when news of the "Tea Party" reached London. People talked wildly of flattening Boston with heavy artillery. This, fortunately, was only talk. However, nearly everyone agreed that the colonists must be taught a lesson. As George III himself put it: "We must master them or totally leave them to themselves." What particularly infuriated the British was the certain knowledge that no American jury would render a judgment against the criminals; the memory of the *Gaspee* affair was fresh in everyone's mind in England, as undoubtedly it was in the minds of those Bostonians who, wearing the thinnest of disguises, brazenly destroyed the tea before thousands of witnesses.

PRINT DEPARTMENT, METROPOLITAN MUSEUM OF ART

Colonies in Revolt

Parliament responded in the spring of 1774 by passing three Coercive Acts. The Boston Port Act closed the harbor of Boston to all commerce until its citizens paid for the tea. The Administration of Justice Act provided for the transfer of cases to courts outside Massachusetts when the governor felt that an impartial trial could not be had within the colony. The Massachusetts Government Act revised the colony's charter drastically, strengthening the power of the governor, weakening that of the local town meetings, making the council appointive rather than elective, and changing the method by which juries were selected. These were unwise laws of course, for they cost Great Britain an empire, but all of them, and especially the Port Act, were unjust laws as well. Parliament was punishing a whole people for the crimes of individuals. These were acts of tyranny, a denial of English principles of justice.

The Americans named these laws (together with a new, more extensive Quartering Act and the Quebec Act, an unrelated measure that attached the area north of the Ohio River to Canada and gave the whole region an authoritarian and centralized government) the "Intolerable Acts." The British answer to the crisis was coercion, and this the Americans found unendurable. Revolution was the inevitable result.

Who must bear the blame for the rupture of more than a century and a half of friendly relations? Both sides in part, but the major share belongs on British shoulders. Although no one had really thought it through in detail, the Americans were trying to work out a federal system, with certain powers centered in London and others in the colonial capitals. Nearly every colonist was willing to see Great Britain continue to control large areas of American affairs. Parliament, however, and in the last analysis George III and most Englishmen, insisted in the face of much evidence to the contrary that their authority over the colonies was unlimited. Behind their stubbornness lay the arrogant psychology of the

COLONIAL WILLIAMSBURG; OTHERS: CHICAGO HISTORICAL SOCIETY

The "American question" was a constant topic of conversation in London, especially after news of the Tea Party crossed the Atlantic. Violence and property destruction dismayed even those Englishmen who were in sympathy with the colonists. These three caricatures, by the London printmakers Sayer and Bennett, are expressions of the hardening of attitudes toward the rebellious colonies. "The Alternative of Williamsburg" (above) portrays the plight of Virginia loyalists coerced into signing nonimportation agreements under the threat of violence or tarring and feathering. The two prints at the right are acid comments on the situation in Boston. At the top, Sons of Liberty brutalize a tax collector against a backdrop of the Tea Party. In "The Bostonians in Distress" (right), residents caged by the Port Act devour fish supplied by fellow colonists.

European colonizer, a psychology that, before 1774 and since, has brought much suffering to the world—along with much material and moral progress. "*Colonists are inferior. . . . We own you . . .*"—in essence, these were the British views. That they resulted from ignorance and prejudice more than malice does not excuse them.

Lord North directed the Coercive Acts at Massachusetts rather than at all the colonies, in part because he hoped that the others, profiting from Massachusetts's discomfiture, would stand aside and allow the British to act as they wished, and in part because of the British tendency to think of the colonies as separate units connected only through London. His strategy failed because his assumption was incorrect: the colonies began at once to act in concert.

In June 1774 Massachusetts called for a meeting of delegates from all the colonies to consider common action. When this First Continental Congress met at Philadelphia in September only Georgia did not send delegates. Various points of view were represented, but the general sentiment was radical. Even the so-called conservatives, in a plan introduced by Joseph Galloway of Pennsylvania, called for a thorough overhaul of the empire. Galloway suggested an *American* government, consisting of a president general appointed by the king and a grand council chosen by the colonial assemblies, that would manage intercolonial affairs and possess a veto over parliamentary acts affecting the colonies.

This was not what the majority wanted. Prolonged thought and discussion had produced a marked shift in the radical position. If taxation without representation was tyranny, so was all other legislation. Parliament, therefore, had no right to legislate in any way for the colonies. James Wilson, born in Scotland and a resident of America for less than a decade, made this argument in a pamphlet, *Considerations on the . . . Legislative Authority of the British Parliament*, published in the summer of 1774 and known to many of the delegates at the Congress. "All the different members of the British empire are distinct states, independent of each other, but connected together under the same sovereign," Wilson insisted. John Adams, a cousin of Samuel's and a Boston lawyer, while still prepared to *allow* Parliament to regulate colonial trade, now felt that Parliament had no inherent right to control it. "The foundation . . . of all free government," he declared, "is a right in the people to participate in their legislative council." Americans "are entitled to a free and exclusive power of legislation in their several provincial legislatures."

Propelled onward by the reasoning of Wilson, Adams, and a number of others, the Congress passed a declaration of grievances and resolves, amounting to a complete condemnation of Britain's actions since 1763. A Massachusetts proposal that the people take up arms to defend their rights was endorsed. The delegates also organized a "Continental Association" to boycott all British goods and to stop all exports to the empire. To enforce this boycott, committees were appointed locally "to observe the conduct of all persons touching this association" and to expose violators to public scorn.

To the extent that the Continental Congress reflected public opinion, and there is no reason to suspect that it did not, it may be said that by the fall of 1774 the American Revolution had already begun. Few Americans as yet sought outright independence. Indeed, when it came to that in 1776, many among those who desired fundamental alterations in the structure of the empire still preferred submission to total rupture. However, events had forced the colonists to think out their relation to Great Britain, and they had decided overwhelmingly that drastic changes must be made.

Fumblingly but inexorably, they were also becoming aware of their common interests, their *Americanism.* It was not merely a question of mutual defense against the threat of British power, not only, in Franklin's aphorism, a question of hanging together lest they hang separately. A nation was being born.

Looking back many years later, one of the delegates to the First Continental Congress made exactly these points. He was John Adams of Massachusetts, and he said: "The revolution was complete, in the minds of the people, and the Union of the colonies, before the war commenced. . . ."

SUPPLEMENTARY READING The fullest analysis of the structure of the British imperial system can be found in the early volumes of L.H. Gipson's *British Empire Before the American Revolution* (1936–1968), while the British political system is described in L.B. Namier, *The Structure of Politics at the Accession of George III** (1929) and *England in the Age of the American Revolution** (1930). For a briefer account, see J.H. Plumb, *England in the 18th Century** (1950). O.M. Dickerson, *American Colonial Government* (1912), is a standard work, as is L.W. Labaree, *Royal Government in America* (1930). J.P. Greene, *The Quest for Power: The Lower Houses of Assembly in the Southern Royal Colonies* (1963), throws light on the process by which the colonists extended their control of political affairs, while R.L. Schuyler, *Parliament and the British Empire* (1929), argues that Great Britain's authority over the colonies was always extensive.

The best broad study of mercantilism is Eli Heckscher, *Mercantilism* (1935); the fullest analysis of the Navigation Acts is G.L. Beer, *The Origins of the British Colonial System* (1908) and *The Old Colonial System* (1912). O.M. Dickerson, *The Navigation Acts and the American Revolution** (1951), takes the position that mercantilism did not injure the colonial economy, but L.A. Harper, *The English Navigation Laws* (1939), concludes that it did. T.C. Barrow, *Trade & Empire: The British Customs Service in Colonial America* (1967), adopts a middle position. C.P. Nettels, *The Money Supply of the American Colonies Before 1720* (1934), is an important study.

The colonial wars are vividly described in Parts V–VII of Francis Parkman's *France and England in North America* (1877–1892); the best modern account is H.H. Peckham, *The Colonial Wars** (1963). On the French and Indian War, L.H. Gipson's multivolume work is particularly useful; but a brief, popular account is Brian Connell, *The Savage Years* (1959). Washington's role receives full treatment in Volume II of D.S. Freeman, *George Washington* (1948). On the problems posed for the British by the acquisition of French Canada, C.W. Alvord, *The Mississippi Valley in British Politics* (1916), may be supplemented with T.P. Abernethy, *Western Lands and the American Revolution* (1937), and J.M. Sosin, *Whitehall and the Wilderness* (1961).

On the causes of the Revolution, two brief treatments are L.H. Gipson, *The Coming of the Revolution** (1954), and E.S. Morgan, *The Birth of the Republic** (1956), a better balanced analysis. Fuller discussions can be found in Merrill Jensen, *The Founding of a Nation* (1968), J.C. Miller, *Origins of the American Revolution** (1943), a most entertaining volume, and in Bernhard Knollenberg, *Origin of the American Revolution** (1960), which is more argumentative but at some points more penetrating. Volumes IV–VII of George Bancroft's *History of the United States* (1834–1874) are still useful, and modern historians are coming back increasingly to his general view that British tyranny was the major cause of the revolt. Bernard Bailyn's *The Ideological Origins of the American Revolution* (1967), and *The Origins of American Politics* (1968), are brilliant analyses of the political thinking and political structure of 18th-century America, while his edition of the *Pamphlets of the American Revolution* (1965), should be sampled by every student.

Important special studies of the period include A.M. Schlesinger, *The Colonial Merchants and the American Revolution** (1918), E.S. and H.M. Morgan, *The Stamp Act Crisis** (1953), B.W. Labaree, *The Boston Tea Party** (1964), John Shy, *Toward Lexington: The Role of the British Army in the Coming of the American Revolution** (1965), J.M. Sosin, *Agents and Merchants: British Colonial Politics and the Origins of the American Revolution* (1965), and M.G. Kammen, *The Colonial Agents, British Politics, and the American Revolution* (1968).

*Available in paperback.

WEDGWOOD

PORTFOLIO

II *Benjamin Franklin*

"The history of our Revolution will be one continued lie from one end to the other," wrote John Adams in 1790. "The essence of the whole will be that Dr. Franklin's electrical rod smote the earth and out sprang General Washington. That Franklin electrified him with his rod—and thence forward these two conducted all the policy, negotiations, legislatures, and war." Sour as it may be, Adams' assessment reflects the exalted position occupied by Benjamin Franklin at the time of his death. To contemporaries, his face was "as well known as that of the moon." Among the scores of likenesses produced in his lifetime is the Wedgwood medallion above, notable for the fact that it was issued in England during the fourth year of the Revolution.

Born in 1706 a subject of Queen Anne, Franklin lived to see independence and federal union, and he participated in the decisive events of this transformation. He has often been called the first American, partly because of his political concepts and partly because he, the tenth son of a Boston soap boiler and tallow chandler, confirmed America's faith in individual opportunity. Originally admired as the very epitome of the Enlightenment, then reduced in the 19th century to a rather stuffy symbol of thrift and frugality (which he seldom practiced), Franklin was in point of fact the most cosmopolitan American of his age, a universal figure dedicated to reason and the natural rights of man.

LIBRARY COMPANY OF PHILADELPHIA

In the 1760's and 70's cabinetmaker Benjamin Randolph rendered fashionable Chippendale, rococo, and Gothic styles. His trade card bears engravings from English design books.

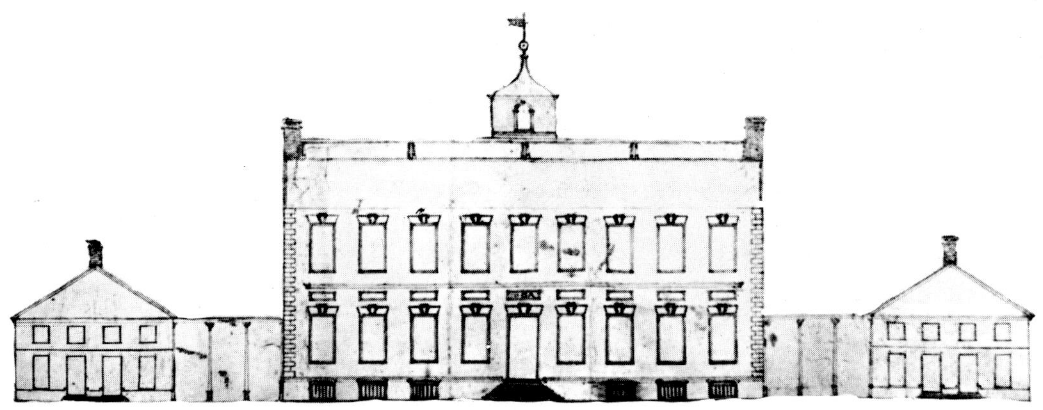

HISTORICAL SOCIETY OF PENNSYLVANIA

Shown in a 1732 plan, the Pennsylvania State House (now Independence Hall) exemplifies Philadelphia's maturing architectural style.

LIBRARY COMPANY OF PHILADELPHIA

Penn's City

The "green countrie towne" that William Penn established on the west bank of the Delaware was rich in opportunity when Franklin arrived from Boston in 1723 to seek work as a journeyman printer. In the 40 years since its founding, Philadelphia had developed into the burgeoning center of commerce depicted (below) about 1720 by a local sign painter named Peter Cooper. In the next half century the rapid growth continued, and on the eve of the Revolution Philadelphia was the largest and richest town in the colonies. Indeed, with 40,000 inhabitants by 1775, Penn's city ranked second only to London in the British Empire.

The Enlightenment came early to Philadelphia, infecting gentry and "leather apronmen" alike with a passion for knowledge. A widespread interest in education, both public and private, was but one example of this drive for self-improvement. Not only the gentry, but many common tradesmen treasured volumes of Locke, Hume, and Voltaire in their libraries. The flowering of the arts, particularly painting, was nurtured by generous patronage awarded to promising young talent, and the search for functional beauty in architecture was another reflection of the new spirit of the age.

In this heady atmosphere ("We are a people, thrown together from various quarters of the world," noted one resident, "differing in all things—language, manners, and sentiments"), pre-Revolutionary Philadelphia fostered a galaxy of notable figures, numbering among them painters Benjamin West and Charles Willson Peale, botanist William Bartram, astronomer David Rittenhouse, and physician Benjamin Rush, in addition to the universal figure of Franklin.

HISTORICAL SOCIETY OF PENNSYLVANIA

Philadelphia's commercial orientation, apparent in Cooper's view below, was soon supplemented by the pursuit of culture. Sketched above by Benjamin West are two of the "young geniuses" of the 1750's: the composer Francis Hopkinson and Elizabeth Graeme, who, "all eye, all ear, and all grasp," was overseer of the first literary salon in America.

NEW YORK PUBLIC LIBRARY

HISTORICAL SOCIETY OF PENNSYLVANIA

Juſt Publiſhed,
And to be ſold by B. FRANKLIN, the follow ing BOOKS,

I. THe POCKET ALMANACK, for the Year 1745.

II. *PAMELA: or* VIRTUE *rewarded. In a Series of FAMILIAR LETTERS from a beautiful young Damſel, to her Parents. Now firſt Publiſhed, in order to cultivate the Principles of* Virtue *and* Religion *in the Minds of the* Youth *of* both Sexes.
A Narrative which has its Foundation in Truth *and* Nature; *and at the ſame time that it agreeably entertains, by a Variety of* curious *and* affecting INCIDENTS, *is intirely diveſted of all thoſe Images, which, in too many Pieces, calculated for Amuſement only, tend to* inflame *the Minds they ſhould* inſtruct. Price 6 s.

III. A Preſervative from the Sins and Follies of Childhood and Youth, *written by way of Queſtion and Anſwer. To which are added, ſome Religious and Moral Inſtructions, in Verſe.* By I. Watts, D. D. Price 8 d.

LIBRARY COMPANY OF PHILADELPHIA

The Anatomy of Man's Body as govern'd by the Twelve Conſtellations.

♈ The Head and Face.

♓ The Feet.

To know where the Sign is.

First Find the Day of the Month, and againſt the Day you have the Sign or Place of the Moon in the 6th Column. Then finding the Sign here, it ſhews the Part of the Body it governs.

The Names and Characters of the Seven Planets.

☉ Sol, ♄ Saturn, ♃ Jupiter, ♂ Mars, ♀ Venus, ☿ Mercury, ☽ Luna, ☊ Dragons Head and ☋ Tail.

The Five Aſpects.

☌ Conjunction, ☍ Oppoſition, ⚹ Sextile, △ Trine, □ Quartile.

For 20 years Franklin's press (top left) issued highly salable titles. Although he published Samuel Richardson's Pamela *(advertisement at left), his output consisted largely of moral discourses, psalm books, and gentlemen's instructors. His greatest moneymaker was* Poor Richard's Almanack, *filled with "scraps from the table of wisdom" and emphemera such as the astrological chart at right.*

ALL: PHILADELPHIA MUSEUM OF ART

Diligence, counseled Poor Richard, and . . .

. . . industry earn large rewards, but . . .

The Way to Wealth

Besides a strong sense of morality, the youthful printer possessed a streak of calculating ambition. In 1728, at the age of 22, Franklin was in business for himself, and within the year he was scheming to gain control of the liveliest of Philadelphia's two newspapers, *The Universal Instructor in All Arts and Sciences: and Pennsylvania Gazette.* To the rival *American Weekly Mercury*, he submitted a series of anonymous satires that attracted scores of new readers. The *Gazette*'s circulation plummeted, and its publisher, "a little knavish withal," sold out to Franklin for a pittance.

To improve his business, Franklin carefully cultivated a proper image. "I took care," he recalled in his *Autobiography*, "not only to be in *Reality* Industrious and frugal, but to avoid all *Appearances* of the contrary. I drest plainly; I was seen at no Places of idle Diversion . . . to show that I was not above my Business, I sometimes brought home the Paper I purchas'd . . . thro' the Streets on a Wheelbarrow." In 1730 he married, partly to curb the passions that had led to what he described as "Intrigues with low Women."

In addition to the *Gazette*, which proved "extreamly profitable," by 1734 Franklin held the government printing contracts for Pennsylvania, Delaware, and New Jersey. The publication of books and pamphlets brought him handsome earnings as well. But his greatest profits came from *Poor Richard's Almanack*. First published for the year 1733, it ran through 26 editions under Franklin's direction and sold, he estimated, 10,000 copies annually. The success of the *Almanack* derived from its proverbs and maxims, the "Sayings of Poor Richard." Franklin wove many of them into the form of a speech by a "plain, clean old man" which served as a preface to his last edition of the *Almanack*. Known as "The Way to Wealth," this sermon gave expression to the prevailing American faith in economic opportunity and individual effort. By 1748 Franklin had practically withdrawn from business, but his many partnerships provided him a yearly income of well over a thousand pounds. He wished to have time "to read, study, [and] make Experiments . . . on such Points as may produce something for the common Benefit of mankind. . . ."

. . . the vices of wine, low women, gaming . . .

. . . and extravagance lead straight to ruin.

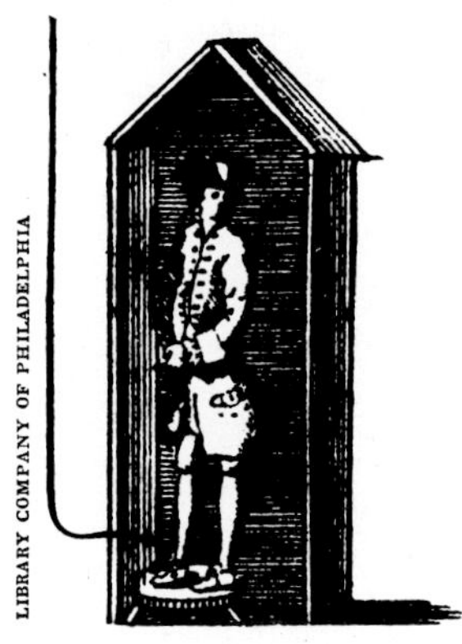

LIBRARY COMPANY OF PHILADELPHIA

A New Prometheus

One of the precepts of the Enlightenment held that science should be esteemed for its utility, its contribution to man's material well-being—a view that Franklin embraced with vigor. As the 1740's wore on, he increasingly applied his energies to research. At first meteorology captured his interest, but soon he was completely absorbed in unraveling the mysteries of electricity.

Although 3,000 miles of ocean separated him from the mainstream of scientific research, Franklin made rapid headway with his experiments. By early 1747 he was far enough along to challenge the accepted theory that there were two kinds of electricity, one that attracted and one that repelled. Later that year, using the recently invented Leyden jar that condensed electricity, he formulated a brilliant hypothesis that opened the door to other fundamental discoveries. Franklin's concept allowed for only a "single fluid," existing in lesser (negative) or greater (positive) amounts.

Franklin then set out to prove that electricity and lightning were one and the same. In 1750 he outlined a plan for building on "some high Tower or Steeple . . . a Kind of Sentry Box" (left) from which the necessary observations could be made. In May of 1752 the French scientist Thomas-François D'Alibard, who had read a published account of the proposed test, performed it successfully at Marly-la-Ville near Paris. Franklin, unaware of the Frenchman's accomplishment and at last despairing of finding a suitable tower, achieved the same feat with his kite a month later.

Franklin's experiments quickly won him an international reputation. The kite experiment and the related invention of the lightning rod assured the New Prometheus, as Immanuel Kant called him, an immediate place in popular legend. The world of learning, represented in part by Harvard, Yale, Oxford, and the Royal Society, was scarcely slower in acknowledging his genius.

AMERICAN ACADEMY OF ARTS AND SCIENCES

David Colden, son of New York's lieutenant governor, sent Franklin this crude rendering of his own experiment with the Leyden jar, noting that the charge drawn from point B left a mere "pricling in the ends of my fingers."

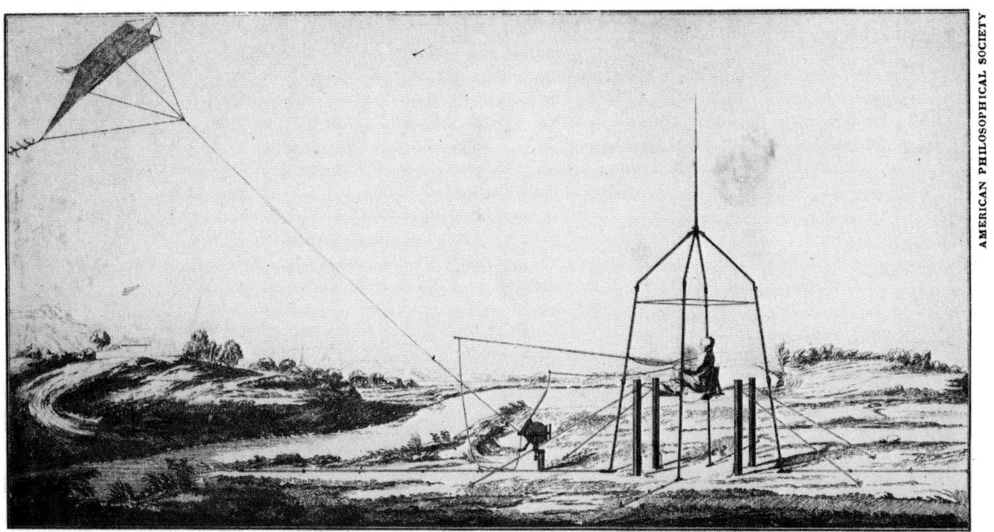

AMERICAN PHILOSOPHICAL SOCIETY

Franklin's feat of drawing "electrical fire" from the clouds prompted imitators. The engraving above, once owned by Franklin, represents the safeguarded method of a French nobleman. Despite refinements, the experiment was basically the same as Franklin's. Lightning striking a pointed rod on the kite traveled down the rain-moistened string and was drawn off by various means into a condenser. The lack of practical applications for electricity—witness the parlor game depicted below, in which static charges were produced—left Franklin "chagrined."

LIBRARY COMPANY OF PHILADELPHIA

Inventions and Promotions

Franklin's head was full of notions for the enjoyment of life, and if he often complained of too little leisure, it was because of his ceaseless tinkering. Drafts that rushed through his house "so strongly as to make a continual Whistling or Howling" led to the Franklin stove, which circulated heated air to make his living room "twice as warm as it used to be." The stove, he boasted, also protected women from head colds "which fall into their Jaws and Gums, and have destroy'd early many a fine Set of Teeth in these Northern Colonies."

Over the years Franklin's passion for tinkering resulted in ideas for bifocal spectacles, an odometer, a copying machine, various pieces of nautical equipment, and a tool (later adapted for use by grocers) for removing books from high library shelves. He once proposed to hold an electrical picnic featuring as the main course a turkey killed by electrical shock. After dining, Franklin and his friends were to drink toasts to famous "Electricians" from "Electrified Bumpers [of wine] under the Discharge of Guns from the Electrical Battery."

"Have you consulted Franklin on this business? And what does he think of it?" asked Philadelphians when urged to consider some new project for their city. Either by direct action or by his forceful pen, Franklin supported nearly every worthy cause undertaken in Philadelphia in his time. In 1751 he helped found the academy now known as the University of Pennsylvania. When Indians or French threatened, he personally organized the defenses of the colony. As Philadelphia postmaster he brought efficiency to the city's mails, and after his appointment in 1753 as His Majesty's Deputy Postmaster General for all of North America, he reorganized the entire colonial postal system.

Out of the Junto, a debating club of tradesmen Franklin established in 1727, emerged the city's first subscription library (1731) and the first fire company (1736). The Junto also served as model for the American Philosophical Society, which he set up in 1743–44 as an intercolonial organization for the exchange of "useful knowledge."

YALE UNIVERSITY LIBRARY

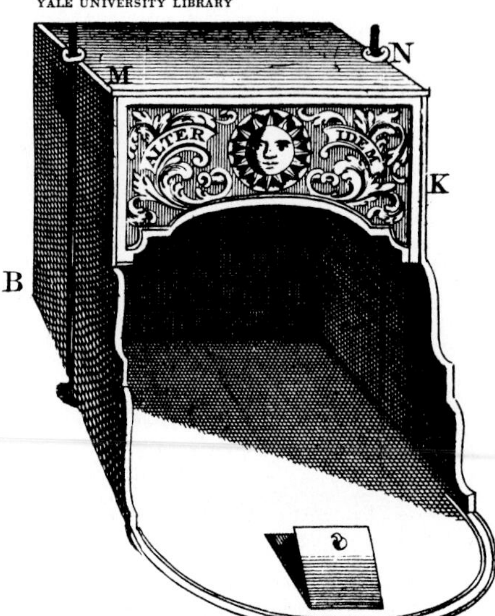

LIBRARY COMPANY OF PHILADELPHIA

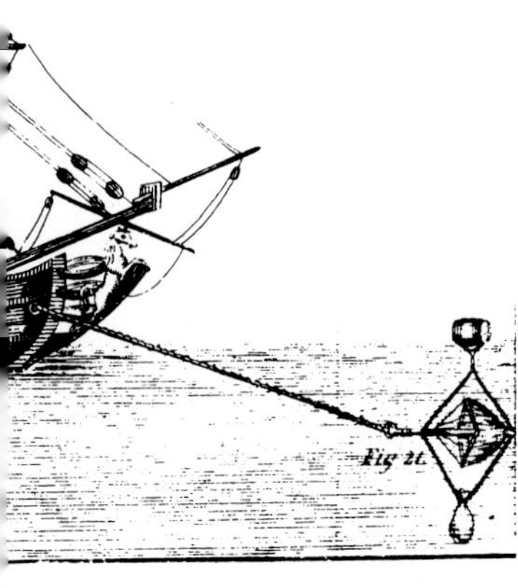

BOTH: LIBRARY COMPANY OF PHILADELPHIA

When it opened its doors in 1756, the new Pennsylvania Hospital (above right) ranked among the best in the world. Franklin's signal contribution to its construction was squeezing financial aid from the balky colonial assembly. Of all his "political maneuvers" he recalled none that gave greater pleasure or more excuse for cunning.

Above left is a sea anchor that the aged diplomat designed on the homeward journey from France, his eighth crossing of the Atlantic, in 1785. At the left is the famous stove, engraved for an edition of Franklin's papers.

Franklin's "armonica" (below left), played by rubbing rotating glass hemispheres, counted Marie Antoinette among its devotees. However, it was given to severe, disturbing vibrations and dropped from vogue about 1800.

STOKES COLLECTION, NEW YORK PUBLIC LIBRARY

The "riots and fool's play" occasioned by Philadelphia's fires largely disappeared with the formation of the Union Fire Company. As in the 18th-century engraving above, the members were divided into disciplined water and rescue teams. Franklin next reformed the city watch and improved the lighting, paving, and cleaning of the streets.

A Plan for Union

Sometime during 1751 Franklin found time to write a provocative essay entitled *Observations concerning the Increase of Mankind, Peopling of Countries, &c.* Set in cool, carefully reasoned prose, it expressed his imperial vision. In America, he explained, there existed something that almost none of the countries of crowded Europe possessed—room for expansion. America was like a vast unplanted field. Plow the lands to the west, he urged, sow them with transplanted Englishmen, and the population would double every 25 years. Not Anglo-American competition, but an ever-expanding market would be the result: "What an Accession of Power to the British Empire! . . . What an Increase of Trade and Navigation!" America's destiny lay with the empire, Franklin asserted, but it must be free to supervise its own internal development.

In 1754 representatives of seven colonies met at Albany for the purpose of "burying the hatchet and renewing the covenant chain" with the Iroquois. Franklin, sent by Pennsylvania, came prepared with some "short hints" for advancing his grand design. This "Albany Plan" called for the creation of an intercolonial council for defense, with powers to tax its members, purchase Indian lands, raise an army, construct fortifications, and organize and develop new western settlements. The presiding officer, who was to be Crown-appointed, would have the right to veto all council actions.

The delegates at Albany approved Franklin's proposals with minor changes; however, the individual assemblies rejected them. Late in life Franklin still believed that his plan could have prevented the Revolution. "But," he remarked, "history is full of errors of states and princes. . . ."

In 1757 the Pennsylvania assembly sent Franklin (a member since 1751) to London to present its case in a financial dispute with the proprietary government of the Penns, a mission that occupied him for five years. Still in London at the end of the French and Indian War, he helped persuade the British to keep Canada instead of the French sugar islands. "Providence," he had written some years before, "seems to require various duties of me."

WITHOUT.
10
11
12
The word WITHOUT is proper to be regarded.
1. Supreme Majestey ——— Power.
2. Counsellors ——— Abilities.
3. Bishops ——— Religion.
NB The Introduction of the word WITHOUT is necessary to the
Publish'd According to Act of Parliament June 17 1757

·om the London Evening Post of Saturday June 11·1757.

1. Meditations for every Hour in ye Day is now very Publick. The true state of a Nation in Europe 1757

——— Honour.	7. Colonies ——— Protection.	10. Great Armies ——— Use.
——— Honesty.	8. Seamen ——— Encouragment.	11. The Common People ——— Money.
s ——— Trade.	9. Parading Fleets ——— Fighting.	12. The Poor ——— Bread!

Prayers have been Offer'd up in proper Congregations for the due Guidance of the Greatest Man in Power. —
St Martins Lane in the Strand. Price Six Pence.

JOHN CARTER BROWN LIBRARY, BROWN UNIVERSITY

The theory of strength by union enunciated at Albany and given dramatic urgency by Franklin's famous rattlesnake woodcut of 1754 (right) was ignored even as disasters mounted in the Seven Years' War. The mood in London during the long, grave months of 1757 before Pitt assumed power is summarized in the cartoon above—hunger stalks the people, the colonies are aflame, the nation's industry stands idle, the monarch sits befogged. The captions for the 12 dismal scenes have a blank for the word without.

LIBRARY OF CONGRESS

The Paxton Boys

Discontent had been long building in the Pennsylvania back country over what westerners regarded as the failure of the Quaker-dominated assembly to provide adequate defense against Indian attack, and it finally spilled over in the winter of 1763–64. The specter of 500 Paxton Boys—"white savages," Franklin called them—marching on Philadelphia greatly alarmed the gentry. The call to arms, undertaken by Franklin, had its embarrassing moments. In one episode, lampooned in the contem-

porary cartoon above, troops answering a frantic summons discovered just in time that they had trained their cannon on a company of German butchers (far right) coming to their aid.

The Paxton affair laid bare the antagonisms within Philadelphia itself, and in the ensuing pamphlet war the city population split into religious, political, and social factions, in many respects presaging the divisions the Revolutionary era. Although Franklin's conservative position cost him his seat in the assembly, late in 1764 Pennsylvania again sent him to England, somewhat wiser for the experience.

Thursday, October 31, 1765. THE NUMB. 1195.

PENNSYLVANIA JOURNAL;

AND

WEEKLY ADVERTISER.

EXPIRING: In Hopes of a Resurrection to LIFE again.

New Jersey's Constitutional Courant, *an underground sheet allegedly printed "at the sign of* the Bribe refused, *on* Constitutional Hill, North-America," *revived Franklin's snake device to protest against the tax. Rather than purchase stamps, William Bradford devised a tombstone display for his* Pennsylvania Journal *and ceased publication.*

JOIN OR DIE.

SATURDAY, September 21, 1765. [NUMB. 1.]

The Constitutional COURANT:

Containing Matters interesting to LIBERTY, and no wise repugnant to LOYALTY.

Stamp Act Crisis

The Stamp Act crisis very nearly ruined Franklin's reputation in America. Clinging to his faith in imperial unity, he underestimated the fury Grenville's measure would provoke in the colonies. Americans resented the mildness of his opposition to the act; to make matters worse, he had a hand in the appointment of two friends as stamp masters. His enemies mentioned bribery, and the rumor spread that he himself was author of the new stamp plan.

By mid-1765 Franklin, at last aware of his awkward position, had thrown himself into the struggle for repeal. He labored behind the scenes, seeking to rouse British public opinion with propaganda in the newspapers and winning friends among the mercantile interests in Parliament. Commerce, that most sensitive of British nerves, was the key to his campaign. In February 1766 Franklin was called before Commons to testify on the Stamp Act. Repeal was in Britain's own best interest, he declared, reminding the House that an internal tax was not only a burden on the colonies but a hindrance to British commerce as a whole. The session ended with two questions Franklin had probably rehearsed with his allies in Commons. "What used to be the pride of the Americans?" he was asked. "To indulge in the fashions and manufactures of Great Britain." "What is now their pride?" "To wear their old cloaths over again, till they can make new ones." On March 4 Commons voted 250–122 for repeal.

LIBRARY COMPANY OF PHILADELPHIA

Franklin pressed his attack on the Stamp Act, the "mother of mischief," with a graphic portrayal of Britannia shorn of her colonies. The ships in the background have brooms tied to their masts, indicating they are being sold for lack of trade. He had his drawing engraved on small cards and "employed a Waiter to put one of them in each Parliament [member's] hand as he entered the house the day preceding the great debate. . . ."

JOHN CARTER BROWN LIBRARY, BROWN UNIVERSITY

A British cartoon applauding repeal shows Grenville (left center) conveying the coffin of his dead brainchild to the "Family Vault," while on the Thames, merchantmen weigh anchor for America. The print was published in March 1766 at the behest of the Rockingham ministry—Grenville had fallen the previous July—and became the most popular cartoon of the Revolutionary era. Pirated versions alone sold over 16,000 copies.

E Pluribus Unum

The explosions at Lexington and Concord in April 1775 found Franklin at sea, returning home after a decade of political activity in London. England now seemed to him an "old rotten state." Reason dictated a final break, even if the heart did not. The morning after arriving in Philadelphia, Franklin was elected to the Second Continental Congress. In subsequent months

HISTORICAL SOCIETY OF PENNSYLVANIA

he served on some 15 committees, most notably those for exploring treaty prospects with European powers and for drafting a declaration of independence. (These appointments perplexed acerbic John Adams, who observed that during deliberations his colleague was often "fast asleep in his chair.") Artists Robert Edge Pine and Edward Savage depicted members of Congress voting for independence on July 2; in the center foreground of their painting is Franklin, sitting pensively (or asleep?) in his chair.

An Innocent Abroad

Declarations of independence, as the representatives at Philadelphia realized, do not win revolutions. General Howe's Redcoats held New York, and there was the galling matter of money. To win foreign support, Congress turned to its most seasoned diplomat, and on October 27, 1776, Franklin embarked for France on the armed sloop *Reprisal.* His mission was to effect a "Treaty of Commerce and Amity." Though implied, the fateful word "alliance" was nowhere in his instructions.

Franklin's arrival in Paris on December 21 precipitated an outburst of public adulation. Preceded by his fame as scientist and homely philosopher, the man from Philadelphia was welcomed as the symbol of New World virtue. In his fur cap, somber "Quaker" garb, and long, unclubbed hair, he epitomized Rousseau's "natural man." All of France vied for his favor. To his niece he wrote: "Somebody, it seems, gave it out that I lov'd Ladies; and then every body presented me their Ladies. . . ." The "kissing of Lips or Cheeks" was not the mode in France, he explained, but "the French Ladies have however 1000 other ways of rendering themselves agreeable. . . ."

Franklin's social activities belied the furious pace of that first year of diplomacy. He was badgered by Congress for stepped-up aid, besieged by applications for positions in the American army (he approved those of Lafayette and Von Steuben)—all the while playing a game for far higher stakes.

BRITISH MUSEUM

Howe's occupation of Philadelphia in 1777, forcing Congress to flee, inspired the cartoon above. American political and military leaders are sharply satirized, and Howe's Hessian mercenaries are represented by the German eagle at upper left. The owl winging off to "Louis Baboon" (upper right) represents Franklin's mission to Paris. John Trumbull's 1778 portrait opposite was copied from a French print honoring "le Bonhomme Richard."

Forging an Alliance

The fall of 1777 was a time of acute distress for the American commission in Paris. Pitfalls appeared in the form of British spies and intrigue in the French court. The Comte de Vergennes, Louis XVI's shrewd foreign minister, granted loans but no alliance. Though eager to recoup the losses of the Seven Years' War, he was not prepared to back a losing cause. The situation was aggravated by undisguised hatred between Arthur Lee and Silas Deane, Franklin's associates.

Then, on the morning of December 4, a courier just off a ship from Boston presented Franklin with spectacular news: Burgoyne and his entire army had been captured at Saratoga. Now it seemed certain that the French, who so far had held back from a formal alliance, would come in on the American side.

Franklin presented the French with a new draft for the proposed alliance on December 8. Still hesitating, Louis agreed to sign only if Spain also announced for the Americans. To force his hand, Franklin now agreed to confer with a British agent sent to Paris to sound out the Americans on prospects for a negotiated peace. The meeting had its desired effect. Vergennes reported to his king with rumors of a possible truce between the combatants and of a joint Anglo-American assault on the French West Indies. The alliance at last received royal assent.

In the event of hostilities with Britain—a virtual certainty—France would guarantee American independence and promise to continue fighting until that aim had been achieved. America pledged to defend the French West Indies and agreed not to make a separate peace. On February 6, 1778, the alliance was signed in Vergennes' chambers. Putting aside the plain garb he affected, Franklin appeared in a coat of figured blue Manchester velvet, telling Deane that he had worn it four years earlier during an abusive session in Commons. Now he was giving the coat "a little revenge."

YALE UNIVERSITY LIBRARY

PRINTS DIVISION, NEW YORK PUBLIC LIBRARY

Above: A harsh appraisal of the alliance shows Britannia, armed solely with the sword of justice, outweighing the combined power of America, France, and two late-coming allies, Spain and Holland.

Left: The French fondness for allegory is apparent in this view of Franklin and Louis XVI come together to succor the infant republic. To America, Louis granted military and financial aid, to Franklin, a portrait studded with 408 diamonds.

Right: In a 1781 Dutch gibe, John Bull, his war chest empty, despairs as Cornwallis gives up. A Frenchman, a Dutchman, and a Spaniard mock Britain's cow of commerce.

PIERPONT MORGAN LIBRARY

HENRY FRANCIS DU PONT WINTERTHUR MUSEUM

A Just Peace

The meaning of Yorktown was quickly revealed. In March of 1782 Lord North's ministry fell, to be replaced by a coalition highly disposed toward peace. Franklin promptly established communications with the new Rockingham ministry, which in April asked for terms.

Congress already had appointed Franklin to a peace commission, but until his associates reached Paris–one, Henry Laurens, a prisoner of war in London, was freed in exchange for General Cornwallis–Franklin acted alone. His task was made doubly difficult by instructions to consult with France at every step and by British attempts to wean America away from her ally.

The request for terms revived Franklin's expansionist dreams of years gone by. The voluntary cession of Canada would, he suggested, "have an excellent effect" on his countrymen. He handed the British a list of specific points: recognition of independence, fishing rights on the Grand Banks, access to the Mississippi Valley, and a northern boundary set above the Great Lakes, or better yet, the whole of Canada.

In the fall of 1782 illness forced Franklin out of the negotiations for nearly two months. During his absence John Jay pushed the British hard for a settlement. To gain a satisfactory accommodation on the Mississippi Valley, which was vital to his country's interests, Jay withdrew the American demand for Canada. Franklin's recovery coincided with the arrival of commissioner John Adams in Paris, and the three men continued the talks independently of the French. A preliminary treaty was signed on November 30 that, except for Canada, conformed generally with Franklin's original demands. Only then was Vergennes informed of the terms, but Franklin managed to smooth his ruffled feathers and even to negotiate a new French loan.

The day for signing the formal articles did not come until September 3, 1783. Benjamin West had already started work on a commemorative painting. He began with portraits (from left) of Jay, Adams, Franklin, Laurens, and Franklin's grandson, who was secretary to the American commission, but the British refused to pose and West never finished the picture.

The Elder Statesman

In 1756 Franklin wrote George Whitefield, "Life, like a dramatic Piece, should not only be conducted with Regularity but methinks it should finish handsomely. Being now in the last Act, I begin to cast about for something fit to end with." In the summer of 1785, 29 years and a revolution later, the prodigal son returned home the most widely revered man of the age. Not only Philadelphia, which staged a week-long celebration upon his arrival, but the world embraced him as the apostle of liberty. "The glory of this father of American independence will continue to receive an increase of effulgence," exclaimed the *Pennsylvania Packet*. "Latest posterity will be wrapt in admiration at the prodigious efforts of [his] native genius which . . . shone forth the bright luminary of the western hemisphere."

Still, Franklin's "last Act" was yet not quite finished. Six weeks after landing, he became "president," or governor, of Pennsylvania, and then in 1787 he was elected to the Constitutional Convention. Just passed his 81st birthday, he was a generation or more removed from the Washingtons, the Madisons, the Hamiltons. Yet this "short, fat, trunched old man" by the mere weight of his prestige contributed greatly to the forging of the Constitution.

It was his last public service. Suffering from gout and the "stone," Franklin was confined to bed for most of the remaining months of his life. He died in his Philadelphia home during the night of April 17, 1790.

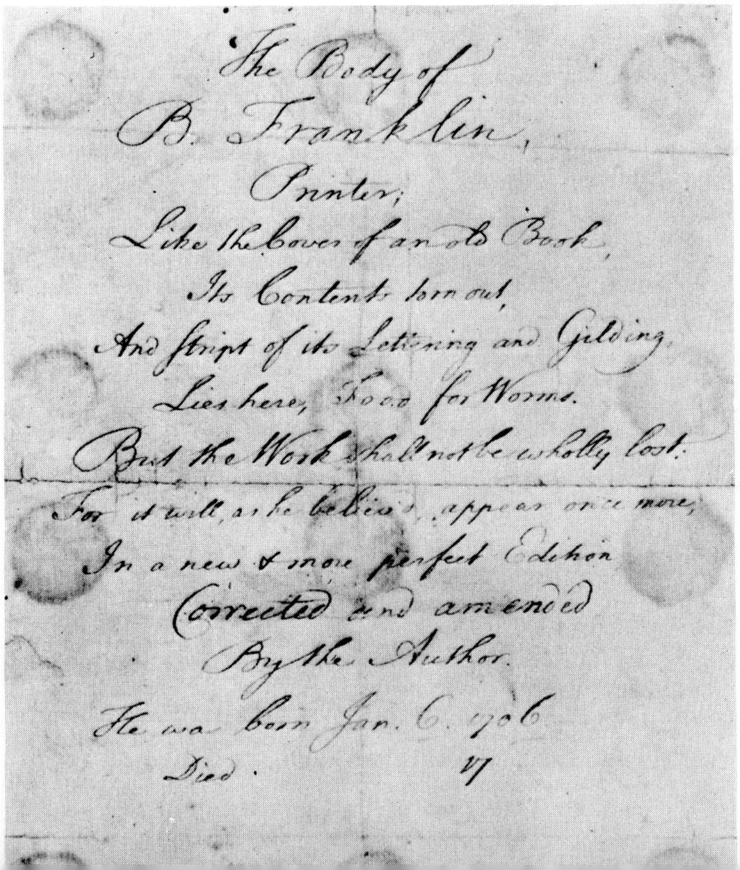

The Body of
B. Franklin,
Printer;
Like the Cover of an old Book,
Its Contents torn out,
And stript of its Lettering and Gilding,
Lies here, Food for Worms.
But the Work shall not be wholly lost:
For it will, as he believ'd, appear once more,
In a new & more perfect Edition
Corrected and amended
By the Author.
He was born Jan. 6. 1706
Died 17

At the age of 22 Franklin composed his own epitaph (left), predicting a resurrection of the author "In a new & most perfect Edition." Jean Honoré Fragonard's 1778 allegory (opposite) depicts the apotheosis of the venerable patriot. It was inspired by the epigram of finance minister Turgot: Eripuit caelo fulmen, mox sceptra tyrannis—*"He snatched lightning from the sky, the scepter from tyrants."*

AMER

4

The American Revolution

The actions of the First Continental Congress led the British authorities to force a showdown with their bumptious colonial offspring. "The New England governments are in a state of rebellion," George III announced. "Blows must decide whether they are to be subject to this country or independent." Already General Thomas Gage, veteran of Braddock's ill-fated expedition against Fort Duquesne and now commander in chief of all British forces in North America, had been appointed governor of Massachusetts. New red-coated regiments poured into Boston, camping on the town common, once peacefully reserved for the citizens' cows. Parliament echoed with demands for a show of force in America. The First Lord of the Admiralty predicted that the colonials would flee in terror at the thunder of the first British cannon. General James Grant (who was to learn otherwise in New Jersey at Christmastime in 1776) announced that with a thousand men he "would undertake to go from one end of America to the other, and geld all the males, partly by force and partly by a little coaxing." Some Englishmen opposed the idea of crushing the Americans, and others did not believe that it could be so easily managed, but they were a small minority. The House of Commons listened to Edmund Burke's magnificent and sensible speech on conciliating the colonies and then voted 270 to 78 against him. When Lord North, a peace-loving man, suggested a compromise that would preserve the principle of parliamentary supremacy but in effect surrender the tax power to the colonies, his associates "turned pale with shame and disappointment."

"The Shot Heard Round the World"

The decision to use troops against Massachusetts was made in January 1775, but the order did not reach General Gage until April. In the interim both sides were active. Parliament voted new troop levies, declared Massachusetts to be in a state of rebellion, and closed the Newfoundland fisheries and all seaports except those in Great Britain and the British West Indies, first to the New England colonies and then to most of the others. The Massachusetts "Patriots," as they were now calling themselves, formed an extralegal provincial assembly, organized a militia, and began

The Retreat
From Concord to Lexington of the Army of Wild Irish Asses Defeated by the Brave American Militia
Mr. Deacon Mr. Loeings Mr. Mulikens Mr. Bonds Housses and Barn all Plunder'd and Burnt on April 19th

JOHN CARTER BROWN LIBRARY, BROWN UNIVERSITY

The colonists were quick to make propaganda capital of Gage's foray to Lexington and Concord. The burning of several houses and barns by the Redcoats (to flush out snipers) and reports of looting inspired this cartoon. The British were led by Major John Pitcairn (mounted, second from right), who was later killed at Breed's Hill.

training "Minute Men" and other fighters. Soon companies of men were drilling on town commons all over Massachusetts, and in other colonies too.

When Gage received his orders on April 14, he acted swiftly. The Patriots had been accumulating arms at Concord, some 20 miles west of Boston. On the night of April 18 Gage dispatched 700 crack troops to seize these supplies. The Patriots were forewarned. Paul Revere set out on his famous ride* to alert the countryside and warn John Hancock and Sam Adams, leaders of the provincial assembly, whose arrest had been ordered. When the Redcoats reached Lexington early the next morning, they found the common occupied by about 70 Minute Men. After an argument, the Americans began to withdraw. Then someone fired a shot. There was a flurry of gunfire and the Minute Men fled, leaving 8 dead.

The British marched on to Concord, where they destroyed whatever supplies the Patriots had been unable to carry off. Now militiamen were pouring into the area from all sides. A hot skirmish at Concord's North Bridge forced the Redcoats to yield that position. Somewhat alarmed, they began to march back to Boston. Soon they were being subjected to a withering fire from American irregulars along their line of march, and Gage was obliged to send out an additional 1,500 men to secure their retreat. When the first day of the Revolutionary War ended, the British had sustained 273 casualties, the Americans less than a hundred.

For a brief moment of history tiny Massachusetts stood alone at arms against an empire that had humbled France and Spain. Yet Massachusetts assumed the offensive! The provincial government chose Artemas Ward, a veteran of the French and Indian War, to command its army, and organized an expedition that captured unsuspecting British garrisons at Fort Ticonderoga and Crown Point, on Lake Champlain. Valuable supplies were taken, including some excellent cannon. However, the other colonies rallied quickly to Massachusetts' cause, sending reinforcements to

*William Dawes and Dr. Samuel Prescott also helped spread the alarm.

the Massachusetts army. Everywhere men could be seen drilling, refurbishing old guns, casting shot, and making saltpeter for gunpowder.

The Second Continental Congress

Philadelphia Patriots decorated their streets with banners reading "Liberty or Death." On May 10 (the day Ticonderoga fell) the Second Continental Congress met in that city. It was a distinguished group, more radical than the First Congress at which John Adams had felt himself surrounded by "Trimmers and Timeservers." In addition to the bluff but brilliant Adams—a staunch advocate of colonial rights yet fair-minded and courageous enough to defend the British officer accused of responsibility for the Boston Massacre—there was his cousin Sam Adams, Patrick Henry and Richard Henry Lee of Virginia, and Christopher Gadsden of South Carolina, all holdovers from the First Congress.

Among the newcomers was a quiet, lanky, sandy-haired young planter from Virginia named Thomas Jefferson, an indifferent debater but a brilliant writer. Jefferson had recently published *A Summary View of the Rights of British America,* an essay criticizing the institution of monarchy and warning George III that "Kings are the servants, not the proprietors of the people." Virginia had also sent George Washington, who could neither write well nor make good speeches, but who knew more than any other colonist about commanding men and wore his buff-and-blue colonel's uniform to indicate his willingness to place his skill at the disposal of the Congress. The renowned Benjamin Franklin was also a delegate and moving rapidly to the radical position. And there were many other prominent men, including the Boston merchant John Hancock, who was chosen president of the Congress.

This Congress was in a difficult position. It had no legal authority. Yet it had to make agonizing decisions under the pressure of rapidly unfolding military events, with the future of every American depending on its actions. Delicate negotiations and honeyed words might yet persuade king and Parliament to change their ways, but precipitate, bold effort was essential to save Massachusetts.

In this predicament Congress naturally dealt with the military crisis first. It formed the forces gathering around Boston under General Ward's command into a Continental Army and appointed George Washington as commander in chief. Ward, Charles Lee, an English convert to the Patriot cause who possessed a wealth of military experience, and several others were named major generals under him. After Washington and his assistants left for the front on June 23, the Congress turned to the task of requisitioning men and supplies.

Meanwhile, in Massachusetts the first major battle of the war had been fought. The British position on the peninsula of Boston was impregnable to direct assault, but high ground north and south, at Charlestown and Dorchester Heights, could be used to pound the city with artillery. When the Patriots seized Bunker Hill and Breed's Hill at Charlestown and constructed a redoubt on the latter, Gage determined at once to drive them off. This was accomplished on June 17, but at frightful cost and only after the Americans had exhausted their powder. Over a thousand Redcoats fell in a couple of hours, out of a force of some 2,200; the Patriots lost only 400 men. The British thus cleared the Charlestown peninsula, but the victory was really the Americans', for they had proved themselves against professional

EMMET COLLECTION, NEW YORK PUBLIC LIBRARY

A British officer's water color shows the fight for Breed's Hill as seen from Boston. Charlestown is enveloped in flames as British reinforcements row ashore (far right) and two frigates shell the American redoubt on Breed's Hill, just beyond the town.

soldiers and had exacted a terrible toll. "The day ended in glory," a British officer wrote, "but the loss was uncommon in officers for the number engaged."

The Battle of Bunker Hill, as it was called for no good reason, greatly reduced whatever hope remained for a negotiated settlement. The spilling of so much blood left each side determined to force the other's submission. The British recalled General Gage, replacing him with General Sir William Howe. George III formally proclaimed the colonies to be "in open rebellion," and a little later instructed the Royal Navy to seize colonial ships on the high seas. The Continental Congress dispatched one last plea to the king (the Olive Branch Petition), but this was a sop to the moderates. Immediately thereafter it adopted the "Declaration of the Causes and Necessity of Taking Up Arms," which condemned everything the British had done since 1763. Americans were "a people attacked by unprovoked enemies"; the time had come to choose between "submission" to "tyranny" and "resistance by force." Congress then ordered an attack on Canada, created a special committee to seek out foreign aid, and another to buy munitions abroad. It also authorized the outfitting of a navy under Commodore Esek Hopkins of Rhode Island.

The Congress, however, and the bulk of the people hung back from a final break with the Crown. Up to this point they knew the British were willing to forgive and forget in return for submission, but to declare for independence would be to burn the last bridge, to become traitors in the eyes of the mother country. Aside from the word's ugly associations, everyone was familiar with the fate meted out to traitors when their efforts failed. Moreover, it was sobering to think of casting off everything that being an Englishman meant: love of king, the traditions of a great nation, pride in the power of a mighty empire. "Where shall we find another Britain?" John Dickinson asked at the time of the Townshend Acts crisis. "Torn from the body to which we are united by religion, liberty, laws, affections, relation, language and commerce, we must bleed at every vein." Then, too, rebellion might end in horrors worse than submission to *British* tyranny. The disturbances following the Stamp Act and the Tea Act had revealed an alarming fact about American society. Protest meetings and mob actions had brought out every thief, every ne'er-do-well, every demagogue in the colonies. Property had been destroyed, not all of it owned by Loyalists and British officials. Too much exalted talk about "rights" and "liberties" might well give the poor (to say nothing of the slaves) an exaggerated impression of their importance. Once unleash the full force of a rebellion, thus officially encouraging resistance to the established order, and no one could be sure where the rebellion would stop. Finally, the 18th century was an age of kings. Could a handful of colonials, spread thinly over so huge an area, maintain a unified system without the cement of hereditary monarchy? Could men *really* govern themselves? The most ardent defender of American rights might well hesitate after considering all these implications of independence.

The Great Declaration

Nevertheless, independence was probably inevitable by the end of 1775. In any case, two events in January 1776 pushed the colonies a long step toward it. First came the news that the British were employing foreign mercenaries to fight against them. Why it seemed more callous for Russian or German troops to shoot at Americans than regiments of Yorkshiremen or Scotsmen is not exactly clear, but so it appeared to the colonists. After the announcement that thousands of hired Hessian soldiers were on the way to America, reconciliation seemed out of the question.

The second decisive event was the publication of *Common Sense*. This tract was written by Thomas Paine, a one-time English corsetmaker and civil servant turned pamphleteer, a man who had been in America scarcely one year. *Common Sense* called forthrightly for complete independence, boldly attacking not only George III but the idea of monarchy itself. Paine had a gift for words, and he applied the uncomplicated logic of the zealot to the recent history of America. Where the colonists had been humbly petitioning George III and swallowing their resentment when he ignored them, Paine called George a "Royal Brute." Where many Americans had wanted to control their own affairs but feared the instability of untried republican government, Paine stated plainly that monarchy was a corrupt institution. "A government of our own is our natural right," he insisted. "O! ye that love mankind! Ye that dare oppose not only tyranny but the tyrant, stand forth!" The time had come to make America "an asylum for mankind."

Practically everyone in the colonies must have read *Common Sense* or heard it explained and discussed. About 150,000 copies were sold in the critical period between January and July.*

The tone of the great debate changed sharply as Paine's slashing attack had its effect. The Continental Congress began to act more boldly. In March it unleashed American privateers against British commerce; in April it opened American ports to foreign shipping; in May it urged the provincial assemblies to frame constitutions and establish state governments.

Then, on June 7, Richard Henry Lee of Virginia introduced a resolution of independence:

> RESOLVED: That these United Colonies are, and of right ought to be, free and independent States, that they are absolved from all allegiance to the British Crown, and that all political connection between them and the State of Great Britain is, and ought to be, totally dissolved.

This momentous resolution was not passed at once; Congress first appointed a committee consisting of Thomas Jefferson, Benjamin Franklin, John Adams, Roger Sherman, and Robert Livingston to frame a suitable justification of independence. Of this group Livingston was the laggard. A member of one of the great New York landowning families, he hesitated to approve a final break with the Crown. He was put on the committee in an effort to push New York toward independence. Sherman, who was a self-educated Connecticut lawyer and merchant, was also a conservative, but strongly opposed to any parliamentary control over colonial affairs. He was, in John Adams' words, "as honest as an angel and as firm in the cause of American Independence as Mount Atlas." But he had no literary gift, being verbose and rather dull, and evidently took no larger part than Livingston in the work of the

*If a comparable portion of today's population purchased any such work, its sale would be in the neighborhood of 10 million copies!

committee. Franklin, as the best-known of all Americans and an experienced writer, was a natural choice, and so was John Adams, whose devotion to the cause of independence combined with his solid conservative qualities made him perhaps the typical man of the Revolution.

Thomas Jefferson was probably placed on the committee because politics required that a Virginian be included and because of his literary skill and the quality of mind. He was far from being a leading member of the Congress, and aside from writing *A Summary View of the Rights of British America,* he had done little to attract notice. At 33 he was the youngest member of the Continental Congress and only marginally interested in the deliberations of the group. He had been slow to take his seat in the fall of 1775 and had gone home to Virginia before Christmas. He put off returning several times and arrived back in Philadelphia only on May 14. Had he delayed another month, someone else would have written the Declaration of Independence. Nevertheless, the committee asked Jefferson to prepare the draft. (Jefferson wanted John Adams to do it, but Adams refused, saying: "You can write ten times better than I can.") And his draft, with a few amendments made by Franklin and Adams and somewhat toned down by the whole Congress, was officially adopted by the delegates on July 4, 1776.

Jefferson's Declaration consisted of two parts. The first was by way of introduction: it justified the abstract right of any people to revolt and described the theory on which the Americans were basing their creation of a new, republican government. The second, much longer, section was a list of the "injuries and usurpations" of George III, a bill of indictment explaining why

YALE UNIVERSITY ART GALLERY

A detail from John Trumbull's Declaration of Independence *(reproduced here in actual size) portrays the five-man drafting committee presenting its handiwork to the Congress. From left, Massachusetts' John Adams, Connecticut's Roger Sherman, New York's Robert Livingston, Virginia's Thomas Jefferson, and Pennsylvania's Benjamin Franklin. Trumbull's skillful composition "ranks" the contributors, with Jefferson dominating.*

the colonists felt driven to exercise the rights outlined in the first part of the document. Here Jefferson stressed George's interference with the functioning of representative government in America, his harsh administration of colonial affairs, his restrictions on civil rights, and his maintenance of troops in the colonies without their consent. The king was also blamed for Parliament's efforts to tax the colonies and to restrict colonial trade. Jefferson included a number of exaggerated charges, accusing George of having incited the slaves to revolt and having urged "the merciless Indian Savages" to attack the frontier. "He has plundered our seas, ravaged our Coasts, burnt our towns, and destroyed the Lives of our people." Naturally enough, in the light of the passions of the times, Jefferson sought to marshal every possible evidence of British perfidy and to make the king, rather than Parliament, the villain. He held George III responsible for many actions by subordinates that George had never deliberately authorized. This long bill of particulars covers every possible reason for the rebellion, but it reads more like a lawyer's brief than a careful analysis. It holds relatively little interest for the modern reader.

Jefferson's general statement of the right of revolution has, however, inspired oppressed peoples all over the world for nearly 200 years:

> We hold these truths to be self-evident, that all men are created equal, that they are endowed by their Creator with certain unalienable Rights, that among these are Life, Liberty and the pursuit of Happiness. That to secure these rights, Governments are instituted among Men, deriving their just powers from the consent of the governed, That whenever any Form of Government becomes destructive of these ends, it is the Right of the People to alter or to abolish it, and to institute new Government....

Why has this statement had so much influence on modern history? Not, certainly, because the thought was original with Jefferson. As John Adams later pointed out—Adams viewed his great contemporary with a mixture of affection, respect, and jealousy—the basic idea was commonplace among 18th-century liberals, being derived chiefly from the writings of John Locke. "I did not consider it any part of my charge to invent new ideas," Jefferson explained, "but to place before mankind the common sense of the subject, in terms so plain and firm as to command their assent. . . . It was intended to be an expression of the American mind."

But if the idea lacked originality, it had never before been put into practice on such a scale. Revolution was not a new thing, of course, but the spectacle of a people solemnly explaining and justifying their right, in an orderly manner, to throw off their oppressors and establish a new system on their own authority was almost without precedent. Soon the French would be drawing upon this example in their great revolt, and ever since rebels everywhere have done likewise. And if Jefferson did not create the concept, he gave it a nearly perfect form. As the French historian Gilbert Chinard has said: "The Declaration of Independence is not only a historical document, it is the first and to this day the most outstanding monument in American literature."

1776: The Balance of Forces

A formal declaration of independence merely cleared the way for tackling the problems of founding a new nation and maintaining it in defiance of Great Britain. Lacking both traditions and any authority based in law, the Congress had to create new political institutions and a new national spirit, and all in the midst of war.

Always the military situation took precedence over other tasks, for a single disastrous setback might make everything else meaningless. At the start the Americans had a great military advantage, for they already possessed their lands except for the few square miles occupied by British troops. An attempt to organize an army of men loyal to Britain in the South had been crushed in February 1776 at the Battle of Moore's Creek Bridge in North Carolina. Although thousands of colonists fought for George III, the British soon learned that to put down the American rebellion they would have to bring in men and supplies from bases on the other side of the Atlantic, a formidable task.

Meanwhile, the initiative remained with the Americans. An expedition under General Richard

Montgomery had captured Montreal in November 1775, and another small force under Benedict Arnold advanced to the gates of Quebec after a grueling march across the wilderness from Maine. Montgomery and Arnold attempted to storm the Quebec defenses on December 31, 1775, but were repulsed with heavy losses. Even so, the British troops in Canada could not drive the isolated remnants of the American army—perhaps 500 men in all—out of the province until reinforcements arrived in the spring of 1776.

Certain long-run factors also operated in America's favor. Although His Majesty's soldiers were brave and well-disciplined, the army was as inefficient and ill-directed as the rest of the British government. Whereas nearly everyone in Great Britain had been willing to crack down hard on Boston after the Tea Party, many boggled at engaging in a full-scale war against all the colonies. Aside from reluctance to spill so much blood, there was the question of expense. Finally, the idea of dispatching the cream of the British army to America while powerful enemies on the Continent still smarted from past losses seemed extremely dangerous. For all these reasons, the British approached the task of subduing the rebellion gingerly. When Washington, strengthened by the acquisition of cannon captured at Ticonderoga, fortified Dorchester Heights overlooking Boston, General Howe withdrew his troops to Halifax rather than risk another Bunker Hill. On March 17, 1776, Washington marched his troops into the city. For the moment, the 13 colony-states were clear of Redcoats.

Awareness of Britain's problems undoubtedly spurred the Continental Congress to the bold actions taken during the spring of 1776. However, on the very day that Congress voted for independence (July 2), General Howe was back on American soil, landing in force on Staten Island in New York harbor in preparation for an assault on the city. Soon Howe had at hand 32,000 well-equipped troops and a powerful fleet commanded by his brother, Richard, Lord Howe.

Suddenly, the full strength of the empire seemed to have descended on the Americans. Superior British resources (a population of 9 million to the colonies' 2.5 million, large stocks of war materials and the industrial capacity to boost them further, mastery of the seas, and a highly centralized and, when necessary, ruthless government) were now all too evident. This demonstration of British might accentuated American military and economic weaknesses: both money and the tools of war were continually in short supply in a predominantly agricultural country. In addition, the country was far from united. Whereas nearly all colonists had objected to British policies after the French and Indian War, many still hesitated to take up arms against the mother country. Even Massachusetts harbored many Loyalists, or Tories, as they were called; about a thousand Americans fled Boston with General Howe, abandoning their homes rather than submit to the rebel army.

No one knows exactly how the colonists divided on the question of independence; what is certain is that the people did divide and that the divisions to some extent cut across geographic, social, and economic lines. The most explicit estimate places Tory strength between 7.6 and 18 per cent of the white population; the "hard-core" Tories, those who left America when the war ended, numbered about 100,000. The Patriots were much more numerous, but large elements were more or less indifferent to the whole conflict or, in Tom Paine's famous phrase, were summer soldiers and sunshine patriots, who supported the Revolution when all was going well and lost their enthusiasm in difficult hours. A high proportion of men holding royal appointments and many Anglican clergymen remained loyal to King George, as did numbers of merchants with close connections in Britain. There were important pockets of Tory strength in rural sections of New York, in the North Carolina back country, and among persons of non-English origin and other minority groups who tended to count on London for protection against the local majority.

Many became Tories simply out of distaste for change or because they were temperamentally pessimistic about the possibility of improving the world. "What is the whole history of human life," wrote the Tory clergyman and schoolmaster Jonathan Boucher of Virginia, "but a series of disappointments?" Still others believed that the actions of the British, however unfair and misguided, did not justify rebellion. Knowing that they possessed a remarkably free and equitable system of government, they could not stomach shedding blood merely to avoid paying a few new taxes or to escape from what they considered minor restrictions on their activities. "The Annals of no Country can produce an Instance of so virulent a Rebellion . . . originating from such trivial Causes," one Loyalist complained.

The Tories lacked organization; many of their "leaders" did not even know one another, and they had no central committee to lay plans or coordinate their efforts. They waited for instructions from the mother country, which were slow in coming. The British, overestimating both the number of Loyalists and their own ability to crush the rebels, supplied little support or direction to the Tories before 1778. The leading Patriots, of course, worked closely together, but many of them also suffered from a lack of *national* feeling. This was true even of some of the most enthusiastic revolutionaries. As in the colonial wars against the French, men who would fight stoutly when their own district was threatened frequently refused to make sacrifices to help Americans in other regions.

But if the differences separating Patriot from Loyalist are unclear, feelings were nonetheless bitter, battles between Tory units and the Continental Army often exceptionally bloody. "Neighbor was against neighbor, father against son and son against father," one Connecticut Tory reported. "He that would not thrust his own blade through his brother's heart was called an infamous villain."

General Howe's campaign against New York brought to light still another American weakness —the lack of military experience. Washington, expecting Howe to attack New York, had moved south to meet the threat, but both he and his men failed badly in this first major test. Late in August Howe crossed from Staten Island to Brooklyn. In the Battle of Long Island he easily outflanked and defeated Washington's army. Had he acted decisively, he could probably have ended the war on the spot, but Howe, who could not decide whether to be a peacemaker or a conqueror, was never decisive. When he hesitated in consolidating his gains, Washington managed to withdraw his troops to Manhattan Island. (Contrary winds had kept Admiral Lord Howe's men-of-war from entering the East River; without this lucky chance Washington's escape would have been impossible and the destruction of his army inevitable.)

Howe could still have trapped Washington simply by using his fleet to land troops on the northern end of Manhattan; instead he attacked New York City directly, leaving the Americans an escape route to the north. Again Patriot troops proved unable to resist British regulars. Though Washington threw his hat to the ground in a rage and threatened to shoot cowardly Connecticut soldiers as they fled from the battlefield, he could not stop the rout and had to fall back on Harlem Heights in upper Manhattan. Once more, however, Howe failed to pursue his advantage promptly.

Still Washington refused to see the peril in remaining on an island while the enemy commanded the surrounding waters. Only when Howe shifted a powerful force to Westchester, directly threatening his rear, did Washington move north to the mainland. Even then he left a large detachment on Manhattan at Fort Washington, which the British soon overwhelmed. Finally, after several more narrow escapes, he crossed over into New Jersey, where the British could not use their naval superiority against him.

The battles in and around New York City seemed to presage an easy British triumph. Yet somehow Washington salvaged a moral victory from these ignominious defeats. He himself learned rapidly; seldom thereafter did he place his troops in such vulnerable positions. And his men, in spite of repeated failure, had become an army. In November and December 1776 they retreated across New Jersey and into Pennsylvania. General Howe then abandoned the campaign, going into winter quarters in New York but posting garrisons at Trenton, Princeton, and other strategic points. The troops at Trenton were hated Hessian mercenaries and Washington decided to attack them. Crossing the ice-clogged Delaware River on Christmas night during a

STOKES COLLECTION, NEW YORK PUBLIC LIBRARY

NEW YORK-NEW JERSEY CAMPAIGNS 1776-1777

American Forces
British Forces
0 5 10 15
Miles

Peekskill
NEW YORK
Hudson R.
White Plains
28 Oct 1776
HOWE
Hackensack
Ft. Lee
Ft. Washington
Morristown (Winter Quarters)
Harlem Heights 16 Sept 1776
East R.
Newark
New York
NEW JERSEY
Passaic R.
WASHINGTON
CORNWALLIS
Long Island 27 Aug 1776
Staten Island
SIR WILLIAM HOWE
ADMIRAL LORD HOWE
Raritan R.
New Brunswick
CLINTON
3 Jan 1777 Princeton
Newton
Trenton 26 Dec 1776
ATLANTIC OCEAN
PENNSYLVANIA
Allentown
Delaware R.

The events in and around New York, so nearly disastrous to Washington and his army, are detailed at the left. Tom Paine's famous pamphlet The Crisis *was written during Washington's hairsbreadth escape across New Jersey. The aquatint above pictures an American attempt, by means of fire ships, to challenge the Royal Navy's control of the Hudson in August of 1776. The crew of the frigate* Phoenix *fends off one of the fire ships; neither it nor the* Rose *(center) were damaged in the attack.*

wild storm, he took the Hessians completely by surprise, capturing over 900 prisoners. A few days later he outmaneuvered British General Cornwallis and the braggart James Grant and won another battle at Princeton. These engagements had little strategic importance, since both armies then went into winter quarters; nonetheless, they bolstered American morale. Without them there might not have been an army to resume the war in the spring.

Forming State Governments

The efforts of the states and of the Continental Congress to establish new governments can only be understood against the background of these military events. For example, when the British invaded New Jersey, Congress fled from Philadelphia to Baltimore, greatly disrupting its activities. Defeats led to confusion and bickering, and hopes for the rapid establishment of a legal central government were soon dashed. A draft constitution prepared by John Dickinson in July 1776 ran into trouble: the larger states objected to equal representation of all the states, and the states with large western land claims refused to cede these to the central government. It was not until November 1777 that the Articles of Confederation were finally submitted to the states for ratification.

Besides struggling to frame a constitution, the Congress had to run the war and perform all the executive functions of government, for there were no departments or other administrative organizations. It did so through a host of committees—the indefatigable John Adams served on over 80. Congress managed to carry on fruitful diplomatic negotiations with France and other powers, borrow large sums, issue Continental currency, requisition money and supplies from the states, organize a postal system, and supervise Washington's conduct of the war.

One great difficulty in the way of establishing a central government was the lack of precedent: there had never been an *American* government. Another was suspicion of authority imposed from above, resulting from British behavior after the French and Indian War. British oppression had forced the colonies to combine, but it had also strengthened their conviction that local control of political power was vital. Remembering Parliament's treatment of them, they refused to give any central authority the right to tax.

Fortunately, neither of these problems blocked the creation of effective state governments. In an important sense the *real* revolution occurred when the separate colonies declared their independence; they, rather than the extralegal Continental Congress, formally broke the official ties with Great Britain. Using their colonial charters as a basis, the states soon framed new constitutions. By the end of 1776 all but Georgia and New York had taken this decisive step.

The new governments were all quite similar and not drastically different from those they replaced. Each provided for an elected legislature, an executive, and a system of courts. In general the powers of the governor and of judges were closely limited—a natural result of past experience, if somewhat illogical now that these officials were no longer appointed by an outside authority. The theory appeared to be that elected rulers no less than those appointed by kings were subject to the temptations of authority, that, as one Patriot put it, all men are "tyrants enough at heart." The typical governor, therefore, was more an administrator than a head of state, and what authority he had he shared with an elected council. He had no voice in legislation and little in appointments. "Rulers must be conceived as the creatures of people," a North Carolina constitution-maker wrote. Pennsylvania went so far as to eliminate the office of governor, replacing it with a 12-man elected council.

The locus of power was in the legislature, which the people had come to count upon to defend their interests. In addition to the lawmaking authority exercised by the colonial assemblies, the state constitutions gave the legislatures the power to declare war, conduct foreign relations, control the courts, and perform many other essentially executive functions. While continuing to confine the suffrage to property owners—even the liberal Pennsylvania charter limited the right to vote to "free men having a sufficient evident common interest with, and attachment to the community"—the constitution-makers remained suspicious even of the legislature. The British concept of virtual representation they of course rejected out of hand. They saw legislators as representing very specific local areas and as being *representatives*, that is, agents carrying out the wishes of the voters, rather than as superior persons chosen to decide public issues according to their own best judgment. Gordon S. Wood, whose book *The Creation of the American Republic* throws much light on the political thinking of the period, describes the concept as "acutely actual representation." Where political power was involved, the common American principle was every man for himself. The constitutions also contained bills of rights protecting the peoples' civil liberties against all branches of the government. In Britain such guarantees checked only the Crown; the Americans now invoked them against their own elected representatives as well.

In general the state governments combined the best of the British system, including its respect for fairness and due process, with the uniquely American stress on individualism and a healthy dislike of too much authority. The idea of drafting written frames of government—contracts between the people and their representatives, carefully spelling out the powers and duties of the latter—grew out of the experience of the colonists after 1763, when the vagueness of the unwritten British Constitution had caused so much controversy, and from the compact principle described in the Declaration of Independence. It represented one of the most important innovations of the Revolutionary era: a peaceful method for altering the political system. In the midst of violence the states changed their frames of government in an orderly, legal manner, a truly remarkable achievement that became a beacon of hope to future reformers all over the world.

Many states seized the occasion of constitution-making to introduce important reforms.* For example, in Pennsylvania, Virginia, North Carolina, and certain other states the seats in the legislature were reapportioned in order to give the western districts their fair share. Primogeniture, entail (the right of an owner of property to prevent his heirs from ever disposing of it), and quitrents were abolished wherever they had existed. Steps toward greater freedom of religion were also taken, especially in those states where the Anglican Church had enjoyed a privileged position. While most states continued to support religion after the Revolution, they usually distributed the money roughly in accordance with the numerical strength of the various Protestant denominations. Prison reform, the abolition of harsh punishments, and the improvement of education were also undertaken in many states. A few tried, without much success, to stamp out the aristocratic practice of dueling.

Many of the states also moved tentatively against slavery. In attacking British policy after 1763, colonists had frequently claimed that Parliament was trying to make slaves of them; no less a personage than George Washington, for example, wrote in 1774: "We must assert our rights, or submit to every imposition, that can be heaped upon us, till custom and use shall make us tame and abject slaves." However exaggerated the language, such reasoning led naturally to general denunciations of slavery, often vague but nonetheless significant in their effects on men's beliefs. The fact that practically every important thinker of the European Enlightenment had criticized slavery on moral and economic grounds (Montesquieu, Voltaire, Diderot, and Rousseau in France, David Hume, Dr. Johnson,* and Adam Smith in England, to name only a few) also had an impact on educated opinion. Then, too, the flat statements in the Declaration of Independence about liberty and equality seemed impossible to reconcile with slaveholding. Gradually, some Americans began to realize that blacks were not inherently inferior to whites, that the degrading environment of slavery was responsible for their low state.

*Actually the process of constitution-making and reform took many years and was not completed until well after the Revolution had ended.

*"How is it," asked Dr. Johnson, who opposed independence vehemently, "that we hear the loudest *yelps* for liberty among the drivers of negroes?"

The war itself opened up direct paths toward freedom for some slaves. As early as November 1775 Lord Dunmore, the royal governor of Virginia, proclaimed that all slaves "able and willing to bear arms" for the British would be liberated. In general, however, the British treated slaves as captured property, seizing them by the thousands in their campaigns in the South. The fate of these blacks is obscure; some ended up in the West Indies, still slaves. But others were eventually evacuated to Canada as free men, and some of these eventually settled the British colony of Sierra Leone, in West Africa, founded in 1787. Probably many more escaped from bondage by running away during the confusion accompanying the British campaigns in the South.

Other slaves won freedom by serving in the Patriot army and navy—an official report of 1778 counted 755 Negroes in arms. Most were from the northern states, however, and many were already free. In any case, black men fought—many with conspicuous bravery—in every major battle from Lexington to Yorktown.

More significant gains resulted from the legal changes in the status of Negroes effected by the state governments. Beginning with Pennsylvania in 1780, the northern states all provided for the emancipation of their slaves. In most cases the process was gradual—slaves born after a certain date were to become free upon reaching maturity. Since New Jersey did not pass its emancipation act until 1804, this meant that there were numbers of slaves in the so-called free states well into the 19th century, over 3,500 as late as 1830. But at least the institution was on its way toward extinction. After the outbreak of the Revolution, all the states prohibited the further importation of slaves from abroad, and except for Georgia and South Carolina, the southern states passed laws making it easier for individual owners to free their slaves. The greatest success of voluntary emancipation came in Virginia, where between 1782 and 1790, 10,000 blacks were freed.

These advances encouraged foes of slavery to hope that the institution would soon disappear. But their hopes were dashed. Slavery died only where it was already moribund, and except for owners whose Negroes were "carried off" by the British, only in Massachusetts were men deprived of existing slave property against their will.

Speaking more generally, little of the social or economic upheaval usually associated with revolutions occurred after 1776. The property of Tories was frequently seized by the state governments, but almost never with the idea of redistributing wealth or providing the poor with land. While some large Tory estates were broken up and sold to small farmers, others passed intact to rich men or groups of speculators. After all, in most cases those who framed the new constitutions had held power even before the Revolution.

That the new governments were liberal but moderate reflected the spirit of the times, best typified by a man like Jefferson, who had great faith in the democratic process but who owned a great estate and many slaves and had never suggested a drastic social revolution. The framers wanted to create a new and better world but had no desire to overturn a privileged class. More men of middling wealth were elected to the legislatures than in colonial times because the Revolution stimulated popular interest in politics, and republican forms subtly undermined the tendency of farmers and artisans to defer automatically to great planters and merchants. Conflicts of course erupted over economic issues involving such matters as land and taxation, but no single class or interest triumphed in all the states or in the national government. In Pennsylvania where the western radical element was strong, the constitution was extremely democratic; in South Carolina the conservative tidewater planters maintained control handily. Many great landowners were ardent Patriots; others became Tories—yet so did many small farmers.

In some cases the state legislatures wrote the new constitutions, but in a number of instances the legislatures ordered special elections to choose delegates to conventions empowered to draft these charters. This convention method was a further important product of the Revolutionary era, an additional illustration of the idea that constitutions are contracts between the people and their leaders. Massachusetts even required that its new constitution be ratified by the people after it was drafted.

Financing the Revolution

All internal conflicts save the political one between Tory and Patriot were muted by the presence of British troops on American soil. The Continental Congress and the states carried on the war cooperatively. General officers were appointed by the Congress, lesser ones locally. The Continental Army, small but increasingly effective, was the backbone of Washington's force, whereas the states raised militia chiefly for short-term service. Militiamen fought well at times but often proved unreliable. Washington continually fretted about their "dirty, mercenary spirit" and their "intractable" nature, yet he could not have won the war without them.

Problems of finance and supply were also handled by both national and local authorities. The fact that Congress' requisitions of money often went unhonored by the states does not mean that the states failed to contribute heavily to the war effort. Altogether, they contributed about $5.8 million in hard money, and also met Congress' demands for beef, corn, rum, fodder, and other essential supplies. In addition, Congress raised large sums by borrowing. Americans bought bonds worth between $7 and $8 million during the war, while foreign governments lent another $8 million, most of this furnished by France. Congress also issued over $240 million in paper money, the states over $200 million more. This currency fell in value rapidly, resulting in an inflation that caused much hardship and grumbling. The people, in effect, paid much of the cost of the war through the depreciation of their savings, but it is hard to see how else it could have been financed, given the prejudice of the populace against paying taxes to fight a war against British taxation.

Other help in the struggle came from France and Spain. Both these powers still smarted from their defeat in the Seven Years' War and were eager to discommode Great Britain whenever possible. Beginning in the 1760's France, hoping for trouble between the British and their American colonies, had maintained secret agents in America to report on developments. When trouble did come, the Comte de Vergennes, French foreign minister, hastened to take advantage of it. By early May 1776 he had persuaded Louis XVI to authorize the expenditure of a million livres for munitions for America, and more was added the next year. Spain also contributed to the cause. Soon vital supplies were being funneled secretly to the rebels through a dummy trading company, Rŏderigue Hortalez et Cie. Most of its gunpowder and many other essentials reached the Revolutionary army in this way. This aid was at first totally unsolicited (for many months the colonial leaders hoped to be able to afford the luxury of maintaining their traditional hatred of France and Spain), but without it, the fight would have been almost impossible to carry on.

HISTORICAL SOCIETY OF PENNSYLVANIA

By His Excellency
GEORGE WASHINGTON, Esquire,
GENERAL and COMMANDER in CHIEF of the Forces of the United States of America.

BY Virtue of the Power and Direction to Me eſpecially given, I hereby enjoin and require all Perſons reſiding within ſeventy Miles of my Head Quarters to threſh one Half of their Grain by the 1ſt Day of February, and the other Half by the 1ſt Day of March next enſuing, on Pain, in Caſe of Failure, of having all that ſhall remain in Sheaves after the Period above mentioned, ſeized by the Commiſſaries and Quarter-Maſters of the Army, and paid for as Straw.

GIVEN *under my Hand, at Head Quarters, near the Valley Forge, in Philadelphia County, this 20th Day of December*, 1777.

G. WASHINGTON.

By His Excellency's Command,
Robert H. Harrison, Sec'y.

LANCASTER: Printed by JOHN DUNLAP.

Washington issued this blunt requisition order the day after his army limped into its Valley Forge encampment. The army's supply problems were intensified by the weakness of its transportation system.

Saratoga and the French Alliance

When spring reached New Jersey in April 1777, Washington had fewer than 5,000 men under arms. Great plans—far too many of them and too complicated, as it turned out—were afoot in the British camp. To his superiors in England, General Howe

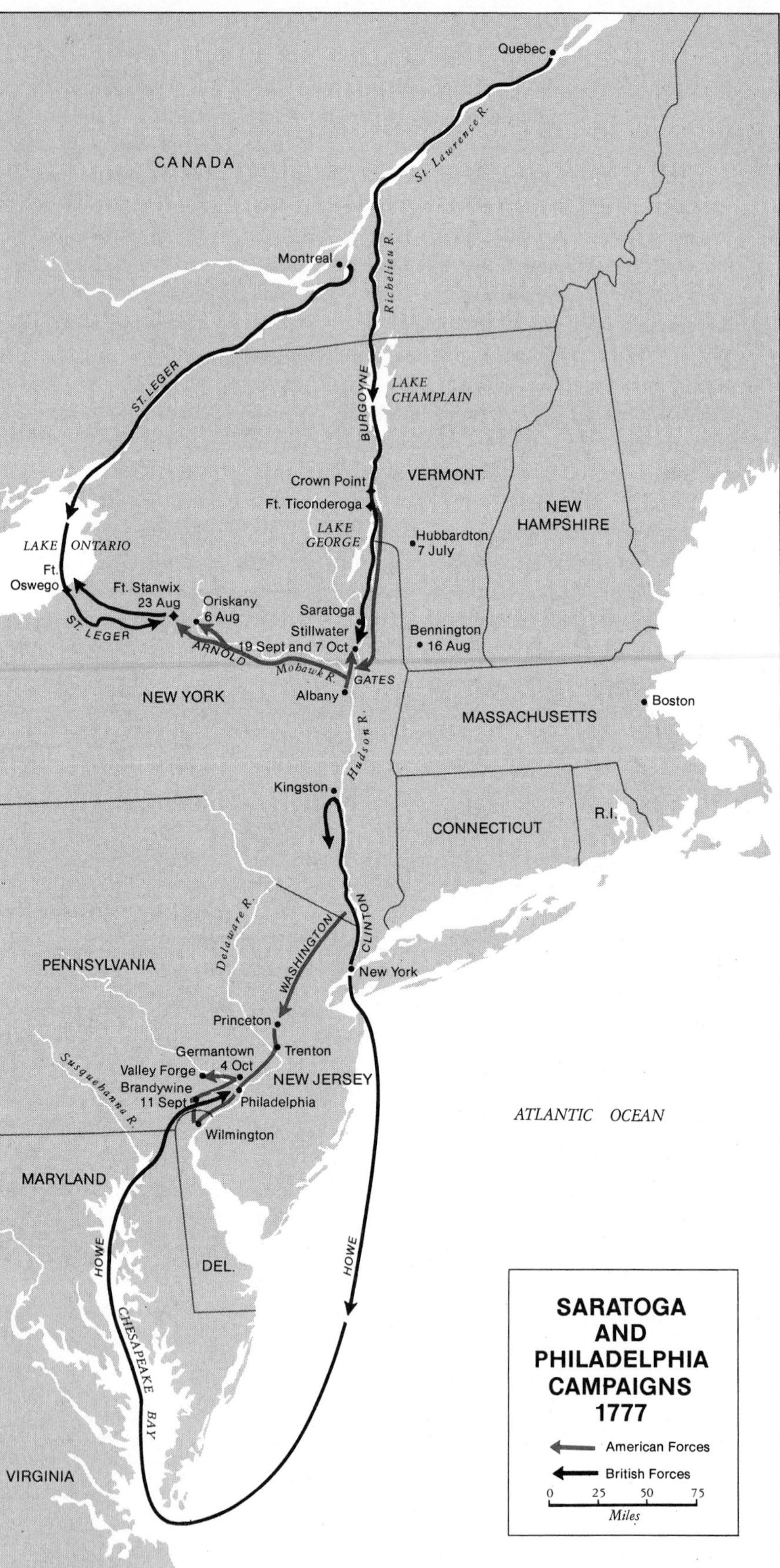

Howe's attack on Philadelphia and Burgoyne's simultaneous fatal essay at grand strategy are detailed here. In the absence of definite orders from London to participate in Burgoyne's campaign, and already resentful that his own strategic plans were ignored, Howe set sail for the Chesapeake, leaving behind in New York a mere token force to cooperate with Burgoyne to the north.

proposed three different strategies for winning the war. (The most ambitious would have required 15,000 additional men, which was out of the question from London's point of view.) General John Burgoyne offered still another. As finally determined, the strategy called for Burgoyne to lead a large army from Canada down Lake Champlain toward Albany, while a smaller force under Lieutenant Colonel Barry St. Leger pushed eastward toward Albany from Fort Oswego on Lake Ontario. Howe was to lead a third force north up the Hudson. Patriot resistance would be smashed between these three armies, and the New England states isolated from the rest. Before participating in this campaign, Howe decided to attack Philadelphia. He hoped that, besides keeping Washington fully occupied, the presence of Redcoats in Pennsylvania would encourage local Tories to rise, thus speeding the disintegration of the American forces.

As a venture in coordinated military tactics the British campaign of 1777 was a fiasco. Burgoyne began his march from Canada in mid-June. By early July he had reached the vicinity of Fort Ticonderoga, at the southern end of Lake Champlain. The fort fell to him on July 6, and he quickly pushed beyond Lake George but thereafter bogged down. Burdened by a huge baggage train that included no less than 52 cannon, he could advance at but a snail's pace through the dense woods north of Saratoga. Patriot forces, mainly militia, impeded his way by felling trees across the forest trails. General Howe, in the meantime, wasted valuable weeks trying to trap Washington into exposing his army in New Jersey. This enabled Washington, who by June had 9,000 regulars and large militia elements at his disposal, to send off some of his regulars to buttress the militia forming in Burgoyne's path. Finally, on July 23, Howe sailed from New York with the bulk of his army to attack Philadelphia, reaching the Chesapeake Bay area on August 25. Only a small force under General Sir Henry Clinton, a brilliant but mentally unstable commander, remained in the New York area to aid Burgoyne.

St. Leger had also been most dilatory in carrying out his part of the grand design. He did not move east from Fort Oswego until July 26, and then he too bogged down at Fort Stanwix, about a third of the way to Albany. He placed the fort under siege early in August, but General Benedict Arnold marched westward with a thousand men from the army resisting Burgoyne and forced St. Leger to fall back to his base at Oswego. A sortie by some of Burgoyne's men into Vermont was smashed at Bennington by Patriot militia on August 16.

Thus, by the end of August, the British plan had been completely disrupted. The drive from Canada had stalled, the push from the west had been turned back, that from New York City had been stillborn. American militiamen were filtering into the area north of Albany. Although he was too smug to realize it, Burgoyne was in serious trouble.

With magnificent disregard for the rest of the war, Howe now proceeded, in a series of well-planned but ponderously executed maneuvers, to move against Philadelphia from his new base on Chesapeake Bay. He taught Washington, who had moved south to oppose him, a series of lessons in tactics, defeating him at the Battle of Brandywine on September 11, feinting him out of position before Philadelphia, and moving unopposed into that city on September 26. Yet he failed to destroy Washington's army, which attacked him sharply at Germantown early in October. This attack was almost successful, and when Howe finally repelled it, winning another useless victory, Washington was still able to retreat in an orderly fashion.

Meanwhile, utter disaster befell General Burgoyne. The American forces under Philip Schuyler and later under Horatio Gates and Benedict Arnold had erected formidable defenses immediately south of Saratoga near the town of Stillwater. Burgoyne struck at this position on September 19 and was stopped cold. With militiamen threatening his flanks in increasing numbers, Burgoyne desperately assaulted the American position again on October 7. Once more he was thrown back, with losses four times those of the Americans. By this time General Clinton had finally started up the Hudson from New York. He got as far as Kingston, about 80 miles below Saratoga, and then, on October 16, decided to return to New

HENRY FRANCIS DU PONT WINTERTHUR MUSEUM

A widely circulated European cartoon (this is a Dutch version), inspired by the events of 1777. England's cow of commerce is milked by France, Spain, and Holland, while America saws off its horns and John Bull fails to rouse the British lion. Behind them, the Howe brothers drowse over a punch bowl in Philadelphia.

York for reinforcements. The next day, at Saratoga, Burgoyne surrendered. Some 5,700 British prisoners were marched off to Virginia.

This overwhelming triumph probably decided the Revolution, for when news of the victory reached France, Louis XVI immediately recognized the United States. By February 1778 Vergennes and three American commissioners in Paris, Benjamin Franklin, Arthur Lee, and Silas Deane, had drafted a commercial treaty and a formal treaty of alliance. The two nations agreed to make "common cause and aid each other mutually" should war "break out" between France and Great Britain. Meanwhile, France guaranteed "the sovereignty and independence absolute and unlimited" of the United States.

When the news of Saratoga reached England, Lord North realized that a Franco-American alliance would probably follow. He moved to forestall it by proposing to give in completely on all the issues that had agitated the colonies before 1775. Both the Coercive Acts and the Tea Act would be repealed. Parliament would pledge itself never to tax the colonies. Indeed, Lord North was ready to repeal every act passed after 1763 if necessary to conciliate the Americans. But once again the insensitivity and ponderous inefficiency of the British government killed whatever small chance existed for a peaceful settlement at this date. Instead of implementing this proposal promptly, Parliament did not act until March 1778. Royal Peace Commissioners did not reach Philadelphia until June, a month after Congress had ratified the French treaty. The British proposals were icily rejected, and while the commissioners were still in Philadelphia war broke out between France and Great Britain.

The Revolution, however, was far from won. After the Battle of Germantown, Washington had settled his army for the winter at Valley Forge, 20 miles northwest of Philadelphia. The site was ill-chosen and foraging in the area unproductive. The supply system collapsed; thousands of men reported unfit for duty simply because they had no shoes. For months everyone was on short rations. The army, Washington said at one point, must either "starve, dissolve, or disperse" unless aid were provided. To make matters worse, there was grumbling in Congress over Washington's failure to win victories, and some disorganized talk of replacing him as commander in chief with Horatio Gates, the "hero" of Saratoga. (Actually Gates was an indifferent soldier, lacking in decisiveness and unable to instill confidence in his subordinates. "Historical accounts of the Saratoga campaign have given abundant reasons for the American victory other than the military skill of Horatio Gates," one of his biographers has confessed.) As the winter dragged on, the Continental Army melted away, some soldiers returning to their homes, others—perhaps 2,000—stumbling half-frozen and in rags into Philadelphia to sign up with the British. General Howe, taking his ease in comfortable quarters in Philadelphia, could easily have routed the Americans had he been willing to march out in force in February or March. He did nothing. In May 1778 he was finally replaced by General Clinton.

The War in the South

Spring brought a revival of American hopes in the form of more supplies, new recruits, and, above all, word of the French alliance. Clinton at this point decided to transfer his base back to New York, and while he was moving across New Jersey, Washington attacked him at Monmouth Court House. The fight was inconclusive, but the Americans held the field when the day ended and were able to claim a victory. Clinton marched on to New York. Thereafter, British strategy changed. Fighting in the northern states practically ceased. Instead, relying on sea power and the supposed presence of many Tories in the South, the British concentrated their efforts in South Carolina and Georgia. Savannah fell late in 1778 and most of the settled parts of Georgia were overrun during 1779. In 1780 Clinton himself led a massive expedition against Charleston. When the city surrendered in May, more than 5,000 soldiers were captured, the most overwhelming American defeat of the war. Leaving General Cornwallis and some 8,000 men to carry on the campaign, Clinton then sailed back to his New York headquarters.

The Tories of South Carolina and Georgia came closer to meeting British expectations than did those of any other region. Nevertheless, the callous behavior of the British troops rapidly persuaded large numbers of hesitating citizens to join the Patriot cause. Guerrilla bands led by men like Francis Marion, the "Swamp Fox," and Thomas Sumter, after whom Fort Sumter, famous in the Civil War, was named, provided a nucleus of resistance in areas that had supposedly been subdued.

In June 1780 Congress placed the highly regarded Horatio Gates in charge of a southern army consisting of these irregular militia units and a hard core of Continentals transferred from Washington's command. Moving south, Gates encountered Cornwallis at Camden, South Carolina. He was outmaneuvered and badly defeated and had to fall back. Congress then recalled him, sensibly permitting Washington to replace him with General Nathanael Greene, a first-rate officer, adaptable, sensible, and steady. Already a band of militiamen had trapped a contingent of Tories at King's Mountain and forced its surrender. Now Greene, cleverly avoiding a major engagement against Cornwallis' superior numbers, divided his forces and staged a series of raids on scattered points. In January 1781, at the Battle of Cowpens in northwestern South Carolina, troops under General Daniel Morgan inflicted a costly defeat on Colonel Banastre Tarleton, one of Cornwallis' best officers. Cornwallis pursued Morgan hotly, but the American rejoined Greene and together they inflicted heavy losses on the Britisher at Guilford Court House. Then Cornwallis, alarmed by the stiffness of American resistance and disappointed by the failure of Tories to flock to his

Cornwallis Retreating!

PHILADELPHIA, April 7, 1781.

Extract of a Letter from Major-General *Greene*, dated CAMP, at *Buffelo Creek, March* 23, 1781.

"ON the 16th Instant I wrote your Excellency, giving an Account of an Action which happened at Guilford Court-House the Day before. I was then persuaded that notwithstanding we were obliged to give up the Ground, we had reaped the Advantage of the Action. Circumstances since confirm me in Opinion that the Enemy were too much gauled to improve their Success. We lay at the Iron-Works three Days, preparing ourselves for another Action, and expecting the Enemy to advance: But of a sudden they took their Departure, leaving behind them evident Marks of Distress. All our wounded at Guilford, which had fallen into their Hands, and 70 of their own, too bad to move, were left at New-Garden. Most of their Officers suffered-- Lord Cornwallis had his Horse shot under him--- Col. Steward, of the Guards was killed, General O Hara and Cols. Tarlton and Webster, wounded. Only three Field-Officers escaped, if Reports, which seem to be authentic, can be relied on.

Our Army are in good Spirits, notwithstanding our Sufferings, and are advancing towards the Enemy; they are retreating to Cross-Creek.

In South-Carolina, Generals Sumpter and Marian have gained several little Advantages. In one the Enemy lost 60 Men, who had under their Care a large Quantity of Stores, which were taken, but by an unfortunate Mistake were afterwards re taken.

Published by Order,
CHARLES THOMSON, Secretary.

§†§ Printed at N. Willis's Office.

In a report to Washington released to the nation in broadside form, Nathanael Greene neatly summed up his campaign of attrition in the Carolinas: "the Enemy were too much gauled to improve their Success."

colors in large numbers, withdrew to the seaport of Wilmington, North Carolina, where he could rely upon the fleet for support and reinforcements. Greene's Patriots quickly regained control of the Carolina back country.

Victory at Yorktown

Seeing no future in further activity in the Carolinas but unwilling to sit idly at Wilmington, Cornwallis pushed north into Virginia where he joined forces with troops under Benedict Arnold, who had sold out to the British. (Disaffected by what he considered unjust criticism of his generalship, Arnold had attempted in 1780 to betray the bastion of West Point, on the Hudson River. But the scheme was foiled when incriminating papers were found on the person of a British spy, Major John André. Arnold fled to the British and André was hanged.) As in the Carolina campaign, the British had numerical superiority at first but lost it rapidly when local militia and Continental forces under generals Lafayette and Von Steuben—the most skilled of the European volunteers serving under Washington—concentrated against them. Again Cornwallis sought to renew his strength by falling back on the sea. This time he chose his base unwisely, establishing himself at Yorktown, on a peninsula extending into Chesapeake Bay.

At this point the French and Americans, by acting decisively and boldly while the British vacillated and delayed, won a great victory that effectively destroyed England's will to fight. Everyone realized that the rebellion could not be suppressed unless Britain could maintain control of the Atlantic. The Saratoga campaign, as well as those of Cornwallis and others, demonstrated that once out of range of their warships, British troops ran into hard going. They might win pitched battles, but they found it next to impossible to hold large areas of land while Patriot militia ranged along their flanks and harried their communications. As General Clinton said in 1780 after the capture of Charleston, "[If] a superior fleet shews itself . . . I despair of ever seeing peace restored to this miserable country." The British navy in American waters far outnumbered American and French vessels, but the Atlantic is wide, and in those days communication was slow. The French had a fleet in the West Indies under Admiral De Grasse and another squadron at Newport, Rhode Island, where a French army was also stationed. Washington, in conjunction with De Grasse and the Comte de Rochambeau, commander of French land forces, decided in the summer of 1781 upon a flexible plan to either bottle up Cornwallis, or attack Clinton in New York, or both.

The British navy in the West Indies and at

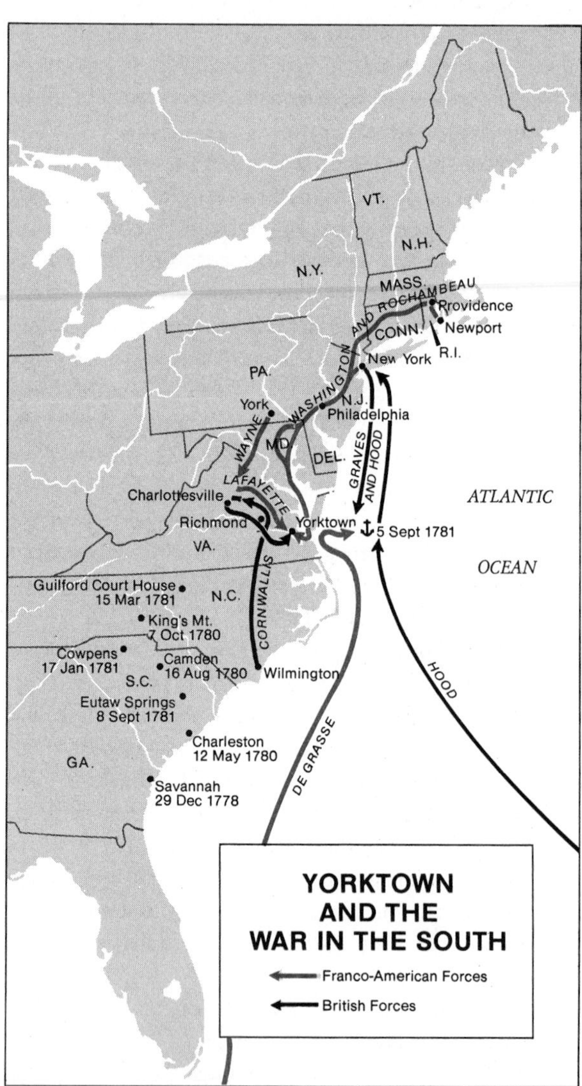

In an era when communications were slow and erratic at best, the coordination between the American and French land and naval forces that sealed up Cornwallis in Yorktown was nothing short of remarkable.

New York might have forestalled this scheme if it had moved promptly and in force. But Admiral Sir George Rodney sent only part of his Indies fleet. (He dispatched two ships to Jamaica on convoy duty and reserved three to escort him back to England.) As a result, De Grasse, after a battle with a British fleet commanded by Admiral Thomas Graves, won control of the Chesapeake and cut Cornwallis off from the sea.

The next move was up to Washington, and this was his finest hour as a commander of troops. Acting in conjunction with Rochambeau, he tricked Clinton into thinking he was going to strike at New York and then pushed rapidly south. By late September he had nearly 17,000 French and American veterans in position before the defenses of Yorktown. Cornwallis was helpless. He held out until October 17 and then asked for terms. On the 19th more than 7,000 British soldiers marched out of their lines and laid down their arms.

The Articles of Confederation

Although there were no major battles after Yorktown, the signing of a peace treaty still lay well in the future. Meanwhile, the nation struggled to establish itself. A great forward step had been taken in March 1781, when the Articles of Confederation were finally ratified. The long delay was occasioned by interstate rivalries. When the Articles were first submitted in November 1777, the states had offered a host of petty objections and suggestions, but when Congress sensibly stood firm, most of them fell in line and accepted the document as submitted. By the beginning of 1779 only Maryland had not ratified it. Maryland held out in order to force a change that would authorize Congress to determine the western limits of states with land claims beyond the Appalachians. There were many good reasons why this should be done. The state claims to the West were overlapping, vaguely defined, in some instances preposterous, extending in a number of cases to the Pacific Ocean. To have permitted a few states to monopolize the West would have unbalanced the union from the start. If actual possession of these regions was to be wrested from the British and Indians, it would require a common, *national* effort.

Many fair-minded men in the "landed" states recognized the justice of Maryland's suggestion, but Maryland was acting also from a more selfish motive. Land speculators in the state had obtained rights from the Indians to large tracts in the Ohio Valley. Virginia had a powerful claim to this area. If it was controlled by Virginia, the Maryland titles would be worthless, but under national administration they might be made to stand up. Naturally, Virginia resented its neighbor's efforts to grasp these valuable lands by indirection.

Finally, with the British about to advance into the state, Virginia agreed to surrender its claim to territory west and north of the Ohio River, but thwarted the Maryland speculators by insisting that all titles based on Indian purchases be declared void. Maryland then had no recourse but to ratify the Articles, and the new government was officially proclaimed on March 1, 1781.

In general the Articles of Confederation merely provided a legal basis for authority that the Continental Congress had already been exercising. It stated plainly that each state, regardless of size, would have but one vote; the union was only a "league of friendship." Article II defined the limit of national power: "Each state retains its sovereignty, freedom, and independence, and every Power, Jurisdiction, and right, which is not by this confederation expressly delegated to the United States, in Congress assembled." Time would prove this an inadequate arrangement, chiefly because the central government had no way of enforcing its authority. As the contemporary historian David Ramsay explained in 1789: "No coercive power was given to the general government, nor was it invested with any legislative power over individuals."

However, the central government had been strong enough to carry on the Revolution, and the ratification of this charter added somewhat to its prestige. At about the same time Congress also increased its effectiveness by establishing departments of Foreign Affairs, War, and Finance, with individual heads responsible to it. The most important of these new department heads was the superintendent of finance, a Philadelphia mer-

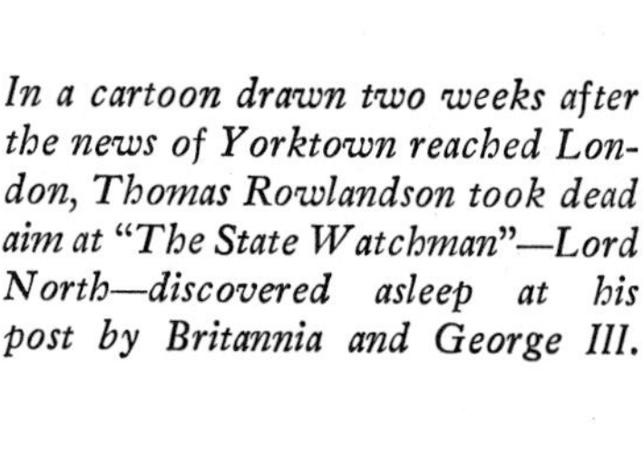

In a cartoon drawn two weeks after the news of Yorktown reached London, Thomas Rowlandson took dead aim at "The State Watchman"—Lord North—discovered asleep at his post by Britannia and George III.

Am I thus Protected?
The State Watchman discovered by the Genius of Britain:
studying plans for the Reduction of America.

BRITISH MUSEUM

chant named Robert Morris. When Morris took office, the Continental dollar was worthless, the system of supplying the army chaotic, the credit of the government exhausted. He set up a more efficient method of obtaining food and uniforms for the army, persuaded Congress to charter a national Bank of North America, and somehow—aided by the slackening of military activity after Yorktown—got the country back on a specie basis. New foreign loans were also obtained, partly because Morris' efficiency and industry inspired confidence.

The Peace of Paris

These developments strengthened the new United States, but the event that confirmed its existence was the signing of a peace treaty with Great Britain. Although Yorktown dealt a heavy blow to British pride, it failed to stir Parliament to greater effort. The mother country's will to continue the struggle vanished. Actually Yorktown was only one of a string of defeats suffered at this time by British arms. The Spanish had captured Pensacola in West Florida in May 1781, and in February 1782 they took Minorca in the Mediterranean. In the same period the French captured St. Eustatius, Nevis, and a number of other British bastions in the West Indies. In Africa and Asia this latest world war was also going badly for Great Britain. The state of the Treasury was precarious, for the national debt had doubled again since 1775. In March 1782 Lord North resigned after Parliament had renounced all further efforts to coerce the colonies. At once the new ministry of Lord Rockingham attempted to negotiate a peace settlement with America.

The problem of peacemaking, however, was extremely complicated, for, as Samuel Flagg Bemis wrote in his authoritative *Diplomacy of the American Revolution*, "the peace which fixed American independence was a major European settlement involving the interests of all the great powers." The United States and France had solemnly pledged not to make a separate peace. Spain, at war with Great Britain since 1779, was allied with France but not with America. Although eager to profit at British expense, the Spanish hoped to limit American expansion beyond the Appalachians, for they had large ambitions of their own in the eastern half of the Mississippi Valley. France, while ready enough to back American independence, had no wish to see the new country become *too* powerful, and in a conflict of interest between America and Spain, France tended to support Spain.

The Continental Congress, grateful for French aid, overestimated both French power and French loyalty to America. As early as 1779 it had appointed John Adams as minister plenipotentiary to conduct peace negotiations. Almost from the moment of his arrival in Paris, Adams came into conflict with Foreign Minister Vergennes. "He means to keep his hand under our chin to prevent us from drowning, but not to lift our heads out of the water," the shrewd Adams noted. When Vergennes, a subtle, intelligent, but somewhat unscrupulous diplomat eager to manipulate the interests of all parties for the benefit of his own country, discovered that Adams was neither pliable nor naive, he used his influence to have him replaced by a five-man commission, consisting of—in addition to Adams—Franklin, Jefferson, John Jay, and Henry Laurens.* Congress went so far as to instruct the commissioners to rely entirely upon the advice of Vergennes in negotiations, subject only to the limitation that they must hold out at all costs for independence. This occurred in June 1781.

Fortunately, the commissioners were intelligent and independent-minded men. When they discovered that Vergennes was not the perfect friend of America that Congress believed, they did not hesitate to violate their instructions. Franklin, perhaps because he was so truly a man of the world and so benign, was neither aggressive nor suspicious enough to press the American point of view fully. John Jay, who had spent two years dealing with Spanish duplicity as unacknowledged American minister in Madrid, was more tough-minded. When he realized that Spain and France were less than entirely committed to American interests, he took Franklin aside and convinced him they must forge ahead on their own without consulting Vergennes at every step. They then hinted to the British representative, Richard Oswald, with whom Franklin had already been dickering, that they would consider a separate peace if it were a generous one and suggested that Great Britain would be far better off with America, a nation that favored free trade, in control of the trans-Appalachian region than with a mercantilist power like Spain. They agreed also that American independence need not be recognized explicitly before beginning their talks; it would suffice if Oswald were empowered to deal with commissioners of the "thirteen United States."

The British government reacted favorably, authorizing Oswald "to treat with the Commissioners appointed by the Colonys, under the title of Thirteen United States." Soon the Americans were deep in negotiations with Oswald, informing Vergennes of what they were doing but not discussing with him the details of their talks. The Englishman was friendly and cooperative, and the Americans drove a hard bargain. One scrap of conversation will reveal the tenor of the talks.

OSWALD: We can never be such damned sots as to disturb you.

ADAMS: Thank you. . . . But nations don't feel as you and I do, and your nation, when it gets a little refreshed from the fatigues of the war, and when men and money become plentiful, and allies at hand, will not feel as it does now.

OSWALD: We can never be such damned sots as to think of differing again with you.

ADAMS: Why, in truth I have never been able to comprehend the reason why you ever thought of differing with us.

By the end of November 1782 a preliminary treaty had been signed. "His Britannic Majesty," Article I began, "acknowledges the said United States . . . to be free, sovereign and independent States." Other terms were equally in line with American hopes and objectives. The boundaries of the nation were set at the Great Lakes, the Mississippi River, and 31° north latitude, roughly the northern boundary of Florida. Britain also recognized the right of Americans to take fish on the Grand Banks off Newfoundland, and—far more important—to dry and cure their catch on un-

*Jefferson did not take part in the negotiations, and Adams and Laurens played relatively minor roles. Franklin and Jay did most of the work of drafting the treaty.

settled beaches in Labrador and Nova Scotia. The British agreed to withdraw their troops from American soil "with all convenient speed." Where the touchy problem of Tory property seized during the Revolution was concerned, the Americans agreed only that Congress would "earnestly recommend" that the states "provide for the restitution of all estates, rights and properties which have been confiscated." They also promised to prevent further property confiscation and prosecutions of Tories, certainly a wise as well as a humane policy, and they agreed not to impede the collection of debts owed British subjects. Vergennes was flabbergasted by the success of the Americans. "The English buy the peace more than they make it," he wrote. "Their concessions . . . exceed all that I should have thought possible."

The American commissioners obtained such favorable terms because they were shrewd diplomats, but also because of the rivalries that existed between all the great European powers. In the last analysis, Britain preferred to have a weak nation of English-speaking people in command of the Mississippi Valley rather than France or Spain. From their experience at the peace talks, the American leaders learned the importance of playing one power against another without committing themselves completely to any. This policy became the basis of what later was known as American isolationism, whereas, of course, in the 1780's it was anything but that. It demanded a constant contact with European affairs and skill at adjusting policies in accordance with changes in the European balance of power. And it enabled the United States, a young and relatively feeble country, to grow and prosper.

Growth of American Nationalism

American independence and control of a wide and rich domain were the most obvious results of the Revolution. Changes in the structure of society, as we have seen, were relatively minor. Economic developments, such as the growth of new trade connections and the expansion of manufacturing in an effort to replace British goods, were also of only moderate significance. By far the most important social and economic changes involved the Tories, and thus were by-products of the political revolution rather than a determined reorganization of a people's way of life. Yet there was another extremely important result of the Revolution: the growth of American nationalism. Most modern revolutions have been *caused* by nationalism and have *resulted* in independence. In the case of the American Revolution the desire to be free antedated any very intense national feeling. The colonies entered into a political union not because they felt an overwhelming desire to bring all Americans under one rule, but because unity seemed to offer the only hope of winning a war against Great Britain. That they remained united after throwing off British rule reflects the degree to which nationalism had developed during the conflict.

By the middle of the 18th century the colonists had begun to think of themselves as a separate breed of men with a society distinct from Europe and even from Britain. To cite a trivial example, in 1750 a Boston newspaper urged its readers to drink "American" beer in order to free themselves from being "beholden to Foreigners" for their alcoholic beverages. Little political nationalism existed before the Revolution, however. When Franklin spoke of "American patriots" in *Poor Richard's Almanack* in the 1750's, he meant no more than when he used the expression "American Subjects of the King." Local ties remained predominant. A few men might say, with Patrick Henry in 1774, "The distinctions between Virginians, Pennsylvanians, New Yorkers, and New Englanders are no more. I am not a Virginian, but an American." But such people were rare before the final break with Great Britain.

The new nationalism rose from a number of causes and expressed itself in different ways. Common sacrifices in war certainly played a part. Although militiamen often melted away when required to fight outside their own states, some units performed notably far from home, while the regulars of the Continental Army fought in the summer heat of the Carolinas for the same cause that had led them to brave the ice floes of the Delaware in order to surprise the Hessians. Such men lost interest in state boundary lines. They became Americans. John Marshall of Fauquier County, Virginia, for example, was a 20-year-old militiaman in 1775. The next year he joined the Continental Army. He served in Pennsylvania, New Jersey, and New York and endured the winter of 1777–78 at Valley Forge. As a result, he later wrote, "I was confirmed in the habit of considering America as my country and Congress as my government." Andrew Jackson, child of the Carolina frontier, was only nine when the Revolution broke out. One brother was killed in battle, another died as a result of untreated wounds. Young Andrew took up arms himself and was captured by the Redcoats. A British officer ordered Jackson to black his boots and when the boy refused, struck him across the face with the flat of his sword. Jackson bore the scar to his grave—and became an ardent nationalist on the spot. He and Marshall had very different ideas and came to be bitter enemies in later life. Nevertheless, they were both American nationalists, and for the same basic reason.

Civilians as well as soldiers reacted in this way. A Carolina farmer whose lands were protected against British looters by men who spoke with the harsh nasal twang of New England adopted a broader outlook toward politics. When the news came that thousands of Redcoats had stacked their arms in defeat at Yorktown, few people cared what state or section had made the victory possible—it was an American triumph.

The war caused many people to move from place to place. Naturally, soldiers traveled as the tide of war fluctuated; so too—far more than in earlier times—did prominent leaders. Members of Congress from every state had to travel to Philadelphia; in the process they saw much of the country and the people who inhabited it. Listening to their fellows and serving with them on the innumerable congressional committees almost inevitably broadened these men, most of them intelligent, public-spirited, and highly influential in their local communities.

With its 13 stars and 13 stripes representing the states, the American flag symbolized national unity and also reflected the common feeling that such a symbol was necessary. After much experimentation (one version pictured the Union as a snake made up of 13 segments), the Continental Congress adopted the basic pattern in June 1777.

Certain practical problems that demanded common solutions also drew the states together. No one seriously considered 13 postal systems, for example. The British, angry at having been forced to recognize American independence, refused for a time to establish full diplomatic relations with the United States, replying contemptuously to one American suggestion that to do so would require the sending of not one minister but 13. This was nonsensical, as the British soon had to admit. The states were united from the start in their foreign relations. Every new diplomatic appointment, every treaty of friendship or commerce signed, committed all to a common policy and thus bound them more closely together. Economic developments also had a unifying effect. The cutting off of English goods stimulated local manufacturing, making America more nearly self-sufficient and stimulating both interstate trade and national pride. During the war Congress tried to encourage native industries, while in every community many persons attempted to make do with homespun clothing and other local products as a form of patriotism.

The Great Land Ordinances

The western lands, which had divided the states in the beginning, became a force for unity once they had been ceded to the national government. Everyone realized what a priceless national asset they were, and while many greedily sought to possess them by fair means or foul, all now understood that no one state could determine the future of the West. Men argued hotly about how these lands should be disposed of. Some advocated selling the land in township units in the traditional New England manner to groups or companies; others favored letting individual pioneers stake out their own farms in the helter-skelter manner common in the colonial South. The decision was a compromise. The Land Ordinance of 1785 provided for surveying western territories into six-mile-square townships before sale. Every other township was to be further subdivided into 36 sections of 640 acres (one square mile) each. The land was sold at

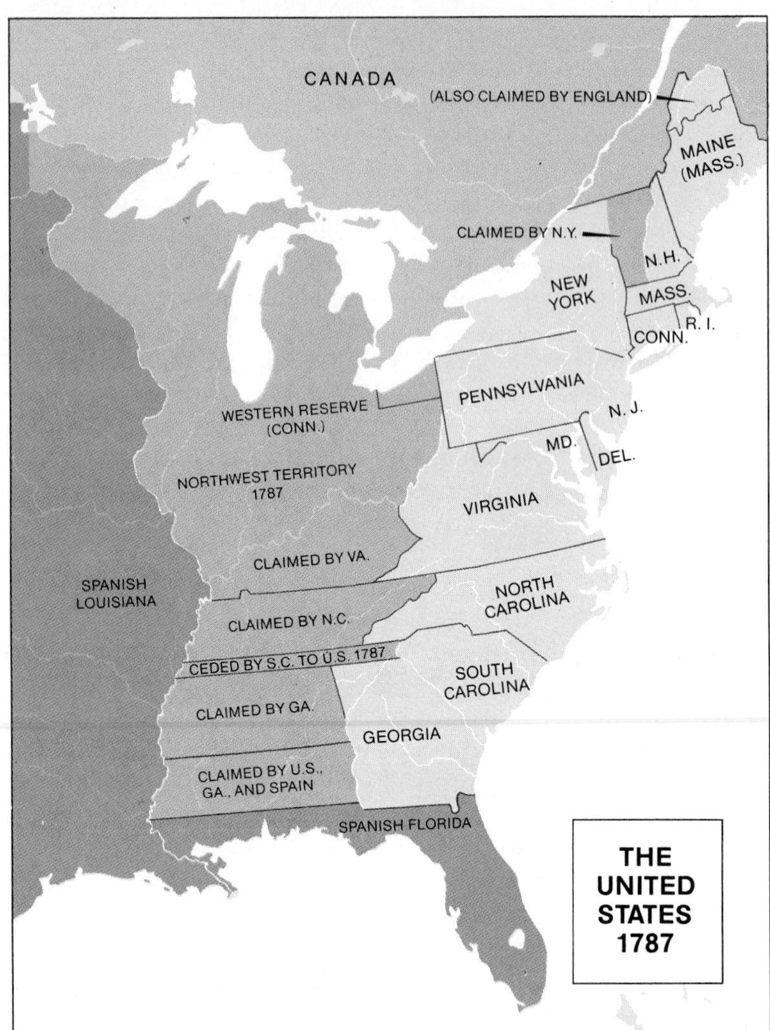

The cession by New York and Virginia of their claims to the vast area that became the Northwest Territory set the precedent for trans-Appalachian land policy. By 1802 the various state claims indicated here had been ceded to the national government.

auction at a minimum price of one dollar an acre. The law favored speculative land-development companies, for even the 640-acre units were far too large and expensive for the typical frontier family. But the fact that the land was to be surveyed and sold by the central government was another nationalizing force. Congress set aside the 16th section of every township for the maintenance of schools, another important and farsighted decision.

Still more significant was the Northwest Ordinance of 1787, which established governments for the West. As early as 1780 Congress had resolved that all lands ceded to the nation by the states should be "formed into distinct republican States" with "the same rights of sovereignty, freedom and independence" as the original 13. In 1784 a committee headed by Thomas Jefferson worked out a basic plan for doing this, and in 1787 it was enacted into law. The area bounded by the Ohio, the Mississippi, and the Great Lakes was to be carved into not less than three nor more than five territories. Until the adult male population of the entire area reached 5,000, it was to be ruled by a governor and three judges, all appointed by Congress. Acting together, these officials would make and enforce the necessary laws. When 5,000 men of voting age had settled in the territory, the ordinance authorized them to elect a legislature and send a nonvoting delegate to Congress. Finally, when 60,000 persons had settled in any one of the political subdivisions it was to become a state. It could draft a constitution and operate in any way it wished, save that the government had to be "republican" and that slavery was prohibited.

Seldom has a legislative body acted more wisely. That the western districts must become states everyone conceded from the start, for the people had had their fill of colonialism under British rule. The rebellious temper of frontiersmen also made it impossible even to consider maintaining the West in a dependent status. For instance, when North Carolina ceded her trans-Appalachian lands to the United States in 1784, the settlers there, uncertain about how they would fare under federal control, hastily organized an extra-legal "State of Franklin," and it was not until 1789 that the national government obtained control. On the other hand, it would have been unfair to turn the territories over to the first comers, who would have been unable to manage such large domains and who would surely have taken advantage of their priority to dictate to later arrivals. A period of tutelage was necessary, a period when the "mother country" must guide and nourish its growing offspring. Thus the intermediate territorial governments corresponded almost exactly to the governments of British royal colonies. The appointed governors could veto acts of the assemblies and could "convene, prorogue, and dissolve" them at their discretion. The territorial delegates to Congress were not unlike colonial agents. Yet it was vital that this intermediate stage end, and that its end be determined in advance so that no arguments could develop over when the territory was ready for statehood. This the Northwest Ordinance provided. The system worked well and was eventually applied to nearly all the new regions absorbed by the nation as it advanced westward. Together with the Ordinance of 1785, which branded its checkerboard pattern on the physical shape of the West, this law gave the growing country a basic unity essential for the growth of a national spirit.

National Heroes

Finally, the Revolution fostered nationalism by giving the people their first commonly revered heroes. Every colony had had its leaders, many of them wise, colorful, and popular men, but none widely known in other regions. However, out of the drama and hardships of the Revolutionary era came a few truly national figures. Benjamin Franklin was widely known before the break with Great Britain through his experiments with electricity, his immensely successful annual, *Poor Richard's Almanack*, and because of his invention of the Franklin stove. However, his staunch support of the Patriot cause, his work in the Continental Congress, and his diplomatic successes in France, where he was extravagantly admired, added greatly to his fame. Franklin demonstrated, not only to Europeans but to Americans themselves, that all Americans need not be ignorant rustics. Thomas Jefferson was also a national figure by the 1780's. His writing of the Declaration of Independence (to which, it will be recalled, Franklin also contributed) was enough to make him a hero to all Americans. Especially in retrospect, when the boldness of the document and its felicity of expression could be fully appreciated and when the success of the revolt made it even more significant, the Declaration and its author were revered in every state.

And then, most notable of all, there was Washington, "the chief human symbol of a common Americanism." Stern, cold, inarticulate, the great Virginian did not seem a likely candidate for hero worship. But he had qualities that made him truly "the Father of his County": his personal sacrifices in the cause of independence, his unyielding integrity, his devotion to duty, his commanding presence, and above all, perhaps, his obvious desire to retire to his Mount Vernon estate (for many Americans feared *any* powerful leader and worried lest Washington seek to become a dictator). As a general, Washington was not a brilliant strategist like Napoleon, although his design for the complicated Yorktown campaign was superb. Neither was he a tactician of the quality of Caesar or Robert E. Lee. His lack of genius made his achievements all the more impressive. He held his forces together in adversity, avoiding both useless slaughter and catastrophic defeat. He learned from experience and won the respect—if not the love—of his men and the cooperation of Congress and his French allies. Men of all sections, from every walk of life, looked upon Washington as the embodiment of American virtues: a man of deeds rather than words; a man of substance accustomed to luxury, yet capable of enduring great hardships stoically and as much at home in the wilderness as a wild Indian; a bold Patriot, quick to take arms against British tyranny, yet eminently respectable. The Revolution might have been won without Washington, but it is unlikely that the free United States would have become so easily a true nation had he not existed.

A National Culture

The new American nationalism took many forms. Breaking away from the empire accentuated certain trends toward social and intellectual independence, and strengthened the national desire to create an *American* culture. Even so unworldly a subject as religion was affected. The Anglican Church in America had to form a new organization once the connection with the Crown was severed; in 1786 it became the Protestant Episcopal Church. The Dutch and German Reformed churches also became independent of their European connections. Roman Catholics in America had been under the administration of the vicar apostolic of England; after the Revolution Father John Carroll of Baltimore assumed these duties, and in 1789 became the first American Roman Catholic bishop. In addition, national sentiment led to increased centralization within many sects. Originally there were three autonomous Episcopal dioceses in America. They soon created a central organization. The Presbyterians and the Methodists also formed national bodies.

The impact of post-Revolutionary nationalism on American education was best reflected in the immense success of the textbooks of Noah Webster, later famous for his American dictionary. The first of these, the famous *Spelling Book*, which appeared in 1783 when Webster was a young schoolteacher in Goshen, New York, emphasized American forms and usage and contained a patriotic preface urging Americans to pay proper respect to their own literature. Webster's *Reader*, published shortly thereafter, included selections from the speeches of Revolutionary leaders who, according to the compiler, were the equals of Cicero and Demosthenes as orators. Some 15 million copies of the *Speller* were sold in the next five decades, several times that number by 1900. The *Reader* was also a continuing best-seller.

YALE UNIVERSITY ART GALLERY

In his patriotic version of the triumph at Yorktown (of which this is a detail), John Trumbull arranged Washington and his generals in noble poses to take the British surrender. In the Capitol rotunda are 900 square feet of Trumbull's Revolutionary history.

Webster's work was not the only sign of nationalism in education. In 1787 John M'Culloch published the first American history textbook. The colleges saw a great outburst of patriotic spirit. King's College (founded in 1754) received a new name, Columbia, in 1784.* Everywhere colleges began to change if not their curricula, at least their focus, for it was widely recognized that the republic required educated and cultivated

* However, Queen's College (founded in 1766), was not renamed Rutgers until 1825. The other colleges existing at the time of the Revolution were Harvard and William and Mary, both founded in the 17th century; Yale (1701); the College of New Jersey, now Princeton (1746); Franklin's Academy, now the University of Pennsylvania (1751); Rhode Island, now Brown (1764); and Dartmouth (1769).

leaders. Many new colleges were founded in the two decades or so following the Revolution, among them the future state universities of Maryland, Georgia, South Carolina, and North Carolina, and such other institutions as Georgetown, St. John's of Annapolis, Williams, and Bowdoin.

Nationalism affected the arts and even the sciences in the years after the Revolution. The American Academy of Arts and Sciences, founded at Boston during the Revolution, was created "to advance the interest, honor, dignity and happiness of a free, independent and virtuous people." Jedidiah Morse's popular *American Geography* (1789) was a paean in praise of the "astonishing" progress of the country, all the result of the "natural genius of Americans."

American painters of the period usually chose extremely patriotic themes. The artist John Trumbull, for example, helped capture Dorchester Heights and force the evacuation of Boston, took part in the defense of northern New York against Burgoyne, and fought also in Pennsylvania and Rhode Island. When he took up painting he studied in Europe, but he produced such pictures as *The Battle of Bunker's Hill*, *The Surrender of Lord Cornwallis at Yorktown*, and *The Declaration of Independence*, referring to these and similar efforts as his "national work." Most of the literary productions of the era also dealt with patriotic subjects and glorified the nation. Joel Barlow intended his *Vision of Columbus*, written between 1779 and 1787, to prove that America was "the noblest and most elevated part of the earth." Ancient empires, Barlow boasted,

> Shall soon behold, on this enlighten'd coast,
> Their fame transcended. . . .

The poems of Philip Freneau dealt with themes like the horrors of British prison camps and the naval triumphs of John Paul Jones, and predicted a great future for the United States. Royall Tyler's play *The Contrast*, which was produced in New York in 1787, compared American virtue (the hero was called Colonel Manly) with British vice, and contained such chauvinistic lines as:

> Why should our thoughts to distant countries roam
> When each refinement may be found at home?

And another poet of the period wrote:

> This land her Swift and Addison shall view,
> The former honors equalled by the new;
> Here shall some Shakespeare charm the rising age,
> And hold in magic chain the listening stage.

Timothy Dwight, later president of Yale and a member of a group of literary lights who were called (for reasons that escape most modern readers) the "Hartford Wits," wrote patriotic songs during the Revolution. In the early 1780's he produced a long, tedious poem, *The Conquest of Canaan*, supposedly a New World epic. A decade later he wrote *Greenfield Hill*, an attempt to glorify America.

The United States in the 1780's was far from the powerful centralized nation it has since become. Probably the typical citizen still gave his first loyalty to his state. In certain important respects the Confederation was pitifully ineffectual. However, people were increasingly aware of their common interests and increasingly proud of their common heritage. The motto of the new nation, *E pluribus unum*—"from many, one"—perfectly describes a process that was rapidly taking place in the years after Yorktown.

SUPPLEMENTARY READING The best brief survey of the Revolutionary years is E.S. Morgan, *The Birth of the Republic** (1956), but Esmond Wright, *Fabric of Freedom** (1961), is also useful. A more detailed (and very lively) treatment is J.C. Miller, *Triumph of Freedom** (1948). J.R. Alden, *A History of the American Revolution* (1969), provides an up-to-date account of the military aspects of the Revolution, as does H.H. Peckham, *The War for Independence** (1958). H.S. Commager and R.B. Morris (eds.), *The Spirit of Seventy-Six* (1958), is a rich collection of source materials. For Washington's role, see D.S. Freeman, *George Washington* (1948–57), and C.P. Nettels, *George Washington and American Independence* (1951). S.E. Morison's biography, *John Paul Jones** (1959), is useful for some of the naval aspects of the struggle, while Piers Mackesy, *The War for America* (1964), treats the conflict from the British point of view.

On the Continental Congress and the Articles of Confederation, see E.C. Burnett, *The Continental Congress** (1941), Lynn Montross, *The Reluctant Rebels* (1950), and two books by Merrill Jensen, *The Articles of Confederation** (1940) and *The New Nation** (1950). The classic analysis of the Declaration of Independence is C.L. Becker, *The Declaration of Independence** (1922). Jefferson's ideas are thoughtfully analyzed in Gilbert Chinard, *Thomas Jefferson: The Apostle of Americanism** (1929), and Adrienne Koch, *Jefferson and Madison** (1950). The formation and early history of the state governments is covered in Elisha Douglass, *Rebels and Democrats** (1955), but Allan Nevins, *The American States During and After the Revolution* (1924), is still indispensable. The development of political ideas during the Revolutionary era is admirably described and analyzed in G.S. Wood, *The Creation of the American Republic* (1969), and in D.J. Boorstin, *The Genius of American Politics** (1953). The financial problems of this period are covered in E.J. Ferguson, *The Power of the Purse** (1968), and Clarence Ver Steeg, *Robert Morris, Revolutionary Financier* (1954). For the development of federal policy toward western lands, see B.H. Hibbard, *A History of Public Land Policies* (1924), R.M. Robbins, *Our Landed Heritage** (1942), and W.D. Pattison, *The Beginnings of the American Rectangular Land Survey* (1957). There is no adequate modern study of the Northwest Ordinance.

The classic account of the social and economic effects of the Revolution is J.F. Jameson, *The American Revolution Considered as a Social Movement** (1926), but the student should also examine the critiques of the Jameson thesis by F.B. Tolles in the *American Historical Review* (1954) and R.B. Morris in the *William and Mary Quarterly* (1962). E.B. Greene, *The Revolutionary Generation* (1943), also contains a wealth of material on social and economic developments. The already mentioned study of Massachusetts in the Revolutionary period by R.E. Brown takes issue with Jameson's view, as does R.P. McCormick, *Experiment in Independence: New Jersey in the Critical Period* (1950). J.T. Main, *The Social Structure of Revolutionary America** (1965), provides a general picture against which to evaluate the views of Jameson and his critics. On the fate of the Tories, see W.H. Nelson, *The American Tory** (1962), and Wallace Brown, *The King's Friends* (1965). P.H. Smith, *Loyalists and Redcoats** (1965), treats the fumbling efforts of the British to make use of their American supporters. The effects of the Revolution on slavery are treated in W.D. Jordan, *White Over Black** (1968), Arthur Zilversmit, *The First Emancipation: The Abolition of Slavery in the North* (1967), and Benjamin Quarles, *The Negro in the American Revolution* (1961).

On the diplomacy of the American Revolution, see S.F. Bemis, *The Diplomacy of the American Revolution** (1935). The definitive account of the peace treaty is R.B. Morris, *The Peacemakers* (1965).*

On the emergence of American nationalism and cultural history generally, see E.B. Greene's abovementioned *The Revolutionary Generation,* and also R.B. Nye, *The Cultural Life of the New Nation** (1960). R.L. Merritt, *Symbols of American Community* (1966), concludes from a study of colonial newspapers that a sense of national identity was well developed before 1763. P.C. Nagel, *One Nation Indivisible: The Union in American Thought* (1964), discusses the various views of the nature of the Union advanced in this period, and Paul Varg, *Foreign Policies of the Founding Fathers* (1963), is also instructive.

*Available in paperback.

5

Nationalism Triumphant

The nationalism spawned by the Revolution grew so rapidly that large elements in the population soon began to resent the constraints imposed by the Articles of Confederation on the power of the central government. Modern research has modified the thesis, advanced by John Fiske in *The Critical Period of American History* (1888), that Congress was demoralized and inadequate. If the government, as Washington said, moved "on crutches . . . tottering at every step," it *did* move. But the country's evolution placed demands upon it that its creators had not anticipated.

Western Tensions

For one thing, the government had to struggle to win actual control over the territory granted the United States in the treaty ending the Revolution. Both Great Britain and Spain stood in the way of this objective. The British had promised to withdraw all their troops from American soil promptly, and so they did within the settled portions of the 13 states. Beyond the frontier, however, they had established a string of seven military posts, running along the St. Lawrence and the Great Lakes from the northern end of Lake Champlain through Niagara and Detroit to the tip of the Michigan peninsula (map, page 203). These, despite the Treaty of Paris, they refused to surrender. Pressing against America's exposed frontier like hot coals, these posts seared national pride. They also threatened to set off another Indian war, for the British intrigued constantly to stir up the tribes against the Americans, hoping either to win the West back for themselves or to fashion an Indian buffer state under their domination. The great prize was the rich fur trade of the region, which the British now controlled but which would probably be drained off through Albany and other American centers if British military influence was removed.

The British justified holding on to these positions by citing the failure of the Americans to live up to some of the terms of the peace treaty. The United States had agreed not to impede British creditors seeking to collect prewar debts in America and to "earnestly recommend" that the states restore Tory property confiscated during the revolt. The national government complied with both these requirements, which it will be noted called for nothing more than words on Congress' part, but the separate states did not cooperate. Many passed laws making it impossible for British creditors to collect debts, and in general the property of Tory *émigrés* was not returned. Yet these violations of the peace terms, which resulted more from the state of public opinion than from the weakness of the central authority, had little to do with the continued presence of the British on American soil. They would not have evacuated the posts at this time even if every farthing of the debt had been paid and every acre of confiscated land restored. Not internal dissension nor the absence of congressional determination but rather the lack of military might accounts for the failure of the United States to compel the British to withdraw. Although Britain had been unable to conquer the colonies, it was a much simpler task to hold posts far removed from centers of American power and in a region swarming with Indians hostile to settlers but perfectly willing to deal with white men interested in buying furs.

Americans found the continued presence of British troops galling, even in the western wilderness. When the French had pushed a line of forts into the Ohio country in the 1750's, it had seemed to most colonists only a matter of local concern, to be dealt with by Virginia or Pennsylvania. Three decades later, inability to eject the British seemed a national disgrace.

Then there was the question of the Spanish in the Southwest. Spain had been a co-belligerent, not an ally, in the war against Great Britain. In the peace negotiations it had won back Florida and the Gulf Coast region east of New Orleans. Spanish troops had also captured Natchez during the war, and although the post lay north of the boundary, Spain refused to turn it over to the United States. Far more serious, the Spaniards also closed the lower Mississippi River to American

MRS. WARREN M. SARIS COLLECTION

The Mississippi teems with commerce in Christophe Colomb's view of about 1790. Two flatboats and a keelboat are in the improbably narrow river; in the foreground Colomb sketches his father-in-law's plantation house.

commerce. Because of the prohibitive cost of moving bulky farm produce over the mountains, settlers beyond the Appalachians depended upon the Mississippi and its network of tributaries to get their corn, tobacco, and other products to eastern and European markets. If Spain closed the river, or even if it denied them the right to "deposit" goods at New Orleans while awaiting oceangoing transportation, the westerners could not sell their surpluses.

Frontiersmen fumed when Congress failed to win concessions from Spain. A few of the unscrupulous and shortsighted among their leaders, such as General James Wilkinson, a handsome, glib, hard-drinking veteran who had moved to Kentucky after the Revolution, accepted Spanish bribes and tried to swing the Southwest into the Spanish orbit. They never came even close to success. Westerners sometimes played along with the Spanish to obtain special trade concessions and to exert pressure on the American Congress, but the majority preferred being part of the United States to being independent and certainly to union with the Spanish, whom they regarded with a mixture of fear and contempt.

A stronger central government might have ameliorated but could not have eliminated these foreign problems. United or decentralized, America was too weak in the 1780's to challenge any major European nation. Until the country grew more powerful or until the Europeans began to clash among themselves, the United States was bound to suffer at their hands. On the domestic scene, however, difficulties arose that only common action could meet. The Confederation strove to meet them but lacked the authority to surmount them. As a result, increasingly large elements in the population came to believe that the authority of the central government should be widened—one more aspect of the growth of American nationalism.

Foreign Trade

The fact that the Revolution freed American trade from the restrictions of British mercantilism proved a mixed blessing in the short run. Americans could now trade directly with the continental powers, and general commercial treaties were negotiated with a number of them. Beginning in 1784, when the 360-ton *Empress of China* reached Canton with a cargo of furs and cotton to be exchanged for oriental silks, tea, and spices, a valuable Far Eastern trade sprang up where none had existed before. On the other hand, exclusion from Britain's imperial trade union brought serious losses.

Immediately after the Revolution, a controversy broke out in Great Britain over fitting the former colonies into the mercantilistic system. Some thoughtful men were beginning to believe generally in free trade, much influenced by Adam Smith's brilliant exposition of the subject in *The Wealth of Nations*, published in 1776. Others, while remaining mercantilists, realized how important the American trade was for British prosperity and argued that special treatment should be afforded the former colonists. Unfortunately, a proud empire recently humbled in war could hardly be expected to exercise such forbearance. Persuaded in part by the reasoning of Lord Sheffield, who claimed that Britain could get all the American commerce it wished without making concessions, Parliament voted to try building up exports to America while holding imports to a minimum, all according to the best tenets of mercantilism.

The British attitude hurt American interests severely. In the southern states the termination of royal bounties hit North Carolina producers of naval stores and South Carolina indigo planters hard, and a new British duty on rice reduced the export of that product by almost 50 per cent. Both rice and tobacco growers were also afflicted by a labor shortage in the 1780's because of the wartime British seizure of so many slaves.

British Orders in Council in 1783 barring American cured meat, fish, and dairy products from the British West Indies and permitting other American products to enter the islands only in British ships struck at the northern states. The British hoped that Canada and Newfoundland would replace New England as the supplier of food for their sugar islands, and they counted upon their own merchant fleet to carry the rich commerce of the region. Although this hope proved illusory, American fishing and shipping interests certainly suffered. Fishermen lost the lucrative West Indian market, merchants a whole host of profitable opportunities. Shipbuilding slumped because of these facts and also because British merchants stopped ordering American-made vessels. Before the war Massachusetts yards were launching about 125 ships a year. In 1784 they built only 45, in the next few years even fewer.

At the same time British merchants, eager to regain markets closed to them during the Revolution when British exports to America fell to five per cent of the prewar figure, poured manufactured goods of all kinds into the United States at low prices. Soon American imports of British goods were approaching the levels of the early 1770's, while exports to the empire reached no more than half their earlier volume. Americans, long deprived of British products, rushed to take advantage of the bargains.

Of course America had always imported more than it exported. The economy was essentially colonial. The people produced bulky raw materials and consumed expensive manufactured goods of all sorts voraciously. In the first three-quarters of the 18th century, historians estimate that imports exceeded exports by more than £20 million. The growth and development of the country had been greatly aided by the investment of huge amounts of foreign capital, chiefly British. The constant shortage of hard money in colonial times was one result of this condition, since gold and silver tended to flow to Europe to pay interest on loans and to purchase manufactured goods.

However, the great influx of British goods after the Revolution aggravated the situation just when the economy was suffering a certain dislocation as a result of the ending of the war. From 1784 to 1786 the country went through a period of bad times. The inability of the central government to pay its debts undermined confidence and caused grave hardships for veterans and others dependent upon the Confederation. In some regions crop failures compounded the difficulties. The depression made the states stingier than ever about supplying the requisitions of Congress; at the same time many of them levied heavy property taxes in order to pay off their own war debts. In 1785 South Carolina devoted £94,000 (roughly 90 per cent of the public revenue) to the payment of interest on its bonds. Everywhere people were hard pressed for cash. "As Money has ever been considered the root of all evils," one Massachusetts man commented sourly, "may we not presage happy times, as this source is almost done away?"

This depression of the mid-1780's was not a major economic collapse by any stretch of the imagination, and by 1786 all signs were pointing toward a revival of good times. Nevertheless, dislike of British trade policy remained widespread in America. The Confederation did its best to improve the situation, dispatching John Adams to London as minister. But Adams failed to exact any concessions. The obvious tactic would have been to place tariffs on British goods in order to limit imports or force the British to open the West Indies to all American goods, but the Confederation lacked the authority to do this. When individual states erected tariff barriers, British merchants easily got around them by bringing their goods in through states that did not. The fact that American consumers delighted in the flood of high-quality British manufactured products at low prices and were therefore of two minds about any plan to bar them, much complicated the problem. That the central government lacked the power to control commerce gravely disturbed not only merchants and other businessmen but also the ever-increasing number of national-minded citizens in every walk of life.

Thus a movement developed to give the Confederation the power to tax imports. As early as 1781 Congress sought authority to levy a five per cent tariff duty. Eleven states agreed, a remarkable indication of the growth of national feeling when one recalls that local control of taxation and trade had been primary objectives of the Revolution. However, the measure required the unanimous consent of the states and therefore failed. Another request for the same power made in a more moderate form actually won the approval of all the states by 1786, but certain conditions imposed by New York were unacceptable to Congress, and again the measure failed. Defeat of the "impost" pointed up the need for revising the Articles of Confederation, for here was a case where a very large percentage of the states were ready to increase the power of the national government yet were unable to do so. Although many individuals in every region were worried about creating a centralized monster that might gobble up the sovereignty of the states, the practical needs of the times convinced most that this risk must be taken. Not a *general* devotion to local sovereignty but the existence of pockets of resistance—as in Rhode Island—to a broader, more national outlook hamstrung the Confederation.

Inflation and Deflation

The depression and the unfavorable balance of trade also led to increased pressures in the states for the printing of paper money and the passage of laws designed to make life easier for debtors. Before the Revolution the colonists had grappled with the chronic shortage of hard money in many ways, declaring various staple products like furs and tobacco and even Indian wampum to be legal tender, deliberately overvaluing foreign coins to discourage their export, making it illegal to ship coins abroad, and printing paper money. In response to wartime needs, both the Continental Congress and the states issued large amounts of paper money during the Revolution, with inflationary results. To cite some examples, the Continental dollar became utterly worthless by 1781, and Virginia eventually called in its paper money at 1,000 to 1. After the war, some of the states set out to restore their credit, imposing heavy taxes and restricting new issues of money severely. Combined with the postwar depression and the great increase in imports, this policy had a powerful deflationary effect on both prices and wages. Soon debtors, especially farmers, were crying for "relief," both in the form of stay laws designed to make it difficult to collect debts (these laws were popular also because of the anti-British feeling of the times) and through the printing of more paper money.

More than half the states yielded to this pressure in 1785 and 1786. In South Carolina, where £100,000 was issued, businessmen willingly accepted the paper, and it eventually came to be preferred to specie. Issues in New York and Pennsylvania were conservatively handled and also succeeded. However, in some states the money depreciated rapidly: Georgia's paper lost 75 per cent of its value in one year; issues in North Carolina and New Jersey also failed.

The most disastrous experience was that of Rhode Island, where the government attempted to legislate public confidence in £100,000 of paper. Any landowner could borrow a share of this money from the state for 14 years, using his property as security. Creditors feared that these loans would never be repaid and had no confidence in the money, but the legislature established a system of fines in cases where men refused to accept it. When creditors fled the state to avoid being confronted, the legislature authorized debtors to discharge their obligations merely by turning the necessary currency over to a local judge. Of course these measures only further weakened public confidence in the money. While many individuals managed to unburden themselves of debts painlessly, no one accepted the currency freely. The Rhode Island Supreme Court, in *Trevett v. Weeden,* declared that it was unconstitutional to fine a creditor for refusing money and soon there was a reaction.* The element of compulsion was withdrawn, and then the paper depreciated rapidly.

Although the Rhode Island experience was atypical, it greatly alarmed conservative and responsible citizens. Then, close upon its heels, came a disturbing outbreak of violence in Massachusetts. The Massachusetts legislature had been almost fanatical in its determination to pay off the state debt and maintain a sound currency. Taxes amounting to almost £1.9 million were levied between 1780 and 1786, the burden falling most heavily on farmers and other men of moderate income. Historian Merrill Jensen estimates that the average Massachusetts farmer paid about a third of his income in taxes during this period. Bad times and deflation led to many foreclosures, and the prisons were crowded with honest men unable to pay their debts. When farmers peti-

*This was the first case in which an American court declared a legislative act void on constitutional grounds.

tioned for stay laws and paper money issues, the General Court refused to budge.

In the summer of 1786 mobs in the western communities began to stop foreclosures by forcibly preventing the courts from holding their sessions. Under the leadership of Daniel Shays, veteran of Bunker Hill, Ticonderoga, and Saratoga, the "rebels" marched on Springfield and prevented the state supreme court from meeting. But when they attacked the Springfield arsenal somewhat later, they were routed. The uprising then collapsed and Shays fled to Vermont.

In itself, "Shays' Rebellion" did not amount to much. As Thomas Jefferson wittily observed, it was only "a *little* rebellion" and as such "a medicine necessary for the sound health of government." Shays was a poor leader, inarticulate and not very intelligent. But he and his fellows were genuinely exasperated by the refusal of the government even to try to provide relief for their troubles. By taking up arms they forced the authorities to heed them. At its next session the legislature made some concessions to their demands. Soon good times returned and the uprising was forgotten. Just the same, the episode had an impact far beyond the borders of Massachusetts and all out of proportion to its intrinsic importance. Unlike Jefferson, most responsible Americans were shocked by the violence of the Shaysites. "What, gracious God, is man! that there should be such inconsistency and perfidiousness in his conduct?" the usually unexcitable George Washington asked when news of the riots reached Virginia. "We are fast verging to anarchy and confusion!" During the crisis, private persons had had to subscribe funds to put the rebels down, and when Massachusetts had appealed to Congress for help there was little Congress could legally do. The lessons seemed plain: liberty must not become an excuse for license. Greater authority must be vested in the central government.

Moreover, the reaction to both the Rhode Island excesses and the uprising in Massachusetts illustrated the continued growth of American nationalism. Citizens everywhere were concerned with what was going on in other parts of the country. Newspapers in all the states followed the bizarre spectacle in Rhode Island of debtors avidly pursuing their creditors with fistfuls of paper money. The tragicomic revolt of Daniel Shays worried planters in far-off Virginia and the Carolinas almost as much as the merchants of Boston. All were becoming more conscious of their common interests, their national identity. Bacon's Rebellion, in every way a far more serious affair, had invoked no such reaction in the 17th century, nor had the Regulator War in North Carolina as late as 1771.

Drafting the Constitution

The country was clearly ready to take another step toward centralized government; agreement on the length of the step or the method of taking it was another matter. Most people wanted to increase the power of Congress, but many were afraid to shift the balance too far, lest they destroy the sovereignty of the states. The machinery for change established in the Articles of Confederation, which required the unanimous consent of the states for all amendments, posed a particularly delicate problem. Experience had shown it unworkable, yet to by-pass it would be revolutionary and therefore dangerous.

The first fumbling step toward reform was taken in March 1785 when representatives of Virginia and Maryland, meeting at the home of George Washington to settle a dispute over the improvement of navigation on the Potomac River, suggested a conference of all the states to discuss common problems of commerce. In January 1786 the Virginia legislature sent out a formal call for such a gathering, to be held in September at Annapolis. During the summer of 1786, Congress debated various suggested amendments to the Articles, although none was submitted to the states, and the Massachusetts legislature passed a resolution calling for a general revision of the Articles. However, the September meeting at Annapolis was disappointing to the friends of reform; delegates from only five states appeared, and being so few they did not feel it worthwhile to propose changes.

Nevertheless, the tide was running strong for reform. Even Washington, always a nationalist but slow to involve himself in political matters, was now arguing for change. "The discerning part of the community," he wrote, "have long since seen the necessity of giving adequate powers to Congress for national purposes, and the ignorant and designing must yield to it ere long."

Among the delegates at Annapolis was a young New York lawyer named Alexander Hamilton, a brilliant, imaginative, and daring man who was convinced that only drastic centralization would save the nation from disintegration. Instead of accepting the failure of the meeting meekly, he proposed another convention to meet at Philadelphia to deal generally with constitutional reform. The regulation of trade was inextricably involved with other vital powers of government, he argued. Delegates to the new convention should be empowered to work out a broad plan for correcting "such defects as may be discovered to exist" in the Articles of Confederation.

These aggressive tactics worked perfectly, for events were marching in Hamilton's direction. The Annapolis group approved his suggestion, and Congress endorsed it officially. This time all the states but Rhode Island sent delegates. On May 25, 1787, 29 men from nine states having arrived at the State House in Philadelphia, the convention opened its proceedings and unanimously elected George Washington its president. When it adjourned four months later, it had drafted the Constitution.

The Philadelphia Convention

As the decades have passed and the Constitution has grown more and more venerable and tradition-encrusted without losing any of its flexibility, each generation has tried to explain how a people so young and inexperienced, so free-swinging and unruly, could have produced it. One reason was the quality of those who drafted it. The Founding Fathers were indeed remarkable men. Jefferson, who along with John Adams was on a foreign assignment and did not attend the convention, called them "demigods," although he later had reason to quarrel with certain aspects of their handiwork. Collectively they possessed a rare combination of talents. Amazingly youthful—President John F. Kennedy, 43 at the time of his inauguration, was older than the average delegate in 1787—they escaped the weaknesses so often associated with youth: instability, half-cocked radicalism, and the refusal to heed the suggestions of others. The times made them mature beyond their years, by and large, for the whole Revolutionary generation had been inspired by the uniqueness of its opportunities. People of every sort gloried in being part of this great experiment in republican government, and the delegates at Philadelphia, the best products of the age, were acutely aware of their responsibilities. "We . . . decide for ever the fate of republican government," Madison said at one point during their deliberations, and if this was an overstatement, it nonetheless represented the opinion of most of those present.

Fortunately, they were nearly all of one mind on basic questions. That there should be a federal system, with sovereignty somehow divided between the states and the central government, was accepted by all but one or two of them. Republican government, drawing its authority from the people and eventually responsible to them, was also a universal assumption. A measure of democracy followed inevitably from this principle, for even the most aristocratic delegates agreed that the ordinary citizen should share in the process of selecting those who were to make and execute the laws. All also agreed, however, that no group within society, no matter how numerous, should have *unrestricted* authority, for they looked upon political power much as we today view nuclear energy: a force with tremendous potential value for mankind, but one easily misused and therefore dangerous to unleash. Man meant well and he had limitless possibilities, these constitution-makers believed, but he was selfish by nature and could not be counted upon to consider the interests of others. The poor, therefore, should have a say in government so as to be able to protect themselves against those who would exploit their individual weakness, but somehow the majority must be prevented from plundering the rich, for property must be secure or no government could be stable. No single state or section must be allowed to predominate either, nor should the legislature be supreme over the executive or the courts. Power, in short, must be divided, and then the segments must be balanced one against the other.

Although the level of education among them was high and a number might fairly be described as learned in matters pertaining to law and government (one thinks of Franklin and Gouverneur Morris of Pennsylvania, Rufus King of Massachusetts, and the Virginia triumvirate of James Madison, George Wythe, and George Mason), the delegates' approach was pragmatic rather than theoretical. They combined, as the historian Adrienne Koch has said, "an uncanny aptitude for political analysis" with a talent "for the adaptation of theories to practice." This was perhaps their most useful asset, for their task called for reconciling clashing interests, and could never have been accomplished without compromise and an acute sense of what was possible as distinct from what was ideally best.

Early in their deliberations they made two vital decisions. One was to keep their discussions secret. This encouraged a franker and freer exchange of ideas and also prevented extreme states'-righters and various pressure groups outside the convention from exciting and confusing public opinion before the convention's work could be seen as a whole and fairly judged. The delegates also decided to go beyond their instructions to revise the Articles of Confederation and draft an entirely new frame of government. This was a bold, perhaps illegal act, but in no way immoral, because nothing the convention might recommend was binding on anyone. Alexander Hamilton, eager to scrap the Confederation in favor of a truly national government, captured the mood of his fellow delegates when he said: "We can only propose and recommend—the power of ratifying or rejecting is still in the States. . . . We ought not to sacrifice the public Good to narrow Scruples."

The delegates voted on May 30 that "a *national* Government ought to be established" and then set to work hammering out a specific plan. Two big questions had to be answered. The first—*What powers should this national government be granted?*—occasioned relatively little discussion. The right to levy taxes and to regulate interstate and foreign commerce was assigned to the central government almost without debate. So was the

ALBERT E. LEEDS COLLECTION

James Madison, one of the key figures at the Convention; miniature by Charles Willson Peale, c. 1783.

power to raise and maintain an army and navy and to summon the militia of the states to enforce national laws and suppress insurrections. With equal absence of argument, the states were deprived of their right to issue money—coin or paper—to make treaties, and to tax either imports or exports without the permission of Congress. Thus, in summary fashion, was brought about a massive shift of power, made practicable by the new nationalism of the 1780's.

The second major question—*Who shall control the national government?*—proved far more difficult to answer in a manner satisfactory to all. Various interests pressed their claims vigorously. Led by Virginia, the larger states pushed for representation in the national legislature based on population, whereas the smaller ones wished to maintain the existing system of equal representation for all. The large states rallied behind the Virginia Plan, drafted by James Madison and presented to the convention by Edmund Randolph, governor of the state. The small states supported the New Jersey Plan, prepared by William Paterson, a former attorney general of that state. The question was important; equal state representation would have been undemocratic, while a proportional system would have pretty effectively destroyed the influence of all the states *as states*. But the delegates saw it in terms of combinations of large or small states, and this was unrealistic:

when the states did combine they did so on geographic, economic, or social grounds that had nothing to do with size. Nevertheless, the debate was long and hot, and for a time it threatened to disrupt the convention. Finally, in mid-July, the delegates agreed to what has been called the "Great Compromise." In the lower house of the new legislature—the House of Representatives—places were to be assigned according to population and filled by popular vote. In the upper house—the Senate—each state was to have two members, elected by the state legislatures.

Then a complicated struggle took place between northern and southern delegates occasioned by the institution of slavery and the differing economic interests of the regions. Northerners contended that slaves should be counted in deciding each state's share of direct federal taxes. The southerners, of course, wanted to exclude slaves from the count. On the other hand, the southerners wished to include slaves when determining their representation in the House of Representatives, although they had no intention of permitting the slaves to vote. In the "Three-Fifths Compromise" it was agreed that "three-fifths of all other Persons" should be counted for both purposes. Settlement of the knotty issue of the African slave trade was postponed by a clause making it illegal for Congress to outlaw the trade before 1808. Questions involving the regulation of less controversial commerce also caused some sectional disagreement. Southerners disliked export taxes, since their great staple products were largely sold abroad. In return for a clause prohibiting such taxes, they dropped their demand that all laws regulating foreign commerce be approved by two-thirds of both houses of Congress. Many other differences of opinion were resolved by the give-and-take of practical compromise.

The final document, signed on September 17, established a legislature of two houses, an executive consisting of a President with wide powers and a Vice President whose only function was to preside over the Senate, and a national judiciary consisting of a Supreme Court and such "inferior courts" as Congress might decide to create. The lower, popularly elected branch of the Congress was supposed to represent especially the mass of ordinary citizens. It was given the sole right to introduce bills for raising revenue. The 26-man Senate was looked upon by many as a sort of advisory council similar to the upper houses of the colonial legislatures. Its consent was required before any treaty could go into effect and for major Presidential appointments. The Senate also served an essential legislative function, for the Founding Fathers intended it to represent in Congress the interests not only of the separate states but also of what Hamilton called "the rich and the well-born" as contrasted with "the great mass of the people."

The creation of a powerful President was the most drastic departure from past experience, and it is doubtful if the Founding Fathers would have gone so far had everyone not counted upon Washington, a man universally esteemed for character, wisdom, and impartiality, to be the first to occupy the office. Besides giving him general responsibility for executing the laws, the Constitution made the President commander in chief of the armed forces of the nation and general supervisor of all its foreign relations. He was to appoint federal judges and other officials, and he might veto any law of Congress, although his veto could be overridden by a two-thirds majority of both houses. While not specifically ordered to submit a program of legislation to Congress, he was to deliver periodic reports on the "State of the Union" and recommend "such Measures as he shall judge necessary and expedient." Most modern Presidents have interpreted this requirement as authorizing them to submit detailed plans for new laws and to employ every means of persuasion to get Congress to enact them.

Looking beyond Washington, whose choice was sure to come about under any system, the Constitution established a cumbersome method of electing Presidents. Each state was to choose a number of "electors" equal to its representation in Congress. The electors, meeting separately in their own states, were to vote for two persons for President. Supposedly, the procedure would prevent anyone less universally admired than Washington from getting a majority in this "Electoral College," in which case the House of Representatives would choose the President from among the five leading candidates, each state having but one vote. However, the swift rise of national political parties prevented the expected fragmentation of the electors' votes, and only two elections have ever gone to the House for settlement.

The national court system was set up to adjudicate disputes under the laws and treaties of the United States. No such system had existed under the Articles, a major weakness. Although the Constitution did not specifically authorize the courts to declare laws void when they conflicted with the terms of the Constitution, the courts soon exercised this right of "judicial review" in cases involving both state and federal laws.

That the Constitution reflected the commonly held beliefs of its framers is everywhere evident in the document. It greatly expanded the powers of the central government, yet did not seriously threaten the independence of the states. Foes of centralization, at the time and ever since, have predicted the imminent disappearance of the states as sovereign bodies. But despite a steady trend toward centralization, probably inevitable as American society has grown ever more complex, the states remain powerful political organizations and absolutely sovereign in many areas of government.

The Founders believed also that since the new powers of government might easily be misused, each should be held within safe limits by some countervailing force. The Constitution is full of ingenious devices ("checks and balances") whereby one power controls and limits another, without reducing it to impotence. The separation of legislative, executive, and judicial functions is, of course, the fundamental example of this principle. Others are the President's veto; Congress' power of impeachment, cleverly divided between House and Senate; the Senate's power over treaties and appointments; judicial review; and the balancing of Congress' right to declare war against the President's control of the armed forces.

Ratification of the Constitution

Influenced by the widespread approval of Massachusetts' decision to submit its state constitution of 1780 to the voters for ratification, the framers of the Constitution provided that their handiwork be ratified by special state conventions. This procedure gave the Constitution what Madison called "the highest source of authority"—the endorsement of the people, expressed through representatives chosen specifically to pass upon it. The framers may also have been motivated by a desire to by-pass the state legislatures, where many members might resent the reductions being made in state authority, but this was not of central importance, because the legislatures could have blocked ratification by refusing to call conventions. Only Rhode Island did so, and since the Constitution was to go into operation when nine states had approved, Rhode Island's stubbornness did no vital harm.

Such a complex and controversial document as the Constitution naturally excited argument throughout the country. Those who favored it were called Federalists, their opponents, Antifederalists.* As with most American political alignments, it is difficult to generalize about the members of these groups. The Federalists tended to be substantial men, members of the professions, well-to-do, active in commercial affairs—more interested, perhaps, in orderly and efficient government than in safeguarding the maximum freedom of individual choice, but not necessarily opposed to popular government. The Antifederalists were more often small farmers, debtors, and men to whom free choice was more important than power. But many rich and worldly men opposed the Constitution and many poor and obscure persons were for it. It seems likely that most persons did not support or oppose the new system for narrowly selfish reasons. The contemporary judgment of David Ramsay that "the great body of independent men who saw the necessity of an energetic government" swung the balance in favor of the Constitution is probably correct.

Whether the Antifederalists were more democratic than the Federalists is an interesting question. Those who are loud for local autonomy do not necessarily believe in equal rights for all the locals. Many Antifederalist leaders (more than half, according to the best recent research) had

*The Antifederalists, however, were those who really favored a federal system. The Federalists should more logically have been called Centralists or Nationalists.

reservations about democracy; only among "the more obscure and the less well-to-do" were democratic ideas very strongly held. On the other hand, even Hamilton, no admirer of democracy, believed that the humblest citizen should have *some* say about his government. In general, practice still stood well ahead of theory when it came to popular participation in politics.

Various Antifederalists criticized many of the specific grants of authority in the new Constitution, some concocting far-fetched arguments to show what disasters might ensue should it be put into effect. The routine clause (Article I, Section 4) giving Congress the power to regulate "the times, places, and manner of holding elections" threatened to "destroy representation entirely," a North Carolina Antifederalist claimed. But the chief force behind the opposition was a general, rather vague fear that the new system would destroy the independence of the states. It is important to keep in mind that the country was large and sparsely settled, that communication was primitive, and that the central government did not influence the lives of most people to any great degree. A farmer in New Hampshire or Georgia might live for years without seeing or dealing directly with an employee of the United States. Many persons believed that a centralized republican system would not work in a country so large and with so many varied interests as the United States. The fact that Congress could pass all laws "necessary and proper" to carry out the functions assigned it and legislate for the "general welfare" of the country seemed alarmingly all-inclusive. The first sentence of the Constitution, beginning "We the *people* of the United States" rather than "We the states," convinced many that the document represented centralization run wild. "As I enter the Building I stumble at the Threshhold," Samuel Adams remarked.

Many members of the Convention were well-to-do and stood to profit from the establishment of a sound and conservative government that would honor its obligations, foster economic development, and preserve a stable society. Since the Constitution was designed to do all these things, it has been suggested that the Founders were not true patriots but merely selfish men out to protect their own interests. Charles A. Beard advanced this thesis over half a century ago in *An Economic Interpretation of the Constitution*, arguing that most of the members of the Convention owned large amounts of depreciated government securities that were bound to rise if the Constitution was approved. His work has been thoroughly discredited by Robert E. Brown and other historians. Certainly the Founders wanted to advance their own interests, as every normal human does. Most of them, however, had no special involvement in securities, being far more concerned with land. Furthermore, there is abundant evidence that the closest thing to a general spirit at Philadelphia was a public spirit. To call men like Washington, Franklin, and Madison self-seeking is simply absurd. Beard's book was and is important, for it provided a necessary corrective to the 19th-century tendency to deify the Founding Fathers, and it called attention to the role of economic motivation in the framing of the Constitution and in other aspects of American history too. But it ought not to obscure the greatness either of the Constitution or the men who made it.

Very little of the opposition to the Constitution grew out of economic issues. Most people wanted the national debt paid off; nearly everyone opposed an unstable currency; most favored uniform trade policies. Aside from a few doctrinaires and an indeterminate but fortunately uninfluential minority of individuals lost in the backwaters of American life, most people were ready to give the new government a chance if they could be convinced that it would not destroy the states. When it was suggested that a series of amendments be added promptly to the document, guaranteeing the civil liberties of the people against invasion by the national government and specifically reserving all unmentioned power to the states, much of the opposition disappeared. Sam Adams, for example, ended up voting for the Constitution in the Massachusetts convention after these additions had been promised.

No one knows exactly how public opinion divided on the question of ratification. In nearly every state a large majority of the more articulate people favored the Constitution. The Federalists were usually able to create an impression of

NEW-YORK HISTORICAL SOCIETY

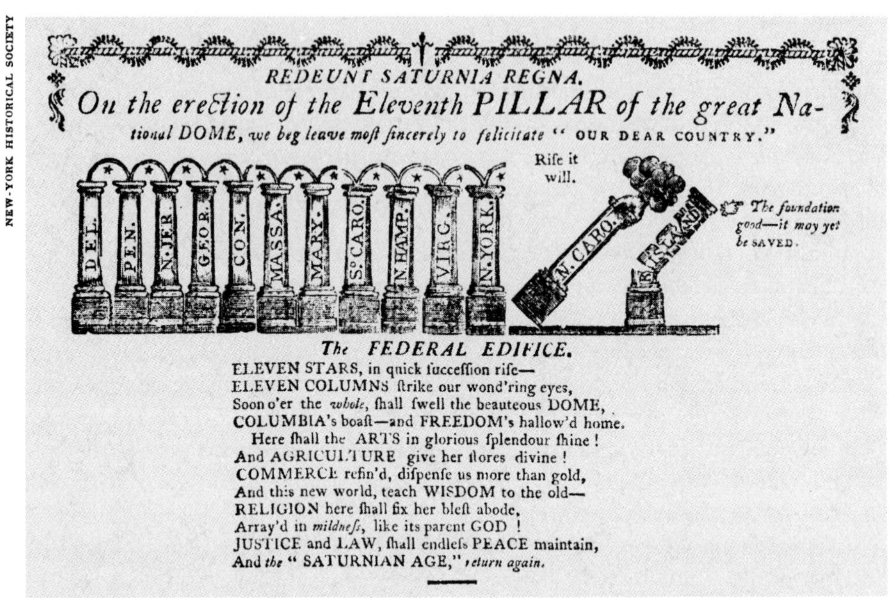

REDEUNT SATURNIA REGNA.

On the erection of the Eleventh PILLAR *of the great National* DOME, *we beg leave moſt ſincerely to felicitate* "OUR DEAR COUNTRY."

The FEDERAL EDIFICE.

ELEVEN STARS, in quick ſucceſſion riſe—
ELEVEN COLUMNS ſtrike our wond'ring eyes,
Soon o'er the *whole*, ſhall ſwell the beauteous DOME,
COLUMBIA's boaſt—and FREEDOM's hallow'd home.
Here ſhall the ARTS in glorious ſplendour ſhine!
And AGRICULTURE give her ſtores divine!
COMMERCE refin'd, diſpenſe us more than gold,
And this new world, teach WISDOM to the old—
RELIGION here ſhall fix her bleſt abode,
Array'd in *mildneſs*, like its parent GOD!
JUSTICE and LAW, ſhall endleſs PEACE maintain,
And *the* "SATURNIAN AGE," *return again.*

New York's approval of the Constitution on July 26, 1788, inspired this comment in the Massachusetts Centinel. *Hope was high that North Carolina would "rise" to ratify, but prospects in Rhode Island were considered less sanguine—and rightly so.*

strength far beyond their actual numbers and to overwhelm doubters with the mere mass of their arguments. They excelled in political organization and in persuasiveness. James Madison, for example, demolished the thesis that a centralized republican government could not function efficiently in a large country. In rule by the majority lay protection against the "cabals" of special interest groups. "Extend the sphere," Madison argued, "and you take in a greater variety of parties and interests; you make it less probable that a majority of the whole will have a common motive to invade the rights of other citizens." Moreover, the management of national affairs would surely attract men of higher ability and sounder character to public service than the handling of petty local concerns ever could in a decentralized system.

In any case, the Constitution met with remarkably little opposition in most of the state ratifying conventions, considering the importance of the changes it instituted. Delaware acted first, ratifying unanimously on December 7, 1787. Pennsylvania followed a few days later, voting for the document by a 2-to-1 majority. New Jersey approved unanimously on December 18, and so did Georgia on January 2, 1788. A week later Connecticut fell in line, 128 to 40.

The Massachusetts convention provided the first real contest, but early in February, by a vote of 187 to 168, the delegates decided to ratify. In April Maryland accepted the Constitution by nearly 6 to 1 and in May South Carolina approved, 149 to 73. New Hampshire came along on June 21, voting 57 to 47 for the Constitution. This was the ninth state, making the Constitution legally operative, and on June 25, before the news from New Hampshire had spread throughout the country, Virginia also voted for ratification, 89 to 79.

Aside from Rhode Island, this left only New York and North Carolina outside the Union. New York politics presented a complex and baffling picture during the whole Revolutionary Era. Resistance to independence had been strong there in 1776, and Tory feeling was a problem all through the war. Although New York was the third largest state, with a population rapidly approaching 340,000, it sided with the small states at Philadelphia, and two of its three delegates (Hamilton being the exception) refused to sign the final document and took the lead in resisting ratification. A handful of great landowning and mercantile families dominated politics, but these were divided into shifting rival factions. In general, New York City favored ratification, whereas the rural areas upstate were against it.

The Antifederalists, well-organized and competently led in New York, won 46 of the 65 seats at the ratifying convention. Fortunately, the Federalists had one great asset in the tide of events in the rest of the country and another in the person of Alexander Hamilton. Although contemptuous of the *weakness* of the new Constitution, Hamilton supported it with all his energies as incomparably stronger than the old government. Working with Madison and John Jay, he produced the *Federalist Papers*, a brilliant series of essays explaining and defending it. These were published in the local press, and later in book form. Although generations of judges and lawyers have treated them almost as parts of the Constitution, their impact on contemporary public opinion was probably slight. Open-minded members of the convention were undoubtedly influenced, but many of the delegates were anything but open-minded. Hamilton therefore became almost a one-man army in defense of the Constitution, plying hesitating delegates with dinners and free drinks, facing obstinate ones with the threat that New York City would secede from the state if the Constitution were rejected. He spoke, one of the leading Antifederalists at the convention remarked, "frequently, very long, and very vehemently" on every aspect of the Constitution, posing as a devoted supporter of republican government and scoffing at the idea that the Constitution represented a threat to liberty. Once New Hampshire and Virginia had ratified, opposition in New York became a good deal less intransigent. In the end, by promising to support a call for a second national convention to consider amendments, the Federalists carried the day by the narrow margin of 30 to 27. With New York in the fold, the new government was free to get under way.*

*North Carolina did not ratify until November 1789, and Rhode Island held out until May 1790.

Washington as President

During January and February of 1789 elections took place in the states, and by early April enough of the new congressmen had gathered in New York, the temporary national capital, to commence operation. The ballots of the Presidential electors were officially counted in the Senate on April 6, Washington being the unanimous choice. John Adams, with 34 electoral votes, won the Vice Presidency. On April 30 Washington took the oath of office at Federal Hall.

Washington made a firm, dignified, conscientious, but cautious and unaggressive President. His acute sense of responsibility and his sensitivity to the slightest criticism made it almost impossible

STOKES COLLECTION, NEW YORK PUBLIC LIBRARY

His hand on the Bible, Washington takes the Presidential oath administered by Robert Livingston on the portico of New York's Federal Hall. Engraving by Amos Doolittle, after a drawing by Peter Lacour.

for him to relax and enjoy himself while in office. "The eyes of Argus are upon me," he complained, "and no slip will pass unnoticed." Each Presidential action must of necessity establish a precedent, and every observer noted what historian Joseph Charles called Washington's "conscious effort to set the tone for the new government." Hoping to make the Presidency appear respectable in the eyes of the world, he saw to it that his carriage was drawn by six cream-colored horses, and when he rode himself (he was a magnificent horseman), it was upon a great white charger, with the saddle of leopardskin and the cloth edged in gold. Twenty-one servants attended his needs at the Presidential mansion on Broadway, and when guests arrived for state functions, they were met at the entry by powdered lackeys.

Washington meticulously avoided treading upon the toes of Congress, for he took the principle of the separation of powers very seriously. Never would he speak for or against a candidate for Congress, nor did he think that the President should push or even propose legislation. When he knew a controversial question was to be discussed in Congress, he avoided all mention of the subject in his annual message. The veto, he believed, should only be employed when the President considered a bill unconstitutional. Once, in 1790, a formal letter arrived from the French government addressed to the President and members of Congress. Washington refused even to open it, sending it on instead to the legislators.

In selecting his Cabinet of advisers,* he sought first ability and loyalty to the new Constitution. Beyond that, geographical considerations carried some weight with him. He made no effort to bring together men of one particular faction, or even men who agreed with his own views. He picked Hamilton for secretary of the treasury, Jefferson for secretary of state, General Henry Knox of Massachusetts for secretary of war, and Edmund Randolph for attorney general. He called upon them for advice according to the logic of his particular needs and frequently without regard for their own specialities. Thus he sometimes consulted Jefferson about financial matters and Hamilton about foreign affairs. This system caused resentment and confusion, especially when rival political factions began to coalesce around Hamilton and Jefferson. Nevertheless, Washington persisted in acting as though no political organizations existed, for he wished to minimize conflict.

Despite his respect for the opinions of others, Washington was a strong Chief Executive. As Hamilton put it, he "consulted much, pondered much, resolved slowly, resolved surely." He had a policy, and he pursued it vigorously. His great stress on the dignity of his office suited the needs of a new country whose people tended to be perhaps too informal. It was indeed important that the *first* President be particularly concerned about establishing precedents. His scrupulous care lest he overstep the bounds of Presidential power helped erase the prejudices of those who feared that republican government must inevitably succumb to dictatorship and tyranny. When each step is an experiment, when foreign dangers loom at the end of every errant path, it is surely wise to go slowly. And no one should forget that Washington's devotion to duty did not always come easily. Occasionally he exploded. Jefferson has left us a picture of him at a Cabinet meeting, in a rage because of some unfair criticism, swearing that "by god he had rather be on his farm than to be made *emperor of the world*."

The Bill of Rights

The first Congress also had the task of setting precedents and constructing the machinery of government. By September 1789 it had created the State, Treasury, and War departments and passed a Judiciary Act establishing 13 federal district courts and three circuit courts of appeal. The number of Supreme Court justices was set at six, and Washington named John Jay chief justice. True to Federalist promises—for a large majority of both houses was friendly to the Constitution—Congress prepared a list of a dozen amendments (ten were ratified) guaranteeing the people's civil liberties. These amendments, known as the Bill of

*The Cabinet was not provided for in the Constitution, but Washington established the system of calling his department heads together for general advice, a practice that was generally followed by his successors.

Rights, provided that Congress should make no law infringing freedom of speech, the press, or religion. The right of trial by jury was reaffirmed. No one was to be subject to "unreasonable" searches or seizures, nor compelled to testify against himself in a criminal case, nor was anyone to "be deprived of life, liberty, or property, without due process of law." The Tenth Amendment, not, strictly speaking, a part of the Bill of Rights, was designed to mollify those who feared the states would be destroyed by the new government. It provided that powers not delegated to the United States or denied specifically to the states by the Constitution were to reside either in the states or in the people.

As experts pointed out, these amendments were not logically necessary, because the federal government had no authority to act in such matters to begin with. But many persons had wanted to be reassured. If only, as Madison put it, to separate "the well-meaning from the designing opponents" of the Constitution, the amendments seemed desirable. Experience has proved repeatedly that whatever the strict logic of the situation, the protection afforded individuals by the Bill of Rights has been anything but unnecessary.

The Bill of Rights did much to convince doubters that the new government would not become too powerful. More complex was the task of proving that it was powerful enough to deal with those national problems that the Confederation had not been able to solve: the threat to the West posed by the British, Spaniards, and Indians; the disruption of the pattern of American foreign commerce resulting from independence; the collapse of the financial structure of the country.

Hamilton and Financial Reform

Of these problems, the last was the most pressing. One of the first acts of Congress in 1789 was to employ its new power to tax. The simplest means of raising money seemed to be that first attempted by the British after 1763, a tariff on foreign imports. Congress levied a flat tax of five per cent on all goods entering the United States, applying higher rates to certain products, such as hemp, glass, and nails, as a measure of protection for American producers. Many southern congressmen opposed this bill as benefiting the northern states exclusively, but it passed easily, for Americans were beginning to learn that independence did not mean freedom from responsibility. The Tariff Act of 1789 also placed heavy tonnage duties on all foreign shipping, a mercantilistic measure designed to stimulate the American merchant marine.

Raising money for current expenses was only a small and relatively simple aspect of the financial problem faced by Washington's administration. The nation's debt was large, its credit shaky, its economic future uncertain. In October 1789 Congress deposited upon the slender shoulders of Secretary of the Treasury Alexander Hamilton the task of straightening out the fiscal mess and stimulating the country's economic development.

Although only 34, Hamilton had already proved himself a remarkable man. Born in the British West Indies, the illegitimate son of a shiftless Scot who was little better than a beachcomber, and raised by his mother's family he came to New York in 1773 to attend King's College. When the Revolution broke out, he joined the army. At 22 he was a staff colonel, aide-de-camp to Washington; later, at Yorktown, he led a line regiment, displaying a bravery approaching foolhardiness. He married the daughter of Philip Schuyler, a wealthy and influential New Yorker, and after the Revolution he practiced law in that state. As we have seen, he played an important role in the movement that resulted in the drafting of the Constitution.

Hamilton was a bundle of contradictions. Witty, charming, possessed of a mind like a sharp knife, he was sometimes the soul of practicality, sometimes an incurable romantic. No more hard-headed realist ever lived, yet he was quick to resent any slight to his honor, even—tragically—ready to fight a duel although he abhorred the custom of dueling. A self-made man, he admired aristocracy and disparaged the abilities of the common run of mankind who, he said, "seldom judge or determine right." Although granting that Americans must be allowed to govern themselves, he was as apprehensive of the "turbulence" of the masses as a small boy passing a graveyard in the

NEW-YORK HISTORICAL SOCIETY

"To confess my weakness," Hamilton wrote when he was only 14, "my ambition is prevalent." This pencil portrait was probably copied from a sculpture.

dark. Fear of demagogues was his bugaboo. "No popular government was ever without its Catilines and its Caesars," he pontificated. On the other hand, in some matters he was remarkably liberal. While the great democrat Jefferson could expound movingly upon the sinfulness of slavery without abandoning the comforting belief that Negroes were inferior beings, Hamilton said plainly: "Their natural faculties are probably as good as ours," a rare insight in the 18th century. "The contempt we have been taught to entertain for the blacks," he also said, "makes us fancy many things that are founded neither in reason nor experience."

The chief political need of the country, Hamilton believed, was a strong national government. A system of divided sovereignty could only end in confusion and weakness. "A great Federal Republic," he said, is a "noble and magnificent" thing, whereas "there is something proportionably diminutive and contemptible in the prospect of a number of petty states, with the appearance only of union, jarring, jealous, perverse, without any determined direction." He wished to reduce the states to mere administrative units, like English counties.

As secretary of the treasury, Hamilton was both a remarkable executive (Leonard D. White, the leading expert on the history of public administration in the United States, called him "the greatest administrative genius in America, and one of the greatest administrators of all time") and a farsighted economic planner. He called the United States a "Hercules in the cradle." Its chief economic need was for capital to develop its vast untapped material and human resources. To persuade investors to commit their funds in America, the country would have to convince them that it would meet every obligation in full. His *Report on the Public Credit* outlined the means for accomplishing this objective. The United States owed more than $11 million to foreigners and over $40 million to its own citizens. Hamilton suggested that this debt be funded at par, which meant calling in all outstanding securities and issuing new bonds to the same face value in their stead, and establishing an untouchable sinking fund to assure payment of interest and principal. Furthermore, a large part of the debts of the states, over $21 million, should be assumed (taken over) by the United States on the same terms.

While most congressmen agreed, albeit somewhat grudgingly, that the debt should be funded at par, many believed that at least part of the new issue should go to the original holders of the old securities: the soldiers, farmers, and merchants who had been forced to accept them in lieu of cash for goods and services rendered the Confederation during the Revolution. Many of these people had sold their securities for a fraction of their face value to speculators; under Hamilton's proposal, the speculators would now make a killing. To the argument for divided payment, Hamilton answered coldly: "[The speculator] paid what the commodity was worth in the market, and took the risks. . . . He . . . ought to reap the benefit of his hazard."

Hamilton was essentially correct, and in the end Congress had to go along. After all, the speculators had not caused the securities to fall in value; indeed, as a group they had favored sound money and a strong government. And the best way to restore the nation's credit was to convince investors that the government would honor all obligations in full. What infuriated his contemporaries and still attracts the scorn of many historians was Hamilton's motive. He deliberately intended his plan to give a special advantage to the rich. The government would be strong, he thought, only if the well-to-do enthusiastically supported it. What better way to win them over than to make it worth their while financially to do so? Furthermore, although Hamilton did not personally profit, he allowed news of his plan to "leak" to certain friends, who plunged heavily in government bonds and profited immensely as a result.

In part, opposition to the funding plan was sectional, for citizens of the northern states held more than four-fifths of the national debt. The scheme for assuming the state debts aggravated the controversy, since most of the southern states had already paid off much of their Revolutionary War obligations. For months Congress was deadlocked, but finally, in July 1790, Hamilton worked out an arrangement with Representative James Madison of Virginia and Secretary of State Jefferson. The two Virginians swung a few southern votes to Hamilton, and he in turn induced some of his followers to support the southern plan for locating the permanent capital of the Union on the Potomac River. Jefferson later claimed that he had been hoodwinked by Hamilton. Having only recently returned from Europe, he said, "I was really a stranger to the whole subject." Hamilton had persuaded him to "rally around" by the false tale that "our Union" was threatened with dissolution. This story was almost certainly nonsense: Jefferson agreed to the compromise because he expected that Virginia and the rest of the South would profit greatly from having the capital so near at hand.

In any case, the assumption bill passed, and the entire funding plan was a great success. Soon the United States had the highest possible credit rating in the world's financial centers. Foreign capital poured into the country.

Next, Hamilton proposed that Congress charter a national bank. Such an institution would provide a safe place for storing government funds, and it would serve as an agent for the government in the collection, movement, and expenditure of tax money. Most important of all, it would issue bank notes, thus providing a vitally needed medium of exchange for the specie-starved economy. This Bank of the United States was to be partly owned by the government, but 80 per cent of the $10-million stock issue was to be sold to private individuals.

The country had much to gain from such a bank, but again—Hamilton's devilish cleverness was never more in evidence—the well-to-do commercial classes would gain still more. Government balances in the bank belonging to all the people would earn dividends for a handful of rich investors. Manufacturers and other capitalists would profit from the bank's credit facilities. Public funds would be invested in the bank, but control would remain in private hands, since the government would appoint only 5 of the 25 directors. Nevertheless, the bill creating the bank passed both houses of Congress with relative ease in February 1791.

President Washington, however, hesitated to sign it, for the bill's constitutionality had been questioned during the debate in Congress. Nowhere did the Constitution specifically authorize Congress to charter corporations or engage in the banking business. As was his wont when in doubt, Washington called upon Jefferson and Hamilton for advice.

Of course Hamilton defended the legality of the bank. If a logical connection existed between the purpose of a bill and some power clearly stated in the Constitution, he wrote, the bill was constitutional. "A bank has a natural relation to the power of collecting taxes—to that of regulating trade—to that of providing for the common defence." Jefferson disagreed. Congress could only do what the Constitution specifically authorized, he said. The "elastic clause" granting it the right to pass "all Laws which shall be necessary and proper" to carry out the specified powers must be interpreted literally or Congress would "take possession of a boundless field of power, no longer susceptible to any definition." Since a bank was obviously not *necessary*, it was not authorized.

Although not entirely convinced, Washington accepted Hamilton's reasoning and signed the bill. He could just as easily have followed Jefferson, for the Constitution is not clear. If one stresses *proper* in the "necessary and proper" clause, one ends up a Hamiltonian; if one stresses *necessary*, then Jefferson's view is correct. Historically, and this is the important point, men have nearly always adopted the position that has suited their interests. Jefferson disliked the bank. Therefore he claimed it was unconstitutional. Had he approved, he doubtless would have taken a different tack. In 1819 the Supreme Court officially sanctioned Hamilton's broad construction of the "necessary and proper" clause, and in general that interpretation has prevailed. Since the majority tends naturally toward an argument that increases its freedom of action, the pressure for this view has been continual and formidable. Of course this does not make the Constitution clear or the broad construction "right."

The Bank of the United States succeeded from the start. When its stock went on sale, investors snapped up every share in a matter of hours. People eagerly accepted its bank notes at face value. Business ventures of all kinds found it easier to raise new capital. Soon other, state-chartered banks entered the field. There were only 3 state banks in 1791; by 1801 there were 32.

Still Hamilton had not finished. In December 1791 he submitted the most brilliant of his state papers, the *Report on Manufactures*, a bold call for economic planning. Through a system of tariffs, subsidies, and awards, Congress was to en-

HENRY FRANCIS DU PONT WINTERTHUR MUSEUM

New York No.
These are to Certify that ... was by a Majority of Votes regularly admitted a Member of the New York Mechanick Society at a Meeting held the ... day of ... A.D. 1791 Given under my hand and the Seal of the Society this 3 day of ... AnnoqueDomini 179
Chairman.
Secy.
Abr. Godwin del. et Sculp. N.Y.

A 1791 certificate of membership in the New York Mechanick Society, a social and fraternal association of skilled workers, reveals in its motto ("By Hammer & Hand, all Arts do stand") the pride of craftsmanship.

courage American manufacturing, changing an essentially agricultural nation into one with a complex, self-sufficient economy. Once again, of course, the business and commercial interests would benefit especially since they would be protected against foreign competition and otherwise subsidized, whereas the general taxpayer, particularly the farmer, would pay the bill in the form of higher taxes and higher prices on manufactured goods. Hamilton argued that in the long run every interest would profit, and he was undoubtedly sincere, being too much the nationalist to favor one section at the expense of another. A majority of the Congress, however, balked at so broad-gauged a scheme. Besides the almost solid opposition of the agriculturally minded southerners, the representatives of northern merchants feared that high tariffs would discourage foreign trade. Hamilton's *Report* was pigeonholed, although many of the specific tariffs he recommended were enacted into law in 1792.

Nevertheless, the secretary of the treasury had managed to transform the financial structure of the country and prepare the ground for an economic revolution. The constitutional reforms of 1787 made this possible, but Hamilton turned possibility into reality.

Foreign Problems

The western problems and those related to international trade proved more difficult because foreign powers were involved. The British showed no disposition to evacuate the posts on American soil simply because the American people had decided to strengthen their central government, nor did the western Indians suddenly agree to abandon their hunting grounds to the white invaders. Military campaigns against the Indians were at first unsuccessful, and when a bill was introduced in Congress to bring economic pressure on the British by placing discriminatory tonnage duties on British ships, it foundered on the opposition of northern business interests.

However, events that had nothing to do with the new Constitution enabled the United States to achieve most of its objectives. In 1789 a revolution broke out in France. By 1793 a republic had been proclaimed, King Louis XVI had been beheaded, and France had become embroiled in a war with the chief European nations. The war caused much trouble for the United States, but by dividing the powers it also presented the United States with an opportunity to play one off against another for its own benefit.

With France fighting Great Britain, the question at once came up of America's obligations under the Alliance of 1778. That treaty required the United States to defend the French West Indies "forever against all other powers." Suppose the British attacked Martinique; must America then go to war? Morally the United States was surely so obligated, but no responsible American statesman urged such a policy. Instead, in April 1793, Washington issued a proclamation of neutrality. Nevertheless, the French sent a special representative, Edmond Charles Genêt, to the United States to seek out support.

The French Revolution had excited much enthusiasm in the United States, for it seemed to indicate that American democratic ideas were already engulfing the world. The increasing radicalism in France tended to dampen some of the enthusiasm, but when "Citizen" Genêt landed at Charleston, South Carolina, the majority of Americans probably still wished the revolutionaries well. As Genêt, a charming, ebullient young man, made his way northward to present his credentials, cheering crowds welcomed him in every town. Quickly concluding that the American people disliked Washington's neutrality policy, he began, in plain violation of American law, to license American vessels to operate as privateers against British shipping and to grant French military commissions to a number of American adventurers in order to mount expeditions against Spanish and British possessions in North America.

This conduct naturally irritated Washington; when Genêt presented his credentials, the President received him coolly, and soon thereafter he ordered him flatly to stop his illegal activities. Genêt, losing all sense of perspective, appealed to public opinion over the President's head and continued to commission privateers. Washington then demanded his recall. The incident ended on a ludicrous note. When Genêt left France, he had been in the forefront of the Revolution. Now

Citizen Genêt, his revolutionary days long past, was painted by the Albany portraitist Ezra Ames.

events had marched swiftly leftward, and the new leaders in Paris considered him a dangerous reactionary. His replacement arrived in America with an order for his arrest. To return might well mean the guillotine, so Genêt asked the government that was expelling him for political asylum! Washington agreed, for he was not a vindictive man, and a few months later the bold revolutionary married the daughter of the governor of New York and settled down as a farmer on Long Island.

The Genêt affair, however, was only incidental to a far graver problem. Although the European war greatly increased the foreign demand for American products, it also led to attacks on American shipping by both France and Great Britain. Each power captured American vessels headed for the other's ports whenever it could. In 1793 and 1794 perhaps 600 United States ships were seized. The British attacks caused far more damage, both physically and psychologically, because the British fleet was much larger than France's, and France at least professed to be America's friend and to favor freedom of trade for neutrals. In addition the British issued secret orders late in 1793 turning their navy loose on neutral ships headed for the French West Indies. Pouncing without warning, British warships captured about 250 American vessels and took them off as prizes to British ports. The merchant marine, one American diplomat declared angrily, was being "kicked, cuffed, and plundered all over the Ocean."

These attacks roused a storm in America, reviving hatreds smoldering since the Revolution. The continuing presence of British troops in the Northwest (in 1794 the British actually began to build a *new* fort in the Ohio country) and the restrictions imposed on American trade with the British West Indies raised tempers still further. To try to avoid a war, for he wisely believed that the country should not become embroiled in the Anglo-French conflict, Washington sent Chief Justice John Jay to London as minister plenipotentiary to seek a general settlement with the British.

Jay's Treaty

Jay spent months in England in 1794 discussing various issues. The British genuinely wanted to keep the peace —as one minister quipped, the Americans "are so much in debt to this country that we scarcely dare to quarrel with them." Still, they were concerned about American intentions. Despite Washington's neutrality proclamation, the United States was technically allied with France, and the British feared that the two new republics would draw together in a battle with Europe's monarchies. Furthermore, the British were riding the crest of a wave of important victories in the war, whereas the United States was pitifully unprepared. Little wonder that the British drove a hard bargain with Jay.

The treaty that Jay brought home contained one major concession: the British agreed to evacuate the posts in the West. They also promised to compensate American shipowners for the seizures recently made in the West Indies and to open up their colonies in Asia to American ships. The British conceded nothing, however, to American demands that their rights as neutrals on the high seas be respected; in effect, Jay submitted to the "Rule of 1756," which was a British regulation stating that neutrals could not trade in wartime with ports normally closed to them by mercantilistic restrictions in time of peace. A provision opening the British West Indies to American commerce was so hedged with qualifications limiting the size of American vessels and the type of goods allowed that the United States refused to accept it. Jay assented to a "most-favored nation" arrangement that prevented the United States from imposing discriminatory duties on British goods, which a number of anti-British congressmen had proposed as a means of forcing Great Britain to treat American commerce more gently. Furthermore, he committed the United States government to pay pre-Revolutionary debts still owed British merchants, a slap in the face to many of the states whose courts had been impeding their collection. Yet nothing was said about the British paying for the slaves they had "abducted" during the fighting in the South.

From a practical point of view this was a valuable treaty for the United States, but it was also a humiliating one. Most of what the Americans gained already legally belonged to them, and they sacrificed principles of tremendous importance to a nation so dependent upon foreign trade. Jay, although perhaps too pro-British to have driven the hardest possible bargain, was unjustly con-

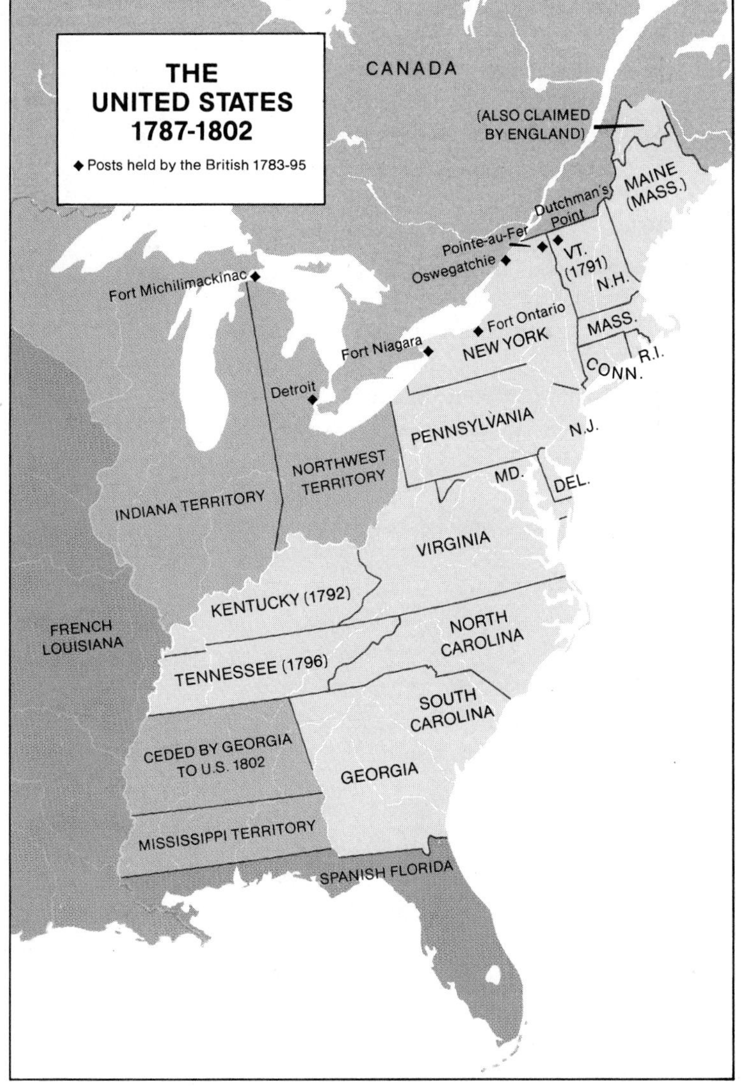

The United States on the eve of the Louisiana Purchase. In 1804 Georgia's cession became part of the Mississippi Territory. The seven British western forts were evacuated as a result of Jay's Treaty (1795).

In October of 1794 at Fort Cumberland, Maryland, Washington reviewed the troops called up to suppress the Whisky Rebellion. The painting is attributed to Charles Willson Peale's brother James, of the artistic clan known as the "Painting-Peales."

demned by people all over the country. The treaty seemed certain to be rejected. But Washington realized that he must accept it or fight. Swallowing his disappointment, he submitted the treaty to the Senate, which, after a difficult contest, ratified it on June 24, 1795.

Washington's decision was one of the wisest—and luckiest—of his career. The treaty marked a long step toward the pacification and regularization of Anglo-American relations, essential for both the economic and political security of the nation. The alternative might well have been to make the United States a French satellite. Unexpectedly—this was the luck of the decision—the treaty also enabled the United States to solve its problems in the Southwest. The Spanish, wishing to withdraw from the anti-French coalition and fearing a British attack on their vulnerable American possessions, interpreted the Jay Treaty as a prelude to a wider Anglo-American entente. A series of plots and conspiracies hatched by Americans seeking to seize the disputed regions of the Southwest alarmed them, especially since their own schemes for organizing Indian resistance to the Americans and bringing large numbers of Spanish settlers into the region had failed. To prevent a complete collapse of their position, they quickly agreed to a treaty (negotiated by Thomas Pinckney) that granted the United States the free navigation of the Mississippi River and the right of deposit at New Orleans, and accepted the American version of the disputed Florida boundary.

Federalism Victorious

Jay's and Pinckney's treaties, signed within a year of each other, finally cleared the United States' title to the vast region between the Appalachians and the Great River. At the same time the long struggle with the Indians, which had consumed a major portion of the government's revenues and had held back settlement of the Northwest Territory, was finally ended. The Indians, determined to hold this country at all costs, had inflicted a series of humiliating defeats on American forces. As late as the winter of 1791–92 they dominated the whole region, reducing the area of American control to two beachheads at Marietta and Cincinnati on the Ohio. But in August 1794, while Jay was dickering in London for the evacuation of the British forts, General Anthony Wayne defeated the Indians at the Battle of Fallen Timbers, near present-day Toledo. When the British at Fort Miami, who had egged the tribesmen on with promises of aid, now coldly refused to help, the Indians' will to resist was at last broken. In the Treaty of Greenville, signed the following summer, they abandoned their claims to much of the Northwest Territory.

After these events of 1794–95, settlers poured into the West as water bursts through a broken

METROPOLITAN MUSEUM OF ART, EDGAR WILLIAM AND BERNICE CHRYSLER GARBISCH GIFT

dike. Kentucky had become a state in 1792; now, in 1796, Tennessee was admitted. Two years later Mississippi Territory was organized, and at the very end of the century, Indiana Territory. The great westward flood reached full tide.

Another event that took place in the West while Jay was negotiating with the British offered a further example of the growth of American nationalism. This was Washington's prompt and overwhelming suppression of the Whisky Rebellion. To help pay for the cost of assuming the state debts, Hamilton had persuaded Congress to put a stiff excise tax on whisky. This hurt western farmers, who turned much of their grain into alcohol in order to cope with the high cost of transportation. When Hamilton frivolously replied to western complaints by suggesting that farmers drank too much to begin with and should cut down on their consumption if they found the tax oppressive, resentment only increased. Finally, in the summer of 1794, rioting broke out in western Pennsylvania. Much like the Shaysites a few years earlier, the "rebels" interfered with judicial proceedings and terrorized local law enforcement officers. But the new Constitution made possible prompt and effective action against them. Washington called up 12,000 militiamen (more men than he had ever commanded during the Revolution) and marched westward. At this tremendous show of force the rebels simply vanished. There was no fighting whatsoever. A few hapless minor figures were rounded up and thrown in jail, and thereafter the tax was peaceably collected until it was repealed during Jefferson's administration. The contrast with Shays' Rebellion warmed the hearts of all who feared "anarchy." Thus the events of the mid-1790's seemed to demonstrate that independence had been truly established and that the United States had become at last a true nation.

SUPPLEMENTARY READING John Fiske's view of what he called the "critical period" can be found in his *Critical Period of American History* (1888). A sounder and more detailed treatment is Allan Nevins, *The American States During and After the Revolution* (1924). The volumes of Merrill Jensen, *The Articles of Confederation** (1940) and *The New Nation** (1950), constitute a most powerful attack on the Fiske thesis. For the western problems of this period, see B.W. Bond, *The Foundations of Ohio* (1941), A.P. Whitaker, *The Spanish American Frontier** (1927), and J.A. James, *Life of George Rogers Clark* (1928). On economic problems, E.J. Ferguson, *The Power of the Purse** (1968), R.A. East, *Business Enterprise in the American Revolutionary Era* (1938), and T.C. Cochran, *New York in the Confederation* (1932), are useful, while C.P. Nettels, *The Emergence of a National Economy** (1962), puts this subject in the broader perspective of the period 1775–1815. A lively treatment of Shays' Rebellion is M.L. Starkey, *A Little Rebellion* (1955).

The political thinking of the period is discussed lucidly in G.S. Wood, *The Creation of the American Republic* (1969). As for the making of the Constitution, the records kept by Madison and other delegates to the Constitutional Convention are reprinted in C.C. Tansill (ed.), *Documents Illustrative of the Formation of the Union . . .* (1927). A good general account of the convention is Clinton Rossiter, *1787: The Grand Convention** (1966). The best treatment of Alexander Hamilton's connection with the Constitution and of his political views generally is Clinton Rossiter, *Alexander Hamilton and the Constitution* (1964). For Madison, Irving Brant, *James Madison: Father of the Constitution* (1950), provides the fullest account.

C.A. Beard, *An Economic Interpretation of the Constitution** (1913), caused a veritable revolution in the thinking of historians about the motives of the Founding Fathers, but recent studies have caused a major reaction away from the Beardian interpretation; see especially R.E. Brown, *Charles Beard and the Constitution** (1956), and a more detailed critique, Forrest McDonald, *We the People: The Economic Origins of the Constitution** (1958). Two books by R.A. Rutland, *The Birth of the Bill of Rights** (1955) and *The Ordeal of the Constitution: The Anti-Federalists and the Ratification Struggle* (1966), and also J.T. Main, *The Antifederalists** (1961), are helpful in understanding the opposition to the Constitution, while the *Federalist Papers** of Hamilton, Madison, and Jay, available in many editions, are essential for the arguments of the supporters of the new government.

On the organization of the federal government and the history of the Washington administration, see L.D. White, *The Federalists* (1948), an administrative history, and J.C. Miller, *The Federalist Era** (1960), a more general history of the period. Nathan Schachner, *The Founding Fathers** (1954), is a somewhat fuller study of these years. Washington himself is treated in great detail in the latter volumes of D.S. Freeman, *George Washington* (1948–1957). Joseph Charles, *Origins of the American Party System** (1961), is very thought-provoking, and the early chapters of W.N. Chambers, *Political Parties in a New Nation** (1963), are also useful.

Hamilton's *Reports* as secretary of the treasury are conveniently collected in Samuel McKee, Jr. (ed.), *Papers on Public Credit, Commerce, and Finance by Alexander Hamilton**(1934). The best of the many biographies of Hamilton are Nathan Schachner, *Alexander Hamilton** (1946), Broadus Mitchell, *Alexander Hamilton* (1957), and J.C. Miller, *Alexander Hamilton: A Portrait in Paradox** (1959). For foreign affairs during the Washington administration, see Alexander De Conde, *Entangling Alliance: Politics and Diplomacy under George Washington* (1958), Felix Gilbert, *To the Farewell Address* (1961), and two volumes by S.F. Bemis, *Jay's Treaty** (1923) and *Pinckney's Treaty** (1926). C.D. Hazen, *Contemporary American Opinion of the French Revolution* (1897), is still useful, while Hannah Arendt, *On Revolution** (1963), provides an interesting discussion of the relative influence of the French and American revolutions on later history.

*Available in paperback.

6

Jeffersonian Democracy

No one had a better right to rejoice in the course of events in the mid-1790's than Alexander Hamilton. His major financial reforms had achieved a dramatic success. Jay's Treaty had extinguished the danger of war with Great Britain, a conflict that in his opinion would have been catastrophic. And the Mississippi had been opened, another vital advance toward the national greatness he so eagerly desired. Yet Hamilton was far from content with the state of national affairs, for a formidable opposition to himself and to everything he most deeply believed in had developed. By the middle of the decade this opposition was coalescing into a political party under the leadership of Thomas Jefferson. A savage struggle for power was under way, the prize being the mantle of Washington, who was determined to retire at the end of his second term in 1797.

Thomas Jefferson: Political Theorist

Jefferson hardly seemed cut out for politics. Although in some ways a typical pleasure-loving southern planter, there was also in him something of the Spartan. He grew tobacco but did not smoke, and he partook only sparingly both of meat and alcohol. Unlike most planters, he never hunted or gambled, although he was a fine horseman and enjoyed dancing, music, and other social diversions. He preferred thought to action; although his practical interests ranged enormously—from architecture and geology to natural history and scientific farming—he displayed little interest in managing men. Personal controversy dismayed him, and he tended to avoid it by assigning to some thicker-skinned associate the task of attacking his enemies. Nevertheless, he was not without ambition. He wanted to have a say in shaping the future of the country, and once engaged he fought stubbornly and at times deviously to get and hold power.

While a fellow member of Washington's Cabinet, Jefferson often disagreed with Hamilton. Like Hamilton, he thought human beings basically selfish. "Lions and tigers are mere lambs compared with men," he once said. Yet he believed that men could be improved by education, and that unless they were free to follow the dictates of reason, the march of civilization would

NEW-YORK HISTORICAL SOCIETY

The Federalists repeatedly attacked Jefferson for his pro-French attitudes. A cartoon of about 1790 shows Washington in the national chariot leading troops against an invasion of bloodthirsty French "Cannibals" at the left. The figures trying to halt the chariot are, from left, Albert Gallatin, Citizen Genêt, and Jefferson.

grind quickly to a halt. "To preserve the freedom of the human mind," he wrote, "every spirit should be ready to devote itself to martyrdom." Democracy seemed to him not so much an ideal as a practical necessity. If men could not govern themselves, how could they be expected to govern their fellows? He had no patience with Hamilton's fondness for magnifying the virtues of the rich and the well-born. "The mass of mankind," he was to write when a very old man, "has not been born with saddles on their backs, nor a favored few booted and spurred, ready to ride them legitimately, by the grace of God."

Actually, Jefferson believed *all* government a necessary evil at best, for by its very nature it restricted the freedom of the individual. For this reason, he wanted the United States to remain a society of small independent farmers.* Such a nation did not need much political organization of any kind. Jefferson's main objection to Hamilton was that Hamilton wanted to commercialize and centralize the country. This he feared, for it would mean the growth of cities, which would make society complicated and corrupt, and hence require more regulation. "When we get piled upon one another in large cities, as in Europe," he wrote Madison in 1787, "we shall become corrupt as in Europe, and go to eating one another as they do there." He distrusted city workers;

*To Jefferson, agriculture was both the fundamental and the noblest calling of mankind. "The greatest service which can be rendered to any country is to add a useful plant to its culture," he once said.

since they did not own property, they seemed to have no stake in orderly government. Like Hamilton he believed such people easy prey for demagogues. "I consider the class of artificers as the panders of vice, and the instruments by which the liberties of a country are usually overturned," he said. "Those who labor in the earth," he also said, "are the chosen people of God, if ever He had a chosen people."

Jefferson further objected to what he considered Hamilton's pro-British orientation. Despite his ardent support of the Revolution, Hamilton admired English society and the orderliness of the British government, and he modeled much of his financial program on the British example. To the author of the Declaration of Independence, these attitudes passed all understanding. Jefferson thought English society immoral and decadent, the British system of government fundamentally corrupt. Toward France, the two took opposite positions. Jefferson was in Paris when the French Revolution broke out. He was delighted to see another blow struck at tyranny. Leading French liberals consulted him at every turn. When he returned to America as secretary of state, he continued to be sympathetic. Though he did not necessarily approve, he excused the excesses of the French upheaval far more than most Americans. To Hamilton, the violence and social disruption caused by the Revolution were anathemas.

The political conflict between Hamilton and Jefferson came to a head slowly. Despite their philosophical differences they did not disagree about practical matters at the start. Each disliked certain aspects of the Constitution, but both supported it. Jefferson went along with Hamilton's funding plan and, as we have seen, traded the assumption of state debts for a capital on the Potomac. However, when Hamilton proposed the Bank of the United States and the Whisky Tax, he dug in his heels. These measures seemed designed to benefit the northeastern commercial classes at the expense of southern and western farmers. Sensing a dastardly plot to milk the producing masses for the benefit of a few capitalists, and suspecting that Hamilton wanted to turn America into a monarchy, Jefferson joined the opposition. Late in the spring of 1791 he and James Madison, who was the real founder of the anti-Hamilton party, began to sound out other politicians. Next he appointed a friend of Madison's, the poet Philip Freneau, to a minor State Department post. Settling in Philadelphia, the new temporary capital, Freneau established a newspaper, the *National Gazette*, and was soon flailing away editorially at Hamilton and his policies. Furious, Hamilton hit back hard at Jefferson through the columns of another Philadelphia paper, John Fenno's *Gazette of the United States*.

As their quarrel became more and more personal, first Jefferson and then Hamilton appealed to Washington for support. The poor President, who hated controversy, tried to get them to bury their differences but to no avail. The only thing the two now agreed upon was that Washington, who was in ill health and wished desperately to retire, must serve a second term.

Federalists and Republicans

Around the striking personalities of these quarreling leaders, two political camps began to gather. Congressional supporters of Hamilton, taking the name "Federalists," acted increasingly in concert on important questions, while Jefferson's friends, called "Democratic Republicans," did likewise. Why national political parties emerged after the ratification of a Constitution that made no provision for such organizations is a question that has long intrigued historians. Probably the main reason for the appearance of parties was the obvious one: by creating a strong central government the Constitution produced national issues and a focus for national discussion and settlement of these issues. Furthermore, by failing to create machinery for nominating candidates for federal offices, the Constitution left a vacuum which informal party organizations promptly filled.

In the early stages, neither the Federalist nor the Democratic Republican was a party in the modern sense; there were no national committees, no conventions, no state "machines." In large measure the two parties were alliances of local and state groups, greatly influenced by parochial issues and the personalities of local leaders. Over time, however, closer-knit organizations developed; the Democratic Republicans, directed more by Madison than by Jefferson, proved more energetic and imaginative in this regard.

What determined a man's party allegiance in the 1790's is hard to pin down. No simple dichotomy between Hamiltonian business interests and Jeffersonian agrarian interests makes sense. The divisions were close, and since 90 per cent of the voters were farmers, a sharp commercial-agrarian split would have produced an overwhelming victory for the Democratic Republicans. Farmers who produced for outside markets were more likely to respond to Federalist arguments; frontiersmen and others in remote areas, to those of the Democratic Republicans. A majority of the privileged group that Hamilton appealed to especially voted Federalist, but numbers of merchants and other businessmen supported the Jeffersonians. As in the divisions over ratifying the Constitution, men of status with established interests tended to be Federalists, those on the periphery of society (and those on the make) were more often on the other side. The problem is enormously complicated by varying conditions and traditions in the separate states, many of which have not yet been studied in sufficient detail to warrant precise conclusions.

In short, no clear-cut social or economic alignments appeared, although social and economic issues were certainly discussed by the politicians. The parties stood for their leaders rather than for principles, and these men, dealing with a series of practical problems, were not always consistent in their attitudes.

The personal nature of early American political controversies, incidentally, goes far toward explaining why the party battles of the era were so bitter. So does the continuing anxiety that plagued men of both persuasions about the supposed frailty of a republican government. The United States, even to its most ardent supporters, was still very much an experiment; leaders who sincerely proclaimed their own devotion to its welfare suspected that their opponents wanted to undermine its institutions. Federalists feared that the Jeffersonians sought a dictatorship based on mob rule, Democratic Republicans that the Hamiltonians intended to make the United States into a monarchy dominated by "aristocrats."

The growing controversy over the French Revolution and the resulting war between France and Great Britain widened the split between the parties. In 1789 Hamilton had welcomed the uprising in France, telling Jefferson that he felt as elated as when the colonies had taken up arms against Great Britain. However, the execution of the king and queen, the spreading violence and social disruption, quickly disillusioned him. Soon he was complaining that the French revolt lacked the "decorum" and "dignity" of the American Revolution, and by 1793 he could speak of it only with horror. The more Hamilton and his followers attacked what they called "the French disease," the more the Republicans defended the Revolution. Slaveowners could be heard singing the praises of *liberté*, *égalité*, *fraternité*, and great southern landlords, whose French counterparts were losing their estates—some even their heads—were extolling "the glorious successes of our Gallic brethren." In the same way the Federalists began to idealize the British, whom they considered the embodiment of the forces resisting French radicalism.

This created an explosive situation. Enthusiasm for a foreign power might tempt Americans, all unwittingly, to betray their own country. Hamilton came to believe that Jefferson was so prejudiced in favor of France as to be unable to conduct foreign affairs rationally, and Jefferson could say contemptuously: "Hamilton is panick struck, if we refuse our breech to every kick which Great Britain may choose to give it."

Actually, Jefferson never lost his sense of perspective. When the Anglo-French war erupted, he recommended neutrality. In the Genêt affair, although originally sympathetic to the young envoy, Jefferson ended by characterizing him as "hotheaded, all imagination, no judgment, passionate, disrespectful and even indecent." He cordially approved Washington's decision to send him packing. Although he objected strongly to the Jay Treaty, he did so not out of fondness for France but because he believed peace with Great Britain could not be purchased by surrendering American rights. "Acquiescence under insult is not the way to escape war," he wrote in 1795.

Hamilton went a little too far in his friendliness to Great Britain. While the Jay Treaty was being negotiated in London, he weakened Jay's bargaining power by revealing to the British minister in Philadelphia that the United States had no intention of joining the League of Armed Neutrality, an organization of most of the neutral European powers, if the British did not yield to all American demands. His excuse was his belief, probably correct, that to gain anything from the proud and suspicious British, the United States must approach them in a frank and friendly manner. The real danger was that some of Hamilton's and Jefferson's excitable and less judicious followers might become so committed as to forget the true interests of the United States.

Washington's Farewell

As long as Washington remained President, the universality of his popularity and his refusal to align himself with either faction inhibited the solidification of party lines. On major questions of finance and foreign policy, he usually sided with Hamilton and thus increasingly incurred the anger of Jefferson. But he was, after all, a Virginian. Only the most rabid partisan could think him a tool of northern commercial interests. He remained as he intended himself to be, a symbol of national unity. Yet he was old and in ill health and determined to put away the cares of office at the end of his second term. In September 1796 he announced his retirement in a "Farewell Address" to the nation.

Washington had found the acrimonious political rivalry between Federalists and Republicans very disturbing. Hamilton advocated national unity, but he seemed perfectly ready to smash any individual or faction that disagreed with his vision of the country's future. Jefferson had risked his neck for independence but would not sanction the kind of economic development needed to make America strong enough to defend that independence. Washington, less brilliant than either Hamilton or Jefferson, saw the world more cearly and appreciated how important it was that the new nation remain at peace—not only with the rest of the world but with itself. In his farewell he tried to show how the North benefited from the prosperity of the South, the South from that of the North, and the East and West also, in reciprocal fashion. "Unity," he wrote, was "a main pillar" of "real independence." He deplored the "baneful effects of the spirit of party" that led honest men to use dishonest means to win a mean advantage over fellow Americans.

He also urged the people to avoid both "inveterate antipathies" and "passionate attachments" to any foreign nation. Nothing had alarmed him more than the sight of Americans dividing into "French" and "English" factions. Furthermore, France had repeatedly interfered in American domestic affairs. First there had been Genêt, childish but exasperating. Later another French minister, Citizen Adet, had tried to prejudice both Congress and public opinion against the Jay Treaty. Ader also attempted to organize on American soil an expedition to conquer Louisiana for France. "Against the insidious wiles of foreign influence," Washington now warned, "the jealousy of a free people ought to be *constantly* awake." America should develop its foreign trade but steer clear of foreign political connections as far as possible. "Permanent alliances" should be avoided, although "temporary alliances for extraordinary purposes" might be sometimes useful.

Election of 1796

Washington's Farewell Address was destined to have a long and important influence upon American thinking, but its immediate impact was small. He had intended it to cool political passions. Instead, in the words of one Federalist congressman, men took it as "a signal, like dropping a hat, for the party racers to start." A few weeks after its publication Citizen Adet was again meddling in American affairs, seeking to influence the election by threatening new attacks on American shipping. All would be well between France and America, he hinted, if the voters threw out the Federalists. By the time the Presidential campaign had ended, many Federalists and Republicans were refusing to speak to one another.

Jefferson was the only Republican candidate seriously considered in 1796. The logical Federalist, of course, was Hamilton, but, as was to happen so often in American history with powerful and active political leaders, he was not considered "available" because his controversial policies had made him many enemies. Gathering in caucus, the Federalists in Congress nominated Vice President John Adams for the top office and Thomas Pinckney, negotiator of the popular Spanish treaty, for Vice President. In the election the Federalists won a majority. But Hamilton, hoping to run the new administration from the wings, preferred Pinckney, a relatively weak character, to the tough-minded Adams, so he arranged for some Federalist electors to vote only for Pinckney. Catching wind of this, a number of Adams' electors retaliated by cutting Pinckney. As a result, Adams won in the Electoral College, 71 to 68, over Jefferson, who had the solid support of the Republican electors, while Pinckney was third. Jefferson thus became Vice President.

This unexpected result seemed to presage a decline in partisanship. Jefferson and Adams regarded each other highly. Indeed, Adams preferred the Virginian to Pinckney for the Vice Presidency, while Jefferson said that if only Adams would "relinquish his bias to an English constitution," he might make a fine Chief Executive. The two had in common a distaste for Hamilton, a powerful bond.

However, the closeness of the election indicated a trend toward the Republicans, who were making constant and effective use of the canard that the Federalists were "monocrats" (monarchists) determined to destroy American liberty. Without Washington to lead them, the Federalist politicians were already quarreling among themselves like starlings over a crust, whereas honest, able, hard-working John Adams was too caustic and too scathingly frank to attract broad support among the voters. The unpopularity of the Jay Treaty hurt the Federalists further. Everything, in March 1797, seemed to indicate a Republican victory at the next election.

The XYZ Affair

At this point came one of the most remarkable revolutions of public feeling in American history. French attacks on American shipping, begun out of irritation at the Jay Treaty and in order to influence the election, continued after Adams took office. Hoping to stop these depredations, Adams appointed three commissioners (Charles Pinckney, United States minister to France and elder brother of Thomas; John Marshall, a prominent Virginia Federalist; and Elbridge Gerry of Massachusetts, a former congressman who was a friend of Jefferson's but not closely identified with either party) to try to negotiate a settlement. Their mission was a complete fiasco. Talleyrand, the French foreign minister, sent three agents (later spoken of as X, Y, and Z) to demand a huge bribe as the price of making a deal. The Americans refused, more because they suspected Talleyrand's good faith than through any distaste for bribery. "No, no, not a sixpence," Pinckney told the agents. The talks broke up, and in April 1798 President Adams released the commissioners' reports.

They caused an immediate sensation. Americans' sense of national honor, perhaps overly tender because the country was so young and insecure, was outraged. Pinckney's laconic refusal to pay a bribe was translated into the grandiose phrase: "Millions for defense, but not one cent for tribute!" and spread broadcast through the land. John Adams, never a man with much mass appeal, suddenly found himself a national hero. Federalist hotheads burned for a fight. Their newspapers overflowed with denunciations of France. Congress unilaterally abrogated the French Alliance, created a Navy Department, and appropriated enough money to build 40-odd warships and triple the size of the army. Washington came out of retirement to lead the forces, with Hamilton, now a general, as second in command. On the seas, American privateers began to attack French shipping.

A call for a declaration of war would have been immensely popular. But perhaps—it is not an entirely illogical surmise about John Adams—the President did not want to be popular. Furthermore, he knew that the United States had only 3,500 men under arms and a navy of exactly three vessels. Instead of calling for war, he contented himself with approving the build-up of American forces.

The Republicans, committed to friendship for France, were thrown into consternation. Although

HISTORICAL SOCIETY OF PENNSYLVANIA

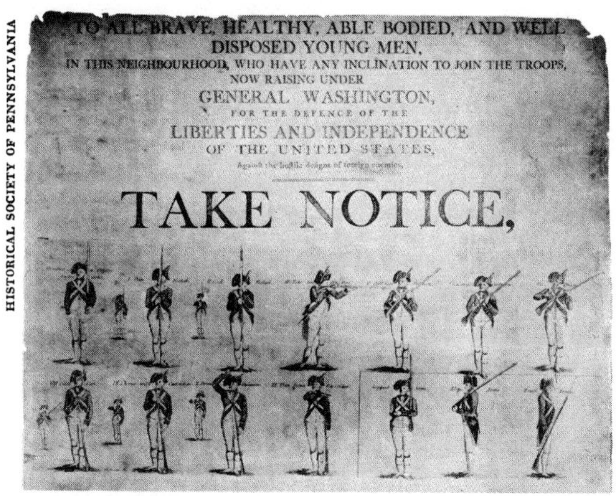

A recruiting poster of 1798 appealed for volunteers to defend the nation "against the hostile designs of foreign enemies," the "enemies" being the French.

angered by the XYZ Affair, they hoped to avoid war and tried, as one angry Federalist put it, "to clog the wheels of government" by opposing the preparedness legislation. Their newspapers, in keeping with the coarse journalistic standards of the day, spewed abuse on Adams and his administration. Benjamin Bache, editor of the Philadelphia *Aurora,* referred to the President as "blind, bald, toothless, querulous," which was three-quarters true, but irrelevant. John Daly Burk of the New York *Time Piece* called him a "mock Monarch," surrounded by a "*court* composed of tories and speculators," which was a flat lie.

Because of this virulent reaction, many Federalists expected the Republicans to side with France if war broke out. Hysterical and near to panic, these Federalists easily persuaded themselves that the danger of subversion was acute. The French Revolution and the resulting war were churning European society to the depths, stirring the hopes of liberals and striking fear in the hearts of conservatives. Refugees of both persuasions were often forced to flee their homes, and many of them came to the United States, always a haven for the dispossessed and the discontented. Suddenly the presence of these foreigners seemed threatening to "native" Americans. Benjamin Bache was a grandson of Benjamin Franklin, but Burk, for example, was Irish-born. The leader of the Republican opposition in Congress was a former Genevan, Albert Gallatin.

Alien and Sedition Acts

Conservative Federalists saw in this situation a chance to smash the liberal opposition. In June and July 1798 they pushed through Congress a series of repressive measures known as the Alien and Sedition Acts. The least offensive of these laws, the Naturalization Act, increased the period a foreigner had to reside in the United States before being eligible for citizenship from 5 to 14 years. The Alien Enemies Act gave the President the power to arrest or expel enemy aliens in time of "declared war," but since the quasi-war with France was never declared, this measure had no practical importance. The Alien Act authorized the President to expel *all* aliens whom he thought "dangerous to the peace and safety of the United States." (Adams never invoked this law, but a number of aliens left the country out of fear that he might.) Finally, there was the Sedition Act. Its first section, making it a crime "to impede the operation of any law" or attempt to instigate a riot or insurrection, was reasonable enough; but the act also made it illegal to publish, or even to utter, any "false, scandalous and malicious" criticism of high government officials.

Although based on English precedents and actually milder than British sedition laws, this proviso rested, as James Madison said, on "the exploded doctrine" that government officials "are the masters and not the servants of the people." To criticize a king is to try to undermine the respect of his subjects for the establishment over which he rules, and that is seditious. To criticize an elected official in a republic is to express dissatisfaction with the way one's agent is performing his assigned task, certainly no threat to the state itself. The fundamental difference between these two modes of thought escaped the Federalists of 1798.

This, of course, is mere theory. Far worse was the Federalists' practice under the Sedition Act. As the election of 1800 approached, they made a systematic attempt to silence the leading Republican newspapers of the country. Twenty-five persons were prosecuted and ten convicted, all in patently unfair trials. In typical cases, editor Thomas Cooper was sentenced to six months in jail and fined $400, editor Charles Holt got three months and a $200 fine, editor James Callender got nine months and a $200 fine. Admittedly, in some instances, the criticisms of the Adams administration had been very raw, yet equally harsh things were being said with impunity by Federalist editors about Vice President Jefferson. When Cooper, a distinguished English-born radical and later president of the University of South Carolina, attempted after serving his sentence to have Hamilton prosecuted for *his* intemperate attacks on President Adams, he got nowhere.

To Thomas Jefferson, the Alien and Sedition Acts went "palpably in the teeth of the Constitution," being in plain violation of the First Amendment's guarantees of freedom of speech and the press and an invasion of the rights of the states.* He conferred with Madison, and they decided to draw up resolutions condemning the laws. Madison's were eventually presented to the Virginia legislature and Jefferson's to the legislature of Kentucky. Since the Constitution was a compact made by sovereign states, each state had "an equal right to judge for itself" when the compact had been violated, the Kentucky Resolves declared. Thus a state could declare a law of Congress unconstitutional. The Virginia Resolves took an only slightly less forthright position.

Actually, neither Kentucky nor Virginia acted to implement these resolves or to interfere with the enforcement of the Alien and Sedition Acts. Jefferson and Madison were protesting against Federalist highhandedness and firing the opening salvo of Jefferson's campaign for the Presidency, not advancing a new constitutional theory of extreme states' rights. "Keep away all show of force," Jefferson advised his supporters.

This was sound advice, for time and the march of events were again playing into the hands of the Republicans. Talleyrand had never wanted war with the United States. When he finally realized how vehemently the Americans had reacted to his little attempt to replenish his personal fortune, depleted during the Revolution, he let Adams know that new negotiators would be properly received.

*Jefferson had no objection per se to state sedition laws.

President Adams quickly grasped the importance of the French change of heart, for like Washington before him, he never forgot that the country needed peace and tranquillity in order to grow stronger and more closely knit. The top Federalists, however, had lost their heads. By shouting about the French danger, they had roused the country against radicalism; they did not intend to surrender this advantage tamely. Hamilton in particular wanted war at almost any price—if not against France, then against Spain. He saw himself at the head of the new American army sweeping first across Louisiana and the Floridas, and then on to the south. "We ought to squint at South America," he suggested. "Our game will be to attack where we can," he added. "Tempting objects will be without our grasp."

The British cleverly played upon Federalist ambitions, hinting at further commercial concessions, talking of convoying American merchant vessels in case of a Franco-American war, even suggesting to the United States minister in London, Rufus King, the idea of a British-American attack on South America. But the Puritan Adams was a specialist at resisting temptation. He would neither go to war merely to destroy the political opposition in America nor follow "the fools who were intriguing to plunge us into an alliance with England . . . and wild expeditions to South America." Without consulting his Cabinet, which Hamilton dominated, he submitted to the Senate the name of a new minister plenipotentiary to France. When the Federalists tried to block the appointment, Adams threatened to resign. That would have made Jefferson President! So the furious Federalists had to give in, although they forced Adams to agree to send three men instead of one.

Napoleon had taken over France by the time the Americans arrived, and he drove a harder bargain than Talleyrand would have, but in the end he signed an agreement (the Convention of 1800) abrogating the Franco-American treaties of 1778. Nothing was said about the damage done to American shipping by the French, but the war scare was over.

Election of 1800

Suddenly the public realized that the furor about war and subversion had been concocted almost out of thin air. Federalist military preparations had necessitated heavy new taxes that now seemed unnecessary. Nevertheless, the Presidential contest between Adams and Jefferson was close. Because of his stand for peace, Adams personally escaped the brunt of popular indignation against the Federalist party. His solid qualities had a strong appeal to conservatives, and fear that the Republicans would introduce wild "French" social reforms did not disappear. Many nationalist-minded voters worried lest the strong government established by the Federalists be disrupted by the Jeffersonians in the name of states' rights.

Under Providence's approving eye, the national bird stops Francophile Jefferson from burning the Constitution on an "Altar of Gallic Despotism." Jefferson's Mazzei letter (1796) charged the government with being reactionary. An 1800 Federalist cartoon.

The economic progress stimulated by Hamilton's financial reforms also seemed threatened. When the electors' votes were counted in February 1801, the Republicans were discovered to have won by the narrow margin of 73 to 65.

But *which* Republican? The Constitution did not distinguish between Presidential and Vice Presidential candidates, providing only that each elector should vote for two men, with the top man becoming President and the runner-up Vice President. The Vice Presidential candidate of the Republicans was Aaron Burr of New York, a former senator and a rival of Hamilton in law and politics. However, Republican party solidarity had been perfect: Jefferson and Burr received 73 votes each. Because of the tie, it devolved upon the House of Representatives (voting by states) to choose between them.

In the House the Republicans could control only 8 of the 16 state delegations. On the first ballot Jefferson got these 8 votes, one short of election, while 6 states voted for Burr. Two state delegations, being evenly split, lost their votes. Through 35 ballots this deadlock persisted; the Federalists, fearful of Jefferson's radicalism, voted solidly for Burr. Great pressures were exerted on both candidates to make deals to win additional support. Officially at least, both refused. Burr put on a great show of remaining above the battle, although had he really been an honorable man, he would have withdrawn, since the voters had clearly intended him for the second spot. Whether Jefferson made any promises is uncertain; there is some evidence that to break the deadlock he assured the Federalists that he would preserve Hamilton's financial system and continue the Washington-Adams foreign policy. Hamilton played an important part in the negotiations behind the scenes; he detested Burr and threw his weight to Jefferson. Finally, on February 17, 1801, the Federalists yielded, and Jefferson was elected. Burr, of course, became Vice President. To make sure that this distressing scene would never be repeated, the Twelfth Amendment was drafted, providing for separate balloting in the Electoral College for President and Vice President. This change was ratified in 1804, shortly before the next election.

The Federalist Contribution

On March 4, 1801, in the raw new national capital on the Potomac River named in honor of the Father of his Country, Thomas Jefferson took the Presidential oath and delivered his inaugural address. The new President believed that a revolution as important as that heralded by his immortal Declaration of Independence had occurred, and for once most of his enemies agreed with him heartily.

Certainly, an era had ended. In the years between the Peace of Paris and Jay's Treaty, the Federalists practically monopolized the political good sense of the nation. In the perspective of history they were "right" in strengthening the federal government, in establishing a sound fiscal system, in trying to diversify the economy, in seeking an accommodation with Great Britain, and in refusing to be carried away with enthusiasm for France despite the bright dreams inspired by the French Revolution. The Federalists had also displayed remarkable self-control and moderation—at least up until 1798. They were nationalists who did not try to destroy local patriotism, aristocrats willing to live with the spirit of democracy. The Constitution is their monument, with its wise compromises, its balance of forces, its restraint, its practical concessions to local prejudices.

But the Federalists were unable to face up to defeat. When they saw the Jeffersonians gathering strength by developing clever new techniques of party organization and propaganda, mouthing slogans about "monocrats," glorifying both the past with its satisfying simplicity and the future with its promise of a glorious day when all men would be free, equal, and brothers, they panicked. Abandoning the sober wisdom of their great period, they fought ignobly to save themselves at any cost. The effort only turned defeat into rout. Jefferson's victory, fairly close in the Electoral College, approached landslide proportions in the congressional elections, where popular feeling could express itself directly. Before the election the Republicans held only 42 seats in the House of Representatives; in the new Congress they held 69 out of a total of 105.

MARYLAND HISTORICAL SOCIETY

Jefferson had entered—unsuccessfully— the competition to design the Executive Mansion into which he moved in March 1801. The winning design, reproduced here, won $500 for Irish-born architect James Hoban. Construction started in 1792, and the building was finished late in John Adams' term; Adams lived there but four months.

Jefferson erred, however, in calling this triumph a revolution. The real upheaval had been attempted in 1798, and it was Federalist inspired, and it failed. In 1800 the voters had expressed a preference for the old over the new. And Jefferson, despite Federalist fears that he would destroy the Constitution and establish a radical new social order, presided instead over a regime that confirmed the great achievements of the Federalist era.

Indeed, what was perhaps most significant about the election of 1800 was that it was *not* a revolution. After a bitter contest the Jeffersonians took power and proceeded to change the policy of the government. They did so peacefully. Thus American republican government passed a crucial test: control of its machinery had changed hands in a democratic and orderly way. And only less significant, the informal party system had demonstrated its usefulness. The Jeffersonians had organized popular dissatisfaction with Federalist policies, formulated a platform of reform, chosen leaders to put their plans into effect, and elected these leaders to office.

WHITE HOUSE COLLECTION

In 1800 Jefferson sat for the most talented of the numerous artistic offspring of his friend Charles Willson Peale, the 22-year-old portraitist Rembrandt.

Jefferson as President

The novelty of the new administration lay in its style and its moderation. Both were apparent in Jefferson's inaugural address. The new President's opening remarks showed that he was neither a demagogue nor a firebrand. "The task is above my talents," he said modestly, "and . . . I approach it with . . . anxious and awful presentiments." The people had spoken, and their voice must be heeded, but the rights of dissenters must also be respected. "All . . . will bear in mind this sacred principle," Jefferson said, "that though the will of the majority is in all cases to prevail, that will to be rightful must be reasonable; that the minority possess their equal rights, which equal law must protect, and to violate would be oppression." Jefferson also spoke at some length about specific policies. He declared himself against "entangling alliances" and for economy in government, and he promised to pay off the national debt, preserve the government's credit, and stimulate both agriculture and its "handmaid," commerce. His main stress was on the cooling of partisan passions. "Every difference of opinion is not a difference of principle. We have called by different names brethren of the same principle. We are all Republicans—we are all Federalists." And he promised the country "a wise and frugal Government, which shall restrain men from injuring one another . . . [and] leave them otherwise free to regulate their own pursuits. . . ."

In office Jefferson quickly demonstrated the sincerity of these remarks. He saw to it that the Whisky Tax and other Federalist excises were repealed, and made sharp cuts in military and naval expenditures to keep the budget in balance. The national debt was reduced from $83 million to $57 million during his eight years. The Naturalization Act of 1798 was also repealed and the old five-year-residence requirement for citizenship restored. The Sedition Act and the Alien Act expired of their own accord in 1801 and 1802. These changes were certainly not drastic. Jefferson made no effort to tear down the fiscal structure that Hamilton had erected. "We can pay off his debt," the new President confessed, "but we cannot get rid of his financial system." Nor did the author of the Kentucky Resolves try to alter the balance of federal-state power.

Yet there was a different tone to the new regime. Jefferson sincerely believed in the worth of the individual and had no desire to surround himself with pomp and ceremony; the excessive formality and punctilio of the Washington and Adams administrations had been distasteful to him. He made sure that his own household was less cluttered by ritualistic displays. From the moment of his election, he played down the ceremonial aspects of the Presidency. He asked that he be officially notified of his election by mail rather than by a committee, and he would have preferred to have taken the oath at Charlottesville, near Monticello, his home, rather than at Washington. After the inauguration, he went back to his boarding house on foot and took dinner in his usual seat at the common table.

In the White House he often wore a frayed coat and carpet slippers, even to receive the representatives of foreign powers when they arrived, all resplendent with silk ribbons and a sense of their own importance, to present their credentials. At social affairs he paid little heed to the status and seniority of his guests. When dinner was announced he offered his arm to whichever lady he was talking to at the moment and placed her at his right; other guests were free to sit wherever they could find an empty chair. During business hours congressmen, friends, foreign officials, and plain citizens coming to call took their turn in the order of their arrival. "The principle of society with us," Jefferson explained, "is the equal rights of all. . . . Nobody shall be above you, nor you above anybody, *pell-mell* is our law."

"Pell-mell" was also good politics, and despite his distaste for controversy and his lack of interest in the routine aspects of administration, Jefferson was a superb politician. He gave dozens of small stag dinner parties for congressmen, serving the food personally from a dumbwaiter connected with the kitchen. The guests, carefully chosen to make congenial groups, were seated at a round table to encourage general conversation; the food and wine were first class. These were ostensibly social occasions—shoptalk was avoided—yet they paid large political dividends. Jefferson learned to know every congressman personally, Democratic Republican and Federalist alike, and not only their political views but their strengths of character, their quirks and flaws. He was also able to work his personal magic upon them; to display the fantastic breadth of his knowledge, his charm and wit, his total lack of pomposity. "You see, we are alone and *our walls have no ears*," he would say, and while the wine flowed and the guests sampled the delicacies prepared by Jefferson's French chef, the President manufactured political capital. "You drink as you please and converse at your ease," one senator-guest reported.

Jefferson also made effective use of his close supporters in Congress, and of Cabinet members as well, in persuading Congress to go along with his proposals. His state papers were models of sweet reason, minimizing conflicts, stressing areas where all honest men must agree. After all, as he indicated in his inaugural address, nearly all Americans *were* both federalists and republicans, no great principle divided them into irreconcilable camps. Jefferson set out to bring them all into *his* camp and succeeded so remarkably in four years that when he ran for re-election against Charles Pinckney, he got 162 of the 176 electoral votes cast. Eventually even John Quincy Adams, son of the second President, became a Jeffersonian. At the same time Jefferson was anything but nonpartisan in the sense that Washington had been. His Cabinet consisted exclusively of men of his own party. He exerted almost continuous pressure on Congress to make sure that his legislative program was enacted into law. He did not actually remove many Federalist officeholders, and at one point he remarked ruefully that government officials seldom died and never resigned; but when he could, he used his power of appointment to reward his friends and punish his enemies.

Attack on the Judiciary

The one area that gave Jefferson serious trouble during his first term involved the courts. Although notably open-minded and tolerant, he had a few stubborn prejudices. One was against kings, another against the British system of government. A third was against judges, or rather, against entrenched judicial power. While recognizing that judges must have a degree of independence, he feared what he called their "habit of going out of the question before them, to throw an anchor ahead, and grapple further hold for future advances of power." The biased behavior of Federalist judges during the trials under the Sedition Act enormously increased this basic distrust. It burst all bounds when the Federalist majority of the dying Congress rammed through the Judiciary Act of 1801 in a last-ditch effort to "protect" the country against Jeffersonian radicalism.

The Judiciary Act created 6 new circuit courts, presided over by 16 new federal judges, and a small army of attorneys, marshals, and clerks. The expanding country needed these judges, but with the enthusiastic cooperation of President Adams the Federalists made shameless use of the opportunity to fill all the new positions with conservative Federalists, and it was this that angered Jefferson. (Adams' action, he said bitterly, was "personally unkind.") Adams also appointed John Marshall of Virginia, whom Jefferson particularly disliked, as chief justice of the Supreme Court. The new appointees were dubbed "midnight justices" because, according to rumor, Adams stayed up till midnight on March 3, his last day as President, feverishly signing their commissions.

The Republicans retaliated as soon as the new Congress met by repealing the Judiciary Act of 1801, but President Jefferson still fumed. Upon taking office he had discovered that in the confusion of Adams' last hours the commissions of a number of justices of the peace for the new District of Columbia had not been distributed. Although these were small fry indeed, Jefferson was so angry that he ordered the commissions held up, even though they had been signed by President Adams. When this happened, one of Adams' appointees, William Marbury, petitioned the Supreme Court for a writ of *mandamus* ordering the new secretary of state, James Madison, to give him his commission.

The case of *Marbury v. Madison* placed Chief Justice Marshall in a most embarrassing position. Marbury certainly had a strong claim. If Marshall refused to issue a *mandamus*, everyone would say he dared not stand up to Jefferson, and the prestige of the Court would suffer. Yet if he issued the writ, he would place the Court in direct conflict with the Executive. Madison would probably ignore the order, and in the prevailing state of public opinion nothing would be done to make him act. This would be a still more staggering blow to the judiciary. What should the chief justice do?

Marshall had studied law only briefly and had no judicial experience, but in this crisis he first displayed the genius that was to mark him as a truly great judge. By right Marbury should have his commission, he announced. However, the Court could not require Madison to give it to him. Marbury's request for a *mandamus* had been based on an ambiguous clause in the Judiciary Act of 1789. That clause was unconstitutional, Marshall declared, and therefore void. Congress could not legally give the Supreme Court the right to issue writs of *mandamus* in such circumstances.

With the skill and foresight of a chess grand master, Marshall turned what had looked like a trap into a triumph. By sacrificing the pawn, Marbury, he established the power of the Supreme Court to invalidate federal laws that conflicted with the Constitution. Jefferson could not check him because instead of throwing an anchor ahead, as Jefferson had feared, Marshall had *refused* power. Yet he had certainly grappled a "further hold for future advances of power," and the President could do nothing to stop him.

The Marbury case made Jefferson still more determined to strike at the Federalist-dominated courts. He decided to press for the impeachment of some of the more partisan judges. First he had the House of Representatives bring charges against District Judge John Pickering. Pickering was clearly insane—he had frequently delivered profane and drunken harangues from the bench—and the Senate quickly voted to remove him. Then Jefferson went after a much larger fish, Samuel Chase, associate justice of the Supreme Court. Chase had been prominent for decades, an early leader of the Sons of Liberty, a signer of the Declaration of Independence, active in the affairs of the Continental Congress. Washington had named him to the Supreme Court in 1796, and he had delivered a number of important opinions. But his handling of cases under the Sedition Act had been outrageously highhanded. Defense lawyers had become so exasperated as to throw down their briefs in disgust at some of his prejudiced rulings. Jefferson made a mighty effort to have the Senate convict him, but Chase's actions had not constituted the "high crimes and misdemeanors" required by the Constitution to remove a judge, and Chase was acquitted. This was a good thing, for the attack on him, as vindictive as his own behavior in the sedition cases, endangered the independence of the courts and thus threatened justice itself.

The Barbary Pirates

Aside from these probably salutary setbacks, Jefferson's first term was a parade of triumphs. Although he cut back the army and navy sharply in order to save money, he temporarily escaped the consequences of leaving the country undefended because of the lull in the European war signalized by the Treaty of Amiens between Great Britain and France in March 1802. Despite the fact that he had only seven frigates in commission, he even managed to fight a small naval war with the Barbary pirates without damage to American interests or prestige.

The North African Arab states of Morocco, Algiers, Tunis, and Tripoli had for decades levied tribute on Mediterranean shipping, the European powers finding it simpler to pay them annual protection money than to crush them. "Bribery and corruption," an American diplomat explained, "answers their purpose better . . . than a noble retaliation." Under Washington and Adams, the United States joined in the payment of this tribute. Such pusillanimity ran against Jefferson's grain—"When this idea comes across my mind, my faculties are absolutely suspended between indignation and impatience," he said—and when the pasha of Tripoli tried to raise the charges he balked. Tripoli then declared war in May 1801, and Jefferson dispatched a squadron to the Mediterranean.

In the words of one historian, the action was "halfhearted and ill-starred." The pirates were not overwhelmed and a major American warship, the frigate *Philadelphia*, had to be destroyed after running aground off the Tripolitanian coast. The payment of tribute continued until 1815. Just the same, America, though far removed from the pirate bases, was the only maritime nation that even tried to resist the shameful blackmail of the Barbary States at this time. Although the war failed to achieve Jefferson's purpose of ending the payments entirely and convincing the pirates "that they mistake their interests in choosing war," its final effect was positive. The pasha agreed to a new treaty more favorable to the United States, and American sailors, led by Commodore Edward Preble, won much valuable experience and a large portion of fame. The greatest hero was Lieutenant Stephen Decatur, who captured two pirate ships, led ten men in a daring raid on another in which he took on a gigantic sailor in a wild battle of cutlass against boarding pike,* and snatched the stricken *Philadelphia* from the pirates by sneaking aboard and setting her afire.

The Louisiana Purchase

The major achievements of Jefferson's first term had to do with the American West, and of these the greatest by far was the acquisition of the huge area between the Mississippi River and the Rocky Mountains. In a sense the purchase of this region, called Louisiana, was fortuitous, an accidental by-product of European political adjustments and of the whim of Napoleon Bonaparte. Certainly Jefferson had not planned it, for in his inaugural address he had expressed the opinion that the country already had all the land it would need for a thousand generations. It was nonetheless perfectly logical, one might almost say inevitable—the result of a long series of events in the history of the Mississippi Valley.

Along with every other American who had even a superficial interest in the West, Jefferson understood that the United States must have access to the mouth of the Mississippi and the

*Decatur killed the pirate by firing a small pistol from his pocket as his opponent was about to skewer him.

city of New Orleans or eventually lose everything beyond the Appalachians. "There is on the globe one single spot, the possessor of which is our natural and habitual enemy," he was soon to write. "It is New Orleans." Thus, when he learned shortly after his inauguration that Spain had given Louisiana back to France, he was immediately on his guard. Control of Louisiana by Spain, a "feeble" country with "pacific dispositions," could be tolerated; control by a resurgent France, now dominated by Napoleon, the greatest military genius of the age, was something entirely different. Did Napoleon have designs on Canada? Did he perhaps mean to resume the old Spanish and British game of encouraging the Indians to harry the American frontier? And what now would be the status of Pinckney's precious treaty? Deeply worried, the President instructed his newly appointed minister to France, Robert R. Livingston, to seek assurances that American rights in New Orleans would be respected and to negotiate, if possible, the purchase of West Florida in case that region had also been turned over to France.

Jefferson's concern was well founded; France was indeed planning new imperial ventures in North America. Ever since the days of Citizen Genêt, the French had been moving in this direction. Immediately after settling their difficulties with the United States through the Convention of 1800, they signed the secret Treaty of San Ildefonso with Spain, which returned Louisiana to France. Napoleon hoped to use this region as a breadbasket for the French West Indian sugar plantations, just as colonies like Pennsylvania and Massachusetts had fed the British sugar islands before the Revolution.

However, the most important French island, Santo Domingo, had slipped from French control. At the time of the French Revolution the slaves of the island had revolted. In 1793 they were granted personal freedom, but they fought on under the leadership of the "Black Napoleon," a

IRVING S. OLDS COLLECTION

The shelling of Tripoli on August 3, 1804, by Commodore Edward Preble's squadron is the subject of this print. Preble's flagship Constitution *(at right) and his gunboats continued their heavy fire for two hours. "The Town of Tripoli, as well as the Shipping in the Harbor has suffered very considerably," Preble reported. Five such bombardments in the fall of 1804 helped persuade the Tripolitanian pirates to modify their tribute demands.*

self-taught genius named Toussaint L'Ouverture, and by 1801 Santo Domingo was entirely in their hands. But the original Napoleon, taking advantage of the slackening of war in Europe, dispatched an army of 20,000 men under General Charles Leclerc to reconquer the island.

When Jefferson learned of the Leclerc expedition, he had no trouble divining its relationship to Louisiana, even though the actual transfer of that territory to France had not yet occurred. His uneasiness became outright alarm. In April 1802 he again urged Minister Livingston to attempt the purchase of New Orleans and Florida or, as an alternative, to buy a tract of land near the mouth of the Mississippi where a new port could be constructed. Of necessity, the mild-mannered idealistic President now became an aggressive realist. If the right of deposit could not be preserved through negotiation, it must be purchased with gunpowder, even if that meant acting in conjunction with the despised British. "The day that France takes possession of New Orleans," he warned, "we must marry ourselves to the British fleet and nation."

Then, in October 1802, the Spanish heightened the tension by suddenly revoking the right of deposit at New Orleans. We now know that the French had no hand in this action, but it was beyond reason to expect Jefferson or the American people to believe it at the time. With the West clamoring for relief, Jefferson appointed his friend and disciple James Monroe as minister plenipotentiary and sent him off to Paris with instructions to offer up to $10 million for New Orleans and Florida. If France refused to make any settlement, he and Livingston should open negotiations for a "closer connection" with the British.

Fortunately, before Monroe reached France the tension was broken. General Leclerc's expedition to Santo Domingo ended in disaster. Although Toussaint surrendered, native resistance continued. Yellow fever raged uncontrolled through the French army. Leclerc himself fell before the fever, which wiped out practically his entire force.

When news of this calamity reached Napoleon early in 1803, he began to have second thoughts about reviving French imperialism in the New World. Without Santo Domingo the wilderness of Louisiana seemed of little value. Napoleon was also preparing to reopen his campaigns in Europe. He could no longer spare troops to win the pestilential jungles of Santo Domingo or hold Louisiana against a possible British attack, and he needed money. For some weeks the commander of the most powerful army in the world mulled over the question without consulting anyone. Then, with characteristic suddenness, he made up his mind. On April 10 he ordered Foreign Minister Talleyrand to offer not merely New Orleans but all of Louisiana to the Americans. The next day Talleyrand summoned Livingston to his office on the rue de Bac and dropped this bombshell. Livingston was almost struck speechless but quickly recovered his composure. When Talleyrand asked what the United States would give for the province, he suggested the French equivalent of about $5 million. Talleyrand pronounced this sum "too low" and urged Livingston to think about the subject for a day or two.

Livingston faced a situation that could never confront a modern diplomat in this world of radio and the jet. His instructions said nothing about buying an area almost as large as the entire United States, but there was no time to write home for new ones. As a good states'-rights Jeffersonian he had grave doubts that such a purchase was even constitutional. Yet the offer staggered the imagination. Luckily, Monroe arrived the very next day to share the responsibility of making a decision. The two Americans consulted, dickered with the French, and finally agreed—they could scarcely have done otherwise—to accept the proposal. Early in May they signed a treaty. For 60 million francs—about $15 million—the United States was to have all Louisiana.

No one knew how large the region was or what it contained. When Livingston asked Talleyrand about the boundaries of the purchase, he replied: "I can give you no direction. You have made a noble bargain for yourselves, and I suppose you will make the most of it." Never, as the historian Henry Adams wrote, "did the United States government get so much for so little."

Napoleon's unexpected concession caused consternation in America, although there was never any real doubt that the treaty would be ratified. Jefferson did not believe that the government had the power under the Constitution to add new territory, or grant American citizenship to the 50,000 residents of Louisiana by executive act, as the treaty required. He even drafted an amendment: "The province of Louisiana is incorporated with the United States and made part thereof," but his advisers convinced him that it would be dangerous to delay ratification until an amendment could be acted upon by three-fourths of the states. Jefferson then suggested that the Senate ratify the treaty and submit an amendment afterward "confirming an act which the nation had not previously authorized." This idea was so obviously illogical that he quickly dropped it. Finally, he came to believe "that the less we say about constitutional difficulties the better." Since what he called "the good sense of our country" clearly wanted Louisiana, he decided to "acquiesce with satisfaction" while Congress overlooked the "metaphysical subtleties" of the problem and ratified the treaty.

Now some of the more partisan Federalists, who had been eager to fight Spain for New Orleans, attacked Jefferson for undermining the Constitution. Even Hamilton expressed some hesitation about absorbing "this new, immense, unbounded world," although he had dreamed of seizing still larger domains himself. In the end, however, Hamilton's nationalism reasserted itself, and he urged ratification of the treaty, as did such other important Federalists as John Adams and John Marshall. And in a way the Louisiana Purchase was as much Hamilton's doing as Jefferson's. Napoleon accepted payment in United States bonds, which he promptly sold to European investors. If Hamilton had not established the nation's credit so soundly, such a large issue could never have been so easily disposed of. It was ironic—and a man as perceptive as Hamilton must surely have recognized the irony—that the acquisition of Louisiana assured Jefferson's re-election and further contributed to the collapse of Federalism. The purchase was popular even in the New England bastions of that party. While the negotiations were progressing in Paris, Jefferson had written of partisan political affairs: "If we can settle happily the difficulties of the Mississippi, I think we may promise ourselves smooth seas during our time." These words turned out to be no more accurate than most political predictions, but the Louisiana Purchase certainly drove another large spike into Federalism's coffin.

Federalism Discredited

The West and South were solid for Jefferson, and the North was rapidly succumbing to his charm. The addition of new western states would soon further reduce New England's power in national affairs. So complete did the Republican triumph seem that certain die-hard Federalists in New England began to think of secession. Led by former Secretary of State Timothy Pickering, a sour, implacable, narrow-minded conservative, a group of these Federalists, known as the Essex Junto, organized in 1804 a scheme to break away from the Union and establish a "Northern Confederacy."

The plan was entirely unrealistic, for even within the dwindling Federalist ranks the Junto had little support. Hamilton flatly rejected Junto advances, and other prominent leaders also refused to participate in the plot. Nevertheless, Pickering and his friends pushed ahead, drafting a plan whereby, having captured political control of New York, they would take the entire Northeast out of the Union. Yet they could not even begin to win New York for anyone in their own ranks. They therefore hit upon the idea of supporting Vice President Aaron Burr, who was running against the "regular" Republican candidate for governor of New York. Although Burr did not promise to bring New York into their confederacy if elected, he encouraged them enough to win their backing. The foolishness of the whole plot was revealed on election day: Burr was overwhelmed by the regular Republican. The Junto's scheme immediately collapsed.

The incident, however, had a tragic aftermath. Hamilton had campaigned against Burr in his most vitriolic style. When he continued after the election to cast aspersions on Burr's character (a not very difficult assignment, since Burr frequently violated both the political and sexual

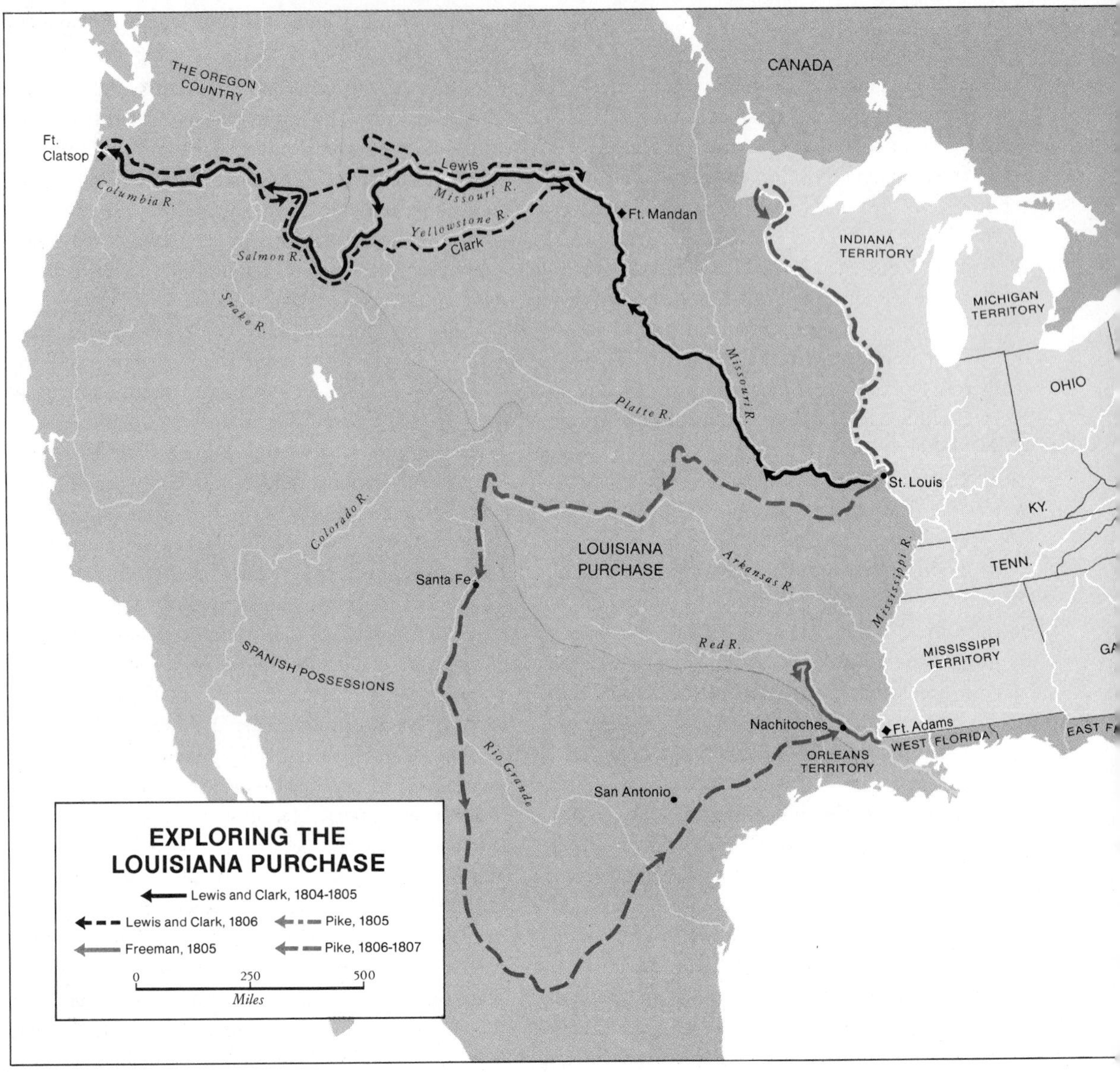

mores of the day), Burr challenged him to a duel. It was well known that Hamilton opposed dueling in principle, his own son having been slain in such an affair, and he certainly had no need to prove his courage. But he believed his honor at stake. The two met with pistols on July 11, 1804, at Weehawken, New Jersey, across the Hudson from New York City. Hamilton contemptuously refused to fire, but Burr took careful aim. Hamilton fell, mortally wounded. Thus a great, if enigmatic, man was cut off in his prime. His work, in a sense, had been completed, and his philosophy of government was being everywhere rejected, but the nation's loss was large.

Lewis and Clark

While Pickering and his clique of disgruntled Federalists were dreaming of secession, Jefferson was serenely planning the exploration of Louisiana and the region beyond. He had always been interested in the West. While American minister to France and again while secretary of state he had encouraged individual adventurers who hoped to penetrate the region. Nothing grew out of these schemes, but soon after he became President, he began to organize an expedition. Early in 1803 he got $2,500 from Congress and obtained the permission of the French to send his exploring party across Louisiana. To command the expedi-

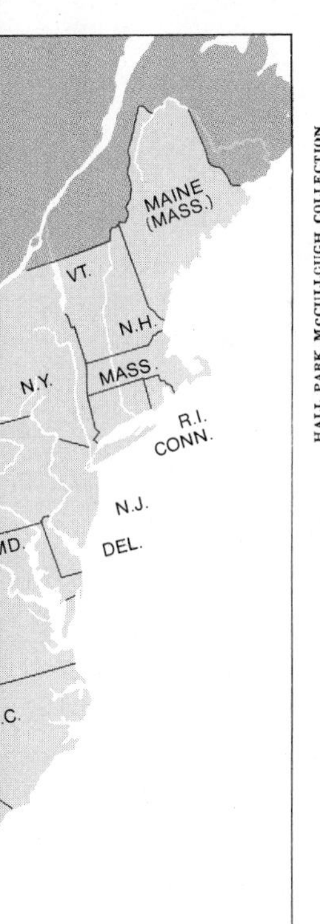

HALL PARK MCCULLOUGH COLLECTION

The explorations of Lewis and Clark, as well as those of Freeman and Pike, are traced at left. The shading shows the Louisiana Purchase as delineated by its "natural" boundaries. On their return journey, Lewis and Clark divided their party to explore more thoroughly the area around the upper Missouri and Yellowstone rivers. The portrait of Meriwether Lewis above was done in 1806 by Charles Saint-Mémin.

tion he appointed his private secretary, Meriwether Lewis, a young Virginian who had seen considerable service with the army in the West. Lewis chose as his companion officer William Clark, an experienced Indian fighter.

Jefferson, whose primary interest in the West was scientific, issued voluminous and minute instructions to Lewis:

> Other objects worthy of notice will be, the soil and face of the country . . . the remains and accounts of any animals which may be deemed rare or extinct; the mineral productions of every kind, but particularly metals . . . volcanic appearances; climate, as characterized by the thermometer, by the proportion of rainy, cloudy, and clear days, by lightning, hail, snow, ice, by the access and recess of frost, by the winds prevailing at different seasons, the dates at which particular plants put forth or lose their flower or leaf, times of appearance of particular birds, reptiles or insects. . . .

Of course, scientific matters were inextricably intertwined with practical ones, such as the fur trade, for in his nature studies Jefferson always concentrated his attention upon "useful" plants and animals. Furthermore, he was haunted by imperialistic visions of an expanding America not really unlike those of Hamilton. After the consummation of the Louisiana Purchase, he instructed Lewis to try to establish official relations with the Indians in the Spanish territories beyond. Lewis should assure the tribes that "they will find in us faithful friends and protectors," Jefferson said. That the expedition would be moving across Spanish territory need not concern the travelers because of "the expiring state of Spain's interests there."

Lewis and Clark gathered a group of 48 experienced men near St. Louis for training during the winter of 1803–04. In the spring they set forth, pushing slowly up the Missouri River by keelboat and pirogue. By late fall they had reached what is now North Dakota, where they built a small station, Fort Mandan, and spent the winter. In April 1805, having shipped back nine boxes of specimens and curios to the President, they struck out again toward the mountains, guided by a Shoshone squaw, Sacagawea, and her French-Canadian husband. They passed the Great Falls of the Missouri and then clambered over the Continental Divide at Lemhi Pass, in southwestern Montana. Soon thereafter, the going became easier, and they descended to the Pacific by way of the Clearwater and Columbia rivers, reaching their destination in November. They had hoped to return by ship, but during the long, damp winter not a single vessel appeared. So in the spring of 1806 they headed back by land, reaching St. Louis September 23.

The country greeted the news of their return with delight. Nothing had been heard of them since Lewis' letters to Jefferson from Fort Mandan had reached the capital some 18 months earlier, and they had been given up for lost. The expedition completely fulfilled Jefferson's hopes. Besides locating several passes across the Rockies, Lewis and Clark established friendly relations with a number of Indian tribes and brought back a wealth of data about the country and its resources. The journals of both leaders, and of many other members of the group, were published and these, along with their accurate map of their route, became major sources for scientists, students, and future explorers of the region. And to Jefferson's great personal satisfaction, Lewis provided him with many specimens of the local wildlife, including two grizzly bear cubs, which he kept for a time in a stone pit in the White House lawn.

But the success of Lewis and Clark did not open very wide the gates of Louisiana. Other explorers sent out by the eager Jefferson accomplished far less. Thomas Freeman, an Irish-born surveyor, led a small party up the Red River but ran into a powerful Spanish force near the present junction of Arkansas, Oklahoma, and Texas and was forced to retreat. Between 1805 and 1807 Lieutenant Zebulon Pike explored both the upper Mississippi Valley and the Colorado region. (He discovered but failed to scale the peak south of Denver that bears his name.) Pike made his way eventually all the way to Santa Fe and the upper reaches of the Rio Grande, but unfortunately he was not nearly so careful and acute an observer as Lewis and Clark were and consequently brought back much less information. By 1808 fur traders based at St. Louis were beginning to invade the Rockies, and by 1812 there were 75,000 people in the southern section of the new territory. That year it was admitted to the Union as the state of Louisiana. The northern region lay almost untouched until considerably later.

Jeffersonian Democracy

With the purchase of Louisiana, Jefferson completed the construction of the political mechanism known as the Republican party and the philosophy of government known as "Jeffersonian Democracy." Federalism was in retreat everywhere as Jefferson swept to a second term with the loss of only two states. How had he done this? From what sort of materials had he constructed his juggernaut? Partly his success was a matter of personality; in the march of American democracy he stood halfway, temperamentally, between Washington and Andrew Jackson, perfectly in tune with the thinking of his times. The colonial American had practiced democracy without really believing in it; hence, for example, the maintenance of property qualifications for voting in regions where nearly everyone owned property. Stimulated by the libertarian ideas of the Revolution, Americans were rapidly adjusting their beliefs to conform with their practices. However, it took a Jefferson, a man of large estates and possessed of the general prejudice in favor of the old-fashioned citizen rooted in the soil, yet also deeply committed to majority rule, to oversee the transition.

Jefferson's marvelous talents as a writer also help to explain his success. He expounded his ideas in such inspired language that few could long resist them. Nevertheless, he was no mere mouther of high-sounding abstractions. He had a remarkable facility for discovering practical arguments to justify his beliefs, as when he suggested that by letting everyone vote, elections would be made more honest because with large numbers going to the polls bribery would become prohibitively expensive.

Jefferson also prepared the country for democracy by proving that a democrat could establish and maintain a stable regime. The Federalist tyranny of 1798 was compounded of selfishness and stupidity, but was also based partly on honest fears that an egalitarian regime would not protect the fabric of society from hotheads and crackpots. The impact of the French Revolution on conservative thinking in the middle 1790's can scarcely be overestimated. America had fought a seven-year revolution without executing a single Tory, yet during the few months that the Terror ravaged France, nearly 17,000 persons were officially put to death for political "crimes," and many thousands more were killed in various civil disturbances. Still worse, in the opinion of many, the French extremists had attempted to destroy Christianity, substituting for it a "Cult of Reason." They discarded the Christian calendar, renaming the days of the week and the months of the year and decreeing a new era, A.D. 1792 becoming the year One. Property was confiscated, strict price controls imposed, slavery abolished in the French colonies. Little wonder that many Americans feared that the Jeffersonians, lovers of France and of *liberté*, *égalité*, and *fraternité*, would try to remodel American society in a similar way.

Jefferson calmed these fears. "Pell-mell" might scandalize the British and Spanish ministers and a few other mossbacks, but it was scarcely revolutionary. The most partisan Federalist was hard put to see a Robespierre in the amiable President, serenely scratching out state papers at his desk or chatting with a Kentucky congressman at a "republican" dinner party. Furthermore, Jefferson accepted Federalist ideas about public finance, even learning to live with Hamilton's bank. As a good democrat, he drew a nice distinction between his own opinions and the wishes of the majority, which he felt must always take priority. Even in his first inaugural he admitted that manufacturing and commerce were, along with agriculture, the "pillars of our prosperity," and while believing that these activities would best thrive when "left most free to individual enterprise," he accepted the principle that the government should interpose its authority when necessary to protect them from "casual embarrassments." Eventually he gave his backing to modest proposals for spending federal money on roads, canals, and other projects that, according to his political philosophy, ought to have been left to the states and private individuals.

During his term the country grew and prospered, the commercial classes sharing in the bounty along with the farmers so close to Jefferson's heart. Blithely, he set out to win the support of all who could vote. "It is material to the safety of Republicanism," he wrote in 1803, "to detach the mercantile interests from its enemies and incorporate them into the body of its friends."

In short, Jefferson undermined the Federalists all along the line. They had said that the country must pay a stiff price for prosperity and orderly government, and they demanded prompt payment in full, both in cash (taxes) and in the form of limitations on human liberty. Under Jefferson these much-desired goals had been achieved cheaply and without sacrificing freedom. A land whose riches could only be guessed at had been obtained without firing a shot and without burdening the people with new taxes. "What farmer, what mechanic, what laborer, ever sees a tax-gatherer in the United States?" the President could ask in 1805, without a single Federalist rising to challenge him. Order without discipline, security without a large military establishment, prosperity without regulatory legislation, freedom without license—truly the Sage of Monticello appeared to have led his countrymen into a golden age.

Republican virtue seemed to have triumphed, both at home and abroad. "With nations as with individuals," Jefferson proudly proclaimed as he took the oath of office at the start of his second term, "our interests soundly calculated, will ever be found inseparable from our moral duties." And he added more complacently still: "Fellow citizens, you best know whether we have done well or ill."

SUPPLEMENTARY READING No student interested in Jefferson's political and social philosophy should miss sampling his writings, of which there are several editions. By far the best, still incomplete, is J.P. Boyd (ed.), *The Papers of Thomas Jefferson* (1950–). A useful compilation of his more important writings is Adrienne Koch and William Peden, *The Life and Selected Writings of Thomas Jefferson* (1944). Miss Koch's *The Philosophy of Thomas Jefferson** (1943) is valuable, as are D.J. Boorstin, *The Lost World of Thomas Jefferson** (1948), Gilbert Chinard, *Thomas Jefferson: The Apostle of Americanism** (1929), and Nathan Schachner, *Thomas Jefferson* (1951). The still-incomplete biography of Jefferson by Dumas Malone (1948–) provides masses of valuable data.

On the Federalist and Democratic-Republican parties, see Joseph Charles, *The Origins of the Amer-*

*ican Party System** (1961), M.J. Dauer, *The Adams Federalists** (1953), N.E. Cunningham, Jr., *The Jeffersonian Republicians** (1958), and W.N. Chambers, *Political Parties in a New Nation** (1963). The best biography of John Adams is still Gilbert Chinard, *Honest John Adams** (1933). Page Smith, *John Adams* (1962), contains a wealth of personal material drawn from the Adams papers, but is almost useless for the politics of Adams' Presidency. S.G. Kurtz, *The Presidency of John Adams** (1957), is a solid study, while much material useful for an understanding of Adams' political philosophy can be found in Zoltán Haraszti, *John Adams and the Prophets of Progress** (1952).

For the diplomatic conflicts of the late 1790's, see Bradford Perkins, *The First Rapprochment: England and the United States* (1967), and Alexander De Conde, *The Quasi-War** (1966). On the Alien and Sedition Acts, both J.M. Smith, *Freedom's Fetters: The Alien and Sedition Laws and American Civil Liberties** (1956), and J.C. Miller, *Crisis in Freedom: The Alien and Sedition Acts** (1951), are excellent. L.W. Levy, *Freedom of Speech and Press in Early American History** (1963), provides valuable background for understanding the acts, for it demonstrates that modern conceptions of civil liberties are very different from those commonly held in the 18th century. Levy's *Jefferson and Civil Liberties: The Darker Side* (1963) is a lawyer's brief for the prosecution.

The standard work on Jefferson's Presidency is Henry Adams, *History of the United States During the Administrations of Jefferson and Madison** (1889–91); this 9-volume study is both a work of art and a magnificent scholarly achievement, although strongly anti-Jefferson in orientation. The most recent general treatment of the Jeffersonian era is Marshall Smelser, *The Democratic Republic** (1968). On the parties of the era, see N. E. Cunningham, Jr., *The Jeffersonian Republicans in Power** (1963), and D. H. Fischer, *The Revolution of American Conservatism: The Federalist Party in the Era of Jeffersonian Democracy** (1965); on the structure of Jefferson's administration, L. D. White, *The Jeffersonians** (1951); on Jefferson's management of the administration and of Congress, J. S. Young, *The Washington Community** (1966), a fascinating book. Older works of value are C. A. Beard, *Economic Origins of Jeffersonian Democracy** (1915), Edward Channing, *The Jeffersonian System* (1906), and C.G. Bowers, *Jefferson in Power** (1936), which is a good corrective to the work of Henry Adams because of its pro-Jefferson bias.

Jefferson's battle with the judges can be followed in A.J. Beveridge, *Life of John Marshall* (1916–19), and Charles Warren, *The Supreme Court in United States History* (1937). For *Marbury v. Madison*, see J.A. Garraty (ed.), *Quarrels That Have Shaped the Constitution** (1964).

The war with the Barbary pirates is covered in R.W. Irwin, *The Diplomatic Relations of the United States with the Barbary Powers* (1931). On the Louisiana Purchase, see Henry Adams' *History*, E.W. Lyon, *Louisiana in French Diplomacy* (1934), A.P. Whitaker, *The Mississippi Question* (1934), Irving Brant, *James Madison: Secretary of State* (1953), and George Dangerfield, *Chancellor Robert R. Livingston of New York* (1960).

Jefferson's interest in the West is discussed in E.T. Martin, *Thomas Jefferson: Scientist** (1952). An excellent general treatment of western exploration is contained in R.A. Billington, *Westward Expansion* (1967). For the Lewis and Clark expedition, see John Bakeless, *Lewis and Clark** (1947), and Bernard De Voto (ed.), *The Journals of Lewis and Clark** (1953). The career of Pike is traced in W.E. Hollon, *The Lost Pathfinder: Zebulon Montgomery Pike* (1949).

*Available in paperback.

7

America Escapes from Europe

Smugness and complacency are luxuries that politicians can seldom afford. Jefferson, beginning his second term with pride in the past and confidence in the future and with the mass support of the nation, soon found himself in trouble both at home and abroad.

Partly, his difficulties rose from the very extent of the Republican victory. In 1805 the Federalists had neither useful ideas, nor intelligent leadership, nor effective numbers. They held only a quarter of the seats in Congress. With Hamilton dead and John Adams retired, they had only the likes of Timothy Pickering to confront Jefferson, Madison, Gallatin (a secretary of the treasury whom even Federalist financiers conceded to be nearly the equal of Hamilton), and a number of other worthy figures. Yet as often happens in such situations, lack of opposition weakened party discipline and encouraged factionalism among the Republicans. At the same time, Napoleon's renewed aggressiveness in Europe, to which the sale of Louisiana had been a prelude, produced a tangle of new problems for the neutral United States. Jefferson could not solve these problems merely by being "just" and "moral" as he had suggested in his second inaugural. At the end of his second term he was suffering from rheumatism and recurrent headaches that were no doubt of psychosomatic origin, and he wrote feelingly to a friend: "Never did a prisoner, released from his chains, feel such relief as I shall on shaking off the shackles of power."

Randolph and the Quids

Jefferson's domestic troubles were not of critical importance, but they were vexing. To a considerable extent, they resulted from the very elements in his make-up that explain his success: his facility in adjusting his principles to practical conditions, his readiness to take over the best of Federalism. This flexibility got him in trouble with some of his disciples, who were less ready than he to surrender principle to expediency. Not every southerner who had made states' rights his gospel modified his thinking as readily as Jefferson did, for example.

The most prominent of these Republican critics and chief figure in a group called the "Quids" was John Randolph of Roanoke, congressman from Virginia and majority leader during

MELLON COLLECTION, NATIONAL GALLERY OF ART

John Randolph of Roanoke (as he signed his name to avoid confusion with his cousin "Possum" John) was painted in 1805, at the age of 32, by Gilbert Stuart.

Jefferson's first term. Randolph was unique. Although he had wit, drive, charm, and imagination, his mind was tragically warped; in later life he was periodically insane. He was apparently sexually impotent, and frustration made him into a sour, vitriolic, and unyielding obstructionist. He made a fetish of preserving states' rights against invasion by the central government. "Asking one of the States to surrender part of her sovereignty is like asking a lady to surrender part of her chastity," he remarked in one of his typical epigrams.

Randolph first clashed with Jefferson in 1804, over an attempted settlement of the so-called Yazoo land frauds. In 1795 the Georgia legislature had sold a huge area in what is now Alabama and Mississippi to four land companies for a tiny fraction of its value, something less than two cents an acre. When it came out that many of the legislators had been corrupted, the next legislature canceled the grants, but not before the original grantees had unloaded large tracts on various third parties. These innocents turned to the federal government for relief when the grants were canceled. Jefferson favored a bill giving 5 million acres to these interests, but Randolph would have none of this. Rising in righteous wrath, he denounced in his shrill soprano all those who would countenance fraud. The compromise bill was defeated.*

By the beginning of Jefferson's second term, Randolph was fretting about how the President's adversaries were taking advantage of his "easy credulity." Then, in December 1805, he broke finally with the administration over a request that Jefferson had made for $2 million to be used in unspecified dealings designed to obtain West Florida from Spain. Randolph suspected some chicanery. By quizzing Secretary of State Madison he discovered that Jefferson wanted the money in order to bribe the French to make their satellite Spain yield the territory. Randolph exploded. He denounced the proposal in his usual unbridled manner and published a full account of his conversation with Madison. Eventually, Congress appropriated the money, although the deal Jefferson had envisioned did not come off. However, from that date forward Randolph could be counted upon to oppose every administration measure. He seldom mustered more than a handful of supporters in Congress, but his stabbing, nerve-shattering assaults grievously disturbed the President's peace of mind.

The Burr Conspiracy

Another Republican who caused much trouble for Jefferson was Aaron Burr, and again the President was partially to blame for the difficulty. He respected Burr's ability but never trusted him. After their contest for the Presidency in 1801, Jefferson pursued him almost vindictively, systematically depriving him of federal patronage in New York, and replacing him as

*The controversy then entered the courts, and in 1810 Chief Justice Marshall held in *Fletcher v. Peck* that in rescinding the grant Georgia had committed an unconstitutional breach of contract. Before Marshall's ruling, however, the federal grant was finally approved by Congress. Had it not been, *Fletcher v. Peck* would have provided the "victims" of the Yazoo frauds with an area considerably larger than the state of Mississippi!

the 1804 Republican Vice Presidential candidate with Governor George Clinton, Burr's chief rival in the state.

While still Vice President, Burr began to flirt with treason. He approached Anthony Merry, the British minister in Washington, and offered to "effect a separation of the Western part of the United States." His price was £110,000 and the support of a British fleet off the mouth of the Mississippi. The British did not fall in with his scheme, but he went ahead nonetheless. Exactly what he had in mind has long been in dispute. Certainly he dreamed of acquiring a western empire for himself; whether he intended to wrest it from the United States or from Spanish territories beyond Louisiana is unclear. He joined forces with General James Wilkinson, whom Jefferson had unfortunately appointed governor of Louisiana Territory, and who, it will be recalled, was secretly in the pay of Spain.

In 1806 Burr and Wilkinson organized a small force at a place called Blennerhassett Island, in the Ohio River. Some six dozen men began to move downriver toward New Orleans under Burr's command. Whether the objective was New Orleans or some part of Mexico, the scheme was clearly illegal. For some reason, however—possibly because he was incapable of loyalty to anyone*—Wilkinson betrayed Burr to Jefferson at the last moment. The President issued a proclamation warning the nation and ordering Burr's arrest. Burr tried to escape to Spanish Florida but was captured in February 1807 and brought to Richmond, Virginia, under guard.

Burr might not have embarked upon his western adventures if Jefferson had not written him out of the Republican party after 1801, but his own strange personality—brilliant, compelling, but unstable—and the fact that he was under indictment for murder in New York and New Jersey because of the Hamilton duel, best explain his singular behavior. Jefferson's actions in the affair were also very odd. He knew about the conspiracy, which was one of the worst-kept secrets of the day, for months before Wilkinson's warning forced him to issue his proclamation. He seemed, indeed, to view the situation with remarkable complacency, which suggests that he might have been willing to look the other way if Burr had concentrated upon attacking *Spanish* holdings.

*John Randolph said of him: "Wilkinson is the only man that I ever saw who was from the bark to the very core a villain."

NEW-YORK HISTORICAL SOCIETY

Aaron Burr was sketched during his 1807 trial for treason by the French expatriate artist Charles Saint-Mémin, who was well known for his profile portraits.

Yet once Burr had been captured, Jefferson sought to have him convicted of high treason. Any President will naturally deal summarily with traitors, but Jefferson's attitude reveals the depth of his hatred of Burr. According to Thomas Perkins Abernethy, the most recent student of the conspiracy, he "made himself a party to the prosecution," personally sending evidence to the United States attorney who was handling the case and offering blanket pardons to associates of Burr who would agree to turn state's evidence. A French adventurer who had been close to Burr was promised a commission in the United States army if he would give evidence "not adverse to the administration." On the other hand, Chief Justice Marshall, presiding at the trial in his capacity as judge of the circuit court, repeatedly showed favoritism to the prisoner, so openly on one occasion that he blushed when called to account for his conduct. The proceedings quickly lost all appearance of impartiality.

In this contest between two great men at their worst, Jefferson as a vindictive executive and Marshall as a prejudiced judge, the victory went to the judge. By defining treason in the narrowest possible sense in his charge to the jury, Marshall made a verdict of not guilty almost mandatory. Organizing "a military assemblage," he said, "was not a levying of war." To "advise or procure treason" was not in itself treason. Unless two independent witnesses testified to an overt act of treason as thus defined, the accused should be declared innocent. In the light of this charge, the jury, after deliberating only 25 minutes, found Burr not guilty.

Burr was also tried and acquitted on the charge of conspiring to invade a friendly power. Throughout his ordeal he never lost his self-possession and seemed to view the proceedings with amiable cynicism. Then, since he was wanted either for murder or treason in six states, he went into exile in Europe. Some years later, however, he returned to New York, where he spent an unregenerate old age, fathering two illegitimate children in his seventies and being divorced by his second wife on charges of adultery when he was 80.

As in his squabble with Randolph and the Quids, Jefferson suffered no vital setback in the Burr affair. Nevertheless, it was a blow to his prestige, it occupied much time that he could have better devoted to pressing international problems, and it left him more embittered than ever against Marshall and the federal judiciary. Certainly the affair added nothing to his reputation as a statesman. Had he acted sooner, when Burr was actually conspiring, and having acted, allowed the courts to proceed in a normal way, something more closely approximating justice would probably have been achieved.

Napoleon and the British

Jefferson's difficulties with both Randolph and Burr may be traced at least in part to the purchase of Louisiana. His easy success in obtaining the region encouraged him to think that West Florida could be snapped up with equal ease, and this error brought down upon him the shrill wrath of Randolph of Roanoke. Louisiana itself, lying fat and empty and unknown athwart the westward march of the Americans, excited the cupidity of men like Burr and Wilkinson. But problems for Jefferson and for the whole country infinitely more serious than these were also related to Louisiana.

Napoleon had jettisoned Louisiana to clear the decks before resuming the battle for control of Europe. This war presented the greatest challenge of Jefferson's Presidency. At first it had the effect of stimulating still further America's prosperity, particularly its foreign trade, for the warring powers needed American goods and American vessels. Shipbuilding boomed; foreign trade, which had already quintupled since 1793, nearly doubled again between 1803 and 1805. By the summer of 1807, however, the situation had changed greatly. A most unusual stalemate had developed in the war. In October 1805 Britain's Horatio Nelson demolished the combined Spanish and French fleets in the Battle of Trafalgar off the coast of Spain. But Napoleon, now at the summit of his powers, quickly redressed the balance, smashing army after army thrown against him by Great Britain's continental allies. First he attacked the Austrians, capturing 50,000 at Ulm in Bavaria. Then he shattered a great Austrian and Russian army in the Battle of Austerlitz (December 1805), perhaps the most brilliant victory of his career. Next, in 1806, he overwhelmed the Prussians at Jena, and the following June, the Russians at Friedland in East Prussia. Thereafter Napoleon was master of Europe, while the British controlled the seas around the Continent. Neither nation could strike directly at the other.

They therefore resorted to commercial warfare, striving to disrupt each other's economy. Napoleon struck first with his Berlin Decree (November 1806), which set up a paper blockade of the British Isles and made "all commerce and correspondence" with Great Britain illegal. The British government retaliated with a series of executive edicts called Orders in Council, blockading most continental ports and barring from them all foreign vessels unless they first stopped at a British port and paid customs duties. Napoleon then issued his Milan Decree (December 1807), declaring any vessel that submitted to the British rules "to have become English property" and thus subject to seizure.

These regulations, with their blockades and counterblockades, seemed designed to stop commerce completely, but this was not the case. Under his "Continental System," Napoleon was willing to sell European products to the British (if the price was right); his chief objective was to deprive them of their continental markets. The British were ready to sell anything on the Continent, and to allow others to do so too, provided they first paid a toll. In effect, this commercial warfare amounted to the organized exploitation of foreign merchants, who, it must be admitted, were enjoying unprecedented opportunities for profit because of the prolonged conflict. The Continental System was, in John Quincy Adams' pithy phrase, "little more than extortion wearing the mask of prohibition," and the British system was equally immoral—a kind of piracy practiced with impunity because of the overwhelming strength of the Royal Navy.

Thomas Jefferson considered these new Anglo-French regulations the final insult in a long series of humiliations. It was becoming impossible to carry on foreign trade, so vital to American prosperity, without running afoul of one or the other of the belligerents. Looking back over the period since 1803, Jefferson could see an increasingly alarming trend.

At first the resumption of hostilities had brought huge profits to American merchants. When war broke out in 1792, the colonial trade of both sides had fallen largely into American hands, because the danger of capture drove many belligerent merchant vessels from the seas. This commerce had engaged Americans in some rather devious practices. Under the Rule of War of 1756, it will be recalled, the British denied to neutrals the right to engage in trade during time of war from which they were barred by mercantilistic regulations in time of peace. If an American ship carried sugar from the French colony of Martinique to France, for example, the British claimed the right to capture it, because such traffic was normally confined to French bottoms by French law. To avoid this risk, American merchants brought the sugar first to the United States, a legal peacetime voyage under French mercantilism. Then they reshipped it to France as *American* sugar. Since the United States was a neutral and sugar not contraband of war, the Americans expected the British to let their ships pass with impunity. Continental products likewise reached the French West Indies by way of United States ports, and the American government encouraged the traffic in both directions by refunding customs duties on foreign products reshipped within a year. Between 1803 and 1806 the annual value of foreign products re-exported from the United States jumped from $13 million to $60 million! In 1806 the United States exported 47 million pounds of coffee, none, of course, of local origin. An example of this type of trade is offered by Samuel Eliot Morison in his *Maritime History of Massachusetts:*

> The brig *Eliza Hardy* of Plymouth enters her home port from Bordeaux, on May 20, 1806, with a cargo of claret wine. Part of it is immediately re-exported to Martinique in the schooner *Pilgrim,* which also carries a consignment of brandy that came from Alicante in the brig *Commerce,* and another of gin that came from Rotterdam in the barque *Hannah* of Plymouth. The rest of the *Eliza Hardy*'s claret is taken to Philadelphia by coasters, and thence re-exported in seven different vessels to Havana, Santiago de Cuba, St. Thomas, and Batavia.

This underhanded commerce naturally irritated the British. In the case of the American ship *Polly* a British court had decided in 1801 that broken voyages (like that of the *Eliza Hardy*) did not violate the rule; however, the increasing frustrations resulting from the long war with Napoleon led to much indignation about broken voyages in Great Britain. Finally, in 1805 and 1806, a British judge, Sir William Grant, reversed the *Polly* decision. In the cases of the *Essex* and the *William* Grant decreed that American ships could no longer rely on "mere voluntary *ceremonies*" to circumvent the Rule of 1756. Thus, just when both Britain and France were cracking down on direct trade by neutrals, Britain also determined to halt the American re-export trade.

The Impressment Controversy

Even more dismaying were the injustices and cruel indignities being visited upon American seamen at this time through the British practice of impressment. Under British law, any able-bodied subject of the king could be drafted for service in the Royal Navy in an emergency. Normally, when the commander of a warship found himself short-handed, he put into a British port and sent a "press gang" ashore to round up the necessary men in harborside pubs, but when far from home waters, he obviously could not do this. He might hail any passing British merchant ship and commandeer the necessary men, although this practice was understandably unpopular in British maritime circles. He might also, however, stop a *neutral* merchantman on the high seas and remove any British subject. Since the United States owned by far the largest merchant fleet among the neutrals, its vessels bore the brunt of this practice.

Impressment had been a cause of Anglo-American conflict for many years; as far back as 1794 John Jay had tried to do something about it when he negotiated his treaty, but without success. American pride suffered every time a vessel carrying the flag was forced to back topsails and heave to at the command of a British man-of-war. Still more galling was the behavior of British officers, contemptuous of Americans and accustomed to absolute obedience to their orders while at sea, when they boarded American ships. They made little effort to be sure they were impressing British subjects; any likely looking lad might be taken when the need was great. Nor was it easy to tell an Englishman or a Scot from an American of English or Scottish descent, especially if the man was determined to conceal his true identity. Furthermore, there were legal questions in dispute. When did an English immigrant become an American? When he was naturalized, the United States claimed. Never, the British retorted; "Once an Englishman, always an Englishman."

America's lax immigration laws compounded this problem. An English-speaking foreigner could enter the United States and become a citizen with ridiculous ease; indeed, those too impatient to wait the required five years for citizenship could purchase false naturalization papers for as little as a dollar. Because working conditions in the American merchant marine were far superior to the British, at all times during the period at least 10,000 British-born tars were serving on American ships. Some of these became American citizens legally; others obtained false papers; some admitted to being British subjects; some were deserters from the Royal Navy. From the British point of view, all were liable to impressment.

The Jefferson administration conceded the right of the British to impress their own subjects from American ships in British ports and would probably not have protested the stopping of vessels in international waters too loudly if only admittedly British subjects had been seized. When legally naturalized Americans were impressed, however, the administration was irritated, and when native-born Americans were taken, it became incensed. Impressment, Secretary of State Madison said in 1807, was "anomalous in principle . . . grievous in practice, and . . . abominable in abuse." Although exact figures are hard to come by, between 1803 and 1812 at least 5,000 sailors were snatched from the decks of United States vessels and forced to serve in the Royal Navy.* Many of these—estimates run as high as three out of every four—were Americans. The British did not claim the right to impress native-born Americans, and when it could be proved that boarding officers had done so, the men in question were released by higher authority. During the course of the controversy, the British authorities actually released 3,800 impressed Americans, which suggests that a much larger number were seized. However, the British rejected outright any proposal that they abandon impressment. "The Pretension advanced by Mr. Madison that the American Flag should protect every Individual sailing under it . . . is too extravagant to require any serious Refutation," one British foreign secretary explained.

The combination of impressment, British interference with the re-export trade, and the general harassment of neutral commerce instituted by both Great Britain and France would have perplexed the most informed and hardheaded of leaders, and Jefferson was neither informed nor hardheaded in dealing with this problem. Funda-

*This is a conservative estimate. Some historians place the number at about 9,000.

mentally, he was an isolationist, being ready "to let every treaty we have drop off without renewal," and he even considered closing down all overseas diplomatic missions. He believed it much wiser to stand up for one's rights than to compromise, yet he hated the very thought of war. While the American merchant fleet passed 600,000 tons and continued to grow at an annual rate of over ten per cent, Jefferson kept only a skeleton navy on active service, despite the fact that the great powers were fighting a no-holds-barred war all over the world. Instead of building a navy that other nations would have to respect, he relied upon a tiny fleet of frigates and a swarm of gunboats that were useless against the Royal Navy—"a macabre monument," in the words of one historian, "to his hasty, ill-digested ideas" about defense.*

The Embargo Act

The frailty of Jefferson's policy became obvious once the warring powers began to attack neutral shipping in earnest. In 1806 Jefferson gave William Pinkney and his favorite diplomatic trouble-shooter, James Monroe—at that time minister to Great Britain—the task of persuading the British to relax their pressures on American commerce. The treaty they negotiated was so unsatisfactory that Jefferson was ashamed to submit it to the Senate. Between 1803 and 1807, the British seized over 500 American ships, Napoleon over 200 more. Yet the United States could do nothing. "We have principles from which we shall never depart," Jefferson stoutly maintained. "Our neutrality should be respected." But he added immediately: "On the other hand, we do not want war, and all this is very embarrassing." The ultimate in frustration came on June 22, 1807, off Norfolk, Virginia, when the British frigate *Leopard* (Captain Salusbury P. Humphreys commanding) insolently hailed the American frigate *Chesapeake* and demanded to be allowed to muster the crew and search for four deserters. When Commodore James Barron refused, the *Leopard* opened fire and the *Chesapeake*, unprepared for action, had to surrender. The suspected deserters were then seized (only one was actually an Englishman) and the crippled *Chesapeake* was turned loose by the British to limp back to port.

Captain Humphreys' action was so grossly in violation of international law that the British disowned it, although they delayed making restitution for many years. The American public clamored for war, but Jefferson, realizing that the country had nothing to fight with, contented himself with ordering British warships out of American territorial waters. However, he was determined to put a stop to the indignities being heaped upon the flag by both Great Britain and France. The result was the Embargo Act, passed by Congress in December 1807, even before news of Napoleon's Milan Decree reached America.

The simplest way to describe the Embargo Act is to say that it prohibited all *exports*. American vessels could not clear for any foreign port, and foreign vessels could do so only in ballast. Importing was not forbidden, but relatively few foreign ships would come to the United States if they had to return without a cargo. Although the law was sure to injure the American economy, Jefferson hoped that it would work in two ways to benefit the nation. By keeping United States merchant ships off the seas it would end all chance of injury to them and to the national honor. By denying both Britain and France American goods and markets, great economic pressure would be put upon them to moderate policies toward American shipping. The fact that boycotts had repeatedly wrested concessions from the British during the crises preceding the Revolution was certainly in Jefferson's mind when he devised the embargo.

Seldom, however, has an American government policy been so bitterly resented and resisted by a large segment of the public. It demanded of the maritime interests far greater sacrifices than they could reasonably be expected to make. The fleet of Massachusetts alone was earning over $15 million a year in freight charges by 1807, and of course Bay State merchants were making

*The gunboats had performed effectively against the Barbary pirates, but Jefferson was enamored of them mainly because they were cheap. A gunboat cost about $10,000 to build, a frigate well over $300,000.

NEW-YORK HISTORICAL SOCIETY

At right, the Ograbme (a palindrome of embargo), *a species of snapping turtle created by cartoonist Alexander Anderson, effectively frustrates an American tobacco smuggler. The embargo's effects are shown graphically below. The brief foreign trade spurt in 1810 was due to congressional passage of Macon's Bill No. 2 (page 238).*

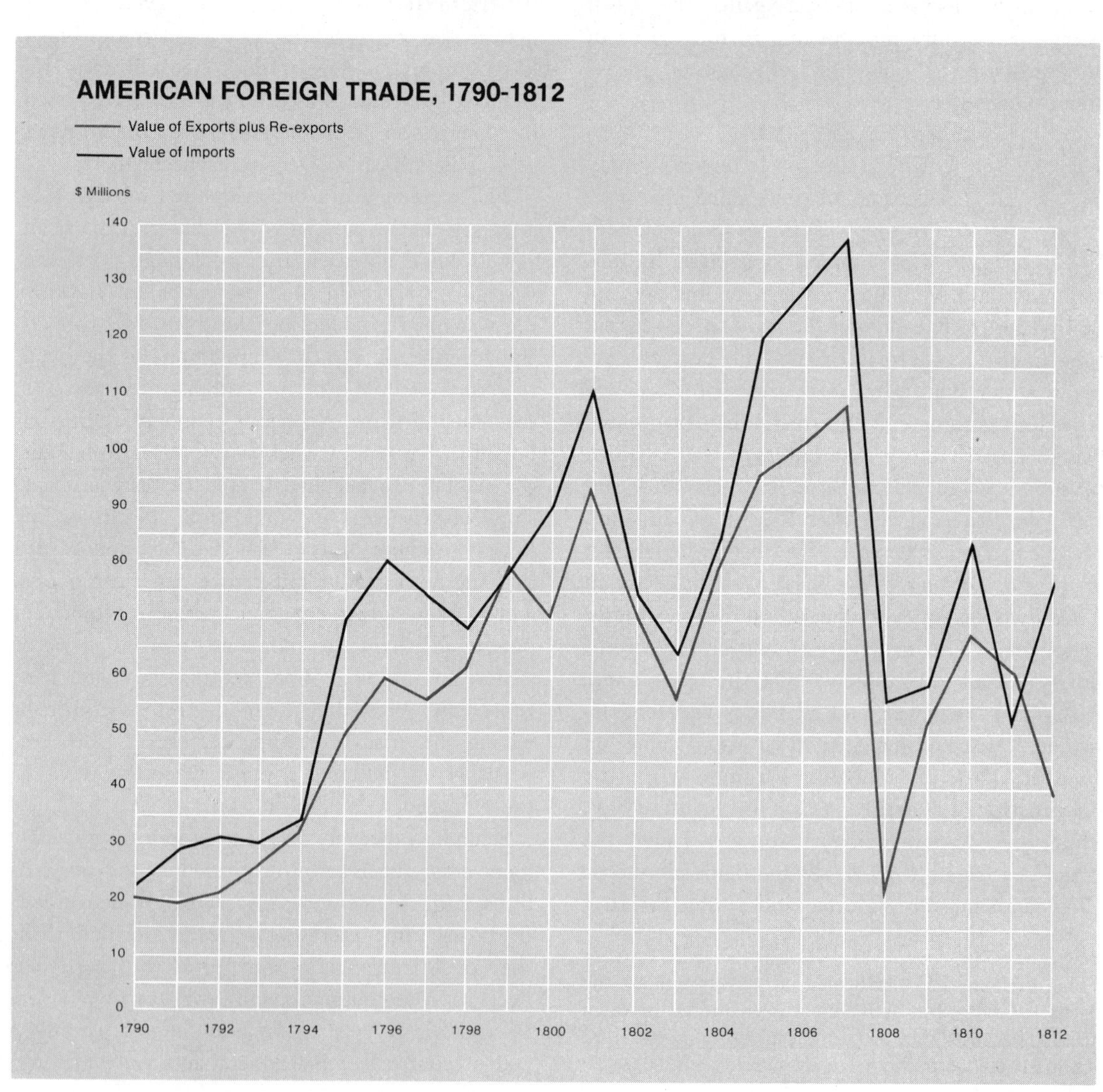

far larger gains from the buying and selling of goods. Indeed, the nation's foreign commerce was the most expansive force in the economy, the chief reason for the prosperity and growth that characterized the years after 1790. Losses through seizure were exasperating, but they could be guarded against by insurance. Impressment excited universal indignation, but it hit chiefly at the defenseless, the disreputable, and the obscure and never caused a labor shortage in the merchant marine. The number of British nationals signing on to work on American ships steadily exceeded the highest estimates of sailors impressed, legally and illegally, into the Royal Navy. The profits of commerce were still tremendous. A Massachusetts senator estimated that if only one vessel in three escaped the blockade, the owner came out ahead. In short, the remedy was more harmful than the disease. As John Randolph remarked in a typical sally, the administration was trying "to cure the corns by cutting off the toes."

The Embargo Act had a catastrophic effect on the American economy. Exports fell from $108 million in 1807 to $22 million in 1808, imports from $138 million to less than $57 million. Prices of farm products and manufactured goods reacted violently; seamen were thrown out of work; merchants found their businesses disrupted. And while British exports to the United States fell off sharply, new markets in South America reduced the losses of British manufacturers and merchants considerably.

The degree to which Americans violated the law is difficult to determine, but that they were ingenious at discovering ways to do so is clear. Many American ships made hastily for blue water before the machinery of enforcement could be put into operation, not to return until the law was repealed. Quantities of goods flowed across the Canadian border illegally. Shipping between American ports had not been outlawed, and coasting vessels were allowed to put into foreign ports when in distress. Suddenly, mysterious storms began to drive experienced skippers leagues off their courses, some as far even as Europe. The brig *Commerce*, en route from Massachusetts to New Orleans, was "forced" by a shortage of water to make for Havana. Having replenished her casks, she also exchanged her cargo for sugar.

The law also permitted merchants with property abroad to send ships to fetch it. About 800 ships went off on such errands. Furthermore, lawbreakers were difficult to punish. In the seaport towns, juries were no more willing to convict men of violating the Embargo Act than their fathers had been to convict those charged with violating the Townshend Acts. A mob at Gloucester, Massachusetts, destroyed a revenue cutter in the same spirit that Rhode Islanders exhibited in 1772 when they burned the *Gaspee*.

Surely the embargo was a bad mistake. The United States ought either to have suffered the indignities heaped upon its vessels for the sake of profits or, by constructing a powerful navy, made it dangerous for the belligerents to treat its merchantmen so roughly. Jefferson was too proud to choose the former alternative, too parsimonious to choose the latter. Moreover, he applied harsher and harsher regulations in a futile effort to accomplish his purpose. Militiamen patrolled the Canadian border; revenuers searched out smuggled goods without proper warrants. Still the illegal trade went on, and in his last months as President, Jefferson simply gave up. Even then he would not admit frankly that the embargo was a fiasco and urge its repeal. Only in Jefferson's last week in office did a leaderless Congress finally abolish it, substituting the Non-Intercourse Act, which forbade trade only with Great Britain and France and authorized the President to end the boycott against either power by proclamation when and if it stopped violating the rights of Americans.

Madison in Power

It is a measure of the great popularity of Jefferson that the Republicans won the election of 1808 handily, despite the embargo. James Madison got 122 of the 173 electoral votes for the Presidency, and the party carried both houses of Congress, although by reduced majorities.

Madison was a small, neat, rather precise person, narrower and less attractive personally to most people than Jefferson but in many ways a deeper thinker and both more conscientious in the performance of his duties and more consistent in adhering to his principles. Ideologically, however, the two were as close as two active and intelligent men could be. Madison had no better solution to offer for the problem of the hour than Jefferson. The Non-Intercourse Act proved difficult to enforce—once an American ship left port, there was no way to prevent the skipper from steering for England or France—and exerted little economic pressure on the British, who continued to seize American vessels. Late in 1809, at the urging of Secretary of the Treasury Gallatin, who was concerned because the government was operating at a deficit, Representative Nathaniel Macon of North Carolina introduced a bill permitting American ships to go anywhere but closing United States ports to the ships of Britain and France. After protracted bickering in Congress, this measure was replaced by another, known as Macon's Bill No. 2, which removed all restrictions on commerce with France and Britain, though French and British warships were still barred from American waters. It also authorized the President to reapply the principle of nonintercourse to either of the major powers if the other should "cease to violate the neutral commerce of the United States." This bill became law in May 1810.

The volume of United States commerce with the British Isles swiftly zoomed to pre-embargo levels. Trade with France remained much more limited because of the British fleet. Napoleon therefore instructed his foreign minister to inform the United States that the Berlin and Milan decrees would be revoked in November on the understanding that Great Britain would abandon its own restrictive policies. Treating this ambiguous proposal as a statement of French policy (which it decidedly was not), Madison reapplied the nonintercourse policy to Great Britain. Napoleon, having thus tricked Madison into closing American ports to British ships and goods, cynically continued to seize American ships and cargoes whenever it suited him to do so.

The British grimly refused to modify the Orders in Council unless it could be shown that the French actually had repealed the Berlin and Milan decrees, and this despite mounting complaints from their own businessmen that the new American nonimportation policy was causing a serious depression by cutting off a major market for their manufactures. Madison, on the other hand, could not afford either to admit that Napoleon had deceived him or to reverse American policy still another time. Years of insults and frustrations had gradually changed the public mood in the United States. Increasingly, people of all sections were talking about war with Britain to vindicate the national honor. A minor clash between the U.S.S. *President* and the British sloop-of-war *Little Belt,* fought off New York harbor in May 1811, greatly stimulated the development of a war psychology.

Tecumseh and the Prophet

This war sentiment, especially noticeable in the agricultural West, was not entirely caused by British violations of neutral rights. For one thing, the Indians were again making trouble, and the frontiersmen believed that the British in Canada were egging them on. This had been true in the past but was no longer the case in 1811–12. American domination of the southern Great Lakes region was no longer in question. While Canadian officials were eager to cultivate the friendship of the tribes, they had no desire to force a showdown between the Indians and the Americans, for that could have but one result. Aware of their own vulnerability, the Canadians wanted to preserve Indian strength in case war should break out between Great Britain and the United States.

As usual, the real cause of the Indian troubles was the greed of the white settlers. Both Federalists and Republicans were on record in favor of what one modern historian has called a policy of "peaceful coexistence based on racial segregation." However, neither Washington nor Adams nor Jefferson had been able to control the frontiersmen, who by bribery, trickery, and force were driving the red men back year after year from the rich lands of the Ohio Valley. General William Henry Harrison, governor of Indiana Territory, a tough, relentless, insensitive soldier, kept a constant pressure on them. He wrested land from one tribe by promising it aid against a traditional enemy, from another as a penalty for having murdered a white man, from others by

CHICAGO NATURAL HISTORY MUSEUM

This portrait, by an unknown artist, is believed to be Tecumseh. "Sell [our] country!" he said. "Why not sell the air, the clouds, and the great sea?"

corrupting a few chiefs. Harrison justified his sordid behavior by citing the end in view—that "one of the fairest portions of the globe" be secured as "the seat of civilization, of science, and of true religion." The "wretched savages" should not be allowed to stand in the path of this worthy objective. As early as 1805 it was clear that unless something drastic was done, Harrison's aggressiveness, together with the corroding effects of the white man's civilization, would soon obliterate the tribes.

At this point the Shawnee chief Tecumseh made a bold and imaginative effort to reverse the trend by binding all the tribes east of the Mississippi into a great confederation. Traveling from the Wisconsin country to the Floridas, he persuaded tribe after tribe to join him. To Tecumseh's essentially political movement his brother Tenskwatawa, known as the Prophet, added the force of a moral crusade, urging the braves to give up white ways and white liquor and reinvigorate their own culture.

The Prophet was a fanatical medicine man who saw visions, burned men as witches, and claimed to be able to control the movement of heavenly bodies. Tecumseh, however, possessed true genius. A powerful orator and a great organizer, he had a deep insight into the needs of his people. Harrison himself said of Tecumseh: "He is one of those uncommon geniuses which spring up occasionally to produce revolutions and overturn the established order of things." Together the two brothers made a formidable team. By 1811 thousands of Indians were organizing to drive the whites off their lands. Alarms swept through the West.

General Harrison marched boldly against the brothers' camp at Prophetstown, where Tippecanoe Creek joins the Wabash, in Indiana. Tecumseh was away recruiting more men, but the Prophet recklessly ordered an assault on Harrison's camp outside the village on November 7, 1811. When the white soldiers held their ground despite the Prophet's magic, the Indians lost confidence and fell back. Harrison then destroyed Prophetstown. While the Battle of Tippecanoe was pretty much a draw, it disillusioned the Indians and shattered their confederation. Frontier warfare continued, but in the disorganized manner of former times. Like all such fighting, it was brutal and bloody. Unwilling as usual to admit that their own excesses were the chief cause of the trouble, the settlers directed their resentment at the British in Canada. Actually, the British had tried to calm Tecumseh's braves and had turned them away when they crossed the border in search of arms, but no American would ever believe that. "This combination headed by the Shawanese prophet is a British scheme," a resolution adopted by the citizens of Vincennes, Indiana, proclaimed. As a result, the cry for war with Great Britain rang along the frontier.

Depression and Land Hunger

Some westerners also pressed for war because they were suffering from an agricultural depression. The prices which they received for their wheat, tobacco, and other products in the markets of New Orleans were falling, and they attributed the downtrend to the loss of foreign markets and the depredations of the British. American commercial restrictions had more to do with the western depression than the British, and in any case, the slow and cumbersome transportation and distribution system that western farmers were saddled with was the major cause of their difficulties. But the farmers were no more inclined to accept these explanations than they were to absolve the British from responsibility for the Indian difficulties. If only the seas were free, they reasoned, costs would go down, prices would rise, and prosperity would return. In urging war, said young Congressman Henry Clay of Kentucky, "we are asserting our right . . . to export our cotton, tobacco and other domestic produce to market."

To some extent, western expansionism also heightened the war fever. The West still contained immense tracts of virgin land, but the westerners wanted more. Canada would surely fall to American arms in the event of war, the frontiersmen believed–and so, apparently, would Florida, for Spain was now Britain's ally. But it was primarily because Canada was nearby and vulnerable that westerners spoke so heatedly about attacking it; had there been no conflict over neutral rights, Canada would not have been an issue. As for Florida, it provided no major cause for a war in itself, being sure to fall into American hands before very long. Already, in 1810, Madison had snapped up the extreme western section without eliciting any effective response from Spain.

Westerners, in short, and many easterners, too, were more patriots than imperialists in 1811 and 1812, although willing enough to seize new territory if the opportunity arose. When the "War Hawks" (their young leaders in Congress) denounced Great Britain, they did so because of the Orders in Council, because of impressment, and because they were ashamed that for so many years their country had been afraid to stand up against British insults. Some of them were so determined to right all national wrongs that they urged a "triangular war" against Great Britain *and* France! The choice seemed to lie between war and surrender of true national independence.

Resistance to War

However, powerful interests in the eastern maritime states were dead set against fighting. Some of this opposition came from Federalists who would have resisted anything the administration proposed, but others based their objections on both economics and a healthy realism. No shipowner could view with equanimity the idea of taking on the largest navy in the world. Such persons complained sincerely enough about impressment and the Orders in Council, but, as with the Embargo Act, war semed worse to them by far. Self-interest led them to urge a policy of patience and fortitude.

Such a policy would have been wise. In the first place, Great Britain did not represent a real threat to the United States. British naval officers were highhanded toward Americans, officials in London complacent and haughty, British diplomats in Washington second-rate and obtuse. But strong economic ties bound the two countries. Language and culture and political traditions united them still more firmly. A powerful pro-American party existed in the mother country and few persons really desired to do the new nation harm, although the bitter memories of the Revolution had not entirely faded. Napoleon, on the other hand, represented a tremendous potential danger to the United States. He had offhandedly turned over Louisiana, but even Jefferson, the chief beneficiary of his largess, hated everything he stood for. Jefferson called Napoleon "the Attila of the age" and "an unprincipled tyrant who is deluging the continent of Europe with blood."

No one understood the Napoleonic threat to America more clearly than the British; part of the stubbornness and arrogance of their maritime policy grew out of their conviction that Napoleon was a threat to all free nations. As the *Times* of London declared almost on the eve of the War of 1812, "The Alps and the Apennines of America are the British Navy. If ever that should be removed, a short time will suffice to establish the headquarters of a [French] Duke-Marshal at Washington." Yet by going to war with Britain, the United States was, of course, aiding Napoleon.

To such lengths had the pursuit of "honor" driven the nation. What made the situation even more unfortunate was the fact that by 1812 conditions had changed in England in a way that made a softening of British maritime policy likely. A business depression caused chiefly by the increasing effectiveness of Napoleon's Continental System was plaguing the country. Manufacturers, blaming the slump on the loss of American markets, were urging repeal of the Orders in Council. Gradually, although with exasperating slowness, the government prepared to yield. On June 23, after a change of ministries, the new foreign secretary, Lord Castlereagh, suspended the orders. Five days earlier, alas, the United States had declared war.

The War of 1812

The illogic of the War Hawks in pressing for a fight was exceeded only by their ineffectiveness in planning and managing the struggle. By what possible strategy could the ostensible objective of the war be achieved? To construct a navy capable of challenging the mighty British fleet would have been the work of many years and a more expensive proposition than even the War Hawks were willing to consider. So hopeless was that prospect that Congress failed to undertake *any* new construction in the first year of the conflict. Several hundred merchant ships lashed a few cannon to their decks and sailed off as privateers to attack British commerce, and the navy's half-dozen first-class warships put to sea, but these forces could not make even a pretense of disputing Britain's mastery of the seas.

For a brief moment the American frigates held center stage, for they were faster, tougher, larger, and more powerfully armed than their British counterparts. Barely two months after the declaration of war, Captain Isaac Hull in the U.S.S. *Constitution* chanced upon H.M.S. *Guerrière* in mid-Atlantic, outmaneuvered her brilliantly, and then gunned her into submission, a hopeless wreck. In October U.S.S. *United States,* captained by Stephen Decatur, hero of the war against the Barbary pirates, caught H.M.S. *Macedonian* off the Madeiras, pounded her unmercifully at long range, and forced her surrender. The *Macedonian* was taken into New London as a prize; over a hundred of her 300-man crew were casualties, while American losses were but a dozen. Then, in December, the *Constitution,* now under Captain William Bainbridge, took on the British frigate *Java* off Brazil. "Old Ironsides" shot away the *Java*'s mainmast and reduced her to a hulk too battered for salvage.

Unfortunately, these victories had little influence upon the outcome of the war. As soon as the Royal Navy could concentrate against them, the American frigates were immobilized, forced to spend the war gathering barnacles at their moorings while powerful British squadrons ranged offshore. The privateering merchantmen were more effective because they were so numerous. The best of them—vessels like the *America,* out of Salem—were redesigned and given more sail to increase their speed, and they were formidably armed. The *America* took 26 prizes valued at more than a million dollars. Privateers captured more than 1,300 British vessels during the war.

From the start, however, it was clear that American aims could be achieved only by indirection, that Great Britain's one weak spot was Canada. The colony had but half a million inhabitants to oppose 7.5 million Americans. Only 2,257 British regulars guarded the entire border from Montreal to Detroit. The Canadian militia was feeble, and many of its members, being of American origin, sympathized with the "invaders." Nevertheless, it quickly developed that the War Hawk talk was mostly brag and bluster. According to congressmen like Clay of Kentucky and Felix Grundy of Tennessee, the West was one solid horde of ferocious frontiersmen, armed to the teeth and thirsting for Canadian blood, but when Congress authorized increasing the army by 25,000 men, only 5,000 volunteered. Kentucky, for example, supposedly eager for the fight, produced but 400 enlistments in response to the first call to the colors.

American military leadership also proved extremely disappointing. Understandably, Madison relied on officers who had served with distinction in the Revolution, but in most cases, as the biographer of one of these men suggested, their abilities "appeared to have evaporated with age and long disuse." Instead of a concentrated strike against Canada's St. Lawrence River lifeline, military leaders planned a complicated three-pronged attack. It was a total failure. In July 1812 General William Hull, veteran of the battles of Trenton, Saratoga, and Monmouth and now governor of Michigan Territory, marched forth with 2,200 men against the Canadian positions facing Detroit.

Hoping that the Canadian militia would desert, he delayed his assault, only to find his communications being threatened by hostile Indians, ably led by Tecumseh. Hastily he retreated to Detroit, and when the Canadians, under General Isaac Brock, pursued him, he surrendered the fort without firing a shot!* Then, in October, another force attempted to invade Canada from Fort Niagara. After an initial success, it was crushed by superior numbers, while a large contingent of New York militiamen watched from the east bank of the Niagara River, unwilling to fight outside their native state. The third arm of the American "attack" was equally unsuccessful. Major General Henry Dearborn, who had fought honorably in the Revolution from Bunker Hill to Yorktown but who had grown so fat that he needed a specially designed cart to get from place to place, set out from Plattsburg, New York, at the head of an army of militiamen. Their objective was Montreal, but when they reached the border, the troops refused to cross. Dearborn meekly marched them back to Plattsburg.

*Hull was court-martialed for cowardice and sentenced to death, but Madison pardoned him in consideration of his brave service during the Revolution.

Meanwhile, the British had captured Fort Michilimackinac in northern Michigan, and the Indians had taken Fort Dearborn (now Chicago), massacring 85 helpless captives. Instead of sweeping triumphantly through Canada, the Americans found themselves trying desperately to keep the Canadians out of Ohio.

Stirred by these disasters, the westerners rallied somewhat in 1813. General Harrison, the victor of Tippecanoe, headed an army of Kentuckians in a series of inconclusive battles against British

CHICAGO HISTORICAL SOCIETY

In Ambroise Louis Garneray's painting, Oliver Hazard Perry's squadron (right) drives through the British line in the Battle of Lake Erie. When Perry's flagship Lawrence *was knocked out of action, he transferred under fire to the* Niagara *and, attacking aggressively, pounded the two largest British vessels into submission.*

troops and Indians led by Tecumseh. He found it impossible to recapture Detroit because a British squadron controlling Lake Erie threatened his communications. President Madison, therefore, assigned Captain Oliver Hazard Perry to the task of building a fleet to challenge this force. In September 1813, at Put-in-Bay near the western end of the lake, Perry destroyed the British vessels in a bloody battle, in which 85 of the 103 men on Perry's flagship were casualties. "We have met the enemy and they are ours," he reported modestly.*

With the Americans in control of Lake Erie, Detroit became untenable for the British, and when they fell back, Harrison gave chase and defeated them at the Thames River, some 60 miles northeast of Detroit. Although little more than a skirmish, this battle had large repercussions. Tecumseh was among the dead (an eccentric American colonel, Richard Mentor Johnson, was to base a long and successful political career upon his claim of having personally done in the great chief), and without him the Indians lost much of their effectiveness. Detroit and the area to the west were thereafter safe.

But American attempts to win control of Lake Ontario and invade Canada in the Niagara region were again thrown back. Another campaign against Montreal also failed. Late in 1813 the British captured Fort Niagara and burned the town of Buffalo. The conquest of Canada was as far from accomplishment as ever.

Furthermore, the British fleet had intensified its blockade of American ports, extending its operations to New England waters, previously spared to encourage the antiwar sentiments of local maritime interests. All along the coast, patrolling cruisers, contemptuous of Jefferson's puny gunboats, captured small craft, raided shore points to commandeer provisions, and collected ransom from port towns by threatening to bombard them. One captain even sent a detail ashore to dig potatoes for his ship's mess.

*About a quarter of Perry's 400 men were Negroes, which led him to remark that "the color of a man's skin" was no more an indication of his worth than "the cut and trimmings" of his coat.

Britain Assumes the Offensive

Until 1814 the British had put relatively little effort into the American war, being primarily concerned with the struggle against Napoleon. However, in 1812 Napoleon had invaded Russia and been thrown back; thereafter one by one his European satellites rose against him. Gradually, he relinquished his conquests; the Allies marched into France, Paris fell, and in April 1814 the emperor abdicated. Then the British, free to strike hard at the United States, dispatched some 14,000 veterans to Canada.

By the spring of 1814, British strategists had devised a master plan for crushing the United States. One army, 11,000 strong, was to march down from Montreal, tracing the route that General Burgoyne had followed to disaster in the Revolution. Another much smaller amphibious force was to make a feint at the Chesapeake Bay area, destroying coastal towns and threatening Washington and Baltimore. A third army was to assemble at Jamaica and sail to attack New Orleans and bottle up the West.

It is necessary, in considering the War of 1812, to remind oneself repeatedly that in the course of the conflict many brave young men lost their lives. Without this sobering reflection it would be easy to dismiss the conflict as a great farce compounded of stupidity, incompetence, and brag. For the British, despite their years of experience against Napoleon, were scarcely more effective than the Americans when they assumed the offensive. The only area where they achieved any significant success was in the diversionary attack in Chesapeake Bay.

While the main British army was assembling in Canada, 4,000 veterans under General Robert Ross sailed for the Chesapeake from Bermuda. After making a rendezvous with a fleet commanded by Vice Admiral Sir Alexander Cochrane and Rear Admiral Sir George Cockburn, which had been terrorizing the coast, they landed in Maryland at the mouth of the Patuxent River, southeast of Washington. A squadron of gunboats "protecting" the capital promptly withdrew upstream, and when the British pursued, their commander ordered them blown up to keep them

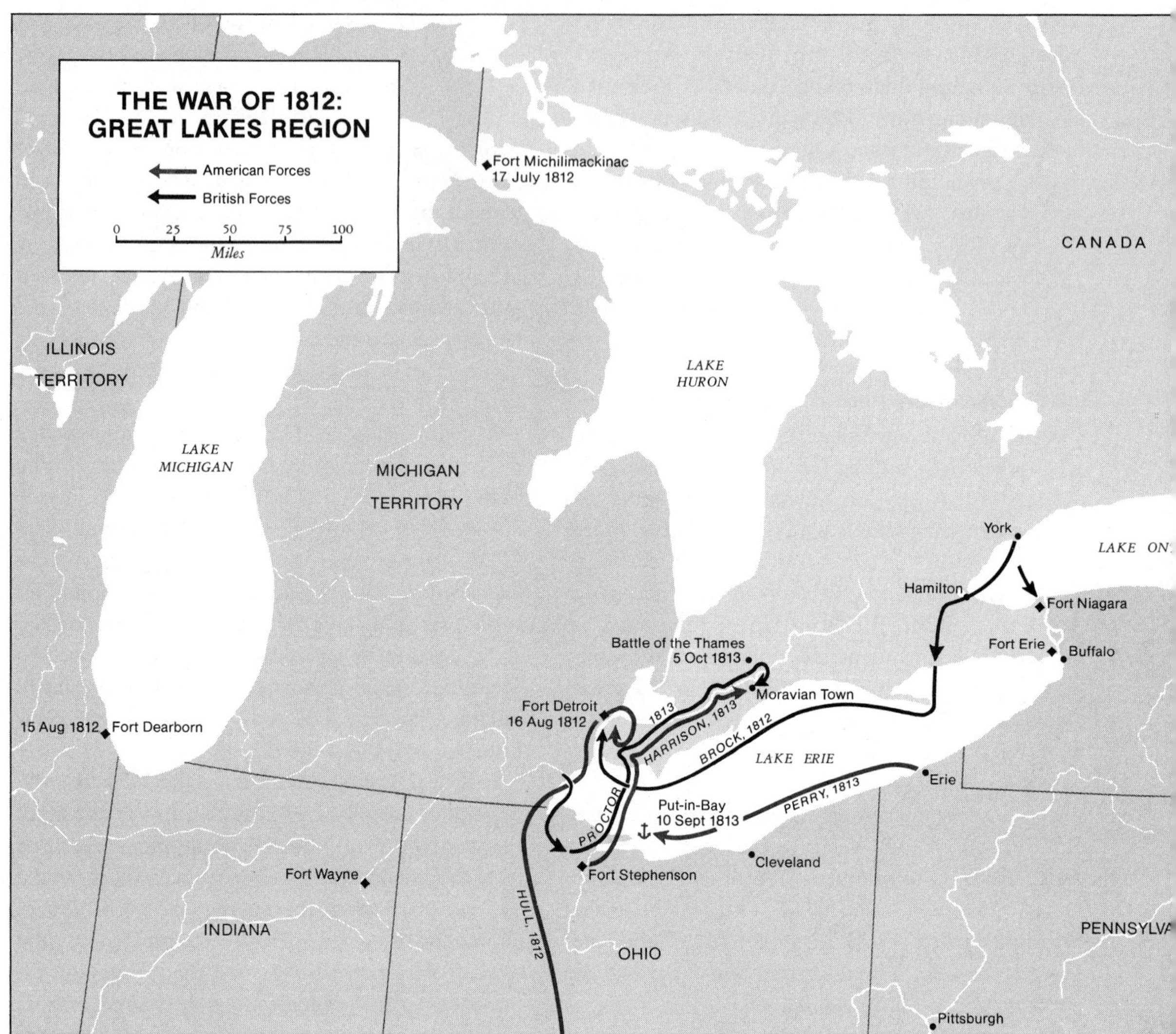

from being captured. The British troops marched rapidly toward Washington. At Bladensburg, on the outskirts of the city, they came upon an army twice their number, commanded by General William H. Winder, a Baltimore lawyer who had already been captured and released by the British in the Canadian fighting. While President Madison and other officials watched, the British charged–and Winder's army turned tail almost without firing a shot. ("No troops could behave worse than they did," a British officer later declared.) The British swarmed into the capital and put most of the public buildings to the torch. Before personally setting fire to the White House, Admiral Cockburn took one of the President's hats and a cushion from Dolley Madison's chair as souvenirs, and, finding the table set for dinner, derisively drank a toast to "Jemmy's health," adding, as an observer coyly recalled, "pleasantries too vulgar for me to repeat."

Yet this was the sum of the British success. When they attempted to take Baltimore, they were stopped by a formidable line of defenses, General Ross falling in the attack. The fleet then moved up the Patapsco River and pounded Fort McHenry with its cannon, raining perhaps as many as 1,800 shells upon it in a 25-hour bombardment on September 13 and 14. While this

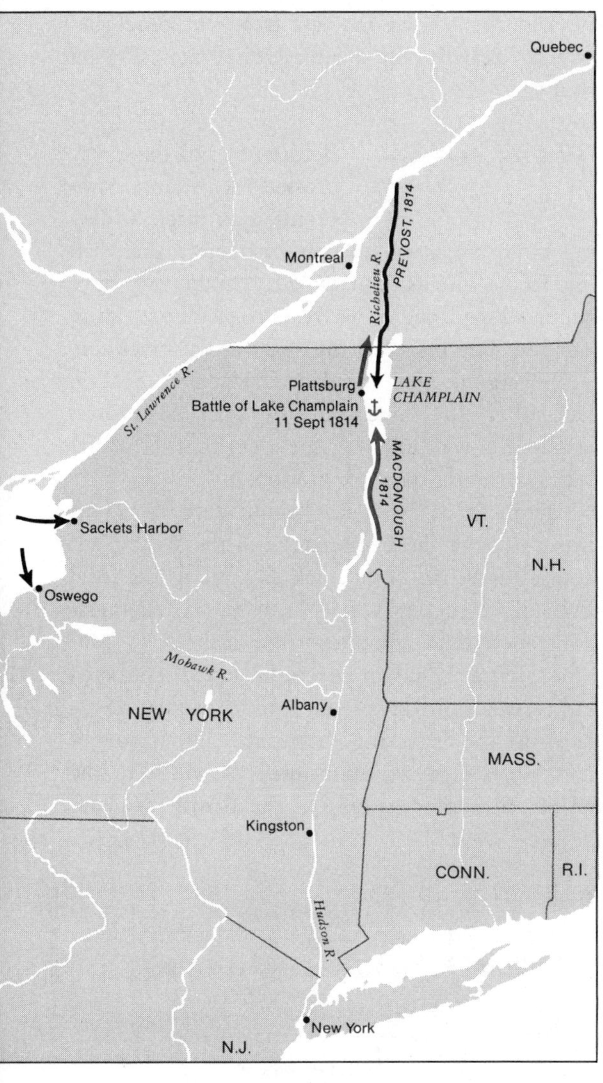

attack was in progress, an American civilian, Francis Scott Key, temporarily detained by the British, watched anxiously through the night. As twilight faded he had seen the Stars and Stripes flying proudly over the battered fort. During the night the glare of rockets and the bursting of bombs gave proof that the defenders were holding out. Then, by the first light of the new day, Key saw again the flag, still waving over Fort McHenry. Drawing an old letter from his pocket, he dashed off the words to "The Star-Spangled Banner," which, when set to music, was to become the national anthem of the United States.

To Key that dawn seemed a turning point in the war. He was roughly correct, for in those last weeks of the summer of 1814 the struggle was indeed being resolved. Unable to crack the defenses of Baltimore, the British withdrew to their ships; shortly after, they sailed off to Jamaica to join with other troops for the attack on New Orleans. The destruction of Washington had been a profound shock; America's will to resist stiffened. Thousands came forward to enlist in the army. This new determination and spirit was strengthened by news from the northern front, where General Sir George Prevost had been leading the main British invasion force south from Montreal. At Plattsburg, on the western shore of Lake Champlain, his 11,000 Redcoats came up against a well-designed defense line manned by 3,300 Americans under General Alexander Macomb. Feeling that he must control the lake before advancing further, Prevost called up his supporting fleet of four ships and a dozen gunboats. An American fleet of roughly similar strength under Captain Thomas Macdonough, a youthful officer who had served with Decatur against the Barbary pirates, came forward to oppose the British. On September 11, in a brutal battle at point-blank range, Macdonough destroyed the British ships and drove off the gunboats. With the Americans now threatening his flank, Prevost lost heart. Despite his overwhelming numerical superiority, he retreated to Canada.

The Treaty of Ghent

The war should have ended with the battles of Plattsburg, Washington, and Baltimore, for later military developments had no effect on the outcome. Earlier in 1814 both sides had agreed to discuss peace terms. Commissioners were appointed and discussions began during the summer at Ghent, in Belgium. The American delegation, one of the most brilliant that has ever represented the United States at an international conference, consisted of former Secretary of the Treasury Gallatin, Speaker Henry Clay of the House of Representatives, James A. Bayard, a former senator, and two veteran diplomats, Jonathan Russell, minister to Sweden, and John Quincy Adams, minister to Russia. Adams was chairman of the delegation. The British commissioners were lesser men by far, partly because they could refer important questions to the Foreign Office in nearby London for decision and partly because Britain's topflight diplomats were all engaged in settling the future of Europe at the Congress of Vienna.

The talks at Ghent were long-drawn-out and frustrating, for the British were in no hurry to sign a treaty, believing that their three-pronged offensive in 1814 would swing the balance in their favor. They demanded at first that the United States abandon practically all the Northwest Territory to the Indians and cede other points along the northern border to Canada. As to impressment and neutral rights, they would make no concessions at all. At one point John Quincy Adams wrote in exasperation: "The causes in which the present war originated . . . will scarce form the most significant item in the Negotiations for Peace." The Americans would yield no territory, for public opinion at home would have been outraged if they had. Old John Adams, for example, told President Madison at this time: "I would continue this war forever rather than surrender an acre. . . ."

Fortunately, the British came to realize that by pressing this point they would only spur the Americans to fight on. News of the defeat at Plattsburg further modified their ambitions, and when the Duke of Wellington advised that from a military point of view they had no case for territorial concessions so long as the United States controlled the Great Lakes, they agreed to settle for *status quo ante bellum*, which is what the Americans were contending for. The other issues, everyone suddenly realized, had simply evaporated. The mighty war triggered by the French Revolution seemed finally over. The seas were free to all ships, and the Royal Navy had no longer any need to snatch sailors from the vessels of the United States or any other power. The Americans decided not to hold out for what would have been meaningless concessions. On Christmas Eve 1814 the treaty, which merely ended the state of hostilities, was signed by all. Although, like other members of his famous family, he was not noted for tact, John Quincy Adams rose to the spirit of the occasion. "I hope," he said, "it will be the last treaty of peace between Great Britain and the United States." And so it was.

The Hartford Convention

Before news of the treaty crossed the Atlantic, two events took place, widely separated in space and in character, that had important effects, but which would not have occurred had the news reached America more rapidly. The first was the Hartford Convention, a meeting of New England Federalists held in December 1814 and January 1815 to protest against the war and plan for a convention of the states to revise the Constitution.

Sentiment in New England had been against the war from the beginning, and the weak Federalist party had been quick to employ the local discontent to revive its fortunes. Federalist-controlled state administrations refused to provide militia to aid in the fight and discouraged individuals and banks from lending money to the hard-pressed national government, which brought it at times close to bankruptcy. Trade with the enemy flourished as long as the British fleet did

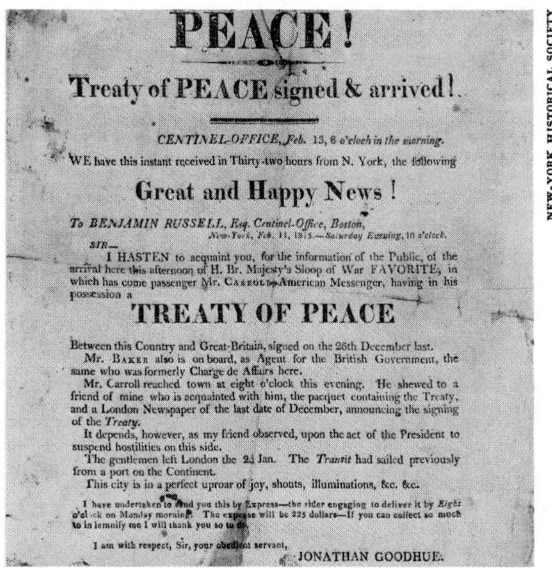

PEACE!

Treaty of PEACE signed & arrived!

CENTINEL-OFFICE, *Feb.* 13, 8 *o'clock in the morning.*

WE have this instant received in Thirty-two hours from N. York, the following

Great and Happy News!

To BENJAMIN RUSSELL, Esq. Centinel-Office, Boston,
New-York, Feb. 11, 1815.—Saturday Evening, 10 o'clock.

SIR—

I HASTEN to acquaint you, for the information of the Public, of the arrival here this afternoon of H. Br. Majesty's Sloop of War FAVORITE, in which has come passenger Mr. CARROLL, American Messenger, having in his possession a

TREATY OF PEACE

Between this Country and Great-Britain, signed on the 26th December last.

Mr. BAKER also is on board, as Agent for the British Government, the same who was formerly Charge de Affairs here.

Mr. Carroll reached town at eight o'clock this evening. He shewed to a friend of mine who is acquainted with him, the pacquet containing the Treaty, and a London Newspaper of the last date of December, announcing the signing of the *Treaty*.

It depends, however, as my friend observed, upon the act of the President to suspend hostilities on this side.

The gentlemen left London the 2d Jan. The *Transit* had sailed previously from a port on the Continent.

This city is in a perfect uproar of joy, shouts, illuminations, &c. &c.

I have undertaken to send you this by Express—the rider engaging to deliver it by *Eight* o'clock on Monday morning. The expense will be 225 dollars—If you can collect so much to indemnify me I will thank you so to do.

I am with respect, Sir, your obedient servant,

JONATHAN GOODHUE.

NEW-YORK HISTORICAL SOCIETY

A ship carrying news of the Treaty of Ghent cleared London January 2, 1815, reaching New York February 11. A post rider delivered it to Boston 32 hours later. This broadside was printed in New Hampshire.

not crack down on New England ports, and goods flowed across the Canadian line in as great or greater volume as during Jefferson's embargo. Their dog-in-the-manger attitude toward the war made the Federalists even more unpopular with the rest of the country, and this in turn encouraged extremists of the Timothy Pickering stripe to talk of seceding from the Union. After Massachusetts summoned the meeting of the Hartford Convention, the fear was widespread that the delegates would propose a New England Confederacy, thus striking at the Union in a moment of great trial.

Luckily for the country, moderate Federalists controlled the convention. They approved a statement that in case of "deliberate, dangerous and palpable infractions of the Constitution" a state has the right "to interpose its authority" to protect itself. This concept, so similar to that expressed in the Kentucky and Virginia resolves by the Republicans when they were in the minority, was accompanied by a list of proposed constitutional amendments designed to make the national government conform more closely to the New England ideal. These would have (1) repealed the three-fifths compromise on representation and direct taxes, which favored the slaveholding states, (2) required a two-thirds vote of Congress for the admission of new states and for declaring war, (3) reduced greatly Congress' power to restrict trade by measures such as an embargo, (4) limited Presidents to a single term, and (5) made it illegal for naturalized citizens to hold national office. Nothing formally proposed at Hartford was treasonable, but the proceedings were kept secret and rumors of impending secession were rife. In this atmosphere came the news from Ghent of an honorable peace. The Federalists had been denouncing the war and predicting a British triumph; now they were discredited.

The Battle of New Orleans

Still more discrediting to them was the second event that would not have happened had communications been more rapid: the Battle of New Orleans. During the fall of 1814 the British had gathered an army of about 7,500 veterans, commanded by Major General Sir Edward Pakenham, at Negril Bay in Jamaica. Late in November an armada of more than 50 ships set out for New Orleans. Instead of sailing directly up from the mouth of the Mississippi as the Americans expected, Pakenham approached the city by way of Lake Borgne, to the east. Proceeding through a maze of swamps and bayous, he advanced close to the city's gates before being detected. Early on the afternoon of December 23, mud-spattered messengers burst into the headquarters of General Andrew Jackson, commanding the defenses of New Orleans, with the news.

For once in this war of error and incompetence the United States had the right man in the right place at the right time. After his Revolutionary War experiences, Jackson had studied law, then moved west, settling in Nashville, Tennessee. He served briefly in both houses of Congress and was active in Tennessee affairs. Jackson was a hard man and fierce-tempered, frequently involved in brawls and duels, but honest and, by western standards, a good public servant. When the war broke out, he was elected major general of volunteers. Almost alone among nonprofessional troops during the conflict, his men won impressive victories over the Indians. In two battles in eastern Alabama they killed nearly a thousand Creeks while losing only 64 of their own number. Jackson's success was due to his toughness and determination rather than to military genius. Discipline, based on fear and respect, made his rough and individualistic frontier militiamen into an army. His men called Jackson "Old Hickory"; the Indians, in contrast, called him "Sharp Knife."

After these victories, Jackson was assigned the job of defending the Gulf Coast against the expected British strike. Although he had misjudged Pakenham's destination at first, he was ready when the news of the British arrival reached him. "Gentlemen," he said at once, "the British are below, we must fight them tonight."

While the British rested and awaited reinforcements, planning to take the city the next morning, Jackson rushed up men and guns. At 7:30 P.M. on December 23 he struck hard, taking the

An engineer in the Louisiana militia named Hyacinthe Laclotte painted the Battle of New Orleans from sketches he made during the action. The main British thrust is shown in progress against the American left. In the foreground a column carrying scaling ladders is caught in a withering fire. In addition to routing the British infantry, Jackson's batteries silenced their artillery as well.

British by surprise. But Pakenham's veterans rallied quickly, and the battle was inconclusive. Jackson then prudently fell back to a point five miles below New Orleans and dug in.

He chose his position wisely. On his right was the Mississippi, on his left an impenetrable swamp, to the front an open field. On the day before Christmas (while the commissioners in Ghent were signing the peace treaty), Jackson's army, which included an excellent, but of course segregated, unit of free Negro militiamen, erected an earthen parapet about ten yards behind a dry canal bed. Here the Americans would make their stand.

For two weeks Pakenham hesitated, probing the American line. Jackson strengthened his defenses daily. At night, patrols of silent Tennesseans slipped out with knife and tomahawk to stalk British sentries. They called this grim game "going hunting." Finally, on January 8, 1815, Pakenham ordered a general assault. The American position was formidable, but his men had defeated Napoleon. Pakenham assumed that the undisciplined Americans—about 4,500 strong—would run at the sight of bare steel. At dawn, through the lowland mists, 5,300 Redcoats moved forward.

The Americans did not run. Perhaps they feared the wrath of their commander more than British bayonets. Artillery raked the advancing British, and when the range closed to about 150 yards, the riflemen opened up. Jackson had formed his men in three ranks behind the parapet. One rank fired, then stepped down as another took its place. By the time the third had loosed its volley, the first had reloaded and was ready to fire again. Nothing could stand against this rain of lead. General Pakenham was wounded

twice, then killed by a shell fragment while calling up his last reserves. During the battle a single brave British officer reached the top of the parapet. When retreat was finally sounded, the British had suffered nearly 2,100 casualties; another 500 were prisoners. Eight Americans lost their lives, and 13 more were wounded.

Fruits of "Victory"

Word of Jackson's magnificent triumph reached Washington almost simultaneously with the good news from Ghent. The public found it easy to confuse the chronology and consider the war a victory won on the battlefield below New Orleans instead of the stand-off it actually was. Jackson became the "Hero of New Orleans." The whole nation rejoiced; one sour Republican complained that the Federalists of Massachusetts had fired off more powder and wounded more men celebrating the victory than they had during the whole course of the conflict. The Senate ratified the peace treaty unanimously, and all the frustrations and failures of the past few years were forgotten. The war, said Albert Gallatin, had "renewed and reinstated" the old nationalism of the Revolution. "The people have now more general objects of attachment with which their pride and political opinions are connected. They are more American; they feel and act more like a nation." Similarly, American success in holding off Great Britain and fighting a war despite internal frictions went a long way toward convincing European nations that both the United States and its republican form of government were here to stay. The powers might accept these truths with less pleasure than the Americans, but accept them they did.

Fortunately, the nation had suffered relatively few casualties, and not much economic loss either, except to the shipping interests. The war had offered another excuse to drive back the Indians, who were the main losers in the contest. When Jackson defeated the Creeks, for example, he forced them to cede 23 million acres to the United States.

The war also completed the destruction of the Federalist party. The success of the Jeffersonians' political techniques had inspired younger Federalists in many parts of the country to imitate them, holding rallies, adopting the rhetoric of democracy, and (more important) perfecting local organizations in most of the states. In 1812 the party made significant gains in the Northeast, electing numbers of congressmen and winning many state and local offices. They did not run a candidate for President, but their support enabled the dissident New York Republican De Witt Clinton to obtain 89 electoral votes to Madison's 128. Their private correspondence reveals that these Young Federalists were no more enchanted by the virtues of mass democracy than their elders, but by mouthing democratic slogans they revived the party in many districts. The results of the war undermined their efforts. They had not supported the war effort; they had argued that the British could not be defeated; they had dealt clandestinely with the enemy; they had even threatened to break up the Union. So long as the issue remained in doubt, these policies won considerable support, but New Orleans made the party an object of ridicule and scorn. Soon after the war, it disappeared even in New England, swamped beneath a wave of confidence and patriotism that flooded the land.

Yet the chief reason for the happy results of the war had little to do with American events. In 1815, after the flurry caused by Napoleon's return from exile had ended at Waterloo, Europe settled down to what was to be a century of relative peace. With peace came an end to serious foreign threats to America and a revival of commerce on a great scale. European emigration to the United States, long held back by the troubled times, soon spurted ahead rapidly, providing the expanding country with its most valuable asset—strong, willing hands to do the work of developing the land. The mood of Jefferson's first term, when democracy had reigned amid peace and plenty, came back with a rush. And the nation, having had its fill of international complications, turned in on itself, as Jefferson had wished it to. With Europe finally quiescent and absorbed in the task of bandaging its own wounds, it could afford to do so.

Anglo-American Rapprochement

There remained a few matters to straighten out with Great Britain and Spain. Since no territory had changed hands at Ghent, neither signatory had reason to harbor a grudge against the other. But neither was there a sudden flowering of Anglo-American friendship. British conservatives continued, in the words of historian George Dangerfield, to view the United States as "little more than a grimy republican thumbprint" on the pages of history, and the device of "twisting the British lion's tail" remained an important tool in the work chest of many an American politician for the rest of the century. Yet for years no serious trouble marred Anglo-American relations. The war had taught the British to respect Americans, if not to love them. As one British naval officer said: "I don't like Americans; I never did, and never shall. . . . I have no wish to eat with them, drink with them, deal with, or consort with them in any way; but let me tell the whole truth, *nor fight* with them. . . ."

In this atmosphere, the two countries worked out peaceful solutions to a number of old problems. In July 1815 they signed a commercial convention ending discriminatory duties and making other adjustments favorable to trade. Boundary difficulties also moved toward resolution. At Ghent the diplomats had created several joint commissions to settle the disputed boundary between the United States and Canada. Many years were to pass before the line was finally drawn, but establishing the principle of defining the border by negotiation was extremely important. Eventually, a line extending over 3,000 miles was agreed to without the firing of a single shot.

Immediately after the war, the British began to rebuild their shattered Great Lakes fleet. Alarmed by this but disinclined to engage in a naval arms race, the United States suggested a mutual demilitarization of the lakes, and the British agreed. The Rush-Bagot Agreement of 1817 limited each power to one 100-ton vessel armed with a single 18-pounder on Lake Champlain and another on Lake Ontario. They were to have two each for all the other Great Lakes. Gradually, as an outgrowth of this decision, the entire border was demilitarized, a remarkable achievement. In 1818 the two countries agreed to the 49th parallel as the northern boundary of the Louisiana Territory between the Lake of the Woods and the Rockies and to the joint control of the Oregon country for ten years. The question of the rights of Americans in the Labrador and Newfoundland fisheries, which had been much disputed during the Ghent negotiations, was also settled amicably.

Transcontinental Treaty

The acquisition of Spanish Florida and the settlement of the western boundary of Louisiana were also accomplished as an aftermath of the War of 1812, but in a far different spirit than that which characterized Anglo-American negotiations. Spain's control of the Floridas was feeble and weakening steadily. United States troops had seized the rest of West Florida in 1813, and frontiersmen in Georgia were eyeing East Florida greedily. The weakness of the Spanish colonial government gave the Georgians legitimate grievances. Marauding Indians struck frequently into American territory, then fled to sanctuary across the line. American slaves who escaped across the border could not be recovered. In 1818 President James Monroe ordered General Andrew Jackson to clear raiding Seminole Indians from American soil and to pursue them into Florida if necessary. Seizing upon these instructions, Jackson marched into Florida and easily captured two Spanish forts. In the process he apprehended and hanged two British subjects who had been inciting the Seminoles against the United States. This rash act caused a momentary war scare in London and Washington, but nothing came of it.

Although Jackson eventually withdrew from Florida, the impotence of the Spanish government made it obvious even in Madrid that if nothing were done, the United States would soon fill the power vacuum by seizing the whole territory. The Spanish also feared for the future of their tottering Latin-American empire, and especially for the northern provinces of Mexico, which stood in the path of American westward expansion. Spain and the United States had never determined where the Louisiana Territory ended and Spanish Mexico began. In return for American acceptance of a boundary as far east of the Rio Grande as possible, Spain was ready to surrender Florida.

For these reasons, the Spanish minister in Washington, Luis de Onís, undertook, in December 1817, to negotiate a treaty with John Quincy Adams, Monroe's secretary of state. Adams understood Onís' objectives perfectly. Realizing that the future of Florida was no longer really an issue, he pressed the minister mercilessly on the question of the western boundary, driving a

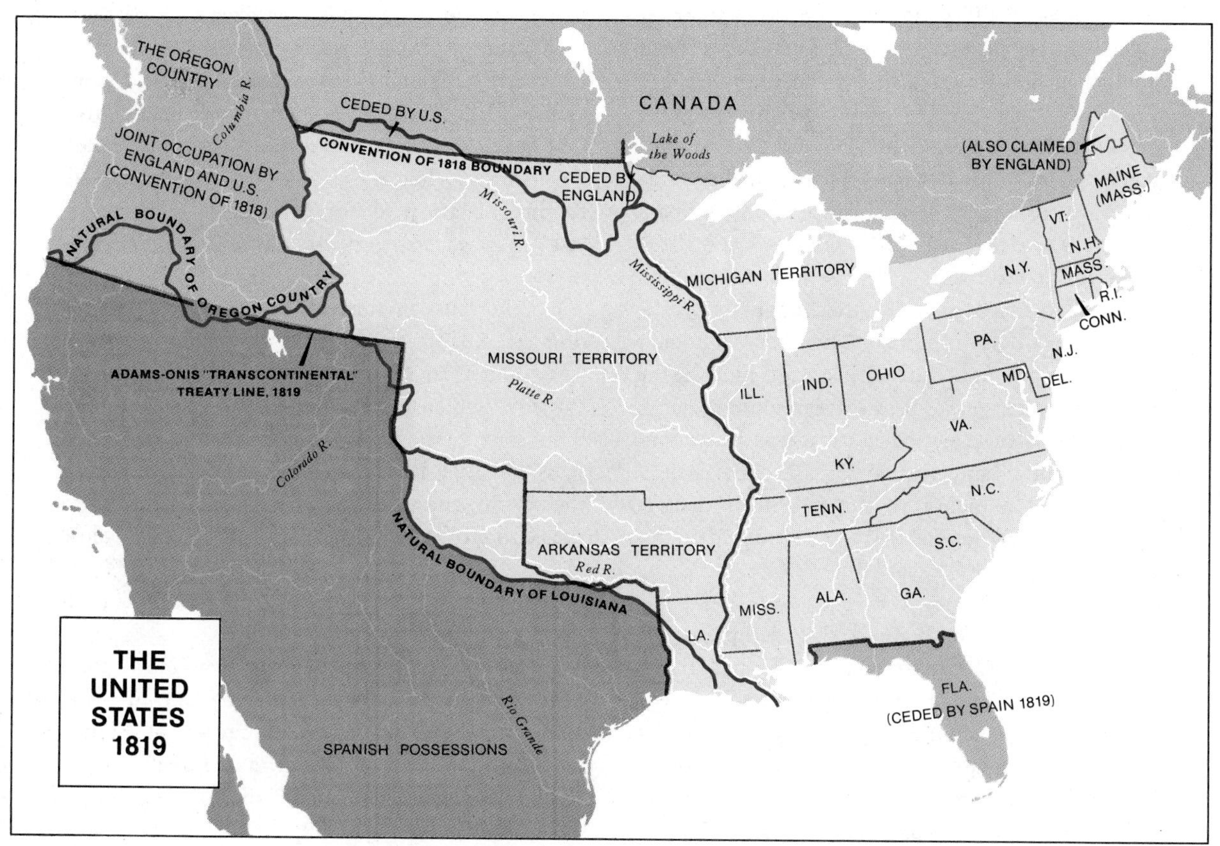

bargain that would have done credit to the most tight-fisted of his Yankee ancestors. Onís opened their talks by proposing a line in the middle of what is now Louisiana, and when Adams countered by demanding a boundary running through present-day Texas, Onís professed to be greatly shocked. Abstract right, not power, should determine the settlement, he said. "Truth is of all times, and reason and justice are founded upon immutable principles." To this Adams relentlessly replied: "That truth is of all times and that reason and justice are founded upon immutable principles has never been contested by the United States, but neither truth, reason, nor justice consists in stubbornness of assertion, nor in the multiplied repetition of error."

In the end Onís could only yield. He saved Texas for his monarch, but accepted a boundary to the Louisiana Territory that followed the Sabine, Red, and Arkansas rivers to the Continental Divide and the 42nd parallel to the Pacific, thus abandoning Spain's claim to a huge area beyond the Rockies that had no connection at all with the Louisiana Purchase. Adams even compelled him to agree that when the boundary followed rivers, United States territory was to extend to the farthest bank, not merely to midstream. The United States also obtained Florida in return for a mere $5 million, paid not to Spain but to Americans who held claims against the Spanish government. This "Transcontinental Treaty" was signed in 1819, although final ratification was delayed until 1821. Most Americans at the time thought the purchase of Florida the most important part of the treaty, but Adams, whose vision of America's future was truly continental, knew better. "The acquisition of a definite line of boundary to the [Pacific] forms a great epoch in our history," he recorded in his diary.

The Monroe Doctrine

Concern with defining the boundaries of the United States was part of a general withdrawal from European affairs; it did not reflect a desire to limit future expansion, being simply a feeling that there should be no more quibbling and quarreling with foreign powers that might distract the people from the great task of national development. The final, classic enunciation of this point of view, the completion of America's withdrawal from Europe, was the Monroe Doctrine.

Two separate strands met in this pronouncement. The first led from Moscow to Alaska, then down the Pacific Coast to the Oregon country. Beginning with the explorations of Vitus Bering in 1741, the Russians had maintained a continuing interest in fishing and fur trading along the northwest coast of North America. In 1821 the czar extended his claim as far south as the 51st parallel and forbade the ships of other powers to enter coastal waters north of this point. This announcement was naturally disturbing to Americans.

The second strand ran from the courts of the western European monarchs to Latin America. Between 1817 and 1822 practically all of the region from the Rio Grande to the Strait of Magellan had won its independence. Spain, former master of all this area except Brazil, was too weak to win it back by force, but Austria, Prussia, France, and Russia decided at the Congress of Verona in 1822 to try to regain the area for Spain in the interests of what they called "legitimacy." There was talk of sending a powerful French army to South America. This possibility also caused very grave concern in Washington.

To the Russian threat, Monroe and Secretary of State Adams responded with a terse warning: "The American continents are no longer subjects for any new European colonial establishments." This statement did not overly impress the Russians, but they had no real intention of colonizing the region, and in 1824 they signed a treaty with the United States abandoning all claims below the present southern limit of Alaska (54°40′ north latitude) and removing their restrictions on foreign shipping.

The Latin-American problem was more complex. The United States was not alone in being alarmed by the prospect of a revival of French or Spanish power in that region. Great Britain, having profited greatly from the breakup of the mercantilistic Spanish empire by developing a thriving commerce with the new republics, had no intention of permitting a restoration of the old order. But the British government preferred not to recognize the new revolutionary South American nations, for England itself was only beginning to recover from a period of social upheaval as violent as any in its history. Bad times and high food prices had combined to cause riots, conspiracies, and angry demands for parliamentary reform. The Coercion Act of 1817 and the so-called Six Acts of 1819 had cracked down viciously on all dissent, causing further resentment. Any admission that rebellion could be legitimized might loose an avalanche. Shelley caught the spirit of the times in "England in 1819":

> Rulers who neither see nor feel nor know,
> But leech-like to their fainting country cling . . .
> A people starved and stabbed in the untilled field—
> An army which liberticide and prey
> Make as a two-edged sword . . .

In any case, in 1823 the British foreign minister, George Canning, suggested to Richard Rush, the American minister in London, that the United States and Britain issue a joint statement opposing any French interference in South America and pledging that they themselves would never annex any part of Spain's old empire, but saying nothing about recognition of the new republics. This proposal of joint action with the British was flattering to the United States but scarcely in its best interests. For one thing, the United States had already recognized the new republics; for another, it had no desire to help Great Britain retain its South American trade. Finally, as Secretary Adams pointed out (and his influence was decisive), to agree to the proposal would be to abandon the possibility of someday adding Cuba or any other part of Latin America to the United States. America should act independently, Adams urged. "It would be more candid, as well as more dignified, to avow our principles explicitly . . . than to come in as a cock-boat in the wake of the British man-of-war."

Monroe heartily endorsed Adams' argument and decided to include a statement of American policy in his annual message to Congress in December 1823. "The American continents," he wrote, "by the free and independent condition which they have assumed and maintain, are henceforth not to be considered as subjects for future colonization by any European powers." Europe's political system was "essentially different" from that developing in the New World and the two should not be mixed. The United States would not interfere with existing European colonies in either North or South America and would avoid involvement in strictly European affairs, but any attempt to extend European control to countries in the hemisphere that had already won their independence would be considered, Monroe warned, "the manifestation of an unfriendly disposition toward the United States" and consequently a threat to the nation's "peace and safety."

This policy statement—it was not dignified with the title "Monroe Doctrine" until decades later—attracted little notice in Europe or Latin America, and not much more at home. Obviously the United States, whose own capital had been overrun by a mere raiding party less than ten years earlier, could not police the whole Western Hemisphere. European statesmen dismissed Monroe's message as "arrogant" and "blustering," worthy only of "the most profound contempt." Latin Americans, while appreciating the intent behind it, knew better than to count on American aid in case of foreign attack. But the principles laid down by President Monroe so perfectly expressed the wishes of the people of the United States that when the country grew powerful enough to enforce them, there was little need to alter or embellish his pronouncement. The depth and permanence of American feeling on the subject has been repeatedly demonstrated, as recently, for example, as in 1962, when Russia attempted to establish missile bases in Cuba.

Later generations saw the Monroe Doctrine as warning Europe: "Hands off Latin America!" In this sense, as George Dangerfield has said, it represented a "valiant committal of the United States to a leading position in *world* politics." At the time, however, the converse of this command—"not," in Monroe's words, "to interfere in the internal concerns" of any European nation—probably seemed more important to most contemporaries. Americans had work to do. They had escaped from European entanglements and wanted nothing better than to be left alone. Better still if Europe could be made to allow the entire hemisphere to follow its own path. This was the heart of Monroe's message.

SUPPLEMENTARY READING Henry Adams' *History of the United States** and most of the other volumes dealing with Jefferson's first administration mentioned in the last chapter continue to be useful for this period. On John Randolph, see Henry Adams, *John Randolph** (1882), and W.C. Bruce, *John Randolph of Roanoke* (1939). C.P. Magrath, *Yazoo: Law and Politics in the New Republic** (1966), is the best treatment of the case of *Fletcher v. Peck.* The best life of Burr is Nathan Schachner, *Aaron Burr** (1937); the most recent studies of his conspiracy are T.P. Abernethy, *The Burr Conspiracy* (1954), and F.F. Beirne, *Shout Treason: The Trial of Aaron Burr* (1959). Raymond Walters, Jr., *Albert Gallatin: Jeffersonian Financier and Diplomat* (1957), is an excellent biography of one of the key figures of the age.

By far the best account of the controversy over neutral rights is Bradford Perkins, *Prologue to War** (1961), which combines careful research with lucid interpretation. Madison's actions can be followed in Irving Brant, *James Madison: The President* (1956). Both L.M. Sears, *Jefferson and the Embargo* (1927), and J.F. Zimmerman, *Impressment of American Seamen* (1925), are solid monographic studies. S.E. Morison, *The Maritime History of Massachusetts** (1921), contains excellent chapters on the embargo and war periods. J.W. Pratt first played up the role of the West in triggering the War of 1812 in his *Expansionists of 1812* (1925). Pratt's thesis is attacked sharply by A.L. Burt, *The United States, Great Britain, and British North America from the Revolution to the Establishment of Peace After the War of 1812* (1940). Perkins deals with this controversy judiciously in *Prologue to War,* but see also Reginald Horsman, *The Causes of the War of 1812** (1962), and R.H. Brown, *The Republic in Peril: 1812* (1963).

For the war itself, see H.L. Coles, *The War of 1812** (1965), a good brief account, and F.F. Beirne, *The War of 1812* (1949), a solid if uninspired volume. Irving Brant, *James Madison: Commander-in-Chief* (1961), vigorously defends Madison's handling of the war. Jackson's part in the conflict is described vividly in Marquis James, *Andrew Jackson: The Border Captain** (1933). Glenn Tucker, *Poltroons and Patriots* (1954), contains much colorful detail. On the Treaty of Ghent, see F.L. Engelman, *The Peace of Christmas Eve* (1962). Bradford Perkins, *Castlereagh and Adams* (1964), S.F. Bemis, *John Quincy Adams and the Foundations of American Foreign Policy* (1949), and George Dangerfield, *The Era of Good Feelings** (1952), also discuss the settlement intelligently. For the Hartford Convention, consult S.E. Morison, *Harrison Gray Otis, 1765–1848* (1969), and Dangerfield's *The Era of Good Feelings.*

For the postwar diplomatic settlements, see Bradford Perkins, *Castlereagh and Adams,* and S.F. Bemis, *John Quincy Adams*; for the Monroe Doctrine specifically, see Dexter Perkins, *The Monroe Doctrine: 1823–1826* (1927), and A.P. Whitaker, *The United States and the Independence of Latin America** (1941).

*Available in paperback.

8

New Forces in American Life

James Monroe, of Westmoreland County, Virginia, was a very lucky man. Neither brilliant nor especially articulate, he was nonetheless an outstanding success. He lived a long life in good health; he was happily married to a beautiful and cultivated wife; he saw close up most of the great events in the history of the young republic and enjoyed the friendship and respect of most of its great figures. Washington looked upon him with favor when he was a youthful soldier and sent him on his first diplomatic mission in 1794. He studied law at the feet of Jefferson, who became his lifelong friend.

Like so many Virginians of his generation, Monroe's chief ambition was to serve his country, and this end he achieved in full measure. At the age of 18 he shed his blood for liberty at the glorious Battle of Trenton. Later he was twice governor of his state, a United States senator, and a Cabinet officer. He was at various times the nation's representative in Paris, Madrid, and London. Finally, in 1816, he was elected President, defeating Rufus King of New York by 183 electoral votes to 34.

The Era of Good Feelings

As President, Monroe's good fortune continued. The world was finally at peace, the country united and prosperous. A pilot who would keep a steady hand on the helm and hold to the present course seemed called for, a man of good feeling rather than of brilliance. Monroe possessed exactly the qualities that the times required. "He is a man whose soul might be turned wrongside outwards, without discovering a blemish," Jefferson said of him, and John Quincy Adams, in general a harsh critic of public men, praised Monroe's courtesy, sincerity, and sound judgment. Courtesy and purity of soul do not always suffice to make a good President, and in more troubled times Monroe might well have brought disaster, for he was not a forceful leader. He originated few policies, presented few important state papers, organized no personal machine. "The existence of parties is not necessary to free government," he told Andrew Jackson in 1816. The Monroe Doctrine, by far the most significant achievement of his administration, was as much the work of Secretary of State Adams as his own. No one ever claimed that Monroe was better than second-rate, yet when his first term ended, he was re-elected without organized opposition. In the absence of a real contest, few persons bothered to vote in the election. In Richmond, Virginia, for example, only 17 persons voted for Presidential electors in 1820.

Monroe seemed to epitomize the final resolution of the conflicts that had divided men politically in the hectic years between the end of the Revolution and the Peace of Ghent. He was no bland exponent of compromise. In his long career he frequently took strong positions on controversial issues: he opposed the ratification of the Constitution; he almost fought a duel with Hamilton; he battled for office with his fellow Virginian James Madison. At one point in his career he appeared to be too pro-French, at another too pro-British. He was even, for a time, the darling of John Randolph and the Quids.

But by 1817 all these issues of earlier days had vanished. Monroe, with a delicate awareness of the public mood, dramatized their disappearance by beginning his first term with a good-will tour of New England, heartland of the opposition. The tour was a triumph. Everywhere the President was greeted with tremendous enthusiasm. After he visited Boston, once the headquarters but now the graveyard of Federalism, a Federalist newspaperman gave the age its name. Pointing out that the celebrations attending Monroe's visit had brought together in friendly intercourse many persons "whom party politics had long severed," he dubbed the times the "Era of Good Feelings."

It has often been said that the harmony of Monroe's administrations was terribly superficial, that beneath the calm lay potentially disruptive political questions that had not yet begun to influence national politics. The dramatic change from the unanimity of Monroe's second election to the factional fragmentation of four years later, when four candidates divided the vote and the House of Representatives had to choose the President, seems to prove the point beyond argument.

Nevertheless, the people of the period had good reasons for thinking it extraordinarily harmonious. Peace, prosperity, liberty, and progress: all flourished in 1817 in the United States. Why should any freeborn American want to change the system? The heirs of Jefferson had accepted, with a varying mixture of resignation and enthusiasm, most of the economic policies advocated by the Hamiltonians. In 1816 Madison put his signature to a bill creating a new national bank almost exactly in the image of Hamilton's, which had expired before the War of 1812, and to a protective tariff which, if less comprehensive than the kind Hamilton had wanted, marked an important concession to the rising manufacturing interests. Monroe accepted the principle of federal aid for transportation projects, even approving a bill authorizing Congress to invest $300,000 in the Chesapeake and Delaware Canal Company.

Furthermore, the Jeffersonian balance between individual liberty and responsible government, having survived both bad management and war, had justified itself to the opposition. The new unity was symbolized by the restored friendship of Jefferson and John Adams. In 1801 Adams had slipped sulkily out of Washington without waiting to attend his successor's inauguration, but after ten years of icy silence, these two old collaborators effected a reconciliation. Although they continued to disagree vigorously about matters of philosophy and government, the bitterness between them disappeared entirely. By Monroe's day, Jefferson was writing long letters to "my dear friend" and receiving equally warm and voluminous replies.

When political divisions appeared again, as they very soon did, it was not because the old balance had been shaky. Few of the new controversies challenged Republican principles or revived old issues. Instead, these controversies were children of the present and of the future—products of the continuing growth of the country.

National unity speeded national expansion, yet expansion, paradoxically, endangered national unity. For expansion, being dynamic, inevitably resulted in change. As the country grew, new differences appeared within its sections even though, at the same time, the threads binding the parts became stronger and more numerous.

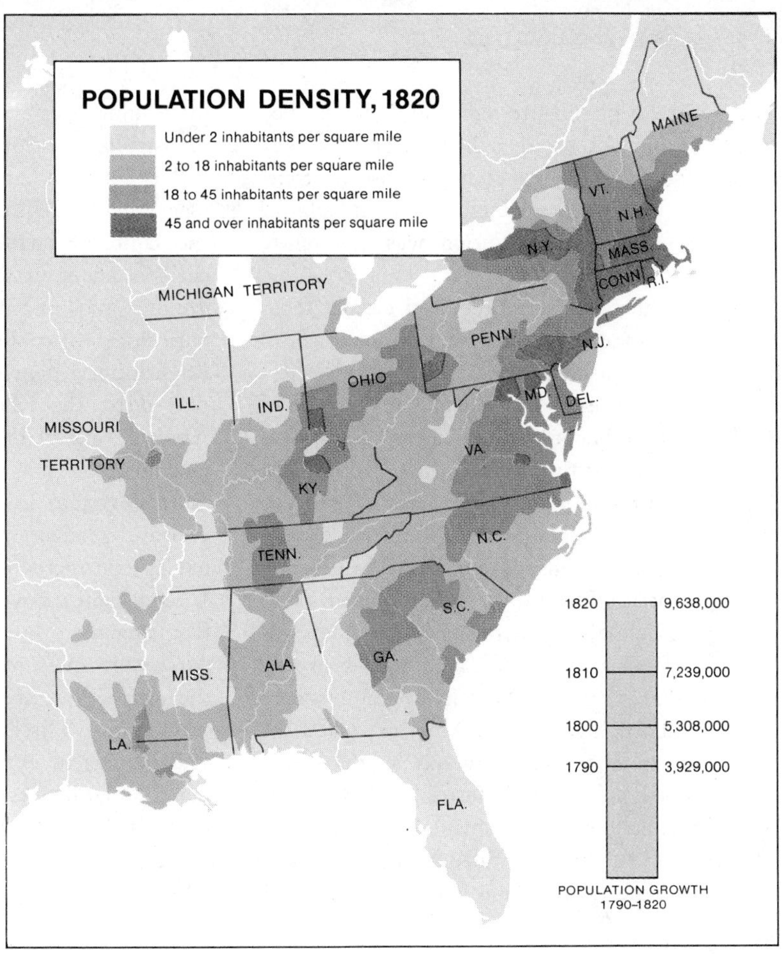

The 1820 census revealed a 33.1 per cent increase in the population nationwide over the previous census, with some of the largest increases in the northwest. The population of the area comprising Illinois, Indiana, and Michigan Territory, for example, grew from 31,000 to over 200,000 during the decade.

Growth in the 30 years after the ratification of the Constitution had been phenomenal even for a country that was accustomed to rapid expansion. The area of the United States doubled, increasing from 888,811 to 1,788,006 square miles, but this figure is deceptive because very little of the Louisiana Purchase had actually been settled by 1820. More significantly, the population of the nation had more than doubled, from 4 million to 9.6 million. Perhaps the most remarkable feature of this growth was that nearly all of it resulted from natural increase of the population. Only about 250,000 immigrants entered the United States between 1790 and 1820, for the turbulent conditions of Europe during the wars had slowed the flow of humanity across the Atlantic to a trickle. The pace of the westward movement had also quickened. In 1790 scarcely 100,000 white men were living beyond the Appalachians. By 1820 more than 2.2 million had settled in the Mississippi Valley, and the moving edge of civilization ran in a long, irregular curve from Michigan to Arkansas.

To the superficial observer, Americans earned their living in the Era of Good Feelings in much the same way as in 1790. The country was still overwhelmingly rural. Less than 700,000 people lived in centers of more than 2,500 souls in 1820, and the percentage of urban dwellers had actually declined in the ten previous years.

Roots of Economic Growth

By the 1820's this seemingly uniform and static condition was changing; the nation was on the brink of a major economic readjustment, for certain obscure seeds planted in the early years of the republic had taken root. Almost unnoticed in a nation that lived by agriculture and maritime commerce, new ways of producing goods and making a living were beginning to take hold. Soon they would be obvious to all; a little later still, they would dominate the economy almost as thoroughly as farming had dominated it in colonial days. The industrial revolution was coming to America with a rush.

The growth of industry required certain technological advances and the development of a new type of business organization. Both these elements already existed in Europe at the time of the Revolution, but it was only after the ratification of the Constitution that they crossed the Atlantic. No doubt they would have come even without the Revolution, for British efforts to prevent the growth of manufactures in the colonies had never been effective. The great advances that followed so closely upon the heels of independence could not have come much earlier in any case, for they were new even in England, where they were born, and colonial America lacked the labor and capital to exploit them. Yet the Revolution helped to trigger industrialization by releasing vast amounts of human energy and by inspiring pride and confidence in so many breasts, and the Constitution added to the effect by making possible the development of the new industry on a national scale.

Between 1790 and 1803 a series of events took place that were basic to the industrialization of the United States and the evolution of a truly national economy. The significance of some was instantly recognized; others seemed merely minor curiosities to contemporaries. In 1790 a young English-born genius named Samuel Slater, employed by the Rhode Island merchant firm of Almy & Brown, began to spin cotton thread by machine, the first effective introduction of the factory system in the United States. In 1800 a youthful graduate of Yale College, Eli Whitney, having contracted to produce 10,000 rifles for the United States government, succeeded in manufacturing them by such precise methods that the parts were interchangeable, a major step toward the perfection of the assembly-line system of production. Three years later Oliver Evans, a Philadelphia inventor, had come close to achieving automation. As early as 1785 he had cut labor costs in half in flour-milling by the use of machines; by 1803 his system had reached a point where a man poured wheat down a chute at one

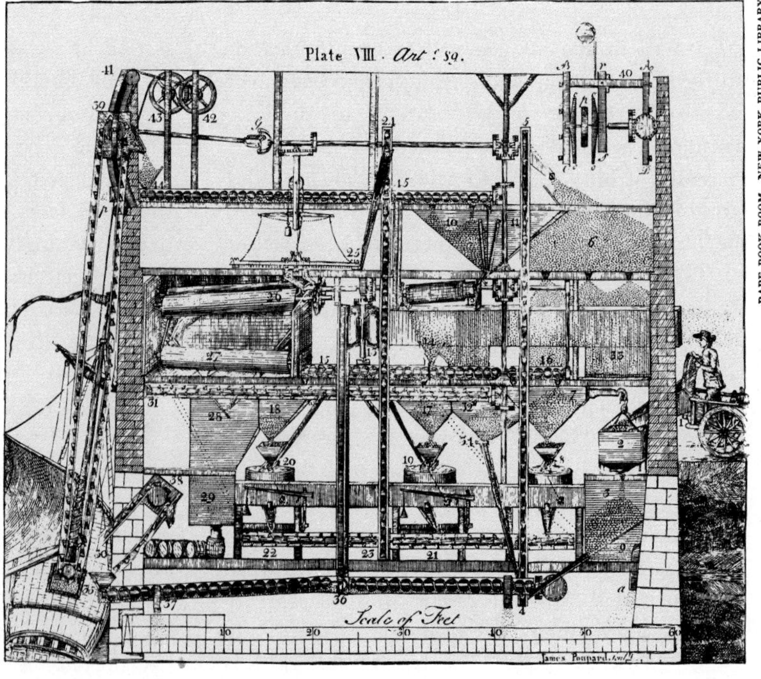

This cross-section plan of Oliver Evans' automated gristmill dates from 1795. A farmer (right) pours wheat into a chute; at the left a "bucket elevator" raises wheat from a ship's hold. Within the mill the grain moved vertically by bucket elevator and horizontally by Archimedes screw. Barrels of flour are at lower left.

end of his plant and a second man headed the barrels of superfine flour which emerged at the other end. All the intervening steps of weighing, cleaning, grinding, and packing were performed by Evans' machines.

Other important technological advances during these same years included John Fitch's construction and operation of the world's first regularly scheduled steamboat in 1790, and the aforementioned Eli Whitney's invention of the cotton gin in 1793. Fitch lacked the financial backing to sustain his venture, and Whitney's invention was so shamelessly pirated that it earned him nothing but fame. But the steamboat and the gin affected American history almost as much as the factory system and mass production. The former, when employed on western waters, cut the cost of transportation dramatically and brought the West into the national economy. The latter made possible the widespread cultivation of cotton, which transformed the South and fed the cotton factories of the world for decades.

Important innovations in the way businesses were organized and financed accompanied these technological developments. The most spectacular step was the sudden flowering of American banking. Here the establishment of the Bank of the United States was of key importance. Aside from aiding all government financial operations, the Bank became a new and important source of credit for business transactions. Its immediate success also led to the founding of many state-chartered banks. When the great Bank was created in 1791, there were only three banks in the entire country. By 1800 there were 29, located in all the major towns and in such minor centers of commerce and industry as Nantucket, Massachusetts, and Hudson, New York.

Less noticeable, but at least as important for the growth of industry in the long run, was the development of the corporation. Although the idea of a specially chartered company was as old in America as the first English colonies, very few were created in America itself before the Revolution. Only 7 existed in 1775. Yet between 1781 and 1801, 326 corporations were chartered by the states. Only a handful of these new companies were involved in manufacturing, the general opinion being that only projects of a quasi-public character, such as roads, canals, insurance companies, and waterworks, were entitled to the privilege of incorporation. Nevertheless, the corporate device was well established by the beginning of the 19th century.

It must be repeated that the sudden appearance of all the elements of modern industrial society did not mean that such a society was created in America overnight. Slater's factory did not signalize the disappearance of the family spinning wheel or even the spread of the factory system to other forms of manufacturing. Interchangeable firing pins for rifles did not lead at once to the spark plug or even to matching pairs of shoes. And, of course, true automation had to wait upon the science of electronics in the 20th century. More than 15 years were to pass after Fitch's steamboat before the invention was widely accepted, and it was the better part of another decade before it found its true home beyond the Appalachians.

Birth of the Factory

Indeed, the first stirrings of America's industrial revolution were slow in coming. By the 1770's, British manufacturers, especially those in textiles, had made astonishing progress in mechanizing their operations, bringing their workers together in buildings called factories where waterpower, and later steam, supplied the force to run new spinning and weaving devices that increased productivity and reduced labor costs tremendously. John Kay's flying shuttle, James Hargreaves' spinning jenny, and Richard Arkwright's perfection of the water frame were the major technological improvements. Arkwright particularly was responsible for the efficient installation of these machines in factories.

Since machine-spun cotton was both cheaper and of better quality than that spun by hand, producers in other countries were eager to adopt the British methods. Americans had been accustomed to depend upon Great Britain for such products, but the Revolution cut off supplies, and the new spirit of nationalism gave further impetus to the development of local industry. A number of state legislatures offered bounties

Maximilian Godefroy's drawing of about 1812 pictures the various buildings of the Union Manufactories textile mill on the Patapsco River in Maryland. Built during Jefferson's embargo, the mill expanded rapidly until by 1825 some 600 millhands were needed to tend its 80,000 spindles. Power was supplied by sixteen water wheels.

to anyone who would introduce the new machinery. The British, however, guarded their secrets carefully. It was illegal to export any of the new machines or to send their plans abroad. Workers skilled in their construction and use were forbidden to leave the country. These restrictions were for a time effective. The principles on which the new machines were based were simple enough, but to construct workable models without plans was another matter. Although a number of persons tried to do so, it was not until Samuel Slater installed his machines in Pawtucket that a really successful factory was constructed.

Slater had been trained by one of Arkwright's partners, but he was more than a skillful mechanic. He possessed what Roger Burlingame, the historian of American invention, called a "truly photostatic mind." Attracted by stories of the rewards being offered in the United States, he slipped out of England in 1789. Not daring to carry any plans, he depended on his memory and his mechanical sense for all the complicated specifications of the necessary machines. When Moses Brown brought him to Rhode Island, he insisted upon scrapping the crude machinery Almy & Brown had assembled. Then, working in extreme secrecy with a carpenter who was "under bond not to steal the patterns nor disclose the nature of the work," he built and installed Arkwright-type water frames and other machinery. In December 1790 all was ready, and the first American factory began production.

Slater's machines made only cotton thread, which Almy & Brown sold in its Providence store and also "put out" to individual craftsmen, who, working for wages, wove it into cloth in their homes. The machines were tended largely by children, for the work was simple and the pace slow. The young operatives' pay ranged from 33 to 67 cents per week, about what a youngster could earn in other occupations. Slater's success was followed by an almost unbroken expansion in the production of factory-made cotton thread. He soon branched out on his own, and others trained by him also opened their own establishments. By 1800 seven mills possessing 2,000 spindles were in operation; by 1815, after production had been stimulated by the War of 1812, there were 130,000 spindles turning in 213 factories. Many of the new factories were inefficient, but the well-managed

ones earned large profits. Slater, for example, began with almost nothing, but at the time of his death in 1835, he owned mill properties in Rhode Island, Massachusetts, Connecticut, and New Hampshire, in addition to other interests, and was by the standards of the day a rich man.

Before long, the Boston Associates, a group of merchants headed by Francis Cabot Lowell, added a new dimension to factory production. Beginning at Waltham, Massachusetts, where the Charles River provided the necessary water-power, they built between 1813 and 1850 a number of large factories that revolutionized the process of textile production. Some early factory owners had set up hand looms in their plants, but these could not keep pace with the whirring jennies. Lowell, after an extensive study of British mills, designed an efficient power loom. His Boston Manufacturing Company at Waltham, capitalized at $300,000, combined machine production, large-scale operation, efficient professional management, and centralized marketing procedures. It concentrated upon the mass production of a standardized product.

Lowell's cloth was durable and cheap, although plain and rather coarse. His profits averaged almost 20 per cent a year during the Era of Good Feelings. In 1823 the Boston Associates began to harness the power of the Merrimack River, setting up a new $600,000 corporation, and by 1826 a booming industrial city, appropriately named Lowell, had sprung up about the sleepy village of East Chelmsford, Massachusetts, where there was a fall of 32 feet in the river.

Nonfactory Production

The efficiency of the "Lowell System" was obvious to all, but it led to no immediate transformation of American manufacturing. While the embargo and the war with Great Britain aided the new factories by limiting foreign competition, they also stimulated nonfactory production. In Monroe's time "the household-handicraft-mill complex" was still dominant nearly everywhere. Accurate statistics for this type of production do not exist, but the volume was very large. In 1816 one authority estimated the value of all textiles manufactured in American homes at $120 million! Traveling artisans and town craftsmen produced goods ranging from hats, shoes, and other articles of clothing to barrels, clocks, pianos, ship's supplies, cigars, lead pencils, and pottery. Neighborhood industries of the mill variety were also ubiquitous. Ironworks, brickyards, flour mills, distilleries, and lumberyards could be found even in the most rural parts of the country. The historian George Rogers Taylor reports that in and about a single tiny Ohio town in 1815 more than 30 craftsmen of the shoemaker-baker-druggist type plied their trades, and that there were at least as many small mills, including (besides the usual flour and lumber mills) a nail factory, a woolens factory, and a number of textile plants.

Nearly all these "manufacturers" produced only to supply local needs, but in some instances large industries, which sold their output over wide areas, grew up without advancing to the factory stage. In the neighborhood of the Connecticut town of Danbury, hundreds of small shops turned out hats by handicraft methods. These hats were sold all over the country, the trade being organized by wholesalers. The shoe industry followed a related pattern, with centers of production in Pennsylvania, New Jersey, and especially in eastern Massachusetts. By the 1820's merchants in these regions had developed a complex and extensive business. They bought leather in wholesale lots, had it cut to patterns in central workshops, and then distributed it to craftsmen who made the shoes in their own homes or workshops on a piecework basis. The finished product was returned to the central shops for inspection and packaging and thence shipped all over the United States. Some very strange combinations of production techniques appeared, none more peculiar than in the manufacture of stockings. Frequently the feet and legs were knit by machine in separate factories and then "put out" to handworkers who sewed the parts together in their own homes.

Since the new technology affected American industry so unevenly, contemporaries found the changes difficult to evaluate. Few persons in the 1820's appreciated how profound the impact of the factory system would eventually be. The city of Lowell seemed remarkable and important but not necessarily a herald of future trends. Yet in nearly every field apparently minor changes were being made. Beginning around 1815, small improvements in the design of water wheels, such as the use of leather transmission belts and of metal gears, made possible larger and more efficient machinery in mills and factories. The woolens industry gradually became as mechanized as the cotton. Iron production, so dependent upon heavy machinery today, advanced beyond the stage of the blacksmith's forge and the small foundry only slowly; nevertheless, improvements were made. By 1810 machines were stamping out nails at a third the cost of the hand-forged type. Shortly after the War of 1812, the development of the rolling mill greatly simplified the manufacture of sheet iron, formerly hammered out laboriously by hand. At about this time the puddling process for refining pig iron made it possible to use coal for fuel instead of expensive charcoal.

In 1817 Thomas Gilpin, a Delaware paper manufacturer, perfected the cylinder process for making paper, prelude to a rapid mechanization of that industry. Improvements were also made in the manufacture of glass and pottery. The commercial canning of sterilized foods in airtight containers, so important for the convenience and health of an urban society, also began about 1820. The invention in that year of a new machine for cutting ice, which reduced the cost by over 50 per cent, had equally important effects on urban eating habits.

Banks and Corporations

Besides the competition of other types of production and the inability of technology to supply instant solutions to every industrial problem, there were many reasons why the factory took hold so slowly in the United States. In most industries mechanization required large capital investments, and capital was chronically in short supply in America. While banks and the device of the corporation existed and were being used increasingly to create and concentrate capital, prejudices against them did not disappear. Bank credit, in historian Bray Hammond's words, "was to Americans a new source of energy, like steam," yet many intelligent citizens failed to understand this truth. "Every dollar of a bank bill that is issued beyond the quantity of gold and silver in the vaults represents nothing and is therefore a cheat upon somebody," John Adams remarked as late as 1809. And in 1813 Jefferson wrote: "My original disapprobation of banks circulating paper is not unknown, nor have I since observed any effects either on the morals or fortunes of our citizens which are any counterbalance to the public evils produced." Prejudice also accounts in part for the slowness with which the corporation invaded the manufacturing field. Throughout this period anyone interested in organizing a corporation had to obtain a special act of a state legislature. Furthermore, even among businessmen there was a tendency to associate corporations with monopoly, with corruption, and with the undermining of individual enterprise. In 1820 the American economist Daniel Raymond wrote:

> The very object . . . of the act of incorporation is to produce inequality, either in rights, or in the division of property. *Prima facie,* therefore all money corporations are detrimental to national wealth. They are always created for the benefit of the rich. . . . The rich have money, and not being satisfied with the power which money itself gives them, in their private individual capacities, they seek for an artificial combination . . . that its force may be augmented.

Such feelings help explain why as late as the 1860's most manufacturing was being done by unincorporated companies.

Industrial Labor

Although the new machines saved immense amounts of labor, a shortage of labor in the United States also hampered the growth of factories. Most Americans preferred not to work for wages if they could gain a livelihood in some other way. Also, since the early factories depended upon waterpower, they were not often located in the towns and were frequently far removed from centers of population. Without efficient means of public transportation, it was difficult for men to reach the machines. Under the household system the labor force could be widely scattered without inconvenience. Part-time work, so easily adapted to household manufacture, was also ill-suited to factory conditions.

Of course in the long run the factory revolutionized the life of the workingman, but as with its effect on production, the immediate impact was uneven and not always clear. The majority of nonagricultural workers in the 1820's were either self-employed craftsmen or part of the apprentice-journeyman structure out of which master craftsmen normally emerged. As in colonial times, the average worker in the trades, whether a tailor, shoemaker, printer, baker, or carpenter, began by apprenticing himself while still a lad to a master. His training period of five to seven years finished, he became a journeyman, working for wages. Eventually, if he was reasonably talented, frugal, and industrious, he could hope to set up a shop of his own.

The changing nature of production subjected this system to severe strain. It was not so much that the new machines were reducing the need for the worker's skills, although in some industries this was certainly a factor. Much more important was the ever-widening spread of markets. As wholesale merchants and budding capitalists took control of the distribution of manufactured goods, they put pressure on producers to decrease costs. In some cases this could be done by lowering wages; more often it was accomplished by cutting corners in the process of manufacture. A cheap, efficient product became more sought after than a finely finished one. The importance of skill (and thus the bargaining power of the worker) declined not so much because machines did the work better, but because in many quarters high-quality work ceased to be valued as it had been. The growing shoe industry, for example, concentrated on producing rough brogans for slaves and western farmers. To achieve efficiency, the merchants who controlled the business broke down the work of the shoemakers into a series of simple tasks. While shoes continued to be made almost entirely by hand, the degree and variety of skill required by each worker declined and with it his prestige and importance.

Most early factory workers, especially in the textile industry, were drawn from outside the regular labor market. Relatively few hand spinners and weavers became factory workers; indeed, most of these continued to work as they had, for it was many years before the factories could even begin to supply the ever-increasing demand for cloth. Nor did immigrants man the new machines. Instead, the operators relied heavily upon the labor of women and children. The machines lessened the need for both skill and strength, while the labor shortage made it necessary to tap some previously unexploited source. By the early 1820's about half the cotton textile workers in the factories were children under 16.

Most people of that generation considered this a good thing, arguing that the work was easy, and that it kept the youngsters busy at useful tasks while providing their families with extra income. Roxana Foote, the mother of Harriet Beecher Stowe, author of *Uncle Tom's Cabin*, came from a solid, middle-class family in Guilford, Connecticut. Nevertheless, she worked full time before her marriage in her grandfather's small spinning mill. "This spinning-mill was a favorite spot," a relative recalled many years later. "Here the girls often received visitors, or read or chatted while they spun." Roxana herself explained her way of life as a "mill girl" in the following quite casual manner: "I generally rise with the sun, and, after breakfast, take my wheel, which is my daily companion, and the evening is generally devoted to reading, writing, and knitting." A society accustomed to seeing the children of even fairly well-to-do farmers put to work full time in the fields was not shocked by the sight of children working all day in mills. In some factories, workers were hired in whole family units. No one member earned very much, but with a couple of adolescent daughters and perhaps a nine- or ten-year-old son helping out, a family could bring in enough to live decently.

The Boston Associates developed the "Waltham System" of employing unmarried girls and housing them in company dormitories. These establishments were strictly supervised; strait-laced New Englanders did not hesitate to permit their daughters to live in them. The regulations laid down by one company, for example, required that all employees "show that they are

YALE UNIVERSITY ART GALLERY, BEQUEST OF S.C. CLARK

Factory girls, lunch pails in hand, begin their working day in Winslow Homer's Morning Bell. *Although Homer's painting was done in 1866, his New England factory scene has the bucolic flavor of an earlier day, of a time three or four decades before when newly industrialized Lowell was proclaimed a "commercial utopia."*

penetrated by a laudable love of temperance and virtue." "Ardent spirits" were "banished" from company property, "games of hazard and cards" prohibited. A ten o'clock curfew was enforced, and the girls were expected to attend church services on Sundays.

For a generation, the thriving factories of cities like Lowell, Chicopee, and Manchester provided the background for a remarkable industrial idyll. Young women came from farms all over New England to work for a year or two in the mills. Not considering themselves part of a permanent labor force, they worked to save for a trousseau, to help educate a younger brother, or simply for the experience and excitement of meeting new people and escaping the confining environment of the farm.

The girls earned about $2.50 or $3 a week and spent perhaps half of that for room and board. Anything but an industrial proletariat, they filled the windows of the factories with flowering plants, organized sewing circles, edited their own literary periodicals, and attended lectures on various edifying subjects. That such activity was possible on top of a 70-hour workweek is a commentary both upon the resiliency of youth and the leisurely pace of the early factories. The English novelist Charles Dickens, though scarcely enchanted by American ways, was impressed by a visit to Lowell, which he compared most favorably to "those great haunts of misery," the English manufacturing towns. "They were all well dressed," he wrote of the factory girls. "They were healthy in appearance, many of them remarkably so, and had the manners and deportment of young women. . . . The rooms in which they worked were as well ordered as themselves."

Although the growth of industry did not suddenly revolutionize American life, it reshaped society in various ways. For many years it acted to depress the importance of foreign commerce, so vital in earlier times. Some relative decline from the lush years immediately preceding Jefferson's embargo was no doubt inevitable, especially in the fabulously profitable re-export trade, but industrial growth reduced the need for foreign products and thus the business of merchants. Only in the 1850's, when the wealth and population of the United States were each more than three times what they had been in the first years of the century, did the value of American exports climb back to the levels of 1807. As the country moved a little closer to self-sufficiency (a point, of course, that it never reached), nationalistic and isolationist sentiments were subtly augmented. During the embargo and the War of 1812 a great deal of capital had been transferred from commerce to industry; afterward new capital continued to prefer industry, attracted by the high profits and growing prestige of manufacturing. The rise of manufacturing affected the farmer too, for as men abandoned agriculture for industry and as cities grew, commercial agriculture flourished. Dairy-farming, truck-gardening, and fruit-growing began to thrive in the areas around every manufacturing center.

Cotton Revolutionizes the South

By far the most important indirect effect of industrialization occurred in the South, which soon began to produce cotton to supply the new textile factories of Great Britain and New England. The possibility of growing large amounts of this crop in America had not been seriously considered in colonial times, but by the 1780's the demand for raw cotton to feed the voracious British mills was so great (consumption increased from 9 million to 28 million pounds between 1783 and 1790) that many American farmers were eager to experiment with the crop. Most of the world's cotton at this time came from Egypt, India, and the East Indies. The plant was generally considered tropical, most varieties being unable to survive the slightest frost. As Hamilton, who missed nothing that related to the economic growth of the country, reported: "It has been observed . . . that the nearer the place of growth to the equator, the better the quality of the cotton."

Beginning in 1786, "sea-island" cotton was grown successfully in the mild, humid lowlands and offshore islands along the coasts of Georgia and South Carolina. This was a high-quality cotton, silky and long-fibered like the Egyptian, but its susceptibility to frost severely limited the area of its cultivation. Elsewhere in the South, green-seed, or upland, cotton flourished, but this plant had little commercial value because the seeds could not be easily separated from the lint. When sea-island cotton was passed between two rollers, its shiny black seeds simply popped out; with upland cotton the seeds were pulled through with the lint and crushed, the oils and broken bits destroying the value of the fiber. To remove the seeds by hand was extremely laborious; a man working all day could clean scarcely a pound of the white fluff. This made it an uneconomical crop even when slave labor was employed. In 1791 the usually sanguine Hamilton admitted in his *Report on Manufactures* that "the extensive cultivation of cotton can, perhaps, hardly be expected," although he added, "with due care and attention, the national cotton may be made to approach nearer than it now does to that of regions somewhat more favored by climate."

Early American cotton manufacturers used the sea-island variety or imported the foreign fiber, paying, in the latter case, a duty of three cents a pound. They believed, as Slater's backer, Moses Brown, explained, that the seeds of upland cotton were so entangled in the fiber "as to discourage the use of it in machines." However, the planters of South Carolina and Georgia, suffering from hard times after the Revolution, were much in need of a new cash crop. Rice production was not expanding, and indigo, the other staple of the area, had ceased to be profitable when it was no longer possible to claim the British bounty. Cotton seemed the obvious answer. All over the South, men were experimenting hopefully with different varieties of the plant and mulling over the problem of how upland cotton could be more easily de-seeded.

This was the situation in the spring of 1793, when Eli Whitney was a guest at Mulberry Grove, the plantation of Catherine Greene, widow of General Nathanael Greene, some dozen miles from Savannah.* Young Whitney had accepted a position as private tutor at 100 guineas a year with a nearby family and had stopped to visit another young Yale man, Phineas Miller, who was overseer of the Greene plantation. While at Mulberry Grove, Whitney, who had never seen a cotton plant before, met a number of the local landowners.

*The property, formerly owned by a prominent Georgia Tory, had been given to Greene by the state in gratitude for his having driven out the British during the Revolution.

> I heard [he wrote his father] much of the extreme difficulty of ginning Cotton, that is, separating it from its seed. There were a number of very respectable Gentlemen at Mrs. Greene's who all agreed that if a machine could be invented that would clean the Cotton with expedition, it would be a great thing both to the Country and to the inventor.

Whitney thought about the problem for a few days and then "struck out a plan of a machine." He described it to Miller, who enthusiastically offered to finance the invention. Since Whitney had just learned that his job as tutor would pay only 50 guineas, he accepted Miller's proposal.

Within ten days he had solved the problem which had baffled the planters. His gin (engine) consisted of a cylinder covered with rows of wire teeth rotating in a box filled with cotton. As the cylinder turned, the teeth passed through narrow slits in a metal grating. Cotton fibers were caught by the teeth and pulled through the slits, but the seeds, too wide for the openings, were left behind. A second cylinder, with brushes rotating in the opposite direction to sweep the cotton from the wires, prevented matting and clogging.

This "absurdly simple contrivance" almost instantly transformed southern agriculture. With a gin a slave could clean 50 times the cotton he could manage by hand; soon larger models driven by mules and horses were also available. The machines were so easy to construct (once the basic idea was understood) that despite years of litigation, Whitney and Miller were never able to enforce their patent rights effectively. Rival manufacturers shamelessly pirated their work, and countless individual farmers built gins of their own. Cotton production figures tell the resulting story: in 1790 about 3,000 bales (the average bale weighed 500 pounds) were produced in the United States. In 1793, 10,000 bales were produced; two years later, 17,000; by 1801, 100,000. The embargo and the War of 1812 temporarily checked this expansion, but in 1816 output spurted ahead by more than 25 per cent as 259,000 bales were ginned, and in the early 1820's annual production averaged well over 400,000 bales.

Despite this avalanche, the price of cotton remained high. During the 1790's it ranged between 26 and 44 cents a pound, a veritable bonanza. In the next decade it was lower (15 to 19 cents), but still provided high profits even for inefficient producers. It was higher again after 1815 and fell below 14 cents in only one year before 1826. With prices at such levels, profits of $50 an acre were not unusual, and the South boomed. Upland cotton would grow wherever there were 200 consecutive days without frost and 24 inches of rain. The crop engulfed Georgia and South Carolina and spread north even into parts of Virginia. After Andrew Jackson smashed the southwestern Indians during the War of 1812, the rich "Black Belt" area of central Alabama and northern Mississippi and the delta region along the lower Mississippi River were rapidly taken over by the fluffy white staple. In 1821 Alabama alone raised 40,000 bales. Central Tennessee in the area below Nashville also became important cotton country.

Cotton greatly stimulated the economy of the rest of the nation as well. Most of it was exported, the sale paying for all kinds of much-needed European products. The transportation, insurance, and final disposition of the crop fell largely into the hands of northern merchants, who profited accordingly. And the surplus corn and hogs of western farmers helped feed the slaves of the new cotton plantations. Indeed, as Douglass North explained in *The Economic Growth of the United States: 1815–1860*, for a generation beginning about 1815 cotton was "the major expansive force" in the economy. "The demands for western foodstuffs and northeastern services and manufactures were basically dependent upon the income received from the cotton trade."

Revival of Slavery

Amid the national rejoicing over this happy prosperity, one aspect both sad and ominous was easily overlooked. Slavery, a declining or at worst stagnant institution in the decade of

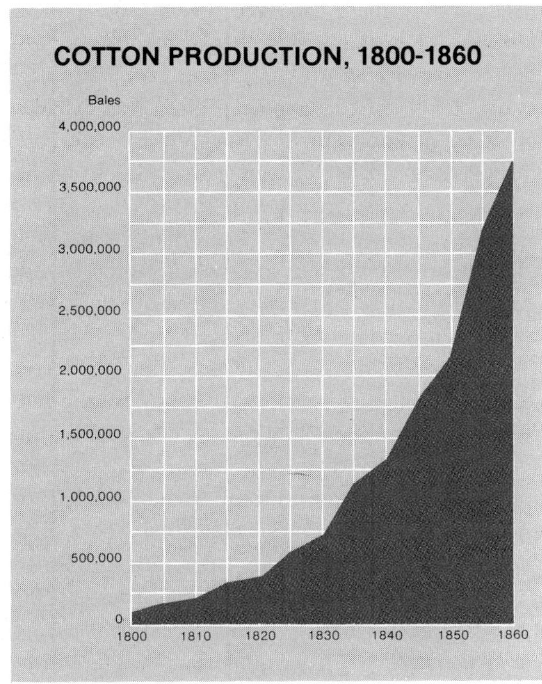

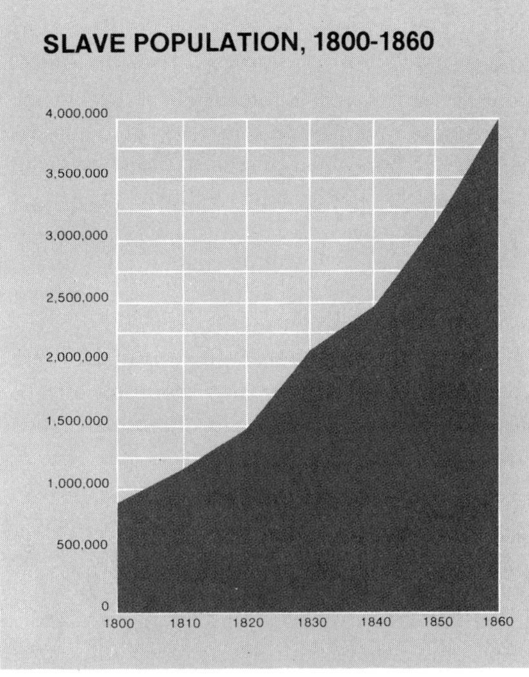

the Revolution, was revitalized in the following years.

Libertarian beliefs inspired by the Revolution ran into the roadblock of race prejudice as soon as some of the practical aspects of freedom for blacks became apparent. As disciples of John Locke, the men of the Revolution had an exaggerated respect for property rights; in the last analysis most white Americans placed these ahead of the personal liberty of black Americans in their constellation of values. Forced abolition of slavery therefore attracted few recruits. Moreover, the rhetoric of the Revolution had raised the aspirations of Negroes. Increasing signs of rebelliousness appeared among them, especially after the slave uprising in Santo Domingo, which culminated, after a great blood bath, in the establishment of the black Republic of Haiti in 1804. This example of a successful slave revolt filled white Americans with fear, irrational (after all the Santo Domingo blacks outnumbered the whites and mulattos combined by seven to one) but nonetheless real. And fear led to violent repression; the exposure of a Negro plot to revolt in Virginia, led by the slave Gabriel, resulted in some three dozen executions, even though no actual rising had occurred.

Still another paradoxical outcome of the Revolution injured southern blacks. The mood of the Revolutionary decade had led to the manumission of many slaves; unfortunately the increased presence of free Negroes in their communities led many whites to have second thoughts about ending slavery. "If the blacks see all of their color slaves, it will seem to them a disposition of Providence, and they will be content," a Virginia legislator, apparently something of an amateur psychologist, discovered early in the 19th century. "But if they see others like themselves free . . . they will repine." As the proportion of free men among the black population rose steeply—from 8 per cent in 1790 to over 13 per cent in 1810—restrictions on free Negroes were everywhere tightened.

In the 1780's, many opponents of slavery began to think of solving the Negro "problem" by colonizing freed slaves in some distant region—in the western districts or perhaps in Africa. This colonization movement had two aspects. One, a manifestation of an embryonic black nationalism, reflected the disgust of black Americans with local racial attitudes and their deep interest in African civilization. Paul Cuffe, a Massachusetts Quaker, managed to finance the emigration of 38 of his fellow blacks to Sierra Leone in 1815, but only a very few others followed. The other colonization movement, led by whites, was humanitarian but paternalistic and essentially racist in character. Some white colonizationists genuinely abhorred slavery but could not stomach living with free Negroes; others were motivated only by the second of these considerations. The colonization idea became popular in Virginia in the 1790's, but nothing was achieved until after the founding of the American Colonization Society in 1817. The society purchased African land and established the Republic of Liberia. However, despite the cooperation of a handful of black nationalists and the patronage of many important white south-

NEW YORK CITY COLONIZATION SOCIETY.

This is to certify
that Rev. A. H. Bishop, Astoria, L. I.
by the contribution of Thirty Dollars
is a Member for Life of the
COLONIZATION SOCIETY OF THE CITY OF NEW YORK.
December 10th 1842.
Anson G. Phelps President.
Corresponding Secretary

OBERLIN COLLEGE

The colonization movement was in decline when this 1842 membership certificate, featuring an inviting African vista, was issued by a colonization society.

erners, including President Monroe and Chief Justice John Marshall, it accomplished little and declined rapidly after about 1830. In fact, few Negroes wished to migrate to a land as alien to their own experience as to their masters'; only about 12,000 went to Liberia, and the toll taken among these by tropical diseases was very large. As late as 1850 the American Negro population of Liberia was only 6,000.

The cotton boom of the early 19th century also acted as a brake on the colonization movement. As cotton production expanded, the need for labor in the South grew apace. The price of slaves doubled between 1795 and 1804. As it rose, the inclination of even the most kindhearted masters to free their Negroes began to falter. Although the importation of slaves from abroad had been outlawed by all the states, perhaps 25,000 were smuggled into the country in the 1790's. In 1804 South Carolina reopened the trade, and between that date and 1808, when the constitutional prohibition of importation became effective, some 40,000 were brought in. Thereafter, this miserable traffic in human souls continued clandestinely.

Equally obnoxious was the interstate slave trade which resulted from the cotton boom. Although it had always been legal for a man to transport his own slaves to a new state if he was himself settling there, many states forbade, or at least severely restricted, interstate commercial transactions in human flesh. A Virginia law of 1778, for example, prohibited the importation of slaves for purposes of sale, and anyone entering the state with Negroes had to swear that he did not intend to sell them. Once cotton became important, these laws were systematically evaded. There was a surplus of slaves in one part of the United States and an acute shortage in another. A migration from the Upper South to the cotton lands quickly sprang up. Slaves from as far north as "free" New York and New Jersey and even from New England suddenly began to appear on the auction blocks of Savannah and Charleston. Early in the so-called Era of Good Feelings, newspapers in New Orleans were carrying reports such as this: "Jersey negroes appear to be particularly adapted to this market. . . . We have the right to calculate on large importations in the future, from the success which hitherto attended the sale." By about 1820 even the letter of the law began to be changed. Soon the slave trade became an organized business, cruel and shameful, frowned upon by the "best" people of the South, managed by the depraved and the greedy, but patronized by nearly anyone who needed labor. "The native land of Washington, Jefferson, and Madison," one disgusted Virginian told a French visitor, "[has] become the Guinea of the United States."

As for the Negroes of the northern states, their lot was almost as bad as that of southern free blacks. Except in New England where there were few Negroes to begin with, most were denied the vote, either directly or by extralegal pressures. They could not testify in court, intermarry with whites, obtain decent jobs or housing, or get a good rudimentary education. Some states prohibited the migration of free Negroes into their territories. Most segregated them in theaters, hospitals, and churches, and on public transportation facilities, and barred them from hotels and restaurants patronized by whites. Only in Massachusetts could Negroes be said to have achieved even political and legal equality, while equality of economic opportunity existed nowhere. However, northern blacks possessed at least the right to protest and to try to convince the white majority of the injustice of their treatment, rights totally denied to their southern brethren. They could and did publish newspapers and pamphlets, organize for political action, petition legislatures and the Congress for redress of grievances—in short, apply methods of peaceful persuasion in an effort to improve their position in society.

Road Building

Inventions and technological improvements were extremely important in the settlement of the West. Upon superficial examination, this may not seem to have been the case, for the hordes of settlers who struggled across the mountains immediately after the War of 1812 were no better equipped than their ancestors who had pushed up the eastern slopes in previous generations. Many plodded on foot over hundreds of miles dragging crude carts laden with their meager possessions: guns, axes, iron plowshares, some household utensils and a few tools, a little spare clothing, blankets, and perhaps a stick or two of furniture. More fortunate pioneers traveled on horseback or in heavy, cumbersome wagons, the best-known being the great, hearselike, canvas-topped Conestoga type, pulled by horses or oxen.

In many cases the pioneer followed trails and roads no better than those of colonial days—quagmires in wet weather, rutted and full of potholes a goodly part of the year. When he settled down, his way of life was no more advanced than that of the Pilgrims two centuries before. At first he was a creature of the forest, feeding upon its abundance, building his shelter and his simple furniture with its wood, clothing himself in the furs of forest animals. He usually planted his first crop in a natural glade; thereafter, year by year, he pushed back the trees with ax and saw and fire and muscle until the land was finally cleared. Any source of power more complicated than an ox was beyond his ken. At least until the population of his territory had grown large enough to support town life, the settler was also as dependent upon crude household manufactures as any earlier pioneer.

But the spread of settlement into the Mississippi Valley created challenges that required technological advances if they were to be met. In the social climate of that age in the United States, these advances were not slow in coming. Mostly they were related to transportation, the major problem for westerners.

The Mississippi River and its vast system of tributaries provided a natural highway for western commerce and communication, but one with grave disadvantages. Heavy farm products could be floated down to New Orleans on rafts and flatboats, but such voyages were slow. It took at least a month to make the descent from Pittsburgh to the Gulf. Transportation upstream was out of the question for anything but the lightest and most valuable products and even for them extremely expensive. Ninety per cent of the tonnage on the western waters moved downstream. The western depression that preceded the War of 1812, which the settlers blamed on the British navy, was actually caused by the high cost and general difficulty of getting western products to salt water. In any case, the natural flow of trade was between East and West. That is why, from early in the westward movement, much attention was given to building roads joining the Mississippi Valley and the eastern seaboard.

Constructing decent roads over the rugged Appalachians was a formidable task. The steepest grades had to be reduced by cutting through hills and filling in low places, all without modern blasting and earth-moving equipment. Drainage ditches were essential if the roads were not to be washed out by the first rains, and a firm foundation of stones, topped with a well-crowned gravel dressing, also had to be provided if they were to

About 1820 a young artist named Joshua Shaw journeyed west to the frontier, sketching the pioneers with whom he shared the rigors of travel. As shown here, many carried everything they owned as they struggled along the rough traces on foot or by mule.

BOTH: MUSEUM OF SCIENCE AND INDUSTRY, CHICAGO

MUSEUM OF FINE ARTS, BOSTON, M. & M. KAROLIK COLLECTION

The crude state of early 19th-century western roads is vividly portrayed in George Tattersall's water color. The expression "to be stumped" stemmed from the frequent plight of wagons and stagecoaches on such roads.

stand up under the pounding of heavy wagons. The skills required for building roads of this quality had been developed in Great Britain and France, and the earliest American examples, constructed in the 1790's, were similar to good European highways. The first such road, connecting Philadelphia and Lancaster, Pennsylvania, was opened to traffic in 1794. Two decades later a fairly extensive network connected most of the principal towns of the Northeast.

Along with improved roads came considerable progress in the design and construction of bridges. Structures built on piles across broad streams were being erected even in the 1790's. The longest, completed in 1800 across Lake Cayuga in central New York, was a full mile from end to end. Substantial stone bridges, such as the one spanning Brandywine Creek at Downingtown, on the Lancaster Pike, were fairly common by the early 19th century, and the wooden truss bridge, based on complicated principles of engineering, also began to appear.

In the most densely populated sections of the country, the volume of traffic made decent roads worth their high cost, which ran to as much as $13,000 a mile where the terrain was difficult, although the average was perhaps half that figure. And in some cases good roads ran out into fairly remote areas. In New York, always a leading state in the movement for improved transportation, an excellent road had been built all the way from Albany to Lake Erie by the time of the War of 1812.

Transportation and the Government

Most of these improved highways, as well as many large bridges, were built as business ventures by private interests. Promoters were authorized to charge tolls, the amounts determined by the states. These tolls were collected at gates along the way, consisting usually of hinged poles suspended across the road which were turned back by a guard after receipt of the toll. Hence these thoroughfares were known as turnpikes, or simply pikes.

The success of a few early turnpikes, such as the one between Philadelphia and Lancaster, caused a boom in private road-building, but in the long run even the most fortunate of the turnpike companies did not make much money. Maintenance was high, traffic spotty. (Ordinary public roads paralleling turnpikes were sometimes called "shunpikes" because penny-pinching travelers used them to avoid the tolls.) Some of the states bought stock to bolster weak companies, and others built and operated turnpikes as public enterprises. By 1806 Pennsylvania had sunk $825,000 in turnpike stock; 20 years later this figure had reached $2 million. State assistance was particularly common in the middle states, but everywhere there was considerable support to be had from local governments, for every town was eager to develop efficient communication with its neighbors.

Despite much talk about individual self-reliance and free enterprise, American governments, local, state, and national, contributed heavily to the development of all sorts of public-utility projects. They served as "primary entrepreneurs," supplying capital for risky but socially desirable enterprises, with the result that a fascinating mixture of private and public energy went into the building of these institutions. At the federal level, even the parsimonious Jeffersonians became deeply involved in constructing what in the jargon of the day were called "internal improvements." In 1808 Secretary of the Treasury Albert Gallatin drafted a comprehensive plan for constructing much-needed roads at a cost of $16 million. This proposal was not adopted, but the government poured money in an erratic but unending stream into turnpike companies and other organizations created to improve transportation. Logically, the major highways, especially those over the mountains, should have been built by the national government. Strategic military requirements alone would have justified such a program. One major artery, the Old National Road, running from Cumberland, Maryland, to Wheeling, in western Virginia, was constructed by the United States between 1811 and 1818 and later gradually extended as far west as Vandalia, Illinois. However, further federal road building was hampered by bitter political squabbles in Congress, usually phrased in constitutional terms, but actually based upon sectional rivalries and other economic conflicts. Over the years the federal government dribbled away many millions of dollars on "internal improvements," but no comprehensive, long-range highway program was undertaken in the 19th century. As Carter Goodrich, an authority on government aid to business, put it, "the primary deficiency of the internal improvement program [was] the failure to develop a workable economic criterion for the selection of projects for government support."

While the National Road, the New York pike, and other, rougher trails such as the Wilderness Road into the Kentucky country were adequate for the movement of settlers, they did not even begin to answer the West's need for cheap and efficient transportation. Wagon freight rates varied considerably but averaged at least 30 cents a ton-mile around 1815. At such rates, to transport a ton of oats from Buffalo to New York would have cost 12 times the value of the oats! To put the problem another way, four horses could haul a ton and a half of oats about 18 or 20 miles a day over a good road. Even assuming that they could obtain half their feed by grazing, the horses would consume about 50 pounds of oats a day. It requires very little mathematics to figure out how much of the oats would be left in the wagon when it reached New York City, almost 400 miles away.

Turnpikes did make it possible to transport goods like clothing, hardware, coffee, and books across the Appalachians, but the expense was still considerable. It cost more to ship a ton of freight 300 miles over the mountains from Philadelphia to Pittsburgh than from Pittsburgh to Philadelphia by way of New Orleans, more than ten times as far. Until the coming of the railroad, which was only just being introduced in England in 1825, cheap land transportation over the great distances common in America was impossible. Enterprising businessmen and inventors concentrated instead upon improving water transport, first of all by designing better boats and then by developing artificial waterways.

This pencil sketch of Robert Fulton was done about 1803 in Paris by the American artist John Vanderlyn, studying abroad under the patronage of Aaron Burr.

Steamboats and the West

Rafts and flatboats were adequate for downstream travel but fairly expensive, since they could be used but once. Sailing ships could navigate upstream on broad rivers like the Hudson and the Mississippi, but head winds and calm periods reduced them to helplessness. It sometimes took oceangoing sailing vessels several weeks to get from the mouth of the Mississippi to the port of New Orleans. Keelboats—narrow craft 40 to 80 feet in length that were poled upstream by men walking back and forth along broad gunwales—could proceed upstream with valuable cargoes, but it took about four months of backbreaking labor to ascend from New Orleans to Pittsburgh in this manner. The only practical solution to upstream travel was the steamboat.

After John Fitch's work around 1790, a number of other men made important contributions to the development of steam navigation. One early enthusiast was John Stevens, a wealthy New Jerseyite, who designed an improved steam boiler for which he received one of the first patents issued by the United States. Stevens got his brother-in-law, Robert R. Livingston, interested in the problem, and the latter used his political influence to obtain an exclusive charter to operate steamboats on New York waters. In 1802, while in France trying to buy New Orleans from Napoleon, Livingston got to know Robert Fulton, a young American artist and engineer who was also experimenting with steam navigation, and agreed to finance his work. In 1807, after returning to New York, Fulton constructed the *North River Steam Boat*, famous to history as the *Clermont*.

The *Clermont* was 142 feet long, 18 feet abeam, and drew 7 feet of water. With her towering stack belching black smoke, her side wheels could push her along at a steady five miles an hour. Nothing about her was radically new, but Fulton brought the various essentials—engine, boiler, paddle wheels, and hull—into proper balance and thus produced an efficient vessel. Over the next few years Fulton built more than a dozen new boats, and he and Livingston obtained another monopoly, on the lower Mississippi. But no one could patent a steamboat; soon the new vessels were plying the waters of every major river from the Mississippi east. After 1815 steamers were making the run from New Orleans as far as Ohio. By 1820 there were at least 60 vessels operating between New Orleans and Louisville, and by the end of the decade there were over 200 steamers regularly plying the Mississippi. The day of the steamboat had dawned, and although it was the next generation that experienced its high noon, even in the 1820's its major effects were clear. The great Mississippi Valley, in the full tide of its development, was immensely enriched. Produce poured down to New Orleans, which soon ranked with New York and Liverpool among the world's great ports. Only 80,000 tons of freight

HERMAN P. DEAN COLLECTION

reached New Orleans from the interior in 1816–17, over 300,000 in 1830–31 and 542,000 in 1840–41. Upriver traffic was affected even more spectacularly. Freight charges plummeted, in some cases to a tenth of what they had been after the War of 1812. For all kinds of goods, the price differential between New Orleans and the cities of the Ohio Valley shrank rapidly. Around 1818, coffee cost 16 cents more a pound in Cincinnati than in New Orleans, a decade later only 2.6 cents more. The Northwest emerged from self-sufficiency with a rush and became part of the national market.

Steamboats were inherently far more comfortable than any contemporary form of land transportation, and competition soon led builders to make them positively luxurious. The *General Pike*, launched in 1819, set the fashion. Marble columns, thick carpets, mirrors, and crimson curtains adorned her cabins and public rooms. Soon the finest river steamers were floating palaces where passengers could dine, drink, dance, and gamble in luxury as they sped smoothly to their destinations. Raft and flatboat traffic actually *increased*, for farmers, lumbermen, and others with goods from upriver could float down in the slack winter season and return quickly and in comfort by steamer after selling their produce—and their rafts as well, for lumber was in great demand in New Orleans. Every January and February New Orleans teemed with westerners and Yankee sailors, their pockets jingling, bent on a fling before going back to work. The shops displayed everything from the latest Paris fashions to teething rings made of alligator teeth mounted in silver, and the streets were crowded with every sort from all over the world. During the carnival season the city became one great festival, where every human pleasure could be tasted, every vice indulged. "Have you ever been in New Orleans?" one visiting bard sang in the late 1820's.

. . . If not you'd better go,
It's a nation of a queer place; day and night a show!
Frenchmen, Spaniards, West Indians, Creoles,
  Mustees,
Yankees, Kentuckians, Tennesseeans, lawyers and
  trustees.
Clergymen, priests, friars, nuns, women of all
  stains;
Negroes in purple and fine linen, and slaves in rags
  and chains.
Ships, arks, steamboats, robbers, pirates, alligators,
Assassins, gamblers, drunkards, and cotton
  speculators;
Sailors, soldiers, pretty girls, and ugly
  fortunetellers;
Pimps, imps, shrimps, and all sorts of dirty fellows;
White men with black wives, *et vice-versa* too,
A progeny of all colors—an infernal motley
  crew! . . .
Snapping turtles, sugar, sugar-houses, water-snakes,

Left: The passing scene on the Ohio River in 1821, painted by Félix Saint-Aulaire, who included himself (foreground) in his composition. Moving downstream are flatboats (left) and a keelboat; an early steamboat chugs upstream. French naturalist Charles Lesueur made the sketch at right, of a rough-and-tumble dance hall in the river town of Natchez in the 1820's.

MUSEE D'HISTOIRE NATURELLE, LE HAVRE

Molasses, flour, whiskey, tobacco, corn, and
johnny-cakes,
Beef, cattle, hogs, pork, turkey, Kentucky rifles,
Lumber, boards, apples, cotton, and many other
trifles. . . .

The Canal Boom

While the steamboat was conquering the western rivers, canals were being constructed which further improved the nation's transportation network. Since the midwestern rivers all emptied eventually into the Gulf of Mexico, they did not provide a direct link with the eastern seaboard. If an artificial waterway could be cut between the great central valley and some navigable stream flowing into the Atlantic, all sections would profit immensely.

No one conceived of using steamboats on canals. Goods moved through them on barges drawn by horses walking on towpaths along the banks. Yet it was spectacularly cheaper to ship by canal than by the finest road. Because there is less friction to overcome, a team plodding along a path beside a canal can tow a barge loaded with a hundred tons of produce and make better time over long distances than it could pulling a single ton in a wagon.

Although canals were as old as Egypt, only about 100 miles of them existed in the entire United States as late as 1816. They cost a great deal to build, and in a rough and mountainous country they presented engineering problems that American technology seemed unprepared to handle. To link the Mississippi Valley and the Atlantic meant somehow circumventing the Appalachian Mountains, and most persons thought this impossible. However, Mayor De Witt Clinton of New York believed that such a project was feasible in New York State. Clinton, a man of much political experience, was also a man of vision. In 1810, while serving as canal commissioner, he traveled across central New York and convinced himself that it would be practicable to dig a canal from Buffalo, on Lake Erie, to the Hudson River. The Mohawk Valley cuts through the Appalachian chain just north of Albany, and at no point along the route to Buffalo does the land rise more than 570 feet above the level of the Hudson. Marshaling a mass of technical, financial, and commercial information (and using his political influence cannily), Clinton placed his proposal before the New York legislature. In its defense he was eloquent and farsighted:

As an organ of communication between the Hudson, the Mississippi, the St. Lawrence, the great lakes of the north and west, and their tributary rivers, [the canal] will create the greatest inland trade ever witnessed. The most fertile and extensive regions of America will avail themselves of its facilities for a market. All their surplus . . . will concentrate in the

> city of New York. . . . That city will, in the course of time, become the granary of the world, the emporium of commerce, the seat of manufactures, the focus of great moneyed operations. . . . And before the revolution of a century, the whole island of Manhattan, covered with habitations and replenished with a dense population, will constitute one vast city.

The legislators were convinced, and in 1817 the state began construction along a route 363 miles long, most of it across a densely forested wilderness. At the time, the longest canal in the United States ran less than 28 miles!

The construction of this Erie Canal, as it was called, was a remarkable accomplishment. The chief engineer, Benjamin Wright, a surveyor-politician from Rome, New York, had almost no previous experience with canal-building. One of his chief associates, James Geddes, possessed only an elementary school education and knew virtually nothing about surveying. But both learned rapidly by trial and error. Fortunately, Wright also proved to be a good organizer and a remarkable judge of engineering talent. He quickly spotted young men of ability among the workers and pushed them forward. One of his finds, Canvass White, was sent to study British canals. White became an expert on the design of locks, and also discovered an American limestone that could be made into waterproof cement, a vital product in canal construction that previously had been imported at a substantial price from England. Another of Wright's protégés was the youthful, untrained John B. Jervis, who began as an axman and rose in two years to resident engi-

NEW-YORK HISTORICAL SOCIETY

The widespread interest in the Erie Canal resulted in a flood of illustrations. The busy scene at the approach to one of the locks was portrayed by J.W. Hill about 1830. The English-born Hill was a leading aquatinter of the day; this is a trial proof, which he then tinted in water color as a guide for the printmaker.

neer in charge of a whole section of the project. Jervis went on to become probably the outstanding American civil engineer of his time. These men, and many others who learned their business digging the "Big Ditch," constructed dozens of canals all over the country in later years.

The Erie, completed in 1825, was immediately a financial success. Together with the companion Champlain Canal, which linked Lake Champlain and the Hudson, it brought in over half a million dollars in tolls in its first year. Soon its entire $7 million cost had been recovered, and it was earning profits of about $3 million a year. The effect of this prosperity on New York was, of course, enormous. Buffalo, Rochester, Syracuse, and half a dozen lesser towns along the canal flourished.

New York City had already become the largest city in the nation, thanks chiefly to its enterprising merchants who had established a reputation for their rapid and orderly way of doing business. In 1818 the Black Ball Line opened the first regularly scheduled transatlantic freight and passenger service between New York and Liverpool. Previously, shipments might languish in port for weeks while a skipper waited for additional cargo. Now merchants on both sides of the Atlantic could count upon the Black Ball packets to move their goods to and from New York on schedule whether or not the transporting vessel had a full cargo. This great improvement brought much new business to the port. In the same year New York enacted a new auction law, requiring that imported goods having once been placed on the block could not be withdrawn if a bid satisfactory to the seller was not forthcoming. This, too, was a boon to businessmen, who could be assured that if they outbid the competition, the goods would be theirs. Now the canal cemented New York's position as the nation's metropolis. Most of the European manufactured goods destined for the Mississippi Valley entered the country at New York and passed on to the West over the canal.

The success of the Erie sparked a nationwide canal-building boom. Most of the canals were constructed either directly by the states, as in the case of the Erie, or as "mixed enterprises" where public and private energies were combined.

No state profited as much from this construction as New York, for none possessed New York's geographical advantages. In New England the terrain was so rugged as to discourage all but fanatics. Canals were built connecting Worcester and Northampton, Massachusetts, with the coast, but they were failures financially. The Delaware and Hudson Canal, running from northeastern Pennsylvania across northern New Jersey and lower New York to the Hudson, was completed by private interests in 1828. It managed to earn respectable dividends by barging coal to the eastern seaboard but made no attempt to compete with the Erie for the western trade. Pennsylvania engaged in an orgy of construction, desperate to keep up with New York in the fight for western trade. In 1834 the state finally completed a complicated system, part canal and part railroad, over the mountains to Pittsburgh. This Mainline Canal cost a staggering sum for that day, but with its 177 locks and its cumbersome "inclined-plane railroad" it was slow and expensive to operate and never competed effectively with the Erie. Efforts of Maryland to link Baltimore with the West by water failed utterly.

Beyond the mountains there was perhaps still greater zeal for canal construction in the 1820's and still more in the 1830's. Once the Erie opened the way across New York, farmers in the Ohio country demanded that links be built between the Ohio River and the Great Lakes so that they could ship their produce directly by water to the East. Local feeder canals seemed equally necessary; with corn worth 20 cents a bushel at Columbus selling for 50 cents at Marietta, on the Ohio, the value of cheap transportation became obvious to Ohio farmers.

Even before the completion of the Erie, Ohio had begun construction of the Ohio and Erie Canal running from the Ohio River to Cleveland. Another, from Toledo to Cincinnati, was begun in 1832. Meanwhile, Indiana had undertaken the 450-mile Wabash and Erie Canal. These canals were well conceived, but the western states greatly overextended themselves building dozens of feeder lines, trying, it sometimes seemed, to supply every farmer west of the Appalachians with direct water connections from his barn to the New York docks. Politics made such programs almost inevitable, for in order to win support for their pet projects, legislators had to back the schemes of their fellows. The result, however, was frequently financial disaster. There simply was not enough traffic to pay for all the waterways that were dug. Nevertheless, these canals were a great boon both for the western farmer and for the national economy. By the end of the 1820's over 1,200 miles of canals had been built, mostly by the state governments, and this was only the beginning.

Government Aid to Business

Throughout this period, both the United States and the states were active in other areas that directly affected the economy. Federal banking, tariff, and land legislation, for example, had much influence on economic expansion. These political activities, which also contributed to the growth of sectional conflicts in the nation, will be considered in the next chapter, but a number of legal and judicial developments require some consideration here.

Although prejudice against corporations in the manufacturing field continued, the device was such a useful means of bringing together the substantial amounts of capital needed for building roads and canals and for organizing banks and insurance companies that a steadily increasing number of promoters applied for charters. Bills authorizing incorporations became so numerous in states like Massachusetts and New York that legislators found themselves devoting a disconcertingly large portion of their time to them. Therefore they were tempted to issue blanket, though restricted, authorizations simply to save time. In 1809, for example, Massachusetts passed a law establishing standard rules for manufacturing corporations in the state. These rules were strict; one of them even made shareholders individually liable for their company's debts beyond their actual investment. While still requiring separate authorizations for each charter, the Massachusetts legislature could thereafter dispose of applications in a more routine fashion. Two years later New York enacted the first general incorporation

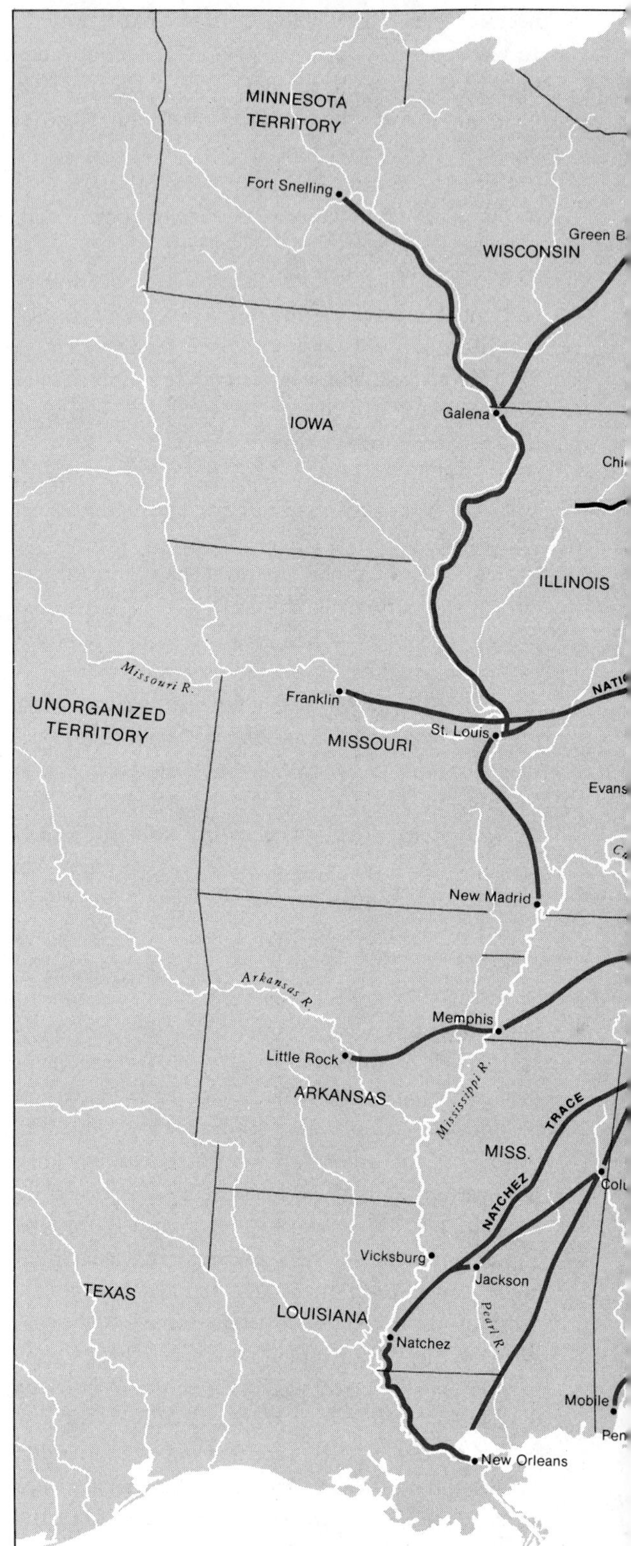

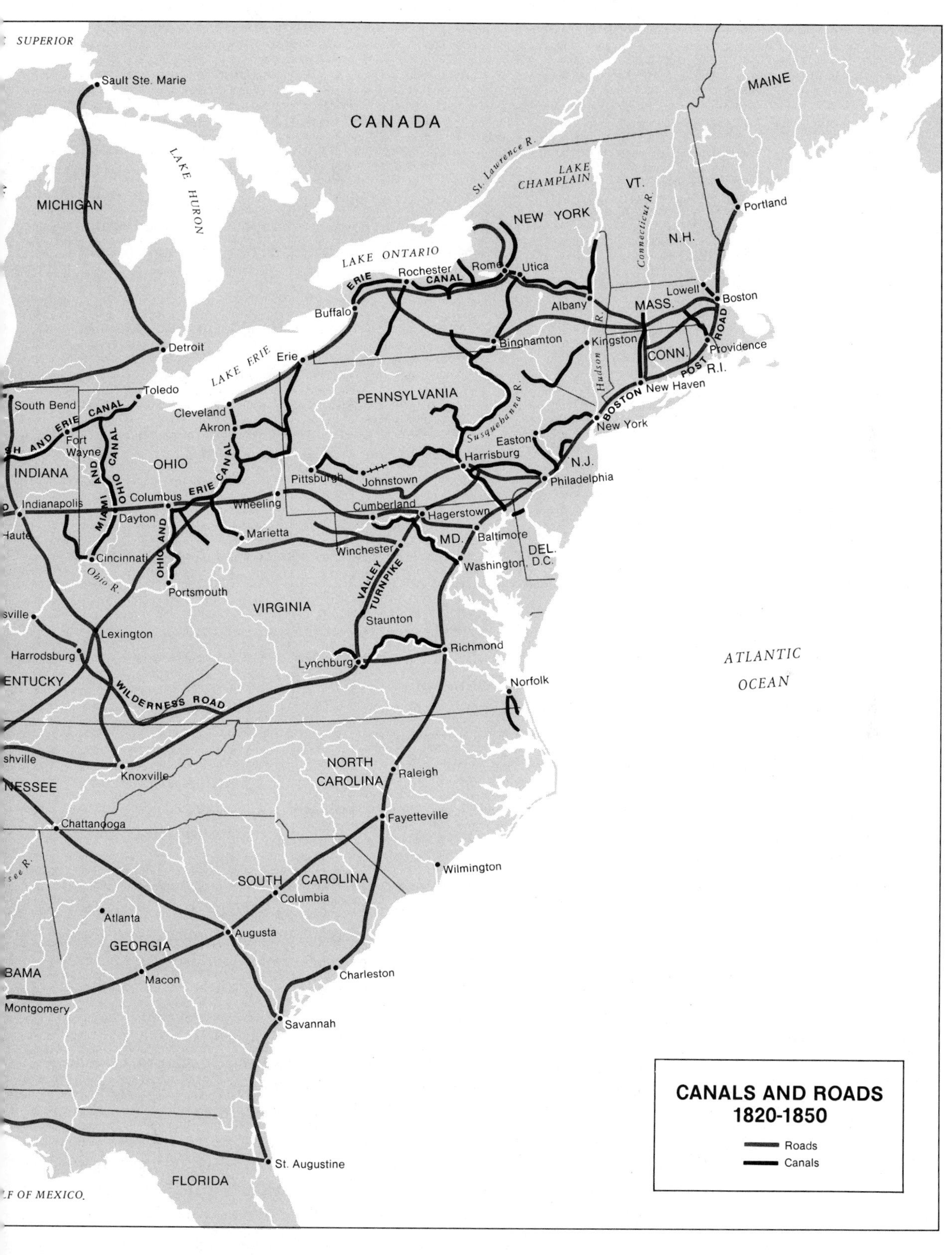
SUPERIOR
Sault Ste. Marie
CANADA
MAINE
LAKE HURON
St. Lawrence R.
LAKE CHAMPLAIN
VT.
MICHIGAN
NEW YORK
N.H.
Portland
Connecticut R.
LAKE ONTARIO
Rochester
Rome
Utica
ERIE CANAL
Lowell
Boston
Buffalo
Albany
MASS.
Detroit
Binghamton
Kingston
Providence
Erie
CONN.
R.I.
LAKE ERIE
Hudson R.
POST ROAD
Toledo
PENNSYLVANIA
New Haven
South Bend
Cleveland
BOSTON
Akron
Susquehanna R.
New York
WABASH AND ERIE CANAL
Fort Wayne
Easton
OHIO
Harrisburg
N.J.
INDIANA
MIAMI AND OHIO CANAL
OHIO AND ERIE CANAL
Pittsburgh
Johnstown
Philadelphia
Columbus
Indianapolis
Dayton
Wheeling
Cumberland
Hagerstown
Marietta
MD.
Baltimore
Cincinnati
Winchester
DEL.
Ohio R.
Washington, D.C.
Portsmouth
VALLEY TURNPIKE
VIRGINIA
Staunton
Lexington
Richmond
Harrodsburg
Lynchburg
ATLANTIC OCEAN
KENTUCKY
Norfolk
WILDERNESS ROAD
Knoxville
NORTH CAROLINA
Raleigh
TENNESSEE
Chattanooga
Fayetteville
Wilmington
SOUTH CAROLINA
Columbia
Atlanta
Augusta
GEORGIA
ALABAMA
Macon
Charleston
Montgomery
Savannah
St. Augustine
FLORIDA
GULF OF MEXICO
CANALS AND ROADS 1820-1850
Roads
Canals

law, permitting the issuance of charters without specific legislative action in each case. Although they held stockholders liable only "to the extent of their respective shares in the . . . company," which was the basic privilege sought by all incorporators, these general charters were not available to companies capitalized at more than $50,000, and they ran for only five years. This was not very satisfactory. After an initial period of enthusiasm (122 charters were issued under the law between 1811 and 1816), the law became very nearly a dead letter. In 1824 only two general charters were issued in New York, while 40 companies were incorporated by special act of the legislature. Other states did not begin to allow for general incorporation until 1837, and businessmen continued to seek, and obtain, special charters for decades thereafter.

Manufacturers in some states received valuable tax benefits. In Vermont no industrial concern paid local taxes. A New York law of 1817 exempted textile mills, and in 1823 Ohio extended similar privileges to textile, iron, and glass companies. Manufacturers also benefited from the protection granted inventors by the United States Patent Office, created in 1790. The original act gave patent holders the exclusive right to make, use, and sell their inventions for 14 years. During the 1790's an average of 27 patents a year were granted. By 1815 the figure was 166, and in the 1820's it rose to 535. The attitude of most courts and juries toward labor unions and strikes also favored employers in this period. Before the end of the 1820's craft unions had become both numerous and active, but judges tended to consider strikes unlawful conspiracies and to find against workingmen when they tried to establish the closed shop. Though the public's attitude toward organized labor was beginning to change, even the legal right of unions to exist was not fully established until the 1840's.

The Marshall Court

The most important legal advantages bestowed upon businessmen in the period were the gift of Chief Justice John Marshall. Historians have tended to forget that he had six colleagues on the Supreme Court, but it is easy to understand their attitude. Marshall's particular combination of charm, logic, and forcefulness made the Court during his long reign, if not a rubber stamp, remarkably submissive to his view of the Constitution. Fundamentally, Marshall's belief in a powerful central government explains his tendency to hand down decisions favorable to the manufacturing and business interests, but he also thought that "the business community was the agent of order and progress" and tended to interpret the Constitution in a way that would advance its interests.

A series of extremely important cases came before the Court between 1819 and 1824, and in each one Marshall's decision was applauded by most of the business community. These cases involved two major principles: the "sanctity" of contracts, and the supremacy of federal legislation over the laws of the separate states.

Marshall shared fully the conviction of the Revolutionary generation that property had to be protected against arbitrary seizure if liberty was to be preserved. Contracts, either between private individuals or between individuals and the government, must always be strictly enforced, he believed, or chaos will result. He therefore gave the widest possible application to the constitutional provision that no state could pass any law "impairing the Obligation of Contracts." Two controversies settled in February 1819 illustrate Marshall's views on the subject of contracts. In *Sturges v. Crowninshield* he declared a New York bankruptcy law unconstitutional. States could pass such laws, he conceded, but they could not make them applicable to debts incurred before the laws were passed, for debts were contracts. In the second suit, *Dartmouth College v. Woodward*, he held that a charter granted by a state was a contract and might not be canceled or altered without the consent of both parties. Contracts could scarcely be made more sacred than Marshall made them in this Dartmouth College case, which involved an attempt by New Hampshire to alter the charter granted to Dartmouth by King George III back in 1769. The state had not sought to destroy the college but merely to change it from a private to a public institution, yet Marshall held that to do so would violate the contract clause. In the light of this decision, corporations licensed by the states seemed immune against later attempts to regulate their activities, although, of course, restrictions imposed at the time of the actual chartering were not affected.* As a result, states began to spell out the limitations of corporate charters in greater detail.

Marshall's decisions concerning the division of power between the federal government and the states were even more important. The question of the constitutionality of a national bank, first debated by Hamilton and Jefferson, had not been submitted to the courts during the life of the first Bank of the United States. By the time of the second Bank there were many state banks, and some of these felt that their interests were threatened by the national institution. Responding to pressure from local banks, the Maryland legislature placed an annual tax of $15,000 on "foreign" banks. The Maryland branch of the Bank of the United States refused to pay, whereupon the state brought suit against its cashier, John W. McCulloch. *McCulloch v. Maryland* was crucial to the Bank, for five other states had levied taxes on its branches, and still others would surely follow suit if the Maryland law were upheld. But Marshall, only a few weeks after his decision in the Dartmouth College case, extinguished the threat. The Bank was constitutional, he announced in phrases taken almost verbatim from Hamilton's 1791 memorandum to Washington on the subject; its legality was implied in many of the powers specifically granted to Congress. Full "discretion" must be allowed Congress in deciding exactly how its powers "are to be carried into execution." Since the Bank was legal, the Maryland tax was unconstitutional. Marshall found a "plain repugnance" in the thought of "conferring on one government a power to control the constitutional measures of another." Indeed, he put this idea in the simplest possible language: "The power to tax involves the power to destroy . . . the power to destroy may defeat and render useless the power to create." The long-range significance of this decision lay in its strengthening of the implied powers of Congress and its confirmation of the Hamiltonian or "loose" interpretation of the Constitution, but by establishing the legality of the Bank it also aided the growth of the economy.

In 1824 Marshall handed down another important decision, one involving the regulation of interstate commerce. This was the "steamboat case," *Gibbons v. Ogden.* In 1815 Aaron Ogden, former United States senator and governor of New Jersey, had purchased the right to operate a ferry between Elizabeth Point, New Jersey, and New York City from Robert R. Livingston, holder of a New York monopoly of steamboat navigation on the Hudson. When Thomas Gibbons, who held a federal coasting license, set up a competing line, Ogden sued him. Ogden argued, in effect, that Gibbons could operate his boat (the captain of which, incidentally, was Cornelius Vanderbilt, later a famous railroad magnate) on the New Jersey side of the Hudson, but that he had no right to cross into New York waters. After complicated litigation in the lower courts, the case finally came to the Supreme Court on appeal. Marshall decided in favor of Gibbons, effectively destroying the New York monopoly. A state can regulate commerce which begins and ends within its own territory but not when the transaction involves crossing a state line, for then the national authority takes precedence. "The act of Congress," he said, "is supreme; and the law of the state . . . must yield to it."

This decision threw open the interstate steamboat business to all comers, and since an adequate 100-ton vessel could be built for as little as $7,000, dozens of small operators were soon engaged in it. Their competition tended to keep rates low and service efficient, to the great advantage of the country. Even more important in the long run, however, was the fact that in order to include the ferry business within the federal government's power to regulate interstate commerce, Marshall had given the word the widest possible meaning. "Commerce, undoubtedly, is traffic, but it is something more,—it is intercourse." By construing the "commerce clause" so broadly, he

*It was in the course of defending Dartmouth's charter that Daniel Webster made his famous, emotion-charged remark: "It is, sir, as I have said, a small college. And yet there are those who love it."

BOSTON ATHENAEUM

The self-taught Chester Harding painted John Marshall in 1828, during the Chief Justice's 27th year on the Court. "The unpretentious dignity [and] the sober factualism" of Harding's style (as art historian Oliver Larkin describes it) was well suited to capturing Marshall's character.

made it easy for future generations of judges to extend its coverage still further to include the control of interstate electric power lines and even of radio and television transmission.

Many of Marshall's decisions in this period aided the economic development of the country in various specific ways, but his chief contribution lay in his broadly national view of economic affairs. When he tried consciously to favor business by making contracts inviolable, his influence was important but limited and, as it worked out, impermanent. In the steamboat case and in *McCulloch v. Maryland,* where he was really deciding between rival property interests, his work was more truly judicial in spirit and far more lasting. In such matters his nationalism enabled him to add form and substance to Hamilton's vision of the economic future of the United States. At the same time, he and his colleagues firmly established the principle of judicial limitation on the power of legislatures, and made the Supreme Court a vital part of the American system of government. In an age plagued by narrow sectional jealousies, Marshall's contribution was of immense influence and significance, and upon it rests his claim to greatness.

SUPPLEMENTARY READING Two splendid works by George Dangerfield provide the best introduction to the Era of Good Feelings: *The Era of Good Feelings** (1952) and *The Awakening of American Nationalism** (1965). The best biography of Monroe is W.P. Cresson, *James Monroe* (1946). Shaw Livermore, Jr., *The Twilight of Federalism* (1962), is also useful.

On the forces changing the American economy and stimulating the development of industry, see Stuart Bruchey, *The Roots of American Economic Growth** (1965), and D.C. North, *The Economic Growth of the United States** (1961). G.R. Taylor, *The Transportation Revolution** (1951), a book far broader in scope than its title indicates, also discusses this subject intelligently. On government aid to business, see Oscar and M.F. Handlin, *Commonwealth: A Study of the Role of Government in the American Economy* (1947), Louis Hartz, *Economic Policy and Democratic Thought: Pennsylvania** (1948), and E.M. Dodd, *American Business Corporations Until 1860* (1954). F.J. Turner, *Rise of the New West** (1906), is still the best volume on the expansion of the West during the Era of Good Feelings, but see also the appropriate chapters of R.A. Billington, *Westward Expansion* (1967).

J.L. and Barbara Hammond's *The Rise of Modern Industry** (1937) provides an excellent account of the background of the Industrial Revolution in Great Britain. For American developments, see V.S. Clark, *History of Manufactures in the United States* (1929), T.C. Cochran and William Miller, *The Age of Enterprise** (1942), Roger Burlingame, *March of the Iron Men** (1938), C.F. Ware, *The Early New England Cotton Manufacture* (1931), and M.T. Parker, *Lowell: A Study in Industrial Development* (1940). R.M. Tryon, *Household Manufactures in the United States* (1917), documents the persistence of one type of production into the 19th century. On the early history of labor, J.R. Commons, *et al., History of Labour in the United States* (1918–1935), is the standard work.

On the spread of cotton cultivation in the South, see L.C. Gray, *History of Agriculture in the Southern United States* (1933). There are two excellent biographies of Eli Whitney: Allan Nevins and Jeannette Mirsky, *The World of Eli Whitney** (1952), and C.McL. Green, *Eli Whitney and the Birth of American Technology** (1956). W.D. Jordan, *White over Black** (1968), and L.F. Litwack, *North of Slavery: The Negro in the Free States** (1961), discuss the fate of Negroes in the North and South. On the colonization movement, see P.J. Staudenraus, *The African Colonization Movement* (1961).

Taylor's *Transportation Revolution,* mentioned above, is the best introduction to the changes in transportation that took place during the period. P.D. Jordan, *The National Road* (1948), is useful, as are L.D. Baldwin, *The Keelboat Age on Western Waters* (1941), and Walter Havighurst, *Voices on the River: The Story of the Mississippi Waterways* (1964). George Dangerfield, *Chancellor Robert R. Livingston of New York* (1960), contains an excellent account of the planning and operation of the *Clermont,* while L.C. Hunter, *Steamboats on the Western Rivers* (1949), is good on later developments. No student should miss Mark Twain, *Life on the Mississippi** (1883).

A good popular history of canal building is A.F. Harlow, *Old Towpaths* (1926). On the Erie Canal, see R.E. Shaw, *Erie Water West: A History of the Erie Canal* (1966), Nathan Miller, *The Enterprise of a Free People* (1962), and R.G. Albion, *The Rise of New York Port* (1939), which argues that the canal merely cemented New York's position as the leading commercial city of the nation. Albion's *Square-Riggers on Schedule* (1938) is also good on the growth of New York City, while Blake McKelvey, *Rochester: The Water-Power City* (1945), discusses the impact of the Erie on that community. Carter Goodrich (ed.), *Canals and American Economic Development* (1961), describes the role of government aid in canal construction authoritatively.

The most important of the decisions of the Marshall Court in this period are discussed in J.A. Garraty (ed.), *Quarrels That Have Shaped the Constitution** (1964). The fullest general account of the Court is Charles Warren, *The Supreme Court in United States History* (1937). Marshall's career is described in laudatory terms in A.J. Beveridge, *The Life of John Marshall* (1916–19); a more critical account is to be found in E.S. Corwin, *John Marshall and the Constitution* (1919).

*Available in paperback.

9

The Emergence of Sectionalism

The nationalism and buoyant optimism of the Era of Good Feelings obscured, but could not repress, the many abrasive conflicts that economic growth and political expansion were creating. Three sectional coalitions, each held together by certain common interests, were giving American political life a new pattern in the 1820's. The richest and most populous group consisted of the states north and east of Maryland. On certain issues Ohio and even Kentucky tended to ally themselves with this region, and in some respects New England was a subgroup with its own special concern. The key to the political unity of this region was manufacturing, although the people and their representatives were of course deeply concerned with agriculture, commerce, and other matters as well.

The southern states made up a second political unit. The cement that held these states together was an amalgam of slavery (as a social institution) and the great southern staples, especially cotton. Thus the entire Southwest, including Kentucky and Tennessee, tended to become part of the South when the so-called "peculiar institution" or matters concerned with cotton were under consideration.

The third political section was the West. Only just beginning to be important enough in Monroe's time to influence national affairs decisively, the region between the Appalachians and the Mississippi was a sprawling, rapidly changing, immensely varied zone. It had less political cohesiveness than either North or South, tending to be pulled abruptly one way and then the other by questions that found the other sections solid and unyielding.

But westerners were acutely aware of their region's special character. When "western issues" like internal improvements, Indian affairs, or land policy came up for discussion, its representatives quickly united. As the West grew, it became powerful in national affairs out of proportion to its population, for it could usually swing the balance on matters in dispute between the North and the South. Furthermore, people realized increasingly that the future belonged to the West. More and more, therefore, this region influenced the tone and spirit of American politics.

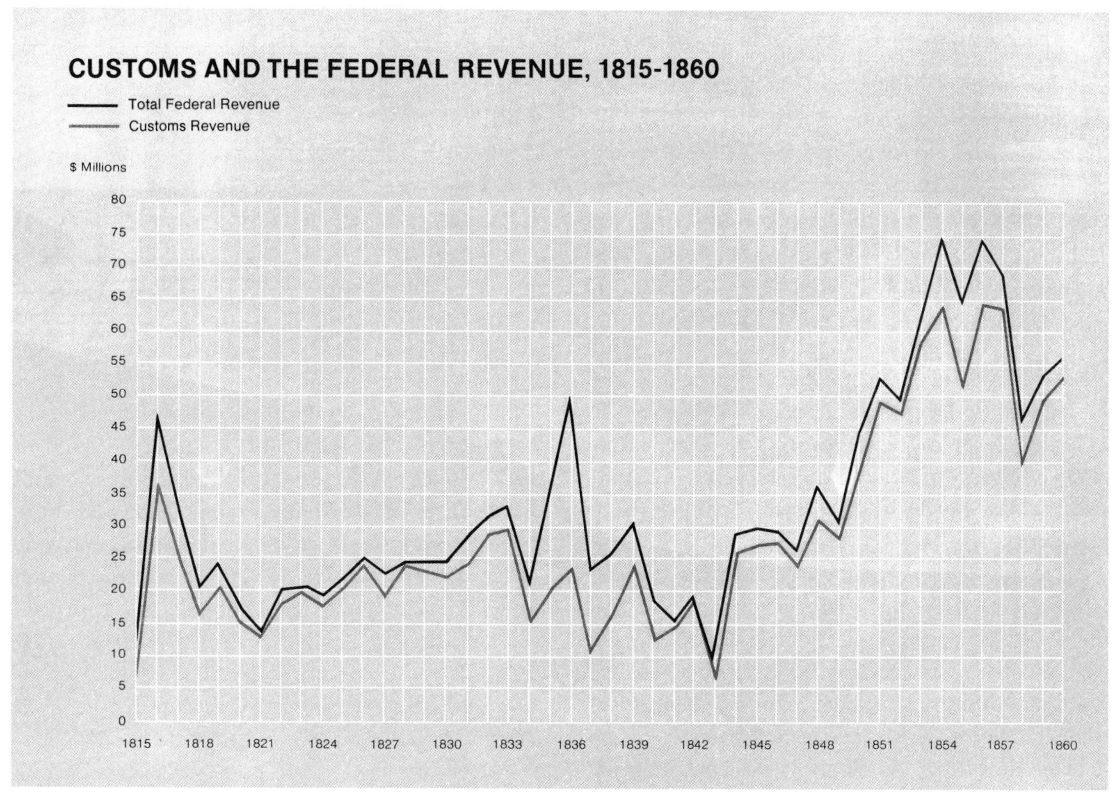

Why the tariff was a political and sectional issue between the War of 1812 and the Civil War is amply demonstrated here. The jump in federal revenues in the mid-1830's was due largely to increased public land sales.

Sectional Political Issues

Two major events, the War of 1812 and the depression that struck the country in 1819, shaped many of the controversies that agitated political life during the Era of Good Feelings. The tariff question, for example, was much affected by both. Before the War of 1812 the level of duties averaged about 12.5 per cent of the value of dutiable products, but to meet the added expenses occasioned by that conflict, Congress doubled all tariffs. In 1816, although the revenue was no longer needed, a new act kept duties fairly close to wartime levels. Infant industries which had grown up during the years of embargo, nonintercourse, and war were able to exert much pressure, for they could show that imports had rocketed from $12 million in 1814 to $113 million in 1815 and were still on the rise. The act especially favored textiles because the British were dumping cloth in America at bargain prices in an attempt to regain lost markets. Then the serious depression at the end of the decade added to the strength of the protectionists. In addition to the manufacturers, unemployed workers and even many farmers became convinced that prosperity would return only if American industry was shielded against foreign competition.

Except for New England, where the shipping interests favored free trade and where the booming mills of the Boston Associates were not being seriously injured by foreign competition, the North solidly favored protection. However, at least in 1816, there was some backing for high duties in every section. A few southerners hoped that textile mills would spring up in their region; more supported protection on the ground that national self-sufficiency was necessary in case of future war. In the West small manufacturers in the towns added their support and so did farmers, who were counting upon workers in the new eastern factories to consume much of their wheat and corn and hogs. But with the passage of time the South rejected protection almost completely. Industry failed to develop, and since they exported most of their cotton and tobacco, southerners soon concluded that besides increasing the cost of nearly everything they bought, high duties on imports would limit the foreign market for southern staples by inhibiting international exchange. As this fact became clear, the West tended to divide on the tariff question: the Northwest and much of Kentucky, which had a special interest in protecting its considerable hemp production, favored high duties; the Southwest, where cotton was the major crop, favored low duties.

National banking policy was another important political issue much affected by the war and the depression. Both Presidents Jefferson and Madison had managed to live with the Bank of the United States despite its supposed unconstitutionality, but its charter was not renewed when it expired in 1811. Aside from the constitutional question, the major opposition to recharter came from state banks eager to take over the business of the Bank for themselves. The fact that Englishmen owned most of the Bank's stock (the government itself had sold 2,200 shares to the British banking house of Baring Brothers in 1802) was also used as an argument against recharter.

The war played havoc with American banking. Many more state banks were created after 1811, and most extended credit recklessly. When the British raid on Washington and Baltimore in 1814 sent panicky depositors scurrying to convert their deposits into gold or silver, the overextended financiers could not oblige them. All the banks outside New England suspended specie payments, that is, they stopped converting their bank notes into hard money on demand. Paper money immediately fell in value; a paper dollar, for example, was soon worth only 85 cents in coin in Philadelphia, still less in Baltimore. Government business also suffered from the absence of a national bank. As early as October 1814 Secretary of the Treasury Alexander J. Dallas submitted a plan for a second Bank of the United States, and after considerable wrangling over its exact form, the institution was authorized in April 1816.

The new Bank differed from its predecessor chiefly in size, being capitalized at $35 million. However, unlike Hamilton's creation, it was badly managed at the start. Its first president, William Jones, who had formerly been secretary of the navy and of the treasury, was inept and easygoing. He displayed, according to the historian George Dangerfield, "a kindheartedness which, in his new position, was tantamount to corruption." All kinds of chicanery went on under Jones's nose. According to the charter, no shareholder could have more than 30 votes, regardless of the size of his holdings, but one director who owned 1,172 shares registered each in a different name, with himself as "attorney" for all, and successfully cast 1,172 votes at meetings. More important, Jones allowed his institution to join merrily in the irresponsible creation of new credit. By the summer of 1818 the Bank's 18 branches had issued notes in excess of ten times their specie reserves, twice the ratio authorized by law. When depression struck the country in 1819, the Bank of the United States was as hard pressed as many of the state banks. Jones resigned.

The new president, Langdon Cheves of South Carolina, was as conservative as Jones had been liberal. During the bad times following the panic, when easy credit was needed, he pursued a policy of stern curtailment. The Bank thus regained a sound position but at the expense of much hardship to debtors. "The Bank was saved," the contemporary economist William Gouge wrote somewhat hyperbolically, "and the people were ruined." Just at the time when John Marshall was establishing its legality, it reached a low point in public favor. Irresponsible state banks resented it, and so did the advocates of hard money.

Regional lines were much less sharply drawn on the Bank issue than on the tariff. Northern congressmen voted against the Bank 53 to 44 in 1816—but many of them because they objected to the particular proposal, not because they were against *any* national bank. Those from other sections favored it by 58 to 30. The collapse occasioned by the Panic of 1819, however, produced much additional opposition to the institution in the West.

Land policy also caused sectional controversy. No one wished to eliminate the system of survey and sale, but there was continuous pressure, beginning before 1800, to reduce both the price of public land and the minimum unit offered for sale. The Land Act of 1800 set $2 per acre as the minimum price and 320 acres (a half section) as the smallest unit. Buyers could pay for the land in four annual installments, which meant that a man needed only $160 to take possession of a good-sized farm. In 1804 the minimum unit was cut to 160 acres, which could be had for about $80 down. Since, in addition, banks were pursuing an easy-credit policy, land sales boomed. The outbreak of the War of 1812 caused a temporary slump, but by 1814 sales had reached an all-time high and were increasing rapidly. In 1818 the government sold nearly 3.5 million acres (graph, page 328). Postwar prices of agricultural products were excellent, for the seas were now free, and European agriculture had not yet recovered from the ravages of the Napoleonic Wars. Thereafter, continuing expansion and the rapid shrinkage of the foreign market as European farmers resumed production led to disaster. Prices fell, the panic struck, and western debtors were forced to the wall by the hundreds. "Crops rotted in the field, trade stood still, and helpless farmers watched miserably as a numbing paralysis settled upon the section," Ray Allen Billington, historian of the West, has written.

Sectional attitudes toward the public lands were fairly straightforward. The West wanted cheap land; the North and South tended to look upon the national domain as an asset that should be converted into as much cash as possible. Northern manufacturers feared that cheap land in the West would drain off surplus labor and force wages up, while southern planters were concerned about the competition that would develop when the virgin lands of the Southwest were put to the production of cotton. The West, however, was ready to fight to the last line of defense over land policy, while the other regions would usually compromise on the issue to gain support for their own vital interests. Sectional alignments on the question of internal improvements were almost identical, but this issue, soon to become very important, had not greatly agitated national affairs before 1820. As we have seen, the only significant federal internal improvement project undertaken before that date was the National Road.

Finally, there was the most divisive of all issues: slavery. After the compromises affecting the peculiar institution made at the Constitutional Convention, it caused remarkably little conflict in national politics before 1819. Congress abolished the African slave trade in 1808 without major incident, and as the nation expanded, free and slave states were added to the Union in equal numbers, Ohio, Indiana, and Illinois being balanced by Louisiana, Mississippi, and Alabama. In 1819 there were 22 states, 11 slave and 11 free. The expansion of slavery occasioned by the cotton boom led southerners to support it much more aggressively, which tended to irritate many northerners, but most persons considered slavery mainly a local issue. To the extent that it *was* a national question, the North opposed it and the South defended it ardently. The West leaned toward the southern point of view, for in addition to the southwestern slave states, the Northwest was also sympathetic, partly because much of its produce was sold on southern plantations and partly because at least half of the early settlers in that area came from Virginia, Kentucky, and other slave states.

By 1824 the giants of the Revolutionary generation had completed their work. Washington, Hamilton, Franklin, Samuel Adams, Patrick Henry, and most of their peers were dead. John Adams (88), Thomas Jefferson (81), and James Madison (73) were passing their declining years quietly on their ancestral acres, full of memories and sage advice, but no longer active in national affairs. In every section new leaders had come forward, men shaped by the past but chiefly concerned with the present. Quite suddenly, between the war and the panic, they had inherited power. They would shape the future of the United States.

NEW-YORK HISTORICAL SOCIETY

Asher B. Durand's portrait of an uncompromising John Quincy Adams dates from 1834, when the ex-President was a congressman from Massachusetts.

Northern Leaders

John Quincy Adams, the best-known political leader of the North in the early 1820's, was a transitional figure, in one sense part of the Revolutionary generation, in another a member of the new group. Just completing his brilliant work as secretary of state under Monroe, he had behind him a record of public service dating back to the Confederation period. All his life had been spent in close contact with public affairs. At 11 he was giving English lessons to the French minister to the Continental Congress and his secretary. ("He shows us no mercy and makes us no compliments," the minister remarked.) While still in his teens he had served as secretary of legation in Russia and Great Britain. After graduating from Harvard in 1787, he became American minister to the Netherlands and to Prussia. Chosen United States senator from Massachusetts in 1803 as a Federalist, he gradually switched to the Republican point of view, even supporting the Embargo Act. Madison sent him back to Europe as minister to Russia in 1809. His work at Ghent on the Peace Commission has already been mentioned.

Adams was farsighted, imaginative, hard-working, and extremely intelligent, one of the most accomplished persons ever to play a major role in American politics, but he was utterly inept in his relations with his fellow men. He had all the virtues and most of the defects of the Puritan, being suspicious both of others and of himself. He suffered in two ways from being his father's child. Naturally, the fact that he was the son of a President put him under severe pressure to live up to the Adams name. Furthermore, his father expected a great deal of him, which added to the burden. When the boy was only seven, John Adams wrote his wife: "Train [the children] to virtue. Habituate them to industry, activity, and spirit. Make them consider vice as shameful and unmanly. Fire them with ambition to be useful. . . . Fix their ambition upon great and solid objects, and their contempt upon little, frivolous and useless ones." Such training made John Quincy an indefatigable worker. Even in winter he normally rose at five o'clock, and he could never really convince himself that most of his associates were not lazy dolts. But it also made him tense, compulsive, conscience-ridden. He set a standard no man could meet and was therefore destined to be continually dissatisfied with himself. As one of his grandsons shrewdly remarked, "he was disappointed because he was not supernatural." Adams had what one Englishman called "a vinegar aspect," passing through life "like a bull-dog among spaniels." Toward enemies he was merciless and overwhelming, toward friends inspiring but demanding.

Like his father and the other great men of the preceding generation, John Quincy Adams was a strong nationalist. While New England was still antiprotectionist, he was at least open-minded on the subject of high tariffs. He supported the second Bank of the United States and, unlike most easterners, he believed that the federal government should spend freely in order to develop roads and canals in the West. To slavery he was, like most northerners, personally opposed. As Monroe's second term drew toward its close, Adams seemed one of the most likely candidates to succeed him. At this period his ambition to be President was his greatest failing, for it led him to make certain compromises with his principles, which in turn plagued his oversensitive conscience and had a corrosive effect upon his peace of mind.

Daniel Webster was far less prominent in the 1820's than Adams, but he was recognized as one of the coming leaders of New England. Born in New Hampshire in 1782, he was graduated from Dartmouth College in 1801, and by the time of the War of 1812 he had made a local reputation as a lawyer and orator. After serving two terms in Congress during the conflict, he moved to Boston to concentrate on his legal practice, quickly becoming one of the leading constitutional lawyers of the country, prominent in the Dartmouth College controversy, *McCulloch v. Maryland,* and a number of other important cases. In 1823 he was again elected to Congress.

Webster owed much of his reputation to his formidable presence and his oratorical skill. Dark, large-headed, craggy of brow, with deep-set, brooding eyes and a firm mouth, he projected a remarkable appearance of moral strength. His thunderous voice, his resourceful vocabulary, his manner—all backed by the mastery of every oratorical trick—made him unique. "He . . . is never averse, whilst traversing the thorny paths of political disputation, to scatter the flowers of rhetorical elegance around him," one contemporary admirer recorded. Webster had also a first-rate mind, powerful and logical. His faults were largely those of temperament. He was too fond of good food and fine broadcloth, of alcohol and adulation. Hard work over an extended period of time was beyond him; generally he bestirred himself only with great effort and too often simply to advance his own cause. Webster could have been a lighthouse in the night, guiding his fellow men to safe harbor. More often he was a weather vane, shifting to accommodate the strongest current breeze. The good opinion of "the best people" meant so much to him that he rarely used his great gifts to shape and guide that opinion in the national interest.

Unlike the independent-minded Adams, Webster nearly always reflected the beliefs of the

DARTMOUTH COLLEGE

Eyes like "anthracite furnaces," remarked the historian Thomas Carlyle of Daniel Webster; this is the "Black Dan" portrait by Francis Alexander.

dominant business interests of New England. His opposition to the embargo and the War of 1812 got him into Congress, and there he faithfully supported the views of the New England merchants. He opposed the high tariff of 1816 because the merchants favored free trade and voted against establishing the Bank chiefly on partisan grounds. (His view changed when the Bank hired him as its lawyer.) He was against both cheap land and federal construction of internal improvements. His opposition to slavery also accorded with the opinion of most of his constituents, but on this question he stood more solidly for principle. Basically he was a nationalist (as was seen in his arguments before the Supreme Court), yet he sometimes allowed political expediency and the prejudices of New England to obscure his feelings. Ahead of him lay fame, considerable constructive service, but also bitter frustration. And, near the end, one hour of greatness.

Elsewhere in the North there were few outstanding figures among the younger politicians.

De Witt Clinton of New York had served briefly in the United States Senate and had run unsuccessfully for the Presidency against Madison in 1812, but he was primarily concerned with state and local affairs, especially during the early 1820's when the Erie Canal was being constructed. New York's man of the future was a little sandy-haired politico named Martin Van Buren. "The Red Fox," as people sometimes called him, was one of the most talented politicians ever to play a part in American affairs. He was born in 1782, and while still in his teens campaigned for Thomas Jefferson. He studied law and prospered, for he was clever and hard-working, but his ambitions were always political. From 1812 to 1820 he served in the state legislature; in 1820 he was elected United States senator.

Van Buren had great charm and immense tact. By nature affable, he never allowed partisanship to mar his personal relationships with other leaders. The members of his political machine, known as the Albany Regency, were almost fanatically loyal to him, and even his enemies could seldom dislike him as a man. Nevertheless, he could be a deadly foe, as many a politician learned to his sorrow. Somehow Van Buren could reconcile deviousness with honesty. He "rowed to his objective with muffled oars," as Randolph of Roanoke said, but he was neither crooked nor venal. Politics for him was like a game or a complex puzzle: the object was victory, but one must play by the rules or lose all sense of achievement. Only a fool will cheat at solitaire, and despite his gregariousness, Van Buren was at heart a solitary operator.

His positions on the issues of the 1820's are hard to determine because he never took a position if he could avoid doing so. Partly this was his politician's desire to straddle every fence, but it also reflected his quixotic belief that issues were means rather than ends in the world of politics. He opposed rechartering the first Bank, yet was not conspicuous among those who fought the second. As a speaker he possessed, as one historian said, "an enormously complicated and diffuse style, which enabled him to say many intelligent things for and against a policy without conveying a very clear idea of his own sentiments." He did not oppose internal improvements, but De Witt Clinton was his political enemy. No one could say with assurance what he thought about the tariff, and since slavery did not arouse much interest in New York, it is safe to suppose that at this time he had no opinion at all about the institution. Any intelligent observer in the 1820's would have predicted that "the Little Magician" would go far, for he was obviously a master of his craft. How far, and in what direction, no one could have guessed.

Southern Leaders

The most prominent southern leader, at least as strong a Presidential candidate as Adams and far more popular among politicians, was William H. Crawford, Monroe's secretary of the treasury. Born in 1772 in the shadow of Virginia's Blue Ridge, he was taken to the Deep South while still a lad, settling finally in Georgia. For a brief time he taught school, then studied law. A giant of a man, rugged, ruddy-faced, with strong, handsome features and shrewd intelligence, he prospered in the law and became a leader of the conservative faction in the state, speaking for the large planters against the interests of the yeomen farmers. After service in the legislature, he was elected to the Senate in 1807. Later he put in a tour of duty as minister to France, and in 1816 he was appointed secretary to the treasury.

Crawford was direct and friendly, a marvelous storyteller, and a superb manipulator of men. He was one of the few persons in Washington who could teach the fledgling senator Martin Van Buren anything about politics, and Van Buren supported him enthusiastically in the contest for the 1824 Presidential nomination. (So, strangely enough, did Thomas Jefferson.) Crawford was one of the first politicians to try to build a national machine. "Crawford's Act" of 1820, limiting the term of minor federal appointees to four years, was passed largely through his efforts, for he realized before nearly anyone else that a handful of petty offices, properly distributed, could win the allegiance of thousands of voters.

Crawford had something interesting to say on most of the important issues of the times. Although predisposed toward the states'-rights posi-

NATIONAL PORTRAIT GALLERY, SMITHSONIAN INSTITUTION

John C. Calhoun is a handsome and striking figure in Rembrandt Peale's portrait, painted during Calhoun's War Hawk period before the War of 1812.

tion, he favored recharter of the Bank and was willing to go along with a moderately protective tariff. During the depression that began in 1819 he devised an excellent relief plan for farmers who were unable to meet installment payments due on land purchased from the government. He even suggested a highly original scheme for a flexible paper currency not convertible into hard money, although it is true that he lacked the political courage to press for its adoption. Crawford was controversial. Many of his contemporaries considered him no more than a cynical spoilsman, although his administration of the Treasury was first-rate. Yet he had many friends. His ambition was vast, his power great. Fate, however, was about to strike Crawford a crippling blow.

John C. Calhoun, the other outstanding southern leader, was born in South Carolina in 1782 and graduated from Yale in 1804. He studied law at Tapping Reeve's remarkable law school in Litchfield, Connecticut, which in half a century turned out 15 future United States senators, 10 governors, 2 Supreme Court justices, and a large number of other men prominent in public affairs. After returning to South Carolina, Calhoun served in the state legislature and in 1811 went to Washington as congressman. A prominent War Hawk, he took a strong nationalist position on all the issues of the day. In 1817 Monroe made him secretary of war.

Although devoted to the South and its institutions, Calhoun took the broadest possible view of political affairs. John Quincy Adams, seldom charitable in his private opinions of colleagues (he called Crawford, for example, "a worm"), praised Calhoun's "quick understanding" and "enlarged philosophic views." "He is above all sectional and factional prejudices," Adams wrote. Charles M. Wiltse has summarized Calhoun's views in the early 1820's as follows:

> Ever since its weakness had been exposed by the War of 1812, Calhoun had consciously striven to guide the Government of the United States into the path of power. . . . To this end he had supported a moderate tariff, a national bank, a large Navy, a well-equipped and well-officered Army, and a unified system of transportation by road and canal; and he had consistently argued that the Constitution granted all the powers necessary to bring these things to fruition.

"Our true system is to look to the country," Calhoun said in 1820, "and to support such measures and such men, without regard to sections, as are best calculated to advance the general interest."

Calhoun was intelligent, bookish, and given to the study of abstractions. Although basically a gentle person, he was cold and restrained in most of his relationships. He had no hobbies and was utterly humorless. In an age when the average politician drank prodigiously, Calhoun would never do more than sip a glass or two of light wine. He neither smoked nor played cards. Legend has it that he once tried to write a poem but after putting down the word "Whereas," gave it up as beyond his powers. Some obscure failing made it impossible for him to grasp the essence of the human condition. Yet he burned to lead his fellows. Few contemporaries could maintain themselves in debate against his powerful intelligence, yet that mind—so sharp, so penetrating—was the blind bondsman of his ambition.

Western Leaders

The outstanding western leader of the 1820's was Henry Clay of Kentucky, one of the most charming and colorful of all American statesmen. Tall, lean, gray-eyed, Clay was the kind of person who made men cheer and women swoon. On the platform he ranked with Webster; behind the political scenes he was the peer of Van Buren. In every environment he was warm and open—what a modern political scientist might call a charismatic personality. Clay loved to drink, swear, tell tales, and play poker. It was characteristic that at one sitting he won $40,000 from a friend and then cheerfully told him that a note for $500 would wipe out the obligation. He was a reasonable man, skilled at arranging political compromises, but he possessed a reckless streak: like so many westerners, his sense of honor was exaggerated. Twice in his career he called men out for having insulted him. Fortunately, all concerned were poor shots.

CHICAGO HISTORICAL SOCIETY

Henry Clay was House Speaker when he posed for Matthew Jouett in 1824. Jouett worked in Lexington, Kentucky, the self-styled "Athens of the West."

Virginia-born, Clay moved to Lexington, Kentucky, in 1797 at the age of 20 and developed a thriving law practice. After some years in the state legislature, he won a seat in Congress in 1810. He led the War Hawks in 1811–12 and was Speaker of the House from 1811 to 1820 and from 1823 to 1825.

Intellectually second-rate when compared to Adams or Calhoun, or even to Webster, Clay had few original ideas. But he had a perfect temperament for politics. He loved power but knew that in the United States it had to be shared to be exercised. His great gift was in seeing national needs from a broad perspective and fashioning a program that could inspire ordinary men with something of his vision. In the early 1820's he was just developing his "American System." In return for eastern support of a program of federal aid in the construction of roads and canals, the West would back the protective tariff, he argued. He justified this scheme on the widest national grounds. By stimulating manufacturing, it would increase the demand for western raw materials, while western prosperity would lead to greater consumption of eastern manufactured goods. Washington did not describe the interdependence of the sections better in his Farewell Address than did Clay, repeatedly, in Congress and upon the stump. And like Washington, Clay was conservative. He opposed the national bank in 1811 on constitutional grounds but supported the new one in 1816 and thereafter, saying, with typical candor and shrewdness, that "the force of circumstance and the lights of experience" had convinced him that he had previously misread the Constitution. His view of slavery, as his biographer Glyndon Van Deusen has said, was "a combination of theoretical dislike and practical tolerance." He would have preferred to ignore the subject. Nevertheless, slavery repeatedly played a crucial role in his career.

The West had other spokesmen in the 1820's. One was Thomas Hart Benton, elected to the Senate by the new state of Missouri. Benton was an expansionist and a hard-money man of the uncompromising sort, suspicious of paper currency and therefore of all banks. He championed the small western farmer, favoring free homesteads for pioneers and an extensive federal internal improvements program. Although opposed in principle to high tariffs, he tended to vote for them "with repugnance and misgiving" to obtain protection for Missouri's lead and furs. Poor workers should cast aside their tools and head west, he believed. For 30 years Benton advocated his ideas in the Senate in bluff, colorful language. "Nobody opposes Benton but a few black-jack prairie lawyers," he would roar. "Benton and democracy are one and the same, sir; synonymous terms, sir; synonymous terms, sir." A large-hearted man, though vain and pompous, he remained essentially a sectional rather than a national figure.

Another western leader was General William Henry Harrison. Although he sat in the Ohio legislature and in both houses of Congress between 1816 and 1828, Harrison was primarily a military man. During the Panic of 1819 he took an anti-Bank and pro-high tariff stand, but he did not identify himself closely with any policy except the extermination of the Indians and had little to do with the newly developing political alignments of the 1820's. Much like Harrison was Andrew Jackson, the "Hero of New Orleans," except that his popularity greatly exceeded Harrison's. He also had many friends, shrewd in the ways of politics, who were working devotedly, if not entirely unselfishly, to make him President. No one knew his views on most questions, but few cared. His military reputation and his forceful personality were his chief assets.

Northern Social and Cultural Life

New issues and new men reflected, in addition to economic change, important alterations in the structure of society and the thinking of the people. Despite the expansion of its industry, New England's population increased scarcely at all when compared to the rest of the country. The best land was already under cultivation, and the price of a farm was, by American standards, high. The region attracted few immigrants, and much of the natural growth of the native population was siphoned off by the West. Between 1790 and 1820 the population of Connecticut rose by only 10 per cent, that of Rhode Island and Massachusetts by little more. The other northern states, especially New York, where development had been relatively slow in the colonial period because of restrictive land policies and the domination of the western districts by the Iroquois, expanded rapidly. In 1790 New York ranked fifth among the states with a population of 340,000, only 20,000 more than Maryland. By 1820 it had more than quadrupled and was the most populous state in the Union.

Throughout the North the urban population was increasing at a faster pace than in other sections. Boston, for example, had only 18,000 inhabitants in 1790. As a result of its rich foreign commerce, its population doubled by 1815, despite the stagnation resulting from the embargo and the war. New England towns like Salem, Providence, and New Haven grew at a similar rate, New York and Philadelphia even more rapidly.

The manners and attitudes of the people of the northern states were changing too, especially after the War of 1812. Society remained anchored to British roots, and socially ambitious people tended, quite self-consciously, to ape what they took to be the modes and manners of London. Books like the *Friendly Instructor, or Companion for Young Ladies and Gentlemen* were widely popular. But by 1820 "republican" manners, which meant generally a stress on equality, informality, directness (some foreigners called it rudeness), and a disregard for the privacy of others were coming everywhere into fashion. However, local differences existed. Each major city had its distinctive qualities. Boston, for example, was like a provincial English town both in appearance and population. Most citizens had been Boston-bred for generations, and nearly all had British ancestors. New York still displayed a strong Dutch influence (observable in its gabled, yellow brick houses set sideways to the streets and in the preponderance of Dutch names), but it had already become, with the possible exception of New Orleans, the most cosmopolitan city in the land, as well as its greatest mercantile

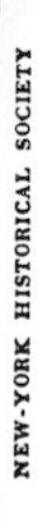

New York's 2,500-seat Park Theatre was depicted in water color by John Searle in 1822, the year after it opened. Searle included many prominent New Yorkers of the time in the audience, who are watching a performance of a popular farce called Monsieur Tonson.

center. Every European tongue could be heard on its busy streets. Philadelphia retained its Quaker character, with a strong admixture of German. No city was so public-spirited, none better supplied with clubs, charitable organizations, and cultural opportunities.

These northern cities were not yet great centers of industry. Although relatively free from slums, they were dirty, crowded, and crude. Police and fire protection scarcely existed, sewage disposal was generally an individual problem. In Boston street-cleaning was left until the 1820's to farmers, who collected the sweepings for fertilizer. Philadelphia, although by far the cleanest and most orderly, lacked a decent water system until 1822.

The North was the center of American art and culture. All the major towns supported theaters, where the works of Shakespeare and other great dramatists were performed along with a remarkable number of American plays. Perhaps as many as 200 works by American authors were produced before 1830. Since transportation was slow and expensive, decentralization was essential even in intellectual matters. Towns as small as Worcester and Albany had active publishing businesses, although New York, Boston, and Philadelphia outdistanced all other cities in this field. By 1825 the House of Harper in New York, organized in 1817, was the largest book publisher in the nation. Public libraries existed in many cities before 1800, but they were very small. Thereafter, however, some grew rapidly. In the 1820's Cambridge, Boston, and Philadelphia had the best public libraries, New York lagging far behind. Every town of any size had at least a weekly newspaper, and magazines of various kinds proliferated. Most were short-lived, but Boston's *North American Review,* founded in 1815, was destined to live for more than a century and to have an influence far out of proportion to its small circulation.

Architecture also flourished in the northern cities, chiefly as a result of the work of Charles Bulfinch and some of his disciples. Bulfinch

ESSEX INSTITUTE

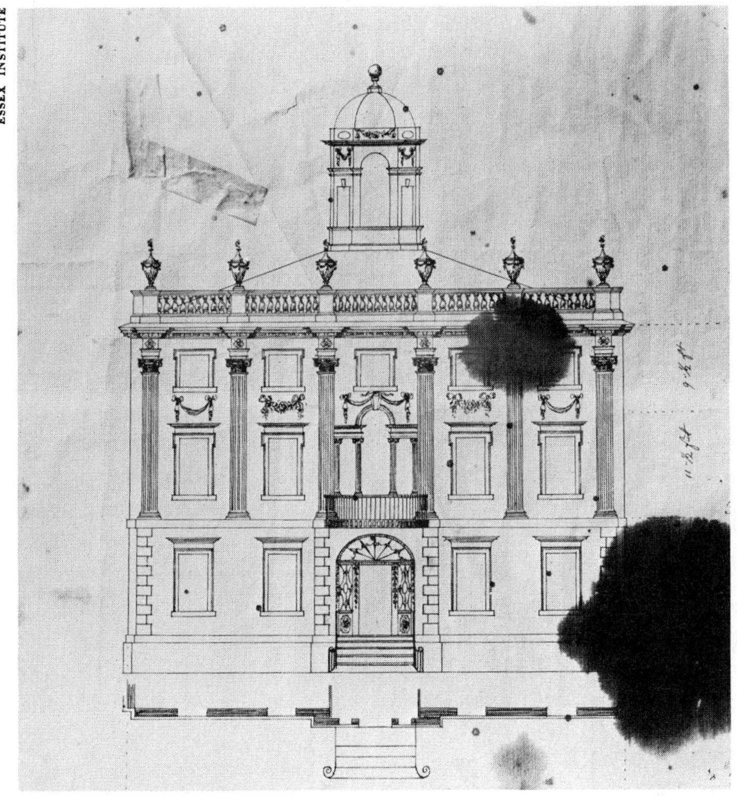

This graceful, Federal-style mansion of the merchant prince Elias Hasket Derby in Salem, Massachusetts, was primarily the work of the architect Samuel McIntire; the front elevation shown here, however, has been credited to McIntire's mentor, Charles Bulfinch.

studied in England and was much influenced by the work of the Adam brothers and other British architects, but he developed a manner all his own. Thanks to his "Federal" style, parts of Boston achieved a dignity and charm equal to the finest sections of London. The State House, many other public buildings, and, best of all, many of Bulfinch's private houses—austere yet elegant, solid yet airy and graceful—gave the town a distinction it had lacked before the Revolution. His Colonnade Row, 19 joined façades fronting on the Boston Common, and his Franklin Crescent, with 16 houses curving along a semioval park, were particular triumphs. Bulfinch and a few of his followers, most notably Samuel McIntire and Asher Benjamin, equaled the achievements of the best European architects of their day. Soon their work was affecting building all over the North and in the West as well. Benjamin wrote a number of books, such as *The Rudiments of Architecture* (1814), which helped to spread interest in the Federal style.

Literature and Painting

Most of the nation's writers in this era also lived in the northern states. These men were greatly preoccupied with trying to produce a distinctively American literature. The *North American Review* set out to "foster American genius," and literary clubs such as Boston's Anthology Club and the Friendly Club in New York sprang up to encourage native authors. American themes, particularly incidents drawn from history, were commonly employed. According to the literary historian Russel B. Nye, in the period between the Revolution and 1830, "every author of note made at least one attempt to use American history in a major literary work." Yet as Nye confessed, in nearly every case "nothing of consequence appeared."

Of novelists before 1830, only James Fenimore Cooper made really successful use of the national heritage. Beginning with *The Spy* (1821), *The Pioneers* (1823), and *The Last of the Mohicans* (1826), he wrote a long series of tales of Indians and settlers which presented a vivid if highly romanticized picture of frontier life. (Cooper's Indians, Mark Twain once quipped, belonged to "an extinct tribe that never existed.") Cooper's work marked a shift from the classicism of the 18th century, which emphasized reason and orderliness in writing, to the romanticism of the early 19th century, with its stress on highly subjective emotional values and its concern for the beauties of nature and the freedom of the individual.

Most novelists of the period slavishly imitated British writers. Some looked to the sentimental novels of Samuel Richardson for a model, others aped satirical writers like Defoe and Tobias Smollett. Most popular of all were historical romances done in the manner of the Waverley Novels of Sir Walter Scott. None approached the level of the best British writers, and as a result, American novelists were badly outdistanced in their own country by the British, both in prestige and popularity. Since foreign copyrights were not recognized in the United States, British books could be shamelessly pirated and sold very cheaply. Half a million volumes of Scott were sold in America before 1823. This benefited American readers but not American writers. Cooper even encouraged a rumor that his first novel, *Precaution* (1820), had been written by an Englishman because he thought this a good way to get it a fair hearing. For a similar reason the playwright James Nelson Barber spread the story that one of his dramas was of English origin.

New York City was the literary capital of the country during the first three decades of the century. Its leading light was Washington Irving, but his "Knickerbocker group" also included the novelist James Kirke Paulding, the poets Joseph Rodman Drake and Fitz-Greene Halleck, and a number of others. They first attracted attention with the *Salmagundi Papers*, published in 20 numbers in 1807 and 1808. These whimsical papers on New York affairs, done in imitation of the 18th-century English *Spectator* essays, were followed in 1809 by Irving's comical *Diedrich Knickerbocker's History of New York*, which made its young author famous on both sides of the Atlantic. Yet Irving soon abandoned the United States for Europe. Even *The Sketch Book* (1819), which included "Rip Van Winkle" and his other well-known tales and legends of the Dutch in the Hudson Valley, was composed while the author was residing in Birmingham and London. Outside New York there was much less literary activity. New England was only on the verge of its great literary flowering. The Massa-

MELLON COLLECTION, NATIONAL GALLERY OF ART

The tales of Washington Irving furnished subject matter for many illustrators and artists, most notably the genre painter John Quidor; no less than 16 of his 35 known canvases are Irving scenes. Reproduced at left is Quidor's The Return of Rip Van Winkle.

In 1801 Charles Willson Peale masterminded the first American scientific expedition, to "exhume" the bones of a prehistoric mastodon found on a New York farm. Peale set up a treadmill to remove muck from the diggings and painted the whole operation (at right), including himself gesturing in the group at far right.

chusetts-born poet William Cullen Bryant made a stir with "Thanatopsis," published in the *North American Review* in 1817, but he soon moved to New York where he became editor of the *Evening Post.* In Philadelphia Philip Freneau continued to write some excellent verse, and, before his premature death in 1810, Charles Brockden Brown produced some mildly interesting novels, but that was all that was worthy of even passing mention.

However, American painting in this period reached a level comparable to contemporary European work. Like the writers, nearly all American artists came from the North. All received most of their training in Europe. Benjamin West of Philadelphia, the first and in his day the most highly regarded, went to Europe before the Revolution and never returned; he can scarcely be considered an American. John Singleton Copley, whose stern, straightforward portraits display a more distinctly American character than the work of any of his contemporaries, was a Bostonian. No one so well captured the vigor, integrity, and sense of individual worth of the Revolutionary generation. Charles Willson Peale was born in Maryland, but after studying under West in London, he settled in Philadelphia, where he established a remarkable museum containing fossils, stuffed animals, and various natural curiosities as well as paintings. Peale also

THE PEALE MUSEUM, GIFT OF MRS. HARRY WHITE

helped found the Pennsylvania Academy of the Fine Arts, and he did much to encourage American painting, not the least of his achievements being the production of a large brood of artistic children to whom he gave names like Rembrandt and Titian and Rubens. The most talented of Peale's children was (appropriately) Rembrandt, whose portrait of Jefferson, executed in 1800, is one of the finest likenesses of the Sage of Monticello that we have (page 217).

Another outstanding artist of this generation was Gilbert Stuart of Rhode Island, best known for his many studies of George Washington. Stuart studied in England with Benjamin West, and his brush was much in demand in London. In America he worked in New York, Philadelphia, and Boston. Stuart was probably the finest of the early American portrait painters, although he lacked sufficient depth to be a truly great artist. He was fond of painting his subjects with ruddy complexions (produced by means of a judicious mixture of vermilion, purple, and white pigment), which made many of his elderly sitters appear positively cherubic. Stuart once remarked that the pallid flesh tones used by a rival looked "like putrid veal a little blown with green flies."

John Vanderlyn of New York was one of the first Americans to study in Paris, where the icy neoclassicism of Jacques Louis David influenced him greatly. Originally a portraitist, in later life he painted a number of curious panoramas covering thousands of square feet of canvas. Henry Inman, who learned his trade as an apprentice to the prolific miniaturist-engraver John Wesley Jarvis, lived most of his life in New York and Philadelphia. Among the many prominent men who sat for Inman were Chief Justice Marshall, President Van Buren, the artist-naturalist John Audubon (whose *Birds of America* [1827–1838] was itself an ornament in the history of American art), the writer Nathaniel Hawthorne, and Nicholas Biddle, president of the second Bank of the United States (page 324).

Still another painter of the period, Washington Allston, was southern-born but no exception to the generalization that the talented artists of the day gravitated to the northern states. After the usual period of study abroad, he did most of his painting in Boston. Similarly, Thomas Sully, another skillful portrait painter, spent all his mature years in the North, although he grew to manhood in Charleston, South Carolina.

In general the painting of this period, while not innovative, was less obviously imitative of European models than the national literature and of far higher quality. In a society that stressed the importance of the individual, wealthy merchants, manufacturers, and planters wished their likenesses preserved, and the demand for portraits of the nation's still-living Revolutionary heroes seemed insatiable. Since paintings could not be reproduced as books could be, American artists did a flourishing business. Yet they remained unmistakably in the European tradition.

Exceptions to this generalization can be found in the work of a number of self-trained artists, men like Jonathan Fisher, Charles Octavius Cole, and J. William Jennys. These primitive painters supplied rural and middle-class patrons in the same way that men like Copley and Stuart catered to the tastes of the rich and prominent. Jennys, for example, received $24 in 1801 for portraits of Dr. William Stoddard Williams of Deerfield, Massachusetts, and his wife. Cole specialized in New England sea captains, whom he often painted holding the brass-bound spyglasses of the mariner's profession. One historian has discovered traces of more than 20 artisan-painters within the single state of Maine in the 1830's and 1840's. Some of these primitive canvases have great charm and distinction, and all show little sign of European influence. Yet they are not especially American either, reflecting rather the characteristics of all primitive art: simplicity and distinctness.

Religion and Education

The religious views of the people of the North in the first decade of the 19th century presented no drastic break with past trends. The region remained overwhelmingly Protestant, but most sects took a somewhat more tolerant attitude toward those who disagreed with them than they had in colonial times. After the Revolution, religion seemed to play a less prominent role in life in all parts of the

OBERLIN COLLEGE

The evangelist Charles Grandison Finney, a prime mover of the "Second Great Awakening," was president of Oberlin College from 1851 to 1866, when the school was caught up in the abolitionist movement.

MUSEE D'HISTOIRE NATURELLE, LE HAVRE

This bizarre scene, of a quarreling New Bedford, Massachusetts, congregation reaching a literal parting of the ways, was drawn in 1816 by Charles Lesueur, a French naturalist touring the United States.

country. Deism remained popular, at least among intellectuals, until about 1800.

Early in the new century a "Second Great Awakening" broke out sporadically in various sections. The new revivals were as emotionally charged as those of the earlier awakening. Preachers described the tortures awaiting unrepentant sinners just as graphically. But the new evangelists took a more optimistic view of men's chances for salvation. Charles Grandison Finney, for example, probably the most influential preacher of the movement, described a benevolent Deity presiding over a democratic heaven not unlike the United States of America. If men would only see the light and behave honestly toward one another, the millennium would (literally) arrive promptly. "God always allows his children as much liberty as they are prepared to enjoy," Finney declared.

Pessimistic Calvinistic religions tended to decline nearly everywhere. After deism began to lose its force, the liberal Unitarian wing of the Congregational churches of New England absorbed many of its major ideas. A man like William Ellery Channing, pastor of the Federal Street Church in Boston, rejected a God of Vengeance. Channing taught that Christ was merely an exceptionally fine human being and he decried the emotional aspects of the Puritan approach to God. The Unitarians, however, retained the Bible as a prime source of religious truth, although not all of them believed it more important than pure reason. They also preserved a Puritan concern for moral earnestness and for social improvement.

Conservative Calvinists did not abandon the field to the Unitarians in New England, but after 1805, when they "captured" Harvard, the liberals were dominant. Unitarianism remained, like deism, pretty difficult going for an untrained mind, but a simpler form, called Universalism, which stressed the comforting belief that God would provide salvation for all men, attracted a wide segment of the population. Although the Presbyterians of the North also suffered from internal dissension, dividing into "old" and "new" schools, the great religious battles of the era were fought in the West.

No spectacular progress was made in education in the northern states until the 1830's and 1840's. Boston established the nation's first public high school in 1821, and in 1824 Massachusetts required all towns of more than 500 families to establish similar institutions, but only an insignificant fraction of the youth of the country enrolled in such schools. Massachusetts also led in opening the public schools to Negroes. By 1845 only Boston of the major Massachusetts towns and cities segregated black students, and in 1855 the legislature outlawed religious and racial discrimination in schools throughout the state. Elsewhere, however, segregation was the rule, except in a few small school districts.

Secondary and higher education remained primarily for the rich and for those of middling wealth willing to make financial sacrifices to advance their children's opportunities. Rousseau's idea that education must be especially adapted to the level of development of the growing child and the Swiss Johann Pestalozzi's belief in the importance of teacher training caused much discussion in the United States but produced little immediate change. The curricula of the schools remained about what they had been in colonial America. Much of the teaching was simply out of date; as late as 1810 some widely used arithmetic texts still employed problems based on shillings and pence and systems of weights and measures that had no practical application for Americans. Salaries were low and many teachers were ill-prepared for their jobs. Turnover was high, both among teachers and their charges. Yet the country as a whole was beginning to accept Jefferson's thesis that in a democracy a decent system of public education was a necessity.

At the college level the great expansion took place in the South and West, but the older northern colleges supplied most of the administrators and teachers for the new institutions and thus made their mark upon them. College teaching was not very distinguished, great emphasis being placed on rote learning. Classical studies were always emphasized heavily, along with rhetoric, mathematics, and philosophy. After 1800 science and "political economy" appeared, but first-class work in these fields was rare. On the whole, academic standards declined, for enrollments were rising without a corresponding increase in the number of teachers or in the financial resources of the colleges. Few professors took any serious interest in research. However, a few students were beginning to go to Germany for advanced work. At least 25 Americans studied at Göttingen, Leipzig, and other German universities before 1830; eventually, their influence on higher education would be strong.

Society and Culture in the South

Social change in the South chiefly resulted from the reinvigoration of slavery and the spread of cotton. The Upper South grew relatively slowly, but the cotton regions expanded almost as rapidly as states like New York and Pennsylvania. Between 1790 and 1820, South Carolina doubled and Georgia quadrupled in population. The South remained predominantly rural, however; the only city in the region that grew rapidly was Baltimore, and its economy was tied to the North rather than to the South. As late as 1810 Charleston, the one truly southern city, had but 24,000 inhabitants.

Superficially, Charleston seemed prosperous and cultivated, with its attractive Georgian houses done in stucco and tile and its procession of concerts and balls. But when the great planters returned to their estates after the social season, Charleston became an empty shell. The small southern towns were both shabby—with rutted streets, open sewers, and unpainted houses—and culturally sterile.

The great slaveowners dominated southern society although they made up only a tiny fraction of the population. Slavery bred a paternalistic point of view, which helps explain why the small farmers usually accepted planter leadership even when they had the political power to overthrow it. The alternative seemed to be identification with the Negroes, and even the lowliest white southerner found that unthinkable. The opportunity to rise in the South was almost as great as in the North, and most people preferred making their way by joining rather than by fighting the establishment. In a slaveholding society a kind of artificial chivalry flourished. Dueling was common; the military arts were highly valued; white women were idealized. This explains the immense popularity of the novels of Sir Walter Scott in the South. Thirty-five towns in the region were named Waverley, and hundreds of girl babies were christened Rowena in honor of the heroine of *Ivanhoe*. Although many small colleges were founded, chiefly by the various religious sects, primary and secondary education lagged and illiteracy was high. The most interesting architectural developments in the area were the graceful homes of the planters, mostly done in classic style, with tall white columns and broad porches. Jefferson's Monticello is an outstanding example.

Like the North, the South was overwhelmingly Protestant, but the religious trend there ran in a different direction. In colonial and Revolutionary times southern planters were notoriously easygoing about religion. That Jefferson was a deist might be expected in the light of his thorough commitment to the rational point of view, but even a man of few intellectual interests like Washington, although he attended Episcopal services, looked upon the Deity as a sort of impersonal first cause and did not make religion an important part of his life. Around 1800, however, while Unitarianism was undermining orthodoxy in New England, southern churches were becoming much more authoritarian and emotional. The expansion of slavery explains this, for freedom of religious thought—of all thought, for that matter—might lead to conclusions dangerous to existing institutions. A stern, paternalistic God made sense to a society determined to convince a large proportion of the population that obedience to authority was a fact of existence and that this life was but a time of trial in preparation for the next. It may also be argued that the white southerner's unconscious guilt at his oppression of the Negro predisposed him to the belief that men are mostly sinners, but such a conclusion must perforce be speculative.

The culture of the southern slaves has been the subject of much recent study. The most interesting questions concern the extent to which their rich and complex African heritage survived the shocking disruption of their forced transit to the New World and the numbing pressures of slavery. White historians long argued that slaves swiftly lost all but the vaguest awareness of their origins, that the typical American Negro, slave or free, was "a man without a past." Ulrich B. Phillips put it this way in *Life and Labor in the Old South* (1929). "Foulahs and Fantyns, Eboes and Angolas begat American plantation Negroes to whom a spear would be strange but a 'languid hoe' familiar, the tomtom forgotten but the banjo inviting." It is now, however, clear that much more of African culture was retained than these historians realized. Aside from such obvious cultural elements as music, dances, names, and folklore, subtle motor habits, speech patterns (although not, of course, the languages themselves), concepts of time and family organization, methods of treating illnesses, to say nothing of religious attitudes and values, persisted among American Negroes, generation after generation.

Beyond the question of African survivals among the Negroes is the question of cultural assimilation generally. It would be anthropologically naive to assume that the culture of white Americans, especially in the South, was not in part African, just as it was partly Indian. Every culture is an amalgam, the American more than most. The extent to which African and evangelical Christian elements "explain" the religious practices of slaves can be asked with equal cogency of the practices of many of their masters.

None of this is to deny the enormous impact of white culture on the slaves, especially after the cutting off of mass importations early in the 19th century. One need only recall how white immigrants lost or "forgot" large elements of their European heritage in America, and then consider how much more difficult it would be for most Africans, forcefully deracinated, scattered, deprived of all formal means of preserving and transmitting their culture, to retain their old ways.

Western Life

The civilization of the new West was a mixture of North and South and at the same time something distinct in itself. The "great migration" from Connecticut and Massachusetts into Ohio gave that state a New England cast, both in the appearance of its towns and farms and in the community spirit and general point of view of the people. Settlers in the Southwest and in the southerly parts of the Old Northwest, being mostly southerners, also brought their own ways along with their baggage. It has been said that if a town possessed a Congregational church and a college, it had been founded by New Englanders, but that if it had a Presbyterian church and a distillery, the settlers had come from some place like Virginia or Kentucky. Many historians have noticed how life in Indiana and Illinois made one boy from the Kentucky border country an Abraham Lincoln, and how moving to Mississippi made another Kentucky lad a Jefferson Davis.

But few western communities were mere extensions of North or South; the frontier left its mark upon them all. The untapped riches, the huge expanse of the West, made the people restless, prodigal, optimistic, boastful, and also industrious and resourceful. Its rawness and remoteness made them tough and crude, but open-hearted and hospitable, too. Even more than other Americans, westerners believed in equality and democracy, although by some alchemy they convinced themselves that Negroes and Indians had no right to these blessings. Great variations in wealth and influence sprang up, but no true westerner accepted inferiority as either his due or his fate.

The West expanded at an enormous pace. The population of Ohio increased more than tenfold between 1800 and 1820; by the latter date it was already the fifth-largest state, with nearly 600,000 residents. Although far more sparsely populated, Mississippi grew almost as swiftly, and the "older" regions of Kentucky and Tennessee were also surging ahead. Although the West remained primarily agricultural, its towns grew as fast as its farms. The expansion of New Orleans after the invention of the steamboat has already been mentioned. Cincinnati had nearly 10,000 inhabitants in 1820, Pittsburgh 8,000, Lexington more than 5,000, and all despite the depression of 1819 which severely checked urban growth. Especially after the appearance of the steamboat, western cities served as the harbors and depots of the inner continent, but local manufacturing quickly appeared. As early as 1810, a resident described Pittsburgh as "a large workshop"; by 1815 the value of its manufactures exceeded $2.6 million. Western cultural life centered in the cities as well. Lexington's claim to be the "Athens of the West" was preposterous, but the town did offer a remarkably varied intellectual fare for such a small community. Cincinnati possessed an important book publishing industry, and most towns of any size had subscription libraries before 1815. Both amateur and professional theaters existed in Lexington, Louisville, Cincinnati, St. Louis, and of course New Orleans, although it could not be said that most of them flourished. By 1820 Cincinnati could boast of its Western Museum, founded by the "Franklin of the West," Dr. Daniel Drake, that indefatigable civic booster and herald of culture who helped also to establish a library, various clubs and educational institutions, and even a medical journal.

Most westerners were undoubtedly uncouth and intellectually naive. Much of their "culture" was inferior even to the low level existing in the eastern regions. But all the towns had what Louis B. Wright has called in *Culture on the Moving Frontier* "a saving remnant" eager to civilize the community. "Often their efforts were pathetic," Wright admits, "but the dream was there and the dream was important."

The western combination of low standards and high zeal can be seen in the educational and religious life of the region. Everyone admitted the need for schools, but despite the provision in the early land ordinances that a section of each township be devoted to educational purposes, schools were poor and not very numerous. Most of the Protestant sects established colleges in the West. In 1820 the Baptists adopted the slogan: "Every state its own Baptist college," and the Methodists and Congregationalists were almost as active. There was a widespread conviction that, as one young teacher said, "it is *baptized intelligence* which alone can save this beautiful valley," but aside from a few fairly good institutions like Transylvania College in Lexington, most of the western colleges were pitifully inadequate by any intellectual standard. Their religious connections hindered these colleges by committing them to the production of devout members of a particular

ALL: *Domestic Manners of the Americans*

Mrs. Frances Trollope, mother of novelist Anthony Trollope, came to the United States in 1827 and with her husband opened a "bazaar," or fancy-goods shop, in Cincinnati. Its failure may have had something to do with her sour attitude toward everything American, for in her Domestic Manners of the Americans *(1832) she was savagely caustic about what she had seen. These sketches for her book are by Auguste Hervieu. At top is Nashoba, Tennessee, a settlement of freed slaves. The scruffy family above left eaked out a living selling firewood to passing steamboats. Hervieu's drawing above right was captioned simply, "The solemnity of justice."*

church rather than young men devoted to the pursuit of knowledge. The reaction of the evangelical religions against the 18th-century rationalism of the deists further crippled their intellectual life. It is significant that Transylvania achieved its greatest distinction under the presidency of a Unitarian, Horace Holley of Boston.

Since westerners preferred plenty of emotion and hellfire in their religion, the Methodists and Baptists attracted the widest support. Episcopalians were rare among them, and even Presbyterians, so numerous among pre-Revolutionary frontiersmen, were not especially common. The Second Great Awakening swept through the region beyond the mountains with special force. The George Whitefield of this movement was James McGready, a preacher who "could so array hell before the wicked that they would tremble and quake, imagining a lake of fire and brimstone yawning to overwhelm them."

McGready, and others inspired by his example, preached a simple message: sin (which included drinking, gambling, and disbelief in Christianity as well as the standard vices) was wrong; salvation (through repentance and church membership) could be had by all. An energetic and essentially simple people, surrounded by the dangers and uncertainties of the frontier, took eagerly to McGready's type of exhortation. Their religious camp meetings lasted for days and attracted thousands. Mass hysteria often swept these earnest throngs. Men sobbed, shrieked, barked like animals, and were seized by the "jerks," transported with what they conceived to be the divine spirit. Inspired by these outbursts, people flocked to the evangelical faiths. Between 1800 and 1803 the Baptists added 10,000 converts in Kentucky alone, and the Methodists were equally successful. Disciples of McGready such as Finis Ewing (so-named because he was the last of 12 children) traveled endlessly through the West, bringing their message to isolated farms, holding camp meetings, converting sinners by the thousands. Others were like Peter Cartwright, a reformed gambler, totally uneducated, who took his Methodist "exhorter's license" and traveled a broad circuit through the West. "His self-reliance, his readiness with tongue and fist, his quick sense of humor, all made him dear to the hearts of the frontier," a biographer explained. "If, as not infrequently happened, intruders attempted to break up his meetings, he was quick to meet force with force and seems to have been uniformly victorious in these physical encounters."

The importance of sociocultural differences among the sections can be exaggerated. The Second Awakening actually began in New England, and a number of Unitarians did live in the West. The average easterner was only a little less crude and brash than most frontiersmen; his view of the Negro differed from those of his slaveholding cousins only slightly. Patriotism of the spread-eagle variety flourished everywhere; loyalty to section did not seem to diminish it. The comments of dozens of foreign observers testify to the existence of an *American* character common to every region. As one visitor wrote: "Over confused diversity there broods a higher unity." Americans North, South, and West paid little heed to social differences among men, they believed in the future progress and prosperity of the country, they worked hard, pampered their children, honored their womenfolk, opened wide their doors to strangers. They loved the dollar mightily, exercising remarkable ingenuity in acquiring it, but donated generously to public causes. They were at once vain and pitifully eager to please, tough fighters but sentimental, proud of America but sedulous apers of European "culture." Nevertheless, they *were* northerners and southerners and westerners too. In the decades following the Era of Good Feelings, this fact became increasingly significant.

The Missouri Compromise

The impact of sectional conflicts on politics in the 1820's was heavy and repeated. The depression of 1819–1822 increased tensions by making people feel more strongly about the issues of the day. For example, manufacturers who wanted a high tariff in 1816 were even more vehemently in favor of protection in 1820 when their business fell off. But even when economic conditions improved, geographical alignments on key issues tended to solidify.

One of the first and most critical of these sectional contests concerned the admission of Missouri as a slave state. When Louisiana entered the Union in 1812, the rest of the Louisiana Purchase was organized as the Missouri Territory. Building upon a nucleus of Spanish and French inhabitants, the region west and north of St. Louis grew rapidly, until by 1817 the Missourians were petitioning for statehood. A large percentage of the settlers—the population exceeded 60,000 by 1818—were southerners who had moved into the valleys of the Arkansas and Missouri rivers. Since many of them owned slaves, Missouri would become a slave state.

The admission of new states had always been routine, in keeping with the admirable pattern established by the Northwest Ordinance, but during the debate on the Missouri Enabling Act in February 1819, Congressman James Tallmadge of New York introduced an amendment prohibiting "the further introduction of slavery" and providing that all slaves born in Missouri after the territory became a state should be freed at age 25.

Although Tallmadge was merely seeking to apply in the territory the pattern of race relations that had developed in the states immediately east of Missouri, his amendment represented, at least in spirit, something of a revolution. The Northwest Ordinance had prohibited slavery in the land between the Mississippi and the Ohio, but that area had only a handful of slaveowners in 1787 and little prospect of attracting more. Elsewhere, no effort to restrict the movement of slaves into new territory had been attempted. If one assumed (as white men always had) that the slaves themselves should have no say in the matter, it appeared democratic to let the settlers of Missouri decide the slavery question for themselves. Nevertheless, the Tallmadge amendment passed the House, the vote following sectional lines closely. The Senate, however, resoundingly rejected it. The less populous southern part of Missouri was then organized separately as Arkansas Territory, and an attempt to bar slavery there was stifled. However, the Missouri Enabling Act failed to pass before Congress adjourned.

When the next Congress met in December 1819, the Missouri issue came up at once. The vote on Tallmadge's amendment had shown that the rapidly growing North controlled the House of Representatives. It was vital, southerners felt, to preserve a balance in the Senate. Yet northerners objected to the fact that Missouri extended hundreds of miles north of the Ohio River, which they considered slavery's natural boundary. Angry debate raged in Congress for months.

This debate did not turn upon the morality of slavery or the rights of Negroes. Northerners objected to adding new slave states because under the Three-fifths Compromise these states would be overrepresented in Congress, since 60 per cent of their slaves would be counted in determining the size of the states' delegations in the House of Representatives, and because they did not relish competing with slave labor. Since no moral issue was involved, a compromise was eventually worked out in 1820. Missouri entered the Union as a slave state and Maine, having been separated from Massachusetts, was admitted as a free state to preserve the balance in the Senate.

To prevent further conflict, Congress also adopted the proposal of Senator Jesse B. Thomas of Illinois which "forever prohibited" slavery in all other parts of the Louisiana Purchase north of 36° 30′ north latitude, this line marking a westward extension of Missouri's southern boundary. Although this division would keep slavery out of most of the territory, the southerners accepted it cheerfully: the land south of the line, the present states of Arkansas and Oklahoma, seemed ideally suited for the expanded plantation economy, and most persons considered the treeless northern regions little better than a desert. One northern senator, decrying the division, contemptuously described the land north and west of Missouri, today one of the world's richest agricultural regions, as "a prairie without food or water."

The Missouri Compromise, however, did not end the crisis. When Missouri submitted its constitution for approval by Congress, the final step in the admission process, the document, besides authorizing slavery and prohibiting the emancipation of any slave without the consent of his owner, *required* the state legislature to pass a law barring free Negroes and mulattos from entering the state "under any pretext whatever." This provision plainly violated Article IV, Section 2 of the United States Constitution: "The Citizens of each State shall be entitled to all Privileges and Immunities of Citizens in the several States." It did not, however, represent any more of a break with established racial patterns, North or South, than the Tallmadge amendment: the states east of Missouri, it will be remembered, also barred free Negroes without regard for the Constitution.

Nevertheless, northern congressmen hypocritically refused to accept the Missouri constitution. Once more the debate raged. But again, since few northerners cared to defend the rights of Negroes seriously, the issue was compromised. In March 1821 Henry Clay found a face-saving formula: out of respect for the "supreme law of the land," Congress accepted the Missouri constitution with the demurrer that no law passed in conformity to it should be construed as contravening Article IV, Section 2 of the United States Constitution. Of course, this was pure cant.

Although the moral issue had been shamelessly avoided, every thinking man recognized the political dynamite inherent in the Missouri controversy. The sectional line-up had been terrifyingly compact. The major compromise passed the House 90 to 87. Every slave-state representative voted one way, all but 15 of the free-state representatives the other. What meant the Union if so trivial a matter as one new state could so divide the people? Moreover, despite the timidity and hypocrisy of the North, everyone realized that the immorality of slavery lay at the heart of the conflict. "We have the wolf by the ears, and we can neither safely hold him, nor safely let him go," Jefferson wrote a month after Missouri became a state. The dispute, he said, "like a fire bell in the night, awakened and filled me with

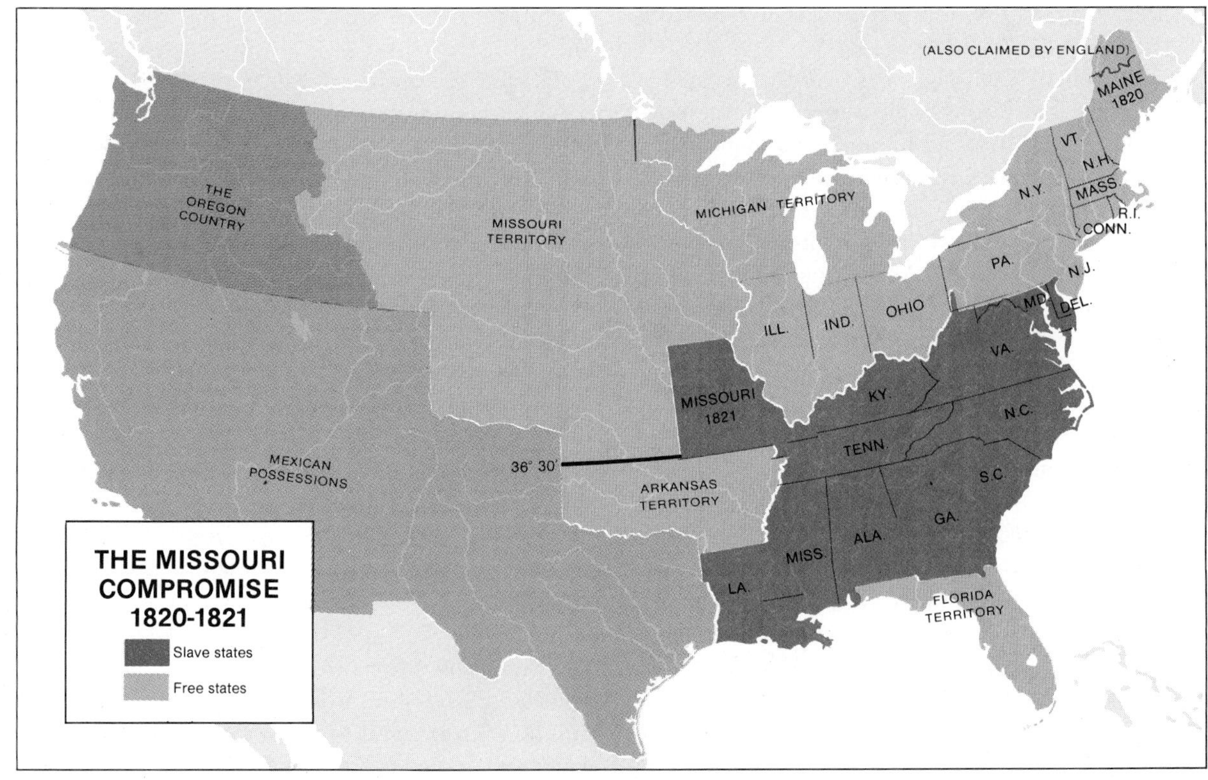

This was the line-up of the slave and free states resulting from the Missouri Compromise. The Compromise was repealed by the Kansas-Nebraska Act (1854) and declared unconstitutional in the Dred Scott case (1857).

terror." Jefferson well knew that the compromise had not permanently quenched the flames ignited by the Missouri debates. "This is a reprieve only," he said. John Quincy Adams called it the "title page to a great tragic volume."

Yet the issue had been settled peaceably, if ignobly. Tempers subsided. Although other controversies also aroused strong feelings, they did not seem to divide the country so deeply. The question of federal internal improvements, for example, caused endless debate that split the country on geographical lines. As early as 1816 the nationalist-minded Calhoun had pressed a plan to set up a $1.5 million fund for roads and canals. Congress approved this despite strong opposition in New England and a divided South. In 1822 a bill providing money for the upkeep of the National Road caused another sectional split. Both these measures were vetoed, but in 1824 Monroe approved a somewhat differently worded internal improvement act. Such proposals excited intense reactions. John Randolph, opposing the 1824 bill with his usual ferocity, threatened to employ "every . . . means short of actual insurrection" to defeat it. Yet other prominent southerners favored internal improvements, and no one—not even Randolph, it will be noted—threatened the Union on this issue.

The tariff also continued to divide the country. When a new, still higher tariff was enacted in 1824, the slave states voted almost unanimously against it, the North and Northwest in favor, and New England remained of two minds. But Clay, who expounded the case for his American System brilliantly in the debates, provided arguments for the tariff that his foes found hard to counter. Webster, continuing to speak for the merchants of New England (he conducted a poll of business leaders before deciding how to vote), made a powerful speech against the act, but the measure passed without creating a major storm.

The Adams Administration

The divisions on these questions were not severely disruptive, in part because the major politicians, hotly competing for the Presidency, did not dare risk alienating any section by taking too extreme a position. Calhoun, for example, had changed his mind about protective tariffs by 1824, but he avoided declaring himself because of his Presidential ambitions. Another reason was that the old party system had broken down; the Federalists had disappeared as a national party and the Jeffersonians, lacking an organized opposition, had become both less aggressive and more troubled by factional disputes.

The Presidential fight was therefore waged on personal far more than party grounds, although the heat generated by the contest began the process of re-energizing party politics. Besides Calhoun, the active candidates were Jackson, Crawford, Adams, and Clay. The maneuvering among them was complex, the infighting savage. In March 1824 Calhoun, who was young enough to wait for the White House, withdrew and declared for the Vice Presidency, which he won easily. Crawford, who had the support of congressional leaders, seemed the likely winner, but he suffered a series of paralytic strokes which gravely injured his chances. Despite the uncertainty and bitterness of the contest, it attracted relatively little public interest; barely a quarter of those eligible took the trouble to vote. In the Electoral College Jackson led with 99, Adams had 84, Crawford 41, and Clay 37. Since no one had a majority, the contest was thrown into the House of Representatives, which, under the Constitution, had to choose from among the three leaders, each state delegation having one vote. By employing his great influence in the House, Clay swung the balance. Not wishing to advance the fortunes of a rival westerner like Jackson and feeling, with reason, that Crawford's health made him unavailable, Clay gave his support to Adams, who was thereupon elected.

Although deeply marked by his New England heritage, Adams was a man of the broadest experience and interests. He took a Hamiltonian view of the future of the country and hoped to use the national authority to foster all sorts of useful projects. He asked Congress for a federal program of internal improvements so vast that even Clay boggled when he realized its scope, and he came out for aid to manufacturing and agriculture, a variety of scientific and educational

PRINTS DIVISION, NEW YORK PUBLIC LIBRARY

A comment by David Claypoole Johnston on the 1824 Presidential "foot race" has Adams leading by a head, trailed by Crawford and Jackson. Clay (far right, hand on head), well behind, pulls up in dismay. The many figures and the dreadful puns ("How is Clay now?" "Oh dirt cheap") are typical of the cartoons of the era.

projects (including expeditions to explore the West, a national university, and an astronomical observatory), and many administrative reforms. For a nationalist of unchallengeable Jeffersonian origins like Clay or Calhoun to have pressed for so extensive a program would have been politically risky. For the son of John Adams to do so was disastrous; every doubter remembered his Federalist background and decided that he was trying to overturn the glorious "Revolution of 1800."

Adams also proved to be his own worst enemy, for he was as inept a politician as ever lived. To persuade Americans, who were almost pathological on the subject of monarchy, to support his road-building program, he cited with approval the work being done abroad by "the nations of Europe and . . . their rulers," which revived fears that all Adamses were royalists at heart. He was insensitive to the ebb and flow of public feeling, and even when he wanted to move with the tide, he seldom managed to dramatize and publicize his stand effectively. There was wide support in the country for a federal bankruptcy law, but instead of describing himself in plain language as a friend of poor debtors, Adams called for the "amelioration" of the "often oppressive codes relating to insolvency" and buried the recommendation at the tail end of a dull state paper. He also refused to use his power of appointment to win support for his administration. "I will not dismiss . . . able and faithful political opponents to provide for my own partisans," he said. This attitude was traditional at the time, but Adams carried it to extremes—in four years he removed only 12 men from office. Nevertheless, by appointing Henry Clay secretary of state, he laid himself open to the charge that he had won the Presidency by a "corrupt bargain." Thus, despite his politically suicidal attitude toward federal jobs, he was subject to the annoyance of a congressional investigation of his appointments out of which came no less than six bills designed "to reduce the patronage of the executive."

To be sure, Adams had inherited a chaotic political situation. Contending sectional interests clashed angrily, uncurbed by loyalty to a national party. Yet he would neither bend to the prevailing winds, nor, by using his power as President, attempt to build an effective party based on the

American System and backed by broad public support. He was soon under attack from every side and miserable. As his grandson Brooks Adams later wrote, his service as President made him doubt the existence of God and the purposefulness of life.

The battle to succeed Adams began almost on the day of his election. Jackson quickly established himself as the candidate of what can best be characterized as the "opposition." Especially after Adams made Clay secretary of state, Jackson felt that he, the man with the largest vote, had been cheated of the Presidency, and he burned for revenge. Relying heavily on his military reputation and on Adams' talent for making enemies, Jackson avoided standing on issues as much as possible. Senator Benton of Missouri, for example, urged Jackson to shrink from any "particular confession" on internal improvements and on other questions where his views might displease certain voters. The political situation, therefore, became monumentally confused, one side unable to marshal support for its policies, the other unwilling to adopt policies for fear of losing support.

"Tariff of Abominations"

The tariff question added to the political confusion. High duties, so repulsive to the export-conscious South, attracted more and more favor in the North and West. Besides the manufacturers, lead miners in Missouri, hemp raisers in Kentucky, woolgrowers in New York, and many other interests demanded protection against foreign competition. The lack of party discipline provided an ideal climate for "logrolling" in Congress. Legislators like Senator Benton who opposed high tariffs in principle found themselves under constant pressure from their constituents to raise the duties on products of local importance; to satisfy these demands, they traded votes with other congressmen similarly situated, and thus massive "support" for protection was generated. In 1828 a new tariff was hammered into shape by the House Committee on Manufactures. Northern and western agricultural interests were in command; they wrote into the bill very high duties on raw wool, hemp, flax, fur, and liquor. New England manufacturers protested vociferously, for although their products were also protected, the proposed law would greatly increase the cost of their raw materials. This gave the southerners, hopelessly in the minority now on the tariff question, a chance to block the bill. When the New Englanders proposed amendments lowering the duties on raw materials, the southerners voted nay, hoping to force them to reject the measure on the final vote. This desperate strategy failed. New England had by this time committed its future to manufacturing, a change signalized by the somersault of Webster, who, responsive to local pressures, now voted for protection. After winning some minor concessions in the Senate, largely through the intervention of Van Buren, enough New Englanders accepted the so-called "Tariff of Abominations" to assure its passage.

Vice President John C. Calhoun, who had watched the debate from the vantage point of his post as president of the Senate, now came to a great turning point in his career. He had thrown in his lot with Jackson, whose running mate he was to be in the coming election, and been assured that the Jacksonians would oppose the bill. Yet northern Jacksonians had been responsible for drafting and passing it. The new tariff would impoverish the South, he believed. Something must be done. "The system is getting wrong," he wrote ex-President Monroe, and he warned Jackson plainly that relief must soon be provided or the Union would be shaken to its foundations. Then he returned to his South Carolina plantation and wrote an essay, the *South Carolina Exposition and Protest*, repudiating the nationalist philosophy he had previously championed.

The South Carolina legislature released this document to the country in December 1828, along with eight resolutions denouncing the protective tariff as unfair and unconstitutional. A theorist like Calhoun, however, was not content with outlining the case against the tariff. His *Exposition* provided also an ingenious defense of the right of the people of a state to reject a law of Congress. Starting with John Locke's revered concept of government as a contractual relationship, he argued that since the states had created

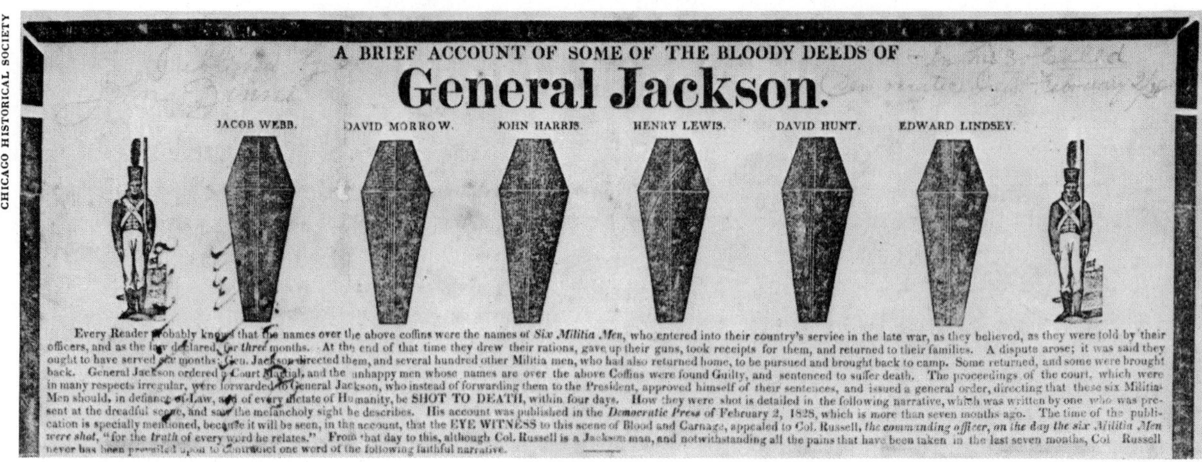

A BRIEF ACCOUNT OF SOME OF THE BLOODY DEEDS OF

General Jackson.

JACOB WEBB. DAVID MORROW. JOHN HARRIS. HENRY LEWIS. DAVID HUNT. EDWARD LINDSEY.

Every Reader probably knows that the names over the above coffins were the names of *Six Militia Men*, who entered into their country's service in the late war, as they believed, as they were told by their officers, and as the law declared, for *three* months. At the end of that time they drew their rations, gave up their guns, took receipts for them, and returned to their families. A dispute arose; it was said they ought to have served six months; Gen. Jackson directed them, and several hundred other Militia men, who had also returned home, to be pursued and brought back to camp. Some returned, and some were brought back. General Jackson ordered a Court Martial, and the unhappy men whose names are over the above Coffins were found Guilty, and sentenced to suffer death. The proceedings of the court, which were in many respects irregular, were forwarded to General Jackson, who instead of forwarding them to the President, approved himself of their sentences, and issued a general order, directing that these six Militia Men should, in defiance of Law, and of every dictate of Humanity, be **SHOT TO DEATH**, within four days. How they were shot is detailed in the following narrative, which was written by one who was present at the dreadful scene, and saw the melancholy sight he describes. His account was published in the *Democratic Press* of February 2, 1828, which is more than seven months ago. The time of the publication is specially mentioned, because it will be seen, in the account, that the **EYE WITNESS** to this scene of Blood and Carnage, appealed to Col. Russell, *the commanding officer, on the day the six Militia Men were shot*, "for the *truth* of every word he relates." From that day to this, although Col. Russell is a Jackson man, and notwithstanding all the pains that have been taken in the last seven months, Col Russell never has been prevailed upon to contradict one word of the following faithful narrative.

CHICAGO HISTORICAL SOCIETY

An example of the sordid tactics of the 1828 campaign is the so-called Coffin Handbill, published by the Adams forces. It attacks Jackson for ordering the execution of six militiamen for desertion shortly after the Battle of New Orleans in 1815 and goes on to specify several more of the general's alleged "bloody deeds."

the Union, logic dictated that they be the final arbiters of the meaning of the Constitution which was its framework. If a special state convention, representing the sovereignty of the people, decided that an act of Congress violated the Constitution, it could interpose its authority and "nullify" the law within its boundaries.

Calhoun did not seek to implement this theory in 1828, for he hoped that the next administration would lower the tariff and make nullification unnecessary.

Election of 1828

The new President was to be Jackson, who had defeated Adams handily, although by no means overwhelmingly, in a contest disgraced by character assassination and lies of the worst sort on both sides. Administration men denounced Jackson as a bloodthirsty military tyrant, a drunkard, and a gambler. His wife Rachel, ailing and shy, was dragged into the campaign, her good name heartlessly besmirched. She had been previously married to a cruel, unbalanced man named Lewis Robards. Two years after her marriage to Jackson they discovered that her divorce had never been legally completed, and when the mistake was corrected, she and Jackson had been forced to go through a second wedding ceremony. Seizing upon this fact, an Adams pamphleteer wrote: "Ought a convicted adulteress and her paramour husband be placed in the highest offices of this free and christian land?" Furiously, the Jacksonians (now calling themselves Democrats) replied in kind. They charged that Adams had lived with his wife before marriage, and that, while American minister to Russia, he had supplied a beautiful American virgin for the delectation of the czar. Discovering that the President had purchased a chess set and a billiard table for the White House, they accused him of squandering public money on gambling devices. They translated his long and distinguished public service into the statistic that he had received over the years a sum equal to $16 for every day of his life in government pay. The great questions of the day were largely ignored.

It was all inexcusable, and both sides must share the blame. When inauguration day arrived, Adams refused to attend the ceremonies because Jackson had repeatedly accused him of making a "corrupt bargain" with Clay, but the Old Puritan may have been equally if unconsciously motivated by shame at tactics he had countenanced during the campaign. In any case, deep personal feelings were uppermost in everyone's mind at the formal changing of the guard. The real issues, however, remained. Andrew Jackson would now have to deal with them.

SUPPLEMENTARY READING George Dangerfield, *The Era of Good Feelings** (1952) and *The Awakening of American Nationalism** (1965), and F.J. Turner, *The Rise of the New West** (1906), continue to be useful for this period. On the tariff, see F.W. Taussig, *The Tariff History of the United States** (1923); on banking, Bray Hammond, *Banks and Politics in America from the Revolution to the Civil War** (1957); on land policy, R.M. Robbins, *Our Landed Heritage** (1942).

The outstanding study of the career of Adams is S.F. Bemis, *John Quincy Adams* (1949–1956). R.N. Current, *Daniel Webster and the Rise of National Conservatism** (1955), is an excellent brief biography; a fuller treatment is C.M. Fuess, *Daniel Webster* (1930). On Clinton, see W.W. Campbell, *The Life and Writings of De Witt Clinton* (1933). Van Buren's early career is treated in R.V. Remini, *Martin Van Buren and the Making of the Democratic Party* (1959). Van Buren's *Autobiography* (1920), edited by J.C. Fitzpatrick, is candid and amusing.

There is no adequate life on Crawford. On Calhoun, the standard study of his early career is C.M. Wiltse, *John C. Calhoun: Nationalist* (1949), an excellent work. Richard Hofstadter, *The American Political Tradition** (1948), contains a thought-provoking essay on Calhoun, and see also R.N. Current, *John C. Calhoun** (1963), and G.M. Capers, *John C. Calhoun, Opportunist* (1960). The best biography of Clay is G.G. Van Deusen, *The Life of Henry Clay** (1937), while Clement Eaton, *Henry Clay and the Art of American Politics** (1957), is a stimulating and judicious brief account of his career. W.N. Chambers, *Old Bullion Benton: Senator from the New West* (1956), is first-rate, but see also Benton's *Thirty Years' View* (1854–56). Freeman Cleaves, *Old Tippecanoe* (1939), covers the life of William Henry Harrison adequately.

Social and cultural trends are discussed in R.B. Nye, *The Cultural Life of the New Nation** (1960), J.A. Krout and D.R. Fox, *The Completion of Independence* (1944), M.E. Curti, *The Growth of American Thought* (1951), and Harvey Wish, *Society and Thought in Early America* (1950). Van Wyck Brooks, *The World of Washington Irving* (1944), discusses the principal literary figures, while O.W. Larkin, *Art and Life in America* (1949), is excellent on painting and architecture. On religion, see Perry Miller, *The Life of the Mind in America from the Revolution to the Civil War* (1965), W.G. McLaughlin, *Modern Revivalism* (1959), Conrad Wright, *The Beginnings of Unitarianism in America** (1955), W.R. Cross, *The Burned-Over District** (1950), and B.A. Weisberger, *They Gathered at the River** (1958). Rush Welter, *Popular Education and Democratic Thought in America** (1962), is a good introduction to the subject.

Southern life is discussed in Clement Eaton, *The Mind of the Old South** (1964) and *The Growth of Southern Civilization** (1961), and also in U.B. Phillips, *Life and Labor in the Old South** (1929), and T.P. Abernethy, *The South in the New Nation* (1961). Melville Herskovits, *The Myth of the Negro Past** (1941), is the standard study of African survivals in the culture of American Negroes. On the West, L.B. Wright, *Culture on the Moving Frontier** (1955), and R.C. Wade, *The Urban Frontier** (1959), are very useful.

On the Missouri Compromise, see Glover Moore, *The Missouri Controversy** (1953). The election of 1824 can be studied in the biographies of Adams, Clay, and Calhoun mentioned above and in Dangerfield's volumes. See also Marquis James, *The Life of Andrew Jackson** (1938), and Shaw Livermore, *The Twilight of Federalism* (1962). On the Presidency of John Quincy Adams, in addition to the Bemis biography, both Henry Adams, *The Degradation of the Democratic Dogma* (1919), and J.H. Powell, *Richard Rush: Republican Diplomat* (1942), are enlightening. R.V. Remini, *The Election of Andrew Jackson** (1964), provides an excellent scholarly survey of the election of 1828.

*Available in paperback.

10

The Age of Jackson

On the 4th of March, 1829, Andrew Jackson, dressed severely in black, left his quarters at Gadsby's Hotel and, accompanied by a few close associates, walked up Pennsylvania Avenue to the Capitol. Skirting the dense crowd waiting on the Hill, he entered the Capitol by a basement door. A few moments later he emerged on the portico, acknowledged the cheers of the multitude, took the oath of office, and delivered an almost inaudible and thoroughly commonplace inaugural address. The first man to congratulate him was Chief Justice Marshall, who had administered the oath; the second was "Honest George" Kremer, a little Pennsylvania congressman best known for the leopardskin coat that he affected, who brushed past the barricade and scrambled up the Capitol steps to wring the new President's hand while the crowd cheered.

Jackson then shouldered his way through the crush, mounted a horse, and rode off to the White House. A reception had been announced, to which "the officially and socially eligible as defined by precedent" had been invited. The day was unseasonably warm after a hard winter, and the streets of Washington were muddy. As Jackson splashed down Pennsylvania Avenue, the crowds that had turned out to see the Hero of New Orleans followed—on horseback, in rickety wagons, and on foot. Nothing could keep them from pursuing him into the Executive Mansion, and the result was chaos. Long tables laden with cakes, ice cream, and orange punch had been set up in the East Room, but these scarcely deflected the mob of well-wishers. Jackson was pressed back helplessly as men tracked mud across valuable rugs and clambered up on delicate chairs to catch a glimpse of him. The White House shook with their shouts, glassware splintered, furniture was overturned, women fainted. Jackson was a thin old man despite his toughness, and soon he was in real danger. Fortunately, some friends formed a cordon and managed to extricate him through a rear door. The new President spent his first night in office back at Gadsby's.

Only a generation earlier Jefferson had felt obliged to introduce "pell-mell" to encourage informality in the White House. Now, a man whom John Quincy Adams called "a barbarian" held Jefferson's office, and, as one Supreme Court justice complained, "The reign of King 'Mob' seemed triumphant."

Jacksonian Democracy Some historians claim that Andrew Jackson was not a democrat at all and anything but a consistent friend of the weak and underprivileged. They point out that he was a wealthy land speculator, owner of a fine Tennessee plantation, the Hermitage, and of many slaves. Before becoming President, it is true, he had opposed cheap-money schemes, favored the big speculators, pressed suits against more than a hundred men who owed him money. Although his supporters liked to cast him as the political heir of Jefferson, he was in many ways like the conservative Washington: a soldier first of all, an inveterate speculator in western lands, a man with few intellectual interests and only sketchily educated.

Nor was Jackson quite the roughhewn frontier character he sometimes seemed. He could not spell (again, like Washington), he possessed the unsavory habits of the tobacco chewer, and he had a violent temper. But his manners were those of a southern planter, his judgment intuitive but usually sound. Even his reputation for unbridled irascibility was not really deserved. His frequent rages were often feigned—designed to accomplish some carefully thought-out purpose. "He would sometimes extemporize a fit of passion in order to overwhelm an adversary," one contemporary noted, "but his self-command was always perfect." Once, after scattering a delegation of protesters with an exhibition of Jovian wrath, he turned to an observer with a chuckle and said impishly, "They thought I was mad."

Actually, it is of small importance to anyone concerned with the study of Jacksonian Democracy to know exactly how "democratic" Jackson was or how sincere his interest in the welfare of the "common man." For whatever his personal convictions, he stood as the symbol for a popular movement supported by a new, democratically oriented generation that had grown up under the spell of the American and French revolutions. The fact that he was both a great hero and in many ways a very ordinary man helps explain his mass appeal. He had defeated a mighty British army and killed hosts of Indians, but he acted on hunches and not always consistently, shouted and pounded his fist when angry, put loyalty to old comrades above efficiency in making appointments, distrusted "aristocrats" and all special privilege. Perhaps he was rich, perhaps conservative, but he was a man of the people, born in a frontier cabin, familiar with the problems of the average citizen.

CORCORAN GALLERY OF ART

Thomas Sully's interpretation of the warrior Jackson captures perhaps better than any other portrait Old Hickory as he was viewed by the common man.

Jackson also epitomized many American ideals. He was independent-minded, natural and democratic in manner (at home alike in the forest and in the ballroom of a fine mansion). He admired good horseflesh and beautiful women, yet no sterner moralist ever lived; he was a tough fighter, a relentless foe, but a gentleman in the best American sense. That some special providence watched over him (as over the United

States) appeared beyond argument to those who had followed his career. He seemed, in short, both an average and an ideal American, one the people could identify with and still revere.

For these reasons, Jackson drew support from every section and every social class: western farmers and southern planters, many—but by no means all—urban workingmen, numerous bankers and merchants flocked to his standard. In this sense, he was profoundly democratic, and in the sense, too, that whatever his position on public issues, he believed firmly in equality of opportunity, distrusted entrenched status of every sort, and rejected no man because of low birth or inadequate education.

Rise of the Common Man

Having been taught by Jefferson that all men are created equal, the Americans of Jackson's day found it easy to believe that every man was as good as his neighbor. The difference between Jeffersonian Democracy and the Jackson variety was one of attitude rather than of practice. Jefferson had believed that ordinary men could be educated to determine right, while Jackson insisted that they knew what was right by instinct. Jefferson's "pell-mell" encouraged the average citizen to hold up his head. By the time of Jackson, this "common man" had become so proud of himself that he gloried in his very ordinariness and made mediocrity a virtue. The slightest hint of either distinctiveness or servility became suspect. That President Washington required his footmen to wear uniforms was taken as a matter of course in the 1790's, but the British minister in Jackson's day found it next to impossible to find American servants willing to don his splendid livery. The word *servant* itself fell into disrepute, being replaced by the egalitarian *help*. The Englishwoman Frances Trollope, who lived in America during this period, commented repeatedly on the "uncouth advances" and "violent intimacy" of people with whom she came in contact.

The Founding Fathers had not foreseen all the implications of political democracy for a society like that which existed in the United States. They believed that the ordinary man should have political power in order to protect himself against the superior man, but they assumed that the latter would always lead. The people would naturally choose the best men to manage public affairs. In Washington's day and even in Jefferson's this was generally the case, but the inexorable logic

MUSEUM OF FINE ARTS, BOSTON, M. & M. KAROLIK COLLECTION

This Jackson montage, "cut with scissors and painted by J.H. Whitcomb in 1830," as its inscription reads, is an unabashed and charming example of hero worship.

of democracy gradually produced a change. The new western states, unfettered by systems created in a less democratic age, drew up constitutions that eliminated property qualifications for voting and holding office, while the eastern states revised their own frames of government to accomplish the same purpose. More public offices were made elective rather than appointive.

Even the Presidency, originally designed to be far removed from direct public control, felt the impact of the new thinking. By Jackson's day only two states, Delaware and South Carolina, still provided for the choice of Presidential electors by the legislature; in all the others they were selected by popular vote. The system of permitting the congressional caucus to name the candidates for the Presidency also came to an end before 1828. Jackson and Adams were put forward by state legislatures, and soon the still more democratic system of nomination by national party conventions was adopted.

Certain social changes also reflect a new way of looking at political affairs. The final disestablishment of churches reveals a dislike of special privilege. The beginnings of the free-school movement, the earliest glimmerings of interest in adult education, the slow spread of secondary education all bespeak a concern for improving the knowledge and judgment of the ordinary citizen. The rapid increase in the number of newspapers, their declining prices (the first successful penny papers appeared in the 1830's), and their ever greater concentration upon political affairs indicate that an effort was being made to bring political news to the common man's attention.

All these changes emphasized the idea that every citizen was equally important and the conviction that all should participate actively in government. Officeholders began to stress the fact that they were *representatives* as well as leaders and to appeal more frankly and much more intensively for votes. The public responded with a surge of interest in voting. For 20 years after 1820, at each succeeding Presidential election, a larger percentage of the population went to the polls.

As voting became more important, so did party politics, for it took organized effort to direct the campaigns and get out the vote. Parties became powerful institutions; as a result, they attracted men's loyalties powerfully. This development took place first at the state level and at different times in different states. According to Richard P. McCormick, whose book, *The Second American Party System*, describes the process, the 1828 election stimulated party formation because it pitted two well-known men against each other, forcing local leaders to make a choice and then convince local voters to accept their judgment. This was especially true in states where neither Adams nor Jackson had a preponderant edge. Thus the new system established itself much faster in states like New York and Pennsylvania than, say, in New England, where Adams was strong, or Tennessee, where the "native son" Jackson had overwhelming support.

Like most institutions, the parties created bureaucracies to keep them running smoothly. Devoted party workers were rewarded with political office when their efforts were successful, a necessary and desirable result if the people were to be served by men committed to the policies for which the majority had voted. However, sometimes the preservation and prosperity of the party became an end in itself, and sometimes party workers looked upon office as a means of support instead of an opportunity to serve. "To the victors belong the spoils," said the New York politician William L. Marcy, and the image, drawn from war and piracy, was appropriate. Although the vigorous wooing of the voter constituted a recognition of his importance and a commitment to keeping him informed, campaigning—another military term—frequently degenerated into demagoguery of the rankest sort. The most effective way to attract the average voter, politicians soon decided, was to flatter him.

Andrew Jackson was the first product of this newly developing system to become President. He was chosen because he was popular, not because he was experienced in government. Despite his considerable political service, Jackson had never been very interested in legislation. During six months in the Senate, for example, he spoke only four times for a total of 20 minutes. No one knew for sure where he stood on such subjects as the tariff and internal improvements because he did not really know himself, having never been much concerned with them. But he was valiant, honest, patriotic, and willing to do his duty—qualities the office has always required.

The Spoils System

Jackson took up his duties with the firm intention of punishing the "vile wretches" who attacked him so viciously during the campaign. (Rachel Jackson had died shortly after the election, and her devoted husband was convinced that the indignities heaped upon her by the Adams men had speeded her decline.) Furthermore, the concept of political office as a reward for victory seemed to justify a complete house-cleaning in Washington. Henry Clay captured the fears of anti-Jackson government workers. "Among the official corps here there is the greatest solicitude and apprehension," he said. "The members of it feel something like the inhabitants of Cairo when the plague breaks out; no one knows who is next to encounter the stroke of death."

Eager for "the spoils," an army of politicians quickly invested Washington. "I am ashamed of myself," one such character confessed when he met a friend on the street. "I feel as if every man I meet knew what I came for." "Don't distress yourself," replied his friend, "for every man you meet is on the same business." There was nothing especially innovative about this invasion, for the principle of filling offices with one's partisans was almost as old as the republic. However, the long lapse of time since the last real political shift, and the recent most untypical example of John Quincy Adams, who rarely removed or appointed anyone for political reasons,* made Jackson's policy appear revolutionary. His removals were not entirely unjustified, for many government workers had grown senile on the job and others corrupt. The fourth assistant auditor of the Treasury was found to be subscribing to 20 newspapers at public expense. A number of other officials were short in their accounts, a few were hopeless drunks. Clearly the time had come, as one Jacksonian said, to scrape these "barnacles" off the "Ship of State." Even John Quincy Adams admitted that some of the men Jackson dismissed deserved their fate.

Aside from going along with the "spoils system" and eliminating incompetents, Jackson advanced another reason for turning experienced government employees out of their jobs—the principle of rotation. "No man has any more intrinsic right to official station than another," he said. Those who hold government jobs for a long time "are apt to acquire a habit of looking with indifference upon the public interests and of tolerating conduct from which an unpracticed man would revolt." By "rotating" jobholders periodically, more citizens could participate in the task of self-government, an obvious advantage in a democracy. The danger of creating an entrenched bureaucracy would also be eliminated. The problem, of course, was that rapid turnover might result in confusion—the constant replacing of trained men by novices is not likely to increase the efficiency of any organization. Jackson's response to this argument was typical: "The duties of all public officers are . . . so plain and simple that men of intelligence may readily qualify themselves for their performance."

This contempt for expert knowledge, combined with the belief that ordinary Americans can do anything they set their minds to, was a fundamental tenet of Jacksonian Democracy. To apply it to present-day government would be to court disaster, but in the early 19th century it was not such a preposterous point of view, for the role that government played in American life was simple and nontechnical. Furthermore, Jackson did not rotate men in fields like the War and Navy departments, where to do so might have been harmful. In general he left what a modern administrator would call "middle management," the backbone of every organization, pretty much alone; during his two terms he dismissed fewer than 20 per cent of the 10,000-odd government workers.

Nevertheless, the spoilsmen roamed the capital in force during the spring of 1829, seeking, as the

*Perhaps he was trying to expiate the "sins" of his father, who had made such partisan use of the federal courts with his "midnight" appointments.

Jackson's spoils system policies were repeatedly attacked by opposition cartoonists. "Office Hunters for the Year 1834," for example, portrays the President as a demon dangling the spoils of his office, including banquets, money, weapons, appointments, and for some obscure reason, millinery, above his greedy supporters.

forthright Jackson said, "a tit to suck the treasury pap." Their philosophy was well summarized by a New Yorker: "No d - - - - d rascal who made use of his office . . . for the purpose of keeping Mr. Adams in, and Genl. Jackson out of power is entitled to the least lenity or mercy. . . . Whether or not I shall get anything in the general scramble for plunder, remains to be proven, but I rather *guess* I shall."

President of all the People

President Jackson was not cynical about the spoils system. As a strong man who intuitively sought to increase his authority, the idea of making government workers dependent upon him made excellent sense. His opponents had pictured him as a simple soldier fronting for a rapacious band of politicians, but he soon proved he would exercise his authority directly. Except for Martin Van Buren, the secretary of state, his Cabinet was not distinguished, and he did not rely on it for advice. He turned instead to an informal "Kitchen Cabinet," which consisted of the influential Van Buren, a few close friends such as William B. Lewis of Tennessee and Andrew Jackson Donelson, the President's nephew and private secretary, plus a number of newspaper men, including Amos Kendall of Kentucky, who wrote many of Jackson's speeches, and Francis P. Blair, editor of the powerful Washington *Globe*. But these men were advisers, not directors; Jackson was clearly master of his own administration.

More than any earlier President, he conceived of himself as the direct representative of all the people, and therefore the embodiment of national power. From Washington to John Quincy Adams, his predecessors had vetoed altogether only 9 bills and always on the ground that the measures were unconstitutional. Jackson vetoed

12, and sometimes simply because he thought the proposed legislation inexpedient. He was also the first President to employ the "pocket veto," the device of killing a bill at the tag end of a session of Congress by refusing either to sign or veto it. Yet he had no ambition to make himself a dictator or to expand the scope of federal authority at the expense of the states. Furthermore, he was a poor administrator, given to penny-pinching and lacking in imagination. His strong prejudices and his contempt for expert advice, even in fields like banking where his ignorance was all but complete, did him no credit and the country considerable harm.

Jackson's great success (not merely his popularity) was primarily the result of his personality. A shrewd French observer, Michel Chevalier, after commenting upon "his chivalric character, his lofty integrity, and his ardent patriotism," pointed out what was probably the central element in Jackson's appeal. "His tactics in politics, as well as in war," wrote Chevalier in 1824, "is to throw himself forward with the cry of *Comrades, follow me!*" Sometimes he might be wrong, but always he was a leader.

Sectional Tensions Continue

Although Jackson drew support from widely scattered parts of the country, his election did not quiet the sectional conflicts of the period. In office he had to say something about western lands, the tariff, and other issues. He tried to steer a moderate course, urging a slight reduction of the tariff, "constitutional" internal improvements, and suggesting that once the rapidly disappearing federal debt had been paid off, the surplus revenues of the government might be "distributed" among the states. Even these cautious proposals caused conflict, so complex were the interrelations of sectional disputes. If the federal government turned the expected surplus over to the states, it could not afford to reduce the price of public land without going into the red. This disturbed some westerners, most notably Senator Thomas Hart Benton of Missouri. Western anxiety in turn suggested to southern opponents of the protective tariff an alliance of South and West. These southerners argued that a low tariff, levied for purposes of revenue only, would increase foreign imports, bring more money into the Treasury, and thus make it possible to reduce the price of public land.

The land question came up in the Senate in December 1829, when an obscure Connecticut senator, Samuel A. Foot, suggested that the sale of government land should be sharply restricted. Benton promptly denounced this proposal as a plot concocted by eastern manufacturers to check the westward migration of their workers. On January 19, 1830, Senator Robert Y. Hayne of South Carolina, a spokesman for Vice President Calhoun, supported Benton vigorously, suggesting an alliance of South and West for cheap land and low tariffs as outlined above. Daniel Webster then rose to the defense of the northeastern interests, cleverly goading Hayne by accusing South Carolina of advocating disunionist policies. Responding to this attack, the South Carolinian, a glib speaker but a rather imprecise thinker, launched into an impassioned exposition of the states'-rights doctrine while Calhoun, observing the debate from his post as president of the Senate, indicated his approval by occasional nods and smiles.

Webster then took the floor again and for two days, before galleries packed with the elite of Washington society, he cut Hayne's argument to shreds with a magnificent display of grandiloquence, patriotism, and common sense. The Constitution was a compact of the American people, not merely of the states, he insisted, the Union perpetual and indissoluble. Nullification could lead only to civil war. Webster's defense of nationalism made the states'-rights position appear close to treason and effectively prevented the formation of a West-South alliance. Nominally directed at Hayne, his attack was actually aimed at bigger game: Calhoun and the doctrine of nullification. Generations of schoolchildren have memorized his concluding paean in praise of the Union, a remarkable example of extemporaneous volubility, in which the flag becomes "the gorgeous ensign of the republic" bearing, in Webster's vivid imagination, the motto: "Liberty *and* Union, now and forever, one and inseparable!"

Jackson and Calhoun

Of course, the attention focused on the Webster-Hayne debate revived discussion of the idea of nullification. Although southern-born, a cotton planter, and a personal friend of Senator Hayne, Jackson had devoted too much of his life to fighting for the entire United States to countenance disunion on any terms. Therefore, when the states'-rights faction invited him to a dinner to celebrate the anniversary of Jefferson's birth, he came prepared. The evening reverberated with speeches and toasts of a states'-rights tenor, but when the President was called upon to volunteer a toast, he raised his glass, fixed his eyes grimly on John C. Calhoun, and said: "Our *Federal* Union: It must be preserved!" Calhoun took up the challenge at once. "The Union," he retorted, "next to our liberty, most dear!"

It is difficult to measure the importance of the animosity between Jackson and Calhoun in the grave crisis to which this clash was a prelude. Calhoun wanted very much to be President. He had failed to inherit the office from John Quincy Adams and had accepted the Vice Presidency again under Jackson in hopes of succeeding him at the end of one term, if not sooner, for Jackson's health was known to be frail. Yet Old Hickory showed no sign of passing on or of retiring. Jackson also seemed to place special confidence in the shrewd Van Buren, who, as secretary of state, also had claim to the succession. A silly social fracas in which Calhoun's wife appeared to take the lead in the systematic snubbing by all the ladies of the administration of Peggy Eaton, wife of the secretary of war, had also estranged the two. (Peggy was supposed to have had an affair with Eaton while she was still married to another man, but Jackson, undoubtedly sympathetic because of the slanders he and Rachel had endured, stoutly defended her good name.) Then, shortly after the Jefferson Day dinner, Jackson discovered that back in 1818, when he had invaded Florida and executed the two Englishmen who had been inciting the Indians, Calhoun, secretary of war at the time, had recommended to President Monroe that he be summoned before a court of inquiry and charged with disobeying orders. Since Calhoun had repeatedly led Jackson to believe that he had supported him at the time, this revelation convinced the President that Calhoun was not a man of honor.

These personal difficulties are worth stressing because ideologically Jackson and Calhoun were not very far apart except on the ultimate issue of the right of a state to resist federal authority. Jackson was a strong President, but he did not believe that the area of national power was large or that it should be expanded. His interests in government economy, the distribution of federal surpluses to the states, and in interpreting the powers of Congress narrowly were all similar to Calhoun's. Like most westerners, he favored internal improvements. While President he approved a greatly enlarged program of federal aid to road and canal companies. But he preferred that local projects be left to the states. In 1830 he vetoed a bill providing aid for the construction of the Maysville Road because it was wholly within Kentucky. There were political reasons for this veto, which was a slap at Kentucky's hero, Henry Clay, but it could not fail to please Calhoun.

Indian Problems

The President also took a states'-rights position in the controversy between the Cherokee Indians and Georgia. Although he shared most of the typical westerner's feelings about Indians, Jackson was not a blind hater of the red men. Ideally he would have liked them to abandon their "savage" ways and become farmers. Since few were willing to do so, as President he pushed the traditional policy of "removing" them from the path of western settlement, a policy that seems heartless to modern critics but which most contemporaries thought the only humane solution if the nation was to continue to expand. Jackson was well aware that removal would impose hardships on what he called "this unhappy race—the original dwellers in our land." He insisted that the Indians receive fair prices for their lands and that the government bear the expense of moving and resettling them. But he believed that shifting them to the unsettled area beyond the Mississippi would protect them from the "degradation and destruction to which they were rapidly hastening . . . in the States."

H. LEWIS, *Das Illustrierte Mississippithal*, 1857

Many of the tribes resigned themselves to removal without argument; a few, such as Black Hawk's Sac and Fox in Illinois and Osceola's Seminoles in Florida, resisted and had to be subdued by troops. However, one Indian nation, the Cherokees, made a courageous and intelligent effort to hold on to their lands by adjusting to white ways. The took up farming and cattle-raising and cultivated the household arts. They even developed a written language, drafted a constitution, and tried to establish a state within a state in northwestern Georgia. Several treaties with the United States seemed to establish the legality of their government. But Georgia would not recognize the Cherokee Nation. It passed a law in 1828 declaring all Cherokee laws void and the region part of Georgia. Another law of 1830 required all white men in the Cherokee country to procure licenses and take an oath of allegiance to the state.

The Indians challenged both these laws in the Supreme Court. In *Cherokee Nation v. Georgia* (1831) Chief Justice John Marshall refused to rule on Georgia's nullification of the Cherokee laws. In *Worcester v. Georgia* (1832), however, he decided in the Indians' favor. Later, when a Cherokee named Corn Tassel, convicted in a Georgia court of the murder of another Indian, appealed on the ground that the crime had taken place in Cherokee territory, Marshall also declared this Georgia action unconstitutional. But Jackson backed Georgia's position. No independent nation could exist within the United States, he insisted. Neither red man nor white "may claim exemption from the . . . laws of the state." As for *Worcester v. Georgia*, he said: "John Marshall has made his decision. Now let him enforce it." Georgia thereupon hanged poor Corn Tassel and destroyed the Cherokee Nation.

Jackson's willingness to allow Georgia to "nullify" decisions of the Supreme Court persuaded the extreme southern states'-righters that he would not oppose the doctrine of nullification should it be formally applied to a law of Con-

MUSEE D'HISTOIRE NATURELLE, LE HAVRE

In 1832, fighting to retain tribal lands in Illinois, Black Hawk and his followers were attacked by militia. Henry Lewis' lithograph (opposite page) depicts their slaughter as they fled across the Mississippi. At left is Charles Lesueur's 1830 study of a Choctaw, one of the southeastern peoples removed to Indian Territory in what is now Oklahoma.

gress. They deceived themselves egregiously. Jackson did not challenge Georgia because he approved of the state's position. He spoke of "the poor deluded . . . Cherokees" and called William Wirt, the lawyer who defended their cause, a "truly wicked" man. He was not one to be bound by principle in such matters or to worry overmuch about being inconsistent. In any case, when South Carolina revived the talk of nullification in 1832, he acted in quite a different manner.

The Nullification Crisis

The proposed alliance of South and West to reduce both the tariff and the price of land had not materialized, partly because Webster had discredited the South in the eyes of western patriots, and partly because the planters of South Carolina and Georgia, fearing the competition of fertile new cotton lands in Alabama and Mississippi, opposed the rapid exploitation of the West almost as vociferously as did northern manufacturers. When a new tariff law was passed in 1832, it lowered duties much less than the southerners desired. At once, talk of nullifying the acts of both 1828 and 1832 began to be heard in South Carolina.

The situation in South Carolina was truly explosive. In addition to the economic woes of the upcountry cotton planters, the great planter-aristocrats of the rice-growing Tidewater, although relatively prosperous, had become hypersensitive to northern criticisms of slavery. The rice region contained the densest concentration of blacks in the United States, and thousands of these slaves were African-born—brought in during the burst of importations before the trade was outlawed by Congress in 1808. Controlled usually by overseers of the worst sort, these slaves seemed to the master race like savage beasts straining to rise up against their oppressors. In 1822 the exposure of a planned revolt in Charleston organized by Denmark Vesey, who had bought his freedom with money won in a lottery, had given the whites a massive case of the jitters. Thereafter, discussion of *future* emancipation was anathema in South Carolina. News of a far more serious uprising in Virginia led by the slave Nat Turner in 1831, just as the tariff controversy was coming to a head, seemed the last straw. Radical South Carolinians saw protective tariffs and agitation against slavery as two sides of the same coin; against both aspects of what seemed to them the tyranny of the majority, nullification seemed the logical defense. Yield on the tariff, editor Henry L. Pinckney of the influential *Charleston Mercury* warned, and "abolition will become the order of the day."

Endless discussions of Calhoun's doctrine after the publication of his *Exposition and Protest* in 1828 had produced much interesting theorizing without clarifying the issue. William H. Freehling, a modern student of the controversy, sums it up aptly: "The theory of nullification was a veritable snarl of contradictions." Admirers of Calhoun praised his "power of analysis & profound philosophical reasonings," but his idea was ingenious rather than profound. Plausible at first glance, it was based on false assumptions: that the Constitution was subject to definitive interpretation; that one party to a compact could interpret the agreement unilaterally without destroying it; that a minority of the nation could reassume its sovereign independence but that a minority of a state could not.

President Jackson was in this respect Calhoun's exact opposite. The South Carolinian's mental gymnastics he brushed aside; intuitively he realized the central truth: if a state could nullify a law of Congress, the Union could not exist. "Tell . . . the Nullifiers from me that they can talk and write resolutions and print threats to their hearts' content," he warned a South Carolina representative when Congress adjourned in July 1832. "But if one drop of blood be shed there in defiance of the laws of the United States, I will hang the first man of them I can get my hands on to the first tree I can find."

This warning was not taken seriously in South Carolina. In October the state legislature provided for the election of a special convention, which, when it met, proved to contain a solid majority of nullifiers. On November 24, 1832, this

PRINTS DIVISION, NEW YORK PUBLIC LIBRARY

An 1833 comment on the implications of nullification has Calhoun reaching for despotism's crown while Jackson (far right) restrains South Carolina governor Robert Hayne and threatens to string up all the nullifiers.

convention passed an Ordinance of Nullification, prohibiting the collection of tariff duties in the state after February 1, 1833. The legislature then authorized the raising of an army and appropriated money to supply it with weapons.

Jackson quickly began military preparations of his own, telling friends that he would have 50,000 men ready to move in a little over a month. But he also made a statesmanlike effort to end the crisis peaceably. First he suggested to Congress that it lower the tariff further. Then, on December 10, he addressed a thoughtful but determined "Proclamation to the People of South Carolina." Nullification could only lead to the destruction of the Union, he said. "The laws of the United States must be executed. I have no discretionary power on the subject. . . . Those who told you that you might peaceably prevent their execution deceived you." Old Hickory then added sternly: "Disunion by armed force is *treason.* Are you really ready to incur its guilt?"

Attention now shifted to Congress where administration leaders introduced both a new tariff bill and a Force Bill granting the President additional authority to execute the revenue laws. Calhoun, having resigned as Vice President to accept appointment as senator from South Carolina, led the fight against the Force Bill. Jackson was eager to see the tariff reduced but absolutely determined to enforce the law. As the February 1 deadline approached, he claimed that he could raise 200,000 men if needed to suppress resistance. Should the governor of Virginia try to block the movement of federal soldiers toward South Carolina, "I would arrest him at the head of his troops," Jackson warned. "Union men, fear not," he said. "*The Union will be preserved.*"

Jackson's determination sobered the South Carolina radicals. Their appeal for the support of other southern states brought further discouragement: without exception these states rejected the idea of nullification. The unionist minority in South Carolina added to the radicals' difficulties by threatening civil war if federal authority were defied. Calhoun, although a brave man, was really alarmed for his own safety, for Jackson had threatened to "hang him as high as Haman" if nullification were attempted. He was suddenly eager to avoid a showdown. Ten days before the deadline, South Carolina postponed nullification pending the outcome of the tariff debate. Then Calhoun joined forces with Henry Clay to push a compromise tariff through Congress. Its passage, early in March 1833, marked the willingness of the North and West to make concessions in the interest of national harmony. Senator Silas Wright of New York, closely affiliated with Van Buren, explained the situation: "People will neither cut throats nor dismember the Union for protection. There is more patriotism and love of country than that left yet. The People will never balance this happy government against ten cents a pound upon a pound of wool."

And so the Union weathered the storm. Having approached the brink of civil war, the nation had drawn hastily back. The South Carolina legislature professed to be satisfied with the new tariff (actually, it made few immediate reductions, providing for a gradual lowering of rates over a ten-year period), and repealed the Nullification Ordinance, saving face by nullifying the Force Bill, which was now a dead letter. But the radical South Carolina planters—although not Calhoun, who continued to count himself a nationalist—were rapidly becoming convinced that only secession would protect slavery. A few years after the crisis, a visitor in Columbia, South Carolina, amused by the talk of local "patriots," asked one man if he thought of himself as an American. "If you ask *me* if I am an American," the fellow replied, "my answer is, No Sir, I am a South Carolinian." To men of this stripe, the nullification fiasco had proved only that they could not succeed without the support of other slave states, and they devoted themselves ceaselessly thereafter to obtaining it.

The Bank War

Jackson's strong stand against South Carolina was the more effective because in the fall of 1832 he had been overwhelmingly re-elected President, defeating Henry Clay by over 150,000 votes and winning a 219 to 49 majority in the Electoral College. The main issue in this election, aside from Jackson's personal popularity, was the second Bank of the United States, or rather the

President's determination to destroy the Bank. In this "Bank War" Jackson won as complete a victory as in his battle with the nullifiers but with far less justice, for the effects of his triumph were anything but beneficial to the country.

After *McCulloch v. Maryland* had presumably established its legality and the conservative Langdon Cheves had gotten it on a sound footing, the Bank of the United States had flourished. In 1823 Cheves was replaced as president by Nicholas Biddle, who managed it with real brilliance. A charming and talented Philadelphian, only 37 when he took over the Bank, Biddle was experienced in the law and in diplomacy as well as in finance. Almost alone in the United States, he realized that his institution could act as a rudimentary central bank, regulating the availability of credit all over the nation by controlling the lending policies of the state banks. Small banks, possessing limited amounts of gold and silver, tended sometimes to overextend themselves, making large amounts of bank notes available to borrowers in order to earn interest. All this paper money was legally convertible into hard cash on demand, but in the ordinary run of business, people seldom bothered to convert their notes so long as they thought the issuing bank was sound. These bank notes passed freely from hand to hand and from bank to bank all over the country.

Eventually, much of the paper money of the local banks came across the counter of some branch of the Bank of the United States. By collecting these notes and presenting them for cor version into specie, Biddle could compel the loca banks to maintain adequate reserves of gold and silver—in other words, make them hold their lending policies within bounds. "The Bank of the United States," he explained, "has succeeded in keeping in check many institutions which might otherwise have been tempted into extravagant and ruinous excesses." By exerting what he called "a mild and gentle but efficient control," he forced local banks to operate upon "a scale . . . commensurate with their real means."

Biddle's policies in the 1820's were good for his own institution, for the state banks, and probably for the country at large. The pressures on local bankers to make loans freely were enormous. The

BRIG. GEN. NICHOLAS BIDDLE COLLECTION

This miniature of Nicholas Biddle, president of the Bank of the United States, is by Henry Inman, considered in his day the nation's finest portraitist.

nation had an insatiable need for money and the general mood of the people was optimistic. Everyone wanted to borrow, and everyone expected values to rise, as, *in general*, they did. By making liberal loans to produce merchants, for example, rural bankers indirectly stimulated farmers to expand their output beyond current demand, which eventually led to a decline of prices and agricultural depression. In every field of economic activity, reckless lending caused inflation and greatly exaggerated the ups and downs of the business cycle. It can be argued, however, that by restricting the lending of state banks, Biddle was slowing the rate of economic growth and that in a predominantly agricultural society an occasional slump was a small price to pay for rapid economic development.

Thus Biddle's policies acted to stabilize the economy of the nation but they roused a great deal of opposition. Partly this opposition originated in pure ignorance: the distrust of paper money and of bankers, common in the time of John Adams and Jefferson, did not disappear, and those who disliked *all* paper saw the Bank as merely the largest (and thus the worst) of many bad institutions. At the other extreme, small bankers chafed under Biddle's restraints because by discouraging them from lending freely, he was limiting their profits. Few financiers realized what Biddle was trying to accomplish. Bray Hammond, whose researches have thrown much light on the history of American banking, estimated that in this period no more than one banker in four actually understood what was happening when he made a loan. What *was* "sound" banking practice? Honest men disagreed, and many turned against the ideas of Nicholas Biddle. This was the case particularly in the West, where capital and credit were in short supply.

Many among the sophisticated minority of financiers who *did* understand what Biddle was doing also resisted him. Especially in New York City, bankers resented the fact that a Philadelphia institution could wield so much power over their affairs. New York was the nation's largest importing center; huge amounts of tariff revenue were collected there. Yet, since this money was all deposited to the credit of the Bank of the United States, Biddle controlled it from Philadelphia. Finally, some persons objected to the Bank because it was a monopoly. The general distrust of all chartered corporations as agents of special privilege tended to focus on the Bank, which had a monopoly of public funds but was managed by a private citizen and controlled by a handful of rich men. Biddle's wealth and social position only aggravated this feeling. Like many brilliant men, he sometimes appeared arrogant. He was unused to criticism and disdainful of ignorant and stupid attacks, failing to see that these were the most dangerous of all.

Jackson's Bank Veto

This formidable opposition was diffuse and unorganized until Andrew Jackson brought it together. When he did, the Bank was quickly destroyed. Jackson belonged among the ignorant enemies of the institution, being a hard-money man suspicious of all commercial banking. "I think it right to be perfectly frank with you," he told Biddle in 1829. "I do not dislike your Bank any more than all banks. But ever since I read the history of the South Sea Bubble I have been afraid of banks."

Naturally, Jackson's attitude dismayed Biddle. But it also mystified him, since the Bank was the country's best defense against a speculative mania like the 18th-century "South Sea Bubble" in which hundreds of naive British investors had been fleeced. Almost against his will, he found himself gravitating toward Clay and the National Republicans, offering advantageous loans and retainers to politicians and newspaper editors in order to build up a following. Thereafter events moved inevitably toward a showdown, for the President's combative instincts were easily aroused. "The Bank," he told Van Buren, "is trying to kill me, *but I will kill it!*"

Henry Clay, Daniel Webster, and other prominent National Republicans hoped to use the Bank controversy against Jackson. The institution was so important to the country that Jackson's opposition to it would destroy his popularity; so, at least, they reasoned. They therefore urged Biddle to ask Congress to renew the Bank's charter. The charter would not expire until 1836, but by pressing the issue before the 1832 Presidential election they could force Jackson either to approve the recharter bill or veto it (which would give candidate Clay a lively issue in the campaign). The banker yielded to this strategy reluctantly, for he would have preferred to postpone the showdown, and a recharter bill passed Congress early in July 1832. Jackson promptly vetoed it.

Jackson's veto message explaining why he had rejected the bill was immensely popular and no doubt swelled his majority in the election. But it adds nothing to his reputation as a statesman. Being a good Jeffersonian—and no friend of John Marshall—he insisted that the Bank was unconstitutional. (*McCulloch v. Maryland* he brushed aside, saying that as President he had sworn to uphold the Constitution as *he* saw it.) The Bank was also inexpedient, he argued, being a dangerous private monopoly that allowed a handful of rich men to accumulate "many millions" of dollars that "must come directly or indirectly out of the earnings of the American people." Furthermore, many of its stockholders were foreigners: "If we must have a bank . . . it should be *purely American*." Little that he said made any more

TENNESSEE STATE LIBRARY & ARCHIVES

A cartoonist's view of the Bank War. Jackson (the "Jack ass") happily tramples the branch banks to the plaudits of newspaper hounds chained to administration policies. Vice President Van Buren, the "Red Fox," stalks the mother bank. The rooster is Major Jack Downing, a political sage invented by a commentator of the time.

sense than this absurdity.* Nowhere did Jackson mention his fundamental distrust of *all* banks. However, by stressing the argument that the Bank enabled a few plutocrats to fatten themselves at public expense, he convinced the country.

The most unfortunate aspect of Jackson's veto was that he could easily have reformed the Bank instead of destroying it. The central banking function was too important to be left in private hands. Biddle boasted at one point that he could destroy nearly any bank in the United States simply by forcing it to exchange specie for its bank notes. He thought he was demonstrating his forbearance, but he was actually revealing a dangerous flaw in the system. When the Jacksonians called him "Czar Nicholas," they were not far from the mark. Private bankers, furthermore, *were* making profits that in justice belonged to the people, for the government received no interest from the large sums it kept on deposit in the Bank.

Jackson would not consider such reforms. Government aid to business was one thing, government regulation quite another. At one point early in his administration he toyed with the idea of establishing an institution owned jointly by the national and state governments simply to handle public financial matters, but he recoiled from the suggestion that this institution be allowed to engage in commercial banking, and the proposal was dropped. Thus, the President set out to smash the Bank of the United States without any real idea of how to replace it—a most foolhardy act.

Destroy it he would. "Until I can strangle this hydra of corruption, the Bank, I will not shrink

*The country needed all the foreign capital it could attract. Foreigners actually owned only $8 million of the $35 million stock, and in any case, they could not vote their shares.

from my duty," he said. Shortly after the start of his second term, he decided to withdraw the government's money from its vaults. Under the law, only the secretary of the treasury could remove the deposits. When Secretary Louis McLane refused to do so, feeling that the alternative depositories, the state banks, were less safe, Jackson promptly "promoted" him to secretary of state and appointed William J. Duane, a Pennsylvania lawyer, to the Treasury post. Foolishly, he failed to ask Duane his views on the deposits before appointing him. Too late he discovered that the new secretary agreed with McLane! It would not be "prudent" to entrust the government's money to "local and irresponsible" banks, Duane said.

Believing that Cabinet officers should obey the President as automatically as a colonel obeys a general, Jackson dismissed Duane, replacing him with Attorney General Roger B. Taney, who had been advising him closely on Bank affairs. Taney carried out the order, simply by depositing new federal receipts in seven state banks in eastern cities while continuing to meet government expenses with drafts on the Bank of the United States.

The situation was both confused and slightly unethical. Set on winning the "Bank War," Jackson lost sight of his fear of unsound paper money. Taney, however, knew exactly what he was doing. "The business of banking . . . should be open as far as practicable to the most free competition," he believed, but he granted special advantages to banks in which he had special interests. One of the state banks favored with federal funds was the Union Bank of Baltimore. Taney owned stock in this institution, and its president was his close friend. Little wonder that Jackson's enemies were soon calling the favored state banks "pet" banks. This charge was not entirely fair, because by 1836 the government's funds had been spread out reasonably equitably in about 90 banks. Neither was it entirely unfair; the administration certainly favored institutions that were politically sympathetic to it.

When Taney began to remove the deposits, the government had $9,868,000 to its credit in the Bank of the United States; within three months the figure fell to about $4 million. Faced with the withdrawal of these funds, Biddle had to contract his operations. He decided, however, to exaggerate the contraction, pressing the state banks hard by presenting all their notes and checks that came across his counter for conversion into specie and drastically limiting his own business loans. He hoped that the resulting shortage of credit would be blamed on Jackson and that it would force the President to return the deposits. "Nothing but the evidence of suffering . . . will produce any effect," he reasoned.

For a time this strategy appeared to be working. Paper money became scarce, specie almost unobtainable. A serious panic threatened. New York banks were soon refusing to make any loans at all. "Nobody buys; nobody can sell," a French visitor to the city observed. Memorials and petitions poured in on Congress. Worried and indignant delegations of businessmen began trooping to Washington seeking "relief." Clay, Webster, and Calhoun thundered in the Senate against the administration.

Jackson would not budge. "I am fixed in my course as firm as the Rockey Mountain," he assured Vice President Van Buren. No "frail mortals" who worshiped "the golden calf" could change his mind. To others he swore he would sooner cut off his right arm and "undergo the torture of ten Spanish inquisitions" than restore the deposits. When delegations came to him, he roared at them harshly: "Go to Nicholas Biddle. . . . Biddle has all the money!" And in the end—because he was right—business leaders began to take the old general's advice. Pressure on Biddle then mounted swiftly, and in July 1834 he suddenly reversed his policy and began to lend money freely. The artificial crisis ended.

Boom and Bust

But Biddle had lost his power to restrain the state banks. Although the United States Bank continued to do business under a Pennsylvania charter after 1836, it no longer could act as a central bank. Freed from the clutches of "the Monster," state banks also began to offer credit on easy terms, aided by a large increase in their specie reserves resulting from causes unconnected with the policies of either the government or Biddle's

Bank.* Bank notes in circulation jumped from $82 million in January 1835 to $120 million in December 1836. Bank deposits rose even more rapidly.

Much of this new money flowed into speculation in land; a mania to invest in property swept the country. The increased volume of currency caused prices to soar 15 per cent in six months, buoying men's spirits and making them ever more optimistic about the future of the nation. By the summer of 1835 one observer estimated that in New York City, which had about 250,000 residents, enough house lots had been laid out and sold to support a population of 2 million. Chicago at this time had only 2 or 3 thousand inhabitants, yet most of the land for 25 miles around the village had been sold and resold in small lots by speculators anticipating the growth of the area. All over the West, farmers borrowed money from local banks by mortgaging their land, used the new bank notes to buy more land from the government, and then borrowed still more money from the banks on the strength of their new deeds.

*A decline in the Chinese demand for Mexican silver led to increased exports of the metal to the United States, and the rise of American interest rates attracted English capital into the country. Heavy English purchases of American cotton at high prices also increased the flow of specie into American banks.

So long as prices rose, the process could be repeated endlessly. In 1832, while the Bank of the United States still regulated the money supply, federal income from the sale of land was $2.6 million. In 1834 it was $4.9 million, in 1835, $14.8 million. In 1836 it rose to $24.9 million, and the government found itself totally free of debt* and with a surplus of $20 million!

*Actually, the debt still existed, but it had been transferred to private hands by the huge sales of land.

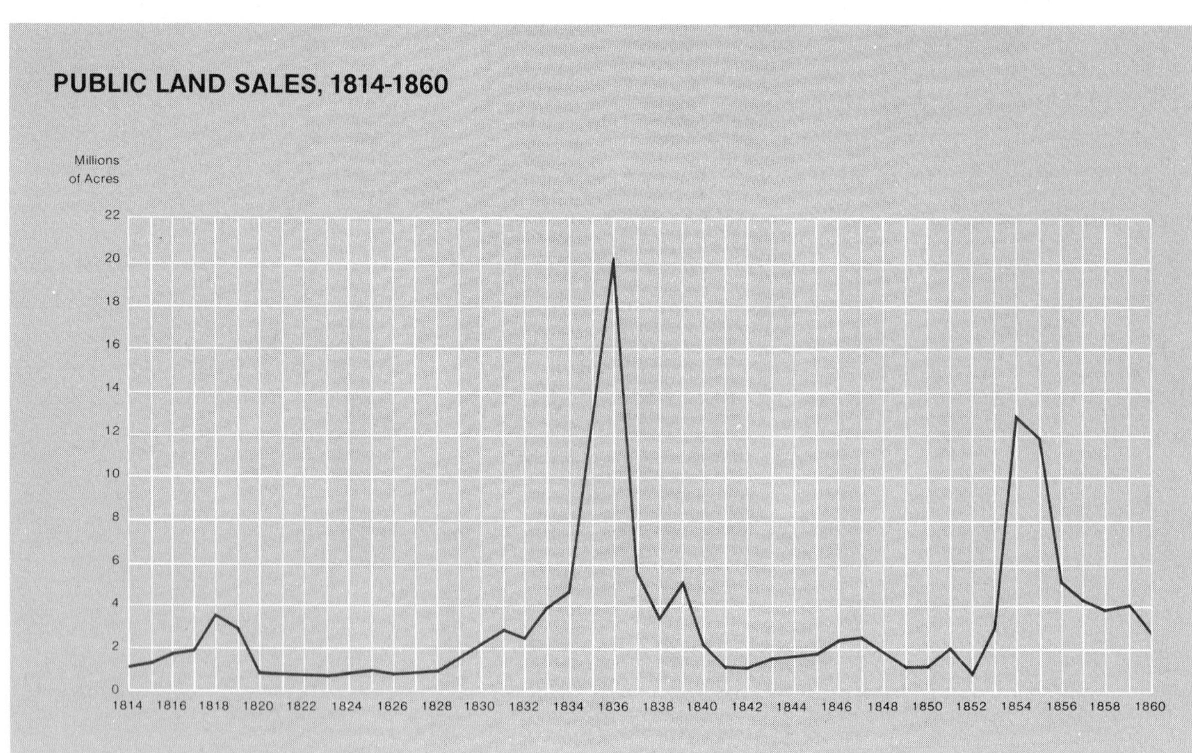

During most of the period covered here, the minimum price of public land was $1.25 an acre. In 1854, however, the price on long-unsold acreage was reduced to as low as 12.5 cents for land 30 years or more on the market.

Finally, Jackson became alarmed by the speculative mania, and in the summer of 1836 he issued the Specie Circular, which provided that purchasers must henceforth pay for public land in gold or silver. At once the rush to buy land ground to a halt, and when demand slackened, prices sagged. Speculators unable to dispose of mortgaged holdings had to abandon them to the banks, but the banks could not realize enough on this foreclosed property to recover their loans. Suddenly, the public mood changed. Commodity prices tumbled 30 per cent between February and May. Hordes of depositors sought to withdraw their credits in specie, and soon the banks exhausted their supplies. Panic swept the country in the spring of 1837 as every bank in the nation was forced to suspend specie payments. The boom was over.

Major swings in the business cycle can never be attributed to the actions of a single man, however powerful, but there is no doubt that Jackson's war against the Bank exaggerated the swings of the economic pendulum, not so much by its direct effects as by the impact of his ill-considered and intemperate policies on popular thinking. His Specie Circular, for instance, did not *prevent* speculators from buying land—at most it caused purchasers to pay a premium for gold or silver—but it convinced potential buyers that the boom was going to end and led them to make decisions which in fact ended it. Thus, by a combination of impetuousness, combativeness, arrogance, and ignorance, Old Hickory rendered the nation he loved so dearly a serious disservice. While a great man and an inspiring leader, he lacked, as Glyndon Van Deusen wrote in *The Jacksonian Era*, "the capacity for that slow and often painful balancing of opposite viewpoints, the fruit of philosophic reflection, which is the characteristic of the man of culture." This was his greatest failing, as a President and as a man.

Jacksonian Foreign Policy

Jackson's emotional and dogmatic side also influenced his handling of foreign affairs. When dealing with other nations, his patriotism was often so extravagant as to be ludicrous; indeed, in less peaceful times he might well have embroiled the country in far bloodier battles than his war with Nicholas Biddle produced. By pushing relentlessly for the solution of minor problems, he won a number of diplomatic successes. Several advantageous reciprocal trade agreements were negotiated, including one with Great Britain that finally opened British West Indian ports to American ships. Various American claims dating from the Napoleonic Wars were pressed most vigorously. The most important result of this policy came in 1831, when France agreed to pay about $5 million to compensate for damages done to American property during that long conflict.

This settlement, however, led to trouble because the French Chamber of Deputies refused to appropriate the necessary funds to carry out the government's pledge. When the United States submitted a bill for the first installment in 1833, it was unable to collect. Jackson at once adopted a belligerent stance, his ire further aroused by a bill for $170,041.18 submitted by Nicholas Biddle for the services of the Bank of the United States in attempting to collect the money. When France also ignored the second installment, Jackson sent a blistering message to Congress, full of phrases like "violation of pledges" and "not to be tolerated" and "take redress into our own hands." He asked for a law "authorizing reprisals upon French property" if the money was not paid.

Jackson's case was ironclad, but the matter surely did not merit such vigorous prosecution. Congress wisely took no action. Nevertheless, Jackson suspended diplomatic relations with France and ordered the navy readied. (In an earlier case of an unpaid claim, he had sent five warships to the kingdom of the Two Sicilies to persuade King Bomba to honor his obligations.) The French—in part, no doubt, because they were clearly in the wrong—were highly insulted by Jackson's manner. Irresponsible talk of war was heard in both countries. Fortunately, the French Chamber finally appropriated the money, Jackson moderated his public pronouncements, and the issue subsided. Yet at the height of the crisis, Jackson had arrogantly refused to tone down a single word of his message to Congress. Similarly, when a snag had delayed the negotiation of the West Indian treaty, Jackson had suggested forcing Great Britain to make concessions by imposing a boycott on trade with Canada. In both cases he showed poor judgment, being ready to take monumental risks to win petty victories. Although in the short run his diplomacy succeeded, it reinforced the impression held by foreigners that the United States was a rash young country with a chip on its shoulder and pathologically mistrustful of the good faith of other powers.

The Jacksonians

Jackson's powerful personality also had a big impact upon the shape and tone of American politics. When he came to office, nearly everyone professed to be a follower of Jefferson. But by 1836 being a Jeffersonian no longer meant much; what mattered was how a man felt about Andrew Jackson.

Jackson rode to power at the head of a diverse political army, but he left behind him an organization of men with a fairly cohesive, if not necessarily consistent, body of ideas. This Democratic party contained rich as well as poor, easterners as well as westerners, abolitionists as well as slaveholders. It was not yet a close-knit national organization but rather a coalition of state organizations, often at odds with one another over specific issues. However, always allowing for individual exceptions, the Jacksonians did agree on certain underlying principles. These included suspicion of special privilege and of large business corporations, both typified by the Bank of the United States; freedom of economic opportunity, unfettered by either private or governmental restrictions; absolute political freedom, for white men at least, including the conviction that any ordinary man is capable of performing the duties of most public offices. Jackson's belligerent patriotism also permeated the Democratic party, though pride in country was a strong force in the breasts of those who opposed him as well. Nevertheless, his ability to reconcile his belief in the *supremacy* of the Union with his conviction that the *area* of national authority should be held within narrow limits tended to make the Democrats the party of those who believed that the powers of the states should not be diminished.

Although the "Locofoco,"* or radical, wing of the party particularly championed the idea, nearly all Jacksonians, like their leader, favored giving the small man his chance—by supporting public education, for example, and by refusing to place much weight on his origin, his dress, or his manners. "One man is as good as another" (again we must supply the adjective "white") was axiomatic with them. This attitude helps explain why immigrants, Catholics, and other minority groups usually voted Democratic. However, the Jacksonians showed no tendency either to penalize the wealthy or to intervene actively in economic affairs to aid the underprivileged. The motto "That government is best which governs least" graced the masthead of the chief Jacksonian newspaper, the Washington *Globe*, throughout the era.

Rise of the Whigs

The opposition to Jackson was far less cohesive. Henry Clay's National Republican party provided a nucleus, but Clay never dominated that party as Jackson dominated the Democrats. Basically, its orientation was simply anti-Jackson. It was as though the American people were a great block of granite from which some sculptor had fashioned a statue of Jackson, the chips from his chisel, scattered about the floor of his studio, representing the opposition.

While Jackson was President, the impact of his personality delayed the formation of a true two-party system, but as soon as he surrendered power the opposition, taking heart, began to coalesce. His Bank veto won him much mass support, but it also added to the strength of his foes. Many Democrats could not accept the odd logic of Jacksonian finance. As early as 1834 these men, together with the Clay element, the extreme states'-righters who followed Calhoun, and other dissident groups, were beginning to call

*A locofoco was a type of friction match. The name was first applied in politics when a group of New York Jacksonians used these matches to light candles when a conservative faction tried to break up their meeting by turning off the gaslights.

themselves Whigs, the name, harking back to the Revolution, implying patriotic resistance to the tyranny of "King Andrew." This coalition possessed great resources of wealth and talent. Anyone who understood banking was almost obliged to become a Whig unless he was connected with one of Jackson's "pets." Those spiritual descendants of Hamilton who rejected the strict hands-off attitude of the administration in economic affairs, its general niggardliness, and its refusal to approach economic problems from a broadly national perspective also joined in large numbers. People of culture and social position offended by the coarseness and "pushiness" of the Jacksonians made up another element in the new party. The anti-intellectual and antiscientific bias of the administration (Jackson rejected proposals for a national university, an observatory, and a scientific and literary institute) drove a large percentage of the educated classes into the Whig fold. However, these groups differed among themselves on many questions, making it hard for them to agree on any program more complicated than opposition to Jackson. Furthermore, they stood in conflict with the major trend of their age: the glorification of the common man. The Whigs quickly discovered that being "right" on such issues as the Bank did not win elections.

CHICAGO HISTORICAL SOCIETY

By the 1840's the daguerreotype—"the mirror with a memory," as Oliver Wendell Holmes described it—was all the rage. This is Martin Van Buren about 1848 when he was the Free-Soil nominee for President.

Lacking an outstanding leader in 1836, the Whigs relied on a group of "favorite sons," hoping to throw the Presidential election into the House of Representatives. Daniel Webster ran in New England. For the West and South, Hugh Lawson White of Tennessee, a former friend who had broken with Jackson, was counted upon to carry the fight. General William Henry Harrison was supposed to win in the Northwest and to draw support everywhere from those who liked to vote for military heroes. This sorry strategy failed, and Jackson's hand-picked candidate, Martin Van Buren, won a majority of both the popular and the electoral votes.

Van Buren's Administration

The "Red Fox," the "Little Magician"—Van Buren's brilliance as a political manipulator has tended to obscure his statesmanlike qualities and his engaging personality. High office had sobered Van Buren and improved his judgment. He fought the Bank of the United States as a monopoly, but he also opposed irresponsible state banks. New York's "Safety Fund System," requiring all banks to contribute to a fund, supervised by the state, to be used to redeem the notes of any member bank which failed, was established largely through his efforts. One historian has called the Safety Fund "an innovation of prime importance in American political economy," the first effective example of the kind of independent regulatory agency that has become so important in modern times. Van Buren believed in public construction of internal improvements, but he favored state rather than national programs, and he urged a rational approach: each project must stand on its own as a useful and profitable public utility. He continued to equivocate spectacularly on the tariff—in his *Autobiography* he described two

NEW-YORK HISTORICAL SOCIETY

The Panic of 1837, interpreted by Whig cartoonist Edward Clay for the 1840 campaign. A caricature of Jackson overlooks idle ships and workmen, clamoring bank patrons, and a closed factory. The bank makes no specie payments, the customs house accepts only specie. Only the pawnbroker and liquor dealer (left) are prosperous.

of his supporters walking home after listening to him talk on the tariff, each convinced that it had been a brilliant speech, but neither having obtained the slightest idea as to where Van Buren stood on the subject—but he was never in the pocket of any special interest group or tariff lobbyist. He accounted himself a good Jeffersonian, tending to prefer state action to federal, but was by no means doctrinaire. Basically he approached most questions rationally and pragmatically.

Van Buren had outmaneuvered Calhoun easily in the struggle to succeed Jackson, winning the old hero's confidence and serving him well. In 1832 he was elected Vice President and thereafter was conceded to be the "heir apparent." In 1835 the Democratic National Convention nominated him for President unanimously.

Van Buren took office just as the Panic of 1837 struck the country. Its effects were frightening but short-lived. When the banks stopped converting paper money into gold and silver, they outraged conservatives but in effect eased the pressure on the money market: interest rates declined and business loans again became relatively easy to obtain. In 1836, at the height of the boom in land sales, Congress had voted to "distribute" the new Treasury surplus to the states, and this flow of money, which the states promptly spent, also stimulated the revival. Late in 1838 the banks resumed specie payments.

However, in 1839 a bumper crop caused a sharp decline in the price of cotton. Then a number of state governments that had overextended themselves in road- and canal-building projects were forced to default on their debts. This discouraged investors, particularly foreigners. A general price decline ensued that lasted until 1843.

Van Buren was not responsible for the panic or for the later decline of prices, but his manner of dealing with economic issues was scarcely helpful. He saw his role as being concerned only with problems plaguing the *government*, ignoring the economy as a whole. "The less government interferes with private pursuits the better for the general prosperity," he pontificated. As Daniel Webster scornfully pointed out, Van Buren was following a policy of "leaving the people to shift for themselves," one which many of the Whigs rejected.

Such a "hands-off" approach to the depression seems foolish by modern standards. Without stretching the generally accepted limits of federal authority, the President could have suggested relief rather than punishment for distressed banks, more federal investment in internal improvements, and perhaps some new revision of the tariff.

Van Buren's refusal to assume any responsibility for the general welfare seems to explode the theory that the Jacksonians were deeply concerned with the fate of the common man. In *The Concept of Jacksonian Democracy* Lee Benson argues that the Whigs, rather than the Democrats, were the "positive liberals" of the era, precursors, indeed, of the New Deal. Benson cites many statements by Whigs about giving "free scope to the employment of capital and credit" and applying "the means of the state boldly and liberally to aid . . . public works." This approach helps correct past oversimplifications, but it also involves judging the period by the standards of a later age. The country in the 1830's was still mainly agricultural, and for most farmers the depression, while serious, did not spell disaster. The means, even the statistical information, necessary for regulating the economy effectively did not exist. Indeed, despite rapid development in that direction, the country did not yet have a truly integrated national economy. Many Jacksonians were perfectly willing to see the *states* engage in practices designed to stimulate economic growth in bad times as, indeed, most of them did.

During his four years, Van Buren's main objective was to find an acceptable substitute for the state banks as a place to keep federal funds. The depression and the suspension of specie payments embarrassed the government along with private depositors. The President soon settled on the idea of "divorcing" the government entirely from all banking activities. His Independent Treasury Bill called for the construction of government-owned vaults in various parts of the country, where all federal revenues could be stored until needed. To insure absolute safety, all payments to the government were to be made in hard cash. After a long and bitter battle that lasted until the summer of 1840, the Independent Treasury Act finally passed both the House and the Senate.

Opposition to the Independent Treasury had been extremely bitter and not all of it partisan. Bankers and businessmen objected to the government withholding so much specie from the banks, which needed all the hard money they could get to support loans that were the lifeblood of economic growth. It also seemed irresponsible for the federal government to turn its back completely on the banks, which so obviously performed a semipublic function. These criticisms made good sense, but through a lucky combination of circumstances, the system worked reasonably well for many years.* By creating suspicion in the public mind, officially stated distrust of banks acted as a useful damper on their tendency to overexpand. No acute shortage of specie developed because heavy agricultural exports and the investment of much European capital in American railroads beginning in the mid-1840's brought in large amounts of new gold and silver. After 1849 the discovery of gold in California added another important new source of specie. As a result, the supply of money and of bank credit kept pace roughly with the growth of the economy, but through no fault of the government. Nevertheless, the disordered state of the currency remained a grave problem until corrected by Civil War banking legislation. "Wildcat" banks proliferated. Fraud and counterfeiting were common, and the operation of everyday business affairs was inconvenienced in countless ways.

*Actually, it was abolished in 1841, reconstituted in 1846, and replaced by the National Banking Act in 1863.

Election of 1840

However, it was not his financial policy that led to Van Buren's defeat in 1840. The depression naturally hurt the Democrats, and the Whigs, now a truly national party, were far better organized than in 1836. The Whigs also adopted a different strategy, cynical but effective, copied from their opponents. The Jacksonians had come to power on the coattails of a popular general whose views on public questions they concealed or ignored. They had maintained themselves by shouting the praises of the common man. Now the Whigs seized upon these techniques and carried them to their logical or, rather, illogical, conclusion. Not even bothering to draft a program and passing over statesmen like Clay and Webster, whose views were known and therefore controversial, they nominated General Harrison for President. The Hero of Tippecanoe was counted upon to conquer the party created in the image of the Hero of New Orleans. Then, to "balance" the ticket, the Whigs chose a former Democrat, John Tyler of Virginia, an ardent supporter of states' rights, as their Vice Presidential candidate.

The Whig argument was specious but smooth and convincing: General Harrison is a plain man of the people, who lives in a log cabin (where the latchstring is always out). Contrast him with the suave Van Buren, luxuriating amid "the

CINCINNATI HISTORICAL SOCIETY

A cornerstone of Whig strategy in the 1840 campaign was the mass political rally, such as this one held in Cincinnati a month before Election Day. A "triumphal" arch was erected across Main Street for the occasion, with Harrison banners, flags, and slogans, both patriotic and political, much in evidence. A contemporary etching.

Regal Splendor of the President's Palace." Harrison drinks ordinary hard cider and eats hog meat and grits, while Van Buren consumes expensive foreign wines and fattens on rich concoctions prepared by a French chef. The general's furniture is plain and sturdy; the President dines off gold plates and treads on Royal Wilton carpets that cost the people $5 a yard. In a country where all men are equal, the people will reject an aristocrat like "Martin Van Ruin" and put their trust in a simple, brave, honest, public-spirited common man.

A typical pro-Harrison speech was thus officially summarized in the *Congressional Globe*:

> The speaker entered into a defense of the military and civil services of General Harrison; gave a description of his furniture and cooking utensils, and presented a graphic picture of the exterior appearance of his dwelling, as well as its general interior arrangement, to show his fitness for the Presidency.

Such nonsense created an irrelevant and also a misleading impression. Harrison came from a distinguished family, being the son of Benjamin Harrison, signer of the Declaration of Independence and former governor of Virginia. He was well educated and in at least comfortable financial circumstances, and he certainly did not live in a log cabin. The Whigs ignored these facts. They organized hundreds of parades and barbecues, complete with brass bands, banners, and homespun orators. The log cabin and the cider barrel became their symbols, which every political meeting saw reproduced in a dozen forms. The leading Whig campaign newspaper, edited by a vigorous young New Englander named Horace Greeley, was called the *Log Cabin*. Cartoons, doggerel, slogans, and souvenirs were everywhere substituted for argument.

The Democrats tried to reply in kind, but although using the same methods as the Whigs and equally well organized on national lines, they had little heart for the fight. The President set the tone for their campaign, and the responsibilities of the White House had made him still more a statesman and less a politician. He tried to run on his record and to focus public attention on real issues, but his voice could not be heard above the huzzas of the Whigs. When the Democrats spoke of financial questions, the Whigs chanted: "Tippecanoe and Tyler too!" and "Van, Van, is a used-up man" and rolled out another barrel of hard cider. Election Day demonstrated both the effectiveness of this Whig strategy and the fact that the two-party system had reached maturity. A huge turnout (four-fifths of the eligible voters, more than 2.4 million as against 1.5 million four years earlier) carried Harrison to victory by a margin of almost 150,000. The electoral vote was 234 to 60.

There was, of course, a powerful irony in this result. The Democrats had been blown up by their own bomb. In 1828 they had portrayed John Quincy Adams as a bloated aristocrat and Jackson as a simple western farmer. The lurid talk of Van Buren dining off golden plates was no different from the stories that made Adams out to be a passionate gambler. If Van Buren was a lesser man than Adams, Harrison was a pale imitation indeed of Andrew Jackson.

The Whigs continued to repeat history by rushing to gather up the spoils of victory. Washington was again flooded by office seekers, the political confusion monumental. Harrison had no ambition to be an aggressive leader. He believed that Jackson had misused the veto and professed to put as much emphasis as had Washington on the principle of the separation of legislative and executive powers. Naturally, this delighted the powerful Whig leaders in Congress, who had had their fill of what they called the "executive usurpation" of Jackson. Either Clay or Webster seemed destined to be the real ruler of the new administration, and soon these two were squabbling over their old general like sparrows over a crust.

But at the height of their squabble, less than a month after his inauguration, Harrison fell gravely ill. Pneumonia developed, and on April 4 he died. John Tyler of Virginia, an honest, conscientious, doctrinaire politician, became President of the United States. The political climate of the country changed drastically. Events began to march in a new direction, one that led ultimately to Bull Run, to Gettysburg, and on to Appomattox.

SUPPLEMENTARY READING Of the many biographies of Jackson the best modern study is Marquis James, *The Life of Andrew Jackson** (1938). R.V. Remini's *Andrew Jackson** (1966) is an excellent brief account told by an admiring but not idolizing historian. The nature of Jacksonian Democracy was analyzed brilliantly by Alexis de Tocqueville, *Democracy in America** (1835–1840). Scholarly interpretations of the subject are numerous, for it is a very controversial one. A.M. Schlesinger, Jr., *The Age of Jackson** (1945), stresses the democratic character of Jacksonianism. J.W. Ward, *Andrew Jackson: Symbol for an Age** (1955), pictures Jackson as typifying certain basic aspects of the American character. D.T. Miller, *Jacksonian Aristocracy* (1967), stresses the growth of economic and class distinctions after 1830, while Marvin Meyers' *The Jacksonian Persuasion** (1957) is another interesting attempt to explain the nature of the times. T.P. Abernethy, *From Frontier to Plantation in Tennessee* (1932), portrays Jackson as a conservative, chiefly by stressing his early career. Richard Hofstadter's analysis of Jackson in *The American Political Tradition** (1948) is also important.

A number of contemporary commentaries by foreigners throw much light on Jacksonian Democracy. See especially, in addition to Tocqueville, Frances Trollope, *Domestic Manners of the Americans** (1832); Michel Chevalier (J.W. Ward, ed.), *Society, Manners and Politics in the United States* (1961); Harriet Martineau, *Retrospect of Western Travel* (1838) and *Society in America** (1837); and F.J. Grund, *Aristocracy in America** (1959).

G.G. Van Deusen, *The Jacksonian Era** (1959), provides a convenient scholarly summary of Jackson's Presidency. On his administration of the government and the development of the spoils system, see L.D. White, *The Jacksonians** (1954), and C.R. Fish, *The Civil Service and the Patronage* (1905); on the development of parties, R.P. McCormick, *The Second American Party System** (1966).

For the Indian problem, consult F.P. Prucha, *American Indian Policies in the Formative Years* (1962), and Grant Foreman, *Indian Removal: The Emigration of the Five Civilized Tribes* (1953). The Supreme Court cases involving the Cherokees are discussed in A.J. Beveridge, *The Life of John Marshall* (1916–19). By far the best treatment of the nullification controversy is W.W. Freehling, *Prelude to Civil War: The Nullification Controversy in South Carolina** (1966), which shows the close relationship between the nullifiers and the slavery issue. Also helpful are C.M. Wiltse, *John C. Calhoun: Nullifier* (1949), and Frederic Bancroft, *Calhoun and the South Carolina Nullification Movement* (1928). C.S. Sydnor, *The Development of Southern Sectionalism** (1948), locates the crisis in a broader context. Calhoun's character is well described in M.L. Coit, *John C. Calhoun: American Portrait** (1950).

The struggle with the Bank is discussed in Bray Hammond, *Banks and Politics in America from the Revolution to the Civil War** (1957), but see also Walter Smith, *Economic Aspects of the Second Bank of the United States* (1953), and especially, Peter Temin, *The Jacksonian Economy** (1969), which minimizes the effects of Jackson's policies on economic conditions. Temin also provides an interesting analysis of economic trends through the entire period. T.P. Govan's *Nicholas Biddle: Nationalist and Public Banker* (1959) is excellent on Biddle's view of banking but too apologetic. C.B. Swisher's *Roger B. Taney* (1935) is a good biography of Jackson's third secretary of the treasury.

The political and economic ideas of Whigs and Democrats are discussed in Lee Benson, *The Concept of Jacksonian Democracy** (1961). For Jackson's foreign policy, see R.A. McLemore, *Franco-American Diplomatic Relations* (1941). Walter Hugins' *Jacksonian Democracy and the Working Class** (1960) is a fine scholarly study. On the development of the Whig party, in addition to the biographies of leading Whigs, see E.M. Carroll, *Origins of the Whig Party* (1925), and G.R. Poage, *Henry Clay and the Whig Party* (1936), and McCormick's above-mentioned *Second American Party System.*

The election of 1840 is treated in R.G. Gunderson, *The Log-Cabin Campaign* (1957), Freeman Cleaves, *Old Tippecanoe* (1939), O.P. Chitwood, *John Tyler: Champion of the Old South* (1939), J.A. Garraty, *Silas Wright* (1949), and the various biographies of Clay and Webster.

*Available in paperback.

NORTHERN NATURAL GAS COMPANY COLLECTION, JOSLYN ART MUSEUM

PORTFOLIO

III *Tocqueville's America*

In 1831 two well-born young Frenchmen, Alexis de Tocqueville and Gustave de Beaumont, set sail from Le Havre for America. Ostensibly, they were to study the American prison system, but their real aim was far more ambitious. "We are leaving," wrote Tocqueville, "with the intention of examining, in detail and as scientifically as possible, all the mechanism of that vast American society which everyone talks of and no one knows. . . . We are counting on bringing back the elements of a fine work." In time that "fine work" would become Tocqueville's classic analysis of American society, *Democracy in America;* but first, as Beaumont wrote, they must "see America; . . . its inhabitants, its cities, its institutions, its customs." In the following nine months they did precisely that, traveling virtually the length and breadth of the nation.

Fortunately, the America Tocqueville and Beaumont saw —and they saw a great deal—can be recaptured today not only in their notes and letters, but also in the drawings, prints, and paintings of the period, such as Carl Bodmer's 1832 water color above of a steamboat landing in New Jersey. The America that the artists pictured has of course long since disappeared, yet many of the fundamental traits of the society Tocqueville analyzed may still be observed in the America of today.

City of Commerce

On May 11, 1831, after an Atlantic passage of some 40 days, Tocqueville and Beaumont landed in New York City for a six-week stay. As he looked at the hustle and bustle of New York, Tocqueville saw a city and a society that differed radically from Paris and the still aristocratic society of early-19th-century France. His first impressions were hardly complimentary. "To a Frenchman the aspect of the city is bizarre and not very agreeable," he wrote his mother. "One sees neither dome, nor bell tower, nor great edifice, with the result that one has the constant impression of being in a suburb. In its centre the city is built of brick, which gives it a most monotonous appearance. . . . The streets are very badly paved, but sidewalks for pedestrians are to be found in all of them."

Everywhere he looked, Tocqueville saw one kind of business or another, and he noted that "the whole society seems to have melted into a middle class." Soon he was turning this observation into his first major generalization about American society: "We are most certainly in another world here. Political passions here are only on the surface. The profound passion, the only one which profoundly stirs the human heart, the passion of all the days, is the acquisition of riches." Pressing his analysis a step further, he noted that this "thirst for riches . . . brings in its train many hardly honourable passions, such as cupidity, fraud, and bad faith. . . . In addition, [Americans] consider the bankruptcies which are very frequent in all cities as of no importance or of very little account."

Though Tocqueville found this business society at first "both vulgar and disagreeably uncultivated" and more the product of "accidental circumstances" than "the will of man," he quickly noted that "before my eyes is none the less an immense spectacle. Never before has a people found for itself such a happy and fruitful basis of life. Here freedom is unrestrained, and subsists by being useful to every one without injuring anybody. There is undeniably something *feverish* in the activity it imparts to industry and to the human spirit. But up to now that fever seems only to increase man's power without affecting his reason. In spite of this activity, nature's resources are inexhaustible. What remains to be done seems to increase in proportion to what has already been done. New York, which had 20,000 souls at the moment of the American Revolution, has 200,000 now, and each year adds immense developments to its greatness."

AMERICAN ANTIQUARIAN SOCIETY

STOKES COLLECTION, NEW YORK PUBLIC LIBRARY

Above is an 1834 aquatint of New York's Broadway, looking north from Canal Street. It is easy to see why Tocqueville concluded that he was in the midst of a highly commercial society: practically every building houses two or more businesses, and street peddlers are busy hawking ice, firewood, and boots. While the two visitors were in the city, they put up at a fashionable boarding house on lower Broadway. As the contemporary views at left and right suggest, they found boarding-house life "very agreeable" if informal. "It upsets all our settled habits," Tocqueville admitted. "We were utterly astounded the first day to see the women come to breakfast at 8 o'clock in the morning carefully dressed for the whole day."

MUSEUM OF THE CITY OF NEW YORK

MUSEUM OF FINE ARTS, BOSTON

The Dinner Party *was painted about 1825 by the Boston artist Henry Sargent. Tocqueville tolerated, but rarely praised American* haute cuisine. *After one banquet, he recorded that the dinner represented the infancy of art: "the vegetables and fish before the meat, the oysters for dessert. In a word, complete barbarism."*

High Society

Tocqueville and Beaumont had an unusual opportunity to observe the upper crust of American society, for wherever they went they found that the company of two young French aristocrats was considered a badge of social distinction. Even in the Jacksonian era, democracy was not without its social affectations. In New York Beaumont wrote that "the aristocracy of fortune aims at distinction here as elsewhere. Much is made of the oldness of families. I was astonished to hear these proud champions of equality call themselves *honourable esquires*. They put heraldic arms on their carriages and on their seals. The taste for superiority crops up everywhere. They are besides excessively vain." Tocqueville carried the analysis a step further. "In this republican country they are a thousand times more fond of nobility, of titles, of crosses, and of all the inconsequential distinctions of Europe than we are in France. The greatest equality reigns here in the laws. It is even in appearance in the customs. But I tell you the devil loses nothing by it. And the pride which cannot come out in public finds at the very bottom of the soul a fine corner in which to install itself." The frantic search for emblems of status was fueled, he noted, by the fact that "money is the only social distinction."

Fresh from the excitement of revolution-torn Paris, Tocqueville found social life in mercantile-minded America exceedingly dull. "In the United States," he wrote, "they have neither war, nor pestilence, nor literature, nor eloquence, nor fine arts, nor revolutions; no great excesses. . . . They enjoy there the most insipid happiness which can be imagined." He feared that democracy was leading to mediocrity: "The people grow more enlightened, knowledge is spreading, a middling capacity is becoming common. The outstanding talents, the great characters, are more rare. Society is less brilliant and more prosperous."

A Baltimore horse race like the one at top "wasn't quite the style of Europe." Tocqueville thought "the horses were fine but the jockeys ridiculously clothed." The public's fashions for such occasions, however, as illustrated in the 1836 advertisement above, won Tocqueville's commendation: "The French mode dominates."

The Rigors of Travel

The America that Tocqueville and Beaumont set out to explore was, as Tocqueville put it, "one vast forest, in the middle of which they have carved out some clearings." In 1831 American railroads were still in their infancy, and canals provided only slow and cramped transportation which a gentleman avoided whenever possible. This was instead the heyday of the stagecoach and the steamboat, and it was largely with the aid of these two conveyances that the two Frenchmen made their extensive tour of the United States. In nine months they traveled more than 4,000 miles, a remarkable achievement. They saw something of all 24 states, explored the edge of the western frontier, traveled down the Ohio and the Mississippi from Pittsburgh to New Orleans, and visited almost all of the nation's major cities.

Neither stagecoach nor steamboat seems to have treated the somewhat frail Tocqueville very kindly, but he never lost his sense of humor, his determination to carry on, or his capacity for objective reporting. The stage road might be "infernal" and the carriage "without springs," yet he could still note the "tranquillity of the Americans over all these inconveniences. They seem to bear them as necessary evils." When he nearly lost his life aboard an Ohio steamboat trapped in ice, he remarked mildly, "water journeys do not go well with us." But above and beyond the hazards and inconveniences, Tocqueville had nothing but praise for the nation's rough but remarkably extensive network of communications. "The roads, the canals, and the mails," he noted, "play a prodigious part in the prosperity of the Union. . . . In the Michigan forests there is not a cabin so isolated, not a valley so wild, that it does not receive letters and newspapers at least once a week. . . . America has undertaken and is finishing some immense canals. It already has more railroads than France. . . . Of all the countries of the world," he concluded, "America is the one where the movement of thought and human industry is the most continuous and the most swift."

TOLEDO MUSEUM OF ART, GIFT OF FLORENCE SCOTT LIBBEY

As if he were describing John Lewis Krimmel's painting (above) of a country inn, Tocqueville wrote, "We were introduced into the 'barroom' . . . where the simplest as well as the richest . . . smoke, drink, and talk politics together, on the footing of the most perfect exterior equality."

The engraving at right, from a mail stage broadside, was labeled, "Thirty-nine hours from Boston to New York." Tocqueville noted ruefully that stages were "drawn at full trot on roads as detestable as those of lower Brittany."

The 1832 French lithograph (left) of a bateau à vapeur américain *shows the type of river craft used by Tocqueville and Beaumont in their travels.*

AMERICAN ANTIQUARIAN SOCIETY

Carl Bodmer, a 23-year-old Swiss, painted the above water color of an Indiana farmstead in 1832. Although the pioneer's log cabin was often a crude and unfinished dwelling, Tocqueville viewed it as an "ark of civilization." When his steamboat approached Detroit, shown opposite in an 1834 lithograph, he marveled, "Without transition you pass from wilderness into the streets of a city."

BEINECKE LIBRARY, YALE UNIVERSITY

Beaumont drew this sketch during an excursion to the frontier outpost of Saginaw. Tocqueville relaxes at right while Beaumont gives their Indian guide a water bottle to prevent his desertion.

Edge of the Frontier

Probably no part of his trip provided Tocqueville with as many insights as the two weeks he spent on the edge of the frontier in the forests of Michigan Territory. The deeper he penetrated into the wilderness, the more amazed he was to find that the American was much the same sort of fellow on the frontier as he was in the city. "The man you left in New York," he wrote, "you find again in almost impenetrable solitudes: same clothes, same attitudes, same language, same habits, same pleasures." He attributed this similarity to the fact that "those who inhabit these isolated places have arrived there since yesterday; they have come with the customs, the ideas, the needs of civilization."

If the settler seemed to be trying to shape the frontier in the image of the civilization he had left behind, the frontier was also putting its own stamp on the American character. The pioneer, Tocqueville wrote, "has braved exile, the loneliness and numberless miseries of the savage life, he has slept on the bare ground, he has exposed himself to the forest fevers and the tomahawk of the Indian." Tocqueville was convinced these efforts in pursuit of "the acquisition of riches" would continue "with a perseverance and a scorn for life that one might call heroic, if that name fitted other than virtuous things."

A further effect of pioneering was a remarkable attitude toward change. "The American has no time to tie himself to anything," wrote Tocqueville. "He grows accustomed only to change, and ends by regarding it as the natural state of man. He feels the need of it, more, he loves it; for the instability, instead of meaning disaster to him, seems to give birth only to miracles all about him." In this world of change, asked Tocqueville, how could the American be anything but an optimist? "The same man has given his name to a wilderness which none before him had traversed, has seen the first forest tree fall and the first planter's house rise in the solitude, where a community came to group itself, a village grew, and today a vast city stretches."

STOKES COLLECTION, NEW YORK PUBLIC LIBRARY

Queen City of the West

On their return from Michigan the two Frenchmen resumed touring the older states, then boarded an Ohio River steamboat for Cincinnati, the "Queen City of the West." What they saw, shown in this 1835 painting by an amateur artist named John Caspar Wild, sent them both scurrying to their notebooks. "I don't believe there exists anywhere on earth a town

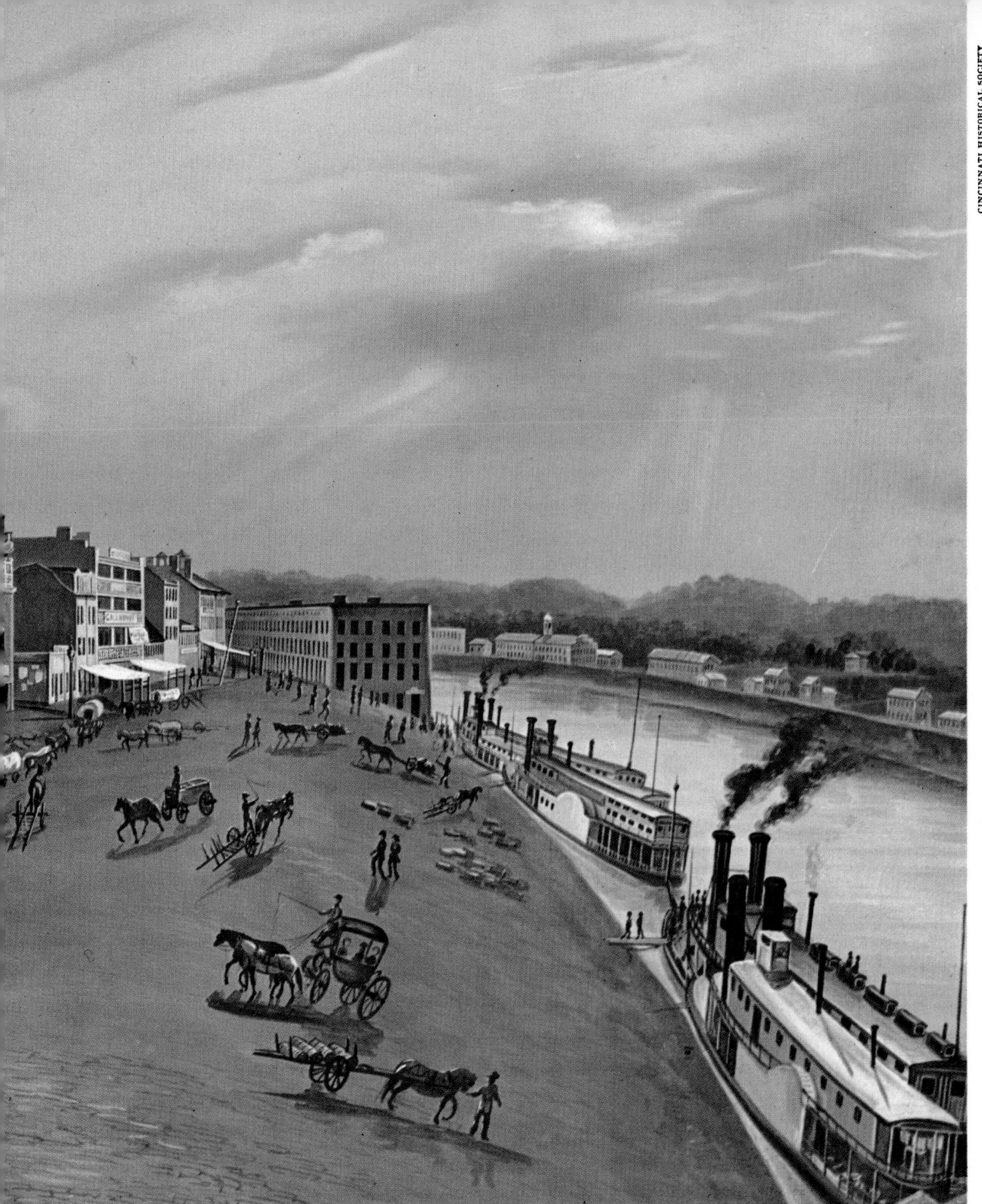

CINCINNATI HISTORICAL SOCIETY

which has had a growth so prodigious," Beaumont wrote. "Thirty years ago the banks of the Ohio were a wilderness. Now there are 30,000 inhabitants." Tocqueville confessed himself astonished by the spectacle of "a city which seems to want to rise too quickly for people to have any system or plan about it. Great buildings . . . houses under construction, no names on the streets, no numbers on the houses, no outward luxury, but the image of industry and labor obvious at every step."

The South and Slavery

Cincinnati demonstrated the vigor of the western frontier, Tocqueville wrote. "Society is growing more rapidly than man." But when their steamboat headed down the Ohio, he was interested to notice how different were Ohio and Indiana, the free states on their right, from the slave state of Kentucky on their left. "For the first time," he wrote his father, "we have had the chance to examine . . . the effect that slavery produces on society. On the right bank of the Ohio everything is activity, industry; labor in honoured; there are no slaves. Pass to the left bank and the scene changes so suddenly that you think yourself on the other side of the world; the enterprising spirit is gone. There, work is not only painful; it's shameful, and you degrade yourself in submitting yourself to it. To ride, to hunt, to smoke like a Turk in the sunshine: there is the destiny of the white. To do any other kind of manual labor is to act like a slave."

Critical as he was of slavery, Tocqueville's aristocratic heart was warmed by southern charm. "The whites, to the South of the Ohio, form a veritable aristocracy which . . . combines many prejudices with high sentiments and instincts. They say, and I am much inclined to believe, that in the matter of honour these men practice delicacies and refinements unknown in the North. They are frank, hospitable, and put many things before money."

But charm alone did not make a strong society. "You see few churches, no schools," he observed. "Society, like the individual, seems to provide for nothing." The South would end "by being dominated by the North. Every day the latter grows more wealthy and densely populated while the South is stationary or growing poor."

Later, after he had returned from New Orleans, he summed up his thoughts in one of those brilliant flashes of insight that would make him famous. Under the heading "Future of the Union," he wrote, "The first result of this disproportionate growth is a violent change in the equilibrium of power and political influence. Powerful states become weak, territories without a name become states. . . . Wealth, like population, is displaced. These changes cannot take place without injuring interests, without exciting violent passions."

KENNEDY GALLERIES

MARYLAND HISTORICAL SOCIETY

The drawing at left by August Köllner and Benjamin Latrobe's water color above portray two aspects of slavery: the leisurely life of the plantation owner and the hard lot of the Negro. Beaumont caustically noted that "in the house of the whites [slaves are] an obligatory furnishing, as is a chair or a table. . . . The convenience of being served . . . makes the white indolent. . . . His customs are feudal; he spends his time hunting, riding, or doing nothing. . . ."

Slavery, observed Tocqueville after witnessing a slave auction like the one below, "brutalizes the black population and debilitates the white." Then, in one blunt sentence, he summed up his two-month tour of the South: "Man is not made for servitude."

CHICAGO HISTORICAL SOCIETY

A Nation of Equals

Despite his disapproval of slavery, Tocqueville believed that equality, both social and political, was the guiding principle of American life. "The great advantage of the Americans," he asserted, "is . . . that they are born equal instead of becoming so." No institution provided proof of this assertion so convincingly as the family. In America, he observed, "the paternal authority is almost reduced to nothing." As soon as the first years of childhood were past, equality, and with it freedom and independence, were given the young—male and female, first-born and last-born alike. Such treatment not only produced the rapid maturing of self-confident men and women ready to extend the frontier but also led to the growth of strong ties between father and son, mother and daughter, brother and brother. Tocqueville felt certain that "in proportion as manners and laws become more democratic . . . rules and authority are less talked of, confidence and tenderness are often increased." In a democracy, he believed, this state of affairs boded well for the family, but it raised serious problems for society as a whole. "Democracy loosens social ties, but tightens natural ones; it brings kindred more closely together, while it throws citizens more apart," he concluded.

In short, it appeared to Tocqueville that outside of the family circle equality tended to isolate men and make them selfish. This dangerous situation might lead either to complete conformity or, at the other extreme, to unrestrained individualism. But happily, Tocqueville noticed, the young democracy had created a veritable abundance of social institutions which managed to generate diversity while providing a framework for communal enterprises. "Americans of all ages, all conditions, and all dispositions constantly form associations," he observed. "They have not only commercial and manufacturing companies, in which all take part, but associations of a thousand other kinds, religious, moral, serious, futile, general or restricted, enormous or diminutive. The Americans make associations to give entertainments, to found seminaries, to build inns, to construct churches, to diffuse books, to send missionaries to the antipodes; in this manner they found hospitals, prisons, and schools. If it is proposed to inculcate some truth or to foster some feeling by the encouragement of a great example, they form a society."

To Tocqueville the centrifugal forces in American life, rather than the centripetal ones, were the most dangerous. It seemed to him that "in proportion as the circle of public society is extended, it may be anticipated that the sphere of private intercourse will be contracted; far from supposing that the members of modern society will ultimately live in common, I am afraid that they will end by forming only small coteries."

The print above, titled The Grand Fantastical Parade, *satirized an 1833 demonstration in New York against the militia system, one of the nation's oldest volunteer organizations. But most Americans were too fond of this highly social institution to be swayed. The sober portrait at the right, c. 1840, of a typically large family is the work of an unknown primitive artist who found painting the human hand beyond his skill.*

MUSEUM OF THE CITY OF NEW YORK

M. & M. KAROLIK COLLECTION, MUSEUM OF FINE ARTS, BOSTON

MR. & MRS. SCREVEN LORILLARD COLLECTION

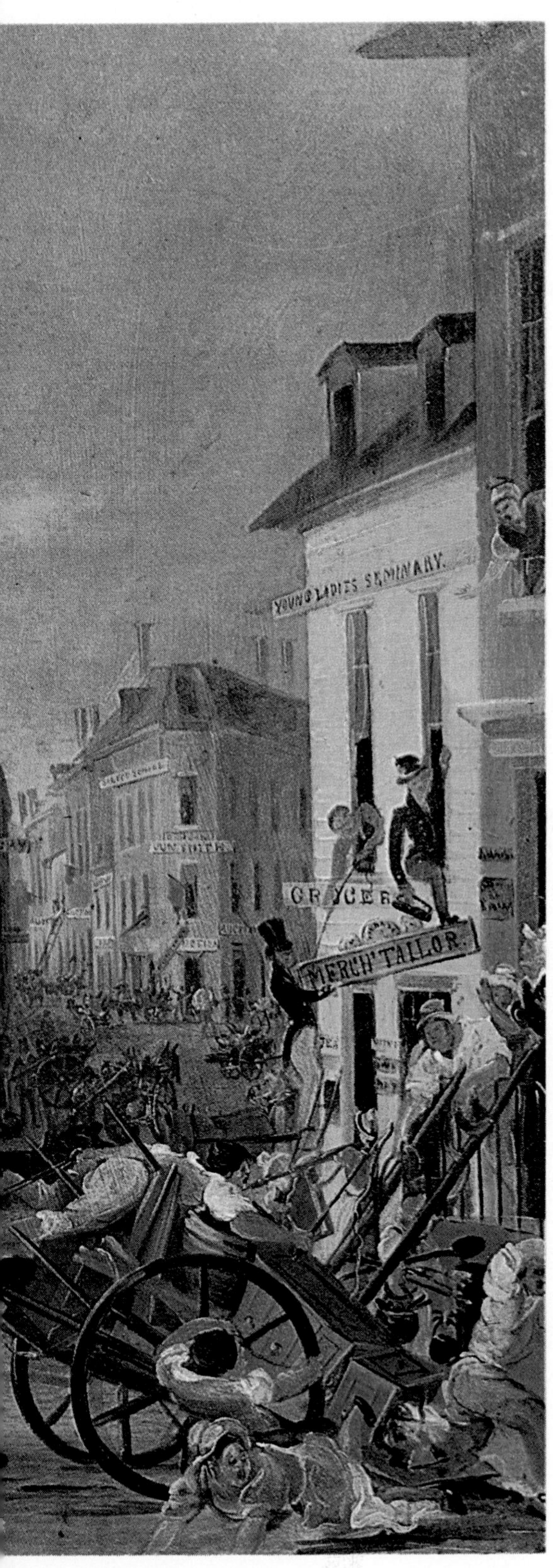

A Restless People

As he penned one of his most telling comments on life in America, Tocqueville observed, "In the United States a man builds a house in which to spend his old age, and he sells it before the roof is on; he plants a garden and lets it just as the trees are coming into bearing; he brings a field into tillage and leaves other men to gather the crops; he embraces a profession and gives it up; he settles in a place, which he soon afterwards leaves to carry his changeable longings elsewhere. If his private affairs leave him any leisure, he instantly plunges into the vortex of politics; and if at the end of a year of unremitting labor he finds he has a few days' vacation, his eager curiosity whirls him over the vast extent of the United States, and he will travel fifteen hundred miles in a few days to shake off his happiness. Death at length overtakes him, but it is before he is weary of his bootless chase of that complete felicity which forever escapes him."

Other eyes, such as those of the unknown artist who painted this view of the clamorous commotion of moving day in New York about 1840 (and included himself at the far left), observed the same phenomenon of restlessness. But Tocqueville went a step further and pinpointed the potential tragedy of such physical and social mobility.

"Equality," he wrote in *Democracy in America*, "leads by a still shorter path to the various effects [of restlessness] I have just described. When . . . the distinctions of ranks are obliterated and privileges are destroyed, when hereditary property is subdivided and education and freedom are widely diffused, the desire of acquiring the comforts of the world haunts the imagination of the poor, and the dread of losing them that of the rich. Many scanty fortunes spring up; those who possess them have a sufficient share of physical gratifications to conceive a taste for these pleasures, not enough to satisfy it. They never procure them without exertion, and they never indulge in them without apprehension. They are therefore always straining to pursue or to retain gratifications so delightful, so imperfect, so fugitive."

The Religious Impulse

Tocqueville had not been in America more than a month when he observed, "Never have I been so conscious of the influence of religion on the morals and the social and political state of a people." A few weeks later he wrote his first long commentary on "American Government and Religion." "Sunday is rigorously observed," he noted. "As for what we generally understand as faiths, such as customs, ancient traditions, the strength of memories . . . I don't see a trace of them." He observed instead that "the immense majority have *faith* in the wisdom and good sense of human kind." America, in other words, had placed its faith in democracy. "In France, I had almost always seen the spirit of religion and the spirit of freedom marching in opposite directions. But in America I found that they were intimately united." United in spirit, but separated in fact, of course; separation spared the church the worldly misfortunes of the state and left it free to be democracy's conscience. Tocqueville concluded that "while the law permits Americans to do what they please, religion prevents them from conceiving, and forbids them to commit what is rash or unjust."

M. & M. KAROLIK COLLECTION, MUSEUM OF FINE ARTS, BOSTON

Tocqueville greatly admired the moral influence of the socially active sects like the Quakers (above). Americans, he thought, had little taste for symbols, ritual, and complicated theology, preferring to have their religion "bared to the light of day."

MUSEUM OF THE CITY OF NEW YORK

NEW-YORK HISTORICAL SOCIETY

In the 1830's pioneers worshiped with unrestrained enthusiasm at camp meetings like the one depicted above by Parisian Jacques Gerard Milbert. Below is Englishman George Harvey's 1837 water color, Night Fall, St. Thomas Church, Broadway. *Tocqueville counted on religion to "purify" and "restrain" American materialism.*

Above is an unknown artist's painting of a girls' school about 1840. Although he was not enthusiastic about equal education for women, Tocqueville concluded that there was "no choice." A good education, he philosophized, was "indispensable to protect women from the dangers with which democratic manners surround them."

MUSEUM OF THE CITY OF NEW YORK

This satirical drawing, also by an unknown artist, shows meteorologist James Pollard Espy delivering a lyceum lecture in New York about 1841. Begun in 1826 and dedicated to the "general diffusion of knowledge," the lyceum movement was a box-office success for years.

Education for Democracy

During most of his tour Tocqueville wrestled with the question: Could a democratic society achieve stable government? Finally, halfway down the Ohio River, he decided that indeed it could. He recorded that "enlightenment," more than anything else, including "virtue," was the prime reason for America's success at self-government: "The Americans are hardly more virtuous than others, but they are infinitely better educated." American education, he continued, was stamped with a democratic character: primary instruction was "within the reach of everybody"; anyone was "free to found a public school and direct it as he pleases"; and education was "an industry like other industries, the *consumers* being the judges and the state taking no hand whatever." Actually state governments did take a hand, but in 1832 education was still largely a local and a private matter. Almost every town outside the South maintained a primary school, and the churches ran a variety of educational institutions.

But schooling was just one part of an American's education. "The citizen of the United States," Tocqueville observed, "does not acquire his practical science and his positive notions from books; the instruction he has acquired may have prepared him for receiving those ideas, but it did not furnish them. The American learns to know the laws by participating in the act of legislation; and he takes a lesson in the forms of government from governing. The great work of society is ever going on before his eyes, and as it were, under his hands." In addition, as Tocqueville observed, the daily newspaper which alone "can drop the same thought into a thousand minds at the same moment," helped to keep Americans informed.

All in all, Tocqueville was immensely impressed and concluded that "the mass of those possessing an understanding of public affairs, a knowledge of law and precedents, a feeling for the best interests of the nation, and the faculty of understanding them, is greater in America than in any place else in the world."

MUSEUM OF ART, RHODE ISLAND SCHOOL OF DESIGN

The informality of the American rural courtroom, as in the painting above, never worried Tocqueville. He was certain the jury system was democracy's best method of adult education— "a gratuitous public school, ever open [that] invests each citizen with a kind of magistracy."

A Sovereign People

John Lewis Krimmel's painting of voting day in Philadelphia pictures the rowdy and colorful confusion which, said Tocqueville, accompanied all American political activity. "No sooner do you set foot upon American ground than you are stunned by a kind of tumult; a confused clamour is heard on every side, and a thousand simultaneous voices demand the satisfaction of

HISTORICAL SOCIETY OF PENNSYLVANIA

their social wants. Everything is in motion around you." By 1832 universal white manhood suffrage was the rule in all but a few states; although only about 60 per cent of those eligible had voted in the Presidential election of that year, this was double the figure for 1824. "King Caucus" had given way to the national nominating convention, and most state offices were now elective. "The people," said Tocqueville "reign in the American political world as the Deity does in the universe."

BOTH: MERCANTILE LIBRARY, ST. LOUIS (© 1959 UNIVERSITY OF OKLAHOMA PRESS)

Democracy in America

A few weeks before Tocqueville returned to France he made his one and only visit to Washington. The capital city, which was then barely 30 years old, did not strengthen his confidence in the vigor of the central government: "Washington offers the sight of an arid plain, burned by the sun, on which are scattered two or three sumptuous edifices and the five or six villages composing the town." He toured Capitol Hill systematically and observed all the institutions of government, including the House of Representatives, shown opposite in a detail from Samuel F.B. Morse's painting of about 1822. He met as many politicians, most notably President Andrew Jackson, as time allowed. He found them, as the two drawings on this page by George Caleb Bingham suggest, clever and ambitious, but lacking in statesmanship. They offered a clear demonstration of the leveling influence of democracy, he decided. The city, the politicians, even the President, lacked the grandeur and the sense of high purpose which Tocqueville had hoped to find. For the time being it did not matter, he wrote, for in the "New World . . . man has no other enemy than himself. . . . In order to be happy and to be free, he has only to determine that he will be so." The challenge would come when America would have to resort "to *conscription* and to *heavy taxation*." "Democracy," he wrote, "does not always perish from weakness and inability to act. It is not in the nature of a democratic power to lack material means, but rather moral force, stability, and skill."

If dark clouds loomed on the horizon, for the present the United States was a "remarkable spectacle." In *Democracy in America* Tocqueville wrote, "Tangible objects and ideas circulate throughout the Union. . . . Nothing checks the spirit of enterprise. The government invites the aid of all who have talents or knowledge to serve it. Inside of the frontiers of the Union profound peace prevails, as within the heart of some great empire; abroad it ranks with the most powerful nations of the earth; two thousand miles of coast are open to the commerce of the world; and as it holds the keys of a new world its flag is respected in the most remote seas. The union is happy and free as a small people, and glorious and strong as a great nation."

11

Expansion and Slavery

Tyler is a political sectarian of the slave-driving, Virginian, Jeffersonian school . . . with talents not above mediocrity and a spirit incapable of expansion," wrote John Quincy Adams in his diary. Like most of Adams' judgments of his contemporaries this was harsh, but it was essentially correct. The new President (his foes called him "His Accidency") was a thin, rather delicate-appearing man with pale-blue eyes and a long nose. Courteous, tactful, soft-spoken, he gave the impression of being weak, an impression reinforced by his professed belief that the President should defer to Congress in the formulation of policy. This was a false impression. John Tyler was stubborn and proud, and these characteristics combined with an almost total lack of imagination to make him worship consistency, as so many second-rate men do. He had turned away from Jackson because of the aggressive way the President had used his powers of appointment and the veto, but he also disagreed with Clay and the northern Whigs about the Bank, protection, and federal internal improvements. Being a typical states'-rights southerner, he considered such measures unconstitutional. Nevertheless, he genuinely admired Clay and hoped to cooperate with him as leader of what he called the "more immediate representatives" of the people, the members of Congress. He asked all of Harrison's Cabinet to remain in office.

The Tyler Administration

Tyler and Clay did not get along, however, and for this Clay was chiefly to blame. He behaved in an arrogant and overbearing manner totally out of keeping with his nature, the best explanation being his resentment at having been passed over by the Whigs in 1840. (When news of Harrison's nomination reached him in Washington he was half drunk. His face darkened and he burst out wrathfully: "I am the most unfortunate man in the history of parties: always run . . . when sure to be defeated, and now betrayed for a nomination when I, or anyone, would be sure of an election." His so-called friends were not worth the powder and shot it would take to kill them, he snarled.) He considered himself the real head of the Whig party and intended to exercise his leadership directly. Harrison had been willing to allow Clay the initiative in policy matters, but Clay was so arbitrary that within a few days after the inauguration the two were at odds. When Harrison died, Clay tried to sweep Tyler out of the way almost contemptuously.

In Congress Clay announced a comprehensive "program" which paid no heed whatsoever to Tyler's states'-rights view of the Constitution. Most important was his plan to set up a new Bank of the United States. A bill to repeal the Independent Treasury Act caused no difficulty, but when Congress passed a new Bank bill, Tyler vetoed it. He would go along with what he called a "Fiscal Bank" in Washington, he said, but not with an institution that could set up branches in the states without their consent. Clay would not settle for this. "Tyler dares not resist," he said. "I will drive him before me." But Tyler dug in his heels, vetoed still a second Bank bill, and the measure died. The entire Cabinet except Secretary of State Webster thereupon resigned in protest. Clay's attitude was so foolish as to appear almost psychopathic in a man of his political experience. At no time could he have hoped to obtain the two-thirds majority needed to overturn Tyler's vetoes, yet he rushed ahead nonetheless to certain defeat.

CHICAGO HISTORICAL SOCIETY

John Tyler posed for a daguerreotypist about 1850, after he had retired from public life. Tyler voted in favor of Virginia's secession ordinance in 1861.

Cast out by the Whigs, Tyler attempted to build a party of his own, and for the remainder of his term the political squabbling in Washington was continuous. Little could be accomplished in Congress, for sectional rivalries added to the confusion. Clay wanted to distribute the proceeds from land sales to the states, presumably to bolster their sagging finances but really to reduce federal revenues in order to justify raising the tariff. To win western votes for distribution, he agreed to support a pre-emption bill legalizing the right of squatters to occupy unsurveyed land and to buy it later at $1.25 an acre without bidding for it at auction. The Pre-emption Act of 1841 put this compromise into effect. However, the southerners insisted upon an amendment pledging that distribution would be stopped if the tariff were raised above the 20 per cent level, and when the Whigs blithely tried to ignore this proviso by pushing a high tariff through Congress without repealing the Distribution Act, Tyler vetoed the bill. Finally, the Distribution Act was repealed and Tyler signed the new Tariff Act of 1842, raising duties to about the levels of 1832. All the debate and maneuvering amounted to little, for the next administration reversed the tariff and banking policies of the Tyler period.

Webster's decision to remain in the Cabinet was partly motivated by his desire to complete certain important negotiations with Great Britain, for an opportunity had arisen to solve several petty but vexing disputes that had been plaguing relations between the two nations. In 1837, during the course of a minor uprising in Canada, some of the rebels took possession of Navy Island, a small vantage point in the Niagara River, whence they hoped to launch an assault on the Canadian mainland. Although Navy Island was Canadian property, the United States became involved. A number of Americans, eager to embarrass the British, were providing the rebels with supplies, which they ferried from the New York shore to Navy Island on the American-owned steamer *Caroline*. One night late in December a party of Canadian militia crossed the Niagara, overpowered the crew of the *Caroline*, cut her loose from her moorings, and set her afire. An American named Amos Durfee was killed in the scuffle. American public opinion was outraged and President Van Buren demanded reparations, but Great Britain refused to assume responsibility.

The issue was hardly worth a war, however, and the tension gradually relaxed, despite a number of further incidents. Then, in 1840, Alexander McLeod, a Canadian deputy sheriff, boasted in an American tavern while in his cups that he had participated in the *Caroline* raid and had personally dispatched Durfee. He was promptly charged with murder and clapped into jail. Now the British protested angrily. McLeod, they insisted, had been acting under military orders. Federal authorities countered by pointing out that they had no jurisdiction since McLeod was charged with violating New York law. Because the incident proved that the attack on the *Caroline* had been officially sponsored, it further exacerbated feelings along the border. If McLeod were actually convicted of murder and executed, a serious international crisis might result.

The still-unsettled boundary between Maine and New Brunswick provided another source of trouble. The intent of the peace treaty of 1783 had been to award the United States all land in the area drained by rivers flowing into the Atlantic rather than the St. Lawrence, but the wording was obscure and the old maps conflicting. In 1827 the king of the Netherlands had agreed to adjudicate the dispute, but he was unable to come to a decision based on evidence. The treaty was "inexplicable and impracticable," he announced in 1831, suggesting a completely arbitrary division that the United States Senate was unwilling to accept. The issue became critical in 1838 when Canadians began cutting timber in the Aroostook Valley, which was claimed by the United States. When Maine sent an agent to remonstrate with the lumberjacks, he was arrested. Maine and New Brunswick each called up militia and the Aroostook "War" followed. Luckily no one was killed, but the danger of a real war was great. Congress appropriated $10 million and authorized the calling of 50,000 men to the colors. Acting with admirable restraint, Van Buren sent General Winfield Scott to the area, and Scott managed to arrange a truce. Both sides agreed to resume diplomatic negotiations, but up to the time that Webster took over the State Department, nothing had been accomplished.

Slavery also caused Anglo-American friction. The British outlawed the slave trade in 1807 and in 1834 abolished slavery throughout the empire. Although the United States also forbade the trade, even providing the death penalty for violators, the American law was only indifferently enforced. Furthermore, American intransigence made it very difficult for the British navy to stifle the slave trade. Suspected slavers often ran up the Stars and Stripes when approached by patrolling British cruisers in order to avoid being searched, for the United States, still touchy because of British aggressiveness before 1812, refused to permit visit and search of American vessels even under such circumstances. This chronic cause of ill feeling was aggravated late in 1841 when the American brig *Creole*, out of Hampton Roads, Virginia, put in at Nassau in the British West Indies. The *Creole* had been en route to New Orleans with a cargo of slaves (a perfectly legal voyage) when the slaves had somehow broken loose. They seized the ship and put into Nassau to claim asylum. The British promptly arrested the ringleaders, charging them with mutiny and murder, but the bulk of the Negroes were given their freedom, despite protests from the State Department.

Webster-Ashburton Treaty

These matters, no one of grave importance, had collectively a most harmful impact on the relations between the two countries, which was made still worse by the fact that the British foreign secretary, Lord Palmerston, was aggressively anti-American. Fortunately, a change in the British government in

1841 brought Lord Aberdeen to the Foreign Office, and he, in the spring of 1842, sent a new minister, Lord Ashburton, to the United States to try to settle all outstanding disputes. Ashburton, head of a great London banking house which had large investments in the United States, made an ideal ambassador. Webster also was fitted for the task at hand, for he liked Lord Ashburton personally and believed in a policy of friendliness toward Great Britain. For example, he arranged to have the attorney general of the United States defend McLeod when the Canadian came to trial in New York. The acquittal of McLeod (it quickly came out that his story was nothing but drunken talk) removed one cause of tension even before Ashburton's arrival.

Working in a friendly and informal atmosphere, Webster and Ashburton found it easy to arrive at a compromise boundary. The British cared relatively little about the Aroostook Valley timber but needed part of the territory to the north to build a military road connecting Halifax and Quebec. Webster, who thought any settlement desirable simply to eliminate a possible cause of war, willingly accommodated Ashburton on this point. The problem of placating Maine and Massachusetts, which claimed title to the land in dispute and wanted every acre of it, Webster solved in an extraordinary manner. It was known that during the peace negotiations ending the Revolution, Franklin had marked the boundary between Maine and Canada on a map with a heavy red line, but no one could locate the Franklin map. Webster therefore obtained an old map of the area and had someone mark off a line in red that followed the British version of the boundary. He showed this document to representatives of Maine and Massachusetts, thus convincing them that they had better agree to his compromise before the British got wind of it and demanded the whole region! Actually, as it later came out, the British had a true copy of the Franklin map, which showed that the whole area rightfully belonged to the United States.

Nevertheless, Webster's generosity made excellent sense. Lord Ashburton, gratified by having obtained the strategic territory he needed, made counterconcessions elsewhere along the Canadian-American border that proved far more valuable than the 5,000 square miles Webster gave up in northern Maine (map, page 386). Through a foolish error, the United States had built a million-dollar fort at the northern end of Lake Champlain on what turned out to be Canadian soil. Ashburton agreed to cede this strip of land along the New York and Vermont border to the United States. He also yielded 6,500 square miles of wild land between Lake Superior and the Lake of the Woods which later proved to contain one of the richest deposits of iron ore in the world. Webster and Ashburton also arranged for the mutual extradition of Canadian and American criminals, and they agreed to maintain separate but cooperating naval squadrons off the African coast to aid in the suppression of the slave trade. Their treaty said nothing officially about the *Caroline*, but Ashburton apologized informally and the incident was written off.

The Senate ratified this Webster-Ashburton Treaty by a vote of 39 to 9 in August 1842. Its importance, more symbolic than practical, was nonetheless great. British dependence on foreign foodstuffs was increasing. America's need for British capital was also on the upgrade. War, or even unsettled relations, would have injured vital business relations and produced no compensating gains. Although no "Era of Good Feelings" between the two nations had yet arrived, the sensible spirit of mutual concession that characterized the Webster-Ashburton negotiations was most encouraging.

The Texas Question

This settlement with Great Britain won support in every section of the United States, but the same could not be said for the other major diplomatic action of Tyler's administration, an attempt to annex the Republic of Texas, for this involved the question of slavery. In the Transcontinental Treaty of 1819 with Spain the boundary of the United States had been drawn in such a way as to exclude Texas. This seemed unimportant at the time, yet within months of the final ratification of the treaty in February 1821, Americans led by Stephen F. Austin had begun to settle in the area, by then part of an

A painting done in 1885 after a study of available sources is probably the most accurate view of the final storming of the Alamo. Mexican troops poured through two breaches pounded in the walls by their artillery; others used scaling ladders to gain the interior of the fort. The Texans made their last stand in the mission at right.

independent Mexico. Cotton flourished on the broad, fertile Texas plains, and the Mexican authorities offered free land to groups of settlers. Soon American farmers were swarming into Texas; by 1830 there were some 20,000 of them, together with about 2,000 slaves. Texas became part of a state in the Republic of Mexico.

John Quincy Adams had offered Mexico $1 million for Texas, and Jackson was willing to pay $5 million, but Mexico would not sell. Nevertheless, as the flood of American settlers continued, the Mexican authorities became alarmed. Since the Texans felt no loyalty to Mexico, they were impossible to assimilate. Most were Protestants, although Mexican law required that all immigrants be Catholics. Few attempted to learn more than a few words of Spanish. When Mexico outlawed slavery, the Texans evaded the law by "freeing" their slaves and then signing them to lifetime contracts as indentured servants. For these reasons Mexico prohibited further immigration of Americans into Texas in 1830, although again the law proved impossible to enforce.

As soon as the Mexican government began to restrict them, the Texans began to seek independence. When their demands for what amounted to local autonomy were rebuffed, they resorted to force. In 1835 a series of armed skirmishes quickly escalated into a full-scale rebellion, the Texans receiving much military and financial aid from American "volunteers." The Mexican president, Antonio López de Santa Anna, marched north with some 6,000 men to subdue the rebels. Late in February 1836 he reached San Antonio, where a tiny force of 187 men under Colonel William B. Travis held the city. Unwilling to surrender, the Texans took refuge behind the stout walls of a former mission called the Alamo. For ten days they beat off Santa Anna's assaults, inflicting terrible casualties on the attackers, but finally, on March 6, the relentless Mexicans carried the walls. Inside they killed everyone, even the wounded, then soaked the corpses in oil and burned them. Among the dead were the legendary Davy Crockett and Jim Bowie, inventor of the Bowie knife. After the Alamo and the slaughter of another garrison at Goliad, southeast of San Antonio, the peaceful settlement of the dispute between Texas and Mexico was impossible.

On March 2, 1836, while the Alamo defenders were still holding out, the rebellious Texans formally declared their independence. Sam Houston, a former congressman and governor of Tennessee and an experienced Indian fighter, was placed in charge of the rebel army. For a time Houston retreated before Santa Anna, but at the San Jacinto River he took a stand. On April 21, 1836, shouting "Remember the Alamo!" his men attacked and routed the Mexican army. All the Mexicans were soon driven from Texas soil, and in October Houston was elected president of the Republic of Texas. Scarcely a month later a plebiscite revealed that an overwhelming majority favored annexation by the United States.

President Jackson hesitated. To take Texas might mean war with Mexico, and it would certainly stir up the sectional controversy over slavery. On his last day in office he recognized the republic, but he made no move to accept it into the Union, nor did Van Buren. Texas thereupon went its own way, developing friendly ties with Great Britain. An independent Texas suited British tastes perfectly, for it could provide an alternative supply of cotton and also a market for manufactures unfettered by tariffs.

These events naturally caused alarm in the United States, especially among southerners, who had hoped to obtain the region for their own expansion and who dreaded the possibility that a Texas dominated by Great Britain might abolish slavery. As a southerner, Tyler shared these feelings, and as a beleaguered politician, spurned by the Whigs and held in contempt by most Democrats too, he saw in the Texas question a chance to revive his fortunes. Webster cleared the way by resigning as secretary of state in the spring of 1843, whereupon Tyler replaced him with a fellow Virginian, Abel P. Upshur, whom he ordered to press for a treaty of annexation. The South, of course, was strong for taking Texas, and in the West and even the Northeast the patriotic urge to add such a magnificent new territory to the national domain was great. Counting noses, Upshur convinced himself that the Senate would approve annexation by the necessary two-thirds majority. He negotiated a treaty with the Texas chargé, Isaac Van Zandt, in February 1844, but before Upshur had signed it he was killed by the explosion of a cannon on the battleship *Princeton* during a weapons demonstration.

Tyler wanted a strong man to insure the winning of Texas, so he appointed John C. Calhoun as the new secretary of state. This was a major blunder, for although Calhoun's own motives were almost certainly unselfish and broadly patriotic, he was so closely associated with the South and with slavery that his appointment alienated thousands of northerners who might otherwise have welcomed annexation. Suddenly, Texas became a hot political issue. Clay and Van Buren, who seemed assured of the 1844 Whig and Democratic Presidential nominations, promptly announced that they opposed annexation, chiefly on the ground that it would probably lead to war with Mexico. With a national election in the offing, northern and western senators refused to vote for annexation, and in June they rejected the treaty, 35 to 16. The Texans were angry and embarrassed, the British eager again to take advantage of the situation. America seemed to have missed a great opportunity.

Manifest Destiny

As it turned out, the Senate, Clay, and Van Buren had all misinterpreted public opinion. John C. Calhoun, whose world was so far removed from that of the average man, in this case came much closer to comprehending the mood of the country than any of its other leaders.

For two centuries Americans had been gradually conquering a continent. Although the first colonists had envisaged a domain extending from the Atlantic to the Pacific, they had not realized the immensities of the New World. By the time their descendants came to appreciate its size, they had been chastened by the experience of battling the Indians for possession of the land and then laboriously constructing upon it a civilized society. The Revolution and its aftermath of nationalism greatly stimulated American expansion, but before the riches of trans-Appalachia had even been inventoried, Jefferson had stunned

NEW-YORK HISTORICAL SOCIETY

his countrymen with Louisiana, an area so big that the mere thought of it left sober men giddy.

The westward march from the 17th century to the 1840's had seemed fraught with peril, the prize golden but to be won only through patient labor and fearful hardships. Wild animals and wild men, mighty forests and mighty foreign powers beset the path. John Adams, for example, wrote of "conquering" the West "from the trees and rocks and wild beasts." He found his heart "enflamed" by the possibilities of "that vast scene which is opening in the West," but to win it he believed the nation would have to "march *intrepidly* on."

However, quite rapidly (as historians measure time) the atmosphere changed. Each year of national growth increased the power and confidence of the people, and every forward step revealed a wider horizon. Now the West seemed a ripe apple, to be plucked almost casually. Where men had once stood in awe before the majesty of the Blue Ridge, then hesitated to venture from the protective shadows of the forest into the open prairies of Illinois, they now shrugged their shoulders at great deserts and began to talk of the Rocky Mountains as "mere molehills" along the road to the Pacific. After 200 years of westward expansion had brought them as far as Missouri and Iowa, Americans now suddenly perceived their destined goal. *The whole continent was to be theirs!* Theirs to exploit, but also theirs to make into one mighty nation, a refuge for the oppressed, a showcase to display the virtues of democratic institutions, living proof that Americans were indeed God's chosen people. A Democratic journalist named John L. O'Sullivan soon captured the new mood in a sentence. Nothing must interfere, he wrote in 1845, with "the fulfilment of our *manifest destiny* to overspread the continent allotted by

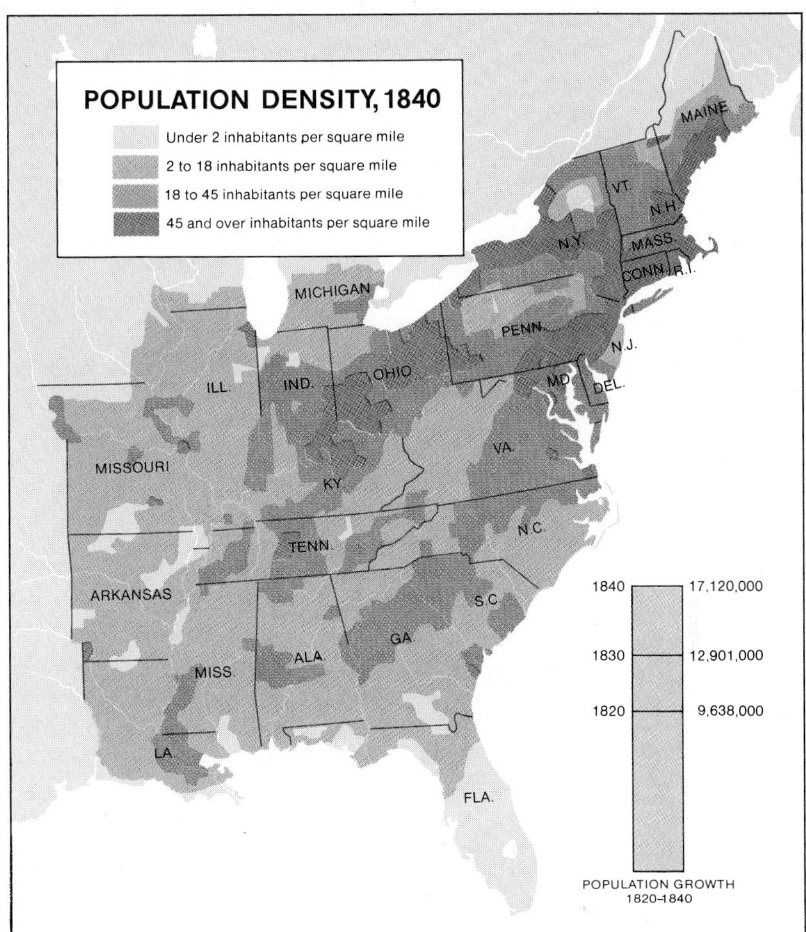

Left: In an 1844 cartoon a slave awaits the outcome of the "Great Prize-Fight" matching the American eagle against Spanish and British contenders, with Texas and California the prize. The spirit of Washington encourages the Republic.

Right: The accelerating westward movement is evident in this map. Arkansas entered the Union in 1836, Michigan in 1837, Texas, Iowa, and Wisconsin in the 1840's. In the 1830's the population of the nation as a whole increased by nearly one-third.

Providence for the free development of our yearly multiplying millions."

The politicians did not sense this new mood in 1844; even Calhoun, who saw the acquisition of Texas as part of a broader program, was thinking of balancing sectional interests rather than of national expansion. But the fact was that the expansion, greatly stimulated by the natural growth of the population and by a revived flood of immigration, was going on in every section and with little regard for political boundaries. New settlers rolled westward in hordes. There were 30,000 people in Arkansas in 1830, nearly 100,000 in 1840. In the same decade the population of Missouri increased by over 200,000; in the next decade Iowa grew from 43,000 to 192,000, Wisconsin from 31,000 to 305,000. Between 1830 and 1835, 10,000 Americans entered "foreign" Texas, and this was but a trickle compared to what the early 1840's were to bring. By 1840 many Americans had also settled far to the west in California, which was unmistakably Mexican territory, and in the Oregon country, jointly claimed by the United States and Great Britain.

California and Oregon

California, a huge and sparsely settled land dominated by cattlemen and mission friars, was first approached by way of the sea. New England captains traded there for sea otter pelts in the late 18th century, and after the region became independent of Spain, a brisk trade in hides and tallow sprang up, the California ranchers taking various manufactured goods in exchange. By the 1830's a handful of Americans had established themselves permanently in California as middlemen, and some of these eventually became ranchers. Few in number but influential, their letters home gradually attracted American settlers, and from the start

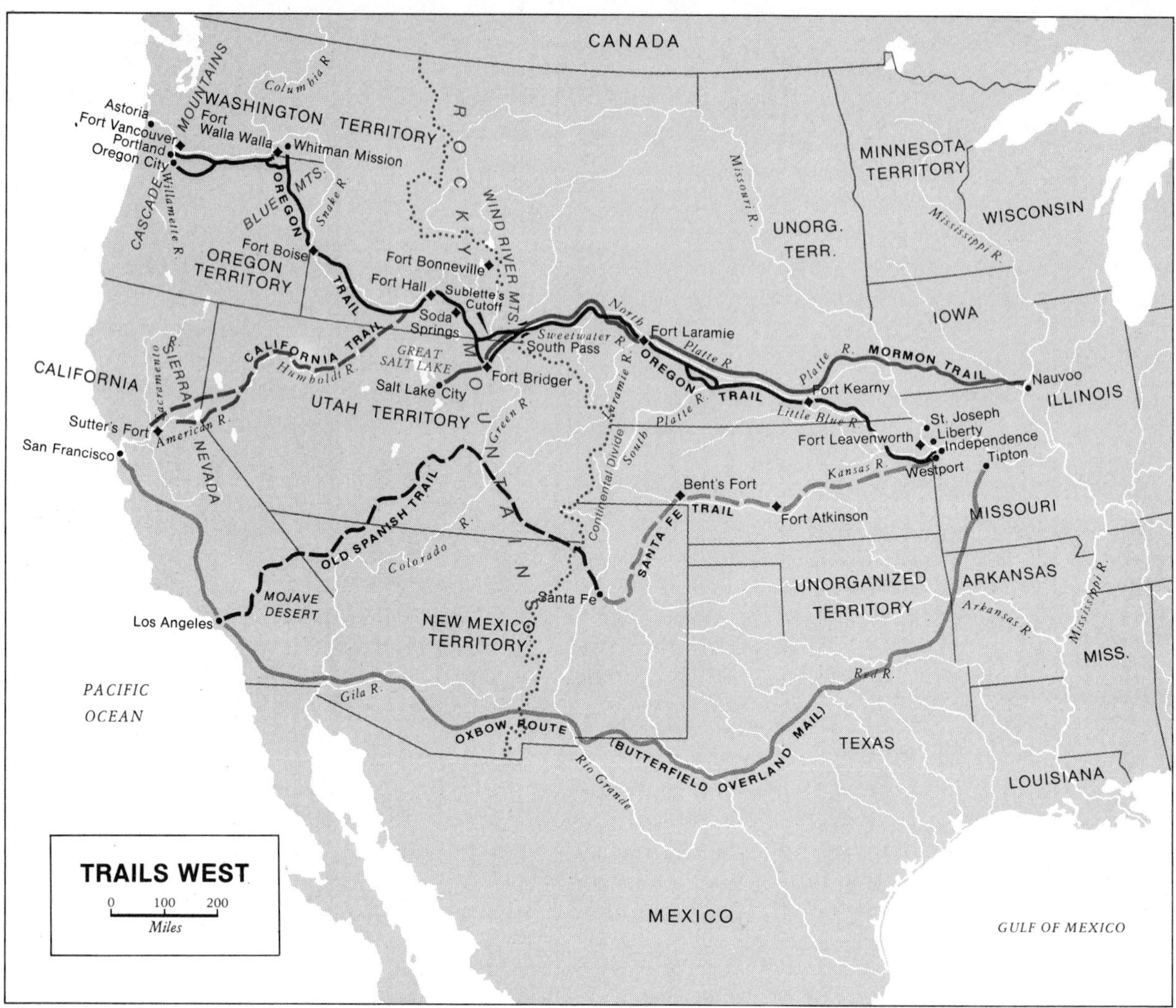

Of the major western trails, the Old Spanish Trail was the earliest; part of it was mapped in 1776 by Father Escalante, a Franciscan missionary. The Santa Fe Trail came into widespread use after 1823. The most famous route, the Oregon Trail, was pioneered by trappers and missionaries. The first party traversed the Mormon Trail in 1847, while the Oxbow Route, developed under a federal mail contract, was in use from 1858 to 1861.

there was hopeful talk of someday bringing California into the Union. Richard Henry Dana's popular *Two Years Before the Mast* (1840), with its graphic description of the hide and tallow trade, further stimulated immigration.

Oregon, a vaguely defined area between California and Russian Alaska, proved still more alluring to Americans. Captain Robert Gray had sailed up the Columbia River in 1792, and Lewis and Clark had visited the region on their great expedition. In 1811 John Jacob Astor's Pacific Fur Company had established trading posts on the Columbia. Some two decades later Methodist, Presbyterian, and Catholic missionaries began to find their way into the Willamette Valley, immediately to the south, and gradually a small number of settlers followed them. Enthusiastic reports appearing in religious periodicals and other sources drew additional pioneers, so that by 1840 there were about 500 Americans in the Willamette area.

In the early 1840's, fired by the spirit of manifest destiny, the country suddenly burned with "Oregon fever." In dozens upon dozens of towns, societies were founded to collect information about the Far West and organize groups to make the march to the Pacific. Land hunger (stimulated by the glowing reports of those on the scene) drew the new migrants most powerfully, but the patriotic, evangelical concept of manifest destiny gave the trek across the 2,000 miles of wilderness separating Oregon from the western edge of American settlement in Missouri the character of a crusade. In 1843 nearly a thousand pioneers made the long trip.

The Oregon Trail began at the western border of Missouri, immediately beyond Independence, and followed the Kansas River, its tributary, the Little Blue, and then the perverse, muddy Platte ("a mile wide and six inches deep") past Fort Laramie to the Rockies. It crossed the Continental Divide by the relatively easy South Pass, veered south briefly to Fort Bridger, on Mexican soil, and then ran north and west through the valley of the Snake River and eventually, by way of the Columbia, to Fort Vancouver, a British post guarding the entrance to the Willamette Valley.

Over this tortuous path wound the canvas-covered caravans with their scouts and their accompanying herds. Each group became a self-governing community on the march, with regulations democratically agreed upon "for the purpose of keeping good order and promoting civil and military discipline." For a party of a thousand-odd like the group of 1843, the Indians posed no great threat, although constant vigilance was necessary, but the five-month trip was full of labor, discomfort, and uncertainty. And at the end still lay the regular tasks of pioneering. The spirit of these trailblazers is caught in this entry from the diary of James Nesmith, who followed the Oregon Trail in 1843:

> Friday, October 27.—Arrived at Oregon City at the falls of the Williamette.
> Saturday, October 28.—Went to work.

News of the successful spanning of the continent by these migrants and the enthusiastic accounts that they were soon sending back further excited the public imagination.

Behind the dreams of the Far West as an American Eden lay the hard fact of the commercial importance of the three major West Coast harbors: San Diego, San Francisco, and the Strait of Juan de Fuca leading into Puget Sound. Eastern merchants considered these harbors the keys to the trade of the Orient. That San Diego and San Francisco were Mexican and the Puget Sound district was claimed by Great Britain did not lessen their desire to possess them. As early as 1835, for example, Jackson tried to buy the San Francisco region. In 1842 Secretary of State Webster also toyed with the idea of obtaining it, and two years later Calhoun called San Francisco the future "New York of the Pacific" and proposed buying all California from Mexico. There was less mass appeal in talk of harbors and foreign trade than in farms and cattle ranches, but prominent and farsighted men had the former clearly in mind, and they had considerable influence on policy-makers and legislators.

Election of 1844

In the spring of 1844, however, expansion did not seem likely to affect the Presidential election. The Whigs nominated Clay unanimously and made no statement about Texas in their party platform. When the Democrats gathered in convention at Baltimore in late May, Van Buren appeared to have the nomination in his pocket, and he, too, wanted to keep Texas out of the campaign. That a politician of Van Buren's caliber, controlling the party machinery, could be upset in a national convention seemed unthinkable. But upset he was. The southern Democrats had never liked him much, and now they rallied round the Calhoun policy of taking Texas to save it for slavery. "I can beat Clay and Van Buren put together on this issue," Calhoun boasted. "They are behind the age." With the aid of a few northern expansionists the southerners forced through a rule requiring that the choice be by a two-thirds majority. This Van Buren did not have, and since he would not modify his anti-Texas position, he could not get it. After a brief deadlock, a "dark horse," James K. Polk of Tennessee, swept the convention.

Polk was a good Democrat by the standards of the Jackson-Van Buren era. He opposed high tariffs and was dead set against establishing another national bank. But he also believed in taking Texas and in expansion generally. To mollify the Van Burenites, the convention nominated Senator Silas Wright of New York for Vice President, but Wright was Van Buren's loyal friend and equally opposed to annexation. When the word was flashed to him in Washington over the new "magnetic telegraph" which Samuel F.B. Morse had just installed between the convention hall in Baltimore and the Capitol, he refused to run. The delegates then picked George M. Dallas of Pennsylvania for the second place on the ticket. The Democratic platform came out solidly for expansion, demanding that Texas be "reannexed" (implying that it had been part of the Louisiana Purchase) and that all of Oregon be "reoccupied" (suggesting that the joint occupation with Great Britain agreed to in the Convention of 1818 be abrogated).

Texas was now in the campaign. The friends of Tyler, also convening in Baltimore, had nominated the President on a "Tyler and Texas" ticket, which threatened to split the expansionist vote; but old Andrew Jackson, who had nothing but contempt for "Tiler," was persuaded to write a letter professing "real regard" for him and praising his "good sense and patriotism." This, together with a little flattery from Polk, convinced Tyler that he should withdraw.

When Clay sensed the new expansionist sentiment of the voters, he tried to hedge on his opposition to annexation, but he probably lost as many votes as he gained by this surrender of principle to expediency, especially among the antislavery element in the northern states. Even so, the election was extremely close. The campaign followed the pattern established in 1840, with much stress on parades, mass meetings, and slogans. Polk was dubbed "Young Hickory" to capitalize on his close friendship with Jackson, and the nation was deluged with hickory "polkers" and a succession of terrible puns about "polking" Whigs. The Whigs retorted by asking derisively, "Who is James K. Polk?" in an attempt to create the impression that the Democratic candidate was an unknown mediocrity, although he had been Speaker of the House of Representatives, governor of Tennessee, and an active candidate for Vice President before the political lightning struck him at Baltimore.

In November Polk carried the country by only 38,000 out of 2.7 million votes. In the Electoral College his margin was 170 to 105. The decisive factor in the contest was the Liberty party, an antislavery splinter group first organized in 1840. Only 62,000 voters supported candidate James G. Birney, a "reformed" Kentucky slaveholder, but nearly 16,000 of them lived in New York, most of these in the western part of the state, a Whig stronghold. Since Polk carried New York by barely 5,000, these votes for Birney probably cost Clay the state. Had he taken New York's 36 electoral votes, he would have been elected, 141 to 134.

Nevertheless, Polk's victory was taken as a mandate for national expansion, since he had indicated plainly his wish to obtain both Texas and Oregon. Seizing upon the election returns for justification, Tyler called upon Congress to take Texas by joint resolution, which would avoid the necessity of obtaining a two-thirds majority in the Senate. This was done a few days before Tyler left the White House. Under the resolution Texas retained title to all the public lands within its boundaries but accepted full responsibility for debts incurred while an independent republic. As many as four new states might be carved from its territory but only with its approval. Polk accepted this arrangement, and in December 1845 Texas became a state.

Polk as President

When he took office, President Polk, a slightly built, erect, handsome man with large, grave, steel-gray eyes, was approaching 50. His mind was not of the first order, for he lacked imagination and was too tense and calculating to allow his intellect free rein. But he was an efficient, hard worker with a strong will and a tough skin, qualities which stood him in good stead in the White House. Polk was an intense partisan who made politics his whole life. Whigs he distrusted and thought incompetent "merely because they were Whigs," as one student of his administration has said. It was typical of the man that he made a careful study of handshaking in order better to cope with the interminable reception lines that every leader has to endure. "When I observed a strong man approaching," he once explained, "I generally took advantage of him by being a little quicker than he was and seizing him by the tip of his fingers, giving him a hearty shake, and thus preventing him from getting a full grip upon me." In four years in office he was away from his desk in Washington for a total of only six weeks.

Polk was uncommonly successful as President. At the beginning of his term he announced that he would not seek re-election (which ought to have handicapped him in carrying out his program but did not). His objectives were anything but timid or limited, yet he accomplished them all. He was determined to lower the Whig-inspired tariff of 1842 and to restore the Independent Treasury, and both these goals he achieved. He opposed federal internal improvements and managed to have his way. He made himself the spokesman of American expansion by committing himself to obtaining, in addition to Texas, both Oregon and the great Southwest. Here again, he succeeded.

Oregon was the first order of business. In his inaugural Polk stated the American claim to the entire region in the plainest terms, but from the American point of view the remote northern half of the Oregon country had little value, and after allowing the British time to digest his demand for everything, he informed the British minister in Washington, Richard Pakenham, that he would accept a boundary following the 49th parallel to the Pacific. However, Pakenham rejected this proposal without even submitting it to London, and Polk thereupon decided to insist again upon the whole area. When Congress met in December 1845, he asked for authority to give the necessary one year's notice for abrogating the 1818 treaty of joint occupation. "The only way to treat John

A cartoonist's view of the new administration: encouraged by Jackson behind him, Polk looks on benignly as expansionists threaten Oregon, and Calhoun rides out of the Cabinet. Spoilsmen and reformers beset the President.

Bull," he told one congressman, "was to look him straight in the eye." Following considerable discussion, Congress complied. It was, Representative Robert Winthrop of Massachusetts proclaimed in the debate, "our manifest destiny to spread over this whole continent." In May 1846 Polk notified Great Britain that he intended to terminate the joint occupation.

The British were now eager to compromise. Officials of the Hudson's Bay Company had become alarmed by the rapid growth of the American settlement in the Willamette Valley. By 1845 there were some 5,000 people there, whereas the country north of the Columbia contained no more than 750 British subjects. A clash between these groups could have but one result; the company decided to shift its base from the Columbia to Vancouver Island. British experts outside the company also reported that the Oregon country could not possibly be defended in case of war. Lord Aberdeen, the foreign secretary, had all along been willing to accept the 49th parallel. When he learned that Pakenham had rejected Polk's compromise offer, he rebuked him for not notifying the government. Thus, when Polk accompanied the one-year notice with a hint that he would again consider a compromise, Aberdeen hastened to suggest dividing the Oregon territory along the 49th parallel. Polk, abandoning his belligerent attitude, agreed. The treaty, ratified in June 1846, followed that line from the Rockies to Puget Sound, but Vancouver Island, which extended below the line, was left entirely to the British (map, page 386). Thus both nations retained free use of the Strait of Juan de Fuca. The British were also guaranteed the right to navigate the Columbia River. Although some expansionists accused Polk of treachery because he had failed to fight for the 54° 40′ boundary, the treaty so obviously accorded with the national interest that the Senate approved it by a large majority.

War with Mexico

One reason for the popularity of the Oregon compromise was that the country was already at war with Mexico and wanted no trouble with Great Britain. Although the expansionist spirit of the United States and the confidence born of its overwhelming advantages of size and wealth certainly encouraged the nation to bully Mexico, this war had broken out in large measure because of Mexico's stubborn pride. Texas had existed as a republic for the better part of a decade without Mexico making any serious effort to reconquer it; nevertheless, the Mexicans promptly broke off diplomatic relations with the United States when Congress voted for annexation. "Victory will perch upon our banners," a leading Mexican newspaper proclaimed belligerently.

Polk, who did not want to fight if he could obtain what he wanted by negotiation, ordered General Zachary Taylor into Texas only to protect the border. However, the location of that border was in dispute. Texas claimed the Rio Grande, while Mexico insisted that the boundary was the smaller Nueces River, which emptied into the Gulf about 150 miles to the north. Taylor reached the Nueces in July 1845 with about 1,500 men and crossed into the disputed territory, but he stopped on the southern bank at Corpus Christi, not wishing to provoke the Mexicans by marching to the Rio Grande.

In November Polk sent an envoy, John Slidell, on a secret mission to Mexico to try to obtain the disputed territory by negotiation. Mexico was in default on some $2 million owed American citizens for losses suffered during past political upheavals in the country. Polk authorized Slidell to cancel this debt in return for recognition of the annexation of Texas and acceptance of the Rio Grande boundary. The President also empowered him to offer as much as $30 million if Mexico would sell the United States all or part of New Mexico and California.

It would have been to Mexico's long-range advantage to have made a deal with Slidell. The country could well have used the money, and the area Polk wanted, lying in the path of American expansion, was likely to be engulfed as Texas had been, without regard for the actions of the American or Mexican governments. Unfortunately, the Mexicans were in no mood to dicker. No one enjoys negotiating with a gun pointed at his head, but in this case the Mexican government did not even dare to receive Slidell. The poverty-stricken Mexican people had little

In this 1846 daguerreotype, the earliest American war photograph, U.S. General John E. Wool poses with his staff in Saltillo, Mexico.

love for the undemocratic regime of President José Herrera. They did love their country, however, and their despair over local conditions exaggerated their patriotism. The mere news that Slidell was in Mexico City hastened the overthrow of Herrera, and the new president, General Mariano Paredes, refusing even to discuss the problem with Slidell, promptly reaffirmed his country's claim to *all* Texas. In March 1846 Slidell returned to Washington convinced that the Mexicans would not negotiate until they had been, as he put it, "chastised."

Taylor then advanced to the Rio Grande. By March 28 his army, swelled to about 4,000 men, was drawn up on the north bank of the river, across from the Mexican town of Matamoros. Polk had already decided to fight; when a Mexican force crossed the river and attacked an American mounted patrol, he had an ideal pretext. His message to Congress treated the matter as a *fait accompli*: "War exists," he stated flatly. On May 13 Congress declared war and authorized the raising and supplying of 50,000 troops.

The outcome of the Mexican War was never in doubt from the moment of the first battles. At Palo Alto, north of the Rio Grande, 2,300 Americans scattered a Mexican force more than twice their number. Then, hotly pursuing, 1,700 Americans routed 7,500 Mexicans at Resaca de la Palma. Fewer than 50 United States soldiers lost their lives in these engagements, while Mexican losses in killed, wounded, and captured exceeded 1,000. Within a week of the declaration of war the Mexicans had been driven across the Rio Grande and General Taylor had his troops firmly established on the southern bank.

The Mexican army was poorly equipped and, despite a surfeit of high-ranking officers, poorly led. The well-supplied American forces, on the other hand, had a hard core of youthful West Pointers eager to make their reputations, and regulars trained in Indian warfare to provide the leadership needed to turn volunteer soldiers into first-rate fighting men. Nevertheless, Mexico was a large, rugged country with few decent roads; conquering it was a formidable task.

Northern Mexico and California

President Polk insisted not only on directing grand strategy (he displayed real ability as a military planner), but on supervising hundreds of petty details, down to the purchase of mules and the promotion of enlisted men. He grumbled with much justice about "old

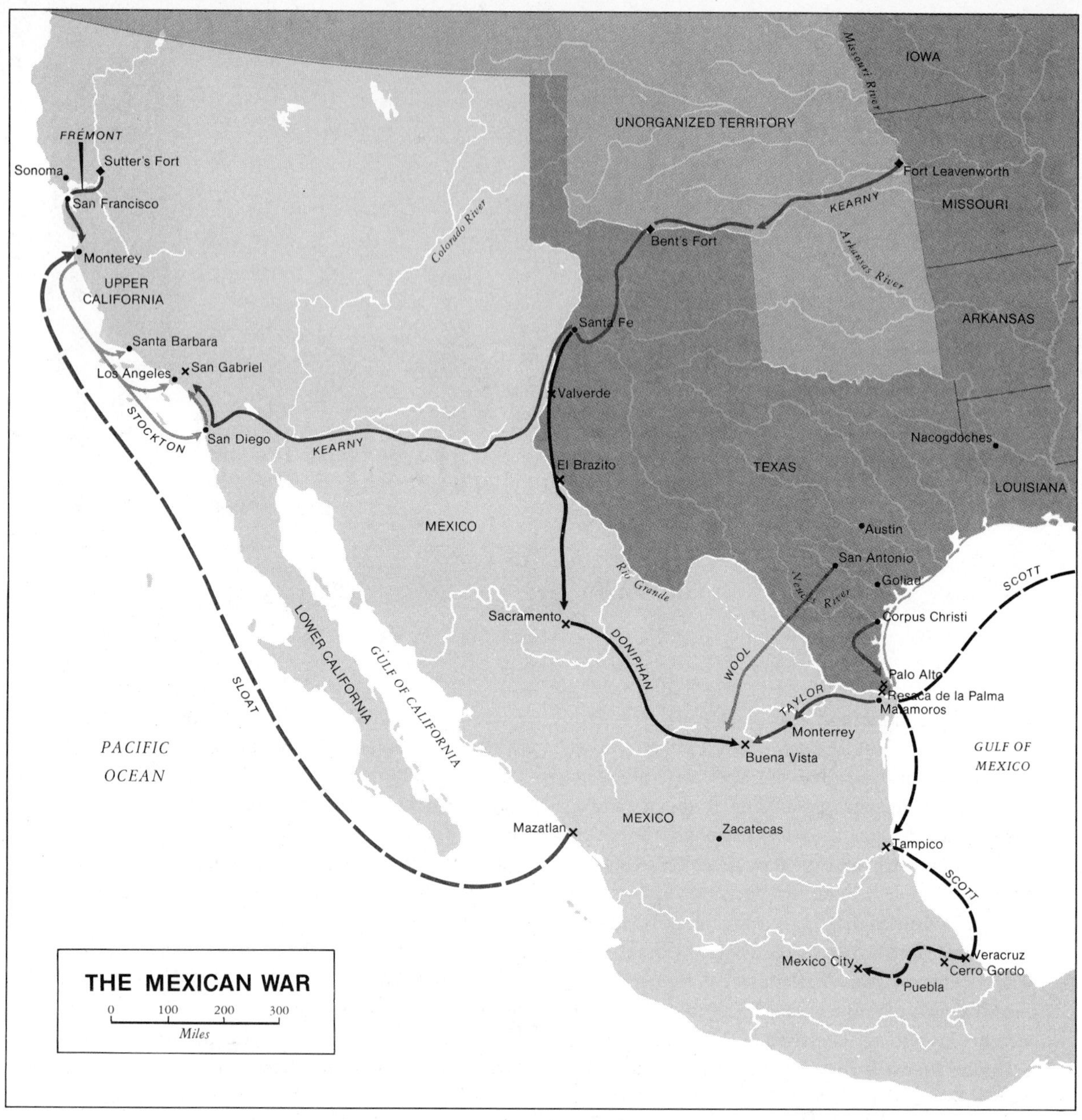

American naval power proved a decisive factor in the Mexican War. The Pacific Squadron, under John D. Sloat and Robert F. Stockton, secured California, and a 200-vessel fleet conveyed Winfield Scott's army to Veracruz.

army officers" content to "jog along in a regular routine" with little thought for winning the war, but his partisanship caused much unnecessary turmoil in army ranks. Try as he might, he could not find a good Democratic general. Both Taylor and Winfield Scott, the commanding general in Washington, were Whigs. Polk feared that one or the other of them would make political capital of his popularity as a military leader. The examples of his hero, Jackson, and of General Harrison loomed large in Polk's thinking. He wanted, as Thomas Hart Benton said, "a small war, just large enough to require a treaty of peace, and not large enough to make military reputations dangerous for the presidency."

Polk's attitude was narrow and almost unpatriotic, but not unrealistic. Zachary Taylor was not a brilliant soldier. Polk believed that he lacked the "grasp of mind" necessary for high command, and General Scott complained of his "comfortable, laborsaving contempt for learning of every kind." But Taylor commanded the love and respect of his men (they called him "Old Rough and Ready" and even "Zack"), and he knew how to deploy them in the field. He had joined the army in 1808 and made it his whole life; he cared so little for politics that he had never even bothered to cast a ballot in an election. Yet the dust had barely settled on the field of Resaca de la Palma when Whig politicians began to pay him court. "Great expectations and great consequences rest upon you," a Kentucky politician explained to him. "People everywhere begin to talk of converting you into a political leader, when the War is done." Polk's concern was also heightened because the Whigs were making the war itself a political issue. The farther from the Rio Grande one went in the United States, the less popular "Mr. Polk's War" became, until in New England opposition was almost as widespread as it had been to "Mr. Madison's War" in 1812.

Polk's design for prosecuting the war consisted of three parts. First, he would clear the Mexicans from Texas and occupy the northern provinces of Mexico. Second, he would take possession of California and New Mexico. Finally, he would march on Mexico City and force the enemy to make peace on American terms. Proceeding west from the Rio Grande, Taylor struck the Mexican fortified town of Monterrey and captured it after a hard, five-day battle in September 1846. The following February he defeated a Mexican army of 15,000 at Buena Vista, effectively ending the war in the northern provinces.

Meanwhile, the entire Southwest was falling into American hands. Four separate forces participated in the conquest. In June 1846 American settlers in the Sacramento Valley seized Sonoma and raised the "Bear Flag" of the Republic of California. Another group, headed by Captain John C. Frémont, leader of an American exploring party which happened to be in the area, clashed with the Mexican authorities around Monterey, California, and then joined with the Sonoma rebels. Most important was a United States naval squadron under Commodore John D. Sloat, which captured Monterey and San Francisco in July 1846 and then moved against the remaining Mexican troops in the southern part of California. The last force was commanded by General Stephen Watts Kearny, who had been ordered by Polk to proceed across the Rockies from his base at Fort Leavenworth to capture New Mexico and California. With 1,700 horsemen, many of them Missouri volunteers, Kearny followed the Arkansas River to Bent's Fort and thence marched over Raton Pass to Santa Fe. The Mexican population of Santa Fe had little will to resist, and when the local governor fled, the city fell without a shot on August 18, 1846. Sending part of his army south and leaving another part to hold Santa Fe, Kearny hurried on with a small contingent of dragoons to California, where he joined with the other American units in mopping-up operations around San Diego and Los Angeles. By February 1847 all organized resistance in the Southwest had been overcome. Thus, after less than nine months of war, the United States had won control of nearly all of Mexico north of the capital city.

On to Mexico City

The campaign against Mexico City was the most difficult of the war but also the best managed. Fearful of Taylor's growing popularity and entertaining certain honest misgivings about his ability to oversee a complicated campaign, Polk decided to put Winfield Scott in charge of this offensive. He tried to persuade Congress to make Thomas Hart Benton a lieutenant general so as to have a Democrat in nominal control, but the Senate displayed enough sense and patriotism to vote this absurd proposal down.

About Scott's competence no one entertained a doubt, but he seemed even more of a threat to the Democrats than Taylor, since he had political ambitions as well as military ability. In 1840 the Whigs had considered running him for President. Scion of an old Virginia family, Scott was a giant of a man, nearly six-and-a-half-feet tall; in uniform his presence was commanding. He was also intelligent, even-tempered, and cultivated, if somewhat punctilious and pompous, as his nickname, "Old Fuss and Feathers," indicated. After a sound but not spectacular record in the War of 1812, he had added greatly to his reputation by helping to modernize military administration and strengthen the professional training of officers. The vast difference between the army of 1812 and that of 1846 was chiefly his doing. On the record, and despite the politics of the situation, Polk really had no choice but to give him this command.

Scott managed the campaign masterfully from start to finish. He landed his army south of Veracruz, Mexico, on March 9, 1847, laid siege to the city, and obtained its surrender in less than three weeks with the loss of only a handful of his 10,000 men. Marching westward through enemy country, he maintained effective discipline, avoiding atrocities that might have inflamed the countryside against him. Finding his way blocked by well-placed artillery and a large army at Cerro Gordo, where the national road rose steeply toward the central highlands, Scott outflanked the Mexican position and then carried it by storm, taking more than 3,000 prisoners and much equipment. By mid-May he had advanced to Puebla, only 80 miles southeast of Mexico City. After delaying until August for the arrival of reinforcements, he pressed on rapidly, won two hard-fought victories at the outskirts of the capital, and on September 14 hammered his way into the city. In every engagement the American troops had been outnumbered, yet they were not once defeated and always exacted a far heavier toll from the defenders than they themselves were forced to pay. In the fighting on the edge of Mexico City, for example, Scott's army sustained about 1,000 casualties, for the Mexicans defended their capital bravely. But 4,000 Mexicans were killed or wounded in these engagements, and 3,000 (including eight generals, two of them former presidents of the republic) were taken prisoner.

The President of the Mexican Republic to the troops engaged in the Army of the United States of America.

The circumstances of war have brought you to the beautiful valley of Mexico; in the midst of a wealthy and fertile country. The American Governement engaged you to fight against a country from which you have received no harm; your companions have after the battle received and shall only receive the contempt of the United States and the scorn of the nations of civilized Europe that, quite surprized, see that that governement seek engagements for their battles in the same manner as they look for beasts to draw their carriages.

In the name of the Nation I represent, and whose authority I exercise, I offer you a reward, if deserting the American standard you present yourselves like friends to a nation that offer you rich fields and large tracts of land, which being cultivated by your industry, shall crown you with happiness and convenience.

The Mexican Nation ouly look upon you as some deceived foreigners and hereby stretch out to you a friendly hand, offer you the felicity and fertility of their territory. Here there is no distinction of races; here indeed there is liberty and not slavery; nature here plentifully sheds its favors and it is in your power to enjoy them. Rely upon what I offer you in the name of a nation; present yourselves like friends and you shall have country, home, lands; the happiness, which is enjoyed in a country of mild and humane customs; civilization, humanity and not fear address you through me.

General Quarters in the Peñon August the 15th 1847.

Antonio Lopez de Santa-Anna.

As Scott's army neared Mexico City in August 1847, Santa Anna's guerrilla forces distributed broadsides such as this one behind American lines, offering deserters the bait of "country, home, and lands."

The Treaty of Guadalupe Hidalgo

The Mexicans were now thoroughly beaten, but they refused to accept the situation. As soon as the news of the capture of Veracruz had reached Washington, Polk had sent Nicholas P. Trist, chief clerk of the State Department, to accompany Scott's army and act as peace commissioner after the fall of Mexico City. Trist, a competent although somewhat pompous man, possessed impeccable credentials as a Democrat, for he had married a granddaughter of Thomas Jefferson and had served for a time as secretary to Andrew Jackson. Long residence as United States consul at Havana had given him an excellent command of Spanish.

Traveling as a "Dr. Taurreau," Trist reached Veracruz in May and at once got in touch with Scott. The two men, each deeply concerned with his *amour propre*, took an instant dislike to each other. Scott considered it a "personal dishonor" to be asked to defer to what he considered a State Department flunky, and his feelings were not salved when Trist sent him an officious, 30-page letter discoursing upon the nature of his assignment. However, Scott was essentially a reasonable man and eager to end the war. He realized that a petty quarrel with the President's emissary would not advance that objective. Trist fell ill and Scott sent him a jar of guava marmalade, and after that gesture, they quickly became good friends.

Because of the confused state of affairs after the fall of Mexico City, Trist could not commence negotiations with Mexican peace commissioners until January 1848. In the meantime Polk, unable to understand the delay, had become impatient. Originally, he had authorized Trist to pay $30 million for New Mexico, Upper and Lower California, and the right of transit across Mexico's narrow Isthmus of Tehuantepec. Now, observing the disorganized state of Mexican affairs, he began to consider demanding more territory and paying less for it. He summoned Trist home. But Trist, with Scott's backing, decided to ignore the order, realizing that unless a treaty were arranged soon the Mexican government might disintegrate completely, leaving no one in authority to sign a treaty. When the opportunity finally came, he proceeded to negotiate, and early in February the Treaty of Guadalupe Hidalgo was completed. By its terms Mexico accepted the Rio Grande as the boundary of Texas and ceded New Mexico and Upper California to the United States. In return, the United States agreed to pay Mexico $15 million and take on the claims of American citizens against Mexico, which by that time amounted to another $3.25 million.

Trist sent this treaty off to Polk in the care of a New Orleans newspaperman. When he learned that Trist had ignored his orders, the President seethed with rage. Trist was "contemptibly base," he thought, an "impudent and unqualified scoundrel." He ordered him placed under arrest and fired him from his State Department job.* Yet he had no choice but to submit the treaty to the Senate, for to have insisted upon more territory would have meant more fighting, and the war had already become very unpopular in many sections. The Senate, subject to the same imperative, ratified the agreement by a vote of 38 to 14.

*Trist was retired to private life without even being paid for his time in Mexico. In 1870, when on his deathbed, Congress finally awarded him $14,299.20.

The Aftermath

The Mexican War, won quickly and at relatively small cost in men and money, brought huge territorial gains. The hopes of all but the most extravagant expansionists had been realized. The whole Pacific coast from south of San Diego to the 49th parallel and all the land between the coast and the Continental Divide had become the property of the American people. Moreover, Great Britain and even Mexico seemed prepared to accept the new dispensation in good temper. Immense amounts of labor and capital would have to be invested before this new territory could be made to yield its bounty, but the country clearly had the capacity to accomplish the job.

The main problem would be one of communication, and fortunately a new means for binding the continent together was at hand in the steam railroad. Already, when the war ended, the nation had some 8,000 miles of track in operation, and imaginative men were confidently planning to build a line across the mountains to California.

In this atmosphere came what seemed a sign from the heavens. In January 1848, while Scott's veterans rested upon their victorious arms in Mexico City, a mechanic named James W. Marshall was building a sawmill on the American River in the Sacramento Valley east of San Francisco. One day, while supervising the deepening of the millrace, he noticed a few flecks of yellow in the bed of the stream. These he gathered up and tested. They were pure gold.

Other strikes had been made in California and been treated skeptically or as matters of local curiosity; since the days of Jamestown, too many pioneers had run fruitlessly in search of El Dorado, too much fool's gold had been passed off as the real thing. Yet this discovery produced a national sensation. The gold, of course, was real and plentiful, but equally important was the fact that the nation was ready to believe the news as never before. The gold rush reflected the heady confidence inspired by Guadalupe Hidalgo; it seemed, indeed, the ultimate justification of manifest destiny. Surely an era of continental prosperity and harmony had dawned.

Slavery in the Territories

Prosperity came in full measure but not harmony, for once again expansion brought the nation face to face with the divisive question of slavery. This giant chunk of North America, most of it completely vacant, its future soon to be determined—should it be slave or free? The question, in one sense, seems hardly worth the national crisis it provoked. Slavery had little future in New Mexico, less in California, none in Oregon. Why did the South fight so hard for the *right* to bring Negroes into a region so unsuited to their exploitation? Why did southern congressmen vote against barring slavery in Oregon Territory, and why, for that matter, did their northern colleagues insist that it be formally barred there, when everyone, North and South, knew that forbidden, encouraged, or ignored, the institution would never gain a foothold in the area?

The answers to these questions are complicated and also tragic. Narrow partisanship is part of the explanation. In districts where slavery was entrenched, a congressman who watched over the institution with the eyes of Argus, ever ready to defend it against the most trivial slight, usually found himself a popular hero. In the northern states the representative who was vigilant in what he might describe as "freedom's cause" seldom regretted it on election day. For many this consideration outweighed the wider national interest or the real merits of each subject under discussion. Then, too, slavery raised a moral question. Most Americans tried to avoid confronting this truth. As patriots, they assumed that any sectional issue could be solved by compromise. However, not many persons, northern or southern, could look upon the ownership of one man by another simply as an alternative form of economic organization and argue its merits as they would those of the protective tariff or a national bank. Twist the facts as they might, slavery was either right or it was wrong; being on the whole honest and moral men they could not, having faced that truth, stand by unconcerned while the question was debated.

Slavery had complicated the Texas problem from the start, and it beclouded the future of the Southwest even before the Mexican flag had been stripped from the staffs at Santa Fe and Los Angeles. The northern, Van Burenite wing of the Democratic party had become increasingly uneasy about the proslavery cast of Polk's policies, which was injuring them in their home districts. Once the likelihood that the war would bring new territory into the Union became clear, they felt compelled to try to check the President and to assure their constituents that they would fight the admission of more slave territory. On August 8, 1846, during the debate on a bill appropriating money for the conduct of the war, one of the Van Burenites, Congressman David Wilmot of Pennsylvania, introduced an amendment which provided "as an express and fundamental condition to the acquisition of any territory from the Republic of Mexico" that "neither slavery nor involuntary servitude shall ever exist in any part of said territory, except for crime, whereof the party shall first be duly convicted." This Wilmot Proviso, as it was called, passed the House but met defeat in the Senate. It caused a good deal of angry discussion, but it did not hold up prosecution of the war, for the issue was not urgent. However, to counter this antislavery proposal, Calhoun, again senator from South Carolina, introduced a series of resolutions the following February which argued that Congress had no right to bar slavery from any territory; since territories belonged to all the states, slave and free, all should have equal rights in them. From this position it was only a step (soon taken) to demanding that Congress not only guarantee the right of slaveowners to bring Negroes into the territories but also establish slave codes in the territories to protect their property after arrival. Most northerners considered this idea as repulsive as southerners found the Wilmot Proviso.

Calhoun's resolutions could never pass the northern-dominated House of Representatives and Wilmot's Proviso had no chance in the Senate. Two possible compromises were offered. One, backed among others by President Polk, would extend the Missouri Compromise line to the Pacific. The majority of southerners were willing to go along with this scheme, although it would not have preserved the balance between free and slave states, but most northerners would no longer agree to the reservation of *any* new territory for slavery. The other possibility, early advocated by Senator Lewis Cass of Michigan, called for organizing new territories without mention of slavery, thus leaving it to the local settlers to determine their own institutions. Cass's "popular sovereignty," known more vulgarly as "squatter sovereignty," had the superficial merits of appearing to be democratic and of enabling the members of Congress to escape the responsibility of deciding the question themselves.

PRINTS DIVISION, NEW YORK PUBLIC LIBRARY

Southerners' efforts to halt the circulation of antislavery publications within their borders inspired this 1848 cartoon. Calhoun is depicted as Joshua commanding the sun, a printing press, to stand still.

Election of 1848

One test of strength occurred in August, before the 1848 Presidential election. After six months of acrimonious debate, Congress passed a bill barring slavery from Oregon. The test, however, proved little. Slavery obviously could not exist in that northwestern corner of the nation; if it required half a year to settle the question for Oregon, how could an answer ever be found for California and New Mexico? Plainly the time had come, in a democracy, to go to the people for the answer, and the coming Presidential election seemed to provide an ideal opportunity.

Alas, in this crisis the politicians failed to meet their responsibilities. Both parties hedged, fearful of losing votes in one section or another. With the issues blurred, the electorate had no real choice. That the Whigs should behave in such a manner was perhaps to be expected of the party of "Tippecanoe and Tyler too," but in 1848 they outdid even their performance in 1840, nominating Zachary Taylor for President. They chose the general despite his total lack of political sophistication and after he had flatly refused to state his opinion on any current subject. The party offered no platform. Taylor was a brave man and a fine general; the Democrats had mistreated him; he was a common, ordinary fellow, unpretentious and warm-hearted. Such was the Whig "argument." Taylor's contribution to the campaign was so naive as to be pathetic. "I am a Whig, *but not an ultra Whig*," he announced. "If elected . . . I should feel bound to administer the government untrammeled by party schemes."

The Democratic party, however, had little better to offer. All the drive and zeal characteristic of it in the Jackson period had gradually seeped away. Polk's espousal of Texas annexation had driven many of the best northerners from its ranks. Men like James Buchanan of Pennsylvania, Polk's secretary of state, and William L. Marcy of New York, his secretary of war—

THE HUNTINGTON LIBRARY

cautious, cynical politicians interested chiefly in getting and holding office—now came to the fore in northern Democratic politics. The Democratic nominee in 1848 was Lewis Cass, the father of popular sovereignty, but the party did not endorse that or any other solution to the territorial question. Cass was at least an experienced politician, having been governor of Michigan Territory, secretary of war, and minister to France, as well as senator. Nevertheless, he was vain, aloof, and conservative, his approach to life being well exemplified by an annoying habit he displayed at Washington social functions. Although a teetotaler, he would circulate among the guests with a glass in hand, raising it to his lips repeatedly but never taking a drop.

The Van Buren wing of the Democratic party, now known as the "Barnburners,"* would not stomach Cass, partly because he was willing to countenance the extension of slavery into new territories and partly because he had led the swing to Polk in the 1844 Democratic convention. Combining with the Liberty party men, they formed the Free-Soil party and nominated Van Buren. Of course Van Buren knew he could not be elected, but he believed the time had come to take a stand. "The minds of nearly all mankind have been penetrated by a conviction of the evils of slavery," the one-time "Fox" and "Magician" declared. This Free-Soil party polled nearly 300,000 votes, about ten per cent of the total, in a very dull campaign. Offered a choice between honest ignorance and cynical opportunism, the voters—by a narrow margin—chose the former, Taylor receiving 1.36 million votes to Cass's 1.22 million. Taylor carried 8 of the 15 slave states and 7 of the 15 free ones, clear proof that the sectional issue had been avoided.

*To call attention to their radicalism—supposedly they would burn down the barn to get rid of the rats.

The Compromise of 1850

Not avoided for long, however. The discovery of gold had brought an army of prospectors into California. By the summer of 1848 San Francisco had become almost a ghost town, and an estimated two-thirds of the adult males of Oregon had hastened south to the gold fields. Quickly,

The hard road to El Dorado, portrayed by J. Goldsborough Bruff, a Washington, D.C. draftsman who led a company "to see the elephant" (in the phrase of the day) in 1849. Above, the gold seekers "circle up" for a night on the Plains. The two self-portraits, from Bruff's diary, neatly sum up the journey.

the rough limits of the gold country had been marked out. For 150 miles and more along the western slope of the Sierras stretched the great Mother Lode. Along this expanse any stream or canyon, any ancient gravel bed might conceal a treasure in nuggets, flakes, or dust. Armed with pickaxes and shovels, with washing pans, even with knives and spoons, men hacked and dug and sifted, accumulating each his horde, some great, some small, of gleaming yellow metal. After President Polk confirmed the "extraordinary character" of the strike in his annual message of December 1848, there was no containing the gold seekers. During 1849, 25,000 made their way to California from the East by ship; more than 55,000 others crossed the continent by overland routes.

Rough, hard men, separated from their women, lusting for gold in a strange wild country where fortunes could be made in a day, gambled away in an hour, or stolen in an instant—the situation demanded the establishment of a territorial government. The new President appreciated this, and in his gruff, simple-hearted way he suggested an uncomplicated answer: admit California directly as a state, letting the Californians decide for themselves about slavery. The rest of the Mexican Cession could be formed into another state. No need for Congress, with its angry rivalries, to meddle at all, he believed. Even to Taylor, it was obvious that both these proposed states would ban slavery, for there were no slaves within their borders, but if they could skip the territorial stage, they could do so without controversy—everyone conceded the right of a *state* to legalize or outlaw the peculiar institution. Thus, Taylor reasoned, the nation could avoid the divisive effects of sectional debate. The Californians reacted promptly and favorably to the President's proposal. By October 1849 they had drawn up a constitution; by December it had been overwhelmingly ratified and a government was functioning. New Mexico was preparing to follow suit.

At this the South stood aghast, the more so because Taylor was himself the owner of a large plantation in Mississippi and many slaves. To admit California would destroy the balance be-

BOTH: METROPOLITAN MUSEUM OF ART, GIFT OF I. N. PHELPS STOKES, EDWARD S. HAWES, ALICE MARY HAWES, MARION AUGUSTA HAWES, 1937

Two of the leading lights of the day, Webster and Clay (below), as they looked about the time they played major roles in the Compromise of 1850. The daguerreotype of Clay dates from the late 1840's, that of Webster (by the noted Boston firm of Southworth & Hawes) from 1851, a year before he died.

tween free and slave states in the Senate; to allow all the new land to become free would doom the South to wither in a corner of the country, surrounded by hostile free states. How long, should that happen, could slavery sustain itself even in South Carolina? Radicals were already saying that the South would have to choose between secession and surrender. Taylor's plan played into the hands of such extremists.

In this crisis, with the South in turmoil and the future of the Union in peril, Henry Clay rose to save the day. He had felt as angry and frustrated when the Whigs nominated Taylor as he had when they had passed him over for Harrison, but now, well beyond 70 and in ill health, he put away his ambition and his resentment and for the last time concentrated his remarkable vision upon a great, multifaceted national problem. California must be free and soon admitted to the Union, but the South must have some compensation. For that matter, why not seize the opportunity to settle every outstanding sectional conflict related to slavery? Why not wipe out, with one stroke, the mean, combative mood of Congress and the country that had delayed even a routine action like the election of a Speaker of the House of Representatives through three weeks and 63 ballots, and bring every American back to a true appreciation of the Union? Clay pondered long and hard, drew up a plan, then consulted his old Whig rival Webster and obtained his general approval. On January 29, 1850, he laid his proposal, "founded upon mutual forbearance," before the Senate. A few days later he defended it on the floor of the Senate in the last great speech of his life.

California should be brought directly into the Union as a free state, he argued. The rest of the Southwest should be organized as a territory without mention of slavery: the southerners would retain the right to bring slaves there, while, in fact, none would do so. "You have got what is worth more than a thousand Wilmot Provisos," Clay pointed out to his northern colleagues. "You have nature on your side." The empty lands in dispute along the Texas border should be assigned to New Mexico Territory,

Clay continued, but in exchange the United States should take over Texas' preannexation debts. The slave trade should be abolished in the District of Columbia (but not slavery itself), and a more effective federal fugitive slave law should be enacted and strictly enforced in the North.

Clay's proposals resulted in one of the most magnificent debates in the history of the Senate. Every important member took part. Calhoun, perhaps more even than Clay, realized that the future of the nation was at stake and that his own days were numbered.* Too feeble to deliver his speech himself, he sat by impassively, wrapped in a great cloak, while Senator James M. Mason of Virginia read it to the crowded Senate. Calhoun thought his plan would save the Union, but his speech was actually an argument for secession; he demanded that the North yield completely on every point, ceasing even to discuss the question of slavery. Clay's compromise was unsatisfactory; he himself had no other to offer. If you will not yield, he said to the northern senators, "let the States . . . agree to separate and part in peace. If you are unwilling we should part in peace, tell us so, and we shall know what to do. . . ."

Three days later, on March 7, Daniel Webster took the floor. He too had begun to fail; the brilliant volubility, the thunder were gone, and when he spoke his face was bathed in sweat and there were strange pauses in his delivery. But his argument was lucid. Clay's proposals should be

*He died on March 31.

WORCESTER ART MUSEUM, GOODSPEED COLLECTION

New Englanders severely criticized Webster for his support of the fugitive slave bill that became part of the Compromise of 1850. In this lithograph, "Conquering Prejudice, or Fulfilling a Constitutional Duty with Alacrity," he is the central figure. "He exceeds my most sanguine expectation," cries a slave catcher (right).

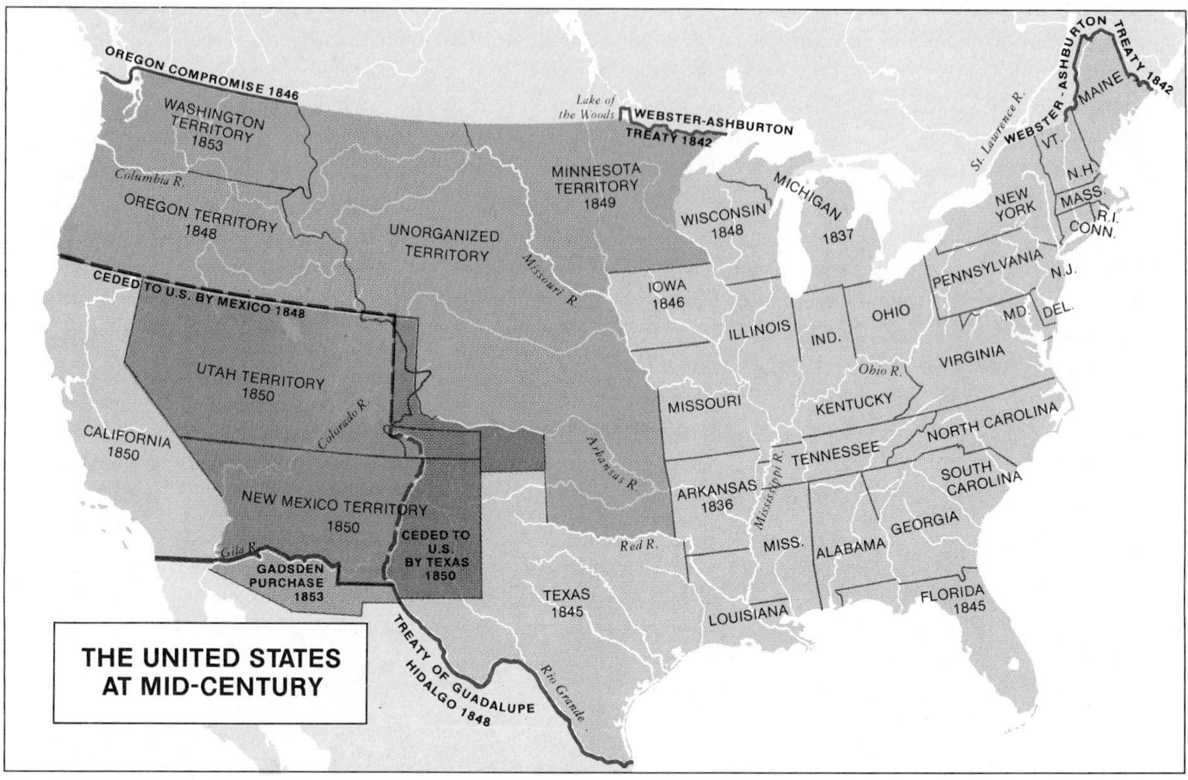

This map indicates the provisions of the Compromise of 1850 that applied to the Mexican Cession. Beginning with the annexation of Texas in 1845 and ending with the Gadsden Purchase in 1853 (sought to furnish a route for a southern transcontinental railroad), the United States added over 869 million acres to its territory.

adopted. Since the future of all the territories had already been fixed by geographical and economic factors, the Wilmot Proviso was unnecessary. The North's constitutional obligation to yield up fugitive slaves, he said, braving the wrath of the New England abolitionists, was "binding in honor and conscience." (A cynic might say that, once again, Webster was placing property rights above human rights, but his sincerity was beyond question.) In any case, he continued, the Union could not be sundered without bloodshed. At the thought of this dread possibility, for a moment the old fire within him flared: "Peaceable secession!" Webster exclaimed, ". . . Heaven forbid! Where is the flag of the republic to remain? Where is the eagle still to tower?"

The debate did not end when the aging giants had had their say. Every possible viewpoint was presented, argued, rebutted, rehashed. Senator William H. Seward of New York, a new Whig leader, close to Taylor's ear, caused a stir while arguing against concessions to the slave interests by saying that despite the constitutional obligation to return fugitive slaves, a "higher law" than the Constitution, the law of God, forbade anything that countenanced the evil of slavery.

The majority clearly favored some sort of compromise. But nothing could have been accomplished except for the death of President Taylor on July 9. Obstinate, probably resentful because few people paid him half the heed they paid Clay and other prominent members of Congress, he had been insisting on his own plan to bring both California and New Mexico directly into the Union. When Vice President Millard Fillmore succeeded him, the deadlock between the White House and Capitol Hill was broken. Even so, each part of the compromise had to be voted upon separately, for too many stubborn congressmen were willing to overturn the whole plan because they objected to minor aspects of it. Senator Benton, for example, announced against Clay's Omnibus Bill because he objected to the fugitive slave provision and the Texas boundary settlement.

The final congressional maneuvering was managed by another relative newcomer, Senator Stephen A. Douglas of Illinois, who took over when Washington's summer heat prostrated the exhausted Clay. Partisanship and economic interests incredibly complicated Douglas' problem. According to rumor, Clay had persuaded an important Virginia newspaper editor to back the compromise by promising him a $100,000 government printing contract. This inflamed many southerners. New York merchants, fearful of the disruption of their southern business, submitted a petition bearing 25,000 names in favor of compromise, a document that had much favorable effect in the South. The prospect of the federal government paying the debt of Texas made ardent compromisers of a horde of speculators. Between February and September, Texas bonds rose erratically from 29 to over 60, while men like W.W. Corcoran, whose Washington bank held more than $400,000 of these securities, entertained legislators and supplied lobbyists with large amounts of cash.

In the Senate and then in the House, tangled combinations pushed through the separate measures, one by one. California became the 31st state. The rest of the Mexican Cession was divided into two territories, New Mexico and Utah, each to be admitted to the Union when qualified, "with or without slavery as [its] constitution may prescribe," and Texas received $10 million to pay off its debt in return for accepting a narrower western boundary. The slave trade in the District of Columbia was abolished as of January 1, 1851. The Fugitive Slave Act of 1793 was amended to provide for the appointment of federal commissioners with authority to issue warrants, summon posses, and compel citizens under pain of fine or imprisonment to assist in the capture of fugitives. These fugitives were to be returned to the South without jury trial merely upon the submission of an affidavit by their "owner," and they could not testify in their own defense.

Only four senators voted for all these bills. In general, the Democrats gave more support to the compromise than the Whigs, but party lines never held very firmly. For example, 17 Democrats and 15 Whigs voted to admit California as a free state. Sectional lines also broke repeatedly, as witness the fact that 11 northern senators and 16 southerners backed the bill creating New Mexico Territory. An extremely large number of congressmen absented themselves when parts of the settlement unpopular in their home districts came to a vote; no less than 21 senators and 36 representatives, for example, failed to commit themselves on the new fugitive slave bill. Senator Jefferson Davis of Mississippi voted for the fugitive slave measure and the bill creating Utah Territory, remained silent on the New Mexico bill, and opposed the other measures. Senator Salmon P. Chase of Ohio, an abolitionist, supported only the admission of California and the abolition of the slave trade. Seward of New York voted for these two bills, did not vote on the fugitive slave and New Mexico bills, and voted against the other parts of the compromise.

In this piecemeal fashion, the Union was preserved. No one was completely satisfied, and extremists in both sections remained unreconciled. The credit belongs to many patriotic men, but mostly to Clay, whose original conceptualization of the compromise enabled lesser men to understand what they must do.

Everywhere, sober and conservative citizens sighed with relief. Mass meetings all over the country "ratified" the result. Hundreds of newspapers gave the compromise editorial approval. In Washington patriotic harmony reigned. "You would suppose that nobody had ever thought of disunion," Webster wrote. "All say they always meant to stand by the Union to the last." When Congress met again in December, it seemed that party asperities had been buried forever. "I have determined never to make another speech on the slavery question," Senator Douglas told his colleagues. "Let us cease agitating, stop the debate, and drop the subject." If this were done, he predicted, the compromise would be accepted as a "final settlement." So, indeed, it seemed, as the year 1850 passed into history.

SUPPLEMENTARY READING G.G. Van Deusen, *The Jacksonian Era** (1959), provides a convenient summary of the period down to the end of the Mexican War. For the Tyler administration, see O.D. Lambert, *Presidential Politics in the United States: 1841–1844* (1936), R.J. Morgan, *A Whig Embattled: The Presidency under John Tyler* (1954), G.R. Poage, *Henry Clay and the Whig Party* (1936), as well as O.P. Chitwood, *John Tyler: Champion of the Old South* (1939), and Robert Seager, *And Tyler Too!* (1963), the latter useful chiefly for its portrayal of Tyler's personal life.

On diplomatic difficulties with the British, see J.S. Reeves, *American Diplomacy under Tyler and Polk* (1907), and A.B. Corey, *The Crisis of 1830–1842 in Canadian-American Relations* (1941). E.C. Barker, *Mexico and Texas* (1928) and *Life of Stephen F. Austin** (1925), discuss the migration of Americans into the Texas region, while W.C. Binkley, *The Texas Revolution* (1952), and Marquis James, *The Raven** (1929), the latter a biography of Sam Houston, are good accounts of the Texans' struggle for independence.

The new expansionism is discussed in A.K. Weinberg, *Manifest Destiny** (1935), and in two books by Frederick Merk, *Manifest Destiny and Mission in American History** (1963) and *The Monroe Doctrine and American Expansionism* (1966). H.N. Smith, *Virgin Land** (1950), is also important for an understanding of this subject. The course of western development is treated in R.A. Billington, *The Far Western Frontier** (1956), and in Billington's more general *Westward Expansion* (1967). On Oregon, see O.O. Winther, *The Great Northwest* (1947), David Lavender, *Westward Vision: The Story of the Oregon Trail* (1963), and Francis Parkman's classic account, *The Oregon Trail** (1849). The history of the American penetration of California is covered in R.G. Cleland, *From Wilderness to Empire* (1944).

For the election of 1844, see J.C.N. Paul, *Rift in the Democracy** (1961). The best biography of Polk is C.G. Sellers' still incomplete *James K. Polk* (1957–1966), but see also E.I. McCormac, *James K. Polk* (1922), C.A. McCoy, *Polk and the Presidency* (1960), and M.M. Quaife (ed.), *The Diary of James K. Polk* (1910). Allan Nevins (ed.), *Polk: The Diary of a President** (1929), is a convenient condensation of this important source. N.A. Graebner, *Empire on the Pacific* (1955), is the fullest analysis of the factors influencing the Oregon boundary compromise. J.W. Schmitz, *Texan Statecraft* (1945), supplements J.H. Smith, *The Annexation of Texas* (1911).

There are a number of good brief accounts of the Mexican War, including A.H. Bill, *Rehearsal for Conflict* (1947), R.S. Henry, *The Story of the Mexican War* (1950), and O.A. Singletary, *The Mexican War** (1960). See also Holman Hamilton, *Zachary Taylor: Soldier of the Republic* (1946), and C.W. Elliott, *Winfield Scott* (1937). Allan Nevins' masterpiece, *The Ordeal of the Union* (1947–1960), commences with 1847 and so covers part of the Mexican conflict. For the discovery of gold in California, in addition to the works of Billington mentioned above, see R.W. Paul, *California Gold: The Beginning of Mining in the Far West** (1947), and J.W. Caughey, *Gold Is the Cornerstone* (1948).

The fullest study of the Compromise of 1850 is Holman Hamilton, *Prologue to Conflict** (1964), a detailed but lucid volume. See also the already mentioned study by Allan Nevins, *Ordeal of the Union*, the biographies of Clay, Calhoun, and Webster cited in earlier chapters, C.B. Going, *David Wilmot: Free-Soiler* (1924), G.F. Milton, *The Eve of Conflict: Stephen A. Douglas and the Needless War* (1934), G.M. Capers, *Stephen A. Douglas: Defender of the Union* (1959), Holman Hamilton, *Zachary Taylor: Soldier in the White House* (1951). Brainerd Dyer, *Zachary Taylor* (1946), and A.O. Craven, *The Growth of Southern Nationalism* (1953).

*Available in paperback.

12

An Era of Economic Change

A nation growing as rapidly as the United States in the middle decades of the 19th century changed continually in hundreds of ways. The country was developing a *national* economy, marked by the dependence of each area upon all the others, the production of goods in one region for sale in all, the increased specialization of both agricultural and industrial producers, and the growth in size of the average unit of production. Even in areas fairly close to the frontier, the small, relatively self-sufficient farmer was becoming far less common than he had been in earlier times.

Basic adjustments within the economy were taking place, although sometimes unnoticed. Cotton remained the most important southern crop and the major American export, but after the mid-forties the mainsprings of national economic growth were the manufacturing of the Northeast and the railroads which revolutionized transportation and communication. The continuing westward movement of agriculture had significant new effects on the country. American foreign commerce changed radically during this period, and the great flood of European immigration had an impact on manufacturing, town life, and farming too. All these changes and others, such as the rich gold strikes in California, had so many ramifications that one can scarcely hope to measure them with accuracy.

Agriculture in the Old South

The South changed less than any other section in the second quarter of the 19th century. Cotton remained "king" of the region, slavery its most distinctive institution. Nevertheless, a number of significant agricultural developments occurred. Cotton continued to march westward until by 1859, 1.3 of the 4.3 million bales grown in the United States came from beyond the Mississippi. In the Upper South, Virginia held its place as the leading tobacco producer, but the states beyond the Appalachians were raising more than half the nation's crop by the 1850's. Early in that decade the introduction of Bright Yellow, a new, mild variety of tobacco that (miraculously) grew best in poor soil, gave a great stimulus to production. The older sections of Maryland, Virginia, and North Carolina shifted to the kind of diversified farming usually associated with the North. Corn was of major importance; the South as a whole raised 60 per cent of all the corn grown in the United States in 1850. But the old Tidewater region also produced wheat and other grains, as well as fruits, vegetables, and livestock in increasing amounts. By 1849 the wheat crop of Virginia was worth twice as much as the tobacco crop. A number of New Englanders migrated to the Upper South in the 1840's and successfully restored worn-out farmlands, but with the intensification of the sectional conflict this "Vandal Invasion," as one prominent Richmond editor called it, tailed off.

Farmers in the Upper South, however, displayed considerable interest in improved farming methods. As early as the time of Washington and Jefferson, progressive Virginia planters had experimented with crop rotation and fertilizers. In the mid-19th century, pressed by the exhaustion of their soils after decades of tobacco cultivation, many Virginia farmers adopted new, advanced methods. The work of Edmund Ruffin, who introduced the use of marl, an earth rich in calcium, to counteract the acidity of worn-out tobacco fields, was of prime importance. Ruffin discovered by experimentation and observation on his own lands that dressings of marl, combined with the use of fertilizers and with proper drainage and plowing methods, doubled and even tripled the yield of corn and wheat. In his *Essay on Calcareous Manures* (1832), which went through five editions, and in his magazine *The Farmers' Register* Ruffin spread the new gospel. In the 1840's some southerners began to import Peruvian guano, a high-nitrogen fertilizer of bird droppings, which also increased yields immensely. Others experimented with contour plowing to control erosion, with improved breeds of livestock, new types of plows, and agricultural machinery.

Slavery as an Economic Institution

The increased importance of cotton in the South strengthened the hold of slavery on the region. The price of Negroes rose, until by the 1850's a prime field hand was worth upward of $1,500, roughly three times his value in the 1820's. Although the prestige value of owning this kind of property affected the price of Negroes, the rise chiefly reflected the increasing value of the South's agricultural output. "Crop value per slave" jumped from less than $15 early in the century to over $100 in 1860.

In the cotton fields of the Deep South slaves brought several hundred dollars per head more than in the older regions; therefore, the tendency to sell them "down the river" continued unabated. Mississippi took in some 10,000 slaves a year throughout the period; as a result, as early as 1830 the black population of the state exceeded the white. Slave-trading became a big business. There were about 50 dealers in Charleston in the 1850's and 200 in New Orleans. The largest traders were Isaac Franklin and John Armfield, who collected slaves from Virginia and Maryland at their "model jail" in Alexandria and shipped them by land and sea to a huge depot near Natchez. Each of the partners cleared half a million dollars before re-

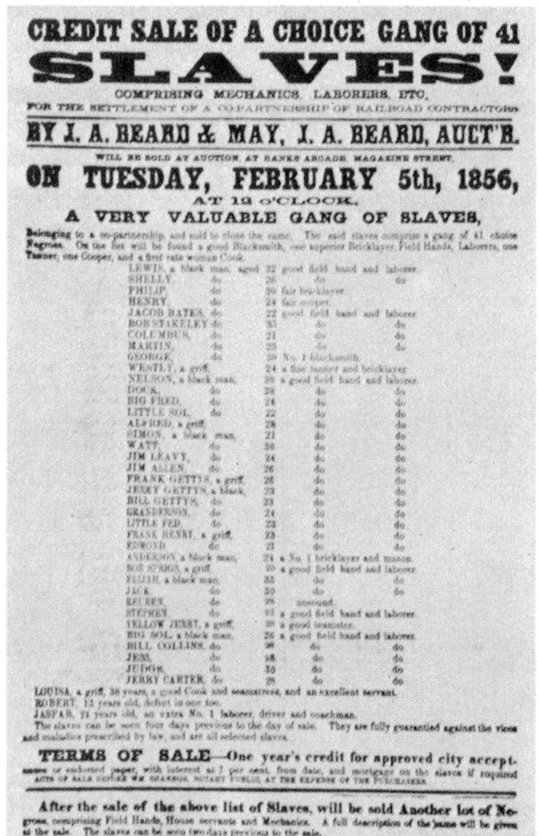

CREDIT SALE OF A CHOICE GANG OF 41

SLAVES!

COMPRISING MECHANICS, LABORERS, ETC.,

FOR THE SETTLEMENT OF A CO-PARTNERSHIP OF RAILROAD CONTRACTORS

BY J. A. BEARD & MAY, J. A. BEARD, AUCT'R.

WILL BE SOLD AT AUCTION, AT BANKS' ARCADE, MAGAZINE STREET,

ON TUESDAY, FEBRUARY 5th, 1856,

AT 12 O'CLOCK,

A VERY VALUABLE GANG OF SLAVES,

Belonging to a co-partnership, and sold to close the same. The said slaves comprise a gang of 41 choice Negroes. On the list will be found a good Blacksmith, one superior Bricklayer, Field Hands, Laborers, one Tanner, one Cooper, and a first rate woman Cook.

LEWIS, a black man, aged	32	good field hand and laborer	
SHELLY, do	26	do	do
PHILIP, do	30	fair bricklayer	
HENRY, do	24	fair cooper	
JACOB BATES, do	22	good field hand and laborer	
BOB STAKELEY do	35	do	do
COLUMBUS, do	21	do	do
MARTIN, do	25	do	do
GEORGE, do	39	No. 1 blacksmith	
WESTLY, a griff	24	a fine tanner and bricklayer	
NELSON, a black man,	30	a good field hand and laborer	
DOCK, do	28	do	do
BIG FRED, do	24	do	do
LITTLE SOL, do	22	do	do
ALFRED, a griff,	28	do	do
SIMON, a black man,	21	do	do
WATT, do	30	do	do
JIM LEAVY, do	24	do	do
JIM ALLEN, do	26	do	do
FRANK GETTYS, a griff,	26	do	do
JERRY GETTYS, a black,	23	do	do
BILL GETTYS, do	23	do	do
GRANDERSON, do	24	do	do
LITTLE FED, do	23	do	do
FRANK HENRY, a griff,	23	do	do
EDMOND do	21	do	do
ANDERSON, a black man,	24	a No. 1 bricklayer and mason	
BOB [illegible], a griff	20	a good field hand and laborer	
ELIJAH, a black man,	35	do	do
JACK do	30	do	do
REUBEN, do	28	unsound	
STEPHEN do	[illegible]	a good field hand and laborer	
YELLOW JERRY, a griff,	38	a good teamster	
BIG SOL, a black man,	26	a good field hand and laborer	
BILL COLLINS, do	[illegible]	do	do
JESS, do	18	do	do
JUDGE, do	30	do	do
JERRY CARTER, do	28	do	do

LOUINA, a griff, 38 years, a good Cook and seamstress, and an excellent servant.
ROBERT, 13 years old, defect in one toe.
JASPAR, 21 years old, an extra No. 1 laborer, driver and coachman.

The slaves can be seen four days previous to the day of sale. They are fully guarantied against the vices and maladies prescribed by law, and are all selected slaves.

TERMS OF SALE—One year's credit for approved city acceptances or endorsed paper, with interest at 7 per cent. from date, and mortgage on the slaves if required. ACTS OF SALE BEFORE WM. SHANNON, NOTARY PUBLIC, AT THE EXPENSE OF THE PURCHASERS.

After the sale of the above list of Slaves, will be sold Another lot of Negroes, comprising Field Hands, House servants and Mechanics. A full description of the same will be given at the sale. The slaves can be seen two days previous to the sale.

AMERICAN ANTIQUARIAN SOCIETY

tiring, and other, smaller operators did proportionately well. With the business so profitable, the prejudice against slave traders tended to disappear; a number of men of high social status became traders, and persons of humble origin who had prospered in the trade had little difficulty in buying land and setting up as respectable planters. In his later years, for example, Franklin owned six plantations in Louisiana and one of the finest properties in the South, "Fairvue," outside Nashville.

As slaves became more expensive, the percentage of the slaveowning population began to decline, until on the eve of the Civil War only one southern family in four owned any at all. On the other hand, few men possessed large numbers. In 1850 only 254 persons owned 200 or more slaves. In 1860 only about 46,000 of the 8 million white residents of the slave states had as many as 20. When one calculates the cost of 20 slaves and the land to keep them profitably occupied, it is easy to understand why this figure is so small. The most efficient size of a plantation worked by gangs of slaves ranged between 1,000 and 2,000 acres. In every part of the South the majority of farmers cultivated no more than 200 acres, in many sections less than 100 acres. A few large plantations and many small farms—this was the pattern. However, the *trend* in the South was toward larger agricultural units. Between 1850 and 1860 the size of the average American farm declined from 203 acres to 194, but it rose sharply in the South: from 289 acres to 346 in Alabama, from 372 to 536 in Louisiana.

Nevertheless, small farmers did grow the staple crops and many of them owned a few slaves, often working beside them in the fields. These yeoman farmers did not seem very remarkable to contemporary chroniclers, but they were the backbone of the South—respectable, hard-work-

MR. & MRS. SAMUEL J. HENRY COLLECTION

"Anderson . . . , 24, a No. 1 bricklayer and mason," brought the top price of $2,700 in a New Orleans slave auction in 1856 (left). The Richmond slave market scene above was painted about 1853 by an Englishman, Eyre Crowe. The quiet dignity of the slave family, the businesslike demeanor of the prospective buyers reminded a commentator on the painting of Hannah Arendt's indictment of Nazi death-camp bureaucracy: "the banality of evil."

These reportorial views of slavery are the work of a young Austrian, Franz Hölzlhuber, an amateur artist who toured much of the South between 1856 and 1860. Above is a rice plantation on the Arkansas River, at center, slave cabins in Tennessee. The slaves at right, harvesting sugar cane in Louisiana, are dressed in striped garb to discourage their attempts at escape.

ing, hospitable, self-reliant, and moderately prosperous, totally unlike the "poor white trash" of the pine barrens and the remote valleys of the Appalachians who scratched a meager subsistence from substandard soils and lived in ignorance and squalor.

Slavery operated increasingly to limit southern development. The relative efficiency of the slave system has been much debated; it seems reasonably certain that well-managed plantations yielded annual profits of ten per cent and more and that, in general, money invested in southern agriculture earned at least a modest return. However, the South failed to develop its own marketing and transportation facilities, and for this slavery was at least partly responsible. In 1840 *Hunt's Merchant Magazine* estimated that it cost $2.85 to move a bale of cotton from the farm to a seaport and that additional charges for storage, insurance, port fees, and freight to a European port exceeded $15. Middlemen from outside the South commonly earned most of this money. New York capitalists gradually came to control much of the South's cotton from the moment it was picked, and a large percentage of the crop found its way into New York warehouses before being sold to manufacturers. These same middlemen supplied most of the foreign goods the planters purchased with their cotton earnings. As one economic historian has summed it up, "The expanding income from the marketing of [southern] staples outside the region induced little growth within the South. Income received there had little multiplier effect."

Southerners complained about this state of affairs but did little to correct it. Capital tied up in the ownership of labor could not be invested in anything else, and social pressures in the South militated against investment in trade and commerce: land and slaves gave men status, a kind of psychic income not available to any middleman. Moreover, the system made underconsumers and underproducers of 4 million southerners. Slaves were nearly always adequately clothed, fed,* and housed, for only a fool or a sadist would fail to protect such valuable property, but as one British visitor pointed out, they were "a nonconsuming class." And no other system could have provided less incentive to hard and efficient labor. Slaves were habitually (and perhaps deliberately) careless of tools and farm machinery, which may explain why on a thousand-acre plantation the value of farm tools seldom totaled $500. The overseer could exact a certain effort with his whip, but

* While slaves received plenty of calories, it has been argued that their diet (chiefly corn and hog fat) was deficient in proteins, which made them disease-prone and lacking in stamina.

ALL: GLENBOW FOUNDATION, CALGARY, ALBERTA

only a limited one. Finally, the enormous reservoir of intelligence and skill that the Negroes represented was almost entirely wasted, as, unfortunately, so much of it is still wasted in America today. Many slave craftsmen worked on the plantations, and a few free Negroes made their way in the South remarkably well, but the amount of talent unused, energy misdirected, and imagination smothered can only be guessed.

Foreign observers in New England frequently noted the alertness and industriousness of ordinary laborers and attributed this, justifiably, to the high level of literacy. Less than one per cent of the population in New England could not read and write. Correspondingly, the stagnation and inefficiency of southern labor could be attributed in part to the high degree of illiteracy, for over 20 per cent of the *white* southerners could not read or write, a tragic squandering of human resources.

Slavery as a Social Institution

As slaves became more valuable and as northern opposition to the institution grew more vocal, the system hardened perceptibly. As in earlier times, slave uprisings occurred very rarely, but southerners made much of the danger of insurrection. Every slave state passed laws restricting the movement and assembling of Negroes. When a plot was discovered or an actual revolt took place, instant and savage reprisals resulted. In 1822, after the conspiracy of Denmark Vesey was exposed by informers, 37 South Carolina Negroes were executed and another 30-odd deported, although no overt act of rebellion had occurred. After a rising in Louisiana, 16 Negroes were decapitated, their heads left to rot on poles along the Mississippi as a grim warning. The Nat Turner revolt in Virginia in 1831 was the most sensational of the slave uprisings; 57 whites lost their lives before it was suppressed. Southerners treated runaways almost as brutally as rebels, although they posed no real threat to the whites. The authorities tracked down fugitives with bloodhounds and subjected captives to merciless lashings.

As the years passed, interest in doing away with slavery simply vanished in the South. The southern states made it increasingly difficult, if not impossible, for masters to free their slaves. During 1859 in all the South only about 3,000 Negroes in a slave population of nearly 4 million were given their freedom, and many of these were elderly and thus of little economic value. Even in Virginia, where the institution was less prosperous than in the Deep South and where manumission was legal, only 277 out of half a million slaves were set free in that year.

Rather than get rid of their slaves, many unscrupulous southerners engaged in smuggling fresh supplies in from Africa. No one knows how many Negroes entered America illegally after the trade was outlawed in 1808. The number was not large relative to the slave population. In *American*

AMERICAN ANTIQUARIAN SOCIETY

SLAVERY RECORD.

INSURRECTION IN VIRGINIA!

Extract of a letter from a gentleman to his friend in Baltimore, dated

'RICHMOND, August 23d.

An express reached the governor this morning, informing him that an insurrection had broken out in Southampton, and that, by the last accounts, there were seventy whites massacred, and the militia retreating. Another express to Petersburg says that the blacks were continuing their destruction; that three hundred militia were retreating in a body, before six or eight hundred blacks. A shower of rain coming up as the militia were making an attack, wet the powder so much that they were compelled to retreat, being armed only with shot-guns. The negroes are armed with muskets, scythes, axes, &c. &c. Our volunteers are marching to the scene of action. A troop of cavalry left at four o'clock, P. M. The artillery, with four field pieces, start in the steam boat Norfolk, at 6 o'clock, to land at Smithfield. Southampton county lies 80 miles south of us, below Petersburg.'

From the Richmond Whig, of Tuesday.

Disagreeable rumors have reached this city of an insurrection of the slaves in Southampton County, with loss of life. In order to correct exaggeration, and at the same time to induce all salutary caution, we state the following particulars:

An express from the Hon. James Trezvant states that an insurrection had broken out, that several families had been murdered, and that the negroes were embodied, requiring a considerable military force to reduce them.

The names and precise numbers of the families are not mentioned. A letter to the Post Master corroborates the intelligence. Prompt and efficient measures are being taken by the Governor, to call out a sufficient force to put down the insurrection, and place lower Virginia on its guard.

Serious danger of course there is none. The deluded wretches have rushed on assured destruction.

The Fayette Artillery and the Light Dragoons will leave here this evening for Southampton; the artillery go in a steamboat, and the troop by land.

We are indebted to the kindness of our friend Lyford for the following extract of a letter from the Editors of the Norfolk Herald, containing the particulars of a most murderous insurrection among the blacks of Southampton County,* Virginia.—*Gaz.*

NORFOLK, 24th Aug. 1831.

I have a horrible, a heart rending tale to relate, and lest even its worst feature might be distorted by rumor and exaggeration, I have thought it proper to give you all and the worst information, that has as yet reached us through the best sources of intelligence which the nature of the case will admit.

A gentleman arrived here yesterday express from Suffolk, with intelligence from the upper part of Southampton county, stating that a band of insurgent slaves (some of them believed to be runaways from the neighboring Swamps,) had turned out on Sunday night last, and murdered several whole families, amounting to 40 or 50 individuals. Some of the families were named, and among them was that of Mrs. Catharine Whitehead, sister of our worthy townsman, Dr. N. C. Whitehead,—who, with her son and five daughters, fell a sacrifice to the savage ferocity of these demons in human shape.

An abolitionist paper, The Liberator, *reprinted southern accounts of the 1831 Nat Turner revolt in Virginia. "Serious danger of course there is none," The Richmond* Whig *hastened to assure its readers.*

Slavers and Federal Law, a fascinating volume, Warren S. Howard estimates that over 30,000 were spirited from the United States and Cuba in the brief period 1857–1860, but he suspects that most of these came to Cuba. British, French, Portuguese, and American naval vessels patrolled the African coast continuously, and the American navy alone seized more than 50 suspected slavers in the two decades before 1860. However, these fast, sharklike pirate cruisers were hard to catch, the anti-slave-trade laws imperfectly worded and unevenly enforced. Many accounts tell of slaves in America long after 1808 with filed teeth, tattoos, and other signs of African origin, yet no one owning such a man was ever charged with the possession of contraband goods.

Psychological Effects of Slavery

The injustice of slavery needs no proof; that it stifled the southern economy is clear. Less obvious is the fact that it had a corrosive effect on the personalities of southerners, slave and free alike. Some slaves found their condition absolutely unbearable. These became the habitual runaways who collected whip scars like medals; the "loyal" servants who struck out in sudden rage against a master knowing that the result would be certain death; the leaders of slave revolts. Denmark Vesey of South Carolina, for example, even after buying his freedom, could not stomach the subservience demanded of Negroes by the system. When he saw Charleston slaves step into the gutter to make way for white men he taunted them: "You deserve to remain slaves!" For years he preached resistance to his fellows, drawing his texts from the Declaration of Independence and the Bible, and promising help from black Santo Domingo. So vehemently did he argue that some of his followers claimed they feared Vesey more than their masters, even more than God. He planned his uprising for five years, patiently working out the details, only to see it aborted at the last moment when a few of his recruits lost their nerve and gave him away to the authorities. For Denmark Vesey, death was probably preferable to living with such rage as his soul contained.

Yet Veseys were rare. Most slaves appeared, if

not contented, at least resigned to their fate. Some seemed even to accept the whites' evaluation of their inherent abilities and place in society. Historian Stanley Elkins has drawn an interesting parallel between the behavior of slaves and that of the inmates of Adolf Hitler's concentration camps, arguing that in both cases such factors as the fear of arbitrary punishment and the absence of any hope of escape led to the disintegration of the victim's personality—to childishness, petty thievery, chronic irresponsibility, and even to a degrading identification with the master race itself. The comparison is somewhat overdrawn, for the plantation was not a concentration camp. In any case, a psychoanalytical explanation is not really necessary. The whole system in the South was intended to make the Negro submissive and childlike and discouraged if it did not entirely extinguish independence of judgment and self-reliance. These qualities are difficult enough to develop in human beings under the best circumstances; when every element in society encouraged slaves to let others do their thinking for them, to avoid questioning the *status quo*, to lead a simple, animal existence, many, probably most, did so willingly enough. Of course this did not mean that they liked being slaves, but it surely undermined their basic human dignity. Was this not slavery's greatest shame?

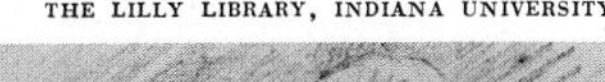
THE LILLY LIBRARY, INDIANA UNIVERSITY

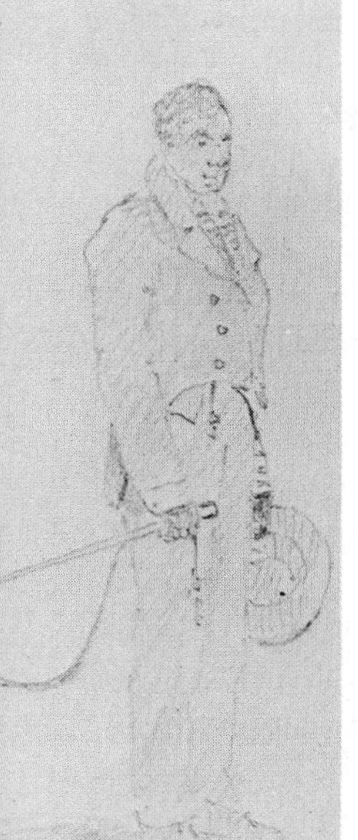

Basil Hall, a touring Englishman, filled his notebooks with sketches of American types, such as these two southerners. At left is a black slave overseer, at right a backwoodsman, posing with his long rifle.

Slavery warped white men almost as severely as black. This subject, too, has attracted the attention of psychoanalytically inclined historians, who have suggested, among other things, that the system encouraged whites to conceal their animal natures from themselves by projecting upon the helpless slaves their own base passions. Many planters, these historians note, took advantage of their position to avail themselves of slave women. Then, to avoid facing the fact that they were rapists, they pictured the *blacks* as lustful, superpotent, and incapable of self-restraint. In a related manner idle slaveowners exacted labor from their slaves by brute force and justified their cruel whips by claiming that not they but the black men were inherently lazy. The harm done to the slaves by such mental distortions is obvious. More obscure is the effect on the masters: self-indulgence is perhaps only contemptible, self-delusion is pitiable.

Such a description of master-slave relations is, to say the least, one-sided. Probably most owners respected the most fundamental personal rights of their slaves. Indeed, so far as sexual behavior is concerned, there are countless known cases of lasting relationships based on love and mutual respect between owners and what law and the community defined as their "property."

But the psychological injury inflicted upon whites by slavery can be demonstrated without resort to Freudian insights. By associating working for others with servility, it discouraged many poor southerners from hiring out to earn a stake. It also provided the weak, the shiftless, and the unsuccessful with a scapegoat that made their own miserable state easier to bear but harder to escape from. A few slaveowning sadists could not resist the temptations that the possession of human beings put before them. "One of the greatest practical evils of slavery," wrote a British traveler in the South, Captain Basil Hall, "arises from persons who have no command over themselves, being placed, without control, in command of others." While growing up in Hannibal, Missouri, Sam Clemens, the future Mark Twain, once saw an angry overseer brain a clumsy slave for some minor ineptitude. "He was dead in an hour," Clemens later recalled. "Nobody in the village approved of that murder, but of course no one said much about it. . . . Considerable sympathy was felt for the slave's owner, who had been bereft of valuable property by a worthless person who was not able to pay for it."

More significant were the countless petty cruelties that the system allowed. "I feel badly, got very angry, and whipped Lavinia," one Louisiana woman wrote in her diary. "O! for government over my temper." But for slavery, she would surely have had better self-control. Similar although more subtle was the interaction of the institution with the American tendency to brag and bluster. "You can manage ordinary niggers by lickin' 'em and by givin' 'em a taste of hot iron once in a while when they're extra ugly," one uncouth Georgian was heard to say at a slave auction shortly before the Civil War. "But if a nigger ever sets himself up against me, I can't never have any patience with him. I just get my pistol and shoot him right down; and that's the best way." The price of Negroes being what it was, this was probably just talk, but bad talk, harmful to speaker and listener alike. Northern braggarts, perforce, were less objectionable.

Still, braggarts are inconsequential in most social situations; historians need seldom pay them much heed. However, the finest southerners were often warped by the institution. While most plantation owners labored endlessly at the management of their estates, their feudal society and the very logic of a system based on the master's exploitation of his slaves encouraged extravagance. One Mississippi planter squandered $10,000 furnishing a single room. Some planters sent their Negro chefs to France for training. The novelist William Gilmore Simms wasted much of his wife's large fortune and his own considerable royalties on lavish entertainment and easy living. The historian Eugene D. Genovese has suggested a practical reason for such "seigneurial display": it helped the great planters to overawe the poor and middle-class whites and thus to assure their hegemony. Nevertheless, as Genovese also notes, it had adverse effects on the economy as well as on the planters as individuals, for it cut down substantially on the accumulation of capital. Furthermore, even men who abhorred slavery sometimes let it corrupt their thinking: "I consider the labor of a breeding woman as no object, and that a child raised every 2 years is of more profit than the crop of the best laboring man." This cold appraisal was written by the author of the Declaration of Independence.

Manufacturing in the South

Although the temper of southern society discouraged business and commercial activity, need and the existence of valuable resources led to considerable manufacturing in this period. Generally, local capital financed these enterprises, and local labor, both slave and free, was employed, sometimes even in the same plant. Small flour and lumber mills flourished all over the South. Both iron and coal were mined in Virginia, Kentucky, and Tennessee, and many foundries existed. The well-known Tredegar Iron Works in Richmond, which did an annual business of about $1 million, was the most important of these. The manufacture of chewing tobacco, centered in Virginia, is another example of a small industry in the South closely related to the exploitation of a local resource.

Logic seemed to require that cotton textiles be manufactured in the South because of the availability of the raw material and the abundance of waterpower along the Appalachian slopes. As early as 1825 a thriving factory was functioning at Fayetteville, North Carolina, and soon others sprang up in North Carolina and in adjoining states.

The most important of the early textile manufacturers was William Gregg of South Carolina. His factory at Graniteville, established in 1846, was a constant moneymaker. An able propagandist as well as a good businessman, Gregg saw the textile business not only as a source of profit, but also as a device for improving the lot of the South's poor whites. He worked hard to weaken the southern prejudice against manufacturing and made his own plant a model of benevolent paternalism. The ignorant hill people who worked for him lived in company houses, traded at a company store, worshiped in company-owned churches. Liquor and even dancing were prohibited in Graniteville. Children under 12 were required to attend the school Gregg built for them, which certainly did them no harm. Gregg's teachings had much influence. On the whole, however, as with every other industry, southern textile manufacturing amounted to very little when compared with that of the North. Gregg employed only about 300 textile workers in 1850, the whole state of South Carolina less than 900. Lowell, Massachusetts, had more spindles turning in 1860 than did the entire South.

Altogether only about ten per cent of the goods manufactured in the United States in 1860 came from the South; in other words, the region did not really develop an industrial society. Its textile manufacturers depended upon the North both for machinery and for skilled workers and technicians. When the English geologist Charles Lyell visited New Orleans in 1846, he was astounded to discover that that thriving city supported not a single book publisher. Even a local guidebook that he purchased bore a New York imprint. Despite the example of a few men like William Gregg, most southerners simply would not make a career of business. Many of the factory owners were transplanted northerners, and those southerners who did engage in business activity were usually planters who, as Clement Eaton has written in *The Growth of Southern Civilization*, "did not regard it beneath their dignity to engage in money-making enterprises" —so long as it was clearly understood that they were primarily planters. "The agrarian ideal," he stresses, "undoubtedly hampered the growth of the business class."

Industrial Expansion

The most obvious change in the North in the decades before the Civil War was the rapid expansion of industry. The best estimates suggest that immediately after the War of 1812 the United States was manufacturing annually less than \$200 million worth of goods. In 1859 the northeastern states alone produced \$1.27 billion of the national total of almost \$2 billion. This rate of growth was accelerating and continued to accelerate for many decades. In 1837 Massachusetts, to take a typical industrial state, turned out manufactured products worth over \$86 million; in 1845, about \$125 million; in 1855, nearly \$300 million.

Manufacturing expanded in so many directions that it is difficult to portray or even to summarize its evolution. By 1852, for instance, there were more than a hundred piano manufacturers in New York City, some running quite large establishments. According to Roger Burlingame, this was a "transition period" in the history of American technological advance. In his *March of the Iron Men*, Burlingame lists half a page of new inventions and processes developed between 1825 and 1850, including—besides such obviously important items as the sewing machine, the vulcanization of rubber, and the cylinder press—the screwmaking machine, the friction match, the lead pencil, and an apparatus for making soda water. Such inventions help explain why industry expanded so fast despite the tremendous demands made by the rapid westward movement on the national supply of labor and capital.

American industry displayed a remarkable receptivity to technological change and to the use of new machinery. "Yankee ingenuity" was perhaps partly an eastern version of the boastfulness common on the frontier, but only partly so. A society in flux put a premium on resourcefulness; an environment that offered so much freedom to the individual encouraged experimentation. The expanding market inspired men to use new techniques. With skilled labor always in short supply, the pressure to create machines that could be substituted for trained hands was great.

As early as the 1820's a foreign visitor noted: "Everything new is quickly introduced here, and all the latest inventions. There is no clinging to old ways; the moment an American hears the word 'invention' he pricks up his ears." By 1850 the United States led the world in the production of goods that required the use of precision instruments, and in certain industries the country was well on the way toward modern mass-production methods. American clocks, pistols, rifles, and locks

LAWRENCE G. ZIMMERMAN COLLECTION

An elaborate 1851 chromolithograph applauds Yankee triumphs at the Crystal Palace Exhibition, ranging from artificial limbs to Hiram Powers' sculpture, The Greek Slave *(page 431). At center is the yacht* America, *winner of the first America's Cup in that year.*

were outstanding. The showing made by American manufacturers of these products at the London Crystal Palace Exhibition of 1851 so impressed the British that they sent two special commissions to the United States to study manufacturing practices. After visiting the Springfield Arsenal, the British investigators placed a large order for gun-making machinery and hired a number of American technicians to help organize what became the Enfield rifle factory. The British visitors were amazed by the lock and clock factories of New England and by the plants where screws, files, and similar metal objects were turned out in volume by automatic machinery. Instead of resisting new laborsaving machines, the British commissioners noted, "the workingmen hail with satisfaction all mechanical improvements." They attributed this enlightened view to the high level of education found among American workers, what they called "the perceptive power so keenly awakened by early intellectual training." Whatever the explanation (and education was certainly a part of it), skilled northern workingmen did display remarkable adaptability to machine-production methods. As one American observer wrote in 1829: "There exists generally among the mechanics of New England a vivacity in inquiring into the first principles of the science to which they are practically devoted." In no way were the intellectual climates of North and South more different.

But invention alone does not account for the industrial advance. Annually, new natural resources were being discovered and made available

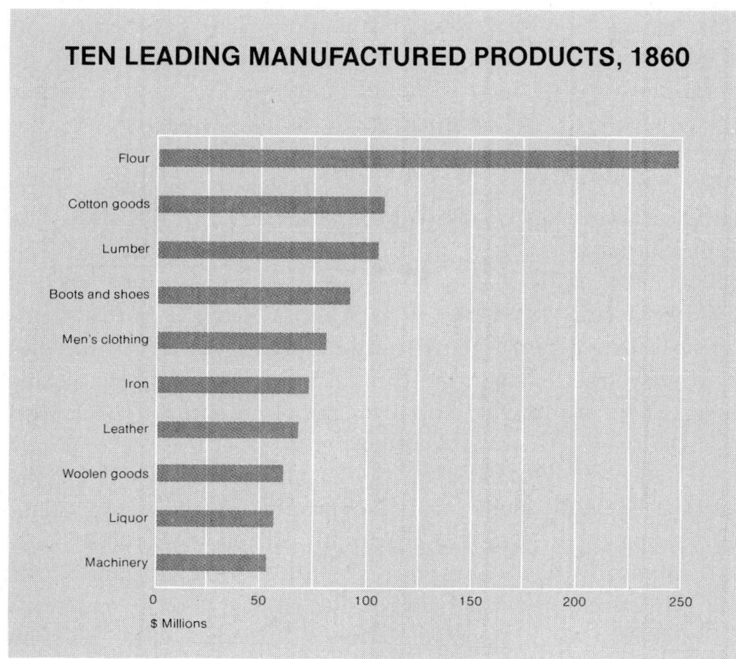

The leading American industries as listed in the 1860 census of manufactures are ranked here by value of product. The boots and shoes industry employed the most workers, 123,000. Next were cotton goods and men's clothing, each with just under 115,000 workmen.

by the westward march of settlement, and the expansion of agriculture produced an ever larger supply of raw materials for the mills and factories. Most of the leading American industries depended directly upon agriculture. First in the United States, from the point of view of the value of its product, was the flour and meal business, which turned out nearly $250 million worth of goods in 1859, more than double that of the second-ranking cotton textile industry. It rested, of course, upon the nation's grain growers, whose $208 million crop fed its mills. Of the ten leading industries in 1860, *eight* (flour, cotton textiles, lumber, shoes, men's clothing, leather, woolen goods, and liquor) relied upon agriculture for their raw materials.

The average American industrial unit was larger, more specialized, and much more mechanized than in the first quarter of the century. In the 1850's the prejudice against the corporation was beginning to break down; by the end of the decade all the northern and northwestern states had passed general incorporation laws. Of course the corporate device made possible larger accumulations of capital. While the federal government did not charter business corporations, two contrasting incidents that occurred in Congress illustrate the shift in public attitudes. In 1840 a group of scientists sought a federal charter for a National Institution for the Promotion of Science. They were turned down on constitutional grounds. If Congress "went on erecting corporations in this way," one legislator said, "they would come, at last, to have corporations for everything." In 1863, however, the bill creating the National Academy of Science went through both houses without debate.

Especially after 1850 the use of steam power in industry made rapid strides, partly because of improvements in the design and power of boilers and steam engines and partly because available supplies of waterpower were already being used to capacity. Many New England textile factories converted to steam to increase output. By 1860 coal-fired steam engines were turning almost a quarter of the spindles in the important Fall River, Massachusetts, region. Steam permitted greater flexibility and speed, freedom from the vicissitudes of drought and freezing weather, and more powerful machinery.

American industrial growth created a great increase in the demand for labor. The effects, however, were mixed. On the one hand, skilled craftsmen, technicians, and toolbuilders earned good wages and found it relatively easy to set themselves up as small manufacturers. Although few industrial workers ever went west to become farmers, the expanding frontier did drain off much agricultural labor that might otherwise have been attracted to industry, and the thriving new towns of the West absorbed large numbers of eastern artisans of every kind. On the other hand, the pay of the unskilled worker never enabled him to support a family decently, and the new machines tended to weaken the bargaining power of the ordinary craftsman by making his skill superfluous.

Many other forces acted to stimulate manufacturing. Immigration increased rapidly during the period; an avalanche of strong backs and willing hands and many thousands of keen, well-trained minds descended upon the country from Europe. New sources of capital also appeared as Europeans invested large sums in the booming American economy. The savings of millions of Americans and the great hoard of new California gold added to the supply. Improvements in transportation, the growth of the population, the absence of internal tariff barriers, and the relatively high per capita wealth of the people all meant an ever-expanding market for manufactured goods.

Self-Generated Expansion

However, the *pace* of the advance is best explained by many interactions, the "backward and forward linkages" resulting from industrial activity. In this respect the cotton textile business was clearly the most important. Samuel Slater built his first machines right in his own little plant, but soon the industry spawned a whole complex of separate companies devoted to the manufacture of looms, spinning frames, and other machines. These, in turn, stimulated the growth of machine-tool production, of metalworking companies, and, eventually, the mining and refining of iron. "For a considerable . . . period," writes George S. Gibb in his study of *Textile Machinery Building in New England, 1813–1849*, "the manufacture of textile machinery appears to have been America's greatest heavy goods industry. . . . From the textile mills and the textile machine shops came the men who supplied

"Damned plague ships and swimming coffins," was the New York Journal of Commerce's *blunt assessment of the transatlantic immigrant vessels crowding into American ports early in the 1850's. This woodcut of immigrant families jammed into the steerage of one of these ships was reproduced in a French newspaper in 1849.*

most of the tools for the American Industrial Revolution. From these mills and shops sprang directly the machine-tool and locomotive industries together with a host of less basic metal fabricating trades." At the same time, the booming mills were stimulating what another historian calls "a vast array of final consumer goods industries to meet the needs of the northeastern urban dweller, the southern slave and planter, and the western farmer."

Similar examples abound of the multiplier effect of industrial growth in these decades. The invention of the sewing machine in 1846 by Elias Howe (who got his early training in a Lowell cotton-machine factory) resulted in the creation of the ready-made clothing industry. The sewing machine also soon revolutionized the shoe industry, speeding the trend toward factory production and triggering the same kind of forward and backward linkages that characterized the textile business. The new agricultural machinery business, besides stimulating other industries, made possible a huge expansion of farm production, which acted in numberless ways to stimulate economic growth.

The New Industrial Society

Rapid industrialization influenced American life in countless ways, none more significant than its effect on the character of the work force and thus on the structure of society. The new jobs created by industrial expansion attracted European immigrants by the tens of thousands. Over 500,000 entered the United States in the 1830's, 1.5 million in the 1840's, and 2.6 million in the 1850's. In proportion to the population, this was the heaviest immigration in all American history; in 1855 about 15 per cent of all residents had arrived within the previous ten years.

During the forties and fifties most of this human tide came from two countries, Ireland and Germany. This was especially true between 1847 and 1854, when the Irish potato blight and a series of crop failures in Germany drove thousands to try their luck in America. In 1849, 159,000 Irish and 60,000 Germans entered the United States; for 1853, another typical year, the corresponding figures are 163,000 and 142,000. By no means did all these immigrants become industrial workers. Many thousands of substantial Germans and Scandinavians pushed on directly into the western regions. But the poorer immigrants could not afford to do this; farming required capital which the majority did not have. The Irish particularly tended to settle in the large eastern seaports, which grew even more rapidly than the country as a whole. In 1830 New York had about 200,000 inhabitants, 20 years later it had 515,000, in 1860 over a million. Whereas only 14 per cent of the population of the Northeast lived in cities in 1830, more than 35 per cent did so in 1860.

Viewed in historical perspective, immigration has stimulated the American economy and increased social mobility. Each increase in the labor force has made possible expanded production, and each new wave of migrants has pushed earlier arrivals up the social scale and on to better jobs. In the short run, however, the great influx of the 1840's and 1850's depressed living standards, weakened the social fabric, and sharpened class divisions. Irish immigrants particularly were so desperately poor that they would accept whatever wage employers offered them. They thus roused resentments among native workers, resentments exacerbated by the Irishmen's unfamiliarity with city ways and their Roman Catholic faith, which the Protestant majority associated with Old World authoritarianism and corruption. The Irish, on the other hand, quickly developed their own prejudices, particularly against Negroes, with whom they competed for work. Even one of their leaders in the old country, Daniel O'Connell, admitted that the American Irish were "among the worst enemies of the colored race." And of course the Negroes responded with equal bitterness. "Every hour sees us elbowed out of some employment to make room for some newly-arrived emigrant from the Emerald Isle, whose hunger and color entitle him to special favor," one of them complained. Anti-Negro prejudice was less noticeable among other immigrant groups but by no means absent; most immigrants adopted the views of the local native majority. Germans in the southern states tended to support slavery, those in the Northwest to oppose it (though they did not necessarily like Negroes).

New York's notorious Five Points district c. 1829. The anonymous artist depicted himself in the left foreground, handkerchief to nose. "Reeking everywhere with dirt and filth," wrote Charles Dickens of Five Points in 1842. "Where dogs would howl to lie, men and women and boys slink off to sleep, forcing the dislodged rats to move."

MR. & MRS. SCREVEN LORILLARD COLLECTION

Social and racial rivalries aside, unskilled immigrants caused serious disruptions of economic patterns wherever they appeared in large numbers. For example, their absorption into the factories of New England inevitably speeded the disintegration of the system of hiring young farm girls and housing them in dormitories. Already competition and technical advances in the textile industry were increasing the pace of the machines and making the life of the young operatives far less pleasant than it had been in the early days. In 1850 the Lowell girls were receiving wages of $2 a week and the companies were spending only 17.5 cents a day to house and feed them. Hours were long—11.5 to 13 a day—life in the boarding houses grim. The Irish, who demanded less coddling and who seemed to provide the mills with a "permanent" working force, were soon taking the places of the girls in large numbers; by 1860 they made up more than 50 per cent of the labor force in the New England mills.

The influx of immigrants does not, however, entirely explain the wretched state of industrial workers during this period. Low wages combined with crowding, resulting from the swift expansion of city populations, produced slums that would make the most noisome modern ghetto seem like a paradise in comparison. A Boston investigation in the late 1840's described one district as "a perfect hive of human beings . . . huddled together like brutes." A Lowell, Massachusetts, newspaper reported a slum family of ten living in a single room along with four boarders. In New York tens of thousands of the poor lived in dark, rank cellars, those in the waterfront districts often invaded by high tides. Tenement houses like great gloomy prisons rose back to back, each with many windowless rooms and often without heat or even running water. The worst of these warrens were boarding houses. Some of these provided what was euphemistically called a three-class system of accommodations. First class, costing about 35 cents a week, consisted of a pile of straw thrown on the floor and first pick at the food. One needs a vivid imagination to grasp what third class, which cost 9 cents a week, was like.

Outside the "home," city life for the poor was almost equally squalid. Slum streets were piled high with garbage and trash, recreational facilities were almost nonexistent, police and fire protection pitifully inadequate. "Urban problems" were less critical than a century later only because they affected a smaller part of the population; for those who experienced them they were, all too often, absolutely crushing.

In the early factory towns most workers maintained small vegetable gardens and a few chickens; low wage rates did not necessarily reflect a low standard of living. In the new industrial slums, even a blade of grass was unusual. In 1851 editor Horace Greeley published a minimum weekly budget for a family of five in his New York *Tribune*. This budget, which allowed nothing for recreation, savings, medical bills, or other amenities—Greeley did include 12 cents a week for newspapers—came to $10.37. Since the weekly pay of a factory hand seldom reached $5, workers had to bring their wives and children into the factories with them merely to survive. And child labor in the factories of the 1850's differed fundamentally from child labor in the early textile mills. The pace was faster, the surrounding environment more depressing.

Relatively few workers in this period belonged to unions. Local federations of craft unions sprang up in the major cities, and for a brief period during the boom that preceded the Panic of 1837, a National Trades' Union, actually representing only a few northeastern cities, managed to hold conventions, although it accomplished nothing very concrete for its members. Early in the Jackson era, "workingmen's" political parties enjoyed a brief popularity, occasionally electing a few local officials. But these organizations were mostly made up of skilled craftsmen, professional reformers, and even businessmen. They soon expired, destroyed by internal bickering over questions that had little or nothing to do with working conditions. By 1832 they had disappeared, and the depression of the late thirties led to the demise of most trade unions. Nevertheless, *skilled* workingmen improved their lot somewhat in the 1840's and 1850's. The average working day declined gradually from about 12.5 hours to 10 or 11. President Van Buren's executive order of 1840 granting the 10-hour day to federal employees was a major step in the achievement of shorter hours. Over the next 10 or 15 years many states passed 10-hour laws, and also laws regulating child labor, although these were seldom enforced. Most states, however, enacted effective mechanic's lien laws, giving workers first call on the assets of bankrupt and defaulting employers, and the Massachusetts court's decision in the case of *Commonwealth v. Hunt* (1842), establishing the basic legality of labor unions, was a judicial landmark since other state courts accepted it as a precedent.

The flush times of the early 1850's caused the union movement to revive. Many strikes occurred, and a few new national organizations appeared. But most unions were mere local institutions, weak and with little control over their membership. The Panic of 1857 dealt the labor movement another body blow. In short, it is difficult to find much indication of a general trend toward the permanent organization of labor between 1820 and the Civil War. For this the workers themselves were partly to blame: craftsmen took little interest in unskilled workers except to keep them down. Even common laborers hesitated to consider themselves part of a permanent working class with different objectives from those of their employers. The traditional individualism of Americans, the fluidity of their society, the constant influx of job-hungry immigrants, and the widespread use of women and children in unskilled jobs made labor organization difficult.

Any investigation of American society before the Civil War reveals a paradox—obvious but difficult to resolve. The United States was a land of opportunity, a democratic society with a prosperous, expanding economy and few class distinctions. Its people had a high standard of living in comparison with the citizens of European countries. Yet within this rich, confident nation there existed a class of miserably underpaid and depressed unskilled workers, mostly immigrants, worse off materially than nearly any southern slave. The literature is full of descriptions of needleworkers earning 12 cents a day, of girls driven to prostitution because they could not earn a living decently, of hunger marches and soup kitchens, of disease and crime, and men sunk into apathy by hopeless poverty. At one point in the 1840's about a quarter of the population of New York City was receiving some form of public relief, and a police drive in the city in 1860 brought in nearly 500 beggars.

Yet the middle-class majority seemed indifferent to or, at best, unaware of these conditions. A handful of reformers conducted investigations, published exposés, and labored to help the victims of urbanization and industrialization. They achieved very little. Great fires burned in these decades to release the incredible energies of America. The poor were the ashes, sifting down silent and unnoticed beneath the dazzle and the smoke. Although the industrial revolution was making the United States the richest nation in the world, it was also creating, as historian Robert H. Bremner has said, "a poverty problem, novel in kind and alarming in size." In the 1840's, almost 50 years before Jacob Riis made the phrase notorious, an American reformer wrote: "One half of the world does not know *how the other half lives.*"

As this statement implies, the change that was occurring had two sides. Industrialization produced poverty (in Marxian terminology a proletarian class) but also a capitalistic aristocracy. Tenements sprang up cheek by jowl with the urban palaces of the new rich; every slum had its counterpart in the tree-lined streets of the prosperous quarters. Beside shocking statistics on crime and vice can be displayed a proud accounting of new theaters, restaurants, and other symbols of urban prosperity and refinement.

What had happened is ironic rather than paradoxical. In colonial times Americans (as we have already seen) believed in a stratified, deferential society, but in practice their civilization became increasingly democratic. After the Revolution, ideology rapidly caught up with practice, and for a brief moment, roughly corresponding to the Presidency of Andrew Jackson, reality and theory were in close accord. Thereafter, the impact of industrial growth shifted the balance in the other direction. Society became more stratified, differences in wealth and status among citizens greater, but the ideology of egalitarian democracy reigned supreme. Before the Revolution Americans assumed that some men were better than others, but the differences between the life of one American and another were relatively slight. By the mid-19th century Americans were convinced that all men were equal, and, indeed, all *white* men did have equal political rights. Socially and economically, however, distances between the top and the bottom were widening. This situation endured at least for the rest of the century, and in some respects it still endures.

Foreign Commerce

Changes in the pattern of foreign commerce were less noticeable than those in manufacturing but nevertheless significant. After increasing erratically during the 1820's and 1830's, both imports and exports leaped forward spectacularly in the next 20 years. The nation remained primarily an exporter of raw materials and an importer of manufactured goods, and in most years it imported more than it exported. Cotton continued to be the most valuable single export, bringing in a record $191 million in 1860 out of a total of $333 million; despite America's own thriving industry, textiles still held the lead among imports, with iron products second. Great Britain, throughout the period as in earlier days, was both the best customer of the United States and its leading supplier.

Certain shifts in emphasis are easily noted. In

ENO COLLECTION, NEW YORK PUBLIC LIBRARY

This minutely detailed, unfinished engraving of New York in the late 1830's, looking across the East River from Brooklyn, is the work of Thomas Horner. Manhattan's wharves are packed solid with merchant ships, and the river teems with vessels of every description, from lighters and ferries to finely depicted steamboats.

earlier times the West Indian trade had been of tremendous importance, but that commerce had long been fully exploited. While it did not decline in value or volume, its relative significance fell off rapidly. The islands consumed nearly 20 per cent of America's exports in the 1820's but only 7 per cent in the years just preceding the Civil War. The re-export trade, so rich in the first decade of the century, also suffered a relative decline in later years. And of course, after the discovery of gold, that metal jumped to prominence as an export, some $450 million being shipped abroad during the 1850's.

The success of sailing packets, those "square-riggers on schedule," greatly facilitated the movement of both passengers and freight. Although other cities tried to compete with New York in founding such lines, few succeeded, except in establishing connections with the metropolis; 52 packets were operating between New York and various European ports by 1845, and many more plied between New York and other coastal cities. This speeded the already growing tendency for trade to concentrate in New York and to a lesser extent in Boston, Philadelphia, Baltimore, and New Orleans. The commerce of smaller towns like Providence and New Haven, which had flourished in earlier days, now languished.

New Bedford and a few other southern New England towns shrewdly saved their prosperity by concentrating on whaling, which boomed between 1830 and 1860. By the mid-fifties, with sperm oil selling at over $1.75 a gallon and the country exporting an average of $2.7 million worth of whale oil and whalebone a year, New Bedford boasted a whaling fleet of well over 300 vessels and a population approaching 25,000. The whalers ranged the oceans of the world; they lived a hard, lonely life punctuated by moments of exhilaration when they sighted the great mammoths of the deep and drove the harpoon home. The also made magnificent profits—to clear 100 per cent in a single voyage was merely routine. However, as Samuel Eliot Morison has written, when merchants could make up at one major port like Boston "an export cargo containing the entire apparatus of civilized life, from cradles and teething-rings to coffins and tombstones," small ports that did not find some specialty like whaling were doomed.

The increase in the volume and value of trade and its concentration at larger ports had a marked effect on the construction of ships. Soon bigger, more efficient vessels were in great demand; by the 1850's the average ship was three times the size of those built 30 years earlier, and some yards were constructing vessels of more than 2,000 tons displacement. Startling improvements in design, culminating in the long, sleek, white-winged clipper ships built in Boston, New York, and Baltimore made possible speeds previously undreamed of. Appearing just in time to supply the need for fast transportation to the California gold fields, these clippers cut sailing time around the Horn to San Francisco from five or six months to three, the record of 89 days being held jointly by the *Andrew Jackson* and by Donald McKay's famous *Flying Cloud*. Another McKay-designed clipper, aptly named *Champion of the Seas,* once logged 465 nautical miles in 24 hours, far in excess of the best efforts of any modern yacht. To achieve such speeds, cargo capacity had to be sacrificed, making clippers uneconomical for carrying the bulky produce that was the mainstay of the nation's commerce. But for specialty products, in their brief heyday the clippers were unsurpassed. Hong Kong merchants, never known for extravagance, willingly paid 75 cents a cubic foot to ship teas by clipper to London, although slower vessels charged only 28 cents. In the early 1850's clippers sold for as much as $150,000, yet with luck they might earn their full cost in a voyage or two.

Steam Conquers the Atlantic

The reign of the clipper ship was destined to be short. Like so many other things, ocean commerce was being mechanized. Steamships conquered the high seas more slowly than the rivers, because early models were unsafe in rough waters and uneconomical. A river boat could depend for fuel upon local stops along its route, whereas an Atlantic steamer had to carry tons of coal across the ocean, greatly reducing its capacity for cargo. However, by the late 1840's steamers were beginning to capture most of the passenger traffic, mail contracts, and first-class freight. Although unable to keep up with the clippers in a heavy breeze, their average speed was faster by far, especially on the westward voyage against the prevailing winds. By 1860 the Atlantic had been crossed in less than ten days. Nevertheless, for really long voyages, such as the 15,000-mile haul around South America to California, fast sailing ships held their own for many years.

The steamship, and especially the iron ship, which had greater cargo-carrying capacity and was both stronger and cheaper to maintain, took away the advantages which American shipbuilders had held since colonial times. American lumber was cheap, but American iron had no such advantage over European; skills acquired by generations of carpenters and shipwrights were of little value when the emphasis shifted to iron and steam. The British excelled in iron technology and quickly made the most of it. Although the United States invested about $14.5 million in subsidies for the merchant marine, these funds were not employed very intelligently and did little good. In 1858 all effort to aid shipping was abandoned.

The American merchant marine did not disappear, however, and for decades the wooden vessels of many nations competed keenly for the world's commerce. The combination of competition, government subsidies, and technological advance drove shipping rates down drastically. Between the mid-twenties and the mid-fifties the cost of moving a pound of cotton from New York to Liverpool fell from one cent to about a third of a cent. Transatlantic passengers could obtain the best accommodations on the fastest ships for under $200 and good accommodations on slower packets for as little as $75. Rates were especially low for European emigrants willing to travel to America on cargo vessels. By the 1840's at least 4,000 ships were engaged in carrying American cotton and Canadian lumber to Europe. On their return trips with manufactured goods they had much unoccupied space, which they converted into rough quarters for passengers and sold at very low rates. It was possible to travel in steerage from Liverpool to New York for £3 (under $15), from an Irish port to Quebec for half that.

Conditions on these ships were terrible: crowded, stuffy, and foul. Frequently, epidemics took a fearful toll among steerage passengers. On one crossing of the ship *Lark,* for example, 158 of 440 passengers died of typhus. Yet without this cheap means of transportation, thousands of poor immigrants would simply have remained at home. Bargain freight rates also help explain the clamor of American manufacturers for high tariffs, since transportation costs added relatively little to the price of European goods.

Railroads and Canals

Perhaps the most dramatic change in the United States in these pre-Civil War years was the shift in the direction of the nation's internal commerce and its immense increase. For as long as the Mississippi Valley had been settled by the white man, the Great River had controlled the flow of goods from farm to market. The completion of the Erie Canal in 1825 heralded a shift, speeded by the feverish canal construction of the following decade.* However, even at the time of the Panic of 1837, which resulted in part from the overbuilding of canals in the western states, the bulk of the trade of the valley flowed down to New Orleans. The Erie Canal boomed, but as late as 1836 four-fifths of its eastward-flowing commerce originated east of Buffalo, within New York State itself.

Nevertheless, each year saw more western produce moving to market through the canals. In 1845 the Erie was still drawing over two-thirds of its west-east traffic from within New York, but by 1847, despite the fact that this local business held steady, more than half of its traffic came from west of Buffalo and by 1851 more than two-thirds. The volume of western commerce over the Erie in 1851 amounted to more than 20 times what it had been in 1836, while the value of western goods reaching New Orleans in this period had increased only two-and-a-half-times.

The canals, however, could not handle the huge exports of the growing West, exports which increased in part because the canals reduced the cost of moving western goods to market. What tied the West to the East once and for all was an entirely new means of transportation—the railroad. The first railroads were built in England in the 1820's, but Americans took up the invention eagerly. Many enterprising businessmen in Boston, Baltimore, Philadelphia, and other cities saw its possibilities at once. "When this great improvement in transportation shall have been extended to Pittsburgh, and thence into the extensive and fertile state of Ohio, and also to the great western lakes, Philadelphia may then become the great emporium of the western country," one early promoter predicted. In 1830 the ambitiously named Baltimore and Ohio Railroad began operations over a 13-mile stretch of track. By 1833 Charleston, South Carolina, had a line reaching 136 miles to Hamburg, on the Savannah River. Two years later the first cars rolled over the Boston and Worcester Railroad. Although the Panic of 1837 slowed construction considerably, by 1840 the United States had 3,328 miles of track, equal to the canal mileage of the country and nearly double the railroad mileage of the entire continent of Europe.

These first railroads did not effectively compete with the canals for intersectional traffic. Although many new lines were built during the 1840's, the through connections needed to move goods economically over great distances materialized slowly. Of the 6,000 miles of track operating in 1848, nearly all lay east of the Appalachians, and little of it had been coordinated into railroad *systems.* The intention of most early builders had been to monopolize the trade of surrounding districts, not to establish connections with competing centers. Frequently roads used different gauges deliberately to prevent other lines from tying into their tracks.

Engineering problems also held back growth, for the distances were great, the topography rugged. Steep grades and sharp curves—unavoidable in many parts of the country if the cost of the roads was not to be prohibitive—required more powerful and flexible engines than as yet existed. Sparks from wood-burning locomotives caused fires; wooden rails topped with strap iron wore out quickly and broke loose under the weight

* In 1830 there were 1,277 miles of canal in the United States. By 1840 there were 3,326 miles.

and vibration of heavy cars. Gradually, hard work and ingenuity solved these difficulties. The iron T-rail and the use of crossties set in loose gravel to reduce vibration increased the durability of the tracks and made heavier, more efficient equipment possible. Modifications in the design of locomotives enabled the trains to negotiate sharp curves. Engines that could burn hard coal appeared, thus eliminating the danger of starting fires along the right of way and reducing fuel costs. The cowcatcher (an improvement based on a model designed by one Isaac Dripps which had impaled the cow on prongs) reduced still another early hazard.

With the ending of the Mexican War a tremendous spurt of construction began. In four years mileage nearly doubled, three years later it had doubled again, and by 1860 the nation had 30,636 miles of track. The laying of this network of rails was "the greatest economic fact of the fifties," Allan Nevins has written.

During this extraordinary burst of activity, four companies drove their lines of gleaming iron from the Atlantic seaboard to the great interior valley. In 1851 the Erie, longest road in the world, with 537 miles of track, linked the Hudson River north of New York City with Dunkirk on Lake Erie. Late the next year the Baltimore and Ohio reached the Ohio River at Wheeling, and in 1853 a banker named Erastus Corning consolidated eight short lines connecting Albany and Buffalo to form the New York Central, soon to be known as "the best-equipped and most efficient road of the day." Finally, in 1858 the Pennsylvania Railroad completed a line across the mountains from Philadelphia to Pittsburgh. At the same time, the states beyond the Appalachians were building at an even more feverish pace. In the 1850's Ohio laid more than 2,300 miles of track, Indiana more than 1,900, Illinois more than 2,600, Tennessee over 1,200, Wisconsin nearly 900. Even in the South, where construction was slower, Mississippi laid about 800 miles, Alabama over 600. By 1855 passengers could travel from Chicago or St. Louis to the East Coast entirely by railroad at a cost ranging from about $20 to $30, the trip taking, with luck, less than 48 hours. A generation earlier such a trip required between two and three weeks.

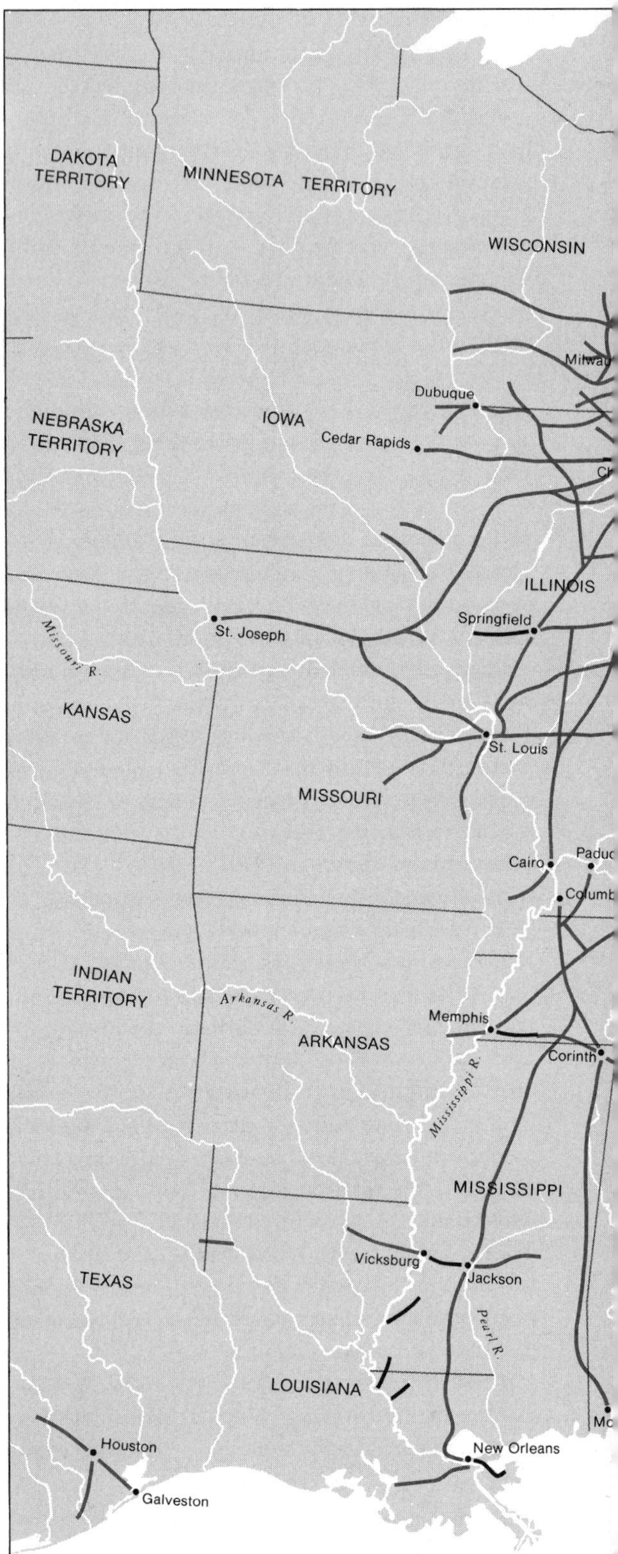

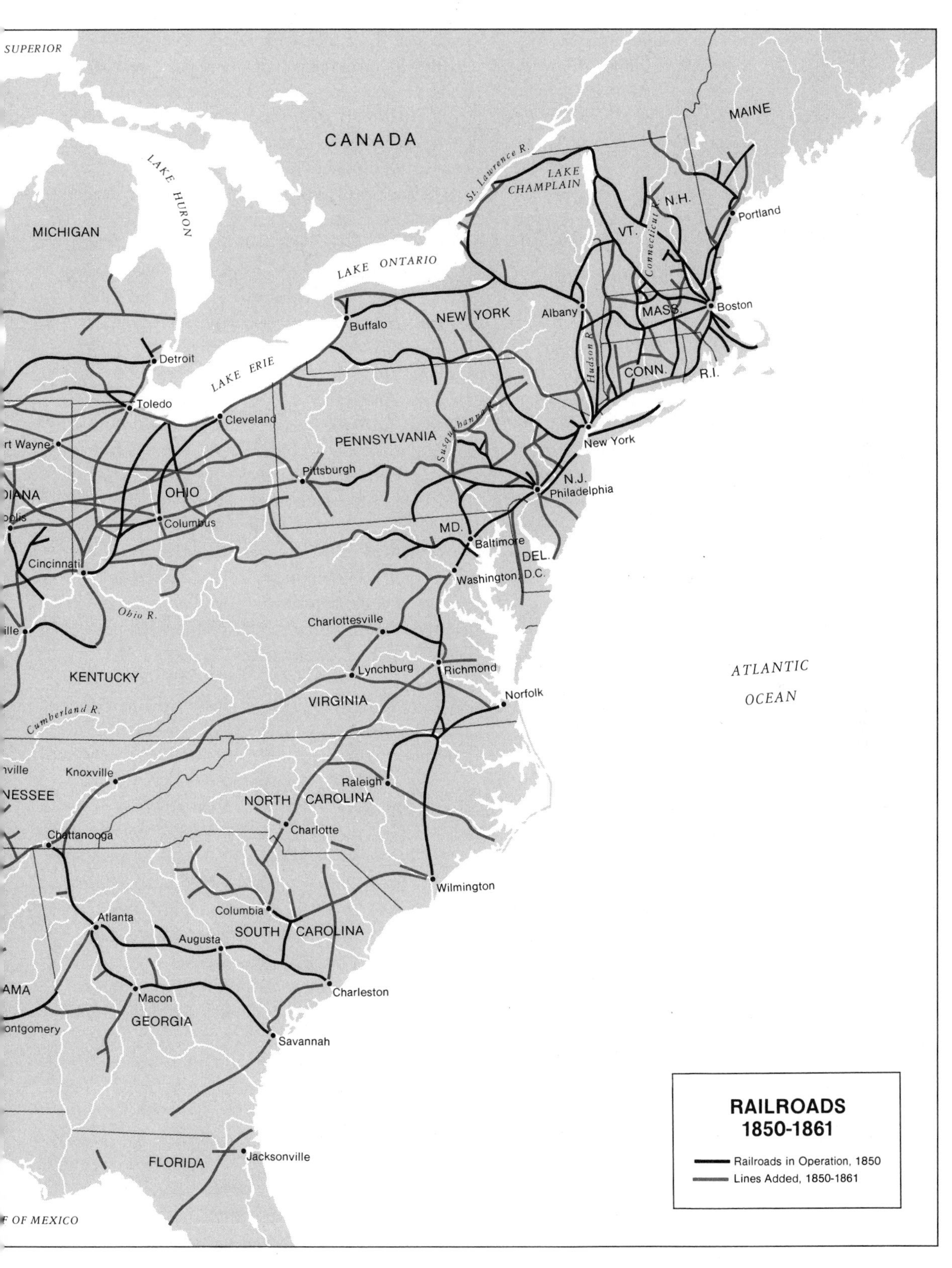

SUPERIOR
CANADA
MAINE
LAKE HURON
St. Lawrence R.
LAKE CHAMPLAIN
N.H.
Portland
MICHIGAN
VT.
Connecticut R.
LAKE ONTARIO
Albany
MASS.
Boston
NEW YORK
Buffalo
Detroit
Hudson R.
LAKE ERIE
CONN.
R.I.
Toledo
Cleveland
Susquehanna R.
rt Wayne
PENNSYLVANIA
New York
Pittsburgh
N.J.
Philadelphia
IANA
OHIO
olis
Columbus
MD.
Baltimore
DEL.
Cincinnati
Washington, D.C.
Ohio R.
ille
Charlottesville
Lynchburg
Richmond
ATLANTIC
OCEAN
KENTUCKY
Norfolk
VIRGINIA
Cumberland R.
ville
Knoxville
Raleigh
NESSEE
NORTH CAROLINA
Charlotte
Chattanooga
Wilmington
Columbia
Atlanta
SOUTH CAROLINA
Augusta
Charleston
AMA
Macon
GEORGIA
ontgomery
Savannah
RAILROADS
1850-1861
Railroads in Operation, 1850
Lines Added, 1850-1861
FLORIDA
Jacksonville
F OF MEXICO

Financing the Railroads

This building program required an immense investment of labor and capital at a time when the United States faced many other demands for these resources. Recent immigrants, or, in the South, slaves, did most of the heavy work. Raising the necessary money proved a more complex task. The Erie and the New York Central each cost about $23 million, the Pennsylvania $18 million. During the height of construction, the labor bill of the Baltimore and Ohio was running at $200,000 a month.

Private investors supplied about three-quarters of the money invested in railroads before 1860. Much of this capital, especially in the early days, came from local merchants and businessmen and from farmers along the proposed rights of way. Farmers hoping to gain from rail connections with eastern markets frequently exchanged mortgages on their lands for railroad stock. In Wisconsin during the 1850's some 6,000 farmers traded mortgages worth between $4.5 and $5 million for shares in local lines. Funds were quite easy to raise because subscribers seldom had to lay out the whole price of their stock at one time; instead they were subject to periodic "calls" for a percentage of their commitment as construction progressed. If the road made money, much of the additional mileage could be paid for out of earnings from the first sections built. The Utica and Schenectady Railroad, one of the lines that eventually went into the making of the New York Central, was capitalized in 1833 at $2 million (20,000 shares at $100). Only $75 per share was ever called for by the directors. Nevertheless, in 1844 the road had been completed, the stock was selling at $129, and the shareholders were receiving handsome cash dividends.

The Utica and Schenectady was a short road in a rich territory; for less favorably situated lines, stocks were harder to sell and bonds, backed by the property of the line, were more commonly used to raise money. In the West where the population was very thin, the distances great, and property values relatively low, outside capital had to be found. Much of it came from New England, where men like the China merchant John Murray Forbes were increasingly active in railroad finance. Such men dealt mainly in bonds; they used stock chiefly to maintain control of the companies whose bonds they held. Foreign investors also preferred bonds over stocks by a large margin; by 1853 Europeans owned about a quarter of all American railroad bonds.

However, by no means all the capital needed to build railroads came from private sources. Of the lines connecting the seaboard with the Middle West, the New York Central alone received no public aid, chiefly because it ran through prosperous, well-populated country and across level terrain. The others were all "mixed enterprises," drawing about half their capital from state and local governments.

Public aid took many forms. Towns, counties, and the states themselves lent money to railroads and invested in their stock. Between 1845 and 1860 the states borrowed over $90 million to finance railroads, and local governments added a sum that was probably even larger. Special privileges, such as exemption from taxation and the right to condemn property, were often granted. In a few cases, states actually built and operated roads as public corporations. Georgia's Western and Atlantic line, running from Atlanta to Chattanooga, was the longest of these. Michigan undertook an ambitious program of public construction in 1837, and two lines, the Michigan Central and the Michigan Southern, were partly completed. However, the strain on the treasury of the state proved too great, and both lines were sold to private interests. Taken all in all, the proportionate contribution of state and local governments to the cost of railroad-building was much less than to canals, and it declined steadily as the rail network expanded and matured.

As with earlier internal improvement proposals, federal financial aid to railroads was usually blocked in Congress by a combination of eastern and southern votes. But in 1850 a scheme for granting federal lands to the states to build a line from Lake Michigan to the Gulf of Mexico won considerable southern and eastern support and passed both houses. The main beneficiary was the Illinois Central Railroad, which received a 200-foot right of way and alternate strips of land along the track one mile wide and six miles deep, a total of almost 2.6 million acres. By mortgaging this land and by selling portions of it to farmers, the Illinois Central raised nearly all the $23.4 million spent on construction. The success of this operation led to additional grants of some 18 million acres in the 1850's, benefiting more than 40 railroads. Far larger federal grants were made, however, after the Civil War, when the great transcontinental lines were built.

Frequently, the capitalists who promoted railroads were more concerned with making money out of the *construction* of the lines than in operating them. Erastus Corning was a good railroad man; his lines were well maintained and efficiently run. Yet he was also a banker and a manufacturer of iron. He accepted no salary as president of the Utica and Schenectady, "asking only that he have the privilege of supplying all the rails, running gear, tools and other iron and steel articles used." When he could not himself produce rails of the proper quality, he purchased them in England, charging the railroad a commission for his services. When he became interested in the Michigan Central, he paid himself similar commissions, which at least one associate thought too large. Corning's actions while president of the New York Central led to stockholder complaints, and a committee was appointed to investigate. He managed to control this group easily enough, but it did report that "the practice of buying articles for the use of the Railroad Company from its own officers might in time come to lead to abuses of great magnitude," a prediction that proved all too accurate in the generation after the Civil War.

Corning, it must be repeated, was an honest man; his only mistake, if mistake it was, lay in overestimating his own impartiality a little. But some men in the business were unashamedly crooked and avidly took advantage of the public passion for railroads. So long as the belief persisted that any railroad was certain to make money, unscrupulous promoters were bound to appear. Some officials issued stock to themselves without paying for it and then sold the shares to gullible investors for hard cash. Others manipulated the books of their corporations, used inside information to make killings in the stock market, and set up special construction companies and paid them exorbitant returns out of railroad assets. These practices did not become widespread until after the Civil War, but all of them first sprang up in the period now under discussion. At least one western governor was complaining angrily in 1861 of "bold, open, unblushing frauds."

Railroads and the National Economy

Although recent researchers have tended to discount earlier extravagant impressions of the importance of railroads to the pre-Civil War economy, the effects of so much railroad construction were certainly profound. While the main thing that led farmers to put more land under the plow was an increase in the price of agricultural products, the railroad helped determine just what land was utilized and how profitably it could be farmed. Much of the fertile prairie through which the Illinois Central ran had been available for settlement for many years before 1850, but development had been slow because it was remote from navigable waters and had no timber. In 1840 the three counties immediately northeast of Springfield had a population of about 8,500. They produced about 59,000 bushels of wheat and 690,000 bushels of corn. In the next decade the region grew slowly by the standards of that day: the three counties had about 14,000 people in 1850 and produced 71,000 bushels of wheat and 2.2 million bushels of corn. Then came the railroad and with it an agricultural revolution. By 1860 the population of the three counties had soared to over 38,000, wheat production had topped 550,000 bushels, and corn 5.7 million bushels. "Land-grant" railroads like the Illinois Central also stimulated agricultural expansion by making every effort to attract settlers to their lands, advertising widely and selling farm sites at low rates on liberal terms.

Access to world markets gave farmers on the fertile prairies of the upper Mississippi Valley a real incentive to increase output. Land was plentiful and cheap, but farm labor was scarce; consequently agricultural wages rose sharply, especially after 1850. Fortunately, new tools and machines appeared in time to ease the labor shortage. First came improvements in the design of plows, necessary because the prairie sod was tough and sticky.

John Roebling's railroad bridge at Niagara Falls, the first to be suspended from wire cables, was memorialized by a Currier lithograph upon its completion in 1855. "No one is afraid to cross," Roebling happily reported.

The cast-iron plow, invented early in the century by Jethro Wood, a New York farmer, was effective in the East but less than satisfactory in the West. Its parts broke under the strain of ripping through the matted roots of the native grasses, and the adhesive soil clung to its rough and pitted surface. John Deere, a Vermont blacksmith who had settled in Illinois in 1837, discovered that steel plowshares were both stronger and smoother. In 1839 he made ten such plows in his little shop. Soon he had a large factory and by 1857 was selling 10,000 a year.

Even more important was the perfection of the mechanical reaper, for the real limit on wheat production was set by the amount that farmers could handle during the brief harvest season. Although many inventors made significant contributions and no single company monopolized production, the major figure in the development of the reaper was Cyrus Hall McCormick. McCormick's horse-drawn reaper bent a swath of grain against the cutting knife and then deposited it neatly on a platform, whence a man could rake it easily into windrows. With this machine, two workers could cut 14 times as much wheat as with scythes.

Displaying remarkable foresight, McCormick, in 1848, located his factory in Chicago, at that time little more than a village. He prospered, but he could not keep other manufacturers out of the business, despite his patents. Competition led to continual improvement of the machines and kept prices within the reach of most farmers. Installment selling also added to demand. Trials and contests at agricultural fairs convinced thousands of skeptics. By 1860 nearly 80,000 reapers had been sold; their efficiency helps explain why wheat output rose by nearly 75 per cent in the 1850's.

The railroad had an equally powerful impact on American cities. Naturally, the great seaports that formed the eastern terminuses of the network benefited, but so did countless intermediate centers like Buffalo and Cincinnati. Most especially Chicago advanced. In 1850 not a single line had reached there. Only five years later it was terminal for 2,200 miles of track and controlled the commerce of an imperial domain. By extending half a dozen lines west to the Mississippi, it drained off nearly all the river traffic north of St. Louis. A bushel of corn raised in the northwestern corner of Illinois could now be shipped by rail to Chicago for about 15 cents less than it cost to move it to St. Louis by barge. The Illinois Central sucked the expanding output of the prairies into Chicago as well. Most of this freight went eastward over the new railroads or on the Great Lakes and the Erie Canal. Nearly 350,000 tons of shipping plied the lakes by 1855.

Of course the railroads, like the textile industry, greatly stimulated other kinds of economic activity. They transformed agriculture, as we have seen; both real-estate values and buying and selling of land increased whenever the iron horse puffed into a new district. Although they apparently did not have a very great effect on general manufacturing before the Civil War, the roads consumed large amounts of iron, thus helping both the mining and smelting industries. New foundries sprang up to turn out locomotives. In 1860 railroads purchased about $15 million worth of bar and sheet iron, nearly half the nation's output. Railroad demands also led to technological advances that were of great importance in the iron industry.

Although the financing of railroad companies meant profits for bankers and opportunities for men with capital, probably more men and more capital were occupied in economic activities *resulting* from the development of railroads than in the roads themselves, which is another way of saying that the railroads were immensely valuable internal improvements. Railroads benefited every section in a thousand ways. Viewed in this perspective, the willingness of communities to invest public funds in railroad companies is perfectly understandable.

However, the railroads were not an unmixed blessing. In their hurry to link distant areas, promoters often laid track carelessly and without sufficient attention to safety. The national eagerness for cheap and rapid transportation led to the granting of privileges to railroad corporations that were not always in the public interest, such as the right to operate lotteries. The New Jersey legislature even gave the Camden and Amboy Railroad a monopoly of rail traffic between Philadelphia and New York. The land-grant system led to abuses, for some companies withheld choice land from the market for speculative purposes.

The proliferation of trunk lines and the competition of the canal system (for many products the slowness of canal transportation was not a serious handicap) led to a sharp decline in freight and passenger rates. Periodically, railroads engaged in "wars" to capture business. At times a man could travel from New York to Buffalo for as little as $4. Anthracite was being shipped from the Pennsylvania mines to the coast for $1.50 a ton. The Erie Canal reduced its toll charges by more than two-thirds in the face of railroad competition, and the roads, in turn, cut their own rates drastically, until, on the eve of the Civil War, it cost less than one cent per ton-mile to send produce through the canal and only slightly more than two cents a mile on the railroads. By that time one could ship a bushel of wheat all the way from Chicago to New York by railroad for less than 35 cents.

Cheap transportation had a revolutionary effect upon western agriculture. Farmers in distant Iowa could now raise grain to feed the factory workers of Lowell and even of Manchester, England. Two-thirds of the meat consumed in New York City was soon arriving by rail from beyond the Appalachians. Swiftly, the center of American wheat production shifted westward to Illinois, Wisconsin, and Indiana. When the Crimean War (1853–56) and European crop failures increased foreign demand, these regions boomed. Success bred success, both for farmers and for the railroads. Profits earned carrying wheat enabled the roads to build feeder lines which opened up still wider areas to commercial agriculture and made it easy to bring in lumber, farm machinery, household furnishings, and the settlers themselves at very low cost. "Immigration, settlement, farm development, and railroad construction were all dependent upon each other," Paul W. Gates writes in *The Farmer's Age*.

Railroads and the Sectional Conflict

Increased production and cheap transportation boosted the western farmer's income and thus his standard of living. The days of isolation and self-sufficiency, even for the man on edge of the frontier, rapidly disappeared. The frontiersman became a businessman and also, to a far greater extent than his forebears, a consumer, buying all sorts of manufactured articles that his ancestors had made for themselves or done without. This was not entirely beneficial. Like the southern planters he now became dependent upon middlemen in a host of ways. Conditions utterly beyond his control could have a drastic effect upon his well-being; therefore, he lost some of his feeling of self-reliance. Overproduction became a problem.

Furthermore, it began to take more capital to buy a farm, for as profits increased, so did the price of land. Machinery was an additional expense. Inevitably, the percentage of farm laborers and tenants tended to rise.

The linking of East and West had fateful effects on politics. Although difficult to prove in detail, it is nonetheless obvious that the increased ease of movement from section to section and the ever more complex social and economic integration of East and West stimulated nationalism and thus became a force for the preservation of the Union. Without the railroads and canals, states like Illinois and Iowa would scarcely have dared to side against the South in 1861. After the Mississippi ceased to be essential to them, citizens of the upper valley could afford to be more hostile to slavery and especially to its westward extension. Economic ties with the Northeast reinforced cultural connections.

The South might have preserved its influence in the Northwest if it had pressed forward its own railroad-building program, but for various reasons it failed to do so. There were a good many southern lines but nothing like a southern *system.* As late as 1856 one could get from Memphis to Richmond or Charleston only by very indirect routes. As late as 1859 the land-grant road extending the Illinois Central to Mobile, Alabama, was not complete, nor did any economical connection exist between Chicago and New Orleans. This state of affairs could be accounted for in part by the scattered population of the South, the paucity of passenger traffic, the seasonal nature of much of the freight business, and the absence of large cities. Southerners placed too much reliance on the Mississippi: the fact that traffic on the river continued heavy throughout the 1850's blinded them to the precipitous rate at which their *relative* share of the nation's trade was declining. But the fundamental cause of the South's backwardness in railroad construction was the attitude of its leading men. Southerners of means were no more interested in commerce than in industry; their capital found other outlets. Allan Nevins' explanation of the failure of New Orleans quickly to build a line north to Illinois applies equally well to all the South: "Planters were indifferent, merchants skeptical; natural obstacles were many; capital was timid."

The Economy on the Eve of Civil War

Between the mid-forties and the mid-fifties the United States had experienced one of the most remarkable periods of growth in its entire history. The territorial expansion resulting from the Mexican War set the stage. Manufacturing output increased an astounding 69 per cent in ten years. Every economic indicator surged forward: grain and cotton production, population, gold production, sales of public land. The building of the railroads further stimulated business, and by making transportation cheaper the completed lines still further energized the nation's economy. The "American System" that Henry Clay had dreamed of arrived with a rush just as Clay was passing from the scene.

Inevitably this growth caused dislocations, these aggravated by the boom psychology that once again infected the popular mind. In 1857 there was a serious collapse. The return of Russian wheat to the world market after the Crimean War caused grain prices to fall. This checked agricultural expansion, which hurt the railroads and cut down on the demand for manufactures. People called this abrupt downturn the "Panic of 1857" and worried about a depression. Yet such was the basic vigor of the economy that the bad times did not last long. The upper Mississippi Valley suffered most, for so much new land had been opened up that supplies of farm produce greatly exceeded demand, and the world situation remained unhelpful. Elsewhere conditions improved rapidly. Gold-mad California had escaped the depression entirely. The South, somewhat out of the hectic rush to begin with, was affected very little by the collapse of 1857, for cotton prices continued high. Manufacturers experienced a moderate revival as early as 1859.

Before a new upward swing could become well established, however, the sectional crisis between North and South shook men's confidence in the future. Then the war came, and a new set of forces began to shape economic development.

SUPPLEMENTARY READING Most of the volumes dealing with economic developments mentioned in Chapter 8 continue to be useful for this period. See especially G.R. Taylor, *The Transportation Revolution** (1951), P.W. Gates, *The Farmer's Age** (1960), D.C. North, *The Economic Growth of the United States** (1961), and Stuart Bruchey, *The Roots of American Economic Growth** (1965). Allan Nevins has interesting chapters on economic developments in *The Ordeal of the Union* (1947).

An excellent survey of the ante-bellum South is Clement Eaton, *The Growth of Southern Civilization** (1961). For more detailed coverage, see C.S. Sydnor, *The Development of Southern Sectionalism** (1948), and A.O. Craven, *The Growth of Southern Nationalism* (1953). The standard works on slavery have also been mentioned. In addition to U.B. Phillips, *American Negro Slavery** (1918), and K.M. Stampp, *The Peculiar Institution** (1956), S.M. Elkins, *Slavery** (1959), E.D. Genovese, *The Political Economy of Slavery** (1965), and A.H. Conrad and J.R. Meyer, *The Economics of Slavery and Other Econometric Studies* (1964), should also be consulted. Among more specialized volumes, P.D. Curtin, *The Atlantic Slave Trade* (1970), is a careful investigation of mortality rates on the slave ships and on the conditions of the trade in general, while W.S. Howard's *American Slavers and the Federal Law* (1963) is an excellent monograph on the illegal slave trade. On the internal trade, see Frederic Bancroft, *Slave-Trading in the Old South* (1931), and W.H. Stephenson, *Isaac Franklin: Slave Trader and Planter of the Old South* (1938). The fullest study of slave insurrections is Herbert Aptheker's *American Negro Slave Revolts** (1943), but this book exaggerates the overt rebelliousness of the slaves. Arna Bontemps, *Great Slave Narratives* (1969), and Gilbert Osofsky, *Puttin' Ole Massa Down** (1969), throw light on slave attitudes, while William Styron's controversial novel, *The Confessions of Nat Turner** (1967), is a fine example of how historical research can be put to effective use by a writer of fiction. R.C. Wade, *Slavery in the Cities* (1964), contains much interesting material, as does W.K. Scarborough, *The Overseer: Plantation Management in the Old South* (1966). A.M. Schlesinger's edition of F.L. Olmstead's contemporary accounts of southern life, *The Cotton Kingdom* (1953), is worthy of study. On southern manufacturing, see Broadus Mitchell, *William Gregg: Factory Master of the Old South* (1941).

On industrial developments, in addition to the above-mentioned volumes of Taylor and Nevins and the books mentioned in Chapter 8, see A.C. Cole, *The Irrepressible Conflict* (1934), Roger Burlingame, *March of the Iron Men** (1938), H.J. Habbakuk, *American and British Technology in the Nineteenth Century** (1962), and G.S. Gibb, *The Saco-Lowell Shops: Textile Machinery Building in New England* (1950). On labor history, F.R. Dulles, *Labor in America* (1960), is a good introduction. N.J. Ware, *The Industrial Worker, 1840–1860** (1924), and W.A. Sullivan, *The Industrial Worker in Pennsylvania* (1955), are more specialized. For workingmen's political activities, see Edward Pessen, *Most Uncommon Jacksonians: The Radical Leaders of the Early Labor Movement* (1967). Immigration is dealt with generally in M.A. Jones, *American Immigration** (1960), and M.L. Hansen, *The Immigrant in American History** (1940). More specialized works include Hansen's *The Atlantic Migration** (1940), Oscar Handlin, *Boston's Immigrants* (1941), and Robert Ernst, *Immigrant Life in New York City* (1949). Poverty in America is examined by R.H. Bremner, *From the Depths** (1956).

Taylor's *Transportation Revolution* is outstanding on developments in commerce and communication, but for more detail, consult E.R. Johnson *et al.*, *History of Domestic and Foreign Commerce* (1915). On the age of sail, see A.H. Clark, *The Clipper Ship Era* (1911), S.E. Morison, *The Maritime History of Massachusetts** (1921), C.C. Cutler, *Greyhounds of the Sea* (1960), and Robert Carse, *The Moonrakers* (1961). Among the useful specialized studies of railroad development are T.C. Cochran, *Railroad Leaders* (1953), P.W. Gates, *The Illinois Central Railroad and Its Colonization Work* (1934), E.C. Kirkland, *Men, Cities, and Transportation* (1948), A.D. Chandler, Jr., *Henry Varnum Poor* (1956), R.W. Fogel, *Railroads and American Economic Growth* (1964), and Albert Fishlow, *American Railroads and the Transformation of the Ante-Bellum Economy* (1965).

*Available in paperback.

13

The Romantic Age

As the United States grew larger, richer, and more centralized, it also made great strides toward achieving a distinctive culture. Still the child of Europe, by mid-century it was more clearly the offspring rather than a mere imitation of the parent society. American literature and art, American intellectual activity of every sort, became with each passing decade more reflective of American experiences. Jefferson, for example, drew most of his ideas from classical authors and 17th-century English thinkers. He gave to these doctrines an American cast, as when he stressed the separation of church and state or the pursuit of happiness instead of property in describing the "unalienable rights" of men. His ideas, however, were primarily European. On the other hand, Ralph Waldo Emerson, whose views were roughly similar to Jefferson's and served later generations of liberals in much the way that Jefferson's did, was an *American* philosopher, despite the fact that he also drew inspiration from European thinkers.

The Romantic View of Life

In the western world the romantic movement was a revolt against the bloodless logic of the Age of Reason. It was a noticeable if unnamed point of view in Germany, France, and England as early as the 1780's and in America a generation later; by the second quarter of the 19th century few if any intellectuals were unmarked by it. "Romantics" emphasized feeling and intuition rather than thought, stressed the differences between individuals and societies rather than their similarities. Ardent love of country was characteristic of the movement; individualism, ingenuousness, emotion were its bywords.

Romanticism so obviously fitted the mood of 19th-century America that one is tempted to think of it as an American way of looking at life despite its European origins. Interest in raw nature and in primitive peoples, worship of the individual, praise of the common folk culture, the subordination of intellect to feeling—were these primarily romantic ideas or American ideas? Jacksonian Democracy with its self-confidence, careless prodigality, contempt for learning, glorification of the ordinary—

was it a product of the American experience or a reflection of a wider world view?

Such questions cannot be answered definitively, nor need they be. Many of the early European romantics, such as Goethe, Chateaubriand, Byron, and Coleridge were much influenced by what they knew of America, and educated Americans were steeped in the writings of the great European romantics. Romanticism found a congenial home in the United States in any case, and Americans in many fields produced works that, while typically romantic, were also original and typically American. Coincidental with the great economic expansion described in the last chapter, the United States experienced a period of remarkable literary productivity. Between 1850 and 1855, among other important works, Nathaniel Hawthorne published *The Scarlet Letter* and *The House of the Seven Gables,* Herman Melville *Moby Dick*, Henry David Thoreau *Walden*, and Walt Whitman *Leaves of Grass.* As F.O. Matthiessen wrote in his excellent study, *American Renaissance: Art and Expression in the Age of Emerson and Whitman,* "You may search all the rest of American literature without being able to collect a group of books equal to these in imaginative vitality." This is not to say that these writers approved of the rapid economic changes they saw taking place all around them, or that they sympathized with the acquisitive spirit of the age, typified by the gold rush, then at its most extravagant height. In general, they did neither. But the romantic movement influenced them all, and all discovered in the American experience much that made the assumptions of the romantics seem plausible.

The Transcendental Spirit

The romantic way of thinking found its best expression in the United States in the transcendentalist movement. Transcendentalism, a New England creation, is difficult to describe because it emphasized the indefinable and the unknowable; it was a mystical, intuitive way of looking at life. Man was truly divine, the transcendentalists believed, because he was part of nature, itself the essence of divinity. Man's intellectual capacity did not define his capabilities, for he could "transcend" reason by having faith in himself and in the fundamental benevolence of the universe. Transcendentalists were complete individualists, seeing the social whole as no more than the sum of its parts. Organized religion, indeed all institutions, were unimportant if not actually counterproductive; what mattered was the single man, and that he aspire, stretch himself *beyond* his known capabilities. In truth, since each human being was part of the great "Over-Soul," his capacities had no limits. Failure resulted only from lack of effort. The expression "hitch your wagon to a star" is of transcendentalist origin.

The individuals most closely connected with this way of thinking were all members of the Transcendental Club, an informal discussion group that began meeting in Boston in 1836 at the home of George Ripley, a Unitarian minister. Its leading figure was Ralph Waldo Emerson. Born in 1803 and Harvard-educated, Emerson became a minister, but in 1832 he gave up his pulpit, deciding that "the profession is antiquated." After traveling to Europe, where he met many of the leading romantic writers, including Coleridge, William Wordsworth, and (especially important) Thomas Carlyle, he settled in Concord, Massachusetts, to a long career as essayist, lecturer, and sage.

Emerson managed to restore to what he called "corpse-cold" Unitarianism the fervor and purposefulness of 17th-century Puritanism without accepting the pessimistic Puritan view of man's fate. His philosophy was at once buoyantly optimistic and rigorously intellectual, self-confident and conscientious. In a notable address at Harvard in 1837 on "The American Scholar," he urged his countrymen to put aside their devotion to things European and seek inspiration in their immediate surroundings. He saw himself as pitting "spiritual powers" against "the mechanical powers and the mechanical philosophy of this time." The new industrial society of New England disturbed him profoundly.

Emerson favored change and believed in progress. "What is man born for," he wrote, "but to be a Reformer?" Temperamentally, however,

"men in the world of today are bugs." p. 24.

Christopher Pearse Cranch was a young convert to transcendentalism who apparently could not suppress a faint sense of skepticism and a barbed sense of humor. His drawings, from a scrapbook he compiled about 1844, Illustrations of the New Philosophy, *interpret literally pompous passages from Emerson.*

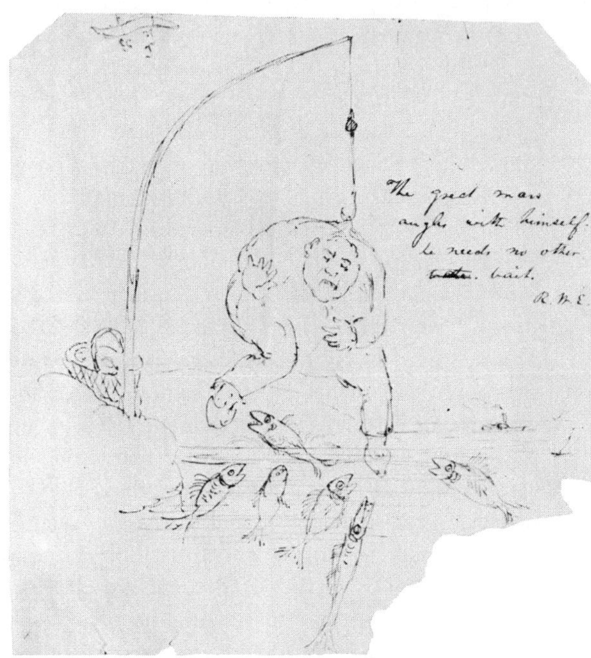

he was too serene and too much his own man to engage actively in the fight for the causes other reformers espoused, and too idealistic to accept the compromises that most reformers make to achieve their ends. Too many reformers were fanatics, he also believed, "narrow, self-pleasing, conceited men [who] affect us as the insane do."

Because he put so much emphasis on self-reliance (the individual who trusted in himself could make "the huge world . . . come round to him"), Emerson disliked strong government of any kind. "The less government we have the better," he said. In a sense he was the prototype of some modern alienated intellectuals, so repelled by the world as it was that in spite of his high ideals he would not actively try to change it. Nevertheless, he thought strong leadership essential, perhaps being influenced in this direction by his friend Carlyle's glorification of the role of great men in history. "The wise man is the State," he argued. Yet, despite a certain ethereal quality coupled with his idealism (utilitarianism, he wrote, was a "stinking philosophy"), Emerson had a strong practical streak. He made his living by lecturing, tracking back and forth tirelessly across the country every year, talking before every type of audience for a fee of $50 per performance.

Closely identified with Emerson was his Concord neighbor Henry David Thoreau, another member of the Transcendental Club. After graduating from Harvard in 1837, Thoreau taught school for a time and helped out in a small pencil-making business run by his family. He was a strange man, gentle, a dreamer, content to absorb the beauties of nature almost intuitively, yet also stubborn and individualistic to the point of selfishness. "He is the most unmalleable fellow alive," one acquaintance wrote. The hectic scramble for wealth that he saw all about him he found disgusting and also alarming, for he believed it was destroying both the natural and the human resources of the country. "Most men," he wrote, "are so occupied with the factitious cares and superfluously hard labors of life, that its finer fruits cannot be plucked by them."

Like Emerson, Thoreau objected to many of society's restrictions on the individual. "That government is best which governs not at all,"

"Standing on the bare ground, — my head
bathed by the blithe air, & uplifted into
infinite space, — all mean egotism
vanishes. I become a transparent
Eyeball."
Nature, p. 13.

I expand and live in the warm day,
like corn & melons.
Nature, p. 73.

he said, going both Emerson and the Jeffersonians one better. He was perfectly prepared to see himself as a majority of one. "When were the good and the brave ever in a majority?" he asked. "If a man does not keep pace with his companion," he wrote on another occasion, "perhaps it is because he hears a different drummer." In 1845 Thoreau decided to put to the test his theory that men need not depend upon society for a satisfying existence. He built a cabin at Walden Pond on some property owned by Emerson and lived there alone for two years. He did not try to be entirely self-sufficient: he was not above returning to his family or to Emerson's for a square meal upon occasion, and he generally purchased the building materials and other manufactured articles that he needed. Instead he set out, by experimenting, to prove that, *if necessary*, an individual could get along without the products of civilization. For example, he used manufactured plaster in building his Walden cabin, but he also gathered a bushel of clamshells and made a small quantity of lime himself, to prove that it could be done.

At Walden Thoreau wrote a book, *A Week on the Concord and Merrimack Rivers* (1849), which utilized an account of a trip he had taken with his brother as a vehicle for a discussion of his ideas about life and literature. He also spent much time observing the quiet world around the pond, thinking, and writing in his journal. The best fruit of this period was *Walden* (1854), one of the most extraordinary books ever written by an American. Superficially *Walden* is the story of Thoreau's experiment, moving and beautifully written. But it is also an acid indictment of the social behavior of the average man. Although not an anarchist, Thoreau argued against unthinking conformity, against subordinating one's own judgment to that of the herd.

The most graphic illustration of his confidence

in his own values occurred while he was living at Walden. He believed that the Mexican War was immoral because it advanced the cause of slavery. To protest against it he refused to pay his Massachusetts poll tax. For this he was arrested and lodged in jail, although only for one night because one of his aunts promptly paid the tax for him. His challenging essay "Civil Disobedience," explaining his view of the proper relation between man and the state, resulted from this experience. Like Emerson, however, Thoreau refused to participate actively in reform movements, preferring to devote his time to thought and writing rather than to action.

Edgar Allan Poe

The work of all the imaginative writers of the period also reveals romantic influences, and it is possibly an indication of the affinity of the romantic approach to American conditions that for the first time a number of excellent writers of poetry and fiction appeared in the 1830's and 1840's. Edgar Allan Poe, one of the most remarkable of these, seems almost a caricature of the romantic image of the tortured genius. Poe was born in Boston in 1809, the son of poor actors, both of whom died before he was three. He was raised and then rejected by a wealthy Virginian, John Allan, and wasted much of his life trying to re-establish himself in Allan's good graces in hopes of inheriting his fortune. Few persons as neurotic as Poe have been able to produce first-rate work. In college he ran up debts of $2,500 in less than a year and had to withdraw. He won an appointment to West Point but was discharged after a few months for disobedience and "gross neglect of duty." He was a lifelong alcoholic, an occasional taker of dope, and probably also impotent. He married a child of 13 and became utterly dependent upon his mother-in-law. At one point in his sad life he attempted to poison himself; repeatedly he was down and out even to the verge of starvation. He was haunted by melancholia and hallucinations. Yet he was an excellent magazine editor, a fresh, honest, and penetrating critic, a poet of unique if somewhat narrow talents, and a fine short-story writer. Although he died of acute alcoholism at 40, he turned out a remarkably large volume of serious, highly original work.

Poe responded strongly to the lure of romanticism. In his youth he aped Lord Byron, and Coleridge profoundly influenced his approach to writing. His works abound with examples of wild imagination and fascination with mystery, fright, and the occult. He was not, however, a mere imitator. If he did not actually invent the detective story, he perfected it, as seen in tales like "The Murders in the Rue Morgue" and "The Purloined Letter." He called such stories, which stressed the thought processes of a clever detective in solving a mystery by reasoning from evidence, "tales of ratiocination." Poe was also one of the earliest writers to deal with what are today called science-fiction themes, and he was a master of the horror tale, such as "The Pit and the Pendulum" and "The Cask of Amontillado."

Contemptuous of American provincialism, Poe ruthlessly criticized the second- and third-rate native works that so many contemporary critics praised. Although dissolute in his personal life, when he touched pen to paper, he became a disciplined craftsman. The most fantastic passages in his works are actually the result of careful, reasoned selection. As Howard Mumford Jones has said, Poe used "vague, yet vivid, words . . . to create a dream world, the world of the surrealist painter."

Despite his poverty, his disreputable habits, and his rejection of most of the values prized by middle-class America, Poe was widely read in his own day. He won a number of literary awards. His "MS. Found in a Bottle" took the prize in the first American short-story contest, run by the *Baltimore Saturday Visiter* in 1833, and his famous poem "The Raven" won instantaneous popularity when it was published in 1845. If he had been a little more stable, he might have made a good living with his pen, but in that case he might not have written as he did.

Nathaniel Hawthorne

Far different from Poe but also influenced by the prevailing romanticism was Nathaniel Hawthorne of Salem, Massachusetts. Hawthorne was born in 1804. When he was a

NEW-YORK HISTORICAL SOCIETY

Both Poe (above, in a portrait by Samuel Osgood) and Hawthorne (below) won popular acclaim in their day. Poe's The Raven and Other Poems *(1845) sold widely, while Hawthorne's* The Scarlet Letter *(1850) achieved best-sellerdom the year it was published.*

CULVER PICTURES

small child, his father died and his grief-stricken mother became a recluse. Left largely to his own devices, he grew to be a lonely, introspective person, bookish and imaginative. He had few contacts with people until he was well over 30. Wandering about New England by himself in summertime, he soaked up much local lore, which he drew upon in writing short stories. For a time he lived in Concord where he came to know most of the leading transcendentalists, but of the group only Thoreau became a friend. Hawthorne disliked the egoism of the transcendental point of view and rejected its bland optimism outright. "Emerson," he said, was an "everlasting rejector of all that is, and seeker for he knows not what." Emerson, for his part, could not enjoy Hawthorne's writings because of their pervasive air of gloom.

Hawthorne was fascinated by the past, particularly by the Puritan heritage of New England and its continuing influence on the people of his own generation. He was also a romantic in his deep love of nature, in his almost morbid satisfaction in being alone, and also in his fondness for the common man. He greatly admired Andrew Jackson, praising his intelligence and his stalwart character. Three Democratic Presidents—Van Buren, Polk, and Franklin Pierce, the last a classmate of his at Bowdoin College—appointed him to minor political offices.

Hawthorne's early stories, originally published in magazines, were brought together in *Twice-Told Tales* (1837). They made excellent use of New England culture and history for background, but in most of them the author concerned himself chiefly with describing the struggles of individuals with sin and guilt, and especially with the pride and isolation that is often man's fate when he places too great reliance upon his own judgment. His greatest works were two novels written in a brief period after the Whigs turned him out of his government job in 1849, following the election of Zachary Taylor. *The Scarlet Letter* (1850), a grim yet sympathetic analysis of adultery, condemned not the sin itself but the people who presumed to judge the sinner. *The House of the Seven Gables* (1851) was a gripping account of the decay of

During the creative surge that produced Moby Dick, *Melville overflowed with new ideas, asking a friend for "fifty fast-writing youths with an easy style."*

an old New England family.

Like Poe, Hawthorne was appreciated in his own day and widely read; unlike Poe, he made a modest amount of money from his work. But he was never very comfortable in the society he inhabited. Thoreau considered him "simple and childlike," and another writer spoke of his "tenderness" and "boundless sympathy with all forms of being." Nevertheless, despite this sensitivity and his acute perception of the tragic element in man, there was a certain gruffness in him too. He had no patience with the second-rate. And despite his success in creating word pictures of a somber, mysterious world, he considered America too prosaic a country to inspire good literature. "There is no shadow, no antiquity, no mystery, no picturesque and gloomy wrong, nor anything but a commonplace prosperity," he complained.

Herman Melville

In 1850, while writing *The House of the Seven Gables,* Hawthorne was introduced by his publisher to another writer in the midst of a novel. This was Herman Melville, the book *Moby Dick.* The two became good friends at once, for despite their very dissimilar backgrounds, they had a great deal in common. Melville was a New Yorker, born in 1819, one of eight children of a merchant of distinguished lineage. His father, however, lost all his money and died when the boy was 12. Herman left school at 15, worked briefly as a bank clerk, and in 1837 went to sea. For 18 months, in 1841–42, he was a crewman on the whaler *Acushnet.* Then he jumped ship in the South Seas. For a time he lived among a tribe of cannibals in the Marquesas; later he made his way to Tahiti, where he remained for nearly a year as a beachcomber. In August 1843 he secured a berth on a passing American warship, the frigate *United States.* After another year at sea, he was honorably discharged when the *United States* reached American waters at Boston in the fall of 1844.

Although he had never before attempted any serious writing, he decided to record the story of his adventures, and in 1846 published *Typee,* an account of his life in the Marquesas. The book was a great success, for Melville had visited a part of the world almost unknown to the white man, and his descriptions of his bizarre experiences among South Sea primitives suited the taste of a romantic age. "The man who had lived among the cannibals" became suddenly a well-known figure. Success inspired him to write a sequel, *Omoo* (1847); other books followed quickly.

However, Melville was not content with being a professional travel writer. As he wrote he became conscious of deeper powers. He read widely, thought profoundly. In 1849 he began a systematic study of Shakespeare, pondering over the bard's intuitive grasp of man's perverse nature. *Antony and Cleopatra* and *King Lear* particularly intrigued him. Like Hawthorne, Melville could not accept the prevailing optimism of his generation. But unlike his friend, he admired Emerson, seconding the Emersonian demand that Americans reject European ties and develop their own literature. "Believe me," he wrote, "men not very much inferior to Shakespeare are this day being born on the banks of the Ohio." Yet he considered Emerson's vague talk about striving and the inherent goodness of mankind complacent nonsense. The individualism that Emerson valued so highly, he said, concealed "a self-conceit so intensely intellectual and calm that at first one hesitates to call it by its right name."

Experience made Melville too acutely aware of the evil in the world to be a transcendentalist. His novel *Redburn* (1849), based on his adventures on a Liverpool packet, was, as F.O. Matthiessen put it, "a study in disillusion, of innocence confronted with the world, of ideals shattered by facts." Yet Melville was anything but a cynic; in his writings he expressed deep sympathy for the Indians and for immigrants, crowded like animals into the holds of transatlantic vessels. He denounced the brutality of discipline in the United States navy in *White-Jacket* (1850). His essay "The Tartarus of Maids," a moving if somewhat overdrawn description of young girls working in a paper factory, protested against the subordination of human beings to machines.

Meeting Hawthorne, whose dark view of human nature coincided with his own, encouraged Melville to press ahead with *Moby Dick,* which he published in 1851. Against the background of a whaling voyage (and no better account of whaling has ever been written), he dealt subtly and symbolically with the problems of good and evil, of man's courage and cowardice, his faith, his stubbornness, his pride. In Captain Ahab, driven relentlessly to hunt down the huge white whale, Moby Dick, which had destroyed his leg, Melville created one of the great figures of imaginative literature; in the book as a whole, he produced probably the finest novel written by an American, comparable to the best in any language.

Melville's greatness escaped most of his contemporaries. As his work became more profound, it lost its appeal to the average reader, and its originality and symbolic meaning escaped most of the critics. *Moby Dick,* his masterpiece, received little attention and most of that unfavorable. Melville had not expected the book to be popular. "Dollars damn me," he told Hawthorne, to whom *Moby Dick* was dedicated. "What I feel most moved to write, that is banned,–it will not pay." He kept on writing until his death in 1891 but was virtually ignored. Only in the 1920's did the critics rediscover him and give him his merited place in the history of American literature.

WALT WHITMAN FOUNDATION

A daguerreotype of Whitman, taken during the late 1840's when he was a journalist in New York and for a brief period the editor of the Brooklyn Eagle.

Walt Whitman

Walt Whitman, whose *Leaves of Grass* (1855) was the last of the great literary works of this brief outpouring of American genius, also wrote in the romantic vein, but he was by far the most original and distinctly American writer of his age. He was born on Long Island, outside New York City, in 1819. At 13 he left school and became a printer's devil; thereafter he held a succession of newspaper jobs in the metropolitan area. He was an ardent Jacksonian and later a Free-Soiler, which got him into hot water with a number of the publishers for whom he worked.

Although genuinely a "common man," thoroughly at home among tradesmen and laborers, Whitman was surely not an ordinary man. Deeply introspective, he read omnivorously, if in a rather disorganized fashion, soaking up

Shakespeare, Goethe, Carlyle, Scott, and many others. He turned out a number of sentimental, melodramatic stories of no particular distinction that were published in magazines like the *Democratic Review*, the leading political monthly of the times. Meanwhile, he was working out a new, intensely personal mode of expression. Probably the most important formative influence on his thinking was the writing of Emerson. During the early 1850's, while he was employed as a carpenter and composing the poems that made up *Leaves of Grass*, he regularly carried a book of Emerson's in his lunch box. "I was simmering, simmering, simmering," he later recalled. "Emerson brought me to a boil." The transcendental idea that inspiration and aspiration are at the heart of all achievement captivated him. A poet could best express himself, he believed, by relying uncritically on his natural inclinations without regard for rigid metrical forms. In this sense Whitman was the opposite of Poe, the careful literary craftsman, whose work, incidentally, he characterized as "brilliant and dazzling, but with no heat."

Leaves of Grass consisted of an Emersonian preface, in which Whitman made the extraordinary statement that the Americans had "probably the fullest poetical nature" of any people in history, and 12 strange poems in free verse: rambling, uneven, appearing to most readers shocking both in the commonplace nature of the subject matter and the coarseness and plainness of the language. Emerson, Thoreau, and a few others saw a fresh talent in these poems, but most readers and reviewers found them offensive. Indeed, the work was so undisciplined and so much of it had no obvious meaning that it was easy to miss the many passages of great beauty and originality that were scattered throughout. Nevertheless, Whitman continued to write, revising and greatly expanding *Leaves of Grass* in a number of editions.

Part of Whitman's difficulty arose because there was much of the charlatan in his make-up; often his writing did not ring true. He actually wrote and published three fulsome anonymous reviews of *Leaves*—one in the *American Phrenological Journal!* Although in reality a sensitive, effeminate person, he tried to pose as a great, rough character. Later in his career he bragged of fathering no less than six illegitimate children, which was assuredly untrue. He never married, and his work suggests that his strongest emotional ties were with men rather than with women. He displayed a great deal of the American love of show and bombast. Thomas Carlyle once remarked shrewdly that Whitman though he was a big man because he lived in a big country. He loved to use foreign words and phrases, and since he had no more than a smattering of any foreign tongue, he frequently sounded pretentious and sometimes even downright foolish when he did so.

However, Whitman's work *was* authentically American, more so than that of any contemporary. His egoism—he entitled one of his finest poems "Song of Myself"—was tempered by his genuine belief that he was merely typical of all mankind.

I celebrate myself, and sing myself,
And what I assume you shall assume,
For every atom belonging to me as good
  belongs to you.

He had a remarkable ear for rendering common speech poetically, for employing slang, for catching the breezy informality of Americans and their faith in themselves.

Earth! you seem to look for something at my
  hands,
Say, old top-knot, what do you want?

I bequeath myself to the dirt to grow from the
  grass I love,
If you want me again look for me under your
  boot-soles.

Because of these qualities and because in his later work, especially during the Civil War, he occasionally struck a popular chord, Whitman was never as neglected as Melville. In his declining years he collected many disciples and even a Boswell, Horace Traubel, to whom we are indebted for knowledge of much of the poet's later conversation and opinions. When he died in 1892, he was, if not entirely understood, at least widely appreciated.

"The Flowering of New England"

These were the great men of American literature before the Civil War. A number of others, if they lacked genius, are still worth reading. One of these was Henry Wadsworth Longfellow, whose romantic poetry has brought pleasure to generations of readers. In 1835, while still in his twenties, Longfellow became professor of modern languages at Harvard. Although he published a fine translation of Dante's *The Divine Comedy* and was expert in many languages, his fame came from poems like "The Village Blacksmith," "Paul Revere's Ride," *The Courtship of Miles Standish,* a sentimental tale of Pilgrim days, and *The Song of Hiawatha,* the romantic retelling of an Indian legend. These brought him excellent critical notices and considerable fortune; his work was widely translated and reprinted. Though musical, polished, full of vivid images, Longfellow's poetry lacked profundity, originality, and force, as he did himself, but it was neither cheap nor trivial. He was an exquisite craftsman, a popular writer in the best sense, and a man universally praised for his sweetness and nobility. When Longfellow wrote

> Life is real! life is earnest!
> And the grave is not its goal . . .

he expressed the heartfelt belief of most of his generation. In this sense he captured the spirit of his times better than any of his great contemporaries, better even than Whitman.

Longfellow was but the most talented of a group of minor New England writers who collectively gave that section great intellectual vitality in the pre-Civil War decades. Prominent in this "flowering of New England" was John Greenleaf Whittier, a poet nearly as popular as Longfellow in his own day. Whittier believed ardently in the abolition of slavery and worked actively in politics and journalism. By nature he was somewhat like Walt Whitman, although not nearly of Whitman's stature as a writer. A few of his poems can still be read with pleasure, such as "The Barefoot Boy," dealing with his own rural childhood. His abolitionist writing continues to have historical significance. Somewhat more weighty was the achievement of James Russell Lowell, successor to Longfellow as professor of modern languages at Harvard. The first editor of the *Atlantic Monthly,* founded in Boston in 1857, Lowell produced a great deal of undistinguished poetry and criticism, but his first series of *Biglow Papers* (1848), humorous stories satirizing the Mexican War, written in the New England dialect, made an original and influential contribution to the national literature. Dr. Oliver Wendell Holmes, professor of medicine at Harvard, was also widely known as a poet and essayist. A few of his poems, such as "The Chambered Nautilus" and "Old Ironsides," are interesting examples of American romantic verse, and his "Autocrat of the Breakfast-Table" series in the *Atlantic Monthly* became a regional if not a national institution.

All these minor writers were blessed with splendid constitutions and lived almost to the end of the century; their greatest influence came after the Civil War, although most of their best work dates from before 1860. Collectively, they had a salutary effect upon American culture, for if rather smug and narrow, they were also serious and industrious. If they did not often soar, at least they fixed their gaze upward and tried to encourage their readers to do likewise.

This may also be said of several important historians of the period, all of whom were also New Englanders. George Bancroft, one of the first Americans to study in Germany, began in 1834 to publish a ten-volume *History of the United States* based on extensive research in the sources. William Hickling Prescott, although almost blind, wrote extensively on the history of Spain and Spain's American empire, his *Conquest of Mexico* (1843) and *Conquest of Peru* (1847) being his most important works. John Lothrop Motley, another German-trained historian, published his *Rise of the Dutch Republic* in 1856, and Francis Parkman began his great account of the struggle between France and Great Britain for the control of North America with his *Conspiracy of Pontiac* in 1851.

The public read all these histories avidly, for they suited the taste of the times, and all were written with a mass audience in mind. Bancroft saw a divine providence guiding his country along the path to greatness, a view that readers found easy to accept. Prescott was almost obsessed with the importance of re-creating a living past peopled by real men. "Keep in view the most important, stirring, affecting incidents," he wrote in his journal. "Above all, keep *character,*–& especially the pervading, dominant character of the hero in view." Motley excelled even Prescott at sharp characterizations based on masses of detail, as in his brilliant if one-sided interpretation of Philip II of Spain, the archvillain of his history. (Motley wrote of Philip II: "If there are vices . . . from which he was exempt, it is because it is not permitted by human nature to attain perfection even in evil.") Parkman appealed to readers through his gripping descriptions of the wilderness and his mastery of forest lore (both based on his own observations and experiences) and by his narrative power. Parkman's prejudices against the Indian–"man, wolf, and devil, all in one"–and against the Catholic French, which conformed to the preconceptions of most of his readers, also added to the popularity of his work.

These historians were thoroughly in the romantic tradition. As David Levin has said in his important study *History as Romantic Art*, "they all shared an 'enthusiastic' attitude toward the Past, an affection for grand heroes, an affection for Nature and the 'natural.'" But their work, particularly Parkman's, has endured, partly because they were talented and conscientious writers, partly because they chose great themes of lasting human interest, and partly because they were good scholars. They, too, managed to point their sights at an unspecialized audience without aiming downward.

Southern Writers

Southern literature was even more markedly romantic than that of New England but much less voluminous. John Pendleton Kennedy of Baltimore wrote several novels with regional historical themes, much in the manner of Sir Walter Scott. The most important of these were *Swallow Barn* (1832), treating plantation life in Virginia after the Revolution, and *Horse-Shoe Robinson* (1835), which dealt with the Revolutionary Battle of King's Mountain. Kennedy recognized Poe's genius before most people and got him an editorial job on the *Southern Literary Messenger.* He was also a Whig politician of some importance, serving several terms in Congress. In 1852 he became secretary of the navy in the Fillmore Cabinet.

More versatile and influential than Kennedy was William Gilmore Simms of South Carolina. Simms wrote nearly two dozen novels as well as several volumes of poetry and a number of biographies. At his peak in the 1830's he earned as much as $6,000 a year with his pen. His favorite theme was the South Carolina frontier, which he portrayed in novels like *The Partisan* (1835), one of a series dealing with the Revolution, and *The Yemassee* (1835), the story of an early 18th-century Indian war. His poetry was Byronic; his novels, like Kennedy's, were written in the style of Scott, to whom his admirers liked to compare him. Simms was a gentleman, as Carl Van Doren put it, "a man of letters if not of genius." His novels seem too melodramatic for modern tastes; the plots lack variety, the style lacks discipline. His portraits of the planter class are too bloodless and reverential to be convincing, and his female characters are nearly all pallid and fragile. Only when he wrote of the frontier life and its people did his work possess much power, yet, along with Kennedy, he contributed largely to the glamorous legend of the Old South.

The Spread of Culture

As the population grew larger and more concentrated and as society, especially in the North, was permeated by a middle-class point of view, popular concern for "culture" in the formal sense increased rapidly. A literate and prosperous people, committed to the idea of education but not generally well educated, became devoted to "self-improvement," to being "refined" and "civilized." Industrialization made it easier to satisfy this demand for culture, although at the same time the new machines tended to make the artifacts of culture more stereotyped. More efficient printing techniques reduced the cost of books, magazines, and newspapers. By the late 1850's one publisher was able to offer a

50-volume set of the ever-popular Sir Walter Scott for $37.50. Booksellers flourished: there were more than 2,000 in the United States by 1859.

The penny newspaper put in its appearance with the New York *Sun* (1833). In 1835 James Gordon Bennett founded the New York *Herald* and brought the new cheap journalism to perfection. The penny papers depended on sensation, crime stories, and society gossip to attract readers, but they contained important news too, leading the masses to a greater awareness of the world around them.

In the 1850's the moralistic, sentimental "domestic" novel was in its prime. Scott remained popular and Charles Dickens became perhaps even more so after the astonishing success of the pirated American edition of *David Copperfield* (1850). Scott and Dickens were master craftsmen, but their skill at portraying the "gentler" emotions best explains their large following in the United States. Dickens also appealed to democratic tastes by his disparagement of the British aristocracy, his heart-rending accounts of the plight of the poor, and his humorous and colorful descriptions of ordinary people. A number of American authors achieved great popularity with this type of work. Most of them were women, which led Hawthorne to complain bitterly that "a d - - - - d mob of scribbling women" was taking over American writing. Susan Warner's *The Wide, Wide World* (1850), a sad tale about a pious, submissive little girl who cried "more readily and more steadily than any other tormented child in a novel of the time," and Maria Cummins' *The Lamplighter* (1854), the story of little Gerty, an orphan rescued by a kindly lamplighter named Trueman Flint, were typical. *The Lamplighter* sold 70,000 copies within a year of publication. As Carl Bode puts it in *The Anatomy of American Popular Culture*, works like these were "the great-grandmother" of the modern soap opera.

Poetry was also very popular; according to Bode, "housewives, merchants, ministers, and clerks often had a little volume of verse handy at their table or bedside." Between 1839 and 1861, 179,000 volumes of Longfellow's poems were sold. Sentimental poetesses like the English Felicia Hemans and the American Lydia Huntley Sigourney found a wide audience for their sticky-sweet treatments of such themes as the death of a child and mother love and also for poems on historical subjects. Mrs. Sigourney, a shrewd businesswoman and a tireless publicizer of her own work, produced 14 volumes of verse in the 1840's alone, all of them very popular. The banality of her work can be seen in these lines from a poem about Anne Boleyn and Henry VIII:

> For him she prays in seraph tone,
> "Oh! be his sins forgiven!
> Who raised me to an earthly throne,
> And sends me now, from prison lone,
> To be a saint in heaven."

Besides reading countless volumes of such sentimental nonsense (the books of another lady novelist, Mary Jane Holmes, sold over a million copies in these years), Americans consumed many volumes of religious literature. In 1840 the American Tract Society disposed of 3 million copies of its various publications; in 1855 the total exceeded 12 million. The society had hundreds of missionary-salesmen called "colporteurs" who roamed the country preaching the gospel and selling or giving away tracts and religious books. These publications avoided denominational controversies and advocated an evangelical brand of Christianity. They bore titles such as "Quench Not the Spirit" (over 900,000 copies distributed by 1850) and "The Way to Heaven." The American Bible Society also flourished in this era, issuing hundreds of thousands of copies of the Old and New Testaments each year. Americans also devoured many books on self-improvement. Some aimed at uplifting the reader's character, others, which would today be called "how-to-do-it" books, at teaching him everything from raising chickens to carving tombstones.

Of course many people found the banality of much of the popular literature of this age appalling. Poe was a vitriolic critic of Mrs. Sigourney and her school, and the *North American Review* maintained decent critical standards. A few men tried to cultivate an appreciation of good literature among the masses. Rufus W. Griswold was one of these. He published an edition of John

Milton's work and an anthology of 19th-century English poetry, as well as an edition of Poe's writings (together with an extremely critical biography of Poe). Griswold's taste, however, was capricious. An advocate of "Americanism" in literature, he often gave the support of his considerable prestige to third- and fourth-rate writers. Far more salutary if more limited was the influence of the New York editor Evert A. Duyckinck, whose magazine, *Literary World,* set a high standard of criticism. Duyckinck was an early friend and admirer of Melville, turning the young adventurer loose in his large private library and printing his critical notices in the *Literary World.* Duyckinck introduced Melville to Hawthorne, whom he also admired. He also edited a *Library of Choice Reading* and many of the works of Thackeray, Irving, Freneau, and others. Together with his brother, he prepared a *Cyclopaedia of American Literature* (1855), which went through many editions.

Education and Art

The popular thirst for knowledge and culture led to some improvement in education, although no spectacular progress was made. Most of the states had some public elementary schools by the 1850's, and by the end of that decade there were free secondary schools in Massachusetts, New York, and Ohio. The idea that public schools were only for paupers was gradually dying. Even in the South, where many planters employed tutors for their children and had little interest in public education, the trend was toward more and better schooling at state expense. Governors like Andrew Johnson of Tennessee and Joseph E. Brown of Georgia, men of humble origins, led the fight. During the 1850's school attendance in the section increased by 40 per cent, the number of schools by 50 per cent, public money spent for education by almost 100 per cent. However, *compulsory* education was everywhere still almost nonexistent. Men like Horace Mann, first secretary of the Massachusetts Board of Education, and Henry Barnard of Connecticut, editor of the *American Journal of Education* and in later years the first United States commissioner of education, were laying the foundations for the development of teaching as a true profession. Professional educational journals were established in many states.

But much remained to be accomplished. Many conservatives objected to public education on the ground that it undermined individual self-reliance. Some of these, however, gave generous support to private schemes designed to help the masses gain knowledge. Rich men such as John Jacob Astor of New York and George Peabody of Massachusetts endowed libraries and colleges. The Lowell Institute, established in Boston in 1836 to sponsor free public lectures, and the Cooper Union, set up by the industrialist Peter Cooper in the late 1850's to offer courses in practical subjects for workingmen, were but the most important of many successful institutions designed to aid the common man to improve himself. When the scientist Benjamin Silliman lectured on chemistry at the Lowell Institute in 1837, the rush for tickets caused a bad traffic jam. Mechanics' libraries sprang up in every industrial center and attracted so many readers that pressure was soon applied to grant them state funds. In 1848 Massachusetts led the way by authorizing the use of public money to back the Boston Public Library, and soon several states had authorized local communities to found tax-supported libraries.

The surge of desire for knowledge and culture in America is well illustrated by the success of mutual improvement societies, known as "lyceums." The movement began in Great Britain; in the United States its father was Josiah Holbrook, an itinerant lecturer and sometime schoolmaster from Connecticut. Holbrook founded the first lyceum in 1826 at Millbury, Massachusetts; within five years there were over a thousand scattered across the country. These were organized into the National American Lyceum, which coordinated the activities of local groups. The lyceums conducted discussions, established libraries, and lobbied for better schools. Soon they began to sponsor lecture series on topics of every sort, and many of the nation's political and intellectual leaders, such as Emerson, Webster, Holmes, Lowell, and Silliman, regularly graced their platforms. Not all the lectures were on important and serious topics, however, and too often the less demanding speakers attracted the largest audiences. Still, the movement had a generally beneficial impact on American life. Holbrook made a career of supplying lyceum groups with mathematical and scientific apparatus of his own manufacture. He also acted as a sort of clearing house in the organization of lecture tours and school aid programs.

Improvements in education both for children and for adults further raised the aspirations of the people for culture of all kinds. Interest in art increased greatly. Industrial and mechanical developments were very important in this connection. In the 1830's and 1840's new techniques made it possible to weave colored patterns into cloth by machine, to manufacture wallpaper printed with complicated designs, and to produce rugs and hangings that looked like tapestries. Combined with the use of machine methods in the furniture business (the output of factory-made furniture quadrupled between 1840 and 1860), these inventions transformed the American home and had a powerful impact on public taste. This impact, at least in the short run, was aesthetically unfortunate, for manufacturers were carried away by the possibilities opened up by their new machinery. As Russell Lynes writes in his entertaining study *The Tastemakers*, "Styles ran riot. The new mechanical methods of making furniture gave designers a free hand to indulge their delight in ornamentation. . . . The new chairs and sofas, bedecked with fruit, flowers, and beasties and standing on twisted spindles, crowded into living rooms and parlors."

The new wood-turning machinery added to the popularity of the elaborately decorated "Gothic" style of architecture. The irregularity and uniqueness of Gothic buildings suited the prevailing romanticism; their upward-aspiring towers, steeples, and arches and their flexibility (a new wing or extension could always be added without spoiling the effect) made them especially attractive to a people so enamored of progress. Although the convoluted, curlicued trimmings and the multitude of joints and angles made the Gothic house relatively expensive,* well-to-do

*A simple seven-room house could be built in this period for about $2,000.

This front elevation of a Gothic "ornamented cottage" is taken from The Model Architect: A Series of Original Designs for Cottages, Villas, Suburban Residences, etc., *published in Philadelphia by Samuel Sloan in 1868.*

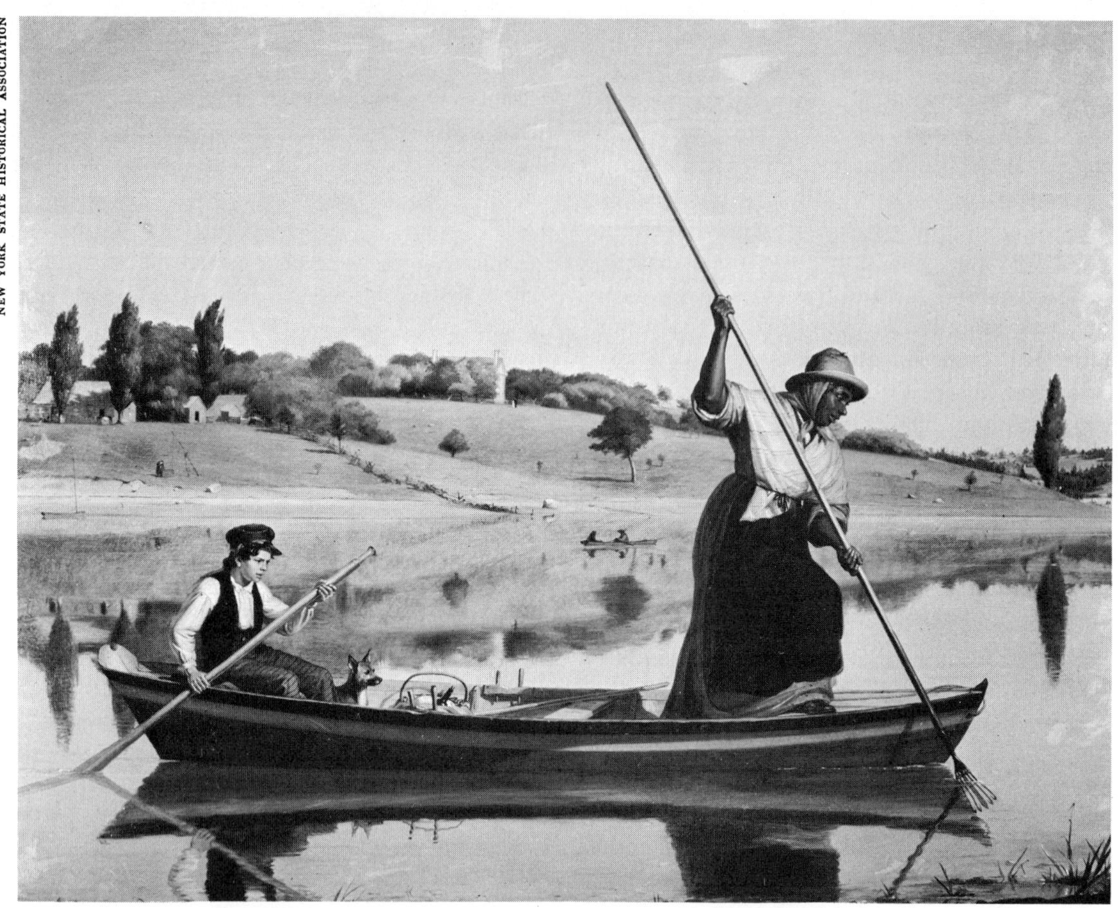

NEW YORK STATE HISTORICAL ASSOCIATION

A native and lifelong resident of rural Long Island, William Sidney Mount took the everyday life of that small corner of America as his inspiration. Eel Spearing at Setauket *(1845) is one of his most characteristic canvases. Mount's subject matter had enough of a universal appeal to sell widely in engraved form in Europe.*

Americans doted on the style. The huge pile of pink masonry of the Smithsonian Institution in Washington, with its nine distinct types of towers, represents American Gothic at its most advanced and lugubrious stage. Designed in 1846 by James Renwick, the building confounded generations of architects, but at last, with the passage of time, it came to seem the perfect setting for the vast collection of mementoes that fill "the nation's attic."

The best of the Gothic designers was probably Andrew Jackson Downing, author of *The Architecture of Country Houses* (1850). "Greek" and "Italian" styles also flourished in this period, the former especially in the South, but elsewhere the Gothic was by all odds the most popular. With a few minor exceptions, however, the architecture of the era was undistinguished, "a collection of tags, thrown at random against a building," as Lewis Mumford has said, "held in place by neither imagination nor logic."

The average American's interest in the fine arts increased considerably after about 1830. There were no real art museums before that date. Enterprises such as Charles Willson Peale's museum in Philadelphia all contained Indian relics, fossils, and other *curiosa* as well as paintings and sculpture. The most popular, like the museum of the famous mountebank and showman Phineas T. Barnum, were more like freak shows than cultural institutions. But in 1832 Luman Reed, a retired merchant and an ardent collector of American art, opened his private gallery in New York City to the public one day a week. This was the first true art museum in the country. In 1853 another New York art enthusiast, Thomas

Jefferson Bryan, made his excellent collection of old masters available to public inspection at a nominal fee.

Increasingly, Americans were purchasing native art. "Never before had so warm an encouragement supported painters and sculptors," Oliver Larkin writes in his account of this period in *Art and Life in America.* George Catlin, who painted hundreds of pictures of Indians and their surroundings, all rich in authentic detail, displayed his work before admiring crowds in many American cities. Outstanding genre painters (artists whose canvases told stories, usually drawn from everyday life), such as William Sidney Mount of New York and George Caleb Bingham of Missouri, were very successful with both their genre paintings and their portraits. Rumor had it that Luman Reed paid Mount $1,000 for his first important canvas; Bingham's paintings commanded excellent prices; and the public bought engravings of the work of both men in enormous numbers. Mount described his approach to art as follows: "Paint pictures that will take with the public—never paint for the few, but for the many."

The more academic artists of the period were also popular with the masses. Members of the highly romantic Hudson River school, who specialized in grandiose pictures of wild landscapes, usually disposed of their canvases at good prices. In the 1840's Thomas Doughty regularly collected $500 each for his paintings. The works of Asher B. Durand and particularly of Thomas Cole were also in demand. The New York merchant Philip Hone bought some of Cole's early Catskill Mountain scenes for $125 each, and by the late 1840's he could congratulate himself that they had appreciated in value to six times that figure. Luman Reed commissioned five large Cole canvases for an allegorical series, *The Course of Empire*, and huge crowds flocked to see another of Cole's series called *The Voyage of Life* when it was exhibited in New York.

In 1839 the American Art-Union was formed in New York to encourage native art. The Art-Union hit upon the ingenious device of selling what were in effect lottery tickets and using the proceeds to purchase paintings, which became the prizes in the lottery. Annual "memberships" sold for $5; 814 subscribed in 1839, ten years later nearly 19,000. Soon, in addition to distributing the canvases of men like Durand, Cole, Mount, and Bingham, the Art-Union was giving every member an engraving of one of its principal prizes. The organization had to disband after a New York court outlawed the lottery in 1851, but in 1854 a new Cosmopolitan Art-Union was established in Ohio. In the years before the Civil War it boomed, reaching a peak of 38,000 members and paying as much as $6,000 for an individual work of art—the sculptor Hiram Powers' daring but boneless female nude, *The Greek Slave.* It also distributed an art magazine and established a grant of a gold medal and $2,000 for foreign study to be given annually to a young artist.

NEWARK MUSEUM, GIFT OF FRANKLIN MURPHY, JR., 1926

Miniature copies of Hiram Powers' The Greek Slave, *said Henry James, stood "exposed under little glass covers" in parlors from Boston to San Francisco.*

The art-unions made little effort to encourage innovators or to improve public taste, but they were a great boon to many serious artists. The American Art-Union paid out as much as $40,000 for its prizes in a single year. By distributing thousands upon thousands of engravings and colored prints, they also introduced competent American works of art into middle-class homes. Beginning in the late 1850's the prints of the firm of Currier and Ives brought a crude but charming kind of art to a still wider audience. Currier and Ives lithographs portrayed subjects like horse racing, trains, rural landscapes, and "every tender domestic moment, every sign of national progress, every regional oddity, every private or public disaster from a cut finger to a forest fire." They sold for as little as 15 cents or a quarter and were issued in very large editions.

An Age of Reform

In the mid-century decades Americans favored the idea of reform as never before in their history. Why reform movements proliferated at this particular time can be explained in a number of ways, none entirely satisfactory but all enlightening. The new optimism of revivalistic religion, with its emphasis on the idea that eternal salvation was available to all good Christians, obviously made men confident that life on earth was also potentially rewarding for all. The transcendentalists' stress on striving played a role as well, and so did the Jeffersonian faith in the power of reason, and the belief in progress shared by frontiersmen and middle-class eastern businessmen alike. The question is complicated by the varying motives of different reformers, some of whom interpreted change as meaning a return to an older, golden age rather than a march toward a new utopia. Not all reforms were democratic in spirit, not all reformers optimists about human nature.

Belief in progress, however, was almost axiomatic among Americans; people who had accomplished so much found it easy to believe that nothing was impossible. At the same time, progress led to social dislocations that stimulated interest in reform. Industrialization posed problems affecting labor, city life, economic organization, and so on. The more society improved, the more it seemed to require still further tinkering, or so it seemed in the 1840's.

The same sense of destiny that had influenced the decisions of the Founding Fathers when they shaped the country's political institutions now possessed the minds of persons interested in social institutions. George Washington had been acutely aware that his every Presidential action would set a precedent; reformers 50 years later hoped to fix social patterns in well-shaped molds. The fact of rapid growth lent an air of urgency to the reform spirit. For the moment all was in flux, society was indeed malleable, but for how long? In discussing educational reform in 1848, Horace Mann spoke of "a futurity, now fluid" but soon "to be struck into adamant." "Society in the West is in a plastic state," a religious reformer in the same decade wrote. "*Now is the time when the West can be saved; soon it will be too late!*"

Both the general belief that America was in the process of creating new institutions and the transcendental, individualistic distrust of all institutions (combined with the easy availability of land) led many reformers to test their theories by establishing experimental communities. The "communitarian" point of view aimed at "commencing a wholesale social reorganization by first establishing and demonstrating its principles completely on a small scale." The first communitarians were religious reformers. In a sense the Pilgrims fall into this category, along with a number of other groups in colonial times, but only in the 19th century did the idea flourish. One of the earliest significant groups was founded by George Rapp, a German zealot, who brought some 600 of his followers to western Pennsylvania in 1804. Originally they had pooled their assets in order to buy land and get started, and with time, a primitive communism became part of their faith. Rappites renounced marriage and sex and took every word in the Bible literally. They believed that the millennium was at hand; everyone must have his affairs constantly in order so as to be ready to meet his Maker on short notice. Industrious, pious, and isolated from other Americans by their language and beliefs, the Rappites prospered but had little influence on their neighbors.

"The Follies of the Age" satirized issues that agitated mid-century America, including (clockwise from lower left) drinking, free love, quack medicine, Mormon polygamy, railroad safety, land speculation, religious revivalism, "natural" bathing, immigration restriction, steamboat disasters, a tour by European singer Jenny Lind, and abolition. At center are gibes at politicians ("I only want to see my country happy") and inept militia.

AMERICAN ANTIQUARIAN SOCIETY

Far more important were the Shaker communities founded by a remarkable English woman, Ann Lee. Ann came to America in 1774, poor and illiterate, but so effective was her preaching that her movement won many adherents. Although she died in 1784, by the 1830's her followers had established about 20 successful Shaker communities with a total of 6,000 members. Like the Rappites, the Shakers practiced celibacy; believing that the millennium was imminent, they saw no reason for perpetuating the human race. Each group lived in a large Family House, strictly segregated as to sex. Property was held in common but controlled by a ruling hierarchy. So much stress was placed on equality of labor and reward and on voluntary acceptance of the rules, however, that the system does not seem to have been oppressive. The Shaker religion, joyful and fervent, was marked by much singing and dancing, which provided the members with necessary emotional release from their tightly controlled regimen. An industrious, skillful people, they made a special virtue of simplicity; some of their designs for buildings and especially for furniture achieved a classic beauty seldom equaled among untutored craftsmen. Despite their odd customs, the Shakers were universally tolerated and even admired; most were courteous, hospitable, temperate, and charitable to a fault. No tramp was ever turned away from one of their Family Houses, and they made a specialty of caring for orphans. "Remember the cries of those who are in need and trouble," Ann Lee preached.

There were many other religious colonies, such as the Amana Community, which flourished in New York and Iowa in the 1840's and 1850's, and John Humphrey Noyes' Oneida Community, where the members practiced "complex" marriage—a form of promiscuity based on the principle that every man in the group was married to every woman—and prospered by developing a number of manufacturing skills. Brook Farm, the famous retreat of the transcendentalists, founded by George Ripley "to combine the thinker and the worker" and "do away with the necessity of menial services," was also essentially a religious experiment at the start. In a way Brook Farm experimenters tried to accomplish through cooperation what Thoreau sought to do at Walden by himself, "to impart," as their constitution stated, "a greater freedom, simplicity, truthfulness, refinement, and moral dignity, to our mode of life." Hawthorne resided briefly at Brook Farm and wrote a novel, *The Blithedale Romance*, about it. He poked a good deal of fun at the experiment but confessed nonetheless that it was a "beautiful scheme of a noble and unselfish life."

By far the most important of the religious communitarians were the Mormons. A remarkable Vermont farm boy, Joseph Smith, founded this new religion in western New York in the 1820's. Smith saw visions; he claimed to have discovered and translated an ancient text, the *Book of Mormon*, written on plates of gold, which described the adventures of a tribe of Israelites that had populated America from Biblical times until their destruction in a great war in 400 A.D. With a small band of followers, Smith founded a community in Ohio in 1831. The Mormons' dedication and economic efficiency attracted large numbers of converts, but their unorthodox religious views and their exclusivism, product of their sense of being a chosen people, roused resentment among unbelievers. They were forced to move first to Missouri and then back to Illinois, where in 1839 they founded Nauvoo, on the Mississippi.

Nauvoo flourished—by 1844 it was the largest city in the state with a population of 15,000. However, once again the Mormons ran into local trouble. They quarreled among themselves, especially after Smith secretly authorized polygamy (he called it "celestial marriage") and a number of other unusual rites for members of the "Holy Order," the top leaders of the church.* They also created a paramilitary organization, the Nauvoo Legion, headed by Smith as lieutenant general, a

* The justification of polygamy, paradoxically, was that marriage was a sacred, eternal state. If a man remarried after his wife's death, eventually he would have two wives in heaven. Therefore why not on earth?

rank previously held in America only by George Washington. They envisaged themselves as a kind of semi-independent state within the federal Union. Rumors circulated that they intended to take over the entire Northwest for their "empire." Once again local "gentiles" rose against them. Smith was arrested, then murdered by a mob.

Under a new leader, Brigham Young, the Mormons decided to seek a haven beyond the frontier. In 1847 they marched westward, pressing through the mountains until they reached the desolate wilderness on the shores of Great Salt Lake, beyond the Wasatch range. There, at last, they established their Zion and began to make their truly significant impact on American history. Young was a forceful and imaginative leader. Irrigation made the desert flourish, precious water being wisely treated as a community asset. Trades and industries were quickly introduced. Hard, cooperative, intelligently directed effort spelled growth and prosperity; over 11,000 people were living in the area when it became part of Utah Territory as a result of the Compromise of 1850. Eventually the communal Mormon settlement broke down, but the religion has remained, along with a distinctive Mormon culture which has been a major force in the shaping of the intermontane West. The Mormon Church is still by far the most powerful single influence in Utah and a thriving organization in many other parts of the United States and in Europe.

Despite their many common characteristics, these religious communities varied enormously; subordination of the individual to the group did not destroy group individualism. Their sexual practices, for example, ranged from the "complex marriage" of the Oneidans through Mormon polygamy and the ordinary monogamy of the Brook Farmers to the reluctant acceptance of sexual intercourse by the Amana Community and the absolute celibacy of the Rappites and Shakers. The communities are more significant as reflections of the urgent reform spirit of the age than

These scenes are from a canvas scroll illuminating the early history of the Mormons, painted by C.C.A. Christensen. At left, a mob attacks a Mormon settlement in Missouri in the 1830's. Moving to Illinois, Joseph Smith organized the Nauvoo Legion (center) to defend his people. Below, the Saints cross the frozen Mississippi, seeking a Zion in the West.

ALL: BRIGHAM YOUNG UNIVERSITY, UTAH, CHRISTENSEN FAMILY MEMORIAL GIFT

they are for their accomplishments. But they did have some influence on certain other reformers who wished to experiment with social organization. For example, when Robert Owen, a British utopian socialist who believed in economic as well as political equality and who considered competition debasing, decided to create an ideal community in America, he purchased the Rappite settlement at New Harmony, Indiana.

As his son later confessed, Owen gathered about him "a heterogeneous collection of radicals, enthusiastic devotees to principle, honest latitudinarians, and lazy theorists, with a sprinkling of unprincipled sharpers thrown in." His advocacy of free love and "enlightened atheism" did not add to the stability of his group or to its popularity among outsiders. The colony was a costly failure.

More significant were the American followers of Charles Fourier, a French utopian socialist who proposed that society should be organized in cooperative units called phalanxes. Fourierism did not seek to tamper with sexual and religious mores. Its advocates included Albert Brisbane, author of *Social Destiny of Man* (1840) and *A Concise Exposition of the Doctrine of Association* (1843), important journalists such as Horace Greeley of the New York *Tribune* and Parke Godwin of the New York *Evening Post*, and many of the leading Massachusetts transcendentalists. In the 1840's several dozen Fourierist colonies were established in the northern and western states; Brook Farm, in its last years, became one of them. Members were supposed to work at whatever tasks they wished and only as much as they wished. Wages were paid according to the "repulsiveness" of the tasks performed; a man who "chose" to clean out a cesspool would receive more than someone hoeing corn or mending a fence or engaging in some task requiring complex skills. As might be expected, none of these communities lasted very long.

Practical Reformers

The communitarians were the most colorful of the reformers, their proposals the most spectacular. More effective, however, were the many individuals, some sensible, some fanatical, who worked for limited practical goals. Something has already been said of the great educational administrator Horace Mann. At a humbler level, many teachers tried to improve the schools by introducing new ideas drawn principally from the work of European educators. The writings of the Swiss Johann Pestalozzi were especially influential. Pestalozzi stressed adapting the curriculum to the changing needs of the growing child. Knowledge should be acquired in a logical and orderly pattern, rote learning de-emphasized. The child should be prepared to take his place in society, Pestalozzi taught, not stuffed drum-tight with useless facts. The Owenites established a Pestalozzian school at New Harmony; there was one at Brook Farm and others elsewhere. Improved education for women also got a start in this period. Emma Hunt Willard's Female Seminary at Troy, New York, was established in 1821. Mary Lyon opened Mount Holyoke College in 1837; four years earlier Oberlin had admitted girl students and became the first co-educational college.

The work of Thomas Hopkins Gallaudet in developing methods for educating the deaf, culminating by 1851 in the establishment of special schools in 14 states, also reflects the spirit of the times, for hundreds of individuals contributed from their private means to aid these public institutions. Dr. Samuel Gridley Howe did similar work for the blind, devising means for making books with raised letters* that the blind could "read" with their fingers, and heading a school for the blind in Boston, the pioneering Perkins Institution. Howe, who was also interested in trying to educate the mentally defective and in other causes, seems one of the most attractive of the reformers from the perspective of modern times. "Every creature in human shape should command our respect," he insisted. "The strong should help the weak, so that the whole should advance as a band of brethren."

Humanitarianism took many forms, for unlike 18th-century reformers who advocated change

* The Braille system of raised dots, invented in France, was not introduced in the United States until later in the century.

for cold-blooded, logical reasons, the people of this romantic age were moved by their feelings perhaps even more than by ideas. Beginning in 1841 Dorothea Dix, with almost saintlike selflessness, devoted 30 years to improving the care of the insane. Her first major effort was a powerful summary of conditions addressed to the Massachusetts legislature: "Insane persons confined within the Commonwealth [are] in *cages*, *closets*, *cellars*, *stalls*, *pens*," she wrote, "*Chained*, *naked*, *beaten with rods*, *and lashed into obedience!*" Massachusetts responded by building a new mental hospital, and Miss Dix went on to press for reforms in state after state. By 1860 more than a dozen had acted to improve conditions. Her efforts to obtain federal support for her work, however, failed.

Even criminals received much sympathy in these years, although the "prison reform" of this era seems scarcely humanitarian today. The highly regarded Philadelphia prison system, for example, was based on strict solitary confinement. Each prisoner had adequate quarters but saw *no one* but prison officials for the duration of his term. Visits from relatives, even letters were forbidden. This formidable and extremely expensive system was supposed to lead the culprit to reflect upon his sins and then reform his ways. The prison, in other words, was literally a penitentiary, a place to repent. In actual fact, this system often drove men mad, and soon a rival "Auburn System" was developed in New York State, which allowed for some social contact and for work in shops and stone quarries. This system was also incredibly harsh by modern standards. Absolute silence was required at all times. Men were herded about in lock step and punished by brutal flogging for the slightest infraction of the rules. Nonetheless, considerable "moral and religious instruction" was provided, and the authorities sincerely intended the system to reform the inmates. When Alexis de Tocqueville and his companion Gustave de Beaumont visited the United States in the 1830's, they made a thorough study of American prisons for the French government. The Philadelphia System, they concluded, produced "the deepest impression on the soul of the convict." The Auburn System made the convict "more conformable to the habits of man in society." While both systems now seem heartless, we must realize that, along with most humanitarians of the period, these intelligent and enlightened young French observers considered American prisons the best in the world by far.

Reformers must of necessity interfere in the affairs of others; thus there is often something of the busybody and arrogant meddler in them. How they are regarded usually depends upon the observer's own attitude toward their objectives. This applies particularly to one of the most conspicuous of the reform causes of the period—the temperance movement. Since Americans consumed huge amounts of liquor, it was natural that efforts should be made to restrain them. Dr. Benjamin Rush's study *An Inquiry into the Effects of Spiritous Liquors on the Human Mind and Body* (1784) had a great influence—by 1850 the American Tract Society alone had distributed 172,000 copies. But most of the foes of alcohol opposed drinking on moral and religious rather than medical grounds, and the temperance crusade was conducted in a spirit of religious revivalism which would suggest to a psychologist that the reformers found in this activity the same emotional release that the drunkard finds in alcohol. In any case, evangelical preachers were very prominent in the temperance movement.

The foundation of the American Temperance Union in 1826 signalized the start of a great crusade. Employing lectures, pamphlets, rallies, essay contests, and many other techniques, the union set out to persuade people to "sign the pledge" not to drink liquor. Primitive sociological studies of the effects of drunkenness (as early as 1833 statisticians had discovered a high correlation between alcoholic consumption and crime) added to the effectiveness of the campaign. Soon the union claimed a million members. In 1840 an organization of reformed drunkards, the Washingtonians, began a campaign of its own to reclaim alcoholics. One of the most effective of its workers was John B. Gough, rescued by the organization in 1842 after seven years in the gutter. Gough became a tireless and convincing orator for the cause. "Crawl from the slimy ooze, ye drowned drunkards," he would shout, "and with suffocation's blue and livid lips speak out against the drink!"

Both the methods and the objectives of the temperance men, most of whom were demanding complete abstinence rather than restraint, roused bitter opposition. They made little real headway in their effort to change the drinking habits of the nation. As was true of the converts at religious camp meetings, many impressionable characters were overwhelmed by the fervor of the reformers and signed the pledge, only to backslide the first time they passed a tavern. Nevertheless, the temperance crusaders were a powerfully organized minority, and in a number of states they obtained first strict licensing systems, heavy liquor taxes, and local option laws, and then outright prohibition. In 1846 Maine passed the first statewide law making alcoholic beverages illegal. The leader of the campaign was Mayor Neal Dow of Portland, a businessman who became interested in the liquor problem after seeing the damage done by drunkenness among his employees. By 1855 a dozen other states had followed Maine's lead.

A still more dubious reform movement of the era was the Protestant "crusade" against the Catholic Church in America. In the name of freedom, democracy, and "true" Christianity, certain Protestant groups deluged the country with tracts and sermons, and at times resorted to violence against worshipers of what they called "the whore of Babylon." Hatred of Roman Catholics, of course, antedated the first English settlements in America and had much to do with the long colonial conflict with the French in Canada. It flared up about 1830 chiefly because for the first time significant numbers of Catholics were coming into the country, most of them from Ireland and Germany. Between 1830 and 1860 the Catholic population of the United States multiplied almost tenfold, rising from 318,000 to 3,100,000. Distaste for Catholics was related to dislike of cities and of industrialization, for large numbers of the new immigrants, especially the Irish, settled in cities and found jobs in the new factories. While bigotry hardly seems related to reform, the anti-Catholics certainly *believed* they were reformers. To them the Pope was the Antichrist, a tyrant seeking to take over the United States.

The Abolitionist Crusade

No reform movement of this era was more significant, more ambiguous in character, or more provocative of later historical investigation than the drive to abolish slavery. That slavery should have been a cause of indignation to reformers was inevitable. Indeed, to the modern temperament, the idea of owning another human being seems so utterly evil that the wonder is that abolition had not become a mass movement by the middle of the century. Humanitarians were outraged by the master's whip and by the practice of disrupting families; democrats protested the denial of political and civil rights to slaves; perfectionists of all kinds deplored the fact that slaves had no chance to improve themselves. Long before reform became a fad, men of good will had criticized the institution.

Nevertheless, for many years the abolition movement attracted few followers, for there seemed no way to get rid of slavery in the United States short of revolution; the institution was beyond federal control since it depended entirely on state laws. To most Americans, especially after the Missouri Compromise crisis of 1820, the slavery controversy appeared explosive enough even when limited to the question of the expansion of the institution into the territories. Those who advocated any kind of *forced* abolition seemed completely irresponsible. Most early foes of slavery therefore confined themselves to urging "colonization" or persuading slaveowners to treat their property humanely. "We consider slavery your calamity, not your crime," the Unitarian clergyman William Ellery Channing told southerners. "We will share with you the burden of putting an end to it."

To black men these abolitionists promised that somehow, someday, wrongs would be righted. Meanwhile, they should "cultivate feelings of piety and gratitude" for the "blessings" they enjoyed. What these blessings were, they seldom specified. As the historian Benjamin Quarles has remarked acidly, their advice was: "bear and forbear."

But in the highly charged atmosphere of the 1830's and 1840's a few zealots would not listen to

METROPOLITAN MUSEUM OF ART, GIFT OF I.N. PHELPS STOKES, EDWARD S. HAWES, ALICE MARY HAWES, MARION AUGUSTA HAWES, 1937

For 35 years The Liberator, *edited by William Lloyd Garrison (above), was one of the nation's leading antislavery organs. Theodore Dwight Weld (below) helped make Ohio a seedbed of abolitionism, first at the Lane Theological Seminary and later at Oberlin.*

NEW YORK SOCIETY LIBRARY

reason. Concepts like equality and progress had become so great a part of their mental baggage that the logic of circumstances had little influence upon them. "If we express frankly and freely our opinions," one of these men pontificated, "they will give up their slaves." Another stern believer in principle was the Quaker Benjamin Lundy, editor of a paper called *The Genius of Universal Emancipation.* Lundy was no fanatic, and he urged the use of persuasion in the South rather than interference by the federal government, but he refused to mince words and was consequently subject to frequent harassment. Even more provocative, however, was his youthful assistant, William Lloyd Garrison of Massachusetts, who seemed in southern eyes the embodiment of everything that was hateful in the antislavery camp. Garrison believed in "immediate" abolition. A mild-mannered man, humanitarian in outlook, backer of many reforms, a pacifist, he was absolutely unyielding in his opposition to slavery. The Negro must be freed and treated as an equal by all white men, he preached. Compensated emancipation would be criminal, colonization unthinkable. Because the government countenanced slavery, Garrison refused to engage in political activity to achieve his ends. He openly burned a copy of the Constitution—he called it an "agreement with hell"—to show his contempt for a system that tolerated human bondage. His method was to denounce and demand; he would neither compromise, nor negotiate, nor wait.

In 1831 Garrison established his own paper, *The Liberator.* "I am in earnest," he announced in the first issue. "I will not equivocate—I will not excuse—I will not retreat a single inch—and *I will be heard.*" Working incessantly for the cause, he organized the New England Anti-Slavery Society (1831) and the American Anti-Slavery Society (1833).

Few white Americans found Garrison's line of argument convincing. More influential in attracting recruits was Theodore Dwight Weld, a young graduate of Lane Theological Seminary in Cincinnati, who had been converted to evangelical Christianity by Charles Grandison Finney (page 299). While just as dedicated to emancipation as Garrison, Weld was willing to advance

PRIVATE COLLECTION

Frederick Douglass posed for this daguerreotype in the 1840's, when he was one of the most effective spokesmen of the Massachusetts Anti-Slavery Society.

step by step (he spoke of "immediate" emancipation "gradually" achieved) and eager to engage in political activity to achieve his ends, but he was also more emotional in his approach. He used the methods of the evangelist to win converts; his antislavery meetings sometimes ran for days. On one occasion, according to an eyewitness, he "held increasing audiences at fever pitch, with his flashing eye, his clarion tones and marvelous eloquence, without manuscript or note, for sixteen successive evenings." Largely through the activities of recruiters like Weld, about 200,000 Americans had joined antislavery societies by 1850, and many hundreds of thousands more had become what would today be called "fellow travelers," unwilling to stand up and be counted but generally sympathetic to the movement. Of course many Negroes were active abolitionists long before the white movement began to attract attention; some 50 black antislavery societies existed in 1830, and thereafter these groups grew in size and influence, being generally associated with the Garrisonian wing. White leaders of the movement eagerly used black speakers, especially runaway slaves, whose heart-rending accounts of their experiences roused sympathies and who, merely by speaking clearly and with conviction, stood as living proof that black men were neither animals nor fools.

By far the most influential black abolitionist was Frederick Douglass, one of the most remarkable Americans of that generation. Douglass was a slave who had escaped from Maryland in 1838. Although slavery had brought him a full portion of beatings and other indignities, he had been taught to read and write and had learned a trade, opportunities denied the vast majority of bondsmen. Douglass was also extremely intelligent and, even while still a slave, thoroughly his own man. Settling in Massachusetts, he attracted the attention of abolitionists and became an agent of the Massachusetts Anti-Slavery Society. A tall, majestically handsome man who radiated power, determination, and indignation, he quickly won fame as a speaker at abolitionist meetings. "He stood there," one witness recalled, "like an African prince, conscious of his dignity and power."

In 1845 Douglass published his autobiography, *Narrative of the Life of Frederick Douglass*, one of the most gripping accounts of a slave's life in the literature. The book attracted wide attention in America and in Europe. Douglass insisted that freedom for blacks required not only emancipation but full equality, social and economic as well as politicial. Not many northerners accepted his reasoning, but few who heard him or read his works could maintain the illusion that all Negroes were dull-witted or resigned to inferior status.

At first Douglass was, in his own words, "a faithful disciple" of Garrison, prepared to tear up the Constitution and destroy the Union to gain his ends. In the late 1840's, however, he changed his mind, deciding that the Constitution, created to "establish Justice, insure domestic Tranquility . . . and secure the Blessings of Liberty," as its preamble states, "could not well have been designed at the same time to maintain and perpetuate a system of rapine and murder like slavery." Thereafter he was prepared to fight against slavery and race prejudice from within the system. This Garrison was never willing to do.

Yet Garrison's importance and his understanding of the problem of slavery cannot be measured by the number of his followers. He recognized that abolitionism was a truly radical movement, not a mere reform; that achieving racial equality, not simply "freeing" the slaves, was the only way to reach the professed objective: justice for the blacks. And he saw crystal clear how few American whites, even among the abolitionists, believed that blacks were their equals. This understanding led him to the conclusion, so totally out of keeping with the view of most reformers of that day, that American society was rotten to the core; hence his contempt for compromise, for political action, for any concession to the existing establishment.

This is not to deny that Garrison was an opinionated fanatic. He was a perfectionist, a trafficker in moral absolutes of the most rigid sort. Nevertheless, the totality of his commitment impressed many persons in spite of themselves. And events played into his hands. The passage of time demonstrated that the moderates were not making headway or even winning the right to be heard. Abolitionists in the North were repeatedly insulted, jailed, manhandled, and prevented from expressing their views. One, Elijah Lovejoy, editor of an abolitionist paper in Alton, Illinois, was killed trying to defend his press against a mob. Soon many "moderates" were taking positions not far removed from Garrison's and by the late 1850's, as one student of the movement has said, "the veteran agitator was . . . in good and almost reputable standing in the North."

For this development, the extremist southern defenders of slavery were chiefly responsible. The bloody Nat Turner slave rebellion, occurring shortly after *The Liberator* began to appear, fired southern tempers against Garrison. Whereas he had only a handful of readers in the North, southern editors, by denouncing him at length, gave his views much publicity in their own region. This was bad tactics but understandable, for "immediate" abolitionists like Garrison were utterly indifferent to what effect the sudden freeing of the slaves would have on the South. Indeed, historian David Donald has suggested that white abolitionist leaders may have been acting from essentially selfish and ignoble motives. Most came from a class of society that had once dominated the nation but was rapidly losing out in the race for status to the new, crass, industrial tycoons of the North and West. They represented, according to this analysis, a sort of displaced elite, their

Abolitionist publications were frequent targets of mob action. A woodcut depicts the destruction of James G. Birney's Philanthropist *press in Cincinnati.*

abolitionism being only "the anguished protest of an aggrieved class against a world they never made."

Such a thesis is difficult to prove, but it makes us take a fresh look at the abolitionists. What we see is disturbing. Certainly they adopted an oversimplified and distorted view of the problem of slavery. They made all southern whites villains, all blacks saints. Garrison said he would rather be governed by "the inmates of our penitentiaries" than by southern congressmen, whom he characterized as "desperadoes" outside "the pale of Christianity." The life of a slaveowner, he wrote, "is but one of unbridled lust, of filthy amalgamation, of swaggering braggadocio, of haughty domination, of cowardly ruffianism, of boundless dissipation, of matchless insolence, of infinite self-conceit, of unequalled oppression, of more than savage cruelty." Rather than accept slavery, another abolitionist raved, "let races be swept from the face of the earth—let nations be dismembered—let dynasties be dethroned—let laws and governments, religions and reputations be cast out." "Slavery and cruelty cannot be disjoined," still another wrote, "consequently every slaveholder must be inhuman." Such specious reasoning was typical and, in the charged atmosphere of the times, destructive.

Defense of Slavery

But to question the motives of white abolitionists is not to defend the slaveholding class in the South. Goaded by criticism and also by the political controversy over slavery in the territories, southerners began to crack down unmercifully on every kind of dissent. They tried unsuccessfully to force the post office to bar antislavery literature from the mails and then accomplished their purpose by passing state laws making it illegal for postmasters to accept such material.* Southern congressmen objected even to the routine reception of petitions urging the abolition of the slave trade in the District of Columbia. In 1836 they managed to pass a "gag rule" in the House of Representatives under which such petitions were automatically laid on the table without "further action whatever." This denial of the right of petition outraged John Quincy Adams, now congressman from Massachusetts. Although not an abolitionist, "Old Man Eloquent" battled furiously against the gag rule. Timorous opponents quailed before his indignation and his remorseless logic, and he succeeded in rousing the North. Petitions poured into Washington, 225,000 of them in a single session. In 1844 the gag rule was finally rescinded, but the long struggle pointed up the southerners' willingness to suppress the liberties of white men as well as those of Negroes. Perhaps it also reflected their guilt feelings, for their policy was self-destructive—bound to attract sympathy to the very ideas they opposed. The gag rule accomplished what can only be called a political miracle: it made a popular hero of John Quincy Adams.

Within the South itself, freedom of expression practically disappeared. Slaves could not legally be taught to read and write except in Maryland, Kentucky, and Tennessee, and even the education of whites was strictly controlled. Schoolbooks were censored, dissident teachers fired. After about 1830 southerners who spoke out against slavery were whipped, beaten, driven away. Any northern abolitionist who appeared openly in the region would have taken his life in his hands. Although humanitarian southerners participated in movements to improve prisons, aid the blind and the insane, and similar causes, in an age when the rest of the nation teemed with social experiments, the South remained a bastion of conservatism. Of the scores of utopian settlements in the country, only two were established in the slave states. Free labor was almost as tightly checked as slave. "The courts were openly antagonistic to striking workers," Richard B. Morris has written. Southerners considered "that strike action, like anti-slavery agitation, was an attack on their 'peculiar' institution."

The South also took the offensive, presenting an interesting and remarkably varied justification of slavery. The most sophisticated presentation of the southern position was *The Pro-Slavery Argu-*

*A determined President could, of course, have ordered the mail delivered, but Jackson refused to do this when the issue first came up in 1835–36 and his successors followed his policy.

ment (1853), the work of several authors, which rejected the Jeffersonian theory that all men were created equal as a pernicious abstraction. Men *differed* in natural endowments of all kinds—strength, intelligence, race. A high civilization depended upon social order, "which implies distinctions and differences of conditions." Equality was in this sense unnatural. Writers such as George Fitzhugh, a Virginia lawyer and philosopher, and William J. Grayson, a South Carolina planter, argued that slavery was *better* than freedom for the laboring man. "Wage slaves" in northern factories, they said, suffered far more than southern slaves, both materially and psychologically. "Liberty and equality throw the whole weight of society on its weakest members," Fitzhugh wrote in *Sociology for the South* (1854). "A Southern farm is the beau ideal of Communism; it is a joint concern, in which the slave consumes more than the master, of the coarse products, and is far happier, because . . . he is always sure of a support." Describing the lot of the Negroes in his poem "The Hireling and the Slave" (1856), Grayson wrote:

> Secure they toil, uncursed their peaceful life,
> With labor's hungry broils and wasteful strife.
> No want to goad, no faction to deplore,
> The slave escapes the perils of the poor.

Other propagandists, tossing about pseudoscientific language with confident abandon, stressed the theory that Negroes were racially inferior. The Negro belonged to the "prognathous" species of mankind, one "authority" proclaimed. He had a nervous system "somewhat like the ourang outang." Even men of the cloth contributed their mite to the cause, quoting the Bible ("Both thy bondmen and thy bondmaids, which thou shalt have, shall be of the heathen that are round about you . . . and they shall be your possession."—Leviticus) and adding such comments as this, from the pen of the Reverend Thornton Stringfellow of Virginia: "Job himself was a great slaveholder, and, like Abraham, Isaac, and Jacob, won no small portion of his claims to character . . . from the manner in which he discharged his duty to his slaves." By 1860 it was possible for a Louisiana minister to deliver a sermon entitled "Slavery, a Divine Trust."

An "advertisement" for the Underground Railroad, from an abolitionist journal. Escapes via the so-called Liberty Line reached a peak during the decade of the 1850's. The most successful of the 3,200 "conductors" who have been identified was Harriet Tubman, herself an escaped slave, who guided some 300 to freedom in the North.

LIBERTY LINE.

NEW ARRANGEMENT---NIGHT AND DAY.

The improved and splendid Locomotives, Clarkson d Lundy, with their trains fitted up in the best style of commodation for passengers, will run their regular ps during the present season, between the borders of e Patriarchal Dominion and Libertyville, Upper Canada. ntlemen and Ladies, who may wish to improve their ...alth or circumstances, by a northern tour, are respectfully invited to give us their patronage.

SEATS FREE, *irrespective of color.*

Necessary Clothing furnished gratuitously to such as have "*fallen among thieves.*"

"Hide the outcasts—let the oppressed go free."—*Bibl*

☞For seats apply at any of the trap doors, or t the conductor of the train.

J. CROSS, *Proprietor.*

N. B. For the special benefit of Pro-Slavery Polic Officers, an extra heavy wagon for Texas, will be fu nished, whenever it may be necessary, in which the will be forwarded as dead freight, to the "Valley of Rascals," always at the risk of the owners.

☞Extra Overcoats provided for such of them as are afflicted with protracted *chilly-phobia.*

The self-serving character of such arguments is clear enough, but those who made them, and indeed many ordinary southerners, were not necessarily hypocrites or cynics. Many planters really were concerned for the welfare of their slaves, and if their assumptions about Negro inferiority had been correct, their philosophy would not have been entirely indefensible. Theirs was a paternalistic view of life, one that imposed heavy responsibilities on those who held power. We can reject their view without condemning those who espoused it. And their criticism of the crass, grasping competitiveness of northern capitalism had much to recommend it. Their difficulty, of course (aside from their fundamental errors about the capacities of Negroes), came in living up to their ideals. Many paid lip service to the gracious, aristocratic, nonmaterialistic values of a neofeudal society; few actually practiced what they preached.

While a large majority of the people, North and South, rejected the positions of both the abolitionists and the fanatical defenders of slavery, events in both sections played into the hands of the extremists. Abolitionist exaggerations angered moderate southerners and made them more receptive to the talk of their own hotheads. The plight of fugitive slaves, hounded relentlessly across the land, often by professional slave catchers, aroused many northerners who might otherwise have avoided commitment. The famous "Underground Railroad," a loose-knit organization of individuals who helped to spirit fugitives to safety in the North or in Canada, was neither as important nor as successful as it has sometimes been portrayed; but only the most heartless northerner could turn a hunted runaway from his door, and once involved, a "conductor" on the Railroad became an accomplice, thus committed to the movement against slavery. After the Supreme Court decided, in the case of *Prigg v. Pennsylvania* (1842), that the states did not have to enforce the federal Fugitive Slave Act, the northern states passed "personal liberty" laws barring state officials from aiding in the capture and return of fugitives. Southern resentment of these acts led to the much more stringent federal act of 1850, part of the Great Compromise, which in turn drove more northern moderates to abolitionism.

Despite the aggressiveness of the reformers and the extremity of some of their proposals, little social conflict blighted these years. Occasionally some zealot was jailed or even killed, like the Mormon prophet Joseph Smith, but reform found too many safety valves to build up explosive pressure. The public readily accepted the need for improving society and at the same time was prepared to shrug off impractical schemes as the work of harmless visionaries. For example, when Sylvester Graham, inventor of the graham cracker, traveled up and down the land praising the virtues of hard mattresses, cold showers, and homemade bread, he was mobbed by the professional bakers, but in general, as his biographer says, "he was the subject of jokes, lampoons, and caustic editorials" rather than violence. Americans argued about everything from women's rights to phrenology, from prison reform to mesmerism, but they seldom came to blows. Even the abolitionist movement might not have caused serious social strife if the conflict over the western territories had not repeatedly dragged the slavery issue into the political arena. When that happened, the romantic age of reform came to an end.

SUPPLEMENTARY READING Useful surveys of cultural and intellectual currents in this period are contained in Merle Curti, *The Growth of American Thought* (1951), V.L. Parrington, *Main Currents in American Thought** (1927–1930), and Harvey Wish, *Society and Thought in Early America* (1950). C.R. Fish, *The Rise of the Common Man* (1927), and A.C. Cole, *The Irrepressible Conflict* (1934), deal more specifically with these years, while Clement Eaton, *The Mind of the Old South* (1964), contains thoughtful and interesting essays on a number of representative southern intellectual leaders. R.B. Davis, *Intellectual Life in Jefferson's Virginia* (1964), is also helpful. F.O. Matthiessen, *American Renaissance: Art and Expression in the Age of Emerson and Whitman** (1941), is especially valuable, both for the intellectual spirit of the time and for the work of its leading literary figures.

The standard treatment of transcendentalism is still O.B. Frothingham, *Transcendentalism in New England** (1876). R.L. Rusk, *The Life of Ralph Waldo Emerson* (1949), and J.W. Krutch, *Henry David Thoreau** (1948), are first-rate biographies. On American literature, Van Wyck Brooks, *The Flowering of New England** (1936), and Lewis Mumford, *The Golden Day** (1926), are useful surveys. Outstanding biographies of the great writers of the age include A.H. Quinn, *Edgar Allan Poe* (1941), Mark Van Doren, *Nathaniel Hawthorne** (1949), Newton Arvin, *Herman Melville** (1950), G. W. Allen, *The Solitary Singer: A Critical Biography of Walt Whitman** (1955), and Newton Arvin, *Longfellow: His Life and Work** (1963). Of course the student should also sample the works of all these writers and of the great romantic historians, which are available in many editions. David Levin, *History as Romantic Art** (1959), is an excellent analysis of the assumptions and attitudes of the historians, but see also the appropriate chapters of Harvey Wish, *The American Historian** (1960), and Michael Kraus, *A History of American History* (1937).

Popular culture is discussed in Carl Bode, *The Anatomy of American Popular Culture* (1959), and Russell Lynes, *The Tastemakers** (1954). Bode's *The American Lyceum** (1956) is also useful. On education, see S.L. Jackson, *America's Struggle for Free Schools* (1941), Merle Curti, *The Social Ideas of American Educators** (1935), and T.R. Sizer (ed.), *The Age of the Academies** (1964). O.W. Larkin, *Art and Life in America* (1949), surveys American painting and architecture from an aesthetic perspective, while Neil Harris, *The Artist in American Society* (1966), puts art in its social setting.

Books treating the reform movements of these years include A.F. Tyler, *Freedom's Ferment** (1944), R.E. Riegel, *Young America* (1949), and A.M. Schlesinger, *The American as Reformer** (1950). H.S. Commager (ed.), *The Era of Reform** (1960), provides a convenient sampling of the writing of reformers. A.E. Bestor, *Backwoods Utopias* (1950), is excellent, but see also Charles Nordhoff, *The Communistic Societies** (1875). F.M. Brodie's biography of Joseph Smith, *No Man Knows My History* (1945), is a good introduction to the study of Mormonism, but see also R.B. Flanders, *Nauvoo: Kingdom on the Mississippi* (1965). Volumes helpful for the understanding of specific reform movements include H.E. Marshall, *Dorothea Dix* (1937), Blake McKelvey, *American Prisons* (1936), F.L. Byrne, *Prophet of Prohibition: Neal Dow and His Crusade* (1961), and R.A. Billington, *Protestant Crusade** (1938).

The abolition movement is considered in Louis Filler, *The Crusade Against Slavery** (1960), D.L. Dumond, *Antislavery** (1961), Benjamin Quarles, *Black Abolitionists* (1969), and G.H. Barnes, *The Anti-Slavery Impulse** (1933). R.B. Nye, *Fettered Freedom* (1949), discusses the impact of slavery on civil liberties. Nye's *William Lloyd Garrison and the Humanitarian Reformers** (1955) is an excellent brief biography. For a more detailed account of Garrison's careers, consult J.L. Thomas, *The Liberator: William Lloyd Garrison* (1933); for a stimulating interpretation, stressing his conscious radicalism, see A.S. Kraditor, *Means and Ends in American Abolitionism: Garrison and His Critics on Strategy and Tactics* (1969). W.S. Jenkins, *Pro-Slavery Thought in the Old South* (1935), and E.L. McKitrick (ed.), *Slavery Defended** (1963), cover the arguments of the southern slaveholders, while Harvey Wish (ed.), *Slavery in the South** (1964), contains a useful sampling of the ideas of contemporary observers with widely differing points of view. See also E.D. Genovese's previously mentioned *Political Economy of Slavery,** and Frederick Douglass' autobiography, *Life and Times of Frederick Douglass** (1962).

*Available in paperback.

14

The Coming of the Civil War

The political settlement between North and South designed by Henry Clay in 1850 lasted only four years. One specific event, the passage of the Kansas-Nebraska Act, upset it, although it was probably doomed in any case. The issues it had hoped to resolve neither died nor faded away. Americans continued to migrate westward by the thousands, and as long as slaveholders carried their human property into federally controlled territories, northern resentments would smolder, no matter how many politicians might join with Senator Douglas in praise of the "final settlement." Slaves continued to seek freedom north of the Mason-Dixon Line, and the stronger federal Fugitive Slave Act did not automatically guarantee their capture and return. Abolitionists intensified their propaganda, and southern extremists defended the peculiar institution as vociferously after 1850 as they had before that date. With wisdom and forbearance, perhaps trouble could have been avoided and a real reconciliation of the sections negotiated, but the historian who searches for examples of intelligent and tolerant statesmanship in the period 1850–54 seeks almost in vain.

Enforcing the Fugitive Slave Act

Large numbers of Americans simply refused to accept the Compromise of 1850. The new fugitive slave law caused a sharp increase in the efforts of southerners to recover escaped slaves. Something approaching panic reigned in the Negro communities of northern cities, with hundreds of former slaves—some of them long-time residents—fleeing to Canada. Many more defiantly remained. Frederick Douglass drew cheers when he urged a meeting of Boston blacks to stand pat even if it meant seeing "the streets of Boston running with blood." Only a few of these were arrested, but some were, generally without undue incident. However, not all these captives were in fact runaways, and northerners frequently refused to stand aside while men of any color were dragged off in chains. Shortly after the passage of the act, a New York City Negro, James Hamlet, was seized, convicted, and rushed off to slavery in Maryland without even being allowed to communicate with his wife and children. The New York Negro com-

PICTURE COLLECTION, NEW YORK PUBLIC LIBRARY

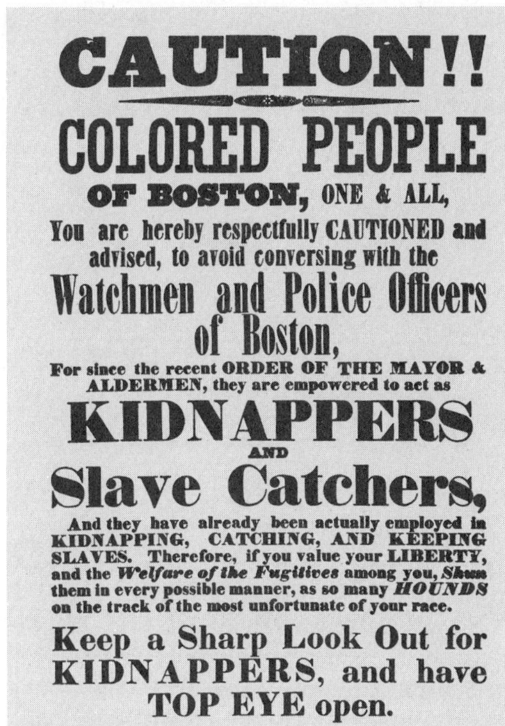

CAUTION!!
COLORED PEOPLE
OF BOSTON, ONE & ALL,
You are hereby respectfully CAUTIONED and advised, to avoid conversing with the
Watchmen and Police Officers of Boston,
For since the recent ORDER OF THE MAYOR & ALDERMEN, they are empowered to act as
KIDNAPPERS
AND
Slave Catchers,
And they have already been actually employed in KIDNAPPING, CATCHING, AND KEEPING SLAVES. Therefore, if you value your LIBERTY, and the Welfare of the Fugitives among you, Shun them in every possible manner, as so many HOUNDS on the track of the most unfortunate of your race.
Keep a Sharp Look Out for KIDNAPPERS, and have TOP EYE open.

A broadside written in 1851 by Boston abolitionist Theodore Parker alerted the city's black community to the dangers posed by the new Fugitive Slave Act.

munity was outraged, and with help from white neighbors swiftly raised $800 to buy his freedom. When he returned to the city, a crowd of 5,000 greeted him with cheers. In 1851 Euphemia Williams, who had lived for years as a free woman in Pennsylvania, was seized, her presumed owner claiming also her six children, all Pennsylvania-born. A federal judge released Mrs. Williams, but the case created much alarm in the North.

On the other hand, abolitionists often interfered with the enforcement of the law in cases where the Negro was unquestionably a runaway. When two Georgians came to Boston to reclaim William and Ellen Craft, admitted fugitives, members of an abolitionist "Vigilance Committee" jeered at them in the streets, threatened them with lynching, and finally forced them to go home empty-handed. The Crafts, however, prudently, or perhaps in disgust, decided to leave the United States for England. A slaveowner pursuing some fugitives in Lancaster County, Pennsylvania, was murdered when he tried to claim them. Early in 1851 a Virginia agent captured Frederick "Shadrach" Wilkins, a waiter in a Boston coffee house. While Shadrach was being held for deportation, a mob of Negroes broke into the courthouse and carried him off to freedom. That October a slave named Jerry, who had escaped from Missouri, was arrested in Syracuse, New York. Within minutes the whole town had the news. Crowds surged through the streets, and when night fell, a mob smashed into the building where Jerry was being held and spirited him away to safety.

Incidents of both these types exacerbated feelings all out of proportion to their significance. Southerners charged the North with reneging on one of the main promises made in the Compromise, while the sight of harmless human beings being hustled off to a life of slavery disturbed many northerners who were neither abolitionists nor even friends of the Negro. In some states it became next to impossible to enforce the Fugitive Slave Act. Massachusetts passed a very strong personal-liberty law. When a newspaperman in Wisconsin was arrested for rousing a mob to free a captured runaway, the state court released him on a writ of habeas corpus and declared the Fugitive Slave Act unconstitutional. After long delays, the United States Supreme Court overruled this decision (*Ableman v. Booth*, 1859), but in the meantime the act was a dead letter in Wisconsin and in other states as well.

Uncle Tom's Cabin

Tremendously important in increasing sectional tensions was Harriet Beecher Stowe's novel *Uncle Tom's Cabin* (1852). Mrs. Stowe, the daughter of Lyman Beecher, president of Lane Theological Seminary in Cincinnati, was neither a professional writer nor an abolitionist and had almost no firsthand knowledge of slavery or of the South. But her conscience was roused by the Fugitive Slave Act, which she called a "nightmare abomination." She dashed off her book quickly; as she later recalled, it seemed to write itself. Its success was immediate and astounding, the first printing being exhausted in two days. Ten thousand copies were sold in a week, 300,000 in a year. Pirated English editions ran to over a million copies, and soon it was being translated into dozens of languages. Dramatized versions were staged in countries all over the world.

The popularity of *Uncle Tom's Cabin* had little to do with its literary merit, for Mrs. Stowe was a second-rate writer. Her approach to the subject explains the book's success. This tale of the pious, patient slave Uncle Tom, the saintly white child Eva, and the callous slave driver Simon Legree appealed to an audience far wider than that reached by the abolitionists. It avoided the vindictive and self-righteous tone found in most abolitionist tracts and was thus infinitely more persuasive. Mrs. Stowe made many of her southern characters fine, sensitive people, while the cruel Simon Legree was a transplanted Yankee. She filled her pages with heart-rending scenes of pain, self-sacrifice, and heroism. The story proved especially effective on the stage: the slave Eliza crossing the frozen Ohio River to freedom, the death of Little Eva, Eva and Tom ascending to heaven—such scenes left countless audiences in tears. *Uncle Tom's Cabin* suited the romantic, humanitarian spirit of the times even without its indictment of slavery, and this accounts for its great success abroad. After it appeared, thousands of British women addressed a plea to the women of the South urging that the separation of slave children from their parents be stopped and that proper attention be paid to the religious training of slaves.

The South, of course, was stung hard by Mrs. Stowe's lash. Critics pointed out, correctly enough, that her picture of plantation life was distorted, her Negro characters completely atypical. They called her a "quack," a "cutthroat," and a "coarse, ugly, long-tongued woman," and accused her of trying to "awaken rancorous hatred and malignant jealousies" that would undermine national unity. The book, one reviewer concluded, was a "criminal prostitution of the high functions of the imagination to the pernicious intrigues of sectional animosity." Most northerners, having little basis on which to judge the accuracy of the book, tended to discount southern criticism as biased. In any case, *Uncle Tom's Cabin* raised questions in many minds that transcended the issue of Mrs. Stowe's accuracy.

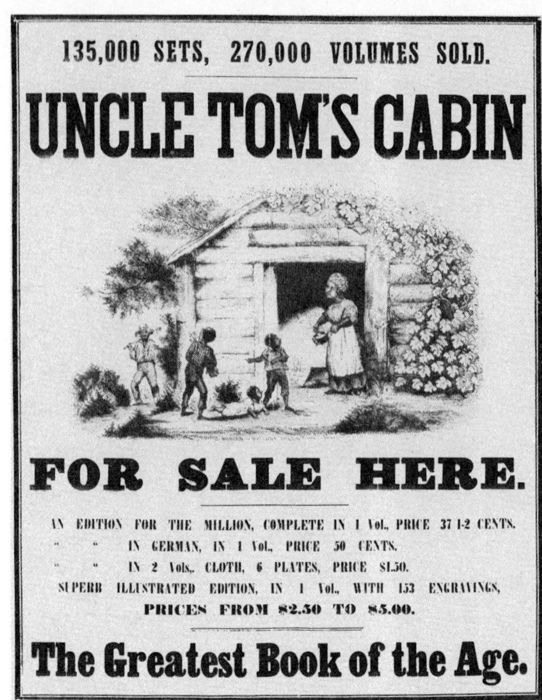

135,000 SETS, 270,000 VOLUMES SOLD.
UNCLE TOM'S CABIN
FOR SALE HERE.
AN EDITION FOR THE MILLION, COMPLETE IN 1 Vol., PRICE 37 1-2 CENTS.
" " IN GERMAN, IN 1 Vol., PRICE 50 CENTS.
" " IN 2 Vols., CLOTH, 6 PLATES, PRICE $1.50.
SUPERB ILLUSTRATED EDITION, IN 1 Vol., WITH 153 ENGRAVINGS,
PRICES FROM $2.50 TO $5.00.
The Greatest Book of the Age.

NEW-YORK HISTORICAL SOCIETY

Mrs. Stowe's novel was issued in a wide variety of editions and languages, and prepublication newspaper serialization whetted book buyers' appetites.

Did it matter if all slaves were not as kindly as Uncle Tom, as determined as George Harris? What if only *one* master was as evil as Simon Legree? No earlier American writer had looked at Negroes as *people*.

Uncle Tom's Cabin touched the hearts of millions. Some became abolitionists. Countless others, still hesitating to step forward, asked themselves as they put the book down: "Is slavery just?" Thereafter, such persons could no longer swallow the politicians' compromises on issues dividing the sections.

It would be wrong, however, to conclude that in the early fifties most Americans were ready to break up the Union over slavery. The overwhelming majority was not. Even among the multitude moved by *Uncle Tom's Cabin,* most, understanding the dangers, stifled qualms of conscience, a least for a time.

"Young America"

But a distraction was needed to help keep the lid on sectional troubles. Some hoped to find one in foreign affairs, for American diplomacy in the fifties was both active and aggressive. The spirit of manifest destiny explains this in large part; once the United States had reached the Pacific on a broad front, expansionists began to seek new worlds to conquer—south to Latin America, west to the islands of the Pacific, even north to Canada. In the late 1840's vague talk began to be heard about transmitting the dynamic, democratic spirit of the United States to other countries, aiding local revolutionaries, opening up new markets, perhaps annexing foreign lands so that their people might enjoy the benefits of the American system.

To an extent this "Young America"' spirit was purely emotional. At the time of the European revolutions of 1848, Americans talked freely about helping the liberals in their struggles against autocratic governments. When the Austrians crushed a rebellion in Hungary, Secretary of State Daniel Webster addressed an insulting note to the Austrian chargé in Washington full of vague threats phrased in the language of his special brand of spread-eagle patriotism. Hungarian revolutionary hero Louis Kossuth visited the United States in search of aid in 1851–52; President Fillmore put a warship at his disposal, and great crowds turned out to cheer him.

The United States had no intention of going to war to win independence for the Hungarians, as Kossuth soon learned to his sorrow. However, the same democratic-expansionist sentiment that brought thousands to cheer for Kossuth led others to dream of actual conquests in the Caribbean area. Between 1849 and 1851, a Venezuelan soldier of fortune, Narciso López, organized on American soil three filibustering expeditions against Cuba. None had any chance of success. In the last of them López and many of his men, including a number of Americans, were captured and executed. In 1855 a freebooter named William Walker, backed by an American company engaged in transporting migrants to California across Central America, seized control of Nicaragua and elected himself president. He was ousted two years later but made repeated attempts to regain control until, in 1860, he died before a Honduran firing squad. Another would-be dictator, "General" George W.L. Bickley, claiming that he was disturbed by that "crookedest of all boundary lines, the Rio Grande," tried to organize an expedition to conquer Mexico in this period.

Although many northerners suspected them of engaging in dastardly plots to obtain more territory for slavery, men like Walker and Bickley were primarily adventurers trying to use the prevailing mood of buoyant expansionism for selfish ends. They did attract some southern recruits by suggesting that slavery might follow in their wake—Bickley proposed that Mexico be divided into no less than 25 slave states—but no important southern leader except Governor John A. Quitman of Mississippi gave men of this type any encouragement.

Nevertheless, the aggressive talk of the period was not all mere bombast. The rapid development of California created a need for improved communication with the West Coast. A canal across Central America would cut weeks from the sailing time between New York and San Francisco. In 1850 Secretary of State John M. Clayton and the British minister, Henry Lytton Bulwer, negotiated a treaty providing for the demilitarization and joint Anglo-American control of any future canal across the isthmus. Although no canal was built at the time, America thus officially staked out its interest in the region.

As the Caribbean began to assume strategic importance to the United States, the desire to obtain Cuba grew stronger. Polk had been ready to pay Spain $100 million for the island. In 1854 President Franklin Pierce instructed his minister to Spain, Pierre Soulé of Louisiana, to offer $130 million. Since Soulé was a hotheaded and bungling diplomat, the administration arranged for him first to confer in Belgium with the American ministers to Great Britain and France, James Buchanan and John Y. Mason, to work out a plan for persuading Spain to part with the island. Out of this meeting came the so-called Ostend Manifesto, a confidential dispatch to the State Department proposing that the United States try to buy Cuba but suggesting that if Spain refused to sell, "the great law of self-preservation" might justify "wresting" it from Spain by force. News of the manifesto leaked out, and it had to be published. The North rose up in arms at once, protesting this "slaveholders' plot." The government had to disavow it, and any hope of obtaining Cuba vanished.

Although the northern opposition made the purchase of Cuba impossible, it would be misleading to consider this incident primarily as part of the slavery controversy. The goals of Young America were the driving force behind the move to obtain Cuba. They also explain President Fillmore's dispatching of an expedition under Commodore Matthew C. Perry to try for commercial concessions in the isolated kingdom of Japan in 1852. Perry's expedition was a great success. The Japanese, impressed by American naval power, agreed to establish diplomatic relations. In 1858 an American envoy, Townsend Harris, negotiated a commercial treaty, opening up six Japanese ports to American ships. President Pierce's negotiation of a Canadian reciprocity treaty with Great Britain in 1854 and the unsuccessful attempt, also made under Pierce, to annex the Hawaiian Islands are further illustrations of the vigorous foreign policy of this period.

UNITED STATES NAVAL ACADEMY MUSEUM

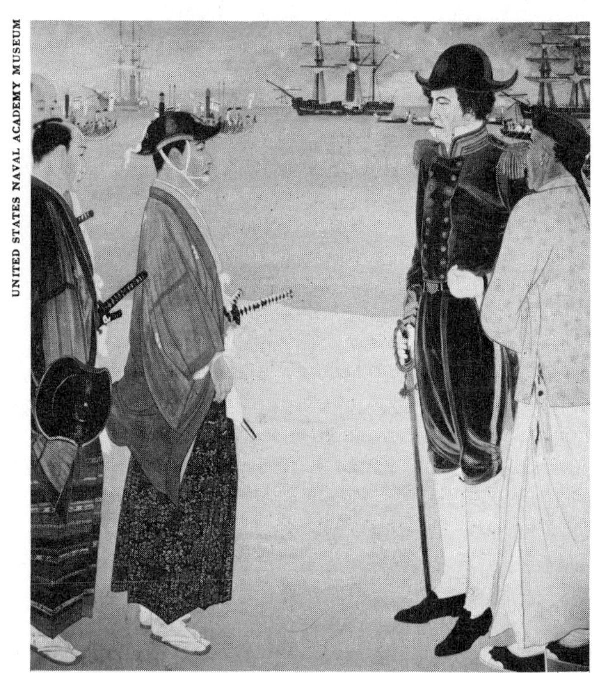

Commodore Perry confronts Japanese leaders in 1853. The "black ships" of Perry's squadron are in the background. A water color by a Japanese artist.

Stephen A. Douglas

The most prominent spokesman of the Young America movement was Stephen A. Douglas. The senator from Illinois was the Henry Clay of his generation, a man of good if not exceptional intellect, gregarious, an excellent politician, and capable of seeing the United States and its national needs in the broadest perspective. He was born in Vermont in 1813 but moved to Illinois when barely 20. There he studied law and was soon deep in Democratic politics. From 1835 to 1843 he held a succession of state offices; then he was elected to Congress. In 1847, after two terms in the House, he was chosen United States senator.

Douglas succeeded at almost everything he attempted; rarely has a man seemed so closely attuned to his time and place in history. His law practice was large and prosperous. He dabbled in Chicago real estate and made a large fortune. Politics suited him to perfection. Although very short, his appearance was so imposing that men called him the "Little Giant." He had powerful shoulders, a large head, strong features, deep-set, piercing eyes. His high forehead was made to appear even bolder by the way he wore his long hair, swept back in a pompadour and hanging over his collar. Aggressive and determined, yet at the same time flamboyant, facile, and dynamic —this was Douglas, a hard-drinking, tobacco-chewing politician. "I live with my constituents," he once boasted, "drink with them, lodge with them, pray with them, laugh, hunt, dance, and work with them. I eat their corn dodgers and fried bacon and sleep two in a bed with them." Yet he was more than a blackslapper. He read widely, wrote poetry, financed a number of young American artists, served as a regent of the Smithsonian Institution, and was interested in scientific farming.

The foundations of his politics were expansion and popular sovereignty. He had been willing to fight for all of Oregon in 1846, and he supported the Mexican War to the hilt in Congress. That local settlers should determine their own institutions in a democratic manner was, to his way of thinking, axiomatic. Arguments over the future of slavery in the territories he believed a foolish waste of energy and time since natural conditions would keep the institution out of the entire West. He therefore considered the Wilmot Proviso unnecessary and disruptive, as well as undemocratic. The main thing, he insisted, was to get on with the development of the United States. Let the nation build railroads, acquire new territory, expand its trade. Like most of his white contemporaries, he believed Negroes inferior beings, but he was definitely not proslavery—he called the institution "a curse beyond computation" for both blacks and whites. He refused, however, to admit that any moral issue was involved. "I do not know any tribunal on earth," he said, "that can decide the . . . morality of slavery." An utter cynic (it was his greatest failing), he cared not, he boasted, whether slavery was voted up or voted down. As a shrewd politician he could see that the question was interfering with the rapid exploitation of the continent; all he really cared about it was that it should be settled so that the country could get on with more important matters.

LIBRARY OF CONGRESS

"By God, sir, I made James Buchanan, and by God, sir, I will unmake him!" Douglas (above) remarked characteristically during the debate over Kansas.

Douglas' success in steering the Compromise of 1850 through Congress added to his already considerable reputation, and in 1851, although only 38, he set out to win the Democratic Presidential nomination. He began to travel about the country making speeches attacking the European monarchs and demanding the annexation of Cuba, and incidentally buttonholing local bigwigs. His main rivals were Lewis Cass, still formidable despite his defeat in 1848, and James Buchanan. They and others like them considered that age and experience entitled them to priority, but Douglas reasoned that since he was the brightest, most imaginative, and hardest-working Democrat around, he had a right to press his claim. His brash aggressiveness proved his undoing. He expressed open contempt for Buchanan and said of Cass, who had served in the diplomatic corps, that his "reputation was beyond the C." While these characterizations were accurate as well as amusing, they did not add to the Little Giant's political strength. His foes combined against him, and he had no chance.

The 1852 Democratic convention, however, was deadlocked between Cass and Buchanan and finally settled upon a dark horse, Franklin Pierce of New Hampshire. The Whigs, rejecting the colorless President Fillmore, nominated General Winfield Scott. In the campaign both sides supported the Compromise of 1850, but the Democrats won an easy victory, 254 electoral votes to 42, with Scott carrying only Vermont, Massachusetts, Kentucky, and Tennessee. The popular vote, however, was fairly close: Pierce 1,601,000, Scott 1,387,000.

So handsome a triumph seemed to insure stability, but in fact it was a prelude to political chaos. The Whig party was crumbling fast. The "Cotton Whigs" of the South, alienated by the antislavery attitude of their northern brethren, were flocking into the Democratic fold, while the radical "Conscience" and the conservative "Silver Gray" factions in the North found themselves more and more at odds with each other. Congress fell overwhelmingly into the hands of southern Democrats, many of them fanatical exponents of the expansion of slavery, a development profoundly disturbing to most of their northern colleagues. Trouble was not inevitable in 1853, but the atmosphere in Washington was explosive. Much depended upon Franklin Pierce and how he chose to lead the nation.

Kansas-Nebraska Act

The new President was a youthful-appearing 48 when he took office. Handsome, gregarious, engaging, he was generally well liked by men of both parties. His career had included service in the New Hampshire legislature and in both houses of Congress. Alcohol had become a problem for him in Washington, however, and in 1842 he had resigned from the Senate. As Roy F. Nichols, his biographer, explained it, his "convivial nature was on occasion too much stimulated by the gay life of the capital." But the setback proved temporary; his New Hampshire law practice boomed, and he added to his reputation by serving as a brigadier general during the Mexican War. Although his nomination had been a surprise, once made, it had appeared perfectly reasonable. Great things were expected of his administration, especially after he surrounded himself with men of all factions: to balance his appointment of a radical states'-rights Mississippian, Jefferson Davis, as secretary of war, for example, he named a staunch conservative and ardent Unionist, William L. Marcy of New York, as secretary of state.

Only a strong man, however, can manage a ministry of all talents, and Pierce was weak. His aggressive foreign policy accomplished little. At home it soon became clear that he could not control the extremists. He followed, as Allan Nevins has written, a "policy of smiling on everybody but specially favoring both ends against the middle." The ship of state was soon drifting; Pierce seemed incapable of holding firm the helm.

This was the situation in January 1854 when Senator Douglas, chairman of the Committee on Territories, introduced what looked like a routine bill organizing the land west of Missouri and Iowa as Nebraska Territory. Since settlers were beginning to trickle into the area, the time had arrived to set up a civil administration, but Douglas also acted because a territorial government was essential to railroad development. For some time he had been urging federal aid for the construction of a transcontinental railroad. As a director of the Illinois Central and as a land speculator, he hoped to make Chicago the terminus of such a line, but construction could scarcely begin until the entire route was cleared of Indians and brought under some kind of civil control. Southerners, wishing to bring the transcontinental line to Memphis or New Orleans, pointed out that a right of way through organized territory already existed across Texas and New Mexico Territory. In 1853 the United States minister to Mexico, James Gadsden, a prominent southern railroad executive, had engineered the purchase of additional Mexican territory south of the Gila River which provided an easy route over the mountains for such a railroad.* Douglas, whose vision of the economic potentialities of the nation was Hamiltonian, would have been perfectly willing to support the construction of two or even three transcontinental railroads, but he knew that Congress would not go that far. In any case, he felt that the Nebraska region must be organized promptly.

Douglas found at once that the powerful southern faction in Congress would not go along with his proposal as it stood. The railroad question aside, Nebraska would presumably become a free state, for it lay north of latitude 36° 30′ in a district from which slavery had been excluded since 1820 by the Missouri Compromise. To win over the southerners, Douglas agreed first to divide the region into two territories, Kansas and Nebraska, and then—a most fateful concession—to the repeal of the part of the Missouri Compromise excluding slavery from the land north of 36° 30′. Whether the new territories should become slave or free, he argued, should be left to the decision of the actual settlers in accordance with the principle of popular sovereignty.

Blind to the moral implications of his action, Douglas reasoned that no one could legitimately object to so democratic a procedure, especially

*The United States obtained through this Gadsden Purchase over 29,000 square miles of land for $10 million.

since the region, unsuited to plantation agriculture, would almost surely become free. The fact that he might advance his Presidential ambitions by making concessions to the South must have influenced him, as must the local political situation in Missouri, where the fear of being "surrounded" on three sides by free states was great.

Douglas' miscalculation of northern sentiment was monumental. Word that the West was to be reopened to slavery caused an indignant outcry. A group of abolitionist congressmen issued an "Appeal of the Independent Democrats" (actually, they were all Free-Soilers and Whigs) denouncing the Kansas-Nebraska bill as "a gross violation of a sacred pledge" and calling for a campaign of letter-writing, petitions, and public meetings to prevent its passage. The North responded vigorously, businessmen, clergymen, lawyers, and editors taking the lead. The unanimity and force of the reaction was like nothing in America since the days of the Stamp Act and the Intolerable Acts.

But these protests could not defeat the bill. Southerners in both houses backed it regardless of party. Douglas, his competitive instincts aroused, pushed it with all his power. The authors of the "Appeal," he charged, were "the pure unadulterated representatives of Abolitionism, Free Soilism, [and] Niggerism." President Pierce added whatever force the administration could muster. As a result, the northern Democrats split, and the bill became law late in May 1854. As finally worded, it declared the Missouri Compromise "inoperative and void" and left the settlers of the new territories "perfectly free to form and regulate their domestic institutions in their own way, subject only to the Constitution of the United States." Thus the nation took its greatest single step in its blind march toward the abyss of secession and civil war.

Bleeding Kansas

The repeal of the Missouri Compromise struck the North like a slap in the face—at once shameful and challenging. Presumably the question of slavery in the territories had been settled forever; now, without justification, it had been reopened. Two days after the Kansas-Nebraska bill passed the House of Representatives, Anthony Burns, a slave who had escaped from Virginia by stowing away on a ship, was arrested in Boston. A mob tried to free him but was thrown back. Troops were rushed to the scene. During the extended examination of the prisoner, armed men ringed the courthouse to restrain the ever-swelling crowds. Burns was without question a runaway, and the federal commissioner finally ruled that he should be returned to his master. This was done, but, as one eyewitness scornfully pointed out, it required two companies of artillery and a thousand police and marines to take "one trembling colored man to the vessel which was to carry him to slavery." As the grim parade marched past buildings festooned with black crepe, the crowd shouted "Kidnapers! Kidnapers!" at the soldiers. Estimates of the cost of returning this single slave to his owner ran as high as $100,000. In previous cases the conservative majority had tended to hold back; after the Kansas-Nebraska Act, nearly everyone opposed the return of fugitive slaves.

The Democratic party lost heavily in the North as a result of the Kansas-Nebraska Act. Douglas was burned in effigy in every free state, and even in Chicago crowds hooted him from the platform when he tried to explain his position. With the Whig partly already moribund, dissidents flocked into two new parties. One was escapist in orientation. Originally a secret organization (its members used the password "I don't know"), this American, or "Know-Nothing," party put forward an ultranationalistic program based on opposition to immigration and to Catholics and sought to beguile voters into forgetting about the slavery question. The Know-Nothings won a string of local victories in 1854 and elected more than 40 congressmen. They appealed strongly to the Young America faction of the Democrats and did well in northern cities, where immigration was creating social problems. Far more important, however, was the new Republican party, made up of former Free-Soilers, Conscience Whigs, and "Anti-Nebraska" Democrats. The Know-Nothing party made a pretense at being a national organization, but the Republican party was purely sectional. It sprang up spon-

KANSAS STATE HISTORICAL SOCIETY, TOPEKA

An 1856 indictment (right) of the administration's handling of the Kansas crisis has Buchanan and Secretary of State William L. Marcy plundering a body, Lewis Cass and a drunken President Pierce ogling Miss Liberty, and Douglas scalping a settler—all against a backdrop of general mayhem. That by 1856 force of arms was seen as the one effective law in Kansas is evident from the daguerreotype at left. This gun crew was protecting Topeka, the seat of the free-state government.

taneously all over the Old Northwest and caught on with a rush in New England. Republicans did not want to avoid the issue: their one major demand was that slavery be kept out of the territories. In the 1854 elections they won over a hundred seats in the House of Representatives, together with control of many state governments.

Still the furor might have died down if settlement of the new territories had proceeded in an orderly manner, but this was not the case. Although most of the men who flocked to Kansas had strong opinions about slavery, almost none owned slaves. Like nearly all frontiersmen, they wanted first land, and secondly local political office, lucrative government contracts, and other business opportunities. Yet when Congress opened the gates to settlement in May 1854, *none* of the land in the territory was available for sale. Treaties extinguishing Indian titles had yet to be ratified, and public lands had not been surveyed. In July Congress finally authorized squatters to occupy unsurveyed federal lands, but much of this property was far to the west of the frontier and practically inaccessible. This situation led to confusion over property boundaries, to graft and speculation, and to general uncertainty among settlers, exacerbating the difficulty of establishing an orderly government.

The legal status of slavery in Kansas became the focus of all these other conflicts. Both North and South were determined to have Kansas. They made of the territory first a testing ground and then a battlefield, thus exposing the fatal flaw in the Kansas-Nebraska Act and the idea of popular sovereignty. The law said that the people of Kansas were "perfectly free" to decide the slavery question, but the citizens of territories were *not* entirely free; by definition, territories were not sovereign political units. The act had created a political vacuum, which its vague statement that the settlers must establish their domestic institutions "subject . . . to the Constitution" did not adequately fill. It seemed plausible to argue that Kansans should be allowed to choose their own institutions, but when should they make the choice? Was it really democratic to let a handful of early arrivals make decisions that would affect the lives of the thousands soon to follow? The virtues of the time-tested system of congressional control established by the Northwest Ordinance only became fully apparent when the system was discarded.

More serious was the fact that outsiders, North and South, refused to permit the Kansans to work out their own destiny. During the debate on the Kansas-Nebraska bill, the radical Senator Seward

LIBERTY, THE FAIR MAID OF KANSAS_IN THE HANDS OF THE "BORDER RUFFIANS".

PRINTS DIVISION, NEW YORK PUBLIC LIBRARY

of New York said to his southern colleagues: "Gentlemen . . . we will engage in competition for the virgin soil of Kansas, and God give the victory to the side that is stronger in numbers as it is in right." The contest began at once as settlers flocked into Kansas. A New England Emigrant Aid Society was formed, with grandiose plans for transporting antislavery settlers to the area. The society was mostly bluff. Of its supposed capital of $5 million, only $100,000 was subscribed and not all of that actually paid in. Only a handful of New Englanders went to Kansas, but they were very conspicuous and undoubtedly encouraged other antislavery settlers to make the move. They also stirred southerners to fight back, and in the early days the proslavery forces had many advantages. The first settlers in frontier regions nearly always came from lands immediately to the east. In this case these were proslavery Missourians. When word spread that "foreigners" from New England were seeking to "steal" the country from them, these men rushed to protect their "rights."

As early as November 1854 an election was held in Kansas to pick a territorial delegate to Congress. A large band of Missourians, who crossed over specifically to elect a proslavery man and then returned to their homes, carried it easily. In March 1855 some 5,000 of these "Border Ruffians" descended upon Kansas again and elected a territorial legislature, which promptly enacted a slave code and passed strict laws against abolitionist agitation. Antislavery settlers refused to recognize this regime and held elections of their own. By January 1856 two governments existed in Kansas, one based on fraud, the other extralegal.

By denouncing the free-state government, located at Topeka, President Pierce encouraged the proslavery settlers to assume the offensive. In May they sacked the antislavery town of Lawrence. This inspired a psychopathic freesoiler named John Brown to take the law into his own hands in retaliation. Together with six companions (four of them his sons) he stole into a proslavery settlement on Pottawatomie Creek in the dead of night, dragged five unsuspecting settlers from their rude cabins, and murdered them. This senseless slaughter brought men on both sides to arms by the hundreds. Irregular fighting broke out and continued for months, until, by the end of 1856, some 200 persons had lost their lives. Exaggerated accounts of "Bleeding Kansas" filled the pages of northern newspapers, and the total effect was to exacerbate already tense sectional animosities. Popular sovereignty in Kansas had proved a disastrous failure.

Unquestionably, northern agitators were partially responsible for the trouble. They shipped arms into Kansas and stirred up passions with distorted descriptions of the fighting. A certain amount of violence was inevitable in any frontier community, but it suited the political interests of the Republicans to make the situation in Kansas seem worse than it was. The Missourians were also partly to blame. Although residents of nearby states often tried to influence elections in new territories, the Border Ruffians made a mockery of the democratic process. But the main responsibility must be borne by the Pierce administration in Washington. Under popular sovereignty the national government was supposed to see that elections were orderly and honest. Instead, the President, who by 1856 was almost completely in the hands of his southern advisers, acted as a partisan. When the first governor of the territory objected to the manner in which the proslavery legislature had been elected, Pierce replaced him with a man who backed the southern group without question. At no time did he make an honest effort to hold a fair election in the territory.

BRADY-HANDY COLLECTION, LIBRARY OF CONGRESS

Charles Sumner remained a senator from 1851 until his death in 1874. Throughout his career he considered himself, he said, "in morals, not politics."

Charles Sumner

As counterpoint to the fighting in Kansas there rose an almost continuous cacophony in the halls of Congress, where red-faced legislators traded insults and threats. For two months early in 1855 the House of Representatives was so torn by factionalism that it could not elect a Speaker. Every event in Kansas brought forth tirades in the Capitol. Epithets like "liar" were freely tossed about. Prominent among the new personalities engaging in these angry outbursts was Senator Charles Sumner of Massachusetts. Brilliant, learned, handsome, and articulate, he had made a name for himself in New England as a reformer, interested in the peace movement and prison reform as well as the abolition of slavery. Sumner possessed great magnetism and was, according to the tastes of the day, an accomplished orator, but he suffered inner torments of a complex nature that warped his personality. He was egotistical and humorless. His unyielding devotion to his principles was less praiseworthy than it seemed upon superficial examination, for it resulted from his complete lack of respect for the principles of others. Reform movements evidently provided him a kind of emotional release; he became combative and totally lacking in objectivity when espousing a cause.

In the Kansas debates Sumner displayed a vindictiveness and an icy disdain for his foes that made him the most hated man in the Senate. Colleagues threatened him with assassination, called him a "filthy reptile" and a "leper." He was impervious to such hostility. In the spring of 1856 he loosed a dreadful blast at "the crime against Kansas," which was, he said, "the rape of a virgin territory, compelling it to the hateful embrace of slavery." Characterizing administration policy as tyrannical, imbecilic, absurd, and infamous, he demanded that Kansas be admitted to the Union at once as a free state. Then he began a long and intemperate personal attack on both Douglas and Senator Andrew P. Butler of South Carolina, who unfortunately was not present to defend himself.

While Sumner was still talking, Douglas, who

shrugged off such language as part of the game, was heard to mutter: "That damn fool will get himself killed by some other damn fool." And indeed, such a "fool" quickly materialized in the person of Congressman Preston S. Brooks of South Carolina, a nephew of Senator Butler. Since Butler was absent from Washington, Brooks, who was probably as mentally unbalanced as Sumner, assumed the responsibility of defending his kinsman's honor. A southern romantic par excellence, he decided that caning Sumner would reflect his contempt more effectively than challenging him to a duel. Two days after the speech, Brooks entered the Senate as it adjourned. Sumner remained at his desk writing. After waiting with exquisite punctilio until a talkative woman in the lobby had left so that she would be spared the sight of violence, Brooks walked up to Sumner and rained blows upon his head with a gutta-percha cane until he fell, unconscious and bloody, upon the floor. "I . . . gave him about 30 first-rate stripes," Brooks later boasted. "Towards the last he bellowed like a calf. I wore my cane out completely but saved the head which is gold." The physical damage suffered by Sumner was relatively superficial, but for obscure psychological reasons the incident so affected him that he was unable to return to his seat in Congress until 1859.

Both sides made much of this disgraceful incident. When the House censured him, Brooks resigned, returned to his home district, and was triumphantly re-elected. A number of well-wishers even sent him souvenir canes. Northerners viewed the affair as illustrating the brutalizing effect of slavery on Southern whites and made a hero of Sumner.

Buchanan Tries his Hand

Such was the atmosphere surrounding the 1856 Presidential election. The Republican party now dominated much of the North, and it must be emphasized that it stood not for abolition but for restricting slavery to areas where it already existed. It nominated the explorer and soldier John C. Frémont, "the Pathfinder," one of the heroes of the conquest of California. Frémont fitted the Whig tradition of Presidential candidates: a popular military man with almost no political experience. However, he was sound and articulate on the issue of slavery in the territories. Although men of diverse interests had joined the party, Republicans expressed their objectives in one simple slogan: "Free soil, free speech, and Frémont." The Democrats cast the ineffectual Pierce aside, but they did not dare nominate Douglas because he had raised such a storm in the North. They settled upon James Buchanan, chiefly because he had been out of the country serving as minister to Great Britain during the long debate over Kansas! The Know-Nothing party, seeking to rally conservatives and those fearful of disunion, nominated ex-President Fillmore, a choice the remnants of the Whigs ratified.

Counting upon solid southern support, the Democrats concentrated on winning votes in the North by presenting the Republicans as a sectional party that threatened to destroy the Union. On this issue they carried the day. Buchanan won only a minority of the popular vote in the three-cornered battle, but he received 174 electoral votes to Frémont's 114 and Fillmore's 8. The significant contest took place in the populous states just north of slave territory, Pennsylvania, Ohio, Indiana, and Illinois. Buchanan carried all of these but Ohio, although by narrow margins.

No one could say that James Buchanan lacked political experience. He had entered the Pennsylvania legislature in 1815 when only 24. He served for well over 20 years in Congress and had been minister to Russia, then Polk's secretary of state, then minister to Great Britain under Pierce. His career had been undistinguished but respectable; while clearly a spoilsman, a complacent conservative, a seeker after the Presidency, he was also honest and devoted to the Union.

Personally, Buchanan was a quixotic figure, a bundle of contradictions. Dignified in bearing and cautious, even suspicious, by nature, he could consume enormous amounts of liquor without showing the slightest sign of inebriation. A big, heavy man, he was nonetheless remarkably graceful and light on his tiny feet, of which he was inordinately proud. He wore a very high collar to conceal a scarred neck, and because of an eye defect he habitually carried his head to one side and slightly forward, which gave him, as his most recent biographer says, "a perpetual attitude of courteous deference and attentive interest" that sometimes led individuals to believe they had won a greater share of his attention and support than was actually the case. Buchanan was popular with women and attracted to them as well, but although he contemplated marriage on more than one occasion, he never took the final step. There was an old-womanish streak in him; he could be stubborn, fussy, and vindictive. Over the years many strong men in politics had held him in contempt. Yet, on balance, his career had not been without merit. He had intelligence and a powerful faith in the Constitution; he was patriotic, conscientious, moderate. Although Republican extremists called him a "Doughface"—meaning that they believed he lacked the force of character to stand up against southern extremists—many reasonable men in 1856 thought they saw in him the qualities necessary to steer the nation through to calmer waters.

The Dred Scott Decision

Kansas provided the first real test of Buchanan's statesmanship, but before he could fairly take that problem in hand, an event occurred that drove another deep wedge between North and South. Back in 1834 Dr. John Emerson of St. Louis joined the army as a surgeon and was assigned to duty at Rock Island, Illinois. Later he was transferred to Fort Snelling, in Wisconsin Territory. In 1838 he returned to Missouri. Accompanying him on these travels was his body servant, Dred Scott, a slave. In 1846, after Emerson's death, Scott, with the help of a friendly lawyer, brought suit in the Missouri courts for his liberty, arguing that residence in Illinois, where slavery was barred under the Northwest Ordinance, and in Wisconsin Territory, where the Missouri Compromise outlawed it, had made him a free man.

Of course the future of Dred Scott mattered not at all to the country or the courts. At issue was the question of whether Congress or the local legislatures had the power to outlaw slavery in the territories. Both sides employed top-notch lawyers to argue the case, which after many years of litigation finally reached the Supreme Court. On March 6, 1857, two days after Buchanan's inauguration, the high tribunal acted. Negroes, the Court declared, were not citizens; therefore Scott could not sue in a federal court. This was dubious legal logic, but it effectively settled Scott's fate. However, the Court went further. Since the plaintiff had returned to Missouri, the laws of Illinois no longer applied to him. His residence in Wisconsin Territory—and this was the most controversial part of the decision—did not make him free because the Missouri Compromise was unconstitutional. According to the Fifth Amendment, the federal government cannot deprive any person of life, liberty, or property without due process of law. Therefore, Chief Justice Roger B. Taney reasoned, "an Act of Congress which deprives a person . . . of his liberty or property merely because he came himself or brought his property into a particular

NEW-YORK HISTORICAL SOCIETY

Buchanan "never made a witty remark, never wrote a memorable sentence, and never showed a touch of distinction," according to historian Allan Nevins.

Territory . . . could hardly be dignified with the name of due process of law." And if Congress could not legally take such action, it was obvious that a territorial legislature authorized under the laws of Congress could not do so either.

The Dred Scott decision has been widely criticized on legal grounds. Each justice filed his own opinion, and in several important particulars there was no line of argument that any five of the nine agreed upon. "When the student finds six judges arriving at precisely the same result by three distinct processes of reasoning," one modern authority, E.S. Corwin, has written, "he is naturally disposed to surmise that the result may have induced the processes rather than the processes compelling the reasoning." Some critics have also argued that the justices should not have gone beyond the minimum of argument necessary to settle the case itself, and many have made much of the fact that a majority of the justices were southerners. It would be going too far, however, to accuse the Court of plotting to extend slavery. By expressing their convictions the judges hoped to settle the vexing question of slavery in the territories once and for all. If this admirable objective could only be accomplished by fuzzy reasoning—well, it would not be the first time in the history of jurisprudence that an important result rested on shaky logic.

While Douglas, along with millions in the North, believed that the Kansas-Nebraska Act had provided a method for keeping slavery out of the territories, its language, as we have seen, was distressingly vague. The Court, for whatever reason, had taken advantage of this vagueness to destroy not only the Missouri Compromise, which the Kansas-Nebraska Act had repealed in any case, but also Douglas' treasured principle of popular sovereignty. Now, apparently, the people of a territory could *not* decide for themselves whether to vote slavery up or down! Until statehood was granted, slavery would remain as inviolate as freedom of religion or speech or any other civil liberty guaranteed by the Constitution.

The irony of employing the Bill of Rights to keep men in chains did not escape northern critics. Many believed the decision part of a dastardly plot to extend slavery to the far corners of the Union, for under it slaves could be brought into Minnesota Territory, even into Oregon. In his inaugural address Buchanan had sanctimoniously urged the people to accept the forthcoming ruling—"whatever this may be"—as a final settlement. Many persons assumed (indeed, it was true) that certain of the judges had "leaked" word of the decision to him in advance of his speech. If this "greatest crime in the judicial annals of the Republic" were allowed to stand, northerners argued, the Republican party would have no reason to exist: its program had been declared unconstitutional! Coming on top of the Kansas troubles, the Dred Scott decision convinced thousands in the northern states that the South was engaged in an aggressive attempt to extend the peculiar institution so far that it could no longer be considered peculiar.

The Lecompton Constitution

Kansas soon provided a test for northern suspicions. Initially, Buchanan handled the problem of Kansas well by appointing Robert J. Walker of Mississippi as governor. Although a southerner, Walker had no desire to foist slavery on the territory against the will of its inhabitants. He was a small man but a courageous one, patriotic, vigorous, tough-minded, much like Douglas in temper and belief. A former senator and Cabinet officer, he had more political stature by far than any previous governor. The proslavery leaders in Kansas soon came to detest him. They had managed to convene a constitutional convention at Lecompton, but the free-soil forces had refused to participate in the election of delegates. When this rump body, meeting amid scenes of appalling disorder, drafted a proslavery constitution and then refused to submit it to a fair vote of all the settlers, Walker denounced their work and hurried back to Washington to explain the situation to Buchanan.

The President refused to face reality. He owed his office largely to southern votes. His prosouthern advisers were clamoring for him to "save" Kansas. Instead of backing Walker and rejecting the Lecompton constitution, he decided to ask Congress to admit Kansas to the Union with this document as its frame of government. "Seldom in the history of the nation," Allan Nevins writes of this act, "has a President made so disastrous a blunder."

Buchanan's decision brought him head on against Stephen A. Douglas, and the repercussions of their clash soon shattered the Democratic party. Principle and self-interest (an irresistible combination!) forced Douglas to oppose the leader of his party. If he stood aside while Congress admitted Kansas before the people of the territory had had an opportunity to vote on its proslavery constitution, he would not only be abandoning his cherished belief in popular sovereignty but would also be committing political suicide. He was up for re-election to the Senate in 1858. Fifty-five of the 56 newspapers in Illinois had declared editorially against the Lecompton constitution; if he supported it, defeat was certain. In a dramatic confrontation at the White House he and Buchanan argued the question at length, tempers rising. Finally, the President tried to force him into line. "Mr. Douglas," he said, "I desire you to remember that no Democrat ever yet differed from an Administration of his own choice without being crushed." "Mr. President," Douglas replied contemptuously, "I wish *you* to remember that General Jackson is dead!" And he stalked out.

Buchanan then compounded his error by putting tremendous political pressure on Douglas, cutting off his Illinois patronage on the eve of his re-election campaign. Of course Douglas persisted, openly joining with the Republicans in the fight, and in the end Congress rejected the admission bill.

Meanwhile, the extent of the fraud perpetrated at Lecompton became entirely clear. In October 1857 a new legislature had been chosen in Kansas, for the first time in a fair election. This body ordered a referendum on the Lecompton constitution. On January 4, 1858, some 10,388 voters went to the polls. Of these, 10,226 flatly rejected the constitution. Even in the face of this landslide, Buchanan persisted. Congress finally ordered another referendum on the Lecompton constitution. To slant the case in favor of approval, the legislators stipulated that if the constitution was voted down, Kansas could not be admitted until it had a population of 90,000. Nevertheless, the Kansans rejected it by a margin of six to one.

More than opposition to slavery influenced this vote, for the mass of settlers were by 1858 totally alienated from the Democratic administration in Washington because of its bungling and corrupt management of the public lands. Hard lines between proslavery and antislavery Kansans blurred when land and Indian policy were under discussion. After delaying land sales unconscionably, Buchanan, in 1858, suddenly put 8 million acres of Kansas land up for auction. Squatters on this land were faced, in the midst of a depression, with finding $200 in cash to cover the minimum price of their quarter sections or losing their improvements. Local protests forced a delay of the sales, but Kansans by the thousands were convinced that Buchanan had thrown the land on the market out of pique at their rejection of the Lecompton constitution.

The Emergence of Lincoln

These were indeed dark days. During the summer of 1857 a panic struck the New York stock market, heralding the onset of a brief but very sharp downturn of the economy. This depression was probably unavoidable considering the feverish expansion and speculation of the previous ten years, but northerners tended to blame the southern-dominated Congress, which had just cut tariff duties to the lowest levels in nearly half a century. As prices plummeted and unemployment rose, they attributed the collapse to foreign competition and accused the South of having sacrificed the prosperity of the nation as a whole for its selfish advantage. The South, in turn, read in the panic proof of the superiority of the slave system, for the depression had very little effect on the southern economy, chiefly because the world price of cotton remained high. Both arguments, fallacious but tenaciously held, created still more intersectional ill-feeling.

Dissolution threatened the Union. To many Americans Stephen A. Douglas, despite his cynicism, seemed to offer the best hope of preserving it. For this reason unusual attention was focused on his campaign for re-election to the Senate in 1858. The importance of the contest and Douglas' national prestige also put great pressure on the Republicans of Illinois to nominate someone who could make a good showing against him. The man they chose was Abraham Lincoln.

After a towering figure has passed from the stage, it is always difficult to discover what he was like before his rise to prominence. This is especially true of a man like Lincoln, who changed greatly when power and responsibility and fame came to him. Lincoln was not unknown in 1858, but his career before the time of the Kansas crisis had not been distinguished. He was born in Kentucky in 1809, and the story of his early life can be condensed, as he once said himself, into a single line from Gray's *Elegy*: "The short and simple annals of the poor." His illiterate, ne'er-do-well father, Thomas Lincoln, was a typical frontier wanderer. When Abraham was seven, the family moved to Indiana. In 1830 they pushed west again into southern Illinois. The boy received almost no formal schooling, but he had a good mind and was extremely ambitious. He cut loose from his family, made a trip to New Orleans, and for a time managed a general store in New Salem, Illinois. When barely 23, he won a seat in the state legislature as a Whig. He studied law and was admitted to the bar in 1836.

However, unlike Douglas, his Democratic contemporary, Lincoln prospered only moderately. He remained in the legislature until 1842, displaying a perfect willingness to adopt the Whig position on all issues, and in 1846 was elected to a single term in Congress. While not engaged in politics he worked at the law, maintaining an office in Springfield and following the circuit, taking a variety of cases, few of much importance. He earned a decent but by no means sumptuous living. After 1848 his political career had petered out, and he seemed fated to pass his remaining years as a typical small-town lawyer-politician.

Even during this period Lincoln displayed many remarkable characteristics. His personality was enormously complex. His rough, bawdy sense of humor and his endless fund of stories and tall tales made him a legend first in Illinois and then in Washington during his brief service in the House. Yet he was subject to periods of melancholy so profound as to appear almost psychopathic. Friends spoke of him as having "cat fits," and he wrote of himself at one point in the early 1840's: "I am now the most miserable man living. If what I felt were equally distributed to the whole human family, there would not be one cheerful face on earth." He was admired in Illinois as a powerful and expert axman and a champion wrestler. He was thoroughly at home with toughs like the "Clary's Grove Boys" of New Salem and in the convivial atmosphere of a party caucus. But in a society where most men

CHICAGO HISTORICAL SOCIETY

Alexander Hesler's portrait, taken in Springfield on June 3, 1860, shortly after the Republican national convention, is generally considered to be the finest of the pre-Civil War photographs of Lincoln.

drank heavily, he never touched liquor of any sort. In a region swept by repeated waves of religious revivalism, Lincoln managed to be at once a man of calm spirituality and a skeptic without appearing offensive to conventional believers. He was a party wheel horse, a corporation lawyer, even a railroad lobbyist, but his reputation for integrity was stainless. It is actually true that from the time he first ran for office in the 1830's, he was familiarly known as "Honest Abe."

The revival of the slavery controversy in 1854 stirred Lincoln deeply. No abolitionist, he had always tried to take a realistic view of the problem. Upon occasion he had even handled the cases of slaveowners seeking to reclaim runaways in Illinois. However, the Kansas-Nebraska bill led him to see the moral issue more clearly. "If slavery is not wrong, nothing is wrong," he stated with the clarity and simplicity of expression for which he later became famous. Past compromises made for the sake of sectional harmony had always sought to preserve as much territory as possible for free men. To open Kansas and Nebraska to the peculiar institution would be a bad mistake. Yet unlike most northern free-soilers, he did not blame the southerners for slavery. "They are just what we would be in their situation," he confessed. He read widely, spent many hours trying to think the problem through. Then he began to make speeches.

Hundreds of politicos were expounding upon slavery in the middle fifties, but Lincoln quickly stood out in this windy crowd. The fairness and moderation of his position combined with its moral force won Lincoln many admirers in the great body of citizens who were trying to reconcile their generally low opinion of the Negro and their patriotic desire to avoid an issue that threatened the Union with their growing conviction that slavery was sinful. *Anything* that aided slavery was wrong, Lincoln argued. There must be no more concessions; no single additional acre of free soil should be corrupted. Popular sovereignty was a snare and a delusion. But before casting the first stone, every northerner should look into his own heart: "If there be a man amongst us who is so impatient of [slavery] as a wrong as to disregard its actual presence among us and the difficulty of getting rid of it suddenly in a satisfactory way . . . that man is misplaced if he is on our platform." And Lincoln confessed:

> If all earthly power were given to me, I should not know what to do as to the existing institution. But . . . [this] furnishes no more excuse for permitting slavery to go into our free territory than it would for reviving the African slave trade.

Thus Lincoln was at once compassionate toward the slaveowner and stern toward the institution. " 'A house divided against itself cannot stand,' " he warned. "I believe this government cannot endure permanently half slave and half free." Without minimizing the difficulties or urging a hasty and ill-considered solution, Lincoln demanded that the people look toward a day, however remote, when not only Kansas but the whole country would be free.

The Lincoln-Douglas Debates

As Lincoln developed these ideas his reputation grew. In 1855 he almost won the Whig nomination for senator. The next year, at the first Republican National Convention, he received 110 votes in the balloting for the Vice Presidential nomination. He seemed the logical man to pit against Douglas in 1858.

In July Lincoln challenged Douglas to a series of debates and the senator accepted. Since the candidates had already spoken in Chicago and Springfield, they agreed to meet once in each of Illinois' seven other congressional districts. These debates were well attended, closely argued, and widely reported. The idea of a direct confrontation between candidates for an important office captured the imagination of thousands of people all over the land. The two candidates* presented a sharp physical contrast that must have helped ordinary men in sorting out their differing points

*The actual choice of the next senator lay, of course, in the hands of the state legislature. Technically, Douglas and Lincoln were campaigning for candidates for the legislature who were pledged to support them for the Senate seat.

of view. Douglas was short and stocky, Lincoln long and lean. Douglas gave the impression of irrepressible energy. While speaking, he roamed all over the platform; he used colorful language, broad gestures, bold, exaggerated arguments. He did not hesitate to call "Honest Abe" a liar. Lincoln on his part was slow and deliberate of speech. His voice was curiously high-pitched, yet it carried well enough to hold a large open-air audience. He seldom used gestures or oratorical tricks, trying rather to create an impression of utter sincerity to add force to his remarks.

Moreover, the two had completely different styles as politicians, each calculated to project a particular public image. Douglas epitomized efficiency and success. He dressed in the latest fashion, favoring flashy vests and the finest broadcloth. Ordinarily he arrived in town for a debate in a private railroad car, to be met by a brass band, then to ride at the head of a parade to the appointed place. Lincoln appeared before the voters as a man of the people. He wore ill-fitting black suits and a stovepipe hat—repository for letters, bills, scribbled notes, and other scraps—that exaggerated his great height. He presented a worn and rumpled appearance, partly because he traveled from place to place on the day coach, accompanied by only a few advisers. When local supporters came to meet him at the station, he preferred to walk with them through the streets to the scene of the debate.

Above all, Lincoln and Douglas maintained a remarkably high intellectual level in their speeches. As the New York *Tribune* reported, this was "not merely a passage at arms between two eminent masters" but a debate that touched "some of the most vital principles of our political system." Nevertheless, these were *political* debates, the speakers politicians. They were not seeking to influence future historians (although these have pondered over their words endlessly), but to win the votes of the hard-bitten farmers of Illinois.

To do so they tended to exaggerate their differences, which were not in fact enormous. Neither liked slavery, nor wanted to see it established in the territories, nor thought it economically efficient, but neither sought to abolish it by political action or force. Both believed black men congenitally inferior to white.

Douglas' strategy was to make Lincoln look like an abolitionist. He accused the Republicans of favoring racial equality and of refusing to abide by the decision of the Supreme Court in the Dred Scott case. Himself he pictured as a heroic champion of democracy, attacked on one side by the "black" Republicans and on the other by the Buchananites but ready to fight to his last breath for popular sovereignty. Lincoln, in turn, tried to picture Douglas as proslavery and a *defender* of the Dred Scott decision. His speeches sparkled with fine, hard-hitting passages. "Slavery is an unqualified evil to the negro, to the white man, to the soil, and to the State," he said. "Judge Douglas," he also said, "is blowing out the moral lights around us, when he contends that whoever wants slaves has a right to hold them." However, he often weakened the force of his arguments, being perhaps too eager to demonstrate his conservatism. "I am not, nor ever have been, in favor of bringing about in any way the social and political equality of the white and black races," he insisted. Only *constitutional* methods should be used to "prevent the evil from becoming larger." Emancipation would come "in God's good time." He took a fence-sitting position on the question of abolition in the District of Columbia and stated flatly that he did not favor repeal of the Fugitive Slave Act.

In the debate at Freeport, a town northwest of Chicago near the Wisconsin line, Lincoln cleverly asked Douglas if, considering the Dred Scott decision, the people of a territory could exclude slavery *before* the territory became a state. Unhesitatingly Douglas replied that they could, simply by not passing the local laws essential for holding men in bondage. "It matters not what way the Supreme Court may hereafter decide as to the abstract question," he said. "The people have the lawful means to introduce or exclude it as they please, for the reason that slavery cannot exist . . . unless it is supported by local police regulations."

This argument saved Douglas in Illinois. The Democrats carried both houses of the legislature by a narrow margin, whereas it is almost certain that if Douglas had accepted the Dred Scott decision outright, the balance would have swung to the Republicans. But the "Freeport Doctrine" cost him heavily two years later when he made his bid for the Democratic Presidential nomination. "It matters not what way the Supreme Court may hereafter decide"!—southern extremists would not accept a man who suggested that the Dred Scott decision could be circumvented, although in fact Douglas had only stated the obvious. Probably Lincoln had not thought beyond the senatorial election when he asked the question. He was merely hoping to keep Douglas on the defensive and perhaps injure him in southern Illinois, where considerable proslavery sentiment existed. In any case, defeat did Lincoln no harm politically. He had more than held his own against one of the most formidable debaters in politics. His name was now known over a wide area, his distinctive personality and point of view had impressed themselves upon thousands of minds. Indeed, his political career was revitalized.

The campaign of 1858 marked Douglas' last triumph, Lincoln's last defeat. Elsewhere the elections in the North went heavily to the Republicans. The Democrats dropped 7 seats in New York, 11 in Pennsylvania, 3 each in Indiana and Ohio. When the old Congress convened in December, northern-sponsored economic measures (a higher tariff, the transcontinental railroad, river and harbor improvements, a free homestead bill) were all blocked by southern votes. Whether the South could continue to prevent the passage of this legislation in the new Congress was problematical. By early 1859 even many moderate southerners were beginning to feel uneasy about the future of their section, while the radicals, made panicky by Republican victories and their own failure to win in Kansas, spoke openly of secession if a Republican was elected President in 1860. Lincoln's "house divided" speech was quoted out of context, while Douglas' Freeport Doctrine added to southern woes. When Senator William H. Seward of New York spoke of an "irrepressible conflict" between freedom and slavery, southerners became still more alarmed. Naturally they struck back. Led by men like William L. Yancey of Alabama and Senators Jefferson Davis of Mississippi, John Slidell of Louisiana, and James H. Hammond of South Carolina, they demanded a federal slave code for the territories, talked of annexing Cuba, reviving the African slave trade. Vindictive southern Democrats even deprived Douglas of his chairmanship of the Senate Committee on Territories. "Issues were becoming emotionalized," historian David Donald writes in discussing these unhappy times. "Slogans were reducing public sentiment to stereotyped patterns; social psychology was approaching a hair-trigger instability."

John Brown's Raid

In October 1859, with feelings North and South already tense, John Brown, the scourge of Kansas, made his second tragic contribution to the evolving sectional drama. Gathering a group of 18 devoted followers, white and black, he staged a mad attack on Harpers Ferry, Virginia, a town on the Potomac upstream from Washington. He planned to seize the federal arsenal there, arm the slaves who he thought would flock to his side, establish a Negro republic in the mountains of Virginia, and then press ahead with a sort of private war against the South. Of course the attack was a fiasco. Simply by overpowering a few night watchmen, Brown and his men occupied the arsenal and a nearby rifle factory. They also captured several hostages. But no slaves came forward to join them. Federal troops, sent quickly from Washington, trapped Brown's men in an engine house of the Baltimore and Ohio Railroad. After a grueling two-day siege in which the attackers picked off ten of his men, Brown was captured.

John Brown's raid generated intense excitement in all parts of the country; no incident so well illustrates the role of emotionalism and irrationality in the sectional crisis. Brown's whole career epitomized blind passion and unreason. Over the years before his Kansas escapade, he had been a drifter, horse thief, and swindler, several times a bankrupt, a failure in everything he attempted. His maternal grandmother, his mother, and five of his aunts and uncles were certifiably insane, as were two of his own children and many collateral relatives. That his ghastly

METROPOLITAN MUSEUM OF ART, GIFT OF MR. & MRS. CARL STOECKEL, 1897

ESTAMPES, BIBLIOTHEQUE NATIONALE

The image of John Brown as martyr was memorialized in art as well as in song and story. Here are two examples. The sketch at right was made in 1860 by the French literary giant Victor Hugo. At left is a conventional interpretation, The Last Moments of John Brown, *painted in 1884 by American genre artist Thomas Hovenden.*

Pottawatomie murders were more than political crimes should have been obvious to anyone: some of the victims were hacked to bits. Yet numbers of intelligent and supposedly high-minded northerners, including Emerson and Thoreau, had supported him and his antislavery "work" after 1856, and some, the "Secret Six" as they were called, contributed directly and knowingly to his Harpers Ferry enterprise. After Brown's capture, Thoreau compared his execution to Christ's crucifixion, and Emerson, in an essay on "Courage," called him a martyr who would "make the gallows as glorious as the cross."

Many southerners reacted to Harpers Ferry with an equal lack of public responsibility and good sense, some with an insane rage similar to Brown's. Rumors flew across the land of other planned uprisings. Dozens of hapless northerners in the southern states were arrested, beaten, or driven off. One, falsely suspected of being an accomplice of Brown, was lynched.

Brown's fate lay in the hands of the Virginia authorities. Ignoring his obvious derangement, they charged him with treason, conspiracy, and murder. He was speedily convicted and hanged. It would have been both wiser and more just to have committed him to an asylum. Then his dreadful act could have been seen in proper perspective.

Yet it would be expecting too much of Virginia and of the nation to have exercised such forbearance. Furthermore, "Old Brown" had still one more contribution to make to the developing sectional tragedy. Despite the furor he had created, cool heads everywhere called for calm and denounced his attack. Most leading Republican politicians repudiated him and tried to reassure the South that they would never condone the use of violence against slavery. Even execution would probably not have made a martyr of Brown had he behaved like a madman after his capture. Instead, an enormous passive dignity descended upon him as he lay in his Virginia jail awaiting death. "If it is deemed necessary that

I should forfeit my life for the furtherance of the ends of justice, and mingle my blood further with the blood of . . . millions in this slave country whose rights are disregarded by wicked, cruel, and unjust enactments," he said before the judge pronounced sentence, "I say, let it be done."

This John Brown, with his patriarchal beard and sad eyes, so apparently incompatible with the bloody terrorist of Pottawatomie and Harpers Ferry, led thousands in the North to ignore his past and their own better judgment and treat him as a martyr, thus a saint. Naturally, southerners reacted with horror and scorn, concluding that the whole North approved his behavior.

In this way a megalomaniac became to the North a hero and to the South a symbol of northern stop-at-nothing ruthlessness. The historian C. Vann Woodward, whose essay on Brown brilliantly analyzes the whole affair, puts it this way: "Paranoia continued to induce counter-paranoia, each antagonist infecting the other reciprocally, until the vicious spiral ended in war." Soon, as the popular song put it, Brown's body lay "a-mouldering in the grave," but the memory of his bloody act did indeed go "marching on."

Election of 1860

By 1860 the nation was teetering on the brink of disunion, perhaps even of civil war. Radicals, North and South, were heedlessly provoking one another. When a disgruntled North Carolinian, Hinton Rowan Helper, published *The Impending Crisis of the South*, an attempt to demonstrate statistically that slavery was ruining the South's economy and corrupting its social structure, the Republicans flooded the country with an abridged edition, although they knew that southerners considered the book an appeal for social revolution. "I have always been a fervid Union man," one southerner wrote in 1859, "but I confess the [northern] endorsement of the Harpers Ferry outrage and Helper's infernal doctrine has shaken my fidelity." In the Deep South more and more people talked of leaving the Union, and in February 1860 the legislature of Alabama formally resolved that the state ought to secede if a Republican was elected President in November.

Extremism was more evident in the South, and to any superficial observer that section must have seemed the aggressor in the crisis. Yet even when making their most outrageous demands, such as the reopening of the African slave trade, southern radicals believed they were defending themselves against attack. They felt surrounded by an ever-mounting hostility. The North was growing at a much faster rate; if nothing were done, they feared, a flood of new free states would soon be able to amend the Constitution and emancipate the slaves. The decline of slavery in border states from Maryland to Missouri seemed to be bringing that day closer, and the increasing worldwide condemnation of the institution added a further psychological burden. John Brown's raid, with its threat of black insurrection, reduced them to a state of panic. Perhaps, by seceding from the Union, the South could raise a dike against the tide of abolitionism and thus preserve its way of life. Secession seemed to make political sense. It also provided an emotional release—a way of dissipating tension by striking back at criticism. Thus, when legislatures in state after state in the South cracked down on freedom of expression, made the manumission of slaves illegal, banished free Negroes, and took other steps that northerners considered blatantly provocative, the advocates of these policies believed that they were only defending the *status quo.*

Stephen A. Douglas was probably the last hope of avoiding a rupture between North and South, but when the Democrats met in April 1860 to choose their Presidential candidate at Charleston, South Carolina, it soon became clear that the southern delegates would not accept him unless he promised not to disturb slavery in the territories. Indeed, they went further in their demands. The North, William L. Yancey of Alabama insisted, must accept the proposition that slavery was not merely tolerable but *right.* Of course the northerners would not go so far. "Gentlemen of the South," said Senator George E. Pugh of Ohio in replying to Yancey, "you mistake us—you mistake us! We will not do it!" When southern proposals were voted down, most of the delegates from the Deep South walked out

Without them, Douglas could not obtain the required two-thirds majority and the convention adjourned without naming a candidate.

In June the Democrats reconvened at Baltimore but failed again to reach agreement. The two wings then met separately, the northerners nominating Douglas, the southerners John C. Breckinridge of Kentucky, Buchanan's Vice President. On the question of slavery in the territories, the northerners promised to "abide by the decision of the Supreme Court," which meant, in effect, that they stood for Douglas' Freeport Doctrine. The southerners announced their belief that neither Congress nor any territorial government could prevent citizens from settling "*with their property*" in any territory. The party of Jefferson and Jackson had split asunder.

Meanwhile, in mid-May, the Republicans had met in Chicago. Skillfully they drafted a platform attractive to all classes and all sections of the northern and western states. For manufacturers they proposed a high tariff, for farmers a homestead law providing free land for actual settlers. Internal improvements "of a National character," most notably a railroad to the Pacific, should receive federal aid. No restrictions should be placed on immigration. As to slavery in the territories, the Republicans did not equivocate: "The normal condition of all the territory of the United States is that of freedom." Neither Congress nor local legislature could "give legal existence to Slavery in any Territory."

In choosing a Presidential candidate the convention displayed equally shrewd political judgment. Seward was the front runner, but he had taken too extreme a stand and made too many enemies. He led on the first ballot but could not get a majority. Then the delegates began to look closely at Abraham Lincoln of Illinois. His thoughtful and moderate views on the main issue of the times attracted many, and so did his political personality. "Honest Abe," the "Railsplitter," a man of humble origins (born in a log cabin), self-educated, self-made, a common man but by no means an ordinary man—the combination seemed unbeatable.

Lincoln also had an excellent team of convention managers. They packed the gallery with leather-lunged ward heelers assigned the task of shouting for their man and made a series of deals with the leaders of state delegations to win additional votes. "I authorize no bargains and will be bound by none," Lincoln telegraphed the convention. "Lincoln ain't here and don't know what we have to meet," one of his managers remarked and proceeded to trade off two Cabinet posts for the votes of key states. On the second ballot Lincoln drew shoulder to shoulder with Seward, on the third he was within two votes of victory. Before the roll could be called again, delegates began to switch their votes and in a landslide, soon made unanimous, Lincoln was nominated. Hannibal Hamlin of Maine was named for the second place on the ticket.

A few days earlier, die-hard Whigs and the remnants of the Know-Nothing organization had formed the Constitutional Union party and nominated John Bell of Tennessee for President. "It is both the part of patriotism and of duty," they resolved, "to recognize no political principle other than the Constitution of the country, the union of the states, and the enforcement of the laws." Ostrichlike, the Constitutional Unionists tried to ignore the conflicts rending the nation, but only in the border states, where the consequences of disunion were sure to be most tragic, did their argument make much headway.

With four candidates in the field, no one could win a popular majority, but it soon became clear that Lincoln was going to be elected. Breckinridge had most of the slave states in his pocket and Bell would run strong in the border regions, but the populous northern and western states had a large majority of the electoral vote, and there the choice lay between the Republicans and the Douglas Democrats. In such a contest the Republicans, with their attractive economic program and their strong stand against slavery in the territories, were sure to come out on top. Douglas grasped this truth quickly, accepted his fate, and for the first time in his career rose above ambition and achieved real greatness. "Mr. Lincoln is the next President," he said. "We must try to save the Union. I will go South." Everywhere, even in the heart of the Cotton Kingdom, he denounced secession and appealed to the voters to stand by the Union whoever was elected. Neither threats, nor snubs, nor an occasional pelting with eggs and vegetables could deter him.

When the votes were counted, Lincoln had only 1,866,000, almost a million fewer than the combined total of his three opponents, but he swept the North and West, which gave him 180 electoral votes and thus the Presidency. Douglas received 1,383,000 votes, but so distributed that he carried only Missouri and part of New Jersey, winning 12 electors. Breckinridge, with 848,000 popular votes, won most of the South (72 electors), and Bell, with 593,000, carried Virginia, Tennessee, and Kentucky for a total of 39 electors. Lincoln was thus a minority President,* but his title to the office was unquestionable. Even if all his opponents could have combined, he would still have won.

*However, the pro-Union candidates with strength in the South, Douglas and Bell, received far more popular votes in the slave states than Breckinridge.

The Secession Crisis

Would the South abide by the result? The answer came quickly. A few days after Lincoln's victory, the South Carolina legislature ordered an election of delegates to a convention to decide the state's future course. On December 20 the convention voted unanimously to secede, basing its action upon the logic of Calhoun. "The State of South Carolina has *resumed* her position among the nations of the world," the delegates announced.

By February 1, 1861, all the other states of the Lower South had followed suit. A week later, at Montgomery, Alabama, a provisional government of the Confederate States of America was established. Virginia, Tennessee, North Carolina, and Arkansas did not leave the Union but warned the

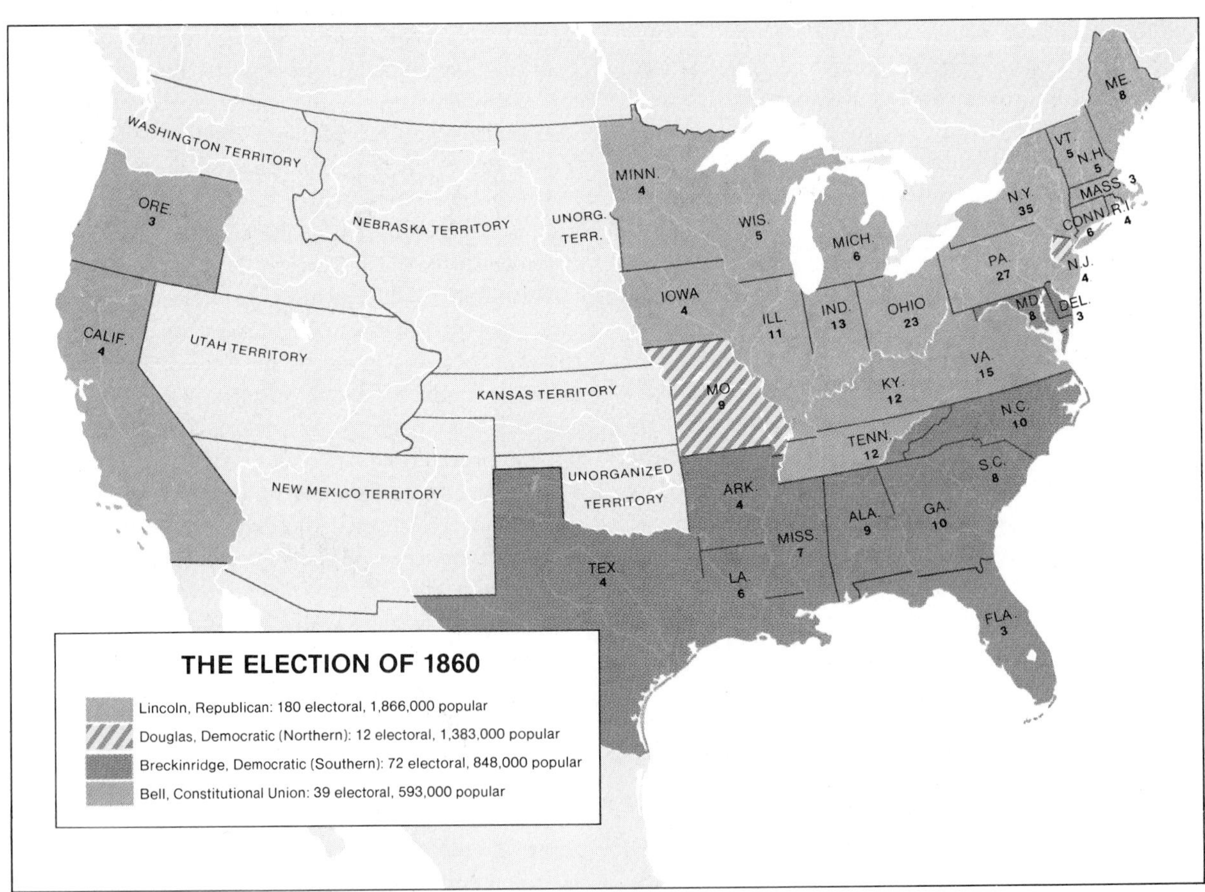

federal government that if it attempted to use force against the Confederacy, they, too, would secede.

In some of the southern states many persons opposed secession, but in all of them a solid majority approved. Why were the southerners willing to wreck the Union their grandfathers had put together with so much love and labor? No simple explanation is possible. The danger that the expanding North would overwhelm them was neither for today nor tomorrow. Lincoln had assured the South he would respect slavery where it existed. The Democrats had retained control of Congress in the election; the Supreme Court was firmly in their hands as well. If the North *did* try to destroy slavery, *then* secession was perhaps a logical tactic, but why not wait until the threat materialized? To leave the Union meant abandoning the very objectives for which the South had been contending for over a decade: a share of the federal territories and an enforceable fugitive slave act.

Two major reasons help to explain why the South rejected this line of thinking. One was the fact that the tremendous economic energy generated in the North seemed to threaten the South's independence. As we have seen, the slave system had much to do with the South's dependence upon the North for manufactures, but few southerners would admit it. Instead they complained about Yankee domination:

> From the rattle with which the nurse tickles the ear of the child born in the South to the shroud which covers the cold form of the dead, everything comes from the North [one southerner complained at a commercial convention in 1855]. We rise from between sheets made in Northern looms, and pillows of Northern feathers, to wash in basins made in the North. . . . We eat from Northern plates and dishes; our rooms are swept with Northern brooms, our gardens dug with Northern spades . . . and the very wood which feeds our fires is cut with Northern axes, helved with hickory brought from Connecticut and New York.

Secession, southerners argued, would "liberate" the South and produce the kind of balanced economy that was proving so successful in the North.

The other reason was purely emotional. The years of sectional conflict, the growing northern criticism of slavery, perhaps even an unconscious awareness that this criticism was well founded, had undermined and in many cases destroyed the patriotic feelings of southerners. Because of the constant clamor set up by the New England antislavery groups, the South tended to identify all northerners as "Yankee abolitionists" and to resent them with increasing passion. "I look upon the whole New England race as a troublesome unquiet set of meddlers," one Georgian wrote. Although states' rights provided the legal justification for leaving the Union and southerners expounded the strict-constructionist interpretation of the Constitution with great fervor and ingenuity, these economic and emotional factors were far more basic. By early 1861 the Lower South had decided to go ahead with secession regardless of the cost. "Let the consequences be what they may," an Atlanta newspaper proclaimed. "Whether the Potomac is crimsoned in human gore, and Pennsylvania Avenue is paved ten fathoms in depth with mangled bodies . . . the South will never submit. . . ."

Not every southerner, it must be repeated, could contemplate secession with such bloodthirsty equanimity. Many accepted it only after the deepest examination of conscience and with much pain and sorrow. Lieutenant Colonel Robert E. Lee of Virginia, who had fought brilliantly and bravely for the Stars and Stripes in the Mexican War, was typical of many thousands. "I see only that a fearful calamity is upon us," he wrote during the secession crisis. "There is no sacrifice I am not ready to make for the preservation of the Union save that of honour. If a disruption takes place, I shall go back in sorrow to my people & share the misery of my native state, & save in her defense there will be one less soldier in the world than now."

In the North there was a foolish but understandable reluctance to believe the South really intended to break away permanently, in the South, an equally unrealistic expectation that the North would not resist secession forcibly. President-elect Lincoln was inclined to write secession off as a bluff designed to win concessions on slavery in the territories which he was determined not to make. Lincoln also showed a lamentable

[Special Despatch to the Morning News.]

IMPORTANT FROM WASHINGTON!

Address of Senator Toombs to the People of Georgia.

PROPOSITIONS FOR NEW GURANTEES REJECTED!

THE SOUTH TREATED WITH DERISION AND CONTEMPT!

Senator Crittenden's Amendments Unanimously Voted Down!

Secession the last and only Resort!

Washington, Dec. 23.—Senator Toombs telegraphs this morning the following, addressed to the people of Georgia:

Fellow-Citizens of Georgia:—I came here to secure your constitutional rights, or to demonstrate to you that you can get no guarantees for these rights from your Northern confederates.

The whole subject was referred to a Committee of thirteen in the Senate yesterday. I was appointed on the Committee and accepted the trust. I submitted propositions, which so far from receiving decided support from a single member of the Republican party on the Committee, they were all treated with either derision or contempt. The vote was then taken in Committee on the amendments to the Constitution proposed by Hon. J. J. Crittenden, of Kentucky, AND EACH AND ALL OF THEM WERE VOTED AGAINST UNANIMOUSLY BY THE BLACK REPUBLICAN MEMBERS OF THE COMMITTEE.

In addition to these facts, a majority of the Black Republican members of the Committee DECLARED DISTINCTLY THAT THEY HAD NO GURANTEES TO OFFER, which was silently acquiesced in by the other members.

The Black Republican members of this Committee of Thirteen are representative men of their party and section, and, to the extent of my information, truly represent the Committee of Thirty-Three in the House, which on Tuesday adjourned for a week without coming to any vote, after solemnly pledging themselves to vote on all the propositions then before them on that date.

That Committee is controlled by Black Republicans, your enemies, who only seek to amuse you with delusive hope until your election, in order that you may defeat the friends of secession. If you are deceived by them it shall not be my fault. I have put the test fairly and frankly. It is decisive against you; and now I tell you upon the faith of a true man that all further looking to the North for security for your constitutional rights in the Union ought to be instantly abandoned. It is fraught with nothing but ruin to yourselves and your posterity.

Secession by the fourth of March next should be thundered from the ballot box by the unanimous voice of Georgia on the second day of January next. Such a voice will be your best guarantee for LIBERTY, SECURITY, TRANQUILITY AND GLORY.

ROBERT TOOMBS.

For the Federal Union.

Senator Robert Toombs reported the failure of the Crittenden Compromise to his Georgia constituents in this angry dispatch, blaming the "Black Republicans" and urging secession as the only recourse.

political caution in refusing to announce his plans or to cooperate with the outgoing Democratic administration before taking over on March 4. As for Buchanan, who still held official power during that grim winter, he deplored secession but professed himself powerless to counteract it. He urged making concessions to the South but lacked the forcefulness to take the situation in hand. Of course he faced unprecedented difficulties. His term was about to run out, and since he could not commit his successor, his influence was minuscule. Yet even in the light of these circumstances, he behaved weakly. A bolder man might still have rallied the Unionists of the South by some dramatic stroke. And Buchanan ought to have denounced secession in uncompromising terms. Instead he tolerated secessionists in his own Cabinet and vacillated between a policy of compromise and one of aimless drift. As his friendly biographer, Philip Klein, has written: "Importuned, threatened, warned, begged, pushed, pulled, and shoved in every direction . . . the president at length became distraught and despaired of achieving a solution."

Appeasers, well-meaning believers in compromise, and those prepared to use force to preserve the Union were alike incapable of successful action. A group of moderates headed by Henry Clay's disciple, Senator John J. Crittenden of Kentucky, proposed a constitutional amendment in which slavery would be "recognized as existing" in all territories south of latitude 36° 30′. The amendment also promised that no future amendment would tamper with the institution in the slave states, and offered other guarantees to the South. But when Lincoln refused to consider any arrangement that would open new territory to slavery, the Republican moderates lost interest, and this Crittenden Compromise got nowhere. While the new southern Confederacy set vigorously to work drafting a constitution, choosing Jefferson Davis as provisional president, seizing arsenals and other federal property within its boundaries, and preparing to dispatch diplomatic representatives to enlist the support of foreign powers, Buchanan bumbled helplessly in Washington and, out in Illinois, Abraham Lincoln juggled Cabinet posts and grew a beard.

SUPPLEMENTARY READING The events leading to the Civil War have been analyzed by dozens of historians. Of modern authorities, Allan Nevins provides the fullest and most magisterial treatment in his *The Ordeal of the Union* (1947) and in *The Emergence of Lincoln** (1950). An excellent briefer summary is J.G. Randall and David Donald, *The Civil War and Reconstruction* (1961), but see also the interpretation of A.O. Craven, more sympathetic to the South, in *The Coming of the Civil War** (1942) and *Civil War in the Making** (1959). R.F. Nichols, *The Disruption of American Democracy** (1948), discusses the political developments of 1856–1861 exhaustively and perceptively.

The works on the abolitionists mentioned in Chapter 13 cover the enforcement of the Fugitive Slave Act and *Uncle Tom's Cabin.** R.F. Wilson, *Crusader in Crinoline* (1941), is a satisfactory biography of Mrs. Stowe. E.L. McKitrick (ed.), *Slavery Defended** (1963), contains a typical southern review of *Uncle Tom's Cabin.* Two recent studies stress the anti-Negro feelings of whites in the western states and their relation to the sectional crisis: E.H. Berwanger, *The Frontier Against Slavery: Western Anti-Negro Prejudice and the Slavery Extension Controversy* (1967), and V.J. Voegeli, *Free but Not Equal: The Midwest and the Negro During the Civil War* (1967).

For the foreign policy of the 1850's, see Dexter Perkins, *The Monroe Doctrine: 1826–1867* (1933), A.J. May, *Contemporary American Opinion of the Mid-Century Revolutions in Central Europe* (1927), Basil Rauch, *American Interests in Cuba* (1948), R.F. Nichols, *Advance Agents of American Destiny* (1956), E.S. Wallace, *Destiny and Glory* (1956), Arthur Walworth, *Black Ships Off Japan* (1946), I.D. Spencer, *The Victor and the Spoils: A Life of William L. Marcy* (1959), and P.S. Klein, *President James Buchanan* (1962).

On Stephen A. Douglas, see G.F. Milton, *The Eve of Conflict* (1934), and G.M. Capers' briefer *Stephen A. Douglas* (1959). Nevins is particularly good on the whole Kansas controversy, but see also R.F. Nichols' biography of Franklin Pierce, *Young Hickory of the Granite Hills* (1931), P.W. Gates, *Fifty Million Acres: Conflicts over Kansas Land Policy** (1954), H.H. Simms, *A Decade of Sectional Controversy* (1942), and J.C. Malin's *The Nebraska Question* (1953) and *John Brown and the Legend of Fifty-Six* (1942).

Sumner's role in the deepening crisis is brilliantly discussed in David Donald, *Charles Sumner and the Coming of the Civil War* (1960). Klein's life of Buchanan, mentioned above, is a careful and judicious analysis. On the Dred Scott case, see C.B. Swisher, *Roger B. Taney* (1935), Vincent Hopkins, *Dred Scott's Case** (1951), and the essay by Bruce Catton in J.A. Garraty (ed.), *Quarrels That Have Shaped the Constitution** (1964).

One can only sample the enormous literature on Lincoln. The outstanding one-volume biography is B.P. Thomas, *Abraham Lincoln* (1952). On his early career, see A.J. Beveridge, *Abraham Lincoln* (1928), and D.E. Fehrenbacher, *Prelude to Greatness** (1962). Other useful biographies include Carl Sandburg, *Abraham Lincoln: The Prairie Years** (1926), moving but inaccurate, and R.H. Luthin, *The Real Abraham Lincoln* (1960). The text of the Lincoln-Douglas debates is conveniently reprinted in R.W. Johannsen (ed.), *The Lincoln-Douglas Debates of 1858** (1965). The best analysis of the debates is H.V. Jaffa, *Crisis of the House Divided* (1959).

The best biography of John Brown is O.G. Villard, *John Brown* (1910), but Nevins' *Ordeal of the Union* provides the finest account of the raid on Harpers Ferry. C.V. Woodward's essay, "John Brown's Private War," in his *The Burden of Southern History** (1960), is excellent on the effects of the Harpers Ferry raid. Nichols' *The Disruption of American Democracy** is excellent on the breakup of the Democratic party and the election of 1860. For the secession crisis and the outbreak of the Civil War, consult K.M. Stampp, *And the War Came** (1950), D.M. Potter, *Lincoln and His Party in the Secession Crisis** (1950), J.G. Randall, *Lincoln, the President** (1945–1955), and D.L. Dumond, *The Secession Movement* (1931).

*Available in paperback.

15

The War to Save the Union

The nomination of Lincoln had worked well for the Republicans, but had his election been a good thing for the country? As March 4 approached, many Americans had their doubts. "Honest Abe" was a clever politician and had spoken well about the central issue of the times, but would he act decisively in this crisis? His behavior between November and March was not reassuring. He offered no clue to his future policy and spent much time closeted with politicians. Was he too obtuse to understand the grave threat to the Union posed by secession? Perhaps the thought of assuming so much responsibility had paralyzed him. Men remembered uneasily that he had never held an executive office, that his congressional career had been short and undistinguished. When finally he uprooted himself from Springfield in February 1861, his occasional speeches while en route to the capital were vague, almost flippant in tone. He kissed babies, shook hands, mouthed platitudes. Some thought it downright cowardly that he would let himself be spirited in the dead of night through Baltimore, where feeling against him ran high.

The Lincoln Administration

Everyone waited tensely to see whether he would oppose secession by force, or, as many persons such as the influential Horace Greeley of the New York *Tribune* were suggesting, allow the "wayward sisters" to "depart in peace." But Lincoln seemed only concerned with organizing his Cabinet. The final slate was not ready until the morning of inauguration day, and shrewd observers found it alarming, for the new President had chosen to construct a "balanced" Cabinet representing a wide range of opinion instead of putting together a group of harmonious advisers who could help him face the crisis.

William H. Seward, the secretary of state, was the ablest and best known of the appointees. Despite his reputation for radicalism, the hawk-nosed, chinless, tousle-haired Seward hoped to conciliate the South and was thus in bad odor with the Radical, or "iron-back," wing of the Republican party. Eventually, Seward proved himself Lincoln's strong right arm, but at this time he badly underestimated the President and confidently expected to dominate him. Representing the iron-backs was Senator

Salmon P. Chase, a bald, square-jawed, antislavery leader from Ohio, whom Lincoln named secretary of the treasury. Chase was humorless and vain, but able; he detested Seward, agreeing with him only in thinking Lincoln a weakling. Simon Cameron of Pennsylvania, the secretary of war, was a politician of dubious integrity; in selecting him Lincoln honored a deal made at the convention by his managers. Likewise, the appointment of Secretary of the Interior Caleb B. Smith was a reward for Smith's work in swinging Indiana to Lincoln at Chicago. The other Cabinet members were Secretary of the Navy Gideon Welles of Connecticut, originally a Democrat; Attorney General Edward Bates of Missouri, chosen to represent the border states; and Postmaster General Montgomery Blair of Maryland, another former Democrat, whose father had been an intimate of Andrew Jackson.

Lincoln's selections worried many thoughtful people. The national emergency explained his desire to conciliate all factions, but could the awkward, somewhat indecisive-appearing President unite and then master such a varied group? Would he be a Washington—or a Franklin Pierce?

Lincoln's inaugural address was conciliatory but firm. Southern institutions were in no danger from his administration. Secession, however, was not merely illegal but impossible. Federal property in the South would be held and protected. "A husband and wife may be divorced," Lincoln said, employing one of his homely and according to the Victorian standards of the day slightly risqué metaphors, "but the different parts of our country cannot. . . . Intercourse, either amicable or hostile, must continue between them." Yet throughout, the tone was both calm and warm. His concluding words catch the spirit of the inaugural perfectly:

> I am loath to close. We are not enemies, but friends. We must not be enemies. Though passion may have strained, it must not break, our bonds of affection. The mystic chords of memory, stretching from every battlefield and patriot grave to every living heart . . . will yet swell the chorus of the Union when again touched, as surely they will be, by the better angels of our nature.

Border state moderates found the speech encouraging but so did the fiery Charles Sumner, who shared the opinion of many intellectuals that Lincoln was a dolt. "I do not suppose Lincoln had it in his mind, if indeed he ever heard of it," Sumner said to a friend, "but the inaugural seems to me best described by Napoleon's simile of 'a hand of iron and a velvet glove.' " The Confederates, however, read it as justifying their decision to secede.

Fort Sumter

Actually, while stoutly denying the legality of secession, Lincoln had taken a temporizing position. The Confederates had already seized most United States property in the Deep South. Lincoln admitted frankly that he would not attempt to reclaim this property or send in "obnoxious strangers" to carry on the functions of officials who had resigned. However, two federal strong points, Fort Sumter, on an island in Charleston harbor, and Fort Pickens, at Pensacola, Florida, were still in loyal hands. Although not especially important, these forts had attracted a great deal of attention, and Lincoln did not want to abandon them without a show of resistance. Yet to reinforce them might mean bloodshed that would make reconciliation impossible. After weeks of indecision, he finally took the moderate step of sending a naval expedition to supply the beleaguered Sumter garrison with food. Unwilling to countenance this, the Confederates opened fire on the fort early on the morning of April 12, before the supply ships arrived. After holding out against the bombardment of shore batteries for 34 hours, Major Robert Anderson and his men surrendered.

This attack precipitated a great outburst of patriotic indignation in the North. Lincoln promptly issued a call for 75,000 volunteers, which in turn caused Virginia, North Carolina, Arkansas, and Tennessee to secede. After years of compromise and quarrels, the nation chose to settle the great conflict between the sections by force of arms. Southerners considered Lincoln's call for troops an act of naked aggression. They were seeking to exercise what a later generation would call the right of self-determination; how, they asked, could the North square its professed belief in

THE WAR.

Highly Important News from Washington.

Offensive War Measures of the Administration.

The President's Exposition of His Policy Towards the Confederate States.

A WAR PROCLAMATION.

Seventy-five Thousand Men Ordered Out.

Thirteen Thousand Required from New York.

Call for an Extra Session of Congress.

Preparations for the Defence of the National Capital.

The Great Free States Arming for the Conflict.

Thirty Thousand Troops to be Tendered from New York.

Strong Union Demonstrations in Baltimore.

THE BATTLE AT CHARLESTON.

EVACUATION OF FORT SUMTER.

Major Anderson to Sail for New York.

IMPORTANT NEWS FROM MONTGOMERY.

On April 15, 1861, the New York Herald *summarized the events triggered by the bombardment of Fort Sumter. Lincoln based his proclamation on a law dating from Washington's administration, giving the President the power to federalize state militia to counter "combinations too powerful to be suppressed."*

democratic free choice with its refusal to permit the southern states to leave the Union peaceably when a majority of their citizens wished to do so? Lincoln took the position, however, that secession was a *rejection* of democracy. If the South could refuse to abide by the result of an election in which it had freely participated, then everything that monarchists and other conservatives had said about the instability of republican governments would be proved true. "The central idea of secession is the essence of anarchy," he said. The United States must "demonstrate to the world" that "when ballots have been fairly and constitutionally decided, there can be no successful appeal except to ballots themselves, at succeeding elections."

This was the proper ground for Lincoln to take, both morally and politically. A war against slavery would not have been in keeping with his many previous pronouncements, and it would not have been supported by a majority of the people. Slavery was patently the root cause of secession, but not of the North's determination to resist secession, which resulted from the people's love of the Union. Although abolition was to be one of the major results of the Civil War, the war was fought for nationalistic reasons, not to destroy slavery. Lincoln made this plain beyond argument when he wrote, more than a year after the outbreak of hostilities: "I would save the Union. . . . If I could save the Union without freeing *any* slave, I would do it; and if I could save it by freeing *all* the slaves, I would do it; and if I could do it by freeing some and leaving others alone, I would also do that." He added, however, "I intend no modification of my oft-expressed *personal* wish that all men, everywhere, could be free."

The Blue and the Gray

In any test between the United States and the 11 states of the Confederacy, the former possessed tremendous advantages. There were 20.7 million people in the northern states (excluding Kentucky and Missouri, where opinion was divided), only 9 million in the South, and of these about 3.5 million were Negro slaves, whom the southerners were unwilling to trust with arms. The North's economic capacity to wage war was even more preponderant, for it had seven times as much manufacturing and a far larger and more efficient railroad system than the South. In 1860 the North produced firearms valued at $2.27 million; the South's output was only worth $73,000. Northern control of the merchant marine and the navy made possible a blockade of the Confederacy, a particularly potent threat to a region so dependent upon foreign markets.

The Confederates discounted these advantages. Many doubted that public opinion in the North would sustain Lincoln if he attempted to meet secession with force. Northern manufacturers needed southern markets, and merchants depended heavily upon southern business as well. Many western farmers were still sending their produce down the Mississippi. War would threaten the prosperity of all these groups, southerners maintained. Should the North try to cut Europe off from southern cotton, the powers, particularly Great Britain, would descend upon the land in their might, force open southern ports, and provide the Confederacy with the means of defending itself forever. "You do not dare to make war on cotton," Senator Hammond of South Carolina had taunted his northern colleagues as early as 1858. "No power on earth dares to make war upon it. Cotton is king."

The Confederacy also counted upon certain military advantages. Amid northern confusion and inactivity during the "interregnum" between November and March, it had accomplished its major objective: secession was a fact before the first shell burst against stout Fort Sumter. The new nation need only hold what it had; it could fight a defensive war, less costly in men and materiel and of great importance in maintaining morale and winning outside sympathy. Southerners would be defending not only their social institutions but also their homes and families. When asked by a northern invader why he was fighting against the Union, one southerner said simply: "Because y'all are down here."

To some extent the South also benefited from superior military leadership. Both armies relied upon West Pointers for their top commanders. Since most of these professionals followed the decisions of their home states when the war broke out, about 300 West Pointers became northern generals, about 180 southern. But among officers of lesser rank, the southerners probably excelled in the first years of the struggle, for the military tradition was strong in the South, and many young men had attended military academies. Luck played a part too; the Confederacy quickly found a great commander, while the highest-ranking northern generals in the early stages of the war proved either bungling or indecisive. In battle after battle, Union armies were defeated by forces equal or inferior in size. Since all the evidence that has been amassed to date indicates that there was little to choose between northern and southern common soldiers, superior generalship clearly made some difference.

Both sides faced massive difficulties in organizing for a war long feared but never properly anticipated. In the first days after Sumter, while the Confederate secretary of war was boasting that Washington would be overrun before May 1, Pennsylvania and other states rushed troops to protect the capital. No attack came, however, and soon the number of soldiers in Washington greatly exceeded the facilities available for quartering and supplying them. These troops were nearly all raw recruits. After southern defections, the regular army consisted of only 13,000 officers and men, far too few to absorb the 186,000 who had joined the colors by early summer. Recruiting was left to the states, each being assigned a quota; there was little central organization. Natty companies of "Fire Zouaves" and "Garibaldi Guards" and "Irish Volunteers" in gorgeous uniforms rubbed shoulders with slovenly units composed of toughs and criminals and with regiments of farm boys from Iowa, Illinois, and Michigan. Few knew even the rudiments of soldiering. The hastily composed high command, headed by the elderly Winfield Scott, debated endlessly about overall strategy, while regimental commanders lacked even decent maps of Virginia. Gradually, the ragged companies began to master close-order drill, but they received almost no effective field training.

The nation mustered its economic and administrative resources slowly because it had little experience with war, and none with civil war. But Lincoln must also share in the blame. The Whig prejudice against a too-powerful President was part of his political heritage; consequently he controlled neither Congress nor his own administration with the firmness of a Jackson or a Polk. He failed to develop either an efficient team of advisers or a central agency to collect information and coordinate the work of government departments. His faction-ridden Cabinet did not supply the kind of central guidance needed. Fortunately, in the early stages of the war, Congress was cooperative. Douglas, while critical of Lincoln before the attack on Sumter, devoted all his energies to rallying the Democrats as soon as war broke out. His death in June 1861 was a great loss to the country.

Without providing dynamic leadership in these early stages, Lincoln proved himself capable of handling heavy responsibilities. From beginning to end, his great strength lay in his ability to think problems through, to accept all their implications, and then to act unflinchingly. Anything but a tyrant by nature, he boldly exceeded the conventional limits of Presidential power in the national emergency, expanding the army without congressional authorization, suspending the writ of habeas corpus, even emancipating the slaves when he thought military necessity demanded such action. He also displayed a remarkable patience and depth of character: despite his high office, he willingly accepted snubs and insults from lesser men in order to advance the cause. Yet he was anything but a weakling. He kept a close check on every aspect of the war effort and quickly demonstrated that neither Seward nor any other man could dominate him. He labored endlessly to master the details of complicated government business, yet found time for thought too. His young secretary John Nicolay reported seeing him sit sometimes for a whole hour like "a petrified image," lost in contemplation. Gradually, his stock rose—first with men like Seward who saw him close up and experienced both his steel and his gentleness, and then with the people at large, who sensed his compassion, his humility, his wisdom. He was only 52 when he became President, but already men were calling him Old Abe. Before long they would call him Father Abraham.*

The South faced far greater problems than the North, for it had to create an entire administration under pressure of war, with the additional handicap of the states'-rights philosophy to which it was committed. The Confederate Constitution did not differ substantially from the United States Constitution and incorporated a few valuable improvements, such as the clause permitting the President to veto separate items in appropriation bills, but it explicitly recognized the sovereignty of the states and contained no broad authorization for laws designed to advance the general welfare. The Confederate Congress was limited in its ability to handle problems of many kinds. State governments repeatedly defied the central administration, located at Richmond after Virginia seceded, even with regard to military affairs. Of course the South made heavy use of the precedents and administrative machinery taken over from the United States. The government quickly decided that all federal laws would remain in force until specifically repealed by the Confederate Congress, and many former federal officials continued to perform their duties under the new auspices.

The call to arms produced a turnout in the Confederacy perhaps even more impressive than that in the North. So many men volunteered that during the early months about 200,000 had to be sent home because there were neither equipment nor facilities to be had for them. Even so, by July 1861 the Confederacy had about 112,000 men under arms. As in the North, men of every type enlisted, and morale was high. Ordinary militia companies sporting names like "Tallapoosa Thrashers," "Cherokee Lincoln Killers," and "Chickasaw Desperadoes" marched in step with elite companies of "Richmond Howitzers" and "Louisiana Zouaves" in exotic uniforms. (A "Zouave" mania swept both North and South, prospective soldiers evidently considering the broad sashes and baggy red breeches the very embodiment of military splendor.)

*Like all strong leaders in critical times, Lincoln had many detractors and was vilified mercilessly by the opposition press.

This battered but still clear daguerreotype portrait of Jefferson Davis was probably taken in Washington about 1860, when Davis was senator from Mississippi.

President Jefferson Davis represented the best type of southern slaveowner. A graduate of West Point, he was both a fine soldier and a successful planter, noted for his humane treatment of his slaves. In politics he had pursued a somewhat unusual course. While senator from Mississippi, he opposed the Compromise of 1850 and became a leader of the southern radicals. After Pierce made him secretary of war, however, he took a more nationalistic position, close to that of Douglas. He supported the transcontinental railroad idea and spoke in favor of the annexation of Cuba and other Caribbean areas. He rejected Douglas' position during the Kansas controversy but tried to close the breach that Kansas had opened in Democratic ranks. In the crisis after the 1860 election, he supported secession only reluctantly, preferring to give Lincoln a chance to prove that he meant the South no harm.

A lean, erect, handsome man with high cheekbones, deep-set, sensitive eyes, and fine features, Davis was courageous, industrious, and intelligent but rather too reserved and opinionated to make either a good politician or a popular leader. As President he devoted too much time to details and failed to delegate authority effectively; he was a worse administrator even than Lincoln. He fancied himself a military expert because of his West Point training and his Mexican War service, often neglecting pressing administrative problems to concentrate on devising strategy. At times he dictated the tactics employed by his generals. Unfortunately for the South, he was only a mediocre military thinker. Unlike Lincoln, he quarreled frequently with his subordinates, held grudges, and allowed personal feelings to influence his judgment, often to the detriment of the southern cause. "He was abnormally sensitive to disapprobation," his wife admitted. "He felt how much he was misunderstood, and the sense of mortification and injustice gave him a repellent manner." Men respected him for his devotion to the Confederacy, but few could feel for him the affection that Lincoln inspired.

The Test of Battle

As summer approached, the two nations prepared for battle, full of pride and enthusiasm and ignorant of the enormity of the tragic confrontation that was beginning. Vainglorious shouts of "Forward to Richmond!" and "On to Washington!" propelled the troops into battle long before they were properly trained. On July 21 at Manassas Junction, Virginia, some 20 miles below Washington, on a branch of the Potomac called Bull Run, 30,000 men under General Irwin McDowell attacked a roughly equal force of Confederates commanded by the "Napoleon of the South," Pierre G.T. Beauregard. McDowell's inexperienced men swept back the Confederate left flank. Victory seemed sure. But a Virginia brigade under Thomas J. Jackson, rushed to the field by rail from the Shenandoah Valley in the nick of time, held doggedly to a key hill, and the advance was checked. (A South Carolina general, seeking to rally his own men, pointed to the hill and shouted: "Look, there is Jackson with his Virginians, standing like a stone wall against the enemy." Thus "Stonewall" Jackson received his famous nickname.) The southerners then counterattacked, driving the Union soldiers back. As often happens with green troops, retreat quickly turned to rout. McDowell's men fled toward the defenses of Washington, abandoning their arms, stumbling through lines of supply wagons, trampling over foolish sightseers who had come out to watch the battle. Panic engulfed Washington while Richmond exulted, both sides expecting the northern capital to fall within hours.

Actually, the inexperienced southern troops were too disorganized to follow up their victory. Casualties on both sides were light, and the battle had little direct effect on anything but morale. Southern confidence increased, while in the North sensible men began to realize how immense the task of subduing the Confederacy would be.

After Bull Run, Lincoln quickly devised a new, broader, more systematic strategy for winning the war. For one thing, he decided to clamp a tight naval blockade on all southern ports. To accomplish this, warships on foreign station were recalled, old vessels reconditioned, a building program begun. Operations in the West designed to gain control of the Mississippi would also be undertaken. And most important of all, a new army would be mustered at Washington to invade Virginia. The men and money for all this were at hand, for the nation had responded nobly in defeat. Congress promptly authorized the enlistment of 500,000 three-year volunteers. To lead this great new army and—after General Scott's retirement in November—to command all the Union forces, Lincoln appointed a 34-year-old major general, George B. McClellan.

McClellan was the North's first military hero. Units under his command had driven the Confederates from the pro-Union western counties of Virginia, clearing the way for the admission of West Virginia as a separate state. The fighting had been on a small scale, but McClellan, an incurable romanticizer and something of an egomaniac, managed to inflate its importance. "You have annihilated two armies," he proclaimed in a widely publicized message to his troops, and few Americans noticed that there were only about 250 victims of this "annihilation."

Despite his penchant for self-glorification, Mc-

M. & M. KAROLIK COLLECTION, MUSEUM OF FINE ARTS, BOSTON

A pencil sketch by an unknown artist, obviously done in haste, captures the panic that swept through the Union ranks after the Bull Run defeat. The scene is the main road leading through Centreville to Washington.

Clellan had many solid qualifications for command. One was experience. After graduation from West Point in 1846, he had served in the Mexican War. During the Crimean War he spent a year in Europe as an observer, talking at length with British officers and studying fortifications. In 1857 he resigned his commission to become chief engineer of the Illinois Central Railroad, only to return to the colors after the attack on Fort Sumter.

To his new command McClellan also brought a fine military bearing, a flair for the dramatic, the ability to inspire his troops, remarkable talent as an administrator and organizer, and a sublime faith in his own destiny. He liked to concoct bold plans, dreamed of striking swiftly at the heart of the Confederacy to capture Richmond, Nashville, even New Orleans, yet he was sensible enough to insist upon massive logistical support, thorough training for the troops, iron discipline, and meticulous staff work before making a move. "I shall take my own time to make an army that will be sure of success," he said.

Behind the Lines

After Bull Run, this policy was exactly right. By the fall of the year a real army was taking shape along the Potomac: disciplined, confident, adequately supplied. All over the North, shops and factories were producing guns, ammunition, wagons, uniforms, shoes, and the countless other supplies needed to fight a great war. Most manufacturers operated on a small scale. There were, for example, 239 concerns making firearms in 1860 and 74 turning out sewing machines. But with the armed forces soon wearing out 3 million pairs of shoes and 1.5 million uniforms a year and with men leaving their jobs by the hundreds of thousands to fight, the tendency of industry to mechanize and to increase the size of the average manufacturing unit became ever more pronounced.

Such changes took time. At the beginning of the war Secretary of the Treasury Chase, inexperienced in monetary matters, greatly underestimated both the financial needs of the government and the probable duration of the conflict. He failed to ask Congress for enough money to fight the war properly. In August 1861 Congress passed an income tax law (3 per cent on incomes over $800, later raised to a top of 10 per cent on incomes over $10,000) and also assessed a direct tax on the states. Loans amounting to $140 million were also authorized. As the war dragged on and expenses mounted, new excise taxes on every imaginable product and service were passed, and still further borrowing was necessary. In 1863 the banking system was overhauled. The financier Jay Cooke became the government's agent for selling war bonds. He set up a network of subagents and advertised in the newspapers to stimulate sales. The program was successful but costly, for Cooke's profits were large and the rate of interest on government bonds ranged as high as 7.3 per cent.

During the war the federal government borrowed a total of $2.2 billion and collected $667 million in taxes, but these unprecedentedly large sums proved inadequate. Some obligations had to be met by printing paper money unredeemable in coin. About $431 million in "greenbacks"—a term used to distinguish this fiat money from the redeemable yellowback bills—were issued during the course of the war.

Printing-press money roused heated emotions; some considered it plain fraud, others a necessary way of mobilizing the national wealth in an emergency. From the modern point of view the latter position seems clearly correct. The greenbacks caused inflation, but it would have been impossible to remain on a specie standard even if they had not been issued. Public confidence in all paper money vacillated with each change in the fortunes of the Union armies. Whenever the war seemed to be going badly, citizens rushed to convert their paper money into gold. Long before the first greenbacks were issued, the banks had been forced to suspend specie payments on their notes—a fortunate thing since it enabled them to ease their lending policies and thus to finance necessary industrial expansion.

On balance, the heavy emphasis on borrowing and currency inflation was expensive but not irresponsible. In a country still chiefly agricultural, people had relatively low cash incomes and therefore could not easily bear a heavy tax load. Many Americans also considered it reasonable to expect future generations to pay part of the dollar cost of saving the Union when theirs was contributing so heavily in labor and blood.

Partisan politics was altered by the war but not suspended. The secession of the southern states left the Republicans with large majorities in both houses of Congress, and the Democratic minority loyally supported most measures necessary for the conduct of the war. The sharpest conflicts came when slavery and race relations were under discussion, the Democrats adopting a conservative stance and the Republicans dividing into Moderate and Radical wings. Political divisions on economic issues such as tariffs and land policy tended to cut across party lines, and so far as the Republicans were concerned, to bear little relation to men's views on slavery and race.

As the war progressed, the Radical faction became increasingly influential. By 1861 the most prominent senator was Charles Sumner, finally recovered from his caning by Preston Brooks and brimful of hatred for slaveholders. In the House, Thaddeus Stevens of Pennsylvania was the rising power. Sumner and Stevens represented the extreme left wing on all questions relating to Negroes; they insisted not merely on abolition but on granting full political and civil rights to blacks. Moderate Republicans objected vehemently to treating Negroes as equals and opposed making abolition a war aim, but even many of the so-called Radicals disagreed strongly with the Sumner-Stevens position on race relations.

As a matter of fact, the Radicals were not a close-knit group in Congress or out, either ideologically or in terms of political organization. They agreed only in wishing to make the abolition of slavery a main objective of the war. Some of the most extreme antislavery men among them found Negroes personally repulsive; many favored the essentially racist policy of colonizing the freedmen after emancipation. Senator Benjamin Wade of Ohio, for example, was a lifelong opponent of slavery, yet he had convinced himself that Negroes (he habitually called them "niggers") had a distinctive and unpleasant smell. He wanted to have nothing to do with them personally and considered the common white prejudice against blacks perfectly understandable. But prejudice, he insisted, gave no one the right "to do injustice to anybody"; he insisted that Negroes were at least as intelligent as white men and that they were entitled not merely to freedom but to full political equality.

At the other end of the political spectrum stood a peace party, dominated by Democrats in the border states and in Ohio, Indiana, and Illinois. These "Copperheads" (the reference was to the poisonous snake of that name) opposed all measures in support of the war and organized secret societies, such as the Knights of the Golden Circle, in an effort to win control of Congress and force a negotiated peace. Few were actually disloyal, but their activities at a time when thousands of men were risking their lives in battle infuriated many northerners.

Lincoln treated dissenters with a curious mixture of repression and tolerance. He suspended the writ of habeas corpus in critical areas and applied martial law freely. Over 13,000 persons were arrested and held without trial, many, as it later turned out, unjustly. Overly enthusiastic Union commanders sometimes employed martial law as a weapon against all criticism. The general in charge of the Department of the Ohio outlawed even the expression of "sympathies" for the Confederacy. "Treason," he decreed in direct violation of the constitutional definition of treason as an overt act, "expressed or implied will not be tolerated." The President argued that the government dared not stand on ceremony in a national emergency. His object, he insisted, was not to punish but to *prevent.* Arbitrary arrests were not made for directly political purposes, and elections were held in complete freedom throughout the war. The federal courts compiled an admirable record in defending civil liberties, although when in conflict with the military, they could not enforce their decrees. In *Ex parte Merryman* (1861), for instance, Chief Justice Taney held General George Cadwalader in contempt for failing to produce a prisoner for trial when ordered to do so, but Cadwalader went unpunished, and the prisoner continued to languish behind bars. After the war, in *Ex parte Milligan* (1866), the Supreme Court declared military trials of civilians in areas where the regular courts were functioning illegal, but by that time the question was only of academic interest.

The suppression of habeas corpus and restrictions on freedom of expression made some new enemies for the administration among civil libertarians who generally favored its war aims, and further embittered those who opposed its objectives. The most notorious domestic foe of the administration was Clement L. Vallandigham of Ohio. In 1863, after he had made a speech urging that the war be ended by negotiation, Vallandigham was seized by the military and thrown into jail. Of course his many followers protested indignantly. Lincoln ordered him released and banished to the Confederacy. Later, when Vallandigham slipped back into the North and campaigned openly against Lincoln in the 1864 election, he was not molested.

David Donald's judgment of Lincoln's policy toward dissenters is worth quoting at length:

> The arbitrary arrests cannot be passed over lightly: to do so would allow too small a value to civil guarantees. On the other hand a search of the full record will show that anything like a drastic military régime was far from Lincoln's thoughts. The harshness of war regulations was often tempered by leniency. . . . The word "dictator" in its twentieth-century connotation would be utterly inappropriate if applied to the Civil War President.

The South also revised its strategy after Bull Run. Although it might have been wiser to risk everything on a bold invasion of the North, President Davis relied primarily on a strong defense to wear down the Union's will to fight. When volunteering slackened in 1862, the Confederate Congress passed a conscription act which contained many glaring inequities. It permitted the hiring of substitutes and exempted many classes of people (including college professors and mail carriers) whose work could hardly have been deemed essential. A provision deferring the owners of 20 or more slaves led many to grumble sourly about "a rich man's war and a poor man's fight."

Although the Confederacy did not develop a two-party system, there was plenty of internal political strife. President Davis made enemies easily, beginning with his diminutive Vice President, the caustic Alexander H. Stephens of Georgia, and his tenure was marked by much bickering and needless argument. The widespread southern devotion to states' rights and individual liberty (for white men) caused endless trouble, especially when Davis found it necessary to suspend the writ of habeas corpus under certain circumstances. Throughout the war, conflicts were continually erupting between Davis and various southern governors, who were jealous of their prerogatives as heads of "sovereign" states.

Finance was the Confederacy's most vexing problem. The blockade made it impossible to raise money through tariffs. The Confederate Congress passed an income tax together with many excise taxes, but the most effective levy was a tax-in-kind, amounting to one-tenth of each farmer's production. The South borrowed as much as it could ($712 million), even mortgaging cotton undeliverable because of the blockade in order to gain European credits. But it relied mainly on printing paper currency. Over $1.5 *billion* poured from the presses during the war. Considering the amount issued, this currency held its value remarkably well until late in the war, when the military fortunes of the Confederacy began to decline. Then the bottom fell out, and by early 1865 the Confederate dollar was worth only 1.7 cents in gold.

Because of the shortage of manufacturing facilities, the task of keeping the army supplied strained southern resources to the limit. Field armies are never noted for sartorial elegance, but the ragged southern troops, as one observer put it, often "looked more like the bipeds of pandemonium than beings of this earth." Large supplies of small arms (some 600,000 weapons during the entire war) came in from Europe through the blockade, along with other valuable supplies. As the blockade became more efficient, however, it became increasingly difficult to obtain European goods. Whereas no more than one blockade runner in ten was captured in 1861, one out of two was being taken in 1865. The Confederates did manage to build a number of munitions plants, and they captured huge amounts of northern equipment. The brilliant administration of the

The Confederate commerce raider Nashville, *assisted by two small steamers, runs the blockade in 1862. The northern navy began the war with far too few warships to effectively blockade the 3,500-mile southern coastline.*

Confederate chief of ordnance, Josiah Gorgas, greatly helped to compensate for the paucity of all kinds of material. In any case, no battle was lost because of a lack of guns or other military equipment, although shortages of shoes and uniforms did handicap the Confederate forces on some occasions.

Foreign policy loomed large in Confederate thinking, for the "Cotton is King" theory presupposed that the great powers would break any northern blockade to get cotton for their textile mills. Southern expectations were not realized, however. The European nations would have been delighted to see the United States broken up, but none was prepared to support the Confederacy directly. The attitude of Great Britain was decisive. The cutting off of cotton did not hit the British as hard as the South had hoped. They had a large supply on hand when the war broke out, and when that was exhausted, alternative sources in India and Egypt took up at least part of the slack. Furthermore, British crop failures necessitated the importation of large amounts of northern wheat, providing a powerful reason for not antagonizing the United States. The fact that the mass of ordinary people in Great Britain favored the North was also of great importance in determining British policy.

Nevertheless, the Civil War hurt the British economy, and the government gave serious thought to recognizing the Confederacy. Had it done so, the result would almost certainly have been war with the United States, and in that event the South might well have won its independence. Several times the two nations came to the brink of war. In November 1861 the American warship *San Jacinto* (Captain Charles Wilkes commanding) stopped a British vessel, the *Trent*, on the high seas off Havana and forcibly arrested two Confederate envoys, James M. Mason and John Slidell, who were en route to London. This violation of international law would probably have led to war if Lincoln had not decided to disavow the arrests and turn the southerners loose. In 1862 two powerful cruisers, the *Florida* and the *Alabama*, were built for the Confederates in English shipyards under the most transparent of subterfuges. Despite American protests, they were permitted to put to sea and were soon wreaking havoc among northern merchantmen. When two ironclad "rams" were also built for the Confederates in Britain, the United States made it clear that it would declare war if they were delivered. Fortunately, the British government confiscated these vessels, thus avoiding a showdown.

The northern cause was greatly aided by the brilliant diplomacy of Charles Francis Adams, the son of John Quincy, who served as American minister in London throughout the conflict. In the last analysis, however, the military situation determined British policy; once the North obtained a clear superiority on the battlefield, the possibility of intervention on behalf of the South vanished.

War in the West: Shiloh

This superiority was achieved only slowly, and at enormous cost. After Bull Run, no heavy fighting took place until early 1862. Then, while McClellan continued his deliberate preparations to attack Richmond, Union forces in the West, led by a shabby, cigar-smoking West Pointer named Ulysses S. Grant, invaded Tennessee from a base at Cairo, Illinois. Making effective use of armored gunboats, Grant captured forts Henry and Donelson, strong points on the Tennessee and Cumberland rivers in northern Tennessee, taking 14,000 prisoners. Next he marched toward Corinth, Mississippi, an important railroad junction.

To check Grant's invasion the Confederates massed 40,000 men under Albert Sidney Johnston, one of the best southern commanders. At dawn on April 6, while Grant slowly concentrated his forces in preparation for an attack, Johnston struck him suddenly at Shiloh, a country church 20 miles north of Corinth. For the moment all was chaos in the Union camp. Some soldiers were caught half-dressed, others in the midst of brewing their morning coffee. A few died in their blankets. "We were more than surprised," one Illinois officer later admitted. "We were astonished." However, Grant's men stood their

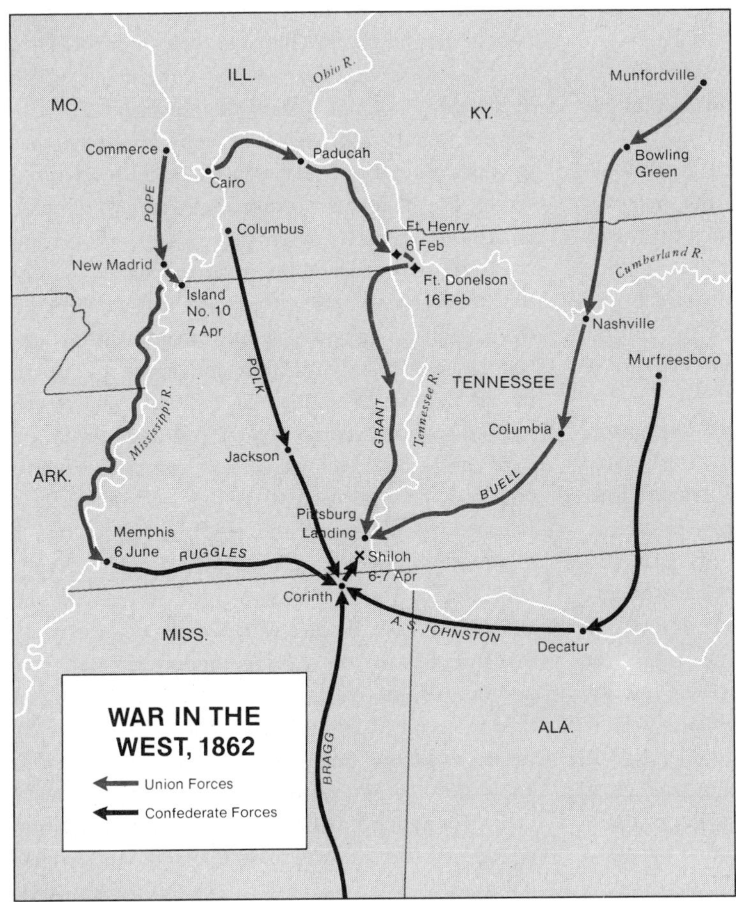

The Confederacy massed its western forces at Corinth for an unavailing counterstroke at Shiloh. The South's Mississippi River defenses also crumbled; by June of 1862 the river was open to Yankee gunboats as far south as Memphis.

ground. At the end of a day of incredible carnage the Confederates held the advantage, but fresh Union troops under General Don Carlos Buell poured in during the night, and in the course of the second day of battle the tide turned. The Confederates fell back toward Corinth, exhausted and demoralized.

Nevertheless, Grant was too shaken by the unexpected attack and too appalled by his huge losses to apply the *coup de grâce* that might have ended Confederate resistance in the West. He allowed the enemy to escape. This cost him the fine reputation he had won in capturing Fort Henry and Fort Donelson. He was relieved of his command by Henry W. Halleck, whose nickname, "Old Brains," was one of the great misnomers of history. Grant's battle-tested army was broken up, its strength dissipated in a series of uncoordinated campaigns. Although Corinth eventually fell and New Orleans was captured by a naval force operating in the Gulf of Mexico under the command of Captain David Farragut, Vicksburg, key to control of the Mississippi, remained firmly in Confederate hands. A great opportunity had been lost.

Grant had been caught off balance at Shiloh—he was still learning his trade—but the decision to punish him by reducing his authority was a major blunder. No one of comparable ability rose to take his place. Eventually, he would prove that Shiloh had not been a fair test of his ability, but in the meantime the war in the West was far from over.

Shiloh had other results still more important. The staggering casualties suffered by both sides shook the confidence of both belligerents. More Americans fell there in two days than in all the battles of the Revolution, the War of 1812, and the Mexican War combined. Union losses exceeded 13,000 out of 63,000 engaged. The Conderates lost 10,699, including General Johnston. The generals began to reconsider their tactics and to experiment with field fortifications and other defensive measures. And the people, North and South, stopped thinking of the war as a romantic test of courage and military guile. Each side developed a new respect—and a new hatred—for the other.

McClellan v. Lee

Meanwhile, attention shifted back to the Virginia front, where General McClellan, after unaccountable delays, was finally moving against Richmond. Instead of trying to advance across the difficult terrain of northern Virginia, he decided to transport his army by water to the tip of the peninsula formed by the York and James rivers and to attack Richmond from the southeast. After the famous battle (March 9, 1862) between U.S.S. *Monitor* and the Confederate *Merrimack*, the first fight in history between armored warships, control of these waters was securely in northern hands.

Although McClellan's battle plan alarmed many congressmen because it seemed to leave Washington relatively unprotected, it was soundly conceived, for it simplified the problem of keeping the army supplied in hostile country. But McClellan now displayed the weaknesses that eventually ruined his career. His view of warfare better suited the 18th century than the 19th. To him the Civil War was not a mighty struggle in which whole peoples contended over fundamental beliefs but a sort of complex game that generals played at a leisurely pace and for limited stakes. He believed it more important to capture Richmond than to destroy the army protecting it. With their capital in northern hands, surely the southerners (outwitted and outmaneuvered by a brilliant general) would abandon the contest in gentlemanly fashion and agree to return to the Union. The idea of crushing the South seemed to him wrong-headed and uncivilized.

Beyond this, McClellan was temperamentally unsuited for a position of so much responsibility. Beneath the swagger and the charm, he was a profoundly insecure man. He talked like Napoleon, but he did not like to fight. Repeatedly he called for more men, and when he got them, he demanded still more. He underestimated the number of his own effectives and at the same time convinced himself that the foe had larger forces available than was actually the case. He knew how to get ready, but he was never ready in his own mind. Allan Nevins' characterization is apt: McClellan was "the General who would not dare."

Of course no one knew this when McClellan began the Peninsula campaign in mid-March. Proceeding deliberately, he floated a huge army of 112,000 men down the Potomac to Fort Monroe, on the tip of the peninsula opposite Norfolk. Yorkstown was captured, and by May 14 McClellan had established a base at White House Landing, on a branch of the York less than 25 miles from Richmond. A swift thrust might have ended the war quickly, but McClellan delayed, despite the fact that he had 80,000 men in striking position and large reserves. As he pushed forward slowly, constantly calling upon Washington to send him more troops, the Confederates caught part of his force separated from the main body by the rain-swollen Chickahominy River and attacked. This Battle of Seven Pines was indecisive but resulted in over 10,000 casualties altogether, another ominious indication of the price to be paid before this Brothers' War was done.

At Seven Pines the Confederate commander, General Joseph E. Johnston, was severely wounded; leadership of the Army of Northern Virginia then fell to Robert E. Lee. Although no enthusiast about secession, Lee was a superb soldier. During the Mexican War his gallantry under fire inspired the most lavish praise from hardened professionals. General Scott called him the bravest man in the army; another officer rhapsodized over his "daring reconnaissances pushed up to the cannon's mouth." He also displayed an almost instinctive mastery of tactics. Admiral Raphael Semmes, who accompanied Scott's army on the march to Mexico City, recalled in 1851 that Lee "seemed to receive impressions intuitively, which it cost other men much labor to acquire."

As a leader he was the antithesis of McClellan, being gentle, courtly, tactful, and entirely without McClellan's swagger and vainglorious belief that he was a man of destiny. McClellan seemed almost deliberately to avoid understanding his foes, acting as though every southern general was an Alexander. Lee, a master psychologist on the battlefield, cleverly took the measure of each Union general and devised his tactics accordingly. Whereas McClellan was complex, egotistical, perhaps even unbalanced, Lee was a man of almost perfect character. Yet on the battlefield Lee's boldness skirted the very edge of foolhardiness. He was an imaginative tactician—crafty, decisive, relentless.

LIBRARY OF CONGRESS

Lee in 1863, by Julian Vannerson. "So great is my confidence in General Lee," remarked Stonewall Jackson, "that I am willing to follow him blind-folded."

Already as a staff officer he had planned a brilliant maneuver to relieve the pressure on Richmond, sending Stonewall Jackson, soon to be his most trusted lieutenant, on a diversionary raid in the Shenandoah Valley, west of Richmond and Washington. Jackson struck hard and swiftly at scattered Union forces in that region, winning a series of battles and capturing vast stores of equipment. Rumor flew before his marching troops: *Soon he would be at Harpers Ferry and then over the Potomac into Maryland. Was he intending to attack Washington?* Lincoln dispatched 20,000 reserves to the Shenandoah to check him, to the dismay of McClellan, who wanted these troops to move against Richmond

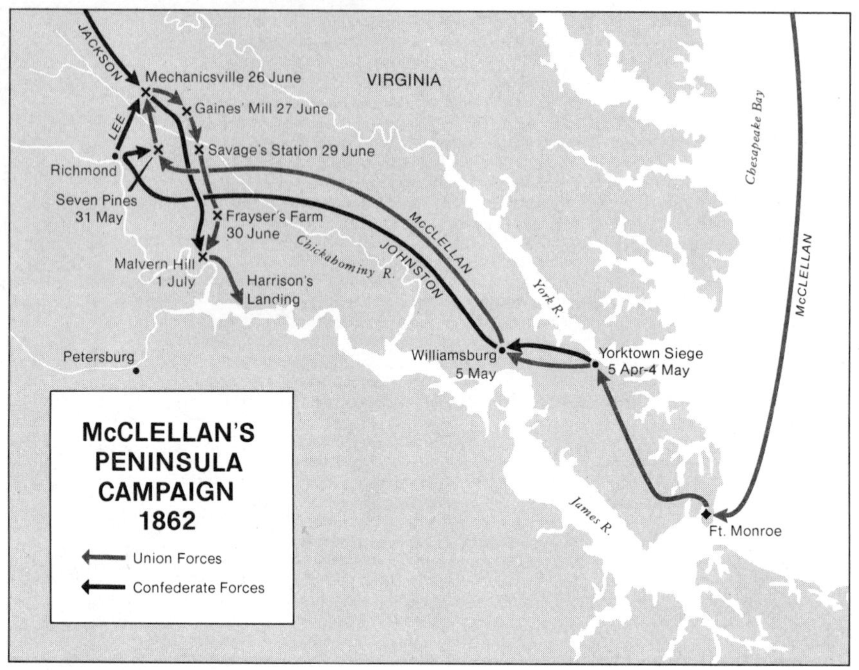

On June 1 Lee succeeded Joseph E. Johnston as head of the Army of Northern Virginia. On June 26 he attacked McClellan and by July 2 had pushed him back to the James.

from the north. But after Seven Pines, Lee ordered Jackson back to Richmond. While Union armies streamed toward the valley, Jackson slipped stealthily between them. On June 25 he reached Ashland, directly north of the Confederate capital.

Before that date McClellan had possessed a clear numerical superiority, yet he had only inched ahead; now the advantage lay with Lee. The very next day he hit the Union army in a massive surprise attack. For seven days the battle raged. Lee's plan was brilliant but too complicated for an army yet untested: the full weight of his force never hit the northern army at any one time. Nonetheless, the shock was formidable. McClellan, who excelled in defense, fell back but held his lines intact, exacting a fearful toll. Under extremely difficult conditions, he transferred his men to a new base on the James River at Harrison's Landing, where the powerful guns of the navy could shield his position. Again the loss of life was terrible. In this Seven Days' campaign, northern casualties totaled 15,800, those of the South nearly 20,000.

Lee Counter-Attacks

McClellan had the better of the fight. He was still within easy striking distance of Richmond, in an impregnable position with secure supply lines and a force of 86,000 men ready to resume the battle. Lee had absorbed heavy losses without winning any significant advantage. Yet Lincoln was exasperated with McClellan for having surrendered the initiative, and after much deliberation, reduced his authority by placing him under the supervision of General Halleck. Halleck called off the Peninsula campaign and ordered McClellan to move his army from the James to the Potomac near Washington. He was to join General John Pope, who was gathering a new army between Washington and Richmond.

For the President to have lost confidence in McClellan was understandable; nevertheless, to allow Halleck to pull back the troops was a very bad mistake, perhaps the worst of his career. Had the federal army poised at Harrison's Landing made any aggressive thrust, Lee would not have dared to move from the defenses of Richmond.

When it withdrew, Lee quickly seized the initiative. With typical decisiveness and daring, he marched rapidly north against Pope. Before McClellan's men could arrive in force—as usual their commander had moved like a snail when speed was of the essence—the Confederates confronted Pope at the line of the Rappahannock River. Even without McClellan's troops, the Union army outnumbered them by 65,000 to 54,000. Yet General Lee coolly *divided* his forces in order to outmaneuver his enemy. He gave Stonewall Jackson three divisions (25,000 men) and sent him racing in a wide arc to the west and north around Pope's unsuspecting army. Marching without wagons or knapsacks in order to move swiftly, these troops skirted the headwaters of the Rappahannock. Then, debouching suddenly from Thoroughfare Gap in the Bull Run Mountains, they seized Manassas Junction, severing Pope's rail connection with Washington and capturing quantities of arms and supplies. Pope wheeled to his rear and tried to trap Jackson, but Stonewall easily evaded him. While the Union regiments groped blindly in his wake, the main Confederate army marched toward Thoroughfare Gap. On August 29 pursuing Union forces struck a series of uncoordinated blows that failed to budge Jackson. Next day Lee's reunited army counterattacked. With bayonets fixed, the Confederates drove Pope's tired and confused troops from the field. It was the same ground, Bull Run, where the first major engagement of the war had been fought. Thousands of brave men paid with their lives for the ineptness of the northern generals.

Thirteen months had passed since the first failure at Bull Run, and despite the expenditure of so many lives and hundreds of millions of dollars the Union army stood as far from Richmond as ever. Dismayed by Pope's incompetence, Lincoln turned in desperation back to McClellan. When his secretary protested that McClellan had expressed contempt for the President, Lincoln replied gently: "We must use what tools we have."

McClellan proceeded to regroup the shaken army, but he reckoned without Robert E. Lee. The Virginian reasoned that no number of individual southern triumphs could destroy the enormous material advantages of the North. Unless some dramatic blow, delivered on northern soil, persuaded the people of the United States that military victory was impossible, the South would surely be crushed in the long run by the weight of superior resources. He therefore marched rapidly northwestward around the defenses of Washington.

Acting with even more than his usual boldness, Lee divided his army of 60,000 into a number of units. One, under Stonewall Jackson, descended upon weakly defended Harpers Ferry, capturing more than 11,000 prisoners. Another pressed as far north as Hagerstown, Maryland, nearly to the Pennsylvania line. McClellan pursued with his usual deliberation, until a captured dis-

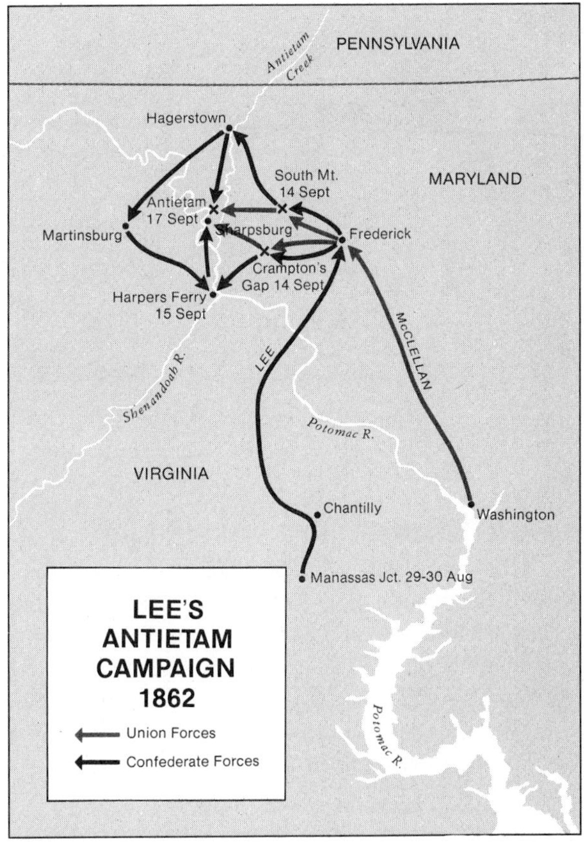

Delaying actions at South Mountain and Crampton's Gap, east of Sharpsburg, bought Lee enough time to pull together his forces to meet McClellan's host.

Part of the human wreckage left by the armies at Antietam. Alexander Gardner took this photograph of Confederate dead by the Cornfield, a nondescript piece of ground that earned a grim fame on September 17, 1862.

patch revealed to him Lee's dispositions. Then he acted more swiftly, forcing Lee to stand and fight on September 17 at Sharpsburg, Maryland, between the Potomac and Antietam Creek.* On a field that offered Lee no room to maneuver, 70,000 Union soldiers clashed with 40,000 Confederates. When darkness fell, over 22,000 of these men lay dead or wounded upon the bloody field. Although casualties were evenly divided and the Confederate army still held its lines, Lee's position was perilous. His men were exhausted, whereas McClellan had not yet thrown in his reserves and new units were arriving hourly. A bold northern general would have continued the fight without respite through the night. One of ordinary aggressiveness would have waited for the first light and then struck with every man who could hold a rifle, for with the Potomac at his back, Lee could not retreat while under fire without inviting disaster. McClellan, however, did nothing. For a whole day, while Lee

*Southerners tended to identify battles by nearby towns, northerners by bodies of water. Thus Manassas and Bull Run, Sharpsburg and Antietam, Murfreesboro and Stone's River, etc.

scanned the field in futile search of some weakness in the Union lines, he held his fire. That night the Confederates slipped back across the Potomac into Virginia.

Lee's invasion had failed, his army had been badly mauled, the gravest threat to the Union in the entire war had been checked. But McClellan had let real victory slip through his fingers. Soon Lee was back behind the shelter of the defenses of Richmond, rebuilding his army .

Once again, this time finally, Lincoln dismissed McClellan from his command.

The Emancipation Proclamation

Nevertheless, Antietam provided Lincoln with an excuse to take a step that changed the whole character of the war. As we have seen, when the fighting started, only a few extremists wanted to free the slaves by force. The fear of alienating the border states alone provided reason enough for not making emancipation a war aim. However, pressures to act against the peculiar institution mounted steadily. Such action would win foreign friends by the thousands and would probably end once and for all the dread possibility that Britain and France would recognize the Confederacy. Public opinion was shifting too. Slavery had divided the nation; now it was driving men to war within themselves. Love of country led Americans to fight to save the Union, but the fighting roused hatreds and caused many to desire to smash the enemy. Sacrifice, pain, and grief made abolitionists of many who had no love for Negroes—these sought to free the bondsman only to injure his master. To make abolition an object of the war promised a direct military advantage: it might encourage the slaves to revolt. Lincoln disclaimed this objective; nonetheless, the possibility existed. Already the slaves seemed to be looking to the North for freedom: whenever Union troops invaded Confederate territory, Negroes flocked into their lines. For a time Lincoln tried to check the enthusiasm of certain generals who issued proclamations freeing these slaves, but in fact little could be done to prevent the disintegration of slavery in captured territory.

As the war progressed, the Radicals in Congress gradually chipped away at slavery. In April 1862 they pushed through a bill abolishing it in the District of Columbia; two months later another measure outlawed it in the territories; in July a Confiscation Act "freed" all slaves owned by persons in rebellion against the United States. In fighting for these measures and in urging general emancipation, some of the Radicals made statements harshly critical of Lincoln; but while he carefully avoided being identified with them or with any other faction, the President was never very far from their position. He resisted emancipation because he feared it would divide the country and injure the war effort, not because he personally disapproved. Indeed, he frequently offered Radical pressure as an excuse for doing what he wished to do on his own, this being an excellent device for keeping reluctant Moderates and war Democrats in line.

Lincoln would have preferred to see slavery done away with by state law, with compensation for slaveowners and federal aid for all freedmen willing to leave the United States. He tried repeatedly to persuade the loyal slave states to adopt this policy, but without success. Moving cautiously, by the summer of 1862 he had become convinced that both for military reasons and to win the support of liberal opinion in Europe, the government should adopt an antislavery policy. "The moment came when I felt that slavery must die that the nation might live," he said. He delayed temporarily, fearing that a statement in the face of military reverses would be taken as a sign of weakness. Antietam gave him his opportunity, and on September 22 he made public the Emancipation Proclamation. After January 1, 1863, it ran, all slaves in areas in rebellion against the United States "shall be then, thenceforward, and forever free."

Of course no single slave was freed directly by Lincoln's announcement, which did not apply to the border states or even to those sections of the Confederacy, like New Orleans and Norfolk, Virginia, that had already been overrun by federal troops. As it specifically stated, those districts were "for the present, left precisely as if this proclamation were not issued." It differed

M. & M. KAROLIK COLLECTION, MUSEUM OF FINE ARTS, BOSTON

The genesis of the Emancipation Proclamation, seen from diametrically opposed viewpoints. The drawing above is by Adalbert Johann Volck, a Baltimore dentist and vitriolic propagandist for the Confederate cause. A satanical Lincoln, one foot on the Constitution, is inspired by a portrait of John Brown and a depiction of the alleged excesses of the Santo Domingo slave revolt of the 1790's. David Gilmour Blythe, a staunch administration supporter, left no doubt in his painting below that the sources of Lincoln's inspiration were of a much higher order.

CARNEGIE-MELLON UNIVERSITY, PITTSBURGH

in philosophy, however, from the Confiscation Act in striking at the institution, not at the property of rebels. Henceforth every Union victory would speed the destruction of slavery, without regard for the attitudes of individual masters.

Some of the President's advisers thought the Proclamation inexpedient and others considered it illegal. Lincoln, however, believed it a justifiable means of weakening the enemy. He drew upon his power as commander in chief of the nation's armed forces for the necessary authority. The Proclamation is full of phrases like "as a fit and necessary war measure" and "warranted by the Constitution upon military necessity."

Nearly two years later, Congress passed a bill that abolished slavery. Lincoln refused to sign it. A Radical Republican protested. "It is no more than you have done yourself!" he said. Lincoln answered: "I conceive that I may in an emergency do things on military grounds which cannot be done constitutionally by Congress."

Naturally enough, southerners considered the Proclamation an incitement to slave rebellion and resolved to fight still harder. Jefferson Davis called it "a measure by which millions of human beings of an inferior race, peaceful and contented laborers in their spheres . . . are encouraged to a general assassination of their masters." The Proclamation, he announced, made restoration of the Union "forever impossible." On the other hand, most antislavery groups approved but thought it did not go far enough. Foreign opinion was mixed: liberals tended to applaud, conservatives to react with alarm or contempt. "The principle is not that a human being cannot justly own another," the London *Spectator* sneered, "but that he cannot own him unless he is loyal to the United States." The mass of ordinary people, however, especially in Great Britain, interpreted the Proclamation as a blow struck for human freedom and dignity everywhere and cheered. Recognition of the Confederacy by the British government was thereafter politically impossible.

As Lincoln anticipated, the Proclamation had a subtle but continuing impact in America. In many ways its immediate effect was to aggravate racial prejudices, for it brought out into the open many deep-seated ambivalences. Millions of white Americans disapproved of slavery but also abhorred the idea of equality for blacks. To some of these, emancipation seemed to threaten an invasion of the North by freedmen who would compete with them for jobs, drive down wages, commit crimes and spread diseases, and—eventually—destroy the "purity" of the white race.* The Democrats spared no effort to make political capital of these fears and prejudices during the congressional election campaign of 1862, and they made large gains, especially in the Northwest. So strong was the anti-Negro feeling that most of the Republican politicians who defended emancipation did so with racist arguments. Far from encouraging southern blacks to move north, they claimed, the ending of slavery would lead to a mass migration of northern blacks to the South. Even Secretary of the Treasury Salmon P. Chase, a long-time abolitionist, claimed that after emancipation "the blacks of the North will slide southward."

When the Emancipation Proclamation began actually to free slaves, the government pursued a policy of "containment," that is, of keeping the freedmen in the South. Panicky fears of an inundation of blacks subsided in the North. Nevertheless, emancipation remained a cause of social discontent. In March 1863, volunteering having fallen off, Congress passed a conscription act. The law applied to all men between 20 and 45, but it allowed draftees to hire substitutes and even to buy exemption for $300, provisions patently unfair to the poor. Moreover, it represented an enormous expansion of national authority, since in effect it gave the government the power of life and death over individual citizens. Draft riots erupted in scattered parts of the nation.

By far the most serious of these occurred in New York City, in July 1863. Many workingmen resented conscription in principle and were embittered by the $300 exemption fee (which represented a year's wages). The idea of being forced to risk their lives to free slaves who would, they believed, then compete with them for jobs infuriated them. On July 13 a mob attacked the office where the names of conscripts were being drawn. Most of the rioters were Irish laborers who were Negrophobes to begin with.

J. CLARENCE DAVIES COLLECTION, MUSEUM OF THE CITY OF NEW YORK

A woodcut taken from Leslie's Illustrated *shows a Negro orphanage destroyed by a mob during the New York draft riots. The rioters were dispersed by combat troops fresh from the Battle of Gettysburg.*

Once they had unleashed their passions, they ran amuck, burning, looting, and killing. For four days the city was an inferno. Public buildings, shops, and private residences were put to the torch. What began as a protest against the draft became a campaign to exterminate Negroes. Dozens—no one knows the exact number—were run down "as hounds would chase a fox" and beaten to death, some even burned alive. Order was restored only after the government temporarily suspended the draft in the city.

The Emancipation Proclamation does not, of

*The word *miscegenation* was coined in 1863 by David G. Croly, an editor of the New York *World*, directly as a result of the Emancipation Proclamation. Its original meaning was: "The mingling of the white and black races on the continent *as a consequence of the freedom of the latter.*" Of course miscegenation in its current, more general meaning long antedated the freeing of any slave.

course, entirely account for the draft riots. The new policy neither reflected nor triggered a revolution in white thinking about the race question, either pro or con. Its significance was subtle but real; both the naive view that Lincoln freed the slaves on January 1, 1863, and the cynical one that his action was a meaningless propaganda trick are incorrect. Northern hostility to emancipation rose from fear of change more than from hatred of blacks, while liberal disavowals of any intention to treat Negroes as equals were in large measure designed to quiet this fear. To a degree the racial blacklash that the Proclamation inspired reflected the public's awareness that a change *had occurred*, frightening but irreversible.

Most white men did not surrender their comforting belief in Negro inferiority, and Lincoln was no exception. Yet Lincoln was evolving. He talked about deporting freedmen to the tropics, but he did not actually send any there. And he began to receive black leaders in the White House and to allow Negro groups to hold their meetings on the grounds. After conferring with the President in 1864, the militant Frederick Douglass remarked simply: "Lincoln treated me as a man."

In spite of themselves many of Lincoln's countrymen were also changing. The brutality of the New York riots horrified many white citizens. Over $40,000 was swiftly raised to aid the victims, and some conservatives were so appalled by the Irish rioters that they began to talk of giving blacks the vote. As the influential *Atlantic Monthly* commented: "It is impossible to name any standard . . . that will give a vote to the Celt and exclude the negro."

A far more revolutionary shift occurred in white thinking about using black men as soldiers. Although Negroes had fought in the Revolution and in the Battle of New Orleans during the War of 1812, a law of 1792 barred them from the army. During the early stages of the rebellion, despite the eagerness of thousands of free Negroes to enlist, this prohibition remained in force. Northern public opinion was unready to face the idea of using black men to save the Union. By 1862, however, the need for manpower was creating great pressure for change. Reluctantly the government yielded. In August 1862 Secretary of War Edwin M. Stanton, who had replaced the incompetent Simon Cameron, authorized the military government of the captured South Carolina sea islands to enlist slaves in the area. In January 1863 Stanton also allowed the governor of Massachusetts to organize a black regiment, the famous Massachusetts 54th. Swiftly thereafter, other states began to recruit black soldiers, and in May 1863 the federal government established a Bureau of Colored Troops to supervise the enlistment of Negroes. By the end of the war one soldier in eight in the Union army was a Negro. These troops were, of course, segregated and commanded by white officers. At first they received only $7 a month, whereas whites were paid nearly double that sum. But they soon proved themselves in battle; 38,000 were killed, a rate of loss about 40 per cent higher than that among white troops. At the very least, their bravery and determination under fire convinced thousands of white soldiers that Negroes were not by nature childish or cowardly. Even southerners were impressed. The Confederates threatened to kill or enslave Negro soldier-prisoners, but they almost never did. Fear of reprisals undoubtedly restrained them, but so did the grudging respect that southern soldiers had to yield to men taken while charging fixed positions under fire and otherwise demonstrating their courage.

To black men slave and free, the Emancipation Proclamation served as a beacon. If it failed immediately to liberate one bondsman or to lift the burdens of prejudice from one free Negro's back, it stood as a promise of future improvement. Perhaps Lincoln was by modern standards a racist, but his most militant black contemporaries respected him deeply. The *Anglo-African*, an uncompromising Negro newspaper, the position of which is revealed in an 1862 editorial which asked: "Poor, chicken-hearted, semi-barbarous Caucasians, when will you learn that 'the earth was made for MAN?' " referred in 1864 to Lincoln's "many noble acts" and urged his reelection. Frederick Douglass said of him: "Lincoln was not . . . either our man or our model. In his interests, in his associations, in his habits of thought and in his prejudices, he was a white man." But he also spoke of Lincoln as "one whom I could love, honor, and trust without reserve or doubt." Douglass wrote in his autobiography: "I took the proclamation for a little more than it purported, and saw in its spirit a life and power far beyond its letter."

As for the slaves of the South, after January 1, 1863, whenever the "Army of Freedom" approached, black men laid down their plows and hoes and stole away. "We-all knows about it," one freedman confided to a northern clergyman early in 1863. "Only we darsen't let on. We *pretends* not to know." As Secretary of State Seward said: "The army acts . . . as an emancipating crusade."

Antietam to Gettysburg

It was well that Lincoln seized upon Antietam to release the Proclamation; had he waited for a more impressive victory, he would have waited nearly a year. To replace McClellan, he chose General Ambrose E. Burnside, a most engaging man, best known to history for his magnificent side whiskers, ever after called "sideburns." Burnside, a West Pointer, had compiled a fine record as a corps commander, but he lacked the self-confidence essential to any man who takes responsibility for major decisions. He knew his own limitations and tried to avoid high command, but patriotism and his sense of duty compelled him, when pressed, to accept leadership of the Army of the Potomac. He prepared to march on Richmond.

Unlike McClellan, Burnside was aggressive—too aggressive. He planned to force the Rappahannock at Fredericksburg. Supply problems and bad weather delayed him until mid-December, however, giving Lee ample time to concentrate his entire army and place it in impregnable positions behind the town. Although he had over 120,000 men against Lee's 75,000, Burnside should have called off the attack when he saw Lee's advantage; instead he ordered his men forward. Crossing the river over pontoon bridges, his divisions occupied Fredericksburg. Then, in wave after wave, they charged the Confederate defense line, while Lee's artillery riddled them from nearby Marye's Heights. They were stopped with frightful losses. Watching the battle from his command post on the heights, General Lee was deeply moved. Turning to General James Longstreet, he said: "It is well that war is so terrible—we should grow too fond of it!" On December 14, the day following this futile assault, General Burnside, tears streaming down his cheeks, ordered the evacuation of Fredericksburg. Shortly thereafter, General Joseph Hooker replaced him.

Unlike Burnside, "Fighting Joe" Hooker was ill-tempered, vindictive, and devious, a lover of intrigue. In naming him to command the Army of the Potomac, Lincoln sent him a letter, now famous for what it reveals of the President's character, which ran as follows:

> I think that during Gen. Burnside's command of the Army, you have taken counsel of your ambition, and thwarted him as much as you could, in which you did a great wrong to the country. . . . I have heard, in such a way as to believe it, of your recently saying that both the Army and the Government need a Dictator. Of course it is not *for* this, but in spite of it, that I have given you the command. Only those generals who gain successes, can set up dictators. What I now ask of you is military success, and I will risk the dictatorship. . . . Beware of rashness, but with energy and sleepless vigilance, go forward, and give us victories.

Unfortunately, Hooker proved no better at this task than his predecessor. By the spring of 1863 he had 125,000 men ready for action. Late in April he forded the Rappahannock and quickly concentrated at Chancellorsville, about ten miles west of Fredericksburg. His army outnumbered the Confederates by more than two to one. He should have forced a battle at once; instead he delayed, convinced that Lee would never stand and fight against such odds. Lee, however, acted with daring. A report came in that the Union right was exposed. Quickly, he called again upon Stonewall Jackson. Taking his whole corps (28,000 men), Jackson sped in broad daylight across tangled countryside to a position directly athwart the unsuspecting Union flank. With magnificent aplomb, he deployed his men and then, at six o'clock on the evening of May 2, attacked.

Completely surprised, the Union right crumbled, brigade after brigade overrun before it could wheel to meet the charge. At the first sound of firing, Lee had struck along the entire front to impede Union troop movements. If the battle had begun earlier in the day, the Confederates might have won a decisive victory; as it happened, nightfall brought a lull, and the next day the Union troops rallied and held their ground. Heavy fighting continued until May 5, when Hooker abandoned the field and retreated in good order behind the Rappahannock.

The victory cost the Confederates dearly, for their losses, in excess of 12,000, were almost as heavy as the North's and harder to replace. They also lost Stonewall Jackson, struck down by the bullets of his own men while returning from a reconnaissance in the confusion following the first evening's charge. Nevertheless, the Union army had suffered another fearful blow to its morale. How could this endless war be won if no northern general could approach the skill of Robert E. Lee?

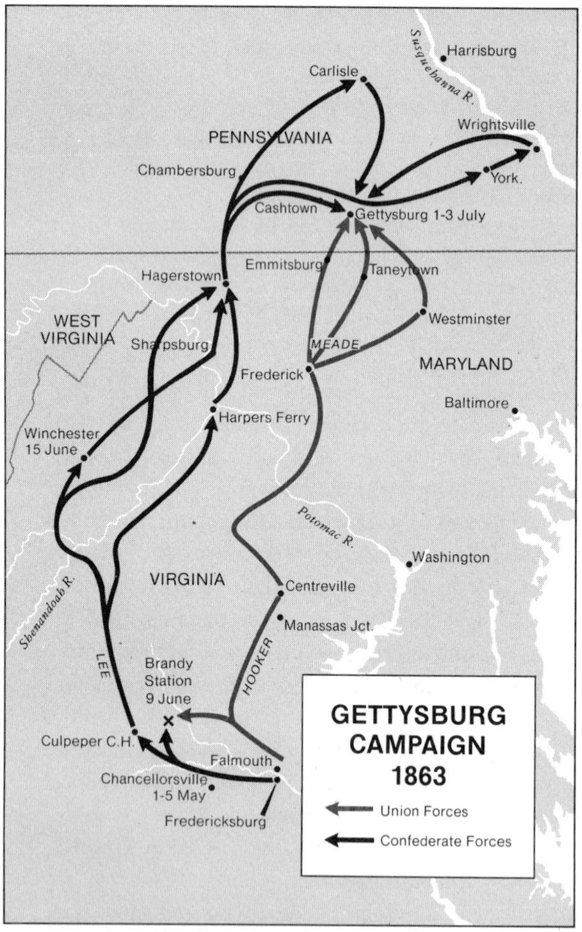

George Meade, the fifth man to head the Army of the Potomac in less than a year, had to challenge Lee at Gettysburg just two days after assuming command.

Seizing upon this psychological advantage and still hoping to win foreign support by a victory on northern soil, Lee now took the offensive. He knew that time was still on the side of the North. To defend Richmond was not enough. Already federal troops in the West were closing in on Vicksburg, thus threatening to cut Confederate communications with Arkansas and Texas. Now was the time to strike, while the morale of the northern people was at low ebb. With 75,000 soldiers, he crossed the Potomac again, a larger Union force dogging his right flank. By late June his army had fanned out across southern Pennsylvania in a 50-mile arc from Chambersburg to the Susquehanna. Gray-clad soldiers ranged 50 miles *northwest* of Baltimore, less than 10 miles from Harrisburg. Then, on July 1, Confederate troops looking for shoes in the town of Gettysburg clashed with a Union cavalry unit stationed there. Both sides sent out calls for reinforcements. Like iron filings drawn to a magnet, the northern and southern armies converged on the town.

On July 1 the Confederates won control of Gettysburg, but the Union army, now commanded by General George G. Meade, took a strong position on Cemetery Ridge, a hook-shaped stretch of high ground just to the south. Lee's men occupied Seminary Ridge, a parallel position one mile west of Cemetery Ridge. On this field the fate of the Union was probably decided. For two days the Confederates attacked Cemetery Ridge from every angle, pounding it with the heaviest artillery barrage ever seen in America and sweeping bravely up its flanks in repeated assaults. General George E. Pickett's famous charge of 15,000 men actually carried the Union lines on the afternoon of July 3, but his men were overwhelmed when reserves closed in before they could consolidate their position. By nightfall the Confederate army was spent and bleeding, the Union lines unbroken.

CAP HISTORICAL PHOTO COLLECTION

U.S. Grant, photographed by Mathew Brady in 1863. As a strategist, Grant was an utter realist. His conquest of Vicksburg was as bold and imaginative a campaign as the war produced, yet in Virginia in 1864–65 he adjusted to different circumstances and fought a slow and grinding battle of attrition.

On the next day the two weary forces rested on their arms. Had the Union army attacked in force at this point, the Confederates might have been totally crushed, but just as McClellan had hesitated after Antietam, now Meade let the opportunity pass. On July 5 Lee retreated to safety. Nevertheless, for the first time he had been clearly bested on the field of battle.

Vicksburg: Lincoln Finds a General

On that same Independence Day, far to the west, federal troops won another great victory. When General Halleck was called east in July 1862, Ulysses S. Grant reassumed command of Union troops in western Tennessee. Grant was one of the most controversial officers in the army. At West Point he had compiled an indifferent record, ranking 21st in a class of 39 at graduation. During the Mexican War he served well, but when he was transferred to a lonely post in Oregon, apart from his wife, he took to drink and was forced to resign his commission. Thereafter he failed at a number of civilian occupations. In 1861, rapidly approaching 40, he seemed headed for a life of frustration and mediocrity.

The war gave him a second chance. Back in service, however, his reputation as a ne'er-do-well and his unmilitary bearing worked against him, as did the heavy casualties suffered by his troops at Shiloh. But the fact that he knew how to manage a large army and win battles did not escape Lincoln. When a gossip tried to poison the President against him by referring to his drinking, Lincoln remarked that if he knew what brand Grant favored, he would send a barrel of it to some of his other generals. Actually, Grant never used alcohol as a substitute for courage.

Grant's major aim was to capture Vicksburg, a city of tremendous strategic importance. Together with Port Hudson, a bastion north of Baton Rouge, Louisiana, it guarded a 150-mile

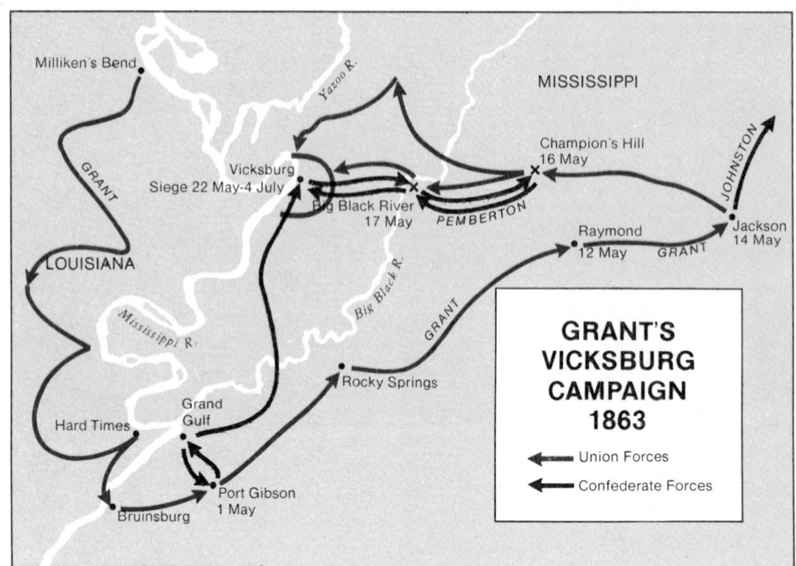

The Union navy played a key role in Grant's Vicksburg plan, slugging its way past the city's guns to transport the federals across the Mississippi. Grant reestablished his supply line via the Yazoo River when he laid siege to Vicksburg.

stretch of the Mississippi. The river between these points was, as Bruce Catton has said, "Confederate water," inaccessible to federal gunboats. So long as Vicksburg remained in southern hands, "the trans-Mississippi region could send men, livestock, grain and foreign imports to the East."

Vicksburg sits on a high bluff overlooking a sharp bend in the river. When it proved unapproachable from either west or north, Grant devised an audacious scheme for getting at it from the *east*. He descended the Mississippi from Memphis to a point a few miles north of the city. Then, leaving part of his force behind to create the impression that he planned to attack from the north, he crossed to the west bank and slipped quickly southward. Recrossing the river below Vicksburg, he abandoned his communications and supply lines and struck at Jackson, the capital of Mississippi. In a series of swift engagements he captured Jackson, cutting off the army of General John C. Pemberton, defending Vicksburg, from other Confederate units. Turning next on Pemberton, he defeated him in two battles and drove him inside the Vicksburg fortifications. By mid-May the city was under siege. Grant applied relentless pressure, and on July 4 Pemberton surrendered. More than 30,000 soldiers laid down their arms. With Vicksburg in Union hands, federal gunboats could range up and down the entire length of the Mississippi.* Texas and Arkansas were isolated, for all practical purposes lost to the Confederacy.

Grant's victory had another result, almost as important for the future of the country. Lincoln had disliked the plan for capturing Vicksburg. Now he generously confessed his error, and promoted Grant to command of all federal troops west of the Appalachians. Grant promptly took over control of the fighting around Chattanooga, in south-central Tennessee, where Confederate advances, beginning with the Battle of Chickamauga (September 19–20) were threatening to develop into a major disaster for the North. Shifting corps commanders and bringing up fresh units, he won another decisive victory at Chattanooga in a series of battles ending on November 25, 1863 and thus cleared the way for an invasion of Georgia. Suddenly this unkempt, stubby little man, who looked more like a tramp than a general, emerged as the great military leader the North had been so desperately seeking. In March 1864 Lincoln summoned him to Washington, named him lieutenant general, and gave him supreme command of the armies of the United States.

*Port Hudson, isolated by Vicksburg's fall, surrendered on July 9.

Economic Effects, North and South

Though much blood would yet be spilled, by the end of 1863 the Confederacy was on the road to defeat. Northern military pressure, gradually increasing, was eroding its most precious resource, manpower. An ever-tightening naval blockade, certainly a major cause of its eventual defeat, was reducing its economic strength. Shortages developed, which, combined with the flood of currency pouring from the presses, led to a drastic inflation that added to the difficulties of doing business. By 1864 a good officer's coat cost $2,000 in Confederate money, cigars sold for $10 each, butter at $25 a pound, flour at $275 a barrel. The southern railroad network gradually wore out, the major lines maintaining operations only by cannibalizing less vital roads. Imported products like coffee disappeared; even salt became scarce, the price leaping from 65 cents a sack to $20. Efforts to increase manufacturing were only moderately successful because of the shortage of labor, capital, and technical knowledge. In general, southern prejudice against centralized authority prevented the Confederacy from making very effective use of its scarce resources. Even blockade-running was left in private hands until 1864, so that precious cargo space that should have been reserved for medical supplies and arms was often devoted to high-priced luxuries.

In the North, after a brief depression in 1861 caused by the uncertainties of the situation and the loss of southern business, the economy boomed. Government purchases greatly stimulated certain lines of manufacturing; the railroads operated at close to capacity and with increasing efficiency; a series of bad harvests in Great Britain and throughout western Europe boosted agricultural prices. Congress passed a number of economic measures long desired but held up in the past by southern opposition: (1) the Homestead Act (1862) gave 160 acres to any settler who would farm the land for five years; (2) the Morrill Land Grant Act of the same year provided the states with land at the rate of 30,000 acres for each member of Congress to support state agricultural colleges; (3) various tariff acts raised the duties on manufactured goods to an average rate of 47 per cent in order to protect domestic manufacturers against foreign competition; (4) the Pacific Railway Act (1862) authorized subsidies in land and money for the construction of a transcontinental railroad; (5) the National Banking Act of 1863 gave the country, at last, a uniform currency. Under this last act, banks could obtain federal charters by investing at least one-third of their capital in United States bonds. They might then issue currency up to 90 per cent of the value of these bonds. A 10 per cent tax on the issues of state banks quickly drove state bank notes out of circulation. The Banking Act had the short-range advantage of bolstering the demand for bonds, but it also produced incalculable benefits for the whole economy.

All these laws stimulated economic activity and added to public confidence. Whether the overall effect of the Civil War on the economy was beneficial is less clear. It was mostly fought with rifles, light cannon, horses, and wagons, rather than masses of heavy artillery, tanks, and trucks. Consequently, it had much less effect than later wars on heavy industry. The production of pig iron increased only moderately, and while the new petroleum business flourished, it was not much dependent upon military demand. As for the economy as a whole, a study of economic indicators for the period 1840–1900 shows a mixed pattern for the Civil War decade. The rate of increase of total commodity output was lower during the 1860's than in the decades preceding and following. Prices soared beginning in 1862, averaging about 80 per cent over the 1860 level by the end of the war. Wages, however, did not even begin to keep pace; they increased only 43 per cent during the period. This condition did not make for a healthy economy. Nor, on the other hand, did the fact that there were chronic shortages of labor in many fields, which were aggravated by a drastic decline in the number of foreign immigrants entering the country.

The war also had a demoralizing effect on many businessmen. Inflation and shortages stimulated all kinds of speculation and fostered a selfish, materialistic attitude toward life. "The intense desire to buy almost any kind of securities amounted almost to insanity," one observer commented as early as January of 1862. Cotton, by 1864, was worth $1.90 a pound in New England and could be had for just 20 cents a pound in the South; although it was illegal to traffic in the staple across the lines, unscrupulous operators did so and made huge profits. Many contractors took advantage of wartime confusion to sell the government "shoddy" goods and swindle the public in other ways. "Governmental transactions with private firms permitted 'legitimate' profits all out of proportion to service rendered," David Donald writes. Lobbying for war contracts, even by highly placed government officials, was common. "Downright swindling was a serious evil which took many diabolical forms," Donald also points out.

However, the war undoubtedly helped prepare the way for modern, industrial society in the United States. It posed problems of organization and planning, both military and civilian, that challenged the talents of many creative persons and thus led to a more complex and efficient economy. The mechanization of industry, the growth of large corporations, the creation of a better banking system, and the emergence of energetic new business leaders attuned to these conditions would surely have occurred in any case, for the industrialization of the nation was well under way long before the South seceded. Nevertheless, the war greatly speeded economic change.

Grant, Sherman, and Victory

Grant's strategy as supreme commander was simple, logical, and ruthless. He would attack Lee and try to capture Richmond; meanwhile General William Tecumseh Sherman would push from Chattanooga toward Atlanta, Georgia. Like a giant claw, the two armies could then close to crush all remaining resistance. Early in May 1864 Grant and Sherman commenced operations, each with over 100,000 men.

Grant marched the Army of the Potomac directly into the tangled wilderness area south of the Rappahannock, where Hooker had been routed a year earlier. Lee, with only 60,000 men, forced the battle in the roughest possible country, where Grant found it difficult to make efficient use of his huge force. For two days (May 5–6) this Battle of the Wilderness raged amid the utmost confusion. When it was over, the North had sustained another 18,000 casualties, far more than the Confederates. But unlike his predecessor, Grant did not fall back after being checked, nor did he expose his army to the kind of devastating counterattack at which Lee was so expert. Instead he shifted to the southeast, attempting to outflank the Confederates. Divining his intent, Lee rushed his divisions southeastward and disposed them behind hastily thrown up earthworks in well-placed positions around Spotsylvania Court House. Nevertheless, Grant attacked. After five more days, the Union army had lost another 12,000 men, and the Confederate lines were still intact.

Grant remained undaunted. He had grasped the fundamental truth that the war could be won only by grinding the South down beneath the weight of numbers. His own losses of men and equipment could be replaced, those of Lee could not. When critics complained of the cost, he replied doggedly that he intended to fight on in the same manner even if it took all summer. Once more he pressed southeastward in an effort to outflank the enemy. At Cold Harbor, only nine miles from Richmond, he found the Confederates once more in strong defenses. At dawn on June 3 he attacked and was thrown back with frightful losses. It was a battle as foolish and almost as one-sided as General Pakenham's assault on Jackson's line outside New Orleans in 1815. "At Cold Harbor," the forthright Grant confessed in his memoirs, "no advantage whatever was gained to compensate for the heavy losses we sustained."

Sixty thousand casualties in less than a month! The news sent a wave of dismay through the North. There were demands that "Butcher" Grant be removed from command. Lincoln, however, stood firm. Although the price was fearfully high, Grant was gaining his objective. At Cold Harbor, Lee had to fight without a single regiment in general reserve, whereas Grant's army was larger than at the start of the offensive. When Grant next swung round his flank, striking south of the James toward Petersburg, Lee had to rush his troops to that city to hold him. As the Confederates dug in, Grant put Petersburg under siege. Soon both armies had constructed complicated lines of breastworks and trenches, running for miles in a great arc south of Petersburg, much like the fortifications that would be used so extensively in World War I in France. Methodically, the Union forces extended their lines, seeking to weaken the Confederates and cut the rail connections supplying Lee's troops and the city of Richmond. Grant could not overwhelm him, but by late June, Lee was pinned to earth. Moving again would mean abandoning Richmond, tantamount, in southern eyes, to surrender.

Nevertheless, the summer of 1864 saw the North submerged in pessimism. The Army of the Potomac held Lee at bay but appeared powerless to defeat him. In Georgia General Sherman inched forward methodically against the wily Joseph E. Johnston, but when he tried a direct assault at Kennesaw Mountain on June 27, he was thrown back with heavy casualties. In July daring Confederate raiders under General Jubal Early dashed suddenly across the Potomac from the Shenandoah Valley to within five miles of Washington before being forced to turn back. A draft call for 500,000 additional men did not improve the public temper. Huge losses and the absence of decisive victory were taxing the northern people's will to continue the fight.

In June Lincoln had been renominated on a National Union ticket, with the staunch Unionist Andrew Johnson of Tennessee, a former Democrat, as his running mate. He was under attack not only from the Democrats, who nominated George B. McClellan and came out for a policy that might almost be characterized as peace at any price, but also from the Radical Republicans, many of whom had wished to dump

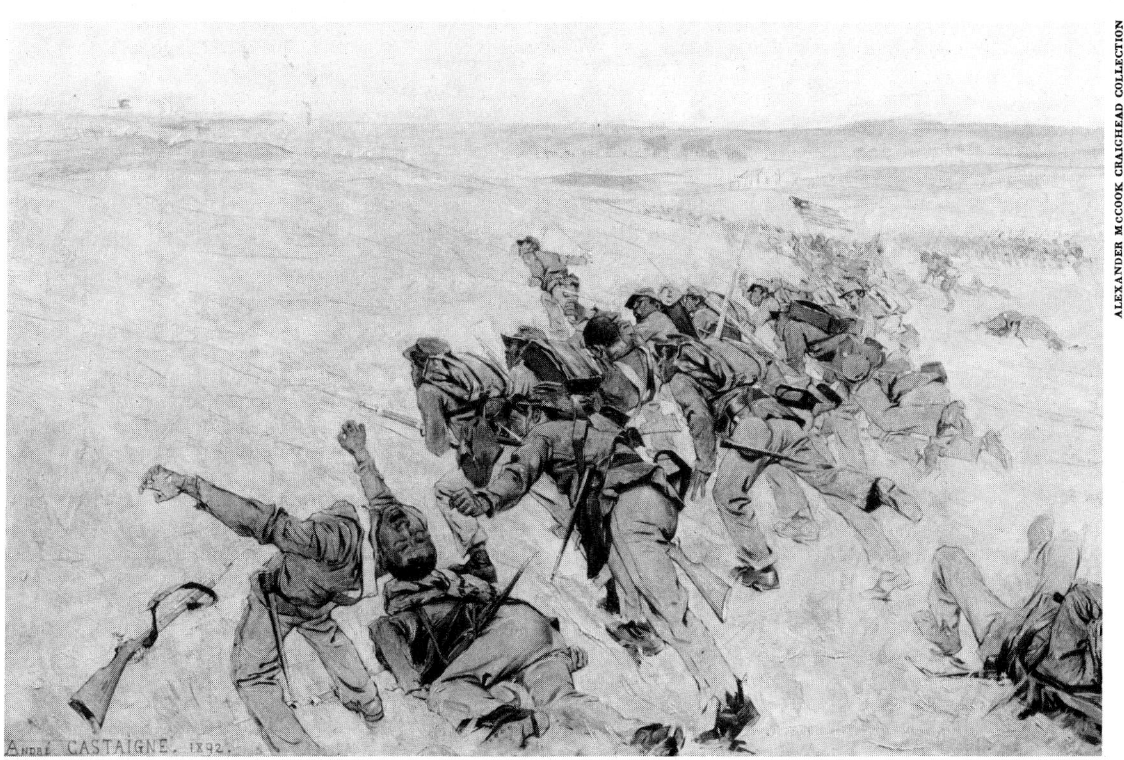

ALEXANDER MCCOOK CRAIGHEAD COLLECTION

Black troops of the 22nd Colored Infantry spearheaded an attack on Petersburg on June 16, 1864, that narrowly failed to overrun the Confederate lines before Lee's reinforcements arrived. Painting by Andre Castaigne.

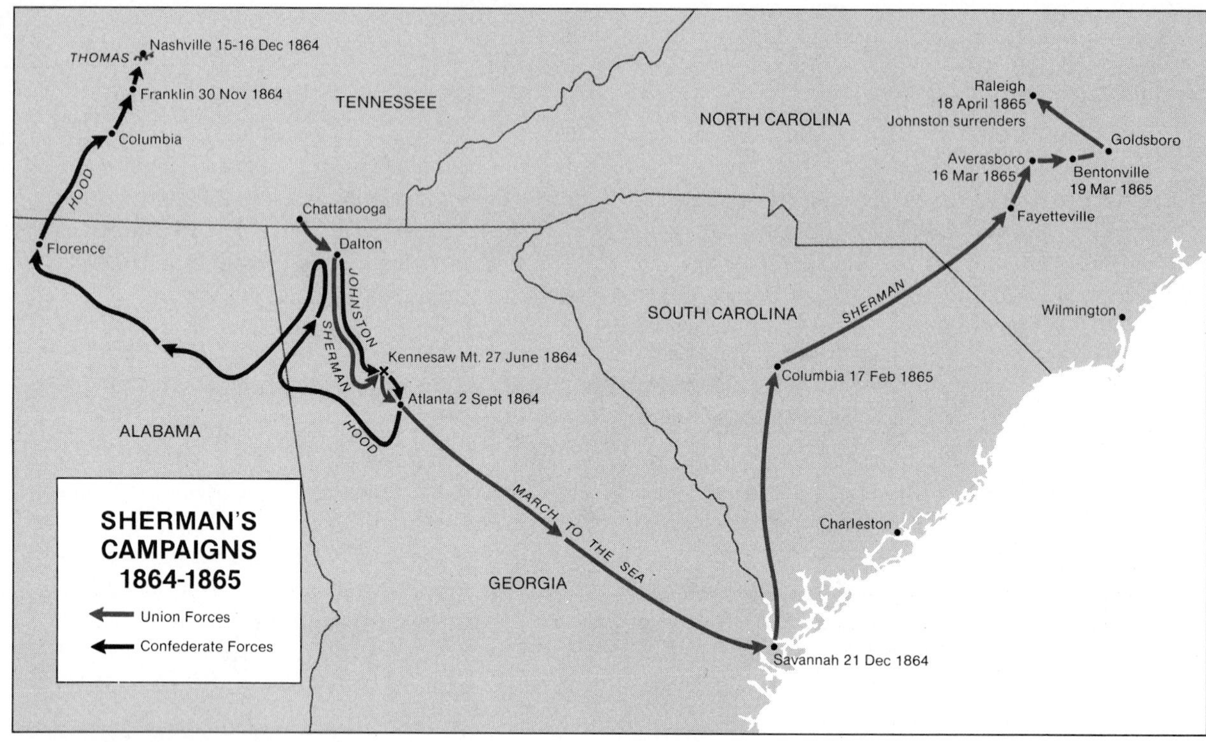

Confederate John B. Hood's "forlorn hope" offensive toward Nashville failed to deter Sherman from marching through Georgia. Joseph E. Johnston could offer little resistance to Sherman's drive through the Carolinas.

him in favor of Secretary of the Treasury Chase. The future looked so dark that Lincoln expected to be defeated and quietly made plans for co-operating with his successor in a last-ditch effort to save the Union.

Then, almost overnight, the atmosphere changed. On September 2 General Sherman's army fought its way into Atlanta. When the Confederates countered with an offensive northward toward Tennessee,* Sherman did not follow. Instead he abandoned his communications with Chattanooga and marched unopposed through Georgia—"from Atlanta to the sea." Far more completely than most military men of his generation, Sherman believed in total war—in appropriating or destroying everything that might help the enemy continue the fight. "War is cruelty, and you cannot refine it," he said. Even before taking Atlanta he wrote his wife: "We have devoured the land. . . . All the people retire before us and desolation is behind. To realize what war is one should follow our tracks." Now, totally dependent upon the countryside for provisions, his army drove across Georgia like a harvester through a field of ripe wheat. "I suppose Jeff Davis will now have to feed the people of Georgia instead of collecting provisions of them to feed his armies," he said coldly.

Sherman's victories staggered not only the Confederacy but also the anti-Lincoln forces in the North. In November the President was easily re-elected, 212 electoral votes to 21.

This demonstration of the North's determination to carry the fight to a conclusion broke the South's will to resist at last. Sherman, having denuded a strip of Georgia 60 miles wide, entered Savannah on December 22. Early in January 1865 he began to march northward, leaving behind him "a broad black streak of ruin and desolation—the fences all gone; lonesome smoke-stacks, surrounded by dark heaps of ashes and

*This force was crushed before Nashville in December by a Union army under General George Thomas.

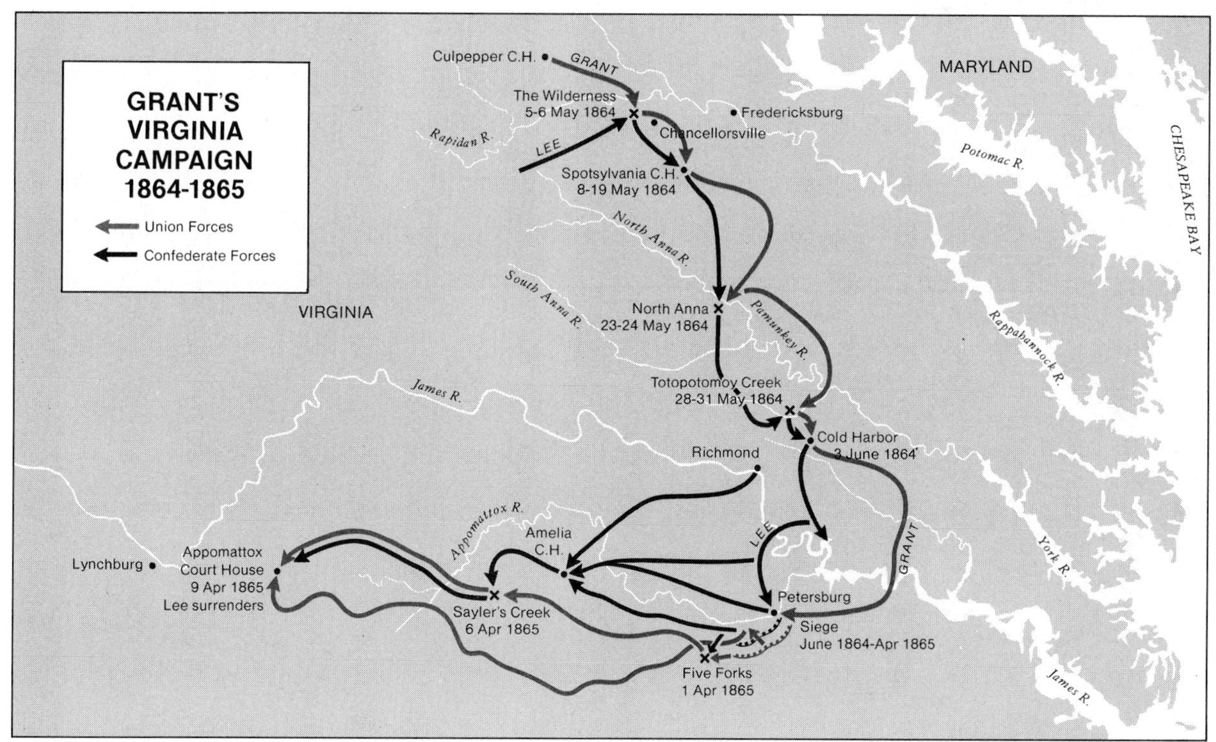

Grant's repeated and costly attempts (60,000 casualties the first month) to outflank Lee are detailed here. At Five Forks the long siege of Petersburg was broken; Richmond was evacuated, and a week later Lee surrendered.

cinders, marking the spots where human habitations had stood." In February his troops captured Columbia, South Carolina; soon thereafter they were in North Carolina, driving ahead relentlessly. In Virginia, Grant's vise grew daily tighter, the Confederate lines thinner and more ragged.

On March 4 Lincoln took the Presidential oath and delivered his second inaugural address. Photographs taken at about this time show clearly how four years of war had marked him. Somehow he had become both gentle and steel-tough, both haggard and inwardly calm. With victory sure, he spoke for tolerance, mercy, and reconstruction. "Let us judge not," he said after stating again his personal dislike of slavery, "that we be not judged." Then he urged all Americans to turn without malice to the task of mending the damage and to make a peace between the sections that would be both just and lasting.

Now the Confederate troops around Petersburg could no longer withstand the federal pressure. Desperately, Lee tried to pull his forces back to the Richmond and Danville Railroad, but the swift wings of Grant's army soon enveloped him. Richmond fell on April 3. With fewer than 30,000 effectives to oppose Grant's 115,000, Lee recognized the futility of further resistance. On April 9 he and Grant met by prearrangement at Appomattox Court House.

It was a scene at once pathetic and inspiring. Lee was noble in defeat, Grant, despite his roughhewn exterior, sensitive and magnanimous in victory. "I met you once before, General Lee, while we were serving in Mexico," Grant said after they had shaken hands. "I have always remembered your appearance, and I think I should have recognized you anywhere." They talked briefly of that earlier war, and then, acting upon Lincoln's instructions, with which he was in full accord, Grant outlined his terms. All that would be required was that the Confederate soldiers lay down their arms. They could return to their homes in peace. When Lee hinted (he was too proud to ask outright for the concession) that

The men of Lee's Army of Northern Virginia march between Union ranks to lay down their arms at Appomattox, sketched by northern combat artist J.R. Chapin. Describing the scene, a federal officer wrote in his diary: "On our part [there was] not a sound of trumpet . . . nor roll of drum; not a cheer . . . but an awed stillness rather. . . ."

his men would profit greatly if allowed to retain possession of their horses, Grant generously offered to let them do so.

Costs and Prospects

And so the war ended. It cost the nation 600,000 lives. More than 110,000 Union soldiers were killed in battle and 250,000 more died of disease and other causes. An additional 275,000 were wounded, many of them permanently disabled. Total Confederate deaths came to about 258,000.

The price in dollars is hard to compute, but if such items as pensions and the rebuilding of civilian property damaged or depleted because of the war are included, it ran into the tens of billions. Two-thirds of the railroad mileage of the South was destroyed, and as late as 1880 the agricultural output of the region had not yet recovered to the levels of 1860. The psychological cost is even more difficult to assay, but it, too, was enormous. Aside from the anguish suffered by relatives and friends of the wounded and the dead, there was the eroding hatred and bitterness that the war implanted in millions of honest hearts. The corruption, the gross materialism, and the selfishness generated by wartime conditions were other disagreeable by-products of the conflict. Such sores fester in any society, but it is certain that the Civil War provided conditions which inflamed and multiplied them. The war produced many examples of charity, self-sacrifice, and devotion to duty as well, yet if the general moral atmosphere of the postwar generation can be said to have resulted from the experiences of 1861–65, the effect overall was definitely bad.

What had been obtained at this great price? Negro slavery was dead, its formal demise accepted everywhere in the South. The concept of an indissoluble Union also won almost universal acceptance: secession was no longer possible after Appomattox. The people of both sections had learned to appreciate how much this great sprawling land and all its associations meant to them. In a strictly political sense, as Lincoln had predicted from the start, the northern victory heartened friends of republican government and democracy all over the world. A better integrated society and a more technically advanced and productive economic system also resulted from the war.

The men of 1865 estimated the balance between cost and profit according to their individual fortunes and prejudices. Only the wisest of them, however, realized that no final accounting could be made until the American people had decided what to do with the fruits of victory. That the physical damage would be repaired no one could reasonably doubt; that even the loss of human resources would be restored in short order was equally apparent. But would the nation make good use of the *opportunities* the war had made available? What would the Negro do with his freedom? How would white men, northerners and southerners, react to emancipation? To what end would the new technology and social efficiency be directed? Would the people be able to forget the recent past and fulfill the hopes for which so many brave men had given their "last full measure of devotion"?

SUPPLEMENTARY READING Allan Nevins, *Ordeal of the Union* (1947–1960), continues to be the fullest and most judicious interpretation of the period down to 1863. It excels both as an account of the fighting and as an analysis of political, social, and economic developments. J.G. Randall, *Lincoln, the President** (1945–1955), is an excellent scholarly study; the last volume of this work was completed after Randall's death by R.N. Current. The best one-volume survey of the period is J.G. Randall and David Donald, *The Civil War and Reconstruction* (1961), while Donald's collection of essays, *Lincoln Reconsidered** (1956), is original and thought-provoking.

Political and constitutional problems are dealt with in J.G. Randall, *Constitutional Problems Under Lincoln** (1926). Lincoln's dealings with the Radicals have been extensively investigated, most recently in H.L. Trefousse, *The Radical Republicans: Lincoln's Vanguard for Racial Justice* (1969), which praises Lincoln's management of the Radicals and minimizes his differences with them. See also, however, T.H. Williams, *Lincoln and the Radicals** (1941). H.J. Carman and R.H. Luthin, *Lincoln and the Patronage* (1943), W.B. Hesseltine, *Lincoln and the War Governors* (1948), F.L. Klement, *The Copperheads in the Middle West* (1960), and Wood Gray, *The Hidden Civil War** (1942), consider other aspects of the political history of the period.

For the movement to make abolition a war aim and the reaction to it, see J.M. McPherson, *The Struggle for Equality: Abolitionists and the Negro in the Civil War and Reconstruction** (1964), G.M. Frederickson, *The Inner Civil War: Northern Intellectuals and the Crisis of the Union** (1965), and V.J. Voegeli, *Free but Not Equal: The Midwest and the Negro During the Civil War* (1967). The activities and attitudes of Negroes during the war are summarized in D.T. Cornish, *The Sable Arm: Negro Troops in the Union Army* (1956), Benjamin Quarles, *The Negro in the Civil War** (1969), and B.I. Wiley, *Southern Negroes** (1938). J.M. McPherson (ed.), *The Negro's Civil War** (1965), is a convenient collection of source material on this subject.

For various aspects of economic and social history, see P.W. Gates, *Agriculture and the Civil War* (1965), and R.P. Sharkey, *Money, Class, and Party: An Economic Study of Civil War and Reconstruction** (1959). E.D. Fite, *Social and Industrial Conditions in the North During the Civil War* (1910), is still useful, and so is Margaret Leech, *Reveille in Washington** (1941).

Clement Eaton, *A History of the Southern Confederacy** (1954), is an excellent brief account of the South during the war, but see also R.S. Henry, *The Story of the Confederacy** (1957), and E.M. Coulter, *The Confederate States of America* (1950). The fullest biography of Jefferson Davis is Hudson Strode, *Jefferson Davis* (1955–1964). Other useful volumes on the Confederacy include C.W. Ramsdell, *Behind the Lines in the Southern Confederacy* (1944), R.W. Patrick, *Jefferson Davis and His Cabinet* (1944), and B.J. Hendrick, *Statesmen of the Lost Cause* (1939).

The voluminous literature on the military history of the Civil War can only be sampled. K.P. Williams, *Lincoln Finds a General* (1949–1952), is exhaustive and judicious. T.H. Williams, *Lincoln and His Generals** (1952), is briefer and more lively. Bruce Catton, *The Centennial History of the Civil War* (1961–65), is vivid and detailed, as are Catton's volumes on the war in the eastern theater, *Mr. Lincoln's Army** (1951), *Glory Road** (1952), and *A Stillness at Appomattox** (1953). The famous *Battles and Leaders of the Civil War,* written during the 1880's by participants, is available in condensed form in Ned Bradford (ed.), *Battles and Leaders of the Civil War* (1956). H.S. Commager (ed.), *The Blue and the Gray* (1951), is an exciting collection of contemporary accounts of the fighting. R.M. Ketchum (ed.), *The American Heritage Picture History of the Civil War* (1960), is excellent. B.I. Wiley, *The Life of Billy Yank** (1952), discusses the role of the common soldier. For the naval side of the conflict, see V.C. Jones, *The Civil War at Sea* (1960–62), and R.S. West, Jr., *Mr. Lincoln's Navy* (1957).

For books dealing with the Confederate military effort, see Frank Vandiver, *Rebel Brass* (1956), A.B. Moore, *Conscription and Conflict in the Confederacy* (1942), D.S. Freeman, *Lee's Lieutenants* (1942–44), and B.I. Wiley, *The Life of Johnny Reb** (1943); see also David Donald (ed.), *Why the North Won the Civil War** (1960).

Among the biographies of Civil War generals, northern and southern, the following are especially noteworthy: Bruce Catton, *Grant Moves South* (1959), J.F.C. Fuller, *Grant and Lee* (1957), W.W. Hassler, Jr., *General George B. McClellan* (1957), Lloyd Lewis, *Sherman, Fighting Prophet* (1932), D.S. Freeman, *R.E. Lee* (1934–35), and Frank Vandiver, *Mighty Stonewall* (1957), U.S. Grant, *Personal Memoirs** (1885–86), should not be missed.

The diplomacy of the Civil War period is covered in H.D. Jordan and E.J. Pratt, *Europe and the American Civil War* (1931), Jay Monaghan, *Diplomat in Carpet Slippers** (1945), E.D. Adams, *Great Britain and the American Civil War* (1925), M.B. Duberman, *Charles Francis Adams** (1961), and F.L. Owsley, *King Cotton Diplomacy* (1931).

*Available in paperback.

16

Reconstruction and the South

On April 5, 1865, Abraham Lincoln visited the fallen capital of Richmond. The center of the city lay in ruins, sections of it blackened by fire, but the President was able to walk the streets unmolested and almost unattended; the townspeople seemed to have accepted defeat without resentment. A few days later, back in Washington, he delivered an important speech on reconstruction, urging that the subject be approached with compassion and open-mindedness. Then, on April 14, he held a Cabinet meeting at which postwar readjustment was considered at length. That evening, however, while he was watching a performance of the play *Our American Cousin* at Ford's Theater, a half-mad actor, John Wilkes Booth, slipped into his box and shot him in the back of the head with a small pistol. Early the next morning, without ever having regained consciousness, Lincoln died.

The murder was part of a complicated and senseless plot organized by die-hard pro-southerners. Seldom have fanatics displayed so little understanding of their own interests, for with Lincoln perished the South's best hope for a mild peace. After his body had been taken home to Illinois for burial, the national mood hardened. It was not a question of avenging the beloved Emancipator; rather a feeling took possession of the public mind that the years of pain and suffering were not yet over, that the awesome drama was still unfolding, that retribution and a final humbling of the South were inevitable.

Presidential Reconstruction

Despite its bloodiness, the Civil War had caused less intersectional hatred than might have been expected. Although civilian property was often seized or destroyed, the invading armies treated the southern population with remarkable forbearance, both during the war and after Appomattox. Not even the top leaders of the Confederacy were punished harshly. While he was ensconced in Richmond behind Lee's army, northerners boasted that they would "hang Jeff Davis to a sour apple tree," and when he was captured in Georgia in May 1865, he was at once taken to Fort Monroe and clapped into irons preparatory to being tried for treason and murder.

But feeling against him subsided quickly. Soon he was given the run of the fort, and then, in 1867, the military turned him over to the civil courts, which released him on bail. He was never brought to trial. A few other high Confederate officials spent short periods behind bars, but the only southerner executed for war crimes was Major Henry Wirz, the commandant of Andersonville military prison.

The legal questions related to bringing the defeated states back into the Union were extremely complex. Since they believed that secession was legal, logic should have compelled southerners to argue that they were out of the Union and would thus have to be formally readmitted. Northerners should have taken the contrary position, since they had fought to prove that secession was illegal. Yet the people of both sections did exactly the opposite. Men like Senator Charles Sumner and Congressman Thaddeus Stevens, in 1861 uncompromising expounders of the theory that the Union was indissoluble, now declared that the Confederate states had "committed suicide" and should be treated like "conquered provinces." Erstwhile states'-rights southerners now argued that their states were still within the Union. Lincoln, believing the issue a "pernicious abstraction," wisely tried to ignore it, and, in fact, during the reconstruction period theoretical or purely legal considerations never determined official policy toward the southern states.

The process of readmission began as early as 1862, when Lincoln appointed provisional governors for those parts of the South already occupied by federal troops. Then, on December 8, 1863, he issued a proclamation setting forth a general policy. He based his right to control reconstruction on the Presidential pardoning power. With the exception of high Confederate officials and a few other special groups, all southerners could reinstate themselves as United States citizens by taking a simple loyalty oath. When, in any state, a number equal to ten per cent of those voting in the 1860 election had taken this oath, they could set up a state government. Such governments had to be republican in form, must recognize the "permanent freedom" of Negroes, and provide for Negro education. The plan, however, did not require that Negroes be given the right to vote.

This "ten per cent plan" reflected Lincoln's moderation and lack of vindictiveness, and also his political wisdom. He realized that any government based on such a small minority of the population would be, as he put it, merely "a tangible nucleus which the remainder . . . may rally around as fast as it can," a sort of puppet regime, like the paper government established in those sections of Virginia under federal control.* The regimes established under this plan in Tennessee, Louisiana, and Arkansas bore, in the President's mind, the same relation to finally reconstructed states that an egg bears to a chicken. "We shall sooner have the fowl by hatching it than by smashing it," he shrewdly remarked. As a politician, and there were few better ones, Lincoln knew that eventually representatives of the southern states would again be sitting in Congress, and he wished to lay the groundwork for a strong Republican party in the section, drawn mainly from former Whigs. Yet he did not see his creations as full-fledged permanent state governments and he well realized that Congress had no intention of seating delegates from these "ten per cent" states at once.

However, the Radicals in Congress disliked the ten per cent plan, partly because of its moderation and partly because it enabled Lincoln to determine Union policy toward the recaptured regions. In July 1864 they passed the Wade-Davis bill, which would have made readmission extremely difficult. It provided for the calling of a constitutional convention only after a *majority* of the voters in a southern state had taken a loyalty oath and barred all Confederate officials and anyone who had "voluntarily borne arms against the United States" from voting in the election or serving at the convention. Besides prohibiting slavery, the new state constitutions would have to repudiate all Confederate debts. Lincoln disposed of the Wade-Davis bill with a

*By approving the separation of the western counties which had refused to secede, this government provided a legal pretext for the creation of West Virginia.

pocket veto and thus managed to retain the initiative in reconstruction for the remainder of the war. Nevertheless, Congress held an important trump in its right to refuse to seat delegates from the "reconstructed" states. There matters stood when Andrew Johnson became President after the assassination.*

Lincoln had picked Johnson for a running mate in 1864 because he was a border-state Unionist Democrat and something of a hero as a result of his courageous service as military governor of Tennessee. From origins even more lowly than Lincoln's, Johnson had risen before the war to be congressman, governor of Tennessee, and United States senator. He was able, efficient, and ambitious but fundamentally unsure of himself, as could be seen in his boastfulness and stubbornness. His political strength came from the poor whites and yeoman farmers in eastern Tennessee, and he was inordinately fond of extolling the common man and attacking "stuck-up aristocrats." Thaddeus Stevens called him a "rank demagogue" and a "damned scoundrel," and it is true that he was a masterful rabble-rouser, but few men of his generation labored so consistently to advance the interests of the small American farmer. Free homesteads, public education, absolute social equality—such were his objectives throughout his career.

His accession posed political problems since officially he was a Democrat, yet that would have mattered very little had it not been for his personality. Because of his record and his reassuring penchant for excoriating southern aristocrats, the Republicans in Congress were ready to cooperate with him. "Johnson, we have faith in you," said Radical Senator Ben Wade, author of the Wade-Davis bill, the day after Lincoln's death. "By the gods, there will be no trouble now in running the government!"

Johnson's reply, "Treason must be made infamous," delighted the Radicals, but the President

*After the collapse of the Confederacy, Lincoln showed signs of moving toward an accommodation with the Radicals. He suggested, for example, that the vote be given to southern blacks who had fought in the Union army and to "very intelligent" freedmen.

BRADY-HANDY COLLECTION, LIBRARY OF CONGRESS

Andrew Johnson, as recorded by Mathew Brady's camera in 1865. Johnson, reported Charles Dickens, radiated purposefulness but no "genial sunlight."

proved temperamentally unable to work with them. As Eric L. McKitrick has said in *Andrew Johnson and Reconstruction,* he was "never really a party man," an "outsider," a "lone wolf" in every way. "The only role whose attributes he fully understood was that of the maverick," McKitrick writes. "For the full nourishment and maximum functioning of his mind, matters had to be so arranged that all the organized forces of society could in some sense, real or symbolic, be leagued against him." Like Randolph of Roanoke, his very antithesis intellectually and socially, opposition was his specialty; he soon alienated every powerful Republican in Washington.

Radical Republicans, listening to Johnson's diatribes against secessionists and the great planters, had assumed that he was anti-southern. Nothing could have been further from the truth. He shared most of his poor white Tennessee constituents' prejudices against Negroes. "Damn the negroes, I am fighting these traitorous aristocrats, their masters," he told a friend during the war. "I wish to God," he said on another occasion, "every head of a family in the United States had one slave to take the drudgery and menial service off his family."

Nor did the new President desire to injure or humiliate the entire South. He had genuinely admired Lincoln; now he followed his predecessor's lead in pushing for a quick return of the southern states to the Union. On May 29, 1865, he issued an amnesty proclamation only slightly more rigorous than Lincoln's. It assumed, correctly enough, that with the war over most southern voters would freely take the loyalty oath and thus it contained no "ten per cent" clause. More classes of Confederates, including those who owned taxable property in excess of $20,000, were excluded from the general pardon. By the time Congress convened in December, all the southern states had organized governments, accepted the new Thirteenth Amendment abolishing slavery, and elected senators and representatives. Johnson promptly recommended these new governments to the attention of Congress.

Republican Radicals

Peace found the Republicans in Congress no more united than they had been during the war. A small group of "ultra"-Radicals insisted on immediate and absolute racial equality; they ignored all practical and political difficulties. Senator Sumner led this faction. A second group of Radicals, headed by Thaddeus Stevens in the House and men like Ben Wade in the Senate, agreed with the ultras' objectives* but were prepared to accept half a loaf if necessary to win the support of less radical colleagues. The moderate Republicans—Senator Lyman Trumbull of Illinois was typical of the group—wanted to protect the freedmen against exploitation and

*When Stevens died, he was buried in a Negro cemetery. Here is his epitaph, written by himself: "I repose in this quiet and secluded spot, not from any natural preference for solitude, but finding other cemeteries limited as to race, by charter rules, I have chosen this that I might illustrate in my death the principles which I advocated through a long life, equality of man before his Creator."

BOTH: BRADY-HANDY COLLECTION, LIBRARY OF CONGRESS

Brady photographed two of the stalwart Radical Republicans, Thaddeus Stevens of Pennsylvania (above) and Benjamin Wade of Ohio. Stevens served in the House from 1859 until his death in 1868. During the Civil War, Senator "Bluff Ben" Wade had chaired the Joint Committee on the Conduct of the War.

guarantee their basic rights but were unprepared to push for full political and social equality for all blacks. A handful of Republicans sided with the Democrats in support of Johnson's approach, but all the rest insisted at least upon the minimum demands of the moderates. Thus Johnsonian reconstruction had no chance of winning congressional approval.

Johnson's proposal that Congress accept reconstruction as completed and admit the new southern representatives was also doomed for reasons having little to do with Negro rights. Although the extremists who wanted harsh punishments were in the minority, if Congress seated the southerners, the balance of power might swing to the Democrats. To expect even the most high-minded Republicans to surrender power in such a fashion was unrealistic. Secondly, northern public opinion remained suspicious of the South and desirous of moving very cautiously toward granting full political rights to ex-Confederates. Former Copperheads gushing with extravagant praise of Johnson's work put Republicans instantly on their guard. Moreover, although most southerners had accepted the result of the war and were eager to re-enter the Union, they were naturally not overflowing with good will toward their conquerors. As a New York *Tribune* reporter who visited the South in 1865 explained, "the people wanted civil government and a settlement," but "they made no hypocritical professions of newborn unionism. . . . The hatred of Yankees . . . had grown and strengthened with the war." Some of the new governments were less than straightforward even about accepting the most obvious results of the war. For example, instead of repudiating secession, South Carolina merely repealed its secession ordinance. A minority of southerners would have nothing to do with amnesties and pardons:

> Oh, I'm a good old rebel,
> Now that's just what I am;
> For the "fair land of freedom,"
> I do not care a dam.
> I'm glad I fit against it—
> I only wish we'd won
> And I don't want no pardon
> For anything I done.

Furthermore, southern voters had provoked northern resentment by their choice of congressmen. Georgia elected Alexander H. Stephens, Vice President of the Confederacy, to the Senate, although he was still in a federal prison awaiting trial for treason! Several dozen men who had served in the Confederate Congress had been elected to either the House or Senate, together with four generals and many other high officials of the defunct Confederate administration. The southern people understandably selected locally respected and experienced leaders, but it was equally reasonable that these choices would sit poorly with many northerners.

Finally, the so-called "Black Codes" enacted by the new southern governments to control the freedmen alarmed the North. These varied from state to state in severity. When seen in historical perspective, even the strictest codes represented a considerable improvement over slavery. Most permitted Negroes to sue and to testify in court, at least in cases involving members of their own race. Negroes were allowed to own certain kinds of property; marriages were made legal; other rights were guaranteed. However, the codes also placed formidable limitations on the freedom of Negroes. They could not bear arms, be employed in occupations other than farming and domestic service, or leave their jobs without forfeiting back pay. The Louisiana code required all Negroes to sign labor contracts for the year during the first ten days of January. In Mississippi the term *vagrant* was made to apply to such varied categories of persons as jugglers, "common night-walkers," and individuals who "habitually misspend their time by frequenting houses of ill-fame, gaming-houses, or tippling shops." Any "vagrant" who could not pay the stiff fine assessed was to be "hired out . . . at public outcry" to the white person who would take him for the shortest period in return for paying his fine. Such laws, apparently designed to get around the Thirteenth Amendment, outraged even moderate northerners.

For all these reasons, the Republicans in Congress strongly opposed Johnsonian reconstruction. Quickly, the two houses established a joint committee on reconstruction, headed by Senator

William P. Fessenden of Maine, a moderate Republican, to study the question of readmitting the southern states. This committee held extensive public hearings, which produced much evidence of the mistreatment of Negroes. Colonel George A. Custer, stationed in Texas, testified: "It is of weekly, if not of daily occurrence that freedmen are murdered." The nurse Clara Barton told a gruesome tale about a pregnant colored woman who had been brutally whipped. Others described the intimidation of Negroes by poor whites. The hearings came as a shock to the North; they played into the hands of the Radicals, who had been claiming all along that the South was perpetuating slavery under another name.

President Johnson's attitude speeded the swing toward the Radical position. While the hearings were in progress, Congress passed a bill expanding and extending the Freedmen's Bureau, which had been established in March 1865 to care for refugees. The bureau, a branch of the War Department, was already exercising considerable coercive and supervisory influence in the South. Now Congress sought to add to its authority in order to protect the Negro population. The bill had wide support even among the moderates. Nevertheless, Johnson vetoed it, arguing that it was an unconstitutional extension of military authority in peacetime. Congress then passed a Civil Rights Act, which, besides declaring that Negroes were citizens of the United States, denied the states the power to restrict their rights to testify in court and to hold property. Enforcement of these rights was entrusted to federal rather than state authority.

Once again the President refused to go along, although his veto was sure to drive more moderates into the arms of the Radicals. "I have lost faith entirely in the President," an important Ohio Republican wrote at this time. "He intends in my judgment to betray us." On April 9 Congress repassed the Civil Rights Act by a two-thirds majority, the first time in American history that a major piece of legislation became law over the veto of a President.

This event marked a revolution in the history of reconstruction. Thereafter Congress, not President Johnson, had the upper hand, and progressively stricter controls were placed upon the South. Instead of a quick return to self-government, much of the South remained under federal domination for more than a decade.

In the clash between the President and Congress, Johnson was his own worst enemy. His language was often intemperate, his handling of men incredibly inept, but above all his analysis of southern conditions was utterly incorrect. He had assumed that the small southern farmers who made up the majority in all the states of the Confederacy shared his prejudices against the planter class. They did not, as their free choices in the postwar elections demonstrated. As a matter of fact, events seemed to indicate that his own hatred of the southern aristocracy might have been based more on jealousy than on principle. Under the reconstruction plan, persons excluded from the blanket amnesty could apply individually for the restoration of their rights. When men of wealth and status flocked to Washington, hat in hand, he found their flattery and humility exhilarating. He began to issue pardons in wholesale lots, saying: "I did not expect to keep out all who were excluded from the amnesty. . . . I intended they should sue for pardon, and so realize the enormity of their crime."

The President also misread northern public feeling. He believed that Congress had no right to pass laws affecting the South before representatives of the southern states had been readmitted to Congress. In the light of the complete refusal of most southern whites to grant any real power or responsibility to the freedmen, an attitude that Johnson did not condemn, the public would not accept this point of view. Johnson placed his own judgment over that of the overwhelming majority of northern voters, and this was a great error, not merely morally but also tactically. It encouraged southerners to resist all efforts to improve the lot of the freedmen and therefore played into the hands of northern extremists.

However, the Radicals encountered grave problems in fighting for their program. Northerners might object to the Black Codes and to seating "rebels" in Congress, but few believed in granting Negroes true equality. Few northern states, it will be remembered, permitted blacks to vote. Between 1865 and 1868 Wisconsin, Minnesota, Connecticut, Nebraska, New Jersey, Ohio, Michigan, and Pennsylvania all rejected bills granting the suffrage to Negroes. Most northerners did not really disagree with the southern belief that the black man was basically inferior.

Like the abolitionists before the war, the Radicals lacked scientific arguments to prove that Negroes were equal to whites in intelligence and character. Moreover, they were, in effect, demanding not merely equal rights for freedmen but *extra* rights: not merely the right to vote but special protection of that right against the pressure that the dominant southern whites would surely apply to undermine it. This idea flew in the face of conventional American beliefs in equality before the law and individual self-reliance. Such protection would furthermore involve drastic interference by the federal government in local affairs, a concept totally at variance with previous American practice. Experience has repeatedly shown that the Radicals were correct—that what amounted to a political revolution in state-federal relations was essential if Negroes were to achieve real equality. But in the climate of that day their proposals encountered bitter resistance, and not only from southerners.

Thus, while the Radicals sought partisan advantage in their battle with Johnson and sometimes tried to play upon war-bred passions in achieving their ends, they were also taking large political risks in defense of genuinely held principles. Many of them went down to defeat in local elections because of their support of Negro rights.

The Fourteenth Amendment

However, events, and President Johnson, played into the Radicals' hands. In June 1866 Congress passed and submitted to the states a new amendment to the Constitution. This Fourteenth Amendment marked a major milestone along the road to the centralization of political power in the nation, for it greatly reduced the power of *all* the states. In this sense it confirmed the great change wrought by the Civil War: the growth of a more complex, more closely integrated social and economic structure requiring closer national supervision. Few persons understood this aspect of the amendment at the time.

First of all, to cope with the possibility that the Supreme Court might find the Civil Rights Act unconstitutional, the amendment supplied a broad definition of American citizenship: "All persons born or naturalized in the United States, and subject to the jurisdiction thereof, are citizens of the United States and of the State wherein they reside." Obviously this included Negroes. Then it struck at discriminatory legislation like the Black Codes: "No State shall make or enforce any law which shall abridge the privileges or immunities of citizens of the United States; nor shall any State deprive any person of life, liberty, or property, without due process of law." The next section attempted to force the southern states to permit Negro voting. If a state denied the vote to any class of its adult male citizens, its representation was to be reduced proportionately. Under another clause, former federal officials who had served the Confederacy were barred from holding either state or federal office unless specifically pardoned by a two-thirds vote of Congress. Finally, the Confederate debt was repudiated.

These provisions were not as drastic as the Radicals had wished. The amendment did not specifically outlaw segregation or prevent a state from disfranchising Negroes if it was willing to see its representation in Congress reduced. Nevertheless, the South would have none of it. Except for Tennessee, all the former Confederate states refused to ratify. Without them, the necessary three-fourths majority of the states could not be obtained.

President Johnson, vociferous in his opposition, vowed to make the choice between the Fourteenth Amendment and his own policy the main issue of the 1866 congressional elections. He embarked upon "a swing around the circle" to rally the public to his cause. He failed dismally, for by this time northern public opinion had hardened; without changing their personal attitudes toward Negroes, a large majority was determined that blacks must have at least formal legal equality, even if it took federal interference to give it to them. The Republicans won better than two-thirds of the seats in both houses, together with control of all the northern state governments. Johnson emerged from the campaign discredited, the Radicals greatly increased in strength.

Since the South had refused to accept their terms voluntarily, the Radicals prepared to impose them by force. The southern states, said Congressman James A. Garfield of Ohio in February 1867, "with contempt and scorn [have] flung back into our teeth the magnanimous offer of a generous nation. It is now our turn to act."

The Reconstruction Acts

Framing effective reconstruction legislation was very difficult. No precedents existed to build upon, and differences of opinion among Republican congressmen were wide. Moderate Republicans clung stubbornly to the hope that at least a semblance of local autonomy could be preserved in the South. Had the southern states been willing to reconsider their rejection of the Fourteenth Amendment, coercive measures might still have been avoided. Their recalcitrance and the continuing indications that local authorities were persecuting Negroes finally led to the passage, on March 2, 1867, of the First Reconstruction Act.

This law divided the former Confederacy—exclusive of Tennessee, which had ratified the Fourteenth Amendment—into five military districts, each controlled by a major general. It gave these officers almost dictatorial power to protect the civil rights of "all persons," maintain order, and supervise the administration of justice. To rid themselves of military rule, the former states were required to frame and adopt new constitutions guaranteeing Negroes the right to vote and disfranchising the same broad classes of ex-Confederates excluded under the proposed amendment. If these new constitutions proved satisfactory to Congress, and if the new governments ratified the amendment, their representatives would be admitted to Congress and military rule ended. This stern measure passed the House of Representatives by 135 to 48 and the Senate by 38 to 10. Johnson's veto was thus easily overridden.

Although drastic, the Reconstruction Act was so vague that it quickly proved unworkable. Military control was easily established, for in practice federal bayonets were already exerting considerable authority all over the South. But in deference to moderate Republican views, the law had not spelled out the process by which the new constitutions were to be drawn up. Southerners, resenting the requirements and hoping that the Supreme Court would declare the act unconstitutional, preferred the status quo, even under army control, to enfranchising the Negro and retiring their own respected leaders. They made no effort to follow the steps laid down in the law. Congress, therefore, passed a second act, requiring the military authorities to register voters and supervise the election of delegates to constitutional conventions. A third act further clarified procedures.

Still, white southerners resisted. The laws provided that the new constitutions must be approved by a majority of the registered voters. Simply by staying away from the polls, the southerners defeated ratification in state after state. At last, in March 1868, a full year after the First Reconstruction Act was passed, Congress changed the rules again. The constitutions were to be ratified by a majority of the *voters*. In this way, at last, the will of Congress was carried out. In June 1868 Arkansas, having fulfilled the requirements, was readmitted to the Union. But it was not until July 1870 that the last southern state, Georgia, qualified to the satisfaction of Congress.

Congress v. the President

To carry out this program in the face of determined southern resistance required a degree of single-mindedness over a long period seldom demonstrated by American legislatures. This persistence resulted partly from the suffering and frustrations of the war years. The refusal of the South, although crushed on the field of battle, to accept the spirit of even the mild reconstruction designed by Johnson goaded the North to ever more overbearing efforts to bring the ex-Confederates to heel. President Johnson's stubbornness also influenced the mood of Congress; Republican leaders became obsessed with the desire to defeat him. The unsettled times and the large Republican majorities, always threatened by the possibility of a Democratic resurgence if "unreconstructed" southern congressmen were readmitted, sustained their determination.

Indeed, these considerations led the Republicans to attempt a kind of grand revision of the federal government, one which almost destroyed the balance between judicial, executive, and legislative power established in 1789. A series of measures passed between 1866 and 1868 increased the authority of Congress over the army, over the process of amending the Constitution, and over the Cabinet and lesser appointive officers. Congress arrogated to itself the right to summon its membership into extra sessions, a power exercised in the past only by Presidents. Even the Supreme Court felt the force of this congressional drive for power. Its size was reduced and also the range of its jurisdiction over civil rights cases. Some Radicals talked of abolishing it altogether. The justices handed down some notably courageous decisions in the face of Radical pressure, but when their powers were reduced by legislation in a way that many lawyers considered unconstitutional, they meekly accepted the restriction. Generally speaking, the Court avoided taking a stand that might have challenged the constitutionality of the Reconstruction Acts, being disinclined, according to one judge, to "run a race with Congress."

Finally, in a showdown caused by emotional conflicts more than by practical considerations, the Republicans attempted to remove President Johnson from office. Johnson was a poor President and out of touch with public opinion. Had he been a prime minister and the United States a parliamentary democracy, he would quickly have been forced to resign. But he had done nothing to merit ejection from office under the Constitution. Although he had a low opinion of Negroes, his opinion was so widely shared by whites that it is unhistorical to condemn him as a reactionary on this ground. Johnson believed that he was fighting to preserve constitutional government. He was sincere, honest, devoted to his duty, and his record easily withstood the most searching examination of his enemies. When Congress passed laws taking away powers granted him by the Constitution, he refused to submit.

The chief issue was the Tenure of Office Act of 1867, which prohibited the President from removing officials who had been appointed with the consent of the Senate without first obtaining senatorial approval. In February 1868 Johnson "violated" this act by dismissing Secretary of War Edwin M. Stanton, who had been openly in sympathy with the Radicals for some time. The House, acting under the procedure set up in the Constitution for removing the President, promptly impeached him before the bar of the Senate, Chief Justice Salmon P. Chase presiding.

This "great act of ill-directed passion," as it has been characterized by one historian, would have been farcical had it not been conducted in so partisan and vindictive a manner. Johnson's lawyers easily established that he had removed Stanton only in an effort to prove the Tenure of Office Act unconstitutional. They also demonstrated that the act did not protect Stanton to begin with, since it gave Cabinet members tenure "during the term of the President by whom they may have been appointed," and Stanton had been appointed by Lincoln! Nevertheless, the Radicals pressed the charges (11 separate articles) relentlessly. To the argument that Johnson had committed no crime, the learned Senator Sumner retorted that the proceedings were "political in character" rather than judicial. Thaddeus Stevens, directing the attack on behalf of the House, warned the senators that although "no corrupt or wicked motive" could be attributed to Johnson, they would "be tortured on the gibbet of everlasting obloquy" if they did not convict him. Tremendous pressure was applied to the handful of Republican senators who were unwilling to disregard the evidence.

Fortunately, seven of them resisted to the end. As a result, the Radicals failed by a single vote to convict Johnson. Had they not, it is more than likely that in future controversies between Congress and the President, the weapon of impeachment would have been freely used, with the result that the independence of the Executive would have been destroyed. Then the legislative branch would have become supreme.

The Fifteenth Amendment

The failure of the impeachment, however, had little effect on the course of reconstruction. The President was finally acquitted on May 16. A few days later the Republican National Convention nominated General Ulysses S. Grant for the Presidency. At the Democratic convention, Johnson received considerable support, but the delegates finally nominated Horatio Seymour, a former governor of New York. In November Grant won an easy victory in the Electoral College, 214 to 80, but the election was not actually a runaway for him. The popular vote was 3 million to 2.7 million. Although he would probably have carried the Electoral College in any case, it is an interesting fact that Grant's margin in the popular vote was supplied by southern Negroes enfranchised under the Reconstruction Acts. Of the estimated 500,000 Negro voters in 1868, about 450,000 supported Grant. In other words, a majority of the white voters probably preferred Seymour. Indeed, since many citizens undoubtedly voted Republican because of personal admiration for Grant, the election statistics suggest that a substantial majority of the white voters were opposed to the policies of the Radicals.

The ratification of the Fourteenth Amendment was finally completed in July 1868. Combined with the Reconstruction Acts it achieved the purpose of enabling southern Negroes to vote. The Radicals, however, were not satisfied; despite the unpopularity of the idea in the North, they wished to guarantee the right of Negroes to vote in every state. Amending the Constitution seemed the only way to accomplish this objective, but passage of such an amendment seemed on the surface utterly impossible. In 1867 and 1868 the voters of New York had rejected a proposal to remove the $250 property qualification for voting imposed on Negroes in the state, and the voters of several middle western states had turned down new constitutional provisions authorizing Negro voting. The Republican platform in the 1868 Presidential election smugly distinguished between Negro voting in the South ("demanded by every consideration of public safety, of gratitude, and of justice") and in the North (where the question "properly belongs to the people").

However, the result of that election, which demonstrated how crucial Negro block voting could be, caused a sudden shift in Republican strategy. Grant had carried Indiana by less than 10,000 votes and lost New York by a similar number. If Negroes in these and other closely divided states had voted, Republican strength would have been greatly enhanced. Suddenly both houses of Congress blossomed with suffrage amendments. After considerable bickering over details, the Fifteenth Amendment was passed and sent to the states for ratification in February 1869. It forbade *all* the states to deny the vote to anyone "on account of race, color, or previous condition of servitude."

Most of the southern states, still under federal pressure and already committed to Negro voting, ratified the amendment swiftly. The same was true in most of New England and in some of the western states. Bitter battles were waged in Connecticut, New York, Pennsylvania, and the states immediately north of the Ohio River, but by March 1870, most of these had ratified the amendment and it became part of the Constitution. The debates precipitated by these contests show that partisan advantage was not the only reason why the voters approved Negro suffrage at last. The unfairness of a double standard of voting, North and South, the contribution of black soldiers during the war, and a general hope that by passing the amendment the strife of reconstruction could be finally ended all played a part.

When the Fifteenth Amendment went into effect, President Grant called it "the greatest civil change and . . . the most important event that has occurred since the nation came to life." Negroes and former abolitionists rejoiced—the American Anti-Slavery Society formally dissolved itself, its work apparently completed. One prominent Radical Republican called this victory over northern prejudice "hardly explicable on any other theory than that God willed it." Of course many of the celebrants lived to see the amendment subverted in the South; indeed, that it could be evaded by literacy tests and other restrictions was apparent at the time and may even have influenced some persons in voting for it. But a stronger amendment, one, for instance, that positively granted the right to vote to all men and put the supervision of elections under national control, could not have been ratified.

"Black Republican" Reconstruction

For the moment, at least, the Radicals had succeeded in imposing their will upon the South. Throughout the region, in the late sixties and early seventies, former slaves voted, held office, and, in general, exercised the "privileges" and enjoyed the "immunities" guaranteed them by the Fourteenth Amendment. Almost to a man they voted Republican.

The spectacle of Negroes not five years removed from slavery in positions of power and responsibility attracted much attention at the time and has since been examined exhaustively by historians. The subject is controversial, but certain facts are beyond argument. For one thing, Negro officeholders were neither numerous nor inordinately influential. No Negro was ever elected governor of a state; fewer than a dozen and a half during the whole period served in Congress; only one (in South Carolina) rose to be a justice of a state supreme court. Negroes held many minor offices and were influential in southern legislatures, although except for a brief period in South Carolina, when they controlled the lower house, they never made up a majority. Certainly they did not share the spoils of office in proportion to their numbers. The real rulers of these "black Republican" governments were white: the "carpetbaggers"—northerners who had come to the South as idealists eager to help the freedmen, as employees of the federal government, or as enterprising adventurers seeking money and power—and the "scalawags"—southerners will

Frank Leslie's Illustrated Newspaper, JANUARY 6, 1877

South Carolina's House of Representatives in session during reconstruction, from Frank Leslie's Illustrated Newspaper. *Negroes were in the majority in South Carolina, and seven were elected to the federal Congress.*

ing to cooperate with the Negro out of principle or to advance their own interests. Far from being the dregs of society, many of the scalawags were well-to-do planters and merchants who had been Whigs until the great crises of the 1850's had destroyed that party in the South.

That the Negroes should fail to assert leadership is certainly understandable. They lacked experience in politics and were both poor and uneducated. They were also, even in the South, a minority. It would have been remarkable indeed if they had dominated the reconstruction governments. Those Negroes who did hold high office during reconstruction proved in the main able and conscientious public servants: able because the best tended to rise to the top in such a fluid situation and conscientious because most of those who achieved importance sought eagerly to demonstrate the capacity of their race for self-government. Extensive studies of states such as Mississippi have shown that even at the local level, where the quality of officials was usually poor, there was little difference in the degree of competence displayed by white and Negro officeholders. In power, the Negroes displayed remarkably little vindictiveness; by and large, they did not seek to restrict the rights of ex-Confederates.

It is true that waste and corruption flourished in some of these governments. Legislators paid themselves large salaries and surrounded themselves with armies of useless, incompetent clerks. Half the budget of Louisiana in some years went for salaries and "mileage" for representatives and their staffs. In South Carolina the legislature ordered an expensive census in 1869, only one year before the regular federal census was to be taken. Large sums were appropriated for imposing state capitols and other less-than-essential buildings. As for corruption, in *The South During Reconstruction* Professor E. Merton Coulter has described dozens of defalcations of various sorts that occurred during these years. One Arkansas Negro took $9,000 from the state for repairing a bridge that had cost only $500 to build. A South Carolina legislator was voted an additional $1,000 in salary after he had lost that sum on a horse race. A judge in Louisiana contrived to sell a state-owned railroad worth several millions for $50,000.

However, to be understood, this corruption must be seen in perspective. First of all, not every reconstruction government was dishonest. In Mississippi fraud was almost nonexistent during the period that Negroes participated in public affairs. In other states the big thieves were nearly always white men, who obtained huge tracts of public land by fraud and siphoned off the proceeds of state bond sales. Blacks, as one historian puts it, got merely the "crumbs" while the "loaf" was divided among carpetbaggers, scalawags, and the Democrats. "If any Negro Radical retired wealthy during or after the Reconstruction, he covered his tracks well." Furthermore, graft and callous disregard of the public interest characterized government in every section and at every level during the decade after Appomattox. Big-city bosses in the North made off with sums which dwarfed the most brazen southern frauds. The defalcations of the New York City Tweed Ring probably amounted to a larger sum than all the southern thefts combined. The crimes of officials in Louisiana and South Carolina appear trivial when compared with the depravity in Washington during President Grant's administrations. While this evidence does not justify the southern corruption, it suggests that the unique features of reconstruction politics—Negro suffrage, military supervision, carpetbagger and scalawag influence—do not explain it.

The "black Republican" governments did display qualities that grew directly from the ignorance and political immaturity of the freedmen. There was a tragicomic aspect to the South Carolina legislature during these years, its many Negro members—some dressed in old frock coats, others in rude farm clothes—rising to points of order and personal privilege without reason, discoursing ponderously on subjects they did not understand. "A wonder and a shame to modern civilization," one northern observer called this spectacle.

The whole country might have been better served if the Negro had been enfranchised only gradually, as Lincoln had suggested, and if a real effort had been made to educate him to the responsibilities of citizenship. Neither northerners nor southerners were willing to adopt such a solution to the problem. Two and a half centuries of

MALCOLM F.J. BURNS COLLECTION

The Freedmen's Bureau established 4,329 schools, attended by some 250,000 ex-slaves, in the South in the postwar period. Harper's Weekly *artist Alfred Waud did this sketch of a Freedmen's Bureau school in Vicksburg, Mississippi, in 1866.*

slavery and the absence of the kind of psychological and sociological studies of Negro intelligence now available made it almost impossible for the best-intentioned southerners to see the Negro as a potential equal. Most simply guffawed and made crude jokes about the stupidity of "nigras." Even intelligent and well-meaning southern whites could not often view the freedman objectively. Robert E. Lee, no lover of slavery, testified that Negroes were an "amiable and social" people who loved "ease and comfort" and looked "more to their present than to their future condition." He did not realize that he was describing qualities found in human beings of all kinds, not merely in Negroes. Northerners refused to recognize that a problem existed, shared the prejudices of their southern cousins, or cynically tried to manipulate the Negro vote for their own ends.

Southerners who complained about the ignorance and irresponsibility of Negro voters conveniently forgot that the whole tendency of 19th-century American democracy was away from educational, financial, or any other restrictions on the franchise. Thousands of white southerners were as illiterate and uncultured as the freedmen, yet no one suggested depriving them of the ballot. Some northern states allowed immigrants to vote before they became citizens, even before they had learned English.

Despite the corruption, confusion, and conflict, the Radical southern governments did accomplish a great deal, instituting many long-needed reforms. They spent money freely—the debt of the former Confederate states increased by more than $100 million—but not entirely wastefully. Tax rates zoomed, but the proceeds were used to finance the repair and expansion of the South's dilapidated railroad network, to rebuild crumbling levees, to care for the poor, and generally to expand social services. Before the Civil War, public education in the South had lagged far behind the rest of the country, and as for Negro education, it was not only nonexistent but illegal. During reconstruction an enormous gap had to be filled, and it took a great deal of money to fill it. The Freedmen's Bureau made a start at the task, and northern religious and philanthropic organizations also did important work. Eventually, however, the state governments established and supported systems of free public education that greatly benefited all the people, whites as well as Negroes.

Freedmen grasped eagerly at the opportunity to learn. Nearly all appreciated the immense importance of knowing how to read and write; the sight of elderly Negroes poring laboriously over elementary texts beside their grandchildren was common everywhere. Of course many were too old, others lacked the time and the sustained interest to master even the three *R*'s. Nevertheless, about 600,000 Negroes were attending public schools by 1877. Schools and other institutions were supported chiefly by property taxes, and these, of course, hit well-to-do white farmers hard. Hence much of the complaining about the "extravagance" of reconstruction governments concealed selfish objections to necessary public expenditures. Eventually, the benefits of expanded government services to the whole population became clear to all classes, and when the period finally ended and white supremacy was re-established, most of the new services, together with the corruption and inefficiency inherited from the carpetbagger governments, were retained.

Southern Economic Problems

The South's grave economic problems complicated the rebuilding of its political system. Taken as a whole, the section had never been as prosperous as the North. Wartime destruction left it desperately poor by any standard. In addition to the physical damage, the South had suffered staggering financial losses. All Confederate bonds and currency became worthless. While freeing the slaves did not deprive the South of their labor, it cost slaveowners dearly, and these were the men accustomed by training and experience to develop and manage the resources of the region. Most of the 5 million bales of cotton on hand in the Confederacy when the war ended, an asset that might have gone a long way toward getting the area back on its feet, were seized and sold by agents of the federal government—much of the proceeds, indeed, being siphoned into their own pockets. The government also placed a heavy tax on cotton, which drained off another $68 million from the South in the immediate postwar years.

The war also disorganized the southern economy. In the long run, the abolition of slavery released immeasurable quantities of human energy previously stifled, but the immediate effect was to create confusion. Understandably enough, many former slaves tended to equate legal freedom with freedom from having to earn a living, a tendency reinforced for a time by the willingness of the Freedmen's Bureau to provide rations and other forms of relief in war-devastated areas.

Many Negroes expected that freedom would also mean free land, and the slogan "forty acres and a mule" achieved wide popularity in the South in 1865. This idea was most forcefully supported by the irascible, relentless Congressman Thaddeus Stevens, whose hatred of the planter class was pathological. "The property of the chief rebels should be seized," he stated. If the lands of the richest "70,000 proud, bloated and defiant rebels" were confiscated, the federal government would obtain 394 million acres. This Stevens would divide into "convenient" farms. Every adult male Negro could easily be supplied with 40 acres, and there would still remain millions of acres for the government to sell at auction, bringing in an immense sum that might be used to pension veterans and reduce the national debt. The beauty of his scheme, Stevens insisted, was that "nine-tenths of the [southern] people would remain untouched." Dispossessing the great planters would also make the South "a safe republic," its lands cultivated by "the free labor of intelligent citizens." If the plan drove the planters into exile, "all the better."

Although Stevens' figures were faulty and his logic shaky, many Radicals agreed with him. "We must see that the freedmen are established on the soil," Senator Sumner declared. "The great plantations, which have been so many nurseries of the rebellion, must be broken up, and the freedmen must have the pieces." Stevens, Sumner, and others who wanted to give land to the freedmen weakened their case by associating it with the idea of punishing the former rebels; the average American had too much respect for property rights to tolerate a policy of confiscation. But aside from its vindictiveness, the extremists' view was too simplistic. Land without capital for tools, seed, and other necessities would have done the freedmen little good. Congress did throw open 46 million acres of poor-quality federal land in the South to Negroes under the Homestead Act, but few settled upon it. Yet a scheme for establishing freedmen on small farms with adequate guidance and financial aid would have been of incalculable benefit to them and to the nation. The country, however, was no more ready for an economic revolution of this type than for the

Among the few blacks to emigrate to the West and obtain land under the provisions of the Homestead Act was the Shores family. S.D. Butcher took this family portrait in Custer County, Nebraska, in the 1880's. Negro homesteaders received limited aid from the Freedmen's Relief Association and eastern philanthropists.

kind of political revolution that would have properly protected the Negroes' political rights.

The freedmen, therefore, had to work out their destiny within the already established framework of southern agriculture. In the beginning, they usually labored for wages. Most southerners soon came to the conclusion that a free Negro produced no more than a third to a half as much as a slave and paid them far less than white workers could command. This was not entirely unjust. Freedmen often quit their jobs at harvest time when the work was hard, leaving the crops to rot in the fields, and went off with a few dollars, wandering aimlessly, reveling in their new right to travel without a pass. This explains in part why the Black Codes contained provisions forcing the Negroes to sign long-term labor contracts.

The payment of wages, however, even under contracts, did not work out well in the postwar South. Money was extremely scarce, and banking capital, never adequate even before the collapse of the Confederacy, accumulated very slowly. As late as 1872 the total capitalization of the banks of Georgia was only $2 million. Interest rates were extremely high. This situation made it difficult for large landowners to meet their labor bills and also for freedmen and poor whites to obtain the funds necessary to buy land. In the same state of Georgia, as late as 1880, Negroes owned fewer than 600,000 of the state's 37,700,000 acres. Planter and freedman attempted to solve their difficulties by developing the system known as sharecropping. Instead of cultivating his lands by gang labor as in ante-bellum times, the planter broke his estate up into small units and established on each a Negro family. He provided housing, agricultural implements, and other supplies, and the family provided labor. The crop was divided between them, usually on a 50–50 basis. If the laborer supplied tools or other equipment, he received a larger share. This system created the incentive needed to keep the sharecropper on the job in all seasons and also gave him the chance to rise in the world. He became the independent manager of his own acres; if successful, he could save money and eventually buy land of his own. Of course the profit in personal dignity and self-confidence for the ex-slave was immense, but the economic benefit was also large. The Negro continued to labor much as he had under slavery, but now he kept a far larger proportion of what his labor produced.

All would have been well had the planters possessed enough capital to finance the system. They did not. Like their colonial ancestors and their fathers in the prewar era, they had to borrow against October's harvest to pay for April's seed. Thus the crop-lien system developed, and to protect his investment, the lender tended to insist that the grower concentrate on the readily marketable cash crops: tobacco, sugar, and especially cotton. Overproduction and soil exhaustion inevitably resulted. The system injured everyone connected with southern agriculture—the big planter, the Negro sharecropper, and the small independent operator, who was also usually in debt. Diversified farming would have reduced the farmers' need for cash, preserved the fertility of the soil, and, by placing a premium on imagination and shrewdness, aided the best of them to rise in the world. Under the crop-lien system, both landowner and sharecropper depended upon credit supplied by local bankers, merchants, and storekeepers for everything from seed, tools, and fertilizer to blue jeans, coffee, and salt. Crossroads stores proliferated, and a new class of small merchants appeared. The prices of goods sold on credit were high, adding to the burden borne by the rural population. These small southern merchants were almost equally victimized by the system, for they also lacked capital, bought their goods on credit, and had to pay high interest rates.

Seen in broad perspective, the situation is not difficult to understand. The South, drained of every resource by the exhausting war, was now competing for funds with the North and West, both vigorous and expanding and therefore vora-

SOUTHERN AGRICULTURE, 1850-1900

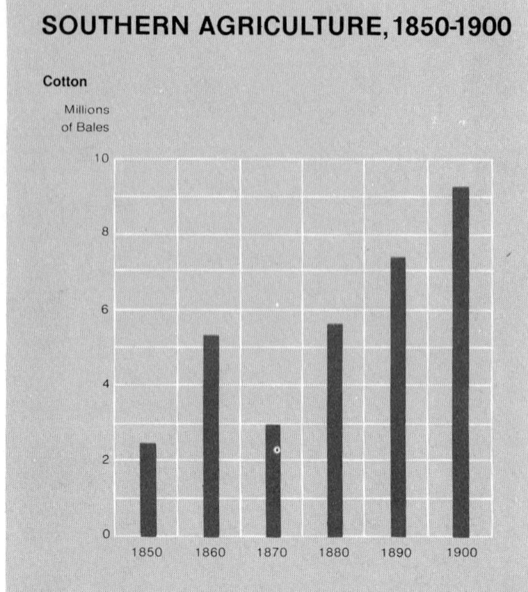

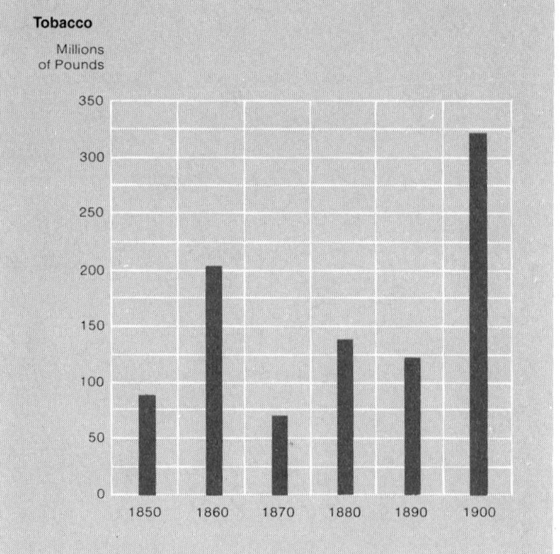

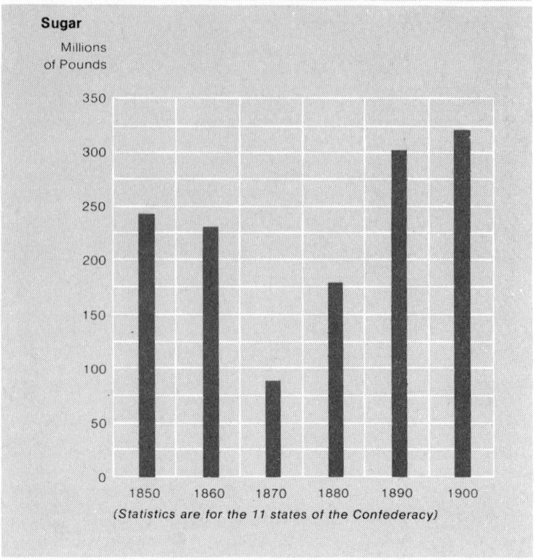

(Statistics are for the 11 states of the Confederacy)

cious consumers of capital. Reconstruction, in the literal sense of the world, was accomplished chiefly at the expense of the standard of living of the producing classes. The crop-lien system and the small storekeeper were only agents attending to the functioning of an economic process dictated by national, perhaps even worldwide conditions.

This does not mean that the South's economy was paralyzed by the shortage of capital or that recovery and growth did not take place. But compared with the rest of the country, progress was slow. In the years just before the Civil War, cotton production averaged about 4 million bales. After the war, the former Confederate states did not enjoy a 4-million-bale year until 1870, and only after 1874 did the crop begin to top that figure consistently. The prewar production record of 5.3 million bales was not broken until 1879. In contrast, national wheat production in 1859 was 175 million bushels and in 1878, 449 million. About 7,000 miles of railroad were built in the South between 1865 and 1879, but in the rest of the nation, nearly 45,000 miles of track were laid.

In manufacturing the South made important gains. The tobacco industry, stimulated by the sudden popularity of the cigarette, expanded rapidly. The town of Durham, North Carolina, home of the famous Bull Durham pipe and cigarette tobacco, flourished. So did Virginia tobacco towns like Richmond, Lynchburg, and Petersburg. The exploitation of the coal and iron deposits of northeastern Alabama in the early 1870's made a boom town of Birmingham. The manufacture of cotton cloth also increased, productive capacity nearly doubling between 1865 and 1880. Yet the mills of Massachusetts alone had eight times the capacity of the entire South in 1880. Despite gains in many fields, the South's share of the national output of manufactured goods declined sharply during the reconstruction era.

The White Counter-Revolution

Although economic conditions improved and federal troops supplied sporadic aid, the Radical governments of the southern states could sustain themselves only so long as they held the support of a significant proportion of the white population, for except in South Carolina and Louisiana, the Negroes were neither numerous nor powerful enough to win elections alone. The key to Radical survival lay in the hands of the wealthy merchants and planters, mostly former Whigs, who had chosen to go along with the carpetbag governments in the interest of harmony and economic recovery. Men of this sort had nothing to fear from Negro economic competition. Taking a broad view, they could see that improving the lot of the former slave would benefit all classes.

These southerners exercised a restraining influence on the rest of the white population. Poor white farmers, the most "unreconstructed" of all southerners, bitterly resented the freedmen, whose every forward step seemed to weaken their own precarious economic and social position. When the carpetbaggers arrived and began to organize and manipulate the new Negro voters much the way big-city bosses were managing the masses of the North, these poorer whites seethed with resentment.

The carpetbaggers used the Union League of America, a patriotic club founded during the war, to control the Negro vote. Employing secret rituals, exotic symbols, and other paraphernalia calculated to impress the Negroes' untutored imaginations, they enrolled the freedmen in droves, made them swear to support the League list of candidates at elections, and then marched them to the polls en masse. Powerless to check the League by open methods, dissident southerners established a number of secret terrorist societies, bearing such names as the Ku Klux Klan, the Knights of the White Camelia, and the Pale Faces.

The most notorious of these was the Klan, which was strong in the Upper South. Its members, sporting awesome titles like Grand Wizard, Hydra, Cyclops, and Night-Hawk, were dedicated to driving the Negro out of politics. In 1868 they opened a campaign of intimidation on a broad front. Sheet-clad nightriders roamed the countryside, frightening the impressionable and chastising the defiant. Klansmen, using a weird mumbo jumbo and claiming even to be the ghosts of Confederate soldiers, spread horrendous rumors, burned crosses, and published terrifying broadsides designed to persuade the freedmen that it was unhealthy for them to participate in politics:

Niggers and Leaguers, get out of the way,
We're born of the night and we vanish by day.
No rations have we, but the flesh of man—
And love niggers best—the Ku Klux Klan;
We catch 'em alive and roast 'em whole,
Then hand 'em around with a sharpened pole.
Whole Leagues have been eaten, not leaving a man,
And went away hungry—the Ku Klux Klan. . . .

Congress struck at the Klan by passing three Force Acts (1870–71) to protect Negro voters. These laws placed elections under federal jurisdiction and imposed fines and prison sentences on persons convicted of interfering with any citizen's exercise of the franchise. Federal troops were dispatched to areas where the Klan was strong. But the main reason the Klan failed to intimidate many Negroes was that very few important white southerners cooperated with it. Planters and merchants accepted the tactics of the Union League as politically necessary and were repelled by the violence and underhandedness of the nightriders. As a result, the Klan had influence only in isolated areas dominated by riffraff and poor whites; by 1871 it had almost disappeared.

However, with the passage of time, the planters and merchants began to reconsider their alliance with the Radicals. Few of them had a very high opinion of Negroes to begin with, and close contact in politics did not improve this opinion, especially when the freedmen, growing accustomed to independence and political power, began demanding more than even a broad-minded southerner thought seemly. The constant pressure of other southerners, who treated every scalawag as a traitor, also had a gradually increasing effect.

As this better type of scalawag became disaffected, the Radical governments began to crumble. Suddenly it became respectable to intimidate Negro voters. Beginning in 1874 a number of movements, such as the "Mississippi plan," spread through the South. Instead of hiding behind masks and operating in the dark, these terrorists donned red shirts, organized into military companies, and paraded openly. The Mississippi red-shirts seized militant Negroes and whipped them publicly. Killings were frequent. When the Negroes dared to fight back, the well-organized whites easily put them to rout. In other states similar organizations sprang up. Negroes soon learned to stay home on election day. Thereafter, one by one, "Conservative" parties—Democratic in national affairs—took over southern state governments. Angry northern Radicals attributed these Democratic victories entirely to the intimidation of Negro voters, but this was only a partial explanation. The increasing solidarity of the whites was equally significant.

No degree of southern white unity could have led to the overthrow of the carpetbag governments if northern public opinion had remained as determined to defend the Negro's political rights as it had been in 1867. By the mid-seventies this was clearly not the case, and for a number of reasons. Many northerners had supported the Radical policy only out of irritation with President Johnson. After his retirement, their enthusiasm waned. The war was fading into the past and with it the worst of the bad feeling it had generated. Northern voters could still be stirred by references to the sacrifices Republicans had made to save the Union and by reminders that the Democratic party was the organization of rebels, Copperheads, and the Ku Klux Klan. Yet nostalgic emotional appeals could not push legislation through Congress nor convince northerners that it was still necessary to maintain large armed forces in the South. Nationalism was reasserting

ALABAMA DEPARTMENT OF ARCHIVES AND HISTORY

A graphic warning by the Alabama Klan to scalawags and carpetbaggers, "those great pests of Southern society"; from the Tuscaloosa Independent Monitor.

itself. Men began to recall that Washington and Jefferson had been Virginians, that Andrew Jackson was Carolina-born. Since most northerners had little real love or respect for the Negro, their interest in his welfare flagged once they felt reasonably certain that he would not actually be re-enslaved if left to his own devices in the South.

Grant as President

Other matters increasingly occupied the attention of northern voters. The expansion of industry and the continued rapid development of the West, much stimulated by a new wave of railroad building, loomed more important to many than the fortunes of Negroes and "rebels." Growth did not mean universal prosperity; beginning in 1873, when a stock market panic struck at public confidence, economic difficulties plagued the country for nearly a decade. Heated controversies arose over the tariff, with western agricultural interests seeking to force reductions from the high levels established during the war, and over the handling of the wartime "greenback" paper money, with debtor groups and aggressive new manufacturers favoring expansion of the supply of dollars still further and conservative merchants and bankers tending to argue for retiring the greenbacks in order to get back to a "sound" currency. These controversies cut across party lines somewhat, but they tended to weaken the Republicans or at least to divert their attention from conditions in the South.

Still more damaging to the Republicans was the failure of Ulysses S. Grant to live up to expectations as President. Qualities that had made Grant a fine military leader for a democracy—his dislike of political maneuvering and his simple belief that the popular will could best be observed in the actions of Congress—made him a poor Chief Executive. Part of his appeal to the politicians had been their conviction that he would not try to dominate Congress. The drive to make the legislative branch of the government supreme had not ended when the Senate acquitted Andrew Johnson. "The executive department of a republic like ours should be subordinate to the legislative department," said Senator John Sherman of Ohio, brother of the conqueror of Atlanta. "The President should obey and enforce the laws, leaving to the people the duty of correcting any errors committed by their representatives." Grant accepted this point of view. When Congress failed to act upon his suggestion that the quality of the civil service needed improvement, he announced meekly that if Congress did nothing, he would assume the country did not want anything done and dropped the subject. Grant remained independent-minded and honest, but his independence took such forms as appointing his Cabinet without consulting the politicians and thus saddling himself with men who added almost nothing to the political weight of his administration, and his honesty was of the naive type that made him the dupe of unscrupulous friends and schemers.

His most serious weakness as President was his failure to develop a coherent program to deal with economic and social problems, but the one that injured him and the Republicans most was his inability to cope with corruption in government. Grant, of course, did not cause the corruption, nor did he participate in the remotest way in the rush to "fatten at the public trough," as the reformers of the day might have put it. Corruption flourished, in part because the times conspired to encourage materialism: people tended to consider the accumulation of wealth more important than the means used to acquire wealth. Furthermore, many persons were reacting against the idealism and self-sacrifice of the war years, which had cost the nation so dearly. Nevertheless, Grant did nothing to prevent the scandals that disgraced his administration and, out of a misplaced belief in the sanctity of friendship, he protected some of the worst culprits and allowed calculating tricksters to use his good name and the prestige of his high office to advance their own interests at the country's expense.

The worst of the scandals—such as the Whiskey Ring affair, which implicated Grant's private secretary, Orville E. Babcock, and cost the government millions in tax revenue, and the defalcations of Secretary of War William W. Belknap in the management of Indian affairs—did not become public knowledge during Grant's first term. However, in 1872 a reform group in the Repub-

Harper's Weekly, AUGUST 24, 1872

Thomas Nast was a staunch Grant man; in a Harper's Weekly *cartoon, done during the 1872 campaign, Greeley (center) and Charles Sumner urge a Negro to "clasp hands" with a Klansman and a Tammany Hall instigator of Civil War draft riots.*

lican party, alarmed by rumors of corruption and disappointed by the failure of the President to achieve civil service reform, organized the Liberal Republican party and nominated Horace Greeley, the able but eccentric editor of the New York *Tribune*, for President. The Democrats also nominated Greeley, although he had devoted his whole political life to flailing that party in the *Tribune*, and the obvious expediency of this, together with Greeley's temperamental unsuitability for the Presidency, made the campaign a fiasco for the reformers. Grant triumphed easily, with a popular majority of nearly 800,000. Greeley carried only six states, none north of Maryland and Kentucky. Had the Liberal Republicans nominated a stronger candidate–Charles Francis Adams, the distinguished former minister to Great Britain, was a possibility–they would probably have lost the election in any case but might have been able to gather strength in defeat for future contests. The choice of Greeley marked them, unfairly, as "impractical visionaries."

Nevertheless, the defection of the Liberal Republicans hurt the Republican party in Congress. And when, no longer hampered as in the Presidential contest by Greeley's notoriety and Grant's fame, the Democrats carried the House of Representatives in the 1874 elections, it was clear that the days of military control in the South were ending. The trend toward white solidarity therefore speeded up, until by the end of 1875 only three states, South Carolina, Florida, and Louisiana, were still under Republican control. As a middle western newspaperman admitted to Carl Schurz, a prominent Liberal Republican, the Republican party in the South was "dead as a doornail." The reporter reflected the thinking of thousands when he added: "We ought to have a sound sensible republican . . . for the next President as a measure of safety; but only on the condition of absolute noninterference in Southern local affairs, for which there is no further need or excuse."

The Disputed Election of 1876

Against this background, the Presidential election of 1876 took place. Since corruption in government was the most widely discussed issue, in choosing their Presidential candidate the Republicans passed over their most attractive political personality, the dynamic James G. Blaine, Speaker of the House of Representatives, for Blaine had been connected with some chicanery involving railroad securities. Instead they nominated Governor Rutherford B. Hayes of Ohio, a former general with an unsmirched reputation. The Democrats picked Governor Samuel J. Tilden of New York, a prominent lawyer who had attracted national attention for his part in breaking up the Tweed Ring in New York City.

In November Tilden triumphed easily in all the southern states from which the carpetbagger regimes had been ejected. He also carried New York, New Jersey, Connecticut, and Indiana. In the three "unredeemed" southern states, Florida, South Carolina, and Louisiana, he also won apparent majorities. This seemed to give him 203 electoral votes to Hayes's 165, with a popular plurality in the neighborhood of 250,000 out of over 8 million votes cast.

However, Republican leaders had anticipated the possible loss of Florida, South Carolina, and Louisiana and were prepared to use their control of the election machinery in these states to throw out sufficient Democratic ballots to alter the results if doing so would change the national outcome. Realizing that the 19 electoral votes of these states were exactly enough to elect their man, they telegraphed their henchmen on the scene to go into action. The board of canvassers in each of these states invalidated Democratic ballots in wholesale lots (13,000 in Louisiana, for example) and filed returns showing Hayes the winner. Naturally enough, the local Democrats protested vigorously and filed their own returns.

The Constitution provides that Presidential electors must meet in their respective states to vote and forward the results to "the Seat of the Government." There, it adds, "the President of the Senate shall, in the Presence of the Senate and House of Representatives, open all the Certificates, *and the Votes shall then be counted.*" But who was to do the counting? The House was Democratic, the Senate Republican; neither would agree to allow the other to do the job. Finally, on January 29, 1877, scarcely a month before inauguration day, Congress created an Electoral Commission to decide the disputed cases. The commission consisted of five senators (three Republicans and two Democrats), five representatives (three Democrats and two Republicans) and five justices of the Supreme Court (two Democrats, two Republicans, and one "independent" judge, David Davis). Since it was a foregone conclusion that the others would vote for their party no matter what the evidence, Davis would presumably swing the balance in the interest of fairness.

Unfortunately at this crucial moment, the Illinois legislature elected Davis senator! He had to resign from the commission. Since, in those partisan times, independents were rare even on the Supreme Court, no neutral was available to replace him. The vacancy went to Associate Justice Joseph P. Bradley of New Jersey, a Republican.

Evidence presented before the commission revealed a disgraceful picture of election shenanigans. On the one hand, in all three disputed states Democrats had clearly cast a majority of the votes; on the other, it was equally unquestionable that many Negroes had been forcibly prevented from voting. South Carolina "rifle clubs," at least one supported by a battery of artillery, had presented so overwhelming a display that the Negroes were completely cowed. In Florida and Louisiana intimidation was almost as effective. The evidence also showed, however, that all three Republican election boards had completely disregarded the facts in voiding Democratic votes.

The sordid truth was that both sides had been at fault in each of the states. Lew Wallace, a northern politician later famous as the author of the novel *Ben Hur*, visited Louisiana and Florida shortly after the election. "It is terrible to see the extent to which all classes go in their determination to win," he wrote his wife from Florida. "Money and intimidation can obtain the oath of white men as well as black to any required statement. . . . If we win, our methods are subject to impeachment for possible fraud. If the enemy win, it is the same thing." The governor of Louisiana was reported willing to sell his state's electoral votes for $200,000. The Florida election board was supposed to have offered itself to Tilden for the same price. "That seems to be the standard figure," Tilden remarked ruefully to a friend.

Most modern authorities take the view that in a fair election the Republicans would have carried South Carolina and Louisiana, but that Florida would have gone to Tilden, thus giving him the election by 188 electoral votes to 181. In the last analysis, this opinion has been arrived at simply by counting white and black heads: Negroes were in the majority in South Carolina and Louisiana. Amid the excitement and confusion of early 1877, however, even a Solomon would have been hard pressed to judge rightly amid the mass of rumors, lies, and contradictory statements, and the Electoral Commission was not composed of Solomons. Although shaken by the news of Davis' election to the Senate, the Democrats had some hopes that Justice Bradley would be sympathetic to their case, for he was known to be opposed to harsh reconstruction policies. On the eve of the commission's decision in the Florida controversy, he was apparently ready to vote in favor of Tilden. But the Republicans subjected him to tremendous political pressure. When he read his opinion on February 8, it was for Hayes. Thus, by a vote of 8 to 7, the commission awarded Florida's electoral votes to the Republicans.

The rest of the proceedings were routine. Vote after vote, both upon details and in the final decisions in the other cases, went exactly according to party lines. The atmosphere of judicial injuiry and deliberation was a façade. With the spitefulness common to rejected suitors, the Democrats assailed Bradley until, as the New York *Times* put it, he seemed like "a middle-aged St. Sebastian, stuck full of Democratic darts." Unlike Sebastian, however, Bradley was protected against the arrows by the armor of his Republican faith. On February 28 the commission completed its work, having assigned all the disputed electoral votes (including one in Oregon, where the Democratic governor had seized upon a technicality to replace a single Republican elector with a Democrat) to Hayes.

To such a level had the republic of Jefferson and John Adams descended! The American democratic tradition, shaken by the South's refusal to go along with the majority in 1860, and also by the suppression of civil rights during the rebellion, further weakened by both military intervention and the intimidation of Negroes in the South during reconstruction, seemed now completely destroyed, a mere farce. Cynics claimed that American politics had become "Mexicanized." Democrats talked of not being bound by so obviously partisan a judgment. According to Tilden's campaign manager, the respected iron

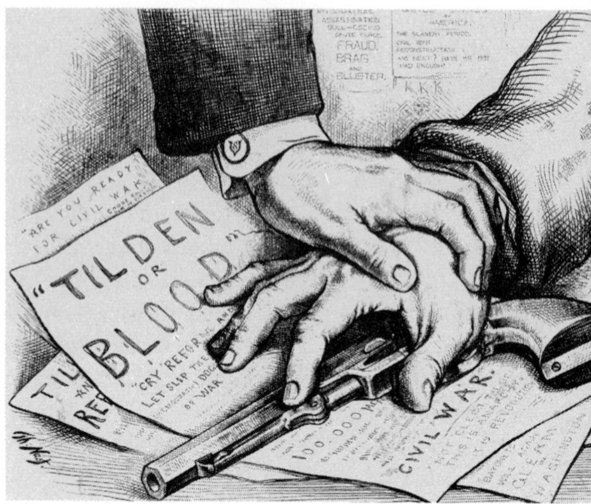

Cartoonist Nast applauded Tilden's statement that the decision of the Electoral Commission must be accepted, staying the threat of civil war in 1877.

manufacturer Abram S. Hewitt, angry Democrats in 15 states, chiefly war veterans, were readying themselves to march on Washington to force the inauguration of Tilden. Tempers flared in Congress, where some spoke ominously of a filibuster that would prevent the recording of the electoral vote and leave the country, on March 4, with no President at all.

The Compromise of 1877

Fortunately, forces for compromise had been at work behind the scenes in Washington for some time. While northern Democrats threatened to fight to the last ditch, many southern Democrats were willing to accept Hayes if they could gain something in exchange. Nearly all the southern congressmen were more interested in ridding their section once and for all of federal interference than in electing a Democratic President. If Hayes would promise to remove the troops and allow the southern states to manage their internal affairs by themselves, these men would be sorely tempted to go along with his election. A more specialized but extremely important group consisted of the ex-Whig planters and merchants who had reluctantly abandoned the carpetbag governments and who were always uncomfortable when in alliance with the poor whites. If Hayes would agree to let the South alone and perhaps appoint a conservative southerner to his Cabinet, these men would support him willingly, eventually hoping to restore the two-party system that had been destroyed in the South during the 1850's.

Other southerners had economic interests congenial to Republican policies. The Texas and Pacific Railway Company, chartered to build a line from Marshall, Texas, to San Diego, had won wide support in the South, and friends of Hayes were quick to point out that a Republican administration would be more likely to help the Texas and Pacific than a retrenchment-minded Democratic one. Ohio Congressman James A. Garfield urged Hayes to find "some discreet way" of showing these southerners that he favored "internal improvements." Hayes replied: "Your views are so nearly the same as mine that I need not say a word."

Tradition has it that a great compromise between the sections was worked out during a dramatic, eleventh-hour meeting at the Wormley Hotel in Washington on February 26. Actually, as C. Vann Woodward has demonstrated in his important book *Reunion and Reaction*, the negotiations were long-drawn-out and informal, and the Wormley conference was but one of many. At any rate, with the tacit support of many Democrats, the electoral vote was formally counted by the president of the Senate on March 2, and Hayes was declared elected, 185 votes to 184.

Like all compromises, this agreement was not entirely satisfactory, and like most, it was not honored in every detail. Hayes recalled the last troops from South Carolina and Louisiana in April. He appointed a former Confederate general, David M. Key of Tennessee, as his postmaster general and delegated to him the congenial task of finding southerners willing to serve their country as officials of a Republican administration. The new alliance of ex-Whigs and northern Republicans did not flourish, however, and the South remained solidly Democratic. The hoped-for federal aid for the Texas and Pacific did not materialize. The major significance of the compromise, one of the great intersectional political accommodations of American history, has been well summarized by Professor Woodward:

> The Compromise of 1877 marked the abandonment of principles and force and a return to the traditional ways of expediency and concession. The compromise laid the political foundation for reunion. It established a new sectional truce that proved more enduring than any previous one and provided a settlement for an issue that had troubled American politics for more than a generation. It wrote an end to Reconstruction and recognized a new regime in the South. More profoundly than Constitutional amendments and wordy statutes it shaped the future of four million freedmen and their progeny for generations to come.

For most of the former slaves, this future was to be gloomy. The period following 1877 marks what one historian has aptly called "the nadir" of the history of the Negro in the United States. Forgotten in the North, manipulated and then callously rejected by the South, rebuffed by the Supreme Court, voiceless in national affairs, he and his descendants were condemned in the interests of sectional harmony to lives of poverty, indignity, and little hope. Meanwhile, the rest of the United States continued its golden march toward wealth and power.

SUPPLEMENTARY READING J.G. Randall and David Donald, *The Civil War and Reconstruction* (1961), is as excellent a brief treatment of postwar readjustments as it is of the war years, but there are a number of longer studies that the student will find rewarding. Of recent works, K.M. Stampp, *The Era of Reconstruction** (1964), and J.H. Franklin, *Reconstruction: After the Civil War** (1961), are outstanding. E.M. Coulter, *The South During Reconstruction* (1947), presents a pro-southern point of view and is strong on economic developments. The older approach to the period, stressing the excesses of Negro-influenced governments and criticizing the Radicals, derives from the seminal work of W.A. Dunning, *Reconstruction, Political and Economic** (1907). W.E.B. Du Bois, *Black Reconstruction in*

*America** (1935), militantly pro-Negro, was the pioneering counterattack against the Dunning view.

Lincoln's ideas about reconstruction are analyzed in W.B. Hesseltine, *Lincoln's Plan of Reconstruction** (1960), and in many of the Lincoln volumes mentioned in earlier chapters. There is no satisfactory biography of Andrew Johnson: both G.F. Milton, *The Age of Hate: Andrew Johnson and the Radicals* (1930), and Milton Lomask, *Andrew Johnson: President on Trial* (1960), are far too sympathetic in approach. Of the special studies of Johnson's battle with the congressional Radicals, H.K. Beale, *The Critical Year* (1930), takes Johnson's side, but recent studies have been very critical of the President. See especially H.L. Trefousse, *The Radical Republicans: Lincoln's Vanguard for Racial Justice* (1969), E.L. McKitrick, *Andrew Johnson and Reconstruction** (1960), LaWanda and J.H. Cox, *Politics, Principle, and Prejudice: 1865–1866* (1963), and W.R. Brock, *An American Crisis: Congress and Reconstruction** (1963), the last a particularly thoughtful analysis of the whole era.

A number of biographies provide information helpful in understanding the Radicals. These include B.P. Thomas and H.M. Hyman, *Stanton* (1962), F.M. Brodie, *Thaddeus Stevens** (1959), R.N. Current, *Old Thad Stevens* (1942), and H.L. Trefousse, *Benjamin Franklin Wade* (1963), J.M. McPherson, *The Struggle for Equality: Abolitionists and the Negro in the Civil War and Reconstruction** (1964), is also valuable. On the Fourteenth Amendment, see Joseph James, *The Framing of the Fourteenth Amendment** (1956); on the Fifteenth Amendment, see William Gillette, *The Right to Vote: Politics and the Passage of the Fifteenth Amendment* (1965).

Conditions in the South during reconstruction are discussed in all the works cited in the first paragraph. Of special studies, W.L. Fleming, *Civil War and Reconstruction in Alabama* (1905), and J.W. Garner, *Reconstruction in Mississippi** (1901), represent the best of those adopting the Dunning approach. More recent "revisionist" state studies include V.L. Wharton, *The Negro in Mississippi** (1947), C.E. Wynes, *Race Relations in Virginia* (1961), W.L. Rose, *Rehearsal for Reconstruction: The Port Royal Experiment** (1964), and Joel Williamson, *After Slavery: The Negro in South Carolina During Reconstruction** (1965). G.R. Bentley, *A History of the Freedmen's Bureau* (1955), discusses the work of that important organization, but see also W.S. McFeely, *Yankee Stepfather: General O.O. Howard and the Freedmen* (1968). On the Ku Klux Klan, see S.F. Horn, *The Invisible Empire* (1939).

F.A. Shannon, *The Farmer's Last Frontier** (1945), is good on southern agriculture during reconstruction. For the growth of industry, see Broadus Mitchell, *The Rise of Cotton Mills in the South* (1921), and J.F. Stover, *The Railroads of the South* (1955).

The standard treatment of Grant's Presidency is W.B. Hesseltine, *Ulysses S. Grant: Politician* (1935), but Allan Nevins, *Hamilton Fish: The Inner History of the Grant Administration* (1936), and Matthew Josephson, *The Politicos** (1938), contain much additional information. On the election of 1868, see C.H. Coleman, *The Election of 1868* (1933), and Stewart Mitchell, *Horatio Seymour* (1938); on the reform movement of the period within the Republican party, see E.D. Ross, *The Liberal Republican Movement* (1919), J.G. Sproat, *"The Best Men": Liberal Reformers in the Gilded Age* (1968), and M.B. Duberman, *Charles Francis Adams** (1961). For the disputed election of 1876 and the compromise following it, consult C.V. Woodward, *Reunion and Reaction** (1951), Harry Barnard, *Rutherford B. Hayes and His America* (1954), and Allan Nevins, *Abram S. Hewitt* (1935). P.H. Buck, *The Road to Reunion** (1937), traces the gradual reconciliation of North and South after 1865.

*Available in paperback.

PORTFOLIO

IV *The Plains Indians*

The history of the plains Indians, those undying if often-killed favorites of American entertainment, is testimony that the truth is stranger and more interesting than the fiction. For about a century, from roughly 1780 to 1880, the plains tribes maintained a unique and colorful existence, living in the midst of an immense grassland, feeding upon the numberless buffalo, mobile and free on their fleet ponies. Much of the vitality of this culture, however, was a direct result of the Indians' adoption of such elements of the white man's civilization as horses, guns, and metal tools. And in the end the white man's lust for land, his diseases, and the deadly efficiency of his mechanical genius devastated the plains civilization.

Fortunately, at the height of this cultural flowering in the middle decades of the 19th century, artists such as George Catlin, Carl Bodmer, Paul Kane, Friedrich Kurz, and Alfred Jacob Miller, as well as the Indians themselves, created a vivid, accurate pictorial record of plains life. For example, Bodmer's 1832 portrait above of the Mandan chief Mato-Tope (Four Bears) is both a skillful work of art and a finely detailed reproduction of war paint patterns—even to the yellow hand painted over Mato-Tope's heart, which was meant to protect him during hand-to-hand combat.

Horse Indians

In 1834 the western painter George Catlin wrote, "A Comanche on his feet is out of his element, . . . almost as awkward as a monkey on the ground, without a limb or a branch to cling to; but the moment he lays his hand upon his horse, his face even becomes handsome, and he gracefully flies away like a different being." Before the coming of the horse, the plains were populated by a few scattered tribes who found hunting buffalo on foot a risky business at best. For almost a century and a half after Coronado's trek from Mexico into the plains in the 1540's, the Spaniards were largely successful in keeping their horses out of Indian hands. But after a bloody revolt by the Pueblos in 1680 loosened Spain's grip on the Southwest, the horse spread northward rapidly. By 1780 the plains tribes were making full use of this highly efficient means of pursuing the buffalo, and the population of the region had tripled to an estimated figure of 150,000.

KENNEDY GALLERIE

MUSEUM OF THE AMERICAN INDIAN, HEYE FOUNDATION

The elkskin painting above of a buffalo hunt is the work of a Crow artist and dates from about 1895. Three cowboys (upper left) suggest that by this time Indians no longer hunted alone.

George Catlin's painting at left, c. 1835, shows a Crow chieftain and his horse in full battle array. It is evident from Catlin's portrait why historian Walter Prescott Webb spoke of plains warriors as "The Red Knights of the Prairie."

At right is an 1862 sketch of a Cree saddle made of buffalo skin and stitched with buffalo sinew. Women's saddles had both a pommel and a cantle.

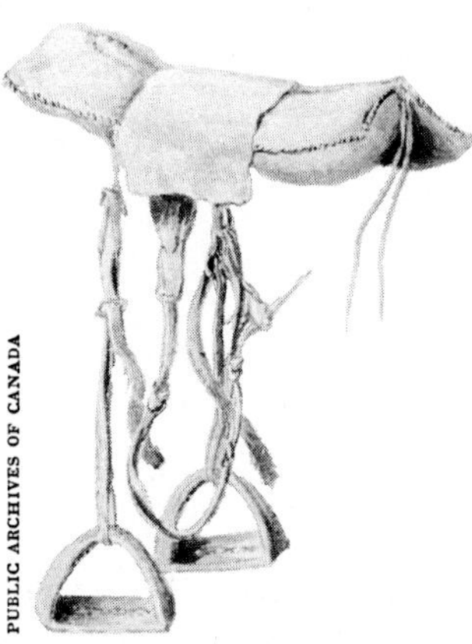

PUBLIC ARCHIVES OF CANADA

Sioux Camp

This remarkable photograph by J.H.C. Grabill shows a large Sioux encampment near the Pine Ridge Reservation in South Dakota. It was probably taken in March 1891 after the "battle" of Wounded Knee, in which some 150 Hunkpapa Sioux, including 44 women and 18 children, were massacred by the Seventh Cavalry. An encampment as extensive as this was rare until the plains tribes became wards of

LIBRARY OF CONGRESS

the government and were confined on reservations. Except for special occasions—a tribal festival, a full-scale buffalo hunt, a war council—food was too scarce to permit an entire tribe to camp in one spot. The making, moving, and caring for the tepee was woman's work. In camp the men did little except feast, attend tribal councils and meetings of warrior societies, and decorate their tepees with figures and symbols based on highly valued dreams and visions and on past hunting and martial exploits.

The Nomadic Life

The plains Indian is best known as a wanderer who traveled by horse to follow the buffalo. He was indeed a nomad, but it should not be forgotten that the horse was a late-comer to the plains and that for thousands of years a few tribes had been farming the more fertile parts of the region as well as hunting buffalo. In the 18th and 19th centuries this pattern persisted. Along the upper Missouri in present-day North Dakota, for example, the Hidatsas and the Mandans continued to live in permanent earthen lodges, to farm, and to hunt buffalo only part-time, even after acquiring the horse.

But for most plains Indians farther west, such as the Arapahos, Crow, Comanches, Cheyenne, Apaches, Blackfeet, Sioux, and Kiowas, life was truly nomadic, spent ever on the move. They might pursue the roaming buffalo for hundreds of miles, taking food, clothing, and shelter with them packed on their travois. While traveling they subsisted on pemmican, an odoriferous but nourishing preserve concocted of dried meat, berries, bone marrow, and melted fat. The hunting grounds of the various tribes were only vaguely defined and intertribal contact was frequent, especially for trading purposes. On these occasions the nomads would barter their buffalo pelts and meat for corn and other agricultural products raised by the more sedentary peoples who made their homes on the fringes of the plains.

SMITHSONIAN INSTITUTION

Above: As Alfred Jacob Miller's Migration of the Pawnees *shows, nomadic life imposed a grueling routine. With the travois, dogs could drag 40-pound loads 5 or 6 miles a day.*

Left: Frederick Kurz drew these Hidatsas portaging their bullboats on the upper Missouri in 1851. The bullboat was made of buffalo hide stretched over a willow framework.

Right: A Mandan woman carrying a pack leads a loaded dog sled on which her child rides across the frozen Missouri in what is now North Dakota. A Bodmer water color, 1834.

COE COLLECTION, YALE UNIVERSITY LIBRARY

NORTHERN NATURAL GAS COMPANY COLLECTION, JOSLYN ART MUSEUM

The Buffalo

"Again and again that morning rang out the same welcome cry of *buffalo, buffalo!* . . . At noon the plain before us was alive with thousands of buffalo—bulls, cows, and calves—all moving rapidly as we drew near. . . . In a moment I was in the midst of a cloud, half suffocated by the dust and stunned by the trampling of the flying herd; but I was drunk with the chase and cared for nothing but the buffalo." That was how historian Francis Parkman was affected by a buffalo hunt in 1846, the year before H.G. Hines painted the scene below. For Parkman the hunt was an exhilarating experience, but for the plains Indian it was the central act of his life, combining necessity, passion, and sport. Alfred Jacob Miller's *Yell of Triumph* (right) captures something of this feeling.

Once killed and butchered, there was little the buffalo did not provide. From the carcass came fresh meat for feasting and dried meat for lean times. The skin provided blankets, moccasins, mittens, shirts, leggings, dresses, and underclothes—and a "canvas" for the artist. Sinew was turned into thread and bowstrings; bones into farming tools; horns into cups, ladles, and spoons; the stomach into a water bottle. Even vanity was served. The rough side of a buffalo tongue was used as a hairbrush and the oily fat became a plains hair tonic.

WALTERS ART GALLERY (© 1951 UNIVERSITY OF OKLAHOMA PRESS)

ROYAL ONTARIO MUSEUM, UNIVERSITY OF TORONTO

Religion and the Hunt

In common with many primitive peoples, the plains Indians drew no clear distinction between the natural and the supernatural. They paid as much attention to the one as to the other, believing that all things had spirits and that these spirits controlled the natural world. No aspect of plains life reflects this harmonious fusion of natural and supernatural better than the buffalo hunt.

A hunt was as carefully organized and as skillfully managed as a modern military operation. In early spring the various bands of the tribe would gather at a predetermined place. There the chiefs and the elders convened a council and deliberated their strategy and tactics. To ensure that plans were followed precisely, one of the warrior societies policed the hunt while scouts kept tabs on the movements of the herd. Once the "battle" was joined, the animals were slaughtered until all needs were met. Little seemed left to chance.

Yet however effective and well organized the hunters were, they believed that without the assistance of the spirits the herds would not come within range, the hunters would lack courage and skill at the crucial moment, and ultimately the harmonious relationship between the shaggy "four-leggeds" and the "two-leggeds" would be destroyed. To insure the overall success of the hunt, the tribesmen therefore devoted as much attention to religious ceremonies and "medicine signs" as they did to planning, discipline, and the perfection of their hunting skills.

Devices for luring the buffalo varied from tribe to tribe. Carl Bodmer's water color of Assiniboin "magic" (lower left) was painted in 1834.

Of grimmer composition is the Mandan "medicine sign" for attracting the herds reproduced at the right.

For centuries before the plains Indians obtained the horse, a favorite method of buffalo hunting was impounding, as illustrated below by Canadian artist Paul Kane in 1845.

NORTHERN NATURAL GAS COMPANY COLLECTION, JOSLYN ART MUSEUM

SMITHSONIAN INSTITUTION

ROYAL ONTARIO MUSEUM, UNIVERSITY OF TORONTO

Bodmer's painting of a Mandan Bull Society dance, held periodically to draw the herds close to the village, reflects the plains Indians' intense feelings toward the buffalo.

After the Hunt

Plains life was not all buffalo hunting. There were days to be spent around the domestic hearth, children to be raised, ceremonies to be performed, games to be played. Work, other than hunting and making war, was generally for women. Education was in the school of experience—a boy learned his role by riding alongside his father, while a girl's mother was her tutor in the arts of the tepee. Elaborate rituals at the onset of puberty were rare, although in most tribes young men did go off on a lonely vigil in search of a vision to guide them. A young man could marry when he possessed the requisite number of horses to give to the girl's family as tokens of his esteem. Courtship largely consisted of the lover playing a flute to his sequestered sweetheart. There was no elaborate marriage ceremony in the modern sense, although custom demanded certain ceremonial observances. The bride, while very much the servant of her husband, was not considered an inferior being.

Hunting and war were in part sport, but they did not exhaust the plains Indians' delight in recreation. Horse racing and dice gave free rein to their love of chance; lacrosse and foot races provided tests of their athletic skills; storytelling presented the central myths of their culture; and clowning gave vent to a Rabelaisian wit.

WALTERS ART GALLERY (© 1951 UNIVERSITY OF OKLAHOMA PRESS)

NEW YORK PUBLIC LIBRARY

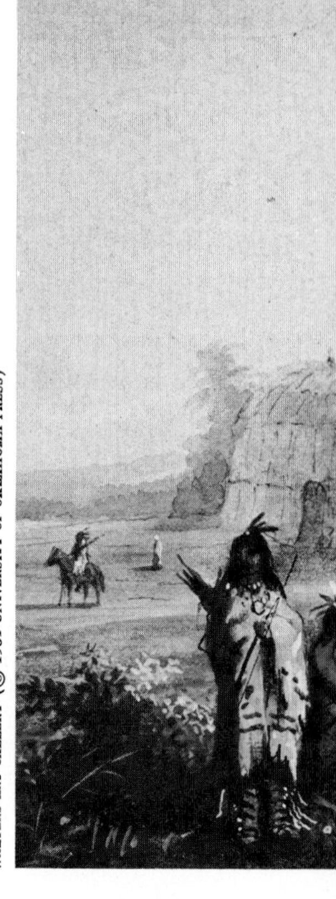

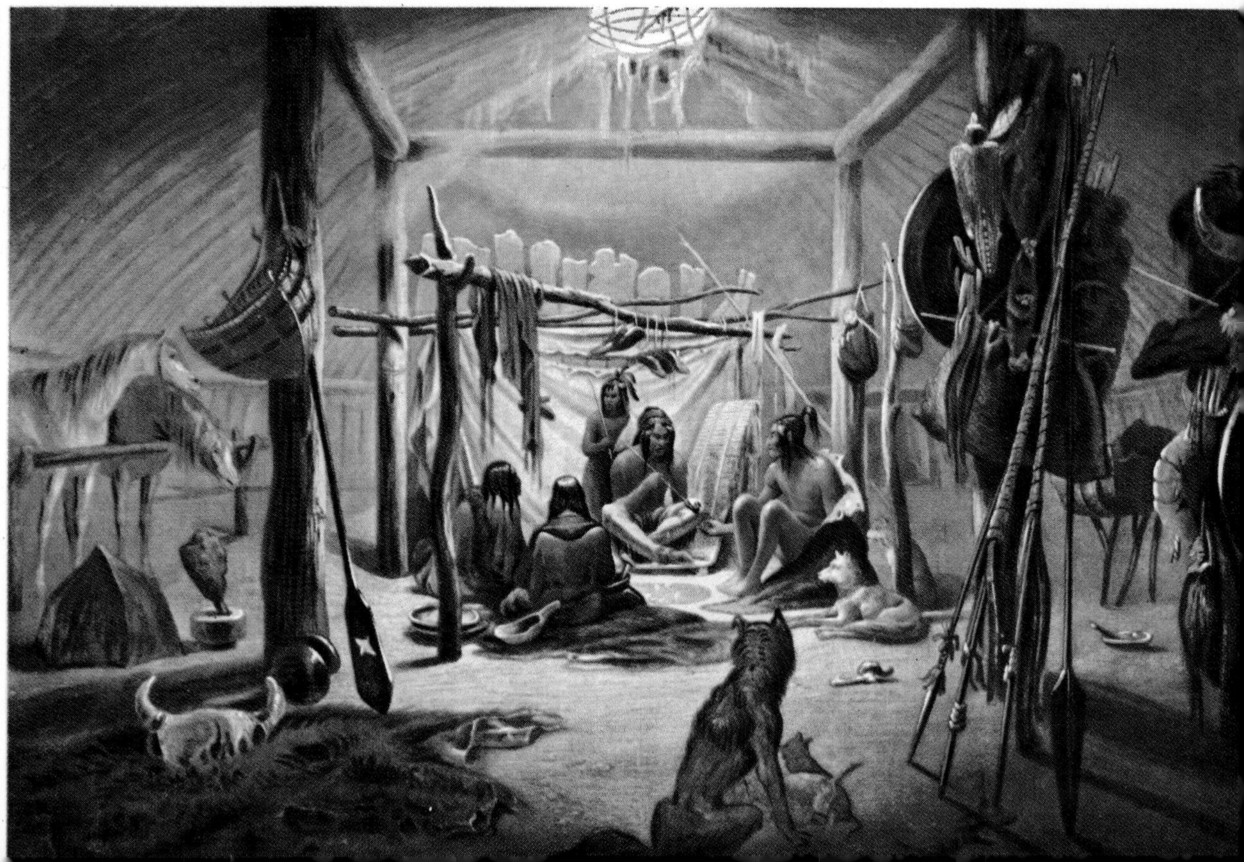

Not all horse-riding, buffalo-hunting plains Indians lived in tepees. The earthen lodges of the Mandans (at left, by Miller, and opposite, by Bodmer) each housed several families, a few favorite horses, a number of dogs, and a wide range of equipment for cooking, hunting, and ceremonial observances. The plains tribes enjoyed rough stick and ball games such as lacrosse (sketches on this page) and shinny, an early rugged form of field hockey favored by plains women. But naturally enough, as Paul Kane's painting below of a Blackfoot horse race suggests, equestrian games took the spotlight. Since Indians loved a sporting bet, games were carefully refereed to ensure fair play.

ROYAL ONTARIO MUSEUM, UNIVERSITY OF TORONTO

The Road to Glory

War was the greatest game of all; it was also the plains Indian's career, hobby, and the touchstone of his honor and prestige. He was told from childhood, as a Blackfoot litany put it, that "It is bad to live to be old. Better to die young fighting bravely in battle." Young boys listened to the elaborate recountings of the valor of a successful war party or to the derisive mocking directed at a man unlucky enough to be accounted a coward as though they were hearing sermons on heaven and hell. They longed for the day when they could join a warrior society and embrace its Spartan discipline. In their teens they fasted alone in the hope of seeing a vision of the spirit of their adoptive father (usually an animal or an impressive natural phenomenon). This spirit would confirm the warrior's identity and give instructions for the "medicine bundle" that was to protect him in battle.

On occasion tribal war did have an economic motive, as in the defense of hunting grounds, but its usual objective was glory and all its trappings. Honor was quantified by the system of counting coups, which were won not just by mere slaughter, but also by such feats as stealing an enemy's favorite horse or touching an armed foe with the hand or with nothing more wounding than a decorated coup stick.

LIBRARY OF CONGRESS

LIBRARY OF CONGRESS

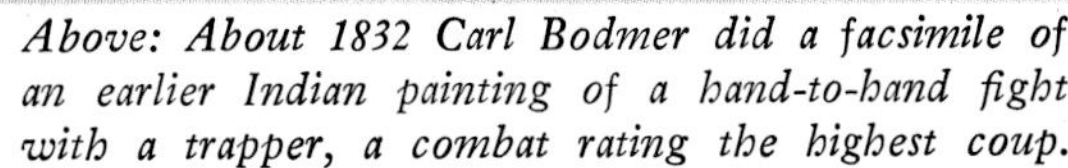

Above: About 1832 Carl Bodmer did a facsimile of an earlier Indian painting of a hand-to-hand fight with a trapper, a combat rating the highest coup.

NEW YORK PUBLIC LIBRARY

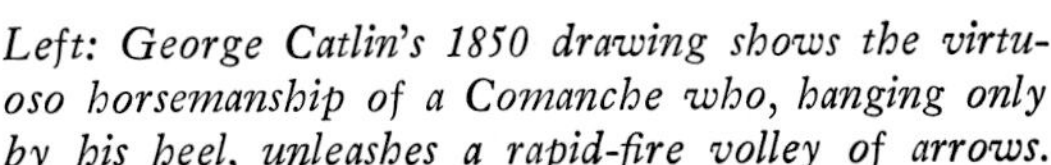

Left: George Catlin's 1850 drawing shows the virtuoso horsemanship of a Comanche who, hanging only by his heel, unleashes a rapid-fire volley of arrows.

Opposite: Among the artifacts in Bodmer's print is a coup stick, complete with feathers for the number of coups, above the arrow at right. The edged weapon at right is a type of tomahawk, and at lower center is a war shield decorated with "medicine."

OKLAHOMA HISTORICAL SOCIETY

This Apache skin painting shows a blending of plains and southwestern cultural elements. The ceremony in progress is a girl's puberty rite, rare in the northern plains but much observed in the Southwest. The rest of the tribe watches from in front of their tepees (a plains element) while the girls, paired with older women who are their guardians and accompanied by posturing medicine men (wearing southwestern-style headdresses), perform a dance around the purifying fire.

Alfred Jacob Miller's painting above, Snake Indian Council *(c. 1840), pictures a tribal powwow as a dignified, ceremonious affair.*

Lovers of Ceremony

Few people have been as self-sufficient as the plains Indians while at the same time professing to be so dependent upon forces outside themselves. The plains resembled the ocean (a metaphor repeatedly appearing in the accounts of white explorers)—vast and mysterious, inspiring both humility and a feeling of what might be called "cosmic togetherness." Far from seeing himself as master of his environment, the Indian felt adrift on a great sea of whispering prairie grass, endlessly searching for the life-giving buffalo that symbolized for him and his people the miraculous world of nature.

Under such circumstances it is hardly surprising that the plains Indian believed himself to be dwelling within a web of supernatural powers. His survival depended upon maintaining contact with these powers; thus he became a seeker of visions and a practicer of rituals, devoted to ceremonies that would bring him into partnership with the cosmos. The primacy of this relationship helps explain the general lack of scientific curiosity in the plains cultures, but it also accounts for an estimable sense of humility and of awe.

MUSEUM OF THE AMERICAN INDIAN, HEYE FOUNDATION

A Shoshoni skin painting that dates from the 1880's portrays in careful detail a ritualistic sun dance as seen from above a tepee.

An Indian Horse Dance.

Art and Artifacts

The artifacts of the plains Indian, like so much else in his culture, combined art with utility. Textiles were poorly developed, pottery limited, and wood carving and stone sculpture almost absent, all for good reasons—cotton was unknown, pottery easily broken in transit, trees few and far between, and stone too heavy to transport. But when it came to making clothes and utensils decorated with quills, beads, paint, feathers, and the fur from that all-purpose beast the buffalo, the plains artisan was in his element. The women dressed and prepared buffalo hides, and then, from beaded moccasin to feathered headdress, made the tribe's clothing, such as the girl's dress at the right. They also cut, fitted, and sewed buffalo hides to make the covering for the tepee, but it was the man's prerogative to decorate the tepee's exterior with his own paintings. The painting reproduced opposite, by Kills Two, an Oglala Sioux, is a striking demonstration of the skill and technical virtuosity of these plains artists.

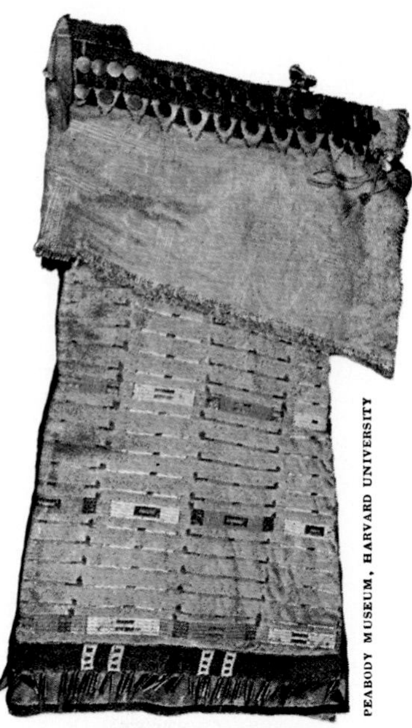

PEABODY MUSEUM, HARVARD UNIVERSITY

The examples below of porcupine quillwork include an Arapaho disk used as a tepee ornament, a Sioux knife sheath, a quill pouch made from an elk bladder, and a decorated tobacco pouch.

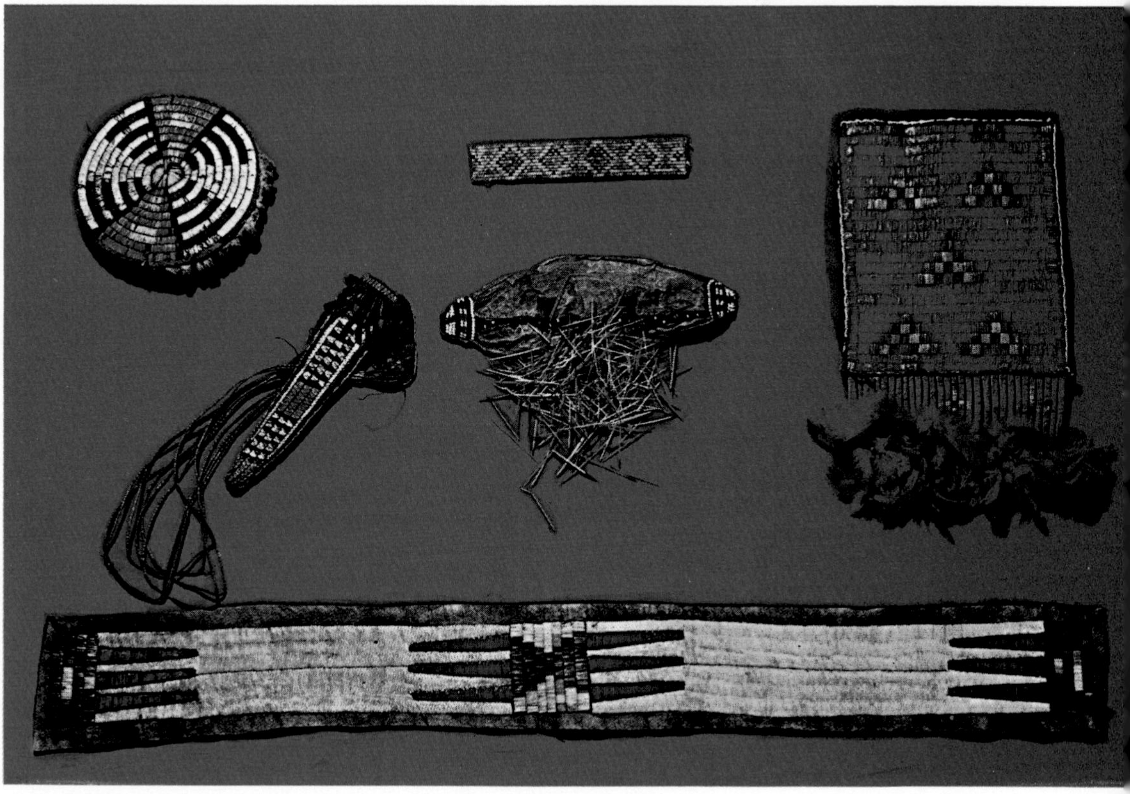

MUSEUM OF THE AMERICAN INDIAN, HEYE FOUNDATION

Changing Ways

In just about 50 years, from 1840 to 1890, the plains civilization reached its apogee and then plunged to the verge of extinction. In his 1885 painting *Caught in the Act*, Charles Russell, the "cowboy artist," depicted a starving Indian family reduced to stealing ranchers' cattle. By this time the plains tribes had suffered the ravages of the white man's diseases, the debasing effects of his whisky, the

MONTANA HISTORICAL SOCIETY

harassment of his army, and the grim hardship resulting from his senseless slaughter of the buffalo. Having smashed the Indian's way of life beyond repair, the government confined him to the reservation. Just before committing suicide, Satanta, a Kiowa chief, spoke for all the plains tribes when he said, "I don't want to settle. I love to roam the prairie. . . . These soldiers cut down my timber, they kill my buffalo, and when I see that, it feels as if my heart would burst with sorrow."

COE COLLECTION, YALE UNIVERSITY LIBRARY

Reproduced above, in a detail, is a heroic Sioux version of the Battle of the Little Big Horn, in which Crazy Horse (center) leads the slaughter of Custer's men. L.A. Huffman's portrait of the Cheyenne scout Red Panther (opposite) offers testimony to the true nobility of the "noble red man."

The Legacy

Although by the end of the 19th century the civilization of the plains tribesmen was "fast traveling to the shades of their fathers, towards the setting sun," the very conquerors who had been unable to live in peace with the Indians surrounded their memory with romance and myth. In defeat the Indian became the "noble savage"; Custer's Last Stand will be remembered as long as Gettysburg or Pearl Harbor. Yet the real importance of the plains Indian stems from his attitude toward life, not merely from his courage and his war skills.

In 1947 John Collier, former Commissioner of Indian Affairs, spoke out for another interpretation of Indian culture. "They had what the world has lost," Collier wrote, ". . . the ancient, lost reverence and passion for human personality, joined with the ancient, lost reverence and passion for the earth and its web of life. . . . They had . . . this power for living . . . as world-view and self-view, as tradition and institution, as practical philosophy dominating their societies, and as an art supreme. . . ."

17

An Age of Exploitation

As Americans turned from fighting and making weapons to more constructive occupations, a surge of activity transformed agriculture, trade, manufacturing, mining, and communication. Immigration, checked somewhat during the war, increased rapidly. Modern America was emerging; expansion was the order of the day. Cities grew in size and number, exerting upon every aspect of life an influence at least as pervasive as that exercised on earlier generations by the frontier. More and more Americans were abandoning the farm for the town and city, supporting themselves by laboring at machines or by scratching out accounts in ledgers, yet such was the expansive force of the time that agriculture did not actually decline. Farm production rose to new heights, and rural society was invigorated by new marketing methods and by the increased use of machinery. At the same time, railroad construction was stimulating and unifying the economy, helping to make possible still larger and more efficient industrial and agricultural enterprises. A continuing flow of gold and silver from western mines excited men's imaginations and their avarice too, while petroleum, the "black gold" discovered in Pennsylvania shortly before the war, gave rise to a new industry soon to become one of the most important in the nation.

"Root, Hog, or Die"

These developments amounted to more than a mere change of scale; they altered the basic structure of society. For nearly a decade after Appomattox, boom conditions existed everywhere outside the South. To some observers, Americans seemed to have abandoned completely all restraints on selfishness in a mad race for personal gain.

The immense resources of the United States, combined with certain aspects of the American character, such as the high value assigned to work and achievement, made the people strongly materialistic. From colonial times onward, they had assumed that prosperity was the natural state of things and shown an inordinate respect for wealth. "When he asked what a man was worth," Henry Steele Commager writes in describing the typical 19th-century American, "he meant material worth, and he was impatient of any but the normal yardstick."

Although the Civil War had many nonmaterialistic aspects—love of country, hatred of slavery, devotion to democratic principles—it greatly encouraged the glorification of material values by demonstrating the relationship between economic power and political and military success. The North's capacity to produce the tools of war had helped preserve the Union; the role of businessmen and manufacturers in winning the struggle was clear to every soldier from General Grant to the lowliest private.

During the emotional letdown that followed the war, Americans became even more enamored of material values. They were tired of sacrifice, eager to act for themselves. Except in their attitude toward the South, still psychologically "outside" the United States, they came to believe more strongly than ever before in a governmental policy of noninterference, or laissez faire. "'Things regulate themselves' . . . means, of course, that God regulates them by his general laws," wrote Professor Francis Bowen of Harvard in his *American Political Economy* (1870). "The progress of the country," said another economist, "is independent of legislation."

Impressed by such logic, Americans, always imbued with the entrepreneurial spirit and never especially noted for their sophistication, taste, or interest in preserving the resources of the country, now tolerated the grossest kind of waste and seemed to care little about corruption in high places, so long as no one interfered with their own pursuit of profit. The writer Mark Twain, raised in an earlier era, called this a "Gilded Age," dazzling on the surface, base metal below. A later student, Vernon L. Parrington, named the period the "Great Barbecue," a time when everyone rushed to get his share of the national inheritance like hungry picnickers crowding around the savory roast at one of the big political outings common in those years. Twain, Parrington, and other critics took too dark a view of the era. Never, perhaps, did the American people display more vigor, more imagination, or greater confidence in themselves and the future of their country. Indeed, in his novel *The Gilded Age*, written with Charles Dudley Warner, Twain portrayed this aspect of the period along with its cheapness and corruption.

However, certain intellectual currents strengthened the exploitative drives of the people. Charles Darwin's *Origin of Species* was published in 1859, and by the seventies his theory of evolution was beginning to influence opinion in the United States. That nature had ordained a kind of inevitable progress, governed by the natural selection of those individual organisms best adapted to survive in a particular environment, seemed eminently reasonable to most Americans, for it fitted well with their own experiences. Some thinkers extended Darwin's strictly biological concept of the survival of the fittest to the activities of men in society, finding in this "Social Darwinism" further justification for aggressive and acquisitive activities. If left to themselves, unhampered by government regulations or other restrictions, the most efficient would "survive" in every field of human endeavor, be it farming, manufacturing, or even—according to one of the most enthusiastic exponents of the theory, William Graham Sumner—teaching Yale undergraduates.

"Professor," one student asked Sumner, "don't you believe in any government aid to industries?" "No!" Professor Sumner replied, "it's root, hog, or die." The student persisted: "Suppose some professor of political science came along and took your job away from you. Wouldn't you be sore?" "Any other professor is welcome to try," Sumner answered. "If he gets my job, it is my fault. My business is to teach the subject so well that no one can take the job away from me." "Let the buyer beware; that covers the whole business," the sugar magnate Henry O. Havemeyer told an investigating committee. "You cannot wet-nurse people from the time they are born until the time they die. They have to wade in and get stuck, and that is the way men are educated."

Few men of practical affairs, and certainly not Havemeyer, went so far as Sumner. Few, indeed, were directly influenced by Darwin's ideas, which did not percolate down to the middle-class mass until late in the century. Most eagerly accepted any aid they could get from the government, many were active in philanthropy, some felt a deep sense of social responsibility. Nevertheless, most were sincere individualists. They believed in open competition, being convinced that the nation would best prosper if everyone were free to seek his personal fortune by his own methods. With such ideas ascendant, exploitation and complacency became the hallmarks of the postwar decades.

The Plains Indians

The force of this drive to possess, combined with monumental self-satisfaction, is well illustrated by the fate of the Indians after the Civil War. For 250 years they had been driven back steadily, yet on the eve of the Civil War they were still free to roam over roughly half the area of the United States, a region much of which was then considered practically worthless —"the Great American Desert." By the time of Hayes's inauguration the Indians had been shattered as an independent people; in another decade the survivors were penned up on reservations, with the government committed to a policy of extinguishing their nomadic way of life. To have done otherwise, a Wyoming editor proclaimed, would have been "mawkish sentimentalism . . . unworthy of the age."

In 1860 the survivors of most of the eastern tribes were living docilely on reservations in what is now Oklahoma. Out in California the forty-niners had made short work of the local tribes. Elsewhere in the West—in the deserts of the Great Basin between the Sierras and the Rockies, in the mountains themselves, and on the semiarid, grass-covered plains between the Rockies and the edge of white civilization in eastern Kansas and Nebraska—nearly a quarter of a million Indians dominated the land. By far the most important lived on the High Plains. From the Blackfeet of southwestern Canada and the Sioux of Minnesota and the Dakotas to the Cheyenne of Colorado and Wyoming and the Comanche of northern Texas, these tribes possessed a generally uniform culture, although they differed considerably in temperament and language. All lived by hunting the hulking American bison, or buffalo, which ranged over the plains by the millions. The buffalo provided the Indians with food, clothing, even shelter, for the famous Indian tepee was covered with hides. On the treeless plains, dried buffalo dung was used for fuel. The buffalo was also an important symbol in Indian religion.

Although they seemed the very epitome of freedom, pride, and self-reliance, the plains tribes had already begun to fall under the sway of the white man. They eagerly adopted the products of the more technically advanced culture—cloth, metal tools, weapons, cheap decorations—but the most important thing the white man gave them was the horse. The geological record shows that the genus *Equus* was native to America, but it had become extinct in the Western Hemisphere long before Cortés brought the first modern horses to American in the 16th century. Multiplying rapidly thereafter, the animals soon roamed wild from Texas to the Argentine. By the 18th century the Indians of the plains had acquired them in large numbers and had made them a vital part of their culture. Horses thrived on the plains and so did their masters. Mounted Indians could run down the buffalo instead of stalking them on foot. They could roam more widely over the country and fight more effectively too. They could acquire and transport more possessions and increase the size of their tepees, for horses could drag heavy loads, heaped on A-shaped frames (called *travois* by the French), whereas earlier Indians had only dogs to depend on as pack animals. The frames of the travois, when disassembled, served as poles for tepees. The Indians also adopted modern weapons, both the cavalry sword, which they especially admired, and the rifle. Both added still more to their effectiveness as hunters and fighters. However, like the white man's liquor and diseases, to which they also quickly succumbed, horses and guns caused problems. The buffalo herds began to diminish, and warfare became bloodier and more frequent.

In a familiar, tragic pattern the majority of the western tribes greeted the first white men to enter their domains in a friendly fashion. As late as the 1820's and 1830's, white hunters and trappers ranged freely over most of the West, trading with the Indians and often taking Indian wives.

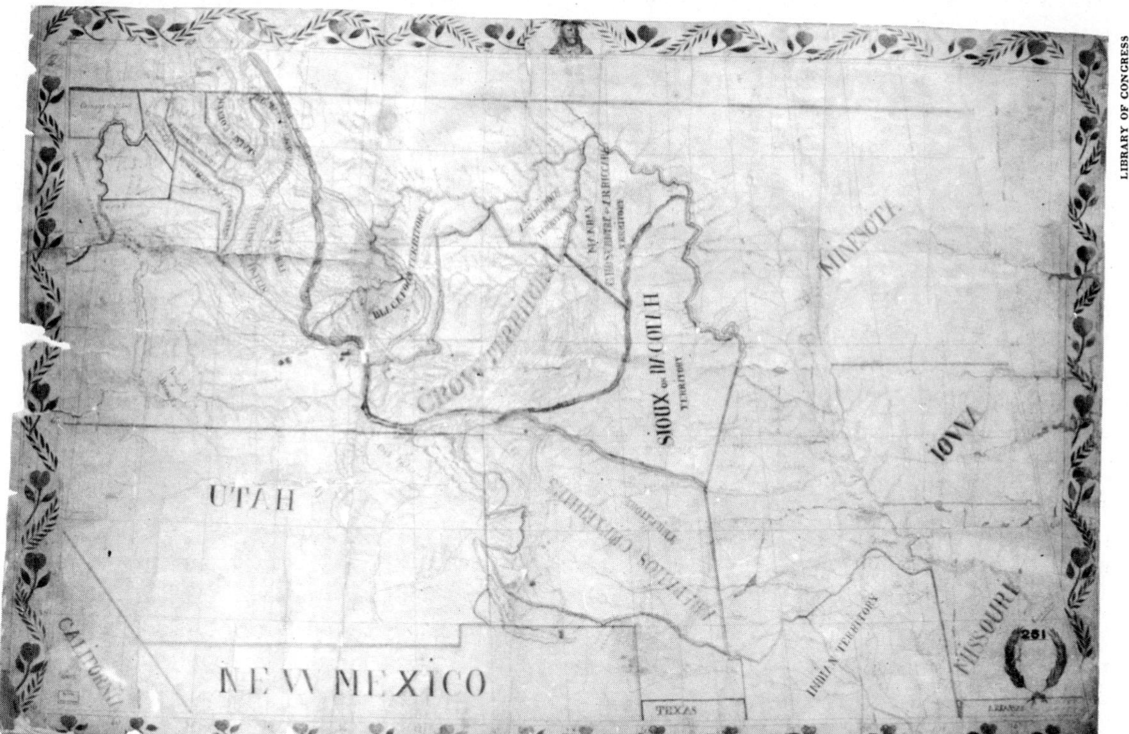

LIBRARY OF CONGRESS

This manuscript map delineating the hunting grounds of the plains tribes was used at the Horse Creek Indian council held in 1851. It was drawn by a Jesuit missionary, Father Pierre-Jean de Smet. Father de Smet had founded a mission among the Flatheads in western Montana in 1841 and was widely respected by the plains tribes.

Settlers pushing cross-country toward Oregon in the 1840's also met with relatively little trouble, although at times bands of braves on the warpath molested small groups or indulged in a certain amount of petty thievery that the migrants found annoying.

Nevertheless, after the start of the gold rush, the whites began to undermine the Indian empire in the West. The need to link the East with California meant that the tribes would have to be pushed aside. Deliberately, the government in Washington prepared the way. In 1851 Thomas Fitzpatrick, an experienced mountain man, a founder of the Rocky Mountain Fur Company, scout for the first large group of settlers to Oregon in 1841 and for General Kearny's forces in their march to Santa Fe and California during the Mexican War, and now an Indian agent, summoned a great "council" of the tribes. About 10,000 Indians, representing nearly all the plains tribes, gathered that September at Horse Creek, 37 miles east of Fort Laramie, in what is now Wyoming. Fitzpatrick was an intelligent and sensible man whom the Indians respected. He had recently married a girl who was half Indian. At Horse Creek he persuaded each tribe to accept definite limits to its hunting grounds. For example, the Sioux nations were to keep north of the Platte, and the Cheyenne and Arapaho were to confine themselves to the Colorado foothills. In return, the Indians were promised gifts and various annual payments. This policy, known as "concentration," was designed to cut down on intertribal warfare and—far more important—to enable the government to negotiate separately with each tribe. It was the classic strategy of divide and conquer.

Although it made a mockery of diplomacy to treat with Indian tribes as though they were European powers, the United States maintained that each was a sovereign nation, to be dealt with as an equal in solemn treaties. Both sides knew that this was not the case. When Indians agreed to meet in council, they were tacitly admitting defeat. They seldom drove very hard bargains or broke off negotiations. Moreover, tribal chiefs had only limited power; young braves frequently refused to respect agreements made by their elders. On the other hand, the United States failed dismally to keep its own pledges.

In Indian relations even more than in most fields, 19th-century Americans displayed a grave lack of talent for administration. After 1849 the Department of the Interior supposedly had charge of tribal affairs. Most of its agents were corrupt placeholders who systematically cheated the Indians. To cite a single example, one agent, heavily involved in mining operations on the side, systematically diverted supplies intended for his charges to his private ventures. When an inspector looked into his records, he sold him shares in a mine. That worthy, in turn, protected himself by sharing some of the loot with the son of the commissioner of Indian Affairs. Also the army, influential in the West as long as the Indians were capable of fighting, continually made trouble for the civilian authorities. Officers squabbled frequently with Indian agents over policy. Congress aggravated the situation by its niggardliness in appropriating funds.

Indian Wars

Worst of all, the government and the people showed little interest in honoring treaties with Indians. No sooner had the Kansas-Nebraska Bill become law when tribes like the Kansa, Omaha, Pawnee, and Yankton Sioux began to feel the pressure for further concessions of territory. By 1860 most of Kansas and Nebraska had been cleared; the Indians had lost all but 1.5 million of their 19-odd million acres. A gold rush into Colorado in 1859 sent thousands of greedy prospectors across the plains to drive the Cheyenne and Arapaho from land guaranteed them in 1851. Other trouble developed in the Sioux country. Thus it happened that in 1862, after federal troops had been pulled out of the West for service against the Confederacy, most of the plains Indians rose up against the whites. For the next five years, intermittent but bloody clashes kept the whole area in a state of alarm.

This was guerrilla warfare, with all its horrors and treachery. In 1864 a party of Colorado militia fell upon an unsuspecting Cheyenne community at Sand Creek and killed an estimated 450. "Kill and scalp all, big and little," Colonel J.M. Chivington, a minister in private life, told his men. "Nits make lice." As a white observer described the scene, "They were scalped, their brains knocked out; the men used their knives, ripped open women, clubbed little children, knocked them in the head with their guns, beat their brains out, mutilated their bodies in every sense of the word." General Nelson A. Miles called this "Chivington Massacre" the "foulest and most unjustifiable crime in the annals of America," but it was no worse than many incidents in earlier conflicts with Indians or than what was later to occur in guerrilla wars involving American troops in the Philippines and (more recently) in Vietnam.

In turn the Indians wiped out dozens of isolated white families, ambushed small parties, and fought many successful skirmishes against troops and militia. They achieved their most notable triumph in December 1866, when the Oglala Sioux, under their great chief Red Cloud, completely wiped out a party of 82 soldiers under Captain W.J. Fetterman. Red Cloud fought ruthlessly, but only when goaded by the construction of the Bozeman Trail, a road through the heart of the Sioux hunting grounds in southern Montana.

Finally, in 1867, the government evolved a new strategy. The "concentration" policy had evidently not gone far enough. All the plains Indians would be confined to two small reservations, one in the Black Hills of Dakota Territory, the other in Oklahoma, and forced to abandon their wild habits and become farmers. At two great conclaves held in 1867 and 1868 at Medicine Lodge Creek and Fort Laramie, the principal chiefs yielded to the government's demands.

However, many of the tribesmen refused to abide by these agreements. With their whole way of life at stake, they raged again across the plains, like a prairie fire and almost as destructive. General Philip Sheridan, Grant's great cavalry commander, explained the situation accurately: "We took away their country and their means of support, broke up their mode of living, their habits of life, introduced disease and decay among them, and it was for this and against this that they made war. Could anyone expect less?"

That a relative handful of "savages," without central leadership or plan, could hold off the cream of the army, battle-hardened in the Civil War and commanded by men of the caliber of Sheridan, can be explained by the character of the vast, trackless country and the skill and bravery of the Indians. Every observer called them the best horse fighters in the world. Armed with stubby, powerful bows quite capable of driving an arrow clear through a bull buffalo, they were a fair match for disciplined troops equipped with carbines and Colt revolvers. Expertly they led pursuers into traps, swept down on unsuspecting supply details, stole up on small parties the way a mountain lion stalks a grazing lamb. They could sometimes be rounded up, as Sheridan herded the tribes of the Southwest into Indian Territory in 1869, but once the troops withdrew, braves began to melt away into the emptiness of the surrounding grasslands. The distinction between "treaty" Indians, who had agreed to live on the new reservations, and the "nontreaty" variety shifted almost from day to day. Trouble flared here one week, next week somewhere else, perhaps 500 miles away. No less an authority than General William Tecumseh Sherman testified that a mere 50 Indians could often "checkmate" 3,000 soldiers. The expense of military operations was enormous, considering the meager results. It cost $2 million a year to maintain a single regiment on the plains, and according to one estimate, the federal government spent a million dollars for each Indian actually killed in battle. Moreover, the continuing bloodshed angered both western settlers and eastern humanitarians.

If one concedes that no one could reverse the direction of history or stop the invasion of Indian lands, then some version of the "small reservation" policy would probably have been the best solution to the problem. If the Indians had been given a reasonable amount of land together with adequate subsidies and allowed to maintain their way of life, they might have accepted the situation and ceased to harry the whites. But whatever chance the policy had was greatly weakened by the government's maladministration of Indian affairs. Indian agents in the field were required to drive off trespassers, confiscate liquor found on the reservations, and keep the Indians in line, but they had no means of enforcement under their command. An "Indian Ring" in the Department of the Interior, much like the "Whiskey Ring" and the other rapacious gangs in Washington, systematically stole funds and supplies intended for the reservation Indians. "No branch of the national government is so spotted with fraud, so tainted with corruption, so utterly unworthy of a free and enlightened government, as this Indian Bureau," Republican Congressman James A. Garfield charged in 1869.

About this time a Yale paleontologist, Professor Othniel C. Marsh, who wished to dig for fossils on the Sioux reservation, asked Red Cloud for permission to enter his domain. The chief agreed on condition that Marsh, whom the Indians called "Big Bone Chief," take back with him samples of the mouldy flour and beef that government agents were supplying to his people. Appalled by what he saw on the reservation, Marsh took the rotten supplies directly to President Grant and prepared a list of charges against the agents. General Sherman, in overall command of the Indian country, claimed in 1875: "We could settle Indian troubles in an hour, but Congress wants the patronage of the Indian bureau, and the bureau wants the appropriations without any of the trouble of the Indians themselves."

Grant, well-intentioned as usual, wanted to place the reservations under army control, but even the Indians opposed this. In areas around army camps Indians fared no better than on the reservations. A quartermaster in the Apache country in New Mexico sequestered 12,000 pounds of corn from the meager supplies set aside for Indian relief. Some soldiers gave liquor to the Indians, and according to one late-19th-century historian, "officers at those camps where the Indians were fed habitually used their official position to break the chastity of Indian women." In 1869 Congress created a distinguished nonpolitical Board of Indian Commissioners to oversee Indian affairs, but the bureaucrats in Washington stymied the commissioners at every turn.

"Their recommendations were ignored . . . gross breaking of the law was winked at, and . . . many matters were not submitted to them at all," the biographer of one commissioner has written. "They decided that their task was as useless as it was irritating."

Nevertheless, the majority of the Indians might have eventually submitted had they been allowed to hold even the lands granted them under the "small reservation" policy, for they knew they could never really eject the whites from their country. This was not to be. Gold was discovered in the Black Hills in 1874. For a season the army tried to keep prospectors out; then the government threw up its hands. By the next winter thousands of miners had invaded the reserved area. Already alarmed by the approach of crews building the Northern Pacific Railroad, the Sioux once again went on the warpath. Joining with nontreaty tribes to the west, they concentrated in the region of the Bighorn River, in southern Montana Territory. The summer of 1876 saw three columns of troops in the field against them. The commander of one of these, General Alfred H. Terry, sent a small detachment of the Seventh Cavalry under Colonel George A. Custer ahead with orders to locate the Indians' camp and then block their escape route into the inaccessible Bighorn Mountains.

Custer was a vain and rash commander, and vanity and rashness were especially grave handicaps in Indian fighting. Grossly underestimating the number of the Indians, he decided to attack directly with his tiny force of 264 men. At the Little Bighorn he found himself surrounded by 2,500 Sioux under Rain-in-the-Face, Crazy Horse, and Sitting Bull. He and his men fought bravely, but every one of them died on the field. Because it was so one-sided, "Custer's Last Stand" (June 26, 1876) was not a typical battle, but it may be taken as symbolic of all the Indian warfare of the period in the sense that it was characterized by bravery, foolhardiness, and a tragic waste of life. It greatly heartened the Indians but did not gain them their cause. That autumn, short of rations and hard pressed by overwhelming numbers of soldiers, they surrendered and returned to the reservation.

Destruction of Tribal Life

Thereafter, the plains fighting slackened. For this the destruction of the buffalo rather than the effectiveness of the army was chiefly responsible. An estimated 13 to 15 million head had roamed the plains in the mid-sixties. Then the slaughter began. Thousands were butchered to feed the gangs of laborers engaged in building the Union Pacific Railroad, and thousands more fell before the guns of sportsmen. Buffalo hunting became a fad, and a brisk demand developed for mounted buffalo heads and for buffalo rugs. Railroads ran excursion trains for hunters; even the shameful practice of gunning down the beasts directly from the cars was allowed. In 1871–72 the Grand Duke Alexis of Russia engaged in a gigantic hunt, supported by "Buffalo Bill" Cody, most famous of the professional buffalo killers, the Seventh United States Cavalry under General Sheridan, and hundreds of Indians.

The discovery in 1871 of a way to make commercial use of buffalo hides completed the tragedy. In the next three years about 9 million were killed; after another decade the animals were almost extinct. At the height of the carnage, hides sold for less than a dollar each; by 1894 the shortage was so acute that buffalo robes in New York retailed for between $75 and $175. "Probably no great American resource has ever been quite so wantonly and completely destroyed within so brief a time," Allan Nevins has written.

BELLA C. LANDAUER COLLECTION, NEW-YORK HISTORICAL SOCIETY

SIXTEENTH ANNUAL CIRCULAR.

BUFFALO ROBES!

HART, TAYLOR & CO.

BOSTON.

COLLECTION OF

BUFFALO ROBES 1876.

UNLINED ROBES.		LINED BUFFALO ROBES.	
No. 1 Seasonable, Sewed Robes,	$9.00	Medium and Small Lined Buffalo, $8, and	$9.00
" 2 " " "	8.00	" Lined "	11.00
" 3 " " "	7.00	" X " "	12.00
" 1 " XX whole "	12.00	Large " "	13.50
" 1 " " "	10.50	" X " "	15.00
" 2 " " "	9.00	" XX " "	16.50
" 3 " " "	8.00	Extra Lined Robes, with superior Linings and Trimmings,	18.00 to 24.00
Calf, according to size,	4.00 to 8.00		
Choice Whole and Split Robes,	12.00 to 15.00		

Buffalo robes for carriages and sleighs were enormously popular in the eastern states, as were buffalo overcoats that sold for less than $20. Hides were also widely used as belts on power-driven machinery.

MUSEUM OF THE AMERICAN INDIAN, HEYE FOUNDATION

After his surrender in 1886, the celebrated Chiricahua Apache Geronimo posed with a fellow chief, Naiche (left), at an army post in Arizona Territory. Geronimo and the Chiricahuas were eventually settled in Oklahoma.

No more efficient way could have been found for destroying the plains Indians. The disappearance of the bison left them starving, homeless, purposeless. All that remained for them was to submit. In 1887 Congress passed the Dawes Severalty Act, designed to put an end to tribal life and convert the Indians to the white man's way of living. Tribal lands were split up into small units, each head of a family being given a quarter section (160 acres). In order to keep unscrupulous speculators from wresting it from the Indians during the period of adjustment, this land could not be disposed of for 25 years. Indians who accepted allotments, took up residence "separate and apart from any tribe," and "adopted the habits of civilized life" were granted United States citizenship. The government also set aside funds for educating and training the Indians. Now that their spirit had been broken, many persons became interested in helping them, stimulated by books like Helen Hunt Jackson's aptly titled *A Century of Dishonor* (1881), a somewhat romantic but essentially just denunciation of past policy.

Although intended as a humane reform, the Dawes Act had disastrous results. Devised in an age that knew almost nothing about anthropology or social structure, it assumed that Indians could be transformed into small agricultural capitalists by act of Congress. It shattered what was left of the Indians' culture without enabling them to adapt to white ways. Moreover, unscrupulous white men systematically tricked the tribesmen into leasing their allotments for a pittance, while local authorities often taxed Indian lands at excessive rates. In 1934, after about 86 million of the 138 million acres assigned under the Dawes Act had passed into white hands, the government went back to a policy of encouraging tribal ownership of Indian lands, but by that time irreparable damage had been done.

By 1887 the tribes of the mountains and deserts beyond the plains had also given up the fight. Typical of the heartlessness of the government's treatment of these peoples was that afforded the Nez Percé of Oregon and Idaho who were led by the remarkable Chief Joseph. After outwitting federal troops in a campaign that ranged across more than a thousand miles of rough country, Joseph finally surrendered in October 1877. He and all his people were then uprooted from their lands and settled on "the malarial bottoms of the Indian Territory" in far-off Oklahoma. The last Indians to abandon the unequal battle were the bitter, relentless Apaches of the Southwest, who carried on the fight until the capture of their fanatical chief, Geronimo, in 1886.

The Plight of Minorities

Americans shunted the Indian aside merely because he stood in their way. Other minorities were treated with equal callousness and contempt in the postwar decades. That the South would deal harshly with the former slaves once federal control was relaxed probably should have been expected, although men like Governor Wade Hampton of South Carolina had piously promised to respect Negro civil rights. "We . . . will secure to every citizen, the lowest as well as the highest, black as well as white, full and equal protection in the enjoyment of all his rights under the Constitution," Hampton said in 1877. Hampton's pledge, which had been repeated by supposedly honorable southerners in other states, was not kept. President Hayes, expecting the South to treat the freedmen fairly, had urged Negroes to trust the southern whites. A new "Era of Good Feelings" had dawned, he announced after making a good-will tour of the South shortly after his inauguration. By December 1877 he had been sadly disillusioned. "By state legislation, by frauds, by intimidation, and by violence of the most atrocious character, colored citizens have been deprived of the right of suffrage," he wrote in his diary. However, although he had written earlier, "My task was to wipe out the color line," he did nothing to remedy the situation except, as his biographer Harry Barnard says, "to scold the South and threaten action." Frederick Douglass called Hayes's policy "sickly conciliation."

Hayes's successors in the 1880's did no better. "Time is the only cure" for the Negro problem, President Garfield said, thus confessing that he had no policy at all. President Arthur gave federal patronage to extreme anti-Negro groups in an effort to split the solidly Democratic South. In President Cleveland's day the Negro had scarcely a friend in high places North or South. In 1887 Cleveland explained to a correspondent why he opposed "mixed schools." Expert opinion, the President said, believed "that separate schools were of much more benefit for the colored people."

Hayes, Garfield, and Arthur were Republicans, Cleveland a Democrat; party made little difference as far as the Negro was concerned. *Both* parties subscribed to hypocritical statements about equality and constitutional rights, but neither did anything to implement them. For a time Negroes were not totally disfranchised in the South. Rival white factions tried to manipulate Negro votes in their struggle for power, and corruption flourished as widely in the South as in the machine-dominated wards of the northern cities.

In the nineties, however, the southern states, led by Mississippi, began to deprive Negroes of the vote systematically. Poll taxes, often cumulative, raised a formidable economic barrier, one that also disfranchised many poor white men. Literacy tests completed the work, a number of states providing a loophole for illiterate whites by including an "understanding" clause whereby an illiterate person could qualify by demonstrating an ability to explain the meaning of a section of the state constitution when an election official read it to him. Of course Negroes who attempted to take this subjective test were uniformly declared to have failed it. This was done with unctuous hypocrisy, the white southerners insisting that they loved "their" blacks dearly and wished only to protect them from "the machinations of those who would use them only to further their own base ends." "We take away the Negroes' votes," a Louisiana politician explained, "to protect them just as we would protect a little child and prevent it from injuring itself with sharp-edged tools."

Practically every Supreme Court decision after 1877 that affected the Negro somehow "nullified or curtailed" his rights, Professor Rayford W. Logan writes. In *Hall v. De Cuir* (1878) the Court even threw out a state law *forbidding* segregation on river boats, arguing that it was an unjustifiable interference with interstate commerce. The Court's most important decision in this area was handed down in the *Civil Rights Cases* (1883), which declared unconstitutional the Civil Rights Act of 1875 barring segregation in public facilities. Negroes who were refused equal accommodations or privileges by hotels, theaters, and other privately owned facilities had no recourse at law, the Court announced. The Fourteenth Amendment guaranteed their civil rights against invasion by the states, not by individuals.

Finally, in *Plessy v. Ferguson* (1896), the Court decided that even in places of public accommodation, such as railroads and, by implication, schools, segregation was legal so long as "separate but equal" facilities were provided. "If one race be inferior to the other socially, the Constitution of the United States cannot put them upon the same plane." In a noble dissent Justice John Marshall Harlan protested against this line of argument. "Our Constitution is color-blind," he said. "The arbitrary separation of citizens, on the basis of race . . . is a badge of servitude wholly inconsistent with civil freedom and the equality before the law established by the Constitution." Alas, more than half a century was to pass before the Court came around to Harlan's reasoning and reversed the Plessy decision. Meanwhile, total segregation was imposed throughout the South. Separate schools, prisons, hospitals, recreational facilities, and even cemeteries were provided for Negroes, and these were almost never equal to those available to whites.

Most northerners supported the government and the Court in their attitude toward Negroes. Nearly all the newspapers commented favorably on the decision in the *Civil Rights Cases*. In news stories, papers presented a stereotyped, derogatory picture of blacks, no matter what the actual circumstances. Northern magazines, even high-quality ones such as *Harper's*, *Scribner's*, and the *Century*, repeatedly made Negroes the butt of crude jokes. Even educated, intelligent northerners believed Negroes inferior. "They are gregarious and emotional, rather than intelligent," Richard Watson Gilder, editor of the *Century*, wrote in 1883, "and are easily led in any direction by white men of energy and determination." James Bryce, the brilliant Englishman whose study of the United States at this time, *The American Commonwealth*, has become a classic, saw much of men of this type and often absorbed their point of view. Negroes, Bryce wrote, were docile, pliable, submissive, lustful, childish, impressionable, emotional, heedless, "unthrifty," with "no capacity for abstract thinking, for scientific inquiry, or for any kind of invention." Being "unspeakably inferior" to white men, they were "unfit to cope with a superior race." Like Bryce, most Americans did not especially wish the Negroes ill; they simply refused to consider them quite human and consigned them complacently to oblivion, along with the Indians. A vicious circle was established. "The negro is not discriminated against on account of his race," an Alabaman explained, "but on account of his intellectual and moral condition." Thus, by denying black men decent educational opportunities and good jobs, the dominant race could use their resultant ignorance and poverty to justify the inferior facilities offered them.

Southern Negroes reacted to this deplorable situation in a variety of ways. Some sought redress in racial pride and what would later be called black nationalism. Men of this type founded a number of all-black communities in Oklahoma Territory and led the great "exodus" of 1879, when, to the consternation of southern whites, thousands of Negroes suddenly migrated to Kansas.* A few became so disaffected with American life that they tried to revive the African colonization movement. "Africa is our home," Bishop Henry M. Turner, a huge, plain-spoken man who had served as an army chaplain during the war and as a member of the Georgia legislature during reconstruction, insisted. "Every man that has the sense of an animal must see there is no future in this country for the Negro." Another militant, T. Thomas Fortune, editor of the New York *Age* and founder of the Afro-American League (1887), called upon Negroes

*When a congressman asked Henry Adams, a leader of the exodus, why he and his followers had left the South, Adams replied: "We seed there was no way on earth . . . that we could better our condition there. . . . The white people . . . treat our people so bad in many respects that it is impossible for them to stand it."

to demand full civil rights, better schools, and fair wages, and to fight against discrimination of every sort. "Let us stand up like men in our own organization," he urged. "If others use . . . violence to combat our peaceful arguments, it is not for us to run away from violence."

Militancy and black separatism, however, won few adherents among southern Negroes. The forces of repression were too strong. The late 19th century saw more lynchings in the South than in any other period of American history. This helps explain the tactics of Booker T. Washington, one of the most extraordinary Americans of that generation.

Washington had been born a slave in Virginia in 1856. Laboriously, he obtained an education, supporting himself while a student by working as a janitor. In 1881, with the financial help of northern philanthropists, he founded Tuskegee Institute in Alabama, which specialized in vocational training. His experiences in the South convinced Washington that the Negroes must lift themselves by their own bootstraps, but that they must also accommodate themselves to white prejudices. A persuasive speaker and a brilliant fund raiser, he soon developed a national reputation as a "reasonable" champion of his race. (As early as 1891, Harvard awarded him an honorary degree.) But his greatest fame and influence followed his speech to a mixed white and black audience in Atlanta in 1895. To the blacks he said: "Cast down your bucket where you are," that is, stop fighting segregation and second-class citizenship and concentrate upon learning useful skills. "Dignify and glorify common labor," he urged. "Agitation of questions of racial equality is the extremest folly." Progress up the social and economic ladder for Negroes would come not from "artificial forcing" but from self-improvement. "There is as much dignity in tilling a field as in writing a poem."

BROWN BROTHERS

Booker T. Washington about 1901, when his autobiography, Up from Slavery, *was published. He wrote his memoirs in the hope of gaining aid for Tuskegee.*

Washington asked the whites of what he called "our beloved South" to lend the Negroes a hand in their efforts to advance themselves. If you will do so, he promised, you will be "surrounded by the most patient, faithful, law-abiding, and unresentful people that the world has seen."

This "Atlanta Compromise" delighted white southerners and won Washington still more influence and financial support in every section. He became one of the most powerful men in the United States, consulted by Presidents, in close touch with business and philanthropic leaders, and capable of influencing in countless unobtrusive ways the fate of millions of Negroes.

Blacks, of course, responded to the Compromise with mixed feelings. Accepting Washington's approach would relieve them of many burdens and dangers and bring them considerable material assistance. But the cost was high in surrendered personal dignity and lost hopes of obtaining real justice.

Washington's career illustrates the terrible dilemma that American Negroes have always faced: the choice between confrontation and accommodation. This choice was particularly difficult in the late 19th century. Washington chose accommodation. It is easy to condemn him as a toady, but difficult to see how, at that time, a more aggressive policy could have succeeded.

One can even interpret the Atlanta Compromise as a subtle form of black nationalism; in a way, Washington was urging his fellows not to *accept* inferiority and racial slurs but to *ignore* them. His own behavior lends force to this view, for his method of operating was indeed subtle, even devious. Publicly, he minimized the importance of civil and political rights, accepted separate but equal facilities—if they were truly equal. Behind the scenes he lobbied against restrictive measures, marshaled large sums of money to fight test cases in the courts, and worked hard in northern states to organize the Negro vote and make sure that Negro political leaders got a fair share of the spoils of office. As one black militant put it, Washington knew the virtue of "sagacious silence." He was perhaps not personally an admirable man, but he was a useful one. His defects point up more the unlovely aspects of the age than of his own character.

Other minority groups also suffered from the contempt and disdain of the majority. Beginning in the mid-fifties a steady flow of Chinese had migrated to the United States, most of them finding work in the California gold fields. The annual influx had averaged only about 4 or 5 thousand however, until the negotiation of the Burlingame Treaty of 1868, the purpose of which was to provide cheap labor to fill out the construction crews building the Central Pacific Railroad. Thereafter, the number of annual immigrants from China more than doubled, although before 1882 it exceeded 20,000 only twice. Yet when the railroads were completed and the Chinese began to compete with native workers, a great cry of resentment went up on the West Coast. Riots broke out in San Francisco as early as 1877. Chinese workers were called "groveling worms," "more slavish and brutish than the beasts that roam the fields." When the migration suddenly increased in 1882 to nearly 40,000,* protests reached such a peak that Congress prohibited Chinese immigration for ten years. Later, legislation extended the ban.

*This was still only about five per cent of the immigration of that year. From Germany alone, in 1882, over 250,000 people came to the United States.

The Chinese in the West created genuine social problems. Most did not intend to remain in the United States and therefore made little effort to accommodate themselves to American ways. Their attachment to gambling, opium, and prostitutes—over 90 per cent of the Chinese in America at this time were males—alarmed respectable citizens. But the attitudes of westerners toward Chinese differed only in degree from that of the rest of the country toward the European immigrants who were flooding into the country in the 1880's. While industrialists wished to keep the gates wide open in order to obtain plentiful supplies of cheap labor, organized workers and many middle-class Americans were beginning to display antiforeign attitudes reminiscent of the 1850's, when Know-Nothingism was at its height. In 1887 the most important antiforeign organization of the era, the American Protective Association, was founded. Especially during hard times and in periods of social unrest, the underlying intolerance of the majority burst forth. For example, the Chicago Haymarket bombing of 1886, supposedly the work of foreign anarchists, produced a wave of denunciations of "long-haired, wild-eyed, bad-smelling, atheistic, reckless foreign wretches."

Black man, red man, or white; aboriginal inhabitant or recent arrival; savage, husbandman, or city worker—anyone who blocked the ambitions of his more powerful fellows received short shrift in post-Civil War America.

Exploiting Mineral Wealth in the West

The inanimate resources of the nation were exploited in these decades as ruthlessly and thoughtlessly as its human resources. Americans had always regarded the West as a limitless treasure to be gobbled up as a rapidly as possible, but after 1865 they engrossed its riches at an even faster pace and in a wider variety of ways. Miners had invaded the western mountains even before the Civil War. For 20 years from the mid-fifties to the mid-seventies they rushed from discovery to discovery, striking each area with the suddenness and concentrated destructiveness of a tornado.

By 1857 the day of the individual prospector panning the streams for gold was finished in California. Large companies had taken over the expensive but still profitable work of extracting the metal from deep veins of quartz rock. Thereafter, thousands of displaced, gold-crazed prospectors fanned out through the Rockies, panning every stream and hacking furiously at every likely outcropping from the Fraser River country of British Columbia to Tucson in southern Arizona, and from the eastern slopes of the Sierras to the Great Plains.

Gold and silver were scattered throughout the area, although usually too thinly to make mining profitable. Whenever anyone made a "strike," men flocked eagerly to the site, drawn by rumors of stream beds gleaming with auriferous gravel and of nuggets the size of men's fists. For a few brief months the area teemed with activity. Towns of 5,000 or more sprang up overnight, improvised roads were crowded with men and supply wagons. Claims were staked out along every stream and gully. Then, usually, expectations faded in the light of reality: high prices, low yields, hardship, violence, and deception. The boom collapsed and the towns died as quickly as they had risen. A few men would have found real wealth, the rest only backbreaking labor and disappointment, until tales of another strike sent them scurrying feverishly across the land on another golden chase.

In the spring of 1858 it was upon the Fraser River in Canada that the horde descended, 30,000 Californians in the van. The following spring, Pikes Peak in Colorado attracted the pack, experienced California prospectors ("yonder siders") mixing with "greenhorns" from every corner of the globe. In June 1859 came the finds in Nevada, where the famous Comstock Lode yielded ores worth nearly $4,000 a ton. In 1861, while men in the settled areas were laying down their tools to take up arms, the miners were racing to the Idaho panhandle, hoping to become millionaires overnight. The next year the rush was to Snake River Valley, then in 1863 and 1864 to Montana. In 1870 Leadville, Colorado, had a brief boom, and in 1874–76 the Black Hills in the heart of the Sioux lands were inundated.

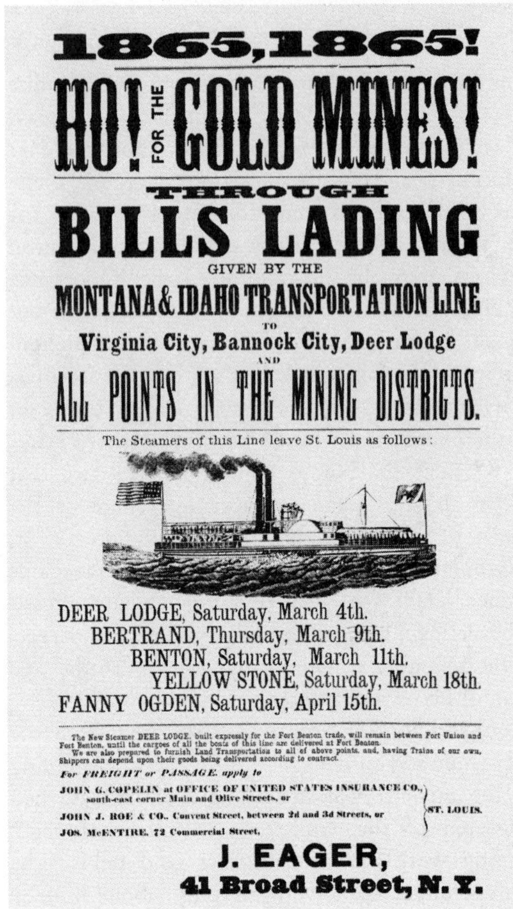

NEW-YORK HISTORICAL SOCIETY

A broadside offering transportation to the Montana gold strikes. It took a steamboat as long as two months to reach Fort Benton on the upper Missouri.

In a sense, the Denvers, Aurarias, Virginia Cities, Orofinos, and Gold Creeks of the West during the war years were harbingers of the point of view that flourished in the East in the age of President Grant and his immediate successors. The miners enthusiastically adopted the get-rich-quick philosophy, willingly enduring privations and laboring hard, but always with the object of striking it rich. Anything that stood in the way of their ambitions, they smashed. They trespassed upon Indian lands without the slightest qualm and "claimed" public land with no thought of paying for it. The idea of reserving any part of the West for future generations never entered their heads. The sudden prosperity of the mining towns attracted every kind of shady character, all bent on extracting wealth from the pockets of the miners rather than from the unyielding earth. Gambling houses, dance halls, saloons, and brothels mushroomed wherever precious metal was found. Around these tawdry palaces of pleasure and forgetfulness gathered thieves, confidence men, degenerates, and desperadoes. Crime and violence were commonplace, law enforcement a constant problem.

The lawless could be controlled when their depredations became too annoying; sooner or later the "better element" in every mining community formed a "vigilance committee" and by a few summary hangings drove the outlaws out of town. Fundamentally, much of the difficulty lay in the antisocial attitudes of the miners themselves. "They were hardened individualists who paid little attention to community affairs unless their own interests were threatened," Ray Allen Billington, historian of the frontier, has written.

Western mining was at its gaudy height during the era of President Grant. Gold and silver dominated everyone's thoughts and dreams, and few paid much attention to the means employed in accumulating this wealth. Storekeepers charged outrageous prices, claim holders "salted" worthless properties with nuggets in order to swindle gullible investors. Ostentation characterized the successful, braggadocio those who failed, while all reveled in liquor and every vulgar pleasure. Virginia City, Nevada, was at the peak of its prosperity, producing an average of $12 million a year in ore. Built upon the richness of the Comstock Lode ($306 million in gold and silver were extracted from the Comstock in 20 years), it had 25 saloons before it had 4,000 people. By the seventies its mountainside site was disfigured by huge, ornate houses in the worst possible taste, where successful mine operators dined off fine china and swilled champagne as though it were water. One tycoon installed silver knobs on every door of his mansion.

In 1873, after the discovery of the Big Bonanza, a rich seam more than 50 feet thick, the future of Virginia City seemed boundless. Other new discoveries shortly thereafter indicated to optimists that the mining boom in the West would continue indefinitely. The finds in the Black Hills district in 1875 and 1876, heralding deposits yielding eventually $100 million, led to the mushroom growth of Deadwood, home of Wild Bill Hickok, Deadwood Dick, Calamity Jane, and such lesser-known characters as California Jack and Poker Alice. In Deadwood, according to Professor Billington, "the faro games were wilder, the hurdy-gurdy dance halls noisier, the street brawls more common, than in any other western town." New strikes in Leadville, Colorado, in 1876 and 1877 caused that ghost town to boom again. In the summer of 1877 it consisted of 20 shanties; by late 1879 it had a population of about 35,000. This, however, was the last important flurry to ruffle the mining frontier. The West continued to yield much gold and silver, especially the latter, but big corporations produced nearly all of it. The mines around Deadwood, for example, were soon controlled by one large company, Homestake Mining.

This was the culminating irony of the history of the mining frontier. The shoestring prospectors, independent and enterprising, made the key discoveries, established local institutions, and supplied the West with much of its color and folklore. But almost none of them was really successful. Stockholders of large corporations, many of whom had never seen a mine, let alone swung a pick or panned gravel from the bed of a mountain stream, made off with the lion's share of the mineral wealth. The men whose worship of gold was so direct and incessant, the actual prospectors who peopled the mining towns and gave the frontier its character, mostly died poor, still seeking a prize as elusive if not as illusory as the pot of gold at the end of the rainbow.

For the mining of gold and silver is essentially like that of coal and iron. To operate profitably, large capital investments, heavy machinery, railroads, and hundreds of hired hands are required. Henry Comstock, the prospector, who gave his name to the Comstock Lode, was luckier than most, but he sold his claims to the lode for a pittance, disposing of what became one valuable mine for $40 and receiving only $10,000 for his share of the fabulous Ophir, the richest concentration of gold and silver ever found. His greatest financial gain from the Comstock came some years later when the owners of the Ophir paid him well to testify in their corporation's behalf in an important lawsuit. More typical of the successful mine owner was George Hearst, senator from California and father of the newspaper tycoon William Randolph Hearst, who, by shrewd speculations, obtained large blocks of stock in both the Ophir and Homestake, as well as other mining properties scattered from Montana to Mexico.

Though marked by violence, fraud, greed, impermanence, and lost hopes, the gold rushes of the 1860's and 1870's had certain valuable results for the country. The most obvious was the new metal itself, which bolstered the financial position of the United States during and after the Civil War. Huge quantities of European goods needed for the war effort and for postwar economic development were paid for with the yield of the new mines. Gold and silver also caused a great increase of interest in the West. A valuable literature appeared, part imaginative, part straightforwardly reportorial, describing the mining camps and the life of the prospectors. These works fascinated contemporaries as they have continued to fascinate succeeding generations when adapted to the motion picture and to television. Mark Twain's *Roughing It* (1872), based in part on his experiences in the Nevada mining country, is the most famous example of this literature.

Furthermore, each new strike and rush, no matter how ephemeral, brought permanent settlers along with the prospectors: farmers, cattlemen, storekeepers, teamsters, lawyers, ministers, and so on. Some saw from the start that a better living could be made supplying the needs of the gold seekers than looking for the elusive metal. Others, abandoning hope of finding mineral wealth, simply took up whatever occupation they could rather than starve or return home empty-handed. In every mining town—along with the saloons and brothels—schools, churches, and newspaper offices sprang up.

The mines also speeded the political organization of the West. Colorado and Nevada were organized as territories in 1861, Arizona and Idaho in 1863, Montana in 1864. Although Nevada was admitted prematurely in 1864 in order to ratify the Thirteenth Amendment and help re-elect Lincoln, most of these territories did not become states for decades, but because of the miners, the framework for future development was early established.

The Land Bonanza

While the miners were engrossing the mineral wealth of the West, other interests were snapping up the region's choice farmland. Presumably the Homestead Act, passed in 1862 after years of agitation, had fundamentally changed federal land policy, ending the reign of the speculator and the large landholder. The West, land reformers had assumed, would soon be dotted with 160-acre family farms. An early amendment to the Homestead Act even prevented husbands and wives from filing separate claims. For a variety of reasons, however, the system did not work out as planned. Most landless Americans were too poor to become independent farmers, even when they could obtain land without cost. The expense of moving a family from the eastern part of the country to the ever-receding frontier exceeded the means of many, and the subsequent costs, from simple hoes and scythes to harvesting machines, fencing, and housing, presented an even more formidable barrier. Nor did the industrial workers for whom the free land was supposed to provide a "safety valve" have either the skills or the inclination to become farmers. Most homesteaders were already farmers, usually from districts not far removed from frontier conditions. And despite the intent of the law, wealthy speculators often used it to obtain large tracts. They hired men to stake out claims, falsely swear that they had fulfilled the conditions laid down in the law for obtaining legal title, and then deed the land over to their employers.

Furthermore, the West was ill-suited to small-scale agriculture. A grant of 160 acres was not large enough for raising livestock or for the kind of commercial agriculture that was developing in the lands west of the Mississippi. Congress made a feeble attempt to make larger holdings available to homesteaders by passing the Timber Culture Act of 1873, which permitted individuals to

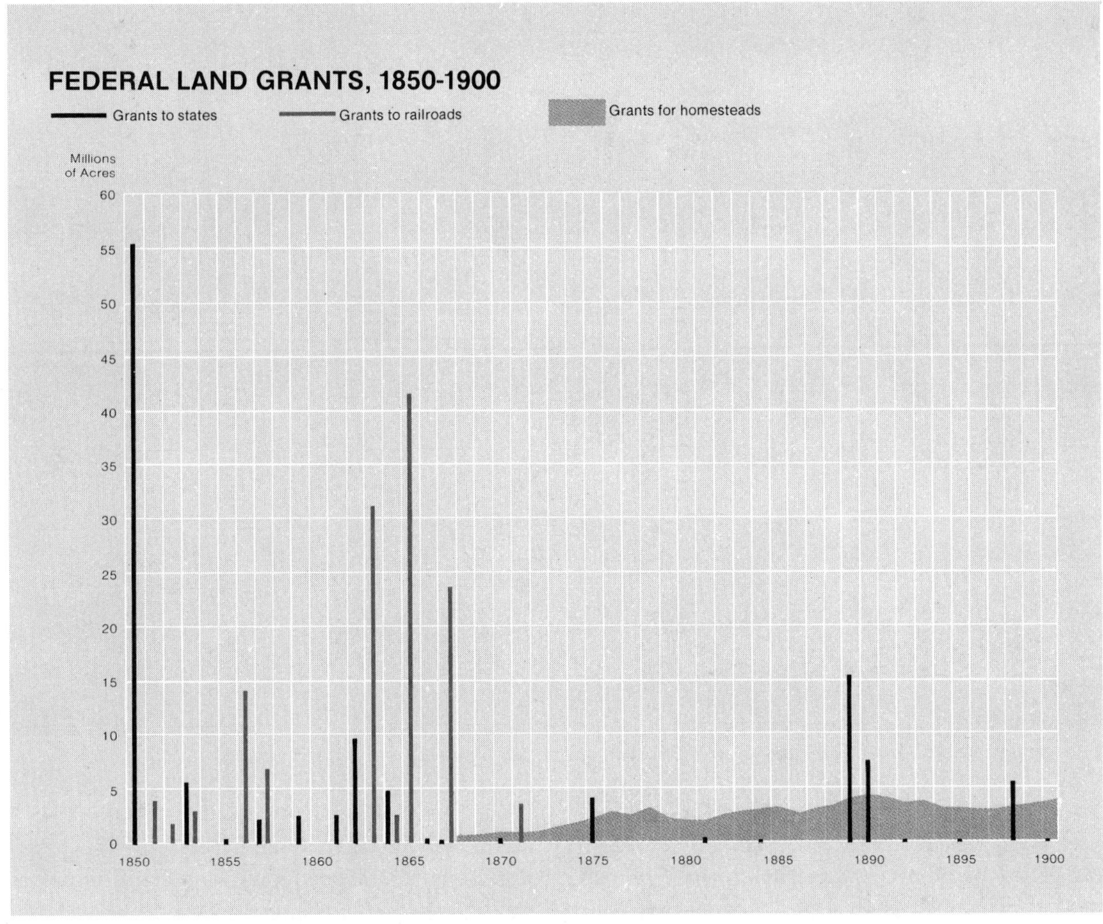

Between 1850 and 1871, grants of federal land to railroads totaled some 130 million acres. The homestead acreage shown indicates land to which homesteaders took title after fulfilling the necessary conditions.

claim an additional 160 acres if they would agree to plant a quarter of it in trees within ten years. This law proved helpful to many farmers in the tier of states running from North Dakota to Kansas. Nevertheless, fewer than 25 per cent of the 245,000 who took up land under this law actually obtained final title to the property. Raising large numbers of seedling trees on the plains was a difficult task.

While futilely attempting to make a forest of parts of the treeless plains, the government permitted private interests to gobble up and destroy many of the great forests that clothed the slopes of the Rockies and the Sierras. The Timber and Stone Act of 1878 allowed anyone to claim a quarter section of forest land for $2.50 an acre if it was "unfit for civilization." This laxly drawn measure enabled lumber companies to obtain thousands of acres by hiring dummy entrymen, whom they marched in gangs to the land offices, paying them a few dollars for their time after they had signed over their claims. "In many instances whole townships have been entered under this law in the interest of one person or firm, to whom the lands have been conveyed as soon as receipts for the purchase price were issued," the commissioner of the General Land Office complained in 1901. "If the act was intended for any other purpose than rapid monopolization of all the valuable timber as yet not patented in the United States," a recent historian has written, "then Congress was very remiss in the phraseology. . . . An acre cost less than the value of one log from one tree where it stood as yet unfelled."

Even if the land laws had been better drafted

The crews of five combines stopped harvesting wheat on a bonanza farm in eastern Washington in 1890 to have their picture taken. Such combines as these reaped, threshed, cleaned, and bagged grain in a single operation.

and more honestly enforced, it is unlikely that the policy of granting free land to small homesteaders would have succeeded. Aside from the built-in difficulties faced by small-scale agriculturalists in the West, too many people in every section were eager to exploit the nation's land for their own profit, without regard for the general interest. Immediately after the war, for example, Congress reserved 47.7 million acres of public land in the South for homesteaders, stopping all cash sales in the region. But in 1876 this policy was reversed, the land thrown open. Speculators flocked to the feast in such numbers that the Illinois Central Railroad began running special trains from Chicago to Mississippi and Louisiana. Between 1877 and 1888 over 5.6 million acres were sold, much of them covered with valuable pine and cypress.

However he attained his acres, the frontier farmer of the 1870's and 1880's grappled with a variety of novel problems as he pushed across the grasslands of Kansas, Nebraska, and the Dakotas. The first settlers took up land along the rivers and creeks, where they found enough timber for home-building, fuel, and fencing. Later arrivals had to build houses of the tough prairie sod and depend upon hay, dried sunflower stalks, even buffalo dung for fuel. The soil was rich, but the climate, especially in the semiarid regions beyond the 98th meridian of longitude, made agriculture frequently difficult and often impossible. Blizzards, floods, grasshopper plagues, and prairie fires caused repeated heartaches, but periodic drought and searing summer heat were the worst hazards, destroying the hopes and fortunes of thousands.

At the same time, the flat immensity of the land combined with newly available farm machinery and the development of rail connections with the East—to be discussed below—encouraged the growth of gigantic, corporation-controlled "bonanza" farms running sometimes into the tens of thousands of acres. One such organization was the railroad-owned empire managed by Oliver Dalrymple in Dakota Territory, which harvested 25,000 acres of wheat in 1880. Dalrymple employed 200 pairs of harrows to prepare his soil, 125 seeders to sow his seed, and 155 binders to harvest his crop. Such farmers could buy supplies wholesale and obtain concessions from railroads and processors, which added to their profits.

Bonanza farmers were the exception in every region, but smaller operators tried to ape their highly commercialized methods, often with disastrous results. Even the biggest organizations could not cope with prolonged drought, however, and most of the bonanza outfits failed in the dry years of the late eighties. Those wise farmers who diversified their crops and cultivated their land intensively fared better in the long run, though even they could not hope to earn a profit in really dry years.

Despite the hazards of plains agriculture, the region became the breadbasket of America in the decades after the Civil War. By 1889 Minnesota topped the nation in wheat production, and ten years later four of the five leading wheat states lay west of the Mississippi. Kansas and Nebraska ranked sixth and eighth among the corn states in 1879, third and fourth at the end of the next decade. The plains also accounted for heavy percentages of the nation's other cereal crops, together with immense quantities of beef, pork, and mutton.

Like other exploiters of the nation's resources, farmers took whatever they could from the soil with little heed for preserving its fertility and preventing erosion. The resultant national loss was less obvious since it was diffuse and slow to assume drastic proportions, but it was very real.

Western Railroad Building

Further exploitation of the land resources of the nation by private interests resulted from the government's policy of subsidizing western railroads. Here was a clear illustration of the conflict between equal opportunity and rapid economic growth, between the idea of the West as a national heritage to be disposed of to deserving citizens and the concept of the region as a boundless prize to be gobbled up in giant chunks by those interests powerful and determined enough to take it. When it came to a choice between giving a particular tract to railroads or to homesteaders, the homesteaders nearly always lost out. To serve a necessary national purpose, the linking of the sections by rail, the land of the West was dispensed wholesale as a substitute for cash subsidies.

Federal land grants to railroads began in 1850 with those allotted the Illinois Central. Over the next two decades about 49 million acres were given to various lines indirectly in the form of grants to the states, but the most lavish gifts of the public domain were those made directly to builders of intersectional trunk lines. These roads received over 155 million acres in this fashion, although about 25 million acres eventually reverted to the government when certain companies failed to construct the required miles of track. About 75 per cent of this went to aid the construction of four transcontinental railroads: the Union Pacific-Central Pacific line, running from Nebraska to San Francisco, completed in 1869; the Atchison, Topeka and Santa Fe, running from Kansas City to Los Angeles by way of Santa Fe and Albuquerque, completed in 1883; the Southern Pacific line, running from San Francisco to New Orleans by way of Yuma and El Paso, completed in 1883; and the Northern Pacific, running from Duluth, Minnesota, to Portland, Oregon, completed in 1883.

Unless the government had been willing to build the transcontinental lines itself, and this was unthinkable in an age so dominated by the spirit of individual exploitation and laissez faire, some system of subsidy was essential; private investors would not hazard the huge sums needed to lay tracks across hundreds of miles of rugged, empty country when traffic over the road could not possibly produce profits for many years. Grants of land seemed a sensible way of financing construction. The method avoided direct outlays of public funds, for the companies could pledge the land as security for bond issues or sell it directly for cash. Moreover, land and railroad values were intimately linked in contemporary thinking. "The occupation of new land and the building of new mileage go hand in hand," the *Commercial and Financial Chronicle* explained in 1886. "There could be no great or continuous opening up of new territory without the necessary facilities in the way of railroads. On the other hand, most new mileage on the borders of our Western territory is prosecuted with the idea and expectation that it is to pave the way for an accession of new settlers and an extension of the area of land devoted to their uses." It even seemed possible that in many cases the value of the land granted might be recovered by the government when it sold other lands in the vicinity, for such properties would certainly be worth more after transportation facilities to eastern markets had been constructed. "Why," asked the governor of one eastern state in 1867, "should private individuals be called upon to make a useless sacrifice of their means, when railroads can be constructed by the unity of public and private interests, and made profitable to all?"

The Pacific Railway Act of 1862 established the pattern for these grants. This law gave the builders of the Union Pacific and Central Pacific railroads five square miles of public land on each side of their right of way for each mile of track laid. The land was allotted in alternate sections, forming a pattern like a checkerboard, the squares of one color representing railroad property, the other government property. Presumably this arrangement benefited the government, since half the land close to the railroad remained in its hands.

However, whenever grants were made to railroads, the adjacent government lands were not opened to homesteaders, the theory being that free land in the immediate vicinity of a line would prevent the road from disposing of its properties at good prices. Since, in addition to the land actually granted, a wide zone of "indemnity" lands was reserved to allow the roads to choose alternative sites to make up for lands that settlers had already taken up within the checkerboard, homesteading was in fact prohibited near land-grant railroads. Grants per mile of track ranged from five alternate sections on each side of the track to the Union and Central Pacific to 40 sections to the Northern Pacific, authorized in 1864. In the latter case, when the indemnity zone was included, homesteaders were barred from an area 100 miles wide, running all the way from Lake Superior to the Pacific. Over 20 years after receiving its immense grant, the Northern Pacific was still attempting to keep homesteaders from filing in the indemnity zone. President Cleveland finally put a stop to this in 1887, saying that he could find "no evidence" that "this vast tract is necessary for the fulfillment of the grant."

Historians have argued at length about the fairness of the land-grant system. No railroad corporation waxed fat directly from the sale of its lands, which were sold at prices averaging between \$2 and \$5 an acre. Collectively the roads have taken in between \$400 and \$500 million from this source, but only over the course of a century. Land-grant lines did a great deal to encourage the growth of the West, advertising their property widely and providing both cheap transportation for prospective settlers and efficient shipping services for farmers. They were also required by law to carry troops and handle government business free or at reduced rates, which has saved the government many millions over the years. At the same time, the system imposed no effective restraints on the railroads in their use of the funds raised with federal aid. Building their lines largely with money obtained from land grants, the operators tended to be extravagant and often downright corrupt.

The Union Pacific, for example, was built by

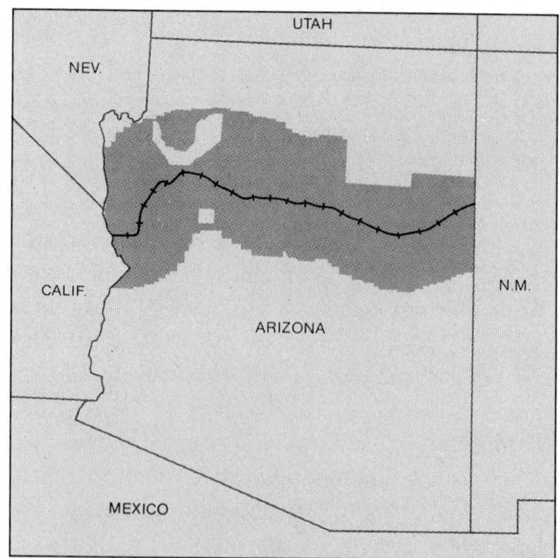

The Atlantic and Pacific's land grant in Arizona on the contemporary map at the right appears as shaded squares on the checkerboard. The grant cut a 100-mile-wide swath across the entire territory (above).

a construction company, the Crédit Mobilier, which was owned by the promoters. These men awarded themselves large contracts at prices that assured the Crédit Mobilier exorbitant profits. When Congress threatened to investigate the Union Pacific in 1868, Oakes Ames, a stockholder in both companies who was also a member of Congress, sold key congressmen and government officials over 300 shares of Crédit Mobilier stock at a price far below its real value. These shares were placed "where they will do the most good," Ames said. "I have found," he also said, "there is no difficulty in inducing men to look after their own property." When these transactions were later exposed, the House of Representatives censured Ames, but such was the temper of the times that neither he nor most of his associates believed he had done anything immoral. According to the president of one western railroad, congressmen frequently tried to use their influence to get railroad land at bargain prices. "Isn't there a discount?" they would ask. "Surely you can give the land cheaper to a friend. . . ." The railroads seldom resisted this type of pressure. Between 1866 and 1872 the Crédit Mobilier dispersed $400,000 for "legal expenses" that were really thinly disguised bribes, and in the period 1875–1885 the Central Pacific spent $500,000 *annually* in a similar manner.

The construction of the Central Pacific in the 1860's illustrates how the system encouraged extravagance. In addition to their land grants, the Central Pacific and the Union Pacific were given loans in the form of government bonds, ranging in value from $16,000 to $48,000 for each mile of track laid, depending upon the difficulty of the terrain. The two competed with each other for these subsidies, the Central Pacific building eastward from Sacramento, the Union Pacific westward from Nebraska. They put huge crews to work grading and laying track, bringing up supplies over the already completed road. The Union Pacific depended upon Civil War veterans and Irish immigrants, the Central upon Chinese immigrants.

This plan, typical of the dog-eat-dog philosophy of the times, favored the Union Pacific—while the Central Pacific was inching upward through the gorges and granite of the mighty Sierras, the Union Pacific was racing across the level plains. Once the Sierras were surmounted, the Central Pacific would have easy going across

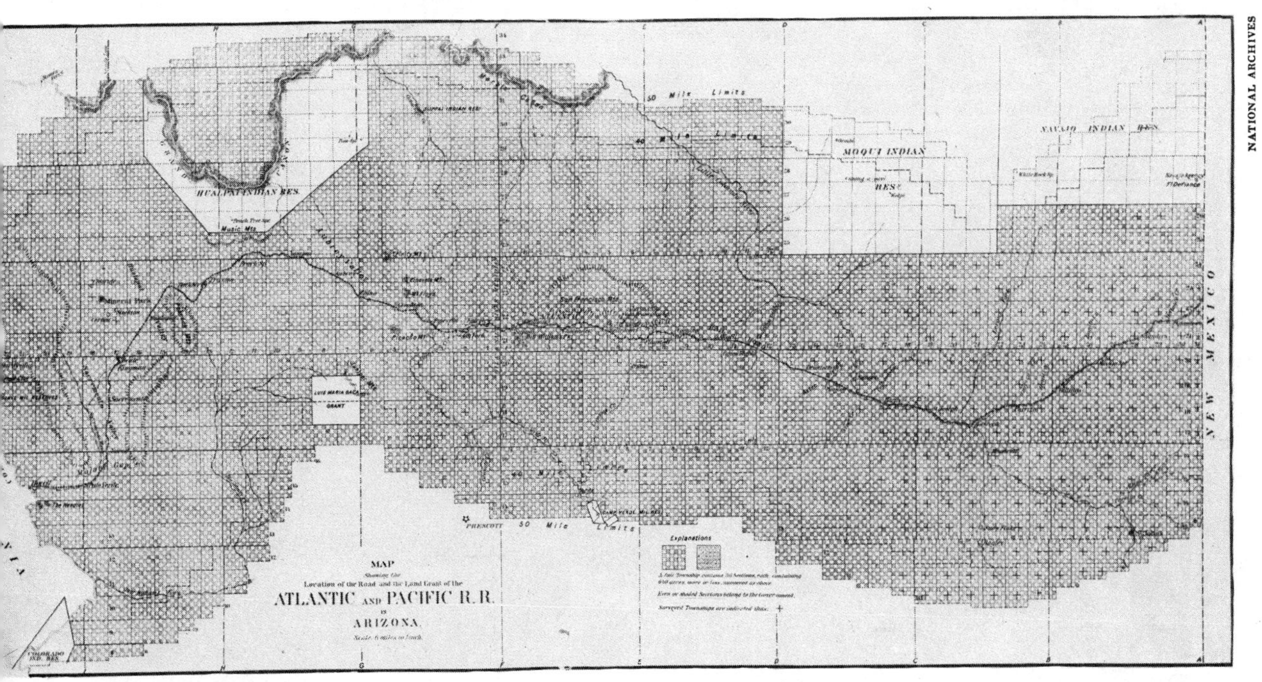

NATIONAL ARCHIVES

the Nevada-Utah plateau country, but by then it might be too late. To prevent the Union Pacific from making off with most of the government aid, the Central Pacific construction crews, headed by Charles Crocker, a hulking, relentless driver of men, who had come to California during the gold rush and made a small fortune as a merchant in Sacramento, wasted huge sums by working right through the winter in the High Sierras. Often the men labored in tunnels dug through 40-foot snowdrifts to get at the frozen ground. To speed construction of the Summit Tunnel, Crocker had a shaft cut down from above so that crews could work out from the middle as well as in from each end. In 1866, over the most difficult terrain, he laid 28 miles of track, but at a cost of over $280,000 a mile. Experts later estimated that 70 per cent of this sum could have been saved had speed not been such a factor. Such prodigality made economic sense to the "Big Four" (Collis P. Huntington, Leland Stanford, Mark Hopkins, and Crocker) who controlled the Central Pacific because of the fat profits they were making through its construction company and because of the gains they could count upon once they reached the flat country beyond the Sierras, where construction costs amounted to only half the federal aid.

Crocker's truly herculean efforts paid off. The mountains were conquered, and then the crews raced across the Great Basin to Salt Lake City and beyond. The final meeting of the rails—the occasion of a tremendous national celebration—took place at Promontory, north of Ogden, Utah, on May 10, 1869, Leland Stanford driving the final ceremonial golden spike with a silver hammer.* The Union Pacific had built 1,086 miles of track, the Central 689.

*A mysterious "San Francisco jeweler" passed among the onlookers, taking orders for souvenir watch chains which he proposed to make from the spike at $5 each. Of course he was an impostor.

The meeting of the rails at Promontory, Utah, May 10, 1869. Andrew J. Russell took this picture from atop the Central Pacific's Jupiter as it moved slowly toward the Union Pacific's No. 119. Dignitaries are gathered for the ceremony of the driving of the golden spike by rail magnate Leland Stanford. Stanford swung and missed.

OAKLAND MUSEUM

However, in the long run the wasteful way in which the Central Pacific was built hurt the road severely. It was ill-constructed, over too-steep grades and too-sharp curves, and burdened with too-heavy debts. Such was the fate of nearly all the railroads constructed with government subsidies. The only transcontinental built without land grants was the Great Northern, running from St. Paul, Minnesota, to the Pacific. Spending private capital, its guiding genius, James J. Hill, was compelled to build economically and to plan carefully. As a result, his was the only transcontinental line to weather the great depression of the 1890's without going into bankruptcy.

The Cattle Kingdom

While the miners were digging out the mineral wealth of the West and the railroads were taking possession of much of its land, another group was avidly acquiring its endless acres of grass. For 20 years after the Civil War, cattlemen and sheep raisers dominated huge areas of the High Plains, making millions of dollars by grazing their herds on lands they did not own. Throughout American history, frontier farmers commonly grazed their livestock on undeveloped public lands, but never on such a scale as on the plains.

Columbus brought the first cattle to the New World in 1493, on his second voyage, and later *conquistadores* took them to every corner of Spain's American empire. Mexico proved to be particularly well-suited to cattle raising. Cortés, for example, called his great Mexican estate Cuernavaca, or Cow Horn. Over the years many Mexican cattle were allowed to roam loose, and they multiplied rapidly in some sections. By the late 18th century what is now southern Texas contained what one observer called "an incredible number of Castilian cattle." These beasts interbred with nondescript "English" cattle, brought into the area by American settlers, to produce the Texas longhorn. Hardy, wiry, ill-tempered, and fleet, with horns often attaining a spread of six feet, these animals were far from ideal as beef cattle and almost as hard to capture as wild horses, but they existed in southern Texas by the millions, most of them unowned.

The lack of markets and transportation explains why Texas cattle were so lightly regarded. But conditions were changing. Industrial growth in the East was causing an increase in the urban population and a consequent rise in the demand for food. At the same time, the expansion of the railroad network made it possible to move cattle cheaply over long distances. As the iron rails inched across the plains, astute cattlemen began to do some elementary figuring. Longhorns could be had locally for $3 or $4 a head. In the northern cities they would bring ten times that much, perhaps even more. Why not round them up and herd them northward to the railroads, allowing them to feed along the way on the abundant grasses of the plains?

In 1866 a number of Texans drove large herds northward toward Sedalia, Missouri, railhead of the Missouri Pacific. This route, however, took the herd through wooded and settled country and across Indian reservations, which provoked many difficulties. The next year the drovers, inspired by a clever young Illinois cattle dealer named Joseph G. McCoy, led their herds north by a more westerly route, across unsettled grasslands, to Abilene, Kansas, on the Kansas Pacific line.

They earned excellent profits, and during the next five years about 1.5 million head made the "Long Drive" over the Chisholm Trail to Abilene. Other shipping points sprang up as the railroads pushed westward. Altogether, before the era ended, about 4 million longhorns were driven from Texas to the central plains across the public lands.

The technique of the Long Drive, which involved guiding herds of two or three thousand cattle slowly across as much as a thousand miles of trackless country, produced the American cowboy, renowned in song, story, and on film. Half a dozen of these men could control several thousand steers. Mounted on wiry ponies, they would range alongside the herd, keeping the animals on the move but preventing stampedes, allowing them time to rest yet steadily pressing them toward the yards of Abilene.

Although the cowboy's life was far more prosaic than it appears in modern legend, con-

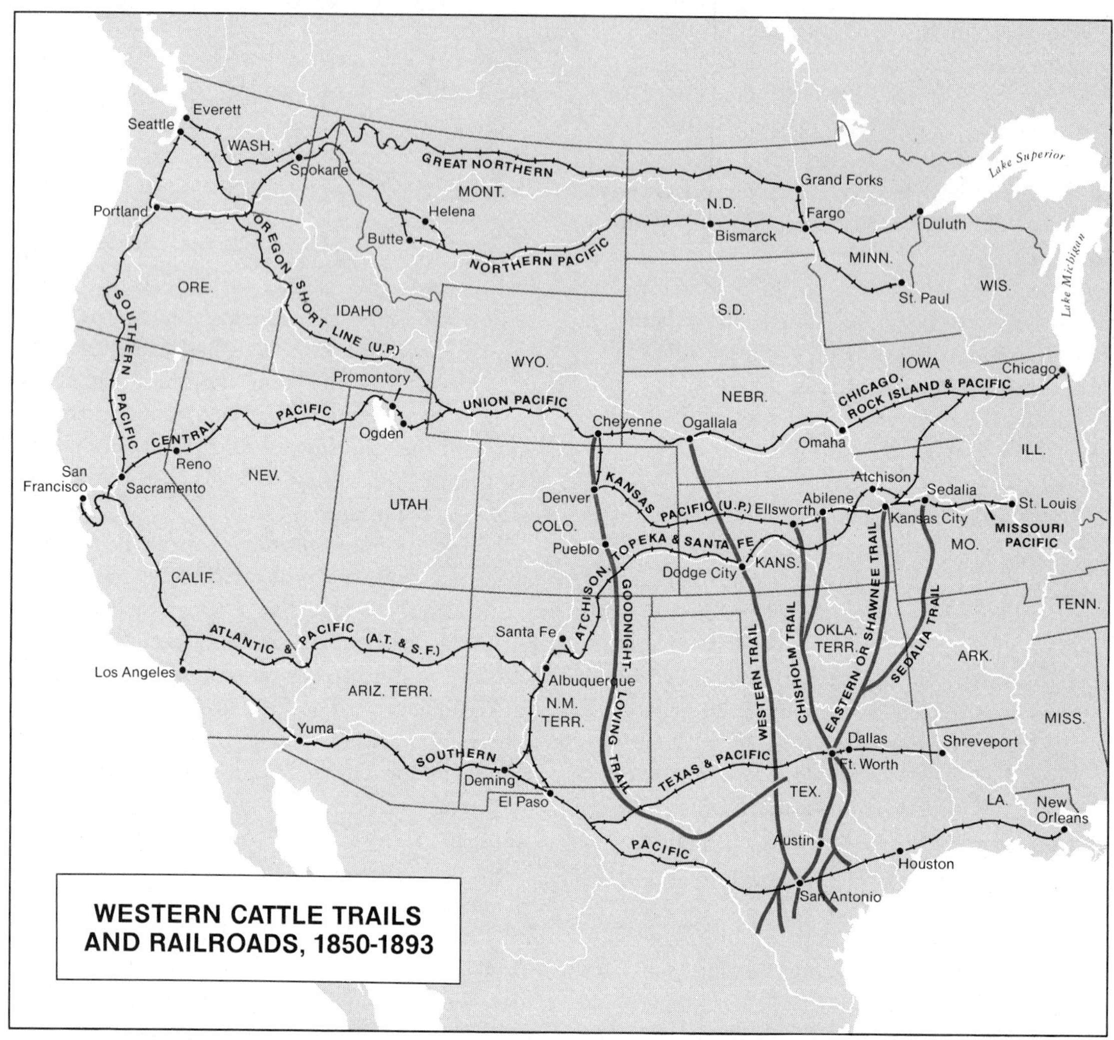

WESTERN CATTLE TRAILS AND RAILROADS, 1850-1893

sisting mainly of endless hours in the saddle surrounded by thousands of bellowing beasts, he was indeed an interesting type, perfectly adapted to his plains environment. Cowboys virtually lived on horseback, for their work kept them far from human habitation for months on end. Most, accustomed to solitude, were indeed "strong, silent men." They were courageous, and expert marksmen, too, for they lived amid many dangers and had to know how to protect themselves. Few grew rich, yet like the miners and other men of the West, they were true representatives of their time—determinedly individualistic, contemptuous of authority, crude of manner, devoted to coarse pleasures.

"Cow towns" like Abilene, Ellsworth, and Dodge City were as riotous and as venal as any mining camp. "I have seen many fast towns," one tough westerner declared, "but Abilene beat them all." A local merchant characterized that town as a "seething, roaring, flaming hell"; its saloons, bearing names like Alamo, Applejack, Longhorn, and Old Fruit, were packed during the season with crowds of rambunctious, gun-toting pleasure seekers. Gambling houses and brothels abounded. When Ellsworth, Kansas, had a population of only a thousand, it had 75 resident professional gamblers. At dance halls like Rowdy Joe's, the customers were expected to buy drinks for themselves and their partners after each dance. Little wonder that McCoy wrote in his *Historic Sketches of the Cattle Trade* (1874): "Few more wild, reckless scenes of abandoned debauchery can be seen on the civilized earth than a dance hall in full blast in one of these frontier towns."

Open-Range Ranching

Soon cattlemen discovered that the hardy Texas stock could survive the winters of the northern plains. Attracted by the apparently limitless forage, they began to bring up herds to stock the vast regions where the buffalo had so recently roamed. By introducing pedigreed Hereford bulls, they improved the stock without weakening its resistance to harsh conditions. By 1869 a million longhorns grazed in Colorado Territory alone, and by 1880 some 4.5 million head had spread across the great sea of grass that ran from Kansas to Montana and west to the Rockies.

The prairie grasses offered cattlemen a bonanza almost as valuable as the gold mines. Open-range ranching required actual ownership of no more than a few acres along some watercourse. In this semiarid region, control of water enabled a man to dominate all the surrounding area back to the divide separating his range from the next stream without investing a cent in the purchase of land. His cattle, wandering freely on the public domain, fattened on grass owned by all the people, to be turned into beefsteak and leather for the profit of the rancher. Theoretically, anyone could pasture stock upon the open range, but without access to water it was impossible to do so. "I have two miles of running water," a cattleman said in testifying before the Public Land Commission. "That accounts for my ranch being where it is. The next water from me in one direction is 23 miles; now no man can have a ranch between these two places. I have control of the grass, the same as though I owned it." By having his cowhands take out homestead claims along watercourses in his region, a rancher could greatly expand the area he dominated. In the late 1870's one Colorado cattle baron controlled an area roughly the size of Connecticut and Rhode Island, although he actually owned outright only 105 small parcels that totaled altogether about 15,500 acres.

Generally, a group of ranchers acted together, obtaining legal title to the lands along the bank of a stream and grazing their cattle over the whole area drained by it. The herds became thoroughly intermixed, each owner's being identified by his individual brand mark. Every spring and fall the ranchers staged a great roundup, driving in all the cattle to a central place, separating them by brand marks, culling steers for shipment to market, and branding new calves.

With the demand for meat rising and transportation relatively cheap (a carload of 20 steers could be shipped from remote Montana to Chicago for less than $200), a princely fortune could be made in a few years with a relatively small investment. Some capitalists from the East and from Europe began to pour funds into the business. By the early 1880's outfits like the Prairie Cattle Company and the Nebraska Land and Cattle Company, controlled by British investors, and the Union Cattle Company of Wyoming, a $3 million corporation, were beginning to dominate the business, just as large companies had taken over most of the important gold and silver mines.

Attracted by what one writer called the "Beef Bonanza"—in a book subtitled *How to Get Rich on the Plains*—Eastern "dudes" like Theodore Roosevelt, a young New York assemblyman who sank over $50,000 in his Elkhorn Ranch in Dakota Territory in 1883, bought up cattle as a sort of profitable hobby. The seemingly limitless range began to be overcrowded. Farmers pushing the frontier westward plowed up the land and fenced off regions where formerly cattle had roamed. Sheep raisers, especially in Montana and the mountain states, were competing with the cattlemen too.

Unlike other exploiters of the West's resources, the ranchers did not at first injure or reduce any public resource. Grass eaten by their stock annually renewed itself, the soil enriched by the droppings of the animals. Furthermore, ranchers poached on the public domain because there was no reasonable way for them to obtain legal possession of the large areas necessary to raise cattle on the plains. Federal land laws made no allowances for the needs of stockmen and the special conditions of the semiarid West. "Title to the public lands [of the West] cannot be honestly acquired under the homestead laws," S.E. Burdett, commissioner of the General Land Office, wrote in an 1875 report. "That cultivation and improvement which are required . . . in the place of price, are impossible. . . . A system of sale should be authorized in accordance with the necessities of the situation."

Such a system was soon devised by Major John Wesley Powell, later the director of the United States Geological Survey. His *Report on the Lands of the Arid Region of the United States* (1879) suggested that western lands be divided into three classes: irrigable lands, timber lands, and "pasturage" lands. On the pasturage lands the "farm unit" ought to be at least 2,560 acres (four sections), Powell urged. Groups of these units should be organized into "pasturage districts" in which the ranchers "should have the right to make their own regulations for the division of lands, the use of the water . . . and for the pasturage of lands in common or in severalty."

However, Congress refused to change the land laws in any basic way, and this had two harmful effects. First, it encouraged fraud: men who could not get title to enough land honestly soon turned to subterfuges. The Desert Land Act (1877) provided well-to-do ranchers with a relatively simple way to do this. It allowed anyone to obtain 640 acres in the arid states for $1.25 an acre provided he irrigated part of it within three years. Since the original claimant could transfer his holding, the ranchers set their cowboys and other hands to filing claims, which were then signed over to them. Over 2.6 million acres were taken up under the act, and according to the best estimate, about 95 per cent of the claims were fraudulent—no sincere effort was made to irrigate the land.

Secondly, because Congress refused to pass laws suited to actual conditions, overcrowding quickly became a problem, leading in turn to serious conflicts, even to shooting, because no one had an uncontestable title to the land. The leading ranchers banded together in cattlemen's

NEBRASKA STATE HISTORICAL SOCIETY

In 1885 masked Nebraskans seeking access to water posed for photographer S.D. Butcher, who captioned the picture, "Settlers taking the law in their own hands: cutting 15 miles of the Brighton Ranch fence."

associations to deal with such problems as quarantine regulations, overcrowding, water rights, and thievery. In most cases these associations devised remarkably effective and sensible rules, but their functions would better have been performed by the government, as such matters usually are.

To keep other men's cattle from those sections of the public domain they considered their own, these associations, and many individual ranchers, began to fence huge areas. This was possible only because of the invention in 1874 of a practical type of barbed wire by Joseph F. Glidden, an Illinois farmer. By the 1880's thousands of miles of the new fencing had been strung across the plains, often across roads, and in a few cases around entire communities. One Texas group ran wire all the way from the Indian Territory to the Rio Grande! "Barbed-wire wars" resulted, fought by rancher against rancher, cattlemen against sheepmen, herder against farmer. The associations tried to police their fences and to punish anyone who cut their wire. Signs posted along lonely stretches gave dire warnings to trespassers. "The Son of a Bitch who opens this fence had better look out for his scalp," one such sign announced, a perfect statement of the philosophy of the age. On the other hand, as one Texas Ranger reported: "Good citizens hold the wire-cutters in dread for they know they would not hesitate a moment to murder them."

By installing these fences the cattlemen were unwittingly destroying their own way of doing business. On a truly open range, cattle could fend for themselves in any weather, instinctively finding water during droughts, drifting safely downwind before the wildest blizzards. Barbed wire prevented their free movement. During winter storms these slender strands became as lethal as high-tension wires: the drifting cattle piled up against them and died by the thousands. "The advent of barbed wire," wrote Walter Prescott Webb in his classic study *The Great Plains* (1931), "brought about the disappearance of the open, free range and converted the range country into the big-pasture country."

The boom times were ending. Overproduction was driving down the price of beef; expenses were on the rise; many sections of the range were becoming badly overgrazed. The dry summer of 1886 left the stock in poor condition as winter approached, and experienced cattlemen were badly worried. The *Rocky Mountain Husbandman* urged its readers to sell their cattle despite the prevailing low prices rather than "endanger the whole herd by having the range overstocked."

Some ranchers took this advice; those who did not made a fatal error. Winter that year came early and with unparalleled fury. Blizzards raged and temperatures plummeted far below zero. Cattle crowded into low places only to be engulfed in giant snowdrifts; barbed wire took a fearful toll. When spring finally came, the streams were choked with rotting carcasses. Between 80 and 90 per cent of all the cattle on the range were dead, many of the survivors in pitiful condition. "We have had a perfect smashup all through the cattle country," Theodore Roosevelt wrote sadly in April 1887 from Elkhorn Ranch.

After that cruel winter, open-range cattle raising quickly disappeared. The large companies were bankrupted, many independent operators, such as Roosevelt, became discouraged and sold out. When the industry revived, it was on a smaller, although more efficiently organized scale. The fencing movement continued, but now each stockman confined himself to enclosing land he actually owned. It then became possible to bring in blooded bulls to improve the breed scientifically. With more valuable, less hardy cattle raised in relatively confined quarters, it was necessary to grow quantities of hay for winter feeding and to sink wells, powered by windmills, to provide water for the animals in all seasons. Cattle-raising, like mining before it, ceased to be an adventure in rollicking individualism and reckless greed and became a business.

Thus, by the late eighties, the bonanza days of the West were over. No previous frontier had caught the imagination of Americans so completely as the Great West, with its wealth, its heroic size, its awesome emptiness, its massive, sculptured beauty. Now the frontier was no more. Most of what Professor Webb called the "primary windfalls" of the region—the furs, the precious metals, the forests, the cattle, and the grass—had been snatched up by first-comers and by men already wealthy. Big companies were taking over all the West's resources. The nation was becoming more powerful, richer, larger, its economic structure more complex and diversified as the West yielded it treasures, but the East, and especially eastern industrialists and financiers, were increasingly dominating the economy of the whole nation.

SUPPLEMENTARY READING The psychology and the political ideas current in this period are covered in Sidney Fine, *Laissez Faire and the General Welfare State** (1956), Richard Hofstadter, *Social Darwinism in American Thought** (1945), and J.W. Hurst, *Law and the Conditions of Freedom in the Nineteenth-Century United States** (1956). C.D. Warner and Mark Twain, *The Gilded Age**

(1873), is a useful and entertaining contemporary impression. On the views of businessmen, see E.C. Kirkland, *Dream and Thought in the Business Community** (1956), Kirkland's edition of Andrew Carnegie's writings, *The Gospel of Wealth* (1962), R.G. McCloskey, *American Conservatism in the Age of Enterprise** (1951), T.C. Cochran, *Railroad Leaders* (1953), and J.D. Rockefeller, *Random Reminiscences of Men and Events* (1909).

R.A. Billington, *Westward Expansion* (1967), is the best introduction to the history of the exploitation of the West. On the Indians, general works include Paul Radin, *The Story of the American Indian* (1944), John Collier, *Indians of the Americas** (1947), and W.T. Hagan, *American Indians** (1961). Of more specialized works, the following are useful: F.G. Roe, *The Indian and the Horse* (1955), L.B. Priest, *Uncle Sam's Stepchildren: The Reformation of United States Indian Policy* (1942), H.E. Fritz, *The Movement for Indian Assimilation* (1963), D.A. Brown, *The Galvanized Yankees* (1963), L.R. Hafen and W.J. Ghent, *Broken Hand: The Life Story of Thomas Fitzpatrick* (1931), and R.G. Athearn, *William Tecumseh Sherman and the Settlement of the West* (1956). The destruction of the buffalo is described in vivid if highly imaginative terms in Mari Sandoz, *The Buffalo Hunters* (1954). H.H. Jackson, *A Century of Dishonor** (1881), is a powerful contemporary indictment of United States Indian policy.

For the fate of other minority groups, see J.H. Franklin, *From Slavery to Freedom* (1956), R.W. Logan, *The Negro in American Life and Thought: The Nadir** (1954), S.P. Hirshson, *Farewell to the Bloody Shirt* (1962), V.P. De Santis, *Republicans Face the Southern Question* (1959), C.V. Woodward, *The Strange Career of Jim Crow** (1966), J.A. Garraty (ed.), *Quarrels That Have Shaped the Constitution** (1964), Gunther Barth, *Bitter Strength: A History of the Chinese in the United States* (1964), R.A. Billington, *The Protestant Crusade** (1938), and John Higham, *Strangers in the Land** (1955).

For the mining frontier, consult R.W. Paul, *Mining Frontiers of the Far West** (1963), W.T. Jackson, *Treasure Hill: Portrait of a Silver Mining Camp** (1963), D.A. Smith, *Rocky Mountain Mining Camps: The Urban Frontier* (1967), and W.J. Trimble, *The Mining Advance into the Inland Empire* (1914). Mark Twain, *Roughing It** (1872), is a classic contemporary account, and W.H. Goetzmann, *Exploration and Empire* (1966), throws much light on all aspects of western development. For federal land policy, see R.M. Robbins, *Our Landed Heritage** (1942), P.W. Gates, *Fifty Million Acres** (1954), and F.A. Shannon, *The Farmer's Last Frontier** (1945), which is excellent on all questions relating to post-Civil War agriculture. Everett Dick, *The Sod-House Frontier* (1937), presents a graphic picture of farm life on the treeless plains. Bonanza farming is described in H.M. Drache, *The Day of the Bonanza* (1964).

The development of transcontinental railroads is discussed in R.E. Riegel, *The Story of the Western Railroads** (1926), Julius Grodinsky, *Transcontinental Railway Strategy* (1962), O.O. Winther, *The Transportation Frontier* (1964), and G.R. Taylor and I.D. Neu, *The American Railroad Network* (1956). For a sampling of the literature on specific roads, see James McCague, *Moguls and Iron Men* (1964), Oscar Lewis, *The Big Four* (1938), J.B. Hedges, *Henry Villard and the Railroads of the Northwest* (1930), and L.L. Waters, *Steel Rails to Santa Fe* (1950). Matthew Josephson, *The Robber Barons** (1934), discusses the chicanery connected with railroad construction at length.

On cattle ranching on the plains, a good account is Lewis Atherton, *The Cattle Kings* (1961), but see also E.S. Osgood, *The Day of the Cattleman** (1929), and Louis Pelzer, *The Cattlemen's Frontier* (1936). For the cowboy and his life, see E.E. Dale, *Cow Country* (1942), Andy Adams, *The Log of a Cowboy** (1902), and J.B. Frantz and J.E. Choate, *The American Cowboy: The Myth and Reality* (1955). W.P. Webb, *The Great Plains** (1931), is a fascinating analysis of the development of a unique civilization on the plains.

*Available in paperback.

18

An Industrial Giant

When the Civil War began, the United States was still a primarily agricultural country; its industrial output, while important and increasing, did not approach that of major European powers. By the end of the century the nation had become far and away the colossus among the world's manufacturers, dwarfing the production of such countries as Great Britain and Germany. The value of manufactured products rose from $1.8 billion in 1859 to $3.3 billion in 1869, $5.3 billion in 1879, $9.3 billion in 1889, and to over $13 billion in 1899. Modern economists estimate that the output of goods and services in the country (the gross national product, or GNP) increased by 44 per cent between 1874 and 1883 and continued to expand, although at a somewhat reduced rate, in succeeding years. According to the economic historian Carter Goodrich, the United States in the 19th century was "the world's greatest example of economic development."

Industrial Growth: an Overview

No radical change explains why industrialization proceeded at such a pace. American manufacturing merely continued to gather momentum. New natural resources were always being discovered and exploited, thus increasing opportunities, attracting the brightest and most energetic of a large, vigorous, and expanding population. The growth of the country added constantly to the size of the national market, while protective tariffs guarded it against foreign competition. However, foreign capital entered the market freely, perhaps in part because tariffs kept out many foreign goods. In a single year, 1871, London absorbed $110 million in American securities; by 1893 foreigners had poured $3 billion into the United States, although, of course, not all of this was invested in industry. The dominant spirit of the time encouraged businessmen to maximum effort by emphasizing progress, glorifying material wealth, and justifying aggressiveness. New European immigrants provided the manpower needed by expanding industry. Two-and-a-half million arrived in the seventies, twice that number in the eighties.

New inventions played a particularly important role in this

growth. It was a period of rapid advance in basic science, and, as one recent student has written, "our capitalists showed a marked appetite for innovations and an unusually progressive spirit. . . . They seemed to grasp thoroughly the importance of investing in scientific research." Scientists and technicians created a bountiful harvest of new machines, processes, and power sources (total horsepower employed in manufacturing increased from 2.3 million in 1869 to 10 million in 1899). These stimulated every branch of the economy. In agriculture, to take but one field, there were James Oliver's chilled iron plow, perfected by 1877, what one contemporary expert called "an endless variety of cultivators," better harvesters, binding machines, and great combines capable of threshing and bagging 450 pounds of grain a minute. An 1886 report of the Illinois Bureau of Labor Statistics claimed that "new machinery has displaced fully 50 per cent of the muscular labor formerly required to do a given amount of work in the manufacture of agricultural implements." Packaged cereals appeared on the American breakfast table at this time, and the commercial canning of food, spurred by improved machinery which cut costs, expanded so rapidly that by 1887 a writer in *Good Housekeeping* magazine could say: "Housekeeping is getting to be ready made, as well as clothing." This profusion of ingenuity in the field of raising and processing food was typical. Statistics of the United States Patent Office show that whereas in the 1850's about 1,000 inventions a year were patented, in the 1870's the average was over 12,000. In 1890 alone 25,322 patents were issued.

The Railroad Network

In 1866, returning from his honeymoon in Europe, 30-year-old Charles Francis Adams, Jr., grandson and great-grandson of Presidents, full of ambition and ready, as he put it, to confront the world "face to face," looked about in search of a career. "Surveying the whole field," he later explained, "I fixed on the railroad system as the most developing force and the largest field of the day, and determined to attach myself to it." Adams' judgment was acute: for the next 25 years the railroads were probably the most significant element in American economic development, railroad executives the most powerful people in the country.

Some historians claim that the railroads were not indispensable to 19th-century economic growth, arguing that the canal and river network could have sustained the post-Civil War expansion and that the motorcar and truck would have been developed sooner if railroads had not existed. In *Railroads and American Economic Growth* Robert W. Fogel insists that "no single innovation was vital" and that the railroads did not make "an overwhelming contribution." In the sense that it warns us against applying the oversimplified "hero theory of history . . . to things," Fogel's work is valuable. It does not, however, suggest that railroads were anything but a major influence.

Railroads were important first of all as an industry in themselves. Less than 35,000 miles of track existed when Lee laid down his sword at Appomattox. In 1870 railroad mileage exceeded 52,000, by 1875 it was over 74,000. In 1880 mileage passed the 93,000 mark, and then, after so much growth, came the real boom: 73,000 miles were laid during the next decade. In 1890 some 166,700 miles of track spanned the United States. Railroads took in over $1 billion in passenger and freight revenues in that year. (The federal government's income in 1890 was only $403 million.) The value of railroad properties and equipment was over $8.7 billion. The national *railroad* debt of $5.1 billion was almost five times as large as the national debt itself, $1.1 billion!

The emphasis in railroad construction after 1865 was on organizing integrated systems. This resulted from sheer necessity. The lines had high fixed costs: taxes, interest on their bonds, maintenance of track and rolling stock, salaries of office personnel. A short train with half-empty cars required almost as many men and as much fuel to operate as a long one jammed with freight or passengers. In order to earn profits the railroads had to carry as much traffic as possible. They therefore spread out feeder lines to draw business to their main lines the way the root network of a tree draws water into its trunk.

Before the Civil War, as we have seen, men and freight could travel by rail from beyond Chicago and St. Louis to the Atlantic coast, but only after the war did true trunk lines appear. In 1861, for example, the New York Central ran across the center of New York from Albany to Buffalo. One could proceed from Buffalo to Chicago, but on a different company's trains. In 1867 the Central passed into the hands of "Commodore" Cornelius Vanderbilt, who had made a large fortune in the shipping business. Vanderbilt already controlled lines running from Albany to New York City; now he merged these properties with the Central. In 1873 he integrated the Lake Shore and Michigan Southern into his empire and two years later the Michigan Central. The Commodore spent large sums improving his properties and buying strategic feeder lines. At his death in 1877 the Central operated a network of over 4,500 miles of track between New York City and most of the principal cities of the Middle West.

While Vanderbilt was putting together the New York Central complex, Thomas A. Scott was making the Pennsylvania Company into a second important trunk line, fusing roads to Cincinnati, Indianapolis, St. Louis, and Chicago to his Pennsylvania Railroad, which linked Pittsburgh and Philadelphia. In 1871 the Pennsylvania also obtained access to New York and soon reached Baltimore and Washington. By 1869 another important system, the Erie, controlled by a triumvirate of railroad freebooters, Daniel Drew, Jay Gould, and Jim Fisk, had extended itself beyond its original route between New York and Buffalo to Cleveland, Cincinnati, and St. Louis. Soon thereafter it, too, tapped the markets of Chicago and other principal cities. The Erie could advertise boastfully: "1,400 miles under one management; 860 miles without a change of cars; the broad-gauge, double-track route between New York, Boston, and New England cities and the West." In 1874 the Baltimore and Ohio also obtained access to Chicago.

The transcontinental lines, of course, were trunk lines from the start; the emptiness of the western country would have made short lines un-

Links in the nation's increasingly interdependent transportation network can be glimpsed in this 1878 painting by a primitive artist, Herman Decker. The scene is the bustling Lonsdale Wharf in Providence, Rhode Island.

EUM OF ART, RHODE ISLAND SCHOOL OF DESIGN

profitable, and builders quickly grasped the need for direct connections to eastern markets and thorough integration of feeder lines and subsidiaries into an efficient transportation system. The dominant systematizer of the Southwest was Jay Gould. A soft-spoken, delicate, unostentatious man who looked, according to one newspaperman, "like an insignificant pigmy," Gould was actually ruthless, cynical, and aggressive. His mere appearance in Wall Street, one Texas newspaper reported in 1890, made "millionaires tremble like innocent sparrows . . . when a hungry hawk swoops down upon them." (A railroad president used a better image when he called Gould a "perfect eel.") With millions acquired in shady railroad and stock market ventures, Gould invaded the West in the 1870's, buying 370,000 shares of Union Pacific stock. He also took over the Kansas Pacific, running from Denver to Kansas City, which he consolidated with the Union Pacific; and the Missouri Pacific, a line from Kansas City to St. Louis, which he expanded through mergers and purchases into a 5,300-mile system. The Texas and Pacific and many other lines became part of his empire. Often Gould put together such properties merely to unload them on other railroads at a profit, but his grasp of the importance of integration was sound. In the Northwest, Henry Villard, a German-born ex-newspaperman, constructed another great railroad complex, based on his control of the Northern Pacific and various properties in Oregon and California. James J. Hill's expansion of the St. Paul and Pacific Railroad into the Great Northern system, absorbing a number of other lines in addition to laying track all the way to Seattle, produced still another western network.

The Civil War had demonstrated the lack of through railroad connections in the South. Shortly after the conflict, this situation began to be corrected as northern capital flowed into southern railroad construction. The Chesapeake and Ohio, organized in 1868, soon opened a direct line from Norfolk, Virginia, to Cincinnati. The Richmond and Danville absorbed some 26 lines after the war, forming a system that ran from Washington to the Mississippi. It in turn became part of the Richmond and West Point Terminal Company, which by the late eighties controlled an 8,558-mile network, largest in the region. Like other southern trunk lines, such as the Louisville and Nashville and the Atlantic Coast Line, this great system was largely controlled by northern capitalists. Gradually over the years the trunk lines had adopted a standard gauge (4 feet 8½ inches) for their tracks. After the southern lines accepted standard gauge in 1886, cars could move freely from system to system all over the country.

The railroads also stimulated the economy indirectly, acting as had foreign commerce and then the textile industry in earlier times as a multiplier speeding development. In 1869 they bought $41.6 million worth of railroad cars and locomotives; thereafter, they expanded their orders in an almost unending progression until in 1889 they bought rolling stock valued at $90.8 million. Such purchases created thousands of jobs, consumed raw materials, and led to countless technological advances. The roads used huge quantities of iron and steel. In 1881, for example, they consumed about 94 per cent of all the rolled steel manufactured in the United States.

Because of their voracious appetite for traffic, railroads in sparsely settled regions and in areas with undeveloped resources devoted much money and effort to stimulating local economic growth. The Louisville and Nashville, for instance, was a prime mover in the expansion of the iron industry in Alabama in the 1880's. The state's output of iron increased tenfold between 1880 and 1889, in considerable part because of the railroad's activities in building spur lines to mines and furnaces and attracting capital into the industry. The president of the Louisville and Nashville during this period, Milton Hannibal Smith, has been called by one historian of the iron industry "the strongest force in the industrial history of Alabama."

The land-grant railroads sought incessantly to speed the settlement of new regions. They sold land cheaply and on easy terms, since sales meant future business as well as quick income. Roads like the Northern Pacific offered special reduced rates to travelers interested in buying farms and

CHICAGO HISTORICAL SOCIETY

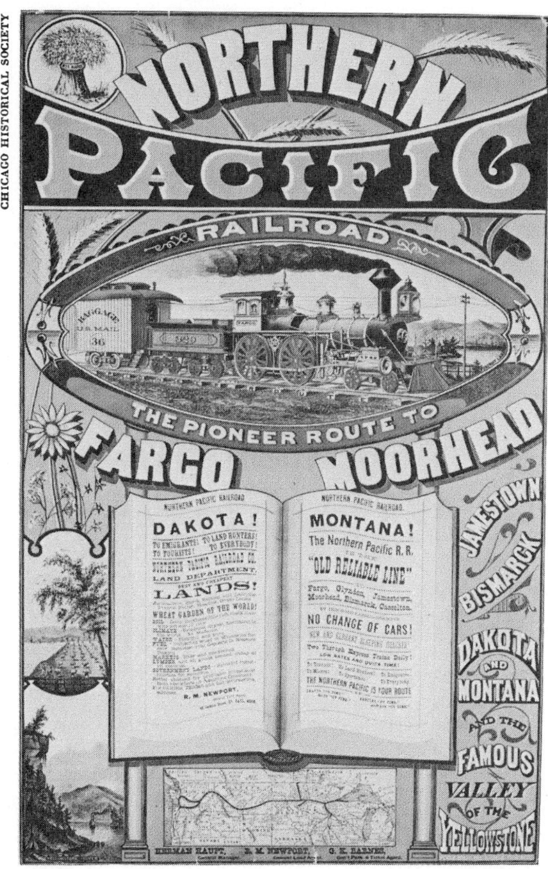

A Northern Pacific poster touts its land offerings as the "best and cheapest" available. By 1917 the railroad had realized $136 million on its land grants.

entertained potential customers with a free hand. Land-grant lines also set up "bureaus of immigration," which distributed elaborate brochures describing the wonders of the new country. Their agents greeted immigrants at the great eastern ports and tried to steer them to railroad property. Overseas branches advertised the virtues of American farmland widely. They sent agents who were usually themselves immigrants—often ministers—all over Europe to drum up prospective settlers, many of whom could be expected to buy railroad land. Occasionally, whole colonies migrated to America under railroad auspices, such as the 1,900 Mennonites who came to Kansas from Russia in 1874 to settle on the land of the Atchison, Topeka and Santa Fe.

Technological advances in railroading also accelerated economic development in complex ways. In 1869 George Westinghouse invented the air brake. By enabling an engineer to apply the brakes simultaneously to all his cars, whereas formerly each car had to be braked separately by its own conductor or brakeman, this invention made possible revolutionary increases in the size of trains and the speed at which they could safely operate. The sleeping car, invented in 1864 by George Pullman, now came into its own.

To pull these heavier trains, more powerful locomotives were needed. These in turn produced a call for stronger and more durable rails to bear the additional weight. Steel, itself reduced in cost because of technological developments, supplied the answer, for steel rails outlasted iron many times despite the use of much heavier equipment. "Steel rails," one expert said in the eighties, "form the very 'cornerstone' of the great improvements which have taken place in railroad efficiency." In 1880 only 50 per cent of the nation's rails were of steel; by 1890 less than 1 per cent were not.

A close tie developed at this time between the railroads and the nation's telegraph network, dominated by the Western Union Company. Commonly, the roads allowed Western Union to string wires along their rights of way, and they transported telegraphers and their equipment without charge. In return they received free telegraphic service, important for efficiency and safety. It is no mere coincidence that the early 1880's, a period of booming railroad construction, also saw a fantastic expansion of Western Union. By 1883 the company was transmitting 40 million messages a year over 400,000 miles of wire. The two industries, as Jay Gould put it, went "hand in hand, . . . integral parts" of American civilization.

Iron, Oil, and Electricity

The transformation of iron manufacturing affected the nation almost as much as railroad development. America was blessed with rich deposits of iron ore and with fuels—first wood and then coal—for smelting and refining it. As we have seen, considerable iron was produced in colonial times. After inde-

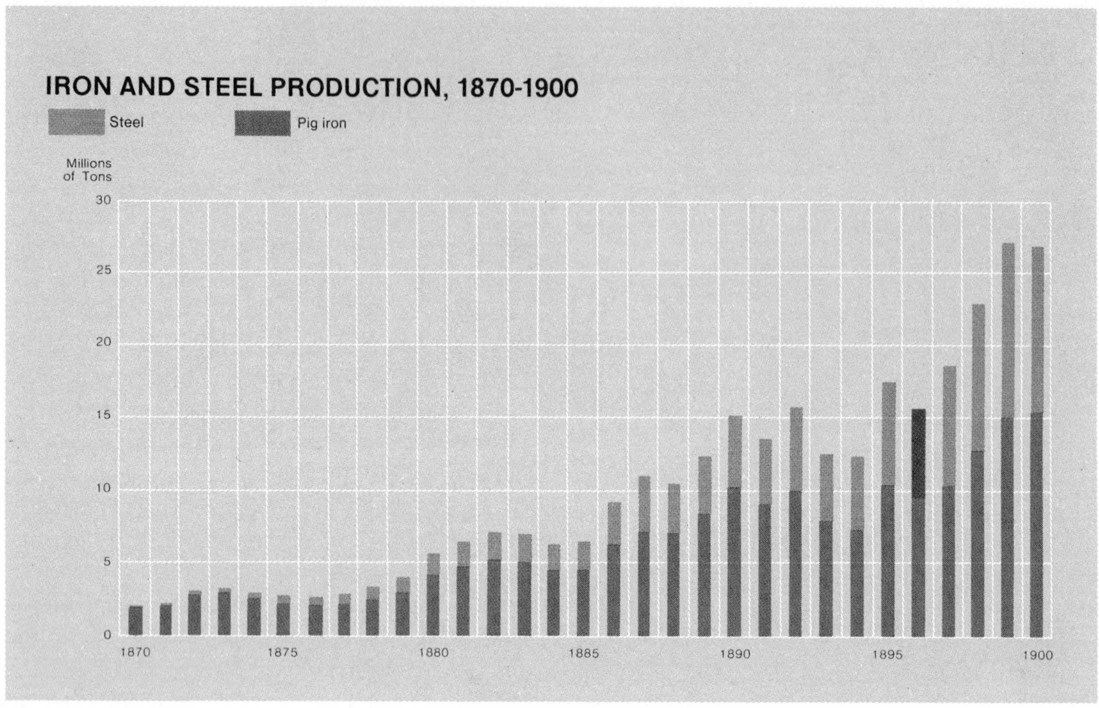

Minnesota's Mesabi Range (right, shown in 1899) was developed largely with Rockefeller money. It shipped 4,000 tons of iron ore in 1892, and within a decade tripled that amount—an increase reflected in the graph above.

pendence, growth was rapid: 22,000 tons in 1820; 185,000 in 1830; 321,000 in 1840; 631,000 in 1850; and 920,000 in 1860. In the postwar era, however, iron production increased still more spectacularly. In 1870 output reached 1.86 million tons. In 1880 it was 4.29 million; in 1890, 10.3 million; in 1900, 15.4 million.

Steel production expanded even more rapidly. Steel is a very special form of iron. In its pure form (wrought iron) the metal is tough but relatively soft. On the other hand, ordinary cast iron, which contains large amounts of carbon and other impurities, is hard but brittle. Steel, which contains one or two per cent carbon, combines the hardness of cast iron with the toughness of wrought iron. For nearly every purpose—structural girders for bridges and buildings, railroad track, machine tools, boiler plate, barbed wire—steel is immensely superior to other kinds of iron. But steel was so expensive to manufacture that it could not be used for bulky products until the invention in the 1850's of the Bessemer process, perfected independently by Henry Bessemer, an Englishman, and William Kelly of Kentucky. Bessemer and Kelly discovered that a stream of air directed into a mass of molten iron caused the carbon and other impurities to combine with oxygen and burn off. When measured amounts of carbon, silicon, and manganese were then added, the whole brew became steel. What had been a rare metal now could be produced by the hundreds and thousands of tons. The Bessemer process and the open-hearth method, a slower but more precise technique which enabled producers to sample the molten mass and thus control quality closely, were introduced commercially in the United States in the sixties. In 1870, 77,000 tons of steel were manufactured, less than four per cent of the volume of pig iron. By 1880, however, 1.39 million tons were pouring annually from the converters. In 1890 production reached 4.79 million tons, by 1900 nearly 11.4 million.

Such growth would have been impossible but for the huge supplies of iron ore in the United States and the coal necessary to fire the furnaces which refined it. In the 1870's the great iron fields rimming Lake Superior started to yield their treasures. The Menominee range in Michigan began production in 1877, followed in 1884 by the Gogebic range, on the Michigan-Wisconsin

MINNESOTA HISTORICAL SOCIETY

border. In each case the completion of rail connections to the fields had been necessary before large-scale mining could take place, another illustration of the importance of railroads in the economic history of the era. The Vermilion range, in the northeast corner of Minnesota, was opened up at about the same time, and somewhat later the magnificent Mesabi region, where the enormous iron concentrations made a compass needle spin like a top. Mesabi ores could literally be mined with steam shovels, almost like gravel. Pittsburgh, surrounded by vast coal deposits, became the iron and steel capital of the country, the Minnesota ores reaching it by way of steamers on the Great Lakes and rail lines from Cleveland. Other cities in Pennsylvania and Ohio were also important producers, and a separate complex, centering around Birmingham, Alabama, developed to exploit local iron and coal fields.

By 1880 the leading iron and steel producer was Andrew Carnegie. His company—atypical in that it was a partnership rather than a corporation—turned out about a quarter of the nation's steel ingots and a larger percentage of certain basic forms, such as rails and armor plate. In 1875 he had opened his J. Edgar Thomson Steel Works, one of the finest and most efficient in the industry, named in honor of a former president of the Pennsylvania Railroad, his best customer. As late as 1880 many hundreds of small producers still existed, but the number declined steadily, Carnegie's share of the market increasing proportionately. Like mining, the iron and steel business was ill-suited to small-scale operation. It required much heavy and expensive equipment, a large labor force, and financial reserves to withstand the buffeting of bad times. By the last years of the century, really small forges had practically disappeared and a few giants controlled the field.

The petroleum industry expanded even more spectacularly than iron and steel. The business had not even existed in pre-Civil War days; Edwin L. Drake drilled the first successful well in Pennsylvania in 1859. During the Civil War, production ranged between 2 and 3 million barrels a year. In 1873 almost 10 million barrels were produced, and in the early eighties annual output averaged over 20 million barrels. A decade later this figure had leaped to about 50 million.

Before the invention of the gasoline engine and the automobile, the most important petroleum product was kerosene. This fuel, burned in lamps, accounted for well over two-thirds of all oil production in the early 1870's when over 6.5 million barrels a year were manufactured. In the early years in Pennsylvania hundreds of tiny refineries, often reminiscent of the ramshackle stills of nearby moonshiners, were engaged in the business. They heated crude oil in large kettles and after the volatile elements had escaped, condensed the kerosene in coils cooled by water. The heavier petroleum tars were simply discarded.

Technological advances came rapidly. By the early 1870's, refiners had learned how to "crack" petroleum by applying high temperatures to the crude in order to break up and rearrange its molecular structure, thus increasing the percentage of kerosene yielded. By-products such as naphtha, gasoline (used in vaporized form as an illuminating gas), rhigolene (a local anesthetic), cymogene (a coolant for refrigerating machines), and many lubricants and waxes began to appear on the market. At the same time a great increase in the supply of crude oil—especially after the chemist Herman Frosch perfected a method for removing sulfur from low-quality petroleum—drove prices down. Naturally, these circumstances put a premium on refining efficiency. Larger plants utilizing expensive machinery and employing skilled technicians became more important in the industry. In the mid-sixties only three refineries in the country could process

DRAKE MUSEUM

A scene on the Oil Creek Railroad in western Pennsylvania in the early 1860's. Initially, crude oil was shipped to refineries in barrels by barge or on railroad flatcars, as shown here. The familiar "boiler-shaped" tank car was invented in 1869, and by the 1870's a network of pipelines was laid to handle the growing oil output.

2,000 barrels of crude a week; by the early seventies plants capable of handling 1,000 barrels a day were common.

By this time the chief oil-refining centers were Cleveland, Pittsburgh, Baltimore, and the New York City area. Of these Cleveland was the fastest growing, chiefly because it enjoyed very low freight rates. Both the New York Central and Erie railroads competed fiercely for its oil trade, and the Erie Canal offered an alternative route. Pittsburgh, on the other hand, depended entirely upon the Pennsylvania Railroad, while New York and Baltimore suffered from being far removed from the oil fields. During the 1870's the Standard Oil Company of Cleveland, whose president was a successful merchant named John D. Rockefeller, rapidly emerged as the giant among the refiners, exploiting every possible new technical advance and employing fair means and foul to persuade competitors first in the Cleveland area and then elsewhere either to sell out or join forces. By 1873 Rockefeller controlled between 30 and 40 per cent of the nation's oil-refining capacity; by 1879 more than 90 per cent was in his hands. He soon owned a network of oil pipelines and added huge reserves of petroleum in the ground to his empire. During the remainder of the century his percentage of the market declined slightly, chiefly because a number of competitors discovered that they could survive by specializing in such items as high-quality lubricating oils, but he dominated the oil industry nonetheless. The existence of this monopoly, together with the remarkable expansion of the entire industry, caused Standard Oil to attract far more attention than its importance warranted in the late 19th century. The period of its greatest growth and economic influence did not come until later. The first 100-million-barrel year was 1903. Thereafter, production really spurted, passing the *billion*-barrel mark in 1929.

Two other important new industries were the telephone and electric light businesses. Both were typical of the period, being entirely dependent upon technical advances and intimately related to the growth of a high-speed, urban civilization that put great stress on communication. The telephone was invented in 1876 by Alexander Graham Bell, who had been led to the study of acoustics through his interest in the education of the deaf. His work with a device for transcribing tone vibrations electrically to aid deaf-mutes in learning to speak encouraged him to experiment with a "speaking telegraph" that used electrified metal disks, acting like the drum of the human ear, to convert sound waves into electrical impulses and electrical impulses back into sound waves. Although considered little more than a clever gadget at first—the Western Union Company passed up an opportunity to buy the invention for $100,000, its president calling the telephone an "electrical toy"—Bell's invention soon proved its practical value. By 1880, 85 towns and cities had local telephone networks. In 1895 there were over 300,000 phones in the country, in 1900 almost 800,000, twice the total for all Europe. By that date the American Telephone and Telegraph Company, a consolidation of over 100 local systems, dominated the business.

When Western Union realized the importance of the telephone, it tried for a time to compete with Bell by developing a machine of its own. The man it commissioned to devise this machine was Thomas A. Edison. Eventually, Bell's patents proved unassailable, and Western Union abandoned the effort to maintain a competing system, but not until Edison had vastly improved telephonic transmission. Not yet 30 when he turned to the telephone problem, Edison had already made a number of contributions toward solving what he called the "mysteries of electrical force," including a multiplex telegraph capable of sending four messages over a single wire at the same time. At Menlo Park, New Jersey, he built the prototype of the modern research laboratory, where specific problems could be attacked on a mass scale by a team of trained specialists. During his lifetime he took out over 1,000 patents, dealing with machines as varied as the phonograph, the motion-picture projector, the storage battery, and the mimeograph. He also contributed substantially to the development of the electric dynamo, ore-separating machinery, and railroad signal equipment.

But Edison's most significant achievement was unquestionably his perfection of the incandescent

EDISON LABORATORY NATIONAL MONUMENT

Edison patented the phonograph in 1878, budgeting $18 for its invention. He was photographed in his laboratory in 1888 working on a wax-cylinder model.

lamp, or electric light bulb. Others before Edison had experimented with the idea of producing light by passing electricity through a thin filament in a vacuum. Always, however, the filaments quickly broke. Edison tried hundreds of fibers before producing, late in 1879, a carbonized filament that would glow brightly in a vacuum tube for as long as 170 hours without crumbling. At Christmastime he decorated the grounds about his laboratory with a few dozen of the new lights. People flocked by the thousands to see this miracle of the "Wizard of Menlo Park." To these admirers of his "bright, beautiful light, like the mellow sunset of an Italian autumn," the inventor boasted that soon he would be able to illuminate whole towns, even great cities like New York.

He was true to his promise. In 1882 his Edison Illuminating Company opened a power station in New York and began to supply current for lighting to 85 consumers, including the New York *Times* and the banking house of J.P. Morgan and Company. Two years later the station had 508 customers using over 10,000 lamps. Soon central stations were springing up everywhere until, by 1898, there were about 3,000 in the country. Edison's manufacturing subsidiaries flourished equally: in 1885 they turned out 139,000 incandescent lamps, by the end of the decade nearly a million a year.

The Edison system employed direct current at low voltages, which limited the distance that power could be transmitted to about two miles. Technicians soon demonstrated that by using alternating current, stepped up to high voltages by transformers, power could be transported over great distances economically and then reduced to safe levels for use by consumers. This encouraged George Westinghouse, inventor of the air brake, to found the Westinghouse Electric Company in 1886. Edison stubbornly refused to accept the superiority of high-voltage alternating current. "Just as certain as death Westinghouse will kill a customer within 6 months," he predicted, and indeed, for a time, the language was graced with the verb "to Westinghouse," meaning to electrocute. But the Westinghouse system quickly proved itself safe as well as efficient, and alternating current became standard. The industry expanded rapidly until by the early years of the 20th century almost 6 billion kilowatt-hours of electricity were being produced annually. Yet this, of course, was only the beginning. In 1927 production exceeded 100 billion kilowatt-hours, by 1963 a *trillion.*

Competition and Monopoly: the Railroads

In all the industries discussed above and in many others, the post-Civil War era saw a similar pattern of development: expansion went hand in hand with concentration; with each passing decade, fewer, larger firms captured an increasing share of the business. The principal cause of this trend, aside from the obvious economies resulting from large-scale production and the growing importance of expensive machinery, was the downward trend of world prices after 1873. This deflation affected agricultural goods as well as manufactures, and it lasted until 1896 or 1897.

Contemporaries believed they were living

through a "great depression," but the name is misleading, since output expanded almost continuously, and at a rapid rate, until 1893, when a "true" depression struck the country. Falling prices, however, kept a steady pressure on profit margins, and this led to increased production and thus to intense competition for markets. Rival concerns battled for business, the strongest, most efficient, and most unscrupulous destroying or absorbing their foes. If no clear victor emerged, the exhausted contenders frequently ended the warfare by combining voluntarily. At least for a time, the government did little about laying down rules for the fighting or preventing the consolidations that seemed to result from it.

According to the theory of laissez faire, competition supposedly advanced the public interest by keeping prices low and assuring the most efficient producer the largest profit. Up to a point it accomplished these purposes in the years after 1865, but it also fathered side effects that injured both the economy and society as a whole.

In railroading, for instance, there were no firmly fixed rates based on mileage and weight for carrying passengers or freight. Besides charging more for transporting valuable manufactured goods than for bulky products like coal or wheat, the lines often made special concessions to shippers to avoid hauling empty cars. In other words, they charged whatever the traffic would bear. Generally speaking, rates became progressively lower as time passed, for as the railroad network expanded, competition naturally intensified. In 1865 it cost from 96 cents to $2.15 per hundred pounds, depending on the class of freight, to ship goods from New York to Chicago. In 1888 rates ranged from 35 cents to 75 cents. In the three decades after the Civil War, the cost of shipping 100 pounds of wheat from Chicago to New York dropped from 65 cents to 20 cents.

Competition cut deeply into railroad profits, causing the lines to seek desperately to increase volume. Paradoxically, they did so chiefly by reducing rates still more, on a selective basis. They gave rebates (secret, unofficial reductions below the published rates) to large shippers in order to capture their business. The granting of some discount to those who shipped in volume made economic sense: it was easier to handle freight in carload lots than in smaller units. Because of the volume of its shipments, Standard Oil received a 10 per cent discount from all the Cleveland carriers merely on the promise that it would divide its business equitably among them. So intense was the battle for business, however, that the roads made concessions to big customers far beyond what the economies of bulk shipment justified. In the 1870's the New York Central regularly reduced the rates charged important shippers by 50 to 80 per cent. One large Utica dry-goods merchant received a rate of 9 cents where others paid 33 cents. Two big New York City grain merchants paid so little that they soon controlled the grain business of the entire city. Between 1877 and 1879, a critical period in the oil business, the major trunk lines carried Standard's petroleum products to the Atlantic seaboard for 80 cents a barrel while charging the independent refiners of Cleveland $1.44½.

Railroad officials disliked rebating but found no way to avoid the practice. "Notwithstanding my horror of rebates," the president of a New England trunk line told one of his executives in discussing the case of a prominent brick manufacturer, "bill at the usual rate, and rebate Mr. Cole 25 cents a thousand." In extreme cases the railroads even gave large shippers drawbacks, which were rebates on the business of the shippers' competitors. For many years Standard Oil collected 20 cents from the Cleveland carriers for each barrel of "independent" oil they transported.

Besides rebating, railroads granted other favors to certain shippers. They issued passes to officials, built sidings at the plants of important companies without charge, and gave freely of their landholdings to attract businesses to their territory. Railroads also battled directly with one another in ways damaging to themselves and to the public. Unscrupulous operators often threw together roundabout, inefficient trunk lines merely to blackmail already established roads, forcing them to buy up the competing properties at inflated prices. Others tried to win control of competing lines in the stock market. Between 1866 and 1868

Vanderbilt of the New York Central fought a futile campaign to win control of the Erie. The raffish Erie directors struck back by issuing themselves thousands of shares of new stock without paying for them, thus gravely overinflating the capitalization of the line. Both roads stooped to bribery in an effort to obtain favorable action in the New York legislature, and there were even pitched battles between the hirelings of each side.

"The force of competition," a railroadman explained, "is one that no carrying corporation can withstand and before which the managing officers of a corporation are helpless." James F. Joy of the Chicago, Burlington, and Quincy made the same point more bluntly: "Unless you prepare to defend yourselves," he advised the president of the Michigan Central, "you will be boarded by pirates in all quarters." Railroad executives are "hardly better than a race of horse-jockeys," Charles Francis Adams, Jr., wrote in *Railroads: Their Origin and Problems* (1879). "The tone among them is indisputably low."

To make up for losses forced upon them by competitive pressures, railroads raised their rates at way points along their tracks where no competition existed. As a result, it sometimes cost more to ship a given product a short distance than a longer one. Rochester, New York, was served only by the New York Central. In the 1870's it cost 30 cents to transport a barrel of flour from Rochester to New York City, a distance of 350 miles. At the same time flour could be shipped from Minneapolis to New York, a distance of well over 1,000 miles, for only 20 cents.* One Rochester businessman told a state investigating committee that he could save 18 cents a hundredweight by sending goods to St. Louis by way of New York, where several carriers competed for the traffic, even though, in fact, the goods might come back through Rochester over the same tracks on the way to St. Louis! Local farmers 165 miles from New York paid 70 cents a tub to ship their butter to the metropolis, while producers as far away as Illinois could ship butter there for only 30 cents.

*During one period of intense competition, the rate on flour from Minneapolis to New York fell to 10 cents a barrel.

MUSEUM OF MODERN ART

Edward Steichen's memorable photographic study of J. Pierpont Morgan, taken in 1903. Looking the formidable Morgan in the eye, Steichen said, was akin to facing the headlights of an onrushing express train.

Although cheap transportation stimulated the economy, few persons really benefited from cutthroat competition. Small shippers, and all businessmen in cities and towns with limited rail outlets, suffered heavily; railroad discrimination against such customers unquestionably speeded the concentration of industry in large corporations located in major centers. The instability of rates troubled even interests like the middle western flour millers who benefited from the competitive situation, for it hampered planning. Nor could manufacturers who received rebates be entirely happy, since few could be sure that some other producer was not getting a still larger reduction.

Probably the worst sufferers were the roads themselves. The loss of revenue resulting from rate-cutting, combined with inflated debts, put most of them in grave difficulty when faced with a downturn in the business cycle. In 1876 two-fifths of all railroad bonds were in default; three years later 65 lines were bankrupt. Since the public would not countenance bankrupt railroads going out of business, these companies were placed in the hands of court-appointed receivers. The receivers, however, seldom provided efficient management and had no funds at their disposal for new equipment. Sometimes they became mere "fronts" for unscrupulous executives looking only for a means of escaping their debts.

A new, strong leadership that would enforce belt-tightening all along the line and bring an end to the chaotic rate wars was sorely needed. This leadership was supplied—at a price—by a handful of important financiers, most notably J. Pierpont Morgan, head of a powerful firm of New York private bankers. Morgan became prominent in railroad affairs in the 1880's when he negotiated "peace settlements" first between the New York Central and the Pennsylvania and then between all the eastern trunk lines. His main contribution came in the mid-nineties, after the depression of those years had brought lines controlling 67,000 miles of track to the wall. The House of Morgan and other private bankers like Kuhn, Loeb of New York and Lee, Higginson of Boston reorganized—critics said they "Morganized"—most of these shattered corporations. The economic historian A.D. Noyes described this method accurately in 1904:

> Bondholders were requested to scale down interest charges, receiving new stock in compensation, while the shareholders were invited to pay a cash assessment, thus providing a working fund. [The bankers] combined to guarantee that the requisite money should be raised. They too were paid in new stock. . . . Though the total capital issues were increased, fixed charges were diminished and a sufficient fund for road improvement and new equipment was provided.

These reorganizations put great trunk lines like the Erie, the Baltimore and Ohio, the Union Pacific, and the Northern Pacific back on their feet. They were kept there by the termination of practices that had toppled them to begin with. Representatives of the bankers sat on the board of every line they saved. Although they generally took no part in handling the everyday affairs of the roads, their influence was predominant, and they consistently opposed rate wars, rebating, and other competitive practices. In effect, control of the railroad network became centralized, even though the companies maintained their separate existences and operated in a seemingly independent manner. When Morgan died in 1913, "Morgan men" dominated the boards of the New York Central, the Erie, the New York, New Haven and Hartford, the Southern, the Pere Marquette, the Atchison, Topeka and Santa Fe, and many other lines.

The Steel Industry: Carnegie

The iron and steel industry was also intensely competitive. Despite the general trend toward higher production, demand varied erratically from year to year, even from month to month. The price of iron products fluctuated wildly. Throughout the mid-seventies, demand was relatively slack. Prices fell, until by 1878 they had reached the lowest levels since colonial times. Then came a revival, but within a three-month period in 1880 the price of pig iron fell from $41 a ton to $25. However, 1881 was again a banner year, the price of pig iron touching $60 a ton. Twelve months later, iron had fallen to $39 a ton.

Such conditions played havoc with many firms. In good times producers tended to build new facilities, only to suffer heavy losses when demand declined and much of their capacity lay idle. The forward rush of technology put a tremendous emphasis on efficiency; expensive plants quickly became obsolete. Improved transportation facilities allowed manufacturers in widely scattered regions to compete with one another in the national market; despite the importance of the Pittsburgh region, in the early nineties multimillion-dollar mills existed in Alabama, Colorado, Illinois, and elsewhere.

The kingpin of the industry was Andrew Carnegie. Born in Dunfermline, Scotland, Carnegie came to the United States in 1848 at the age of 12. His first job as a bobbin boy in a cotton mill brought him $1.20 a week, but his talents perfectly fitted the times, and he rose rapidly: Western Union messenger boy, to telegrapher, to private secretary to a railroad executive. He saved his money, made some shrewd investments, and by 1868 had an income of $50,000 a year. At about this time he decided to specialize in the iron business, saying, in an oft-quoted remark, that he believed in putting all his eggs in one basket and then watching the basket. Carnegie possessed great talent as a salesman, boundless faith in the future of the country, an uncanny knack of choosing topflight subordinates, and enough ruthlessness to survive in the iron and steel jungle. He was a superb competitor, according to one biographer, Burton J. Hendrick, "the most daring man in American industry." Whereas other steelmen built new plants in good times, he preferred to expand in bad times, when it cost far less to do so. During the 1870's, he later recalled, "many of my friends needed money. . . . I . . . bought out five or six of them. That is what gave me my leading interest in this steel business."

Carnegie grasped the importance of technological improvements in his industry. Slightly skeptical of the Bessemer process at first, once he became convinced of its practicality he adopted it enthusiastically. He employed chemists and other specialists freely and was soon making steel from iron oxides that other manufacturers had discarded as waste. He was also a driver of men and a merciless competitor, exhibiting what Robert G. McCloskey has called "a single-minded pursuit of the main chance that left a trail of ruined competitors and 'partners' strewn in the wake." When a plant manager announced: "We broke all records for making steel last week," Carnegie replied: "Congratulations! *Why not do it every week?*" When another informed him of an especially outstanding record compiled by the crew of one furnace, he answered coldly: "What are the other ten furnaces doing?" Carnegie sold rails by paying "commissions" to railroad purchasing agents, and he was not above reneging on a contract if he thought it profitable and safe to do so.

By 1890 the Carnegie Steel Company dominated the industry and its output increased nearly tenfold over the next decade. Profits mounted from $3 million in 1893 to $6 million in 1896, despite the depression of those years, and soared to $21 million in 1899. In 1900 they reached $40 million, Andrew Carnegie's personal share amounting to $25 million. Alarmed by his increasing control of the industry, the makers of finished steel products like barbed wire and tubing began to combine and to consider entering the primary field. Carnegie, his competitive temper aroused, then threatened to turn to finished products himself. A colossal steel war seemed imminent.

However, Carnegie longed to retire in order to devote himself to philanthropic work. He had for years professed the belief that great wealth entailed social responsibilities and that it was a disgrace to die rich. When J.P. Morgan approached him through an intermediary with an offer to buy him out, he assented readily. In 1901 Morgan put together United States Steel, the "world's first billion-dollar corporation." This huge combination included all the Carnegie properties, the Federal Steel Company (Carnegie's largest competitor), and such important fabricators of finished products as the American Steel and Wire Company, the American Tin Plate Company, and the National Tube Company. Vast reserves of Minnesota iron ore and a fleet of Great Lakes ore steamers were also included. U.S. Steel was capitalized at $1.4 billion, about twice the value of its separate properties but not necessarily an overestimation of its profit-earning capacity. The owners of Carnegie Steel received $492 million, of which $250 million went to Carnegie himself.

The Standard Oil Trust

The pattern of fierce competition leading to combination and monoply is well illustrated by the history of the petroleum industry. Irresistible pressures led the refiners into a brutal struggle to dominate the business. Production of crude oil, subject to the uncertainties of prospecting and drilling, fluctuated constantly and without regard for need. In general, output surged ahead in huge bounds, far in excess of demand. Refining capacity also grew beyond the requirements of the day, for it took little capital to erect a new plant and low crude prices encouraged even incompetent manufacturers. As John D. Rockefeller later explained, "all sorts of people . . . the butcher, the baker, and the candlestick-maker began to refine oil."

Rockefeller's Standard Oil Company emerged victorious in the resulting competitive wars because Rockefeller and his associates were the toughest and most imaginative fighters as well as the most efficient refiners in the business. In addition to obtaining rebates from the railroads, Standard Oil cut prices locally to force small independents to sell out or face ruin. One Massachusetts refiner testified that Standard drove down the price of kerosene in his district from 9¼ cents to 5¼ simply to destroy his business. Since kerosene was largely sold through grocery stores, Standard supplied its own outlets with meat, sugar, and other products at artificially low prices to help crush the stores that handled other

BROWN BROTHERS

John D. Rockefeller carried his passion for perfection onto the golf course, hiring a boy to do nothing but intone "keep your head down" on each shot.

brands of kerosene. The company employed spies to track down the customers of independents and offer them oil at bargain prices. Bribery was also a Standard practice, as is illustrated in the quip of the reformer Henry Demarest Lloyd, who said that the company had done everything to the Pennsylvania legislature except refine it. Rockefeller's most sympathetic biographer, Allan Nevins, admits that Standard Oil "committed acts against competitors which could not be defended."

Although a bold planner and a daring taker of necessary risks, Rockefeller was far too orderly and astute to enjoy the free-swinging battles that plagued his industry. Born in an upstate New York village in 1839, he settled in Cleveland in 1855 and became a successful produce merchant. During the Civil War he invested in a local refinery and by 1865 was engaged full time in the oil business.

Like Carnegie, Rockefeller was an organizer; he knew little about the technology of petroleum. He sought efficiency, order, and stability. His forte was meticulous attention to detail: stories are told of his ordering the number of drops of solder used in making oil cans reduced from 40 to 39, and of his insisting that the manager of one of his refineries account for 750 missing barrel bungs. Not miserliness but a profound grasp of the economies of large-scale production explain this behavior; by reducing the cost of refining a gallon of crude oil by a mere .082 cents, Standard Oil increased its annual profit about $600,000. Rockfeller competed ruthlessly not primarily to crush other refiners but to persuade them to join with him, to share the business peaceably and rationally so that all could profit. Competition was obsolescent, he argued, although no more effective competitor than he ever lived. In truth, most of the independent refiners that Standard Oil destroyed by unfair competition had previously turned down offers to merge or sell out on terms that modern students consider generous. Of course this fact does not justify the means used to crush them.

Rockefeller achieved his monopoly by convincing other refiners that resistance would be unprofitable if not suicidal. As we have seen, by 1879 most of them had given up the fight, and

Standard Oil controlled more than 90 per cent of the nation's oil business. He stabilized and structured his monopoly by creating a new type of business organization, the trust. Standard Oil was an Ohio corporation, prohibited by local law from owning plants in other states or holding stock in out-of-state corporations. As Rockefeller and his associates took over dozens of companies with facilities scattered across the country, serious legal and managerial difficulties arose. How could these many organizations be integrated with Standard Oil of Ohio? A rotund, genial little Pennsylvania lawyer named Samuel C.T. Dodd came up with an answer to this question in 1879.* The stock of Standard of Ohio and of all the other companies that the Rockefeller interests had swallowed up was turned over to nine trustees, who were empowered to "exercise general supervision" over all these properties. Stockholders received in exchange trust certificates, on which dividends were paid. Thus order came to the petroleum business. Competition almost disappeared; prices steadied; profits skyrocketed. By 1892 John D. Rockefeller was worth over $800 million.

The Standard Oil Trust was not a corporation. Indeed, it had no charter, no legal existence at all. For many years few people outside the organization knew that it existed. The form chosen persuaded Rockefeller and other Standard Oil officials that without violating their consciences, they could deny under oath that Standard Oil of Ohio owned or controlled other corporations "directly or indirectly through its officers or agents." The *trustees* controlled these organizations—and Standard of Ohio too!

After Standard Oil's secret was finally revealed during a New York investigation in 1888, the word *trust*, formerly signifying a fiduciary arrangement for the protection of the interests of individuals incompetent or unwilling to guard them themselves, immediately became a synonym for monopoly, and Standard Oil became the most hated and feared company in the United States. However, from the company's point of view, monopoly was not the purpose of the trust—that had been achieved before the device was invented. Centralization of the management of diverse and far-flung operations was its chief function. Standard Oil headquarters in New York became the brain of a complex network where information from the field was collected and digested, where decisions were made, and whence orders went out to drillers, refiners, scientists, and salesmen. The resulting advantages explain why the trust device was soon adopted by many other industries.

*The trust formula was not "perfected" until 1882.

Public Utilities

That public utilities like the telephone and electric lighting industries tended to form monopolies is not difficult to explain, for in such fields competition involved costly duplication of equipment and, especially in the case of the telephone, loss of service efficiency. However, competitive pressures were very strong in the early stages of their development. Since these industries depended upon patents, Bell and Edison had to fight mighty battles in the courts against rivals seeking to infringe upon their rights. As Edison's biographer explains it, "a powerful corporation . . . had many ways of getting control of a new product, once it was proved practicable: by imitation; by evasion; or by the erosive effect on the original inventor of lawsuits conducted at enormous costs." Few quibbled over means when so much money hung in the balance. After having turned down a chance to buy Bell's invention for a pittance, Western Union organized the American Speaking Telephone Company, capitalized at $300,000, and employed Edison to invent a device that would enable it to circumvent Bell's rights. In return, the Bell interests challenged Edison's improved telephone transmitter, claiming that it infringed upon patents issued to one Emile Berliner, which they had bought up. Western Union was the victor in this particular battle, but in the end the telegraph company became convinced that the courts would uphold Bell's claims and abandoned the field.

As for Edison himself, much of his time was taken up with legal battles to protect his rights under his many patents. When he first announced his electric light, capitalists, engineers, and inventors flocked to Menlo Park. Edison proudly revealed to them the secrets of his marvelous lamp. Many of them hurried away to turn this information to their own advantage, thinking the "Wizard" a naive fool. When they invaded the field, the law provided Edison with far less protection than he had expected. He had to fight a "Seven Years' War" with Westinghouse over the carbon-filament incandescent lamp. Although he won, his costs were over $2 million, and when the courts finally decided in his favor, only two years remained before the patent expired. "My electric light inventions have brought me no profits, only forty years of litigation," Edison later complained. A patent, he said bitterly, was "simply an invitation to a lawsuit."

The attitude of businessmen toward the rights of inventors and industrial pioneers is illustrated by this early advertisement of the Westinghouse Company:

> We regard it as fortunate that we have deferred entering the electrical field until the present moment. Having thus profited by the public experience of others, we enter ourselves for competition, hampered by a minimum of expense for experimental outlay.... In short, our organization is free, in large measure, of the load with which [other] electrical enterprises seem to be encumbered. The fruit of this . . . we propose to share with the customer.

Competition in the electric-lighting business raged for some years between Edison, Westinghouse, and still another corporation, the Thomson-Houston Electric Company, which was operating 870 central lighting stations by 1890. Finally, in 1892, the Edison and Thomson-Houston companies merged, forming General Electric, a $35 million corporation. Thereafter, General Electric and Westinghouse maintained their domination in the manufacture of bulbs and much other electrical equipment as well as in the distribution of electrical power.

The pattern of competition leading to dominance by a few great companies was repeated in many other businesses. In life insurance, to take a final example, an immense expansion took place after the Civil War, triggered by the perfection of a new variety of group policy, the "tontine," by Henry B. Hyde of the Equitable Life Company.* High-pressure salesmanship prevailed; agents gave rebates to customers by shading their own commissions; companies stole crack agents from their rivals and raided new territories. They sometimes invested as much as 96 per cent of the first year's premiums in obtaining new business. By 1900, after three decades of fierce competition, three giants dominated the industry, Equitable, New York Life, and Mutual Life, each with approximately $1 billion of insurance in force.

Americans React to Big Business

The expansion of industry and its concentration in fewer and fewer hands caused a major shift in the thinking of the people about the role of government in economic and social affairs. As we have seen, the fact that Americans, strongly individualistic, disliked powerful government in general and strict regulation of the economy in particular had never meant that they objected to *all* government activity in the economic sphere. Banking laws, tariffs, internal-improvement legislation, and the granting of public land to railroads are only the most obvious of the economic regulations enforced in the 19th century by both the federal government and the states. Americans saw no contradiction between government activities of this type and the free-enterprise philosophy, because such laws were intended to release human energy and thus *increase* the area in which freedom could operate. Tariffs stimulated industry and created new jobs, railroad grants opened up new regions for development, and so on. As J.W. Hurst has put it in a thought-provoking study, *Law and the Conditions of Freedom in the Nineteenth-Century United States*, the people "resort[ed] to law to enlarge the options open to private individual and group energy."

After about 1870 the public attitude began to

*A tontine policy paid no dividends for a stated period of years. If a policyholder died, his heirs received the face value but no dividends. At the end of the tontine period, survivors collected not only their own dividends but those of the unfortunates who had died or permitted their policies to lapse. This was psychologically appealing, since it stressed living rather than dying and added an element of gambling to insurance.

The Verdict, JANUARY 22, 1900

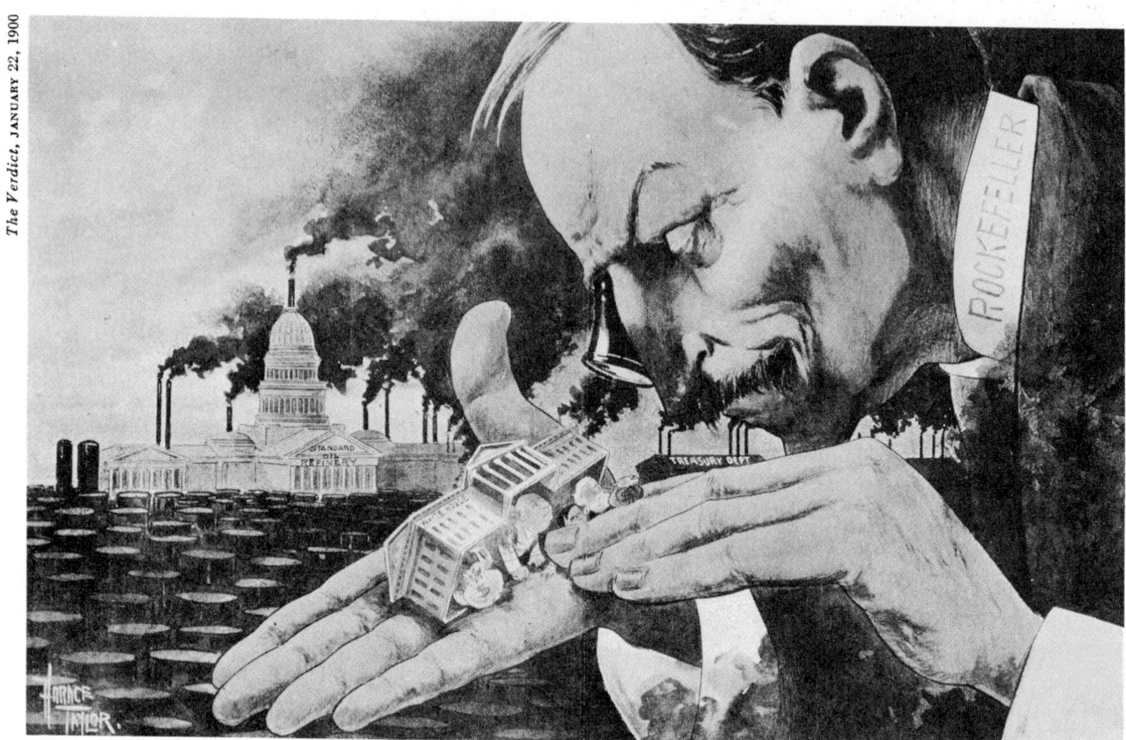

The Verdict, *a cartoon weekly that flourished briefly at the turn of the century, devoted its pages to unremitting attacks on Republicans, big business, and monopolists. In Horace Taylor's drawing above, Rockefeller remarks, "What a funny little government!" George Luks, one of the "ashcan" artists, did the cartoon below.*

NEW-YORK HISTORICAL SOCIETY

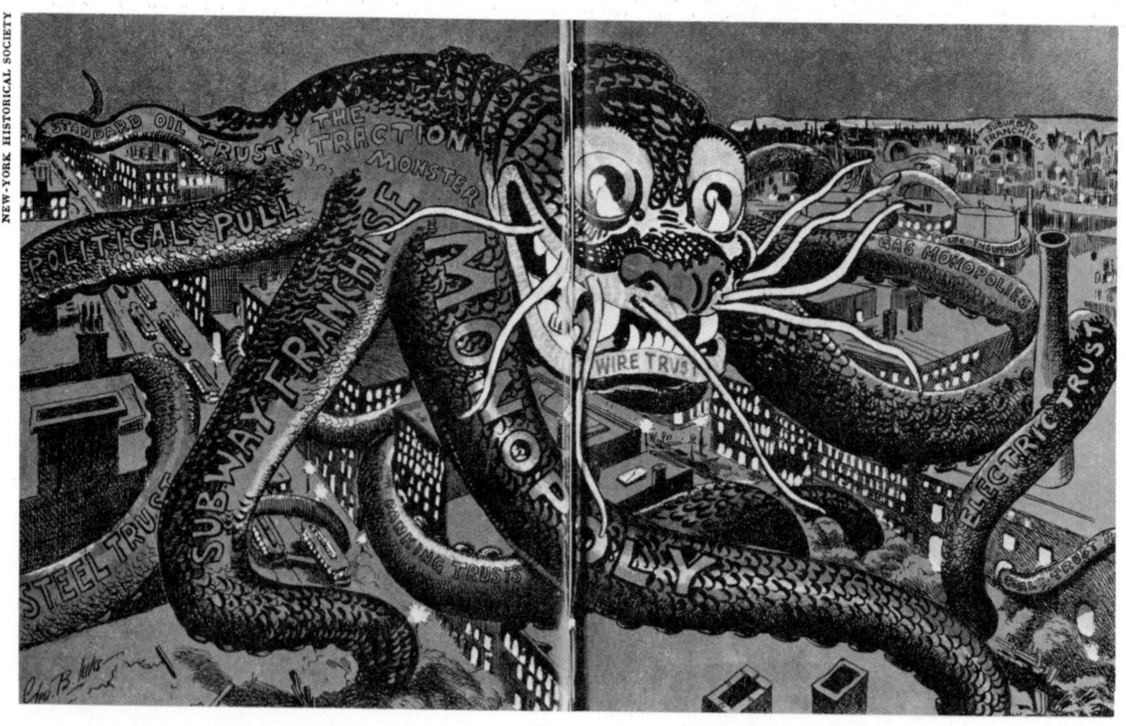

change. The growth of huge industrial and financial organizations and the increasing complexity of economic relations gave people what Hurst calls "a new sense of individual helplessness," yet made them at the same time greedy for more of the goods and services the new society was turning out. To many, the great new corporations and trusts resembled Frankenstein's monster—marvelous and powerful, but a grave threat to society. The astute James Bryce described the changes clearly in *The American Commonwealth*:

> New causes are at work. . . . Modern civilization . . . has become more exacting. It discerns more benefits which the organized power of government can secure, and grows more anxious to attain them. Men live fast, and are impatient of the slow working of natural laws. . . . There are benefits which the law of supply and demand do not procure. Unlimited competition seems to press too hard on the weak. The power of groups of men organized by incorporation as joint-stock companies, or of small knots of rich men acting in combination, has developed with unexpected strength in unexpected ways, overshadowing individuals and even communities, and showing that the very freedom of association which men sought to secure by law . . . may, under the shelter of the law, ripen into a new form of tyranny.

To some extent public fear of the new industrial giants simply reflected concern about monoply. If Standard Oil completely dominated oil refining, it might raise prices inordinately at vast cost to consumers. Charles Francis Adams, Jr., expressed this feeling when he wrote in the 1870's: "In the minds of the great majority, and not without reason, the idea of any industrial combination is closely connected with that of monopoly, and monopoly with extortion."

Although in isolated cases monopolists did raise prices unreasonably, generally they did not; indeed, prices tended to fall, until by the 1890's a veritable "consumer's millennium" had arrived. Far more important in causing resentment against the new corporate giants was the fear that they were destroying economic opportunity, making it difficult for the small man to rise, and threatening democratic institutions. It was not the *wealth* of the new tycoons like Carnegie and Rockefeller and Morgan so much as their *influence* that worried the American people. In the face of the growing disparity between rich and poor—there were over 4,000 millionaires in the United States by the early nineties—could republican institutions survive? Was the avalanche of cheap new products made available by the new corporations worth the sacrifice of the American way of life? "We must place . . . ethics above economics," one foe of monopoly insisted at a great turn-of-the-century conference on trusts at Chicago, and his audience gave him an ovation.

Some observers believed either autocracy or a form of revolutionary socialism to be almost inevitable. In 1890 former President Rutherford B. Hayes pondered over "the wrong and evils of the money-piling tendency of our country, which is changing laws, government, and morals and giving all power to the rich," and decided that he was going to become a "nihilist." Campaigning for the governorship of Texas in 1890, James S. Hogg, a staunch conservative, said: "Within a few years, unless something is done, most of the wealth and talent of our country will be on one side, while arrayed on the other will be the great mass of the people, composing the bone and sinew of this government. . . . The commune threatens us, but it is the legitimate child and offspring of the cormorant." John Boyle O'Reilly, a liberal Catholic journalist, wrote in 1886: "There is something worse than Anarchy, bad as that is; and it is irresponsible power in the hands of mere wealth." William Cook, a New York lawyer, warned in *The Corporation Problem* (1891) that "colossal aggregations of capital" were "dangerous to the republic." Cook added that "a vague and indescribable dread and suspicion of [corporations] pervade[d] the minds of men."

These are typical examples of the reactions of responsible citizens to the rise of industrial combinations. Less thoughtful Americans sometimes went much further in their hatred of entrenched wealth. In 1900 Eddie Cudahy, son of a prominent member of the Beef Trust, was kidnaped. His captor, Pat Crowe, received $25,000 ransom but was apprehended. Crowe's guilt was clear: "I want to start right by confessing in plain English that I was guilty of the kidnapping," he wrote. But a jury acquitted him, presumably on the theory that it was all right to rob a member of the Beef Trust if you could get away with it.

As the volume of criticism mounted, the leaders of the trusts rose to their own defense. Rockefeller described in graphic terms the chaotic conditions that plagued the oil industry before the rise of Standard Oil, making the final monopolistic outcome seem both inevitable and in the public interest: "It seemed absolutely necessary to extend the market for oil . . . and also greatly improve the process of refining so that oil could be made and sold cheaply, yet with a profit. We proceeded to buy the largest and best refining concerns and centralized the administration of them with a view to securing greater economy and efficiency." Carnegie, in an essay published in 1889, insisted that the concentration of wealth was necessary if humanity was to progress, softening this "Gospel of Wealth" by insisting that the rich must use their money "in the manner which . . . is best calculated to produce the most beneficial results for the community." The rich man was merely a trustee for his "poorer brethren," Carnegie said, "bringing to their service his superior wisdom, experience, and ability to administer." Lesser tycoons echoed these arguments.

The voices of the critics were louder if not necessarily more influential. Many clergymen rejected the Social Darwinist view of progress and competition, which they considered unethical and un-Christian. The new class of professional economists (the American Economic Association was founded in 1885) tended to repudiate laissez faire. State aid, wrote Richard T. Ely of Johns Hopkins University, "is an indispensable condition of human progress."

The Radical Reformers

More revealing of the dissatisfaction in the country was the popularity of a number of radical theorists. In 1879 Henry George, a California newspaperman, published *Progress and Poverty*, a forthright attack on the maldistribution of wealth in the United States. George argued that labor was the true and only source of capital. Observing the speculative fever of the West, which enabled landowners to reap profits merely by holding on to property while population increased, the development of surrounding areas causing values to rise, George proposed a "Single Tax" that would confiscate all this "unearned increment" of the owner. The value of land depended upon society and should belong to society; allowing individuals to keep this wealth was the major cause of the growing disparity between rich and poor, George believed. The Single Tax would bring in so much money that no other taxes would be necessary, and the government would have plenty of funds to establish new schools, museums, theaters, and other badly needed social and cultural services. Although the Single Tax was never adopted, George's ideas attracted enthusiastic attention. Single Tax clubs sprang up all over the nation, and more than 2 million copies of *Progress and Poverty* were sold in the next 25 years.

Even more spectacular was the reception afforded *Looking Backward, 2000–1887*, a utopian novel written in 1888 by Edward Bellamy. This book, which sold over a million copies in its first few years, described a future America that was completely socialized, all economic activity carefully planned. Bellamy compared 19th-century society to a great, lumbering stagecoach upon which the favored few rode in comfort while the great mass of the people toiled to haul them along life's route. Occasionally, one of the toilers managed to fight his way onto the coach; whenever a rider fell from it, he had to join the multitude dragging it along. Such, Bellamy wrote, was the working of the vaunted American competitive system. He suggested that the ideal socialist state, in which all men shared equally, would arrive without revolution or violence. The trend toward consolidation would continue, he predicted, until one monstrous trust controlled *all* economic activity. At this point everyone would realize that nationalization was essential.

A third influential attack on the trend toward monopoly was that of Henry Demarest Lloyd, whose *Wealth Against Commonwealth* appeared in 1894. Lloyd, a journalist of independent means, devoted years to preparing a denunciation of the Standard Oil Company. Marshaling masses of fact, presenting his material with patent sincerity, packing his pages with vivid examples, he assaulted the trust at every point. Although in his zeal Lloyd sometimes distorted and exaggerated the evidence to make his indictment more effective—"Every important man in the oil, coal and many other trusts ought to-day to be in some one of our penitentiaries," he wrote in a typical overstatement—as a polemic his book was peerless. His forceful, uncomplicated arguments and his copious references to official documents made *Wealth Against Commonwealth* utterly convincing to thousands. The book was more than an attack on Standard Oil. Lloyd denounced the application of Darwin's concept of survival of the fittest to economic and social affairs, and he condemned the laissez-faire philosophy as leading directly to monopoly.

The popularity of these books indicates that the trend toward monopoly in the United States was worrying many people, but despite the drastic changes suggested in their pages, none of them really questioned the underlying values of the middle-class majority. The popular reformers rejected Marxian ideas, abjured the use of force to achieve their goals, assumed that men were basically altruistic and reasonable and that reform could be accomplished without serious inconvenience to any individual or class. In *Looking Backward* Bellamy pictured the socialists of the future gathered around a radiolike gadget in a well-furnished parlor listening to a minister delivering an inspiring sermon.

Nor did most of their millions of readers seriously consider trying to apply the reformers' ideas. Henry George ran for mayor of New York City in 1886 and lost only narrowly to Abram S. Hewitt, a wealthy iron manufacturer, but even if he had won, he would have been powerless to apply the Single Tax to metropolitan property. Bellamyites founded over 150 "Nationalist Clubs" but steered clear of politics in nearly every case. The national discontent was apparently not very profound. If John D. Rockefeller became the bogeyman of American industry because of Lloyd's attack, no one prevented him from also becoming the richest man in the United States. The writings of these reformers focused American thinking on the monopoly problem and prepared the way for the rejection of laissez faire, but when the government finally took action, the new laws only slightly altered the *status quo*.

Railroad Regulation

Political action came first on the state level and dealt chiefly with the regulation of railroads. Even before the Civil War a number of New England states established railroad commissions to supervise lines within their borders; by the end of the century, 28 states had such boards. The New England type held mere advisory powers, but those set up in the Middle West around 1870 were true regulatory bodies with authority to fix rates and control other railroad activities.

Strict systems of regulation were largely the result of agitation by farm groups, principally the National Grange of the Patrons of Husbandry. The Grange, founded in 1867 by Oliver H. Kelley, was created in order to provide social and cultural benefits for isolated rural communities, but as it spread and grew in influence—14 states had Granges by 1872 and membership reached 800,000 in 1874—the movement became political too. "Granger" political leaders, often not themselves farmers (for many local businessmen resented such railroad practices as rebating), won control of a number of state legislatures in the West and South. Railroad regulation invariably followed, for while farmers were eager boosters of every internal improvement, they tended to become disillusioned when the lines were completed. Intense competition might reduce rates between major centers like Chicago and the East, but most western farm districts were served by only one line. In 1877, for example, the freight charges of the Burlington road were almost four times as high west of the Missouri as they were east of the river. It cost less to ship wheat all the way from Chicago to Liverpool, England, than from some parts of the Dakotas to Minneapolis.

Granger-controlled legislatures tried to correct this kind of discrimination. The Illinois Granger laws were typical. The revised state constitution of 1870 declared railroads to be public highways and authorized the legislature to "pass laws establishing reasonable maximum rates" and to "prevent unjust discrimination." The legislature did so and also set up a commission to enforce the laws and punish violators. The railroads protested, insisting that they were being deprived of property without due process of law, but in *Munn v. Illinois* (1877),* one of the most important decisions in its long history, the Supreme Court upheld the constitutionality of this kind of act in very broad terms. Any business that served a public interest, such as a railroad or a grain warehouse, was subject to state control, the justices ruled. Legislatures might fix maximum charges, and if the charges seemed unreasonable to the parties concerned, they should direct their complaints to the legislatures or to the people, not to the courts.

Regulation of the railroad network by the separate states was inefficient, however, and in some cases the commissions were incompetent and even corrupt. When the Supreme Court, in the Wabash case (1886), declared unconstitutional an Illinois regulation outlawing the long-and-short-haul evil, federal action became necessary. The Wabash, St. Louis and Pacific Railroad had charged 25 cents a hundred pounds for shipping goods from Gilman, Illinois, to New York City and only 15 cents from Peoria, which was 86 miles farther from New York. Illinois judges had held this to be illegal, but the Supreme Court decided that Illinois could not regulate interstate shipments. "If each one of the States through whose territories these goods are transported can fix its own rules," the Court reasoned, "the embarrassments upon interstate transportation . . . might be too oppressive to be submitted to."

Congress had been considering federal railroad regulation for years, so the legislators were not unprepared to fill the gap created by the Wabash decision. A thorough report on railroad malpractices by a Senate committee headed by Shelby M. Cullom of Illinois, released in 1886, provided a further stimulus to action. In February 1887 the

*The Munn case actually involved a grain elevator whose owner had refused to comply with a state warehouse act. It was heard along with seven railroad cases dealing with violations of Illinois regulatory legislation.

CULVER PICTURES

Interstate Commerce Act was passed. All charges made by railroads "shall be reasonable and just," the act stated. Rebates, drawbacks, the long-and-short-haul evil, and other competitive practices were declared unlawful, and so were their monopolistic counterparts—pools and traffic agreements. Railroads were required to publish schedules of rates and forbidden to change them without due public notice. Most important, the law established an Interstate Commerce Commission, the first federal regulatory board, to supervise the affairs of railroads, investigate complaints, and issue "cease and desist" orders when the roads acted illegally.

The Interstate Commerce Act broke new ground, but it was neither a radical nor a particularly effective measure. Railroad stocks rose at the news of its passage. In practice the commission had less power than the law seemed to give it. It could not fix rates, only bring the roads into court when it considered rates unreasonably high. Such cases could be extremely complicated; applying the law "was like cutting a path through a jungle." With the truth so hard to determine

"The Grange Awakening the Sleepers" (left), a Granger attack on railroad practices, dates from 1873. (Ties were called sleepers in the parlance of the day.) Thomas Nast's "The Senatorial Round-House" (right), drawn for Harper's Weekly *in 1886, predicted that any federal legislation passed to regulate railroads would be toothless.*

and the burden of proof on the commission, the courts, in nearly every instance, decided in favor of the railroads.

State regulatory commissions also fared poorly in the Supreme Court in the last years of the century. Overruling part of their decision in *Munn v. Illinois,* the justices declared in *Chicago, Milwaukee and St. Paul Railroad Company v. Minnesota* (1890) that the reasonableness of rates was "eminently a question for *judicial* investigation." In a Texas case, *Reagan v. Farmers' Loan and Trust Company* (1894), the Court held that it had the "power and duty" to decide if rates were "unjust and unreasonable" even when the state legislature itself had established them. Nevertheless, by stating so clearly the right of Congress to regulate private corporations engaged in interstate commerce, the Interstate Commerce Act seriously challenged the philosophy of laissez faire. Later legislation made the commission more effective. The commission also served as the prototype of a host of similar federal administrative authorities, such as the Federal Communications Commission (1934).

Sherman Antitrust Act

As with railroad legislation, the first antitrust laws originated in the states, but these were southern and western states with relatively little industry and most of the statutes were vaguely worded and ill-enforced. As Professor J.W. Jenks of Cornell wrote in his authoritative study *The Trust Problem* (1905), state laws had "practically no effect, as regards the trend of our industrial development." Federal action came in 1890 with the passage of the Sherman Antitrust Act. Any combination "in the form of trust or otherwise" that was "in restraint of trade or commerce among the several states, or with foreign nations," was declared to be illegal. Persons forming such combinations were made subject to fines of $5,000 and a year in jail. Individuals and businesses suffering losses because of actions performed in violation of the law were authorized to sue in the federal courts for triple damages.

Whereas the Interstate Commerce Act sought to outlaw the excesses of competition, the idea behind the Sherman Act was to restore competition. If men formed together to "restrain" (monopolize) trade in a particular field, they should be punished and their work undone. Monopoly was already illegal under the common law, but as Senator George Frisbie Hoar of Massachusetts pointed out during the antitrust debates, no *federal* common law existed.

"The great thing this bill does," Hoar explained, "is to extend the common-law principle . . . to international and interstate commerce." This was important because the states ran into legal difficulties when they tried to use the common law to restrict corporations engaged in interstate activities. The Sherman Act was rather loosely worded—Thurman Arnold, a modern authority, once said that it made it "a crime to violate a vaguely stated economic policy"—and critics have argued that the congressmen were more interested in quieting the public clamor for action against the trusts than in actually breaking up any of the new combinations. This seems unlikely, for the bill passed with only one dissenting vote. *All* the legislators could not have been party to a plot to deceive the people. Congress was trying to solve a new problem and did not know how to proceed. Most Americans assumed that the courts would deal with the details, as they always had in common-law matters.

Actually, the Supreme Court quickly emasculated the Sherman Act. In *U.S. v. E.C. Knight Company* (1895) it held that the American Sugar Refining Company had not violated the law by taking over a number of important competitors. Although the Sugar Trust now controlled about 98 per cent of all sugar refining in the United States, it was not restraining *trade*. "Doubtless the power to control the manufacture of a given thing involves in a certain sense the control of its disposition," the Court said in one of the greatest feats of judicial understatement of all time. "Although the exercise of that power may result in bringing the operation of commerce into play, it does not control it, and affects it only incidentally and indirectly."

If the creation of the Sugar Trust did not violate the Sherman Act, it seemed unlikely that any other combination of manufacturers could be convicted under the law. In *The History of the Last Quarter-Century in the United States* (1896), E. Benjamin Andrews, president of Brown University, presented a strong indictment of the trusts. "The crimes to which some of them resorted to crush out competition were unworthy of civilization," he wrote. Yet he referred only obliquely to the Sherman Act, dismissing it as "obviously ineffectual" and "of little avail."

Little wonder that the years around the turn of the century saw a new surge of mergers and combinations. Excluding railroads, in 1896 less than a dozen American corporations possessed assets of over $10 million. In 1903 over 300 such giants existed. The enormous United States Steel Corporation was put together by J.P. Morgan without a word of protest from the government. When, some years after his retirement, Andrew Carnegie was asked by a committee of the House of Representatives to explain how he had dared participate in the formation of the great Steel Trust, he replied: "Nobody ever mentioned the Sherman Act to me, that I remember."

American industry was flourishing, but each year a larger portion of it seemed to fall under the control of a handful of rich men. As with the railroads, other industries were coming to be strongly influenced, if not completely dominated by investment bankers—the Money Trust seemed fated to become the ultimate monopoly. The firm of J.P. Morgan and Company controlled many railroads, the largest steel, electrical, agricultural machinery, rubber, and shipping companies, two giant life insurance companies, and a number of banks. By 1913 Morgan and the Rockefeller-National City Bank group between them could name 341 directors to 112 corporations worth over $22.2 billion. The public benefited immensely from the productive efficiency and the rapid growth of the new industrial empires. Living standards rose rapidly. But despite decades of protest and much state and federal legislation, the trend toward giantism was continuing unchecked. With ownership falling into fewer and fewer hands, what would be the ultimate effect of big business on American democracy?

SUPPLEMENTARY READING Of general works dealing with industrial growth, E.C. Kirkland, *Industry Comes of Age** (1961), is the most up-to-date and thoughtful, but see also V.S. Clark's detailed *History of Manufactures in the United States* (1929), Allan Nevins, *The Emergence of Modern America* (1927), I.M. Tarbell, *Nationalizing Big Business* (1936), and T.C. Cochran and William Miller, *The Age of Enterprise** (1942). Matthew Josephson, *The Robber Barons** (1934), is highly critical but provocative. Rendigs Fels, *American Business Cycles* (1959), is technical but valuable. On technological developments, in addition to many of the volumes on specific industries cited below, see H.J. Habakkuk, *American and British Technology in the Nineteenth Century** (1962), W.P. Strassmann, *Risk and Technological Innovation: American Manufacturing Methods During the Nineteenth Century* (1959), and Lewis Mumford, *Technics and Civilization** (1934).

For the railroad industry, consult G.R. Taylor and I.D. Neu, *The American Railroad Network* (1956), J.F. Stover, *Amercan Railroads** (1961), T.C. Cochran, *Railroad Leaders* (1953), Julius Grodinsky, *Transcontinental Railway Strategy* (1962) and *Jay Gould* (1957). R.W. Fogel, *Railroads and American Economic Growth* (1964), deals mainly with pre-Civil War events but is also important for this period. C.F. Adams, Jr., *Railroads: Their Origin and Problems* (1879), is a valuable contemporary analysis.

The iron and steel business is discussed in great detail in J.F. Wall, *Andrew Carnegie* (1970), Peter Temin, *Iron and Steel in Nineteenth-Century America* (1964), an economic analysis, J.H. Bridge, *The Inside History of the Carnegie Steel Company* (1903), and in Carnegie's *Autobiography* (1920); there is no solid scholarly history of the industry. For the oil industry, however, a number of excellent volumes exist. See H.F. Williamson and A.R. Daum, *The American Petroleum Industry: Age of Illumination* (1959), Allan Nevins, *Study in Power: John D. Rockefeller* (1953), and R.W. and M.E. Hidy, *Pioneering in Big Business* (1955), the first volume of their *History of Standard Oil Company (New Jersey)* (1955–56). The electrical industry is discussed in an excellent study, H.C. Passer, *The Electrical Manufacturers* (1953), and in an equally good biography, Matthew Josephson, *Edison** (1959). H.G. Prout, *A Life of George Westinghouse* (1921), is also useful.

Many of these volumes deal with the problems of competition and monopoly. See also, however, E.G. Campbell, *The Reorganization of the American Railroad System* (1938), Gabriel Kolko, *Railroads and Regulation* (1965), which is critical of both railroad leaders and of government policy, J.D. Rockefeller, *Random Reminiscences of Men and Events* (1909), H.D. Lloyd, *Wealth Against Commonwealth** (1894), Lewis Corey, *The House of Morgan* (1930), H.W. Laidler, *Concentration of Control in American Industry* (1931), and J.W. Jenks, *The Trust Problem* (1905).

For contemporary discussions of the monopoly problem, see Lloyd's *Wealth Against Commonwealth,* Henry George, *Progress and Poverty* (1879), and Edward Bellamy, *Looking Backward** (1888). The background of government regulation of industry is treated in Sidney Fine, *Laissez Faire and the General-Welfare State** (1956), J.W. Hurst, *Law and the Conditions of Freedom in the Nineteenth-Century United States** (1956), J.A. Garraty, *The New Commonwealth** (1968), and Lee Benson, *Merchants, Farmers, and Railroads* (1955). Other useful volumes include W.Z. Ripley, *Trusts, Pools, and Corporations* (1905), H.B. Thorelli, *The Federal Antitrust Policy* (1954), and S.J. Buck, *The Granger Movement** (1913).

*Available in paperback.

19

The Response to Industrialism

The industrialization that followed the Civil War profoundly affected American life. New machines, improvements in transportation and communication, the appearance of the great corporation with its uncertain implications for the future—all made deep impressions not only on the economy but also on the social and cultural development of the nation. Indeed, the history of the period may be treated, as historian Samuel P. Hays suggests, as a "response to industrialism," the "story of the impact of industrialism on every phase of human life."

The American Workingman

Of course the laboring man felt the full force of the tide; it affected him in countless ways—some beneficial, others unfortunate. As industry became more important in the United States, the number of industrial workers multiplied rapidly: from 885,000 in 1860 to over 3.2 million in 1890. Although these workers lacked much sense of solidarity, they exerted a far larger influence on society at the turn of the century than they had in the years before the Civil War. Furthermore, more efficient methods of production enabled them to increase their output, making possible a rise in their standard of living. David A. Wells, a liberal economist, estimated in 1889 that workers' purchasing power had gone up nearly 40 per cent between 1850 and 1880, and modern economic historians are in rough agreement. Wells also claimed that even the unskilled could provide for the basic needs of their families if they husbanded their resources, and in this he seems to have been incorrect. An unskilled worker could still not maintain a family decently by his own efforts. The weight of the evidence also indicates that industrial workers did not receive a fair share of the fruits of economic growth. Nevertheless, it is incontestable that materially most workers were improving their position.

On the other hand, industrialization created grave problems for those who toiled in the mines, mills, and shops. When machines took the place of handicrafts, jobs became monotonous. Mechanization undermined both the craftsman's pride and his bargaining power vis-à-vis his employer. As expensive machinery became *more* important, the workingman seemed of necessity *less* important. If a machine must operate at high speed to pay for itself, the man who tends it must quicken his pace accordingly. What matter if he is exhausted at the end of the day or if the whirring wheels and clashing gears threaten life or limb? At a discussion of these problems at a New York Workingmen's Lyceum in 1880, men spoke of the "treadmill monotony of . . . existence" and deplored "the tension resulting from the American system of seeking to increase quantity, rather than quality of products." As businesses grew larger, man-to-man contact between employer and hired hand tended to disappear. Relations between them became less human, more businesslike and ruthless. The trend toward bigness also seemed to make it more difficult for men to rise from the ranks of labor to become themselves manufacturers, as Andrew Carnegie, for example, had done during the Civil War era.

It is difficult to generalize about the actual conditions of laborers in the late 19th century. In good times something approaching full employment existed; in periods of depression unemployment caused much hardship. Workers in some industries fared better than others. By and large, skilled workers, always better off than the unskilled, improved their positions relatively, despite the increased use of machinery. Women and children continued to supply a significant percentage of the industrial working force, always receiving lower wages than adult male workers. About 600,000 boys and girls between 10 and 14 were gainfully employed in 1890 in the United States, over 387,000 of them in the southern states.

Furthermore, a great deal depended upon the education, intelligence, and motivation of workers. Early social workers who visited the homes of industrial laborers in this period reported enormous differences in the standard of living of men engaged in the same line of work, differences related to such variables as the wife's ability as a homemaker and the degree of the family's commitment to middle-class values. An Illinois investigator found a family of five living frugally but decently in 1883 on an annual income of only $250. Some families spent most of their income on food, others saved substantial sums even when earning no more than $400 or $500 a year. Family incomes also varied greatly among workers who received similar hourly wages, depending on the steadiness of employment and on the number of family members holding down jobs. Skilled workers with a couple of fully employed grown sons often had family incomes of $2,000 or more, at least five times the national average for this period.

For most laborers, the working day still tended to approximate the hours of daylight, but it was shortening perceptibly by the 1880's. In 1860 the average was 11 hours; by 1880 only one worker in four labored more than 10, and radicals were beginning to talk about 8 hours as a fair day's work. To some extent the exhausting pace of the new factories made longer hours uneconomical, but employers realized this only slowly, and until they did, many workers suffered. In North Carolina, for example, the workday in the textile mills averaged over 11 hours even for women and children, who made up well over half the work force.

Despite the improvement in living standards, there was a great deal of dissatisfaction among industrial workers. Writing in 1885, the labor leader Terence V. Powderly said it was undeniable "that a deep-rooted feeling of discontent pervades the masses," and a few years later a Connecticut official conducted an informal survey of labor opinion in the state and found a "feeling of bitterness" and "distrust of employers" endemic. This discontent rose from many causes. For some, poverty was still the chief problem, but for others, rising aspirations triggered discontent.

Workers everywhere were becoming confused about their destiny; the tradition that no able man need remain a hired hand died hard. They wanted to believe their bosses and the politicians when those worthies voiced the old slogans about a classless society and the community of interest of capital and labor. "Our men," said William Vanderbilt of the New York Central in 1877, "feel that, although I . . . may have my millions and they the rewards of their daily toil, still we are about equal in the end. If they suffer, I suffer, and if I suffer, they cannot escape." "The poor," said another conservative spokesman a decade later, "are not poor because the rich are rich." Instead "the service of capital" softened their lot and gave them many benefits. Statements like these, although self-serving, were essentially correct. The rich were growing richer and more people were growing rich, but ordinary workers were also better off. However, the gap between the very rich and the ordinary citizen was widening. "The tendency . . . is toward centralization and aggregation," the Illinois Bureau of Labor Statistics reported in 1886. "This involves a separation of the people into classes, and the permanently subordinate status of large numbers of them." Thus even a worker whose personal standard of living was rising might find his relative position in society declining.

To study social and economic mobility in a large industrial country is extraordinarily difficult. Late-19th-century Americans believed their society offered great opportunities for individual advancement, and to prove it they could point to men like Andrew Carnegie and dozens of other poor boys who accumulated large fortunes over a short span of time. How general was the rise from rags to riches, or even to modest comfort, is another question.

The most ambitious modern investigation, Stephan Thernstrom's study of the workingmen of Newburyport, Massachusetts, between 1850 and 1880, described in his book *Poverty and Progress*, indicates that few unskilled workers progressed beyond the ranks of the semiskilled, and that their sons did little better. "The barriers against moving more than one notch upward were fairly high." It would be risky to generalize from Thernstrom's evidence, for Newburyport was only one city, and something of a backwater at that. Nevertheless, the evidence is important. Probably contemporaries were overly influenced by spectacular examples such as Carnegie in concluding that American society was highly mobile. The Carnegies, clearly, were the exception.

However, the dissatisfaction of labor may have resulted more from the dashing of unrealistic hopes inspired by such cases than from the absence of real opportunity, which, however difficult to measure, was surely greater than in any other industrial nation at the time. Any conclusion must be tentative, but this one offers a plausible explanation for the coexistence of discontent and rising living standards. In any case, it remains probable that most workers, even when expressing dissatisfaction with their present lot, continued to subscribe to middle-class values like hard work and thrift—that is, they continued to hope. Thernstrom notes that hundreds of poor families in Newburyport, by practicing what he calls "ruthless underconsumption," gradually accumulated enough money to buy their own homes and provide for themselves in their old age.

Growth of Labor Organizations

Discontent with conditions and class consciousness led some workers to join unions, but only a small percentage of the work force was organized and most of this consisted of craftsmen, such as cigarmakers, printers, and carpenters, rather than semiskilled factory hands. Aside from skilled ironworkers, railroad workers, and miners, few industrial laborers belonged to unions. Nevertheless, in a sense, the union was the workingman's response to the big corporation: a combination designed to eliminate competition for jobs and provide efficient organization for labor. "Capital," a Pennsylvania newspaper admitted in 1877, "cannot consistently advocate combination among the employers, and at the same time denounce it among the employed." As one labor leader said: "Modern industry evolves these union organizations out of existing conditions."

After 1865 the growth of national craft unions like the iron molders, the printers, and the cigarmakers, which had been organized in the fifties, quickened perceptibly. By the early 1870's about 300,000 workers belonged to such organizations, and many new trades, most notably in railroading, had been unionized. A federation of such unions, the National Labor Union, was created in 1866. Under the presidency of William Sylvis of the Iron Molders Union, it enjoyed some success, but it remained chiefly a paper organization. Most of its leaders were visionaries out of touch with the practical needs and aspirations of the

A Negro delegate introduces Terence V. Powderly at a Knights of Labor convention held in Richmond. At one point, the union had some 60,000 Negro members.

workers. They opposed the wage system, strikes, and anything that increased the laborers' sense of being members of the working class. A major objective was the formation of worker-owned cooperatives. "By cooperation we will become a nation of employers—the employers of our own labor," Sylvis explained. "The wealth of the land will pass into the hands of those who produce it." Because the union desired basic social reforms that had little to do with bargaining between workers and employers, it eventually became a political organization, the National Labor Reform party. When the election of 1872 proved this venture a fiasco, the organization disappeared.

Far more remarkable than the National Labor Union was the Knights of Labor, a curious organization with one foot in the past, the other in the future. Founded in 1869 by a group of Philadelphia garment workers headed by Uriah S. Stephens, the Knights flourished in the 1880's. Like so many labor organizers of the period, Stephens was a reformer of wide interests rather than a man dedicated to the specific problems of industrial workers. He, his successor as head of the movement, Terence V. Powderly, and many of its other leaders would have been thoroughly at home in any of the labor organizations of the Jacksonian era. Like the Jacksonians, they supported political objectives that had no direct connection with working conditions, such as currency reform, the nationalization of natural resources, and the curbing of land speculation. They rejected the idea that workers must resign themselves to remaining wage earners. By pooling their resources, workingmen could advance up the economic ladder and enter the capitalist class. "There is no good reason," Powderly wrote in his autobiography, *The Path I Trod,* "why labor cannot, through cooperation, own and operate mines, factories, and railroads." He showed no grasp at all of the changing character of the industrial system with its ever-increasing emphasis on amassing large amounts of capital, and on technical and managerial skills. The leading Knights saw no contradiction between their denunciation of "soulless" monopolies and of "drones" like bankers and lawyers, and their talk of "combining all branches of trade in one common brotherhood." Such muddled thinking led the Knights to attack the wage system and also to frown on strikes as "acts of private warfare."

At the same time the Knights supported some startlingly advanced ideas about labor organization. They rejected the traditional grouping of workers by crafts, developing a concept closely resembling modern industrial unionism. "Machinery has so revolutionized the methods of industry that there are practically very few trades remaining." They welcomed Negroes (chiefly in segregated locals), women, and immigrants and accepted unskilled workers as well as craftsmen. The eight-hour day was one of their basic demands, their argument being that increased leisure would give workers time to develop more cultivated tastes and thus higher aspirations. Higher pay would inevitably follow:

> Whether you work by the piece or work by the day
> Decreasing the hours increases the pay.

The growth of the union, however, had little to do with ideology. Stephens had made the Knights a secret organization with an elaborate ritual. Under his leadership, as late as 1879 it had fewer than 10,000 members. Under Powderly, secrecy was discarded. The rising prosperity of the eighties was a boon. Between 1882 and 1886 a series of succesful strikes by local "assemblies" against western railroads, including one against the hated Jay Gould's Missouri Pacific, brought recruits by the thousands. The membership passed 42,000 in 1882, 110,000 in 1885, and then, in 1886, soared beyond the 700,000 mark. Alas, sudden prosperity was too much for the Knights. Its national leadership was ineffective and unable to control local groups. A series of poorly planned strikes failed dismally; public opinion was alienated by sporadic acts of violence and intimidation. Disillusioned recruits began to drift away.

However, circumstances largely fortuitous caused the collapse of the organization. By 1886 the movement for the eight-hour day had gained wide support among workers. Several hundred thousand men (estimates vary) were on strike in various parts of the country by May of that year. In Chicago, an important center of the eight-hour movement, about 80,000 workers were involved, and a small group of anarchists was taking advantage of the excitement to stir up radical feeling. When a striker was killed in a fracas at the McCormick Harvesting Machine Company, the anarchists called a protest meeting on May 4, at Haymarket Square. Police intervened to break up the meeting, and someone—his identity was never established—hurled a bomb into their ranks. Seven policemen were killed and many others injured. While the anarchists were the direct victims of the resulting public indignation and hysteria—seven were condemned to death and four eventually executed—organized labor, and especially the Knights, suffered heavily. No tie between the Knights and the bombing could be established, but the union had been closely connected with the eight-hour movement, and the public tended to associate it with violence and radicalism. Its membership declined as suddenly as it had risen, and soon it ceased to exist as an important force in the labor movement.

The Knights' place was taken by the American Federation of Labor, an organization of national craft unions established in 1886. In a sense the AF of L was a reactionary organization. Its principal leaders, Adolph Strasser and Samuel Gompers of the Cigarmakers Union, were, like the founders of the Knights of Labor, originally interested in utopian social reforms; they even toyed with the idea of forming a workingmen's political party. Experience, however, soon led them to abandon such ambitions and concentrate on organizing skilled workers and fighting for specific "bread-and-butter" issues such as higher wages and shorter hours. "Our organization does not consist of idealists," Strasser explained to a congressional committee. "We do not control the production of the world. That is controlled by the employers. . . . I look first to cigars." Yet

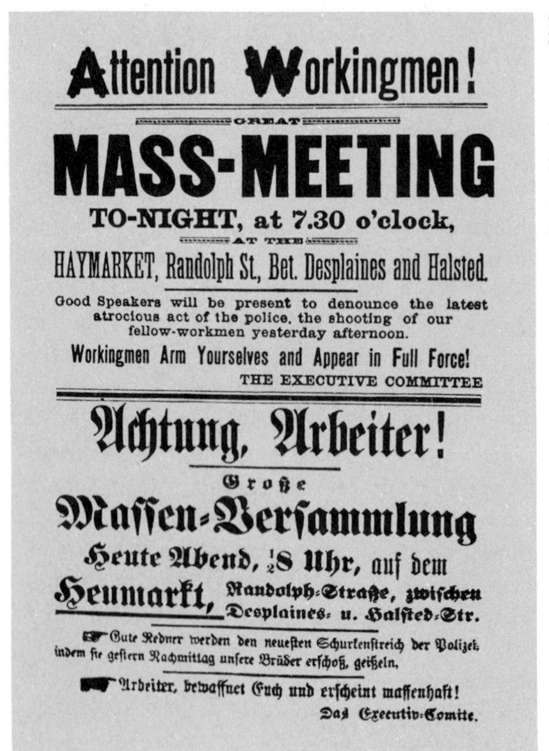

Century Magazine, APRIL, 1893

An anarchist group printed and distributed 20,000 of these bilingual handbills on the day of the Haymarket Square bombing incident in Chicago in 1886.

the AF of L was modern in its view of industrial trends; it accepted the fact that most workers would remain wage earners all their lives and tried to develop in them a sense of common purpose and pride in their skills and station. Strasser and Gompers paid great attention to building a strong organization based on regular dues-paying members committed to unionism as a way of improving their lot.

The chief weapon of the federation was the strike, which it used both to win concessions from employers and to attract recruits to the member unions. Gompers, president of the AF of L almost continuously from 1886 to his death in 1924, encouraged workers to make "an intelligent use of the ballot" in order to advance their own interests, and the federation adopted a "legislative platform" which demanded such things as eight-hour, employers'-liability, and mine-safety laws, but it avoided direct involvement in politics. "I have my own philosophy and my own dreams," Gompers once told a left-wing French politician, "but first and foremost I want to increase the workingman's welfare year by year. . . . The French workers waste their economic force by their political divisions." Gompers' approach to labor problems produced solid, if unspectacular, growth for the AF of L. Unions with a total of about 150,000 members formed the federation in 1886. By 1892 the membership had reached 250,000, and in 1901 it passed the million mark.

Labor Unrest

The stress of the AF of L on the strike weapon reflected rather than caused the increasing militancy of labor. Workers felt themselves threatened from all sides: the growing size and power of their corporate employers, the substitution of machines for human skills, the invasion of foreign workers willing to accept substandard wages. At the same time they had tasted some of the material benefits of industrialization and had learned the advantages of concerted action.

The average employer, on the other hand, behaved like a tyrant when dealing with his workers. He discharged men arbitrarily when they tried to organize unions; he hired scabs to break strikes; he frequently failed to provide the most rudimentary protections against injury on the job. Mine owners who operated company stores in areas remote from towns charged exorbitant prices and sometimes paid their men in scrip so that they would have to patronize the stores. Some employers professed to approve of unions, but almost none of them was really willing to bargain with labor collectively. To do so, they argued, would be to deprive the individual worker of his sacred freedom to contract for his own labor in any way he saw fit.

Of course the industrialists of the period were not all ogres; they were as alarmed by the rapid changes of the times as their workers, and since they had more at stake materially, they were probably more frightened by the uncertainties. The pressures produced by deflation, technological change, and intense competition kept even the most successful under constant strain. The thinking of most employers was remarkably confused. They argued that the interests of capital and labor were identical but refused to allow labor a share in the decision-making that determined their common fate. They considered workers who joined unions "disloyal," but at the same time treated labor as a commodity to be purchased as cheaply as possible. "If I wanted boiler iron," Henry B. Stone, a railroad official, explained, "I would go out on the market and buy it where I could get it cheapest, and if I wanted to employ men, I would do the same." Yet Stone was furious when the men he had "bought" on such terms joined a union. When labor was scarce, employers resisted demands for higher wages by arguing that the price of labor was controlled by its productivity, but when it was plentiful, they justified reducing wages by referring to the law of supply and demand.

Thus both capital and labor were often spoiling for a fight—frequently without fully understanding why. When labor troubles developed, they tended to be bitter, even violent. As early as 1877 a great railroad strike convulsed much of the nation. It began on the Baltimore and Ohio system in response to a wage cut and spread first to other eastern lines and then throughout the West, until about two-thirds of the railroad mileage of the country had been shut down. Violence broke out, rail yards were put to the torch, dismayed and frightened businessmen formed militia companies to patrol the streets of Chicago and other cities. Alarmed citizens began to talk about a revolution triggered by "communist orators" and "designing and mischievous leaders." One clergyman called the leaders of the workers "a junto of men, who stand ready to strike in the dark, from their secret conclave, at everything we hold dear, our very altars and our firesides." Eventually President Hayes, responding to the request of the governors of four states, sent federal troops to the trouble spots to restore order, and the strike collapsed. There had been no real danger of revolution, but the violence and destruction of the strike had been without precedent in America.

The disturbances of 1877 were a response to a business slump, those of the next decade a response to good times. In Boston alone over 550 strikes took place during the "great uprising" of the mid-eighties. Nationally, twice as many strikes occurred in 1886 as in any previous year. Even before the Haymarket bombing centered the country's attention on labor problems, the situation had become so disturbing that President Cleveland, in the first Presidential message devoted to labor problems, had urged Congress to create a voluntary arbitration board to aid in settling labor disputes—a remarkable suggestion for a man of Cleveland's conservative, laissez-faire approach to economic issues.

In 1892 a violent strike broke out among the silver miners at Coeur d'Alene, Idaho, and a far more important clash shook Andrew Carnegie's Homestead steel plant near Pittsburgh when strikers attacked 300 private guards brought in to protect strikebreakers, killing seven of them and forcing the rest to "surrender" and march off ignominiously. The Homestead affair was part of a bitter struggle between capital and labor in the steel industry. The steel men believed that the workers were holding back progress by resisting technological changes, while the workers argued that the company was refusing to share the fruits of more efficient operation fairly. The strike was precipitated by the decision of company officials to crush the union at all costs. The final defeat, after a five-month walkout, of the 24,000-member Amalgamated Association of Iron and Steel Workers, one of the most important elements in the AF of L, destroyed unionism as an effective force in the steel industry and set back the progress of organized labor all over the country.

As in the case of the Haymarket bombing, the activities of radicals on the fringe of the dispute turned the public against the steelworkers. The boss of Homestead was Henry Clay Frick, a tough-minded foe of unions who was determined to "teach our employees a lesson." Frick had made the decision to bring in strikebreakers and employ Pinkerton detectives to protect them. During the course of the strike, Alexander Berkman, an anarchist, burst into Frick's office and attempted to assassinate him. Frick was only slightly wounded, but the attack brought him much sympathy and redounded quite unjustly to the discredit of the strikers.

The most important strike of the period took place in 1894, when the workers at George Pullman's Palace Car factory outside Chicago walked out in protest against a series of wage cuts. (While reducing wages, Pullman insisted on holding the line on rents in the company town of Pullman; when a delegation called upon him to remonstrate, he refused to give in and had three of the leaders fired.) Some Pullman workers belonged to the American Railway Union, an independent union of 150,000 members headed by Eugene V. Debs. After the strike had dragged along for weeks, this group voted to refuse to handle trains with Pullman cars. The resulting railroad strike tied up trunk lines running in and out of Chicago.

The railroad owners, banded together in the General Managers' Association, were, as federal investigators later reported, "determined to crush the strike rather than accept any peaceable solution through conciliation, arbitration, or otherwise." By-passing Governor John Peter Altgeld of Illinois because of his known prolabor views, they appealed to President Cleveland to send troops to preserve order. On the pretext that the soldiers were needed to ensure the movement of the mails,* Cleveland agreed. Thus the strike was broken, and when Debs defied a federal court's injunction, he was jailed for contempt.

The crushing of the Pullman strike demonstrated the power of the courts to break strikes by issuing injunctions. Even more ominous for organized labor, perhaps, was the fact that the government based its request for the injunction on the Sherman Antitrust Act, arguing that the American Railway Union was a combination in restraint of trade. Another result of the strike was to make Eugene V. Debs a national figure. While serving out his sentence for contempt, he was visited by a number of prominent socialists, who sought to convert him to their cause. One gave him a copy of Karl Marx's *Capital,* which he found too dull to finish, but he did study radical works like *Looking Backward* and *Wealth Against Commonwealth,* and in 1897 he became an active socialist. Thereafter, he ran for President five times on the Socialist party ticket.

The "New" Immigration

Industrial expansion increased the need for labor, and this in turn powerfully stimulated immigration; between 1866 and 1915 about 25 million foreigners entered the United States. Industrial growth alone does not explain this influx. The Atlantic crossing, once so hazardous and uncomfortable, became safe and speedy with the perfection of the steamship. Competition between the great packet lines such as Cunard, North German Lloyd, and Holland-America drove down the cost of the passage, and advertising by the lines further stimulated traffic. Improved transportation also wrought changes in the economies of many European countries that caused an increase in the flow of people to America. Cheap wheat from the United States, Russia, and other parts of the world could now be imported into western Europe, bringing disaster to farmers in England, Germany, and the Scandinavian countries. The spreading industrial revolution led to the collapse of the peasant economy of central and southern Europe. For rural inhabitants this meant the loss of self-sufficiency, the fragmentation of landholdings, poverty, and, for many, the decision to make a new start in the New World. Political and religious persecutions pushed still others into the migrating stream. However, the main reason for immigration remained the desire for economic betterment. "In America," as a British immigrant put it, "you get pies and puddings."

While immigrants continued to people the farms of America, industry absorbed an ever-increasing number. As early as 1870 one industrial worker in three was foreign-born. In 1890, 48 per cent of all British immigrants were employed in industry. When congressional investigators examined 21 major industries early in the new century, they discovered that 57.9 per cent of the labor force was foreign-born and that in certain industries, such as iron and steel, the percentage was still higher.

Most of these new millions came into the

After the collapse of his American Railway Union in 1897, Eugene V. Debs (shown here addressing a Socialist party gathering) devoted himself to politics.

UPI

*Actually the union was perfectly willing to handle mail trains. The owners, however, refused to run trains unless they were made up of a full complement of cars. When Pullman cars were added to mail trains, the workers refused to move them.

United States by way of New York City. A Serbian immigrant, Michael Pupin, later a distinguished physicist at Columbia University, has left a moving description of what it was like to enter. He arrived in 1874 on the Hamburg-American liner *Westphalia* amid a great horde of peasants and craftsmen. After disembarking at Hoboken, he was brought by tug to the immigration reception center at Castle Garden on the southern tip of Manhattan. He confessed to the authorities that he had only five cents to his name and knew no Americans except—by reputation—Franklin, Lincoln, and Harriet Beecher Stowe. But he explained in eloquent phrases why he wanted to live in the land of liberty rather than in the aristocratic Austro-Hungarian empire. The officials conferred briefly, then admitted him. After a good breakfast, supplied by the immigration authorities, the Castle Garden Labor Bureau offered him a job as a farm hand in Delaware. Within 24 hours of his arrival he had reached his destination, ready to work.

Before 1882 when—in addition to the Chinese—criminals, idiots, lunatics, and persons liable to become public charges were excluded, entry into the United States was almost unrestricted. A host of private agencies, philanthropic and commercial, served as a link between the new arrivals and employers looking for labor. Until the Foran Act of 1885 outlawed the practice, a few companies brought in skilled craftsmen under contract, advancing them passage money and collecting it in installments from their pay checks. However, ordinary unskilled immigrants were not handled in this way. Various nationality groups assisted, and sometimes exploited, their compatriots by organizing "immigrant banks" which recruited labor in the old country, arranged the necessary transportation, and then housed the newcomers in boarding houses in the United States while finding them jobs. The *padrone* system of the Italians and Greeks was typical. The *padrone,* a sort of contractor who agreed to supply gangs of unskilled workers to companies for a lump sum, usually signed on immigrants unfamiliar with American wage levels at rates that assured him a fat profit.

Beginning in the 1880's, the spreading effects of industrialization in Europe caused a massive shift in the sources of American immigration from northern and western to southern and eastern sections of the Continent. In 1882, when 789,000 immigrants entered the United States, over 350,000 of them came from Great Britain and Germany, only 32,000 from Italy, and less than 17,000 from Russia. In 1907—the all-time peak year, with 1,285,000 immigrants—Great Britain and Germany supplied only 116,000, whereas 285,000 Italians and 258,000 Russians entered.* These "new" immigrants were culturally far different both from "native" stock and the run of earlier immigrants from countries like Germany, France, and Sweden. Poor, isolated, uneducated, more than ordinarily clannish in their strange surroundings, they seemed to contemporaries much harder to assimilate than earlier arrivals. Actually, most of the older immigrant groups had been equally ill-prepared for local conditions when they arrived in the United States; what made the new breed appear to dissolve so slowly in the American "melting pot" was their large number, not their resistance to acculturation. Failing to appreciate this fact, many Americans concluded, wrongly but understandably, that the new immigrants were incapable of becoming good citizens and should be kept out.

The first to show concern about the new trend were reformers, who were worried by the social problems that arose when so many poor immigrants flocked into cities already bursting at the seams because of the flow of population to urban areas. As early as 1883 Henry George, author of *Progress and Poverty,* expressed alarm about the "human garbage" descending upon the nation from foreign parts. During the 1880's large numbers of social workers, economists, and church leaders basically sympathetic to immigrants began to feel that some kind of restriction should be placed on the incoming human tide. The directors of charitable organizations, who bore the burden of aiding the most unfortunate of the

*Throughout history up to 1880, only about 200,000 southern and eastern Europeans had migrated to America. Between 1880 and 1910, approximately 8.4 million arrived.

CULVER PICTURES

During the first decade of the 20th century, when the "new" immigration from southern and eastern Europe was at flood tide (below), Lewis Hine took a notable series of photographs of the human drama at Ellis Island. The immigrants above nervously await the processing of their passports, identification tags, and health certificates.

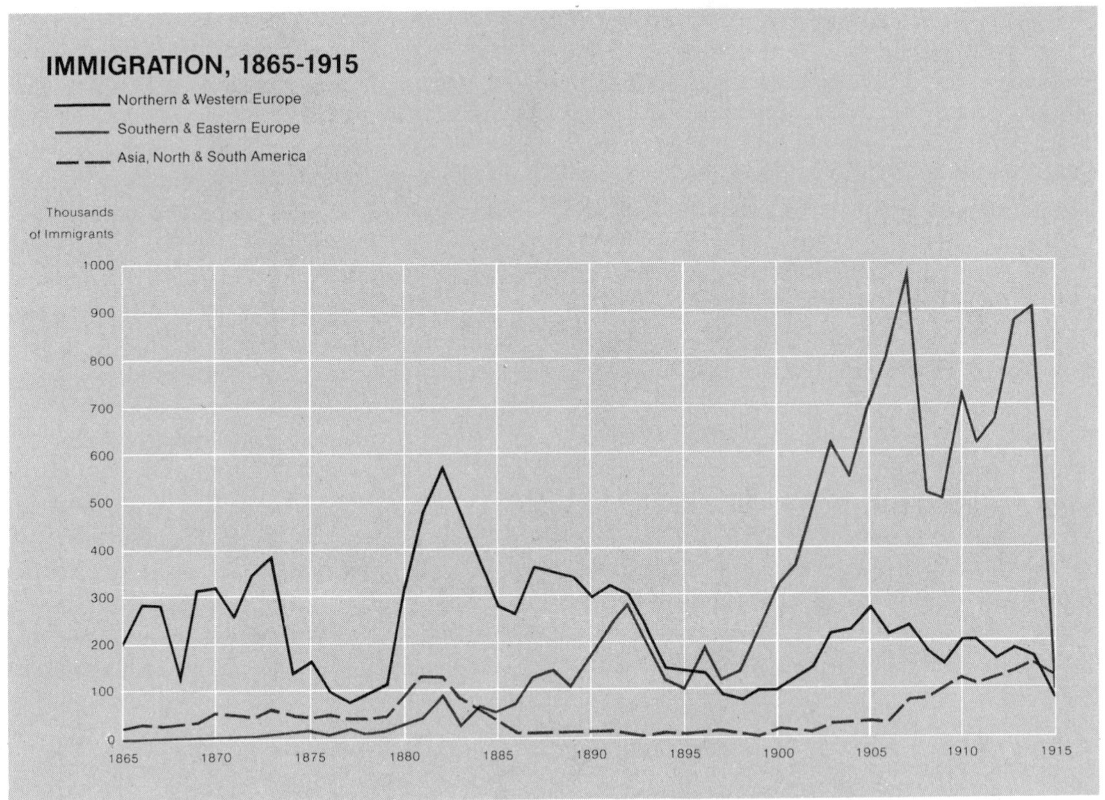

immigrants, were soon complaining that their resources were being exhausted by the needs of the new flood.

Organized labor, fearing the competition of workers with low living standards and no bargaining power, became increasingly vocal against the "enticing of penniless and unapprised immigrants . . . to undermine our wages and social welfare." Some corporations, especially in fields like mining, which employed large numbers of unskilled workers, made use of immigrants as strikebreakers, and this particularly angered union men. According to the historian John Higham, Slavic and Italian miners imported into the Pennsylvania coal fields were "abused in public and isolated in private, cuffed in the works and pelted on the streets." "The Poles, Slavs, Huns and Italians," a labor paper editorialized in 1909, "come over without any ambition to live as Americans live and . . . accept work at any wages at all, thereby lowering the tone of American labor as a whole." David Brody, historian of the steelworkers, describes an "unbridgeable gulf" in the steel industry between native and foreign laborers.

Naturally, employers were not disturbed by the continuing influx of men with strong backs willing to work hard for low wages. Nevertheless, by the late 1880's many of them were becoming alarmed about the supposed radicalism of the immigrants. The Haymarket bombing focused attention on the handful of foreign-born extremists in the country and loosed a flood of unjustified charges that "anarchists and communists" were dominating the labor movement. Nativism, which had waxed in the 1850's under the Know-Nothing banner and waned during the Civil War, now flourished again as a wave of nationalist hysteria swept across the land. Denunciations of "long-haired, wild-eyed, bad-smelling, atheistic, reckless foreign wretches," of "Europe's human and inhuman rubbish," of the "cutthroats of Beelzebub from the Rhine, the Danube, the Vistula and the Elbe" crowded the pages of the nation's press. The Grand Army of the Republic, an organization of Civil War veterans, commenced grumbling about foreign-born radicals. A number of superpatriotic societies, such as the Loyal Legion (1887), began to blast out with what Professor Higham has aptly characterized as "buckshot attacks on immigrants."

This new nativism struck more at Catholics and other minority groups than at immigrants as such; it was primarily a middle-class movement inspired by the social tensions of the time, a "response to industrialism" in the broadest sense. Neither labor leaders nor important industrialists, despite their misgivings about immigration, took a broad antiforeign position. The most powerful nativist organization of the period, the American Protective Association, a secret society founded in 1887, existed primarily to resist what its members called "the Catholic menace." Perhaps as many as 500,000 persons had joined the APA by 1894, most of them middle westerners.

Despite so much thunder, however, very little was done to slow down the pace of immigration. After the Exclusion Act of 1882 and the almost meaningless 1885 ban on importing contract labor, no further laws were passed until the 20th century. Strong support for a literacy test for admission developed in the 1890's, pushed by a new organization, the Immigration Restriction League. Since there was much more illiteracy in the southeastern quarter of Europe than in the northwestern, such a test offered a convenient method of discrimination without seeming to do so on national or racial grounds. After all, an argument could be made that persons unable to read and write could not function effectively as citizens in a democracy. A literacy-test bill passed both houses of Congress in 1897, but President Cleveland vetoed it. Such a "radical departure" from the "generous and free-handed policy" of the past, Cleveland said, was unjustified. He added, perhaps with tongue in cheek, that a literacy requirement would not keep out "unruly agitators," who were only too adept at reading and writing.

The Expanding City and Its Problems

Americans who favored restricting immigration made much of the fact that so many of the newcomers crowded into the cities, aggravating problems of housing, public health, crime and immorality, and a host of other social evils. Immigrants did tend to concentrate in the cities because the new jobs created by expanding industry were located there. So, of course, did native Americans; the proportion of urban dwellers had been steadily increasing since about 1820.

It is important to keep in mind that national population density is not necessarily related to the existence of large cities. In the late 19th century there were areas in Asia as large as the United States that were as densely populated as Belgium and England but still overwhelmingly rural. The United States, on the other hand, was by any standard sparsely populated, but well before the Civil War it had become one of the most urban nations in the world. In 1860 more than 16 per cent of the population lived in cities of 8,000 or more inhabitants.* Industrialization does not entirely explain the growth of 19th-century cities, in the United States or elsewhere. All the large American cities got their start as commercial centers, and the development of huge metropolises like New York and Chicago would have been impossible without an efficient national transportation network. But by the latter decades of the century, the enormous expansion of industry had become the chief cause of city growth. Thus the urban concentration continued; by 1890 one person in three lived in a city, by 1910 nearly one in every two.

Throughout this period a steadily increasing proportion of the urban population was made up of immigrants. In 1890 the foreign-born population of Chicago almost equaled the *total* population of Chicago in 1880, a third of all Bostonians and a quarter of all Philadelphians were immigrants, and four out of every five residents of New York City were either foreign-born or the children of immigrants.

After 1890 the immigrant concentration became even more dense. Like the Irish newcomers of the 1840's and 1850's, these "new" migrants from eastern and southern Europe were desperately poor; they lacked even the resources to travel to the agriculturally developing regions, to say nothing of the sums necessary to acquire land and farm equipment. As the process of concentration progressed it fed upon itself, for all the eastern cities developed many ethnic neighborhoods, in each of which immigrants of one particular nationality congregated. Lonely, confused, often unable to speak a word of English, the Italians, the Greeks, the Polish and Russian Jews, and other ethnic groups naturally tended to settle where their predecessors had settled. Each great American city became a Europe in microcosm, where it sometimes seemed that every language in the world but English could be heard. New York, the great entrepôt, had a "Little Italy," a Polish, a Greek, a Jewish, and a Bohemian quarter—even a Chinatown.

However, the rapidity of urban growth explains the troubles associated with city life far better than the high percentage of foreigners. The cities were suffering from growing pains. Sewer and water facilities frequently could not

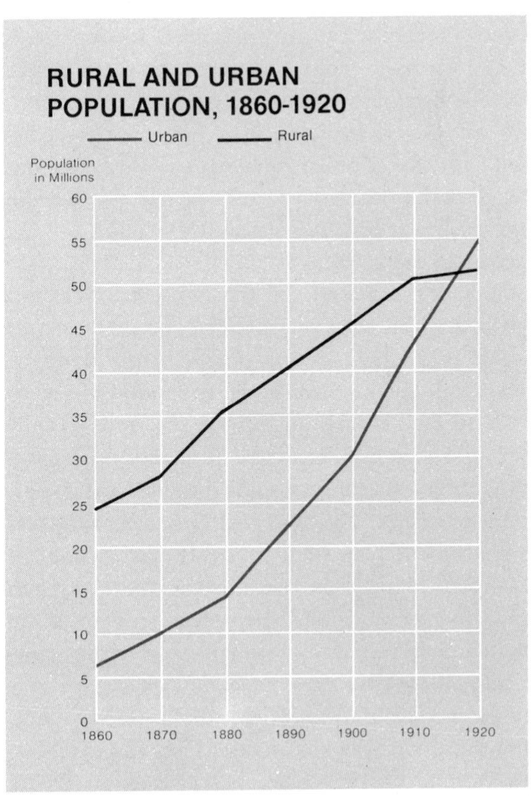

*Yet the population density of the United States in 1860 was only 10.6 per square mile. Even in 1900 it was only 25.6.

keep pace with skyrocketing needs. By the nineties the tremendous growth of Chicago had put such a strain on its sanitation system that the Chicago River had become practically an open sewer, and the city's drinking water contained so many germ-killing chemicals that it tasted like creosote. In the eighties all the sewers of Baltimore emptied into the sluggish Back Basin, and, according to the journalist H.L. Mencken, every summer the city smelled "like a billion polecats." A group of Philadelphia citizens in 1883 characterized the city sewage system as "notoriously bad" and the water supply as unfit even for bathing purposes. This explains why the death rate from typhoid fever in Philadelphia was twice that of New York and Boston, which had decent systems.

Fire protection in most cities became increasingly inadequate, and while there were no conflagrations in the eighties and nineties comparable to the holocausts that devastated Chicago and Boston in 1871 and 1872, the total fire losses in the nation's cities rose sharply, from about $64 million in 1878 to more than $150 million in 1892. Nearly everywhere garbage piled up in streets faster than it could be carted away, and the streets themselves crumbled beneath the pounding of heavy traffic. Urban growth proceeded with such speed that new streets were laid out more rapidly than they could be paved. Chicago, for example, had more than 1,400 miles of dirt streets in 1890.

Housing posed by far the most serious urban problem, for substandard living quarters aggravated other evils, such as disease, the danger of fire, and the disintegration of family life with its attendant mental anguish, crime, and juvenile delinquency. People poured into the great cities faster than apartments could be built to accommodate them. This terrible crowding of areas already densely packed in the 1840's became literally unbearable as rising property values and the absence of zoning laws conspired to make builders utilize every possible foot of space, jamming their structures together, squeezing out light and air ruthlessly in order to wedge in a few additional family units. The bloody New York riots of 1863, although sparked by dislike of the Civil War draft and of Negroes, also reflected the bitterness and frustration of thousands jammed together amid filth and threatened by disease. A citizens' committee seeking to discover the causes of the riots expressed its amazement after visiting the slums "that so much misery, disease, and wretchedness can be huddled together and hidden . . . unvisited and unthought of, so near our own abodes."

The city fathers at last created a Metropolitan Health Board in 1866, and a tenement house law the next year made at least a feeble beginning at regulating city housing. A new tenement house law in 1879 finally placed a limit on the percentage of lot space that could be covered by *new* construction and established minimal standards of plumbing and ventilation. The magazine *Plumber and Sanitary Engineer* sponsored a contest to pick the best design for a tenement that met these specifications. The winner of the competition was James E. Ware, whose plan for a "dumbbell" apartment house managed to crowd from 24 to 32 four-room apartments on a plot of ground only 25 by 100 feet.

> The feat was accomplished [writes Oscar Handlin in *The Uprooted*] by narrowing the building at its middle so that it took on the shape of a dumbbell. The indentation was only two-and-a-half feet wide and varied in length from five to fifty feet; but, added to the similar indentations on the adjoining houses, it created on each side an air-shaft five feet wide. . . . The stairs, halls, and common water closets were cramped into the narrow center of the building so that almost the whole of its surface was available for living quarters.

Despite such "reforms," in 1890 over 1.4 million persons were living on Manhattan Island, and in some sections the population density exceeded 900 persons per acre. Jacob Riis, a New York reporter, captured the horror of these crowded warrens in his classic study of life in the slums, *How the Other Half Lives* (1890):

> Be a little careful, please! The hall is dark and you might stumble. . . . Here where the hall turns and dives into utter darkness is . . . a flight of stairs. You can feel your way, if you cannot see it. Close? Yes! What would you have? All the fresh air that enters these stairs comes from the hall-door that is forever

JACOB A. RIIS COLLECTION, MUSEUM OF THE CITY OF NEW YORK

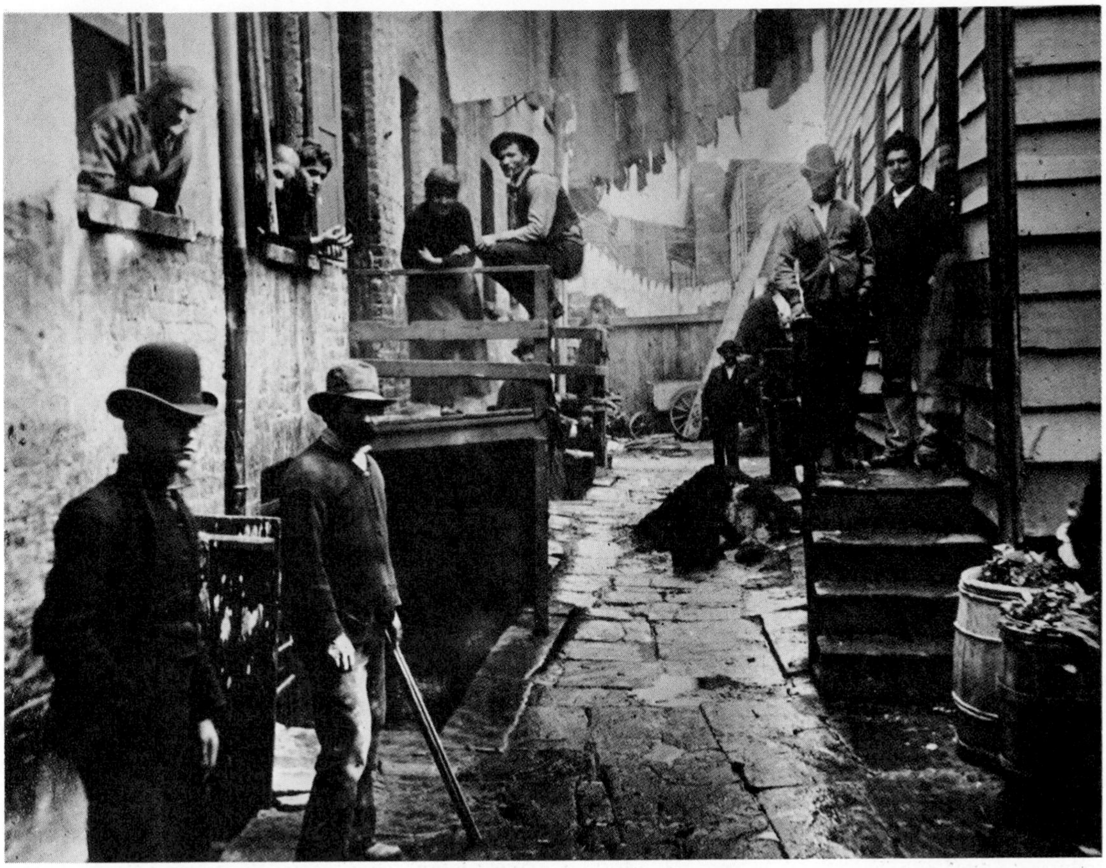

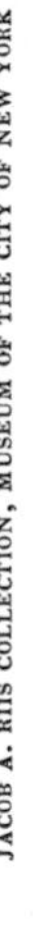

An alley known as "Bandit's Roost," on New York's Lower East Side, photographed for the New York Sun *in 1887 or 1888 by police reporter Jacob Riis, himself an immigrant. "What sort of an answer, think you, would come from these tenements to the question 'Is life worth living?'" Riis asked in his* How the Other Half Lives.

slamming. . . . The sinks are in the hallway, that all the tenants may have access—and all be poisoned alike by their summer stenches. . . . Here is a door. Listen! That short, hacking cough, that tiny, helpless wail—what do they mean? . . . The child is dying of measles. With half a chance it might have lived; but it had none. That dark bedroom killed it.

The unhealthiness of the tenements was notorious; one noxious corner of New York became known as the "lung block" because of the prevalence of tuberculosis among its inhabitants—during a five-year period in the 1890's the Health Department reported over 100 cases there. In 1900 three out of every five babies born in one poor district of Chicago died before their first birthday. Equally frightening was the impact of such overcrowding on the morals of the tenement dweller. Under such conditions, sin proved as contagious as tuberculosis or measles. "The drunkard, the wife or child beater, the immoral woman, and the depraved child infect scores of their neighbors by their vicious acts," one reformer complained in 1885.

Crime also flourished in the slums. The number of prison inmates in the United States increased by 50 per cent in the eighties and the homicide rate nearly tripled, most of the rise occurring in cities. Opponents of unlimited immigration blamed the foreign-born for this crime wave, but most of the new lawbreakers were native Americans—the children of immigrants, reared amid the dirt and chaos of the slums. Driven into the streets by the squalor of their homes, poor, ignorant, and hopeless, the youth of the slum districts formed gangs bearing names like Alley Gang, Rock Gang, and Hell's Kitchen Gang. From petty thievery and shoplifting they graduated to housebreaking, bank robbery, and murder. According to Jacob Riis, when the leader of the infamous Whyo Gang, convicted of murder, finally confessed his sins to a prison chaplain, "his father confessor turned pale . . . though many years of labor as chaplain of the Tombs had hardened him to such rehearsals."

Slums bred criminals—the wonder being that they bred so few. They also drove the well-to-do element to exclusive sections and to the suburbs. From Boston's Beacon Hill and Back Bay to San Francisco's Nob Hill, the rich retired into great cluttered mansions and ignored conditions in the poorer parts of town.

The big-city political bosses, with their corrupt yet useful "machines," filled the vacuum created by upper-class abdication of responsibility. The immigrant masses, largely of peasant stock, had no experience with representative government. Furthermore, the difficulties of life in the slums bewildered and often overwhelmed them. Hopeful, passive, naive, they could not be expected to take a broad view of social problems when so harassed by personal ones. Shrewd urban politicians, most of them of Irish origin—the Irish being the first-comers among the migrants—quickly took command of these immigrants. They shepherded them through the complexities of taking out citizenship papers and then marched them in obedient phalanxes to the polls.

Most city machines were not tightly geared hierarchical bureaucracies ruled by a single leader, but loose-knit neighborhood organizations, each headed by a ward boss. Men like "Big Tim" Sullivan of New York's Lower East Side and "Hinky Dink" Kenna of Chicago were typical of the breed. Such men won the support of the city masses by providing services that no one else seemed willing to supply. They found jobs for new arrivals and distributed food and other help to all in bad times. Anyone in trouble with the law could obtain at least a hearing from the ward boss, and often, if the crime was venial or due to ignorance, the difficulty was quietly "fixed" and the culprit sent off with a word of caution. Sullivan provided turkey dinners for 5,000 or more derelicts each Christmas, distributed new shoes to all the poor children of his district on his birthday, arranged summer boat rides and picnics for young and old alike. At any time of year the victim of some sudden disaster could turn to the local clubhouse for help. Informally, probably without consciously intending to do so, men like Sullivan served to educate the immigrants in the complexities of American civilization, helping them to leap across the gulf between the almost medieval society of their origins and the modern industrial world.

The price of such aid—for the bosses were no altruists—was unquestioning political support, which the bosses converted into cash. In New York Sullivan levied tribute on gambling, had a hand in the liquor business, controlled the issuance of peddlers' licenses. When he died in 1913, he was reputedly worth a million dollars. Yet he and others like him were immensely popular; 25,000 grieving constituents followed Big Tim's coffin to the grave.

The more visible and better-known "city" bosses played less socially justifiable roles than the ward bosses. Their principal technique for extracting money from the public till was the "kickback." In order to get city contracts, suppliers were made to pad their bills and turn over the excess to the politicians. Similarly, operators of streetcar lines, gas and electricity companies, and other public utilities were compelled to pay huge bribes to obtain favorable franchises.

The most notorious—and probably the most despicable—of the major 19th-century city bosses was William Marcy Tweed, whose "Ring" extracted tens of millions of dollars from New York City during the brief period 1869–1871. Tweed, quite properly and relatively swiftly, was lodged in jail. More typical of the city bosses was Richard Croker, who ruled New York's Tammany Hall organization from the mid-1880's to the end of the century. Croker, who came to New York as a child during the great Irish migration of the 1840's, held a number of local offices, but his power rested upon his position as chairman of the Tammany Hall finance committee. Although more concerned than Tweed with the social and economic services that machines provided for the city masses, Croker was primarily a corrupt political manipulator; he accumulated a large fortune, owned a $200,000 mansion and a

Harper's Weekly, AUGUST 19, 1871

Thomas Nast's devastating assaults on the Tweed Ring, printed in Harper's Weekly, *helped bring about its demise. At left, members of the ring (Tweed is at left front) reply "'Twas Him" to the question, "Who stole the people's money?" Below, Tweed and his fellow vultures cower under the storm raised against them. Tweed offered Nast a $500,000 bribe to stop the cartoons.*

PICTURE COLLECTION, NEW YORK PUBLIC LIBRARY

stable of racehorses, one of which was good enough to win the English Derby in 1907.

Despite their welfare work and their admitted popularity with the masses, most bosses were essentially thieves. American city government, as James Bryce wrote in a famous passage in *The American Commonwealth*, was a "conspicuous failure." Efforts to romanticize the bosses as the Robin Hoods of industrial society grossly distort the facts. However, the system developed and survived because too many middle-class city dwellers were indifferent to the fate of the poor. Except spasmodically, during "reform waves," few tried to check the rapaciousness of the politicos. Many substantial citizens shared at least indirectly in the corruption. The owners of tenements, interested only in crowding as many rent payers as possible into their buildings, and utility companies seeking franchises preferred a system that enabled them to buy favors. Honest men who had no selfish stake in the system and who were repelled by the sordidness of city government were seldom sufficiently concerned to do anything about it. When young Theodore Roosevelt decided to seek a political career in 1880, his New York socialite friends laughed in his face. "[They] told me," Roosevelt wrote in his

autobiography, "that politics were 'low'; that the organizations were not controlled by 'gentlemen'; that I would find them run by saloon-keepers, horse-car conductors, and the like."

Indeed, many so-called urban reformers resented the boss system mainly because it gave political power to those who were not "gentlemen," or as one reformer put it, to a "proletarian mob" of "illiterate peasants, freshly raked from Irish bogs, or Bohemian mines, or Italian robber nests." A British visitor in Chicago struck at the root of the urban problem of the era. "Everybody is fighting to be rich," he said, "and nobody can attend to making the city fit to live in."

Urban Improvement

Nevertheless, as American cities grew larger and more crowded, thus aggravating a host of social problems, various practical forces operated to bring about improvements. Once the relationship between polluted water and disease was fully understood, everyone saw the need for decent water and sewage systems. Although some businessmen profited from corrupt dealings with the city machines, more of them wanted efficient and honest government in order to reduce their tax bills. Many businessmen used large amounts of gas, water, and electricity in their plants and thus came to favor cheap and efficient public utilities, and some realized that by lowering the cost of living for their workers, such facilities would make it easier for them to hold wages down. Efficient citywide transportation systems increased the size of the labor pool available to employers, too. City dwellers of all classes resented dirt, noise, and ugliness, and in many communities public-spirited groups formed societies to plant trees, clean up littered areas, and develop recreational facilities. When one city undertook improvements, others tended to follow suit, spurred on by local pride and the booster spirit.

Gradually, in the eighties and nineties, what Arthur M. Schlesinger, Sr., has called "the basic facilities of urban living" were improved. Streets were paved, first with cobblestones and wood blocks and then with smoother, quieter asphalt. Gaslight, then electric arc lights, and finally Edison's incandescent lamps brightened the cities after dark, making law enforcement easier, stimulating night life, and permitting factories and shops to operate after sunset. As we have seen, by the turn of the century about 3,000 central power stations were in operation, some of them municipally owned.

Urban transportation advanced phenomenally during the period. The pre-Civil War horsecars proved unable to handle the crowds of workers and shoppers of the postwar decades. Elevated steam railways helped reduce the congestion, New York leading the way in the 1870's. However, the cheaper, quieter, and less unsightly electric trolley car soon became the principal means of municipal transportation. A retired naval officer, Frank J. Sprague, pioneered in this field, installing his first practical line in Richmond, Virginia, during the winter of 1887–88. At once other cities seized upon the trolley; by 1895 some 850 lines were busily hauling city dwellers over 10,000 miles of track, and mileage more than doubled in the next decade. As with other new enterprises, control of street railways quickly became centralized. Established horsecar lines in the major cities had already fallen into the hands of a few big operators–Charles T. Yerkes in Chicago, P.A.B. Widener and William L. Elkins in Philadelphia, William C. Whitney and Thomas Fortune Ryan in New York. The New York and Philadelphia groups combined, then expanded into other centers, until they controlled the trolleys of over 100 eastern cities and towns. Their various companies were capitalized at about $1 billion.

Streetcars changed the whole character of big-city life. Before their introduction urban communities were limited by the distances men could conveniently walk to work. What historian Sam B. Warner, Jr., calls the "walking city" could not easily extend more than two-and-a-half miles from its center. Streetcars increased this radius to six miles or more, which meant that the *area* of the city expanded enormously. Dramatic population shifts resulted. Rich and poor previously lived close together; now the better-off moved out from the center in search of air and space, abandoning the crumbling, jam-packed older

NEW-YORK HISTORICAL SOCIETY

A view of New York's Herald Square, made about 1900, includes two forms of urban transport that revolutionized city travel. Streetcars crowd Broadway; at right are the tracks of the Sixth Avenue elevated railroad.

neighborhoods to the immigrant poor and the Negroes. Thus economic segregation speeded the growth of ghettos. Older peripheral towns that had maintained some of the self-contained qualities of village life were swallowed up, becoming part of a vast urban sprawl. As time passed, each new area, originally peopled by rising economic groups, tended to become crowded and then to deteriorate. The middle class pushed steadily outward, which helps to explain why this group abandoned its interest in city government so easily.

On the other hand, by extending their tracks *beyond* the city limits, the streetcars enabled city dwellers to escape into the countryside on holidays.

Advances in bridge design, most notably the perfection of the steel-cable suspension bridge by John A. Roebling, also aided the ebb and flow of metropolitan populations. The Brooklyn Bridge—"a weird metallic Apparition under a metallic sky, out of proportion with the winged lightness of its arch, traced for the conjunction of worlds . . . the cables, like divine messages from above . . . cutting and dividing into innumerable musical spaces the nude immensity of the sky"—was Roebling's triumph. Completed by Roebling's son in 1883 at a cost of $15 million, it was soon carrying more than 33 million passengers a year over the East River between Manhattan and Brooklyn.

Even the extremely high cost of urban real estate, which fathered the tenement, produced some beneficial results for the cities in the long run. Instead of crowding squat structures cheek by jowl on 25-foot lots, some imaginative architects began to build upward. The introduction of the iron-skeleton type of construction, which

J. CLARENCE DAVIES COLLECTION, MUSEUM OF THE CITY OF NEW YORK

The Brooklyn Bridge, "the eighth wonder of the world," as it looked from Manhattan in 1889. The bridge took 13 years to build, claimed the life of chief engineer John A. Roebling, and left his son Washington a cripple.

freed the walls from bearing the immense weight of a tall building, was the work of a group of Chicago architects who had been attracted to the metropolis of the Midwest by opportunities to be found amid the ashes of the great fire of 1871. The group included William Le Baron Jenney, John A. Holabird, Martin Roche, John W. Root, and Louis H. Sullivan. Jenney's Home Insurance Building, completed in 1885, was the first metal-frame edifice, employing cast-iron columns and wrought-iron crossbeams. Mere height, however, did not satisfy these innovators; they were determined to create a truly new style, uniquely American, somehow in the spirit of Walt Whitman, whose poetry they much admired. Instead of erecting grotesque enlargements of Romanesque and Gothic structures, they sought a new form that would reflect the structure and purpose of their buildings. Their leader was Louis Sullivan. In an article, "The Tall Office Building Artistically Considered," published in *Lippincott's Magazine* in 1896, Sullivan described his vision. Builders must discard "books, rules, precedents, or any such educational impedimenta" and design functional buildings, he argued. A tall building "must be every inch a proud and soaring thing, rising in sheer exultation . . . from bottom to top . . . a unit without a single dissenting line."

Sullivan's Wainwright Building in St. Louis and Prudential Building in Buffalo, both completed in the early nineties, combined beauty, low construction costs, and efficient use of scarce space in pathbreaking ways. Soon a "race to the skies" was on in all the great cities of America, and the words *skyscraper* and *skyline* entered the language.

Efforts to redesign American cities, much stimulated by the remarkable "White City" built for the Chicago World's Fair of 1893 by Daniel H. Burnham, with its broad vistas and acres of open space, resulted in a "City Beautiful" movement of considerable scope. Burnham and the landscape architect Frederick Law Olmsted, designer of New York's Central Park, gave direction to the movement. Ambitious civic centers were all the rage around the turn of the century, as impressive projects were undertaken in Washington, Cleveland, and other cities. But these never became more than expensive showplaces, broad plazas fringed by pretentious public buildings in the classic style made popular by White City, but surrounded by close-packed, dingy ugliness.

The City Beautiful movement also gave birth to many public parks, and these, of course, brought immense benefits to the people. However, few could be located where they were most needed. In the slums the best that could usually be done was to clear an occasional tiny plot, such as the three-acre Mulberry Bend Park in Manhattan's Lower East Side. Similarly, efforts to relieve the congestion in the slum districts made little headway. In Brooklyn Alfred T. White established Home Buildings, a 40-family model tenement, in 1877; eventually, he expanded the experiment to include 267 apartments. Each unit had plenty of light and air and contained its own sink and toilet. Ellen Collins developed a smaller project in Manhattan's Fourth Ward in the nineties. These model tenements were self-sustaining, but of necessity they yielded only modest returns. The landlords were essentially philanthropists; their work had no significant impact upon urban housing in the 19th century.

Religion Responds to Industrialism

The modernization of the great cities, in short, was not solving most of the social problems of the slums. As this fact became clear in the late 19th century, a number of urban religious leaders began to take a hard look at the situation. Traditionally, American churchmen had insisted that where sin was concerned there were no such things as extenuating circumstances. To the well-to-do they preached the virtues of thrift and hard work, to the poor they extended the possibility of a better existence in the next world, but to all they stressed the individual's responsibility for his own behavior, and thus for his salvation.

Such a point of view brought meager comfort to residents of slums. As a result, the churches lost influence in the poorer sections of the big cities. Furthermore, as better-off citizens followed the streetcar lines out from the city centers, their church leaders followed them. In New York, for example, 17 Protestant congregations abandoned the depressed areas of Lower Manhattan between 1868 and 1888. Catering almost entirely to middle- and upper-class worshipers, they tended to become even more conservative and individualistic in their approach. No more strident defender of reactionary ideas existed than Henry Ward Beecher, pastor of Brooklyn's fashionable Plymouth Congregational Church. Beecher attributed most of the poverty of the slums to the improvidence of laborers, who, he claimed, squandered their wages on liquor and tobacco. "No man in this land suffers from poverty," he said, "unless it be more than his fault—unless it be his *sin*." The best check on labor unrest was a plentiful supply of cheap immigrant labor, he told President Hayes. Unions were "the worst form of despotism and tyranny in the history of Christendom."

Although an increasing proportion of the residents of the blighted districts were Catholics, the Roman Church confined its assistance to distributing alms and maintaining homes for orphans, wayward girls, and old people; church leaders were deeply committed to the idea that sin and vice were personal, poverty an act of God. The release of Pope Pius IX's encyclical *Syllabus of Errors* (1864), which declared every form of liberalism and reform anathema, did nothing to encourage parish priests and Catholic laymen to try to change the status quo. As Arthur Mann has pointed out in his study of late-19th-century Boston reformers, despite the heavy concentration of Catholics in that city, "the Archdiocese of Boston failed to send a single priest into the army of social reform . . . during the period 1880–1900." Catholic leaders deplored the rising trend of crime, disease, and destitution among their co-religionists but failed to see the connection between these evils and the squalor of the slums. "Intemperance is the great evil we have to overcome," wrote the president of the leading Catholic charitable organization, the Society of St. Vincent de Paul. "It is the source of the misery for at least three-fourths of the families we are called upon to visit and relieve." The Church, according to a Catholic historian, Aaron I. Abell, "seemed oblivious to the bearing of civil legislation on the course of moral and social reform." Instead it invested much money and energy in chimerical attempts to colonize poor city dwellers in the West. In the early 1880's, for example, the Irish Catholic Colonization Association of America settled some 35,000 acres in Nebraska and Minnesota. Of course this effort to reverse the national trend from farm to city had little effect on urban conditions.

Like conservative Protestant clergymen, the Catholic hierarchy opposed, or was at best neutral toward, organized labor. Although Terence V. Powderly was a Catholic, a number of priests and bishops looked askance at his Knights of Labor—the liberal Cardinal James Gibbons of Baltimore had to appeal personally to the Vatican to forestall a papal condemnation of the Knights in 1887. The situation changed somewhat after Pope Leo XIII issued his great encyclical *Rerum novarum* (1891), which criticized the excesses of capitalism, defended the right of labor to form unions, and even gave qualified approval to certain aspects of socialism. The workingman was entitled to a wage that would guarantee him a reasonable and frugal comfort, Leo declared, and he committed no sin by seeking government aid to get it. After *Rerum novarum*, one American bishop declared, it was clear that "the mission of the Church [was] not only to save souls, but to save society." Concrete action by American Catholic leaders, however, was slow in coming.

The conservative attitudes of most religious leaders, both Protestant and Catholic, did not prevent some earnest preachers from working directly to improve the lot of the city poor. Some followed the path blazed by Dwight L. Moody, who became famous all over America and Great Britain as a lay evangelist. A gargantuan figure weighing nearly 300 pounds, Moody conducted a vigorous campaign to persuade the denizens of the slums to cast aside their sinful ways. He went among them full of enthusiasm and God's love and made an impact no less powerful than that of George Whitefield during the Great Awakening of the 18th century. Over the years uncounted millions heard him preach. Moody and other evangelists founded mission schools in the worst parts of the slums and tried to provide spiritual and recreational facilities for the unfortunate. Men of this type were prominent in the establishment in the United States of the Young Men's Christian Association (1851) and the Salvation Army (1880).

However, the evangelists paid little heed to the causes of urban poverty and vice. In effect, they depended upon old-fashioned faith in God to enable the poor to transcend the material difficulties of life. For a number of Protestant clergymen who had become familiar with the terrible problems of the slums, a different approach seemed called for. Slum conditions produced the sins and crimes of the cities; the wretched humans who actually committed them could not be blamed, these men argued. They began to preach a "Social Gospel" which focused on trying to improve living conditions rather than on merely saving souls. If men were to lead pure lives, they must have enough to eat, decent homes, opportunities to develop their talents.

Social Gospelers rejected the theory of laissez faire. They advocated civil service reform to break the power of the machines, child labor legislation, the regulation of the trusts, and heavy taxes on incomes and inheritances. The most influential preacher of the Social Gospel was probably Washington Gladden. At the start of his career Gladden, who was raised on a Massachusetts farm, had opposed unions and all governmental interference in social and economic affairs, but his experiences as a minister in Springfield, Massachusetts, and Columbus, Ohio, exposed him to some of the harshness of the poor man's lot in industrial cities, and his views changed. In *Applied Christianity* (1886) and in other works, he defended labor's right to organize and strike and denounced the idea that supply and demand should control wage rates. He favored factory inspection laws, strict regulation of public utilities, and other reforms.

Gladden was a mild-mannered man who never questioned the basic values of capitalism. More radical was R. Heber Newton, a New York Episcopal clergyman. Someday a "co-operative commonwealth" might have to be established in the interest of justice for all men, Newton warned. By the nineties a number of ministers had gone all the way to socialism. The Reverend William D.P. Bliss of Boston, for example, believed in the kind of welfare state envisioned by Edward Bellamy in *Looking Backward.* He founded the Society of Christian Socialists (1889) and edited a radical journal, *The Dawn.* His *Encyclopedia of Social Reform* (1897) summed up admirably the ideas of the Social Gospelers. In addition to nationalizing industry, Bliss and other Christian Socialists, such as George D. Herron and Philo W. Sprague, advocated public unemployment-relief programs, public housing and slum-clearance projects, and other measures designed to ease the lot of the city poor.

Nothing so well reveals the receptivity of the public to the Social Gospel as the fantastic popularity of Charles M. Sheldon's novel *In His Steps* (1896), one of America's all-time best sellers. Sheldon, a minister in Topeka, Kansas, described what happened in the mythical city of Raymond when a group of leading citizens decided to live truly Christian lives, asking themselves "What would Jesus do?" before adopting any course of action. Naturally, the tone of Raymond's society was immensely improved, but basic social reforms also followed quickly. The "Rectangle," a terrible slum area, "too dirty, too coarse, too sinful, too awful for close contact," became the center of a great reform effort. One of Raymond's "leading society heiresses" undertook a slum-clearance project, and a concerted attack was made on drunkenness and immorality. The moral regeneration of the whole community was soon accomplished.

The Settlement Houses

Although millions read *In His Steps*, its effect, and that of other Social Gospel literature, was merely inspirational. On the practical level, a number of earnest souls began to grapple with slum problems directly by organizing what were known as "settlement houses." The prototype of the settlement house was London's Toynbee Hall, founded in the early eighties; the first American example was the Neighborhood Guild, opened on the Lower East Side of New York in 1886 by Dr. Stanton Coit. By the turn of the century nearly a hundred had been established, the most famous being Jane Addams' Hull House in Chicago (1889), Robert A. Woods's South End House in Boston (1892), and Lillian Wald's Henry Street Settlement in New York (1893).

Like the evangelists, settlement-house workers attempted to improve conditions through personal contact with the slum dwellers. They interpreted American ways to the new immigrants and tried to create a community spirit among the rootless and the deprived. At the same time they expected to benefit morally and intellectually themselves by learning about a way of life far different from their own. Idealistic college students and young professional people flocked to the movement in an effort to help bridge the widening gap in American society between the masses and the classes. Lillian Wald, a nurse by training, explained the concept succinctly in *The House on Henry Street* (1915): "We were to live in the neighborhood . . . identify ourselves with it socially, and, in brief, contribute to it our citizenship."

Miss Wald and other leaders soon discovered that practical problems occupied most of their energies. They agitated for tenement house laws, the regulation of the labor of women and children, and better schools, and they employed private resources to establish playgrounds in the slums, along with libraries, classes in arts and crafts, social clubs, and day nurseries. In Boston

Robert A. Woods organized clubs to get the youngsters of the South End off the streets, helped establish a restaurant where a meal could be had for five cents, acted as an arbitrator in labor disputes, and lobbied for laws tightening up on the franchises of public utility companies. In Chicago Jane Addams developed an outstanding cultural program that included classes in music and art and an excellent "little theater" group. Hull House soon boasted a gymnasium, a day nursery, and several social clubs. Miss Addams also worked tirelessly and effectively at the state and local level for improved public services and social legislation of all kinds. She even got herself appointed garbage inspector in her ward and hounded local landlords and the garbage contractor until something approaching decent service was established.

The settlement houses accomplished such miracles that almost everyone appreciated their virtues. By the end of the century even the Catholics, so laggard in entering the arena of practical social reform, were joining the movement, partly because they were losing many communicants to socially minded Protestant churches. The first Catholic-run settlement house was founded in 1898 in an Italian district of New York. Two years later Brownson House in Los Angeles, catering chiefly to Mexican immigrants, threw open its doors. Yet with all their accomplishments, the settlement houses seemed to be fighting a losing battle. "Private beneficence," wrote

Jacob Riis's view of prayer time at the Five Points House of Industry, an orphanage in one of New York's more notorious slum districts. Riis was one of the first to use the camera to document the need for urban reforms.

JACOB A. RIIS COLLECTION, MUSEUM OF THE CITY OF NEW YORK

Jane Addams, of Hull House, "is totally inadequate to deal with the vast numbers of the city's disinherited." As a tropical forest grows faster than a handful of men armed with machetes can cut it down, so the slums, fed by an annual influx of hundreds of thousands, blighted additional areas more rapidly than the intrepid settlement house workers could clean up old ones. It became increasingly apparent that the wealth and authority of the state must be brought to bear in order to keep abreast of the problem.

Social Legislation

State laws aimed at the social problems resulting from industrialism and urbanization date from before the Civil War, but the earlier ones were either so imprecise as to be unenforceable or—like the Georgia law "limiting" textile workers to 11 hours a day and the New York Housing Act of 1867, which set a standard to which the city's dreadful tenements easily conformed—so weak as to be ineffective. As time passed, however, a scattering of workable laws was enacted. In 1874 a Massachusetts law restricted the working hours of women and children to ten per day, and by the 1890's many other states, mostly in the East and Middle West, had followed suit. Illinois even passed an eight-hour law for women workers in 1893. A New York law of 1882 struck at the sweatshops of the slums by prohibiting the manufacture of cigars on premises "occupied as a house or residence." Many states passed fire and sanitary inspection laws that improved conditions in the cities.

As part of this trend, some states established special rules for workers in hazardous industries. In the 1890's Ohio and several other states began to regulate the hours of railroad workers on the ground that fatigue sometimes caused railroad accidents. New York set a ten-hour-per-day limit for brickyard workers (1893) and bakers (1897). Utah restricted the hours of work in mining to eight in 1896; Montana, Colorado, and several other states did the same. California, in 1881, even made it illegal for women to work as waitresses in saloons. In 1901 New York finally enacted an effective tenement house law, greatly increasing the area of open space on building lots and requiring separate toilets for each apartment, better ventilation systems, safer fire escapes, and more adequate fireproofing. New Jersey, Connecticut, Wisconsin, and many other states soon passed laws modeled after New York's.

The collective impact of these laws was not very impressive. Powerful vested interests, such as manufacturers and landlords, threw their weight against many kinds of social legislation, and since such laws ran counter to the American traditions of individualism and laissez faire, they often succeeded in either defeating them or rendering them innocuous. Many of the early laws limiting hours, for example, were made to apply only "in the absence of agreements" to work longer hours.

The federal system itself further complicated the task of obtaining effective legislation. Throughout the 19th century few authorities contested the right of government to protect society and individuals against anything that threatened the general welfare, but these authorities assumed that such problems would be dealt with by the states, not the national government.* As a rule, this "police power" of the states was broadly interpreted; the courts even upheld laws prohibiting the manufacture and sale of liquor on the ground that drunkenness was a social as well as an individual problem, affecting non-imbibers as well as the drinkers themselves.

However, the development of a truly national economy after the Civil War greatly complicated the problem of coping with social and industrial problems at the state level. Obviously, until *all* the states outlawed child labor, that evil could not be completely eradicated, yet once producers all over the country could compete effectively with one another, it became very hard to persuade legislators in one state to prohibit child labor so long as others refused to do so. If they did, they would injure their own manufacturers by giving firms in other states an unfair advantage. For example, the labor legislation of the New England states helps explain why the textile

*Congress enacted an eight-hour law for government workers in 1892.

industry began to shift to the South, where such laws were almost unknown. Yet a federal child labor law seemed out of the question on constitutional grounds.

Furthermore, the enemies of state social legislation soon discovered still another weapon—the Fourteenth Amendment to the Constitution. Although enacted to protect the civil rights of Negroes against southern Black Codes, this amendment imposed a revolutionary restriction on state power, for it forbade the states to "deprive any person of life, liberty, or property without due process of law." This restriction did not abolish the police power of the states, for if it had, the states would have ceased to exist. After all, most laws deprive someone of either life, liberty, or property. But tenement house laws, child labor laws, and other social legislation represented extensions of police power that conservative judges considered dangerous and unwise, and the Fourteenth Amendment gave them an excuse to overturn them. Both state and federal courts began to draw a line beyond which the states could not go in this area. Some measures seemed unexceptionable; the courts did not, for example, interfere with laws requiring fire escapes on tall buildings, although these certainly deprived builders of property by increasing their costs and of the liberty to erect any kind of structure they pleased. Laws regulating the hours and conditions of labor, however, met mixed fates, depending upon the wording of the acts and the prejudices of particular judges.

Laws affecting women and children, and those regulating conditions in dangerous and unhealthy occupations like mining, fared better than those attempting to deal with the population as a whole, but it is very difficult to generalize. The pioneering Massachusetts ten-hour law of 1874, restricting the working day of women and children, was upheld as a valid exercise of the police power by the Massachusetts courts. On the other hand, the Illinois law of 1893 limiting the hours of women employed in manufacturing to eight per day was declared unconstitutional. "The mere fact of sex will not justify the legislature in putting forth the police power," the Illinois court declared in *Ritchie v. People.* "There is no reasonable ground . . . for fixing upon eight hours in one day as the limit within which woman can work without injury to her physique." The New York Court of Appeals threw out the sweatshop law of 1882 on similar grounds. "It cannot be perceived," Justice Earl wrote in a decision so unrealistic that it appears preposterous to anyone who knows a little about slum conditions in the 1880's, "how the cigar maker is to be improved in his health or his morals by forcing him from his home with its hallowed associations and beneficient influences, to ply his trade elsewhere." The United States Supreme Court upheld the Utah mining law of 1896 (*Holden v. Hardy*, 1898), but the nearly identical Colorado act was declared by the state courts to have violated the Fourteenth Amendment by depriving workers of the liberty to work as long as they wished. "That this act infringes both the right to enjoy liberty and to acquire and possess property seems too clear for argument," the justices said.

As stricter and more far-reaching laws were enacted, conservative judges, sensing what they took to be a trend toward socialism and regimentation, adopted an increasingly narrow interpretation of state police power. The severest blow came in 1905, when for the first time the Supreme Court of the United States declared a piece of state social legislation unconstitutional. New York's ten-hour act for bakers, the Court decided in *Lochner v. New York,* deprived bakers of the liberty of working as long as they wished, and thus violated the Fourteenth Amendment. Justice Oliver Wendell Holmes, Jr., wrote a brilliant dissenting opinion in this case, arguing that if a majority of the people of New York believed that the public health was endangered by bakers working long hours, it was not the Court's business to overrule them. "A constitution is not intended to embody a particular economic theory, whether of paternalism . . . or of *laissez faire,*" Holmes said. "The word 'liberty,' in the Fourteenth Amendment, is perverted when it is held to prevent the natural outcome of a dominant opinion." Of course Holmes's sensible doctrine did not alter the decision, which was deplored by all those who hoped to limit the hours of labor through legislation.

Civilization and its Discontents

As the 19th century died, the majority of the American people, especially those comfortably well off, the residents of small towns, the shopkeepers, many farmers, some skilled workingmen, remained confirmed optimists and uncritical admirers of their own civilization. However, Negroes, immigrants, and others who failed to share in the good things of life, along with a growing number of humanitarian reformers, found few reasons to cheer and many to lament the state of affairs in their increasingly industrialized society. Giant monopolies flourished despite federal restrictions. The gap between rich and poor was widening, while the slum spread its poison and the materially successful made a god of their success. Human values seemed in grave danger of being crushed by impersonal materialistic forces, typified by the great corporations.

As early as 1871 Walt Whitman, usually so full of extravagant praise for the American way of life, called his fellow countrymen the "most materialistic and money-making people ever known":

> I say we had best look our times and lands searchingly in the face, like a physician diagnosing some deep disease. Never was there, perhaps, more hollowness of heart than at present, and here in the United States.

By the late eighties a well-known journalist could write to a friend: "The wheel of progress is to be run over the whole human race and smash us all." Others noted an alarming jump in the national divorce rate and an increasing taste for all kinds of luxury. "People are made slaves by a desperate struggle to keep up appearances," a Massachusetts commentator declared, and the economist David A. Wells expressed concern over statistics showing that heart disease and mental illness were on the rise. These "diseases of civilization," Wells explained, were "one result of the continuous mental and nervous activity which modern high-tension methods of business have necessitated."

Wells was a prominent liberal, but pessimism was no monopoly of men of his stripe. A little later, Senator Henry Cabot Lodge of Massachusetts, himself a millionaire, complained of the "lawlessness" of "the modern and recent plutocrat" and his "disregard of the rights of others." Lodge also spoke of "the enormous contrast between the sanguine mental attitude prevalent in my youth and that, perhaps wiser, but certainly darker view, so general today."

Of course intellectuals often tend to be critical of the world they live in, whatever its nature. Thoreau, for example, had denounced materialism and the worship of progress in the 1840's as vigorously as any late-19th-century prophet of gloom. But the voices of the dissatisfied were rising. Despite the many benefits that industrialization had made possible, it was by no means clear around 1900 that the American people were really better off under the new dispensation.

SUPPLEMENTARY READING The idea of interpreting social and economic history in the post-Civil War decades as a broad reaction to the growth of industry is presented in S.P. Hays, *The Response to Industrialism** (1957). Other general treatments of the period include R.H. Wiebe, *The Search for Order** (1968), and Ray Ginger, *The Age of Excess** (1965). J.A. Garraty, *The New Commonwealth** (1968), treats all the subjects covered in this chapter; A.M. Schlesinger, *The Rise of the City* (1933), stresses the importance of urban developments but also provides a wealth of information about social trends. Both H.U. Faulkner, *Politics, Reform, and Expansion** (1959), and Blake McKelvey, *The Urbanization of America* (1962), also contain useful information. An excellent collection of source materials dealing with many aspects of social and economic history in these years may be found in Sigmund Diamond (ed.), *The Nation Transformed** (1963). Henry Adams, *The Education of Henry Adams** (1918), is a fascinating if highly personal view of the period. James Bryce, *The*

*American Commonwealth** (1888), while primarily a political analysis, contains a great deal of information about social conditions, as does D.A. Wells, *Recent Economic Changes* (1889).

The standard history of American labor is J.R. Commons *et al., History of Labour in the United States* (1918–1935), but see also Philip Taft, *Organized Labor in America* (1964), N.J. Ware, *The Labor Movement in the United States** (1929), and the appropriate chapters of E.C. Kirkland, *Industry Comes of Age** (1961). J.A. Garraty (ed.), *Labor and Capital in the Gilded Age** (1968), provides a convenient selection of testimony from the great 1883 Senate investigation of that subject, while David Brody, *Steelworkers in America** (1960), and Stephan Thernstrom, *Poverty and Progress: Social Mobility in a Nineteenth-Century City** (1964), throw much light on the lives of workingmen. Businessmen's attitudes are covered in T.C. Cochran, *Railroad Leaders** (1953), and E.C. Kirkland, *Dream and Thought in the Business Community** (1956). On the growth of unions, see J.P. Grossman, *William Sylvis* (1945), Philip Taft, *The A.F. of L. in the Time of Gompers* (1957), G.N. Grob, *Workers and Utopia** (1961), Samuel Gompers, *Seventy Years of Life and Labor* (1925), and T.V. Powderly, *Thirty Years of Labor* (1889). The important strikes and labor violence of the period are described in R.V. Bruce, *1877: Year of Violence* (1959), Henry David, *History of the Haymarket Affair** (1936), Leon Wolff, *Lockout* (1965), Almont Lindsey, *The Pullman Strike** (1942), and W.G. Broehl, Jr., *The Molly Maguires** (1964).

On immigration, see M.A. Jones, *American Immigration** (1960), M.L. Hansen, *The Immigrant in American History** (1940), and I.S. Hourwich, *Immigration and Labor* (1923). Oscar Handlin, *The Uprooted** (1951), describes the life of the new immigrants with imagination and sensitivity, while John Higham, *Strangers in the Land** (1955), and B.M. Solomon, *Ancestors and Immigrants** (1956), stress the reactions of native Americans to successive waves of immigration. Moses Rischin, *The Promised City: New York's Jews** (1962), T.N. Brown, *Irish-American Nationalism** (1966), Charlotte Erickson, *American Industry and the European Immigrant* (1957), and R.T. Berthoff, *British Immigrants in Industrial America: 1790–1950* (1953), are important monographs.

A brief interpretive history of urban development is C.N. Glaab and A.T. Brown, *A History of Urban America** (1967). For the growing pains of American cities, consult the volumes by Schlesinger and McKelvey mentioned above, and also R.H. Bremner, *From the Depths** (1956), Jacob Riis, *How the Other Half Lives** (1890), Gordon Atkins, *Health, Housing, and Poverty in New York City* (1947), and R.M. Lubove, *The Progressives and the Slums: Tenement House Reform in New York City* (1962). For urban government, see the classic criticisms in Bryce's *American Commonwealth,* and also F.W. Patton, *The Battle for Municipal Reform: Mobilization and Attack* (1940). Urban architecture is discussed in O.W. Larkin, *Art and Life in America* (1949), Lewis Mumford, *The Brown Decades** (1931), and J.E. Burchard and Albert Bush-Brown, *The Architecture of America** (1961). S.B. Warner, Jr., *Streetcar Suburbs** (1962), is an interesting study of Boston's development that is full of suggestive ideas about late-19th-century growth.

The response of religion to industrialism is discussed in H.F. May, *Protestant Churches and Industrial America** (1949), in two books by A.I. Abell, *The Urban Impact on American Protestantism* (1943) and *American Catholicism and Social Action** (1960), Arthur Mann, *Yankee Reformers in the Urban Age** (1954), and C.H. Hopkins, *The Rise of the Social Gospel in American Protestantism** (1940). See also Washington Gladden, *Applied Christianity* (1886), and R.T. Ely, *Social Aspects of Christianity* (1889). For the settlement house movement, see Jane Addams, *Twenty Years at Hull House** (1910), and Lillian Wald, *The House on Henry Street** (1915).

Sidney Fine, *Laissez Faire and the General-Welfare State** (1956), deals with both social and economic thought and with state and federal social legislation, but see also C.G. Groat, *Attitude of American Courts in Labor Cases* (1911), A.M. Paul, *Conservative Crisis and the Rule of Law: Attitudes of Bar and Bench** (1960), and R.G. McCloskey, *American Conservatism in the Age of Enterprise** (1951).

*Available in paperback.

OLD PRINT SHOP

PORTFOLIO

V *A Nation Industrialized*

As the nation turned toward peace in 1865, Senator John Sherman of Ohio wrote: "The truth is, the close of the war with our resources unimpaired gives an elevation, a scope to the ideas of leading capitalists. . . . They talk of millions as confidently as formerly of thousands." A decade later a homespun commentator remarked that the new technology was enough "to run anybody's idees up into majestic heights and run 'em round and round into lofty circles and spears of thought they hadn't never thought of runnin' into before." In 1876, when the United States celebrated its 100th birthday, the great majority of middle-class Americans still considered the industrialization process as an unmixed blessing.

As the decades passed, however, a gradual sense of unease began to erode this happy mood. The graphic representations of the period, as the following pages demonstrate, reflected this change. Where Henry Clay Frick's coke operations were guilelessly portrayed in an 1870's print, the spectacle of young boys laboring as coal breakers shocked the reformer-photographer Lewis Hine in 1910; where once four-color advertising represented real artistic merit, as in the locomotive builder's lithograph above, by 1914 it disfigured nearly every city in the land. With the coming of the new century, a nation industrialized was also a nation troubled.

The New Landscape

Travelers passing through the Monongahela Valley in the 1880's glimpsed a new America in the making. The checkerboard landscape of field and farm was giving way to the age of iron and steel. Nor was this phenomenon limited to western Pennsylvania; indeed, it was transforming much of the nation. At a bend in the Monongahela, several miles upstream from Pittsburgh, lay the Homestead steel mill. In

CHARLES J. ROSENBLOOM COLLECTION

1883 Andrew Carnegie absorbed the mill into his empire, soon adding Bessemer converters and installing one of the revolutionary new open-hearth furnaces. William C. Wall painted Homestead a year after Carnegie took it over. In rendering the mill, the toylike trains, and the company town (right) as integral parts of a pastoral setting, Wall was reflecting the widespread belief—or at least the hope—that this new American landscape would blend painlessly into the old.

Miracles of Industry

"The people have a wonderful appetite for science just now," trumpeted the New York *Tribune* in 1872, reporting that an enthusiastic crowd had braved the worst blizzard to hit the city in years to hear a lecture on light by British physicist John Tyndall. His audience thrilled to the prediction that their everyday lives would soon reflect the latest scientific advances, and within a matter of months Americans bought over 100,000 copies of his lectures. Tyndall returned to England proclaiming, "mechanical ingenuity engages a greater number of minds in the United States than in any other nation. . . ."

There seemed no end to the miracles being wrought by this American ingenuity. Technology surely heralded a golden age; manifest destiny was bound up in each new ore strike, each new mile of railroad track laid, each new bridge raised. Americans boasted of the great Brooklyn Bridge, the four-mile Sutro tunnel in Nevada's silver region, the canal at Sault Ste. Marie that by the mid-1880's was carrying three times the tonnage of the Suez Canal. Thousands flocked to little Wabash, Indiana, in 1880 to celebrate the city's new system of electric arc lamps. When the lights were turned on for the first time, "men fell on their knees . . . and many were dumb with amazement." Walt Whitman, singing of America's "sacred industry," was simply echoing the national mood.

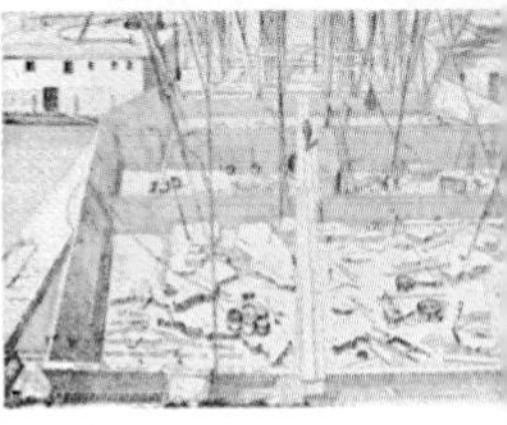

Not surprisingly, Machinery Hall was the central attraction at the Centennial Exposition in Philadelphia in 1876. An *Atlantic Monthly* writer declared that "nowhere else are the triumphs of ingenuity, the marvels of skill and invention so displayed. . . . Surely here, and not in literature, science or art, is the true evidence of man's creative powers. Here is Prometheus unbound."

Steelmaster Andrew Carnegie summarized the growing miracle of production: "Two pounds of ironstone mined upon Lake Superior, and transported nine hundred miles to Pittsburgh; one pound and one-half of coal, mined and manufactured into coke, and transported to Pittsburgh; one-half pound of lime, mined and transported to Pittsburgh; a small amount of manganese ore mined in Virginia and brought to Pittsburgh —and these four pounds of materials manufactured into one pound of steel, for which the consumer pays one cent."

After the Civil War, Americans collected views of the latest industrial miracles with the enthusiasm that an earlier age showed for patriotic prints. Some of these views were given away for advertising purposes, others were sold outright. The Frick coke works, which supplied fuel for Pittsburgh's steel plants, distributed the print at right. Above is a testimonial to the design of James Eads's railroad bridge across the Mississippi at St. Louis.

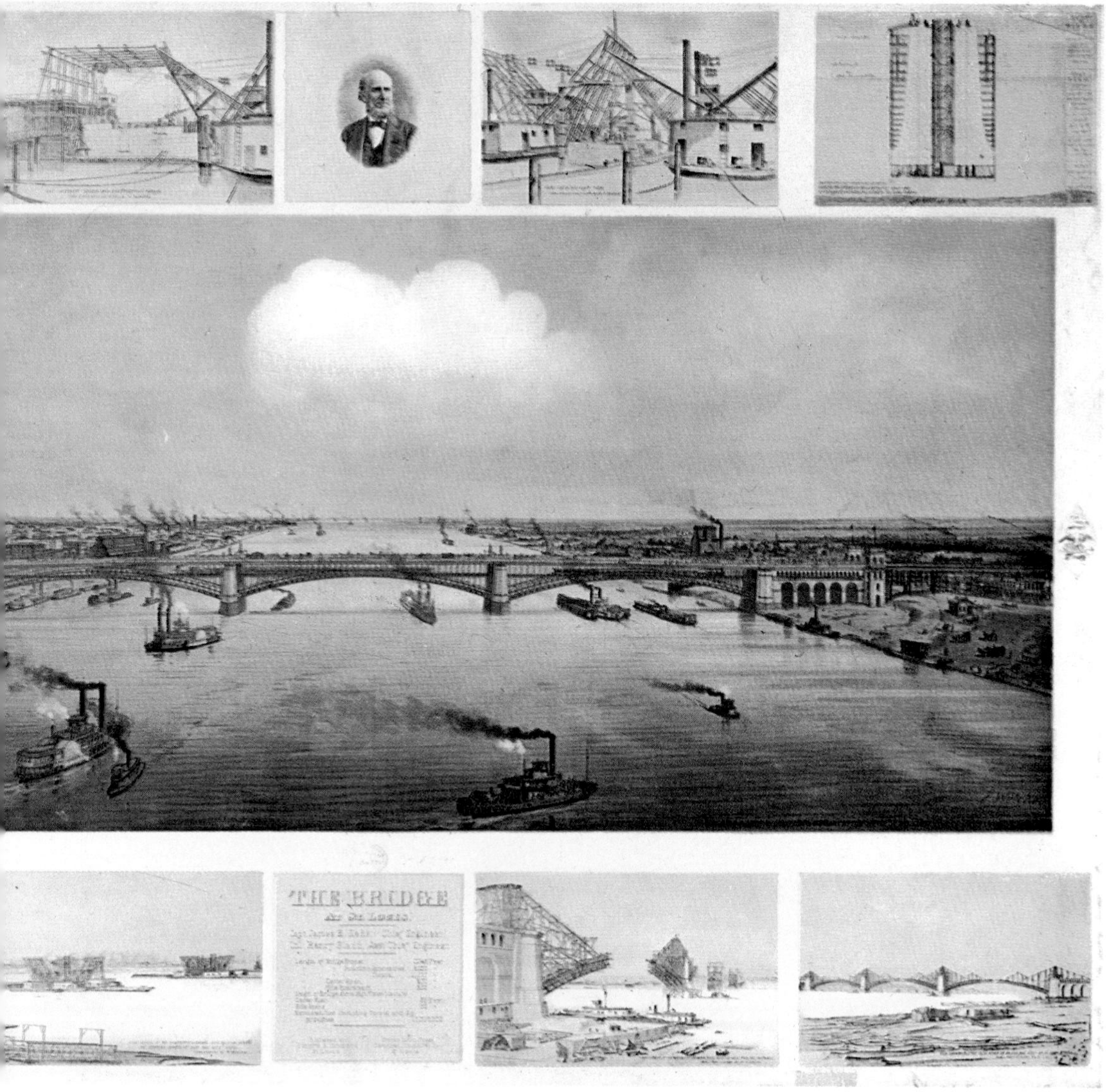

BOTH: LIBRARY OF CONGRESS

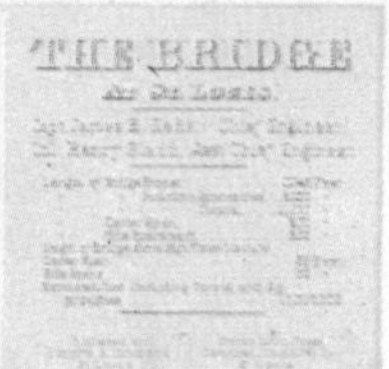
THE BRIDGE

Moving the Goods

Subscribers to the *North American Review* might well have wondered if the civilized world was coming to an end when they received their copies for September 1893. Missing for the fourth time in as many issues was the familiar cover typography; in its place were quarter-page displays for Royal baking powder, W. & J. Sloane carpets, Baker's breakfast cocoa, and Waterbury watches. Inside the magazine, no less than 42 pages were given over to various consumer products, ranging from cement and Londonderry Lithia Spring Water to a remedy for the "Morphine Habit" and a painless cure offered by the Baltimore Hernia Institute. Following the lead already taken by such upstarts as *Harper's*, the *Atlantic Monthly*, and the *Ladies' Home Journal*, the *North American Review*, a veritable national bastion of refinement and culture since 1815, had finally succumbed to the advertising mania.

The rising output of America's factories posed some new and unexpected problems. How were the barons of industry to keep their machines from outracing consumer demand? Or, more specifically, how was a New York sewing machine manufacturer to capture a sizable share of the market in Boston and Chicago? Massive doses of advertising, combined with new marketing techniques, provided the answers. By the eighties advertising was big business. Like the industries that supported it, advertising owed much to new technology, particularly advances in color lithography, stereotyping, and printing that made magazine advertising practicable.

A Russian visitor complained in 1895 that most American newspapers contained "almost nothing but advertisements." Moreover, he said, "the mails are choked with circulars, throwaways, and brochures." Another foreign observer complained that in every part of the country he visited he was confronted by "huge white-paint notices of favorite articles of manufacture." The American people, however, seemed to be taking the onslaught in stride, accepting the logic of the slogan, "If your business isn't worth advertising, advertise it for sale."

Above is the cover of a 1901 Singer sales brochure, while the Ford ad is an example of magazine displays in the early 1900's. The Duluth flour poster made imaginative use of the ballooning craze around the turn of the century. Endorsements appeared early and revealed a relaxed attitude toward the notion of "fair use"; witness the checkers contest at the right between Presidents Cleveland and Harrison.

NEW-YORK HISTORICAL SOCIETY

The FORD
MOTOR CAR
In the eyes of the Chauffeur
is the most satisfactory Automobile made for every-day service. The two cylinder (opposed) motor gives 8 actual horse-power, and eliminates the vibration so noticeable in other machines. The body is luxurious and comfortable and can be removed from the chassis by loosening six bolts.
Price with Tonneau, $900.00
As a Runabout, $800.00
Standard equipment includes 3-inch heavy double tube tires
We agree to assume all responsibility in any action the TRUST may take regarding alleged infringement of the Selden Patent to prevent you from buying the Ford—"The Car of Satisfaction."
We Hold the World's Record
The Ford "999" (the fastest machine in the world), driven by Mr. Ford, made a mile in 39⅖ seconds—equal to 92 miles an hour.
Write for illustrated catalogue and name of our nearest agent.
Ford Motor Co., Detroit, Mich.

Harper's Weekly, FEBRUARY 13, 1904

JARED COFFIN HOUSE

LIBRARY OF CONGRESS

Man and Machine

At a hearing of a Senate committee investigating working conditions in New York City in 1883, Conrad Carl, a tailor, testified that before the Civil War his had been "a very still business, very quiet." Then the sewing machine appeared. "It stitched very nicely, nicer than the tailor could do; and the bosses said: 'We want you to use the sewing machine. . . .'" Asked how this innovation affected the tailors, Carl replied: "We work now in excitement—in a hurry. It is hunting; it is not work at all; it is a hunt."

In Chicago in 1900 an industrial commission heard a Russian immigrant named Abraham Bisno describe the job of a fellow worker, a buzz saw operator. "I asked him how long he had worked there," Bisno related. "He said 10 years. He gets $1.50 a day. He had worked at that buzz saw for 3 years. He has a big stack of rubber plates he must feed into that buzz saw every day, that is, 10 hours." As the operator talked to him he unconsciously repeated the motions of his work, Bisno said, and he added: "It is not hard work. He has not developed his muscles and has not become hardy enough to apply himself to common labor anywhere. . . . He has become a part of that machine he operates."

Mechanization and what one contemporary observer called the "minute subdivision of labor" was to reach near-perfection on Henry Ford's assembly lines by 1914, but the trends had been visible in other industries for decades. As the products of industry grew increasingly complex, the steps in their manufacture were simplified and standardized. This increased output and lowered costs, but it also spawned boredom, unrest, and carelessness among workmen. Frederick W. Taylor, whose time-and-motion studies ("Taylorism") had gained considerable popularity with employers by the turn of the century, pointed out that worker morale was very much a dollar-and-cents matter. Writing in 1895, he listed as one advantage of a new piecework system he was proposing the fact that it "promotes a most friendly feeling between the men and their employers, and so renders labor unions and strikes unnecessary."

J.I. CASE COMPANY

LIBRARY OF CONGRESS

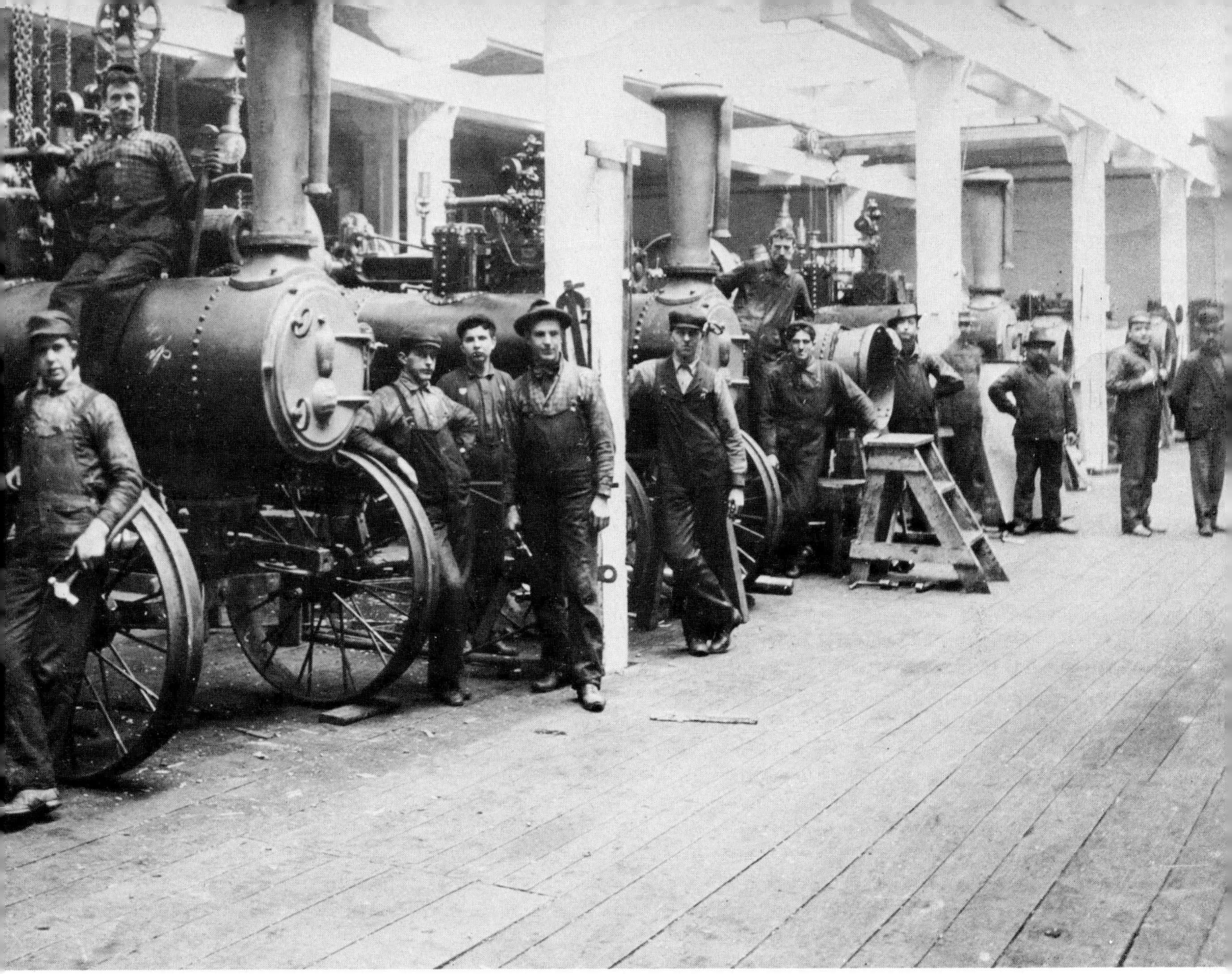

Above, workers at the Case steam tractor factory, photographed in 1902. At lower left is a Cincinnati slaughterhouse gang, depicted in an 1872 lithograph, on an early form of assembly line. At right, spruce Heinz girls bottle olives in about 1907. Specialization posed perplexing problems of status for workingmen. Shoemaking, for example, was divided into 64 steps; hence, asked an economist, was a shoemaker but a 64th as skilled as he once was?

H.J. HEINZ COMPANY

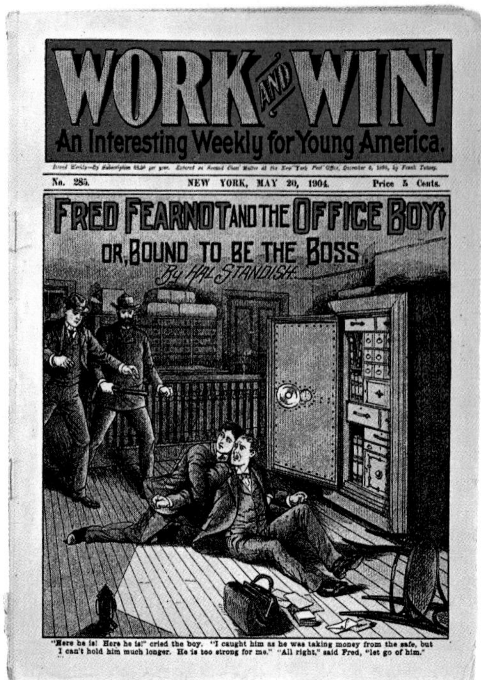

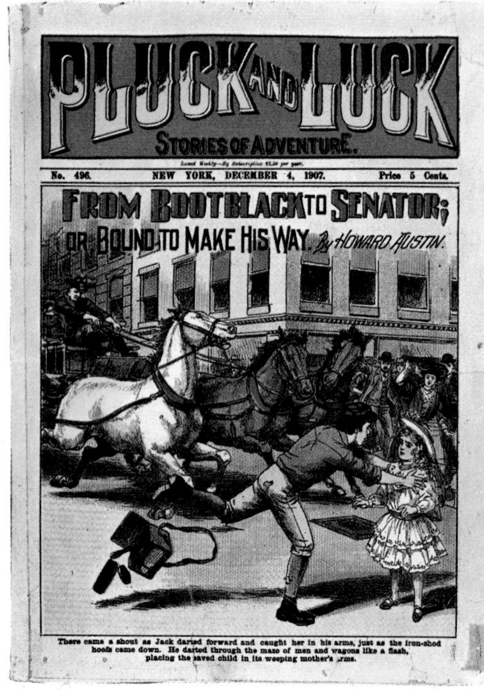

A Gospel of Wealth

Only fools and sluggards, according to the popular American tradition, failed to make their way in the world. Materialism was the common denominator; Americans were constantly reminded that they could and, indeed, they should make every effort to amass a fortune. "Godliness is in league with . . . riches," as Bishop Lawrence of Massachusetts explained it to his congregation.

There was no shortage of success stories on which to set one's sights. Had not Andrew Carnegie arrived from Scotland in steerage and by dint of hard work and virtuous living gained an annual income of $25 million? Examples of other self-made men were easy to find: Vanderbilt and Rockefeller, Swift and Armour, Edison, Marshall Field, the Guggenheims. It was this gospel of success that the tireless Horatio Alger served up to three generations of American youth. With but slight alterations Alger wrote the same tale at least 115 times; between the Civil War and World War I some 200 million copies of his works were sold.

Success bred imitation, and by the end of the century dime novel publishers were churning out a new brand of thriller, the Wall Street success story—or, as *Fame and Fortune Weekly* candidly put it, "Stories of Boys who Make Money." Beneath the lurid covers of dime novels (which competition drove down to a nickel) were oceans of small type that added up to a liberal borrowing on the Alger formula. The surest way to success was still the time-honored ritual of rescuing a tycoon's offspring from certain death, but quick wits paid off in other ways as well. Take, for example, Hal Morton, *Fame and Fortune Weekly*'s "Young Wonder of Wall Street" (above right). Hal, a messenger boy for a brokerage house, developed eavesdropping into a fine art (while still managing to look impressively busy) in order to catch stock tips. Thus forearmed, a few forays into the market brought him a cool $250,000. Only then did the Young Wonder quit his messenger's job and go into business for himself—at the age of 16.

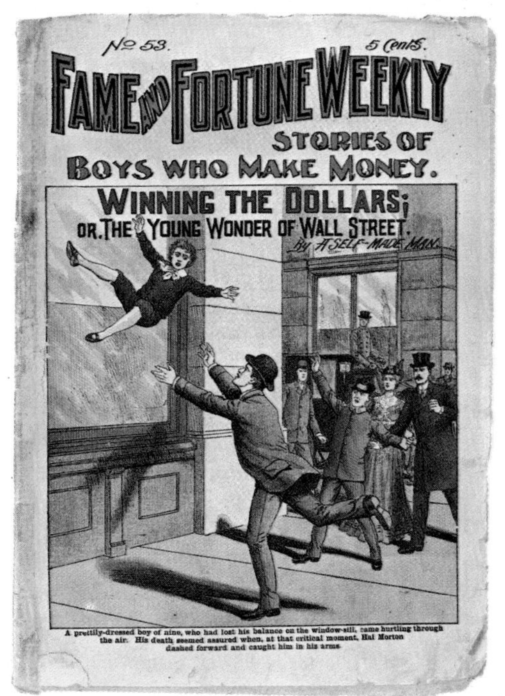

UNDERWOOD & UNDERWOOD

Andrew Carnegie's "The Gospel of Wealth" made provision for generous philanthropy. "Thirty-three and an income of $50,000 per annum!" he wrote in 1868, pleased by his early success. "Beyond this never earn. . . ." The dime novel genre (examples above) is credited to one Erastus Beadle, who began his publishing career labeling grain bags.

ALL: CULVER PICTURES

The wrecks of ruined railroads and bankrupt investors littered the paths of Jay Gould (above) and Jim Fisk (below). Observing their portraits on one of Fisk's Fall River Line steamboats, a stockbroker muttered, "There are the two thieves, but where's Christ?" W.H. Vanderbilt was exposed by Puck *in 1879 (left) as a "Colossus of Roads" monopolizing the routes to New York. Assisting him are two lesser industrial demigods, Cyrus Field, of the city's transit system, and the unsavory Gould.*

The Public Be Damned

Flush times in the postwar era produced a new kind of business titan. Freebooters such as Daniel Drew, Jay Gould, and Jim Fisk swindled each other as well as the public and boasted of the legislatures they bought; not even the Crédit Mobilier nor the worst political corruptionists were more brazen in their pillaging. In their scorn for the public welfare they shared the attitudes of their political ally Boss Tweed ("Well, what are you going to do about it?") and W.H. Vanderbilt, son of "Commodore" Cornelius Vanderbilt ("The public be damned!").

The battle to control the Erie Railroad in 1868, pitting Drew, Gould, and Fisk against the elder Vanderbilt, was the archetype of financial piracy: judges and legislatures in two states corrupted, 50,000 shares of stock illegally printed and sold, a railroad looted of millions. Victorious, Gould and Fisk next embarked on a scheme notable for its audacity—a corner on the nation's gold supply. Possessing enough cash to control the open market, they sought to neutralize the Treasury's stock of gold through the influence of President Grant's brother-in-law. The price of gold shot up at their bidding until September 24, 1869 ("Black Friday"), when Grant belatedly released the government reserves. Gould and Fisk slipped out from under their collapsing scheme, but hundreds of investors were ruined. "Nothing is lost save honor," said the carefree Fisk. "Let everyone carry out his own corpse."

Such depredations, although denounced from the pulpit and cursed in the press, met with only half-hearted government censure. Fisk's flamboyant career was cut short in 1872, not by the law but by two bullets from the gun of a rival suitor. He was accorded a funeral befitting a statesman, and a jaded public sang the sentimental ballad, "Jim Fisk, or He Never Went Back on the Poor." In later years Gould transferred his attentions to such western railroads as the Union Pacific and the Central Pacific; Western Union; and the New York *World*, which he found useful for improving his public image. He left a fortune estimated at $75 million.

Titans of Wall Street

Financial panic, like a plague, made periodic visits to the nation after Appomattox. Barely recovered from Black Friday, Wall Street plunged once more in 1873, then in 1882, in 1893, again in 1907. In each instance, reckless speculation overinflated values. Confidence collapsed, heralding long, cyclical depressions with their attendant business failures and unemployment.

Life, October 26, 1911

Not a few of the victims joined in cursing the titans of Wall Street. Labor and agrarian interests saw themselves being sacrificed to speculation and manipulation. To them, as to Henry Adams, hard times were the work of a "dark, mysterious, crafty, rapacious, and tyrannical power . . . to rob and oppress and enslave the people." One solution was to banish the thieves from the temple, a course that suggested to one cartoonist this intriguing scene: "When We All Get Wise."

The Trusts

Mr. Dooley, Finley Peter Dunne's irreverent philosopher, offered a solution to the trust problem based on his assessment of the trust-busting techniques of Theodore Roosevelt. "Lave us be merry about it an' jovial an' affectionate," he proposed. "Lave us laugh an' sing th' octopus out iv existence." Mr. Dooley's line of attack was not exactly new. For three decades monopolistic combinations, "in the form of trusts or otherwise," as the Sherman Antitrust Act described them, had felt the sting of some of the most savage barbs in the history of American caricature.

Public response to the trusts took a variety of forms, but for sheer ingenuity, the campaigns waged by the cartoonists of *Harper's Weekly*, *Frank Leslie's Illustrated*, *Puck*, and other pictorial weeklies were unsurpassed. *Puck*, the most outspoken and flamboyant of the critics, was founded in New York in 1876 by Joseph Keppler, who made the large colored cartoon his hallmark, printing three of them in each issue. Keppler drew and published his first attack on the evils of monopoly in 1881, and as an avowed Democrat he delighted in regularly jabbing at a group of Republican senators headed by Nelson Aldrich of Rhode Island and Donald Cameron of Pennsylvania, whom he considered the mouthpieces of big business.

The effects of this prolonged, uninhibited barrage by Keppler and his fellow artists is difficult to assess precisely, but it seems likely that they were no less effective in bringing the trusts to bay than the revelations of such reform writers as Ida Tarbell, Upton Sinclair, and Henry Demarest Lloyd. For one thing, the combined circulation of the picture weeklies was enormous; for another, this was an era when cartoonists had greater influence—and maintained higher artistic standards—than at any time before or since. Boss Tweed, who blamed his downfall on Thomas Nast's exposures in *Harper's Weekly*, testified feelingly on the power of the cartoons. He cared little about what reformers wrote, Tweed said, since few of his constituents could read, but they could "look at the damned pictures."

LIBRARY OF CONGRESS

Joseph Keppler's "The Bosses of the Senate" (right) appeared in Puck *in 1889, not long before debate began on the Sherman Antitrust bill. No less devastating was the work of Thomas Nast (below) and W. A. Rogers (below right) of* Harper's Weekly. *Rogers' inspired creation, "the trustworthy beast," was a fixture in his anti-monopoly cartoons. In this example Uncle Sam remarks, "I guess this new breed of cattle has got to go next."*

PRINTS DIVISION, NEW YORK PUBLIC LIBRARY

PEOPLES' ENTRANCE.
CLOSED.
THIS IS A SENATE OF THE MONOPOLISTS BY THE MONOPOLISTS AND FOR THE MONOPOLISTS!
COAL
TIN TRUST
SUGAR TRUST.
IRON TRUST
STANDARD OIL TRUST.
COPPER TRUST.
STEEL BEAM TRUST.
NAIL TRUST.

SUGAR TRUST
STEEL TRUST
OIL TRUST
COAL TRUST
ANARCHY
W. A. Rogers

Workingmen Organize

Something more than real and imagined threats by big business and monopoly caused the embattled common people to close ranks in the last decades of the 19th century. In an age when commerce and the machine were exalted above all else, American workers, whether farmers or factory hands, felt a grievous loss of status. To revive the Jeffersonian image of the yeoman husbandman, to restore the artisan's once-proud position in society, became important although elusive goals.

Agitation alone could not salve injured pride. Thus Uriah Stephens and Terence Powderly committed the Knights of Labor—on principle at least—to education rather than to direct economic action, and even the militant Samuel Gompers hastened to include compulsory public education among the demands of the American Federation of Labor. Self-respect and the dignity of honest toil became the Knights' watchwords. "Respect industry in the person of every intelligent worker," Stephens exhorted his followers. "Unmake the shams of life by deference to the humble but useful craftsman." The secrecy and elaborate ritual of the Knights not only protected the identity of the workers but offered them a sense of solidarity and self-importance.

The agrarian orders, in addition to working to improve the economic position of farmers, went to considerable lengths to improve the outlook of their members. The Grange and the Farmers' Alliance, the chief nationwide organizations, successfully established local study groups, circulating libraries, and newspapers. One prominent Alliance leader looked fondly to that day in the future when a "general system of home culture, somewhat on the plan of Chautauqua" could be established on a broad scale. Even if the wider vision remained unfulfilled, such schemes had a profound and widespread influence. "People commenced to think who had never thought before, and people talked who had seldom spoken," reported a contemporary observer. "Everyone was talking and everyone was thinking. . . ."

NEW-YORK HISTORICAL SOCIETY

"The Purposes of the Grange" (opposite), a lithograph published in Cincinnati in 1873, and the United Mine Workers membership certificate reproduced above, dating from about 1900, celebrate the virtues of the yeoman farmer ("I pay for all," says the central figure in the Granger print) and the inherent dignity of "daily toil in the recesses of the earth."

GIFT FOR THE GRANGERS.
"I PAY FOR ALL."
FAITH,
HOPE,
CHARITY,
FIDELITY
IGNORANCE
SLOTH
P
H
HARVEST DANCE.
RUTH & BOAZ
POWERS & CO. FRATERNITY & FINE ART PUBLISHERS, CIN.TI
STROBRIDGE & CO., LITH. CINCINNATI, O.

The Public Interest

The Pullman strike was in its seventh week when in the early morning hours of July 4, 1894, a special train carrying cavalry, artillery, and infantry regulars rolled into Chicago. The troops were there by order of President Cleveland to enforce an injunction, issued two days earlier, enjoining Eugene Debs and the American Railway Union from continuing a rail boycott. The injunction and the troops clearly dashed whatever hopes the Pullman strikers had for success, but in a real sense the strike was doomed the moment the ARU entered the struggle.

Considerable public sympathy had greeted the walkout of 3,000 Pullman workers in mid-May, but when Debs's union voted to support the strikers by means of a boycott, the full hostility of the press was aroused. The boycott, *Harper's Weekly* reported, was an attempt "to subjugate the people of the United States, to extort from the nation the control and management of its highways, intercourse and commerce. . . ." Newspapers and magazines, paying little heed to facts, depicted Chicago in the hands of a crazed mob bent on destroying private property. The government based its intervention on "uncontrolled violence" and the interruption of the mails. Yet no mail had accumulated in Chicago, and before the arrival of the troops damage to railroad property had not exceeded $6,000.

Serious rioting, however, broke out less than 18 hours after the troops encamped in the city. The press became hysterical: REGULARS POWERLESS BEFORE CHICAGO'S RIOTOUS ARMY; GUNS AWE THEM NOT; MOB WILL IS LAW. Most of the destruction was in the railroad yards, but now the citizenry was thoroughly frightened. "Men must be killed," a clergyman demanded. "The soldiers must use their guns."

At storm center were Debs and Governor John Peter Altgeld, who denounced the federal government's intervention. The mild-mannered Debs was described as "a reckless, ranting, contumacious, impudent braggadocio," while the New York *Times* suggested that "his present conduct is due . . . to the disordered condition of his mind and body, brought out by the liquor habit. . . ."

On July 10 Debs was arrested for conspiracy. That same day the 14,000-man anti-strike force began moving the trains out of Chicago. The strike was crushed, "anarchy" put to rout.

For four consecutive weeks in 1894 Harper's Weekly *devoted most of its editorial columns and picture spreads to the Pullman strike. The magazine made little effort to conceal its bias. Debs and the American Railway Union were the targets of three full-page cartoons by W.A. Rogers; in "The Vanguard of Anarchy" (left), dictator Debs is borne by clownish prolabor politicians led by Governor Altgeld of Illinois. The* Harper's *correspondent on the scene was Frederic Remington, who sent back a steady stream of dispatches and sketches depicting the "rape of government" in Chicago. In "Giving the Butt" (below), Remington demonstrated how infantry regulars dealt with what he described as a "malodorous crowd of anarchistic foreign trash." When the federal troops began moving trains (lower left),* Harper's *hailed the action as a triumph of public opinion.*

CHICAGO HISTORICAL SOCIETY

ALL: GEORGE EASTMAN HOUSE

The Exploited

Even if government was slow to respond to the plight of the exploited worker and the slum dweller, reform-minded citizens were not. Some, such as social workers Jane Addams and Lillian Wald, set a course of direct action and example with their settlement houses. Others, such as Henry George and Edward Bellamy, proposed major revisions of the capitalistic system. Still others, most notably Jacob Riis and Lewis Hine, sought by documentary photography to make Americans *see* the social ills in their midst.

Riis, a Danish immigrant, was a pioneer in the use of the camera to document reporting. His book, *How the Other Half Lives* (1890), and the dozens of newspaper and magazine articles he wrote were instrumental in arousing New Yorkers to conditions within their city. Hine lacked Riis's skill as a writer, but he had few equals as a photographer. Also, printing advances allowed his pictures to reproduce accurately in halftone rather than in the inferior woodblock engraving of Riis's day.

Hine taught himself to use a camera in 1903, and he soon earned a reputation for his studies of immigrants. In 1910 he joined the National Child Labor Committee. According to his biographer, Robert Doty, Hine managed "to smuggle his camera into mills and factories despite threatening foremen. Often he had to pose as an insurance salesman or fire inspector. Winning the confidence of the children, he would interview them while scribbling notes on a pad inside his pocket. These would be rewritten later, in a legible form." He photographed young girls in southern textile mills, boys breaking coal in Pennsylvania mines, women laboring in New York's garment district, and his pictures provided illustration for booklets, articles, and posters, as well as factual documentation for crusading playwrights. He made it possible for the evils of child and sweatshop labor to be "emotionally recognized," said the chairman of the committee. "The work Hine did for this reform was more responsible than all other efforts in bringing the need to public attention."

The Outlook

In 1901 Yale's eminent sociologist William Graham Sumner tried to project America's future by examining the legacy of the past century. "The competition of life is so mild," Sumner decided, "that men are hardly conscious of it. So far as we can see ahead there is every reason for even rash optimism in regard to the material or economic welfare of mankind." Sumner's sunny outlook had substantial basis in fact. Many were certainly reaping the material benefits of invention and industrialization. By 1901, for example, Americans could enjoy "opera at home" through the magic of Thomas Edison's Victrola or make a pictorial record of the good life with George Eastman's Kodak or, if they were particularly adventuresome, take a drive in Ransom Olds's runabout.

Other observers found small comfort in the legacy of the 19th century. They were made apprehensive by evidence of continuing poverty (fewer than 10 per cent of America's families earned more than $380 a year in 1890); by the chaotic growth of cities (New York had grown 460 per cent in 50 years, Chicago 5,500 per cent); by mounting labor discontent (there were some 24,000 strikes and lockouts between 1880 and 1900). "What will be the fate of personal individuality?" asked another sociologist in 1904. Would that "cockleshell, the individual soul" enjoy greater freedom in the future, or would it, "too frail to navigate the vaster expanses, become more and more the sport of irresistible waves and currents?"

PHILLIPS COLLECTION

Six O'Clock Winter, *by the "ashcan" painter John Sloan, is dominated by the thundering presence of New York's Third Avenue el. Sloan's canvas evokes an image of the early 20th-century metropolis that displayed to a contemporary observer "all the signs of the heaped industrial battle-field, all the sounds and silences, grim, pushing, intruding. . . ." Opposite, the new era as proclaimed in the Times Square advertising jungle; a photograph taken in about 1914.*

VICTOR
HOTEL
"MASTERS' VOICE"
"VICTOR"
OFFICE
OPERA AT HOM
The Pierce Arro
Uneeda

20

Intellectual and Cultural Trends

The great forces that governed American economic and social development after the Civil War also shaped American thinking and American culture. Industrialization altered men's ways of looking at life at the same time that it transformed their ways of making a living. Technological advances revolutionized the communication of ideas more drastically than the transportation of goods or the manufacture of iron and steel. The growth of cities provided a favorable environment for intellectual and artistic expression. The materialism that permeated American attitudes toward business also affected contemporary education and literature, while Charles Darwin's theory of evolution influenced American philosophers, lawyers, and historians profoundly. At the same time, older ideologies like romantic individualism and faith in democracy continued to affect American thinking deeply. No really dominant pattern emerged; the American mind, like the people themselves, was too diverse—one might say confused, even incoherent—to be neatly delimited.

Public Education

The history of American education after about 1870 reflects the impact of many social and economic forces. While men like Horace Mann and Henry Barnard had laid the foundations for state-supported school systems back in the Age of Jackson, these systems did not become compulsory until after the Civil War. Only then did the growth of cities provide the concentrated populations necessary for economical mass education; only then did the upward spurt of human productivity resulting from industrialization produce the huge sums that universal education required. In the 1860's about half the children in the country received some formal education, but this did not mean that half the children were attending school at any one time. Sessions were short, and many children dropped out after only two or three years of classes; as late as 1870 the average American had received only four years of schooling.

Thereafter, steady growth and improvement took place. Attendance in the public schools increased from 6.8 million in 1870 to about 10 million in 1880 and 15.5 million in 1900, a remarkable expansion even when allowance is made for the growth of the population. Public expenditures for education rose from $63 million in 1870 to $145 million in 1890 and $234 million in 1902. The national rate of illiteracy declined from 20 per cent in 1870 to 10.7 per cent in 1900.* Nearly all the states outside the South had compulsory education laws by 1900, and over the years these were gradually extended to cover broader age groups and longer school sessions. Most notable was the increase in secondary education: the number of high schools jumped from perhaps 100 in 1860 to 6,000 at the end of the century. At the other extreme, the kindergarten, developed in Germany in the 1830's by Friedrich Froebel, caught on rapidly. The first public kindergarten was opened in St. Louis in 1873; by 1880 there were about 300 in the country, and by the 1890's most systems of any size had adopted the idea.

Southern schools lagged far behind the rest of the nation, partly because the section was poor and still predominantly rural; the factors that made possible improvement elsewhere were lacking in the states of the old Confederacy. The restoration of white rule in the 1870's brought an abrupt halt to the progress in Negro public education that the reconstruction governments had made. Church groups, and private foundations such as the Peabody Fund and the Slater Fund, financed chiefly by northern philanthropists, did support Negro schools after 1877, including two important experiments in vocational training, Hampton Institute (1886) and Booker T. Washington's Tuskegee Institute (1881).

These schools, however, had to overcome considerable resistance and suspicion in the white community; they survived only because they taught a docile, essentially subservient philosophy, preparing students to accept second-class citizenship and become good farmers and craftsmen. Since proficiency in academic subjects might have given the lie to the southern belief that Negroes were intellectually inferior to whites, such subjects were avoided. The southern

*At present, the rate is about 2 per cent.

LIBRARY OF CONGRESS

Tuskegee, said Booker T. Washington, began as "a broken down shanty and an old hen house." As shown here, students built many of the school's buildings, learning a trade and earning their board. A 1903 photograph.

insistence upon segregating white and Negro students in the public schools, buttressed by the "separate-but-equal" decision of the Supreme Court in *Plessy v. Ferguson,* imposed a crushing financial burden on sparsely settled communities, while the dominant white opinion that Negroes were not really educable did not encourage communities to make special efforts in their behalf. Educational expenditures in the South were inadequate by any standard—investment per pupil, teachers' salaries, and so on.

An industrial society created new demands for vocational and technical training. Science courses appeared in the new high schools. In 1880 Calvin M. Woodward opened a Manual Training School in St. Louis, and soon a number of institutions were offering courses in carpentry, metalwork, sewing, and other manual arts. By 1890, 36 American cities had public vocational high schools. Woodward, who was inspired by the work of Victor Della Vos, director of the Russian Imperial Technical School, thought of vocational training as part of a broad general education rather than as preparation for a specific occupation, but manual training also attracted the backing of prominent industrialists with more practical objectives. Their support, in turn, made organized labor suspicious of the new trend. One union leader called the trade schools "breeding schools for scabs and rats," and Samuel Gompers denounced them for "turning out 'botch' workmen who are ready and willing . . . to take the places of American workmen far below the wages prevailing in the trade." Fortunately, the usefulness of such training soon became evident to the unions; by 1910 the AF of L was lobbying side by side with the National Association of Manufacturers for more trade schools.

Foreign influences also triggered a revolution in teaching methods. Traditionally, American teachers had emphasized the three R's and depended upon strict discipline and rote memory to enforce learning. Typical of the pedagogues of the period was the Chicago teacher, described by a reformer in the 1890's, who told her students firmly: "Don't stop to think, tell me what you know!" But the ideas of early-19th-century German educators, most notably Johann Friedrich Herbart, were beginning to attract attention in the United States. According to Herbart, the teacher should arouse the interest of the child by relating new information to what he already knew; good teaching called for skilled professional training, psychological insight, enthusiasm, and imagination, not merely for factual information and a birch rod. At the same time, evolutionists were also pressing for a kind of education that would help children to "survive" by adapting to the demands of their environment.

Forward-looking American educators seized upon these ideas avidly because dynamic social changes were making the old system, never really suited to American conditions, increasingly inadequate. Settlement-house workers, for example, quickly discovered that slum children needed training in handicrafts, good citizenship, and personal hygiene as much as in reading and writing. They were appalled by the local schools, which suffered from the same diseases—filth, overcrowding, rickety construction—that plagued the surrounding tenements, and by the school systems, most of which were controlled by corrupt machine politicians who doled out teaching positions to party hacks and other untrained persons. They also recognized the great value of school playgrounds, kindergartens, adult education programs, and extracurricular clubs. Gradually, they came to regard educational reform as central to the whole problem of improving society. Soon they were advocating the broader kind of schooling that the theoreticians had been long describing. "We are impatient with the schools which lay all stress on reading and writing," Jane Addams declared. This type of education, she added, "fails to give the child any clew to the life about him."

The philosopher who summarized and gave direction to these forces in the educational world was John Dewey, a professor at the University of Chicago. Dewey was concerned with the implications of evolution and indeed of all science for education. Essentially his approach was ethical. Was the nation's youth being properly prepared for the tasks it faced in the modern world? He became interested in Francis W. Parker's remarkable experimental school in Chicago, which was organized as "a model home, a complete community and embryonic democracy." In 1896, together with his wife, Dewey founded the Laboratory School to put his educational ideas to the test. Three years later he published *The School and Society*, describing and defending his theories.

The schools must engage in new activities, Dewey argued, because in an industrial society the family no longer performed many of the educational functions it had carried out in an agrarian society. Farm children learn about nature, about work, about human character and man's fate in countless ways denied to children in cities. The school can fill the gap by becoming "an embryonic community . . . with types of occupations that reflect the life of the larger society." At the same time, education should center on the child, new information should be related to what he already knows. The child's imagination, energy, and curiosity are tools for broadening his outlook and increasing his store of information. Finally, the school should become an instrument for social reform, "saturating [the child] with the spirit of service" and helping to produce a "society which is worthy, lovely, and harmonious." Education, in other words, ought to build character and teach good citizenship as well as transmit knowledge.

The School and Society created a great stir, and Dewey immediately assumed leadership of the movement which, in the next generation, was called "progressive education." Although the gains made in public education before 1900 were more quantitative than qualitative and the philosophy dominant in most schools not very different at the end of the century from that prevailing in Horace Mann's day, change was in the air. The best educators of the period were full of optimism, convinced that the future was theirs.

Keeping the People Informed

The inadequacy of so much of their schooling left many Americans with a hunger for knowledge. As in early times, lecturers toured the country constantly, attracting large audiences. Nothing so well illustrates the mass desire for information as the rise of the Chautauqua movement, founded by John H. Vincent, a Methodist minister, and Lewis Miller, an Ohio manufacturer of farm machinery. Vincent had charge of Sunday schools for the Methodist Church. In 1874 he and Miller organized a two-week summer course for Sunday-school teachers on the shores of Lake Chautauqua in New York. Besides instruction, they offered good food, evening song fests around the campfire, and a relaxing and wholesome atmosphere—all for $6 for the two weeks. The 40 young teachers who attended were delighted with the program, and the idea caught on swiftly.

Soon the leafy shore of Lake Chautauqua became a city of tents each summer as thousands poured into the region from all over the country. The founders expanded their offerings to include instruction in literature, science, government, and economics. Famous authorities, including, over the years, six Presidents of the United States, came to lecture to open-air audiences on every subject imaginable. Eventually Chautauqua even offered correspondence courses leading over a four-year period to a diploma, the program being designed, in Vincent's words, to give "the college outlook" to persons who had not had the opportunity to obtain a higher education. Books were written specifically for the program and a monthly magazine, the *Chautauquan*, was published.

Such success naturally provoked imitation, until, by 1900, there were about 200 Chautauqua-type organizations in existence. Intellectual standards in these programs varied greatly; in general they were very low. By and large, entertainment was as important an objective as enlightenment. Musicians (good and bad), homespun humorists, inspirational lecturers, and assorted quacks shared the platform with prominent divines and scholars. Moneymaking undoubtedly motivated many of the entrepreneurs who operated these centers, all of which, including the original Chautauqua, reflected the prevailing tastes of the American people—diverse, enthusiastic, uncritical, and shallow. Nevertheless, the Chautauqua movement provided wonderful opportunities for thousands of earnest souls seeking stimulation and intellectual improvement.

Still larger numbers profited from the proliferation of public libraries after the Civil War.

By the end of the century nearly all the states were supporting libraries, and private donors, led by the ironmaster Andrew Carnegie, contributed many millions to the cause. In 1900 over 1,700 libraries in the United States had collections of more than 5,000 volumes.

Newspapers and magazines, of course, were also important means for disseminating information and educating the masses. Here the new technology supplied the major incentive for change. The development by Richard Hoe and Stephen Tucker of the web press (1871), which printed simultaneously on both sides of the paper fed into it from large rolls, and Ottmar Mergenthaler's linotype machine (1886), which cast rows of type as needed directly from molten metal, cheapened the cost of printing and speeded the production of newspapers in a revolutionary manner. Machines for making paper out of wood pulp reduced the cost of newsprint to a quarter of what it had been in the 1860's. By 1895 machines existed capable of printing, cutting, and folding 24,000 32-page newspapers an hour. The spread of the telegraph network and the laying of transoceanic cables wrought a similarly basic transformation in the gathering of news. Press associations, led by the New York Associated Press, flourished, the syndicated article appeared, and a few publishers—Edward W. Scripps was the first—began to acquire chains of newspapers.

Population growth and educational improvements created an ever larger demand for printed matter. At the same time, the integration of the economy enabled manufacturers to sell their goods all over the country. Advertising became important, and sellers soon learned that newspapers and magazines were excellent means of placing their products before millions of eyes. Advertising revenues soared just at the time when new machines and general expansion were making publishing a very expensive business. The day of the journeyman printer-editor ended. Magazine and especially newspaper publishing were becoming big business. Rich men like railroad magnates Jay Gould, Henry Villard, and Tom Scott, and mining tycoon George Hearst invested heavily in important newspapers in the postwar decades. Such publishers tended to be conservative, a tendency increased by the needs and prejudices of their businessmen-advertisers. On the other hand, reaching the masses meant lowering intellectual and cultural standards, appealing to the emotions, and adopting popular, and sometimes radical, causes.

Cheap, mass-circulation papers had first appeared in the 1830's and 1840's, the most successful being the *Sun*, the *Herald*, and the *Tribune* in New York, the Philadelphia *Public Ledger*, and the Baltimore *Sun*. None of these, however, much exceeded a circulation of 50,000 before the Civil War. The first publisher to reach a truly massive audience was Joseph Pulitzer, a Hungarian-born immigrant who had learned his trade in St. Louis, where he made a first-rate paper of the St. Louis *Post-Dispatch*. In 1883 Pulitzer bought the New York *World*, a sheet with a circulation of perhaps 20,000. Within a year he was selling 100,000 copies daily, and by the late nineties the *World*'s circulation regularly exceeded 1 million copies.

Pulitzer achieved this brilliant success by casting a wide net among New York's teeming, variegated population. For the educated and affluent, he provided better political and financial coverage than the most respectable New York journals. To the masses he offered bold black headlines devoted to crime (ANOTHER MURDERER TO HANG), scandal (VICE ADMIRAL'S SON IN JAIL), catastrophe (TWENTY-FOUR MINERS KILLED), society and the theater (LILY LANGTRY'S NEW ADMIRER), together with a variety of feature stories, political cartoons, comics, and pictures. Pulitzer also made the *World* a crusader for civic improvement, attacking political corruption, monopoly, and slum problems. In 1886 he organized a campaign among his readers to raise $100,000 for a 100-foot pedestal for the new Statue of Liberty which had been donated to the United States by the people of France. His energetic reporters literally made news, masquerading as criminals and poor workers in order to write graphic accounts of conditions in New York's jails and sweatshops.

"The *World* is the people's newspaper," Pulitzer boasted, and in the sense that it interested men and women of every sort, he was

JOSEPH PULITZER, JR., COLLECTION

Above, J.S. Sargent's portrait of Joseph Pulitzer. Below, an opposition paper's caricature of Hearst as the Yellow Kid, a sleazy comic strip character and inspiration for the phrase "yellow journalism."

The Bee, 1898

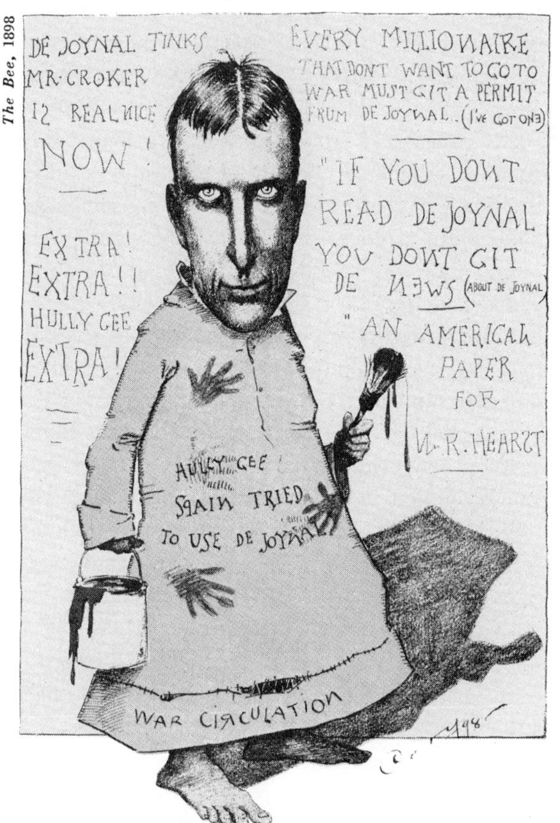

correct. Pulitzer's methods were quickly copied by competitors, most especially by William Randolph Hearst, who purchased the New York *Journal* in 1895 and soon outdid the *World* in sensationalism. But no other newspaperman of the era approached Pulitzer in originality, boldness, and the knack of reaching the masses without abandoning seriousness of purpose and basic integrity.

Growth and ferment also characterized the magazine world. Expansion was almost continuous. In 1865 there were about 700 magazines in the country, 20 years later about 3,300, by the turn of the century over 5,000. Until the mid-eighties, few of the new magazines were in any way unusual. A handful of serious periodicals, such as the *Atlantic Monthly*, *Harper's*, and the *Century* among the monthlies and the *Nation* among the weeklies, dominated the field. They were staid in tone and conservative in political caste. Articles on current topics, a good deal of fiction and poetry, historical and biographical studies, and similar material filled their pages, and many of them justly prided themselves on the quality of their illustrations. Although they had great influence, none even approached a mass circulation because of the limited size of the upper-middle-class audience they aimed at. The *Century* touched a peak in the eighties of about 250,000 when it published a series of articles on Civil War battles by famous commanders, but could not sustain that level. A circulation of 100,000 was considered good for such magazines, and the *Nation*, although extremely influential, seldom sold more than 8,000 copies.

Magazines directed at the average man also existed in the immediate post-Civil War era, but all were of very low quality. The leading publisher of this type of magazine in the sixties and seventies was Frank Leslie, who controlled a variety of periodicals, such as *Frank Leslie's Popular Monthly*, *Frank Leslie's Chimney Corner*, *Frank Leslie's Illustrated Newspaper*, and *Frank Leslie's Jolly Joker*. Leslie specialized in illustrations of current events (he put as many as 34 engravers to work on a single picture in order to bring it out quickly) and on providing what he frankly admitted was "mental pabulum"—a combination of cheap romantic fiction, old-fashioned poetry, jokes, and advice columns. Some of his periodicals sold as many as 300,000 copies per issue.

After about 1885, however, vast changes began to take place. New magazines such as the *Forum* (1886) and the *Arena* (1889) emphasized hard-hitting articles on controversial subjects by leading experts. The weekly *Literary Digest* (1890) offered summaries of press opinion on current events, and the *Review of Reviews* (1891) provided monthly commentary on the news. Even more startling changes revolutionized the mass-circulation field. Between 1883 and 1893 the *Ladies' Home Journal, Cosmopolitan, Munsey's*, and *McClure's* appeared on the scene. Although superficially similar to the Frank Leslie type, these magazines maintained a far higher intellectual level. In 1889 Edward W. Bok became editor of the *Ladies' Home Journal*. Besides advice columns ("Ruth Ashmore's Side Talks with Girls"), he offered articles on child care, gardening, and interior decorating, published fine contemporary novelists, including Rudyard Kipling, William Dean Howells, and Mark Twain, and employed public figures, such as Presidents Grover Cleveland and Benjamin Harrison, to discuss important questions. He printed colored reproductions of art masterpieces—the invention of cheap photoengraving was of enormous significance in the success of mass-circulation magazines—and crusaded for women's suffrage, conservation, and other reforms. Bok did not merely cater to public tastes, he created new tastes. He even refused to accept patent medicine advertising, a major source of revenue for many popular magazines.

Samuel S. McClure and Frank A. Munsey were also masters of popular journalism. *McClure's*, often if somewhat erroneously called the first "muckraking" magazine because it published the work of Lincoln Steffens, the leading reform journalist of the early 20th century, specialized in first-class fiction, serious historical studies, and exciting articles attacking political corruption, monopoly, and other social evils. *Munsey's* adopted the same formula but pitched its appeal somewhat lower.

Bok, McClure, Munsey, and a number of their competitors reached millions of readers. Like Pulitzer in the newspaper field, they found ways of interesting every type: rich and poor, cultivated and ignorant. Utilizing the new printing technology to cut costs and drawing heavily on advertising revenues, they sold their magazines for 10 or 15 cents a copy and still made fortunes. Under Bok, the *Journal* eventually reached a circulation of 2 million. Between 1894 and 1907, Munsey cleared over $7.8 million from his numerous publications. All had an acute sensitivity to the shifting interests of the masses. "I want to know if you enjoy a story," McClure once told Lincoln Steffens. "If you do, then I know that, say, ten thousand readers will like it. . . . But I go most by myself. For if I like a thing, then I know that millions will like it. My mind and my taste are so common that I'm the best editor."*

Colleges and Universities

Improvements in public education and the needs of an increasingly complex society for every type of intellectual skill led to advances in higher education and professional training during the last quarter of the century. Statistical evidence in this area is impressive if somewhat less spectacular than in other fields of human activity in the United States. The number of colleges, for example, rose from about 350 to 500 between 1878 and 1898, and the student body roughly tripled. Although as yet only a mere fraction of the population even contemplated college, the aspirations of the nation's youth were rising, and more and more parents had the financial means necessary for fulfilling them.

More significant than the expansion of the colleges were the alterations that took place in their curricula and in the atmosphere permeating the average campus. In 1870 most colleges were much as they had been in the 1830's: small, impoverished, limited in their offerings, intellectually stagnant. The ill-paid professors were seldom scholars of any stature. Thereafter, change came like a flood tide. State universities flourished; the

*McClure added ruefully: "There's only one better editor than I am, and that's Frank Munsey. If *he* likes a thing, then *everybody* will like it."

federal government's "land-grant" program in support of training in "agriculture and the mechanic arts," established under the Morrill Act of 1862, came into its own; wealthy philanthropists poured fortunes into old institutions and founded new ones; a number of farsighted educators began to introduce new courses and adopt new teaching methods; professional schools of law, medicine, education, business, journalism, and other specialties increased in number.

In the forefront of reform was Harvard, the oldest and most prestigious college in the country. In the 1860's it possessed an excellent faculty, including James Russell Lowell in literature, Benjamin Peirce in mathematics, Wolcott Gibbs in chemistry, and the naturalists Asa Gray and Louis Agassiz. But teaching methods were antiquated, and the curriculum had remained almost unchanged since the colonial period. In 1869, however, a dynamic new president, the chemist Charles W. Eliot, undertook a great transformation of the college. Eliot introduced the elective system, gradually eliminating required courses and expanding offerings in such areas as modern languages, economics, and the laboratory sciences. He did away with the "scale of merit," under which students had received a daily grade in each course based on routine recitals in class, and encouraged his faculty to experiment with new teaching methods. He brought in men with original minds and new ideas like Henry Adams, grandson of John Quincy Adams. Adams made the study of medieval history a true intellectual experience. "The boys worked like rabbits, and dug holes all over the field of archaic society," he boasted. "Mr. Adams roused the spirit of inquiry and controversy in me," one student later wrote; another, the historian Edward Channing, called Adams "the greatest teacher that I ever encountered."

Under Eliot's guidance the standards of the medical school were raised, and the case method was introduced in the law school. He also encouraged the expansion of graduate education. For the first time, students were allowed to borrow books from the library! In some respects he went too far—the elective system eventually led to the fragmentation of the curriculum and encouraged superficiality and laxness in many students—but on balance he transformed Harvard from a college, "a place to which a young man *is sent*," to a university, a place "to which he *goes*."

An even more important development in higher education was the founding of Johns Hopkins in 1876. This university was one of many established in the period by wealthy industrialists; its benefactor, the Baltimore merchant Johns Hopkins, had made his fortune in the Baltimore and Ohio Railroad. Its distinctiveness, however, was due to the vision of its first president, Daniel Coit Gilman. Having observed European universities firsthand, Gilman modeled Johns Hopkins on the great German universities where meticulous research and absolute freedom of inquiry were the guiding principles. In staffing the institution, Gilman aimed in every field of knowledge for scholars of the highest reputation, scouring Europe as well as America in his search for talent and offering outstanding men high salaries for that time—up to $5,000 for a professor. On the other hand, he also employed a number of relatively unknown but brilliant younger scholars, such as the physicist Henry A. Rowland and Herbert Baxter Adams, whom he made an associate in history on the strength of his excellent doctoral dissertation at the University of Heidelberg. Gilman promised his teachers good students and ample opportunity to pursue their own research, which explains why men like Herbert Baxter Adams repeatedly turned down attractive offers from other universities.

Johns Hopkins specialized in graduate education. In the generation after its founding, it turned out a remarkable percentage of the most important scholars in the nation, including Woodrow Wilson in political science, John Dewey in philosophy, Frederick Jackson Turner in history, and John R. Commons in economics. The seminar in political science and history conducted by Herbert Baxter Adams was particularly productive: the Adams-edited *Johns Hopkins Studies in Historical and Political Science*, consisting of the doctoral dissertations of his many students, was both voluminous and influential—"the mother of similar studies in every part of the United States."

The success of Johns Hopkins did not stop the migration of American scholars to Europe—over 2,000 matriculated at German universities during the 1880's—but as Hopkins graduates took up professorships at other institutions and as men trained elsewhere adopted the Hopkins methods, true graduate education became possible in most sections of the country.

The immediate success of Johns Hopkins encouraged other rich men to endow universities offering advanced work. Clark University in Worcester, Massachusetts, founded by Jonas Clark, a merchant and real-estate speculator, opened its doors in 1889. Its president, G. Stanley Hall, had been a professor of psychology at Hopkins, and he built the new university in that institution's image. More important was John D. Rockefeller's creation, the new University of Chicago (1892). Rockefeller's money made Chicago possible, but again Johns Hopkins provided the example. The president of Chicago, William Rainey Harper, was a brilliant Biblical scholar—he received his Ph.D. from Yale at the age of 18—and an energetic and imaginative administrator. The new university, he told Rockefeller, should be designed "with the example of Johns Hopkins before our eyes." Like Daniel Coit Gilman, Harper sought the best men possible for his faculty. He offered such high salaries that he was besieged with over a thousand applications, but he was not content to settle for the best of those who came forward voluntarily. Armed with Rockefeller dollars, he "raided" all the best institutions in the nation. He decimated the faculty of the new Clark University—"an act of wreckage," the indignant President Hall complained, "comparable to anything that the worst trust ever attempted against its competitors." From the start, Chicago offered first-class graduate and undergraduate education. During its first year there were 120 instructors for fewer than 600 students, and despite fears that the mighty tycoon Rockefeller would enforce his social and economic views on the institution, complete academic freedom was the rule.

Also noteworthy during these years was the rapid expansion of state and federal aid to higher education. The Morrill Act granting land to each state at a rate of 30,000 acres for each senator and representative provided princely endowments, especially for the populous states. A few states turned the funds derived from the sale of this land over to private colleges, such as the Massachusetts Institute of Technology and Cornell. Others gave the money to existing state institutions, such as the universities of Vermont and Wisconsin. Most, however, created new "land-grant" colleges. In this way many important modern universities, such as Illinois, Michigan State, and Ohio State, got their start. While the federal assistance was earmarked for specific subjects, all the land-grant colleges offered a full range of courses and all received additional funds from the states. Other state institutions also benefited, for the public was displaying an increasing willingness to support their activities.

In general the land-grant universities adopted new ideas quickly. They were co-educational from the start, and most offered a wide variety of courses, developed professional schools, and experimented with extension work and summer programs. Typical of the better state institutions was the University of Michigan, which reached the top rank among the nation's universities during the presidency of James B. Angell (1871–1909). Like Eliot at Harvard, Angell expanded the undergraduate curriculum and strengthened the law and medical schools. He also encouraged graduate studies, seeking to make Michigan "part of the great world of scholars." He worked hard both to win popular support for the university and to find ways in which the university could serve the general community.

While, on balance, higher education made great strides forward between 1870 and 1900, not all the results were beneficial. On the one hand, the elective system led to superficiality; students gained a smattering of knowledge of many subjects but mastered none. On the other hand, intensive graduate work often produced narrowness of outlook and dry-as-dust research monographs on trivial subjects. Attempts to apply the scientific method in fields such as history and economics often enticed students into making smug claims to objectivity and definitiveness which from the nature of the subjects they could not even approach in their actual work.

The gifts of rich industrialists sometimes came with strings attached; every collegiate benefactor was not as willing as John D. Rockefeller to keep his hands off educational policies. Jonas Clark, for example, meddled constantly in university affairs to the vast annoyance of the Clark faculty. As colleges grew more dependent upon the wealth of private citizens, their boards of trustees tended to be dominated by businessmen, who sometimes attempted to impose their own social and economic beliefs on faculty members. Although few professors lost their positions because their views offended conservative trustees, at many institutions trustees exerted constant nagging pressures that limited academic freedom and scholarly objectivity. At state colleges politicians often interfered in academic affairs, even treating professorships as part of the patronage system.

As Thorstein Veblen pointed out in his caustic study of *The Higher Learning in America* (1918), "the intrusion of businesslike ideals, aims and methods" harmed the universities in countless subtle ways. Mere size—the verbose Veblen called it "an executive weakness for spectacular magnitude"—became an end in itself, and the practical values of education were exalted over the humanistic. As administration became more complicated, the prestige of administrators rose inordinately. At many institutions professors came to be regarded as mere employees of the governing boards. In 1893, for example, the members of the faculty of Stanford University were officially classified as personal servants of Mrs. Leland Stanford, widow of the founder. This was done in a good cause—the Stanford estate was tied up in probate court and this ruling made it possible to pay the professors out of Mrs. Stanford's allowance for household expenses—but that such a procedure was even conceivable must have appalled the scholarly world.

As the number of college graduates increased and as colleges ceased being primarily training institutions for clergymen, the influence of alumni on educational policies began to make itself felt, not always happily. Social activities became more important on most campuses. Fraternities proliferated. Interest in organized sports first appeared as a laudable outgrowth of the general expansion of the curriculum, but soon athletic contests were playing a role all out of proportion to their real significance. Football evolved as the leading intercollegiate sport, especially after Walter Camp, coach of the Yale team, began selecting "All America" squads in 1889. By the early nineties important games were attracting huge crowds (over 50,000 attended the Yale-Princeton game in 1893), and thus the sport became a source of revenue that many colleges dared not neglect. Since students, alumni, and the general public demanded winning teams, college administrators stooped to subsidizing student athletes, in extreme cases even employing players who were not students at all. One exasperated college president quipped that the B.A. degree was coming to mean Bachelor of Athletics.

In short, higher education reflected American needs and values, with all their strengths and weaknesses. A complex society required a more professional and specialized education for its youth. Naturally, the coarseness, the rampant materialism and competitiveness of the era also found expression in the colleges and universities.

Scientific Advances

Much has rightly been made of the crassness of late-19th-century American life, yet the period also produced considerable intellectual activity of the highest quality. If the business mentality dominated society and if the great barons of industry, exalting practicality over theory, tended to look down upon the life of the mind, nonetheless men of intellect, quietly pondering the problems of their generation, created works which eventually affected the country as profoundly as the achievements of industrial organizers like Rockefeller and Carnegie and technicians like Edison and Bell.

In the area of pure science America produced a number of outstanding figures in these years. The giant among these, one whose contributions some experts rank with those of Newton, Darwin, and Einstein, was Josiah Willard Gibbs, professor of mathematical physics at Yale from 1871 to 1903. Gibbs's monograph "On the Equilibrium of Heterogeneous Substances" (1876,

Josiah Willard Gibbs graduated from Yale and took his doctorate there, then studied in Paris, Berlin, and Heidelberg before returning to his alma mater.

1878) created an entirely new science, physical chemistry, and made possible the study of how complex substances respond to changes in temperature and pressure. Purely theoretical at the time, Gibbs's ideas led eventually to vital advances in metallurgy and in the manufacture of plastics, drugs, and other products. Gibbs is often used to illustrate the supposed indifference of the age to its great minds, but this is hardly fair. He was a shy, self-effacing man who cared little for the spotlight or for collecting disciples. He published his major papers in the obscure *Transactions of the Connecticut Academy of Arts and Sciences*. Furthermore, he was so far ahead of his times that only a handful of specialists had the faintest glimmering of the importance of his work. The editors of the *Transactions* frankly admitted that they did not understand his papers.

Of lesser but still major significance was the work of Henry A. Rowland, the first professor of physics at Johns Hopkins University. President Gilman, with characteristic insight, had plucked the youthful Rowland from the faculty of Rensselaer Polytechnic Institute, where his brilliance was not fully appreciated.* Rowland conducted valuable research in spectrum analysis and contributed to the development of electron theory. His work, too, was purely theoretical, but it led to the improvement of transformers and dynamos and laid the basis for the modern electric-power industry.

Still another important American physicist was Albert A. Michelson of the University of Chicago, who made the first accurate measurements of the speed of light. Michelson's researches in the 1870's and 1880's helped prepare the way for Einstein's theory of relativity; in 1907 he became the first American scientist to win a Nobel prize.

Many other scientists of the period deserve mention: the astronomer Edward C. Pickering, director of the Harvard Observatory, a pioneer in the field of astrophysics; Samuel P. Langley of the Smithsonian Institution, an expert on solar radiation who also contributed to the development of the airplane; the paleontologist Othniel C. Marsh, whose study of fossil horses provided one of the most convincing demonstrations of the truth of evolution ever made; John Wesley Powell, director of the U.S. Geological Survey, noted for his studies of the Grand Canyon as well as for important work on the uses of water in arid regions; Benjamin Peirce, the Harvard mathematician who did important work in physics as well; Ira Remsen, whose seminar at Johns Hopkins produced a host of first-rate chemists. These men and many others of only slightly lesser stature give the lie to the myth that late-19th-century Americans were only interested in applied science.

The New Social Sciences

In the social sciences, of course, a close connection existed between the practical issues of the age and the achievements of the leading thinkers. The application of the theory of evolution to every aspect of human relations, the impact of industrialization on so-

*One of Rowland's path-breaking scientific papers had been rejected by a leading American journal on the ground that he was "too young to publish such."

ciety—such topics were of intense concern to American economists, sociologists, and historians. An understanding of Darwin increased the already strong interest of these men in studying the *development* of institutions and their interactions one with another, while controversies over trusts, slum conditions, and other contemporary problems drew scholars out of their towers into practical affairs. Furthermore, social scientists were deeply impressed—too impressed as it turned out—by the astonishing progress being made all about them in the physical and biological sciences. They applied the vaunted scientific method to their own specialties eagerly, hoping thereby to arrive at objective truths in fields which were by their very nature essentially subjective.

Among the economists something approaching a revolution took place in the 1880's. The old classical school, which maintained that immutable natural laws governed all human behavior and used the insights of Darwin only to justify unrestrained competition and laissez faire, was challenged by a group of young economists who had been influenced by the new German "historical" school, which argued that as times changed, economic theories and laws must be modified in order to remain relevant to actual conditions. Richard T. Ely, another of the scholars who made Johns Hopkins such a font of new ideas in the eighties, summarized the thinking of this group in 1885. "The state [is] an educational and ethical agency whose positive aid is an indispensable condition of human progress," Ely proclaimed. Laissez faire was both outmoded and dangerous. Economic problems were basically moral problems; their solution required "the united efforts of Church, state and science." The proper way to study these problems was by induction rather than deduction—by analyzing actual conditions, not by applying abstract laws or principles.

This approach led Henry Carter Adams (Ph.D., Johns Hopkins, 1878) to analyze the circumstances under which the government might regulate competition and even, in certain industries, establish monopolies under strict public control. Simon Patten of the University of Pennsylvania offered a theory justifying state economic planning and vast public works programs. Such ideas gave birth to the so-called "institutionalist school" of economics, whose members made detailed on-the-spot investigations of sweatshops, factories, and mines, studied the history of the labor movement, and conducted similar research activities of a concrete nature. The study of actual institutions would lead both to theoretical understanding and to practical social reform, they believed. John R. Commons, one of Ely's students at Johns Hopkins and later professor of economics at the University of Wisconsin, was perhaps the outstanding member of this school. His ten-volume *Documentary History of American Industrial Society* (1910–11) reveals the institutionalist approach at its best.

A similar revolution struck sociology in the mid-eighties. Once again prevailing opinion up to that time utterly rejected the idea of government interference with the organization of society. The influence of the Englishman Herbert Spencer, who objected even to public schools and the postal system, was immense. As one prominent American sociologist later recalled: "Nearly all of us who took up sociology between 1870, say, and 1890, did so at the instigation of Spencer. His book, *The Study of Sociology* . . . probably did more to arouse interest in the subject than any other publication before or since." Spencer and his American disciples, such as William Graham Sumner of Yale, who "elevated laissez faire into a social and economic law and assigned to it the same standing as the law of gravity," and Edward L. Youmans, editor of *Popular Science Monthly*, twisted the ideas of Darwin to mean that society could only be changed by the force of evolution, which moved, of course, with cosmic slowness. "You and I can do nothing at all," Youmans told the reformer Henry George. "It's all a matter of evolution. Perhaps in four or five thousand years evolution may have carried men beyond this state of things."

Such a point of view had little relevance in America, where society was changing rapidly and the range of government social and economic activity was expanding. The first important challenger of the Spencerians was an obscure scholar employed by the U.S. Geological Survey, Lester

Frank Ward, whose *Dynamic Sociology* was published in 1883. Ward's style was turgid, but his mind was penetrating. He assailed the Spencerians for ignoring the possibility of "the improvement of society by cold calculation." In *The Psychic Factors of Civilization* (1893) he blasted the "law of competition." Human progress, he argued, consisted of "triumphing little by little over this law," as, for example, by interfering with biological processes through the use of medicines to kill harmful bacteria. Government regulation of the economy offered another illustration of man's ability to control his environment. "Nothing is more obvious today," Ward wrote in the *Forum* in 1895, "than the signal inability of capital and private enterprise to take care of themselves unaided by the state." Society must indeed evolve, but it would evolve through careful social planning. Man should not abandon his responsibilities by handing over his future to the forces of nature, which, Ward easily demonstrated, were enormously wasteful and inefficient.

Like the new economists, Ward emphasized the practical and ethical sides of his subject. Sociologists should seek "the betterment of society," he said. "Dynamic Sociology aims at the organization of happiness." He had little direct influence because his writings were highly technical. In six years, only 500-odd copies of *Dynamic Sociology* were sold. However, a handful of specialists, including the economist Ely, president Andrew D. White of Cornell, the Social Gospel preacher Washington Gladden, and the sociologists Albion W. Small and Edward A. Ross—two more products of Johns Hopkins—carried his ideas to a wider audience. By the nineties Small, who considered Ward's work "an immeasurable advance," was advocating public ownership of natural resources, gasworks, and street railways. Ross introduced Ward's ideas to his students at Stanford and Wisconsin and wrote trenchant attacks on "the rapacity of over-grown private interests." The new sociologists' arguments yielded few concrete results before 1900, but they effectively demolished the Spencerians and laid the theoretical basis for the modern welfare state.

Similar currents of thought influenced the other social sciences as well. In his *Systems of Consanguinity* (1871) the pioneer anthropologist Lewis Henry Morgan developed a theory of social evolution and showed how kinship relationships reflected and affected tribal institutions. Morgan's *Ancient Society* (1877–78) stressed the mutability of social and cultural patterns and the need to adjust these patterns to meet altered conditions. Applying his knowledge of primitive societies to modern life, he warned against the current overemphasis of property values. "Since the advent of civilization, the outgrowth of property has been so immense . . . that it has become, on the part of the people, an unmanageable power," he wrote. "The time will come, nevertheless, when human intelligence will rise to the mastery over property, and define the relations of the state to the property it protects."

The new political scientists were also evolutionists and institutionalists. The Founding Fathers, living in a world dominated by Newton's concept of the universe as an immense, orderly machine governed by fixed natural laws, had conceived of the political system as an impersonal set of institutions and principles—a government of laws rather than of men. Nineteenth-century thinkers (John C. Calhoun is the best example) concerned themselves with abstractions, such as states' rights, and ignored the extra-legal aspects of politics, such as parties and pressure groups. In the 1880's, however, political scientists began to employ a different approach. In his doctoral dissertation at Johns Hopkins, *Congressional Government* (1885), Woodrow Wilson analyzed the actual workings of the American system, concluding that the real locus of authority lay in the committees of Congress, which had no constitutional basis at all. Wilson was by no means a radical—he idolized the great English conservative Edmund Burke. Nevertheless, he viewed politics as a dynamic process and offered no theoretical objection to the expansion of state power. In *The State* (1889) he distinguished between essential functions of government, such as the protection of property and the punishment of crime, and "ministrant" functions, such as education, the regulation of corporations, and social welfare legislation. The desirability of any particular state action of the latter type was simply a matter of expediency. "Every means," he wrote, "by which society may be perfected through the instrumentality of government . . . ought certainly to be diligently sought."

Law and History

Even jurisprudence, by its nature conservative and rooted in tradition, felt the pressure of evolutionary thought and the new emphasis on studying institutions as they actually were. In 1881 Oliver Wendell Holmes, Jr., son of the "Autocrat of the Breakfast-Table," published *The Common Law.* Rejecting the idea that judges should limit themselves to the mechanical explication of statutes, that law consisted merely of what was written in lawbooks, Holmes argued that "the felt necessities of the time" rather than precedent should determine the rules by which men are governed. "The life of the law has not been logic; it has been experience," he wrote. "It is revolting," he added on another occasion, "to have no better reason for a rule of law than that so it was laid down in the time of Henry IV."

Holmes went on to a long and brilliant career on the bench, during which he repeatedly stressed the right of the people, through their elected representatives, to deal with contemporary problems in any reasonable way, unfettered by outmoded ideas of the proper limits of governmental authority. Like the societies they regulated, laws should evolve as times and conditions changed, he said. This way of reasoning caused no sudden reversal of judicial practice. Holmes's most notable opinions as a judge tended, as in the Lochner bakeshop case, to be dissenting opinions. But his philosophy reflected the advanced thinking of the late 19th century, and his influence grew with every decade of the 20th.

The new approach to knowledge did not always advance the cause of liberal reform, however. Historians in the new graduate schools became intensely interested in studying the origins and evolution of political institutions. They concluded, after much "scientific" study of old charters and law codes, that the roots of democracy were to be found in the customs of the ancient tribes of northern Europe. This theory of the "Teutonic origins" of democracy, which has since been thoroughly discredited, fitted well with the prejudices of men of British stock, and it provided ammunition for those who favored restricting immigration from other parts of the world as well as for those who argued that Negroes were inferior beings.

Out of this work, however, came the frontier thesis of Frederick Jackson Turner, still another scholar who was trained at Johns Hopkins. Turner's essay, "The Significance of the Frontier in American History" (1893), opened up wide new areas for study. He showed how the frontier experience, through which every section of the country had passed, had affected the thinking of the people and the shape of American institutions. The isolation of the frontier, the need during each successive westward advance to create civilization anew, account, he said, for the individualism of Americans and for the democratic character of their society. Indeed, nearly everything unique in our culture, Turner argued, could be traced to the existence of the frontier.

Turner, and still more his many disciples, made too much of his basic insights. Life on the frontier was not as democratic as Turner believed, and certainly does not "explain" American development as completely as he claimed. Nevertheless, Turner's work showed how important it was to investigate the evolution of institutions and encouraged historians to study social and economic, as well as purely political, subjects. And if the claims of the new historians to objectivity and definitiveness were absurdly overstated, their emphasis on thoroughness, exactitude, and impartiality did much to raise standards in the profession. Perhaps the finest product of the new scientific school, a happy combination of meticulous scholarship and literary artistry, was Henry Adams' nine-volume *History of the United States During the Administrations of Jefferson and Madison.*

Realism in Literature

When what Mark Twain called "The Gilded Age" began, American literature was dominated by the romantic mood. All the important writers of the 1840's and 1850's except

Hawthorne, Thoreau, and Poe were still living and many of the lesser ones as well. Longfellow stood at the height of his fame, and the lachrymose Susan Warner—"tears on almost every page"—continued to turn out stories in the style of her popular *The Wide, Wide World.* Romanticism, however, had lost its creative force; most writing in the decade after 1865 was sentimental trash pandering to the emotions and preconceptions of middle-class readers. There has always been a market for such pap, but at this time even educated audiences accepted it uncomplainingly; magazines like the *Atlantic Monthly* overflowed with stories about fair ladies worshiped from afar by stainless heroes, elderly women coping selflessly with drunken husbands, consumptive school mistresses, perfidious adventurers, and poor but honest youths rising through a combination of virtue and assiduity to positions of wealth and influence. Most writers of fiction in this period tended to ignore both the eternal problems inherent in the perverse nature of man and the particular social problems of the age; polite entertainment and pious moralizing appeared to be their only objectives.

The patent unreality, even dishonesty of contemporary fiction eventually caused a reaction. As early as the mid-sixties, Thomas Wentworth Higginson, essayist, historian, Garrisonian abolitionist, Civil War commander of a Negro regiment, was attacking the sentimentality of American literature and urging writers to concern themselves with "real human life." New antiromantic foreign influence—Emile Zola's first novels appeared in the sixties—also began to affect American interests and tastes. But the most important forces giving rise to the Age of Realism were those which were transforming every other aspect of American life: industrialism, with its associated complexities and social problems; the theory of evolution, which made men more aware of the force of the environment and the basic conflicts of existence; the new science, which challenged old, traditional values and taught men to observe their surroundings empirically, dispassionately.

The decade of the 1870's saw a gradual shift in styles; by the 1880's realism was beginning to flower.* Novelists undertook the examination of current social problems such as slum life, the conflict between capital and labor, and political corruption. They created multidimensional characters, depicted persons of every social class, used dialect and slang to capture the flavor of particular local types, fashioned painstaking descriptions of the surroundings into which they placed their subjects. Some simply used these aspects of the real world as properties for hackneyed dramas, but a few of uncommon talent, managing to treat reality imaginatively, produced real literature.

One early sign of the new realism can be seen in the rise of the "local color" school, for writers seeking to describe real situations quite naturally turned to the regions they knew best for material. Beginning in 1880, Joel Chandler Harris wrote his "Uncle Remus" stories, faithfully reproducing the dialect of Georgia Negroes and incidentally creating a remarkably realistic literary character. The novels of Edward Eggleston, from *The Hoosier Schoolmaster* (1871) to *The Graysons* (1888), drew vivid pictures of middlewestern life. Sarah Orne Jewett's carefully constructed tales of life in Maine, first published in the *Atlantic Monthly* in the mid-seventies, caught the spirit of that region perfectly. Most local colorists could not rise above the conventional sentimentality of the era. By concentrating, as most did, on depicting rural life, they were retreating from current reality. But their concern for exact description and their fascination with local types reflected a growing interest in realism.

Mark Twain

Although it was easy to romanticize the West, that region also lent itself to the realistic approach. Almost of necessity, western writers employed dialect, described coarse characters from the

*It must be emphasized, however, that the romantic novel did not disappear. Books like General Lew Wallace's *Ben Hur* (1880) and Frances Hodgson Burnett's *Little Lord Fauntleroy* (1886) were best sellers. Francis Marion Crawford's shamelessly romantic tales, published in wholesale lots between 1883 and his death in 1909, were very popular. In the nineties a spate of historical romances made the realists fume.

lower levels of society, and dealt with crime and violence. It would have been difficult indeed to write a genteel romance about a mining camp. The outstanding figure of western literature, the first great American realist, was Mark Twain. Born Samuel L. Clemens in 1835, he grew up in Hannibal, Missouri, on the banks of the Mississippi. After having mastered the printer's trade and worked as a river-boat pilot, he went west to Nevada in 1861. The wild, rough life of Virginia City fascinated him, but prospecting got him nowhere, and he became a reporter for the *Territorial Enterprise*. Soon he was publishing humorous stories about the local life under the *nom de plume* Mark Twain. In 1865, while working in California, he wrote "The Celebrated Jumping Frog of Calaveras County," a story which brought him national recognition. A tour of Europe and the Holy Land in 1867–68 led to *The Innocents Abroad* (1869), which made him a famous man.

Twain's greatness stemmed from his acute reportorial eye and ear, his eagerness to live life to the full, his marvelous sense of humor, his ability to be at once "in" society and outside it, to love mankind yet be repelled by man's vanity and perversity. He epitomized all the zest and adaptability of his age, and also its materialism. No contemporary pursued the almighty dollar more assiduously. An inveterate speculator, he made a fortune with his pen and lost it in foolish business ventures. He wrote tirelessly and endlessly about America and Europe, his own times and the feudal past, about tourists, slaves, tycoons, cracker-barrel philosophers—and man's fate. He was equally at home and equally successful on the Great River of his childhood, in the mining camps, and in the eastern bourgeois society of his mature years, but every prize slipped through his fingers and he died a black pessimist, surrounded by adulation, yet alone, an alien and a stranger in the land he loved and knew so well.

Twain excelled every contemporary in the portrayal of character. In his biting satire *The Gilded Age* (1873), he created that magnificent mountebank Colonel Beriah Sellers, purveyor of eyewash ("the Infallible Imperial Oriental Optic Liniment") and false hopes, ridiculous, unscrupulous, but lovable. In *Huckleberry Finn* (1884), his masterpiece, his portrait of the slave Jim, loyal, patient, naive, yet withal a man, is unforgettable. When Huck takes advantage of Jim's credulity merely for his own amusement, the slave turns from him coldly and says: "Dat truck dah is *trash;* en trash is what people is dat puts dirt on de head er dey fren's en makes 'em ashamed." And, of course, there is Huck Finn himself, one of the great figures of all literature, full of deviltry, romantic, amoral—up to a point —but at bottom the complete realist. When Miss Watson tells him he can get anything he wants by praying for it, he makes the effort, is disillusioned, and then concludes: "If a body can get anything they pray for, why don't Deacon Winn get back the money he lost on pork? . . . Why can't Miss Watson fat up? No, I says to myself, there ain't nothing in it."

Whether directly, as in *The Innocents Abroad* and in his fascinating account of the world of the river pilot, *Life on the Mississippi* (1883), or when transformed by his imagination in works of fiction such as *Tom Sawyer* (1876) and *A Connecticut Yankee in King Arthur's Court* (1889), Mark Twain always put much of his own experience and feeling into his work. "The truth is," he wrote in 1886, "my books are mainly autobiographies." A story, he once told a fellow author, "must be written with the blood out of a man's heart." His very inner confusions, the clash between his recognition of the pretentiousness and meanness of human beings and his wish to be accepted by society, added depths and overtones to his writing that together with his comic genius give it lasting appeal. He could not rise above the sentimentality and prudery of his generation entirely, for these qualities were part of his nature. He never dealt effectively with sexual love, for example, and often—even in *Huckleberry Finn*—he contrived to end his tales on absurdly optimistic notes that ring false after so many brilliant pages portraying men and the world as they are. On balance, however, Twain's achievement was magnificent. Rough and uneven like the man himself, his works catch more of the spirit of the age he named than those of any other writer.

William Dean Howells

Mark Twain's literary realism was far less self-conscious than that of his long-time friend William Dean Howells. Like Twain, Howells, who was born in Ohio in 1837, had little formal education. He learned the printer's trade from his father and became a reporter for the *Ohio State Journal*. In 1860 he wrote a campaign biography of Lincoln and was rewarded with an appointment as consul in Venice. His sketches in *Venetian Life* (1866) were a product of this experience. After the Civil War he worked briefly for the *Nation* in New York and then moved to Boston, where he became editor of the *Atlantic Monthly*. In 1886 he returned to New York as editor of *Harper's*.

A long series of novels and much literary criticism poured from his pen over the next 34 years. Although he insisted upon treating his material honestly, at first he was not a critic of society, voting the straight Republican ticket and being content to write about what he called "the smiling aspects" of life. Howells held the sentimental novelists of the sixties and seventies in contempt because they offered the reader saccharine falsehoods and pampered his "gross appetite for the marvellous," not because they avoided controversial subjects. By realism, he meant concern for the complexities of individual personalities and faithful description of the genteel, middle-class world he knew best. Nevertheless, he did not hesitate to discuss what prudish critics called "sordid" and "revolting" subjects, such as the unhappy marriage of respectable people, which he treated sensitively in *A Modern Instance* (1882).

However, besides a sharp eye and an open mind, Howells had a real social conscience. Gradually he became aware of the problems that industrialization was creating. As early as 1885, in *The Rise of Silas Lapham*, he dealt with some of the ethical conflicts faced by businessmen in a competitive society. The harsh public reaction to the Haymarket bombing in 1886 stirred him deeply, and he threw himself into a futile campaign to prevent the execution of the anarchist suspects. Thereafter, he moved rapidly toward the left; soon he was calling himself a socialist. "After fifty years of optimistic content with 'civilization' . . . I now abhor it, and feel that it is coming out all wrong in the end, unless it bases itself anew on a real equality," he wrote.* His great novel *A Hazard of New Fortunes* (1890), in which Howells put his own ideas in the mouth of a magazine editor, Basil March, contained a broad criticism of industrial America—of the slums, of the callous treatment of workers, of the false values of the promoter and the new-rich tycoon.

But Howells was more than a reformer, more than an inventor of utopias like Edward Bellamy, although he admired Bellamy and wrote a utopian novel of his own, *A Traveller from Altruria* (1894). *A Hazard of New Fortunes* attempted to portray the whole range of metropolitan life, its plot weaving the destinies of a dozen interesting and fully realized personalities from diverse sections and social classes. The book represents a triumph of realism, not only in its careful descriptions of various sections of New York and of the ways of life of rich and poor, and in the intricacy of its characters, but also in its rejection of sentimentality and even of romantic love. "A man knows that he can love and wholly cease to love, not once merely, but several times," the narrator says, "but in regard to women he cherishes the superstition of the romances that love is once for all, and forever." And Basil March, himself happily married, tells his wife: "Why shouldn't we rejoice as much at a non-marriage as a marriage? . . . In reality, marriage is dog cheap, and anyone can have it for the asking—if he keeps asking enough people."

Aside from his own works, which were widely read, Howells had an immense impact on American literature. He was the most influential critic of his times. He helped bring the finest contemporary foreign writers, including Tolstoy, Dostoevsky, Ibsen, and Zola, to the attention of readers in the United States, and he encouraged many important young American novelists, such as

*With remarkable self-insight he added immediately: "Meanwhile I wear a fur-lined overcoat, and live in all the luxury my money can buy." Like nearly all American reformers of the era, he was not really very radical.

An 1897 drawing from the comic weekly Life, *titled "Our Popular but Over-advertised Authors," features (from left) William Dean Howells, George W. Cable, John K. Bangs, James Whitcomb Riley, Mark Twain, Mary Freeman, Richard Harding Davis, F. Marion Crawford, Frances Burnett, and Joel Chandler Harris.*

Stephen Crane, Theodore Dreiser, Frank Norris, and Hamlin Garland. Some of these Americans went far beyond Howells' realism to what they called naturalism. Many of them, like Twain and Howells, began as newspaper reporters, which provided excellent training for any realist. Working for a big-city daily in the 1890's taught these naturalists much about the dark side of life. They believed that man was essentially an animal, a helpless creature, whose fate was determined by his environment. Their world was Darwin's world—mindless, without either mercy or justice. They wrote chiefly about the most primitive emotions—lust, hate, greed. In *Maggie, A Girl of the Streets* (1893) Stephen Crane described the seduction, degradation, and eventual suicide of a young girl, all set against the background of a sordid slum; in *The Red Badge of Courage* (1895) he captured the pain and humor of war. In *McTeague* (1899) Frank Norris told the story of a brutal, dull-witted dentist who murdered his greed-crazed wife with his bare fists. In *Main-Travelled Roads* (1891) Hamlin Garland pictured the cruel loneliness of farm life on the plains.

Such stuff was too strong for Howells, but he recognized its importance and befriended these younger writers in many ways. He found a publisher for *Maggie* after it had been rejected many times, and wrote appreciative reviews of the work of Garland and Norris. Even Theodore Dreiser, who was contemptuous of Howells' writings and considered him hopelessly middle-class in point of view, appreciated his aid and praised his influence on American literature. Dreiser's first novel, *Sister Carrie* (1900), treated sex so forthrightly that it was withdrawn after publication.

Henry James

Howells also knew and admired the other great novelist of the time, Henry James. Like Howells, James was very different in spirit and background from the tempestuous naturalists. Born to

PHILADELPHIA MUSEUM OF ART

Thomas Eakins' interest in science nearly equaled his interest in art. In the early 1880's he collaborated with the photographer Eadweard Muybridge in serial-action photographic experiments and later devised a special camera for his anatomical studies; one of his pictures is reproduced at left. The impact of these studies can be seen in The Swimming Hole *(right), painted by Eakins in 1883. He was then director of the Pennsylvania Academy's art school*

wealth, reared in a cosmopolitan atmosphere, twisted in some strange way while still a child and thus unable to achieve satisfactory relationships with women, James spent most of his mature life in Europe, writing novels, short stories, plays, and volumes of criticism. Although far-removed from the world of practical affairs, he was pre-eminently a realist, determined, as he once said to Robert Louis Stevenson, "to leave a multitude of pictures of my time" for the future to contemplate. He admired the European realists greatly and denounced the "floods of tepid soap and water which under the name of novels are being vomited forth" by the romancers. "All life belongs to you," he told his fellow novelists. "There is no impression of life, no manner of seeing it and feeling it, to which the plan of the novelist may not offer a place."

Although he rejected the New World in favor of the Old and lived in the narrow, cultivated surroundings of London high society, James yearned for the recognition of his countrymen almost as avidly as Mark Twain. However, he was incapable of modifying his rarefied, overly subtle manner of writing. Most of the serious writers of the time admired his books and he received many honors, but he never achieved widespread popularity. His major theme was the clash of American and European cultures, his primary interest the close-up examination of wealthy, sensitive, yet often corrupt persons in a cultivated but far from polite society. He dealt with social issues, such as feminism and the difficulties faced by artists in the modern world, but always subordinated these to his interest in his subjects as individuals. *The American* (1877) told the story of the love of a wealthy American in Paris for a French noblewoman who rejected him because her family disapproved of his "commercial" background. *The Portrait of a Lady* (1881) described the disillusionment of an intelligent girl married to a charming but morally bankrupt man and her eventual decision to remain with him nonetheless. *The Bostonians* (1886) was a complicated and psychologically sensitive study of the varieties of female behavior in a seemingly uniform social situation.

James's reputation, far greater today than in his own lifetime, rests more on his highly refined accounts of the interactions of individuals and their environment and his masterful commentaries on the novel as a literary form than on

FORT WORTH ART ASSOCIATION

his ability as a storyteller. Few major writers have been more long-winded, more prone to circumlocution. Yet few have been so dedicated to their art, possessed of such psychological penetration, or so uniformly successful in producing a large body of serious work.

Realism in Art

American painters responded to the times much the way writers did, but with this difference: despite the new concern for realism, the romantic tradition retained its vitality. Pre-eminent among the realists was Thomas Eakins, who was born in Philadelphia in 1844. Eakins studied in Europe in the late sixties and was much influenced by the great realists of the 17th century, Velásquez and Rembrandt. Returning to America in 1870, he passed the remainder of his life teaching and painting in Philadelphia.

The scientific spirit of the age suited Eakins perfectly. He mastered human anatomy; some of his finest paintings, such as *The Gross Clinic* (1875), are graphic illustrations of surgical operations. He was also an early experimenter with motion pictures, seeking to capture exactly the attitudes of human beings and animals in action. Like his friend Walt Whitman, whose portrait is one of his finest achievements, Eakins gloried in the ordinary, but he had none of Whitman's weakness for sham and self-delusion. His portraits are monuments to his integrity as well as to his craftsmanship: never would he touch up or soften a likeness to please his sitter. When the Union League of Philadelphia commissioned a canvas of Rutherford B. Hayes, Eakins showed the President working in his shirt sleeves, which scandalized the club fathers. His work was no mere mirror reflecting surface values. His study of six men bathing (*The Swimming Hole*) is a stark portrayal of nakedness, his surgical scenes catch the tenseness of the situation without descending into sensationalism. His object, as he once said, was "to peer deeper into the heart of American life," and in this he succeeded.

Realism was also characteristic of the work of Eakins' contemporary Winslow Homer, a Boston-born painter best known for his brilliant water colors. Homer was trained as a lithographer and was one of the world's great masters of the water-color medium, but he had almost no formal training. Indeed, he had contempt for academicians and refused to go abroad to study.

HAROLD T. PULSIFER COLLECTION, COLBY COLLEGE

Between the Civil War and the 1880's, when he turned to the sea for artistic inspiration, much of Winslow Homer's work dealt with the New England scene. He painted The Berry Pickers *in 1873.*

Aesthetics did not seem to concern him at all; he liked to shock people by referring to his profession as "the picture line." His concern for accuracy was so intense that as preparation for painting *The Life Line* (1884) he made a trip to Atlantic City to observe the handling of a breeches buoy. "When I have selected [a subject]," he said, "I paint it exactly as it appears."

During the Civil War, Homer worked as an artist-reporter for *Harper's Weekly*, and he continued to do magazine illustrations for some years thereafter. He roamed widely in America, painting scenes of southern farm life, Adirondack campers, and after about 1880, magnificent seascapes and studies of fishermen and sailors. For years he made his home in a cottage at Prout's Neck, in Maine, although he also traveled extensively in the Caribbean region, where some of his finest water colors were executed.

In some ways Homer resembled the local colorists of American literature, and like many of the members of that group there are romantic elements in his work. His *Gulf Stream* (1899), showing a Negro sailor on a small broken boat menaced by an approaching waterspout and a school of sharks, and his *Fox Hunt* (1893), in which huge, ominous crows hover over a fox at bay, express his interest in the violence and drama of raw nature, a distinctly romantic theme. However, his approach, even in these works, was utterly prosaic, although not unimaginative. When some silly women complained about the fate of the poor sailor in *Gulf Stream*, Homer wrote his dealer sarcastically: "Tell these ladies that the unfortunate Negro . . . will be rescued and returned to his friends and home, and live happily ever after."

The outstanding romantic painter of the period was Albert Pinkham Ryder, a strange, neurotic genius haunted by the mystery and poetry of the sea. Ryder was born in New Bedford, Massachusetts, in 1847, during that city's heyday as a whaling port, but spent most of his mature years in New York City, living and working in a dirty, cluttered attic studio. He typified the solitary romantic—brooding, eccentric, otherworldly, mystical. His heavily glazed paintings of dark seas and small boats "bathed in an atmosphere of golden luminosity" beneath a pale moon, and weird canvases like *The Race Track* (*Death on a Pale Horse*), which shows a specter carrying a scythe riding on an empty track under an ominous sky, radiate a strange magic. Yet they are also masterpieces of design.

The careers of Eakins, Homer, and Ryder show that the late-19th-century American environment was not uncongenial to first-rate artists. Nevertheless, at least two major American painters abandoned native shores for Europe. One was James A. McNeill Whistler, whose portrait of his mother, which he called *Arrangement in Grey and Black,* is probably the most famous canvas ever painted by an American. Whistler left the United States in 1855 when he was 21 and spent most of his life in Paris and London. "I shall come to America," he announced grandly, "when the duty on works of art is abolished!" Whistler made a profession of eccentricity, but he was also a remarkably talented and versatile artist. Some of his portraits are triumphs of realism, while his misty studies of the London waterfront, which the critic John Ruskin characterized as pots of paint flung in the face of the beholder, but which Whistler conceived of as visual expressions of poetry, are thoroughly romantic in conception. Paintings like "Whistler's Mother" represent still another expression of his talent. Such pictures, spare and muted in tone, are more interesting as precise arrangements of color and space than as images of particular objects; they have had a tremendous influence on the course of modern art.

The second important expatriate artist was Mary Cassatt, daughter of a wealthy Pittsburgh banker and sister of Alexander J. Cassatt, president of the Pennsylvania Railroad around the turn of the century. She went to Paris originally as a tourist and dabbled in art like many conventional young socialites, but she was caught up in the impressionist movement and decided to become a serious painter. She settled permanently in Paris in 1874. Her work is more French than American and was little appreciated in the United States before the First World War. Once, when she came back to America for a visit, the Philadelphia *Public Ledger* reported: "Mary Cassatt, sister of Mr. Cassatt, president of the Pennsylvania Railroad, returned from Europe yesterday. She has been studying painting in Paris, and owns the smallest Pekinese dog in the world."

If Mary Cassatt was unappreciated and if Whistler had some reasons for considering his fellow countrymen uncultured, it remains true that interest in art was considerable in America. Museums and art schools flourished; settlement-house workers put on exhibitions that attracted large and enthusiastic crowds of workingmen; wealthy patrons gave countless commissions to portrait painters, the most fashionable of whom, a fine craftsman if not a great artist, was John Singer Sargent. Many men of wealth poured fortunes into collecting, and if some were interested only in vain display and others had execrable taste, some were discriminating collectors. Martin A. Ryerson, with a fortune made in lumber, bought the works of the French impressionists when few Americans understood their importance. Charles L. Freer of the American Car and Foundry Company was a friend and admirer of Whistler and a specialist in oriental art. John G. Johnson, a successful corporation lawyer, covered the walls of his Philadelphia mansion with

Of the French impressionists, Mary Cassatt was most influenced by Manet and Degas. She did this gentle study of motherhood, La Toilette, *in Paris in 1891.*

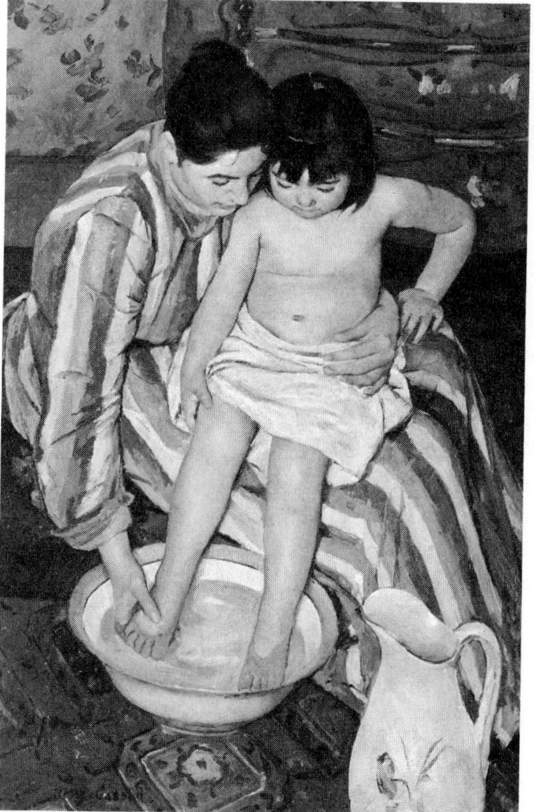

ART INSTITUTE OF CHICAGO

a carefully chosen collection of Italian primitives, accumulated before anyone appreciated them. "You could not even go into a bathroom without making five or six masterpieces rattle back and forth," one of Johnson's guests noted.

Other rich men, most notably the great J.P. Morgan, employed experts to help them put together their collections. Nor were the advanced painters of the day rejected by all wealthy patrons. It is true that only a handful of his contemporaries recognized the talent of the weird, avant-garde Ryder. But while Eakins' work was undervalued, he received many important commissions. Some of Homer's canvases commanded thousands of dollars, and so did those of the radical Whistler.

The Pragmatic Approach

It would have been remarkable indeed if the intellectual ferment of the late 19th century had not affected men's ideas about the meaning of life, the truth of revealed religion, moral values, and similar fundamental problems. In particular, the theory of evolution, so important in altering contemporary views of science, history, and social relations, produced significant changes in American thinking about religious and philosophical questions.

Evolution posed an immediate challenge to religion: if Darwin was correct, the Biblical account of the creation was obviously untrue, and the idea that man had been formed in God's image was highly unlikely at best. A bitter controversy erupted, described by president Andrew D. White of Cornell in *The Warfare of Science with Theology in Christendom* (1896). Although millions of the faithful continued to believe in the literal truth of the Bible, among intellectuals, lay and clerical, victory went to the evolutionists, because in addition to the arguments of the geologists and the biologists, scholars were throwing light on the historical origins of the Bible, showing it to be of human rather than divine inspiration. Philip Schaff's 25-volume summary of this research, *A Commentary on the Holy Scriptures* (1865–1880), was of great importance in resolving the dispute. However, evolution did not permanently undermine the faith of any large percentage of the population. If the account of the creation in Genesis could not be taken literally, the Bible remained a great depository of wisdom and inspiration. Soon books like John Fiske's *The Outlines of Cosmic Philosophy* (1874) were providing religious persons with the comforting thesis that evolution, while true, was merely God's way of ordering the universe. Man's body might have evolved from lower forms, but his soul was nonetheless divine, they concluded.

The effects of Darwinism on philosophy were less dramatic but in the end far more significant. Fixed systems and eternal verities were difficult to justify in a world that was constantly evolving. By the early 1870's a few philosophers had begun to reason that ideas and theories mattered little except when applied to specifics. "Nothing justifies the development of abstract principles but their utility in enlarging our concrete knowledge of nature," wrote Chauncey Wright, secretary of the American Academy of Arts and Sciences. In "How to Make Our Ideas Clear" (1878), Wright's friend Charles S. Peirce, an amazingly versatile and talented albeit obscure thinker, argued that concepts could be fairly understood only in terms of their practical effects. Once the mind accepted the truth of evolution, Peirce also believed, logic required that it accept the impermanence even of scientific laws. There was, he wrote, "an element of indeterminacy, spontaneity, or absolute chance in nature."

This startling philosophy, which Peirce called pragmatism, was presented in language understandable to the intelligent layman by William James, brother of the novelist. James was one of the most remarkable men of his generation. Educated in London, Paris, Bonn, and Geneva as well as at Harvard, he studied painting, participated in a zoological expedition to South America, took a medical degree, and was a professor at Harvard successively of comparative anatomy, psychology, and finally philosophy. His *Principles of Psychology* (1890) may be said to have established that discipline as a modern science; an abridged version was for years the leading college textbook in the field. His widely read *Varieties of Religious Experience* (1902), which treated the subject from both psychological and

BROWN BROTHERS

Psychologist and philosopher William James explored the Amazon with zoologist Louis Agassiz before embarking on his notable 35-year career at Harvard.

philosophical points of view, helped thousands of readers to reconcile their religious faith with their increasing knowledge of man and the physical universe.

Although less rigorous a logician than Peirce, who was his friend, James's wide range and his verve and imagination as a writer made him by far the most influential philosopher of his times. He rejected wholly the deterministic interpretation of Darwinism and all other one-idea explanations of existence. Belief in free will was one of his axioms; environment might influence survival, but so did the *desire* to survive, which existed independently of surrounding circumstances. Truth was relative; it did not exist in the abstract; it *happened* under particular circumstances. What a man thought helped make what he thought occur, or come true. The mind, James wrote in a typically vivid phrase, has "a vote" in determining truth. "It is in the game, and not a mere looker-on." Religion was true, for example, because men were religious. "The ultimate test for us of what a truth means," James said in an important lecture at the University of California in 1898, "is . . . the conduct it dictates or inspires."

The pragmatic approach inspired much of the reform spirit of the late 19th century and even more of that of the early 20th. James's hammer blows shattered the Social Darwinism of Spencer and Sumner. In "Great Men and Their Environment" (1880) he argued that social changes were brought about by the actions of men of genius whom society had selected and raised to positions of power, rather than by the impersonal force of the environment. Such reasoning fitted the preconceptions of the individualists and encouraged those dissatisfied with society to work for change. Educational reformers like John Dewey, the institutionalist school of economists, settlement-house workers, and other reformers accepted pragmatism eagerly. Thus, James's philosophy appealed to both the individualism and the community spirit of Americans. It did much to revive the buoyant optimism that had characterized the pre-Civil War reform movement.

Yet pragmatism also brought Americans face to face with many somber problems. While relativism made men optimistic, it also bred insecurity, for there could be no certainty, no comforting reliance on any eternal value in the absence of absolute truth. Pragmatism also seemed to suggest that the end justified the means, that what worked was more important than what ought to be. At the time of James's death in 1910, the *Commercial and Financial Chronicle* pointed out that the pragmatic philosophy was very helpful to businessmen in making decisions. By emphasizing practice at the expense of theory, the new philosophy also encouraged materialism, anti-intellectualism, and other unlovely aspects of the American character. And what place had conventional morality in such a system? Perhaps pragmatism placed too much reliance on the free will of human beings, ignoring their capacity for selfishness and self-delusion.

In any case, the men of the new century found pragmatism a heady wine. They would quaff it freely and enthusiastically—down to the bitter dregs.

SUPPLEMENTARY READING All the surveys of American intellectual history deal extensively with this period. See, for example, Merle Curti, *The Growth of American Thought* (1943), Louis Hartz, *The Liberal Tradition in America** (1955), and Clinton Rossiter, *Conservatism in America: The Thankless Persuasion** (1962). H.S. Commager, *The American Mind** (1950), and A.M. Schlesinger, *The Rise of the City* (1933), contain much interesting information, and there are useful essays on some aspects of the subject in H.W. Morgan (ed.), *The Gilded Age: A Reappraisal** (1970). Ray Ginger, *The Age of Excess** (1965), is also stimulating.

E.P. Cubberley, *Public Education in the United States* (1934), provides a general introduction to the subject, but L.A. Cremin, *The Transformation of the School: Progressivism in American Education* (1961), is much more penetrating. On education in the South, see C.W. Dabney, *Universal Education in the South* (1936). For the work of Dewey, consult Sidney Hook, *John Dewey* (1939). The best treatment of the Chautauqua movement is Victoria and R.O. Case, *We Called It Culture* (1948). Trends in the history of journalism are discussed in J.M. Lee, *History of American Journalism* (1923), B.A. Weisberger, *The American Newspaperman* (1961), and F.L. Mott, *A History of American Magazines* (1938–1957). George Juergens, *Joseph Pulitzer and the New York World* (1966), W.A. Swanberg, *Citizen Hearst** (1961), and Peter Lyon, *Success Story: The Life and Times of S.S. McClure* (1963), are useful biographies.

On higher education, see L.R. Veysey, *The Emergence of the American University* (1965), and Richard Hofstadter and W.P. Metzger, *The Development of Academic Freedom in the United States** (1955). Of the many histories of particular universities, S.E. Morison, *Three Centuries of Harvard* (1936), and Hugh Hawkins, *Pioneer: A History of the Johns Hopkins University* (1960), are particularly important for this period. E.D. Ross, *Democracy's College* (1942), deals with the land-grant institutions. Henry James, *Charles W. Eliot* (1930), G.S. Hall, *The Life and Confessions of a Psychologist* (1923), and Allan Nevins, *John D. Rockefeller: The Heroic Age of American Enterprise* (1940), also contain valuable information. Thorstein Veblen, *The Higher Learning in America** (1918), is full of stimulating opinions.

For developments in American science, see the excellent essay by P.F. Boller, Jr., in H.W. Morgan (ed.), *The Gilded Age** (1970), and also Bernard Jaffe, *Men of Science in America* (1944). Muriel Rukeyser, *Willard Gibbs** (1942), is a good biography. A good general introduction to the work of the social scientists is Sidney Fine, *Laissez Faire and the General-Welfare State** (1957), but H.S. Commager's above-mentioned *American Mind* is also useful, as is Richard Hofstadter, *Social Darwinism in American Thought** (1944). Biographies of prominent figures include P.G. Rader, *The Academic Mind and Reform: The Inflence of Richard T. Ely in American Life* (1967), H.W. Bragdon, *Woodrow Wilson: The Academic Years* (1967), Samuel Chugerman, *Lester F. Ward: The American Aristotle* (1939), Carl Resek, *Lewis Henry Morgan* (1960), M. DeW. Howe, *Justice Oliver Wendell Holmes: The Proving Years* (1963), and W.H. Jordy, *Henry Adams: Scientific Historian** (1952).

The great literary figures of the age are discussed in Everett Carter, *Howells and the Age of Realism* (1954), Alfred Kazin, *On Native Grounds** (1942), Larzer Ziff, *The American 1890s** (1966), and Van Wyck Brooks, *New England: Indian Summer, 1865–1915** (1940) and *The Confident Years: 1885–1915* (1952). See also, on Twain, Bernard De Voto, *Mark Twain's America** (1932), and Justin Kaplan, *Mr. Clemens and Mark Twain** (1966); on Howells, E.H. Cady, *The Realist at War* (1958); on James, Leon Edel, *Henry James** (1953–1962).

American painting is discussed in O.W. Larkin, *Art and Life in America* (1949). Biographies of leading artists include Lloyd Goodrich, *Thomas Eakins* (1933) and *Winslow Homer* (1944), F.N. Price, *Ryder* (1932), and E.R. and Joseph Pennell, *The Life of James McNeill Whistler* (1911).

On pragmatism, see Hofstadter's *Social Darwinism,* Commager's *American Mind,* and R.B. Perry, *The Thought and Character of William James** (1935).

*Available in paperback.

21

National Politics: 1877–1896

Modern students generally conclude that the political history of the United States in the last quarter of the 19th century was singularly divorced from what now seem the meaningful issues of that day. Most political discussions revolved around essentially trivial matters. On the rare occasions when important, supposedly controversial measures such as the Sherman Antitrust Act, the Interstate Commerce Act, the Pendleton Civil Service Act, and the Dawes Severalty Act were debated, they excited far less argument than they merited.

A graduated income tax, the greatest instrument for orderly economic and social change that a democratic society has devised, was enacted during the Civil War, repealed after that conflict, re-enacted in 1894 as part of the maneuvering over tariff reform, and then declared unconstitutional in 1895 without, in most instances, causing more than a ripple in the world of partisan politics. Proponents of the tax argued only that it offered a fairer way of distributing the costs of government, its foes that it penalized efficiency and encouraged governmental extravagance. Almost no one saw it as a means of redistributing wealth. This was typical. As the English observer James Bryce noted in the late eighties, the politicians were "clinging too long to outworn issues" and "neglecting to discover and work out new principles capable of solving the problems which now perplex the country." Congress, wrote another critic, "does not solve the problems, the solution of which is demanded by the life of the nation."

Yet the public remained intensely interested in politics. Vast sums were spent on political propaganda; huge crowds turned out to hear vapid orators mouth hackneyed slogans and meaningless generalities. Most elections were closely contested and millions of voters turned out enthusiastically to choose, essentially, between Tweedledum and Tweedledee.

The American Commonwealth

A succession of weak Presidents presided over the White House. Although the impeachment proceedings against Andrew Johnson had failed, the executive branch seemed cowed by the attack and Congress dominated the

Joseph Keppler's 1890 Puck *cartoon, "None but millionaires need apply: the coming style of Presidential election," comments acidly on the low status of the Presidency. The tag on the Chief Executive's chair refers to the Cabinet. As the examples in this chapter indicate, the late 19th century was a heyday for political cartoonists.*

government. "There has not been a single presidential candidate since Abraham Lincoln," Bryce wrote in 1888, "of whom his friends could say that he had done anything to command the gratitude of the nation."

Within Congress, the Senate generally overshadowed the House of Representatives. Indeed, in his novel *Democracy* (1880), the cynical Henry Adams wrote that the United States had a "government of the people, by the people, for the benefit of Senators." Critics called the Senate a "rich man's club," and it did contain many millionaires, such as Leland Stanford, founder of the Central Pacific Railroad, James G. "Bonanza" Fair of Nevada, who extracted a fortune of $30 million from the Comstock Lode, Philetus Sawyer, a self-made Wisconsin lumberman, and Nelson Aldrich of Rhode Island, whose wealth derived from banking and a host of corporate connections. However, the true sources of the Senate's influence lay in the long tenure of many of its members, which enabled them to master the craft of politics, in the fact that it was small enough to encourage real debate, and in its long-established reputation for wisdom, intelligence, and statesmanship. The antics of some senators put a severe strain on its prestige, but it still attracted, as Bryce said, "the best ability of the country that has flowed into political life."

The House of Representatives, on the other hand, was one of the most disorderly and inefficient legislative bodies in the world. "As I make my notes," a reporter wrote in 1882 while sitting in the House gallery, "I see a dozen men reading newspapers with their feet on their desks. . . . 'Pig-Iron' Kelley of Pennsylvania has dropped his newspaper and is paring his fingernails. . . . The vile odor of . . . tobacco . . . rises from the two-for-five-cents cigars in the mouths of the so-called gentlemen below. . . . They chew, too! Every desk has a spittoon of pink and gold china beside it to catch the filth from the statesman's mouth."

More serious was the infernal din that rose from the crowded chamber. Desks slammed, members held private conversations, hailed pages, shuffled from place to place, clamored for the attention of the Speaker, and all the while some poor orator tried to discuss the question of the moment. Speaking in the House, one writer said, was like trying to address the crowd on a passing Broadway bus from the curb in front of the Astor House in New York. On one occasion, in 1878, the adjournment of the House was held up for more than 12 hours because most of the members of an important committee—and their clerks—were too drunk to prepare a vital appropriations bill for final passage. President Hayes, who, along with his entire Cabinet, was kept cooling his heels in the President's Room at the Capitol, was naturally furious. "*It should be investigated*," he wrote in his diary.

The great political parties professed undying enmity to each other, but seldom took clearly opposing positions on the questions of the day. Democrats were separated from Republicans more by accidents of geography, religious affiliation, ethnic background, and emotion than by economic issues. Questions of state and local importance, unrelated to national politics, often determined congressional elections, and thus who controlled the federal government. The fundamental division between Democrats and Republicans was sectional, resulting from the Civil War. The South, after the political rights of Negroes had been drastically circumscribed, became heavily Democratic. Most of New England was solidly Republican. Elsewhere the two parties stood in fair balance, although the Republicans tended to have the advantage. A preponderance of the well-to-do, cultured northerners was Republican. "If you find yourself dining with one of 'the best people,'" Bryce noticed, "in any New England city, or in Philadelphia, or in Cincinnati, Cleveland, Chicago, or Minneapolis, you assume that the guest sitting next [to] you is a Republican." Perhaps in reaction to this concentration, immigrants, Catholics, and—except for the Negroes—other minority groups tended to vote Democratic. But there were so many exceptions that these generalizations are of little practical importance. German and Scandinavian immigrants usually voted Republican. Many powerful business leaders supported the Democrats. During the 1888 campaign the vice chairman of the Republican National Committee believed that "the influence and money of the great corporation interest, such as the Vanderbilts and Goulds and the North[ern] Pacific," was being exerted in behalf of the Democrats.

The personalities of political leaders often dictated the voting patterns of individuals and groups. In 1884 J.P. Morgan voted Democratic because he admired Grover Cleveland, while Irish-Americans, traditionally Democrats, cast thousands of ballots for Republican James G. Blaine. In 1892, when Cleveland defeated Benjamin Harrison, a prominent steel manufacturer wrote to Andrew Carnegie: "I am very sorry for President Harrison, but I cannot see that our interests are going to be affected one way or the other." And Carnegie replied: "We have nothing to fear. . . . Cleveland is [a] pretty good fellow. Off for Venice tomorrow." The bulk of the people—farmers, laboring men, shopkeepers, white-collar workers—distributed their ballots fairly evenly between the two parties in most elections; the balance of political power after 1876 was almost perfect—"the most spectacular degree of equilibrium in American history." Between 1856 and 1912 the Democrats elected a President only twice (1884 and 1892), but most of the contests were extremely close. Majorities in both the Senate and the House fluctuated continually. Between 1876 and 1896, the "dominant" Republican party controlled both houses of Congress and the Presidency at the same time for only one two-year period.

Issues of the "Gilded Age"

Four questions obsessed the politicians in these years. One was the "bloody shirt," which historian Paul H. Buck has called "possibly the greatest weapon any American party ever possessed." The term, which became part of the language after a Massachusetts congressman had dramatically displayed to his colleagues in the House the bloodstained shirt of an Ohio carpetbagger who had been flogged by terrorists in Mississippi, referred to the tactic of reminding the electorate of the northern states that the men who had taken the South out of the Union and precipitated the Civil War had been Democrats, and that they and their descendants were still Democrats. Should their party regain power, former rebels would run the government and undo all the work accomplished at such sacrifice during the war. "Every man that endeavored to tear down the old flag," a Republican orator proclaimed in 1876, "was a Democrat. Every man that tried to destroy this nation was a Democrat. . . . The man that assassinated Abraham Lincoln was a Democrat. . . . Soldiers, every scar you have on your heroic bodies was given you by a Democrat." Naturally, every scoundrel or incompetent who sought office under the Republican banner waved the bloody shirt in order to divert the attention of northern voters from his own shortcomings, but the technique worked so well that many decent candidates could not resist the temptation to employ it in close races. Nothing, of course, so effectively obscured the real issues of the day.

Waving the bloody shirt was related intimately to the issue of Negro rights. Throughout this period, the Republicans vacillated between trying to build up their organization in the South by appealing to Negro voters—which incidentally required them to make sure that Negroes in the South could vote—and trying to win conservative white support by stressing economic issues, such as the tariff. When the former strategy seemed wise, they waved the bloody shirt with vigor; in the latter case they piously announced that the Negro's future was "as safe in the hands of one party as it is in the other."

The question of veterans' pensions also bore a close relationship to the bloody shirt. After the Civil War, Union soldiers formed the Grand Army of the Republic, and by 1890 the organization had a membership of 409,000. Beginning in the 1880's, the GAR put immense pressure on Congress, first for aid to veterans with service-connected disabilities, then for those with *any* disability, and eventually for all former Union soldiers. Republican politicians played upon the emotions of the ex-soldiers by waving the bloody shirt, but the tough-minded leaders of the GAR demanded they prove their sincerity by treating in openhanded fashion the warriors whose blood had stained the shirt.

The tariff was another perennial issue in post-Civil War politics. Despite much loose talk about free trade, almost no one in the United States except for a handful of professional economists, most of them college professors, actually believed in eliminating duties on imports. Manufacturers naturally desired protective tariffs, and a majority of their workers were convinced that wage levels would fall sharply if goods produced by cheap foreign labor entered the United States untaxed. Even many farmers supported protection. Congressman William McKinley of Ohio, who reputedly could make a tariff schedule sound like poetry, stated the majority opinion in the clearest terms: high tariffs foster the growth of industry and thus create jobs for workingmen. "Reduce the tariff and labor is the first to suffer," he said. Whatever college professors may say about the virtues of free trade and international competition, "the school of experience" teaches that protection is necessary if America is to prosper. "The 'markets of the world' in our present condition are a snare and a delusion. We will reach them whenever we can undersell competing nations, and no sooner."

Voters found such logic irrefutable. Duties had been raised during the Civil War to an average of about 50 per cent ad valorem. Some slight reductions were made in the seventies and eighties, but in 1890 the McKinley tariff restored these cuts. This law even granted protection to a nonexistent industry, the manufacture of tin plate, and to such agricultural products as eggs and potatoes, which would not have been imported even under free trade. When the legislators decided to remove the duty on raw sugar in order to get rid of an embarrassing revenue surplus, they compensated domestic sugar raisers by awarding them a bounty of two cents a pound on their product.

The tariff could have been a real political issue despite the general belief in protection, for American technology was advancing so rapidly that many industries no longer required protection against foreign competitors. A powerful argument could have been made also for scientific rate-making that would adjust duties to actual conditions and avoid overprotection. The Democrats professed to believe in moderation, but whenever party leaders tried to revise the tariff downward, Democratic congressmen from industrial states like Pennsylvania and New York deserted them and sided with the Republicans. Many Republicans also endorsed tariff reform in principle, but when particular schedules came up for discussion, most of them demanded the highest possible rates for industries in their own districts and traded votes shamelessly with colleagues representing other interests in order to get what they wanted. Every new tariff bill became an occasion for logrolling, lobbying, and outrageous politicking rather than for sane discussion and careful evaluation of the true public interest.

A third political question in this period was currency reform. During the Civil War, it will be recalled, the government, faced with obligations it could not meet by taxing or borrowing, suspended specie payments and issued about $450 million in paper money. These "greenbacks" did not command the full confidence of a people accustomed to money readily convertible into gold or silver. Greenbacks seemed to threaten inflation, for how could one trust the government not to issue them in wholesale lots to avoid passing unpopular tax laws? The experience of the Confederacy, where printing-press money had been issued in such amounts that the Confederate dollar became worthless, stood as a horrible example of this danger. Thus, when the war ended, a strong sentiment developed for withdrawing the greenbacks from circulation and getting back to a bullion standard. "By a law resting on the concurring judgment . . . of mankind in all ages and countries, the precious metals have been the measure of value," one politician wrote in 1878. "That law can no more be repealed by act of Congress than the law of gravitation."

On the other hand, the nation's burgeoning population and the rapid expansion of every kind of economic activity increased the need for currency. In actual fact, prices declined sharply after Appomattox. According to the Bureau of Labor Statistics, the wholesale price index fell from 132 in 1865 to 46.5 in 1896. This deflation increased the real income of bondholders and other creditors but injured debtors. Farmers were particularly hard hit, for many of them had borrowed heavily during the wartime boom to finance expansion.

Here was a question of real significance. Many groups supported some kind of currency inflation. A National Greenback party nominated Peter Cooper, an iron manufacturer, for President in 1876. Although Cooper received only 81,000 votes, a new Greenback Labor party polled over a million in 1878, electing 14 congressmen. However, the major parties refused to confront each other over the currency question. While Republicans professed to be the party of sound money, most western Republicans favored expansion of the currency. And while one wing of the Democrats flirted with the Greenbackers, the conservative, or "Bourbon," Democrats were as strongly in favor of deflation as any of the Republicans.

In 1874 a bill to increase the supply of greenbacks was defeated in a Republican-dominated Congress only by the veto of President Grant. The next year Congress voted to resume specie payments, but in order to avoid a party split on the question, the Republicans agreed to allow $300 million in greenbacks to remain in circulation and to postpone actual resumption of specie payments until 1879. Spurred on by the silver miners as well as by those advocating any measure that would increase the volume of money in circulation, various congressmen introduced proposals to coin large amounts of silver. Neither party took a clear-cut stand on silver, however. Indeed, in debating the money question, the politicians seemed unable to rise above "rusty dogmas, piecemeal expedients, idealistic cure-all nostrums and political jockeying." Although under various administrations steps were taken to increase or decrease the amount of money in circulation, the net effect on the economy was not significant. Few politicians before 1890 considered treating fiscal policy as a device for influencing economic development. The effect of all the controversy was thus, in the words of economist Joseph Schumpeter, "so light as to justify exclusion from the general analysis of the determining factors of the economic process."

The final major political issue of these years was civil service reform. That the federal bureaucracy needed overhauling nearly everyone agreed. As American society grew larger and more complex in an industrial age, the government necessarily took on more functions. The need for professional administration increased. The number of federal employees rose from 53,000 in 1871 to 256,000 at the end of the century. Corruption flourished; waste and inefficiency were the normal state of affairs. The collection of tariff duties offered perhaps the greatest opportunity for venality. The New York Custom House, one observer wrote in 1872, teemed with "corrupting merchants and their clerks and runners, who think that all men can be bought, and . . . corrupt swarms [of clerks], who shamelessly seek their price."

With a succession of relatively weak Presidents and a Congress that squandered its energies on private bills, pork-barrel projects, and other trivia, the whole administration of the government was monumentally ineffective. The land laws, for example, became extremely complicated, yet the General Land Office, according to Leonard D. White, provided a "dismal example of administrative confusion, laxness, and frustration." Since only a handful of ill-paid clerks had any grasp of procedures and precedents, "claims and contests over land ownership multiplied." "The federal system from Grant through McKinley was generally undistinguished," Professor White concluded after an exhaustive study of the period. "Nobody, whether in Congress or in the executive departments, seemed able to rise much above the handicraft office methods that were cumbersome even in the simpler days of the Jacksonians."

Every honest observer could see the need for reform, but the politicians refused to surrender the power of dispensing government jobs to their henchmen without regard for their qualifications. They argued that patronage was the lifeblood of politics, that parties could not function without armies of loyal political workers, and that these men expected and deserved the rewards of office when their efforts were crowned with victory at the polls. Typical was the attitude of the New York assemblyman who, according to Theodore Roosevelt, had "the same idea about Public Life and the Civil Service that a vulture has of a dead sheep." When reformers, most of them eminently respectable and conservative men, suggested establishing even the most modest kind of professional, nonpartisan civil service, politicians of both parties subjected them to every kind of insult and ridicule, although both the Democratic and Republican parties regularly wrote civil service reform planks into their platforms.

Political Strategy and Tactics

The major American parties have nearly always avoided clear-cut stands on controversial questions in order to appeal to as wide a segment of the electorate as possible, but in the last quarter of the 19th century their equivocations assumed abnormal proportions. This was due in part to the precarious balance of power between them: neither dared declare itself too clearly on any question lest by so doing it drive away more voters than it attracted. But the rapid pace of social and economic change in those years also militated against political decisiveness. No one in or out of politics had as yet devised effective solutions for many current problems. When, for example, the party leaders tried to deal with the money question, they discovered that the bankers and the professional economists were as confused as the public at large. "We dabble in theories of our own and clutch convulsively at the doctrines of others," a Philadelphia banker confessed. "From the vast tract of mire by which the subject is surrounded, overlaid, and besmeared, it is almost impossible to arrive at anything like a fair estimate of its real nature." How could mere politicians act rationally or consistently under such circumstances?

The parties stumbled so badly when they confronted the tariff problem because tariffs in a complex industrial economy are not susceptible to solution by counting noses. As modern experience has shown, they are better determined by the executive branch, once broad policies have been laid down by Congress. But in the 19th century specialists had not yet arrived at this conclusion. Reformers could thunder self-righteously against the spoils system, but how could political parties exist without it? They could denounce laissez faire, but who had devised instruments for social and economic control that could be centrally administered with intelligence and efficiency? The embryonic social sciences had not devised the techniques, or even collected the statistical information necessary for efficient social management.

If the politicians steered clear of the "real" issues, they did so as much out of a healthy respect for their own ignorance as out of any desire to avoid controversy. Unable to provide answers to the meaningful questions, they had to turn to other, simpler issues that they and their constituents could understand, merely in order to provide the political system with a semblance of purposefulness, while society, blindly but steadily, accumulated the experience and skills required for dealing with the results of the industrial revolution.

With the Democrats invincible in the South and the Republicans predominant in New England and most of the states beyond the Mississippi, the outcome of Presidential elections was usually determined in a handful of populous states: New York (together with its satellites, New Jersey and Connecticut), Ohio, Indiana, and Illinois. The fact that opinion in these states on important questions like the tariff and monetary policy was sharply divided goes far to explain why the parties hesitated to commit themselves on issues. In every Presidential election, Democrats and Republicans concentrated their heaviest guns on these states.

Campaigns were conducted in a carnival atmosphere, entertainment being substituted for serious debate. Large sums were spent on brass bands, barbecues, uniforms, and banners. Men of national reputation were imported to attract crowds, and spellbinders noted for their leather lungs—this was before the day of the loudspeaker—and their ability to rouse popular emotions were brought in by the dozens to address mass meetings. With so much depending upon so few, the level of political morality was abysmal. Mudslinging, character assassination, and plain lying were standard practice, bribery routine. Men from neighboring states were carried into key states by the trainload to vote on Election Day. Drifters and other dissolute citizens were paid in cash—or more often in free drinks—to vote the party ticket. The names of persons long dead were solemnly inscribed in voting registers, their suffrages exercised by impostors. Since both parties indulged in these tactics, their efforts were often self-canceling, but in some instances Presidents were made and unmade in this sordid fashion.

The Men in the White House

The leading statesman of the period showed as little interest in truly important contemporary questions as the party hacks who made up the rank and file of their organizations. Let us consider first the Presidents. None was evil or stupid; all, indeed, were honest and at least moderately intelligent and energetic. Yet none can be said to have presided over a successful administration or to have left much mark upon the history of the country.

Rutherford B. Hayes, President from 1877 to 1881, came to office with a distinguished record. Born in Delaware, Ohio, in 1822, he attended Kenyon College and the Harvard Law School before settling down to practice in Cincinnati. Although he had a wife and family to support, he volunteered for service within weeks after the first shell fell on Fort Sumter. "This [is] a just and necessary war," he wrote in his diary. "I would prefer to go into it if I knew I was to die . . . than to live through and after it without taking any part."

Hayes fought bravely, even recklessly, through nearly four years of war. He was wounded at South Mountain, on the eve of Antietam, and later served under Sheridan in the Shenandoah Valley campaign of 1864. Entering the army as a major, he emerged a major general. In 1864 he was elected to Congress; four years later he became governor of Ohio, serving three terms altogether. The Republicans nominated him for President in 1876 because of his reputation for honesty and moderation, and his election, made possible by the Compromise of 1877, seemed to presage an era of sectional harmony and political probity.

Hayes was a long-faced man with deep-set blue eyes, a large nose, a broad, smooth forehead, and a full beard. Outwardly he had a sunny disposition, inwardly, in his own words, he was sometimes "nervous to the point of disaster." Despite his geniality, he was utterly without political glamour. Always abstemious, as President he became a total abstainer and refused even to serve wine at state dinners. Politically temperate and cautious, he had never been a vigorous waver of the bloody shirt, although in the heat of a hard campaign he was not above urging others to stress the dangers of "rebel rule" should the Democrats win. He tended to play down the tariff issue whenever possible, favoring protection in principle but refusing to become a mere spokesman for local business interests. On the money question he was conservative. He cheerfully approved the resumption of gold payments in 1879 and vetoed bills to expand the currency by coining silver. He accounted himself a civil service reformer, appointing Carl Schurz, a leader of the movement, to his Cabinet. He opposed the collection of political contributions from federal officeholders and issued an order forbidding them "to take part in the management of political organizations, caucuses, conventions, or election campaigns."

As President, Hayes adopted the Whig approach; he saw himself more as a caretaker than a leader and felt that Congress should assume the main responsibility for settling national problems. According to a recent biographer, "he had no intention of . . . trying to be a President in the heroic mold," and another historian writes that he showed "no capacity for such large-minded leadership as might have tamed the political hordes and aroused the enthusiasm, or at least the interest, of the public." He hated having constantly to make decisions on controversial questions. As we have seen, he complained about the South's failure to treat the Negro decently after the withdrawal of federal troops, but he took no action. "White supremacy was more securely entrenched in the South when he left the White House than it had been when he entered it," a leading authority writes. Hayes fought harder for civil service reform but failed to achieve the "thorough, rapid and complete" change he had promised. In this, as in most other matters, he was content to "let the record show that he had made the requests."

In the eyes of his contemporaries his administration was a failure. Neither he nor they seriously considered him for a second term. "I am not liked as President," he confessed to his diary, and the Republican minority leader of the House admitted that the President was "almost without a friend" in Congress. As early as 1879 Hayes wrote: "I am heartily tired of this life of bondage, responsibility, and toil," and in 1881 he spoke of "the embarrassments, the heartbreaking sufferings . . . and a thousand other drawbacks" of his high office.

Hayes's successor, James A. Garfield, was cut down by an assassin's bullet only four months after his inauguration. Even in that short time, however, his ineffectiveness had been clearly demonstrated. Garfield grew up in poverty on an Ohio farm. He was only 29 when the Civil War broke out, but he helped organize a volunteer regiment and soon proved himself both a fine disciplinarian and an excellent battlefield commander despite his inexperience. He fought at Shiloh and later at Chickamauga, where he was General Rosecrans' chief of staff. He rose in two years from lieutenant colonel to major general. Then, in 1863, he won a seat in Congress, where his oratorical and managerial skills soon brought him to prominence in the affairs of the Republican party.

Garfield was a big, broad-shouldered man, balding, with sharp eyes, an aquiline nose, and a thick, full beard. Studious, industrious, with a wide-ranging, well-stocked mind, he was called by one friend "the ideal self-made man." His one great weakness was indecisiveness—what another of his admirers described as a "want of certainty" and a "deference for other men's opinions." As President Hayes put it, Garfield "could not face a frowning world. . . . His course at various times when trouble came betrayed weakness."

*In one of Keppler's more original—and outrageous—*Puck *cartoons, done for the 1880 campaign, "bride" Garfield is reminded of a shady past. "But it was such a little one!" the bride murmurs (Garfield's alleged link with Crédit Mobilier netted him but $329). GOP worthies Carl Schurz and Whitelaw Reid are the bridesmaids.*

Like many other ex-soldiers, including Hayes and even General Grant, Garfield did not really enjoy waving the bloody shirt, but when hard-pressed politically, as when his name was linked with the Crédit Mobilier railroad scandal, he would lash out hard at the South in an effort to distract the voters. Intellectually he was inclined toward low tariffs. "The scholarship of modern times," he said in 1870, "is . . . leading in the direction of what is called free trade." Nevertheless, he would not sacrifice the interests of Ohio manufacturers for a mere principle. "I shall not admit to a considerable reduction of a few leading articles in which my constituents are deeply interested when many others of a similar character are left untouched," he declared. Similarly, though eager to improve the efficiency of the government and resentful of the "intellectual dissipation" resulting from time wasted listening to the countless appeals of office seekers, he often wilted under pressure from the spoilsmen. "I believe in party government, and that the spirit and doctrines of the Republican party should prevail in the Executive departments," he assured a close associate at the time of his nomination. Only on fiscal policy did he take a firm stand: he opposed categorically all inflationary schemes.

Political patronage proved to be Garfield's undoing. The Republican party in 1880 was split into two factions, the "Stalwarts" and the "Half-Breeds." The Stalwarts, led by the New York politico Senator Roscoe Conkling, believed in the blatant pursuit of the spoils of office. They had only contempt for civil service reformers. The Half-Breeds did not really disagree but behaved more circumspectly, hoping to attract the support of independents. Actually, competition for office was the main reason for their rivalry.

Garfield had been a compromise choice at the 1880 Republican convention; his election precipitated a great battle over patronage, the new President standing in a sort of no man's land between the factions. "I am considering all day whether A or B shall be appointed to this or that office," he moaned. "Once or twice I felt like crying out in the agony of my soul against the greed for office and its consumption of my time." Soon he was complaining to his secretary of state: "My God! What is there in this place that a man should ever want to get into it?"

Garfield did stand up against the most grasping of the politicians, resisting particularly the demands of Senator Conkling. By backing the investigation of a post office scandal, and by appointing a Half-Breed collector of the Port of New York, he infuriated the Stalwarts. In July 1881 an unbalanced Stalwart lawyer named Charles J. Guiteau, who had been fruitlessly haunting Washington offices in search of a consulship or some other minor post, shot Garfield in the Washington railroad station. After lingering for weeks, the President died on September 19.

The assassination of Garfield elevated Chester A. Arthur to the Presidency. Arthur was born in Vermont in 1830. After graduating from Union College, he studied law and settled in New York City. An abolitionist, he became an early convert to the Republican party and rose rapidly in its local councils. In 1871 Grant gave him the juiciest political plum in the country, the collectorship of the Port of New York, which he held until removed by Hayes in 1878 for refusing to keep his hands out of party politics. The only elective position he ever held was the Vice Presidency. Before Garfield's death he had paid little attention to questions like the tariff and monetary policy, being content to collect annual fees ranging upward of $50,000 and oversee the operations of the New York customs office, with its hordes of clerks and laborers. (During Arthur's tenure, the novelist Herman Melville was employed as an "outdoor inspector" by the Custom House.) Of course Arthur was an unblushing defender of the spoils system, although it must be said in fairness that he was personally honest and an excellent administrator.

The tragic circumstances of his elevation to the Presidency sobered Arthur considerably. Although a genial, convivial man, perhaps overly fond of good food and flashy clothes, he comported himself with great dignity as President. He did not cut his ties with the Stalwart faction, but he handled patronage matters with restraint, continuing the investigation of the post office scandals over the objections of important Republican politicians who were involved in them, and he gave at least nominal support to the movement for civil service reform, which had been greatly strengthened by public indignation following the assassination of Garfield. In 1883 Congress passed the Pendleton Act, "classifying" about ten per cent of all government jobs and creating a bipartisan Civil Service Commission to prepare and administer competitive examinations for these positions. The law also made it illegal to force officeholders to make political contributions and empowered the President to expand the list of classified positions at his discretion.

Although many politicians resented the new system bitterly—one senator denounced it as "un-American"—the Pendleton Act opened a new era in government administration. The results have been summed up by historian Ari Hoogenboom: "An unprofessional civil service became more professionalized. Better educated civil servants were recruited and society accorded them a higher place. . . . Local political considerations gave way in civil servants' minds to the national concerns of a federal office. Business influence and ideals replaced those of the politician."

Arthur also took an intelligent and moderate position on the tariff. He urged the appointment of a nonpartisan commission to study existing rates and suggest rational reductions, and after such a commission was created, he urged Congress to adopt its recommendations. He came out for federal regulation of railroads several years before the passage of the Interstate Commerce Act. "Congress should protect the people . . . against acts of injustice which the State governments are powerless to prevent," he said. He vetoed pork-barrel legislation and pushed for much-needed construction of a modern navy. As an administrator he was systematic, thoughtful, businesslike, and at the same time cheerful and considerate. Just the same, he, too, was a political failure. He made no real attempt to push his program through Congress, instead devoting most of his energies to a futile effort to build up his personal following in the Republican party by distributing favors. But the Stalwarts would not forgive his "desertion," and the reform element could not forget his past. At the

CULVER PICTURES

Parodying a popular painting of the day of a beautiful Greek courtesan being unveiled before Athenian statesmen, Puck's *Bernhard Gillam drew James G. Blaine revealed to Republican leaders in 1884. The "Mulligan letters" receive prominent display among the tattoos, and Blaine's renowned personal magnetism is labeled as a fraud.*

1884 convention the politicos shunted him aside.

The election of 1884 brought the Democrat Grover Cleveland to the White House. Born in New Jersey in 1837, Cleveland grew up in western New York. After studying law, he settled in Buffalo. Although somewhat lacking in the social graces and in intellectual pretensions, he had a basic integrity that everyone recognized; when a group of civic reformers sought a candidate for mayor in 1881 who would throw out the corrupt machine that controlled the city, he was a natural choice. His success in Buffalo led to his election as governor of New York in 1882. In the governor's chair his no-nonsense attitude toward public administration endeared him to civil service reformers at the same time that his basic conservatism pleased businessmen. When he vetoed a popular bill to force a reduction of the fares charged by the New York City elevated railway on the ground that it was an unconstitutional violation of the company's franchise, his stock soared. Here was a man who cared more for principle than the adulation of the multitude, a man of courage, honest, hard-working, and eminently sound. As a result, the Democrats nominated him for President in 1884.

The election revolved around personal issues, for the platforms of the parties were almost identical. The Republican candidate, the dynamic James G. Blaine, had an immense following, but his reputation had been soiled by the publication of the "Mulligan letters," which connected him with the corrupt granting of congressional favors to the Little Rock and Fort Smith Railroad. Blaine had defended himself brilliantly in this matter, but the evidence of corruption was strong and his injunction in the Mulligan correspondence, "Burn this letter," counted heavily against him. On the other hand, it came out during the campaign that Cleveland, a bachelor, had fathered an illegitimate child. Instead of debating public issues, the Republicans chanted the ditty

> Ma! Ma! Where's my pa?
> Gone to the White House,
> *Ha! Ha! Ha!*

to which the Democrats countered

> Blaine, Blaine, James G. Blaine,
> The continental liar from the State of Maine,
> *Burn this letter!*

Probably Blaine lost more heavily in this mudslinging than Cleveland. The latter's quiet courage in saying "Tell the truth" when his past was brought to light contrasted favorably with Blaine's glib but unconvincing denials. A significant group of distinguished eastern Republicans, who were known as "Mugwumps,"* campaigned openly for the Democrats. However, Blaine was enormously popular and ran a very strong race against a general pro-Democratic trend; Cleveland won the election by fewer than 25,000 votes. The change of a mere 600 ballots in New York would have given that state, and the Presidency, to his opponent.

Cleveland was a sound-money man and a moderate tariff reformer. As a Democrat, he had no stomach for refighting the Civil War in every campaign, yet he did not overly favor the South when in office, thus quieting Republican fears that a Democratic administration would fill Washington with unreconstructed rebels. Civil service reformers overestimated his commitment to their cause, for he believed in rotation in office, being as convinced as Andrew Jackson that anyone of "reasonable intelligence" could handle most government jobs. He would not summarily dismiss Republicans, but he thought that when they had served four years, they "should as a rule give way to good men of our party." He did, however, insist upon honesty and efficiency regardless of party and scrutinized all applications for patronage. As a result, he made few poor appointments.

Probably no President could have handled patronage problems much better, considering the times. The Democrats, having been out of the White House since before the Civil War, clamored for the spoils of victory. The Mugwumps, who had contributed considerably to Cleveland's election, were dead set against politicking with government jobs. Steering a middle course, Cleveland failed to satisfy either group. He increased the number of civil service posts from 14,000 to 27,000, but before his term ended he had replaced about two-thirds of all government workers with Democrats of his own choosing.

CHICAGO HISTORICAL SOCIETY

Republican cartoonists found a friendly welcome in the weekly Judge. *In this comment on the Democrats' return to power, ungainly Miss Democracy makes her debut, introduced to society by President Cleveland.*

Cleveland had little imagination and too narrow a conception of his powers and duties to be a successful President. His appearance perfectly reflected his character: a squat, burly man weighing well over 200 pounds, he could defend a position against heavy odds, but his mind lacked flexibility and he provided little effective leadership. He took a fairly broad view of the powers of the federal government—he supported the

*The Mugwumps considered themselves reformers, but on social and economic questions nearly all of them were very conservative. They were sound-money men and advocates of laissez faire. Reform to them consisted almost entirely of doing away with corruption and making the government more efficient.

Interstate Commerce Act, agricultural research, and even came out for federal arbitration of labor disputes—but he thought it unseemly to put pressure on Congress, believing in "the entire independence of the executive and legislative branches." To an important Democratic congressman he wrote in 1886: "I am not at all inclined to meddle with proposed legislation while it is pending in Congress."

As a mayor and governor, Cleveland had been best known for his vetoes. Little wonder that he found being President a burdensome duty. Scarcely a year after his inauguration he was complaining of the "cursed constant grind." Later he grumbled about "the want of rest" and "the terrible nagging" he had to submit to. One of his biographers says that he "approached the presidency as though he were a martyr."

Toward the end of his term, Cleveland bestirred himself and tried to provide constructive leadership on the tariff question. The government was embarrassed by a large surplus revenue, which Cleveland hoped to reduce by cutting the duties on necessities and on the raw materials of manufacturing. He devoted his entire annual message of December 1887 to the tariff, thus focusing public attention on the subject. When worried Democrats reminded him that an election was coming up and that the tariff might cause a rift in the organization, he replied simply: "What is the use of being elected or re-elected, unless you stand for something?"

The House of Representatives, dominated by southern Democrats, passed a bill reducing many duties, but the measure, known as the Mills bill, was flagrantly partisan: it slashed the rates on iron products, glass, wool, and other items made in the North, but left those on southern goods almost untouched. The Republican-controlled Senate rejected the Mills bill and the issue was left to be settled by the voters at the 1888 election. However, in a fashion typical of the period, it did not work out this way. The Democrats hedged by nominating a protectionist, 75-year-old Allen G. Thurman, for Vice President and putting another high-tariff man at the head of the Democratic National Committee. Cleveland toned down his attacks on the important protected industries. Other issues also attracted much attention, such as the "Murchison letter," in which Sir Lionel Sackville-West, the British minister at Washington, was tricked into expressing the opinion that the re-election of Cleveland would best advance the interests of Great Britain. This undoubtedly cost the Democrats the votes of many Irish-Americans, who were rabidly anti-British. Corruption was rife in the campaign as well, perhaps more so than in any other Presidential election. Cleveland obtained a plurality of the popular vote, but his opponent, Benjamin Harrison, grandson of President William Henry Harrison, carried most of the key northeastern industrial states by narrow margins, thus obtaining a comfortable majority in the Electoral College, 233 to 168.

The new President was a short, rather rotund but erect man with a full, graying beard, narrow blue eyes, and a broad forehead. Intelligent and able, he was too reserved to make a good politician. He did not suffer fools gladly and kept even his most important advisers at arm's length. One observer called him a "human iceberg," and he admitted himself that he had "few of the elements of a 'leader'" other than "unobtrusive industry" and a willingness to assume responsibilities. Nevertheless, his career, like his ancestry, had been distinguished. After graduating from Miami University in 1852 at the age of 18, he studied law. He settled in Indiana, where for a number of years he was Indiana Supreme Court reporter, editing five volumes of *Reports* with considerable skill. During the Civil War he rose to command a brigade. He fought under Sherman at Atlanta and won a reputation as a stern, effective disciplinarian. In 1876 he ran unsuccessfully for governor of Indiana, but in 1881 he was elected to the Senate.

Harrison believed ardently in the principle of protection, stating firmly if somewhat illogically that he was against "cheaper coats" because cheaper coats seemed "necessarily to involve a cheaper man and woman under the coat." His approach to fiscal policy was conservative, although he was extremely freehanded in the matter of veterans' pensions. He would not use "an apothecary's scale," he said, "to weigh the re-

Cartoonist Keppler finds Harrison not measuring up to the Presidential hat of his grandfather, William Henry Harrison. Raven Blaine croaks, "Nevermore."

wards of men who saved the country." No more flamboyant waver of the bloody shirt existed. "I would a thousand times rather march under the bloody shirt, stained with the lifeblood of a Union soldier," he said in 1883, "than to march under the black flag of treason or the white flag of cowardly compromise." Harrison professed to favor civil service reform, but his biographer, Father Harry J. Sievers, admits that he fashioned a "singularly unimpressive" record on the question. He objected to the law forbidding the solicitation of campaign funds from officeholders. He appointed the vigorous young reformer Theodore Roosevelt to the Civil Service Commission but then proceeded to undercut him systematically. Before long the frustrated Roosevelt was calling the President a "cold blooded, narrow minded, prejudiced, obstinate, timid old psalm singing Indianapolis politician."

Under Harrison, Congress distinguished itself by expending, for the first time in a period of peace, more than $1 billion in a single session. It also raised the tariff to an all-time high. The Sherman Antitrust Act was passed and so was a Silver Purchase Act authorizing the government to coin large amounts of that metal, a measure much desired by mining interests and those favoring inflation. A Federal Elections, or "Force" bill, providing for federal control of elections as a means of protecting the right of southern Negroes to vote, a right increasingly under attack, passed the House, only to be filibustered to death in the Senate. Harrison had little to do with the fate of any of these measures. By and large, he failed, as one historian has said, to give the people "magnetic and responsive leadership." The Republicans lost control of Congress in 1890, and two years later Grover Cleveland swept back into power, defeating Harrison by over 350,000 votes.

Thus none of these Presidents provided the nation with effective leadership. Indeed, in the early nineties, one would have had to look back all the way to Lincoln to find a really successful Chief Executive.

Congressional Leaders

Nor were the lesser politicians of the period able to rise much above the sordid limitations of the age. No one of the stature and influence of Webster, Clay, or Calhoun graced the halls of Congress between 1865 and the end of the century. The most outstanding figure in Congress was unquestionably James G. Blaine of Maine, who served from 1863 to 1881, first in the House and then in the Senate. Blaine had many of the qualities that mark a great leader: personal dynamism, imagination, political intuition, oratorical ability, and a broad view of the national interest. President Lincoln spotted him when he was a freshman congressman, calling him "one of the brightest men in the House" and "one of the coming men of the country." Blaine was essentially a reasonable man, favoring sound money without opposing inflexibly every suggestion for increasing the volume of the currency, supporting the protective system but advocating reciprocity agreements to increase trade, adopting a moderate and tolerant attitude toward the South. Almost alone among the men of his generation, he was deeply interested in foreign affairs. His personal warmth captivated thousands. He never forgot a name. His handshake—he would grasp a visitor's hand firmly at a reception and often hold it throughout a brief conversation with unaffected, manly friendliness—won him hundreds of adherents. This was perhaps calculated, yet he was capable of impulsive acts of generosity and kindness too.

That Blaine, although perennially an aspirant, never became President was partly a reflection of his very abilities and his active participation in so many controversial affairs over the years. Naturally, he aroused jealousies and made many enemies. But some inexplicable flaw marred his character. He had a streak of recklessness entirely out of keeping with his reasonable position on most issues. He waved the bloody shirt with cynical vigor, heedless of the effect on the nation as a whole. He showered contempt on civil service reformers, characterizing them as "noisy but not numerous . . . ambitious but not wise, pretentious but not powerful." The scandal of the Mulligan letters made a dark blot on his record, but there is also reason to doubt his general honesty, for, as one historian has pointed out, he "became wealthy without visible means of support." Sometimes he seemed almost deliberately to injure himself by needlessly antagonizing powerful colleagues. His clashes with the Stalwart leader Roscoe Conkling shook the chambers of Congress, for example. Blaine moved through history amid cheers and won a host of spectacular if petty triumphs, yet his career was barren, essentially tragic.

Roscoe Conkling's was another remarkable but empty career. Handsome, colorful, companionable, and dignified, Conkling served in Congress almost continually from 1859 to 1881 and was a great power, dominating the complex politics of New York for many years. Such was his prestige that two Presidents offered him a seat on the Supreme Court. Yet no measure of importance was attached to his name. He squandered his energies in acrimonious personal quarrels, caring only for partisan advantage. Although he wanted very much to be President, he had no conception of what a President must be, and in the end, even his own hack followers deserted him.

Dozens of other figures of the period merit brief mention; the following are representative types. Congressman William McKinley of Ohio was perhaps the most personally attractive. He was a man of simple honesty, nobility of character, and quiet warmth—and a politician to the core. The tariff was McKinley's special competence, the principle of protection his guiding star. The peak of his career still lay in the future in the early 1890's. Another Ohioan, John Sherman, brother of the famous Civil War general, accomplished the remarkable feat of holding national office continuously for nearly half a century, from 1855 to 1898. Three times a prominent candidate for the Republican Presidential nomination, he had a deserved reputation for expertness in financial matters. However, he was colorless, stiff—he was called "the Ohio Icicle"—and while personally honest, altogether too willing to compromise his beliefs for political advantage. He admired Andrew Johnson and sympathized with his attitude toward reconstructing the South, yet he voted to convict him at the impeachment trial. Repeatedly he made concessions to the inflationists, despite his personal dedication to sound money. Sherman gave his name (and not much else) to the Antitrust Act of 1890 and to other important legislation, but in retrospect left little mark on the history of his country, despite his long service.

Another prominent figure of the age was Thomas B. Reed, Republican congressman from Maine, a witty, widely read man of immense latent energy but ultraconservative and cursed with a sharp tongue that he could never curb. Reed coined the famous definition of a statesman —"a politician who is dead." When one pompous politico said in his presence that he would rather be right than President, Reed advised him not to worry, since he would never be either. In 1890 Reed was elected Speaker of the House and quickly won the nickname "Czar" because of his autocratic way of expediting business.

Since the Republicans had only a paper-thin majority, the Democrats attempted to block action on partisan measures by refusing to answer to their names on quorum calls. Reed coolly ordered the clerk to record them as present and proceeded to carry on the business of the House. His control soon became so absolute that Washington jokesters began to say that representatives dared not even breathe without his permission. Reed had large ambitions and the courage of his convictions, but his vindictiveness kept him from exercising a constructive influence on his times.

One of the most attractive Democratic politicians of the era was Richard P. "Silver Dick" Bland of Missouri, congressman from 1873 until the late nineties. As a young man, Bland had spent ten years as a prospector and miner, and he devoted most of his energies in politics to fighting for the free coinage of silver. Although almost fanatical on this question, he was no mere mouthpiece for special interests, fighting against monopolies and consistently opposing the protective tariff. He lived simply and was immune to the temptations that led so many of his colleagues to use their political influence to line their own pockets. Yet he never emerged as a truly national leader.

More colorful, yet utterly sterile was the career of Benjamin F. Butler of Massachusetts. Butler was a political chameleon. A states'-rights Democrat before the Civil War, he supported Jefferson Davis for the Democratic Presidential nomination in 1860. During the conflict he served as a Union general, during reconstruction as a Radical Republican congressman. In 1878 he came out for currency inflation and won a seat in Congress as a Greenbacker. In 1882 he was elected governor of Massachusetts, this time as a Democrat! Butler had a sharp wit, a vivid imagination, a real feeling for the interests of the laboring man. He detested all kinds of sham and pretense. But he was also a brutal, corrupt demagogue, almost universally hated by men of culture and public spirit. Although by no means a typical politician, Butler typified many aspects of the age—its shaky morality, its extremism, its intense interest in meaningless political controversy.

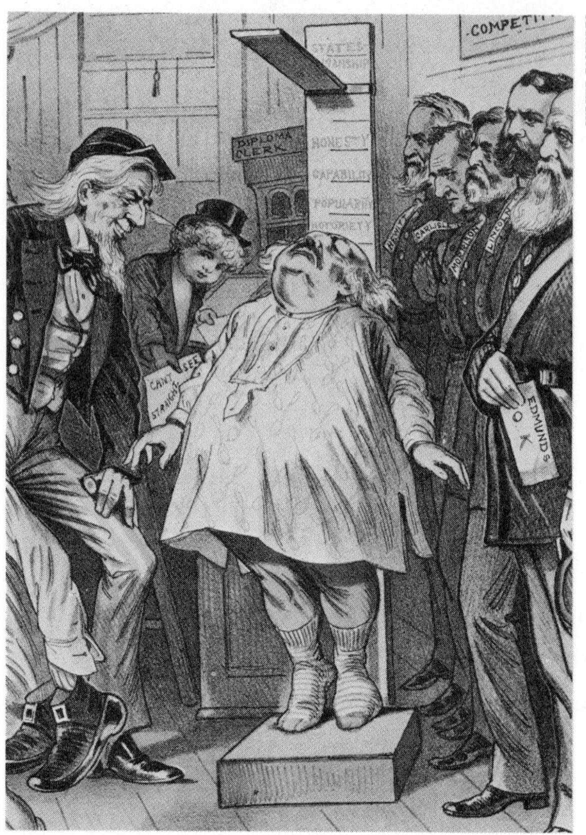

CULVER PICTURES

Benjamin Butler, straining to measure up, attains only Notoriety; from Puck, *1884. The spoons on his nightshirt refer to his wartime military rule in New Orleans, when he allegedly pilfered silver spoons.*

Agricultural Discontent

The vacuity of American politics may well have stemmed from the complacency of the middle-class majority. The country was growing; no foreign enemy threatened it; the poor were mostly recent immigrants, Negroes, and others with little influence, easily ignored by those in comfortable circumstances. However, one important group in society was suffering increasingly as the years rolled by—the farmers. Out of their travail came the force that finally, in the 1890's, brought American politics face to face with the real problems of the age.

Long the backbone of American society, the farmer was rapidly being left behind in the race for wealth and status. The number of farmers and the volume of agricultural production continued to rise, but agriculture's relative place in the national economy was declining steadily.

Between 1860 and 1890 the number of farms rose from 2 million to 4.5 million, wheat output leaped from 173 million bushels to 449 million, cotton from 5.3 million bales to 8.5 million. The rural population increased from 25 million to 40.8 million. But as we have seen, industry was expanding far faster, and the urban population, quadrupling in the period, was soon destined to overtake and pass that of the countryside. Immediately after the Civil War, wheat sold at nearly $1.50 a bushel, and even in the early 1870's it was still worth well over a dollar. By the mid-nineties the average price stood in the neighborhood of 60 cents. Cotton, the great southern staple, which was selling for over 30 cents a pound in 1866 and 15 cents in the early 1870's, at times in the nineties fell below 6 cents. The tariff on manufactured goods appeared to aggravate the farmers' predicament, and so did the domestic marketing system, which enabled a multitude of middlemen to gobble up a large share of the profits of agriculture. Worldwide improvements in transportation at this time made it practicable for farmers in Australia, Canada, Russia, and Argentina to sell their produce in western European markets, thus increasing the competition faced by Americans seeking to dispose of surplus produce abroad.

Along with declining income, farmers suffered a decline in status. Relatively few of the new intellectual currents of the period influenced rural thinking. Compared to city dwellers, farmers seemed increasingly provincial and behind the times. Rural educational standards did not keep pace, modern concepts like evolution were either ignored or rejected, and religious fundamentalism, cast aside by eastern sophisticates, maintained its hold in the countryside. Soon people in the cities began to refer to farmers as "rubes," "hicks," or "hayseeds" and to view them with amused tolerance or even contempt.

This combination of circumstances angered and frustrated the farmers. Repeated waves of radicalism swept the agricultural regions, giving rise to demands for social and economic experiments that played a major role in breaking down rural laissez-faire prejudices dating back to the time of Jefferson. Much of this reform spirit was both illiberal and illogical. Some farmers talked almost paranoiacally about dark conspiracies organized by bloated tycoons to milk them of their hard-earned dollars. Of course no such conspiracies existed. Others claimed to desire a return to the self-sufficient agriculture of frontier days, when every tiller of the soil was an "independent yeoman," whereas, in fact, nearly all of them eagerly adopted the values of a commercial society. They idealized the nonmaterial rewards of farm life, yet pursued their own profit as avidly as any other businessman.

However, many of the farmers' complaints had a firm basis in reality, and whatever their motives and self-delusions, they advanced many practical proposals that would aid nonagricultural elements as well as themselves. As we have seen, in the 1870's, pressure from the Patrons of Husbandry produced legislation regulating railroads and warehouses. This Granger movement also led to many interesting cooperative experiments in the marketing of farm products and in the purchase of machinery, fertilizers, and other goods.

Actually, farmers did not react to economic developments as a unit; in a country so huge, the interests and prejudices of all rural groups never coincided exactly. Because of the steady decline of the price level, farmers in newer settled regions were usually worse off than those in older areas, since they had to borrow money to get started and were therefore burdened with fixed interest charges that became harder to meet with each passing year. In the 1870's farmers in states like Illinois and Iowa suffered most, which accounts for the popularity of the Grangers in that region. Except as a purely social organization, the Grange had little importance in eastern states where farmers were relatively prosperous. However, by the late eighties farmers in the old Middle West had become better established. When prices dipped sharply and a general depression gripped the country, they were able to weather the bad times nicely, as Allan G. Bogue has shown. Illinois farmers took advantage of the new technology to increase output, shifting from wheat to the production of corn, oats, hogs, and cattle, which did not decline so drastically in price.

On the new agricultural frontier in Kansas, Nebraska, and the Dakotas, farmers were less fortunate. Throughout the middle eighties this region had experienced boom conditions. Adequate rainfall produced bountiful harvests, credit was available, and property values rose rapidly. Land near Abilene, Kansas, that had sold for $6.25 an acre in 1867 changed hands in 1887 at $270 an acre. Between 1881 and 1887 farms in parts of Nebraska doubled in value; in eastern Colorado even more spectacular rises occurred. In the decade of the 1880's the population of Kansas increased by 43 per cent, that of Nebraska by 134 per cent, of the Dakotas by 278 per cent.

Such booms occurred periodically in every frontier district, and like all others, this one collapsed when settlers and investors took a more realistic look at the prospects of the region. However, in this case special circumstances turned the slump into a major catastrophe. The bitter winter of 1886–87 dealt a smashing blow to the open-range cattle industry. Then a succession of dry years shattered the hopes of the farmers. The downward swing of the business cycle in the early 1890's completed the devastation. Settlers who had paid more for their lands than they were worth and borrowed money at high interest rates to do so found themselves squeezed relentlessly. Thousands lost their farms and returned eastward, penniless and dispirited. The population of Nebraska increased by fewer than 4,000 persons in the entire decade of the nineties.

The Populist Movement

This profound agricultural depression triggered a new outburst of farm radicalism, the Alliance movement. The alliances were organizations of farmers' clubs, most of which had sprung up during the bad times of the late seventies. Improved conditions in the early eighties held back the growth of these groups, but after about 1885 they expanded

The western land boom reached a climax on April 22, 1889, when parts of Oklahoma were opened to settlers. Within a few hours nearly 2 million acres were claimed by hordes of "boomers." This photograph by Harman T. Swearingen was taken a few weeks later in the boom town of Guthrie, whose sign painter was working overtime.

WESTERN HISTORY COLLECTION, UNIVERSITY OF OKLAHOMA LIBRARY

rapidly. In the perennially depressed South the Agricultural Wheel, originally a debating club, and the Southern Alliance, founded in Texas to round up stray cattle, bring horse thieves to justice, and engage in cooperative purchasing, recruited thousands of new members. In the northern regions, the Northwestern Alliance experienced a similar revival. These organizations adopted somewhat differing policies, but all agreed that agricultural prices were too low, that transportation costs were too high, and that something was radically wrong with the nation's financial system. "There are three great crops raised in Nebraska," an angry rural editor proclaimed in 1890. "One is a crop of corn, one is a crop of freight rates, and one a crop of interest. One is produced by farmers who by sweat and toil farm the land. The other two are produced by men who sit in their offices and behind their bank counters and farm the farmers." All agreed, too, on the need for political action of some kind if the lot of the agriculturalist was to be improved.

Although the state alliances of the Dakotas and Kansas joined the Southern Alliance in 1889, for a time local prejudices and conflicting interests prevented the formation of a single national organization. Northern farmers mostly voted Republican, southerners Democratic, and resentments created during the Civil War lingered in all sections. Cotton-producing southerners opposed the protective tariff, whereas most northerners, fearing the competition of foreign grain producers, favored it. The Southern Alliance was a secret society, a fact offensive to many in the other groups. Railroad regulation and federal land policy seemed the vital questions to northerners, financial reform loomed most important in southern eyes. Northerners were receptive to the idea of forming a third party, while southerners, wedded to the one-party system, preferred working to capture local Democratic machines.

Although unable to unite, the various farm groups entered local politics actively in the 1890 elections. Utterly convinced of the righteousness of their cause, they campaigned with tremendous fervor. In Georgia Tom Watson, a youthful firebrand running for Congress, orated: "Like the thunder that shakes yon sky, the voice of the people has shaken the power from the hands of the political bosses and placed it in the hands of the masses where it belongs." In Kansas, according to one chronicler, "it was a religious revival, a crusade, a pentecost of politics in which a tongue of flame sat upon every man, and each spake as the spirit gave him utterance." The results were most encouraging. In the South, Alliance-sponsored gubernatorial candidates won in Georgia, Tennessee, South Carolina, and Texas; 8 southern legislatures fell under Alliance control; 44 congressmen and 3 senators committed to Alliance objectives were sent to Washington. In the West, Alliance men swept the Kansas elections, captured a majority in the Nebraska legislature, and enough seats in Minnesota and South Dakota to hold the balance of power between the major parties.

Such success, coupled with the reluctance of the Republicans and Democrats to make concessions to their demands, encouraged Alliance men to create a new national party. If they could also recruit industrial workers, perhaps a real political revolution could be accomplished. In February 1892 farm leaders, representatives of the Knights of Labor, and various professional reformers, some 800 in all, met at St. Louis, organized the People's party, and issued a call for a national convention to meet at Omaha in July.

That convention nominated General James B. Weaver of Iowa for President (with a one-legged Confederate veteran as his running mate) and drafted one of the most comprehensive reform programs ever advanced by an important American political party. The platform called for a graduated income tax and national ownership of both railroads and the telegraph and telephone systems. A "subtreasury" plan that would permit farmers to hold nonperishable crops off the market when prices were low was also advocated. Under this proposal the government would make loans to farmers secured by crops held in storage. When prices rose, the farmers could sell their crops and repay the loans. To combat deflation, the platform called for the unlimited coinage of silver and an increase in the money supply "to no less than $50 per capita," and to make the government more responsive to public opinion, it urged the adoption of the initiative and referendum procedures and the election of U.S. senators by popular vote. To win the support of industrial workers—"the interests of rural and civil labor are the same," the platform declared—the use of Pinkerton detectives in labor disputes was denounced, the eight-hour day backed, and the restriction of "undesirable" immigration advocated.

The appearance of the new party was by far the most exciting and significant aspect of the Presidential campaign of 1892, which saw Harrison and Cleveland refighting the election of 1888. The People's party, or Populists, put forth a host of colorful spellbinders: Tom Watson of Georgia, now a congressman, whose temper was such that on one occasion he administered a beating to a local planter with the man's own riding crop; William A. Peffer, senator from Kansas, whose long beard and grave mien gave him the look of a Hebrew prophet; "Sockless Jerry" Simpson of Kansas, unlettered but full of grassroots shrewdness and wit, a former Greenbacker and an admirer of the Single Tax doctrine of Henry George; Ignatius Donnelly, "the Minnesota Sage," who claimed to be an authority on science, Shakespeare—he believed that Francis Bacon wrote the plays—and economics, and who had just published a widely read novel, *Caesar's Column* (1891), which pictured an America of the future wherein a handful of plutocrats tyrannized over masses of downtrodden workers and serfs.

In the South, Populist strategists struck at the very foundations of local society by seeking to unite white and Negro farmers against the ruling Democratic organization. Economic interests, they decided, were more important than race. "You are kept apart that you may be separately fleeced," Watson told the poor farmers of Georgia. Southern Negro farmers had their own Colored Alliance, and even before 1892 their leaders had worked closely with the white alliances. Nearly 100 black delegates had attended the Populist convention at St. Louis. Of course the Negroes would be useless if they could not vote; therefore white Populist leaders opposed the southern trend toward disfranchising blacks and called for full civil rights for all. In the Northwest the Populists assailed the "bankers' conspiracy" in unbridled terms. Ignatius Donnelly, running for governor of Minnesota, wrote another novel of political prognostication, *The Golden Bottle,* made 150 speeches, talked personally with 10,000 voters, vowing to make the campaign "the liveliest ever seen" in the state.

The results, however, proved disappointing. Watson, for example, lost his seat in Congress, and Donnelly ran a poor third in the Minnesota gubernatorial race. The Populists did manage to sweep Kansas. They also carried large numbers of local offices in many other western states and cast over a million popular votes for Weaver. But the effort to unite white and Negro farmers in the South failed miserably. Conservative Democrats played on racial fears cruelly, insisting that the Populists sought to destroy white supremacy. Since most white Populists saw the alliance with Negroes as at most a marriage of convenience—they did not really believe in racial equality, or propose to do anything for black sharecroppers—this argument had a deadly effect. Elsewhere, even in the old centers of the Granger movement, the party made no significant impression. Urban workers remained aloof. By standing firmly for conservative financial policies, Cleveland attracted much Republican support and won a solid victory over Harrison in the Electoral College, 277 to 145. Weaver's electoral vote was 22.

Showdown on Silver

One obvious conclusion that the politicians reached after analyzing the 1892 returns was that the money question, especially the controversy over the coinage of silver, was of paramount interest to the voters. Despite the wide-ranging appeal of the Populist platform, most of Weaver's strength came from the silver-mining states. On the other hand, Cleveland's strong stand for gold proved very popular in the Northeast. Actually, the issue of gold versus silver was superficial; the real question was what, if anything, should be done to check the continuing deflationary spiral. Undoubtedly, the declining price level benefited bondholders and others with fixed incomes, and injured debtors. Industrial workers profited from deflation except during periods of depression when unemployment rose, which helps explain why the Populists made little headway among them. Southern farmers, prisoners of the crop-lien system, and farmers in the plains states were, as we have seen, hit hard by the downward trend.

By the early 1890's, discussion of federal monetary policy revolved around the coinage of silver. Traditionally, the United States had been on a bimetallic standard. Both gold and silver were coined, the numbers of grains of each in the dollar being periodically adjusted to reflect the commercial value of the two metals. An act of 1792 established a 15:1 ratio—371.25 grains of silver and 24.75 grains of gold were each worth one dollar at the Mint. In 1834 the ratio was changed to 16:1, and in 1853 to 14.8:1, the latter reduction in the value of gold reflecting the new discoveries in California. This ratio slightly undervalued silver. In 1861, for example, the amount of silver bullion in a dollar was worth $1.03 in the open market, so no one brought silver to the Mint for coinage. However, an avalanche of silver from the mines of Nevada and Colorado gradually depressed the price, until, around 1874, it again became profitable for miners to coin their bullion. Alas, when they tried to do so, they discovered that the new Coinage Act of 1873, taking account of the fact that no silver had been presented to the Mint in years, had demonetized the metal.

The silver miners denounced this "Crime of 1873" and inflationists, who desired more money regardless of its base, joined them in demanding a return to bimetallism. Conservatives, then still fighting the battle against greenback paper money, resisted strongly. During the seventies and eighties these forces battled sporadically in Congress over the silver issue. The result was a series of compromises. In 1878 the Bland-Allison Act authorized the purchase of $2–4 million of silver a month at the market price, but this had little inflationary effect, since the government consistently purchased only the minimum amount. The commercial price of silver continued to fall, until in 1890 its ratio to gold was 20:1. In that year the Sherman Silver Purchase Act required the government to buy 4.5 million *ounces* of silver monthly, but in the face of increasing supplies and a worldwide trend among governments to adopt a single gold standard, the price of silver fell still further—the ratio reaching 26:1 in 1893 and 32:1 in 1894.

These compromises satisfied no one. The silver miners grumbled because their bullion brought in only half of what it had in the early seventies. Debtors noted angrily that because of the general decline of prices, the dollars they used to meet their obligations were worth more than twice as much as in 1865. Advocates of the gold standard, noting the increasing pressure of the silverites, feared that unlimited coinage would be authorized, "destroying the value of the dollar." When a financial panic brought on by the collapse of the great London banking house of Baring Brothers ushered in a severe industrial depression, the confidence of both silverites and "gold bugs" was further eroded.

President Cleveland believed that the agitation over silver had caused the depression by shaking the confidence of the business community and that all would be well if the country returned to a single gold standard. He summoned a special session of Congress, and by exerting immense political pressure, forced the repeal of the Sherman Silver Purchase Act in October 1893. All that this accomplished was to split the Democratic party, its southern and western wings deserting him almost to a man.

During 1894 and 1895, while the nation floundered in the worst depression it had ever experienced, a series of events further undermined public confidence. In the spring of 1894 an "army" of unemployed led by Jacob S. Coxey, an eccentric Ohio businessman, marched on Washington to demand relief. Coxey wanted the government to undertake a program of federal public works and to authorize local communities to exchange non-interest-bearing bonds with the Treasury for $500 million in paper money, the funds to be used to hire unemployed workers to build roads. The scheme, Coxey claimed, would pump money into the economy, provide work for the jobless, and benefit the whole nation by improving transportation facilities. Such a plan had much to recommend it, but when Coxey's pitiful little group of demonstrators, perhaps 500 in all, reached the Capitol grounds, he and two other leaders were

Harper's Weekly, APRIL 14, 1894

Mutiny aboard the good ship Democracy, *as seen by W.A. Rogers of* Harper's Weekly, *1894. Civil Service and tariff reform (along with one of its advocates) are about to get the deep six, the Tammany tiger gorges himself, and, at the stern, Captain Cleveland determinedly vetoes mutineers promoting a silver-purchase bill.*

arrested, their followers dispersed by a horde of club-wielding policemen. This callous treatment convinced many Americans that the government had little interest in the suffering of the people, an opinion much strengthened when Cleveland, in July 1894, used federal troops to crush the Pullman strike.

The next year the Supreme Court handed down a series of reactionary decisions. First, in *U.S. v. E.C. Knight Company*, it refused to employ the Sherman Antitrust Act to break up the Sugar Trust. Next, in *Pollock v. Farmers' Loan and Trust Company*, it invalidated a federal income tax law, despite the fact that a similar measure levied during the Civil War had been upheld by the Court in *Springer v. U.S.* (1881). The New York *World* called this decision "the triumph of selfishness over patriotism." Finally the Court denied a writ of habeas corpus to Eugene V. Debs of the American Railway Union, who had been imprisoned for disobeying a federal injunction during the Pullman strike.

On top of these indications of official conservatism came a desperate financial crisis. Throughout 1894 the Treasury's gold reserve had dwindled fast as alarmed citizens exchanged greenbacks (now convertible into specie) for hard money and foreign investors cashed in large amounts of American securities. The government tried to float new gold-bond issues to bolster the reserve, but since investors mostly purchased the bonds with gold-backed paper money, in effect withdrawing gold from the Treasury and then returning it for the bonds, the reserve continued to melt away. Early in 1895 it touched a low point of $41 million. At this juncture a syndicate of bankers headed by J.P. Morgan turned the tide by underwriting a new $62 million bond issue, guaranteeing that half the bullion would come from Europe. But this caused a great public outcry; the spectacle of the nation being saved from bankruptcy by a private banker infuriated millions. Morgan's profit was estimated as high as $16 million—it was actually about $250,000—and the silverites even went so far as to accuse Cleveland of profiting personally from the transaction.

All these events, together with the continuing depression, discredited the Cleveland administration. "I haven't got words to say that I think of that old bag of beef," Governor "Pitchfork Ben" Tillman of South Carolina, who had resolutely resisted the Populists in 1892, told a local audience two years later, "If you send me to the Senate, I promise I won't be bulldozed by him."

Increasingly, the silver issue was coming to dominate politics. As the Presidential election of 1896 approached, with the Populists demanding unlimited coinage of silver at a ratio of 16:1, the major parties found it impossible to continue straddling the money question. The Populist vote had increased by 42 per cent in the 1894 congressional elections. Southern and western Democratic leaders feared that they would lose their entire following unless Cleveland was repudiated. Western Republicans, led by Senator Henry M. Teller of Colorado, were threatening to bolt to the Populists unless their party came out for silver coinage. After a generation of political equivocation and hypocrisy, the major parties had to face a real issue squarely. Confusion approaching chaos gripped them both, but in the end each made the inevitable decision to go along with its dominant element.

The Republicans, meeting to choose a candidate at St. Louis in June 1896, announced for the gold standard. "We are unalterably opposed to every measure calculated to debase our currency or impair the credit of our country," the platform declared. "We are therefore opposed to the free coinage of silver. . . . The existing gold standard must be maintained."* The party then nominated Ohio's William McKinley for President. McKinley, best known for his staunch advocacy of the protective tariff but also highly regarded by labor, was expected to run strongly in the Middle West and East.

The Democratic convention met in July at Chicago. Although the pro-gold Cleveland element made a hard fight, the silverites swept them aside. The high point came when a youthful Nebraskan named William Jennings Bryan rose to close the debate on the platform. When he spoke for silver against gold, for western farmers against the industrial East, his every sentence provoked ear-shattering applause.

> We have petitioned [he said] and our petitions have been scorned; we have entreated, and our entreaties have been disregarded; we have begged, and they have mocked when our calamity came. We beg no longer; we entreat no more; we petition no more. *We defy them!*

The crowd responded like a great choir to Bryan's every gesture. "Burn down your cities and leave our farms," he said, "and your cities will spring up again as if by magic; but destroy our farms and the grass will grow in the streets of every city in the country." And he ended with a marvelous figure of speech that set the tone for the coming campaign. "You shall not press down upon the brow of labor this crown of thorns," he warned, bringing his hands down suggestively to his temples. "You shall not crucify mankind upon a cross of gold!" Dramatically, he extended his arms to the side, the very figure of the crucified Christ.

The convention promptly adopted a platform calling for "the free and unlimited coinage of both silver and gold at the present legal ratio of 16 to 1" and went on to nominate Bryan, who was barely 36, for President. This action put tremendous pressure on the Populists. By supporting Bryan they risked losing their party identity, but if they nominated another man, they would insure McKinley's election. Some preferred the latter choice, figuring that in the long run their major goals could best be achieved in this way. "The Democratic idea of fusion," Tom Watson complained, is "that we play Jonah while they play whale." But most Populists, trusting in Bryan's liberal sentiments, were ready to follow the Democratic lead. "We must join with [the Democrats] or be destroyed," one of them explained. Their convention nominated the Nebraskan late in July, seeking to preserve the party identity by substituting Watson for the Democratic Vice Presidential nominee, Arthur Sewall of Maine.

*The party did offer to accept a bimetallic standard if "the leading commercial nations" would do likewise, but in the prevailing state of world opinion this was impossible.

Election of 1896

Never did a Presidential campaign raise such intense emotions or produce such drastic political realignments. The Republicans from the silver-mining states swung solidly behind Bryan, Senator Teller calling him "an able man of high character, a strong friend of silver, and close to the people." The gold Democrats refused to accept the decision of the Chicago convention. Cleveland professed to be "so dazed by the political situation that I am in no condition for speech or thought on the subject," and many others adopted the policy of Governor David B. Hill of New York, who said: "I am a Democrat still—very still." The extreme gold bugs, calling themselves National Democrats, nominated a candidate of their own, 79-year-old Senator John M. Palmer of Illinois. Palmer ran only to injure Bryan. "Fellow Democrats," he announced, "I will not consider it any great fault if you decide to cast your vote for William McKinley."

At the start the Republicans seemed to have everything in their favor. Bryan's extreme youth and his relative lack of political experience—two terms in the House—contrasted unfavorably with McKinley's distinguished war record, his long service in Congress and as governor of Ohio, and his reputation for honesty and good judgment. The severe depression also operated in favor of the party out of power, although by repudiating Cleveland, the Democrats escaped much of the burden of explaining away his errors. Furthermore, the newspapers came out almost unanimously for the Republicans. Important Democratic papers such as the New York *World*, the Boston *Herald*, the Baltimore *Sun*, the Chicago *Chronicle*, and the Richmond *Times* not only supported McKinley editorially, but also slanted their news stories against the Democrats. The New York *Times* even accused Bryan of being insane, his affliction being variously classified as "paranoia querulenta," "graphomania," and "oratorical monomania." The Democrats had almost no money and few well-known speakers to fight the campaign.

Bryan, however, quickly proved himself a formidable opponent. Casting aside tradition, he took to the stump personally, traveling 18,000 miles and making over 600 speeches. Unquestionably, he was one of the very greatest of orators. A big, handsome man with a voice capable of carrying without strain to the far corners of a great hall, yet equally effective before a cluster of auditors at a rural crossroads, he projected an image of absolute sincerity without appearing fanatical or argumentative. At every major stop on his tour, huge crowds assembled. In Minnesota, for example, he packed the 10,000-seat St. Paul Auditorium, while thousands more milled in the streets outside. His energy was amazing, his charm and good humor unfailing. At one whistle stop, while he was shaving in his compartment, a small group outside the train began clamoring for a glimpse of him. Flinging open the window and beaming through the lather, he shook hands cheerfully with each of these admirers. Everywhere he hammered away at the money question, but he did not totally neglect other issues, speaking, he said, for "all the people who suffer from the operations of trusts, syndicates, and combines."

McKinley's campaign was managed by a new type of politician, Marcus Alonzo Hanna, an Ohio businessman. Politics fascinated Hanna, and despite his wealth and wide interests, he was willing to labor endlessly at the routine work of political organization. He aspired to be a king-maker and early fastened upon McKinley, whose honesty and charm he found irresistible, as the vehicle for satisfying his ambition. He spent about $100,000 of his own money on the preconvention campaign. His attitude toward the candidate, one mutual friend observed, was "that of a big, bashful boy toward the girl he loves."

Before most Republicans realized how effective Bryan was on the stump, Hanna perceived the danger and sprang into action. Since the late 1880's the character of political organization had been changing. The Civil Service Act was cutting down on the number of jobs available to reward campaign workers and thus on the sums of money the parties could raise by assessing these workers. At the same time, the new mass-circulation newspapers and the development of nationwide press associations were increasing the pressure on candidates to speak openly and often on national issues. This trend put a premium on party or-

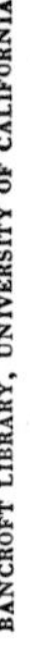

William Jennings Bryan (center) strides to the speaker's platform at a Democratic rally in California in 1896. Delivering as many as 30 speeches a day, Bryan spoke directly to some 5 million people during the campaign.

ganization and consistency—the old political trick of speaking out of one side of the mouth to one audience, out the other to another, no longer worked very well. Moreover, as the federal government became more involved in economic issues, powerful business interests found more reason to be concerned about national elections and willing to spend money freely in behalf of candidates whose views they approved. As early as the campaign of 1888 the Republicans had set up a businessmen's "advisory board" to raise money and stir up enthusiasm for Benjamin Harrison.

Hanna clearly understood what was happening to politics. Certain that money was the key to political power, he set up headquarters at Chicago and New York and began amassing an enormous campaign fund. He demanded, for example, that the Boston Republican leaders raise $400,000. When businessmen hesitated to contribute, he pried open their purses by a combination of persuasiveness and intimidation. Banks and insurance companies were "assessed" a percentage of their assets, big corporations a share of their receipts, until some $3.5 million had been collected. Hanna disbursed these funds with efficiency and imagination. He sent 1,500 speakers into the doubtful districts and blanketed the land with no less than 250 million pieces of campaign literature, printed in a dozen languages. "He has advertised McKinley as if he were a patent medicine," Theodore Roosevelt exclaimed.

Incapable of competing with Bryan as a swayer of mass audiences, McKinley conducted what was known as a "front-porch campaign." This technique also dated from the first Harrison-Cleveland election, when Harrison had regularly delivered off-the-cuff speeches to groups of visitors representing special interests or regions in his home town of Indianapolis. This system conserved the candidate's energies and enabled him to avoid the appearance of seeking the Presidency too openly—which was still considered bad form—and at the same time allowed him to make headlines all over the country. McKinley, guided by the masterful Hanna, now brought the front-porch method to perfection. Superficially the proceedings were delightfully informal. From every corner of the land, groups representing various regions, occupations, and interests descended upon McKinley's unpretentious frame house in Canton, Ohio. Gathering on the lawn—the grass was soon reduced to mud, the fence stripped of pickets by souvenir hunters—the visitors paid their compliments to the candidate and heard him deliver a brief speech, while beside him on the porch his aged mother and adoring invalid wife listened with rapt attention. Then there was a small reception, during which the delegates were given an opportunity to shake their host's hand.

Despite their air of informality, these performances were carefully staged. The delegations arrived on a tightly coordinated schedule worked out by McKinley's staff and the railroads, which operated cut-rate excursion trains to Canton from all over the nation. McKinley was fully briefed on the special interests and attitudes of each group, and the speeches of delegation leaders were submitted in advance. Often his secretary amended these remarks, and upon occasion McKinley even wrote the visitors' speeches himself. Naturally, his own talks were also prepared in advance, each calculated to make a particular point. All were reported fully in the newspapers. Thus, without moving from his doorstep, McKinley met thousands of people from every section. On a single day in October he made 16 speeches to an estimated 30,000 people.

These tactics worked admirably for the Republicans. On election day McKinley carried the East, the Middle West, including even Iowa, Minnesota, and North Dakota, and the Pacific Coast states of Oregon and California, while Bryan won in the South, the plains states, and the Rocky Mountain region. McKinley collected 271 electoral votes to Bryan's 176, the popular vote being 7,036,000 to 6,468,000.

McKinley speaks to the faithful from the front porch of his Canton, Ohio, home. He flattered visitors with his full attention, listening to their prepared speeches, said an observer, "like a child looking at Santa Claus."

OHIO HISTORICAL SOCIETY

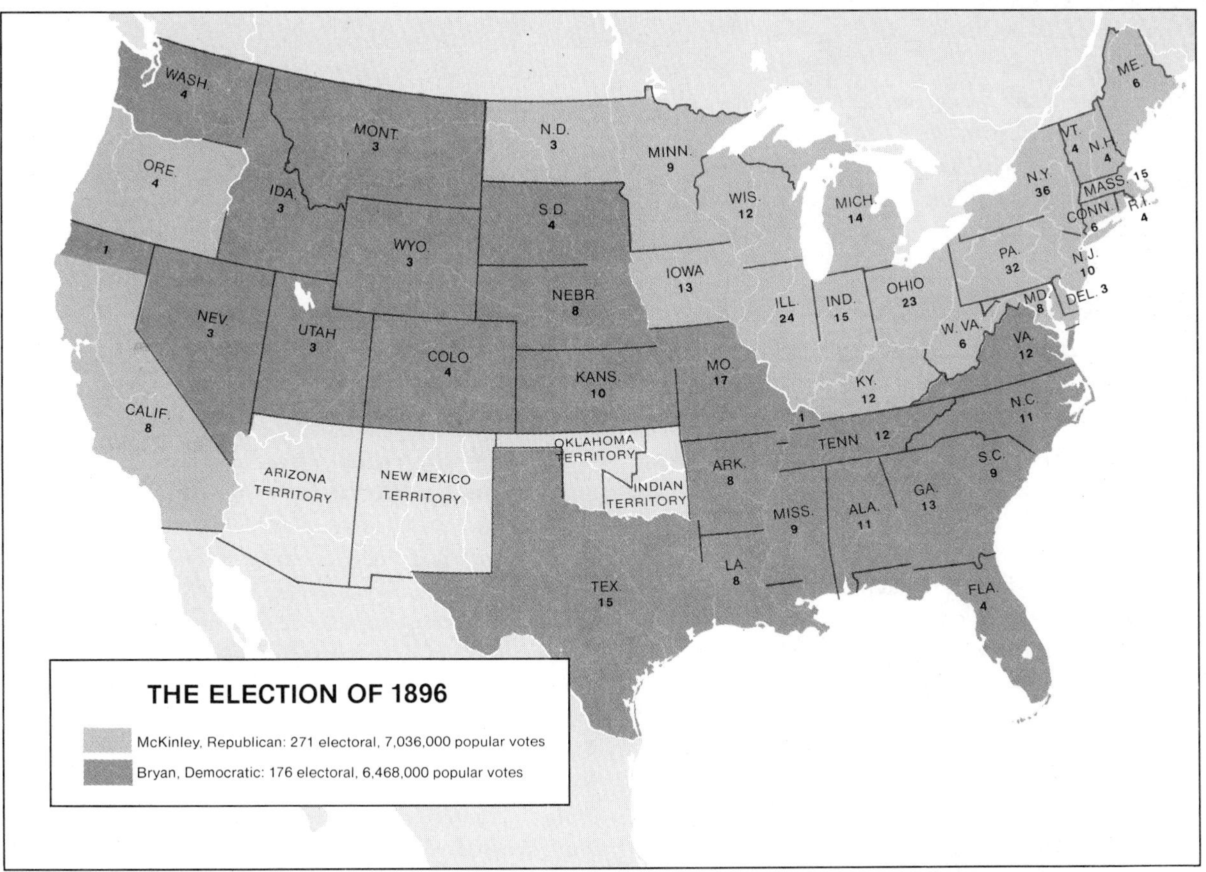

The sharp sectional division indicated that the industrial part of the country had triumphed over the agricultural; it did not, however, represent a division of the nation along economic or social lines. The business and financial interests, it is true, voted solidly for the Republicans, fearing that a Democratic victory would bring economic chaos. When a Nebraska landowner tried to float a mortgage during the campaign, a loan-company official wrote him: "If McKinley is elected, we think we will be in the market, but we do not care to make any investments while there is an uncertainty as to what kind of money a person will be paid back in." Other groups were far from united, however. Many thousands of farmers voted for McKinley, as his success in states such as North Dakota, Iowa, and Minnesota proved. In the East and in the states bordering the Great Lakes, the agricultural depression was not very severe, and farm radicalism practically nonexistent.

A preponderance of the labor vote also went to the Republicans. In part this resulted from the tremendous pressures that many industrialists applied to their workers. "Men," one manufacturer announced, "vote as you please, but if Bryan is elected . . . the whistle will not blow Wednesday morning." A number of companies placed orders for materials subject to cancellation if the Democrats won. But coercion was not a major factor, for McKinley was highly regarded in labor circles. While governor of Ohio, he had advocated the arbitration of industrial disputes and backed a law fining employers who refused to permit workers to join unions. During the Pullman strike he had sent his brother to try to persuade George Pullman to deal fairly with the strikers. He had invariably based his advocacy of high tariffs on the argument that American wage levels would be depressed if foreign goods could enter the country untaxed. Mark Hanna, too, had the reputation of always giving the workingman a square deal. The Republicans ran strongly in all the large cities, and in critical states like Illinois and Ohio this made the difference between victory and defeat.

During the campaign, some frightened Republicans had laid plans for fleeing the country if Bryan were elected, and belligerent ones, such as Theodore Roosevelt, then police commissioner of New York City, readied themselves to meet the "social revolutionaries" on the battlefield. Victory sent such men into transports of joy. Roosevelt, for example, expressed profound relief at having successfully weathered "the greatest crisis in our national fate, save only the Civil War." Most conservatives concluded happily that the way of life they so fervently admired had been saved for all time.

However heartfelt, such sentiments were not founded upon fact. With workers standing beside capitalists, with the farmers divided, and with immigrant groups also split fairly evenly between the parties, it cannot be said that the election divided the nation class against class or that McKinley's victory saved the country from revolution.

Far from representing a triumph for the status quo, the election marked the coming of age of modern America. The battle between gold and silver, which everyone had considered so vital, had very little real significance. The inflationists seemed to have been beaten, but new gold discoveries in Alaska and South Africa and improved methods of extracting gold from low-grade ores soon led to a great expansion of the money supply. In any case, within two decades the whole system of basing the volume of currency on bullion had been abandoned. Bryan and the Populists, supposedly the advance agents of revolution, were oriented more toward the past than the future. Their ideal was the rural America of Jefferson and Jackson. McKinley, on the other hand, for all his innate conservatism was essentially a man of his own times, one even capable of looking ahead toward the new century. His approach was national where Bryan's was basically parochial. While never daring and seldom imaginative, he was capable of dealing pragmatically with current problems. Before long, as America became increasingly an exporter of manufactures, he would even modify his position on the tariff. And no one better reflected the spirit of the age than Mark Hanna, the outstanding political realist of his generation. Far from preventing change, the outcome of the election of 1896 made possible still greater changes as the United States moved into the 20th century.

SUPPLEMENTARY READING The political history of this period is covered in lively and controversial fashion by Matthew Josephson, *The Politicos** (1938), in briefer but equally controversial style by Ray Ginger, *Age of Excess** (1965), and more solidly and sympathetically in H.W. Morgan, *From Hayes to McKinley* (1969). Both H.U. Faulkner, *Politics, Reform, and Expansion** (1959), and J.R. Hollingsworth, *The Whirligig of Politics* (1963), treat the politics of the nineties in some detail, while H.S. Merrill, *Bourbon Democracy of the Middle West* (1953), and C.V. Woodward, *Origins of the New South** (1951) are important regional studies. J.A. Garraty, *The New Commonwealth** (1968), attempts to trace the changing character of the political system after 1877.

There are three superb analyses of the political system of the period written by men who studied it firsthand: James Bryce, *The American Commonwealth** (1888), Woodrow Wilson, *Congressional Government** (1886), and Moisei Ostrogorski, *Democracy and the Organization of Political Parties** (1902). L.D. White, *The Republican Era** (1958), is an excellent study of the government in that period by a modern scholar. D.J. Rothman, *Politics and Power: The United States Senate, 1869–1901* (1966), analyzes the shifting structure of the Upper House. Frances Carpenter (ed.), *Carp's Washington* (1960), is a useful collection of the writings of a perceptive Washington reporter of the 1880's.

The issues of postreconstruction politics are discussed in P.H. Buck, *The Road to Reunion** (1937), S.P. Hirshson, *Farewell to the Bloody Shirt** (1962), J.W. Oliver, *History of the Civil War Military Pensions* (1917), F.W. Taussig, *The Tariff History of the United States** (1914), D.R. Dewey, *Financial*

History of the United States (1918), A.D. Noyes, *Forty Years of American Finance* (1909), Irwin Unger, *The Greenback Era** (1964), Milton Friedman and A.J. Schwartz, *A Monetary History of the United States* (1963), W.T.K. Nugent, *Money and American Society* (1968), Geoffrey Blodgett, *The Gentle Reformers: Massachusetts Democracy in the Cleveland Era* (1966), J.G. Sproat, "*The Best Men*": *Liberal Reformers in the Gilded Age* (1968), Ari Hoogenboom, *Fighting the Spoilsmen** (1961), and in several essays in H.W. Morgan (ed.), *The Gilded Age** (1970).

Among biographies of political leaders, the following are especially worth consulting: Harry Barnard, *Rutherford B. Hayes and His America* (1954), R.G. Caldwell, *James A. Garfield* (1931), G.F. Howe, *Chester A. Arthur* (1934), Allan Nevins, *Grover Cleveland* (1932), H.S. Merrill, *Bourbon Leader: Grover Cleveland and the Democratic Party** (1957), H.J. Sievers, *Benjamin Harrison* (1952–1968), D.S. Muzzey, *James G. Blaine* (1934).

For the farmers' problems, see F.A. Shannon, *The Farmer's Last Frontier** (1945), S.J. Buck, *The Granger Movement** (1913), J.D. Hicks, *The Populist Revolt** (1931), and Theodore Saloutos, *Farmer Movements in the South** (1960). Populism has been the subject in recent years of intensive re-examination. Richard Hofstadter, *The Age of Reform** (1955), takes a dim view of populism as a reform movement, while Norman Pollack, *The Populist Response to Industrial America** (1962), pictures it as a truly radical one. W.T.K. Nugent, *The Tolerant Populists* (1963), leans in Pollack's direction but is more restrained. C.V. Woodward, *Tom Watson: Agrarian Rebel** (1938), and Martin Ridge, *Ignatius Donnelly: Portrait of a Politician* (1962), are excellent biographies of populist leaders. F.E. Haynes, *James Baird Weaver* (1919), is also useful.

On the depression of the 1890's, consult Rendigs Fels, *American Business Cycles* (1959). The political and social disturbances connected with the depression are discussed in G.H. Knoles, *The Presidential Campaign and Election of 1892* (1942), Allan Nevins, *Grover Cleveland,* D.L. McMurry, *Coxey's Army* (1929), Almont Lindsey, *The Pullman Strike** (1942), Ray Ginger, *The Bending Cross: Eugene V. Debs** (1949) and *Altgeld's America** (1958), and F.L. Allen, *The Great Pierpont Morgan** (1949).

For the election of 1896, see S.L. Jones, *The Presidential Election of 1896* (1964), R.F. Durden, *The Climax of Populism: The Election of 1896** (1965), and P.W. Glad, *McKinley, Bryan, and the People** (1964). On Bryan, consult Glad's *The Trumpet Soundeth** (1960), and P.E. Coletta, *William Jennings Bryan* (1964); on McKinley, consult Margaret Leech, *In the Days of McKinley* (1959), and H.W. Morgan, *William McKinley and His America* (1963). Herbert Croly, *Marcus Alonzo Hanna* (1912), is the best life of Hanna.

*Available in paperback.

22

From Isolation to Empire

Americans have always been somewhat confused and ambivalent in their attitudes toward other nations, but at no point in their history has this been more clearly the case than in the decades following the Civil War. Fully occupied with the task of exploiting the West and building their great industrial machine, they gave little thought to foreign affairs. Benjamin Harrison reflected a widely held belief when he said during the 1888 Presidential campaign that the United States was "an apart nation" and thus it should remain. James Bryce made the same point in *The American Commonwealth.* "Happy America," he wrote, stood "apart in a world of her own . . . safe even from menace."

One recent historian, David W. Pletcher, has called the period "the awkward age" of American diplomacy, a time when the foreign service was "amateurish" and "spoils-ridden," when policy was either nonexistent or poorly planned, when treaties were clumsily drafted and state secrets ill kept. More than ever before or since, foreign affairs were the playthings of politics. "The general idea of the diplomatic service," one reporter commented at this time, "is that it is a soft berth for wealthy young men who enjoy court society." An important New York newspaper, the *Sun,* suggested in the 1880's that the State Department had "outgrown its usefulness" and ought to be abolished.

America's Divided View of the World

Of course late-19th-century Americans never ignored world affairs entirely. They had little direct concern for what went on in Europe, but their interest in Latin America was great and growing, in the Far East only less so. And economic developments, especially certain shifts in foreign commerce resulting from industrialization, were strengthening this interest with every passing year. Whether one sees isolation or expansion as the hallmark of American foreign policy after 1865 depends upon what part of the world one looks at.

The disdain of the people of the United States for Europe rested upon a number of historical foundations. Faith in the unique character of American civilization and the converse of that belief—suspicion of Europe's supposedly aristocratic and decadent society—formed the basis of this isolation. Bitter memories of indignities suffered during the Revolution and the Napoleonic Wars and anger at the hostile attitude of the great powers toward the United States during the Civil War strengthened it, as did the dislike of Americans for the traditional pomp and punctilio of European diplomacy. More important still was the undeniable truth that the United States was both practically invulnerable to European attack and incapable of mounting an offensive against any European power. In turning their backs on Europe, Americans were taking no risks and passing up few opportunities—hence their indifference.

When occasional conflicts with one or another of the great powers erupted, the United States pressed its claims hard. It insisted, for example, that Great Britain should pay for the loss of some 100,000 tons of American shipping sunk by Confederate cruisers that had been built in British yards during the rebellion, and some politicians even demanded that the British pay for the entire cost of the war after the Battle of Gettysburg—some $2 billion—on the ground that without British backing the Confederacy would have collapsed at about that point. However, the controversy never became critical, and in 1871 the two nations signed the Treaty of Washington, agreeing to arbitrate these so-called *Alabama* claims. The next year the judges awarded the United States $15.5 million for the ships and cargoes that had been destroyed.

In the 1880's a squabble developed with Germany, France, and a number of other countries over their banning of American pork products, ostensibly because some uninspected American pork was discovered to be diseased. This affair produced a great deal of windy oratory denouncing European autocracy and led to threats of economic retaliation. The indignation was not without justification; the restrictions were inspired by European pig farmers, who were suffering from American competition, and by manufacturers, who resented the American protective tariff. But Congress eventually provided for the inspection of meat destined for export, and in 1891 the European nations lifted the ban. Similarly, there were repeated alarms and outbursts of anti-British feeling in the United States in connection with Great Britain's treatment of Ireland, all, however, motivated chiefly by the efforts of politicians to appeal to Irish-American voters. None of these incidents amounted to very much.

On the other hand, the nation's interest in other parts of the world gradually increased in the period after 1865. During the Civil War France had established a protectorate over Mexico, setting up the Archduke Maximilian of Austria as emperor. In 1866 Secretary of State William H. Seward demanded that the French withdraw, and the government moved 50,000 soldiers to the Rio Grande. Although fear of American intervention was only one of many reasons for their action, the French did pull their troops out of Mexico during the winter of 1866–67. Nationalist rebels promptly seized and executed Maximilian. In 1867, at the instigation of Seward, the United States purchased Alaska from Russia for $7.2 million, thus ridding the continent of another foreign power.

The aggressive Seward also tried to obtain a number of island footholds for the United States in the Caribbean and the Pacific. The distant Midway Islands, far to the west of Hawaii, were acquired in 1867. In the same year Seward negotiated a treaty to purchase the Danish West Indies, now the Virgin Islands, but he could not persuade the Senate to ratify it. He also made overtures toward annexing the Hawaiian Islands and looked longingly at Cuba. As early as 1859 he said of Cuba, displaying a monumental ignorance of historical geology, "every rock and every grain of sand in that island were drifted and washed out from American soil by the floods of the Mississippi, and the other estuaries of the Gulf of Mexico."

But at this date the nation was unready for such grandiose schemes. The purchase of the Danish Indies was defeated in the Senate despite the fact that a plebiscite in the islands showed an overwhelming sentiment in favor of annexation. Seward soon had to admit that there was no significant support in the country for his expansionist plans.

The issue came to a head in 1870, when Presi-

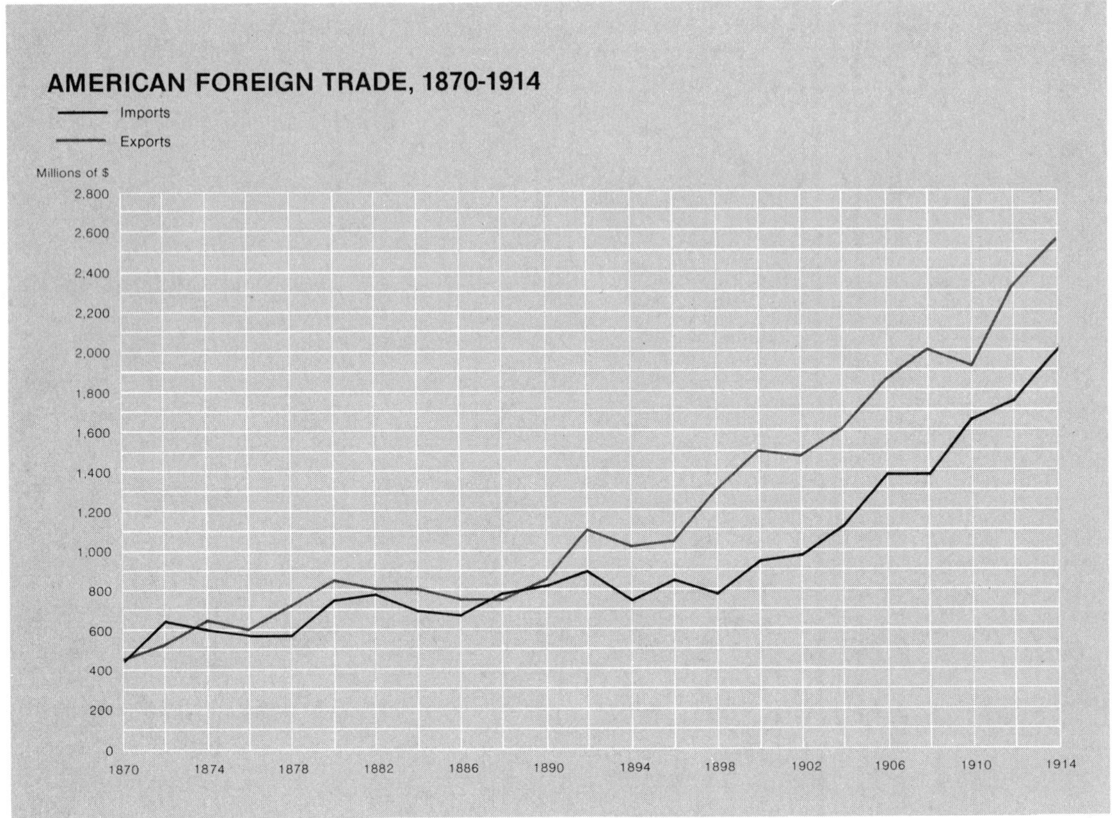

dent Grant submitted a treaty to the Senate annexing the Dominican Republic. He applied tremendous pressure in an effort to obtain ratification, thus forcing a "great debate" on extracontinental expansion. He stressed the wealth and resources of the country, the markets it would provide, even its "salubrious climate." But the arguments of the opposition proved more persuasive. The distance of the Dominican Republic from the continent, its crowded, dark-skinned population of what one congressman called "semi-civilized, semi-barbarous men who cannot speak our language," made annexation appear unattractive. The treaty was rejected, the nation apparently having decided that its destiny was to dominate the continent but to stop at the water's edge. Prevailing opinion was well summarized by a Philadelphia newspaper: "The true interests of the American people will be better served . . . by a thorough and complete development of the immense resources of our existing territory than by any rash attempts to increase it."

However, the very internal growth which distracted Americans from foreign ventures eventually led them to look outward again. By the late 1880's the country was producing enormous amounts of agricultural and industrial goods and exporting an ever larger share of this production. Exports rose in value from $450 million in 1870 to $853 million in 1880 and passed the billion-dollar mark early in the 1890's. Imports increased at an only slightly less spectacular rate.

The character of foreign trade was also changing: manufactures loomed ever more important among exports, until in 1898 the country shipped abroad more manufactured goods than it imported. By this time American steelmakers, for example, could compete with British producers for business anywhere in the world. In 1900 one company received a large order for steel plates from a Glasgow shipbuilder, and an American firm won contracts for structural steel used in constructing bridges for the Uganda Railroad in British East Africa. When a member of Parliament questioned the colonial secretary about the latter deal, the secretary replied: "Tenders [bids] were invited in the United Kingdom . . . [but] one of the American tenders was found to be considerably the lowest in every respect and was therefore accepted." As American industrialists became conscious of their ability to compete with Europeans in far-off markets, they began to take a new interest in world affairs, especially in periods of depression, when domestic consumption fell off.

The shifting intellectual currents of the times further altered the attitudes of Americans toward foreign affairs. Darwin's theories, applicable by analogy to international relations, gave the concept of manifest destiny a new plausibility. Darwinists like the historian John Fiske argued that the American democratic system of government was clearly the world's "fittest" and must spread inevitably over "every land on the earth's surface." In *Our Country*, Josiah Strong found racist and religious justifications for American expansionism, also based upon the theory of evolution. The Anglo-Saxon race, centered now in the United States, possessed "an instinct or genius for colonization," Strong claimed. "God, with infinite wisdom and skill is training the Anglo-Saxon race for . . . *the final competition of races.*" Christianity, he added, had developed "aggressive traits calculated to impress its institutions upon mankind." Soon American civilization would "move down upon" Mexico and all Latin America, and "out upon the islands of the sea, over upon Africa and beyond." "Can anyone doubt," Strong asked, "that the result of this . . . will be 'the survival of the fittest'?"

The completion of the conquest of the American West also encouraged Americans to consider expansion beyond the seas as a means of preserving the vitality of the nation. "For nearly 300 years the dominant fact in American life has been expansion," declared Frederick Jackson Turner, propounder of the frontier thesis. "That these energies of expansion will no longer operate would be a rash prediction." Turner and writers who advanced other expansionist arguments were much influenced by foreign thinking. European liberals had tended to disapprove of colonial ventures, but in the 1870's and 1880's many of them were modifying their positions. English liberals in particular began to talk and write about the "superiority" of English culture, to describe the virtues of the "Anglo-Saxon race" in Darwinist terms, to stress a "duty" to spread Christianity among the heathen, and to advance various economic arguments for overseas expansion.

European ideas were reinforced for Americans by their observations of the imperialist activities of the European powers in what would today be called underdeveloped areas. By swallowing up most of Africa and systematically destroying the independence of the crumbling empire of China, the French, British, Germans, and other colonizers inspired some patriots in the United States to advocate joining the feast before all the choice morsels had been digested. "While the great powers of Europe are steadily enlarging their colonial domination in Asia and Africa," said James G. Blaine in 1884, "it is the especial province of this country to improve and expand its trade with the nations of America." While Blaine emphasized commerce, the excitement and adventure of overseas enterprises appealed to many perhaps more than their economic possibilities or any sense of obligation to fulfill a supposed national or racial destiny.

Finally, military and strategic arguments were advanced to justify adopting a "large" policy. The powerful Union army had been demobilized rapidly after Appomattox; in the 1880's only about 25,000 men were under arms, their chief occupation fighting Indians in the West. Half the navy had been scrapped after the war, and the remaining ships had soon become obsolete. While other nations were building steam-powered iron warships, the United States depended upon a handful of wooden sailing vessels. As early as 1867 a British naval publication accurately described the American fleet as "hapless, broken-down, tattered [and] forlorn."

Although no foreign power menaced the country, the decrepit state of the navy vexed many of its officers. Chief among these was Commodore Stephen B. Luce, who conducted a long campaign for better officer-training facilities and a general strengthening of the service. In 1884 Luce persuaded the Arthur administration to create the Naval War College, and the next year he brought in Captain Alfred Thayer Mahan to lecture there on tactics and naval history. Mahan, who succeeded Luce as president of the college in 1886, used his lectures to develop a startling theory about the importance of sea power, which he explained to the public in two important books, *The Influence of Sea Power upon History* (1890) and *The Influence of Sea Power upon the French Revolution and Empire* (1892). History proved, according to Mahan, that a nation with a powerful navy and the overseas bases necessary to maintain it would be invulnerable in war and prosperous in time of peace. Applied to the current American situation, Mahan explained in a series of magazine articles, this meant that in addition to building a modern fleet, the United States should obtain a string of coaling stations and bases in the Caribbean, annex the Hawaiian Islands, and cut a canal across Central America. Eventually, a more extensive colonial empire might follow, but these defensive bases and the canal they would protect were essential first steps if the United States was to insure its future as a great power.

Writing at a time when the imperialist-minded European nations were showing signs of extending their influence in South America and the Pacific islands, Mahan attracted many influ-

Harper's Weekly, JANUARY 30, 1892

This double-spread engraving from Harper's Weekly, *portraying major units of the United States fleet, appeared in January 1892, at the height of the Chilean "crisis." The cruiser* Baltimore, *whose seamen were attacked by a mob in Valparaiso, triggering the incident, is at right center (number 12). The* Baltimore *later fought under Admiral Dewey in the Battle of Manila Bay in 1898. At center foreground is the ill-fated battleship* Maine.

ential disciples. One of these was Congressman Henry Cabot Lodge of Massachusetts, a prominent member of the Naval Affairs Committee. Lodge had married into a navy family and was intimate with Commodore Luce, whose son had married his wife's sister. He soon became a good friend of Mahan's. He helped push an act through Congress in 1883 authorizing the building of three steel warships and consistently advocated expanding and modernizing the fleet. Elevated to the Senate in 1893, Lodge continually pressed for expansionist policies, basing his arguments on the strategic concepts of Mahan. "Sea power," he repeatedly proclaimed, "is essential to the greatness of every splendid people." Another important follower of Mahan was Benjamin F. Tracy, Harrison's secretary of the navy, who greatly improved the administration of his department and helped persuade Congress to increase naval appropriations. Lodge's close friend Theodore Roosevelt was still another ardent supporter of the "large" policy, but he had little influence until he became assistant secretary of the navy in 1897.

The Course of Empire

The interest of the United States in the Pacific and the Far East dated back to the late 18th century when the first American merchant ship dropped anchor in Canton harbor. After the Treaty of Wanghia (1844), American merchants in China enjoyed many privileges and trade expanded rapidly. Missionaries began to flock into the country in increasing numbers too—in the late eighties, over 500 were established there.

The Hawaiian Islands were an important way station on the route to China, and by 1820 merchants and missionaries were making contacts there. As early as 1854 a movement to annex the islands existed, although this foundered because of Hawaii's insistence on being admitted to the Union as a state. Commodore Perry's expedition to Japan led to the signing of a commercial treaty (1858) which opened several Japanese ports to American traders. In general the United States pursued a policy of cooperating with the European powers in expanding commercial activities in the Far East. In Hawaii the tendency was to claim a special position for America but to accept the fact that the Europeans also had interests in the islands.

This state of affairs did not change radically after the Civil War. Despite Chinese protests over the exclusion of their nationals from the United States after 1882, American commercial privileges in China were not disturbed. American influence in Hawaii increased rapidly, the descendants of missionary families, most of them engaged in raising sugar, dominating the native monarchy. In 1875 a reciprocity treaty admitted Hawaiian sugar to the United States free of duty in return for a promise not to yield any territory to a foreign power. When this treaty was renewed in 1887, the United States obtained the right to establish a naval base at Pearl Harbor. In addition to occupying Midway, America also obtained a foothold in the Samoan Islands in the South Pacific (1878). After a period of rivalry with Germany and Great Britain in these islands, a treaty was negotiated in Berlin in 1889 establishing a tripartite protectorate over the archipelago.

During the 1890's American interest in the Pacific area steadily intensified. Conditions in Hawaii had much to do with this. The McKinley Tariff Act of 1890, discontinuing the duty on raw sugar and compensating American producers of cane and beet sugar by granting them a bounty of two cents a pound, struck Hawaiian sugar growers hard, for it destroyed the advantage they had gained in the reciprocity treaty. Hawaiian sugar fell in value from $100 a ton to $60, an annual loss to the islanders of about $12 million. The next year the death of the complaisant King Kalakaua brought Queen Liliuokalani, a determined nationalist, to the throne. Placing herself at the head of a "Hawaii for the Hawaiians" movement, she abolished the existing constitution under which the white minority had pretty much controlled the islands and attempted to rule as an absolute monarch. The local Americans, alarmed by this threat to their interests and always eager for annexation by the United States, then decided to stage a coup. In January 1893, with the connivance of the United States minister, John L. Stevens, who ordered 150 marines from the cruiser *Boston* into Honolulu, ostensibly to protect American lives and property but actually to overawe the natives, they deposed Queen Liliuokalani and set up a provisional government. Stevens recognized their regime at once, and the new government promptly sent a delegation to Washington to seek a treaty of annexation.

In the closing days of the Harrison administration, such a treaty was negotiated and sent to the Senate, but when Cleveland took office in March, he withdrew it. The new President disapproved of the way American troops had been used to overthrow the native government. He sent a special commissioner, James H. Blount, to Hawaii to investigate. When Blount reported the natives opposed annexation, the President dismissed Stevens and attempted to restore Queen Liliuokalani. Since the provisional government was by that time firmly entrenched, this could not be accomplished peacefully, and Cleveland was unwilling to use force against the Americans in the islands, however much he objected to their actions. Thus he found himself unable to do anything at all. Although unwilling to depart from the "unbroken American tradition" of eschewing overseas dependencies, he could not suggest any method "consistent with American honor, integrity, and morality" of restoring native rule. The revolutionary government of Hawaii remained in power, independent but still eager to be annexed.

The Hawaiian debate continued sporadically over the next four years, providing a thorough airing of the whole question of overseas expansion. Fears that another power—Great Britain or perhaps Japan—might step into the void created by Cleveland's refusal to act greatly alarmed those who favored annexation. It would be "madness" to allow Great Britain to seize the islands, Senator Lodge warned, adding that the Japanese, "a great fighting race at sea," were "in a state of mind when they think they can whip anybody" and looking covetously at Hawaii. When the Republicans came back to power in 1897, a new annexation treaty was negotiated. However, domestic sugar producers now threw their weight against it, and the McKinley administration could not obtain the necessary two-thirds majority in the Senate. Finally, in July 1898, after the outbreak of the Spanish-American War, Congress annexed the islands by joint resolution, a procedure requiring only a simple majority vote.

Most of the arguments for extending American influence in the Pacific applied even more strongly to Central and South America, where the United States had much larger economic interests and where the strategic importance of the region was clearly defined. Furthermore, the Monroe Doctrine had long conditioned the American people to the idea of acting to protect national interests in the Western Hemisphere. Although the post-Civil War plans of Seward and Grant for expansion in the Caribbean were thwarted, support for an aggressive policy in the hemisphere was always considerable.

As early as 1869 President Grant had come out for an American-owned canal across the Isthmus of Panama, in spite of the fact that the United States had agreed in the Clayton-Bulwer Treaty with Great Britain (1850) that neither nation would "obtain or maintain for itself any exclusive control" over an interoceanic canal. In 1880, when the French engineer Ferdinand de Lesseps organized a company to build a canal across the isthmus, President Hayes announced that the United States would not permit any European power to control such a waterway. "The policy of the country is a canal under American control," he announced, another blithe disregard of the Clayton-Bulwer agreement.

In 1888 Congress authorized the convening of a Pan-American Conference in Washington to discuss hemispheric problems. Secretary of State James G. Blaine, who had planned such a conference as early as 1881, hoped to use this meeting to obtain a general reciprocity agreement with the Latin-American countries, for the United States was importing about three times as much from them as they were purchasing in America. Blaine even persuaded the influential protectionist congressman William McKinley to advocate placing hides on the free list in order to get the South Americans to make similar concessions. When they gathered in Washington in 1889, however, the delegates accomplished nothing beyond the establishment of an International Bureau—later known as the Pan-American Union—to promote commercial and cultural exchange. The conference was nevertheless significant, for it marked the first effort by the United States to assume the leadership of all the nations of the hemisphere.

At the Washington meeting the United States posed as a friend of peace; Blaine's proposals included a general arbitration treaty to settle all hemispheric disputes. However, a minor disagreement with the Republic of Chile in 1891 soon demonstrated that the country could quickly be brought to the verge of war with one of its southern neighbors. Anti-*Yanqui* feeling was high at that time in Chile, chiefly because the United States had refused to sell arms to the current government during the revolution that had brought it to power. In October a group of sailors from the U.S.S. *Baltimore* on shore leave in Valparaiso were set upon by a mob. Two of the sailors were killed and more than a dozen others injured. President Harrison, furious at what he called an "insult . . . to the uniform of the United States sailors," demanded "prompt and full reparation." When the Chilean authorities delayed in supplying an appropriate apology and went so far as to issue a statement that "imputed untruth and insincerity" on Harrison's part, the President sent a special message to Congress virtually inviting it to declare war.

The United States had good reason to demand reparations and a formal apology, but the incident was too trivial to fight about. Secretary Blaine labored manfully to calm Harrison, even threatening to resign if he insisted on war, but the rest of the Cabinet, especially the expansionist navy secretary, Benjamin F. Tracy, supported the President. Faced with the alternative of war with the United States, Chile backed down, offering the required apology and agreeing to pay damages to the sailors. Of course Chile's humiliation destroyed much of the good will engendered by the Pan-American Conference.

When Cleveland returned to power in 1893, the possibility of trouble in Latin America seemed remote, for he had always opposed imperialistic ventures. The Latin-American diplomatic colony in Washington greeted him with real warmth after its experience with the hot-tempered Harrison. Yet scarcely two years later the United States was again on the verge of war in South America as a result of a crisis in Venezuela, and before this issue was settled Cleveland had proclaimed the most powerful statement of American hegemony in the hemisphere ever uttered.

The tangled borderland between Venezuela and British Guiana had long been in dispute, with Venezuela demanding more of the region than it was entitled to and Great Britain also submitting exaggerated claims and imperiously refusing to submit the question to arbitration. As early as the Hayes administration, the United States had offered its good offices in trying to settle the argument. What now made a crisis of this controversy was chiefly the political situation in the United States. A recent minor incident in Nicaragua, where the British had temporarily occupied the port of Corinto to force compensation for injuries done British subjects in that country, had alarmed American supporters of the Monroe Doctrine. Cleveland had wisely avoided involvement, but along with his refusal to take Hawaii, the incident had angered expansionists. With his party rapidly deserting him because of his stand on the silver question and with the election of 1896 approaching, the President desperately needed a popular issue.

There was much latent anti-British feeling in the United States. A disagreement over fishing rights off Canada in 1885 had caused a nasty flurry. A clash over seal-hunting in the Bering Sea, during which American revenue cutters had seized Canadian vessels beyond the three-mile limit, had exacerbated Anglo-American relations between 1886 and 1892 and cost the United States nearly $500,000 in damages when it was finally arbitrated. By taking the Venezuelan side in the boundary dispute, Cleveland would be defending a weak neighbor against a great power, a position sure to evoke a popular response. "Turn this Venezuela question up or down, North, South, East or West, and it is a 'winner,' " one Democrat advised the President.

Convinced that Venezuela's cause was just, the stubborn, self-righteous, and harassed Cleveland could not resist the temptation to intervene. In July 1895 he ordered his secretary of state, Richard Olney, to send a near-ultimatum to the British. By occupying the disputed territory, Olney insisted, Great Britain was invading Venezuela and thus violating the Monroe Doctrine. Quite gratuitously, he went on to boast: "To-day the United States is practically sovereign on this continent, and its fiat is law upon the subjects to which it confines its interposition." Unless Great Britain responded promptly by agreeing to arbitration, the President would call the question to the attention of Congress.

The note threatened war, but the British ignored it for months. They did not take the United States seriously as a world power, and with much reason, since the American navy, although now rapidly expanding, could not hope to stand up against the British, which had no less than 50 battleships and 25 armored cruisers, together with many smaller vessels. When Lord Salisbury, the prime minister and foreign secretary, finally replied, he rejected outright the argument that the Monroe Doctrine had any status under international law and refused to arbitrate what he called the "exaggerated pretentions" of the Venezuelans.

If Olney's note had been belligerent, this reply was supercilious and sharp to the point of asperity. Cleveland was furious. On December 17, 1895, he asked Congress for authority to appoint an American commission to determine the correct line between British Guiana and Venezuela. When that had been done, he added, the United States should "resist by every means in its power" the appropriation by Great Britain of any territory "we have determined of right belongs to Venezuela." Congress responded at once, and unanimously, appropriating $100,000 for the boundary commission. Popular enthusiasm was almost equally universal. In Great Britain, on the other hand, government and people suddenly awoke to the seriousness of the situation. No one wanted a war with the United States, certainly not over a remote patch of tropical real estate. Britain's position in Europe was being threatened by a rising Germany; trouble was developing in British South Africa; the Royal Navy was mighty but widely scattered; Canada would be terribly vulnerable in the event of war. Most important of all, the British faced up at last to the immense *potential* strength of the United States. Could they afford to make an enemy of a nation of 70 million, already the richest industrial power in the world? Obviously they could not. To fight with America, the British colonial secretary said, "would be an absurdity as well as a crime."

And so Great Britain backed down and agreed to arbitrate the boundary. At once the war scare subsided; soon Olney was talking about "our inborn and instinctive English sympathies" and offering "to stand side by side and shoulder to shoulder with England in . . . the defence of human rights." When the boundary tribunal awarded nearly all the disputed region to Great Britain, whatever ill-feeling the surrender may have occasioned in that country faded away. Instead of leading to war, the affair marked the beginning of an era of Anglo-American friendship. It had the unfortunate effect, however, of adding to the long-held American conviction that the nation could get what it wanted in international affairs by threats and bluster—a dangerous illusion.

Cuba and the War with Spain

On February 10, 1896, scarcely a week after Venezuela and Great Britain had signed the arbitration treaty ending their dispute, General Valeriano Weyler arrived in Havana from Madrid to take up his duties as governor of Cuba. His assignment to this post was occasioned by the guerrilla warfare that Cuban nationalist rebels had been waging on the island for almost a year. Weyler, a tough and ruthless man, set out to administer Cuba with "a salutary rigor." He began herding the rural population into "reconcentration" camps in order to deprive the rebels of food and recruits. Conditions in these camps were wretched. Resistance in Cuba hardened and the conflict, already bitter, became a cruel, bloody struggle that could not help affecting the American people.

The United States had been interested in Cuba since the time of John Quincy Adams, and except for northern opposition to adding more slave territory might well have taken the island at one time or another before the Civil War. When the Cubans revolted against Spain in 1868, considerable support for intervening on their behalf developed, although the firmness of Hamilton Fish, Grant's secretary of state, held this sentiment in check. Spain managed to pacify the rebels in 1878 by promising reforms, but these were slow in coming—slavery was not abolished until 1886. The worldwide depression of the 1890's hit the Cuban economy hard, and when an American tariff act in 1894 jacked up the rate on Cuban sugar by 40 per cent, the resulting distress precipitated another revolt.

The new uprising caused immediate concern in the United States. Public sympathy naturally went out to the Cubans, who seemed to be fighting for liberty and democracy against an autocratic Old World power, and this sympathy was played upon cleverly by a junta of Cuban propagandists resident in the United States. Most American newspapers supported the Cubans; labor unions, veterans' organizations, many Protestant clergymen, and important politicians in both major parties demanded that the United States aid the rebel cause. Furthermore, rapidly increasing American investments in Cuban sugar plantations, now approaching $50 million, were endangered by the fighting and the social chaos sweeping across the island. When reports, often exaggerated, of the cruelty of "Butcher" Weyler and the horrors of his reconcentration camps began to filter into America, the cry for action intensified. In April 1896 Congress adopted a concurrent resolution suggesting that the revolutionaries be granted the rights of belligerents. Cleveland would not take this unneutral step, but he did exert diplomatic pressure on Spain to remove the causes of the rebels' complaints, and in addition he offered the services of his government as mediator. The Spanish rejected this suggestion flatly.

For a time, however, the issue subsided. The election of 1896 deflected American attention from Cuba, and then the gentle McKinley, recoiling from the thought of war, refused to take any action that might disturb Spanish-American relations. Business interests—except those with holdings in Cuba—backed McKinley, for they feared that a crisis would upset the economy, just beginning to pick up after the long depression. In Cuba General Weyler made some progress toward stifling rebel resistance. American expansionists continued to demand intervention, and the press, especially Joseph Pulitzer's New York *World* and William Randolph Hearst's New York *Journal*, competing fiercely to increase circulation, kept resentments alive with tales of Spanish atrocities. But McKinley remained adamant, and he controlled foreign policy. Although he warned Spain that Cuba must be pacified, and soon, his tone was friendly and he issued no ultimatum. A change in government in Spain in the fall of 1897 further relieved the situation, for the new regime recalled Weyler and promised partial self-government to the Cubans. In a message to Congress in December 1897, McKinley urged that Spain be given "a reasonable chance to realize her expectations" in the island. McKinley was not insensible to Cuba's plight—although far from being a rich man, he made an anonymous contribution of $5,000 to the Red Cross Cuban relief fund—but he genuinely desired to avoid intervention.

His hopes were doomed, primarily because Spain failed to "realize her expectations." Furthermore, the rebels would accept nothing less than independence. The war continued. Riots broke out in Havana in January 1898. To protect American citizens, McKinley ordered the battleship *Maine* to Havana harbor. Then, early in February, Hearst's New York *Journal* printed a letter written to a friend in Cuba by the Spanish minister in Washington, Depuy de Lôme. The letter had been stolen by a spy. De Lôme, an experienced but arrogant and reactionary diplomat, failed to appreciate McKinley's efforts to avoid intervening in Cuba. In this letter he characterized the President as a *politicastro*, or "would-be politician," which was a gross error, and a "bidder for the admiration of the crowd," which was equally insulting, although somewhat closer to the truth. Americans were outraged, and De Lôme's hasty resignation did little to soothe their feelings.

Before the furor over this incident could subside, the *Maine* was blown up in Havana harbor, 260 of her crew perishing in the explosion. Interventionists in the United States immediately accused Spain of having destroyed the ship and clamored for war. The willingness of Americans to blame Spain indicates the extent of anti-Spanish opinion in the United States by 1898; actually, no one has ever discovered what really happened. A naval court of inquiry decided that the vessel had indeed been sunk by a submarine mine, but it was absurd to think that the Spanish government would have been foolish enough to commit an act so likely to bring American troops into Cuba. Probably some fanatical rebel group was responsible.

With admirable courage, McKinley refused to be panicked, but he could not check the public clamor for intervention. Although he might ignore belligerent editorials and the irresponsible warmongering of expansionist politicians, he could not resist the wishes of millions of citizens that something be done to stop the carnage and allow the Cubans to determine their own fate. In the last analysis, Spanish pride and Cuban intransigence had taken the issue of peace or war out of his hands. The Spanish government could not suppress the rebellion, but it would not yield to the nationalists' increasingly extreme demands. To have granted independence to Cuba might have caused the Madrid government to fall, might even have led to the collapse of the monarchy, because the Spanish public was in no mood for abject surrender. The Cubans, sensing that the continuing bloodshed aided their cause, refused to give the Spanish regime any room to maneuver. After the *Maine* disaster, Spain might have agreed to an armistice if the rebels had asked for one and in the resulting negotiations might well have given up the island. The rebels refused to make the first move. The fighting went on, bringing the United States every day closer to intervention.

The President faced a fearful dilemma. Most of the business interests of the country, to which he was particularly sensitive, still opposed intervention. His personal feelings were equally firm. "I have been through one war," he told a friend. "I have seen the dead piled up, and I do not want to see another." Congress, however, seemed determined to act. When he submitted a restrained report on the sinking of the *Maine*, congressional hotheads exploded with wrath. The Democrats, even most of those who had supported Cleveland's policies, now gleefully accused McKinley of timidity. Vice President Hobart warned him that the Senate could not be held in check for long; should Congress decide to declare war on its own, the administration would be discredited. McKinley spent a succession of sleepless nights; even sedatives brought him no repose. Finally, early in April, the President drafted a message asking for authority to use the armed forces "to secure a full and final termination of hostilities" in Cuba.

At the last moment, however, the Spanish government seemed to yield; it ordered its troops in Cuba to cease hostilities. McKinley passed this information on to Congress along with his war message, but he gave it no emphasis and did not try to check the march toward war. It would have been more courageous to seek further delay at this point but not necessarily wiser. Merely to stop fighting was not enough. The Cuban nationalists now insisted upon full independence, and the Spanish politicians were still unprepared to abandon the last remnant of their once-great American empire. If the United States took Cuba, they might save their political skins; if they surrendered the island, they were done for.

On April 20 Congress by joint resolution recognized the independence of Cuba and authorized the use of the armed forces to drive out the Spanish. An amendment proposed by Senator Henry M. Teller disclaiming any intention of adding Cuban territory to the United States passed without opposition. Four days later Spain declared war on the United States.

The Spanish-American War was fought to free Cuba, but the first action took place on the other side of the globe in the Philippine Islands. Weeks earlier, Theodore Roosevelt, whom McKinley had appointed assistant secretary of the

The Bee, MAY 16, 1898

This cartoon appeared in The Bee *after Dewey's Manila Bay victory, but before the destruction of Spain's Caribbean squadron (the* New York *was one of the vessels blockading Santiago); thus its label, a "prophescopic-scoopograph," is appropriate if improbable. The rowboat is a swipe at editor Hearst's reporting from Cuba.*

navy, had alerted the United States Asiatic Squadron under Commodore George Dewey to move against the Spanish base at Manila if war came. Dewey had reacted promptly and efficiently, drilling his gun crews, taking on supplies, giving his gleaming white ships a coat of battle-gray paint, and establishing secret contacts with Filipino nationalist forces under Emilio Aguinaldo. When word of the declaration of war reached him, he steamed from Hong Kong across the South China Sea with four cruisers and two gunboats. On the night of April 30 he entered Manila Bay, and at daybreak opened fire on the Spanish fleet at 5,000 yards. His squadron made five passes, each time slightly reducing the range, and when the smoke had cleared, all ten of Admiral Montojo's ships had been destroyed. Dewey's fleet was intact—not a single American was killed in the engagement.

The American people received the news of Dewey's victory joyfully, although many had never heard of the Philippines before the bold headlines announced his triumph. The commodore asked for troops to take and hold Manila, for now that war had been declared, he could not return to Hong Kong or put in at any neutral port in the Far East. McKinley promptly dispatched some 11,000 soldiers and additional naval support. On August 13 these forces, assisted by Filipino irregulars under Aguinaldo, captured Manila.

Meanwhile, in the main theater of operations, the United States had won a quick and complete victory, more, however, because of the feebleness of the Spanish than because of the power or efficiency of the Americans. When the war began, the regular army consisted of about 28,000 men. This tiny force was bolstered by 200,000 ill-trained and poorly supplied volunteers. In May an expeditionary force began to

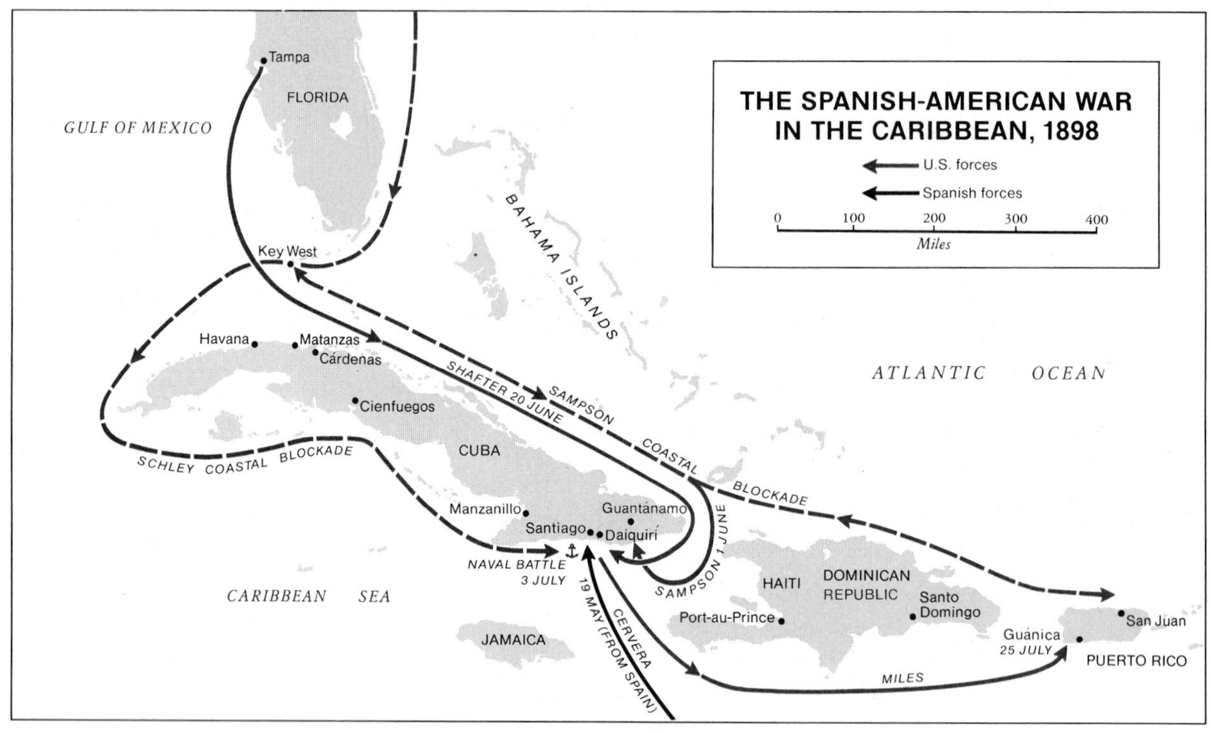

gather at Tampa, Florida. That semitropical hamlet was soon inundated. Rail connections proved totally inadequate to handle the masses of men and supplies that descended upon it; whole regiments sat without uniforms or weapons while hundreds of freight cars lay forgotten on sidings, jammed with equipment. Army staff work was abominable, rivalry between commanders a serious problem. Aggressive units like the regiment of "Rough Riders" that Theodore Roosevelt, now a lieutenant colonel of volunteers, had raised, scrambled for space and supplies, shouldering aside other units to get what they needed. "No words could describe . . . the confusion and lack of system and the general mismanagement of affairs here," the angry Roosevelt complained.

Since a Spanish fleet under Admiral Pascual Cervera was known to be in Caribbean waters, the invading army could not safely embark until it could be located. Finally, on May 29, the American fleet found Cervera at Santiago harbor, on the eastern end of Cuba, and established a blockade. On June 14 a 17,000-man expeditionary force commanded by General William Shafter sailed from Tampa. Landing at Daiquiri, east of Santiago, this army pressed quickly toward the city, handicapped more by its own inadequate equipment than by the enemy, although the Spanish troops resisted bravely. The Americans sweated through Cuba's torrid summer in heavy wool winter uniforms, ate "embalmed beef" out of cans, and fought mostly with old-fashioned rifles using black powder cartridges that marked the position of each soldier with a puff of smoke whenever he fired his weapon. On July 1 they broke through undermanned Spanish defenses and stormed San Juan Hill, the intrepid Colonel Roosevelt in the van. ("Are you afraid to stand up while I am on horseback?" Roosevelt demanded of one soldier pinned down by Spanish fire.)

With Santiago harbor now in range of American artillery, Admiral Cervera had to run the blockade. On July 3 his black-hulled ships, flags proudly flying, steamed forth from the harbor and fled westward along the coast. Like hounds after rabbits, five American battleships and two

WADSWORTH ATHENEUM, HARTFORD

Spanish admiral Cervera evaded the American naval blockade (map at left) to reach Santiago. At the right is the grim aftermath of the storming of San Juan Hill, recorded by William Glackens, a painter later famous as a pioneer of American realism.

cruisers, commanded by Rear Admiral William T. Sampson and Commodore Winfield Scott Schley, quickly ran them down. In four hours the entire Spanish force was destroyed by a hail of 8- and 13-inch projectiles. Damage to the American ships was superficial; only one seaman lost his life in the engagement.

The end then came abruptly. Santiago surrendered on July 17. A few days later, other United States troops completed the occupation of Puerto Rico. On August 12, one day before the fall of Manila, Spain agreed to get out of Cuba and to cede Puerto Rico and an island in the Marianas (Guam) to the United States. The future of the Philippines was to be settled at a formal peace conference, convening in Paris on October 1.

Developing a Colonial Policy

Although the Spanish resisted surrendering the Philippines at Paris, they had been so thoroughly defeated that they had no choice. The decision hung rather upon the outcome of a conflict over policy within the United States. The war, won at so little cost militarily,* produced problems far larger than those it solved. The nation had become a great power in the world's eyes. As a French diplomat wrote a few years later: "[The United States] is seated at the table where the great game is played, and it cannot leave it." European leaders had been impressed by the forcefulness of Cleveland's diplomacy in the Venezuela boundary dispute as well as by the efficiency displayed by the new navy in the war. The annexation of Hawaii and other overseas bases intensified their conviction that the United States was determined to become a major force in international affairs.

Actually, the imagination of Americans had been captured by the *trappings* of empire, not by its essence. It was titillating to think of a world map liberally sprinkled with American flags and of the economic benefits that colonies

*Over 5,000 Americans died as a result of the conflict, but less than 400 fell in combat. The others were mostly victims of diseases like yellow fever and typhoid.

might bring, but few citizens were ready to join in a worldwide struggle for power and influence. They entered blithely upon adventures in far-off regions without facing the implications of their decision realistically.

The debate over taking the Philippine Islands throws much light on the state of American opinion at this time. The expansionists, of course, were eager to annex the entire archipelago. Even before he had learned to spell the name, Senator Lodge was saying that "the Phillipines mean a vast future trade and wealth and power," offering the nation a greater opportunity "than anything that has happened . . . since the annexation of Louisiana." President McKinley adopted a more cautious stance, but he, too, favored "the general principle of holding on to what we can get." A speaking tour of the Middle West in October 1898, during which he experimented with varying degrees of commitment to expansionism, soon convinced him that the public wanted the islands. Business opinion, to which he was especially sensitive, had shifted dramatically during the war, and saw the Philippines as the gateway to the markets of the Far East.

On the other hand, an important minority objected strongly to the United States acquiring colonies. Men as varied in interest and philosophy as the tycoon Andrew Carnegie and the labor leader Samuel Gompers, as the Social Darwinist William Graham Sumner and the pragmatist William James, as the venerable Republican Senator George Frisbie Hoar of Massachusetts and "Pitchfork Ben" Tillman, the southern Democratic firebrand, together with writers like Mark Twain and William Dean Howells, reformers like Lincoln Steffens and Jane Addams, and educators like presidents Charles W. Eliot of Harvard and David Starr Jordan of Stanford united in opposing the annexation of the Philippines. These anti-imperialists insisted that it was unconstitutional to own colonies and a violation of the spirit of the Declaration of Independence to govern a foreign territory without the consent of its inhabitants. Senator Hoar argued that by taking over "vassal states" in "barbarous archipelagoes" the United States was "trampling . . . on our own great Charter, which recognizes alike the liberty and the dignity of individual manhood."

McKinley was not insensitive to this appeal to idealism and tradition, but he rejected it for a variety of reasons. Many anti-imperialists opposed Philippine annexation for selfish and unworthy motives. Pure partisanship led many of the Democrats to object. Most southern anti-imperialists were governed more by race prejudice than by democratic principles. "I strenuously oppose incorporating any more colored men in the body politic," Senator Tillman frankly admitted. Labor leaders like Gompers feared the possible competition of "the Chinese, the Negritos, and the Malays" who presumably would flood into the United States if the islands were taken over.

Even more compelling to McKinley was the absence of any practical alternative to annexation. Public opinion would not sanction restoring Spanish authority in the Philippines or allowing some other power to have them. That the Filipinos were sufficiently advanced and united socially to form a stable government if granted independence seemed highly unlikely. Senator Hoar believed that "for years and for generations, and perhaps for centuries, there would have been turbulence, disorder and revolution" in the islands if they were left to their own devices. Strangely—for he was a kind and gentle man—Hoar faced this possibility with equanimity. McKinley was unable to do so. The President searched the depths of his soul but could find no alternative to annexation. Of course the state of public feeling made the decision easier, and he must have found the idea of presiding over an empire appealing. The commercial possibilities did not escape him either. But in the end it was with a heavy sense of responsibility that he ordered the American peace commissioners to insist upon acquiring the Philippines. To salve the feelings of the Spanish, the United States agreed to pay $20 million for the archipelago, but it was a forced sale, accepted by Spain with bitter resignation.

The peace treaty still faced a hard battle in the United States Senate, where a combination of partisan politics and anticolonialism made it difficult to amass the two-thirds majority necessary for ratification. McKinley had shrewdly appointed three senators, including one Democrat, to the five-man commission, and this predisposed many members of the upper house to approve the treaty, but the vote was very close. William Jennings Bryan, titular head of the Democratic party, could probably have prevented ratification if he had urged his supporters to vote *nay*. Although he was personally opposed to taking the Philippines, he would not do so. The question should be decided, he said, "not by a *minority* of the Senate but by a *majority* of the people" at the forthcoming Presidential election. Perplexed by Bryan's stand, a number of Democrats allowed themselves to be persuaded by the expansionists' arguments and by McKinley's judicious use of patronage; the treaty was ratified in February 1899 by a vote of 57 to 27.

The national referendum that Bryan had hoped for never materialized. Bryan himself confused the issue in 1900 by making free silver a major plank in his platform, thus driving conservative anti-imperialists into McKinley's arms. Moreover, early in 1899, the Filipino nationalists under Aguinaldo, furious because the United States would not withdraw, rose in rebellion. A savage guerrilla war resulted. Like all such conflicts, waged in tangled country, chiefly by small, isolated units surrounded by a hostile civilian population that had little regard for the "rules" of war, this one produced many atrocities. Goaded by sneak attacks and isolated instances of cruelty to captives, American soldiers, many of whom had little respect for Filipinos to begin with, responded in kind. Horrible tales of rape, arson, and murder by United States troops began to filter into the country, providing much ammunition for the anti-imperialists. "You seem to

LIBRARY OF CONGRESS

A photograph taken in 1899 shows guerrilla troops captured during the Philippine Insurrection. Although the guerrilla leader, Emilio Aguinaldo, was seized in March 1901, fighting in the islands did not end until mid-1902.

have about finished your work of civilizing the Filipinos," Andrew Carnegie wrote angrily to one of the American peace commissioners. "About 8,000 of them have been completely civilized and sent to Heaven. I hope you like it." However, so long as the fighting continued it was politically impossible for the United States to withdraw from the islands. A commission appointed by McKinley in 1899 attributed the revolt to the ambitions of the nationalist leaders but recommended that the Philippines be granted independence at some indefinite future date. This seems to have been the wish of most Americans.

In any case, the re-election of McKinley in 1900 settled the Philippine question, although it took the efforts of some 70,000 American soldiers and three years of brutal guerrilla warfare before peace was finally restored. Meanwhile, McKinley sent a second commission headed by William Howard Taft, an Ohio judge, to establish civil government in the islands. Taft, a warm-hearted, affable man, took an instant liking to the Filipinos and soon won from them a large measure of confidence; his policy of encouraging natives to participate in the new territorial government attracted many converts. In July 1901 he became the first civilian governor of the Philippines.

Anti-imperialists claimed that it was unconstitutional to take over territories without the consent of the local population, but their reasoning, while certainly not specious, was unhistorical. No American government had seriously considered the wishes of the American Indians or of the French and Spanish settlers in Louisiana or of the natives of Alaska when it had seemed in the national interest to annex new lands.

Nevertheless, grave new constitutional questions did arise as a result of the acquisitions that followed the Spanish-American War. McKinley had acted with remarkable independence in handling the problems involved in expansion, setting up military governments, for example, in Cuba, Puerto Rico, and the Philippines without specific congressional authority, but eventually both Congress and the Supreme Court took a hand in working out the colonial policy of the country. In 1900 Congress passed the Foraker Act, establishing a civil government for Puerto Rico but granting the Puerto Ricans neither American citizenship nor full local self-government. The law also placed a tariff on Puerto Rican products imported into the United States. The tariff provision was promptly challenged in the courts on the ground that Puerto Rico was part of the United States, but in *Downes v. Bidwell* (1901) the Supreme Court upheld the legality of the duties.

In this and other "insular cases" the reasoning of the judges was more than ordinarily difficult to follow. ("We suggest, without intending to decide, that there may be a distinction between certain natural rights enforced in the Constitution . . . and what may be termed artificial or remedial rights," the Downes opinion ran.) The effect, however, was clear. The Constitution did not follow the flag; Congress could act toward the colonies almost as it pleased, although the Court expressed the pious hope that "ultimately" the "blessings of a free government under the Constitution" could be extended to these possessions. Meantime, as one dissenter put it, a colony could be kept "like a disembodied shade, in an indeterminate state of ambiguous existence for an indefinite period."

Although the most heated arguments raged over Philippine policy, the most difficult colonial problems concerned the relationship between the United States and Cuba, for there idealism and self-interest clashed painfully. Despite the genuine desire of most Americans to see Cuba establish a free and independent government, such a regime could not easily be created. Order and prosperity did not automatically appear when the red-and-gold ensigns of Spain were hauled down from the flagstaffs of Havana and Santiago. The insurgent government was feeble, corrupt, and oligarchic, the Cuban economy in a state of collapse, the social order chaotic. The first Americans entering Havana found the city a shambles, the streets littered with garbage and the corpses of horses and dogs, all public services at a standstill. It was essential for the United States, as McKinley said, to give "aid and direction" until "tranquillity" could be restored.

Yet as soon as Americans landed in Cuba,

trouble broke out between them and the local populace. The first soldiers coming ashore at Daiquiri had been greeted with cheers; almost at once, however, discord developed. Most American soldiers viewed the ragged, half-starved insurgents as "thieving dagoes," and displayed an unfortunate race prejudice against their dark-skinned allies. As the novelist Stephen Crane, who covered the war for Pulitzer's *World*, reported: "Both officers and privates have the most lively contempt for the Cubans. They despise them." General Shafter did not help matters. He believed the Cubans "no more fit for self-government than gun-powder is for hell" and employed the insurgent forces chiefly as labor troops. After the fall of Santiago, he even refused to let rebel leaders participate in the formal surrender of the city. This infuriated the proud and idealistic Cuban commander, General Calixto García. When McKinley established a military government for Cuba late in 1898, it was soon embroiled with local leaders. Then a horde of American promoters descended upon Cuba in search of franchises and concessions. Congress put a stop to this exploitation, however, by forbidding all such grants so long as the occupation continued.

The problems were indeed knotty, for no strong local leader capable of uniting Cuba appeared. Even Senator Teller, father of the Teller Amendment, expressed concern lest "unstable and unsafe" elements get control of the country. European leaders confidently expected that the United States would eventually annex Cuba, and many Americans, including General Leonard Wood, who became military governor in December 1899, considered this the best solution. The desperate state of the people, the heavy economic stake of Americans in the region, and its immense strategic importance militated against withdrawal.

Yet, in the end, the United States did withdraw, after doing a great deal to modernize sugar production, improve sanitary conditions, establish schools, and restore orderly administration. In November 1900 a Cuban constitutional convention met at Havana and proceeded without substantial American interference or direction to draft a frame of government. The chief restrictions imposed by this document on Cuba's freedom concerned foreign relations; at the insistence of the United States, it authorized American intervention whenever necessary "for the preservation of Cuban independence" and "the maintenance of a government adequate for the protection of life, property, and individual liberty." Cuba had also to promise not to make any treaty with a foreign power compromising its independence and to grant naval bases on its soil to the United States. This arrangement, known as the Platt Amendment, was accepted, after some grumbling, by the Cubans. It also had the support of most American opponents of imperialism. The amendment was a true compromise; as David F. Healy, a student of Cuban-American relations, has said, "it promised to give the Cubans real internal self-government . . . and at the same time to safeguard American interests." Finally, in May 1902, the United States officially turned over the reins of government to the new republic. The next year the two countries signed a reciprocity treaty tightening the economic bonds between them.

True friendship did not result. Repeatedly the United States used the threat of intervention to coerce the Cuban government, although American troops occupied Cuba only once, in 1906, and then at the specific request of Cuban authorities. American economic penetration proceeded rapidly but without regard for the well-being of the Cuban peasants, many of whom lived in a state of peonage on great sugar plantations. Furthermore, their good intentions did not make up for the distressing tendency of Americans to consider themselves innately superior to the Cubans and to overlook the fact that Cubans did not always wish to adopt American customs and culture. The admirable reform program instituted during the occupation was marred by attempts to apply American standards at every step. In the new schools American textbooks were translated into Spanish without trying to adapt the material to the experience of Cuban children. General Wood considered the Cubans "inert" because they showed little interest in his plans to grant a large measure of self-government to municipal authorities, failing to understand that the people were accustomed to a highly centralized system with decision-making concentrated in Havana. Wood complained that the Cubans were mired in "old ruts," yet the charge might well have been leveled at him, although he was an efficient and energetic administrator.

If the purpose of the Spanish-American War had been to bring peace and order to Cuba, the Platt Amendment was a logical step. The same purpose soon necessitated a further extension of the principle, for once the United States accepted the role of protector and stabilizer in part of Latin America it seemed desirable, for the same economic, strategic, and humanitarian reasons, to supervise the entire region.

The Caribbean countries were economically underdeveloped, socially backward, politically unstable, and desperately poor. Everywhere a few ruling families owned most of the land and dominated social and political life. The mass of the people were uneducated peasants, many of them little better off than slaves. Rival cliques among the wealthy minority struggled for power, force being the normal method of effecting a change in government. Most of the meager income of the average Caribbean state was swallowed up by the military or diverted into the pockets of the currently ruling party.

Cynicism and fraud poisoned the relations of most of these nations with the great powers. European merchants and bankers systematically cheated their Latin-American customers, who, in turn, frequently refused to honor their obligations. Foreign bankers floated Caribbean bond issues on outrageous terms, while revolutionary Caribbean governments annulled concessions and repudiated debts with equal disdain for the rules of honest business dealing. Because these little countries were so weak, the powers tended to intervene whenever their nationals were cheated or when chaotic conditions endangered the lives and property of foreigners. In one notorious instance, Germany sent two warships to Port-au-Prince, Haiti, and by threatening to bombard the town compelled the Haitian government to pay $30,000 in damages to a German citizen who had been arrested and fined for allegedly assaulting a local policeman. Such actions as this always aroused the concern of the United States.

In 1902, shortly after the United States pulled out of Cuba, troubled erupted in Venezuela, where the local dictator, Cipriano Castro, was refusing to honor debts owed the citizens of European nations. To force him to pay up, Germany and Great Britain established a blockade of Venezuelan ports and destroyed a number of Venezuelan gunboats and harbor defenses. This alarmed the United States, and under pressure from Roosevelt, the Europeans agreed to arbitrate the dispute. At last the great powers were coming to accept the broad implications of the Monroe Doctrine. The British prime minister went so far as to state publicly that "it would be a great gain to civilization if the United States were more actively to interest themselves in making arrangements by which these constantly recurring difficulties . . . could be avoided."

By this time Theodore Roosevelt had become President of the United States, and he quickly capitalized on the new European attitude. In 1903 the Dominican Republic defaulted on bonds totaling some $40 million. When European investors urged their governments to intervene, Roosevelt decided to make a general statement of policy. Under the Monroe Doctrine, the United States could not permit foreign nations to intervene in Latin America. But Latin-American nations should not be allowed to escape their obligations. "If we intend to say 'Hands off' . . . sooner or later we must keep order ourselves," he told Secretary of War Elihu Root. The President did not want to make a colony of the Dominican Republic. "I have about the same desire to annex it as a gorged boa constrictor might have to swallow a porcupine wrong-end-to," he said. He therefore arranged for the United States to take charge of the Dominican customs service—the one reliable source of revenue in that poverty-stricken country. Fifty-five per cent of the customs duties would be devoted to debt payment, the remainder turned over to the Dominican government to care for its internal needs.

Roosevelt defined his policy, known as the

CULVER PICTURES

As the Monroe Doctrine became increasingly significant around the turn of the century, chauvinistic cartoonists used it to taunt European powers. In this example, from a 1901 issue of Puck, *Europe complains, "You're not the only rooster in South America!" to which Uncle Sam retorts, "I was aware of that when I cooped you up!"*

Roosevelt Corollary to the Monroe Doctrine, in a message to Congress in December 1904. "Chronic wrongdoing" in Latin America, he stated with typical disregard for the subtleties of complex affairs, might require outside intervention. Since, under the Monroe Doctrine, no other nation could step in, the United States must "exercise . . . an international police power." In the short run, this policy worked admirably. Dominican customs were honestly collected for the first time and the country's finances put in order. The presence of American warships in the area discouraged revolutionary elements, most of whom were cynical spoilsmen rather than social reformers, providing a much needed measure of political stability. In the long run, however, the Roosevelt Corollary caused much resentment in Latin America, for it added to nationalist fears that the United States wished to exploit the region for its own benefit.

The Open Door Policy

The insular cases, the Platt Amendment, and the Roosevelt Corollary established the framework for American colonial policy. Within this framework, a considerable expansion of activity quickly took place, both in Latin America and in the Far East. Coincidental with the Cuban rebellion of the nineties, a far greater upheaval had convulsed the ancient empire of China. In 1894–95 Japan had easily defeated China in a war over Korea. Alarmed by Japan's new aggressiveness, the European powers hastened to check it by rushing to carve out for themselves new concessions, or spheres of influence, along China's coast. After the annexation of the Philippines, McKinley's secretary of state, John Hay, urged on by businessmen fearful of losing out in the scramble to exploit the Chinese market, tried to prevent the further absorption of China by the great powers. For the United States to join in the dismemberment of China was politically impossible because of anti-imperialist feeling, so Hay sought to protect American interests by clever diplomacy. In a series of "Open Door" notes (1899), he asked the powers to agree to respect the trading rights of all countries and to impose no discriminatory railroad or port duties within their spheres of influence. Chinese tariffs should continue to be collected in these areas and by Chinese officials.

Although the replies to these notes were at best noncommittal, Hay blandly announced in March 1900 that the powers had "accepted" his suggestions! Thus he could claim to have prevented the breakup of the empire and protected the right of Americans to do business freely in its territories. In reality nothing had been accomplished; the imperialist nations did not extend their political control of China only because they feared that by doing so they might precipitate a major war among themselves. Nevertheless, Hay's action marked a revolutionary departure from the traditional American policy of isolation, a bold step into the complicated and dangerous world of international power politics.

Collier's, SEPTEMBER 22, 1900

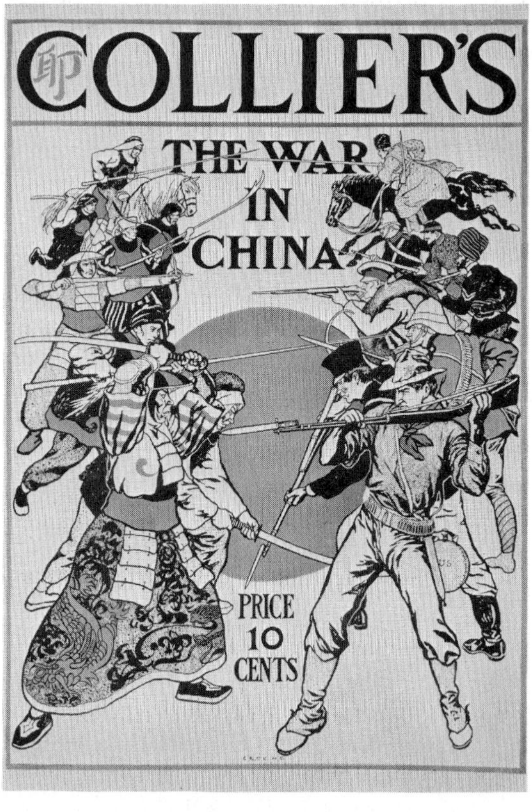

Collier's *devoted a cover story to the Boxer Rebellion in 1900. The international expeditionary force sent to relieve Peking included American, British, French, German, Russian, and Japanese contingents.*

Within a few months of Hay's announcement, the Open Door policy was put to the test. Chinese nationalists, angered by the spreading influence of foreign governments, had launched the so-called Boxer Rebellion, overrunning Peking and driving the terrified foreigners in the capital within the walls of their legations, which were placed under siege. For weeks, until an international rescue expedition, which included 2,500 American soldiers, broke through to free them, their fate was unknown. Fearing that the Europeans would use the rebellion as a pretext for further expropriations, Hay sent off another round of Open Door notes announcing that the United States believed in the preservation of "Chinese territorial and administrative entity" and in "the principle of equal and impartial trade with all parts of the Chinese Empire." This broadened the Open Door policy to include all China, not merely the European spheres of influence.

Hay's diplomacy was superficially successful. Although the United States maintained no important military force in the Far East, American business and commercial interests there were free to develop and to compete with Europeans. But once again European jealousies and fears rather than American cleverness were responsible. When the Japanese, mistrusting Russian intentions in Manchuria, asked Hay how he intended to implement his policy, he replied meekly that the United States was "not prepared . . . to enforce these views on the east by any demonstration which could present a character of hostility to any other power." Willy-nilly, the United States was being caught up in the power struggle in the Far East without having faced candidly the implications of its actions.

Eventually, the country would pay a heavy price for this unrealistic attitude, but in the decade following 1900 its policy of diplomatic

Theodore Roosevelt's high-powered pursuit of personal diplomacy captured wide attention. A Copenhagen paper comments on his mediation of the Russo-Japanese War, which won him the Nobel peace prize.

meddling unbacked by bayonets worked remarkably well. Japan attacked Russia in a quarrel over Manchuria, smashing the Russian fleet in 1905 and winning a series of battles on the mainland. Japan was unprepared for a long war, however, and suggested to President Theodore Roosevelt that an American offer to mediate would be favorably received.

Eager to preserve the nice balance in the Far East which enabled the United States to exert influence without any significant commitment of force, Roosevelt accepted the hint. In June 1905 he invited the belligerents to a conference at Portsmouth, New Hampshire. At the conference the Japanese won title to Russia's sphere around Port Arthur and a free hand in Korea, but when they asked for all of Sakhalin Island and a large money indemnity, the Russians balked. Unwilling to resume the war, the Japanese then settled for half of Sakhalin and no money.

This arrangement was unpopular in Japan, and the government managed to place the blame on Roosevelt, who had supported the compromise. Ill-feeling against Americans increased in 1906, when the San Francisco school board, responding to local opposition to the influx of cheap labor from Japan, instituted a policy of segregating oriental children in a special school. Japan protested, and President Roosevelt persuaded the San Franciscans to abandon segregation in exchange for his pledge to cut off further Japanese immigration. He accomplished this through a "Gentlemen's Agreement" (1907) in which the Japanese promised not to issue passports to laborers seeking to come to America. Discriminatory legislation based specifically on race was thus avoided.

The next year, in the Root-Takahira Agreement, the United States and Japan outlined their "common aim" in the Far East to develop commerce, maintain the status quo in China, and respect each other's interests. However, the atmosphere between the two countries remained charged. Japanese resentment at American race prejudice was great. Many Americans talked fearfully of the "yellow peril."

In most instances Roosevelt was pre-eminently a realist in foreign relations. "Don't bluster," he once said. "Don't flourish a revolver, and never draw unless you intend to shoot." In the Far East, however, he failed to follow his own advice. He considered the situation in that part of the world fraught with peril. The Philippines, he said, were "our heel of Achilles," indefensible in case of a Japanese attack. He bemoaned the fact that the American public would not countenance an adequate military buildup in the islands, and suggested privately that the United States ought therefore "be prepared for giving the islands independence . . . much sooner than I think advisable from their own standpoint." He did not, however, either try to increase American naval and military strength in the Orient appreciably or cease to attempt to influence the course of events in the area, and he took no step toward withdrawing from the Philippines. He sent the fleet on a world cruise to demonstrate its might to Japan but well realized that this was mere bluff. "The 'Open Door' policy," he warned his successor, "completely disappears as soon as a powerful nation determines to disregard it." Nevertheless, he allowed the belief to persist in the United States that the nation could influence the course of Far Eastern history without risk or real involvement.

Caribbean Diplomacy

In the Caribbean region American policy centered on the building of an interoceanic canal across Central America. Expanding interests in both Latin America and the Far East made a canal vitally necessary, a truth pointed up dramatically at the time of the war with Spain by the two-month voyage of the U.S.S. *Oregon* around South America from California waters to participate in the action against Admiral Cervera's fleet at Santiago. The first step was to get rid of the old Clayton-Bulwer Treaty with Great Britain, which barred the United States from building a canal on its own. Great Britain realized after the Spanish-American War that the United States would go ahead with the canal in any case and therefore posed no serious objections. In 1901 Lord Pauncefote, the British ambassador, and Secretary of State John Hay negotiated an agreement abrogating the Clayton-Bulwer pact and giving America the right to build, and by implication fortify, a transisthmian waterway. The United States agreed in turn to maintain any such canal "free and open to the vessels of commerce and of war of all nations."

Next, the location of the canal had to be determined. One possible route lay across the Colombian province of Panama, where the French-controlled New Panama Canal Company had taken over the franchise of the old De Lesseps company. Only 50 miles separated the oceans in Panama. The terrain, however, was rugged and unhealthy—although the French company had sunk much money in the project, it had little to show for its efforts aside from some rough excavations. A second possible route ran across Nicaragua. This route was about 200 miles long but relatively easy, since much of it traversed Lake Nicaragua and other natural waterways.

At first American opinion favored the Nicaraguan route. But the French company in Panama, eager to unload its assets on the United States, employed a New York lawyer, William Nelson Cromwell, as a lobbyist and succeeded in stirring up considerable support. President McKinley appointed a commission to study the alternatives. It reported that the Panamanian route was technically superior but recommended building in Nicaragua because the French company was asking $109 million for its assets, which the commission valued at a mere $40 million. Lacking another possible purchaser, the French company quickly lowered its price to $40 million, and after a great deal of clever propagandizing by Cromwell and Philippe Bunau-Varilla, a French engineer with heavy investments in the company, President Roosevelt settled upon the Panamanian route. Early in January 1903 Secretary of State Hay negotiated a treaty with Tomás Herrán, the Colombian chargé in Washington. In return for a 99-year lease on a zone across Panama six miles wide, the United States agreed to pay Colombia $10 million and an annual rent of $250,000. The Colombian senate, however, unanimously rejected this treaty, partly because it did not adequately protect Colombian sovereignty over Panama and partly for purely materialistic reasons. The Colombians thought it hardly fair

Judge, JUNE 4, 1904

that the New Panama Canal Company should receive $40 million for its frozen assets and they only $10 million. They demanded $15 million directly from the United States, plus $10 million of the company's share.

A little more patience might have produced a mutually satisfactory settlement, but Roosevelt looked upon the Colombians as highwaymen who were "mad to get hold of the $40,000,000 of the Frenchmen." "You could no more make an agreement with the Colombian rulers," he later remarked, "than you could nail currant jelly to a wall." Therefore, when local Panamanians, egged on by the French company, staged a revolution in November 1903, he ordered the cruiser *Nashville* to Panama to cow the Colombian forces. The revolution succeeded, and in a matter of hours Roosevelt recognized the new Republic of Panama. Hay and the new Panamanian minister, Bunau-Varilla, quickly negotiated a treaty granting the United States a zone *ten* miles wide *in perpetuity*, on the same terms as those rejected by Colombia. Within the Canal Zone the United States could act as if it were "the sovereign of the territory . . . to the entire exclusion of . . . the Republic of Panama." The United States also undertook to guarantee the independence of the republic. Of course the New Panama Canal Company then received its $40 million.

Historians have condemned Roosevelt for his actions in this shabby affair, and with good reason. It was not that he fomented the revolution, for he did not. Separated from the government at Bogotá by an impenetrable jungle, the people of Panama province had long wanted to be free of Colombian rule. They had revolted time and again over the years but lacked the force necessary to maintain themselves against government troops. Furthermore, knowing that an American-built canal would bring a flood of dollars and job opportunities to the area, they were prepared to take any necessary steps to avoid having the United States shift to the Nicaraguan route. Nor was it that Roosevelt prevented Colombia from suppressing the revolution, although his excuse for doing so—an 1846 treaty authorizing the United States to protect the freedom of transit across the isthmus—was extremely flimsy. He

NEW YORK *Times*, 1903

Two views of Roosevelt's handling of the Panamanian affair. At left, a drawing from the Republican Judge, *captioned "A crown he is entitled to wear." A New York* Times *cartoonist saw the matter very differently, charging a conspiracy (above). When Bunau-Varilla asked the President to send a warship to Panama "to protect American lives and interests," he got no answer. "But his look was enough for me," Bunau-Varilla recalled.*

sinned, rather, in his disregard of Latin-American sensibilities. He referred to the Colombians as "dagoes" and insisted smugly that he was defending "the interests of collective civilization" when he overrode their opposition to his plans. "They cut their own throats," he said. "They tried to hold us up; and too late they have discovered their criminal error." If somewhat uncharitable, this analysis was not entirely inaccurate; nevertheless, it did not justify Roosevelt's haste in taking Panama under his wing. "Have I defended myself?" Roosevelt asked Secretary of War Elihu Root. "You certainly have, Mr. President," Root retorted. "You were accused of seduction and you have conclusively proved that you were guilty of rape." All over Latin America, especially as nationalist sentiments grew stronger, Roosevelt's intolerance and aggressiveness in the canal incident bred resentment and fear.

Eventually, in 1921, the United States made amends for Roosevelt's actions by giving Colombia $25 million. Colombia, in turn, recognized the independence of the Republic of Panama. Meanwhile, the canal had been built—the first vessels passed through its locks in 1914—and American hegemony in the Caribbean further expanded. Yet even in that strategically vital area, there was more show than substance to American strength. The navy ruled Caribbean waters largely by default, for it lacked adequate bases in the region. In 1903, as authorized by the Cuban constitution, the United States obtained an excellent site for a base at Guantanamo Bay, but before 1914 Congress appropriated only $89,000 to develop it.

The tendency was to try to influence outlying areas without actually controlling them. Roosevelt's successor, William Howard Taft, gave the policy its clearest expression when he called it "dollar diplomacy," his theory being that American economic penetration would bring stability to underdeveloped areas and power and profit to the United States without making it necessary to commit American troops or spend public funds.

Under Taft, the State Department won a place for American bankers in an international syndicate engaged in financing railroads in Manchuria. When Nicaragua defaulted on its foreign debt in 1911, the department arranged informally for a group of bankers to reorganize Nicaraguan finances and take over the operation of the customs service. Although the government truthfully insisted that it did not "covet an inch of territory south of the Rio Grande," dollar diplomacy provoked further apprehension in Latin America. Efforts to establish similar arrangements in Honduras, Costa Rica, and Guatemala all failed. Even in Nicaragua, orderly administration of the finances did not bring internal peace. In 1912, 2,500 American marines and sailors had to be landed to put down a revolution.

On the other hand, economic penetration by private American interests in the Caribbean area proceeded briskly. American investments in Cuba reached $200 million by 1910 and $500 million by 1920, and smaller but significant investments were also made in the Dominican Republic and in Haiti. In Central America the United Fruit Company accumulated large holdings in banana plantations, railroads, and other ventures. Other firms plunged heavily in Mexico's rich mineral resources.

"Non-Colonial Imperial Expansion"

Generally speaking, the United States deserves fair marks for effort in its post-Spanish-American War foreign relations, barely passable marks for performance, and failing ones for results. If one defines imperialism narrowly as a policy of occupying and governing foreign lands, American imperialism lasted for an extremely short time. With trivial exceptions, all the American colonies—Hawaii, the Philippines, Guam, Puerto Rico, the Guantanamo base, and the Canal Zone—were obtained between 1898 and 1903. In retrospect it seems clear that the urge to own colonies was only fleeting; sober second thoughts and the headaches connected with overseas possessions caused a swift change of policy. The objections of protectionists to the lowering of tariff barriers, the shock of the Philippine Insurrection, the worldwide unfavorable reaction of liberals to the costly British war against the Boers of South Africa, and a growing conviction that the costs of colonial administration outweighed the profits all affected American thinking. Hay's Open Door notes (which, incidentally, anti-imperialists praised highly) marked the beginning of the retreat from imperialism thus defined, while the Roosevelt Corollary and dollar diplomacy signaled the consolidation of a new policy. Elihu Root, who became secretary of state in 1905, summarized this policy as it applied to the Caribbean (and by implication to the rest of the underdeveloped world) in these words: "The key to our attitude towards these countries can be put in three sentences: We do not want to take them for ourselves. We do not want any foreign nations to take them for themselves. We want to help them."

Yet imperialism can be given a broader definition than this one. The historian William Appleman Williams, a sharp critic, has described 20th-century American foreign policy as one of "non-colonial imperial expansion." Its object was to obtain profitable American economic penetration of underdeveloped areas without the trouble of owning and controlling them. Its subsidiary aim was to encourage these countries to "modernize," modernize meaning to remake themselves in the image of the United States. The Open Door policy, in Williams' view, was not unrealistic, and by no means a failure—indeed, it was *too* successful. He criticizes American policy not because it did not work or because it led to trouble with the powers, but because of its harmful effects on the underdeveloped countries.

Examined from this perspective, the Open Door policy, the Roosevelt Corollary, and dollar diplomacy make a single pattern of exploitation, "tragic" according to Williams rather than evil, because its creators were not evil but only of limited vision. They did not recognize the contradictions in their ideas and values. They saw American expansion as mutually beneficial to all concerned—and not exclusively in materialistic terms. They genuinely believed that they were exporting democracy along with capitalism and industrialization.

Williams probably goes too far in arguing that American statesmen consciously planned their foreign policy in these terms. American economic interests in foreign nations expanded enormously in the 20th century, but diplomacy had relatively little to do with this. Western industrial society (not merely American) was engulfing the rest of the world, as it continues to engulf it. Yet he is correct in pointing out that western economic penetration has had many unfortunate results for the nonindustrial nations, and that Americans were particularly, although not uniquely, unimpressed by the different social and cultural patterns of people in far-off lands and insensitive to the wish of such people to develop in their own way.

Both the United States government and American businessmen showed little interest in finding out what the poverty-stricken common people of Cuba wanted out of life. They assumed that it was what *everybody* (read, "Americans") wanted, and if by some strange chance this was not the case, that the best thing to do was to give it to them anyway. Dollar diplomacy had as its primary objectives the avoidance of violence and the economic development of Latin America; it paid small heed to how peace was maintained and how the fruits of development were distributed. The policy, therefore, was self-defeating, for in the long run, stability depended upon the support of the masses, which was seldom forthcoming. Internal troubles remained endemic, and they were usually followed by American intervention; this, in turn, always produced a harvest of resentment and suspicion.

By the eve of World War I the United States had become a major world power. But the people had not really learned what that meant. Although they stood ready to extend their influence into distant lands, they did so blithely, with little awareness of the implications of their behavior for themselves or for other peoples. The national psychology, if such a term has any meaning, remained fundamentally isolationist. Americans fully understood that their wealth and numbers made their nation strong, and that geography made it practically invulnerable. They proceeded, therefore, to do what they wanted to do in foreign affairs, limited more by their humanly flexible consciences than by any rational analysis of the probable consequences. This seemed safe enough—in 1914.

SUPPLEMENTARY READING Among the many general diplomatic histories, Alexander De Conde, *A History of American Foreign Policy* (1963), is the most detailed, and R.W. Leopold, *The Growth of American Foreign Policy* (1962), is the most thoughtful and interpretative. F.R. Dulles, *Prelude to World Power* (1965), offers fuller detail, while J.A.S. Grenville and G.B. Young, *Politics, Strategy, and American Diplomacy: Studies in Foreign Policy* (1966), throws new light on many aspects of the period. Post-Civil War expansionism is treated in Dexter Perkins, *The Monroe Doctrine: 1867–1907* (1937), and Allan Nevins, *Hamilton Fish* (1936). Walter LaFeber, *The New Empire* (1963), presents a forceful but somewhat overstated argument on the extent of expansionist sentiment, especially on the part of American businessmen.

The new expansionism is also discussed in A.K. Weinberg, *Manifest Destiny** (1935), J.W. Pratt, *Expansionists of 1898** (1936), and Harold and Margaret Sprout, *The Rise of American Naval Power** (1939). Contemporary attitudes are reflected in Josiah Strong, *Our Country* (1885), while A.T. Mahan, *The Influence of Sea Power upon History: 1660–1783** (1890), provides the clearest presentation of Mahan's thesis. W.D. Puleston, *Mahan* (1939), is a good biography.

D.W. Pletcher, *The Awkward Years: American Foreign Relations Under Garfield and Arthur* (1962), is definitive. Other useful studies include A.F. Tyler, *The Foreign Policy of James G. Blaine* (1927), S.K. Stevens, *American Expansion in Hawaii* (1945), Allan Nevins, *Grover Cleveland* (1932) and *Henry White* (1930), L.M. Gelber, *The Rise of Anglo-American Friendship* (1938), and Henry James, *Richard Olney* (1923).

On the Spanish-American War, a good brief summary is H.W. Morgan, *America's Road to Empire** (1965). For greater detail, consult E.R. May, *Imperial Democracy* (1961), Walter Millis, *The Martial Spirit* (1931), Margaret Leech, *In the Days of McKinley* (1959), and Orestes Ferrara, *The Last Spanish War* (1937). H.W. Morgan, *William McKinley and His America* (1963), is a good modern biography.

On imperialism, see J.W. Pratt, *America's Colonial Experiment* (1950), Richard Hofstadter, *Social Darwinism in American Thought** (1945), E.R. May, *American Imperialism: A Speculative Essay* (1968), and W.A. Williams, *The Tragedy of American Diplomacy** (1962), the last extremely critical of what the author calls "non-colonial imperial expansion." R.L. Beisner, *Twelve Against Empire: The Anti-Imperialists* (1968), contains lively and thoughtful sketches of leading foes of expansion. For colonial problems, see Leon Wolff, *Little Brown Brother* (1961), on the Philippines, D.F. Healy, *The United States in Cuba: 1898–1902* (1963), and D.G. Munro, *Intervention and Dollar Diplomacy in the Caribbean: 1900–1921* (1964). S.F. Bemis, *The Latin American Policy of the United States** (1943), is an excellent general account of the subject. Other useful volumes include D.C. Miner, *The Fight for the Panama Route* (1940), H.K. Beale, *Theodore Roosevelt and the Rise of America to World Power** (1956), A.W. Griswold, *The Far Eastern Policy of the United States** (1938), Tyler Dennett, *John Hay* (1938), C.S. Campbell, Jr., *Special Business Interests and the Open Door Policy* (1951), Thomas McCormick, *China Market* (1967), and H.C. Hill, *Roosevelt and the Caribbean* (1927). R.E. Osgood, *Ideals and Self-Interest in America's Foreign Relations** (1953), and G.F. Kennan, *American Diplomacy: 1900–1950** (1951), are important interpretations of early-20th-century United States policy, more general in scope than May's *American Imperialism* and Williams' *Tragedy of American Diplomacy*, mentioned above.

*Available in paperback.

23

The Progressive Era

The period of the history of the United States marked roughly by the end of the Spanish-American War and American entry into World War I is usually called the Progressive Era. Like all such generalizations about complex subjects, this title involves a great oversimplification. Whether *progressive* is taken to mean "tending toward change," or "improvement," or is merely used to suggest an attitude of mind, it was not a universal characteristic of the early years of the 20th century. Furthermore, progressive elements existed in earlier periods and did not disappear when the first doughboys took ship for France. In many important ways, as Samuel P. Hays has shown, the progressivism of the time was only a continuation of the response to industrialism that began after the Civil War, a response which, of course, has not ended. Historians have scoured the sources trying to define and explain the Progressive Era without devising an interpretation of the period satisfactory to all. Indeed, as their investigations go on, it seems at times that the meaning of the word *progressive* is becoming progressively less clear. Surveying the recent literature in his study *Businessmen and Reform,* Robert H. Wiebe shrewdly remarks: "Over the years historians have gradually closed the door to the progressive club," by which he means that under close examination, most progressives appear far less radical than at first glance. Another writer has called his work on the period *The Triumph of Conservatism*! Nevertheless, the term *progressive* provides a useful description of this exciting and significant period of American history.

Roots of Progressivism

One reason why historians have had so much difficulty in generalizing about progressivism is that the progressives were never a unified group seeking a single objective. The movement sprang from many sources. One of these was the fight against corruption and inefficiency in government, dating back at least to the Grant era. The struggle for civil service reform was only the first skirmish in this contest; the continuing power of corrupt big-city political machines and the growing influence of large corporations and their lobbyists on municipal and state governments outraged thousands of citizens and led them to seek ways of purifying politics and making the machinery of government responsive to the majority rather than to special-interest groups.

Progressivism also had roots in the effort to regulate and control big business, which characterized the Granger and Populist agitation of the 1870's and 1890's. The failure of the Interstate Commerce Act to end railroad abuses and of the Sherman Antitrust Act to check the growth of monopolies became ever more apparent after 1900. The return of prosperity after the great depression of the nineties aggravated these problems by strengthening the big corporations. It also encouraged the opposition by removing the inhibiting fear, so influential in the 1896 Presidential campaign, that an assault on the industrial giants might lead to the collapse of the whole economy. Between 1897 and 1904 the steady trend toward concentration in industry suddenly accelerated. Such new giants as Amalgamated Copper (1899), U.S. Steel (1901), and International Harvester (1902) attracted most of the attention, but even more alarming were the overall statistics. In a single year (1899) over 1,200 firms were absorbed in mergers, the resulting combinations being capitalized at $2.2 billion. By 1904 there were 318 industrial combinations with an aggregate capital of some $7.5 billion in the country, a large majority of them founded no earlier than 1898. Men who considered bigness inherently evil demanded that these huge new "trusts" be broken up or at least strictly controlled.

Settlement-house workers and other reformers concerned about the welfare of the urban poor made up a third battalion in the progressive army. The fight against the manifold evils of slum life—the crowded tenement, the polluted water supply, the filth and disease and moral degradation—was far from won when the new century dawned. The working conditions of slum dwellers also remained abominable. The child labor problem was particularly acute. In 1900 about 1.7 million children under the age of 16 were working full time—more than the total membership of the American Federation of Labor. Laws regulating the hours and conditions of women in industry were also far from adequate, and almost nothing had been done, despite the increased use of dangerous machinery in the factories, to enforce safety rules or provide some kind of compensation or insurance for workers injured on the job. As the number of social workers grew and as they became increasingly competent professionally, the movement for social-welfare legislation gained momentum.

The return of prosperity after the election of McKinley strengthened the political reformers, the antimonopolists, and the social workers, and by attracting additional thousands of sympathizers to the general cause of reform, it produced the progressive movement. Good times made people tolerant and generous, willing to help others, not merely to advance their own interests. So long as his own profits were on the rise, the average businessman did not object if labor improved its position too. Many middle-class Americans who had been prepared to man the barricades in the event of a Bryan victory in 1896 now became conscience-stricken when they compared their own comfortable circumstances with those of the "huddled masses" of immigrants and native poor. Nonmaterialistic, humanitarian motives governed their behavior; they were reformers more "of the heart and the head than of the stomach."

The new industrial and commercial giants threatened not so much the economic well-being as the ambitions and sense of importance of the middle class. What owner of a small mill or shop could now hope to rise to the heights attained by a Carnegie, or by great merchants like John Wanamaker or Marshall Field? The growth of large labor organizations also worried such men. Union membership tripled between 1896 and 1910; bargaining became a clash of massive economic interests; individual relationships between employer and worker no longer counted for much in the industrial world. In general, human character and moral values seemed less influential; organizations—cold, impersonal, heartless—were coming to control business, politics, and too many other aspects of life.

The historian Richard Hofstadter has suggested

still another explanation of the movement. Numbers of established, moderately prosperous businessmen, together with members of the professions and other educated persons, felt themselves threatened and discomfited by the increasing power and status of the new tycoons, many of them coarse, assertive men fond of vulgar display, and by machine politicians, who made a mockery of the traditions of duty, service, and patriotism associated with statesmanship. The comfortably off, middle-level businessman lived in what seemed like genteel poverty compared to a Rockefeller or a Morgan and often found that the influence in the community which he considered his birthright had been usurped by a cynical local boss.

The impact of The Silent War, *a 1906 novel by J. Ames Mitchell which dealt with the growing class struggle in America, was enhanced by William Balfour Ker's graphic illustration, "From the Depths."*

Protestant pastors accustomed to the respect and deference of their flocks found their moral leadership challenged by materialistic vestrymen who did not even pay them decent salaries, while their working-class parishioners drifted from the church. College professors, although growing in numbers and competence, watched their institutions fall increasingly under the sway of wealthy trustees who had little interest in or respect for learning. The law, once the most powerful and independent of professions, was also being affected by the business world. Attracted by fat fees, many lawyers could not resist the blandishments of great corporations, but they resented the loss of freedom involved nonetheless. "The profession is commercialized," one lawyer complained in 1904. "The lawyer today does not enjoy the position and influence that belonged to the lawyer of seventy-five or a hundred years ago." Members of other professions echoed this complaint. In 1902, Hofstadter explains, an architect could look back longingly on the days when the members of his craft "ranked . . . several pegs higher in the social rack than the merely successful merchant or broker."

Such people could support reform measures without feeling that they were being very radical because the intellectual currents of their time harmonized with the ideas of social improvement and the welfare state. The new doctrines of the social scientists, the Social Gospel religious leaders, and the philosophers of pragmatism provided a salubrious climate for progressivism. Many of the thinkers who formulated these doctrines in the eighties and nineties turned to the task of putting them into practice in the new century: for example, the economist Richard T. Ely, the sociologist E.A. Ross, the philosopher John Dewey, the Baptist clergyman Walter Rauschenbusch, who, in addition to his many books extolling the Social Gospel, was active in civic reform movements in Rochester, New York.

The Muckrakers

As the diffuse and unorganized progressive army gradually formed its battalions, a new journalistic fad suddenly brought the movement into focus. For many years maga-

NEW YORK *Telegram*, MAY 5, 1906

"The smile that won't come off": a caricature of muckraker Ida M. Tarbell, the nemesis of Standard Oil, reproduced in the New York Telegram *in 1906.*

zines like *Forum*, *Arena*, *McClure's*, and even the staid *Atlantic Monthly* had been publishing articles describing various political, social, and economic evils. Henry Demarest Lloyd's first blast at the Standard Oil monopoly appeared in the *Atlantic Monthly* as far back as 1881; radicals such as Henry George and Eugene V. Debs had discussed a variety of problems in the pages of *Arena* in the early 1890's; Josiah Flynt had exposed the corrupt relationship between criminals and the New York police for *McClure's* in 1900.

Over the years the tempo and forcefulness of this type of literature steadily increased. Then, in the fall of 1902, *McClure's* began publishing two particularly hard-hitting series of articles, one on Standard Oil by Ida Tarbell, the other on urban political machines by Lincoln Steffens. These evoked much comment. When S.S. McClure decided to include an attack on labor gangsterism in the coal fields in the January 1903 issue along with the next installments of the Tarbell and Steffens series, he called attention to the coincidence in a striking editorial. Something was radically wrong with the "American character," he wrote. These articles showed that large numbers of American employers, workers, and politicians were fundamentally immoral. Furthermore, lawyers were becoming the tools of big business, judges were permitting evildoers to escape justice, the churches were materialistic, the colleges incapable even of understanding what was happening. "There is no one left; none but all of us," McClure concluded. "We have to pay in the end."

McClure's editorial, one of the most influential ever published in an American magazine, summoned "the people" to a moral crusade against the evils of the times and loosed a complicated chain reaction in the intellectual and political world. The January issue sold out quickly. Other editors jumped to adopt the McClure formula. Thousands of readers found their own vague apprehensions brought into focus, some becoming active in progressive movements, more lending passive support.

A small army of skillful professional writers was soon flooding the periodical press with denunciations of the insurance business, the drug business, college athletics, prostitution, sweatshop labor, political corruption, and dozens of other subjects. The typical article was solidly factual and righteously indignant in tone. It appealed to the public conscience while catering to the public's love of scandal and sensation. Many of the authors were active reformers, others simply honest reporters working on assignment, still others cynical hacks capitalizing on the current fad. The intellectual level and the essential honesty of their work varied greatly; much of it was lurid, distorted, designed to titillate and scandalize rather than to inform.

The latter type of article inspired Theodore Roosevelt, with his gift for vivid phraseology, to compare these journalists to "the Man with the Muck-Rake" in Bunyan's *Pilgrim Progress*, whose attention was so fixed on the filth at his feet that he could not notice the "celestial crown" that was offered him in exchange. This characterization grossly misrepresented the more worthy literature of exposure, but the label *muckraking* was thereafter permanently affixed to the type, and despite the connotations, *muckraker* became a term of honor.

The Progressive Mind

The writings of the muckrakers reveal the underlying temper of progressivism. Progressives were essentially middle-class moralists seeking to arouse the conscience of "the people" in order to purify American life. Local, state, and national government must be made more responsive to the will of the unorganized mass of decent citizens who stood for all the traditional virtues. Next, the government (once purified) must *act*. Whatever its virtues, laissez faire was obsolete. Businessmen, especially big businessmen, must be compelled to behave fairly, their acquisitive drives curbed in the interests of universal justice and equal opportunity for all. Finally, the weaker elements in society—women, children, the poor, the infirm—must be protected against unscrupulous power. The people, by which the progressives usually meant the comfortable middle class, must assume new responsibilities toward the unfortunate.

Despite its fervor and democratic rhetoric, progressivism was paternalistic, moderate, and somewhat soft-headed. The typical reformer of the period oversimplified complicated issues and treated his own highly personal values as absolute standards of truth and morality. Thus progressives often acted at cross-purposes; at times some were even at war with themselves. This accounts for the diffuseness of the movement. Cutthroat business practices were criticized by great tycoons seeking to preserve their own positions and by small operators trying to protect themselves against the tycoons. But the former wanted federal regulation of big business and the latter strict enforcement of the antitrust laws. Political reforms like the direct primary election appealed especially to rural progressives but found few adherents among progressive businessmen.

Many persons who genuinely desired to improve the living standards of workingmen rejected the proposition that workingmen could best help themselves by organizing powerful national unions. Union leaders favored government action to outlaw child labor and restrict immigration but adopted a laissez-faire attitude toward wages-and-hours legislation; they preferred to win these objectives through collective bargaining, thus justifying their own existence. Many who favored "municipal socialism," meaning public ownership of streetcars, waterworks, and other local utilities, adamantly opposed the national ownership of railroads. Progressives stressed individual freedom, yet gave strong backing to the drive to deprive the public of its right to drink alcoholic beverages. Few progressives worked more assiduously than Congressman George W. Norris of rural Nebraska for reforms that would increase the power of the ordinary voter, such as the direct primary and popular election of senators, yet Norris characterized the mass of urban voters as "the mob." Theodore Roosevelt fulminated against the "malefactors of great wealth" and denounced men like E.H. Harriman, the railroad king, and "the Standard Oil people," while also speaking of "the immense good effected by corporate agencies [and] . . . their officers and directors."

Finally, it must be emphasized that the progressives never challenged the fundamental principles of capitalism, nor did they attempt any basic reorganization of society. The Socialist party developed considerable strength during the period, capturing control of a dozen or more city administrations, sending a few representatives to state legislatures, and polling nearly 900,000 votes in the 1912 Presidential election. But the progressives would have little to do with the socialist brand of radicalism. Wisconsin was the most progressive of states, but its leaders never cooperated with the Social Democrats of Milwaukee. When socialists threatened to win control of Los Angeles in 1911, California progressives made common cause with their reactionary foes in order to defeat them. Many progressives were also anti-immigrant and only a handful had anything to offer the Negroes, surely the most exploited class in American society.

A good example of the relatively limited radicalism of progressives is offered by the experiences of progressive artists. Early in the century a number of painters, including Robert Henri, John Sloan, and George Luks, tried to develop a distinctively American style, one that would probe the very heart of the world they lived in. These "ashcan" artists were individualists, yet in sympathy with social reform. They turned to city streets and the people of the slums for their models, depended more upon inspiration and inner conviction than careful craftsmanship to achieve their effects. "Technique did you say?" one of them asked. "Who taught Shakespeare technique? Guts! Guts! Life! Life! That's my technique." These men were caught up in the progressive movement. Their idols were socially conscious painters like Hogarth, Goya, and Daumier; they thought of themselves as rebels.

In 1912 they formed the Association of American Painters and Sculptors, determined to press their "radical" ideas on the art world. The next year, in New York's 69th Regiment Armory, they organized a big showing of their work. Almost incidentally, they decided to include a sampling of recent and current European art to add another dimension to the exhibition.

But artistically the ashcan painters were not really very advanced, being uninfluenced by, if not ignorant of, the outburst of post-impressionist activity taking place at the time in Europe. These Europeans almost literally stole the show. For the first time Americans—well over 250,000 of them—were offered a comprehensive view of "modern" art, from Manet and Cézanne through Van Gogh and Seurat to Rouault, Matisse, and Picasso.* Most found the dazzling color and weird distortions of the European "madmen" shocking but fascinating. A relatively unimportant cubist painting, Marcel Duchamp's *Nude Descending a Staircase,* became the focal point of the exhibition, attracting the scorn of conservative critics and the snickers of unschooled observers. One critic proposed renaming it "Explosion in a Shingle Factory"; another wit suggested "Rush Hour at the Subway"; Theodore Roosevelt, reviewing the exhibition for the *Outlook*, compared it unfavorably with a Navaho rug in his bathroom.

Amid the furor the work of the Americans was almost ignored. As a means of demonstrating their daring and originality, the show was an almost total failure. Even Roosevelt, who praised the ashcan painters highly while laughing off the cubist "Knights of the Isosceles Triangle" and other members of the "lunatic fringe," believed that the association had arranged the Armory Show "primarily . . . to give the public a chance to see what has recently been going on abroad." Most of the ashcan painters were confused and disheartened by their show. Some rejected the Europeans out of hand; others tried, mostly without success, to imitate them. As a group, they were shunted aside and their hopes for creating a new American style died.

Neither the confusions nor the limitations of the progressives should, however, obscure their accomplishments. They elevated the tone of politics, raised the aspirations of the American people, and fashioned many valuable practical reforms.

Reforming the Political System

To most progressives, political corruption and inefficiency lay at the root of all the other evils plaguing American society. As the cities grew, their antiquated and boss-ridden administrations became more and more disgraceful. San Francisco may serve as a typical example. After 1901, a clever lawyer named Abe Ruef ruled over one of the most powerful and dissolute organizations in the nation. Only one kind of paving material was used on San Francisco's streets—Ruef was the lawyer for the company that supplied it. When the local gas company asked for a rate increase of ten cents per 100 cubic feet, Ruef, who was already collecting $1,000 a month from the company as a "retainer," demanded and got an outright bribe of $20,000 in return. A streetcar company needed city authorization to install overhead trolley wires. Ruef's approval cost the company $85,000. Prostitution flourished, with Ruef and his henchmen sharing in the profits; there was a brisk and illegal trade in liquor

*Before this exhibition, one art historian has said, "a painting truly modern was only a rumor" in the United States.

licenses and other favors. No deal was too large or too small for the corruptionists; one official accepted a bribe of $26.10 in connection with the sale of some furniture to the city. Similar conditions existed in dozens of communities. For his famous muckraking series for *McClure's* Lincoln Steffens visited St. Louis, Minneapolis, Pittsburgh, New York, Chicago, and Philadelphia and found them all riddled with corruption.

Beginning in the late nineties, progressives mounted a massive assault upon dishonest and inefficient urban governments. In San Francisco a group headed by the newspaperman Fremont Older and Rudolph Spreckels, a wealthy sugar manufacturer, broke the machine and eventually lodged Ruef in jail. In Toledo, Ohio, Samuel M. "Golden Rule" Jones won election as mayor in 1897 and succeeded in arousing the local citizenry against the corruptionists. The signs that Jones placed on the lawns of Toledo's parks admirably reflected the spirit of his administration. Instead of "Keep Off the Grass," they read: "Citizens, Protect Your Property." Other important progressive mayors included Tom L. Johnson of Cleveland, whose administration Lincoln Steffens called the best in the United States, Joseph W. Folk of St. Louis, Seth Low and later John P. Mitchell of New York, and Hazen S. Pingree of Detroit.

In nearly every case, however, city reformers could not permanently destroy the machines without changing urban political institutions. Some cities obtained "home rule" charters which gave them greater freedom from state control in dealing with their problems. Beginning in 1900 the National Municipal League, an organization of some 200 "good government" clubs founded in 1894, offered a model "Municipal Program" for the guidance of groups seeking to improve urban administration. Many cities created research bureaus which investigated governmental problems in a scientific and nonpartisan manner. A number of middle-sized communities (Galveston, Texas, provided the prototype) experimented with a system which integrated executive and legislative powers in the hands of a small elected commission, thus concentrating responsibility and making it easier to coordinate complex activities. Out of this experiment came the city-manager system, wherein still further centralization was achieved by having the commissioners appoint a single professional manager to administer city affairs on a nonpartisan basis. Dayton, Ohio, which adopted the city-manager plan after the town had been devastated by a great flood in 1913, offers the best illustration of the city-manager system in the Progressive Era.

To carry out this kind of change required the support of state legislatures, since all municipal government depends upon the authority of a sovereign state. Such approval was often difficult to obtain, partly because local bosses were usually entrenched in powerful state machines and partly because most legislatures were controlled by rural majorities insensitive to urban needs. The progressives, therefore, had to strike at inefficiency and corruption at the state level too.

Wisconsin provides by far the most successful example of state progressivism. During the first decade of the new century, that state was transformed by Robert M. La Follette, one of the most remarkable figures of the age. La Follette was a reformer in the agrarian tradition, although he had never been a Populist. Born in Primrose, Wisconsin, in 1855, he had served three terms as a Republican congressman (1885–1891) and developed a reputation as an uncompromising foe of corruption and business control of politics before being elected governor in 1900. That the people would do the right thing in any situation if properly informed and inspired was the fundamental article of his political faith. "Machine control is based upon misrepresentation and ignorance," he said. "Democracy is based upon knowledge. . . . The only way to beat the boss and ring rule [is] to keep the people thoroughly informed." His own career seemed to prove his point, for in his repeated clashes with the conservative Wisconsin Republican machine, he won battle after battle by vigorous grassroots campaigning.

As governor, La Follette overhauled the political structure of the state. Over the opposition of conservative Republicans subservient to Wisconsin railroad and lumbering interests, he and his followers obtained a direct primary system for nominating candidates, a corrupt practices act, and laws limiting campaign expenditures and lobbying activities. In power he became something of a boss himself. He made ruthless use of patronage, demanded absolute loyalty of his subordinates, often stretched, or at least oversimplified, the truth in presenting complex issues to the voters. La Follette was also a consummate showman, and he never rose entirely above rural prejudices, being prone to scent a nefarious "conspiracy" organized by what he called "the interests" behind even the mildest opposition to his proposals. But he was devoted to the cause of honest government and, unlike so many rural reformers, he appreciated the importance of intellect and professional training in solving the complex problems of modern government. Realizing that some state functions called for highly technical expert knowledge, he and his supporters pushed for the creation of special commissions and agencies to handle such matters as railroad regulation, tax assessment, conservation, and highway construction. They established a legislative reference library to assist lawmakers in drafting bills. In work of this kind, La Follette made effective use of the faculty of the University of Wisconsin, enticing men like the economist Balthasar H. Meyer and the political scientist Thomas S. Adams into the public service and drawing freely upon the advice of such outstanding social scientists as Richard T. Ely, John R. Commons, and E.A. Ross.

STATE HISTORICAL SOCIETY OF WISCONSIN

Robert M. La Follette speaking to Wisconsin farmers in 1897. After six years as governor of the state, he won election to the Senate, serving four terms.

The success of what became known as the "Wisconsin Idea" led other states to adopt similar programs. Reform administrations swept into power in Iowa and Arkansas (1901), Oregon (1902), Minnesota, Kansas, and Mississippi (1904), New York and Georgia (1906), Nebraska (1909), New Jersey and Colorado (1910). In some cases the reformers were Republicans, in others Democrats, but in all these states and in many others, the example of Wisconsin was very influential. From every section of the country, requests for information and advice flooded in upon Wisconsin administrators. As early as 1910, 15 states had established legislative reference services, most of them staffed by men trained in Wisconsin. The direct primary system soon became almost universal; some states even went beyond Wisconsin in striving to make their governments responsive to the popular will. In 1902 Oregon, under the dynamic leadership of William S. U'Ren, began to experiment with the initiative, a system by which a bill could be forced upon the attention of the legislature by popular petition, and the referendum, a method for allowing the electorate to approve measures rejected by their representatives and to repeal measures that the legislature had passed. Eleven states, most of them in the West, had legalized these devices by 1914. Thirteen states had also given the vote to women by this time.

On the national level, the progressive drive for direct democracy resulted in the Seventeenth Amendment to the Constitution, ratified in 1913, which required the popular election of senators, and the Nineteenth, ratified in 1920, guaranteeing women the right to vote. A group of "insurgent" congressmen also managed to reform the House of Representatives by limiting the power of the Speaker. During the early years of the century, operating under the system established in the 1890's by "Czar" Thomas B. Reed, Speaker Joseph G. Cannon exercised tyrannical authority, appointing the members of all committees and controlling the course of legislation. A representative could seldom even obtain the floor without first explaining his purpose to Cannon and obtaining the Speaker's consent. In 1910, however, the insurgents, led by George W. Norris of Nebraska, stripped Cannon of his control over the House Rules Committee. Thereafter, appointments to committees were determined by the whole membership, acting through party caucuses. The spirit of this change was thoroughly progressive. "We want the House to be representative of the people and each individual member to have his ideas presented and passed on," Norris explained.

These were the only important alterations of the national political system made during the Progressive Era. Although some 20 states passed Presidential primary laws, no basic change in the cumbersome and undemocratic method of electing Presidents was accomplished. An attempt to improve the efficiency of the federal bureaucracy led Congress to create a Commission on Efficiency and Economy in 1911, but it did not act on the commission's recommendations. Congress did, however, pass a law in 1911 requiring representatives to file statements of their campaign expenses.

Social and Economic Reform

Most progressives saw political reform only as a means to an end; once the system had been made responsive to the desires of the people, they hoped to use it to improve society itself. Many cities began to experiment with "gas and water socialism," taking over public utility companies and operating them as departments of the municipal government. By 1915 nearly two-thirds of all city waterworks were publicly owned and so were many gas, electric, and streetcar systems. Progressive mayors achieved a wide range of social and economic improvements as well. Toledo's "Golden Rule" Jones established a minimum wage for city employees, built playgrounds and golf courses, and moderated the city's harsh penal code. Seth Low improved New York's public transportation system and obtained the passage of the tenement house law of 1901. Tom Johnson forced a fare cut to three cents on the Cleveland street railways.

At the state level, progressives continued to battle for legislation based on the police power, despite restrictions imposed by the courts under the Fourteenth Amendment. In general, industrial workers improved their position during the period but mainly because good times kept unemployment down. Real wages rose only slightly in spite of the rapid increase in labor productivity, and the length of the work week declined very slowly—from an average of 59 hours in 1896 to 55 in 1914. Government action did force a significant decline in the employment of children, however. Sparked by the National Child Labor Committee, organized in 1904 to coordinate the drive, reformers over the next ten years obtained laws in nearly every state banning the employment of young children (the minimum age varied from 12 to 16) and limiting the hours of older children to eight or ten per day. Many states also outlawed night work and labor in dangerous occupations by minors. These laws fixed no uniform standards and many were poorly enforced, yet when Congress passed a federal child labor law in 1916, the Supreme Court, in *Hammer v. Dagenhart* (1918), declared it unconstitutional.*

The states also extended increasing protection to female workers. By 1917 nearly all had placed limitations on the hours of women employed in industry, and about ten states also had set minimum wage standards for women. Once again, however, federal action that would have extended such regulations to the entire country did not materialize. Even a ten-hour law for women workers in the District of Columbia was thrown out by the Court in *Adkins v. Children's Hospital* (1923).

*A second child labor law, passed in 1919, was also thrown out by the Court, and a child labor amendment, submitted in 1924, failed to achieve ratification by the necessary three-quarters of the states.

Legislation protecting workers against on-the-job accidents was also enacted by many states. Disasters like the 1911 Triangle fire in New York City, in which nearly 150 women perished because the Triangle shirtwaist factory had no fire escapes, led to the passage of stricter municipal building codes and to many state factory inspection acts. By 1910 most states had modified the old common-law principle that a worker accepted the risk of accident as one of the conditions of his employment and was not entitled to compensation if injured unless he could prove that his employer had been negligent, a costly, uncertain, and time-consuming procedure. Gradually, they adopted accident insurance systems: by 1916 nearly three-quarters of the states had them. Some also began to grant pensions to widows with small children.

The passage of so much state social legislation sent conservatives scurrying to the Supreme Court for redress. Such men believed, quite sincerely in most instances, that *no* government had the power to deprive either workers or employers of the right to negotiate any kind of labor contract they wished. The decision of the Supreme Court in the Lochner bakeshop case (1905) seemed to indicate that the justices would adopt this point of view. But in *Muller v. Oregon* (1908), the Court held that an Oregon law limiting women laundry workers to ten hours a day was a legitimate exercise of the state police power. In arguing the state's case before the Court, Louis D. Brandeis presented a remarkable brief stuffed with economic and sociological evidence indicating that *in fact* long hours damaged both the health of individual women and the health of society. This nonlegal evidence greatly impressed the judges. "It may not be amiss," they declared, "to notice . . . expressions of opinion from other than judicial sources" in determining the constitutionality of such laws. "Woman's physical structure, and the functions she performs in consequence thereof, justify special legislation," they concluded. "The limitations which this statute places upon her contractual powers . . . are not imposed solely for her benefit, but also largely for the benefit of all."

The fact that the Oregon law applied only to women reduced the importance of the Muller case somewhat. The Court did not overrule the Lochner decision, and in some later cases it threw out labor laws based on the police power. Nevertheless, after 1908 the right of states to protect the weaker members of society by special legislation was widely accepted. The use of the "Brandeis brief" technique to demonstrate the need for such action became standard practice.

Progressives also launched a massive if ill-coordinated attack on the economic problems of the times, particularly those related to monopoly and business influence on government. The variety of regulatory legislation passed by the states between 1900 and 1917 was almost endless. In Wisconsin alone the progressives created a powerful railroad commission staffed with nonpartisan experts; they enacted a graduated income tax and strengthened the state tax commission, which then proceeded to force corporations to bear their proper share of the cost of government; they overhauled the laws regulating insurance companies, passing some two dozen acts in a single year (1907) and setting up a small state-owned life insurance company to serve as a yardstick for evaluating the rates of private companies. In 1911, besides creating an industrial commission to enforce the state's labor and factory legislation, they established a conservation commission, headed by Charles R. Van Hise, president of the University of Wisconsin.

A similar spate of legislation characterized the brief reign of Woodrow Wilson as governor of New Jersey (1911–13). Urged on by the relentless Wilson, the New Jersey legislature enacted a number of political and social reforms. It created a strong public utility commission with authority to evaluate the properties of railroad, gas, electric, telephone, and express companies, and to fix rates and set standards for these corporations. The legislature also passed storage and food inspection laws, and in 1913, after Wilson had moved on to the Presidency, it enacted seven bills (the "Seven Sisters" laws) tightening the state's notoriously loose controls over corporations, which had won New Jersey the unenviable reputation of being "the mother of trusts."

Economic reform movements in other states

were less spectacular but impressive in the mass. In New York an investigation of the big life insurance companies led to comprehensive changes in the insurance laws and put Charles Evans Hughes, who had conducted the investigation, in the governor's chair, where he led a drive for other progressive reforms. In Iowa stiff new laws regulating railroads were passed in 1906. In Nebraska the legislature created a system of bank deposit insurance in 1909. Minnesota levied an inheritance tax and built a state harvesting machine factory to combat the harvester trust at about this time. Georgia raised the taxes on corporations. These are but typical examples, plucked almost at random from among hundreds of laws passed by states in every part of the nation. However, as in the area of social legislation, piecemeal state regulation failed to solve the problems of an economy growing yearly more integrated and complex. It was on the national level that the most significant battles for economic reform were fought.

Theodore Roosevelt

On September 6, 1901, an anarchist named Leon Czolgosz shot President McKinley during a public reception at the Pan-American Exposition at Buffalo, New York. Eight days later McKinley died and Theodore Roosevelt became President of the United States. The new President hastened to assure the country that he intended to carry on in his predecessor's footsteps. "It shall be my aim," he said on taking the oath of office, "to continue, absolutely unbroken, the policy of President McKinley for the peace, the prosperity, and the honor of our beloved country." Roosevelt doubtless spoke from the heart, and indeed he instituted no drastic changes in the following months. Nevertheless, his ascension to the Presidency marked the beginning of a new era in national politics.

Although only 42, by far the youngest President in the nation's history up to that time, Roosevelt brought solid qualifications to his high office. Son of a well-to-do New York merchant of Dutch ancestry, he had been graduated from Harvard in 1880 and had studied law briefly at Columbia, although he did not complete his degree. In addition to political experience that included a term in the New York assembly, six years on the United States Civil Service Commission, two years as police commissioner of New York City, another as assistant secretary of the navy, and a term as governor of New York, he had been a rancher in Dakota Territory and a soldier in the Spanish War. He was also a well-known author: his *Naval War of 1812* (1882), begun during his undergraduate days at Harvard, and his four-volume *Winning of the West* (1889–1896) were valuable works of scholarship, and he had written two popular biographies and other books as well. Politically, he had always been a loyal Republican. He rejected the Mugwump heresy in 1884, despite his distaste for Blaine, and he vigorously denounced Populism, Bryanism, and "labor agitators" during the tempestuous nineties.

Nevertheless, his elevation to the Presidency alarmed many conservatives, and not without reason. To begin with, he did not fit their conception, based on a composite image of the Chief Executives from Hayes to McKinley, of what a President should be like. He seemed too undignified, too energetic, too outspoken, colorful, unconventional. It was one thing to have operated a cattle ranch, another to have captured a gang of rustlers at gunpoint, one to have run a metropolitan police force, another to have roamed New York slums in the small hours in order to catch patrolmen fraternizing with thieves and prostitutes, one to have commanded a regiment, another to have killed a Spaniard personally.

Roosevelt had been a weak and sickly child, plagued by asthma and poor eyesight, and he seems to have spent much of his adult life compensating for the sense of inadequacy that these troubles bred in him. Mark Twain called him "the Tom Sawyer of the political world . . . always hunting for a chance to show off." He repeatedly carried his displays of physical stamina and personal courage, and his interest in athletics and big-game-hunting, to preternatural lengths. Once, while fox-hunting, he fell from his horse, cutting his face severely and breaking his left arm. Instead of waiting for help to come or struggling to some nearby house to summon a doctor, Roosevelt clambered back on his horse and resumed the chase. "I was in at the death," he wrote next day. "I looked pretty gay, with one arm dangling, and my face and clothes like the walls of a slaughter house." That evening, after his arm had been set and put in splints, he attended a dinner party.

Roosevelt also worshiped aggressiveness and was extremely sensitive to any threat to his honor as a gentleman. When another young man showed some slight interest in Roosevelt's fiancée, he sent off for a set of French dueling pistols. His teachers found him an interesting student, for he was intelligent and imaginative, but rather annoyingly argumentative. "Now look here, Roosevelt," one Harvard professor finally said to him, "let me talk. I'm running this course."

Few individuals have rationalized or sublimated their feelings of inferiority as effectively as Roosevelt and to such good purpose. And few have been more genuinely warm-hearted, more full of spontaneity, more committed to the ideals of public service and national greatness. As a political leader he was energetic and hard-driving but seldom lacking in good judgment: responsibility usually tempered his aggressiveness. But conservatives and timid souls, sensing his aggressiveness even when he held it in check, distrusted Roosevelt's judgment, fearing he might go off halfcocked in some crisis.

Above all, Roosevelt believed in action. When he was first mentioned as a possible running mate for McKinley in 1900, he wrote: "The Vice Presidency is a most honorable office, but for a young man there is not much to do." It would have been unthinkable for him to preside over a mere caretaker administration devoted to maintaining the status quo. However, the reigning Republican politicos, basking in the sunshine of the prosperity which had contributed so much to their victory in 1900, distrusted anything suggestive of change. Mark Hanna reflected the mood of most of his fellow senators when he urged the country to "stand pat and continue Republican prosperity," and the same sentiment pervaded the House, where Speaker Cannon said that his philosophy could be summed up in the phrase: "Stand by the status."

If Roosevelt had been the impetuous hothead that conservatives like Hanna feared, he would have plunged ahead without regard for their feelings and influence. Instead he moved slowly and won his major victories by using his executive power rather than by persuading Congress to pass new laws. His domestic program, ill-defined at first, included some measure of control of big corporations, more power for the Interstate Commerce Commission, and the conservation of natural resources. By consulting fully with congressional leaders and following their advice not to bring up controversial matters like the tariff and currency reform, with which he was not deeply concerned in any case, he obtained a modest budget of new laws. The Newlands Act (1902) funneled the proceeds from land sales in the West into federal irrigation projects. The Expedition Act (1903) speeded the handling of antitrust suits in the courts. Another 1903 law created a Department of Commerce and Labor, which was to include a Bureau of Corporations, with authority to investigate industrial combines and issue reports. The Elkins Act of 1903 strengthened the Interstate Commerce Commission's hand against the railroads by making the receiving as well as the granting of rebates illegal and by forbidding the roads to deviate in any way from their published rates.

Roosevelt and Big Business

Roosevelt soon became known as a "trustbuster," and in the sense that he considered the monopoly problem the most pressing issue of the times, the title has some meaning. But he did not believe in breaking up big corporations indiscriminately. "Much of the legislation . . . enacted against trusts," he said in 1900 while governor of New York, "is not one whit more intelligent than the mediaeval bull against the comet, and has not been one particle more effective." Industrial giantism, he believed, "could not be eliminated unless we were willing to turn back the wheels of modern progress." Regulation, rather than disruption, seemed the best way to deal with the big corporations.

However, with Congress unwilling to pass a stiff regulatory law—even the bill creating the relatively innocuous Bureau of Corporations ran into much opposition—Roosevelt resorted to the Sherman Act to get at the problem. Although the Supreme Court decision in the Sugar Trust case seemed to have emasculated that law, in 1902 he ordered the Justice Department to bring suit against the Northern Securities Company.

He chose his target wisely. The Northern Securities Company controlled the Great Northern, the Northern Pacific, and the Chicago, Burlington and Quincy railroads. It had been created in 1901, after a titanic battle on the New York Stock Exchange between the forces of J.P. Morgan and James J. Hill and those of E.H. Harriman, who was associated with the Rockefeller interests. In their efforts to obtain control of the Northern Pacific, the rivals had forced its stock up to $1,000 a share, ruining many speculators and threatening to cause a major panic. Neither side could win a clear-cut victory, so they decided to put the stock of all three railroads in a holding company owned by the two groups. Since Harriman also controlled the Union Pacific and the Southern Pacific, a virtual monopoly of western railroads was thus effected. The public had been greatly alarmed, for the merger seemed to typify the rapaciousness of the great tycoons. Few big corporations had more enemies; thus Roosevelt's attack won wide support.

The announcement of the suit caused consternation in the business world. Morgan rushed to the White House. "If we have done anything wrong," he said to the President, "send your man to my man and they can fix it up." Roosevelt was not fundamentally opposed to exactly this sort of agreement, but it was too late to compromise in this particular instance. Attorney General Philander C. Knox pressed the case vigorously, and in 1904 the Court ordered the dissolution of the Northern Securities Company. Although actual ownership of the three railroads was not affected, this decision had extremely important results. It made further prosecutions possible—Roosevelt soon ordered suits against the meat packers, the Standard Oil Trust, and the American Tobacco Company—and served notice on all the great corporations that they could no longer ignore the Sherman Act. Roosevelt's stock among progressives rose, yet he had not embarrassed the conservatives in Congress by demanding new antitrust legislation.

Furthermore, he went out of his way to assure *cooperative* corporation magnates that he had no intention of attacking them. He saw no basic conflict between capital and labor and was not against size per se. "In our industrial and social system," Roosevelt said, "the interests of all men are so closely intertwined that in the immense majority of cases a straight-dealing man who by his efficiency, by his ingenuity and industry, benefits himself must also benefit others." His Bureau of Corporations, headed by James R. Garfield, son of the former President, followed a policy of "obtaining hearty co-operation rather than arousing [the] antagonism of business and industrial interests." At an informal White House conference in 1905, Roosevelt and Elbert H. Gary, chairman of the board of U.S. Steel, reached a "gentlemen's agreement" whereby Gary promised "to co-operate with the Government in every possible way." The Bureau of Corporations would conduct an investigation of U.S. Steel, Gary providing it with full access to company records. Roosevelt, in turn, promised that if the investigation revealed any malpractices on the part of the corporation, he would allow Gary to set matters right voluntarily, thus avoiding an antitrust suit. He reached a similar agreement with the International Harvester Company two years later.

There were limits to the effectiveness of such arrangements; Standard Oil, for example, first agreed to a similar détente and then reneged, refusing to turn over vital records to the bureau. The Justice Department then brought suit against the company under the Sherman Act, and eventually it was broken up at the order of the Supreme Court. Roosevelt would have preferred a more binding kind of regulation, but when he asked for laws giving the government supervisory authority over big combinations, Congress refused to act. Given this situation, his gentleman's agreements seemed the best alternative. Trusts that conformed to his somewhat subjective standards could remain as they were; others must take their chances with the Supreme Court.

Life, MAY 16, 1907

The comic weekly Life *ran a series called "The Teddyssey" in 1907. In this episode Columbia steers T.R. safely past the monopolistic Sirens—Rockefeller, harpist J.P. Morgan, and Carnegie, a Scotch-plaid mermaid.*

Roosevelt also made remarkable use of his executive power during the anthracite coal strike of 1902. In June of that year the United Mine Workers, led by John Mitchell, lay down their picks and demanded higher wages, an eight-hour day, and recognition of their union. Most of the anthracite mines were owned by railroads. Two years earlier the miners had won a ten per cent wage increase in a similar strike, chiefly because the owners feared that labor unrest might endanger the election of McKinley. Now the mine operators were dead set against further concessions; when the men walked out, they shut down their properties and prepared to starve the strikers into submission.

Throughout the summer and early fall the miners held firm. They conducted themselves with great restraint, avoiding violence and offering to submit their claims to arbitration. As the price of anthracite soared with the approach of winter, sentiment in their behalf mounted rapidly. The fact that great railroad corporations closely allied with Wall Street controlled most of the mines and that the owners refused even to discuss terms with the union also predisposed the public in the workers' favor. The operators' spokesman, George F. Baer of the Reading Railroad, proved particularly inept at handling public relations. Baer stated categorically that God was on the side of the owners, but when someone suggested asking an important Roman Catholic prelate to arbitrate the dispute, he replied icily: "Anthracite mining is a business and not a religious, sentimental or academic proposition." He would not surrender, he said, even if it were necessary to "cripple industry, stagnate business or tie up the commerce of the world."

Roosevelt shared the public's sympathy for the miners, and the threat of a coal famine naturally alarmed him. But for months he could think of no legal way to intervene. Finally, early in October, he summoned both sides to a conference in Washington, asking them as patriotic Americans to sacrifice "personal consideration[s]" for the "general good." His action enraged the operators, for they believed he was trying to force them to recognize the union. They refused even to speak to the UMW representatives at the conference and demanded that Roosevelt end the strike by force and bring suit against the union under the Sherman Act. Mitchell, on the other hand, aware of the immense prestige that Roosevelt had conferred upon the union by calling the conference, cooperated fully with the President. He offered to meet with the owners at any time or to submit the workers' claims to a government-appointed arbitral tribunal.

The refusal of the operators to bargain infuriated Roosevelt and strengthened public support of the miners. Even former President Grover Cleveland, who had used federal troops to break the Pullman strike, said that he was "disturbed and vexed by the tone and substance of the operators' deliverances." Encouraged by this state of affairs, Roosevelt took a bold step—he announced that if no settlement were reached promptly, he would order federal troops into the anthracite regions, not to break the strike but to seize and operate the mines.

This threat of government intervention brought the owners to terms. Secretary of War Root worked out the details with J.P. Morgan, whose firm had great interests in the Reading and other railroads, while cruising up and down the Hudson River on Morgan's yacht. The miners would go back to the pits, and all issues between them and the operators would be submitted for settlement to a commission appointed by Roosevelt. After a last-minute crisis over the inclusion of a union man on the commission—solved by Roosevelt's appointing the president of one of the Railroad Brotherhoods but classifying him as an "eminent sociologist" to save the faces of the operators—both sides accepted this arrangement and the men went back to work. In March 1903 the commission granted the miners a ten per cent wage increase and a nine-hour day. The owners, however, were not required to recognize the United Mine Workers.

To the public, the incident seemed a great victory for the miners and for the people as a whole. "Right" had triumphed over the selfishness of the "interests." It seemed a perfect illustration of the progressive spirit—in Roosevelt's words, everyone had received a "square deal." Actually, the results were by no means so clear-cut. The miners gained relatively little and the operators lost still less, for the commission recommended a ten per cent increase in the price of coal, ample compensation for their increased wage costs. Eventually, George F. Baer came to believe that Roosevelt's appointment of the commission was the best thing he ever did. As for the public, it, too, gained less than it thought, for the coal shortage had never been really acute. If the strike had continued through the winter, bituminous coal could have been substituted for anthracite for most purposes. The President was the main winner. The public acclaimed him as a fearless, imaginative, and public-spirited executive. Construing the powers of his office broadly, he had interjected the federal government into a labor dispute, forced both sides to accept his leadership, and established an extralegal committee of neutrals representing the national interest to arbitrate the questions at issue. Without calling upon Congress for support, he had expanded his own authority and hence that of the federal government in order to protect the public interest. His action marked a major forward step in the evolution of the modern Presidency.

Roosevelt's Second Term

By reviving the Sherman Act, settling the coal strike, and pushing a number of moderate but constructive reforms through Congress, Roosevelt insured that he would be elected President in 1904 in his own right. Progressives were pleased by his performance if not yet captivated. Conservative Republicans, impressed by his deference to men like Senator Nelson Aldrich and Speaker Cannon, offered no serious objection to his renomination and supported him loyally during the campaign. Sensing that Roosevelt had won over the liberals, the Democrats nominated a conservative candidate, Judge Alton B. Parker of New York, and bid for the support of eastern industrialists. This strategy failed, for businessmen continued to eye the party of Bryan with intense suspicion. Despite his resentment at Roosevelt's handling of the Northern Securities incident, J.P. Morgan contributed $150,000 to the Republican campaign. Other tycoons gave with equal generosity. As the New York *Sun* put it, most businessmen preferred "the impulsive candidate of the party of conservatism to the conservative candidate of the party which the business interests regard as permanently and dangerously impulsive." Roosevelt swept the country, piling up a majority of more than 2.5 million votes. Even border states like Maryland and Missouri gave him their electoral votes. According to one wit: "Parker ran for the presidency against Theodore Roosevelt and was defeated by acclamation."

Encouraged by this landslide and by the increasing militancy of progressives in the separate states, Roosevelt began to press Congress for reform legislation. His most imaginative proposal was a plan to make the District of Columbia a model progressive community. He suggested a variety of reforms, including a child labor law, a factory inspection law, and a slum-clearance program, but Congress refused to act. Likewise, his request for a minimum wage for railroad workers was rejected.

He had greater success, however, when he urged Congress to increase the power of the Interstate Commerce Commission again. The Elkins Act had proved a bitter disappointment, for the federal courts continued to favor the railroads in most cases. Rebating remained a serious problem. With progressive state governors urging him to act and with farmers and manufacturers, especially in the Middle West, clamoring for relief against discriminatory rates, Roosevelt was ready by 1905 to make railroad legislation his major objective. The ICC should be empowered to fix rates, not merely challenge unreasonable ones, he declared. It should also have the right to inspect the private records of the railroads, since fair rates could not be determined unless the true financial condition of the roads was known.

Since these proposals struck at rights that businessmen considered sacrosanct, many congressmen balked at them. Roosevelt cleverly threatened to call a special session of Congress to revise the tariff unless they agreed, and this proposal so alarmed conservative Republicans that most of them fell in line. Senator Aldrich tried to confuse the issue by putting Senator Tillman of South Carolina, a Democrat personally obnoxious to the President, in charge of the rate bill, but Roosevelt swallowed his distaste for Tillman and worked with him effectively. The conservatives did manage to obtain amendments preserving the right of the roads to challenge ICC rate decisions in the courts. Much to the chagrin of some of his progressive supporters, Roosevelt meekly accepted this compromise, for he remained eager to conciliate his party's right wing. In June 1906 the Hepburn bill became law. It gave the commission the power to inspect the books of railroad companies, to fix rates (subject to judicial review), and to control sleeping car companies, owners of oil pipelines, and other firms engaged in transportation. The roads could no longer issue passes freely, an important check on their political influence. All in all, the Hepburn Act was a major achievement. Although the right of the federal government to regulate interstate carriers had been long recognized, this law made that regulation reasonably effective for the first time.

Roosevelt also obtained passage of meat inspection and pure food and drug legislation in 1906. The question of federal regulation of slaughterhouses was an old one, dating back to the "pork controversy" with the European powers in the 1880's. Feelings about meat inspection in the business world were mixed. The major packers tended to favor it because of their interest in the export market, while most local packers objected. Other businessmen were also divided, some objecting on grounds of principle to any extension of government regulation. In 1906, for example, the president of the National Association of Manufacturers opposed regulating the packers, but the NAM's board of directors voted not to campaign against inspection.

The issue was precipitated by the publication in 1906 of Upton Sinclair's novel *The Jungle*, a devastating exposé of the filthy conditions in the Chicago slaughterhouses. Sinclair was more interested in writing a socialist tract than in meat inspection, but his book, which became a best seller, raised a storm against the packers. When Roosevelt read *The Jungle*, he sent two officials to Chicago to investigate. Their report was so shocking, he said, that its publication would "be well-nigh ruinous to our export trade in meat." He threatened to release the report, however, unless Congress acted. After a hot fight, the meat inspection bill passed. A Pure Food and Drug Act, forbidding the manufacture and sale of adulterated and fraudulently labeled products, rode through Congress on the coattails of this measure.

Roosevelt has probably received more credit

than he deserves for these laws. He had never been deeply interested in pure food legislation and considered Dr. Harvey W. Wiley, chief chemist of the Department of Agriculture and the leader of the fight for this reform, something of a crank. In the case of the meat inspection law, as with the Hepburn Act, he placed accommodating the conservatives above total victory, accepting a halfway measure cheerfully, despite his loud denunciations of the evils under attack. "As now carried on the [meat-packing] business is both a menace to health and an outrage on decency," he said. "No legislation that is not drastic and thoroughgoing will be of avail." Yet he went along with the packers' demand that the government pay the costs of inspection, although he believed that "the only way to secure efficiency is by the imposition upon the packers of a fee." Nevertheless, the end results were positive and generally in line with his conception of the public good.

To advanced liberals, Roosevelt's achievements seemed limited when placed beside his professed objectives and his smug evaluations of what he had done. They did not see how he could be a reformer and a defender of established interests at the same time. Roosevelt, however, found no difficulty in holding such a position. As one historian has said, "he stood close to the center and bared his teeth at the conservatives of the right and the liberals of the extreme left." He also changed with the times; as the progressive movement advanced, he advanced with it, never accepting all the ideas of what he called its "lunatic fringe," but taking steadily more liberal positions. For example, he always insisted that he was not hostile to business interests, but when these interests sought to exploit the national domain, they had no more implacable foe. He placed some 150 million acres of forest lands in federal reserves, and he enforced the laws governing grazing, mining, and lumbering strictly. When his opponents managed to attach a rider to an essential appropriation bill prohibiting the creation of further reserves without the approval of Congress, Roosevelt hurriedly transferred an additional 17 million acres to the reserve before signing the bill. In 1908 he organized a National Conservation Conference, attended by 44 governors and 500 other persons, to discuss conservation matters. As a result of this meeting, most of the states created their own conservation commissions.

As Roosevelt became more liberal, conservative Republicans began to balk at following his lead. The sudden panic that struck the financial world in October 1907 speeded the trend considerably. Government policies had no direct bearing on the panic, which began with a run on several important New York trust companies and spread to the Stock Exchange when speculators found themselves unable to borrow money to meet their obligations. In this emergency Roosevelt acted forcefully, sending Secretary of the Treasury George C. Cortelyou to New York and allowing him to deposit large amounts of government cash in New York banks. Roosevelt also informally authorized the acquisition of the Tennessee Coal and Iron Company by U.S. Steel when the bankers told him that the purchase was necessary to prevent a further spread of the panic. But in spite of his efforts, conservatives referred to the financial collapse as "Roosevelt's Panic" and blamed the President for the depression which followed on its heels. Such men argued that dangerous socioeconomic experiments were undermining the confidence of the business community.

Roosevelt, however, turned left after 1907 rather than right. In 1908 he came out for federal income and inheritance taxes, for wider regulation of interstate corporations, and for reforms designed to help the industrial worker. He denounced "the speculative folly and the flagrant dishonesty" of "malefactors of great wealth," further alienating the conservative, or Old Guard, wing of his party. These men felt that economic reform had gone far enough and that political reforms like the direct primary were destroying the basis of their power. They also resented the attacks on their integrity implicit in many of Roosevelt's statements. When the President began criticizing the courts, the last bastion of conservatism, he lost all chance of obtaining further reform legislation. As he put it himself, during his last months in office "the period of stagnation continued to rage with uninterrupted violence."

William Howard Taft

Nevertheless, Roosevelt remained popular and politically powerful; when his term ended, he chose William Howard Taft, his secretary of war, to succeed him and easily obtained his nomination. William Jennings Bryan was again the Democratic nominee. Campaigning on Roosevelt's record, Taft carried the country by well over a million votes, defeating Bryan by 321 to 162 in the Electoral College.

Taft was intelligent, experienced, and public-spirited; he seemed ideally suited to carry out Roosevelt's policies. Born in Cincinnati in 1857, educated at Yale, he had served as an Ohio judge, as solicitor general of the United States under Harrison, and then as a federal circuit court judge before accepting McKinley's assignment to head the Philippine Commission in 1900. His success as civil governor of the Philippines led Roosevelt to make him secretary of war in 1904. He supported the "Square Deal" loyally. This, together with his mentor's ardent endorsement, won him the backing of most progressive Republicans. Yet the Old Guard liked him too; although outgoing, he had none of the Rooseveltian impetuosity and aggressiveness. His antilabor opinions voiced while on the bench also raised his status among conservatives. His genial nature and his obvious desire to avoid conflict appealed to moderates.

However, Taft was not cut out to be a 20th-century President. In the 1880's his administrative ability and eminent respectability might have seen him through; amid the fervor and conflict of the Progressive Era, he was a failure. He lacked the physical and mental stamina required of a modern Chief Executive. Although not really lazy, he weighed over 300 pounds and needed to rest this vast bulk more than the job allowed. He liked to eat in leisurely fashion, to idle away mornings on the golf course, to take an afternoon nap. Campaigning bored him, speechmaking seemed a needless chore. The judicial life was his real love; intense partisanship dismayed and confused him. He was too reasonable to control a coalition and too unambitious to impose his will on others. He found extremists irritating, persistent men difficult to resist. He supported many progressive measures, but he never absorbed the progressive spirit.

CULVER PICTURES

Taft was the first Presidential golfer, playing enthusiastically despite his bulk. He ended his career happily as Chief Justice of the Supreme Court.

Taft honestly desired to proceed along the path laid out by Roosevelt. He enforced the Sherman Act even more vigorously than his predecessor, and continued Roosevelt's policy of adding to the national forest reserves. He pushed for a postal savings system, and approved a measure—the Mann-Elkins Act of 1910—that further strengthened the Interstate Commerce Commission by empowering it to suspend rate increases without waiting for a shipper to complain, and by establishing a Commerce Court to speed the settlement of railroad rate litigation. An eight-hour day for all persons engaged in work on government contracts, mine-safety legislation, and a number of other reform measures also received his approval. He even summoned Congress into special session specifically to reduce tariff duties—something Roosevelt had not dared to attempt.

In nearly everything he did, however, Taft's

lack of vigor and his political ineptness led to trouble. He had an uncanny ability to aggravate men with views substantially like his own. In the matter of the tariff, he favored a sharp downward revision. When the special session met in 1909, the House promptly passed the Payne bill which was roughly in line with his desires. But Senate protectionists, led by Nelson Aldrich, restored the high rates of the Act of 1897 on most items. A group of "insurgent" senators, led by Robert La Follette of Wisconsin, Jonathan Dolliver of Iowa, and Albert J. Beveridge of Indiana, fought desperately against these changes, producing masses of statistics to show that the proposed schedules on cotton goods, woolens, and other products were unreasonably high. They were fighting the President's battle, but Taft did little to help them; like so many Republican Presidents, he did not relish challenging Congress over legislative details. The fanaticism of the insurgents also annoyed him. In the end, he signed the Payne-Aldrich measure and even called it "the best [tariff] bill that the Republican party ever passed." He had some small justification for this faint praise, since the act did make important reductions in the duties on cotton goods, hides, shoes, and iron ore, but the President's attitude dumbfounded the progressives. "There is developing a most bitter and relentless hostility to Taft," one antitariff Republican senator wrote. "Aldrich has completely captured [him]."

In 1910 Taft got into a similar difficulty with the conservationists. The issue concerned the integrity of his secretary of the interior, Richard A. Ballinger. A less than ardent conservationist, Ballinger returned certain waterpower sites to the public domain which his predecessor in the Roosevelt administration had withdrawn on the legally questionable ground that they were to become ranger stations. Ballinger's action alarmed Chief Forester Gifford Pinchot, the darling of the conservationists, and when Pinchot learned that Ballinger also intended to validate the shaky claim of some powerful mining interests to a vast tract of coal-rich land in Alaska, he launched an intemperate attack on the secretary. In this Ballinger-Pinchot controversy, Taft felt obliged to support his own man. The coal-lands dispute was complex, and Pinchot's charges were both exaggerated and in poor taste. It was certainly unfair to call Ballinger "the most effective opponent the conservation policies have yet had." When Pinchot, whose own motives were partly political, persisted in attacking Ballinger, Taft dismissed him, thus bringing down upon himself the wrath of the conservationists. He had really no choice under the circumstances, but a more adept leader would have found some way of avoiding a showdown.

Breakup of the Republican Party

One ominous aspect of the Ballinger-Pinchot affair was the fact that Pinchot was a close friend of Theodore Roosevelt's. After Taft's inauguration, Roosevelt had gone off on a hunting expedition to Africa, bearing in his baggage an autographed photograph of his protégé and a touching letter of appreciation, in which the new President said: "I can never forget that the power I now exercise was a voluntary transfer from you to me." For months, as he trudged across Africa, guns blazing, Roosevelt remained almost completely out of touch with affairs in the United States. When he emerged from the wilderness in March 1910, bearing over 3,000 trophies, including 9 lions, 5 elephants, and 13 rhinos, he was quickly caught up in the growing squabble between the progressive members of his party and its titular head. Pinchot met him in Italy, laden with injured innocence and a packet of angry letters from various progressives. His close friend Senator Lodge, essentially a conservative, barraged him with messages, the gist of which was that Taft was lazy and inept and that Roosevelt should prepare to become the "Moses" who would guide the party "out of the wilderness of doubt and discontent" into which Taft had led it.

Roosevelt hoped to steer a middle course, but Pinchot's complaints impressed him. Taft had deliberately decided to strike out on his own, he now concluded. "No man must render such a service as that I rendered Taft and expect the individual . . . not in the end to become uncomfortable and resentful," he wrote Lodge sadly. No immediate break took place, but Taft sensed the former President's coolness and was offended by it. He was egged on by his ambitious wife, who wanted him to stand clear of the Rooseveltian shadow and establish his own reputation.

Probably the resulting rupture was inevitable. The Republican party was dividing into two factions, the progressives and the Old Guard. Forced to choose between them, Taft threw in his lot with the Old Guard. When House progressives revolted against the domination of Speaker Cannon, Taft deprived them of patronage, practically reading them out of the party. Rooosevelt, in turn, backed the progressives. Speaking at Osawatomie, Kansas, in August 1910, he came out for a comprehensive program of social legislation, which he called the "New Nationalism." Besides attacking "special privilege" and the "unfair money-getting" practices of "lawbreakers of great wealth," he called for a broad expansion of federal power at the expense of the states. "The betterment we seek must be accomplished," he said, "mainly through the National Government."

The final break between Taft and Roosevelt came in October 1911, when the President ordered an antitrust suit against U.S. Steel. Roosevelt, of course, opposed breaking up large corporations. "The effort at prohibiting all combination has substantially failed," he said in his New Nationalism speech. "The way out lies . . . in completely controlling them." Taft, on the other hand, was prepared "to enforce [the Sherman] law or die in the attempt." What especially enraged Roosevelt, however, was Taft's emphasis in the steel suit on the absorption of the Tennessee Coal and Iron Company by U.S. Steel during the panic of 1907, which Roosevelt had unofficially authorized. The government's antitrust brief made Roosevelt appear to have been either an abettor of monopoly or—far worse—a fool who had been duped by the steel corporation. He began to denounce Taft publicly, and early in 1912 declared himself a candidate for the Republican Presidential nomination.

This dramatic split between the nation's two leading Republicans intensified the progressive-Old Guard conflict within the party. Already the liberal faction had organized (January 1911) a

BOTH : CULVER PICTURES

The Life *cartoon above appeared at the time of the 1912 Presidential nominating conventions. Cartoonists had a field day with Roosevelt as a Bull Moose; below, T.R. enters the political zoo, from* Harper's.

National Progressive Republican League and was pushing Senator La Follette for the Republican nomination. Roosevelt's entry into the race now encouraged the progressives to strike more boldly against the administration. Although some, particularly those from the Middle West, found Roosevelt's position on the Sherman Act unpalatable, in the last analysis the fact that he stood a better chance than La Follette of winning the nomination and carrying the country led most of them to swing to his support.

Roosevelt plunged into the preconvention campaign with typical energy. He was almost uniformly victorious in the states that held Presidential primaries, carrying even Ohio, Taft's home state. However, the President controlled the party machinery and entered the national convention with a small majority of the delegates. Since some of his supporters had been chosen under questionable circumstances, the Roosevelt forces challenged the right of 254 Taft delegates to their seats. Unfortunately for Roosevelt, the Taft-controlled credentials committee, paying little attention to the evidence, gave all but a few of these disputed seats to the President, who won easily on the first ballot.

If Roosevelt had swallowed his resentment and bided his time, Taft would almost certainly have been defeated in the election, and the 1916 Republican nomination would have been Roosevelt's for the asking. But he was understandably outraged by the ruthless manner in which the Taft "steamroller" had overridden his forces. When his leading supporters urged him to organize a third party and when two of them, George W. Perkins, formerly of the House of Morgan, and Frank Munsey, the publisher, offered to finance the campaign, he agreed to make the race. In August, amid scenes of hysterical enthusiasm, the first convention of the Progressive party met at Chicago and nominated him for President. Announcing that he felt "as strong as a bull moose," Roosevelt delivered a stirring "confession of faith," calling for strict regulation of corporations, a tariff commission, national Presidential primaries, minimum-wage and workmen's compensation laws, the elimination of child labor, and many other reforms. Although most professional Republican politicians refused to break with their party, the magnetic Roosevelt and this advanced progressive program would clearly have great popular appeal.

Election of 1912

Meantime, the Democrats were making the most of the opportunity offered by the Republican schism. Had they nominated a conservative or allowed Bryan a fourth chance, they would probably have insured Roosevelt's election. Instead, after battling through 46 ballots at their convention in Baltimore, they nominated Woodrow Wilson, who had achieved a remarkable liberal record as governor of New Jersey.

Although as a political scientist Wilson had sharply criticized the status quo and had taken a pragmatic approach to the idea of government regulation of the economy, he had objected strongly to the Bryan brand of politics; in 1896 he voted the Gold Democratic ticket. But by 1912, influenced partly by ambition and partly by the spirit of the times, he had been converted to progressivism. He called his program the "New Freedom." The federal government could best advance the cause of social justice, he argued, by eradicating the special privileges that had enabled the "interests" to flourish. Where Roosevelt seemed to have lost faith in competition as a way of protecting the public against monopolies, Wilson insisted that competition could be restored. The government must break up the great trusts and establish fair rules for doing business, subjecting violators to stiff punishments; thereafter, the classical checks of the free-enterprise system would protect the public against exploitation without destroying individual initiative and opportunity. "If America is not to have free enterprise, then she can have freedom of no sort whatever," he said. Instead of regulating monopoly as Roosevelt proposed, the nation should regulate competition. Although rather vague in explaining how to do this, he won the approval of thousands of voters who found the growing power of great corporations frightening, but who hesitated to make the thoroughgoing commitment to a welfare state that Roosevelt was advocating.

Thus progressives confronted two fairly clear alternatives in 1912. Roosevelt's reasoning was perhaps theoretically sound. Fear of a powerful national government was an inheritance from the 18th century, when political power had been equated with monarchy and tyranny and when America had been sparsely settled and decentralized. In the 20th century, with democratic institutions firmly established and with a highly integrated economy, citizens had much less reason to fear political centralization and economic regulation. As Herbert Croly pointed out in *The Promise of American Life* (1909), the time had come to employ Hamiltonian means to achieve Jeffersonian ends.* Laissez faire also made less sense than it had in earlier times. Philosophers and scientists had undermined the old view of an orderly society designed by a divine watchmaker and capable of running itself. The complexities of the modern world required a positive approach, a plan, the close application of human intelligence to current social and economic problems.

Yet Wilson's New Freedom, being less drastic and more in line with American experience, had also much to recommend it. The danger that selfish individuals would use the power of the state for their own ends had certainly not disappeared, despite the efforts of progressives to make government more responsive to popular opinion. Any considerable increase in national power would likely create many new difficulties. Furthermore, individual freedom of opportunity surely merited the toleration of a certain amount of inefficiency. To choose between the New Na-

*It is ironic that Jefferson, who provided in the Declaration of Independence the theoretical justification for a government subservient to the people, remained almost as suspicious of his own creation as he had been of George III's Britain.

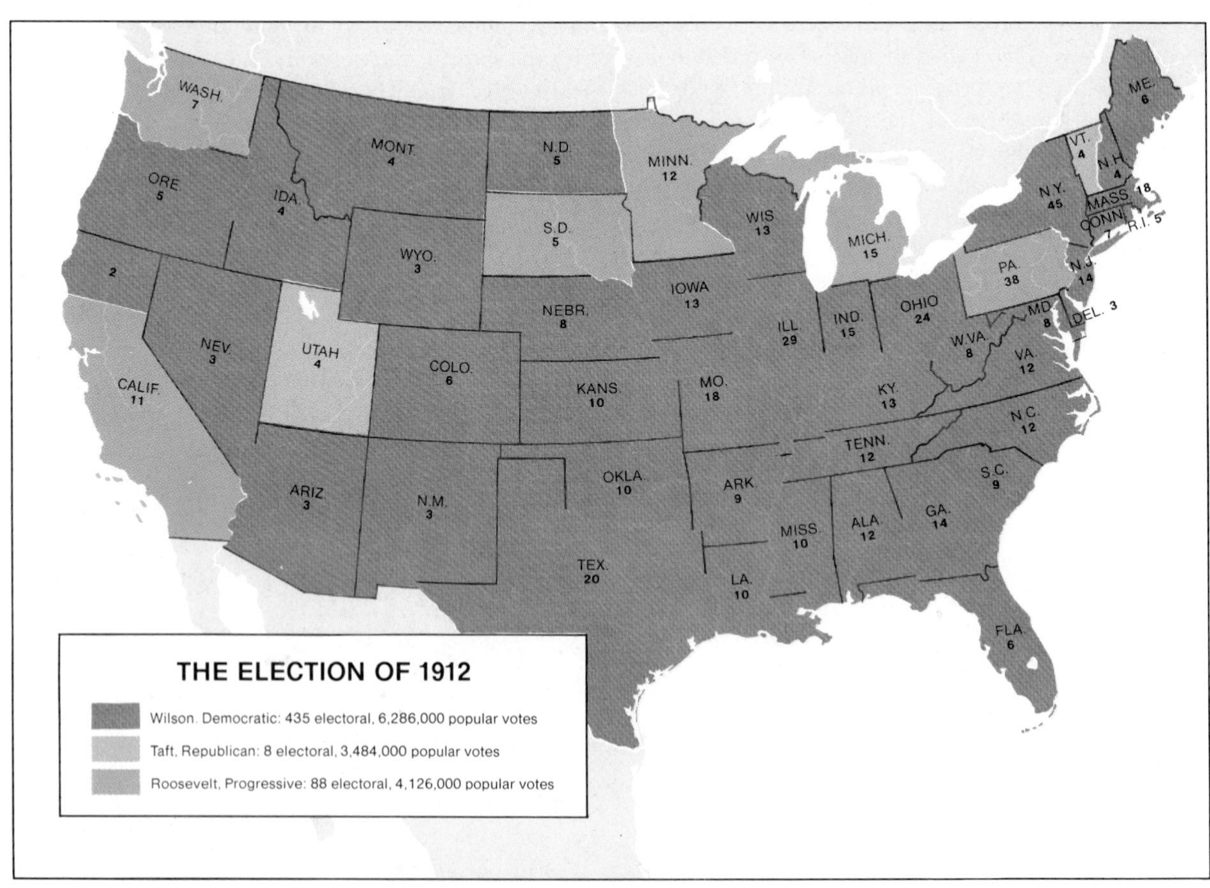

tionalism and the New Freedom, between the dynamic Roosevelt and the idealistic Wilson, was indeed difficult.

While thousands grappled with this problem before going to the polls, partisan politics really determined the outcome of the election. Taft got the hard-core Republican vote but lost the progressive wing of the GOP to Roosevelt. Wilson, on the other hand, had the solid support of both conservative and liberal Democrats. As a result, he won an easy victory in the Electoral College, receiving 435 votes to Roosevelt's 88 and Taft's 8. The popular vote was Wilson, 6,286,000; Roosevelt, 4,126,000; and Taft, 3,484,000. But if partisan politics determined the winner, the election was nonetheless an overwhelming victory for progressivism. The radical temper of the times was shown by the 897,000 votes given Eugene V. Debs, the Socialist candidate. Altogether, professed liberals amassed over 11 million of the 15 million ballots cast. Wilson was a minority President, but he took office with a clear mandate to press forward with further reforms.

Wilson: the New Freedom

No man ever rose more suddenly and spectacularly in American politics than Woodrow Wilson. In the spring of 1910 he was president of Princeton University; he had never held or even run for public office. In the fall of 1912 he was President-elect of the United States. Yet if his rise was unexpected, in a very real sense he had devoted his whole life to preparing for it. Born in Staunton, Virginia, in 1856, son of a Presbyterian minister, Wilson studied political theory avidly as a youth, developing a profound admiration for the British parliamentary system and for such British statesmen as Edmund Burke and William E. Gladstone. While still in college he dreamed of representing his state in the Senate. He studied law solely because he thought it the best avenue to public office, and when he discovered himself temperamentally unsuited for a career at the bar, he took a doctorate at Johns Hopkins in political science.

For years, however, his hopes had seemed doomed to frustration. He taught first at Bryn Mawr, then at Wesleyan, finally at his alma mater, Princeton. He wrote several influential books, including *Congressional Government* and *The State,* and achieved an outstanding success as a teacher and lecturer. In 1902 he was chosen president of Princeton and soon won a place among the nation's leading educators. He revised the curriculum, introducing many new subjects but insisting that students pursue an organized and integrated course of study. He instituted the preceptorial system, which placed the students in close intellectual and social contact with their teachers. He also attracted many outstanding young scholars to the faculty. Eventually, his advanced educational ideas and his overbearing manner of applying them got him in trouble with some of Princeton's alumni and trustees; but though his university career was wrecked, the controversies, in which he appeared to be championing democracy and progress in the face of reactionary opponents, brought him at last to the attention of the politicians. Then, in a great rush, came power and fame.

Wilson was an immediate success as President. Since Roosevelt's last year, Congress had been almost continually at war with the executive branch and with itself. Legislative achievements had been relatively few. Now, although friction persisted, a small avalanche of important new measures received the approval of the lawmakers. In October 1913 came the Underwood Tariff, the first significant reduction of duties since before the Civil War. Food, wool, iron and steel, shoes, agricultural machinery, and other items that could be produced more cheaply in the United States than abroad were placed on the free list, and the rates on most other products were cut substantially, the object being to equalize the cost of foreign and domestic goods in order to make real competition between them possible. To compensate for the expected loss of revenue, the act provided for a graduated tax on personal incomes.*

Two months later the Federal Reserve Act was passed, giving the country a central banking

*The Sixteenth Amendment, ratified in February 1913, authorized the collection of a federal income tax.

system for the first time since Jackson destroyed the Bank of the United States. This measure divided the nation into 12 banking districts, each under the supervision of a Federal Reserve Bank, which was a sort of bank for bankers. All national banks in each district and those state banks that wished to participate had to invest 6 per cent of their capital and surplus in the Reserve Bank, which was empowered to exchange (the technical term is rediscount) paper money, called Federal Reserve notes, for the commercial and agricultural paper that member banks took in as security from borrowers. The new Federal Reserve notes, like the older national bank notes, were convertible into gold, and the law required Federal Reserve Banks to keep 40 per cent of their assets in gold, but the volume of currency was no longer at the mercy of the supply of gold or any other particular commodity.

The crown and nerve center of the system was a Federal Reserve Board in Washington, composed of the secretary of the treasury, the comptroller of the currency, and six financial experts appointed by the President on a nonpartisan basis. The board appointed a majority of the directors of the Federal Reserve Banks and had some control over rediscount *rates* (the commission charged by the Reserve Banks for performing the rediscounting function). Thus a true central banking system was created. When inflation threatened, the Reserve Banks could raise the rediscount rate, discouraging borrowing and reducing the amount of money in circulation. In bad times it could lower the rate, making it easier to borrow and injecting new dollars into the economy. Much remained to be learned about the proper management of the money supply, but the nation finally had a flexible yet safe currency.

In 1914 Congress passed two important laws affecting corporations. One created a Federal Trade Commission to replace Roosevelt's Bureau of Corporations. In addition to investigating interstate corporations and publishing reports, this nonpartisan board could issue "cease and desist" orders against "unfair" trade practices brought to light through its researches. The law did not define the term "unfair," and the commission's rulings could be taken on appeal to the federal courts, but the FTC was nonetheless a powerful instrument for protecting the public against the trusts. The second measure, the Clayton Antitrust Act, made certain specific business practices illegal, including price discrimination that tended to foster monopoly, "tying" agreements–which forbade retailers from handling the products of a firm's competitors–and the creation of interlocking directorates as a means of controlling competing companies. Labor and agricultural organizations were exempted from the antitrust laws, and the use of injunctions in labor disputes was curtailed. Furthermore, the officers of corporations could be held individually responsible when their companies were found guilty of violating the antitrust laws.

While Wilson was not entirely in sympathy with all the terms of these laws, they reflected his desires and could not have been enacted without his hard-driving leadership. The time was ripe for reform. The fact that the Democrats controlled both houses of Congress for the first time since 1890 and were eager to make a good record also helped. But Wilson's imaginative and aggressive use of Presidential power was decisive. He entered office determined, like a British prime minister, to play an active part in the formulation of legislation and the management of Congress. He called the legislators into special session in April 1913, and appeared before them in person to lay out his program, the first President to address Congress since John Adams. Then he followed the course of administration bills closely. He installed a private telephone line between the Capitol and the White House. Administration representatives haunted the cloakrooms and lobbies of both houses. Cooperative congressmen began to receive little notes of praise and encouragement, recalcitrant ones stern demands for support, often written on the President's own portable typewriter. When lobbyists tried to frustrate his plans for tariff reform by bringing pressure to bear on key senators, he made a dramatic appeal to the people. "The public ought to know the extraordinary exertions being made by the lobby in Washington," he told reporters. "Great bodies of astute men seek to create an artificial opinion and to overcome the interests of the public for their private profit." The lobby was imposing "an intolerable burden" on the democratic process, he added. "Only public opinion can check and destroy it." The voters responded to this appeal so strongly that the Senate stood firm and passed the tariff bill substantially as Wilson desired it.

In short, despite his lack of experience, Wilson proved to be a masterful politician as well as an inspiring leader. He explained his success by saying, only half humorously, that running the government was child's play for anyone who had managed the faculty of a university. Responsible *party* government was his objective; he expected individual Democrats to submit to the will of the party majority, and his idealism never prevented him from awarding the spoils of office to city bosses and conservative congressmen, so long as they supported his program.

Nor did his career as a political theorist make him rigid and doctrinaire. In practice the differences between the New Freedom point of view and that of the New Nationalism tended to disappear. The Underwood Tariff and the Clayton Antitrust Act fitted the philosophy Wilson had expounded during the campaign, but the Federal Trade Commission represented a step toward the kind of regulated economy that Roosevelt advocated, and so did the Federal Reserve system. Wilson drew advice from divergent sources—from the lawyer Louis D. Brandeis, ardent foe of monopoly, and from his mysterious, behind-the-scenes alter ego, Colonel Edward M. House, who was close to many prominent business leaders.

There were, however, limits to Wilson's progressivism, limits imposed partly by his temperament and partly by his philosophy of government. He disliked all forms of privilege, objecting almost as strenuously to laws granting special favors to farmers and workers as to those benefiting the tycoons. When a bill was introduced in 1914 placing federal funds at the disposal of rural banks so that they could make low-interest loans to farmers, he refused to support it. "I have a very deep conviction that it is unwise and unjustifiable to extend the credit of the Government to a single class of the community," he said. He considered the provision exempting unions from the antitrust laws equally unsound. Nor would he push for a federal law prohibiting child labor. Such a measure would be unconstitutional, he believed. Wilson also refused to back a constitutional amendment giving the vote to women. Probably he thought it improper for women to mix in politics, but he argued publicly that it was wrong to deprive the states of their control of the suffrage.

Wilson also proved far less unsympathetic to big business than some of his campaign pronouncements had led observers to expect. He appointed men friendly to the corporations to the FTC and conducted no trustbusting crusade. When the business cycle took a turn downward in the fall of 1913, he adopted the Rooseveltian policy of allowing corporation leaders to discuss doubtful practices with Justice Department lawyers, thus arranging informal agreements which protected them against antitrust actions. Delegations of businessmen and bankers were soon trooping through the White House, while the President went out of his way to insist that he had no quarrel with bigness per se in industrial affairs.

On balance, by the end of 1914 the Wilsonian record was positive but distinctly limited. The President himself, justly proud of the results of his forceful leadership, believed that the major progressive goals had been achieved; he had no plans for further reform. Many other progressives felt that a great deal more remained to be done.

The Progressives and the Negro

On one important reform issue—the question of Negro rights—Wilson was distinctly reactionary. Negroes had not, to put it mildly, fared well at the hands of the progressives. In the South the Populist effort to unite white and black farmers led to the imposition of further repressive measures. Segregation became more rigid, white opposition to Negro voting more monolithic. To cite only a few examples, in 1900 the body of a Mississippi Negro was dug up by order

Vigilante justice in Texas, 1893. A Negro accused of killing a white child was captured and condemned to death without benefit of trial after he was said to have confessed. Before a crowd estimated in the thousands he was burned at the stake, but only after the child's family took their revenge with branding irons.

of the state legislature and reburied in a segregated cemetery; in Virginia, in 1902, the daughter of Robert E. Lee was arrested for riding in the Negro section of a railroad car; in Alabama the constitution of 1901 reduced the number of Negro voters to two per cent of the adult Negro males.

Southern so-called progressives argued that disfranchising blacks would "purify" politics by removing from unscrupulous white politicians the temptation to purchase black votes! The typical southern attitude toward the education of blacks was summed up in the folk proverb: "When you educate a Negro, you spoil a good field hand." As late as 1910, only about 8,000 Negroes in the entire South were attending high schools. Yet despite the almost total suppression of Negro rights, the lynching of Negroes continued on a large scale: between 1900 and 1914 more than 1,100 were murdered by mobs, most, but not all, in the southern states, and in the rare cases where local leaders sought to punish the lynchers, juries almost without exception brought in a verdict of not guilty.

Booker T. Washington was shaken by this trend of events, but he could find no way to combat it. The times were passing him by. He appealed to his white southern "friends" to resist Negro disfranchisement but got nowhere. Increasingly, he talked about the virtues of rural life, the evils of big cities, and the uselessness of higher education for Negroes. By the turn of the century a number of young, well-educated blacks, most of them northerners, were beginning to break away from his leadership.

William E.B. Du Bois was the most prominent of the new, militant Negroes. Du Bois was born in Great Barrington, Massachusetts, in 1868. His father, a restless wanderer of Negro and French Huguenot stock, abandoned the family, and young William grew up on the edge of poverty. Neither accepted nor overtly rejected by the overwhelmingly white community, he devoted himself to his studies, showing such brilliance in the local schools that his future education was assured by scholarships: to Fisk University, then to Harvard, then to the University of Berlin. In 1895 he became the first American Negro to earn a Ph.D. from Harvard; his dissertation, *The Suppression of the African Slave Trade to the U.S.A., 1638–1870* (1896), is still a standard work on the subject.

But personal success and "acceptance" by whites did not make the proud and sensitive Du Bois complacent. Outraged by white treatment of Negroes and by the tendency of many blacks to accept second-class citizenship, he set out in the 1890's to make American blacks proud of their color—"beauty is black," he said—and of their African origins and culture. American Negroes should make themselves leaders of the world's 200 million black people. To do so they must organize themselves. They must establish their own businesses, run their own newspapers and colleges, write their own literature—in short, preserve their identity rather than seek to amalgamate themselves into a society that offered them only crumbs and contempt. "Hated here, despised there, and pitied everywhere," he wrote in 1897, "our one haven of refuge is ourselves, [our] one means of advance . . . our own implicit trust in our ability and worth."

Like Washington, Du Bois wanted Negroes to lift themselves up by their own bootstraps, and for a time he cooperated with the head of Tuskegee Institute. But eventually he rejected Washington's limited goals and his accommodating approach to white prejudices. In 1903 in an essay "Of Mr. Booker T. Washington and Others," published in his book, *Souls of Black Folk*, he subjected Washington's "attitude of adjustment and submission" to polite but searching criticism. Washington had asked black men to give up political power, civil rights, and the hope of higher education, not realizing that "voting is necessary to modern manhood, that . . . discrimination is barbarism, and that black boys need education as well as white boys." Washington "apologizes for injustice," Du Bois charged, "belittles the emasculating effects of caste distinctions, and opposes the higher training and ambitions of our brightest minds." This was totally wrong. "The way for a people to gain their reasonable rights is not by voluntarily throwing them away."

Du Bois was not, however, an uncritical admirer of the ordinary American Negro. He believed that "immorality, crime, and laziness" were common Negro vices. "We are diseased," he wrote in 1897, "we are developing criminal tendencies, and an alarming large percentage of our men and women are sexually impure." Quite properly he blamed the weaknesses of blacks on the treatment afforded them by whites, but his approach to the solution of racial problems was frankly elitist. "The Negro race," he wrote, "is going to be saved by its exceptional men," what he called the "Talented Tenth" of the black population. As the Negro historian Benjamin Quarles has put it, Du Bois was "uncomfortable in the presence of the rank and file." After vividly describing how white mistreatment had corrupted his people, Du Bois added loftily: "A saving remnant continually survives and persists, continually aspires, continually shows itself in thrift and ability and character."

Whatever his personal prejudices, however, Du Bois exposed both the weaknesses of Washington's strategy and the callousness of white American attitudes cogently and brilliantly. "Accommodation" was not working. Washington was praised, even lionized by prominent southern whites, but when Theodore Roosevelt casually invited him to stay on for a meal at the White House after a conference, they exploded with indignation, and Roosevelt, who had no personal

L. HUGHES & M. MELTZER, *A Pictorial History of the Negro in America*, 1956

John Henry Adams made this study of William E.B. Du Bois in 1905, the year that Du Bois helped to initiate the Niagara Movement for racial equality.

prejudice against Negroes, meekly backtracked, never repeating his "mistake."

Not mere impatience but despair led Du Bois and a few like-minded Negroes to meet at Niagara Falls in July 1905 and issue a stirring list of black demands: the unrestricted right to vote; an end to every kind of segregation; equality of economic opportunity; the right to higher education for the talented; equal justice in the courts; an end to trade union discrimination. This Niagara Movement did not attract much support among the Negro masses, but it did stir the consciences of some whites, many of them the descendants of abolitionists, who were also becoming disenchanted by the failure of accommodation to provide blacks with real opportunity. In 1909, the centennial of the birth of Abraham Lincoln, a group of these liberals, including Oswald Garrison Villard (grandson of William Lloyd Garrison), the social worker Jane Addams, the philosopher John Dewey, and the novelist William Dean Howells, founded the National Association for the Advancement of Colored People (NAACP). This organization was dedicated to the eradication of racial discrimination. Its leadership was predominantly white in the early years, but Du Bois became a national officer, and editor of its journal, *The Crisis*.

Although the majority of American Negroes were not suddenly made militant by the Niagara Movement and the NAACP, a great turning point had been reached: after 1909 virtually every important leader of the Negroes, black and white alike, rejected the Washington approach. More and more, Negro leaders turned to the study of their past in an effort to stimulate pride in their heritage and to expose the cruelty and injustice of the white treatment of blacks. In 1915, for example, Carter G. Woodson founded the Association for the Study of Negro Life and History, and the next year began editing the *Journal of Negro History*, which swiftly became the major organ for the publishing of scholarly studies of the subject.

However, militancy produced few results in the Progressive Era. Whatever his personal views, Roosevelt behaved on the Negro question no differently than earlier Republican Presidents: he courted blacks when he thought it advantageous to do so, turned his back on them when he did not. When he ran for President on the Progressive ticket in 1912, he adopted a "lily-white" policy, hoping to break the Democrats' monopoly in the South. By trusting in "[white] men of justice and of vision," Roosevelt argued in the face of decades of experience to the contrary, "the colored men of the South will ultimately get justice."

The southern-born Wilson was actively antipathetic to Negroes. During the 1912 campaign he appealed to them for support and promised Villard of the NAACP that he would "assist in advancing the interest of their race" in every possible way. Once elected, he refused even to appoint a privately financed National Race Commission to study the Negro problem. Southerners dominated both his administration and the Congress; as a result, blacks were still further degraded. No less than 35 Negroes in the Atlanta Post Office lost their jobs, while in Washington Negro employees in many government offices were rigidly segregated, those who objected being summarily discharged. These actions roused such a storm that Wilson backtracked somewhat, but he never abandoned his belief that segregation was in the best interests of both races. "Wilson . . . promised a 'new freedom,'" one Negro newspaperman complained. "On the contrary we are given a stone instead of a loaf of bread." Even Booker T. Washington admitted that his people were more "discouraged and bitter" than at any time in his memory.

Du Bois, who had supported Wilson in 1912, attacked administration policy in the *Crisis,* pointing out to the President that "there are 237,942 black voters" in crucial northern states he must carry to be re-elected. In November 1914 the militant editor of the Boston *Guardian,* William Monroe Trotter, a classmate of Du Bois at Harvard and a far more caustic critic of the Washington approach, led a delegation to the White House to protest the segregation policy of the government. When Wilson accused him of blackmail, Trotter lost his temper and an ugly confrontation resulted. The mood of black leaders had changed completely.

By this time the Great War had broken out in Europe. Soon its effects would be felt by every American, by the Negroes perhaps more than by any other group. In November 1915, a year almost to the day after Trotter's clash with Wilson, Booker T. Washington died. For the Negro, one era had ended; a new one was beginning.

SUPPLEMENTARY READING Two excellent volumes trace the political history of the Progressive Era: G.E. Mowry, *The Era of Theodore Roosevelt** (1958), and A.S. Link, *Woodrow Wilson and the Progressive Era** (1954). A number of historians have offered new interpretations of progressivism in recent years. Richard Hofstadter, *The Age of Reform** (1955), stresses the idea of the status revolution. Gabriel Kolko, *The Triumph of Conservatism** (1963), sees the period as dominated by the efforts of big business to attain its objectives with the aid of the government. Other interesting studies include R.B. Nye, *Midwestern Progressive Politics* (1951), and R.H. Wiebe, *Businessmen and Reform** (1962).

The role of muckraking journalism is considered in C.C. Regier, *The Era of the Muckrakers* (1932), Louis Filler, *Crusaders for American Liberalism** (1939), D.M. Chalmers, *The Social and Political Ideas of the Muckrakers** (1964), and Peter Lyon, *Success Story: The Life and Times of S.S. McClure* (1963). Arthur and Lila Weinberg (eds.), *The Muckrakers** (1961), is a convenient collection of writings by the muckrakers. Also useful are Lincoln Steffens, *Autobiography** (1931), and I.M. Tarbell, *All in the Day's Work* (1939).

State and local progressivism are considered in G.E. Mowry, *The California Progressives** (1951), R.S. Maxwell, *La Follette and the Rise of Progressives in Wisconsin* (1956), R.E. Noble, *New Jersey Progressivism Before Wilson* (1946), R.M. Abrams, *Conservatism in a Progressive Era* (1964), H.L. Warner, *Progressivism in Ohio* (1964), Sheldon Hackney, *Populism to Progressivism in Alabama* (1969), Z.L. Miller, *Boss Cox's Cincinnati: Urban Politics in the Progressive Era** (1968), and C.V. Woodward, *Origins of the New South** (1951). The story of the fight for reform in San Francisco is told in W.E. Bean, *Boss Ruef's San Francisco** (1952). Books treating special aspects of progressivism include A.F. Davis, *Spearheads for Reform: The Social Settlements and the Progressive Movement* (1967), Irwin Yellowitz, *Labor and the Progressive Movement in New York State* (1965), J.H. Timberlake, *Prohibition and the Progressive Movement* (1963), and W.L. O'Neill, *Divorce in the Progressive Era* (1967). On the Negro in this period see C.F. Kellogg, *NAACP: A History of the National Association for the Advancement of Colored People* (1970), E.M. Rudwick, *W.E.B. Du Bois: Propagandist of the Negro Protest** (1960), W.E.B. Du Bois, *The Souls of Black Folk** (1903), and August Meier, *Negro Thought* *in America: 1880–1915** (1963).

Many progressives have written autobiographical accounts of their work. See especially Theodore Roosevelt, *Autobiography* (1913), R.M. La Follette, *Autobiography** (1913), W.A. White, *Autobiography* (1946), and G.W. Norris, *Fighting Liberal** (1945).

W.H. Harbaugh, *Power and Responsibility: The Life and Times of Theodore Roosevelt** (1961), is the soundest scholarly treatment of Roosevelt's career, but H.F. Pringle, *Theodore Roosevelt** (1931), is still the most entertaining. G.W. Chessman, *Theodore Roosevelt and the Politics of Power** (1969), is a good brief account, while Chessman's *Governor Theodore Roosevelt: The Albany Apprenticeship* (1965), throws much light on the development of Roosevelt's ideas before 1901. J.M. Blum, *The Republican Roosevelt** (1954), is a brilliant analysis of his political philosophy and his management of the Presidency. The essays on Roosevelt–and on Wilson–in Richard Hofstadter, *The American Political Tradition** (1948), also merit close reading. No student should miss sampling Roosevelt's letters. See E.E. Morison (ed.), *The Letters of Theodore Roosevelt* (1951–54).

For specific events during Roosevelt's Presidency, consult R.J. Cornell, *The Anthracite Coal Strike of 1902* (1957), the essay on the Northern Securities case in J.A. Garraty (ed.), *Quarrels That Have Shaped the Constitution** (1964), E.R. Richardson, *The Politics of Conservation* (1962), S.P. Hays, *Conservation and the Gospel of Efficiency** (1959), and J.R. Hollingsworth, *The Whirligig of Politics* (1963).

The best life of Taft is H.F. Pringle, *The Life and Times of William Howard Taft* (1939). On the Ballinger-Pinchot controversy, see A.T. Mason, *Bureaucracy Convicts Itself* (1941), and M.N. McGeary, *Gifford Pinchot* (1960). The breakup of the Republican party and the history of the Progressive party are discussed in G.E. Mowry, *Theodore Roosevelt and the Progressive Movement** (1946), J.A. Garraty, *Right-Hand Man: The Life of George W. Perkins* (1960), and H.M. Hooker's edition of A.R.E. Pinchot, *History of the Progressive Party* (1958).

The standard biography of Wilson, still incomplete, is A.S. Link, *Wilson* (1947–). A.C. Walworth, *Woodrow Wilson** (1958), is a detailed life. Two briefer biographies are J.M. Blum, *Woodrow Wilson and the Politics of Morality** (1956), and J.A. Garraty, *Woodrow Wilson** (1956).

Among the many biographies of political leaders of the period are J.M. Blum, *Joe Tumulty and the Wilson Era* (1951), C.G. Bowers, *Beveridge and the Progressive Era* (1932), R.M. Lowitt, *George W. Norris* (1963), B.C. and Fola La Follette, *Robert M. La Follette* (1953), P.C. Jessup, *Elihu Root* (1938), J.A. Garraty, *Henry Cabot Lodge* (1953), A.T. Mason, *Brandeis* (1946), and M.J. Pusey, *Charles Evans Hughes* (1951).

Finally, the student should sample some of the political writings of the progressives themselves. See especially Theodore Roosevelt, *The New Nationalism** (1910), Woodrow Wilson, *The New Freedom** (1913), Herbert Croly, *The Promise of American Life** (1909) Walter Weyl, *The New Democracy** (1912), and Walter Lippmann, *Drift and Mastery** (1914).

*Available in paperback.

24

Woodrow Wilson and the Great War

Woodrow Wilson's approach to foreign relations was well intentioned and idealistic, but somewhat confused. He knew that the United States had no wish to injure any foreign state and assumed that all nations would recognize this fact and cooperate. He sincerely desired to help other countries, especially the republics of Latin America, achieve stable democratic governments and improve the living conditions of their people. Imperialism was in his eyes immoral. Yet he also expected to sustain and protect American interests abroad. The maintenance of the Open Door in China and the completion of the Panama Canal, for example, were as important to him as they had been to Theodore Roosevelt.

Moreover, Wilson's view of nations with traditions different from those of the United States was distressingly shortsighted and provincial. His attitude resembled that of 19th-century Christian missionaries: he wanted to spread the gospel of American democracy, to lift up and enlighten the unfortunate and the ignorant—but in his own way. Convinced of his own disinterestedness and the superiority of his value system over all others, he did not hesitate to lecture foreigners about their own best interests. "I am going to teach the South American republics to elect good men!" he told one British diplomat.

Wilson also underestimated the difficulty of conducting foreign relations. He distrusted professional diplomats, whom he thought cynical and hidebound. He appointed William Jennings Bryan as secretary of state, despite the Nebraskan's almost total ignorance of foreign affairs and, as one historian puts it, "entrusted critical diplomatic missions to other innocents." Bryan, bland and benign, filled minor diplomatic posts with what he called "deserving Democrats," most of them inexperienced, many of them incompetent, and some of them corrupt.

"Missionary Diplomacy"

Wilson set out at once to raise the moral tone of American foreign policy by denouncing dollar diplomacy. Encouraging bankers to lend money to countries like China, he said, implied the possibility of "forcible interference" if the loans were not repaid, a policy "obnoxious to the principles upon which the government of our people rests." The practice of seeking economic concessions in Latin America was "unfair" and "degrading." The United States would seek no special favors, exert no special pressures. It would deal with Latin-American nations "upon terms of equality and honor."

In certain small matters, Wilson succeeded in conducting American diplomacy on this idealistic basis. He withdrew the government's support of the international consortium that was arranging a loan to develop Chinese railroads, and the American bankers pulled out of this one-sided arrangement. When the Japanese attempted, in the notorious Twenty-One Demands (1915), to reduce China almost to the status of a Japanese protectorate, he persuaded them to modify their conditions slightly. Congress had passed a law in 1912 exempting American coastal shipping from the payment of tolls on the Panama Canal in spite of a provision in the Hay-Pauncefote Treaty with Great Britain guaranteeing that the canal would be available to the vessels of all nations "on terms of entire equality." Wilson insisted that Congress repeal the law in order to vindicate the national honor. He also permitted Secretary Bryan to negotiate conciliation treaties with some 21 nations. The distinctive feature of these agreements was the provision for a "cooling-off" period of one year, during which signatories agreed, in the event of any dispute, not to engage in hostilities.

Where more vital interests of the United States were concerned, Wilson sometimes failed to live up to his promises. Because of the strategic importance of the Panama Canal, he was unwilling to tolerate "unrest" in the nations of the Caribbean, but good intentions and inspirational oratory alone would not stabilize that backward and dictator-ridden region. Within a matter of months he was pursuing the same tactics that circumstances had forced on Roosevelt and Taft. The Bryan-Chamorro Treaty of 1914, which gave the United States an option to build a canal across Nicaragua, made that country virtually an American protectorate and served to maintain in power an unpopular dictator, Adolfo Díaz. In the Dominican Republic one of Bryan's "deserving Democrats," a former prize fight promoter named James M. Sullivan, engaged in shady financial dealings and helped support a tyrannical and reactionary regime. When a revolution broke out in 1916, United States marines occupied the country. In Haiti, rocked by eight revolutions in four years, American troops also took over and installed a puppet president. By a treaty of September 1915, Haiti became a United States protectorate.

The most perplexing example of missionary diplomacy occurred in Mexico. Once again internal troubles led to American intervention but with far more serious consequences, since the nationalistic Mexican people resented American interference intensely. The dictator Porfirio Díaz had been exploiting the resources and people of Mexico for the benefit of a small class of wealthy landowners, clerics, and military men for many decades, when, in 1911, a liberal coalition overthrew his corrupt and arbitrary government and installed Francisco Madero as president. This revolution was no mere squabble between rival bandit cliques—Madero, although a wealthy landowner, was committed to economic reform and to the drafting of a democratic constitution; a highly moralistic man, he had apparently been much influenced by the progressive movement in the United States. Unfortunately, he was both weak-willed and a terrible administrator. Conditions in Mexico deteriorated rapidly, and less than a month before Wilson's inauguration, one of Madero's generals, Victoriano Huerta, treacherously seized power and had his former chief murdered. An unabashed reactionary, Huerta intended to restore things as they had been under Díaz. Since he seemed capable of maintaining the stability that foreign investors desired, most of the powers, including Great Britain, Germany, and France, promptly recognized Huerta's government.

The American ambassador in Mexico City, together with important American financial and business interests in Mexico and in the United States, urged Wilson to do likewise, but he refused. His sympathies were all with the constitutionalists, and the brutal murder of Madero had horrified him. He had a sufficient practical reason for withholding recognition, for the followers of

Madero remained in control of a large part of the country, but Wilson chose to act on moral grounds. "I will not recognize a government of butchers," he said firmly. This was an unconventional argument, since nations do not ordinarily consider the means by which a foreign regime has come to power before deciding to establish diplomatic relations.

Wilson then proceeded to bring enormous pressure to bear against Huerta. He dragooned the British into withdrawing recognition, dickered with rebellious Mexican factions, and demanded that Huerta hold free elections as the price of American mediation in the continuing civil war. Huerta would not yield an inch. Indeed, he drew strength from Wilson's effort to oust him, for even his internal enemies resented American interference in Mexican affairs. Frustration added to Wilson's moral outrage and weakened his judgment. It became a contest of will between him and the dictator; he subordinated his wish to let the Mexicans solve their own problems to his personal desire to destroy Huerta.

This explosive situation erupted in April 1914, when a small party of American sailors was arrested in the port of Tampico, Mexico. Although a minor Mexican official had been responsible for the arrest and the men had been promptly released by higher authority, the Mexicans refused to supply the apology demanded by the sailors' commander. Wilson fastened upon the affair as an excuse for sending troops into Mexico. Force would be used, he informed Congress, against "General Huerta and those who adhere to him," not against the Mexican people. His only object, he told a reporter, was "to help the [Mexican] people to secure [their] liberty."

The actual invasion took place at Veracruz, whence Winfield Scott had launched the assault on Mexico City in 1847. When he learned that a German merchantman laden with munitions was expected at Veracruz, Wilson ordered the city occupied to prevent these weapons from reaching the Huertistas. But instead of meekly surrendering their city, the Mexicans resisted tenaciously, suffering 400 casualties before falling back. This bloodshed caused dismay throughout Latin America and failed to unseat Huerta. The leader of the constitutionalist armies, General Venustiano Carranza, denounced the Americans vociferously.

The unexpected result of his action shook Wilson to the core. He could not escape the facts. Men had died, an all-out war threatened, and he was doing exactly what American critics of his Mexican policy desired while groups of peace-loving citizens all over the United States deluged him with protests. It appeared that he must either withdraw ignominiously from Veracruz or fight a war against both Huerta and the constitutionalists.

Fortunately, at this point three South American states, Argentina, Brazil, and Chile, offered to mediate the dispute. Wilson accepted eagerly, Huerta also agreed, and the conferees met at Niagara Falls, Ontario, in May. Although no settlement was reached, Huerta, hard pressed by constitutionalist armies, finally abdicated. On August 20, 1914, General Carranza entered Mexico City in triumph.

Carranza's victory allowed Wilson to escape from the consequences of his effort to impose good government on Mexico from the outside,* but the President failed to make the most of his fortune. Carranza proved scarcely more successful than the tyrant Huerta in controlling his turbulent country. Soon one of his own generals, Francisco "Pancho" Villa, rose against him and seized control of Mexico City. At this point Wilson made a monumental blunder. Villa professed to be willing to cooperate with the United States, and Wilson, taking him at his word, gave him his support. However, Villa was little more than an ambitious bandit, "more a force of nature than of politics," one historian has called him, a kind of populist but without definite class interests or any objective more social than personal power. Carranza, while no social revolutionary, was com-

*During the occupation of Veracruz, the American forces cleaned up the city, built roads and bridges, improved public services, and made the city, in the words of historian Robert E. Quirk, "the most efficient, most honestly and justly governed city in all of Mexican history." Yet they succeeded only in arousing "the hatred and the scorn of the Mexicans," and when they withdrew, Veracruz quickly reverted to its old ways.

Troopers of the 10th Cavalry, photographed in Mexico in 1916 during Pershing's pursuit of Villa. Pershing was an advocate of black troops; his nickname, "Black Jack," stemmed from his command of this crack regiment.

mitted to constitutionalism and had wide support among the middle class. Fighting back, he drove the Villistas into the northern provinces.

When Wilson finally realized the extent of Carranza's influence in Mexico, he reversed himself; in October 1915 he recognized the Carranza government. Still, his Mexican troubles were not over, for Villa, seeking to undermine Carranza by forcing the United States to intervene, began a series of unprovoked attacks on Americans. Early in 1916 he stopped a train in northern Mexico and killed 16 American passengers in cold blood. When this failed to rouse Wilson, he crossed into New Mexico and burned the town of Columbus, killing 19. Having learned his lesson, Wilson would have preferred to bear even this assault in silence, but public opinion forced him to send American troops under General John J. Pershing across the border in pursuit of Villa.

On his own ground, Villa proved impossible to catch. Cleverly he drew Pershing deeper and deeper into Mexico, which in turn greatly alarmed Carranza, who insisted that the Americans withdraw. Several clashes occurred between Pershing's men and Mexican regulars, and for a brief period in June 1916 war seemed imminent. Wilson now acted bravely and wisely. He negotiated when it would have been far easier to fight and, in the end, he was big enough to yield. Of course the growing threat of involvement in the European war that was now raging made it easier to do so. Early in 1917 he recalled Pershing's force to American soil.

Thereafter, the Mexicans proceeded to work out their own destiny. Missionary diplomacy had produced mixed, but in the long run essentially beneficial, results. By opposing Huerta, Wilson had surrendered to his prejudices, yet he had also helped the real revolutionaries, although they opposed his acts. His bungling bred anti-Americanism in Mexico, but by his later restraint in the face of stinging provocations, he permitted the constitutionalists to consolidate their power and preserve their self-respect.

Outbreak of the Great War

On June 28, 1914, in the Austro-Hungarian provincial capital of Sarajevo, Gavrilo Princip, a young student, assassinated the Archduke Franz Ferdinand, heir to the imperial throne. Princip, a member of the Black Hand, a Serbian terrorist organization, was seeking to further the cause of Serbian nationalism. Instead, his rash act precipitated a general European war. Within little more than a month, following a complex series of diplomatic challenges and responses, two great coalitions, the Central Powers (chiefly Germany and Austria-Hungary) and the Allied Powers (chiefly Great Britain, France, and Russia), were locked in a combat that brought one era in world history to a close and inaugurated another.

The outbreak of what contemporaries were soon to call the Great War caught the American people psychologically unprepared; few understood the significance of what had happened. President Wilson promptly issued a proclamation of neutrality and even asked the nation to be "impartial in thought." While no one, including the President, had the superhuman self-control that this request called for, the almost unanimous reaction of Americans, aside from dismay, was that the conflict did not concern them. Of course they were wrong, for this was a world war and Americans were sure to be affected by its outcome. Furthermore, the uneasy balance of forces that soon developed between the belligerents could be upset at any time if the United States should decide to commit all its immense resources to one side or the other. To have remained indifferent would have required an act of self-abnegation without precedent in human history.

Yet there were good reasons, aside from a failure to understand the significance of the struggle, why the United States sought to remain neutral. Over a third of its 92 million inhabitants were either foreign-born or the children of immigrants. Sentimental rather than political ties bound these former Europeans to the lands of their ancestors, but most felt strongly, one way or the other, when war broke out. American involvement would create new internal stresses in a society already strained by the task of assimilating so many diverse groups. War was also an affront to the prevailing progressive spirit, which assumed that men were reasonable, high-minded, and capable of settling their disputes peaceably. Along with the traditional American fear of entanglement in European affairs, these were ample reasons for remaining aloof.

Although most Americans hoped to keep out of the war, nearly everyone was partial to one side or the other. People of German or Austrian descent, about 8 million in number, and the nation's 4.5 million Irish-Americans, motivated chiefly by hatred of the British, sympathized with the Central Powers. The majority of the people, however, influenced by their British origins and by the bonds of language and culture, preferred an Allied victory. Also, the aggressiveness of Germany in recent decades, with its stress on colonial expansion and militarism, had antagonized many people. When the war began, the Germans launched a mighty assault across neutral Belgium in an effort to outflank the French armies. This unprovoked attack on a tiny nation whose neutrality the Germans had previously agreed to respect caused a further increase in anti-German feeling in the United States.

As the war progressed, the Allies cleverly exploited these American prejudices by such devices as publishing exaggerated tales of German atrocities against Belgian civilians. A supposedly impartial study of these charges by the widely respected James Bryce, author of *The American Commonwealth*, portrayed the Germans as ruthless and cruel barbarians. The Germans also conducted a shrewd and extensive propaganda campaign in the United States, but they labored under severe handicaps and won few converts.

Freedom of the Seas

Propaganda, in fact, did not basically alter American attitudes; far more important were questions rising out of trade and commerce. Naturally, all the warring nations wanted to draw upon American resources. Under international law, neutrals could trade freely with any belligerent. The Americans were prepared to do so, but because the British fleet dominated the North Atlantic, they could not. Although the specific issues differed somewhat, the situation was similar to that which had prevailed during the Napoleonic Wars. Eager to cut off Germany from foreign products, the British declared nearly all commodities, even foodstuffs, to be contraband of war. They rationed imports to neutral nations such as Denmark and the Netherlands so that they could not transship supplies to Germany. They forced neutral merchantmen into Allied ports in order to search them for goods headed for the enemy. Many cargoes were confiscated, often without payment, and American firms that traded with the Central Powers were "blacklisted," which meant that no British subject could deal with them. When these policies caused angry protests in America, the British answered that in a battle for survival they dared not adhere to old-fashioned rules of international law. "If the American shipper grumbles, our reply is that this war is not being conducted for his pleasure or profit," the London *Daily Graphic* explained.

Had the United States insisted that Great Britain abandon these "illegal" practices, as the Germans demanded, no doubt it could have had its way. It is ironic that an embargo, which failed so ignominiously in Jefferson's day, would have been almost instantly effective if applied at any time after 1914, for American supplies were absolutely vital to the Allies. As the British foreign secretary, Sir Edward Grey, later admitted: "The ill-will of the United States meant certain defeat. The object of diplomacy, therefore, was to secure the maximum of blockade that could be enforced without a rupture with the United States."

Although the British tactics frequently exasperated Wilson, he never considered taking such a drastic step. He faced a true dilemma. To allow the British to make the rules meant being unneutral toward the Central Powers. Yet to insist on the old rules, which had never actually been obeyed in wartime, meant being unneutral toward the Allies, for that would have deprived them of much of the value of their naval superiority. *Nothing* the United States might do would be really impartial. Of course Wilson's own sentiments made it doubly difficult for him to object strenuously to British practices. No American admired British institutions and culture more extravagantly than this disciple of Burke and Gladstone, this worshiper of Wordsworth, Dickens, and Scott. "Everything I love most in the world is at stake," he confessed privately to the British ambassador. A German victory "would be fatal to our form of Government and American ideals."

In any case, the immense expansion of American trade with the Allies made an embargo unthinkable. While commerce with the Central Powers fell off to a trickle, that with the Allies soared from $825 million in 1914 to over $3.2 billion in 1916. An attempt to limit this commerce would have raised a storm; to have eliminated it would have caused a catastrophe. Munitions-makers and other businessmen did not want the United States to enter the war; neutrality suited their purposes admirably, despite the harassments of the Royal Navy. They did, however, profit from the war and wished to continue to do so.

The Allies soon exhausted their ready cash and had to borrow in order to continue their purchases. Pressed by the pacifistic Bryan, Wilson first refused to let American bankers lend them money but soon reversed himself. The bankers first extended commercial credit to their overseas customers and in September 1915 floated a $500 million issue of French and British war bonds. Over the next year and a half, the Allies borrowed an additional $1.7 billion. Although such loans violated no principle of international law, they fastened the United States still more closely to the Allies' cause.

During the first months of the Great War, the Germans were not especially concerned about neutral rights or American goods, for they expected to crush the Allied armies quickly. But when their first swift thrust was blunted along the Marne and the war became a bloody stalemate, they began to plan countermeasures aimed at forcing the Allies to permit neutral goods to enter their territories and at cutting off such goods from Great Britain. Unwilling to risk their battleships and cruisers against the much larger British fleet, they resorted to a new weapon, the submarine (*Unterseeboot*), commonly known as the U-boat.

German submarines played a role in World War I not unlike that of American privateers in the Revolution and the War of 1812: they ranged the seas stealthily in search of merchantmen. However, they could not operate under the ordinary rules of war, which required that a raider stop its prey, examine its papers and cargo, and give the crew and passengers time to get off in lifeboats before sending it to the bottom. When surfaced, U-boats were vulnerable to the deck guns that many merchant ships carried; they could even be sunk by ramming, once they had stopped and put out a boarding party. Therefore they commonly launched their torpedoes from below the surface without warning, and the result was often a heavy loss of life on the torpedoed ships.

In February 1915 the Germans declared the waters surrounding the British Isles a zone of war and announced that they would sink, without warning, all enemy merchant ships encountered in the area. Since Allied vessels sometimes flew neutral flags to disguise their identity, neutral ships entering the zone would do so at their own risk. This statement was largely bluff, for the Germans had only a handful of submarines in operation, but they were building more feverishly. Wilson, perhaps too hurriedly considering the importance of the question, warned the Germans that he would hold them to "strict accountability" for any loss of American life or property resulting from violations of "acknowledged [neutral] rights on the high seas." He did not clearly distinguish between losses incurred through the destruction of *American* ships and those resulting from the sinking of other vessels. If he meant to hold the Germans responsible for injuries to Americans on *belligerent* vessels, he was changing the traditional rules of international law as arbitrarily as the Germans were. Secretary Bryan, who opposed Wilson vigorously on this point, took sound legal ground when he said: "A ship carrying contraband should not rely upon passengers to protect her from attack—it would be like putting women and children in front of an army." Furthermore, Wilson's note was, in effect, an ultimatum: in the long run, "strict accountability" meant war unless the Germans backed down. Yet Wilson was unprepared to fight; he refused even to ask Congress for increased military appropriations at this time, saying that he did not want to "turn America into a military camp."

Correct or not, however, Wilson's position accurately reflected the attitude of most Americans. It seemed barbaric to them that defenseless civilians should be killed without warning, and they refused to surrender their "rights" as neutrals to cross the North Atlantic on any ship they wished. The depth of their feeling was quickly demonstrated when, on May 7, 1915, the submarine *U-20* sank the British liner *Lusitania* off the Irish coast. Nearly 1,200 persons, including 128 Americans, lost their lives in this catastrophe.

The torpedoing of the *Lusitania* caused as profound and emotional a reaction in the United States as that following the destruction of the *Maine* in Havana harbor, except that only a few extremists called for an immediate declaration of war. Wilson, like McKinley in 1898, was shocked, but he kept his head. He demanded that Germany disavow the sinking, indemnify the victims, and promise to stop attacking passenger vessels; but when the Germans quibbled about these points, he responded with further diplomatic correspondence rather than with an ultimatum.

In one sense he acted wisely. The Germans pointed out that they had published warnings in American newspapers saying they considered the *Lusitania* subject to attack, that the liner was carrying munitions, and that on past voyages it had flown the American flag as a *ruse de guerre*. It would also have been very difficult politically for the German government to have backed down completely before an American ultimatum, although after dragging the controversy out for nearly a year, it did eventually apologize and agree to pay an indemnity. Finally, after the torpedoing of the French channel steamer *Sussex* in March 1916 had produced another stiff American protest, the Germans at last promised to stop sinking merchantmen without warning. Furthermore, if Wilson had forced a showdown in 1915, he would have alienated a large segment of American opinion. Even his relatively mild notes resulted in the resignation of Secretary of State Bryan,* who believed it unneutral to treat German violations of international law differently than Allied violations, and Bryan reflected the feelings of thousands.

*Wilson appointed Robert Lansing, counselor of the State Department, to succeed Bryan.

On the other hand, if Wilson had asked for war over the *Lusitania*, a majority of Congress and the country would probably have gone along, and in that event, the dreadful carnage in Europe would have been ended much sooner. This is the reasoning of hindsight, but such a policy would also have been logical, given Wilson's assumptions about the justice of the Allied cause and America's material stake in an Allied victory. However, the President, and most Americans, were not certain enough in their minds in 1915 to act entirely logically. In November 1915, during the long crisis, Wilson at last began to press for increased military and naval expenditures. Nevertheless, he continued to vacillate, dispatching a sharp note of protest against Allied blacklisting of American firms and telling his confidante, Colonel House, that the British were "poor boobs!" His position on preparedness remained so equivocal that his secretary of war, Lindley M. Garrison, resigned in protest.

Election of 1916

Part of Wilson's confusion in 1916 resulted from the grave political difficulties he faced in his fight for re-election. He had won the Presidency in 1912 only because the Republican party had split in two. Now its segments were rapidly reuniting, for Theodore Roosevelt, the chief defector, had become so incensed by Wilson's refusal to commit the United States to the Allied cause that he was ready to support almost any Republican to guarantee the President's defeat. At the same time, many lesser progressives were complaining about Wilson's unwillingness to work for further domestic reforms. Unless he could find some additional support, he seemed sure to lose the election.

He attacked this problem by openly wooing the progressives. In January 1916 he appointed Louis D. Brandeis to the Supreme Court. In addition to being an advanced progressive, Brandeis was Jewish, the first American of that religion ever appointed to the Court, and Wilson's action won him many friends among people who favored fair treatment for minority groups. In July he bid for the farm vote by signing the Farm Loan Act to provide low-cost loans based on agricultural credit. Shortly thereafter, he approved the Keating-Owen Child Labor Act barring goods manufactured by the labor of children under 16 from interstate commerce, and a workmen's compensation act for federal employees. He also persuaded Congress to pass the Adamson Act, establishing an eight-hour day for railroad workers, and he modified his position on the tariff by approving the creation of a tariff commission and accepting "antidumping" legislation designed to protect American industry from cutthroat foreign competition after the war. Each of these actions represented a sharp reversal of policy. In 1913 Wilson had considered Brandeis too radical even for a Cabinet post. The new farm, labor, and tariff laws were all examples of the kind of "class legislation" he had refused to countenance in 1913 and 1914. As Arthur S. Link has pointed out, Wilson was putting into effect "almost every important plank of the Progressive platform of 1912." It would be uncharitable to conclude that he was doing so only to win votes; he had been moving in the direction of the New Nationalism for some time. Nevertheless, his actions paid spectacular political dividends when Roosevelt refused a proffered second nomination of the Progressive party and came out for the Republican nominee, Justice Charles Evans Hughes of the Supreme Court. The Progressive party reluctantly endorsed Hughes, who had earlier compiled an excellent record as governor of New York, but many of Roosevelt's 1912 supporters felt he had betrayed them and voted for Wilson in 1916.

Nevertheless, the key issue in the Presidential election was American policy toward the warring powers. Wilson intended to stress preparedness, which he was at last wholeheartedly supporting. However, during the Democratic convention the delegates responded so enthusiastically whenever orators referred to his success in keeping the country out of the war that he modified his approach. When one spellbinder, for example, pointed out that the President had "wrung from the most militant spirit that ever brooded above a battlefield an acknowledgment of American rights and an agreement to American demands," the convention erupted in a wild

UPI

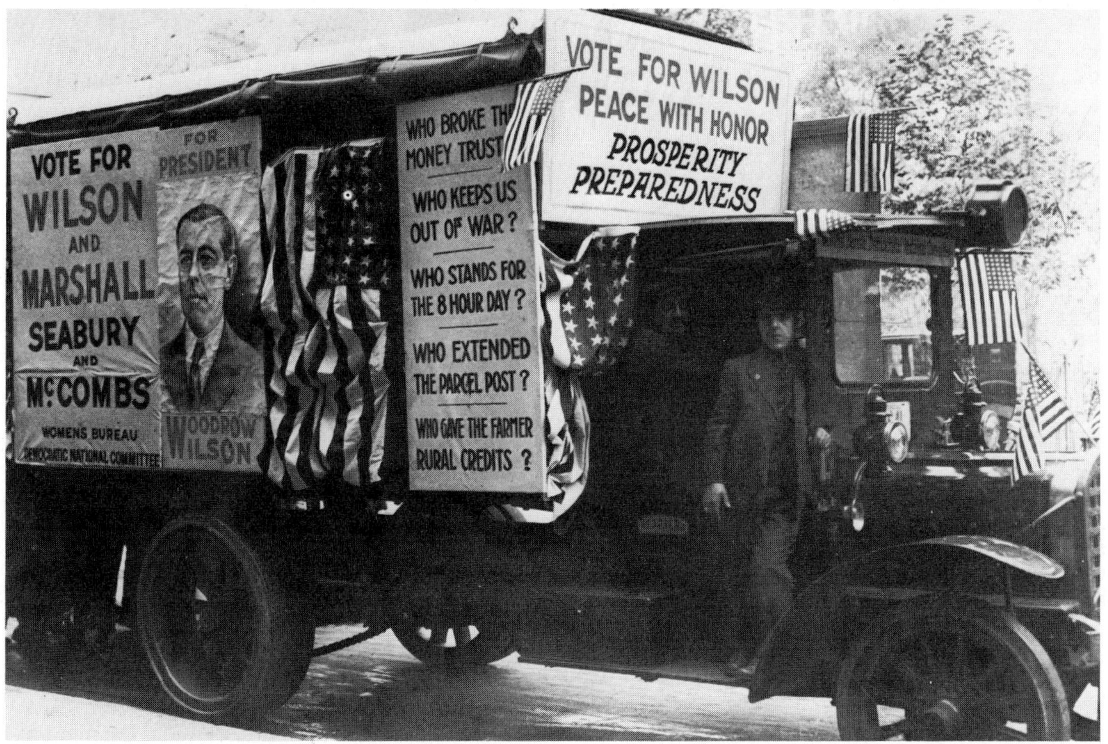

A Wilson campaign truck offered voters in New York City a convenient summary of the Democratic platform in 1916. The eight-hour-day plank refers to the President's support of a federal law for railroad workers.

demonstration of approval that lasted more than 20 minutes. Thus "He Kept Us out of War" became the Democratic slogan.

To his credit, Wilson made no promises. "I can't keep the country out of war," he told one member of his Cabinet. "Any little German lieutenant can put us into the war at any time by some calculated outrage." His attitude undoubtedly cost him the votes of many extremists on both sides, but it won the backing of thousands of moderates. Theodore Roosevelt's unbridled attacks on Wilson for his failure to commit the country to all-out aid to the Allies also alarmed large segments of the population.

The combination of progressivism and the peace issue brought the Democrats on substantially equal terms with the Republicans; thereafter, personal factors probably tipped the balance. Hughes proved a poor campaigner: he was very stiff and a poor speaker; he unintentionally offended a number of important politicians, especially in crucial California, where he inadvertently snubbed the popular progressive governor, Hiram Johnson; and he equivocated on a number of key issues. Nevertheless, on election night he appeared to have won, having carried nearly all the East and Middle West. Late returns gave Wilson California, however, and with it victory by the narrow margin of 277 to 254 in the Electoral College. He led Hughes in the popular vote by 9.1 million to 8.5 million.

The Road to War

Encouraged by his triumph, appalled by the continuing slaughter on the battlefields, fearful that the United States would be dragged into the holocaust, Wilson made one last effort to end the war by negotiation. In 1915 he had sent his friend Colonel House on a secret mission to London, Paris, and Berlin to try to mediate among the belligerents. Everywhere House had been received cordially, but he made little progress and his negotiations were disrupted by the *Lusitania* crisis. A second House mission (January–February 1916) had proved equally fruitless, partly because House had by that time come to favor entering the war on the Allied side, but chiefly because each side still hoped for a clear-cut military victory. Now, after another long season of bloodshed, perhaps the powers would listen to reason.

Wilson's own feelings were more genuinely neutral than at any other time during the war, for the Germans had stopped sinking merchantmen without warning and the British had irritated him repeatedly by their arbitrary restrictions on neutral trade. He drafted a note to the belligerents asking them to state the terms on which they would agree to lay down their arms. Neutrals as well as the warring powers were suffering, he reminded them. Unless the fighting ended soon, all would be so ruined that peace would be meaningless. When neither side responded encouragingly to this appeal, Wilson went before the Senate on January 22, 1917, and delivered a moving, prophetic speech, aimed, as he admitted, at "the *people* of the countries now at war" more than at their governments. Any settlement imposed by a victor, he declared, would breed only hatred and more wars. There must be a "peace without victory," based on the principles that all nations were equal, that every nationality group should determine its own form of government, that it was wrong "to hand peoples about from sovereignty to sovereignty as if they were property." He also mentioned, albeit vaguely, disarmament and freedom of the seas, and he suggested the creation of some kind of international organization to preserve world peace. "There must be not a balance of power, but a community of power," he said, and added, "I am speaking for the silent mass of mankind everywhere."

This noble appeal met a tragic fate. Even as Wilson was addressing the Senate, the Germans were preparing a momentous announcement. They had decided to unleash their submarines against *all* vessels headed for Allied ports. After February 1 any ship in the war zone would be attacked without warning. Possessed now of more than 100 U-boats, the German military leaders had convinced themselves that they could starve the British into submission and reduce the Allied armies to impotence by cutting off American

L. RAEMAEKERS, *The Great War*, 1916

In a 1916 drawing by the Dutchman Louis Raemaekers, one of the most effective of the Allied propagandists, Kaiser Wilhelm is flanked by War and Hunger.

supplies. The United States would probably declare war, but—the Germans reasoned—they could overwhelm the Allies before the Americans could get to the battlefields in force. "The United States . . . can neither inflict material damage upon us, nor can it be of material benefit to our enemies," Admiral von Holtzendorff boasted. "I guarantee that for its part the U-boat war will lead to victory."

In *Tiger at the Gates* the French playwright Jean Giraudoux makes Ulysses say, while attempting to stave off what he considers an inevitable war with the Trojans: "The privilege of great men is to view catastrophe from a terrace."* Surely this is not always true, but in 1917, after the Germans had made this decision, events moved relentlessly, almost uninfluenced by the actors who presumably controlled the fate of the world:

**Le privilège des grands, c'est de voir les catastrophes d'une terrasse.*

February 3: U.S.S. *Housatonic* torpedoed. Wilson announces to Congress that he has severed diplomatic relations with Germany. Secretary of State Lansing hands the German ambassador, Count von Bernstorff, his passport. *February 24:* Walter Hines Page, United States ambassador to Great Britain, transmits to the State Department an intercepted German dispatch (the "Zimmermann Telegram") revealing that Germany has proposed a secret alliance with Mexico, Mexico to receive, in the event of war with the United States, "the lost territory in Texas, New Mexico, and Arizona." *February 25:* Cunard liner *Laconia* torpedoed, two American women perish. *February 26:* Wilson asks Congress for authority to arm American merchant ships. *March 1:* Zimmermann Telegram released to the press. *March 4:* President Wilson takes oath of office, beginning his second term. Congress adjourns without passing the Armed Ship bill, the measure having been filibustered to death by antiwar senators. Wilson characterizes the filibusterers, led by Senator Robert M. La Follette, as "a little group of willful men, representing no opinion but their own." *March 9:* Wilson, acting under his executive powers, orders the arming of American merchantmen. *March 12:* Revolutionary provisional government established in Russia. *Algonquin* torpedoed. *March 15:* Czar Nicholas II of Russia abdicates. *March 16: City of Memphis, Illinois, Vigilancia* torpedoed. *March 21:* New York *World,* a leading Democratic newspaper, calls for declaration of war on Germany. Wilson summons Congress to convene in special session on April 2. *March 25:* Wilson calls up the National Guard. *April 2:* Wilson asks Congress to declare war. Germany is guilty of "throwing to the winds all scruples of humanity," he says. America must fight, not to conquer, but for "peace and justice. . . . The world must be made safe for democracy." *April 4, 6:* Congress declares war—the vote, 82–6 in the Senate, 373–50 in the House.

Thus it had to be, once the Germans loosed their submarines, but the bare record conceals Wilson's agonizing search for an honorable alternative. It had taken him a long time to decide that the war was being fought for no good purpose and he could not abandon this view easily. To admit that Germany posed a threat to the United States meant confessing that rabid interventionists like Roosevelt had been right all along. To go to war, he also realized, meant, besides sending innocent Americans to their death, unleashing the forces of hatred and intolerance in the United States and allowing "the spirit of ruthless brutality [to] enter into the very fibre of our national life." The President's rigid Presbyterian conscience tortured him relentlessly. During the long weeks between the break with Germany and the declaration of war, he lost sleep, appeared gray and drawn. When someone asked him which side he hoped would win, he answered petulantly, "Neither." "He was resisting," Secretary Lansing recorded, "the irresistible logic of events." In the end, he could satisfy himself only by giving the war an idealistic purpose. However sordid the purposes of all the belligerents, the war had become a threat to humanity. Unless the United States threw its weight into the balance, western civilization itself might be destroyed. Out of the long blood bath must come a new and better world; the war must be fought to end, for all time, war itself. Thus finally, in the name not of vengeance and victory but of justice and humanity, he sent his countrymen into battle.

The Home Front

America's entry into the World War determined its outcome. The Allies were rapidly running out of money and supplies; their troops, decimated by nearly three years in the trenches, were disheartened and rebellious. In February and March 1917 U-boats sent over a million tons of Allied shipping to the bottom of the Atlantic. The outbreak of the Russian Revolution in March 1917, although at first lifting the spirits of the western democracies, led to the Bolshevik takeover under Lenin. The Russian armies collapsed, and by December 1917 Russia was out of the war and the Germans were moving huge masses of men and equipment from the eastern front to France. Without the aid of the United States, it is likely that the war would have ended in 1918 on terms dictated from Berlin. Instead American men and supplies helped contain the Germans' last drives and then made it possible to push them back to final defeat.

Even so, it was a very close thing, for the United States entered the war little better prepared to fight than it had been in 1898 and never got its full weight into the fray. For this, Wilson was partly to blame. Because of his devotion to peace he had not tried hard enough to ready either the country or his own administration for war. Even after he espoused the preparedness movement, for example, he never envisioned an army of over half a million, yet by the end of the conflict nearly 5 million Americans were in uniform.

The conversion of American industry to war production had to be organized and carried out without prearrangement. Much confusion and waste resulted. The hurriedly designed shipbuilding program proved an almost total fiasco. The gigantic Hog Island yard, which cost $65 million and employed at its peak over 34,000 men, completed its first vessel only after the Armistice had been signed. The nation's railroads, strained by immensely increased traffic, became progressively less efficient, but only after a monumental tie-up in December and January of 1917–18 did Wilson finally appoint Secretary of the Treasury William G. McAdoo director-general of the railroads, with power to run the roads as a single system. Ambitious airplane, tank, and artillery construction programs developed so slowly that they had no effect on the war. The big guns that backed up American troops in 1918 were made in France and Great Britain. American pilots, such as the great "ace" Captain Eddie Rickenbacker, flew British Sopwiths and De Havillands or French Spads and Nieuports. Theodore Roosevelt's son Quentin was shot down while flying a Spad over Château-Thierry, in July 1918.

Of course the problem of mobilization was complicated and required dramatic alterations in public attitudes that no leader could have accomplished easily. It took Congress six weeks of hot debate merely to decide upon conscription. Only in September 1917, nearly six months after the declaration of war, did the first draftees (men between the ages of 21 and 30) reach the training camps, and it is hard to see how Wilson could have speeded this process appreciably. He wisely supported the professional soldiers, who insisted that he resist the appeals of politicians who wanted to raise volunteer units, even rejecting, at very considerable political cost, Theodore Roosevelt's offer to raise an entire army division.

Wilson was a forceful and inspiring war leader once he grasped what needed to be done. Despite the compelling demand for haste and the countless new activities taken on by the government, no corruption or scandal marred the administration's record. Waste there was, and inefficiency, but Wilson never lost control of the situation. No one in the country worked harder or devoted himself to the task of mobilizing society so intensely or displayed such unfailing patience in the face of frustration and criticism.

The President also displayed remarkable flexibility in fashioning, by trial and error, his wartime administration. Raising an army was only a small part of the job. The Allies had to be supplied with food and munitions, and immense amounts of money had to be collected. Originally, Wilson placed the whole program in the hands of a Council of National Defense, consisting of six Cabinet officers and a seven-man advisory commission. The council attempted to coordinate the manufacture of munitions and other war goods, but it lacked the authority to do the job properly. After a series of experiments, it created (July 1917) the War Industries Board to oversee all aspects of industrial production and distribution.

However, only after Wilson reorganized the WIB under Bernard M. Baruch in March 1918 did it begin to function effectively. Baruch, a daring Wall Street speculator by trade, performed brilliantly, but it was Wilson's decision to make him practically an economic dictator that enabled Baruch to succeed. The WIB allocated scarce materials, standardized production, fixed prices, and coordinated American and Allied purchasing.

The evaluation of this unprecedented and complicated effort raises some interesting historical questions. The antitrust laws were suspended and producers were encouraged, even compelled, to cooperate with one another. The New Freedom variety of laissez faire had no place in a wartime economy. Wilson accepted completely the kind of government-industry ententes developed under Theodore Roosevelt which he had denounced in 1912. Prices were set by the WIB at levels that allowed large profits—U.S. Steel, for example, despite very high taxes, cleared over half a billion dollars in two years. Baruch justified these returns with what seemed to him irrefutable logic: "You could be forgiven if you paid too much to get the stuff, but you could never be forgiven if you did not get it, and lost the war." It is at least arguable that producers would have turned out just as much even if compelled to charge somewhat lower prices.

Another important effect of the Wilsonian system was to foster a close relation between business and the military. At the start of the conflict, army procurement was decentralized and inefficient—as many as eight bureaus were purchasing materiel independently. By 1918 the supply system was in a condition approaching chaos. Nevertheless, the army resisted cooperating with civilian agencies, being, as the historian Paul Koistiner puts it, "suspicious of, and hostile toward civilian institutions." Wilson finally compelled the war department to place officers on WIB committees, and when the army discovered that its interests were not injured by the system, the foundation for what was later to be known as the "industrial-military complex" was laid, the close alliance between business and military leaders that was to cause so much controversy after the Second World War.

In general the history of industrial mobilization was the history of the whole home-front effort in microcosm: prodigies were performed, but the task was so gigantic and unprecedented that a full year passed before an efficient system had been devised, and many unforeseen results occurred.

The problem of mobilizing agricultural resources was solved more quickly, and this was fortunate because in April 1917 the British had on hand only a six-weeks' supply of food. Wilson named Herbert Hoover, a mining engineer who had headed the Belgian Relief Commission earlier in the war, as food administrator. Acting under powers granted by the Lever Act of August 1917, Hoover set the price of wheat at $2.20 a bushel in order to encourage production.* He also established a special government corporation to purchase the entire American and Cuban sugar crop, which he then doled out to American and British refiners. Avoiding compulsory rationing, Hoover organized a campaign to persuade consumers to conserve food supplies voluntarily. "Wheatless Mondays" and "Meatless Tuesdays" were the rule, and although no law compelled their observance, the public responded patriotically. Boy Scouts dug up back yards and vacant lots to plant vegetable gardens, chefs devised new recipes to save on scarce items, restaurants added horsemeat, rabbit, and whale steak to their menus. Chicago housewives were so successful in making use of leftovers that the volume of raw garbage in the city declined from 12,862 tons to 8,386 tons per month in a single year. New York State supplemented federal efforts by establishing a Food Control Commission, with authority to regulate the processing and distribution of food. New York also authorized local communities to buy and sell food in order to stabilize prices. Without subjecting its own citizens to serious personal inconvenience, the United States increased food exports from 12.3 million tons to 18.6 million tons in one year. Farmers, of course, profited greatly: their real income increased nearly 30 per cent between 1915 and 1918. Their increased production, involving as it did the use of much submarginal land, caused grave difficulties during the postwar era, however.

Wilson handled the wartime labor problem in a way that greatly benefited workingmen. The war gave labor many advantages, for it created full employment and a remarkable industrial prosperity. With the army siphoning millions of men from the labor market and with immigration reduced to a trickle, wages rose. This produced unprecedented economic opportunities for disadvantaged groups, especially Negroes. The movement of freedmen from the former slave states began with emancipation, but the mass exodus that many northerners had expected did not materialize. Between 1870 and 1890 only about 80,000 came to the North, most of these settling in the cities. Compared with the urban influx from Europe and from northern farms, this was a trivial increase; the proportion of

*Output rose from 619 million bushels in 1917 to 904 million in 1918.

blacks to the total population of New York, for example, fell from over ten per cent in 1800 to under two per cent in 1900.

Around the turn of the century, as the first post-slave generation reached maturity and as southern repression increased, the northward movement quickened—about 200,000 Negroes migrated between 1890 and 1910. After 1914, however, the war boom drew blacks north in a flood, half a million in five years. In this period the Negro population of New York rose from 92,000 to 152,000, of Chicago from 44,000 to 109,000, of Detroit from 5,700 to 41,000.

However, the war produced disadvantages for workingmen as well. The emergency roused the public against strikers; some conservatives even demanded that war workers be conscripted just as soldiers were. Although he opposed strikes that impeded the war effort, Wilson set great store in preserving the individual worker's freedom of action. It would be "most unfortunate . . . to relax the laws by which safeguards have been thrown about labor," he said. "We must accomplish the results we desire by organized effort rather than compulsion."

The government began regulating the wages and hours of workers building army camps and manufacturing uniforms early in the conflict; then, in April 1918, Wilson created a National War Labor Board, headed by former President Taft and Frank P. Walsh, a prominent lawyer, to settle labor disputes. The board considered more than 1,200 cases and prevented many strikes. A War Labor Policies Board, headed by Professor Felix Frankfurter of the Harvard Law School, made an overall study of the labor market and laid down standard wages-and-hours patterns for each major war industry. Since these were determined in consultation with employers and representatives of labor, the WLPB helped speed the unionization of workers by compelling management, even in antiunion industries like steel, to deal with labor leaders. The administration consciously encouraged the growth of unions and collective bargaining. Union membership rose by 2.3 million during the war; in 1920 the American Federation of Labor could boast a membership of 3.26 million.

Trends in the steel industry reflect the general improvement of the lot of labor in wartime. Wages of unskilled steelworkers had more than doubled by November 1918. Thousands of southern Negroes flocked into the steel towns. Union organizers made inroads in many steel plants, especially after a War Labor Board decision forbidding the companies to interfere with their activities. By the summer of 1918 organized labor was preparing an all-out assault to unionize steel, basing its appeal on the idea that if the world was to be made safe for democracy, there must be "economic democracy [along] with political democracy."

Wilson also managed the task of financing the war effectively, although at first he greatly underestimated the amount of money that would be needed. The struggle cost the United States about $33.5 billion, not counting pensions and other postwar expenses. About $7 billion of this was lent to the Allies,* but since this money was largely spent in America, it contributed to the national prosperity. Over two-thirds of the cost of the war was met by borrowing. Five massive Liberty and Victory Loan drives, spurred by advertising, parading, and appeals to patriotism, persuaded the people to open their purses. Industrialists, eager to inculcate a sense of personal involvement in the war effort in their employees, conducted great campaigns in their plants. Some went so far as to threaten "A Bond or Your Job," but more typical was the appeal of the managers of the Gary, Indiana, plant of U.S. Steel, who printed patriotic advertisements in six languages in order to reach their immigrant workers.

In addition to borrowing, the government collected about $10.5 billion in taxes during the war. A steeply graduated income tax took over 75 per cent of the incomes of the wealthiest citizens. A 65 per cent excess-profits tax, yielding over $2 billion in 1918, and a 25 per cent inheritance tax were also enacted. Thus, while many individuals made fortunes out of the war,

*In 1914 Americans owed foreigners about $3.8 billion. By 1919 they *were owed* $12.5 billion by Europeans alone.

The nation's advertising and entertainment industries were mobilized to promote war-bond drives. This poster was aimed at recent immigrants from Europe.

the cost of the struggle was distributed far more equitably than that of the Civil War. Americans also contributed generously to philanthropic agencies engaged in war work. Most notable, perhaps, was the great 1918 drive of the United War Work Council, an interfaith religious group, which raised over $200 million mainly to finance recreational programs for the troops overseas.

Wilson was pre-eminently a teacher and preacher, a specialist in the transmission of ideas and ideals, and for this reason he excelled at mobilizing public opinion and inspiring men to battle for the better world he hoped would emerge from the Great War. In April 1917 he created a Committee on Public Information, headed by the journalist George Creel, to marshal the nation behind the war effort. Creel organized an army of speakers and writers to blanket the country with propaganda: they pictured the war as a crusade for freedom and democracy, the Germans as a bestial people bent on world domination. Creel worked closely with the press, establishing an effective system of voluntary censorship to prevent the leakage of information helpful to the enemy.

Creel's committee served a practical function, for thousands of persons—German- and Irish-Americans, for example, and men of socialist and pacifist leanings—did not yet believe the war necessary or just. However, the committee, and more especially a number of unofficial patriotic groups, soon allowed their enthusiasm for the conversion of the hesitant to become outright suppression of dissent. Persons who refused to buy war bonds were often exposed to public contempt, even to assault. Opposition to Germany led to attacks on all things German; men with German names were persecuted without regard for their actual views, school boards outlawed the teaching of the German language, sauerkraut was renamed "liberty cabbage." Opponents of the war of unquestionable patriotism were subjected to ridicule and abuse. For example, the cartoonist Rollin Kirby pictured Senator Robert La Follette receiving an Iron Cross from the German militarists,* and the faculty of his own University of Wisconsin voted to censure La Follette.

Despite his understanding of the danger that the war posed for civil liberties, Wilson failed to keep these superpatriots in check. He approved the Espionage Act of 1917, which imposed fines of up to $10,000 and jail sentences ranging to 20 years on persons guilty of aiding the enemy or obstructing recruiting. This law further authorized the postmaster general to ban from the mails any material which he personally considered treasonable or seditious.

In May 1918, again with Wilson's approval, Congress went still further, passing the Sedition Act, which made it a crime even to attempt by persuasion to discourage the sale of war bonds or to "utter, print, write, or publish any disloyal, profane, scurrilous, or abusive language" about the government, the Constitution, or the

*Kirby later expressed his deep regret for having defamed La Follette.

NATIONAL ARCHIVES

In 1917 the Germania Life Insurance Building in St. Paul was renamed the Guardian Building; since Germania herself could not be disguised, down she came.

uniform of the army or navy. Mere criticism became cause for arrest and imprisonment. Socialist periodicals like *The Masses* were suppressed, and Eugene V. Debs was sentenced to ten years imprisonment for making an antiwar speech. A Hollywood producer, Robert Goldstein, received a ten-year sentence because his movie *The Spirit of '76* contained a scene showing British redcoats attacking women and children. The film was "intended to arouse antagonism, hatred, and enmity" between the United States and its ally Britain, the government contended.

While legislation to prevent sabotage and control subversives was justifiable, these laws went far beyond what was necessary to protect the national interest. Especially reprehensible was the way some local officials used them to muzzle liberal opinion. Men were jailed for suggesting that the draft law was unconstitutional and for criticizing private organizations like the Red Cross and the YMCA. One woman received a ten-year sentence for writing: "I am for the people, and the government is for the profiteers." In such an atmosphere, many fanatics sought a kind of private vengeance against anyone whom they considered to be unpatriotic. Conscientious objectors were frequently reviled; labor organizers were attacked by mobs.

The Supreme Court upheld the constitutionality of the Espionage Act in *Schenck v. U.S.* (1919), a case involving a man who had mailed circulars to draftees urging them to refuse to report for induction into the army. Free speech has limits, Justice Oliver Wendell Holmes, Jr., explained. No one has the right to cry *"Fire!"* in a crowded theater. When there is a "clear and present danger" that a particular statement would threaten the national interest, it can be repressed by law. In peacetime Schenck's circulars would be permissible, but not in time of war. This clear-and-present-danger doctrine, however, did not prevent judges and juries from interpreting the Espionage and Sedition acts broadly, and although in many instances their decisions were overturned by higher courts, this usually did not occur until after the war. The wartime hysteria far exceeded anything that happened in Great Britain and France, where the threat to national survival was really acute. In 1916 the French novelist Henri Barbusse published *Le Feu* (*Under Fire*), a graphic account of the horrors and purposelessness of trench warfare. In one chapter Barbusse described a pilot flying over the trenches on a Sunday, observing French and German soldiers at Mass in the open fields, each worshiping the same God. His message, like that of the German Erich Maria Remarque's *Im Westen nichts Neues* (*All Quiet on the Western Front*), written *after* the conflict, was unmistakably antiwar. Yet *Le Feu* circulated freely in France, even winning the coveted Prix Goncourt.

With all its failures and successes, the American mobilization experience was part and product of the Progressive Era and of the American industrial revolution. The work of the progressives at both the national and state levels in expanding government power in order to deal with social and economic problems before the war provided precedents and conditioned the people for the all-out effort of 1917–18. This effort, in turn, had a great influence on national policy in later crises, most notably during the New Deal period and in World War II. The concept of social and economic planning and the management of huge business operations by public boards and committees got their first large-scale practical tests. College professors, technicians, and others with complex intellectual skills entered government service en masse. The expansion of federal powers took another giant step forward as the national government for the first time entered actively and continuously in such fields as housing and labor relations.

Many progressives, especially the social workers, saw the war as creating the sense of common purpose that would stimulate the people to act unselfishly to benefit the poor and to eradicate social evils. Patriotism and public service seemed at last united. Secretary of War Newton D. Baker, a prewar urban reformer, expressed this attitude in supporting a federal child labor law: "We cannot afford, when we are losing boys in France to lose children in the United States." Men and women of this sort worked for a dozen causes only remotely concerned with the war effort. The women's suffrage movement was stimulated, as was the campaign against alcohol. The Red Cross and the YMCA, while focusing their energies on aiding men in uniform, also stepped up their civilian services. Reformers began to talk about health insurance and to press older drives for workmen's compensation laws. A national campaign against prostitution and venereal disease was mounted.*

War-inspired cooperation also brought social benefits to American Negroes to supplement their new economic opportunities. The northern migration worried southern whites and led to some mitigation of conditions. Although there were terrible race riots in a number of northern and southern cities triggered by white resentment of the thousands of migrants who were crowding in to fill war jobs, unprecedented forward steps were taken. The draft law applied to blacks and whites equally, and while it is possible to view this cynically, most Negroes saw it as an important gain, for it implicitly recognized their bravery and patriotism. More important, Negroes were accepted for officer training, as Red Cross nurses, and for high posts in government agencies. W.E.B. Du Bois supported the war enthusiastically. He praised Wilson for making, at last, a strong statement against lynching. He even went along with the fact that black officer candidates were trained in segregated camps. "Let us," he wrote in the *Crisis*, "while the war lasts, forget our special grievances and close ranks shoulder to shoulder with our fellow citizens and the allied nations that are fighting for democracy." Many Negroes condemned Du Bois's accommodationism (which he promptly abandoned when the war ended), but for the moment the prevailing mood among blacks was one of optimism. "We may expect to see the walls of prejudice gradually crumble"—this was the common attitude in 1917–18.

*The effort to wipe out prostitution around military installations was a cause of some misunderstanding with the Allies, who provided licensed facilities for their troops as a matter of course. When the Premier of France graciously offered to supply prostitutes for American units in his country, Secretary of War Baker is said to have remarked: "For God's sake . . . don't show this to the President or he'll stop the war."

"Over There"

All activity on the home front, of course, had one ultimate objective: defeating the Central Powers on the battlefield. This it accomplished. The navy performed with special distinction. In April 1917 German submarines sank over 870,000 tons of Allied shipping; after April 1918, monthly losses never reached 300,000 tons. American destroyers helped control the U-boats, but most important was the decision of Admiral William S. Sims, made at the urging of Wilson and accepted by the British only after intense argument, to send merchantmen across the Atlantic only in convoys screened by warships. Checking the U-boats was essential because of the need to transport millions of soldiers to Europe. This feat was carried out without the loss of a single man.

The first units of the American Expeditionary Force (AEF), elements of the regular army commanded by General John J. Pershing, reached Paris on Independence Day 1917 and took up positions on the front near Verdun in October. Not until the spring of 1918, however, did the "doughboys," as they were called, play a significant role in the fighting, except insofar as their mere presence boosted French and British morale. Pershing, as commander of the AEF, insisted upon maintaining his troops as independent units; he would not allow them to be filtered into the Allied armies as reinforcements. This was part of a perhaps unfortunate general policy, reflecting America's isolationism and suspicion of Europeans, of refusing to accept full membership in the Allied coalition. Wilson always referred to the other nations fighting Germany as "associates," not as "allies."

In March 1918 the Germans launched a great spring offensive, their armies strengthened by thousands of veterans from the Russian front. By late May they had reached a point on the Somme River just 12 miles from Amiens, a key

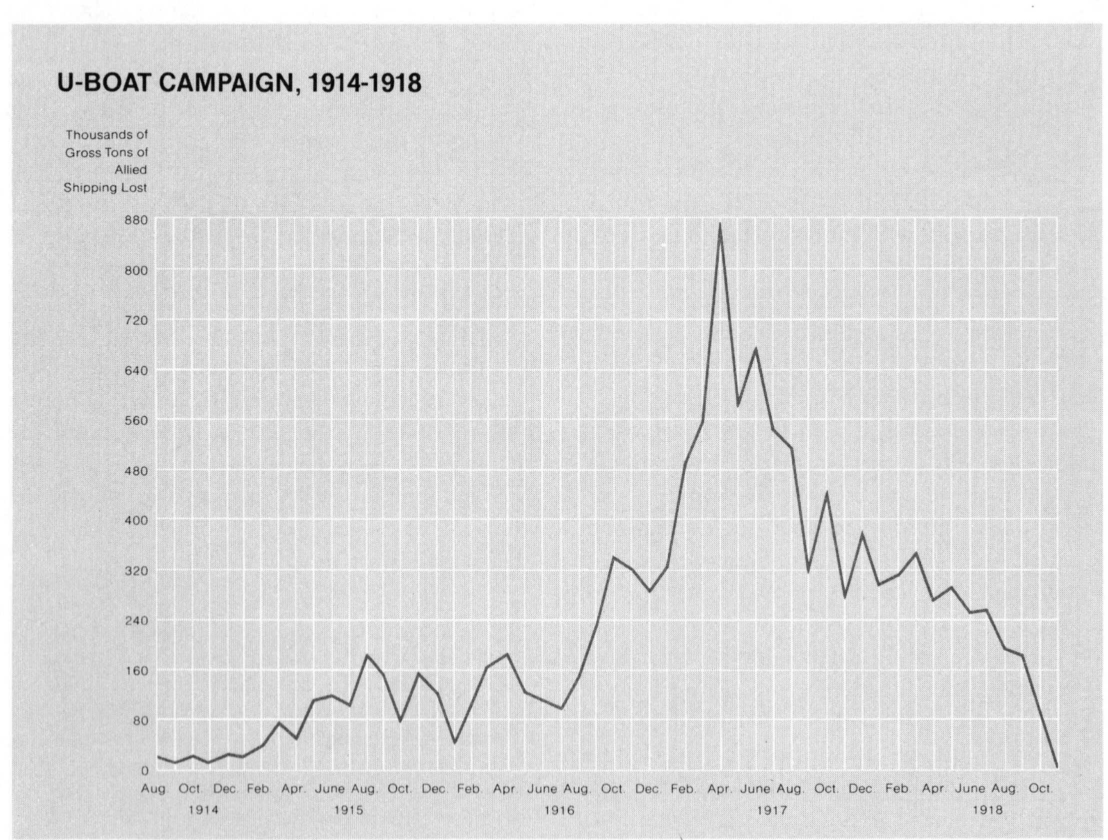

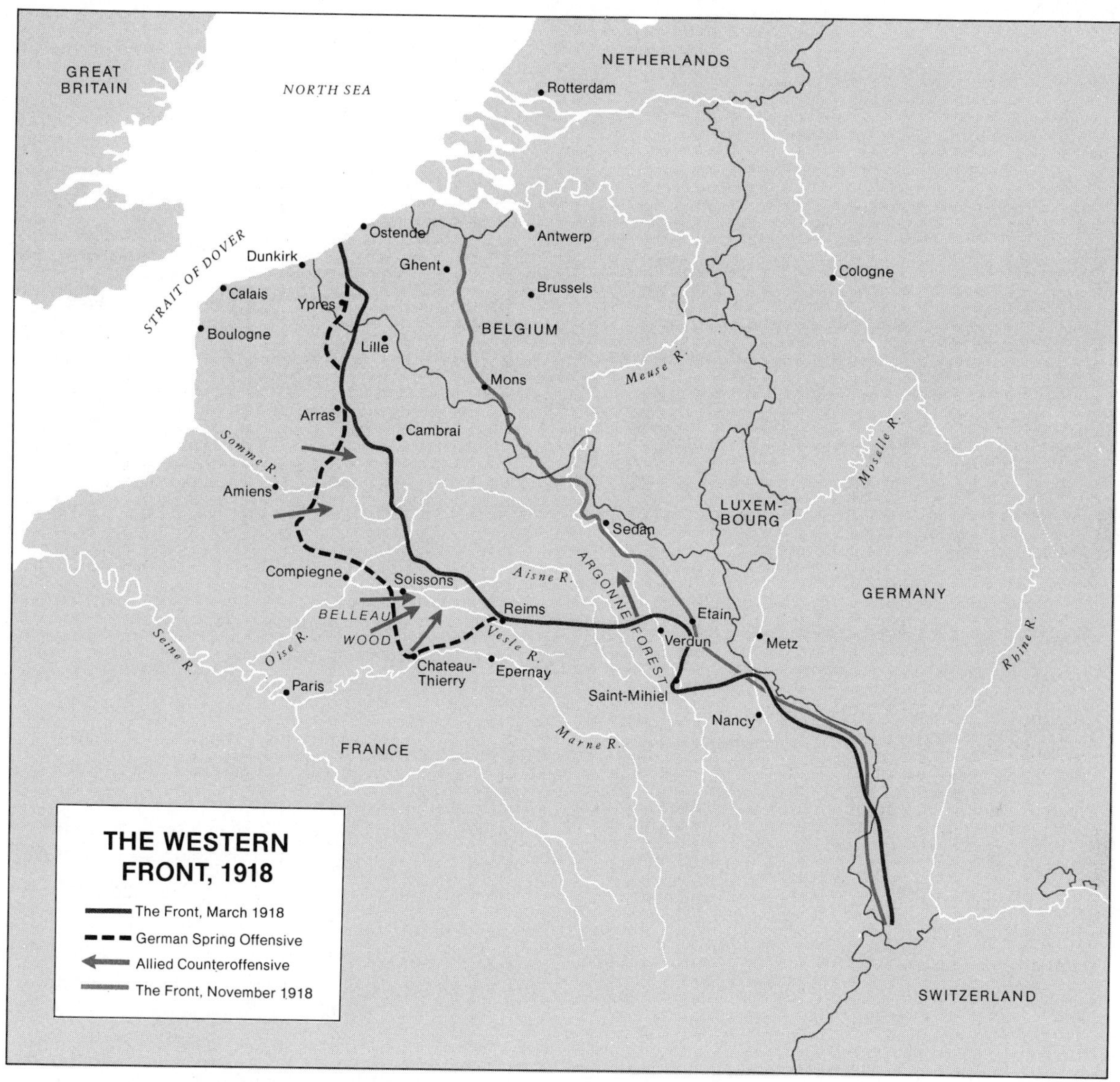

British base, and were only 50 miles from Paris itself, on the Marne River near the town of Château-Thierry. Early in June, the AEF fought its first major engagements, driving the Germans back from Château-Thierry and Belleau Wood.

In this fighting only about 27,500 Americans saw action, but thereafter the number escalated rapidly. When the Germans advanced again in the direction of the Marne in mid-July, 85,000 Americans were in the lines that withstood their charge; when the Allied armies counterattacked a few days later, 270,000 Americans participated, helping to flatten the German bulge between Reims and Soissons. By late August the American First Army, 500,000 men, was poised before the Saint-Mihiel salient, a deep extension of the German lines southeast of Verdun. On September 12 this army, buttressed by French troops, struck and in two days wiped out the salient.

Then, late in September, began the greatest American engagement of the war. No less than 1.2 million doughboys drove forward on a broad front west of Verdun into the Argonne Forest, a region described by one historian as "ten miles

SMITHSONIAN INSTITUTION

A column of American troops, with their walking wounded and their prisoners, was sketched in October 1918 during the Meuse-Argonne offensive by Harvey Dunn, a combat artist attached to the American Expeditionary Force.

of jungle growth, rocky slopes, cliffs, ravines, innumerable brooks, its terrain shell-holed like the moon." For over a month of indescribable horror the Americans inched ahead through the tangle of the Argonne and the formidable defenses of the Hindenburg Line, while to the west, French and British armies staged similar drives. In this one offensive the AEF suffered 120,000 casualties. The Americans' artillery fire was so heavy that 14 trainloads of shells were consumed in a single day. Finally, on November 1, they broke the German center and raced ahead toward the vital Sedan-Mézières railroad. On November 11, with Allied armies advancing on all fronts, the Germans signed the Armistice, ending the fighting.*

*Total American losses in the World War amounted to 112,432 dead and 230,074 wounded. More than half of the deaths, however, resulted from disease. Although severe, these casualties were trivial compared with those of the other belligerents. British Commonwealth deaths amounted to 947,000, French to 1.38 million, Russian to 1.7 million, Italian to 460,000. Among the Central Powers, Germany lost 1.8 million men, Austria-Hungary 1.2 million, Turkey 325,000. In addition, about 20 million men were wounded.

Preparing for Peace

On November 11, 1918, as the echoes of the last thundering artillery salute reverberated across the pockmarked tangle of mud and barbed wire from the Vosges to the North Sea and countless gray and olive-drab helmets rose warily from the opposing trenches in the strange stillness of the Armistice, western civilization stood at a great turning point. The fighting had ended, but the shape of the postwar world remained to be determined. Aside from the immense loss of life and the destruction of so much wealth and property, the structure of European society had been shaken to its foundations. Confusion reigned. Men wanted peace yet burned for revenge. Millions faced starvation, other millions were completely disillusioned by the seemingly purposeless sacrifices of four years of horrible war. Communism—to some an idealistic promise of human betterment, to others a commitment to rational economic and social planning, and to still others a danger to individual freedom, toleration, and democracy—having conquered Russia threatened to envelop Germany and much of the defunct Austro-Hungarian empire, perhaps even the victorious Allies. How could stability be restored? How could victory be made meaningful?

Woodrow Wilson, who had grasped the true significance of the Great War while most statesmen still thought that triumph on the battlefield would settle everything automatically, faced the future on November 11 with determination and sober confidence. As early as January 1917, he had realized that victory would be wasted if the winners permitted themselves the luxury of vengeance, that such a policy would disrupt the balance of power and lead to economic and social chaos. American participation in the struggle had not blurred his vision. The victors must build a better society, not punish those they believed had destroyed the old. In a speech to Congress on January 8, 1918, he outlined a plan, known as the Fourteen Points, designed to make the world "fit and safe to live in." The peace treaty should be negotiated in the full view of world opinion, not in secret. It should guarantee that the seas would be free to all nations, in war as in peacetime; it should tear down barriers to international trade, provide for a drastic reduction of armaments, and establish a colonial system that would take proper account of the interests of the native peoples concerned. European boundaries should be redrawn so that no substantial group would have to live under a government not of its own choosing. More specifically, captured Russian territory should be restored, Belgium evacuated, Alsace-Lorraine given back to France, the heterogeneous nationalities of Austria-Hungary accorded autonomy. Italy's frontiers should be adjusted "along clearly recognizable lines of nationality," the Balkans made free, Turkey divested of its subject peoples, an independent Polish state (with access to the Baltic) created. To oversee the new system, Wilson insisted, "a general association of nations must be formed under specific covenants for the purpose of affording mutual guarantees of political independence and territorial integrity to great and small states alike."

Wilson's Fourteen Points for a fair peace lifted the hopes of well-meaning people everywhere. When the German armies began to crack in the summer of 1918, the plan also helped to undermine the will of the Central Powers to resist, thus hastening the end of the war. After the guns fell silent, however, the vagueness and inconsistencies in the Points became apparent. Complete national self-determination was impossible in polyglot Europe; there were too many regions of mixed population for every group to be satisfied. Self-determination also, like the war itself, fostered the very spirit of nationalism that Wilson's dream of an international organization, a league of nations, was designed to de-emphasize. Furthermore, the Allies had made certain territorial commitments to one another in secret treaties that ran counter to the principle of self-determination, and they were unready to give up all claim to Germany's sprawling colonial empire. Freedom of the seas in wartime posed another problem; the British flatly refused to accept the idea. On the other hand, many Americans were alarmed at the thought of abandoning the principle of protective tariffs. In every Allied country millions repudiated the concept of a peace without indemnities; they expected to make the enemy pay for the war, hoping, as David Lloyd George, the British prime minister, put it, to squeeze Germany "until the pips squeak."

Wilson discounted all these difficulties, or rather, assumed that the practical virtues of his program would compel selfish and shortsighted opponents to fall in line. He had the immense advantage of seeking nothing for his own country and the additional strength of being leader of the one important nation to emerge from the war richer and more powerful than it had been in 1914. Yet this combination of altruism, idealism, and power was his undoing, for it intensified his tendency to be overbearing and undermined his judgment. He had never found it easy to compromise. Once, for example, while at Princeton, he got into an argument over some abstract question with a professor while shooting a game of pool. To avoid acrimony, the professor finally said: "Well, Doctor Wilson, there are two sides to every question." "Yes," Wilson answered, "a right side and a wrong side." Now, believing that the fate of humanity hung on his actions, he became still more unyielding. Always a preacher, he became in his own mind a prophet, almost, one fears, a kind of god.

In the last weeks of the war Wilson proved himself a brilliant diplomat, dangling the Fourteen Points before the German people to encourage them to overthrow the kaiser, Wilhelm II, and sue for an armistice, and then sending Colonel House to Paris to persuade Allied leaders to accept the points as the basis for the peace. When the Allies raised objections, House made certain small concessions, but by hinting that the United States might make a separate peace with Germany, he forced them to agree. Under the Armistice of November 11, Germany had to pull back behind the Rhine and surrender its submarines, together with quantities of munitions and other materials, but it received the assurance of the Allies that the Wilsonian principles would prevail at the peace conference.

Wilson next came to a daring decision: he would personally attend the conference, which convened formally on January 12, 1919, at Paris, as a member of the United States Peace Commission. This was a precedent-shattering step, for no previous President had left American territory while in office. Taft, for example, had a summer home on the St. Lawrence River in Canada but never vacationed there during his term, feeling that to do so would be unconstitutional. Wilson probably erred in going to Paris, but not because of the novelty or possible illegality of the act. By leaving the country, he was turning his back on certain obvious domestic problems, less directly important than those being settled at Versailles to be sure, but ones that demanded his personal attention far more.

To begin with, the 1916 Wilsonian coalition was rapidly falling apart. Western farmers felt that they had been discriminated against during the war, since wheat prices had been controlled while southern cotton had been allowed to rise unchecked, skyrocketing from 7 cents a pound in 1914 to 35 cents in 1919. Businessmen had become disaffected because of the administration's drastic tax program; labor, despite its gains, was restive in the face of reconversion to peacetime conditions. Wilson had greatly increased his political difficulties by making a partisan appeal for the election of a Democratic Congress in 1918. Republicans who had, in many instances, supported his war program more loyally than the Democrats, considered the statement a gross affront. The appeal failed, for the Republicans won majorities in both houses; thus Wilson appeared to have been repudiated at home at the very moment that he set forth to represent the nation abroad. Most important of all, Wilson intended to break with the isolationist tradition and bring the United States into a league of nations. Such a revolutionary change required explanation. He should have undertaken a great campaign to convince the people of the wisdom of this step.

Wilson also erred in his choice of the other commissioners. He selected Colonel House, Secretary of State Lansing, General Tasker H. Bliss, and Henry White, a career diplomat. These men were all thoroughly competent, but none except White was a Republican, and he had no stature as a politician. Since the peace treaty would have to be ratified by the Senate, Wilson should have given that body some representation on the commission, and since the Republicans would have a majority in the new Senate, a Republican senator, or someone who had the full confidence of the Republican leadership, should have been appointed. The wily McKinley, it will be remembered, named *three* senators to the American delegation to the peace conference after the Spanish-American War.

The Paris Peace Conference

This blunder did not affect the actual making of the treaty, however. Wilson arrived in Paris a world hero. He toured England, France, and Italy briefly and was greeted ecstatically almost everywhere. This reception tended to increase his sense of mission and to convince him, in the fashion of a typical progressive, that whatever the European politicians might say about it, "the people" were behind his program.

When the immense conference, consisting of many hundreds of delegates and experts from all over the world, finally settled down to its work, control quickly fell into the hands of the so-called Big Four: Wilson, Lloyd George, Premier Georges Clemenceau of France, and Prime Minister Vittorio Orlando of Italy. Wilson stood out in, but did not dominate, this group. Aside from his dedication, his main advantage in the negotiations was his untiring industry. He alone of the leaders tried to master all the complex details of the task.

The 78-year-old Clemenceau, stooped, white-haired, with a walrus mustache and a powerful jaw, cared only for one thing: French security. He viewed Wilson most cynically, saying that since mankind had been unable to keep God's Ten Commandments, it was unlikely to do better with Wilson's Fourteen Points. "Talking to Wilson is something like talking to Jesus Christ!" Clemenceau once told Colonel House. Lloyd George's approach to the peacemaking was pragmatic and almost cavalier. His baby-pink face, framed by a shock of white hair, radiated charm and informality. He sympathized with much that Wilson was trying to accomplish but found the President's frequent sermonettes about "right being more important than might, and justice being more eternal than force" incomprehensible. "If you want to succeed in politics," Lloyd George advised a British statesman, "you must keep your conscience well under control." Orlando, clever, cultured, a believer in international cooperation but inflexible where Italian national interests were concerned, was not the equal of his three colleagues in influence and left the conference in a huff when they failed to meet all his demands.

The conference labored from January to May 1919, and finally brought forth the Versailles Treaty. Many American liberals whose hopes had soared at the thought of a peace based on the Fourteen Points found the document abysmally disappointing. Ray Stannard Baker, a former muckraker, wrote: "When I read the first proofs . . . it seemed to me a terrible document; a dispensation of retribution with scarcely a parallel in history." Herbert Hoover, one of the American experts, was dismayed by the "hate and revenge" he found in its "political and economic passages."

Liberal critics had sound reasons for their complaints. The peace settlement failed to carry out the principle of self-determination completely. It gave Italy a large section of the Austrian Tyrol, although the area contained 200,000 persons who considered themselves Austrians. Other German-speaking groups were incorporated into the new states of Poland and Czechoslovakia. Japan was allowed to take over the Chinese province of Shantung, and one or another of the Allies swallowed up all the German colonies in Africa and the Far East. The victors also forced Germany

MUSEE DE LA GUERRE, PARIS

Frenchman Edouard Réquin drew the Big Four at Versailles. From left, France's Clemenceau, President Wilson, Britain's Lloyd George, and Italy's Orlando.

to accept full responsibility for having caused the war—an act of senseless vindictiveness as well as a gross oversimplification—and to sign a "blank check" agreeing to pay reparations not only for all damage to civilian properties, but also for future pensions and other indirect war costs. The total reparations bill, as finally determined, amounted to $33 billion, a sum far beyond Germany's ability to pay. Thus, instead of attacking imperialism, the treaty attacked *German* imperialism; instead of seeking a new international social order based on liberty and democracy, it created a new great-power entente designed to crush Germany and exclude Bolshevist Russia from the family of nations. It said nothing about freedom of the seas, the reduction of tariffs, or disarmament. To men who had taken Wilson's "peace without victory" speech and the Fourteen Points literally, the Versailles Treaty seemed an abomination.

The complaints of the critics were individually reasonable, but their conclusions were not entirely fair. The new map of Europe left fewer people on "foreign" soil than in any earlier period of history. Although the Allies seized the German colonies, they were required, under the mandate system, to render the League of Nations annual accounts of their stewardship and to prepare the inhabitants for eventual independence. Above all, Wilson made the powers incorporate the League of Nations directly into the treaty.

Wilson expected this League of Nations to make up for all the inadequacies of the Versailles Treaty. Once the League had begun to function, problems like freedom of the seas and disarmament would solve themselves, he argued, and the relaxation of trade barriers would surely follow. The League would arbitrate international disputes, act as a central body for registering treaties, and, in the last analysis, employ sanctions, military as well as economic, against aggressor nations. Each member promised (Article X) to protect the "territorial integrity" and "political independence" of all other members. No great power could be made to go to war against its will, but—and this Wilson emphasized—all were *morally* obligated to carry out League decisions. Liberal critics of the League were correct in saying that Wilson was seeking to prop up the existing social and economic system, that he was gravely concerned lest communism or even democratic socialism gain the upper hand in central Europe. Any form of class-oriented radicalism appalled him. He hoped, unrealistically as it turned out, to see Europe develop a capitalist-laborer consensus like that which existed in the United States. But by any standard, he had achieved a remarkably moderate peace, one full of hope for the future. Except for the war-guilt clause and the crushing reparations burden imposed on Germany, he could be justly proud of his work.

The Senate and the League of Nations

When Wilson returned from France, he finally directed his attention to the problem of winning his countrymen's approval of his handiwork. Probably a large majority of the people favored the League of Nations in principle, although few understood all its implications or were entirely happy with every detail. Wilson had already persuaded the Allies to accept certain changes in the original draft to mollify American opposition. One provided that no nation could be forced to accept a colonial mandate, another that "domestic questions" such as tariffs and the control of immigration did not fall within the competence of the League. The Monroe Doctrine had also been excluded from League control to satisfy American opinion, and a clause was added permitting members to withdraw from the organization after two years' notice.

Many senators, however, found these modifications insufficient. As early as March 1919, 37 Republican senators had signed a Round Robin, devised by Henry Cabot Lodge of Massachusetts, expressing opposition to Wilson's League and demanding that the question of an international organization be put off until "the urgent business of negotiating peace terms with Germany" had been completed. Wilson rejected this suggestion icily. The Allies had exacted major concessions in return for the changes he had already proposed; further alterations were out of the question. "Anyone who opposes me . . . I'll crush!" he told one Democratic senator. "I shall consent to nothing. *The Senate must take its medicine.*" Thus the stage was set for a monumental test of strength between the President and the Republican majority in the Senate.

Partisanship, principle, and prejudice clashed mightily in this contest. A Presidential election loomed ahead. Should the League prove a success, it was politically essential for the Republicans to be able to claim a share of the credit, yet Wilson had resolutely refused to allow them to participate in drafting the document. This predisposed all of them to favor changes. Politics aside, genuine alarm at the possible sacrifice of American sovereignty to an international authority led many

Republicans to urge modification of the League Covenant, or constitution. Personal dislike of Wilson and his highhanded methods motivated others. On the other hand, the noble purpose of the League made many reluctant to oppose it entirely. The intense desire of the people to have an end to the long war also operated to make GOP leaders hesitate before voting down the Versailles Treaty, and they could not reject the the League without rejecting the treaty too.

Wilson could count on the Democratic senators almost to a man, but he had to win over many Republicans to obtain the two-thirds majority necessary for ratification. Republican opinion divided roughly into three segments. At one extreme were some dozen "irreconcilables," led by the shaggy-browed William E. Borah of Idaho, an able, kindly individualist of progressive leanings but uncompromisingly isolationist and almost congenitally predisposed to resist the will of a powerful executive like Wilson. Borah claimed that he would vote against the League even if Jesus Christ returned to earth to argue in its behalf, and most of his followers were equally inflexible. At the other extreme stood another dozen "mild" reservationists who approved the League in principle but who hoped to alter it in minor ways, chiefly for political purposes. In the middle were the "strong" reservationists, men willing to go along with the League only if American sovereignty were fully protected and if it was made perfectly clear that their party had played a major role in fashioning the final document.

The leader of the Republican opposition was Senator Lodge. A haughty, rather cynical, intensely partisan person, Lodge possessed a keen intelligence, a mastery of parliamentary procedures, and, as chairman of the Senate Foreign Relations Committee, a great deal of power. Although not an isolationist, Lodge had little faith in the League. He also had a profound distrust of Democrats, and especially of Wilson, with whom he had clashed repeatedly. Lodge considered Wilson both a hypocrite and a coward; the President's pious idealism left him cold. While perfectly ready to see the country participate actively in world affairs, he insisted that its right to determine its own best interests in every situation be preserved. He had been a senator since 1893 and an admirer of senatorial independence since early manhood; when a Democratic President tried to ram the Versailles Treaty through the upper house, he fought him with every weapon he could muster.

Lodge belonged to the strong reservationist faction. His own proposals, known as the Lodge Reservations, 14 in number to match Wilson's Fourteen Points, spelled out the limits of the United States' obligations to the League and stated in unmistakable terms the right of Congress to decide when to honor these obligations. Some were mere quibbles. One, for example, exempted the Monroe Doctrine from League jurisdiction, although the treaty had already done so. Others, such as the provision that the United States would not endorse Japan's seizure of Chinese territory, were included mainly to embarrass Wilson by pointing up compromises he had made at Versailles. The most important reservation applied to Article X of the League Covenant, committing signatories to protect the political independence and territorial integrity of all member nations, which Wilson had rightly called "the heart of the Covenant." This reservation made Article X inoperable so far as the United States was concerned "unless in any particular case the Congress . . . shall by act or joint resolution so provide."

Lodge performed brilliantly if somewhat unscrupulously in uniting the diverse factions of his own party behind these reservations. He got the irreconcilables to agree to them by conceding their right to vote against the final version in any case, and held the mild reservationists in line by modifying some of his demands and by stressing the importance of party unity. Since the reservations, as distinct from amendments, would not have to win the formal approval of other League members and since Lodge's proposals (whatever his personal motivation) dealt forthrightly with the problem of reconciling traditional concepts of national sovereignty with the new idea of world cooperation, sincere friends of the League could accept them without sacrifice of principle. Wilson, however, refused to agree. "Accept the Treaty with the *Lodge* reservations," the President snorted when a friendly senator warned him that

Punch, MARCH 26, 1919

Two views of the League of Nations. In London's Punch *(left) the dove of peace looks askance at Wilson's hefty olive branch, asking, "Isn't this a bit thick?" At right, a New York* World *cartoon by Rollin Kirby. The intransigent seat-holders are anti-League senators Borah, Lodge, and Hiram Johnson.*

he must accept a compromise. "Never! Never!"

This foolish intransigence seems almost incomprehensible in a man of Wilson's intelligence and political experience. In part his hatred of Lodge accounts for it, in part his faith in his League. But his physical condition in 1919 also played a role. At Paris he had suffered a violent attack of indigestion that was probably a symptom of a minor stroke. Thereafter, many observers noted small changes in his personality, particularly an increased stubbornness and a loss of judgment. In any case, instead of making further concessions, he set out, early in September, on a nationwide speaking tour to rally support for the League. Although some of his speeches were brilliant, they had little effect on senatorial opinion and the effort drained away his last physical reserves. On September 25, after an address in Pueblo, Colorado, he collapsed. The rest of the trip had to be canceled. A few days later, back in Washington, he suffered a severe stroke, which partially paralyzed his left side.

For nearly two months as he slowly recovered, the President was almost totally cut off from affairs of state, leaving his friends leaderless while Lodge maneuvered the reservations through the Senate. Gradually, popular attitudes toward the League shifted. Italian-, Irish-, and German-Americans, angered by what they considered unfair treatment of their native lands in the treaty, clamored for outright rejection. The arguments of the irreconcilables persuaded many other citizens that Wilson had made too sharp a break with America's isolationist past and that the Lodge Reservations were therefore necessary. Other issues connected with the reconversion of society to a peacetime basis increasingly occupied the public mind.

Yet a coalition of Democrats and moderate Republicans could easily have carried the treaty. That no such coalition was organized was largely Wilson's fault. Lodge obtained the simple majority necessary to pass his reservations merely by keeping his own party united. When the time came for the final roll call on November 19, Wilson, bitter and emotionally distraught, ordered the Democrats to vote for rejection. "Better a thousand times to go down fighting than to dip your colours to dishonourable compromise," he explained to his wife. Thus the amended treaty failed, 35 to 55, the irreconcilables and the Democrats voting against it. Lodge then allowed the original draft to come to a vote. Again the result was defeat: 38 to 53. Only one Republican, Por-

ter J. McCumber, cast his ballot for ratification.

Dismayed but not yet crushed, friends of the League in both parties forced reconsideration of the treaty early in 1920. Neither Lodge nor Wilson, however, would yield an inch. Lodge, who had little confidence in the effectiveness of any league of nations, was under no compulsion to compromise. That Wilson, whose whole being was tied up in the Covenant, would not do so is further evidence of his physical and mental decline. Probably he was incompetent to perform the duties of his office. Almost certainly, had he died or stepped down, the treaty, with reservations, would have been ratified. When the Senate balloted again in March, half the Democrats violated Wilson's orders and voted for the treaty with the Lodge Reservations. The others, mostly southern party regulars, joined with the irreconcilables. Together they mustered 35 votes, 7 more than the one-third that meant defeat.

Wilson still hoped for vindication at the polls in the Presidential election, which he sought to make a "great and solemn referendum" on the League. The election was scarcely a referendum, for while the Democrats, who nominated Governor James M. Cox of Ohio, took a stand for Wilson's Covenant, the Republicans, whose candidate was another Ohioan, Senator Warren G. Harding, equivocated shamelessly on the issue. To a large extent, the result turned on other matters, largely emotional. Disillusioned by the results of the war, many Americans had had their fill of idealism. They wanted, apparently, to end the long period of moral uplift and reform agitation that had begun under Theodore Roosevelt and get back to what Harding called "normalcy." To the extent that the voters were expressing opinions on Wilson's League, they responded overwhelmingly in the negative. Harding had been a strong reservationist, yet he swept the country, winning over 16.1 million votes to Cox's 9.1 million. In July 1921 Congress formally ended the war with the Central Powers by passing a joint resolution.

That the defeat of the League was a tragedy is undeniable, both for Wilson, whose crusade for a world order based on peace and justice ended in failure, and for the world, which was condemned by the result to endure another still more horrible and costly war. Perhaps this dreadful outcome could not have been avoided in any case. The United States, in 1919–1920, was unready to assume the responsibility of preserving peace in other lands. If Wilson had compromised and if Lodge had behaved like a statesman instead of like a politician, America would have joined the League, but it might well have failed to respond when called upon to meet its obligations. As events soon demonstrated, the great League powers themselves acted pusillanimously and even dishonorably when challenged by aggressor nations. Nevertheless, it might have been different had the Senate ratified the Versailles Treaty. America's retreat from international cooperation discouraged supporters of the League in other countries and lessened the dangers that dictators like Mussolini and Hitler had to consider when planning their moves. In the 20-year respite between World War I and World War II, the western democracies might have drawn closer together and become more firm of heart if *all* had been committed to the League. What was lost when the treaty failed in the Senate was not peace, but the *possibility* of peace, a tragic loss indeed.

SUPPLEMENTARY READING Wilson's handling of foreign relations is discussed in several volumes by A.S. Link: *Wilson* (1947–), *Woodrow Wilson and the Progressive Era** (1954), and *Wilson the Diplomatist** (1957), as well as in the Wilson biographies listed in the preceding chapter. See also Harley Notter, *The Origins of the Foreign Policy of Woodrow Wilson* (1937), and N.G. Levin, Jr., *Woodrow Wilson and World Politics: America's Response to War and Revolution* (1968). Latin-American affairs under Wilson are treated in S.F. Bemis, *The Latin American Policy of the United States** (1943), H.F. Cline, *The United States and Mexico** (1953), and D.G. Munro, *Intervention and Dollar Diplomacy in the Caribbean* (1964). R.E. Quirk, *An Affair of Honor: Woodrow Wilson and the Occupation of Veracruz** (1962), is an admirable monograph, and C.C. Clendenen, *The United States and Pancho Villa* (1961), is also interesting.

For American entry into the Great War, see, in addition to the Link volumes mentioned above, E.R. May, *The World War and American Isolation** (1959), E.H. Buehrig, *Woodrow Wilson and the Balance of Power* (1955), Charles Seymour, *American Diplomacy During the World War* (1934) and *American Neutrality* (1935), all essentially favorable to Wilson. For contrary views, see Walter Millis, *The Road to War* (1935), and C.C. Tansill, *America Goes to War* (1938).

The war on the home front is covered in F.L. Paxson, *American Democracy and the World War* (1936–1948), and more briefly in Preston Slosson, *The Great Crusade and After: 1914–28* (1930), and W.E. Leuchtenburg, *The Perils of Prosperity** (1958). Other useful volumes include B.M. Baruch, *American Industry in War* (1941), M.I. Urofsky, *Big Steel and the Wilson Administration* (1969), Zechariah Chafee, *Free Speech in the United States** (1941), Donald Johnson, *The Challenge to American Freedoms* (1963), J.R. Mock and Cedric Larson, *Words That Won the War* (1939), David Brody, *Steelworkers in America* (1960), Herbert Stein, *Government Price Policy During the World War* (1939), D.R. Beaver, *Newton D. Baker and the American War Effort* (1966), and S.W. Livermore, *Politics Is Adjourned: Woodrow Wilson and the War Congress** (1966).

Laurence Stallings, *The Doughboys** (1963), is a good popular account of the American army in France, but see also J.J. Pershing, *My Experiences in the World War* (1931), E.E. Morrison, *Admiral Sims and the Modern American Navy* (1942), and T.G. Frothingham, *The Naval History of the World War* (1924–26).

On the peace settlement, in addition to the biographies of Wilson, consult A.J. Mayer, *Politics and Diplomacy of Peacemaking* (1967), Paul Birdsall, *Versailles Twenty Years After* (1941), Harold Nicolson, *Peacemaking, 1919** (1939), T.A. Bailey, *Woodrow Wilson and the Lost Peace** (1944) and *Woodrow Wilson and the Great Betrayal** (1945), J.A. Garraty, *Henry Cabot Lodge* (1953), H.C. Lodge, *The Senate and the League of Nations* (1925), Allan Nevins, *Henry White* (1930), J.M. Keynes, *The Economic Consequences of the Peace* (1919), and Robert Lansing, *The Peace Negotiations: A Personal Narrative* (1921). On the election of 1920, see Wesley Bagby, *The Road to Normalcy** (1962), and R.K. Murray, *The Harding Era* (1969).

*Available in paperback.

25

The Twenties: The Aftermath of the Great War

The Armistice of 1918 ended the fighting, but the Great War had so shaken the world that for a whole generation every major nation lived in its shadow. Americans sought desperately to escape from its influence, tried almost to deny that it had occurred, yet every aspect of their lives in the postwar years reflected its baneful impact. Convinced that they had made a terrible mistake by going to war, a great many people rejected all the values that had led them to do so. Idealism gave way to materialism, naiveté to cynicism, moral purposefulness to irresponsibility, progressivism to reaction, community spirit to rugged individualism, faith to iconoclasm. Yet this reaction, like so many defense mechanisms, was neurotic, based on unreal and conflicting assumptions, and for this reason unsuccessful.

The nation had put forth an immense effort to win the war, drastically regulating its way of life to increase production and improve social efficiency. Yet when the war ended, all this effort at communal improvement was largely abandoned. The government, in Wilson's words, "took the harness off" at once, blithely assuming that the economy could readjust itself without direction. The army was hastily demobilized, pouring millions of bored trainees and battle-shaken veterans into the job market without plan. Nearly all the controls established by the War Industries Board and other agencies were dropped overnight. Billions of dollars worth of war contracts were suddenly canceled. Despite the obvious benefits that government operation of the railroads had brought and despite the agitation of the railroad unions for the Plumb Plan, a scheme for nationalizing the system, the roads were turned back to private control.*

This return to laissez faire did not lead immediately to a depression. Business boomed in 1919 as consumers invested wartime savings in the purchase of automobiles, housing, and other goods that had been in short supply during the conflict. Unemployment was only briefly a serious problem as industry ex-

*The Esch-Cummins Transportation Act (1920) did, however, further strengthen the Interstate Commerce Commission's power to set rates and oversee railroad financing. It also authorized the pooling of traffic and the consolidation of some lines in the interest of efficiency.

panded to satisfy rising demand. But temporary shortages caused inflation; by 1920 the cost of living stood at more than twice the level of 1913. Inflation, in turn, produced labor trouble. The unions, grown strong during the war, fought for wage increases in order to hold their gains. Successful walkouts by textile workers, longshoremen, telephone operators, and others soon after the Armistice encouraged all workers to adopt more militant attitudes. Work stoppages aggravated shortages, triggering still further inflation and more strikes. Then came one of the most precipitous economic declines in American history. Between July 1920 and March 1922, prices, especially agricultural prices, plummeted, while unemployment soared to 5.75 million in mid-1921. Thus, the unrealistic attitude of the Wilson government toward the complexities of economic readjustment caused much unnecessary strife.

Radicalism and Xenophobia

Far more important than the economic losses, however, were the social effects of these labor difficulties, for they came at the worst possible time. Americans wanted peace, but their wartime tensions did not subside immediately. They continued to need some release for aggressive drives, formerly focused on the Germans, and were unready, as historian John Higham has said, to surrender the "psychic gratifications" the war had provided. They still required, in other words, an enemy. The people had no basic antipathy to labor; most persons recognized the services that industrial workers had contributed to the war effort and sympathized with their aspirations for a better way of life. Nevertheless, they found strikes frustrating and drew invidious comparisons between the lot of the unemployed soldier who had risked his life for a dollar a day and that of the striker who had drawn down fat wages during the war in perfect safety.

Furthermore, the activities of the radical fringe of the labor movement led millions of Americans to associate unionism and strikes with the new threat of communist world revolution. That threat seemed serious in 1919. Although there were only a handful of communists in the United States—no more than 100,000—Russia's experience indicated to many that a tiny minority of ruthless revolutionaries could take over a nation of millions if conditions were right. The leaders of international communism formed the Third International in March 1919 and announced that world revolution was their aim. In Germany and other parts of Europe, the danger that they would succeed appeared very real. Communists made themselves the self-appointed champions of the workers; labor unrest attracted them magnetically. When a wave of strikes, sometimes accompanied by violence, broke out in the United States, many persons interpreted them as communist-inspired preludes to revolution. One businessman wrote the attorney general in 1919: "There is hardly a respectable citizen of my acquaintance who does not believe that we are on the verge of armed conflict in this country." Louis Wiley, an experienced New York *Times* reporter, told a friend at this time that anarchists, socialists, and radical labor leaders were "joining together with the object of overthrowing the American Government through a bloody revolution and establishing a Bolshevist republic."

Organized labor in America had seldom been truly radical. The Industrial Workers of the World (IWW), influential in western mining and among migratory workers in the Progressive Era, had advocated violence and the abolition of the wage system but had made little impression in most industries. However, some labor leaders, such as Eugene V. Debs, had been attracted to socialism, and many Americans failed to distinguish between the common ends sought by communists and socialists and the entirely different methods that they proposed to achieve these ends. Any radical activity tended to be tarred as communist. When a general strike paralyzed Seattle in February 1919, the fact that a pro-communist had helped organize it sent shivers down countless conservative spines. When the radical William Z. Foster began a drive to organize the steel industry for the AF of L at about this time, these fears became more intense. In September 1919, 343,000 steelworkers walked off their jobs, and in the same month the Boston police also struck. Violence marked the steel strike and, of course, the suspension of police protection in Boston led to looting and fighting which only ended when Governor Calvin Coolidge (who might have prevented the strike if he had acted earlier) called out the National Guard.

During the same period a handful of demented anarchists caused a series of alarms by attempting to murder various prominent persons. In April 1919 a servant of Senator Thomas W. Hartwick of Georgia was maimed when an innocent-looking package addressed to the senator exploded while she was unwrapping it. Prompt investigation led to the discovery in a New York post office of 16 similar packages, all containing bombs, addressed to men like John D. Rockefeller and Justice Oliver Wendell Holmes, Jr. On June 2 an explosion shattered the front of the home of Attorney General A. Mitchell Palmer in Washington, and other bombs were set off in seven other cities. Anarchism had little in common with communism except a willingness to use violent methods, but many Americans lumped all extremists together and associated them with a monstrous assault on society.

What aroused the public even more was the fact that nearly all the radicals were immigrants, few of them American citizens. Wartime fear of alien saboteurs transformed itself easily into peacetime terror of foreign radicals, and ugly nativist sentiments that had built up during the Progressive Era as a result of mass immigration and rapid social change erupted. Wartime patriotism became "100 per cent Americanism"; instead of Germany, the enemy became the lowly immigrant, usually an Italian or a Jew or a Slav, and usually an industrial worker, too. In this muddled way radicalism, unionism, and questions of racial and national origins combined to make many Americans think their way of life in danger of imminent attack. That few immigrants were radicals, that most workers had no interest in communism, that the extremists themselves were faction-ridden, disorganized, and irresolute did not affect conservative thinking. From all over the country came demands that radicals be ruthlessly suppressed. Even President Wilson, on his last speaking tour in behalf of the League, warned of the "poison of revolt" that was seeping into "the veins of this free people." Thus the "Big Red Scare" was born.

BOTH: *The Liberator,* FEBRUARY, 1920

During the "Big Red Scare" radical cartoonist William Gropper sharply criticized the tactics of Attorney General Palmer. These drawings appeared in The Liberator *early in 1920. At left, Palmer's agents warn, "Clear the road there, boys—we got a dangerous Red." At right, a suspect faces a loutish, unsympathetic audience.*

The key figure in the resulting purge was A. Mitchell Palmer, Wilson's attorney general. Palmer had been a typical progressive, a supporter of the League of Nations and of many liberal measures, such as women's suffrage and child labor legislation. When the public clamor against alien radicals began, he tried to resist it. Even after his own home had been bombed, he reminded the country of the traditional American policy "that the oppressed of every clime shall find here a refuge." However, continued pressure from Congress and the press, and his growing conviction that the communists really were a menace, led him to change his mind.

When he did, he joined the red hunt with the enthusiasm of the typical convert. Soon he was saying of the radicals: "Out of the sly and crafty eyes of many of them leap cupidity, cruelty, insanity, and crime; from their lopsided faces, sloping brows, and misshapen features may be recognized the unmistakable criminal type."

In August 1919 Palmer established a General Intelligence Division in the Department of Justice, headed by J. Edgar Hoover, to collect information about clandestine radical activities. In November Justice Department agents swooped down upon the meeting places of an anarchist organization known as the Union of Russian Workers in a dozen cities. More than 650 persons, many of them unconnected with the union, were arrested, but in only 43 cases could evidence be found to justify deportation. Nevertheless, the public reacted so favorably that Palmer, thinking now of winning the 1920 Democratic Presidential nomination, abandoned the last shreds of his former tolerance. Quietly he planned an immense roundup of communists. He obtained no less than 3,000 warrants and on January 2, 1920, his agents, reinforced by local police and self-appointed vigilantes, struck simultaneously in 33 cities.

Palmer's biographer, Stanley Coben, has described these "Palmer raids" vividly:

> There was a knock on the door, the rush of police. In meeting houses, all were lined up to be searched; those who resisted often suffered brutal treatment.... Prisoners were put in overcrowded jails or detention centers where they remained, frequently under the most abominable conditions. . . . Police searched the homes of many of those arrested; books and papers, as well as many people found in these residences, were carried off to headquarters. Policemen also sought those whose names appeared on seized membership lists; they captured many of these suspects in bed or at work, searching their homes, confiscating their possessions, almost always without warrants.

All in all, about 6,000 persons were taken into custody, many of them citizens and therefore not subject to the deportation laws, many others totally unconnected with any radical cause. Some were held incommunicado for weeks while the authorities made futile efforts to find evidence against them. In a number of cases, individuals who came to visit prisoners were themselves thrown behind bars on the theory that they, too, must be communists. Hundreds of suspects were jammed into filthy "bullpens," beaten, forced to sign "confessions." Relatives of persons arrested often endured weeks of anxiety, with no knowledge of the victims' whereabouts.

The public tolerated these wholesale violations of civil liberties because of the supposed menance of communism. Gradually, however, protests began to be heard, first from lawyers and from liberal magazines like the *Nation* and the *New Republic* and then from a wider segment of the population. Despite the furor, no revolutionary outbreaks had taken place. Out of 6,000 seized in the Palmer raids, only 556 proved liable to deportation. The widespread ransacking of communists' homes and meeting places produced mountains of inflammatory literature, but only three pistols. In Europe the threat of communism had actually decreased by 1920. The foolish action of the New York legislature in expelling five socialist assemblymen also had a sobering effect, and the publication of the National Popular Government League's shocking report, *Illegal Practices of the United States Department of Justice* (1920), speeded the shift in public thinking.

Palmer, attempting to maintain the crusade, had announced that the radicals were planning a gigantic terrorist demonstration for May Day 1920. In New York and other cities thousands of police were placed on round-the-clock duty; federal troops stood by anxiously. But the day passed without even a riot or a rowdy meeting. Suddenly Palmer appeared ridiculous. His Presidential boom collapsed and the Red Scare swiftly subsided.

The ending of the Red Scare unfortunately did not herald the disappearance of xenophobia. War-stimulated passions continued strong and the dominant public mood remained reactionary. It was perhaps inevitable and possibly even wise that some kind of limitation be placed upon the entry of immigrants into the United States after the Great War. An immense backlog of prospective migrants had piled up during the conflict, and the desperate postwar economic condition of Europe led hundreds of thousands to seek better circumstances in the United States. Immigration rose from 110,000 in 1919, to 430,000 in 1920, and to 805,000 in 1921, with every prospect of continuing upward.

However, instead of setting some general limit on new arrivals, Congress, reflecting a widespread prejudice against eastern and southern Europeans, passed an emergency act establishing a quota system. Each year immigrants equal to three per cent of the number of foreign-born residents of the United States in 1910 might enter the country. Under this law about 350,000 could come in annually, but since each country's quota was based on the number of its nationals in the United States in 1910, only a relative handful of these would be from southern and eastern Europe, because at that time the foreign-born population had still been overwhelmingly of northern- and western-European origin. After further modifications in 1924, Congress established a new system in 1929 which allowed only 150,000 immigrants a year to enter the country. Each national quota was based on the supposed origins of the entire white population of the United States in 1920, not merely upon the foreign-born, a procedure heavily favoring immigrants from Great Britain and northern Europe. The system was complicated and also unscientific, because no one could determine with any real accuracy the "origins" of millions of citizens. It can perhaps best be explained by citing an example:

$$\frac{\text{Italian quota}}{150{,}000} = \frac{\text{Italian-origin population, 1920}}{\text{White population, 1920}}$$

$$\frac{\text{Italian quota}}{150{,}000} = \frac{3{,}800{,}000}{95{,}500{,}000}$$

$$\text{Italian quota} = 6{,}000 \text{ (approximately)}$$

The law actually reduced immigration to far below 150,000 a year, for the favored nations of northern Europe never filled their quotas. Total British immigration between 1931 and 1939, for example, amounted to only 23,000, although the *annual* British quota was over 65,000. Meanwhile, hundreds of thousands of southern and eastern Europeans waited for admission. By 1963 more than 265,000 Italians were in line, and the Greek quota (308) amounted to 1/337 of the number seeking immigration visas.

The United States had not only closed the gates, it had abandoned the theory of the melting pot. Instead of an open, cosmopolitan society eager to accept, in Emma Lazarus' stirring lines, the "huddled masses yearning to breathe free, the wretched refuse" of Europe's "teeming shore," America now became committed to preserving a homogeneous, "Anglo-Saxon" population.*

Urban-Rural Conflict

The war-born tensions and hostilities of the twenties also found expression in other ways, most of them related to an older rift in American society—the conflict between the urban and the rural way of life. It has often been noted that the census of 1920 revealed that for the first time a majority of Americans (54 million in a total population of 106 million) was living in "urban" rather than "rural" places. These figures are somewhat misleading when applied to the study of social attitudes, for the census classified anyone in a community of 2,500 or more as urban. Of the 54 million "urban" residents in 1920, over 16 million lived in communities of fewer than 25,000 persons, and the evidence suggests strongly that a large majority of these held ideas and values more similar to those of rural citizens than to those of city dwellers. But the truly urban Americans, the one person in four who lived in a city of 100,000 or more and especially the nearly 16.4 million who lived in great metropolises of at least half a million, were increasing steadily both in numbers and in influence.

Over 19 million persons moved from farm to

*The injustices of the national-origins system were finally eliminated by the Immigration Act of 1965, which allowed 170,000 persons a year to enter the United States, admission being determined on such grounds as skill and the need for political asylum. However, the law also put a limit of 120,000 on Western Hemisphere immigration, which had previously been unrestricted.

WHITNEY MUSEUM OF AMERICAN ART

In Baptism in Kansas *(1928) John Steuart Curry viewed sympathetically the sincerity and the depth of feeling that marked the revival of religious fundamentalism in much of rural America during the twenties. Curry was a leader of the rural regionalist painters, seeking, he said, to show the "struggle of man against nature."*

city in the 1920's, and the population living in centers of 100,000 or more increased by about a third. To both the scattered millions who still tilled the soil and to the other millions who lived in towns and small cities, the new city-oriented culture seemed sinful, overly materialistic, and unhealthy. But there was no denying its power and compelling fascination. Made even more aware of the appeal of the city by such modern improvements as radio and the automobile, farmers and townspeople coveted the comfort and excitement of city life at the same time that they condemned them. They fulminated against the metropolis, yet watched enviously as their sons and neighbors drifted off to taste its pleasures.

Out of this ambivalence developed some strange social phenomena, all exacerbated by the backlash of wartime emotions. Rural society, at once attracted and repelled by the city, responded by rigidly proclaiming the superiority of its own ways, as much to protect itself against temptation as to denounce urban life. Change, omnipresent in the postwar world, must be desperately resisted, even at the cost of individualism and freedom. The fact that those who held such views were in the majority, yet conscious that their majority was rapidly disappearing, explains their desperation, thus their intolerance.

One expression of this intolerance of modern urban values was the resurgence of religious fundamentalism. Although it was especially prevalent in certain Protestant sects, such as the Baptists and Presbyterians, fundamentalism was primarily an attitude of mind, profoundly conservative, rather than a religious idea. Fundamentalists rejected the theory of evolution, indeed, the whole mass of scientific knowledge about the origins of man and the universe that had been discovered during the 19th century. As we have seen, educated persons had been able to resolve the apparent contradictions between Darwin's theory and religious teachings easily enough, but in rural districts, especially in the southern and border states, this was never the case. Partly, fundamentalism resulted from simple ignorance; where educational standards were low and culture relatively static, old ideas remained unchallenged. Urban sophisticates tended to dismiss the fundamentalists as crude boors and hayseed fanatics, but the persistence of old-fashioned ideas was understandable enough. The power of reason, so obvious to men living in a technologically advanced society, seemed much less obvious to rural people. Even prosperous farmers, in close contact with the capricious, elemental power of nature, tended to have more respect for the force of divine providence than city folk. Beyond this, the majesty and beauty of the King James translation of the Bible, often the only book in rural homes, made it extraordinarily difficult for many persons to abandon their belief in its literal truth.

What made crusaders of the fundamentalists, however, was their resentment of the modern urban culture which had passed them by, and the emotional currents of the age. Although in some cases they did harass liberal ministers, their religious attitudes had little public significance; their efforts to impose their views on public education were another matter. The teaching of evolution must be prohibited, they insisted. Throughout the early twenties they campaigned vigorously for laws banning all mention of Darwin's theory in textbooks and classrooms.

Their greatest asset in this unfortunate crusade was William Jennings Bryan. Age had not improved the "Peerless Leader." Never a profound thinker, after leaving Wilson's Cabinet in 1915 he devoted much time to religious and moral issues without applying himself conscientiously to the study of these difficult questions. He went about charging that "they"—meaning the mass of educated Americans—had "taken the Lord away from the schools" and denouncing the expenditure of public money to undermine Christian principles. Bryan toured the country offering $100 to anyone who would admit that he was descended from an ape; his immense popularity in rural areas assured him a wide audience, and no one came forward to take his money.

The fundamentalists won a minor victory in 1925, when Tennessee passed a law forbidding instructors in the state's schools and colleges to teach "any theory that denies the story of the Divine Creation of man as taught in the Bible." The circumstances surrounding the passage of this law reveal that the fundamentalists possessed an influence all out of proportion to their actual numbers. Although the bill passed both houses by immense majorities, few of the legislators really approved of it. They voted "aye" only because they dared not expose themselves to charges that they disbelieved in the Bible. Educators in the state, hoping to obtain larger school appropriations from the legislature, hesitated to raise their voices in protest. Governor Austin Peay, an intelligent and liberal-minded man, also feared to veto the bill lest he jeopardize other measures he was backing. "Probably the law will never be applied," he predicted when he signed it. "Nobody believes that it is going to be an active statute." Even Bryan, who used his influence to obtain passage of the measure, urged—unsuccessfully—that it include no penalties.

Upon learning of the passage of this act, the American Civil Liberties Union announced that it would finance a test case challenging its constitutionality if a Tennessee teacher would deliberately violate the statute. Urged on by local friends, John T. Scopes, a young biology teacher in Dayton, reluctantly agreed to do so. He was arrested and bound over to the grand jury. After the judge had read the anti-evolution law and the opening chapters of Genesis to the jury, and after a number of high school students had testified as to his teachings, Scopes was indicted. A battery of nationally known lawyers came forward to defend him, while the state obtained the services of Bryan himself. The Dayton "Monkey Trial" became an overnight sensation.

Clarence Darrow, chief counsel for the defendant, stated the issue clearly. "Scopes isn't on trial," he said, "civilization is on trial. The prosecution is opening the doors for a reign of bigotry equal to anything in the Middle Ages. No man's belief will be safe if they win." The comic aspects of the trial obscured this issue. Big-city reporters like H.L. Mencken of the Baltimore *Evening Sun* flocked to Dayton to make sport of the fundamentalists. The town took on a carnival air, simple hill folk mingling with cynical urban sophisticates while back-country preachers delivered impromptu sermons in the courthouse square. The judge, John Raulston, a typical rural magistrate from the hamlet of Fiery Gizzard, Tennessee, was strongly prejudiced against the defendant, even refusing to permit expert testimony on the validity of evolutionary theory. The conviction of Scopes was a foregone conclusion; after the jury rendered its verdict, Judge Raulston fined him $100.

Nevertheless, the trial served to expose both the stupidity and danger of the fundamentalist position on education. The high point came when Bryan agreed to testify as an expert witness on the Bible. In a sweltering courtroom, both men in shirt sleeves, the lanky, roughhewn Darrow, one of the finest trial lawyers in the country, cross-examined the bland, aging champion of fundamentalism, mercilessly exposing his childlike faith and his abysmal ignorance. Bryan admitted to believing literally that the earth had been created in 4004 B.C., that a whale had swallowed Jonah, that Joshua had stopped the sun in its course, and that Eve had been created from Adam's rib.

The Monkey Trial ended in frustration for nearly everyone concerned. Scopes soon moved away from Dayton. Judge Raulston was defeated when he sought re-election to the bench. Bryan departed amid the cheers of his disciples only to die in his sleep a few days later. In 1930 his Dayton admirers founded William Jennings Bryan College in his honor, but the institution did not flourish—35 years later it had only about 250 students. Moreover, in retrospect the heroes of the Scopes trial—science, tolerance, freedom of thought—seem somewhat less stainless than they did to liberals at the time. The account of evolution in the textbook used by Scopes was far from satisfactory, yet it was advanced as unassailable fact. The book also contained statements that to the modern mind seem at least as bigoted as anything that Bryan said at Dayton. In a section on "the Races of Man," for example, it described Caucasians as "the highest type of all . . . represented by the civilized white inhabitants of Europe and America."

Prohibition: the "Noble Experiment"

The conflict between the countryside and the city, between the past and the future, was fought on many fronts, and in one sector the rural forces achieved a quick victory. This was the prohibition of the manufacture, transporting, and sale of alcoholic beverages by the Eighteenth Amendment, ratified in 1919. Although there were some big-city advocates of prohibition, on no issue did urban and rural views divide more clearly. In one key congressional test on prohibition, only 13 of 197 "yea" votes were cast by big-city representatives. The Eighteenth Amendment, in the words of historian Andrew Sinclair, marked a triumph of the "Corn Belt over the conveyor belt."

This rural victory was made possible by a peculiar set of circumstances. The temperance movement had been important since the age of Jackson, and by the Progressive Era many reformers, captivated by the idea that both human nature and society could be improved by law, were eager to prohibit drinking entirely. More than a quarter of the states were dry by 1914. The war also aided the prohibitionists by increasing the nation's need for food. The Lever Act of 1917 outlawed the use of grain in the manufacture of alcoholic beverages, primarily as a conservation measure. The prevailing dislike of foreigners helped the dry cause still more: beer-drinking was associated with Germans, wine consumption with Italians. To a large degree, the country was dry by 1917, although national prohibition did not become official until January 1920.

This "noble experiment," as Herbert Hoover called it, achieved a number of socially desirable results. Undoubtedly it cut down on the national consumption of alcohol; arrests for drunkenness fell off sharply, as did deaths from alcoholism. Fewer workingmen squandered their wages on drink. If the drys had been more reasonable—if they had permitted, for example, the use of beer and wine—the experiment might have worked. Instead, by insisting on total abstinence, they drove millions of moderates to direct violation of the law. In such circumstances, strict enforcement became impossible, especially in the cities.

The Prohibition Bureau had only between 1,500 and 3,000 agents to control the illicit liquor trade, and many of these were inefficient and corrupt. In areas where sentiment favored prohibition strongly, liquor remained very difficult to find. Elsewhere, anyone with sufficient money could obtain it easily; application of the Volstead Act (prohibition's enforcement statute) in such regions was never more than sporadic. Smuggling became a major business along the nation's 18,700-mile perimeter: in a single year the authorities seized $2 million worth of foreign spirits in Detroit alone, a tiny fraction of what actually came in. Private individuals busied themselves learning how to manufacture "bathtub gin," redistillation of industrial alcohol assumed the proportions of a major enterprise, fraudulent druggists' prescriptions for alcohol were issued freely, and illegal stills and breweries sprang up everywhere. *Bootlegger* became a household word. The saloon disappeared, replaced by the speakeasy, a supposedly secret bar or club, op-

MUSEUM OF THE CITY OF NEW YORK

Ben Shahn's Prohibition Alley *is a richly symbolic summary of the seamier side of the "noble experiment." Under a diagram of the workings of a still, bootleggers stack whisky smuggled in by ship, an operation eyed by Chicago gangster Al Capone. At left is a victim of gang warfare, at right, patrons outside a speakeasy.*

erating usually under the benevolent eye of the local police.

Inevitably most of the liquor traffic fell into the hands of gangsters, of whom Alphonse "Scarface Al" Capone of Chicago was only the most notorious. The gangsters hijacked one another's shipments, fought minor but bloody wars for control of their "territories," invested their profits in countless other businesses, legitimate and illegitimate. Their noxious influence pervaded law-enforcement agencies and other organs of government. Americans had never been a particularly law-abiding people, but in the twenties statistics on crime soared. Gangsters gunned down their enemies in broad daylight and bombed rival distilleries and warehouses without regard for passing innocents. Each year more men died violent deaths in Chicago alone than in the entire British Isles. Capone presided over an army of perhaps a thousand hoodlums and gunmen; the gross income of his enterprises, before he was finally jailed for income tax evasion in 1931, reached $60 million.

Prohibition widened already serious rifts in the social fabric of the country; its repressive spirit, interacting darkly with the lingering hostilities and ambivalent feelings characteristic of the times, pitted city against farm, native against immigrant, race against race. In the South, where the dominant whites had argued that prohibition would improve the morals of the ignorant Negro masses, Negroes actually became the chief bootleggers. "Instead of keeping the Negroes from vice," Andrew Sinclair writes in *Prohibition: The Era of Excess*, prohibition "put them in control of it."

Besides undermining public morality by encouraging hypocrisy and lawbreaking, prohibition had a vicious effect on the politics of the 1920's. It almost destroyed the Democratic party as a national organization; Democratic immigrants in the cities hated it, but southern Democrats sang its praises, often while continuing to drink themselves. The humorist Will Rogers quipped that Mississippi would vote dry "as long as the voters could stagger to the polls." The hypocrisy of prohibition had a particularly deleterious effect on politicians, a class seldom famous for candor. Congressmen catered to the demands of the powerful lobby of the Anti-Saloon League, yet failed to grant adequate funds to the Prohibition Bureau. Nearly all the prominent leaders, Democrat and Republican, from Wilson and La Follette to Hoover and Franklin D. Roosevelt, equivocated shamelessly on the liquor question. By the end of the decade almost every competent observer recognized that prohibition had failed, but the well-organized and powerful dry forces continued to reject all proposals for modifying it.

The Ku Klux Klan

By far the most horrible example of the social malaise of the 1920's was the spectacular revival of the Ku Klux Klan. Like its predecessor of reconstruction days, the new Klan began as an instrument for Negro repression in the South. In the reactionary postwar period many white southerners set out to undo the gains blacks had made during the war years. Lynchings increased in number; dreadful race riots broke out in a dozen cities in the summer and fall of 1919. The new Klan, founded in 1915 by William J. Simmons, an alcoholic former preacher with considerable experience as an organizer for fraternal organizations such as the Masons and Knights Templar, expanded rapidly in this atmosphere.

Simmons gave his society the kind of trappings and mystery calculated to attract gullible and bigoted men who yearned to express their frustrations and hostilities without personal risk. Klansmen masked themselves in white robes and hoods, enjoyed a childish mumbo jumbo of magnificent-sounding titles and dogmas (Kleagle, Klaliff, Kludd; kloxology, Kloran) mostly beginning with the letter *K*. They burned crosses, organized mass demonstrations to intimidate Negro voters, brought pressure on businessmen to fire Negro workers from better-paying jobs. When black men resisted, the Klan frequently employed more brutal means to achieve its ends.

By 1920, however, it was expanding into new areas and seeking out other victims. From the start it had admitted only native-born, white Protestants to membership. The distrust of foreigners, Catholics, and Jews implicit in this regulation burst into the open in a social climate that also spawned religious fundamentalism, immigration restriction, and prohibition. In addition, an agricultural depression sent cotton from 35 cents to 15 cents a pound in 1920, and wheat from $2.16 a bushel to $1.03 between 1919 and 1921, psychologically readying millions of potential Klansmen in the South and Middle West to vent their dissatisfactions in a nativist crusade for "100 per cent Americanism."

In 1920 two unscrupulous publicity agents, Edward Y. Clarke and Mrs. Elizabeth Tyler, got control of the movement and organized a massive membership drive, diverting a major share of the initiation fees into their own pockets. In a little over a year they enrolled 100,000 recruits and by 1923 claimed the astonishing total of 5 million.

The Klan had relatively little appeal in the northeast or in the largest metropolitan centers in any part of the country, but it found many members in middle-sized cities as well as in the small towns and villages of middle western and western states like Indiana, Ohio, and Oregon. The scapegoats in such regions were immigrants, Jews, and especially Catholics; the rationale, an urge to get back to an older, supposedly finer America and a desperate desire to stamp out all varieties of nonconformity. Klansmen "watched everybody," always themselves safe from observation behind their masks and robes. Posing as guardians of public and private morality, they persecuted gamblers, loose women, violators of the prohibition laws, as well as respectable persons who happened to differ from them on religious questions or who belonged to a "foreign race." They professed to believe that the pope intended to move his headquarters to the United States, that American bishops were stockpiling arms in their cathedrals, that Catholic traitors had already entrenched themselves in many branches of the government. The Klan also conducted crusades against unfriendly politicians and in some cases controlled the elections of governors and congressmen as well as countless local officials. Since a considerable percentage of its members were secret libertines and corruptionists, the dark, unconscious drives leading men to

A Ku Klux Klan initiation ceremony, photographed in Kansas in the 1920's. During its peak influence at mid-decade, Klan endorsement was essential to political candidates in many areas of the West and Midwest. Campaigning for re-election in 1924, an Indiana congressman testified, "I was told to join the Klan, or else."

KANSAS STATE HISTORICAL SOCIETY

join the organization are not hard to imagine.

Fortunately, the very success of the Klan led to its undoing. Factionalism sprang up and rival leaders squabbled over the large sums that had been collected from the membership. The cruel and outrageous behavior of the organization roused both liberals and decent conservatives in every part of the country. Klansmen themselves began to worry about the misuse of Klan funds. And, of course, its victims joined forces against their tormentors. When the powerful leader of the Indiana Klan, a middle-aged reprobate named David C. Stephenson, was convicted of assaulting and causing the death of a young woman, the rank and file abandoned the organization in droves. It remained influential for a number of years, contributing to the defeat of the Catholic Alfred E. Smith in the 1928 Presidential election, but it ceased to be a dynamic force after 1924. By 1930 it had only some 9,000 members.

Revolt of the Intellectuals

The malaise of postwar society produced dissatisfactions among urban sophisticates too, and among others who looked to the future rather than to the past. To many young people of that generation, the narrowness and prudery of the fundamentalists and the stuffy conservatism of the politicians seemed not merely old-fashioned but ludicrous. The repressiveness of redbaiters and Klansmen made them place an exaggerated importance on their right to express themselves in bizarre ways, the casual attitude of drinkers toward the prohibition laws encouraged

NEW SCHOOL FOR SOCIAL RESEARCH

Thomas Hart Benton, like Curry an artist of the rural regionalist school, found the impact of the "Jazz Age" on urban culture deeply disturbing. In this mural, painted for the New School for Social Research in New York about 1930, he emphasized the brutality and tawdriness of the city, that "coffin for living and thinking."

them to flout other institutions as well. The new psychology of Sigmund Freud, with its stress on man's animal nature and the importance of sex, persuaded many who had never actually read Freud to adopt what they called "emancipated" standards of behavior which Freud, himself a staid, highly moral man, had neither advocated nor practiced.

This was the "Jazz Age," the era of "flaming youth." Young people danced to wildly syncopated African rhythms, swilled bootleg liquor from pocket flasks, careened about the countryside in automobiles in search of pleasure and forgetfulness, made gods of movie stars and professional athletes. Women in particular threw off the restrictions of the past. The "modern" woman, often called a "flapper," wore knee-length skirts, bobbed her hair, smoked cigarettes, and drank cocktails in public places—all examples of behavior that would have marked her mother or grandmother as a prostitute or wanton. "Younger people," one shrewd observer noted as early as 1922, had only "contempt . . . for their elders." As a result, they were attempting "to create a way of life free from the bondage of an authority that has lost all meaning."

Conservatives bemoaned the breakdown of moral standards, the increasing popularity of divorce, the fragmentation of the family, and the decline of parental authority, and with some reason. Nevertheless, society was not collapsing. Much of the rebelliousness of the times was faddish in nature, soon to peter out. An encouragingly large percentage of the flappers and their swains soon settled down to commonplace, middle-class lives devoted to moneymaking and child-rearing.

However, the excesses of the fundamentalists, the xenophobes, the Klansmen, the redbaiters, and the prohibitionists disturbed American intellectuals profoundly—their resentment was not childish, no mere fad. Persons of culture and education found life in the twenties an affront to many deeply held beliefs. More and more they felt alienated from their surroundings, bitter and contemptuous of those who appeared to control the country. Yet their alienation came at the very time that society was growing more dependent

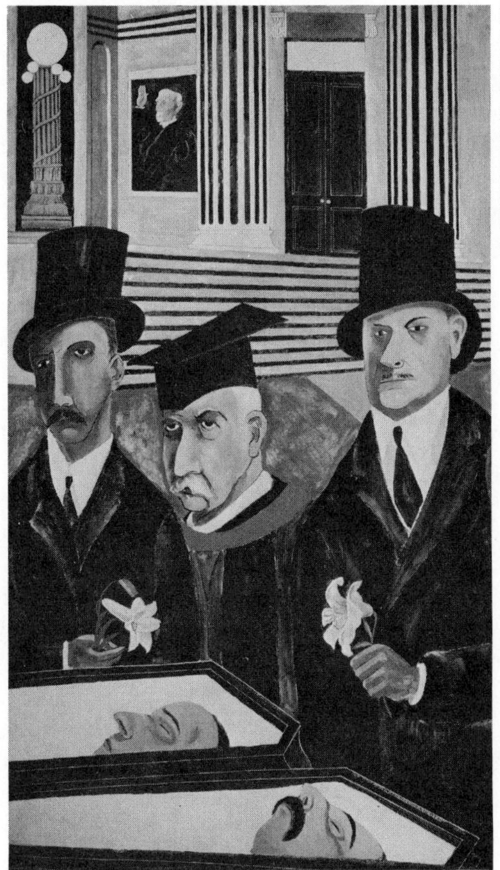

WHITNEY MUSEUM OF AMERICAN ART

In The Passion of Sacco and Vanzetti *Ben Shahn included the Lowell Committee (Harvard president Lowell at center) that "confirmed" the trial's fairness and an approving Judge Thayer (background).*

upon brains and sophistication; this compounded the confusion and disillusionment characteristic of the period.

Nothing demonstrates this fact so clearly as the Sacco-Vanzetti case. In April 1920 two men in South Braintree, Massachusetts, killed a paymaster and a guard in a daring daylight robbery of a shoe factory. Shortly thereafter, Nicola Sacco and Bartolomeo Vanzetti were charged with the crime, and in 1921 they were convicted of murder. Sacco and Vanzetti were anarchists and also Italian immigrants. Their trial was a travesty of justice. The presiding judge, Webster Thayer, conducted the proceedings like a prosecuting attorney; he even referred privately to the defendants as "those anarchist bastards."

The case became a *cause célèbre*. Prominent persons all over the world protested, and for years Sacco and Vanzetti were kept alive by efforts to obtain a new trial. Vanzetti's quiet dignity and courage in the face of death wrung the hearts of millions. "You see me before you, not trembling," he told the court. "I never commit a crime in my life. . . . I am so convinced to be right that if you could execute me two times, and if I could be reborn two other times, I would live again and do what I have done already." When, in August 1927, the two were at last electrocuted, the disillusionment of American intellectuals with current values was profound. Recent historians, impressed by modern ballistic studies of Sacco's gun, now suspect that he, at least, was actually guilty. Nevertheless, the truth and the shame remain: Sacco and Vanzetti paid with their lives for being radicals and aliens, not for any crime.

Literary Trends

The literature of the twenties perfectly reflects the disillusionment of the intellectuals. The prewar period had been an age of hopeful experimentation in the world of letters. Writers, applying the spirit of progressivism to the realism they had inherited from Howells and the naturalists, had been predominantly optimistic. Ezra Pound, for example, talked grandly of an American Renaissance and fashioned a new kind of poetry called Imagism, which, while not appearing to be realistic, abjured all abstract generalizations and concentrated upon concrete word pictures to convey meaning. "Little" magazines and experimental theatrical companies sprang to life by the dozens, each convinced that it would revolutionize its art. New York's Greenwich Village teemed with youthful Bohemians, contemptuous of middle-class values but too fundamentally cheerful to reject the modern world. In Chicago another new school of vigorous, reform-minded writers gathered. They, too, posed as rebels and innovators, yet nearly all expected to succeed in refashioning the world to their liking. The poet Carl Sandburg, best-known representative of the Chicago school, denounced the local plutocrats but sang the praises of the city they had made: "Hog Butcher for the World . . . City of the Big Shoulders." Most writers eagerly adopted Freudian psychology without really understanding it. Freud's teachings seemed only to mean that one should cast off the senseless restrictions of Victorian prudery; almost to a man they ignored his essentially dark view of human nature. Theirs was an "innocent rebellion," exuberant—and rather muddle-headed.

As historian Henry F. May has shown, writers, along with most other intellectuals, began to abandon this view about 1912, and the Great War completed the destruction of their optimism. Then the antics of the fundamentalists, the cruelty of the redbaiters, and the philistinism of the dull politicos of the day turned them into sharp critics of society. Ezra Pound, for example, dropped his talk of an American Renaissance and wrote instead of a "botched civilization." The soldiers, said he,

> walked eye-deep in hell
> believing in old men's lies, then unbelieving
> came home, home to a lie,
> home to deceits,
> home to old lies and new infamy;
> usury age-old and age-thick
> and liars in public places.

Yet out of this negativism came a literary flowering of major importance.

The herald of the new day was Henry Adams, whose autobiography, *The Education of Henry Adams*, was published posthumously in 1918. Adams' disillusionment long antedated the war, but his description of late-19th-century corruption and materialism and his warning that industrialism was crushing the human spirit beneath the weight of its machines appealed powerfully to those whose pessimism was newborn. Soon hundreds of bright young men and women were referring to themselves with a self-pity almost maudlin as the "lost generation," and either seeking refuge in hedonism or flight to Europe or systematically assaulting contemporary American society.

The symbol of the lost generation, in his own mind as well as to his contemporaries and to later critics, was F. Scott Fitzgerald. Born to modest

CHARLES SCRIBNER'S SONS

Ernest Hemingway (above), photographed at Key West, Florida, in 1929, the year that A Farewell to Arms *was published. Like Hemingway, F. Scott Fitzgerald (below) wrote some of his best work when an expatriate in Paris, including* The Great Gatsby.

BETTMANN ARCHIVE

wealth in St. Paul, Minnesota, in 1896, Fitzgerald rose to sudden fame in 1920 when he published *This Side of Paradise,* a somewhat sophomoric but patently accurate description of the mores and attitudes of modern youth. The novel captured the fears and confusions of the lost generation and also the façade of frenetic gaiety that concealed them; as Alfred Kazin has written, it "sounded all the fashionable lamentations" of the age. In *The Great Gatsby* (1925), a more mature work, Fitzgerald dissected a modern millionaire—coarse, unscrupulous, jaded, in love with another man's wife. Gatsby's tragedy lay in his dedication to this woman, who, Fitzgerald made clear, did not merit even his illicit passion. He lived in "the service of a vast, vulgar, meretricious beauty," and in the end, he understood this himself.

The tragedy of *The Great Gatsby* was related to Fitzgerald's own. Like Mark Twain he lusted after the very products of civilization he despised: money, glamour, the sensual satisfactions of the moment. Pleasure-loving and extravagant, he quickly squandered the money earned by *This Side of Paradise.* When *The Great Gatsby* failed to sell as well, he turned to writing potboilers. "I really worked hard as hell last winter," he told the critic Edmund Wilson, "but it was all trash and it nearly broke my heart." Although some of his later work was first class, he descended into the despair of alcoholism, ending his days as a Hollywood scriptwriter.

Many of the younger American writers and artists became expatriates in the twenties, flocking to Rome, Berlin, and especially to Paris, where they could live cheaply and escape what seemed to them the "conspiracy against the individual" prevalent in their own country. The *quartier latin* along the left bank of the Seine was a large-scale Greenwich Village in those days, full of artists and eccentrics of every sort. There the expatriates lived simply and freely, eking out a living as journalists, translators, and editors, perhaps turning an extra dollar from time to time by selling a story or a poem to an American magazine, a painting to a passing tourist.

Ernest Hemingway was the most talented of the expatriates. Born in 1898 in Illinois, Hemingway first worked as a reporter for the Kansas City *Star*. He served in the Italian army during the war, was grievously wounded (in spirit as well as in body), and then, after further newspaper experience, settled in Paris in 1922 to write. His first novel, *The Sun Also Rises* (1926), portrayed the café world of the expatriate and the rootless desperation, amorality, and sense of outrage at life's meaninglessness that obsessed so many in those years. In *A Farewell to Arms* (1929) he drew upon his military experiences to describe the confusion and horror of war.

Hemingway's books were best sellers and he became a legend in his own time, but his style rather than his ideas explain his towering reputation. Few novelists have been such self-conscious craftsmen or capable of suggesting powerful emotions and action in so few words. Mark Twain and Stephen Crane were his models, Gertrude Stein, a queer, revolutionary genius, his teacher, but his style was his own, direct, simple, taut, sparse:

> I went out the door and down the hall to the room where Catherine was to be after the baby came. I sat in a chair there and looked at the room. I had the paper in my coat that I had bought when I went out for lunch and I read it. . . . After a while I stopped reading and turned off the light and watched it get dark outside. (*A Farewell to Arms*)

> Nick opened the door and went into the room. Ole Anderson was lying on the bed with all his clothes on. He had been a heavyweight prize fighter and he was too long for the bed. He lay with his head on two pillows. He did not look at Nick.
>
> "What was it?" he asked.
>
> "I was up at Henry's," Nick said, "and two fellows came in and tied me up and the cook, and they said they were going to kill you."
>
> It sounded silly when he said it. Ole Anderson said nothing. . . . (*The Killers*)

This kind of writing, evoking rather than describing emotion, fascinated readers and inspired hundreds of imitators; it has made a permanent mark on world literature. What Hemingway had to say was of less universal interest. Despite his carefully controlled prose, he was an unabashed, rather muddled romantic, an adolescent emotionally. He wrote about bullfights, hunting, and fishing, violence of all sorts, and while he did so with masterful penetration, these themes placed limits on his work that he never transcended. The critic Kazin has summed him up in a sentence: "He brought a major art to a minor vision of life."

Although neither was the equal of Hemingway or Fitzgerald as an artist, two other writers of the twenties deserve mention: H.L. Mencken and Sinclair Lewis. Each reflected the distaste of intellectuals for the climate of the times. Mencken, a Baltimore-born newspaperman and columnist, founder of one of the great magazines of the era, the *American Mercury*, was a thoroughgoing cynic but never indifferent to those many aspects of American life that roused his contempt. He coined the word "booboisie" to define the complacent, middle-class majority and fired superbly witty broadsides at fundamentalists, prohibitionists, and "Puritans." Politics at once fascinated and repelled him. "The typical lawmaker," he wrote, "is a man wholly devoid of principle—a mere counter in a grotesque and knavish game. If the right pressure could be applied to him, he would be cheerfully in favor of polygamy, astrology, or cannibalism." As a political prognosticator he was frequently wrong, and his basic judgments were not always sound, but he was unfailingly interesting.

He assailed the statemen of his generation with magnificent impartiality:

> BRYAN: If the fellow was sincere, then so was P.T. Barnum. . . . He was, in fact, a charlatan, a mountebank, a zany without sense or dignity.
>
> WILSON: The bogus Liberal. . . . A pedagogue thrown up to 1000 diameters by a magic lantern.
>
> HARDING: The numskull, Gamaliel . . . the Marion stonehead. . . . The operations of his medulla oblongata . . . resemble the rattlings of a colossal linotype charged with rubber stamps.
>
> COOLIDGE: A cheap and trashy fellow, deficient in sense and almost devoid of any notion of honor—in brief, a dreadful little cad.
>
> HOOVER: Lord Hoover is no more than a pious old woman, a fat Coolidge. . . . He would have made a good bishop.

While amusing, Mencken's diatribes were not, of course, very profound. In perspective, he ap-

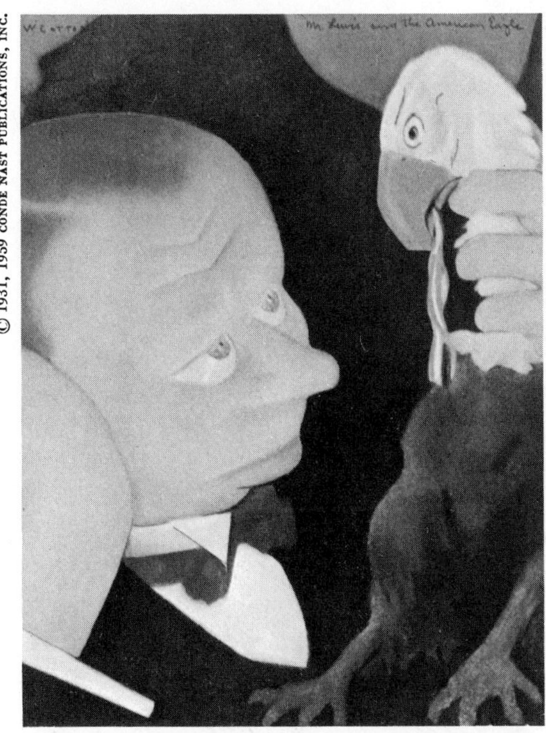

A baleful-looking Sinclair Lewis throttles the American eagle in this caricature by William Cotton that appeared in the magazine Vanity Fair *in 1931.*

peared more a professional iconoclast than a constructive critic; like both Fitzgerald and Hemingway, he was something of a perennial adolescent. He did, however, consistently support freedom of expression of every sort.

Sinclair Lewis was probably the most popular American novelist of the twenties. Like Fitzgerald, his first major work brought him instant fame and notoriety, and for the same reason. *Main Street* (1920) portrayed the smug ignorance and bigotry of the American small town so accurately that even Lewis' victims recognized themselves; his title became a symbol for provinciality and middle-class meanness. Next he created, in *Babbitt* (1922), an image of the businessman of the twenties, a "hustler," a "booster," blindly orthodox in his political and social opinions, slave to every cliché, gregarious, full of loud self-confidence yet underneath a bumbling, rather timid, decent fellow who would like to be better than he was but dared not. From this point Lewis went on to dissect a variety of American attitudes and occupations: the medical profession in *Arrowsmith* (1925), religion in *Elmer Gantry* (1927), fascism in *It Can't Happen Here* (1935), and many others.

Although his indictment of contemporary society rivaled Mencken's in savagery, Lewis was not a cynic. Superficially as objective as an anthropologist, he remained at heart committed to the way of life he was assaulting. His remarkable powers of observation depended upon his identification with the society he described. He was frustrated by the fact that his victims, recognizing themselves in his pages, accepted his criticisms with remarkable good temper and, displaying the very absence of intellectual rigor that he decried, cheerfully sought to reform. At the same time, lacking Mencken's ability to remain aloof, Lewis tended to value his own work in terms of its popular reception. He craved the good opinion and praise of his fellows. When he was awarded the Pulitzer prize for *Arrowsmith,* he petulantly refused it because it had not been offered earlier. He politicked shamelessly for a Nobel prize, which he received in 1930, the first American author to win this honor.

Lewis was pre-eminently a product of the twenties. When times changed, he could no longer portray society with such striking verisimilitude; none of his later novels approached the level of *Main Street* and *Babbitt.* When critics noticed this, Lewis became bewildered, almost disoriented. He died in 1951, a desperately unhappy man.

The New Negro

Both the disillusionment and the naive exuberance of the twenties affected American Negroes strongly. Even more than for white liberals, the postwar reaction brought bitter despair for many blacks. Aside from the obvious barbarities of the Klan, Negroes suffered from the postwar middle-class hostility to labor (and from the persistent refusal of organized labor to admit black workers to its ranks). The increasing presence of southern Negroes in the great northern cities also caused social conflict.

During the decade the exodus of Negroes from

PHILLIPS COLLECTION

Beginning in the 1930's black artist Jacob Lawrence painted a series of powerful "picture-narratives" dealing with the black experience in America. This painting, of southern Negroes crowding onto northbound trains during World War I, is the first of a 60-panel narrative that Lawrence titled "The Migration of the Negro."

the South continued; over 581,000 left the three southern states of Virginia, South Carolina, and Georgia alone. Some 393,000 Negroes settled in the three states of New York, Pennsylvania, and Illinois, most of these in New York City, Philadelphia, and Chicago. The black population of New York City more than doubled between 1920 and 1930, and in the latter year only one Negro in four in the city had been born in the state.

This enormous influx speeded the development of urban ghettos. In earlier periods Negroes in northern cities had tended to live together, but in many small neighborhoods scattered over large areas. Now the tendency was toward concentration. Harlem, a white, middle-class residential section of New York City as late as 1900–1910, had 50,000 blacks in 1914, 73,000 in 1920, and nearly 165,000 in 1930. The restrictions of ghetto life produced a vicious circle of degradation. Population growth and segregation caused a desperate housing shortage; rents in Harlem doubled between 1919 and 1927. Since the average Negro worker was unskilled and ill-paid, tenants were forced to take in boarders. Landlords converted private homes into rooming houses and allowed their properties to fall into disrepair, the process of decay speeded by the influx of what the Negro sociologist E. Franklin Frazier called "ignorant and unsophisticated peasant people" from the rural South, inexperienced in city living. Such conditions caused disease and crime rates to rise sharply. Infant mortality in Harlem was 111 per thousand in the 1920's, 64.5 per thousand for the city as a whole. Similar conditions existed in the Negro quarters of every large northern city.

Coming after the rising hopes inspired by wartime gains, the disappointments of the 1920's produced a new militancy among many Negroes. As early as 1919 W.E.B. Du Bois wrote in the

Crisis: "We are cowards and jackasses if . . . we do not marshal every ounce of our brain and brawn to fight . . . against the forces of hell in our own land." He increased his commitment to black nationalism, organizing a series of Pan African Conferences in an effort—futile as it turned out—to create an international Negro movement.

Du Bois, however, remained somewhat confused in his thinking. He never really made up his mind whether to work for integration or black separatism. Such ambivalence never troubled Marcus Garvey, a West Indian whose Universal Negro Improvement Association attracted hundreds of thousands of followers in the early twenties. Garvey had nothing but contempt for whites, for light-skinned Negroes like Du Bois, and for organizations such as the NAACP which sought to bring whites and blacks together to fight segregation and other forms of prejudice. "Back to Africa" was his slogan; the black man must "work out his salvation in his motherland." (Paradoxically, Garvey's ideas won the enthusiastic support of the Ku Klux Klan and other white racist groups.)

Garvey's message was naive and overly simple, but it served to build racial pride among the masses of poor and unschooled Negroes. He dressed in elaborate braided uniforms, wore a plumed hat, drove about in an expensive limousine. Both God and Christ were black, he insisted. He organized Negro-run businesses of many sorts, including a company that manufactured black dolls for Negro children. He established a corps of Black Cross nurses, and a Black Star Line Steamship Company to transport Negroes back to Africa. Negro leaders like Du Bois detested him, and, in truth, he was something of a charlatan as well as a terrible businessman. In 1923 his steamship line went into bankruptcy and he was convicted of defrauding thousands of his supporters who had invested in its stock and he was sent to prison. Nevertheless, his message, if not his methods, helped to create the "new" Negro, proud of his color and his heritage and prepared to resist both white mistreatment and white ideas: "Up, you mighty race, you can accomplish what you will!"

The new urban ghettos produced certain compensating advantages for Negroes. One effect, not fully utilized until later, was to increase their political power by enabling them to elect representatives to state legislatures and to Congress, and to exert great influence on the parties in closely contested elections. More immediately, city life stimulated Negro self-confidence; despite their horrors, the ghettos offered economic opportunity, political rights, freedom from the day-to-day debasements of southern life, above all a black world where black men and women could be themselves. In the ghettos, Negro writers, musicians, and artists found both an audience and the "spiritual emancipation" that unleashed their cultural capacities. Harlem in particular, the largest Negro city in the world, became a cultural capital, center of the "Harlem Renaissance." Negro newspapers and magazines flourished, along with theatrical companies, libraries, and the like. Du Bois opened the *Crisis* to young Negro writers and artists, and a dozen "little" magazines sprang up. Langston Hughes, one of the finest poets of the era, has described the exhilaration of his first arrival in this city within a city, a "magnet" for every black intellectual and artist. "Harlem! I . . . dropped my bags, took a deep breath, and felt happy again."

For Hughes and for thousands of less talented Negroes, the twenties, despite the persistence of prejudice and the sordidness of the ghettos, was a time of hope. Sociologists and psychologists (to whom, incidentally, the ghettos were indispensable social laboratories), were demonstrating that environment rather than heredity was preventing Negro progress. Together with the achievements of creative Negroes, which were for the first time being appreciated by white intellectuals, these new discoveries seemed to herald the decline and eventual disappearance of race prejudice. The black man, wrote Alain Locke in *The New Negro* (1925), "lays aside the status of beneficiary and ward for that of a collaborator and participant in American civilization." Alas, as Locke and other black intellectuals were soon to discover, this prediction, like so many others made in the 1920's, was to be proved tragically inaccurate.

The Era of "Normalcy"

The men who presided over the government of the United States during this era were Warren G. Harding of Ohio and Calvin Coolidge of Massachusetts. Harding was a newspaperman by trade, publisher of the Marion *Star*, with previous political experience as a legislator and lieutenant governor in his home state and as a United States senator. No President, before or since, looked more like a statesman; few were less suited for running the country. Coolidge, a taciturn New England type with a long record in Massachusetts politics climaxed by his inept but much-admired handling of the Boston police strike while governor, made a less impressive appearance than Harding and did not much excel him as a leader. "Don't hurry to legislate," was one of his slogans. He preferred to follow public opinion and hope for the best. "Mr. Coolidge's genius for inactivity is developed to a very high point," the correspondent Walter Lippmann wrote. "It is a grim, determined, alert inactivity, which keeps Mr. Coolidge occupied constantly."*

Harding won the 1920 Republican nomination because the party convention could not decide between General Leonard Wood, who represented the Roosevelt faction, and Frank Lowden, governor of Illinois. His genial nature and lack of strong convictions made him attractive to many of the politicos after eight years of the headstrong Wilson. During the campaign he exasperated sophisticates by his ignorance and imprecision. He coined the famous vulgarism "normalcy" as a substitute for the word "normality," referred, during a speech before a group of actors, to Shakespeare's play "Charles the Fifth," and committed numerous other blunders. "Why does he not get a private secretary who can clothe . . . his 'ideas' in the language customarily used by educated men?" one Boston gentleman demanded of Senator Lodge, who was strongly supporting Harding. Lodge, ordinarily a stickler for linguistic exactitude, replied acidly that he found Harding a paragon by comparison with Wilson, "a man who wrote English very well without ever saying anything." A large majority of the voters, untroubled by the candidate's lack of erudition, shared Lodge's confidence that he would be a vast improvement over Wilson.

*Coolidge was physically delicate, being plagued by chronic stomach trouble. He required 10 or 11 hours of sleep a day.

Harding was intelligent enough to appreciate his own limitations but lacked the will power to resist when offered the nomination. He paid a high price, both in personal well-being and in reputation, for his weakness. He has often been characterized as lazy and incompetent, but he was actually both hard-working and politically shrewd; his true difficulties were indecisiveness and an unwillingness to offend. He turned the most important government departments over to efficient administrators of impeccable reputation. Charles Evans Hughes, who became secretary of state, conducted the nation's foreign affairs with distinction if not brilliance. Herbert Hoover in the Commerce Department, Andrew Mellon in the Treasury, and Henry C. Wallace in Agriculture also ran their organizations efficiently. Harding kept track of what they did but seldom initiated policy in their areas. However, many lesser offices, and a few of major importance, Harding gave to the unsavory "Ohio Gang," headed by Harry M. Daugherty, whom he made attorney general.

The President was too kindly, too well-intentioned, too unambitious to be dishonest. He appointed corruptionists like Daugherty, Secretary of the Interior Albert B. Fall, Director of the Mint "Ed" Scobey, and Charles R. Forbes, head of the new Veterans Bureau, out of a sense of personal obligation or because they were old friends who shared his taste for poker and liquor. Before 1921 he had greatly enjoyed officeholding; he was a good politician, adept at mouthing platitudes on the stump, at home in the easy good-fellowship of the Senate cloakrooms, a loyal party man who seldom questioned the decisions of his superiors. In the lonely eminence of the White House, whence, as President Harry Truman later said, the buck cannot be passed, he found only misery. "The White House is a prison," he complained. "I can't get away from the men who dog my footsteps. I am in jail."

In domestic affairs Secretary of the Treasury

Mellon, multimillionaire banker and master of the aluminum industry, dominated the Harding administration. Mellon set out to lower the taxes of the rich, reverse the low tariff policies of the Wilson period, return to the laissez-faire philosophy of McKinley, and reduce the national debt by cutting expenses and administering the government more efficiently. In principle, his program had considerable merit. Wartime tax rates, designed to check consumer spending as well as to raise the huge sums needed to defeat the Central Powers, were undoubtedly hampering economic expansion in the early twenties. Certain industries such as chemicals, silks and rayons, and toys, which had sprung up in the United States for the first time during the Great War, were suffering acutely from German and Japanese competition now that the fighting had ended. Rigid regulations necessary during a national crisis could well be dispensed with in peacetime. And efficiency and economy in government are always desirable.

Mellon, however, carried his policies to unreasonable extremes. To reduce the national debt he insisted that the Allies repay the money they had borrowed to the last dollar, not seeing that protective tariffs on European products would deprive them of the means of accumulating dollar credits to meet their obligations. Mellon also proposed eliminating inheritance taxes and reducing the tax on high incomes by two-thirds in order to stimulate investment, but he opposed lower rates for taxpayers earning less than $66,000 a year, apparently not realizing that economic expansion required greater mass consumption as well. Mellon actually suggested increasing the tax burden on the average man by doubling certain excises, raising postal rates, and imposing a federal levy on automobiles. By freeing the rich from "oppressive" taxation, he argued, they would be able to invest in risky but potentially productive enterprises, the success of which would create jobs for ordinary people. Little wonder that Mellon's admirers called him "the greatest Secretary of the Treasury since Alexander Hamilton."

Although the Republicans had large majorities in both houses of Congress, Mellon's proposals were too drastically reactionary to win unqualified approval. Somewhat halfheartedly, Congress did pass a Budget and Accounting Act (1921), creating a director of the budget to assist the President in preparing a unified budget for the government, and a comptroller general to audit all government accounts. A general budget had long been needed; previously Congress had dealt with the requirements of each department separately, trusting largely to luck that income and expenditures would balance at year's end. The appointment of a comptroller general enabled Congress to check up on how the departments actually used the sums granted them.

Mellon's tax and tariff program, however, ran into stiff opposition from middle-western Republicans and southern Democrats, who combined to form the so-called "Farm Bloc." The cause of this alignment was essentially economic. The revival of European agriculture was cutting the demand for American farm produce just when the increased use of fertilizers and machinery was boosting output. As in the era after the Civil War, farmers found themselves burdened with heavy debts while their dollar income dwindled. In the decade after 1919 their share of the national income fell by nearly 50 per cent. The Farm Bloc represented a kind of conservative populism, economic grievances combining with a general prejudice against "Wall Street financiers" and rich industrialists to unite agriculture against "the interests."

Mellon epitomized everything the Farm Bloc disliked. Rejecting his more extreme suggestions, it pushed through the Revenue Act of 1921, which abolished the excess-profits tax and cut the top income tax rate from 73 to 50 per cent, but raised the tax on corporate profits slightly and left inheritance taxes untouched. Three years later Congress cut the maximum income tax to 40 per cent but reduced taxes on lower incomes significantly and raised inheritance levies. The Farm Bloc also overhauled Mellon's tariff proposals, placing heavy duties on agricultural products in 1921 while refusing to increase the rates on most manufactured goods. Although the Fordney-McCumber Tariff of 1922 granted more than adequate protection to the "infant industries" (rayon, china, toys, and chemicals), it held to the Wilsonian principle of moderate protection for most industrial products. Agricultural machinery and certain other items important to farmers remained on the free list. The act also authorized the President, upon the recommendation of the Tariff Commission, to raise or lower any rate by as much as 50 per cent. However, the changes made under this provision by Harding and Coolidge were all trivial.

Mellon nevertheless succeeded in balancing the budget and reducing the national debt. The first director of the budget, Charles G. Dawes, a Chicago banker, cut the requests of the departments drastically; government expenditures fell from $6.4 billion in 1920 to $3.3 billion in 1922 and a low of $2.9 billion in 1927. Throughout the twenties the national debt shrank an average of over $500 million a year. So committed were the Republican leaders to retrenchment that they even resisted the demands of veterans, organized in the politically potent American Legion, for an "adjusted compensation" bonus. Arguing not entirely without reason that they had served for a pittance while war workers had been drawing down high wages, the veterans sought grants equal to a dollar a day for their period in uniform ($1.25 for time overseas). Congress responded sympathetically, but both Harding and Coolidge vetoed bonus bills in the name of economy. Finally, in 1924, a compromise bill granting the veterans paid-up life insurance policies was passed over Coolidge's veto.

The business community heartily approved the policies of Harding and Coolidge, as indeed it should have, since both were uncritical advocates of the business point of view. "We want less government in business and more business in government," Harding pontificated, to which Coolidge added the slogan: "The business of the United States is business." Besides pushing a reluctant Congress as far as it would go on tax and tariff matters, Harding and Coolidge used their executive powers to convert regulatory bodies like the Interstate Commerce Commission and the Federal Reserve Board into pro-business agencies. Harding put a pro-railroad congressman, John J. Esch, on the ICC and Coolidge added Thomas F. Woodlock, another archconservative. Harding made Daniel R. Crissinger, one of his second-rate cronies from Marion, governor of the Federal Reserve Board, and V.W. Van Fleet, a thoroughly mediocre Indiana politician, a member of the Federal Trade Commission. Coolidge named William E. Humphrey, whom Senator George W. Norris called "a fearless advocate of big business," to the FTC. With such men in charge, the regulatory agencies ceased almost entirely to restrict the activities of the industries they were supposed to be controlling. As one bemused academic observer put it, the FTC seemed, throughout the twenties, to be trying to commit hara-kiri. Senator Norris, an uncompromising supporter of progressive ideals, characterized these Harding-Coolidge appointments as "the nullification of federal law by a process of boring from within."

The Harding Scandals

At least Mellon and the other pro-business leaders of this period were honest. The "Ohio Gang," however, used its power in the most blatantly corrupt way imaginable. Jesse Smith, a crony of Attorney General Daugherty, was what today would be called an "influence peddler" extraordinary. When his venality was exposed in 1923, he committed suicide. Charles R. Forbes of the Veterans Bureau siphoned millions of dollars appropriated for the construction of hospitals into his own pocket. When he was found out, Forbes fled to Europe and resigned. Later he returned, stood trial, and was sentenced to two years in prison. His assistant, Charles F. Cramer, committed suicide. Daugherty himself was deeply implicated in the fraudulent return of German assets seized by the Alien Property Custodian to their original owners. He escaped imprisonment only by refusing to testify on the ground that he might incriminate himself. Thomas W. Miller, the alien property custodian, was sent to jail for accepting a bribe.

The worst of these scandals involved Secretary of the Interior Albert B. Fall, a former senator. Although Harding had put Fall in the Cabinet chiefly because he liked him, opposition to the

MEMPHIS *Commercial Appeal*

When the Teapot Dome scandal broke in 1924, a newspaper cartoonist suggested its political repercussions with this drawing, "Assuming definite shape."

appointment had come only from conservationists interested in the national forest reserves; no one considered him morally unfit. However, in 1921, after arranging with the complaisant Secretary of the Navy Edwin Denby for the transfer to the Interior Department of government oil reserves being held for the future use of the navy, Fall leased these properties to private oil companies. Edward L. Doheny's Pan-American Petroleum Company got the Elk Hills reserve in California, and the Teapot Dome reserve in Wyoming was turned over to Harry F. Sinclair's Mammoth Oil Company. When critics protested, Fall announced that it was necessary to develop the Elk Hills and Teapot Dome properties because adjoining private drillers were draining off the navy's oil. Nevertheless, in 1923 the Senate ordered a full-scale investigation, conducted by Senator Thomas J. Walsh of Montana. It soon came out that Doheny had "lent" Fall $100,000 in hard cash, handed over secretly in a "little black bag." Sinclair had given Fall over $300,000 in cash and negotiable securities. Although the three culprits escaped conviction on the charge of conspiring to defraud the government, Sinclair was sentenced to nine months in jail for contempt of the Senate and for tampering with a jury, while Fall was fined $100,000 and given a year in prison for accepting a bribe. In 1927 the Supreme Court revoked the leases and the two big reserves were returned to the government.

The public still knew little of the scandals when, in June 1923, Harding left Washington on a western speaking tour, which included a visit to Alaska. His health was poor, his spirits low, for he had begun to understand how his "God-damn friends," as he put it, had betrayed him. Returning from Alaska late in July, he came down with what his physician, an incompetent crony from Ohio whom he had made surgeon general of the United States, diagnosed as ptomaine poisoning resulting from his having eaten a tainted Japanese crab. Actually, the President had suffered a heart attack. After briefly rallying, he died in San Francisco on August 2.

Few Presidents have been more deeply mourned by the people at the moment of their passing. Harding's kindly nature, his very ordinariness, increased his human appeal. "Our hearts are broken; we are sore stricken with the sense of loss," one minister declared. Three million persons viewed the Presidential coffin as it passed across the country. Soon, however, as the scandals came to light, sadness turned to scorn and contempt. The poet E.E. Cummings came closer to catching the final judgment of Harding's contemporaries than has any historian:

the first president to be loved by his
bitterest enemies" is dead

the only man woman or child who wrote
a simple declarative sentence with seven grammatical
errors "is dead"
beautiful Warren Gamaliel Harding
"is" dead
he's
"dead"
if he wouldn't have eaten them Yapanese Craps
somebody might hardly never not have been
unsorry, perhaps

Coolidge Prosperity

Had he lived, Harding might well have been defeated in 1924 because of the scandals. But Vice President Coolidge, unconnected with the troubles and not the type to surround himself with cronies of any kind, seemed the ideal man to clean out the corruptionists. After he replaced Attorney General Daugherty with the eminently respectable Harlan Fiske Stone, dean of the Columbia Law School, the Harding scandals ceased to be a serious political handicap for the Republicans.

Coolidge soon became the darling of the conservatives. His admiration for businessmen and his devotion to laissez faire knew no limit. "The man who builds a factory builds a temple," he said in all seriousness. "The Government can do more to remedy the economic ills of the people by a system of rigid economy in public expenditure than can be accomplished through any other action." Andrew Mellon, whom he continued in office as secretary of the treasury, was his ideal and mentor in economic affairs.

In 1924 Coolidge won the Republican nomination easily, but the Democrats, badly split, required 103 ballots to choose a candidate. The southern, dry, anti-immigrant, pro-Klan wing had fixed upon William G. McAdoo, Wilson's secretary of the treasury. The eastern, urban, wet element supported Governor Alfred E. Smith of New York, child of the slums, a Catholic, who had compiled a distinguished record in the field of social welfare legislation. After days of futile politicking, the party compromised on John W. Davis, a conservative corporation lawyer closely allied with the Morgan interests. Dismayed by the conservatism of both Coolidge and Davis, the aging Robert M. La Follette, backed by the Farm Bloc, the Socialist party, the American Federation of Labor, and numbers of intellectuals, entered the race as the candidate of a new Progressive party. The progressives adopted a neopopulist platform calling for the nationalization of railroads, the direct election of the President, the protection of labor's right to bargain collectively, and other reforms. La Follette stressed the perennial monopoly issue; his chief objective, he said, was to remove "the combined power of private monopoly over the political and economic life of the American people."

The situation was almost exactly the opposite of 1912, when one conservative had run against two liberals yet been swamped. Coolidge received 15.7 million votes, Davis 8.4 million, La Follette only 4.8 million. In the Electoral College La Follette won only his native Wisconsin, Coolidge defeating Davis by 382 to 136. Conservatism was clearly the dominant mood of the country, not merely of the business classes. A few years later, James M. Beck, one of the nation's most vocal and uncompromising reactionaries, was elected to Congress by a Philadelphia slum district, "a place of endless rows of shabby, featureless houses, inhabited by immigrants and Negroes," by a vote of 60,000 to 2,000.

The glorification of the antedeluvian and inert Coolidge and of the "New Era" over which he presided had its origin in the unprecedented prosperity that the nation enjoyed during his reign. After a brief but sharp slump in 1921 and 1922, business had boomed, real wages increased, and unemployment declined. The number of millionaires rose from about 4,500 in 1914 to 11,000 in 1926. The United States was as rich as all Europe; perhaps 40 per cent of the world's total wealth lay in American hands. Little wonder that thousands came to believe that no one should tamper with the marvelous economic machine that was yielding such bounty.

Prosperity rested on a variety of bases, one of which, it must be admitted, was the friendly, hands-off attitude of the government, which bolstered the confidence of the business community. The Federal Reserve Board, at some risk of inflation, consistently kept interest rates low, a further stimulus to economic growth. Pent-up wartime demand helped also to power the boom. The construction business in particular profited from a series of extremely busy years. The continuing mechanization and rationalization of industry provided a more fundamental stimulus to the economy. From heavy road-grading equipment and concrete mixers to devices for making cigars and glass tubes, from pneumatic tools to the dial telephone, machinery was replacing human hands at an ever more rapid rate, a truth demonstrated by the remarkable fact that industrial output almost doubled between 1921 and 1929 without any substantial increase in the industrial labor force. Greater use of power, especially of electricity, also encouraged expansion—

by 1929 the United States was producing more electricity than the rest of the world combined. Most important of all, American manufacturing was experiencing an amazing improvement in efficiency. The method of breaking down the complex processes of production into many simple operations and the use of interchangeable parts, turned out by precise machine tools, were 19th-century innovations, but in the 1920's they were adopted on an almost universal scale. The moving assembly line which carried the product to the worker, first devised by Henry Ford in his automobile plant in the decade before the Great War, speeded production and reduced costs. The time-and-motion studies of Frederick W. Taylor, developed early in the century, were applied in hundreds of factories after the war. Taylor's minute analyses of each step and movement in the manufacturing process and his emphasis upon speed and efficiency alarmed some union leaders, but no one could deny the effectiveness of his "scientific shop management" methods.

The growing ability of manufacturers to create new consumer demands also stimulated the economy. Advertising and salesmanship were raised almost to the status of fine arts. Bruce Barton, one of the advertising "geniuses" of the era, wrote a best-selling book, *The Man Nobody Knows* (1925), in which he described Jesus as the "founder of modern business," the man who "picked up twelve men from the bottom ranks . . . and forged them into an organization that conquered the world." By 1929 American businessmen were spending over $1.8 billion a year on advertising. Producers concentrated on making their goods more attractive and on changing models frequently to entice buyers into the market. Easy credit, accompanied by an expansion of the practice of selling goods on the installment plan, helped bring expensive items within the reach of the masses. Inventions and technological advances created a host of new or improved products, from radios, automobiles, and electric appliances like vacuum cleaners and refrigerators to gadgets like cigarette lighters and new forms of entertainment like motion pictures, which became, during the twenties, one of the ten largest industries in the country. Materials such as aluminum, synthetic fibers, and plastics gave rise to new industries and led to the development of many more new products.

These factors interacted one with another, serving to increase the effects of each much the way the textile industry in the early 19th century and the railroad industry after the Civil War had been the "multipliers" of earlier eras. Undoubtedly, the automobile had the single most important impact on the nation's economy in the twenties. Although well over a million cars a year were being regularly produced by 1916, the real expansion of the industry came after 1921. Output reached 2.2 million in 1922 and 3.6 million in 1923. It fell below the latter figure only twice during the remainder of the decade. By 1929, 23 million private cars clogged the highways, an average of only slightly less than one per family.

The auto industry also created other industries, such as the manufacture of tires and spark plugs. It consumed immense quantities of rubber, paint, glass, nickel, and, of course, petroleum products. It triggered the most gigantic road-building program in history: there were 387,000 miles of paved roads in the United States in 1921, 662,000 in 1929. Hundreds of manufacturers turned out

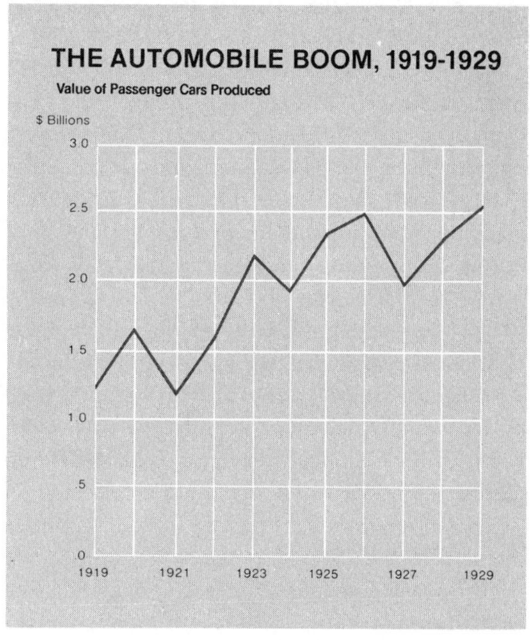

gadgets to decorate, clean, and improve the performance of automobiles; thousands of persons found employment in filling stations, roadside stands, and other businesses catering to the motoring public. The tourist industry profited and the already growing shift of the population from the cities to the suburbs was much accelerated.

Henry Ford The man most directly responsible for the growth of the automobile industry was Henry Ford, a self-taught mechanic from Greenfield, Michigan. Ford was not a great inventor or even one of the true automobile pioneers. He had two great insights. The first, as he said, was "Get the prices down to the buying power." Through mass production, cars could be made cheaply enough to bring them within reach of the ordinary citizen. In 1908 he designed the famous Model T Ford, a simple, tough box on wheels, powered by a light, durable, easily repaired engine. In a year he proved his point by selling 11,000 Model T's. Thereafter, relentlessly cutting costs and increasing efficiency by installing the assembly-line system, he expanded production at an unbelievable rate. By 1914 he could put a car together in his plant in 93 minutes. By 1925 he was turning out over 9,000 cars a day, one approximately every ten seconds, and the price of the Model T had been reduced to below $300.

Secondly, Ford grasped the importance of high wages as a means of stimulating output (and incidentally selling more automobiles). The assembly line simplified the laborer's task and increased the pace of work at the same time that it made each man much more productive. Jobs became both boring and fatiguing, absenteeism and labor turnover serious problems. To combat this difficulty, in 1914 Ford established the $5 day, an increase of about $2 over prevailing wages in the industry. At once the rate of turnover in his plant fell 90 per cent, and although critics charged that he recaptured his additional labor costs by speeding up the line, his policy had a revolutionary effect upon American wage rates. Later he raised the minimum to $6 and then to $7 a day.

Ford's profits soared along with sales, and since he owned the entire company himself, he became enormously wealthy, actually a billionaire. Throughout the twenties he cleared an average of about $25,000 *a day*. He also became an authentic folk hero: his homespun simplicity, his dislike of bankers and sophisticated society, his intense individualism endeared him to millions. He stood as a symbol of the wonders of the American system—he had given the nation a marvelous convenience at a low price, at the same time enriching himself and raising the living standards of his thousands of employees.

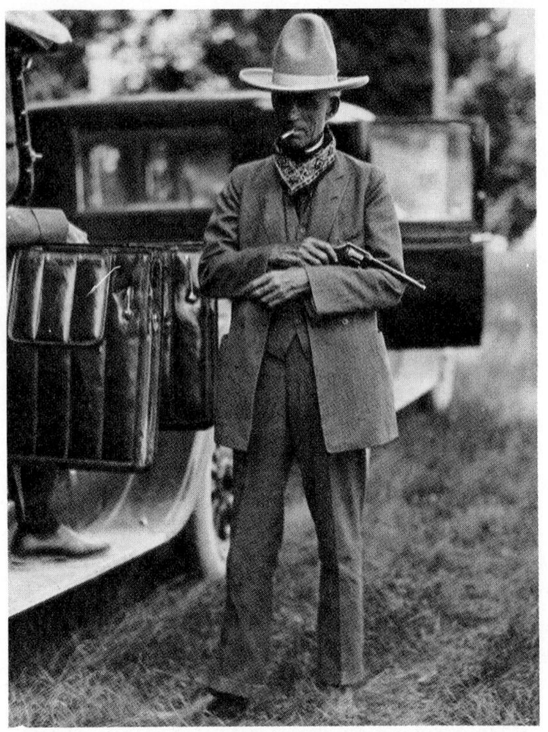
FORD MOTOR COMPANY

According to his biographer, Allan Nevins, Ford's complex personality included the characteristics of "a wry, cross-grained, brilliant adolescent." Here, on a summer outing, Ford poses as a western badman.

Unfortunately, Ford had the defects of his virtues in full measure. He paid high wages but tyrannized over his workers, refusing to deal with any union, employing spies to check up on the private lives of his help and gangsters and bully boys to enforce plant discipline. When he discovered a worker driving any car but a Ford, he had him instantly dismissed. So close was the supervision in the factory that the men devised the "Ford whisper," a means of talking without moving the lips. Success also made Ford stubborn. The Model T remained essentially unchanged for nearly 20 years and although no one could compete with it in terms of price, other companies, most notably General Motors, were soon turning out far better vehicles for very little more money. Customers, increasingly affluent and style-conscious, began to shift to Chevrolets and Chryslers. Gradually Ford's share of the market declined. Finally, in 1927, he shut down all operations for 18 months in order to retool for the Model A, his competitors rushing in during this period to fill the vacuum. Although his company continued to make a great deal of money, Ford never regained the dominant position he had held for so long. In truth, the age of the great individualistic tycoon was ending; he was replaced by the business "team" made up of "organization men."

Ford was enormously uninformed, yet—because of his success and the praise the world heaped upon him—he did not hesitate to speak out on subjects far outside his area of competence, from the evils of drink and tobacco to medicine and international affairs. He developed political ambitions, engaged in virulent anti-Semitic propaganda through his newspaper, the Dearborn *Independent,* said he would not give five cents for all the art in the world. While praising his talents as a manufacturer, historians have not dealt kindly with Ford the man, in part, no doubt, because he once said: "History is more or less the bunk."

Economic Problems

Like Ford, its outstanding success, the American economic system of the twenties had also grave flaws. Certain industries—coal and textiles, for example—did not share in the good times. The coal business, suffering from the competition of petroleum and electricity, entered a period of decline. Textile production lagged, and the industry began to be plagued by falling profit margins and chronic unemployment. In both these businesses, labor troubles multiplied. Moreover, the movement toward consolidation in industry, somewhat checked during the latter part of the Progressive Era, resumed during the twenties. By 1929 the 200 largest corporations controlled nearly half the nation's corporate assets. About 1 per cent of the public utility companies accounted for over 80 per cent of production. General Motors, Ford, and Chrysler turned out nearly 90 per cent of all American cars and trucks. Four tobacco companies produced over 90 per cent of the cigarettes. While banking capital doubled, the number of banks declined: 1 per cent of all financial institutions controlled 46 per cent of the nation's banking business and great concerns like Kuhn, Loeb and Company and the House of Morgan extended their already immense influence over the major industries of the country. Even retail merchandising, traditionally the domain of the small shopkeeper, reflected the trend. The A & P food chain expanded from 400 stores in 1912 to 5,000 in 1922 and 17,500 in 1928. The Woolworth chain of five-and-ten-cent stores flourished. Drug, Incorporated, a holding company, controlled over 10,000 drugstores and several important drug manufacturing concerns by 1929.

Consolidation did not necessarily lead to monopoly, for most great manufacturers, aware that bad public relations resulting from the unbridled use of monopolistic power outweighed any immediate economic gain, sought stability and "fair" prices rather than the maximum profit possible at the moment. "Regulated" competition was the order of the day, oligopoly the typical situation. The trade association movement expanded; producers in various industries formed voluntary organizations to exchange information, discuss policies toward government and the public, and "administer" prices. Usually the largest corporation, such as U.S. Steel in the iron and steel business, became the "price leader," its competitors, some themselves giants, following slavishly.

The success of the trade associations depended partly upon the attitude of the federal government, for such organizations might well have been attacked under the antitrust laws. But Harding and Coolidge considered them desirable. Their secretary of commerce, Herbert Hoover, put the facilities of his department at the disposal of these associations. "We are passing from a period of extremely individualistic action into a period of associational activities," Hoover stated. More important, however, were the good times. With profits high and markets expanding, the most powerful producers could afford to share the bounty with smaller, less efficient competitors. Thus industrial self-restraint and the pro-business attitudes of the Republican administrations account for the lax enforcement of the antitrust laws. The one major action under the Sherman Act during the period, a suit against the National Cash Register Company, resulted only in a $50 fine imposed on one executive of the corporation.

The most important weak spot in the economy was agriculture. In addition to the slump in farm prices caused by overproduction, farmers' expenses mounted steadily in boom times. Besides having to purchase expensive machinery in order to compete, their psychological needs were increasing. Every self-respecting farmer felt he had to own an automobile in the era of the Model T, and conveniences like electricity and good plumbing seemed equally essential. Conditions became steadily worse because per-acre yields rose rapidly, chiefly as a result of the increased use of chemical fertilizers. Although 13 million acres of farmland were withdrawn from cultivation during the decade, output continued to rise. In 1921, 64.5 million acres of wheat land produced about 819 million bushels of wheat. In 1928, 59 million acres yielded 914 million bushels.

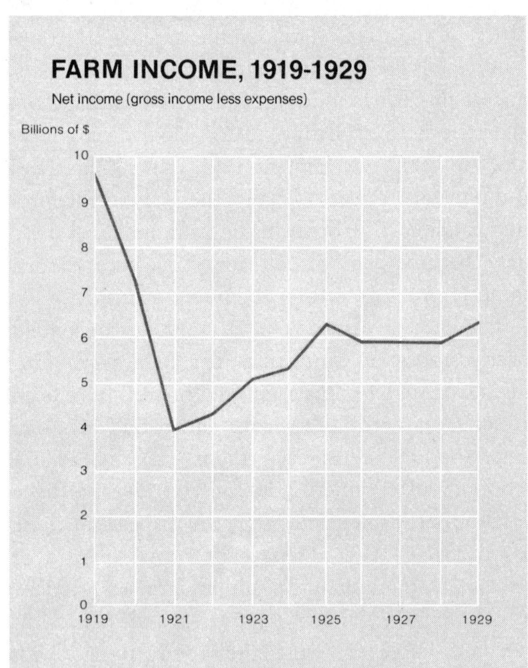

Despite the power of the Farm Bloc, the government did little to improve the situation. President Harding opposed direct aid to agriculture on idealistic grounds. "Every farmer is a captain of industry," he declared. "The elimination of competition among them would be impossible without sacrificing that fine individualism that still keeps the farm the real reservoir from which the nation draws so many of the finest elements of its citizenship." During his administration Congress strengthened the laws regulating railroad rates and grain exchanges and made it easier for farmers to borrow money, but such measures did nothing to increase agricultural income. Nor did the high tariffs on agricultural produce have much effect, for Americans grew more wheat, cotton, and other staples than they consumed and were unlikely to import such products in any case. Being forced to sell their surpluses abroad, they found that world prices depressed domestic prices despite the tariff wall.

The attitude of Claude R. Wickard, a "master farmer" from Carroll County, Indiana, later secretary of agriculture under Franklin D. Roosevelt, typifies the feelings of American farmers during the twenties:

> There were certain people who liked to point out every year that they had made some money in farming, but somehow you got the idea that it was just by chance, like the Irish Sweepstakes. . . . I was disturbed—genuinely disturbed—by the trend of things, and I think, what was most important of all, my hope began to vanish. I became discouraged with agriculture. We didn't know where we were going.

As early as 1921 George N. Peek, a plow manufacturer from Moline, Illinois, advanced a scheme to "make the tariff effective for agriculture." The federal government, Peek suggested in "Equality for Agriculture," should buy up the surplus American production of wheat.* This additional demand would cause domestic prices to rise. Then the government could sell the surpluses abroad at the lower world price, recovering its losses by as-

*He soon extended his plan to cover cotton and other staples.

sessing an "equalization fee" on American farmers.

Peek's plan had flaws, for if the price of staples rose, farmers would tend to increase output, but this problem might have been solved by imposing production controls. It was certainly a most ingenious and promising idea; hundreds of organizations in the farm belt endorsed it. Farm Bloc congressmen took it up and in 1927 the McNary-Haugen bill was passed, only to be vetoed by President Coolidge. Although he raised a number of sound practical objections, Coolidge based his opposition chiefly on constitutional and philosophical grounds. "A healthy economic condition is best maintained through a free play of competition," he insisted, ignoring the fact that the scheme had been devised precisely because competition was proving distinctly unhealthy for American farmers. Congress passed a similar bill again in 1928, but Coolidge again rejected it.

Thus, while most economic indicators reflected an unprecedented prosperity, the boom times rested upon unstable foundations. The problem was mainly one of maldistribution of resources. Productive capacity raced ahead of buying power. Too large a share of the profits went into too few pockets. The 27,000 families with the highest annual incomes in 1929 earned as much money as the 11 million at the bottom of the scale, those with annual incomes of under $1,500, the minimum sum, at that time, required to maintain a family decently. High earnings and low taxes permitted huge sums to pile up in the hands of men who could not spend their profits usefully. The money went into further industrial expansion, which aggravated the problem, or into stock market speculation, which led to the "big bull market" and eventually to the Great Depression. While Coolidge reigned, however, few persons realized the danger. Complacency was the order of the day. "The country," Coolidge told Congress in 1928, "can regard the present with satisfaction, and anticipate the future with optimism."

Election of 1928

The climax of the postwar era in American politics came in 1928, one year before the economy reached its high point. Coolidge—somewhat cryptically, as was his wont—withdrew his name from consideration, and Herbert Hoover, whom he detested, easily won the Republican nomination. Hoover was the intellectual leader, almost the philosopher, of the New Era. He spoke and wrote of "progressive individualism," arguing that American capitalists had learned to curb their selfish instincts and devote themselves to public service and equal opportunity for all. Although stiff and uncommunicative and entirely without experience in elective office, he made an admirable candidate in 1928. His roots in the Middle West and West (Iowa-born, he was raised in Oregon and educated at Stanford University in California) neatly balanced his outstanding reputation among eastern business tycoons. He was very rich, but self-made. His career as a mining engineer had given him a wide knowledge of the world, yet after his experiences at the Versailles Conference, he had become highly critical of Europe, which disarmed the isolationists, who might otherwise have suspected that his long years abroad had made him an effete cosmopolite.

The Democrats, having had their fill of factionalism in 1924, could no longer deny their nomination to Governor Al Smith. Superficially Smith was Hoover's antithesis. Born and raised in New York's Lower East Side slums, affable, witty, determinedly casual of manner, he had been thoroughly schooled in machine politics by Tammany Hall. He was a Catholic, Hoover a Quaker; a wet whereas Hoover supported prohibition vigorously; he dealt easily with men of every race and nationality, while Hoover had little interest in and less knowledge of Negroes and immigrants. However, like Hoover, Smith managed to combine a basic conservatism with his genuine humanitarian concern for the underprivileged. Equally as adept in administration as Hoover, he was also equally uncritical of American capitalism. Indeed, as William E. Leuchtenburg has said, "it was this combination of humanitarianism with economic orthodoxy . . . that accounted for much of [Smith's] appeal."

Unwilling to challenge the public's complacent view of Coolidge prosperity, the Democrats adopted a conservative platform. Smith appointed John J. Raskob, a wealthy automobile executive, to manage his campaign. Franklin D. Roosevelt, who ran for governor of New York at Smith's urging in 1928, actually charged that Hoover's expansion of the functions of the Department of Commerce had been at least mildly socialistic. "Some of Mr. Hoover's regulatory attempts are undoubtedly for the good of our economic system," Roosevelt said, "but I think the policy of Governor Smith to let businessmen look after business matters is far safer for the country." This strategy failed miserably. Smith's Catholicism, his brashness, his criticism of prohibition, his machine connections, and his urban background hurt him badly in rural areas, especially in the South. On the other hand, nothing he could do or say was capable of convincing Republican businessmen that he was superior to Hoover. In the election Hoover won a smashing triumph, 444 to 87 in the Electoral College, 21.4 million to 15 million in the popular vote. All the usually Democratic border states, and even North Carolina, Florida, and Texas, went to the Republicans, along with the entire West and Northeast, save for Massachusetts and Rhode Island.

In November 1928 the Democratic party seemed on the verge of extinction. Nothing could have been further from the truth. The religious question and his big-city roots hurt Smith, but the chief reason he lost was the prosperity of the country. As Professor Leuchtenburg puts it: "If Smith had been Protestant, dry, and born in a log cabin of good yeoman stock, he would still have been defeated." The good times, however, were to be of short duration. Furthermore, Hoover's overwhelming victory concealed a remarkable political realignment that was taking place. The immigrant voters in the major cities, largely Catholic and unimpressed by Coolidge prosperity, had swung heavily to the Democrats. In 1924 the 12 largest cities in the United States had been solidly Republican; in 1928 all of them went Democratic. Even in agricultural states like Iowa, Smith ran far better than Davis had in 1924, for Coolidge's vetoes of the McNary-Haugen bills had caused much resentment. A new coalition of urban workingmen and dissatisfied farmers was in the making. Prosperity, plus Smith's personal disadvantages, held the Republican edifice together in 1928. When the good times ended, it crumbled, suddenly but completely, in one of the greatest political reversals in the nation's history.

SUPPLEMENTARY READING The most recent comprehensive survey of the twenties is J.D. Hicks, *Republican Ascendancy** (1960), but W.E. Leuchtenburg, *The Perils of Prosperity** (1958), is equally broad in coverage and more interpretive. A.M. Schlesinger, Jr., *The Age of Roosevelt: The Crisis of the Old Order** (1957), is rich in detail and sharply anti-Republican in attitude. F.L. Allen, *Only Yesterday** (1931), is an excellent popular account, a modern classic, oriented especially toward social history. Preston Slosson, *The Great Crusade and After* (1930), is a more comprehensive but less entertaining social history. The economic history of the period is covered in George Soule, *Prosperity Decade** (1947), but see also J.W. Prothro, *The Dollar Decade* (1954), and Robert Sobel, *The Great Bull Market: Wall Street in the 1920's** (1968). Other useful volumes include Karl Schriftgiesser, *This Was Normalcy* (1948), and Isabel Leighton (ed.), *The Aspirin Age** (1949).

The labor history of the postwar decade is discussed in Irving Bernstein, *The Lean Years** (1960), and Philip Taft, *Organized Labor in the United States* (1964). David Brody, *The Steel Strike of 1919** (1965), and R.L. Friedheim, *The Seattle General Strike* (1965), are useful special studies. On the Big Red Scare, see R.K. Murray, *Red Scare* (1955), Zechariah Chafee, *Free Speech in the United States** (1941), and Stanley Coben, *A. Mitchell Palmer* (1963). Nativism and immigration restriction are covered in M.A. Jones, *American Immigration** (1960), and John Higham, *Strangers in the Land** (1955). Fundamentalism is treated in N.F. Furniss, *The Fundamentalist Controversy* (1954), the Monkey Trial in Ray Ginger, *Six Days or Forever?** (1958). The fullest and most thoughtful history of prohibition is Andrew Sinclair, *Prohibition: The Era of Excess** (1962), but see also Herbert Asbury, *The Great Illusion* (1950), and Charles Merz, *Dry Decade* (1931), a colorful popular account. On the Klan, consult D.M. Chalmers, *Hooded Americanism: The History of the Ku Klux Klan** (1965), K.T. Jackson, *The Ku Klux Klan in the City** (1967), and A.S. Rice, *The Ku Klux Klan in American Politics* (1961). Sacco and Vanzetti are dealt with sympathetically in G.L. Joughin and E.M. Morgan, *The Legacy of Sacco and Vanzetti** (1948), and in Felix Frankfurter, *The Case of Sacco and Vanzetti** (1927), but Francis Russell, *Tragedy in Dedham* (1962), casts doubt on their innocence.

The literature of the prewar period is discussed in H.F. May, *The End of American Innocence** (1959), that of the twenties in Alfred Kazin, *On Native Grounds** (1942), and F.J. Hoffman, *The Twenties** (1955). On Fitzgerald, see Arthur Mizener, *The Far Side of Paradise** (1951); on Hemingway, C.H. Baker, *Hemingway: The Writer as Artist** (1956); on Mencken, W.R. Manchester, *Disturber of the Peace: The Life of H.L. Mencken** (1951); on Lewis, Mark Schorer, *Sinclair Lewis** (1961).

For the history of the Negro in the period, see, besides the sociologist Gunnar Myrdal's classic *An American Dilemma** (1944), Gilbert Osofsky, *Harlem: The Making of a Ghetto** (1965), E.M. Rudwick, *W.E.B. Du Bois: Propagandist of the Negro Protest** (1960), E.D. Cronon, *Black Moses: The Story of Marcus Garvey* (1955), Alain Locke, *The New Negro: An Interpretation** (1925), J.W. Johnson, *Black Manhattan* (1930), and Harold Cruse, *The Crisis of the Negro Intellectual** (1967).

The best brief biography of Harding is Andrew Sinclair, *The Available Man** (1965), the fullest analysis of his Presidency, R.K. Murray, *The Harding Era* (1969). D.R. McCoy, *Calvin Coolidge: The Quiet President* (1967), is the best life of Coolidge, but see also W.A. White, *A Puritan in Babylon** (1938). Other useful political biographies include B.C. and Fola La Follette, *Robert M. La Follette* (1953), Oscar Handlin, *Al Smith and His America** (1958), Frank Freidel, *Franklin D. Roosevelt: The Ordeal* (1954), and Arthur Mann, *La Guardia: A Fighter Against His Time** (1959). David Burner, *The Politics of Provincialism: The Democratic Party in Transition* (1968), discusses the evolution of the Democratic party in the 1920's.

On Henry Ford, see Allan Nevins and F.E. Hill, *Ford* (1954–57), and Keith Sward, *The Legend of Henry Ford** (1948). Farm discontent is covered in Theodore Saloutos and J.D. Hicks, *Twentieth Century Populism: Agricultural Discontent in the Middle West** (1951), Dean Albertson, *Roosevelt's Farmer* (1961), and G.C. Fite, *George N. Peek and the Fight for Farm Parity* (1954). On the election of 1928, see E.A. Moore, *A Catholic Runs for President* (1956).

*Available in paperback.

26

The Great Depression: 1929–1939

In the spring of 1928 prices on the New York Stock Exchange, already at a historic high point, began to surge ahead. As the Presidential campaign gathered momentum, the market increased its pace, stimulated by Hoover's prediction that "the abolition of poverty" lay just around the corner and by Al Smith's efforts to outdo his rival in praising the marvels of the American economic system. "Glamour" stocks skyrocketed–Radio Corporation of America, for example, rose from under 100 to 400 between March and November. A few conservative brokers expressed alarm, suggesting that most stocks were becoming grossly overpriced, but the majority scoffed at such talk. "Be a bull on America," they urged. "Never sell the United States short."

Through the first half of 1929, despite occasional sharp breaks, the market climbed still higher. A mania for speculation swept the country, thousands of small investors pouring their savings into common stocks, often purchased "on margin."* By September 1929 fantastic heights had been reached. RCA, without ever paying a dividend, topped 500; General Electric, traded at about 128 in March 1928, now approached 400; U.S. Steel zoomed from 138 to 279 during the period, Anaconda Copper from 54 to 162.

Then the market wavered. For over a month, amid volatile fluctuations, the stock averages moved downward. Most analysts, however, contended that the Exchange was simply "digesting" previous gains. A prominent Harvard economist expressed the prevailing view when he said that stock prices had reached a "permanently high plateau" and would soon resume their advance.

Alas, on October 24 a massive wave of selling sent prices spinning downward. Nearly 13 million shares changed hands, a record. Bankers and politicians rallied to check the decline, as they had during the Panic of 1907. J. P. Morgan, Jr., rivaled the

*Margin buyers paid only part of the cost of their stocks, borrowing the rest through brokers. Although the Federal Reserve Board pushed interest rates to as high as six per cent during the summer of 1929, such was the public's confidence that the volume of brokers' loans rose from $4 billion in 1928 to $8.5 billion in October 1929.

efforts of his father in that earlier crisis, and President Hoover assured the people that "the business of the country . . . is on a sound and prosperous basis." But on Tuesday, October 29, the bottom seemed to drop out of the market. Thousands of speculators, forced to put up more margin as prices declined, dumped their holdings in one security to raise money to cover their investments in another. Over 16 million shares were sold, prices plummeting an average of 40 points. The boom was over.

PHILADELPHIA MUSEUM OF ART

To James N. Rosenberg, a New York attorney and amateur artist who sketched this grim view of the Wall Street financial district, October 29, 1929 ("Black Tuesday") was no less than the Day of Judgment.

Hoover and the Depression

The collapse of the stock market did not cause the depression; stocks rallied late in the year and business activity did not begin to decline significantly until the spring of 1930. The Great Depression was caused basically by the industrialization and urbanization of the United States in the course of a century: too much of the wealth of the nation had fallen into too few hands, with the result that consumers were unable to buy all the goods produced. The trouble came to a head mainly because of the easy-credit policies of the Federal Reserve Board and the Mellon tax structure, which favored the rich, and its effects were so profound and prolonged because the government (and for that matter the professional economists) did not fully understand what was happening or what to do about it. A few keen observers had noticed the danger even in the prosperous twenties, but now the underlying weaknesses of the economy suddenly became apparent. The chronic problem of underconsumption operated to speed the downward spiral. Unable to rid themselves of mounting inventories, manufacturers closed down plants and laid off workers, thus causing demand to shrink still further. Automobile output fell from 4.5 million units in 1929 to 2.7 million in 1930 and 1.1 million in 1932. When Ford closed his Detroit plants in 1931, some 75,000 men lost their jobs. The great multiplier industry of the twenties became the divisor of the thirties, for the decline in auto production affected a host of suppliers and middlemen as well as the workers directly involved.

At the same time, the domination of most industries by a few great corporations meant that prices tended to fall more slowly than wages, further unbalancing the situation. The financial system soon began to crack under the strain, more than 1,300 banks closing their doors in 1930, 3,700 more in the next two years. Each failure deprived thousands of persons of funds that might otherwise have gone into consumer goods; when the Bank of the United States in New York City became insolvent in December 1930, 400,000 depositors found their savings immobilized. And of course the industrial depression accelerated the depression in agriculture, since unemployed workers had literally to tighten their belts, cutting down on the already inadequate demand for American foodstuffs. Every economic indicator reflected the collapse. New investments declined from $10 billion in 1929 to $1 billion in 1932, and the national income fell from over $80 billion to under $50 billion in the same brief period. Unemployment rose to about 13 million.

President Hoover was an intelligent man, experienced in business matters and with a good layman's grasp of economics. He was also a forceful leader, capable of thinking through complex problems and acting courageously to carry out his policies. Many ultraconservatives, such as Secretary of the Treasury Mellon, insisted that the economy must be allowed to slide unchecked until the cycle had found its bottom. "Let the slump liquidate itself," Mellon urged. "Liquidate labor, liquidate stocks, liquidate the farmers. . . . People will work harder, live a more moral life. Values will be adjusted, and enterprising people will pick up the wrecks from less competent people." Hoover realized that such a policy would cause unbearable hardship for millions and determined to try to halt the decline by artificial means. Wages should be maintained along with prices, he argued. The Federal Reserve Board should lower interest rates to encourage borrowing and thus industrial expansion. Public works programs should be stepped up, both to stimulate production and make jobs for the unemployed, and taxes should be cut to free money for the purchase of consumer goods. The nation's leaders should act vigorously to restore the confidence both of businessmen and the general public, since fear and discouragement gravely aggravated the depression.

Hoover's program, evolved gradually between 1929 and 1932, called for cooperative action by businessmen, free from fear of antitrust prosecution, to maintain prices and wages; for federal tax cuts, public works programs, and interest rate reductions; for a great increase in state and local building programs; for federal loans to banks and industrial corporations threatened with collapse; and for aid to homeowners unable to meet mortgage payments. The President also proposed measures making it easier for farmers to borrow money, and he suggested that cooperative farm marketing schemes designed to solve the problem of overproduction be supported by the government. Nor did the wartime savior of Belgium ignore the human misery resulting from the depression. He called for an expansion of state and local relief programs and urged all who could afford it to increase their gifts to charitable institutions. Above all he tried to restore public confidence. The depression was only a minor downturn, he said repeatedly. The economy was basically healthy, prosperity was "just around the corner." In short, Hoover rejected classical economics; indeed, many laissez-faire theorists attacked his handling of the depression. The English economist Lionel Robbins, writing in 1934, criticized Hoover's "grandiose buying organizations" and his efforts to maintain consumer income "at all costs." Numbers of "liberal" economists, on the other hand, praised the Hoover program highly.

However, while his plans were theoretically sound, they failed to check the economic slide, partly because of curious limitations in his conception of how they should be implemented. He placed far too much reliance on his powers of persuasion and the willingness of citizens to act in the public interest without legal compulsion. He called a series of industrial conferences to urge manufacturers to maintain wages and keep their factories in operation, but the businessmen, under the harsh pressure of economic realities, soon slashed wages and curtailed output sharply. He permitted the Federal Farm Board (created under

ST. LOUIS *Post-Dispatch*, JANUARY 11, 1931

The anomaly of surplus food and natural resources in a time of want mystified many Americans, a view expressed by cartoonist Daniel Fitzpatrick in 1931.

the Agricultural Marketing Act of 1929) to establish semipublic stabilization corporations with authority to spend millions of dollars supplied by the federal government in an effort to buy up surplus wheat and cotton, but he refused to countenance production controls. As a result, these corporations poured out hundreds of millions of dollars without checking the downward trend of agricultural prices, for farmers increased production faster than the corporations could buy up the excess for disposal abroad. The scheme, one critic said, was only "a first-class way of throwing good money into a bottomless pit."

Hoover also resisted all efforts to shift authority from state and local agencies to the federal government, despite the fact—soon obvious—that these lesser governmental bodies lacked the resources to cope with emergency conditions. For example, by 1932 the federal government, with Hoover's approval, was spending $500 million a year on public works projects, but because of the sharp decline of state and municipal construction, the total public outlay fell nearly $1 billion below what it had been in 1930. More serious was his refusal, on constitutional grounds, to allow federal funds to be used for the relief of individuals. State and municipal agencies and private charities must take care of the needy, he insisted. Unfortunately the depression was drying up the sources of private charities just as the demands upon these organizations were expanding. State agencies were also swamped at a time when their capacities to tax and borrow were shrinking. By 1932 about one-third of the entire population of Pennsylvania was on relief; in Chicago 700,000 persons—40 per cent of the work force—were unemployed. Only the national government possessed the power and credit to deal adequately with the crisis. Yet despite his genuine humanitarianism, Hoover would not act. He set up a committee to coordinate local relief activities but insisted on preserving what he called "the principles of individual and local responsibility."

Federal aid to businessmen was constitutional, he believed, because such assistance took the form of loans that could be put to productive use and eventually repaid. When drought destroyed the crops of farmers in the South and Southwest in 1930, Hoover was willing to grant them federal loans to buy seed and even food for their livestock, but he would provide no direct relief for the farmers themselves. In 1932 he approved the creation of the Reconstruction Finance Corporation, which was authorized to make loans to banks, railroads, and insurance companies. The RFC represented an important extension of federal authority in the economic sphere, but one thoroughly in line with Hoover's philosophy. Its loans, secured by solid collateral, were commercial transactions, not gifts. Aside from the fact that far too much of the $1.5 billion dispersed by the RFC went to a handful of large financial institutions, the agency did almost nothing for individuals in need of personal relief. The same could be said of the Glass-Steagall Banking Act of 1932, which eased the tight credit situation by permitting Federal Reserve banks to accept a wider variety of commercial paper as security for loans. Although the President's sincerity could not be questioned, the public grew increasingly resentful of his doctrinaire adherence to principle while breadlines lengthened and millions of willing workers searched fruitlessly for jobs.

In addition, Hoover overemphasized the importance of balancing the federal budget. In hard times, he reasoned, everyone ought to live within his means, and the government should set a good example. While it is true that his stress on economy bolstered the confidence of businessmen somewhat, the principle of limiting expenses to income hampered all his efforts to stimulate recovery. Revenues fell so sharply that deficits soon became inevitable; the government was nearly $500 million in the red by June 1931. Since Hoover understood the value of pumping money into the stagnant economy, it is difficult to see why he did not make a virtue of this necessity. Instead, as Arthur M. Schlesinger, Jr., has said, "fear of the deficit became an obsession" with the President. "The primary duty of the Government . . . is to hold expenditures within our income," Hoover said. "Prosperity cannot be restored by raids on the public Treasury."

Hoover also allowed his anti-European prejudices to interfere with the implementation of his program. In 1930 Congress passed the Hawley-

A breadline in New York in 1933. The Great Depression, said an English observer, "outraged and baffled" the nation that took it as "an article of faith . . . that America, somehow, was different from the rest of the world."

Smoot Tariff Act, which raised duties on most manufactured products to prohibitive levels. Although over a thousand economists joined in urging Hoover to veto this measure on the grounds that it would encourage inefficiency and stifle world trade, he signed it cheerfully. The new tariff made it impossible for European nations to earn the dollars they needed to continue making payments on their World War I debts to the United States and also helped bring on a financial collapse in Europe in 1931. In that year Hoover wisely proposed a one-year "moratorium" on all international obligations. But the efforts of Great Britain and many other countries to save their own skins by devaluing their currencies in order to encourage foreigners to buy their goods led him to blame them for the depression itself, ignoring the fact that it had started in the United States. He seemed unable to grasp what should have been obvious to a man of his intelligence: that high American tariffs made currency devaluation almost inevitable in Europe and that the curtailment of American investment on the Continent as a result of the depression had dealt a staggering blow to the economies of all the European nations.

No man could have prevented the Great Depression or brought the country back to good times quickly. Much of the contemporary criticism of Hoover and a good deal of that heaped upon him by later historians was unfair. Yet his record as President shows that he was too rigid and doctrinaire, too wedded to a particular theory of government to cope effectively with the problems of the day. Since these problems were in a sense insoluble—no one, after all, possessed enough knowledge and intelligence to understand entirely what was wrong or enough authority to enforce the proper corrective measures—flexibility and a willingness to experiment were essential to any program aimed at restoring prosperity. Hoover lacked these qualities. He was also his own worst enemy, being too uncompromising to get on well with the politicians and too aloof to win the public's confidence and affection. He had too much faith in himself and his plans. When he failed to achieve the results he anticipated, he attracted, despite his devotion to duty and his concern for the welfare of the country, not sympathy but scorn.

The Economy Sounds the Depths

During the spring of 1932, as the economy sounded the depths, thousands of Americans were facing actual starvation. The Detroit Welfare Department found itself $800,000 in debt with no prospect of finding additional funds. In Philadelphia, during an 11-day period when no relief funds at all were available, hundreds of families existed on stale bread, thin soup, and garbage. In Birmingham, Alabama, landlords in poor districts simply gave up trying to collect rents. "Frequently," one Alabama congressman told a Senate committee, "the landlord prefers to have somebody living there free of charge rather than to have the house . . . burned up for fuel [by scavengers]." When Birmingham officials advertised for 750 common laborers at 20 cents an hour, 12,000 men offered their services. In the nation as a whole, only about one quarter of the unemployed were receiving any public aid at all.

In every major city homeless families gathered in ramshackle communities called "Hoovervilles," constructed of packing boxes, rusty sheet metal, and similar refuse on swamps, garbage dumps, and other wasteland. Thousands of hungry tramps roamed the countryside. Yet at the same time, food prices fell so low that farmers were burning corn for fuel. In states like Iowa and Nebraska, farmers organized Farm Holiday movements, refusing to ship their crops to market in protest against 31-cent-a-bushel corn and 38-cent wheat. They blocked roads and rail lines, dumped milk, overturned trucks, and established picket lines to enforce their boycott.

The national mood ranged from apathy to resentment to outright fury. In June and July 1932 unemployed veterans, 20,000 strong, marched on Washington to demand immediate payment of their "adjusted compensation" bonuses. When Congress rejected their appeal, most returned home, but some 2,000 refused to leave, settling down with their families in a jerry-built camp of shacks and tents at Anacostia Flats, a swamp bordering the Potomac. President Hoover, much alarmed, charged incorrectly that the "Bonus Army" was largely composed of criminals and radicals and sent troops into the Flats to disperse it with bayonets, tear gas, and tanks. The veterans' protest had been aimless and not entirely justified, but as the Washington *News* said, the spectacle of the United States government "chasing unarmed men, women, and children with Army tanks" appalled the nation.

The unprecedented severity of the depression led some persons to favor radical alterations of the country's economic and political systems. The disparity between the lots of the rich and the poor, always a challenge to democracy, became more striking and engendered much bitterness. "Unless something is done to provide employment," two labor leaders warned Hoover, "disorder . . . is sure to arise. . . . There is a growing demand that the entire business and social structure be changed because of the general dissatisfaction with the present system." The communists gained few converts among the mass of workingmen, but many intellectuals, already alienated by the trends of the twenties, now found radical causes attractive. Persuaded by their experiences that the old progressive viewpoint was futile and naive, they responded positively to the communists' emphasis on economic planning and the total mobilization of the state to achieve social goals. Even the popular cracker-barrel humorist Will Rogers was impressed by reports of the absence of serious unemployment in Russia. "All roads in our day lead to Moscow," the former muckraker Lincoln Steffens wrote. Communism, John Strachey argued in his widely read *The Coming Struggle for Power* (1932), offered "the one method by which human civilization can be maintained." Only the disdain of the communists for individual rights and the internecine strife within the Russian party organization kept the communist movement from making more headway in America in the dark days of the early thirties.

As the end of his term approached, President Hoover seemed to grow daily more dour, petulant, and pessimistic. The depression, climaxing 12 years of Republican rule, probably insured a Democratic victory in any case, but his attitude as the election neared alienated many voters and turned defeat into rout.

Franklin D. Roosevelt

Confident of victory, the Democrats chose Governor Franklin Delano Roosevelt of New York as their Presidential candidate. Roosevelt owed his nomination chiefly to his success as governor. In 1928, while Hoover was carrying New York against Smith by a wide margin, Roosevelt won election by 25,000 votes. In 1930 he swept the state by a 700,000-vote majority, double the previous record. Under his administration, New York had led the nation in providing relief for the needy and had enacted an impressive program of old-age pensions, unemployment insurance, conservation, and public power projects. The governor also had the advantage of the Roosevelt name (he was a distant cousin of the inimitable T.R.), and his sunny, magnetic personality contrasted favorably with that of the glum and colorless Hoover.

Roosevelt was far from being a radical. Although he had made a good record in the Wilson administration while serving as assistant secretary of the navy and had supported the League of Nations vigorously while campaigning for the Vice Presidency in 1920, during the twenties he had not seriously challenged the basic tenets of Coolidge prosperity. For a time he even served as head of the American Construction Council, a Hoover-type trade association. Indeed, his life before 1932 gave very little indication that he really understood the aspirations of the masses of the American people or had any deep commitment to social reform.

Born to wealth and social status in Dutchess County, New York, in 1882, pampered in childhood by a doting yet domineering mother, he was educated at the exclusive Groton School and then at Harvard, where he proceeded, as his biographer Frank Freidel has written, "from one extracurricular triumph to another." Ambition as much as the desire to render public service motivated his career in politics; even after an attack of infantile paralysis in 1921 left him badly crippled in both legs, he refused to abandon his hopes for high office. During the 1920's he had been a hard-working member of the liberal wing of his party, supporting Smith for President in 1924 and 1928, but he was no extremist and never displayed any difficulty in adjusting his views to the prevailing sentiments of the day.

To some observers he seemed rather a lightweight intellectually. When he ran for the Vice Presidency, the Chicago *Tribune* commented: "If he is Theodore Roosevelt, Elihu Root is Gene Debs, and Bryan is a brewer." Twelve years later many critics judged him too irresolute, too amiable, too eager to please all factions to be a forceful leader. One Democratic editor dismissed him as "another Hoover," and the political analyst Walter Lippmann, in a now-famous observation, called him "a pleasant man who, without any important qualifications for the job, would very much like to be President."

Despite his physical handicap—he could walk only a few steps, and then only with the aid of steel braces and two canes—Roosevelt was a brilliant campaigner: as Al Smith pointed out during the 1928 contest, "a Governor does not have to be an acrobat." He traveled back and forth across the country, radiating confidence and good humor even when directing his sharpest barbs at the Republicans. He spoke effectively if not always clearly and consistently before numberless crowds, and, like every great political leader, he took as much from the people as he gave them, understanding the causes of their confusion, sensing their needs. "I have looked into the faces of thousands of Americans," he told a friend. "They have the frightened look of lost children. . . . They are saying: 'We're caught in something we don't understand; perhaps this fellow can help us out.'" Roosevelt soaked up information and ideas from a thousand sources—from professors like Raymond Moley and Felix Frankfurter, from politicians like James A. Farley and John N. Garner, the Vice Presidential candidate, from social workers, businessmen, and lawyers. Yet he maintained close control over every aspect of the campaign.

To those seeking specific answers to the questions of the day, Roosevelt was seldom very satisfying. On vital matters like farm policy, the tariff, and government spending, he equivocated, contradicted himself, or remained silent. Aided by hindsight, historians have discovered portents of much of his later program in his speeches, but to contemporaries these pronouncements, buried among dozens of conflicting generalities, often passed almost unnoticed. He did say, for example: "If starvation and dire need on the part of any of our citizens make necessary the appropriation of additional funds which would keep the budget out of balance, I shall not hesitate to . . . ask the people to authorize the expenditure of that additional amount," but in the same speech he called for sharp cuts in federal spending and a balanced budget, and he castigated Hoover for presiding over "the greatest spending administration in peace time in our history."

Nevertheless, his basic position was unmistakable. There must be a "New Deal," a "re-appraisal of values." Instead of adhering to old ideas about the scope of federal power, the government should take on any functions necessary to protect the unfortunate and advance the public good. Lacking concrete answers, he advocated a point of view rather than a plan: "The country needs bold, persistent experimentation. It is common sense to take a method and try it. If it fails, admit it frankly and try another. But above all, try something." The effectiveness of this approach was demonstrated in November. Hoover, who had lost only eight states in 1928, won only six, all in the Northeast, in 1932. Roosevelt amassed 22.8 million votes to Hoover's 15.8 million and carried the Electoral College by 472 to 59.

During the interval between the election and Roosevelt's inauguration in March 1933, the Great Depression reached its nadir. The holdover "lame duck" Congress, last of its kind,* proved incapable of effective action. President Hoover, perhaps understandably, hesitated to institute changes without the cooperation of his successor, while Roosevelt, for equally plausible reasons, refused to accept responsibility before assuming power officially. The nation, curiously apathetic in the face of so much suffering, drifted aimlessly, like a sailboat in a flat calm.

*The Twentieth Amendment (1933) provided for convening new Congresses in January instead of the following December. It also advanced the date of the President's inauguration from March 4 to January 20.

Then the banking system disintegrated—no lesser word portrays the extent of the collapse. Starting in the rural West and spreading to major cities like Detroit and Baltimore, a financial panic forced hundreds of banks to close down. All over the country depositors began to line up before the doors of even the soundest institutions, desperate to withdraw their savings. In February, to check the panic, the governor of Michigan declared a "bank holiday," shutting up every bank in the state for eight days. Maryland, Kentucky, California, and other states followed suit; by inauguration day four-fifths of the states had suspended all banking operations. So great was the fear and confusion that the New York Stock Exchange was closed on March 4.

The Hundred Days

This unprecedented emergency proved a blessing in disguise for the new President and for the country. Obviously something drastic had to be done. The most conservative business leaders were as ready for government intervention as the most advanced radicals. Partisanship, while not disappearing, was for once subordinated to broad national needs.

Then Roosevelt provided the spark that reenergized the American people. His inaugural address, delivered in a raw mist beneath dark March skies, reassured the country and at the same time stirred it to action: "The only thing we have to fear is fear itself. . . . Our true destiny is not to be ministered unto but to minister to ourselves and to our fellow men. . . . We cannot merely take but we must give as well. . . . This Nation asks for action, and action now. . . . I assume unhesitatingly the leadership of this great army of our people. . . ." Many such lines punctuated his brief address, which concluded with this stern pledge:

In the event that Congress shall fail . . . I shall not evade the clear course of duty that will then confront me. I shall ask the Congress for the one remaining instrument to meet the crisis—broad Executive power to wage a war against the emergency.

The inaugural captured the heart of the country; almost half a million letters of congratulation poured into the White House. "Your human feeling for all of us in your address is just wonderful," one citizen wrote. "It seemed to give the people . . . a new hold upon life," said another. When Roosevelt summoned Congress into special session on March 9, the legislators outdid one another to enact his proposals into law. "I had as soon start a mutiny in the face of a foreign foe as . . . against the program of the President," one representative declared. In the following 100 days, until Congress adjourned on June 16, opposition, in the sense of an organized group committed to resist the administration, simply did not exist. As a result, an impressive body of new legislation was placed on the statute books. The New Deal was under way.

Roosevelt had the power and the will to act, but no comprehensive plan of action. He and his eager congressional collaborators proceeded in a dozen directions at once, sometimes wisely, sometimes not, often at cross purposes with themselves and one another. Untangling the national financial mess presented the most immediate problem. On March 5 Roosevelt declared a nationwide bank holiday and placed an embargo on the exportation of gold. Within hours after it convened, Congress passed an emergency banking bill, confirming these measures, outlawing the hoarding of gold, and giving the President broad power over the operations of the Federal Reserve system. A plan for reopening the banks under Treasury Department licenses was devised and soon most of them were functioning again, public confidence in their solvency restored. In April Roosevelt took the country off the gold standard. Before the session (the "Hundred Days") ended, Congress had also established the Federal Deposit Insurance Corporation to guarantee bank deposits, forced the separation of investment banking and commercial banking concerns while extending the power of the Federal Reserve Board over both types of institutions, and created the Home Owners Loan Corporation to refinance mortgages and prevent foreclosures. It also passed a Federal Securities Act requiring promoters to make public full financial information about all new stock issues and giving the Federal Trade Commission the right to regulate such transactions.*

After the adjournment of Congress, Roosevelt began buying gold on the open market, hoping thereby to cause a general price rise and increase American world trade. When this policy failed to do much good, Congress, in January 1934, passed the Gold Reserve Act, permitting the President to fix the price of gold by proclamation. Roosevelt promptly set the price at $35 an ounce, about 40 per cent higher than its pre-New Deal level. Roosevelt's monetary policies did not produce any dramatic rise in the price level, but, considering the severity and complexity of the deflation problem, they represented an intelligent and reasonably successful approach.

Problems of unemployment and industrial stagnation also had a high priority during the Hundred Days. Urged on by the President, Congress appropriated $500 million for relief of the needy and created the Civilian Conservation Corps to provide jobs for young men between the ages of 18 and 25 in reforestation and other conservation projects. To stimulate industry, Congress passed one of its most controversial measures, the National Industrial Recovery Act (NIRA), evolved from a bill introduced by Senator Hugo Black of Alabama. Besides establishing the Public Works Administration, with authority to spend $3.3 billion on roads, public buildings, and similar enterprises, this law permitted manufacturers to draw up industry-wide codes of fair business practices in order to raise prices and limit production by agreement, without fear of the antitrust laws. The law also gave workers the protection of minimum-wage and maximum-hours regulations, and guaranteed them the right "to organize and bargain collectively through representatives of their

*In 1934 this task was transferred to the new Securities and Exchange Commission, which also was given broad authority over all the activities of stock exchanges.

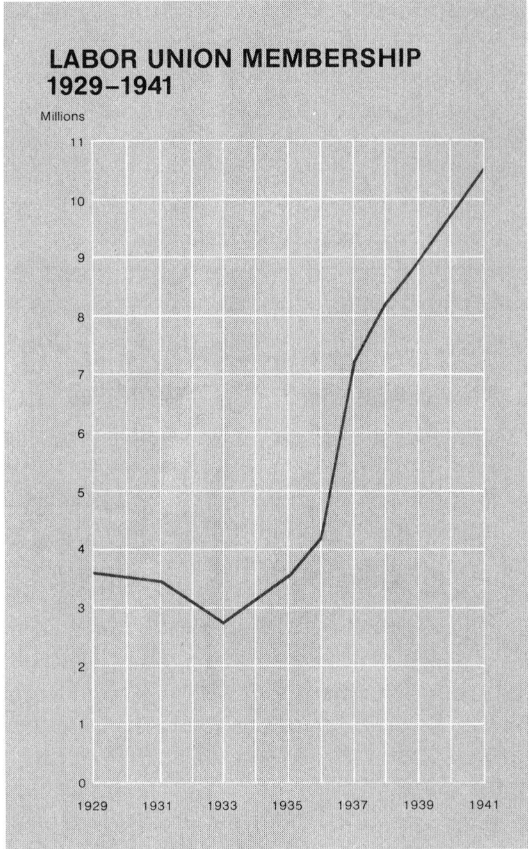

own choosing," an immense stimulus to the labor union movement. The National Recovery Administration (NRA), headed by General Hugh Johnson, supervised the drafting and operation of the business codes, although in practice the largest manufacturers in each industry controlled what went into the agreements. The object, the gruff Johnson explained, was to "eliminate eye-gouging and knee-groining [sic] and ear-chewing in business."

Drafting the codes posed difficult problems, first because each industry insisted on tailoring the agreements to its special needs and second because most manufacturers were unwilling to accept all the provisions of Section 7a of the law dealing with the rights of labor. Although thousands of employers agreed to the pledge "We Do Our Part" in order to receive the Blue Eagle symbol of NRA, many were more interested in the monopolistic aspects of the act than in boosting wages and encouraging unionization. General Johnson was soon fulminating against "chiselers," and his impetuosity and his violent tongue did much to destroy whatever spirit of cooperation the manufacturers possessed. After Johnson had been a year in office, President Roosevelt forced his resignation. There was a brief upturn in the spring of 1933, but the expected revival of industry did not take place; in nearly every case the dominant producers in each industry used their power to raise prices and limit production rather than to increase output.

However, the law did achieve important results. Beginning with the cotton textile code, the agreements succeeded in doing away with the centuries-old problem of child labor in industry. They established the principle of federal regulation of wages and hours and led directly to the organization of hundreds of thousands of workers, even in industries like steel and autos where unions had never before been significant. Within a year John L. Lewis' United Mine Workers expanded from 150,000 members to half a million. About 100,000 automobile workers joined unions, as did a comparable number of steelworkers. Labor boards, established under the act, conducted elections to determine whether or not the men wished to be represented by unions, and forced manufacturers to bargain with their employees in good faith.

Organizers cleverly used the NIRA to persuade workers that the popular President Roosevelt *wanted* them to join unions, which was something of an overstatement. In 1935, after the conservative and craft-oriented AF of L had revealed very little enthusiasm for enrolling unskilled workers on an industry-wide basis, John L. Lewis, together with such forward-looking officials of the garment trade unions as David Dubinsky and Sidney Hillman, formed the Committee for Industrial Organization (CIO) and set out to rally workers in each of the mass-production industries into one union without regard for craft lines, a far more effective method of organization. The AF of L expelled these unions, however, and in 1938 the CIO became the Congress of Industrial Organizations. Soon it rivaled the AF of L in size and importance.

MUSEUM OF MODERN ART

Ben Shahn did this lithograph in 1937 for the government's Resettlement Administration, an agency established to aid victims of "Dust Bowl" conditions.

Roosevelt displayed more concern over the plight of the farmers than over that of any other group in America, for he believed that the nation was becoming overcommitted to industry. The New Deal farm program, incorporated in the Agricultural Adjustment Act of May 1933, combined compulsory restrictions on production with government subsidies of staple commodities like wheat, cotton, tobacco, and pork, paid for by levying processing taxes on middlemen such as flour millers. The object was to lift agricultural prices to "parity" with industrial prices, the ratio in most cases being based on the levels of 1909–1914, when farmers had been reasonably prosperous. In return for withdrawing part of their land from cultivation, farmers received "rental" payments from the Agricultural Adjustment Administration (AAA).

Since the 1933 crops were already growing when the law was passed, Secretary of Agriculture Henry A. Wallace, son of Harding's secretary of agriculture and himself an experienced farmer and plant geneticist, decided to pay farmers to destroy their produce in the field. Cotton planters plowed up 10 million acres of growing crops, receiving $100 million in return. Six million baby pigs and 200,000 pregnant sows were slaughtered. Such ruthlessness appalled observers, especially when they thought of the millions of hungry Americans who could have eaten the destroyed food, but no practical alternative existed during that first year of the program. Thereafter, limitation of acreage proved sufficient to raise agricultural prices considerably, although it must be admitted that a widespread drought in the Middle West and South also acted to reduce output. A far more serious criticism of the program was its failure to help poor farmers, especially tenants and sharecroppers, many of whom lost their livelihoods completely when owners took land out of production to obtain AAA payments.

But in 1933 even farmers with large holdings were in desperate trouble, and these at least were helped. Acreage restrictions and mortgage relief saved thousands. In addition, the farm program was a remarkable attempt to rationalize the chaotic agricultural economy. As one New Deal official put it, the AAA was "the greatest single experiment in economic planning under capitalist conditions ever attempted by a democracy in times of peace."

The most striking achievement of the Hundred Days was the creation of the Tennessee Valley Authority. To provide power for factories manufacturing synthetic nitrate explosives during World War I, the government had constructed a hydroelectric plant at Muscle Shoals, Alabama, where the Tennessee River plunges 130 feet in a 40-mile stretch. After 1920 farm groups and public power enthusiasts, led by Senator George W. Norris of Nebraska, had blocked administration plans to turn these facilities over to private capitalists. But their efforts to have the site operated under federal auspices had been defeated by Presidential vetoes. Roosevelt, however, eagerly pressed to have the whole Tennessee Valley area, one of the poorest in the land, incorporated into a broad experiment in social planning. Besides expanding the hydroelectric plants at Muscle Shoals and developing nitrate manufacturing in order to produce cheap fertilizers, he envisioned a coordinated program of soil conservation, reforestation, and industrialization. Since the Tennessee flowed through seven states, national control of the project was essential.

Over the objections of private power interests, led by Wendell L. Willkie of the Commonwealth and Southern Corporation, Congress passed the TVA Act in May 1933. This law created a three-man board authorized to build dams, power plants, and transmission lines and sell fertilizers and electricity throughout the region to individuals and local communities. The board could also undertake flood control, soil conservation, and reforestation projects, and improve the navigation of the river. While the TVA never became the comprehensive regional planning organization some of its sponsors had anticipated, it greatly improved the standard of living of millions of inhabitants of the valley. In addition to producing quantities of electricity and fertilizers and providing a "yardstick" whereby the efficiency, and thus the rates, of private power companies could be tested, it took on a variety of other functions, ranging from the eradication of malaria to the development of recreational facilities.

The New Deal Spirit

By the end of the Hundred Days, the country had made up its mind about Roosevelt's New Deal, and despite the many vicissitudes of the next decade, it never really changed it. A large majority was ready to label it a solid success. In the first place, considerable industrial recovery had taken place, partly because manufacturers built up inventories in anticipation of higher labor costs under NIRA. The New York *Times* index of business activity rose from 60 in March to 99 in June. This was relatively unimportant, however, for the recovery did not continue. More basic was the fact that Roosevelt, recruiting an army of forceful, intelligent men to staff the new government agencies and barraging Congress with no less than 15 important special messages, had managed to infuse his administration almost instantaneously with a spirit of bustle and optimism. The director of the Presidential Secret Service unit, returning to the White House on inauguration day after escorting Herbert Hoover to the railroad station, found the executive mansion "transformed during my absence into a gay place, full of people who oozed confidence." Within a few weeks Roosevelt's New Dealers had changed the whole atmosphere of Washington. "They have transformed it," one observer noted, "from a placid leisurely Southern town . . . into a gay, breezy, sophisticated and metropolitan center."

Dozens of men who lived through those stirring times have left records that reveal the New Deal spirit. "Come at once to Washington," Senator Robert La Follette, Jr., son of "Fighting Bob," telegraphed Donald Richberg, an old Theodore Roosevelt progressive. "Great things are under way." When Richberg arrived, he found his liberal friends "seething with excitement and anticipation." A seasoned newspaperman, looking back on the Hundred Days, wrote: "It was one of the most joyous periods in my life. We came alive, we were eager." And Justice Harlan Fiske Stone of the Supreme Court recorded: "Never was there such a change in the transfer of government."

Roosevelt himself seemed to have been "transfigured," as one reporter said, "from a man of charm and buoyancy to one of dynamic aggressiveness." During the first days of the New Deal, the financial expert Norman H. Davis, who had known Roosevelt since the time of their joint service under Woodrow Wilson, encountered a mutual friend on the White House steps. "That fellow in there is not the fellow we used to know," he said. "There's been a miracle here."

The New Deal lacked any consistent ideological base. Although the so-called "Brain Trust" (a group of college professors headed by Raymond Moley, a Columbia political scientist, and including Columbia economists Rexford G. Tugwell and Adolf A. Berle, Jr., Felix Frankfurter of the Harvard Law School, and a number of others) attracted a great deal of attention, the-

The proliferation of federal agencies during the New Deal inspired a legion of satirists. In this example, from Vanity Fair, *Uncle Sam becomes Swift's Gulliver besieged by the Lilliputian brain-trusters.*

orists never impressed Roosevelt very much. His New Deal drew upon the old populist tradition as seen in its antipathy to bankers and its willingness to adopt schemes for inflating the currency; upon the New Nationalism of Theodore Roosevelt in such matters as its dislike of competition and its de-emphasis of the antitrust laws; and upon the ideas of social workers trained in the Progressive Era. Techniques developed by the Wilsonians also found a place in the system: Louis D. Brandeis had considerable influence on Roosevelt's financial reforms, and New Deal labor policy grew directly out of the experience of the War Labor Board of 1917–18.

Within the administrative maze that Roosevelt created, rival bureaucrats battled to enforce their views. The "spenders," led by Tugwell of the Brain Trust, clashed with those favoring strict economy, who gathered around Lewis Douglas, director of the budget. Blithely disregarding logically irreconcilable differences, Roosevelt mediated between the factions, deciding this time in favor of one group, next in favor of the other. Washington became a battleground for dozens of special-interest groups: the Farm Bureau Federation, the big unions, the trade associations, the silver miners, and so on. William E. Leuchtenburg has described New Deal policy as "interest-group democracy," another historian, Ellis W. Hawley, as "counterorganization" policy, aimed at creating "monopoly power" among groups previously unorganized, such as farmers and industrial workers. While, as Leuchtenburg says, the system was greatly superior to that of Roosevelt's predecessors, who had allowed one interest group, big business, to predominate, it slighted the unorganized majority. The NRA aimed frankly at raising the prices paid by consumers of manufactured goods; the AAA processing tax came ultimately from the pocketbooks of ordinary citizens. Yet the New Deal found wide acceptance. The public assumed that Roosevelt's ultimate objective was to improve the lot of all classes of society and that he was laboring diligently and imaginatively in pursuit of this goal.

The Unemployed

Although the Great Depression had by no means been conquered and at least 9 million men were still without work, the Democrats confounded the political experts, including their own, by increasing their already large majorities in both houses of Congress in the 1934 elections. All the evidence indicates that even most of the jobless continued to support the administration. Their loyalty can best be explained by Roosevelt's unemployment policies, which, while insufficient to eradicate the problem, were both extensive and imaginative.

In May 1933 Congress had established the Federal Emergency Relief Administration and given it $500 million to be dispensed through state relief organizations. Roosevelt appointed Harry L. Hopkins, an eccentric but brilliant and dedicated social worker, to direct FERA. However, Hopkins insisted that the unemployed needed jobs, not merely handouts. In November he persuaded Roosevelt to create a Civil Works Administration to achieve this objective. Within a month Hopkins had put over 4 million persons to work directly for the federal government, building and repairing roads and public buildings, teaching schools, decorating the walls of post offices with murals, and utilizing their special skills in dozens of other ways. The cost of this program frightened Roosevelt–Hopkins spent about $1 billion in less than five months–and he soon abolished the CWA, but an extensive public works program was continued throughout 1934 under FERA. Despite charges by critics that many of the projects were mere "boondoggles," thousands of roads, bridges, schools, and other valuable structures were built or refurbished, and the morale of several million otherwise jobless workers was immeasurably raised. Even those who did not benefit directly took the program as an indication of Roosevelt's determination to attack the unemployment problem on a broad front.

After the midterm elections, Roosevelt committed himself wholeheartedly to the Hopkins approach. Returning "unemployables" to the care of state and local agencies (where their fate was often miserable), the federal government assumed the task of making work for many of the rest. In May 1935 Roosevelt put Hopkins in charge of a new agency, the Works Progress Administration (WPA). By the time this agency was disbanded in 1943 it had spent $11 billion and found employment for 8.5 million persons. Besides carrying out an extensive public works program, the WPA developed the Federal Theatre Project, which put thousands of actors, directors, and stagehands to work producing plays that entertained a total of 60 million people; the Federal Writers' Project, which turned out valuable guidebooks, collected local lore, and published about a thousand books and pamphlets; and the Federal Art Project, which made work for needy painters and sculptors. These agencies, a writer in *Fortune* pointed out in 1937, accomplished a veritable "cultural revolution" in the nation. In addition, the National Youth Administration created part-time jobs for over 2 million high school and college students and an even larger number of other youths who could not technically be classified as unemployed, but who needed financial help.

Nevertheless, WPA did not reach all the unemployed; like so many New Deal programs, it did not go far enough, chiefly because Roosevelt could not escape from his fear of unbalancing the federal budget too drastically. Halfway measures did not provide the massive stimulus the economy needed. The President also hesitated to pay adequate wages to WPA workers or undertake projects that might compete with private enterprises for fear of offending business. Yet his caution did him no good politically; the very interests he sought to placate were becoming increasingly hostile to the New Deal.

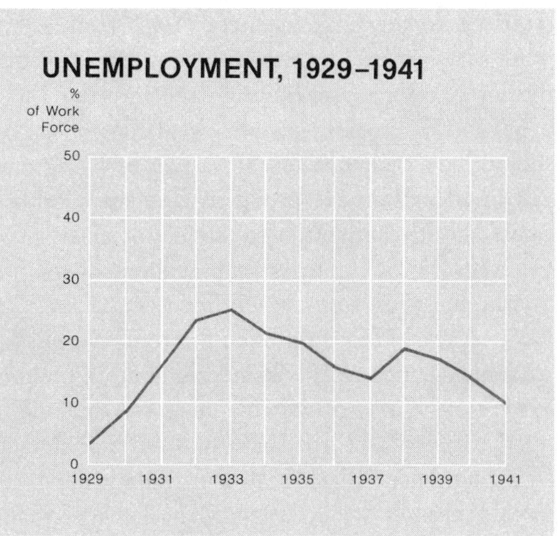

The Extremists

Roosevelt's moderation also roused extremists, both on the left and on the right. Of these, the most formidable was Louisiana's Senator Huey Long, the "Kingfish." Raised on a farm in northern Louisiana, Long was progressively a traveling salesman, a lawyer, state railroad commissioner, governor, and, after 1930, United States senator. By 1933 he ruled Louisiana with the absolutism of an oriental monarch.

Long was a controversial figure in his own day and so he has remained. In many ways he was a typical southern conservative, and he was certainly a demagogue. Yet as his biographer T. Harry Williams has convincingly demonstrated, the plight of all poor people concerned him deeply and—more important—he tried to do something about it. His record in Louisiana is a fascinating mixture of overbearing egotism, sordid politicking, and genuine efforts to improve the lot of poor men, black as well as white. He did not question segregation or white supremacy, nor did he suggest that Louisiana blacks should be allowed to vote. He used the word *nigger* with total unself-consciousness, even when addressing northern Negro leaders. But he treated Negro-baiters with scathing contempt. When Hiram W. Evans, Imperial Wizard of the Ku Klux Klan, announced his intention to campaign against him in Louisiana, Long told reporters: "Quote me as saying that that Imperial bastard will never set foot in Louisiana, and that when I call him a sonofabitch I am not using profanity, but am referring to the circumstances of his birth."

As a reformer, Long stood in the populist tradition; he hated bankers and "the interests." He believed that all poor people, regardless of color, should have a chance to earn a decent living and get an education. He provided free schoolbooks, public health benefits, and other social services to Negroes on a scale unprecedented in the South, and thus won the enthusiastic backing of local blacks. His arguments were simplistic, patronizing, possibly insincere, but effective. "Don't say I'm working for niggers," he told a northern Negro journalist. "I'm for the poor man —all poor men. Black and white, they all gotta have a chance. . . . 'Every Man a King'—that's

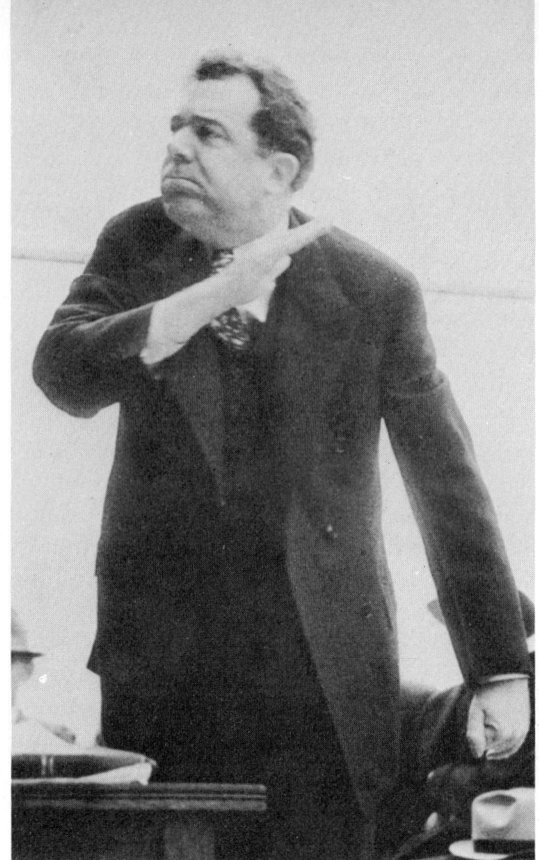

BOTH: UPI

Above, Senator Huey Long explains his "Share-Our-Wealth" plan to an Iowa audience in April of 1935. That same month, Father Charles Coughlin (below), the "Radio Priest," was photographed in Detroit as he promoted his National Union for Social Justice.

my slogan. That means every man, niggers along with the rest, but not specially for niggers."

Raffish, totally unrestrained, yet extremely shrewd—a fellow southern politician called him "the smartest lunatic I ever saw"—Long had supported the New Deal at the start, but partly because he thought Roosevelt too conservative and partly because of his own ambition, he soon broke with the administration. Although Roosevelt was himself more hostile to the big financiers than to any other group, Long denounced him as a stooge of Wall Street. By 1935 he was heading a national "Share-Our-Wealth" movement with a membership of over 4.6 million. His program called for the confiscation of all family fortunes of more than $5 million and a tax of 100 per cent on incomes of over $1 million a year. The money thus collected would provide every family with a "homestead" (including a car and other necessities as well as a house) and an annual income of $2,000–$3,000, plus old-age pensions, educational benefits, and veterans' pensions. In addition, Long proposed to limit the hours of labor to make more jobs, and a farm price-support program. As the 1936 election approached, he was planning to organize a third party to split the liberal vote. He assumed that the Republicans would win the election and so botch the job of fighting the depression that he could himself sweep the country in 1940.

Less powerful than Long but more widely influential was Father Charles E. Coughlin, the "Radio Priest." A big, genial Irishman of Canadian birth, Coughlin began his public career in 1926, broadcasting a weekly religious message over station WJR in Detroit. His mellifluous voice and orotund rhetoric soon won him a huge national audience, and the depression gave him a secular cause. In 1933 he had been an eager New Dealer, but his dislike of New Deal financial policies—he believed that inflating the currency drastically would end the depression—and his need for ever more sensational ideas to hold his public from week to week led him to turn against the New Deal by 1935. Soon he was calling Roosevelt a "great betrayer and liar." Although his National Union for Social Justice was especially appealing to Catholics, it attracted people of every faith, especially in the lower-middle-class districts of the big cities. Some of his more sensational radio talks caused more than a million persons to send him messages of congratulation; contributions amounting to perhaps $500,000 a year flooded into his headquarters. Coughlin attacked bankers, New Deal planners, Roosevelt's farm program, and the alleged sympathy of the administration for communism. His program resembled fascism more than any leftist philosophy, but he posed a serious threat, especially in combination with Long, to the continuation of Democratic rule.

Another rapidly growing movement alarmed the Democrats in 1934–35: Dr. Francis E. Townsend's campaign for "Old-Age Revolving Pensions." Townsend, a retired California physician, differed from Long and Coughlin in that he was colorless and low-keyed, the opposite of a demagogue, but like them he had an oversimplified and thus appealing "solution" to the nation's troubles. He was shocked by the pitiful state of thousands of elderly persons, whose job prospects were even dimmer than those of the mass of the unemployed. "We owe a decent living to the older people," he insisted. Influenced in his youth by Edward Bellamy's *Looking Backward,* he believed that "we ought to plan as a nation for the things we need." He advocated paying every person 60 and over a pension of $200 a month, the only conditions being that the pensioners must give up all gainful employment and spend the entire sum within 30 days. Their purchases, he argued, would stimulate production tremendously, thus creating new jobs for younger men and revitalizing the economy. A stiff transactions tax, collected whenever any commodity changed hands, would pay for the program.

Economists quickly pointed out that with about 10 million persons eligible for the Townsend pensions, the cost would amount to $24 billion a year, roughly half the national income; but among the elderly the scheme proved extremely popular. Local Townsend Clubs, their proceedings conducted in the spirit of revivalist camp meetings, flourished everywhere, and the *Townsend National Weekly* soon reached a circulation of over 200,000. Although the Townsendites were anything but radical in point of view, their plan, like Long's Share-Our-Wealth scheme, would have revolutionized the distribution of wealth in the country. On the one hand, they reflected a reactionary spirit like that of religious fundamentalists, on the other, the emergence of a new force in American society. With medical advances rapidly lengthening the average life span, the percentage of old people in the population was rising steadily. The physical demands placed on workers by the pace of modern industry and the breakdown of close family ties in an increasingly mobile society were causing many of these citizens to be cast adrift to live out their last years poor, sick, idle, and alone. Dr. Townsend's simple-minded program focused the attention of the country on a new problem—one it has not yet entirely resolved.

Like Long and Coughlin, Townsend represented a threat to Roosevelt; his success helped to make the President see that he must move boldly to restore good times or face serious political trouble in 1936. After weeks of hesitation, in the spring of 1935 he finally acted. Political imperatives had much to do with his decision, but the influence of Justice Brandeis and his disciples, most notably Felix Frankfurter, was also great. They urged Roosevelt to abandon his pro-business programs, especially NRA, and put more stress on restoring competition and taxing the big corporations heavily. The fact that most businessmen were turning away from him anyway encouraged the President to accept this advice and so did the Supreme Court's decision in *Schechter v. U.S.* (May 1935), which declared the National Industrial Recovery Act unconstitutional. (This case involved the provisions of the NRA Live Poultry Code; the Court voided the act on the grounds that Congress had delegated too much power to the code authorities and that the defendants, four brothers engaged in slaughtering chickens in New York City, were not engaged in interstate commerce.)

The Second New Deal

Already existing laws had failed to end the depression; extremists were luring away many of Roosevelt's supporters; conservatives had failed to appreciate his moderation; the Supreme Court was undermining his past achievements. For these many reasons, Roosevelt, in June, launched the "Second New Deal," calling upon Congress to enact a spate of new laws.

There ensued the second Hundred Days, one of the most productive periods in the history of American legislation. The National Labor Relations Act—commonly known as the Wagner Act—restored the labor guarantees wiped out by the Schechter decision. It gave workers the right to bargain collectively and prohibited employers from interfering with union organizational activities in their factories. A National Labor Relations Board (NLRB) was established to supervise plant elections and designate successful unions as official bargaining agents when a majority of the workers approved. The board could also conduct investigations of employer practices and issue cease-and-desist orders when "unfair" activities were unearthed. Aside from the great prestige that this official support of unionization provided, the Wagner Act effectively destroyed the ability of employers to harass organizers. Repeatedly the NLRB forced antiunion corporations to rehire men discharged for union activities. It also gave union leaders great control over the rank-and-file, and while in the long run this produced serious problems, its immediate effect was to make labor more powerful.

Still more important was the Social Security Act of August 1935. This law, partly designed to undercut the Townsendites, set up a national system of old-age insurance, financed partly by a tax on wages, partly by a tax on payrolls. It also created a state-federal system of unemployment insurance, financed by another payroll tax. Liberal critics considered this social security system inadequate, for it did not cover agricultural workers, domestics, self-employed persons, and some other groups particularly in need of its benefits. Health insurance was not included either, and since the size of pensions depended upon the amount earned, the lowest-paid workers could not count on much support after reaching 65. But the law was of major significance. Over the years the pension payments were increased and the classes of workers covered expanded. To those who objected to employee contributions,

Roosevelt had a ready answer: "We put those . . . contributions there," he said, "so as to give the contributors a legal, moral, and political right to collect their pensions and their unemployment benefits. With those taxes in there, no damn politician can ever scrap my social security program."

Other important new laws enacted at this time included a new banking act and a Public Utility Holding Company Act. The former strengthened the control of the Federal Reserve Board (renamed the Board of Governors) over member banks and over commercial credit and interest rates; the latter outlawed the pyramiding of control of gas and electricity companies through the use of holding companies and gave various federal commissions the power to regulate strictly the rates and financial practices of these companies. The hotly debated "death sentence" clause of the holding company law provided for the dismemberment of all utility complexes more than twice removed from the actual operating companies and authorized the Securities and Exchange Commission to break up smaller ones that could not demonstrate that their existence served some socially useful purpose.

The Rural Electrification Administration, created by executive order, also began to function during this remarkable period. The REA was authorized to lend money at low interest rates to private utility companies and to farmer cooperatives interested in bringing electricity to rural areas. When the REA went into operation, only one farm in ten had electricity; by 1950 only one in ten did not. Another important measure was the Wealth Tax Act of August 1935, which, while not the "soak the rich" measure both its supporters and opponents claimed, raised taxes on incomes of over $50,000 to as high as 75 per cent. Estate and gift taxes were also increased. A new excess-profits tax, and a modestly graduated tax on corporate profits replacing the existing flat rate, reflected the Brandeis group's desire to penalize corporate giantism. Although this law achieved no drastic redistribution of the tax burden, in the long run it was one of the most important of all New Deal measures, for it began the movement in the direction of "soaking the rich" that was to reach maturity during World War II. Much of the opposition of conservatives to other New Deal legislation rose from the fact that thereafter the well-to-do had to bear a disproportionate share of the cost of *all* governmental activities.

The upper crust plans an evening at the newsreels: "Come along. We're going to the Trans-Lux to hiss Roosevelt." By The New Yorker*'s Peter Arno, 1936.*

Whether the Second New Deal was more radical than the First depends largely on the perspective from which it is considered. Measures like the Social Security Act and the new tax law had a much greater long-range effect on American life than the legislation of the first Hundred Days, but they were fundamentally less revolutionary than laws like the National Industrial Recovery Act and the Agricultural Adjustment Act, which represented a large-scale attempt to establish a planned economy. "Where the First New Deal contemplated government, business, and labor marching hand in hand toward a brave new society," Arthur M. Schlesinger, Jr., has written, "the Second New Deal proposed to revitalize the tired old society. . . . The First New

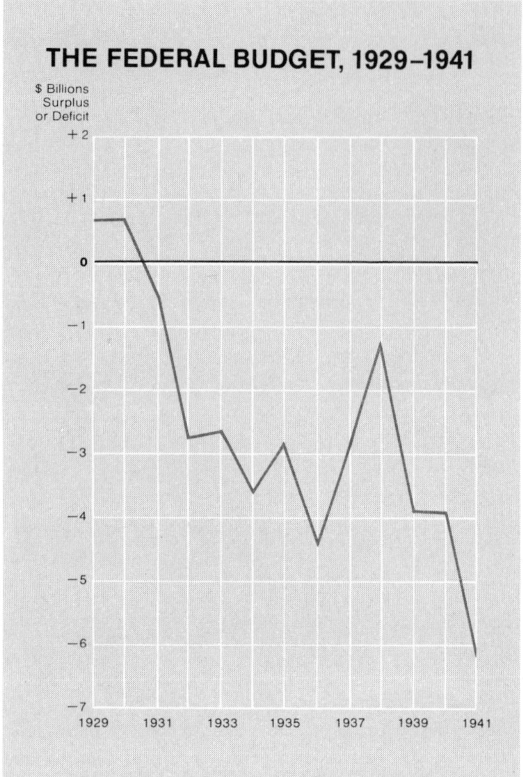

Deal characteristically told business what it must do. The Second New Deal characteristically told business what it must *not* do."

This distinction escaped most of Roosevelt's critics, particularly the businessmen, who felt the impact of his assault on existing conditions most directly. If theoretically the NIRA threatened the free enterprise system, it was still less objectionable to the average manufacturer than laws that increased his taxes and forced him to contribute to old-age pensions for his workers.

Herbert Hoover epitomized the attitude of conservatives when he called the New Deal "the most stupendous invasion of the whole spirit of Liberty that the nation has witnessed." Undoubtedly many opponents of the New Deal sincerely believed that it was undermining the foundations of American freedom. The immense cost of the New Deal also alarmed them. By 1936 some members of the administration had fallen under the influence of the British economist John Maynard Keynes, who was arguing that the world depression could only be conquered if governments deliberately unbalanced their budgets by cutting taxes and increasing expenditures in order to stimulate consumption and investment. Roosevelt never really accepted Keynes's theories; he conferred with the economist as early as 1934 but could not grasp the "rigmarole of figures" with which Keynes deluged him. Nevertheless, the imperatives of the depression forced him to spend more than the government was collecting in taxes; thus he partially adopted the Keynesian approach. Conservative businessmen considered this financially irresponsible, and the fact that deficit spending seemed to be good politics—one cynical New Dealer reputedly said that the administration would "spend, spend, spend" and "elect, elect, elect" until doomsday—made them seethe with rage.

Election of 1936

The election of 1936 loomed as a showdown between orthodoxy and, if not revolution, at least drastic change and a disregard of tradition. "America is in peril," the Republican platform declared. The GOP candidate, Governor Alfred M. Landon of Kansas, was himself reasonably liberal, a former follower of Theodore Roosevelt, a foe of the Ku Klux Klan in the twenties, and a believer in government regulation of business. But he was a poor speaker, colorless, and handicapped by the reactionary views of many of his backers. Against the personal charm and political astuteness of Roosevelt, Landon's arguments—chiefly that he could administer the government more efficiently than the President—made little impression. He won the support of some conservative Democrats, including two former Presidential candidates, Al Smith and John W. Davis, but this was not enough.

The radical fringe put a third candidate in the field, Congressman William Lemke of North Dakota, who ran on the Union party ticket. Father Coughlin, denouncing Roosevelt as the "dumbest man ever to occupy the White House," rallied his National Union for Social Justice behind Lemke. Dr. Townsend also supported him. However, the extremists were losing ground by 1936. Huey Long fell victim of an assassin in

September 1935, and his organization was taken over by the blatantly demagogic rightist, Gerald L.K. Smith. The New Deal, Smith said in 1936, was led by "a slimy group of men culled from the pink campuses of America." The Townsendites fell under a cloud because of rumors that some of their leaders had their hands in the organization's treasury. Father Coughlin's slanderous assaults on Roosevelt caused a powerful backlash; a number of American Catholic prelates denounced him and the Vatican issued an unofficial but influential rebuke. Lemke made little impression on the country, polling only 892,000 votes.

Roosevelt, however, did not win in 1936 because of the inadequacies of his foes. Having abandoned his efforts to hold the businessmen, whom he now denounced as "economic royalists," he appealed openly for the votes of the underprivileged classes. The powerful new labor unions gratefully poured thousands of dollars into the campaign to re-elect him. Negro voters, traditionally Republican, switched to the Democrats in large numbers. Whereas Hoover had won a large majority of the Negro vote in 1932, Roosevelt carried most Negro sections impressively four years later. Cincinnati's 16th Ward gave Roosevelt only 29 per cent of its vote in 1932, more than 65 per cent in 1936.

Farmers liked Roosevelt because of his evident concern for their welfare: when the Supreme Court declared the Agricultural Adjustment Act unconstitutional (*U.S. v. Butler,* 1936), he immediately rushed through a new law, the Soil Conservation and Domestic Allotment Act, which accomplished the same objective by paying farmers to divert land from commercial crops to soil-building plants like clover and soybeans. Countless elderly persons backed him out of gratitude for the Social Security Act. Homeowners were grateful for his program guaranteeing mortgages—eventually about 20 per cent of all urban private dwellings were refinanced by the Home Owners Loan Corporation—and for the Federal Housing Administration, which, beginning in 1934, made available low-cost, long-term loans for modernizing old buildings and constructing new ones. By the spring of 1937 a million and a quarter persons had obtained more than $500 million in home-improvement loans alone through the FHA. A modest upturn, which raised industrial output to the levels of 1930, also played into Roosevelt's hands. For the first time since 1931 U.S. Steel was showing a profit.

On election day the country gave the President a tremendous vote of confidence. He carried every state but Maine and Vermont, swamping Landon by more than 10 million votes. In the entire nation the Republicans elected only 89 representatives; their strength in the Senate fell to 16, an all-time low. Both Roosevelt's personality and his program had captivated the land. His political genius had effected a coalition of diverse elements larger than any previous leader had achieved in a contested election. A few weeks later, when he set out on a good will tour of South America, he seemed irresistible, the most powerfully entrenched President in the history of the United States.

Roosevelt and the Supreme Court

On January 20, in his second inaugural, Roosevelt spoke feelingly of the plight of millions of citizens "denied the greater part of what the very lowest standards of today call the necessities of life. . . . denied education, recreation, and the opportunity to better their lot and the lot of their children." A third of the nation, he added without exaggeration, was "ill-housed, ill-clad, ill-nourished." He interpreted his great victory in 1936 as a mandate for further reforms, and with his personal prestige and his immense congressional majorities, nothing appeared to stand in his way. Nothing, that is, but the Supreme Court.

Throughout Roosevelt's first term, the Court had stood almost immovable against the trend toward increasing the scope of federal authority and broadening the general powers of government, state as well as national, to cope with the exigencies of the depression. Of the nine justices, only Louis Brandeis, Benjamin N. Cardozo, and Harlan Fiske Stone viewed the New Deal sympathetically. Four others, James C. McReynolds, Willis Van Devanter, Pierce Butler, and George

BROWN BROTHERS

Al Hirschfeld titled his mid-thirties caricature of the Supreme Court, "Nine Old Men." From left to right are Justices Owen J. Roberts, Pierce Butler, Louis D. Brandeis, Willis Van Devanter, Charles Evans Hughes (the chief justice), James C. McReynolds, George Sutherland, Harlan Fiske Stone, and Benjamin N. Cardozo.

Sutherland were intransigent reactionaries. Chief Justice Charles Evans Hughes and Justice Owen J. Roberts, while more open-minded, tended to side with the reactionaries on many questions. Besides invalidating both the NIRA and AAA, the Court had voided the federal Guffey-Snyder Act, establishing minimum wages in the coal industry, and also a New York minimum-wage law, thus creating, as Roosevelt remarked, a "no man's land" where neither national nor state government could act. The Court, Roosevelt also noted at the time of the Schechter case, had adopted a "horse-and-buggy" interpretation of the commerce clause of the Constitution, closing off one of the most important avenues for expanding federal power. Worse still, the reactionaries on the Court seemed governed by no consistent constitutional philosophy; they used any reasoning that suited their immediate needs to "protect" the nation against liberal ideas. For example, they tended to limit the police power of the states when wages-and-hours laws came before them but to interpret it very broadly when state laws restricting civil liberties were under consideration. In 1937 all the major measures of the Second New Deal appeared to be doomed. The Wagner Act had little chance of winning approval, experts predicted. Lawyers were advising employers to ignore the Social Security Act, so confident were they that the Court would declare it unconstitutional.

Faced with this situation, Roosevelt took a bold step. To reduce the power of the Court by amending the Constitution would be, if possible at all, too time-consuming. He decided, therefore, to ask Congress to shift the balance on the Court by increasing the number of justices, thinly disguising the purpose of his plan by making it part of a general reorganization of the judiciary. Under Roosevelt's proposal, a member of the Court reaching the age of 70 would have the option of retiring at full pay. If he chose not to retire, the President was to appoint an additional justice, up to a maximum of six, in order to ease the burden of work for the aged jurists who remained on the bench.

Although he knew that this measure would run into strenuous resistance, Roosevelt confidently expected Congress to pass it. The huge Democratic majorities could override any opposition, he believed, and the public would back him solidly. Few except reactionaries would rise to the Court's defense, for it had been widely criticized in recent years by liberals and legal theorists.

No astute politician had erred so badly in estimating the effects of an action since Stephen A. Douglas introduced the Kansas-Nebraska bill in 1854. Although polls showed the public fairly evenly divided on the "court-packing" bill, the opposition was both vocal and influential. To the expected denunciations of conservatives were added the complaints of liberals fearful that the principle of court-packing might in the future be used to subvert civil liberties. What, asked Senator Norris, would have been the reaction if a man like Harding had proposed such a measure? Opposition among congressmen was immediate and intense; many who had cheerfully supported every New Deal bill came out strongly against the plan. The press denounced it, and so did most local bar associations. Judges were almost unanimous against this assault on their independence. Chief Justice Hughes released a devastating critique; even the liberal Brandeis—the oldest judge on the court—rejected the bill out of hand.

In addition, many ordinary voters felt that Roosevelt had tried to trick them. The 1936 Democratic platform had spoken only of a possible amendment "clarifying" the Court's power, and Roosevelt had studiously avoided the issue during the campaign. For months Roosevelt stubbornly refused to concede defeat, thus tying up the rest of his legislative program while Congress wrangled over the court reform bill. Finally, in July 1937, he had to yield. Although minor administrative reforms of the judiciary were enacted, the size of the Court remained unchanged.

Yet the struggle did not result in saving all the important legislation of the Second New Deal. Alarmed by the threat to the Court, Justices Hughes and Roberts, never entirely committed to the conservative position, beat a strategic retreat on a series of specific issues. While the battle raged in Congress, they sided with the liberals in upholding first a minimum-wage law of the state of Washington little different from the New York act the Court had recently rejected, then the Wagner Act, then the Social Security Act. In May Justice Van Devanter retired, Roosevelt replacing him with Senator Hugo Black of Alabama, an advanced New Dealer. The conservative justices thereupon gave up the fight, and soon Roosevelt was able to appoint enough new judges to give the Court a large pro-New Deal majority. No further measure of any significance was declared unconstitutional during his Presidency. The fight, however, hurt him severely. His prestige never fully recovered. The solidity of the New Deal coalition in Congress was forever shattered. Conservative Democrats who had feared to oppose Roosevelt because of his supposedly invulnerable popularity took heart and began to join with the Republicans on key issues. When the President summoned a special session of Congress in November 1937 and submitted a program of "must" legislation, not one of his bills was passed.

The End of the New Deal

Although the Court fight marked the beginning of the end of the New Deal, social and economic developments contributed even more to its decline, and the final blow originated in the area of foreign affairs. With unemployment high, wages low, and workers relatively powerless against their employers, most Americans had adopted a sympathetic attitude toward New Deal legislation and toward the big industrial unions whose growth it stimulated. However, strength made the unions ambitious and aggressive. Massive organizational drives in industries like steel and automobiles changed the power structure within the economy and gave many members of the middle class second thoughts concerning labor's demands.

In 1937 a series of "sit-down strikes" broke out, beginning at General Motors' Flint, Michigan, plant. Striking workers barricaded themselves *inside* the factories; when police and strikebreakers tried to dislodge them, they drove them off with barrages of soda bottles, tools, spare parts, and crockery. The tolerant attitude of the Roosevelt administration and of governors like Frank Murphy of Michigan insured the strikers against government intervention. "It is illegal," Roosevelt said of the General Motors strike, "but shooting it out . . . [is not] the answer. . . . Why can't those fellows in General Motors meet with the committee of workers?" Fearful that all-out efforts to clear their plants would result in the destruction of expensive machinery, most employers soon capitulated to the workers' demands. All the automobile manufacturers except Henry Ford quickly came to terms with the United Automobile Workers.

The major steel companies, led by U.S. Steel, recognized the CIO and granted higher wages and a 40-hour week. The auto and steel unions alone boasted over 725,000 members by late 1937; other CIO units conquered the rubber industry, the electrical industry, the textile industry, and many others. Together with the seizures of property in sit-down strikes, the disregard of unions for the "rights" of nonunion workers, and the violence that accompanied some strikes, this rapid growth alarmed many moderates. The enthusiasm of such people for all reform cooled rapidly after 1937.

While the sit-down strikes and the Court fight were going on, the New Deal suffered still another heavy blow. Despite fluctuations, business conditions had been gradually improving since 1933. Heartened by the trend, Roosevelt, who had never fully grasped the importance of government spending in stimulating recovery, cut back sharply on the relief program in June 1937, with disastrous results. Between August and October the economy slipped downward like sand through a chute. Stocks plummeted, unemployment rose by 2 million, industrial production slumped. This new depression, known as the "Roosevelt recession," further damaged the President's reputation and for many months he aggravated the situation by adopting an almost Hoover-like attitude toward the problem. "Everything will work out all right if we just sit tight and keep quiet," he actually said.

BUTLER INSTITUTE OF AMERICAN ART

The militancy of labor in the late 1930's, particularly in its fight to unionize the steel and auto industries, is symbolized in Joe Jones's We Demand.

While the President hesitated, rival theorists within his administration warred. The Keynesians, led by WPA head Harry Hopkins, Marriner Eccles of the Federal Reserve, and Secretary of the Interior Harold Ickes, clamored for stepped-up government spending; the conservatives, led by Treasury Secretary Henry Morgenthau, Jr., advocated retrenchment. Perhaps confused by the conflict, Roosevelt seemed incapable of decisive action. When Keynes himself sent him "some bird's eye impressions" of the recession in February 1938, urging "large scale recourse to . . . public works and other investments aided by Government funds," he sent him only a routine acknowledgment, drafted by the conservative Secretary Morgenthau.

Finally, in April 1938, Roosevelt committed himself to the spenders. At his urging Congress passed a $3.75 billion public works bill. Two major pieces of new legislation were also enacted at about this time. A new AAA program went into effect (February 1938), setting marketing quotas and acreage limitations for growers of staples like wheat, cotton, and tobacco, and authorizing the Commodity Credit Corporation to lend money to farmers on their surplus crops. These surpluses were to be stored by the government. When prices rose, farmers could repay the loans, reclaim their produce, and sell it on the open market. This "ever-normal granary" idea avoided the need for dumping excess production abroad and protected the country against the danger of wide fluctuations in farm prices.

The second measure, the Fair Labor Standards

Act, besides formally abolishing child labor, established a national minimum wage of 40 cents an hour and a maximum work week of 40 hours, with time-and-a-half for overtime. Although the law failed to cover many of the poorest-paid types of labor, its passage meant wage increases for 750,000 workers. Far more important, it proved to be only a beginning. In later years many new classes of workers were brought within its protection and the minimum wage was repeatedly increased.

These measures further alienated conservatives without dramatically improving economic conditions. The resistance of many Democratic congressmen to further reform hardened. As the 1938 elections approached, Roosevelt decided to go to the voters in an effort to strengthen party discipline and re-energize his New Deal. He singled out a number of conservative Democratic senators, most notably Walter F. George of Georgia, Millard F. Tydings of Maryland, and "Cotton Ed" Smith of South Carolina, and tried to "purge" them by backing other Democrats in the primaries.

The purge failed. Southern voters liked Roosevelt but resented his interference in local politics. Smith dodged the issue of liberalism by stressing the question of white supremacy in South Carolina; Tydings emphasized Roosevelt's "invasion" of Maryland; in Georgia the President's enemies compared his campaign against George to General Sherman's march across the state during the Civil War. All three senators were easily renominated, and re-elected in November. In the nation at large the Republicans made important gains for the first time since Roosevelt had taken office. The Democrats maintained nominal control of both houses of Congress, but the conservative coalition, while unable to muster the strength to do away with already accomplished reforms, succeeded in blocking further reform.*

*This so-called "conservative condition" was never a well-organized group. Its membership shifted from issue to issue; it had no real leaders and certainly no long-range plans. If any common policy united its adherents, it was rural opposition to the New Deal's "overconcern" for the interests of unions, the unemployed, and underprivileged urban minorities.

Significance of the New Deal

By 1939 Roosevelt was ready to abandon further efforts at reform. He would hold the line against the reactionaries effectively, but thereafter foreign affairs dominated his thinking. The mounting danger of war in Europe as a result of the aggressions of the German dictator, Adolf Hitler, required that he devote all his energies to preparing the country to face the coming holocaust strong and united.

After war finally came in 1939, the Great Depression was swept away on a wave of orders from the beleaguered European democracies. Business boomed and unemployment declined. For this Roosevelt received much undeserved credit. His New Deal had not brought the country back to full employment nor really restored prosperity. It is a truth still ominous for the future of the American system that no convincing reply has ever been devised to the argument that modern capitalism cannot flourish without the stimulus of massive military expenditures.

The perspective of a generation points up other inadequacies of the New Deal. Roosevelt's willingness to experiment with different means of combating the depression made sense because no one really knew what to do; his uncertainty about the ultimate objectives of the New Deal, however, was surely counterproductive. He vacillated between seeking to stimulate the economy by deficit spending and trying to balance the budget; between a narrow "America First" economic nationalism and a broad-gauged international approach; between regulating monopolies and trust-busting; between helping the underprivileged and bolstering those already strong. At times he acted on the assumption that the United States had a "mature" economy and that the major problem was overproduction. At other times, he appeared to think that the answer to the depression was more production. He could never really make up his mind whether to try to rally liberals to his cause without regard for party or to run the government as a partisan leader, conciliating the conservative Democrats.

Yet these are criticisms after the fact; they ignore the complexities of the pressures of those

Negro sharecroppers evicted from their tenant farms were photographed by Arthur Rothstein along a Missouri road in 1939. Rothstein was one of a group of outstanding photographers who created a unique "sociological and economic survey" of the nation under the aegis of the Farm Security Administration between 1936 and 1942.

years, the way Roosevelt's thinking evolved during his first two terms, and above all the psychological as distinct from the practical effects of both the New Deal and its chief architect upon the American people. Programs that did not "work" often had totally unanticipated beneficial results.

On balance, the New Deal had an immense constructive impact on the nation. By 1939 the country was committed to the idea that government, especially the federal government, should accept responsibility for the national welfare and act to meet specific problems in every necessary way. What was significant was not the proliferation of new agencies nor the expansion of federal power, for these were but continuations of trends already a century old when the New Deal began. The importance of the "Roosevelt revolution" was that it settled the issue permanently, removing it from the realm of practical politics. "Never again," the Republican Presidential candidate was to say in 1952, "shall we *allow* a depression in the United States," and in 1958 another Republican, Vice President Richard M. Nixon, stated flatly: "The time is past when the Federal Government can stand by and allow a . . . depression without decisive Government action."

Because of New Deal decisions, many areas of American life formerly left unregulated became henceforth subject to federal authority: the stock exchange; agricultural prices and production; labor relations; relief of the needy. In general, after the New Deal years the government accepted its obligation to try to provide all the people with a decent standard of living and to pay some attention to achieving the Jeffersonian goal of happiness for all as well. If the New Deal failed to end the depression, it effected changes that have—so far, at least—prevented later economic declines from degenerating into major catastrophes. Although it is difficult to show conclusively that unionization has affected real wages significantly, by encouraging the growth of labor unions the New Deal probably helped workers obtain a larger share of the profits of industry. By putting a floor under the income of many farmers it checked the decline of the agricultural classes. The social security program, with all its inadequacies, also lessened the impact of bad times on an increasingly large proportion of the population and provided immense psychological benefits to all the people.

Furthermore, the New Deal hastened several major changes in the United States. One of the most dramatic shifts of the era was the movement of Negro voters from the Republican to the Democratic party. Although post-reconstruction Republican administrations had seldom treated them fairly, Negroes had traditionally supported the GOP, partly out of "gratitude" for emancipation, mainly because the Democratic party was so heavily influenced by its southern wing. Before Roosevelt there had been only two Democratic Presidents since James Buchanan left office in 1861: Cleveland, who made the political rehabilitation of southern Democrats one of his major objectives, and Wilson, who had little sympathy for blacks.

However, when Roosevelt became President, the situation was much changed. The great 20th-century migration of Negroes to the northern cities had coincided, in its later stages, with a growing tendency of urban voters to support the Democrats. This shift, noticeable by the election of 1928, had been completed by 1936, and it affected black city dwellers along with white. In large measure, Negroes supported the New Deal for the same reasons that whites did.

How the New Deal affected Negroes and racial attitudes specifically is a more complicated question. Roosevelt did nothing about civil rights before 1941 and little thereafter; in this respect he was as much a prisoner of the southern wing of his party as any earlier Democratic leader. Many New Deal programs treated blacks as second-class citizens. They were often paid at lower rates than whites under NRA codes. The early farm programs inadvertently forced many black tenants and sharecroppers from the land. Negroes were segregated in the Civilian Conservation Corps and in TVA projects. The Social Security Act, by excluding agricultural laborers and domestic servants, did nothing for hundreds of thousands of poor black workers. Negroes did not even get their full share of employment relief funds.

Yet the fact that Negroes got less than they deserved under the New Deal did not keep most of them from becoming New Dealers: half a loaf was far more than any American government had ever given them before. Moreover, aside from the direct benefits, Negroes profited in other ways. Some New Deal officials—Secretary of the Interior Harold L. Ickes was a shining example—gave important places to black executives, such as Clark Foreman, whom Ickes gave the job of stimulating the employment of blacks in other departments, and Robert C. Weaver, a Harvard-trained economist. Eventually, dozens of New Deal agencies employed Negroes in skilled professional posts, not merely as laborers and clerks. Eleanor Roosevelt, truly the first lady of the land in this respect as in so many others, worked steadily for the cause of racial equality. In the labor movement, the new CIO unions accepted black members, and this was particularly significant because these unions were organizing industries—steel, automobiles, mining among others—that employed large numbers of Negroes. Thus, while Negroes suffered horribly from the depression, they gained from New Deal efforts to counteract its effects both some relief and a measure of hope.

Among other important social changes, the TVA and the New Deal rural electrification program made farm life literally more civilized. Urban public housing, while never undertaken on a massive scale, helped rehabilitate some of the nation's worst slums. Government public power projects, such as the giant Bonneville and Grand Coulee dams in the Pacific Northwest, were only the most spectacular parts of a broad New Deal program to develop the natural resources of the country. The NIRA and later labor legislation forced businessmen to re-examine their role in American life and to become far more socially conscious than they had ever been before. The WPA art and theater programs widened the horizons of millions. All in all, the spirit of the New Deal heightened the people's sense of community, revitalized national energies, and stimulated the imagination and creative instincts of countless citizens.

How much of the credit for these achievements belongs personally to Franklin D. Roosevelt is debatable. The researches of careful historians such as Arthur M. Schlesinger, Jr., and William E. Leuchtenburg show that he had very little to do with many of the details and even with some of the broad principles behind the New Deal. His knowledge of economics was shaky, his understanding of many social problems superficial, his political philosophy distressingly vague. Basically a conservative, he did not seek the pervasive social and economic changes over which he presided.

Nevertheless, every aspect of the New Deal bears the brand of his remarkable personality. His political genius constructed the coalition that made the program possible, his fundamental humanitarianism made it a reform movement of truly major significance. Roosevelt rose above his intellectual limitations and prejudices. Although considered by many a terrible administrator because he encouraged rivalry among his subordinates, established countless special agencies often with overlapping responsibilities, failed to discharge many incompetents, and frequently put off making difficult decisions, he was actually one of the most effective Chief Executives in the nation's history. His seemingly haphazard practice of dividing authority among competing administrators unleashed the energies and sparked the imaginations of his aides, giving the ponderous federal bureaucracy a remarkable flexibility and *élan*.

UPI

Well-wishers greet the President at Warm Springs, Georgia, in 1933. The Roosevelt "magic," unfeigned and inexhaustible, amazed his associates. "I have never had contact with a man who was loved as he is," reported Secretary of the Interior Harold L. Ickes.

Like Wilson he was almost a prime minister, taking charge of the administration forces in Congress, drafting bills, buttonholing legislators, deluging the lawmakers with special messages. Like Jackson he maximized his role as leader of all the people. No earlier President used the newspapers so effectively in calling attention to his activities. His informal, biweekly press conferences, a constant source of delight to reporters, proved a matchless means of keeping the public in touch with developments and himself in tune with popular thinking. He made the radio an instrument for communicating with the masses in the most direct way imaginable: his "fireside chats" convinced millions that he was personally interested in their lives and welfare, as indeed he was. At a time when the increasing size and complexity of the federal government made it impossible for any one man to direct the nation's destiny, Roosevelt managed the minor miracle of personifying that government to 130 million persons. "There was a real dialogue between Franklin and the people," Eleanor Roosevelt said after his death, and she did not exaggerate. Under Hoover, a single clerk was able to handle the routine mail that flowed into the office of the President from ordinary citizens. Under Roosevelt, the task required a staff of 50.

While the New Deal was still evolving, contemporaries recognized Roosevelt's right to a place beside Washington, Jefferson, and Lincoln among the great Presidents. The years have not altered their judgment. Yet as his second term drew toward its close, some of his most important work lay still in the future.

SUPPLEMENTARY READING The Great Depression and the New Deal are covered briefly but comprehensively in J.D. Hicks, *Republican Ascendancy** (1960), and W.E. Leuchtenburg, *Franklin Roosevelt and the New Deal** (1963). The first three volumes of A.M. Schlesinger, Jr.'s still incomplete *The Age of Roosevelt** (1957–1960) treat the period to 1936 in vivid fashion. Basil Rauch, *The History of the New Deal** (1944), is also important. Both Dixon Wecter, *The Age of the Great Depression* (1948), and F.L. Allen, *Since Yesterday** (1940), are important for social history, while Broadus Mitchell, *Depression Decade** (1947), is a good economic history of the period.

For the stock market crash, consult Robert Sobel, *The Great Bull Market: Wall Street in the 1920's** (1968), which is highly analytical; John Brooks, *Once in Golconda: A True Drama of Wall Street* (1969), a more lively account; and J.K. Galbraith, *The Great Crash** (1955). The Hoover administration is discussed in H.G. Warren, *Herbert Hoover and the Great Depression** (1959), in A.U. Romasco, *The Poverty of Abundance* (1965), in R.L. Wilbur and A.M. Hyde, *The Hoover Policies* (1937), and in Herbert Hoover's *Memoirs: The Great Depression* (1951–52). Robert Bendiner, *Just Around the Corner** (1968), is full of interesting details. Irving Bernstein, *The Lean Years** (1960), contains an excellent account of the early years of the depression but is perhaps too sharply critical of Hoover.

Franklin D. Roosevelt's early career is treated exhaustively in Frank Freidel, *Franklin D. Roosevelt* (1952–56), but see also Bernard Bellush, *Franklin D. Roosevelt as Governor of New York* (1955). Of the many biographies of Roosevelt, see especially J.M. Burns, *Roosevelt: The Lion and the Fox** (1956), R.G. Tugwell, *The Democratic Roosevelt** (1957), and John Gunther, *Roosevelt in Retrospect** (1950). Daniel Fusfeld, *The Economic Thought of Franklin D. Roosevelt and the Origins of the New Deal* (1958), is also important. Richard Hofstadter has interesting essays on Hoover and Roosevelt in *The American Political Tradition** (1948). E.E. Robinson, *The Roosevelt Leadership* (1955), is highly critical. J.T. Patterson, *Congressional Conservatism and the New Deal** (1967), is a solid study of congressional politics.

Useful special studies of the New Deal include J.M. Blum, *From the Diaries of Henry Morgenthau, Jr.* (1959–1964), Gilbert Fite, *George N. Peek and the Fight for Farm Parity* (1954), C.M. Campbell, *The Farm Bureau and the New Deal* (1962), R.S. Kirkendall, *Social Scientists and Farm Politics in the Age of Roosevelt* (1966), D.E. Conrad, *The Forgotten Farmers: The Story of Sharecroppers in the New Deal* (1965), S.F. Charles, *Minister of Relief: Harry Hopkins and the Depression* (1963), E.E. Witte, *The Development of the Social Security Act** (1962), Roy Lubove, *The Struggle for Social Security* (1968), E.W. Hawley, *The New Deal and the Problem of Monopoly** (1966), J.D. Matthews, *The Federal Theater* (1967), Irving Bernstein, *The New Deal Collective Bargaining Policy* (1950), and two books by Sidney Fine, *The Automobile Under the Blue Eagle* (1963) and *Sit Down: The General Motors Strike of 1936–1937* (1969).

For the activities of the "radical fringe" consult D.R. McCoy, *Angry Voices: Left-of-Center Politics in the New Deal Era* (1958), and D.H. Bennett, *Demagogues in the Depression: American Radicalism and the Union Party* (1969). On Huey Long, see T.H. Williams, *Huey Long: A Biography* (1969).

Of the many published memoirs and diaries of New Deal figures, the following are outstanding: Raymond Moley, *After Seven Years* (1939), Frances Perkins, *The Roosevelt I Knew** (1946), Eleanor Roosevelt, *This I Remember** (1949), H.L. Ickes, *The Secret Diary of Harold L. Ickes* (1953–54), Marriner Eccles, *Beckoning Frontiers* (1951), and D.E. Lilienthal, *Journals: The TVA Years: 1939–1945* (1964).

*Available in paperback.

27

Isolationism and War: 1921–1945

On March 4, 1921, taking office after his overwhelming triumph in the 1920 election, President Warren G. Harding put an end to the brief era of Wilsonian internationalism. "Confident of our ability to work out our own destiny," he said, "we seek no part in directing the destinies of the Old World. We do not mean to be entangled. We will accept no responsibility except as our own conscience and judgment may determine." Twenty years later, almost to the day, President Franklin D. Roosevelt was addressing the awards dinner of the Academy of Motion Picture Arts and Sciences. "We can no longer consider our own problem of defense as a separate interest," he said. "It involves the future of democracy wherever it is imperiled." Between these two statements, so different in spirit, lay two decades of shortsighted diplomacy, a generation of American attempts to ignore world responsibilities, a tragic interlude of self-delusion. Ahead—a scant few months ahead—lay Pearl Harbor.

Peace Without a Sword

Presidents Harding, Coolidge, and Hoover did not handle foreign relations very differently from the way they managed domestic affairs. Harding left policy formulation to his secretary of state, the competent Charles Evans Hughes, and deferred to senatorial prejudice against executive domination in the area. Coolidge, who lacked both interest and energy for such matters, adopted a similar course. Hoover understood his diplomatic problems clearly and constructed intelligent plans for dealing with them, but he would not take legitimate risks and failed to win the confidence either of the American people or of the statesmen who directed the foreign relations of other powers.

In trying to direct the nation's foreign relations, all three faced the obstacle of a resurgent isolationism. The same forces of war-bred hatred, postwar disillusionment, and fear of communist subversion that produced the Red Scare at home also led Americans to turn their backs on the rest of the world. The bloodiness and apparent senselessness of the long conflict combined with an awareness of the fact that war was the ultimate weapon for settling international controversies convinced millions that the only way to be sure it would not happen again was to "steer clear" of "entanglements." That these famous words had been used by Washington and Jefferson in vastly different contexts did not deter isolationists from attributing to them the same authority they gave to Scripture. The country's increasing economic independence of Europe—the Continent's share of American foreign commerce was steadily declining—made it easier for many citizens to ignore European affairs. Vexing problems involving Allied war debts to the United States and competition with the European powers for world markets caused a further deterioration of relations. Americans were so suspicious of internationalism in the early twenties that the Harding administration treated the League of Nations with what the diplomatic historian Richard W. Leopold calls "studied hostility." In 1922 the career diplomat Joseph C. Grew, later ambassador to Japan, was stationed in Switzerland. One day, while waiting for a friend outside the League of Nations headquarters in Geneva, he ran into a reporter from the Chicago *Tribune*. Poor Grew felt obliged to explain at length why he was standing in so incriminating a place and to plead with the reporter not to publicize his "indiscretion." For a time, the State Department refused even to answer letters from the League Secretariat in Geneva.

THE ISOLATIONIST
"AM I MY BROTHER'S KEEPER ?"
AMERICA WILL NEVER ACCEPT
THE CURSE OF CAIN!

A poster issued in 1924, on the tenth anniversary of the outbreak of World War I, suggested an internationalist stance as the only hope for world peace.

While this nonsensical behavior did not long continue, the Presidents of the twenties failed to combat popular isolationism. They did not cease to concern themselves with foreign affairs, but they backed away from responsibility for maintaining world peace and for disabusing the public of its naive belief that foreign affairs did not vitally concern American national interests. Too often the Presidents allowed domestic questions to control American relations with the rest of the world. Their interest in disarmament flowed chiefly from their desire to cut taxes. Philippine policy was determined more by the domestic conflict between American sugar growers and American refiners than by international considerations or the needs of the Filipinos. Tariffs were adjusted to satisfy American manufacturers without regard for their effects on the world political situation.

The first important diplomatic event of the period revealed a great deal about American foreign policy after World War I. In November 1921 delegates representing the United States, Great Britain, Japan, France, Italy, China, and three other nations gathered at Washington to discuss disarmament and the problems of the Far East. By the following February this Washington Armament Conference had drafted three major treaties and a number of lesser agreements. The Four-Power Treaty, signed by the United States, Great Britain, Japan, and France, committed these nations to respect one another's interests in the islands of the Pacific and to confer in the event that any other country launched an attack in this area. The Five-Power Treaty, in which Italy joined these four, committed the signatories to stop building battleships for ten years and to reduce their fleets of capital ships to a fixed ratio, with Great Britain and the United States limited to 525,000 tons, Japan to 315,000 tons, and France and Italy to 175,000 tons. All the conferees signed the Nine-Power Treaty, agreeing to respect

China's independence and maintain the Open Door. In a separate pact they permitted China to raise its tariffs on imports.

On the surface the Washington Conference seemed a remarkable achievement, and, indeed, its effects were certainly salutary. For the first time in history, the major powers accepted certain limitations on their right to arm themselves. The Open Door, never before more than a pious expression of American hopes, received the formal endorsement of all nations with Far Eastern interests except Russia. Japan committed itself to restricting its ambitions in the Pacific area. By taking the lead in drafting the agreements, America regained some of the moral influence it had lost by not joining the League of Nations.

UNDERWOOD & UNDERWOOD

President-elect and Mrs. Hoover aboard the battleship Maryland, *1928. The Washington Armament Conference's halting of battleship construction began the aircraft carrier's rise to capital-ship status.*

However, these gains masked grave weaknesses both in the treaties themselves and in underlying American attitudes toward world affairs. The treaties were uniformly toothless. The signers of the Four-Power pact agreed only to consult in case of aggression in the Pacific; they made no promises to help one another or to restrict their freedom of action in any way. As President Harding assured the Senate: "There [was] no commitment to armed force, no alliance, no written or moral obligation to join in defense." The naval disarmament treaty said nothing about the number of cruisers and other warships that the powers might build, about the far more important question of land and air forces, or about the underlying industrial and financial structures that really controlled the ability of the nations to make war.* Nor did any of the imperialist powers that signed the Nine-Power Treaty actually intend to surrender their special privileges in China and allow that nation to become truly independent.

While basking smugly in the reflected glory of Secretary Hughes's diplomacy, the United States remained fundamentally irresponsible. Congress failed to provide enough money to maintain the navy even at the limit set by the Five-Power pact. Many Americans were also fundamentally anti-Japanese, as seen in the refusal of Congress to grant *any* immigration quota to Japan under the National Origins Act of 1924, although the formula applied to other nations would have allowed only 100 Japanese a year to enter the country. While stressing the fact that they had won overall naval equality with Great Britain, American diplomats failed to make clear that the 5–5–3 ratio permitted the Japanese to dominate the western Pacific. This ratio left the Philippine Islands undefendable and exposed Hawaii to possible attack. They boasted of having "forced" the powers to "recognize" the Open Door principle in China but remained as unwilling as ever to fight to keep the door open when a more determined nation slammed it shut.

*A second disarmament conference, held at London in 1930, attempted to place limits on smaller warships, but no agreement could be reached.

The Americans of the twenties wanted peace, but would neither surrender their prejudices and dislikes nor build the defenses necessary to make it safe to indulge these passions, nor contribute significantly to the building of stable institutions and prosperous economic conditions in other parts of the world. Peace societies flourished: the Carnegie Endowment for International Peace, designed "to hasten the abolition of war, the foulest blot upon our civilization"; the Woodrow Wilson Foundation, aimed at helping "the liberal forces of mankind throughout the world . . . who intend to promote peace by the means of justice"; and many others. In 1923 Edward W. Bok, retired editor of the *Ladies' Home Journal,* offered a prize of $100,000 for the best workable plan for preserving international peace and was flooded with suggestions. But too many lovers of peace were like Senator William E. Borah of Idaho—sincerely opposed to war yet committed to isolationism with equal fervor. When Franklin D. Roosevelt drafted a peace plan for the Bok contest while recovering from his attack of infantile paralysis,* he felt constrained to include in the preamble this statement:

> We seek not to become involved as a nation in the purely regional affairs of groups of other nations, nor to give to the representatives of other peoples the right to compel us to enter upon undertakings calling for a leading up to the use of armed force without our full and free consent, given through our constitutional procedure.

So great was the opposition to international cooperation that the United States refused even to accept membership on the World Court, although this tribunal could settle disputes only when all the nations involved agreed. Probably a majority of the American people favored joining the Court, but its advocates were never able to bring enough pressure on Senate isolationists to prevent them from blocking ratification of the necessary treaty. Too many peace lovers believed that their goal could be attained simply by pointing out the moral and practical disadvantages of war. In their opinion, any attempt to discourage aggressors by building up one's own strength seemed more likely to cause trouble than prevent it.

The culmination of this illusory faith in preventing war by criticizing it came with the signing of the Kellogg-Briand Pact in 1928. This treaty was born in the fertile brain of French Foreign Minister Aristide Briand. France, desperately concerned over its future security, was eager to collect allies against possible attack by a resurgent Germany. In 1927 Briand proposed to Secretary of State Frank B. Kellogg that their countries agree never to go to war with each other. Such a treaty would have been, as historian Robert H. Ferrell has said, "a negative military alliance," and Kellogg found the idea as repugnant as any conventional alliance, but American isolationists as well as pacifists found the suggestion fascinating. They plagued Kellogg with demands that he negotiate such a treaty.

To extricate himself from this situation, Kellogg cleverly suggested that the pact be broadened to include *all* nations. Briand was furious. Like Kellogg, he saw how meaningless such a treaty would be, especially when hedged, as Kellogg insisted, with a proviso that "every nation is free at all times . . . to defend its territory from attack and it alone is competent to decide when circumstances require war in self-defense." Nevertheless, Briand also found public pressures irresistible. In August 1928, at Paris, diplomats from 15 nations bestowed upon one another an "international kiss," condemning "recourse to war for the solution of international controversies" and renouncing war "as an instrument of national policy." Seldom has so unrealistic a promise been made by so many intelligent men. Most Americans, however, considered the Kellogg-Briand Pact a milestone in the history of civilization: the Senate, habitually so suspicious of international commitments, ratified it 85 to 1.

The Good Neighbor Policy

Isolationism did not, however, deter the government from seeking to advance American economic interests abroad. The Open Door concept remained predominant; the State Department worked to obtain opportuni-

*Roosevelt did not submit the plan because his wife Eleanor was named one of the judges.

ties for businessmen and investors in underdeveloped countries, hoping both to stimulate the American economy and to bring stability to "backward" nations in the interests of world peace. Although this policy sometimes roused local resentments because of the tendency of the United States to cooperate with conservative forces abroad, it did result in a further retreat from active interventionism.

The pattern is well illustrated by events in Latin America. "Yankeephobia" had long been a chronic condition south of the Rio Grande. The continued presence of marines in Central America fed this bad feeling, as did the failure of the United States to enter the League of Nations, which all but four of the Latin-American nations had joined. Basic, of course, was the immense wealth and power of the "Colossus of the North" and the feeling of Latin Americans that the wielders of this strength had little respect for the needs and values of their southern neighbors. However, the evident desire of the United States to limit its international involvements had a gradually mollifying effect on Latin-American opinion.

In dealing with this area of the world, Harding and Coolidge performed neither better nor worse than Wilson, while Hoover advanced significantly toward a wiser and more humane position. American interference in Central America declined steadily. In the face of continued radicalism and instability in Mexico, which caused Americans with interests in land and oil rights to suffer heavy losses, President Coolidge acted with forbearance. His decision to appoint his friend Dwight W. Morrow, a patient, sympathetic, and thoughtful lawyer, as ambassador to Mexico in 1927 resulted in a gradual improvement in Mexican-American relations. The Mexicans were able to complete their social and economic revolution in the twenties without significant interference from the United States.

Under Herbert Hoover, the United States began at last to treat Latin-American nations as equals. Hoover reversed Wilson's policy of trying to teach them "to elect good men." The Clark Memorandum (1930), written by Undersecretary of State J. Reuben Clark, disassociated the right of intervention in Latin America from the Roosevelt Corollary. The corollary had been an improper extension of the Monroe Doctrine, Clark declared. The right of the United States to intervene depended rather upon "the doctrine of self-preservation." The distinction seemed slight to Latin Americans, but the underlying reasoning was important. Obviously any nation capable of doing so will intervene in the affairs of another when its own existence is at stake. But the long-established "right" of the United States under the Monroe Doctrine to keep *other* nations out of Latin America as a matter of principle did not give it a similarly broad authority to intervene there itself. President Hoover never officially acknowledged the Clark Memorandum, but did not intervene in Latin America, on the basis of the Roosevelt Corollary or on any other ground.

Hoover's policies were taken over and advanced by Franklin Roosevelt after 1933. At the Montevideo Pan-American Conference (December 1933) his secretary of state, Cordell Hull, voted in the affirmative on a resolution that "no state has the right to intervene in the internal or external affairs of another," a statement scarcely more meaningful than the Kellogg-Briand denunciation of war, but gratifying to sensitive Latin Americans. By 1934 all the marines had been withdrawn from Nicaragua, the Dominican Republic, and Haiti. Roosevelt also, in 1934, renounced the right to intervene in Cuban affairs, thus abrogating the Platt Amendment to the Cuban constitution.

Beyond doubt the "Good Neighbor Policy" of Hoover and Roosevelt* helped to convince many Latin Americans that the United States had no aggressive intentions south of the Rio Grande. Unfortunately, however, the United States took no effective steps to improve social and economic conditions in the region, so that the underlying jealousy and resentment of "rich Uncle Sam" did not disappear. Although isolationism paid some unearned dividends when applied to a part of the world that posed no possible threat to the United States, the essential blindness of the policy meant

*Hoover invented this term, but it was typical of the relative political effectiveness of the two Presidents that Roosevelt got most of the credit.

the loss of many opportunities to advance the national interest by *helping* other countries.

The Fascist Challenge

The futility and danger of isolationism was glaringly exposed in September 1931 when the Japanese invaded Chinese Manchuria. China had been torn by revolution since 1911; by the twenties the Nationalists, led by Chiang Kai-shek, had adopted a policy of driving all "foreign devils" from their country. The western powers, including the United States, offered little resistance to the loss of special privileges in China, but when Chiang attempted to exert full control over Manchuria, which both Japan and Russia considered vital to their interests, he ran into trouble. In 1920 he tried to deprive the Russians of their control of the Chinese Eastern Railway. Russia promptly sent in troops and forced Chiang to back down. Efforts to invoke the new Kellogg-Briand Pact in the conflict demonstrated the ineffectiveness of this agreement, for the Russians insisted they were acting in self-defense and no other power was ready to challenge them. Japan's attack was a far more serious affair, for the Japanese were not satisfied merely to protect rights already held. They speedily overran all Manchuria and converted it into a puppet state called Manchukuo. This clearly violated both the Kellogg-Briand and Nine-Power pacts.

Unable to contain the invaders, China had appealed both to the League of Nations and to the United States for help. Neither would intervene. When the League asked the United States if it would cooperate in any police action—it is far from certain that it would have moved decisively against Japan even if cooperation had been forthcoming—President Hoover refused to consider either economic or military reprisals. Such sanctions, he said "are the roads to war." When pressed to enforce the Nine-Power and Kellogg-Briand treaties, he replied that these were "solely moral instruments."

Thus Japan was allowed to keep a large and valuable territory that it had seized by force. The League sent a commission to investigate, and Secretary of State Henry L. Stimson, unable to persuade President Hoover to take a stronger hand, announced (the Stimson Doctrine) that the United States would never recognize the legality of seizures made in violation of American treaty rights. Unbacked by either force or the support of Great Britain and France, the doctrine served only to irritate the Japanese. They blandly went ahead with their dismemberment of China. In January 1932 they attacked Shanghai, the bloody battle marked by the indiscriminate bombing of residential districts. When the League at last officially condemned their aggressions, they withdrew from the organization, sure that the powers would not back admonitions with action, and extended their control of northern China. The lesson of Manchuria, of course, was not lost upon Adolf Hitler, who became chancellor of Germany on January 30, 1933.

It is easy, in surveying the diplomatic events of 1920–1939, to condemn the western democracies for their unwillingness to stand up for basic principles, their refusal to resist Germany, Italy, and Japan when those nations embarked on the aggressions that led to World War II and cost the world millions of lives and billions of dollars. The democracies failed, until almost too late, to realize that a new ideology, totalitarianism, had arisen in Europe and that unless they resisted it forcefully, it would destroy them.

It is also possible to place some of the blame for the troubles of that era on these same powers: they controlled much of the world's resources and were far more interested in holding on to what they had than in helping other nations to improve the lives of their citizens or in righting international wrongs.

Nevertheless, the new totalitarian states were clearly the aggressors. Their system, involving complete subordination of the individual to the state and the concentration of political power in the hands of a dictator, was made possible by the industrial revolution, which produced tightly integrated national economies and the instruments of power and communication needed to control closely the actions of masses of people. The social and economic dislocations that followed the Great War created the desperate conditions which led millions of Europeans to adopt totalitarian ideas. The doctrine first assumed importance in 1922 in Italy, when Benito Mussolini seized power. Over the next few years Mussolini abolished universal suffrage, crushed every dissenter who dared speak out against him, and established a kind of dictatorial socialism which he called fascism (*fascismo*), the term referring to the Roman *fasces,* a symbol of governmental authority consisting of a bundle of rods bound around an ax. Mussolini blamed all the ills plaguing the Italian people on foreign sources, a convenient way to avoid the responsibilities that should have accompanied power. Since state control of every aspect of social and economic life characterized his regime, his movement was essentially a violent kind of nationalism, epitomized in the person of the leader (*Il Duce*).

Mussolini was an absurd poseur and mountebank whose power in world affairs remained relatively slight. Western leaders could perhaps be excused for failing to take him seriously. But the German fascist dictator Hitler presented a threat that the democracies ignored at their peril. Besides ruthlessly destroying countless innocent Jews whom he blamed for all Germany's troubles, Hitler denounced democracy as a system of government. He established a monolithic police state that crushed every form of dissent, every humane value. He glorified violence and announced plainly that he intended to extend his control over all German-speaking peoples. He dismissed the international agreements made by his predecessors with contempt. Germany possessed a potential for war far greater than Italy's, yet to Hitler's cruelest and most flagrantly aggressive actions, the western nations responded only by making concession after concession, in the vain hope of pacifying him.

In a way the democracies failed to resist totalitarianism because of their very virtues: their faith in man's essential goodness, their willingness to see the other side of complicated questions, their horror of war. Any history of the period that treats the leading figures and their followers as fools or cowards grossly distorts the truth. Nevertheless, an unbiased account must conclude that the western diplomats failed to control events, that they and the citizens of their respective lands should have acted more wisely and courageously than they did. This statement applies as fully to the Americans as to the Europeans.

They did not stand together firmly against the aggressors in part because they disagreed among themselves. Particularly divisive was the controversy over war debts—those of Germany to the Allies and those of the Allies to the United States. During and immediately after the war, the United States lent more than $10 billion to its comrades in arms for munitions and other supplies. Since most of this money had been spent in the United States, it might well have been considered part of America's contribution to the war effort. The public, however, demanded full repayment—with interest—when the war was over. "These were loans, not contributions," the "greatest Secretary of the Treasury since Alexander Hamilton" firmly declared. Even when the Foreign Debt Commission scaled the interest rate down from 5 per cent to about 2 per cent, the total obligation, to be repaid over a period of 62 years, amounted to over $22 billion.

Simplicissimus, JUNE 28, 1922

A German magazine's bitter 1922 comment on the issue of war reparations. American loans intended to restore the German economy go instead, in the form of reparations, to fatten a militaristic Frenchman.

Repayment of such a colossal sum was almost impossible. In the first place, the money had not been put to productive use. Dollars lent to build factories or roads might be expected to earn profits for the borrower, but those devoted to the purchase of shells actually destroyed wealth. Furthermore, the American protective tariff reduced the ability of the Allies to earn the dollars needed to pay the debts.

The Allies tried to load their obligations to the United States, along with all the other costs of the war, upon the backs of the Germans, demanding reparations amounting to $33 billion. If this sum were collected, they declared, they could rebuild their economies and obtain the international exchange needed to pay their debts to the United States. But as John Maynard Keynes had predicted in his *Economic Consequences of the Peace* (1919), Germany could not pay such huge reparations. When Germany defaulted, so did the Allies.

Everyone was bitterly resentful: the Germans because they felt they were being bled white; the Americans, as Senator Hiram Johnson of California put it, because the wily Europeans were treating the United States as "an international sucker"; the Allies because (as the French said) "*l'oncle Shylock*" was demanding his pound of flesh with interest. "If nations were only business firms," Clemenceau wrote Calvin Coolidge in 1926, "bank notes would determine the fate of the world. . . . Come see the endless lists of dead in our villages." Everyone also shared the blame: the Germans because they resorted to a wild inflation that reduced the mark to less than one-*trillionth* of its prewar value, at least in part in hopes of avoiding their international obligations; the Americans because they refused to recognize the connection between the tariff and the debt question; the Allies because they made little effort to pay even a reasonable proportion of their debts.

In 1924 an international agreement, known as the Dawes Plan, attempted to solve the problem by granting Germany a $200 million loan designed to stabilize its currency. Under this arrangement, Germany agreed to pay about $250 million a year in reparations, the hope being that this amount could be increased as the German economy revived. In 1929 the Young Plan scaled down the total reparations bill to a more reasonable $8 billion. In practice, Allied payments to the United States amounted roughly to the sums actually collected from Germany. Since the money Germany paid during the twenties came largely from private American loans, the United States would have served itself and the rest of the world far better if it had written off the war debts at the start. In any case, when the Great Depression struck, Americans stopped lending money to Germany, Germany defaulted on its reparations payments, and the Allies soon gave up all pretense of meeting their obligations to the United States.

In 1931 President Hoover arranged a one-year moratorium on all international obligations. (He was motivated partly by the fear that if Germany continued to pay reparations it would be unable to pay back the money it had borrowed in the twenties from American bankers.) When this period of grace expired, the whole question of reparations and debts expired with it—the last token debt payments were made in 1933. All that remained was a heritage of mistrust and hostility, shared by all concerned. In 1934 Congress passed the Johnson Debt Default Act, banning further loans to nations that had not paid their war debts.

Besides putting an end to the debt question, the worldwide depression of the thirties affected international relations in another way. Faced with declining production and shrinking foreign markets, most of the powers abandoned the gold standard, devaluing their currencies in hopes of increasing their exports. These efforts failed, partly because the nations also raised their tariffs, but mainly because when *everyone* went off the gold standard, the device was self-defeating. Abandoning gold also hampered international commerce, since an inconvertible currency was useless outside the nation issuing it. Any country with a favorable balance of trade soon accumulated large amounts of paper money it could not put to productive use.

President Roosevelt took the United States off the gold standard in April 1933. The next month a World Economic Conference met in London. Delegates from 64 nations sought ways to increase world trade, perhaps by a general reduction of tariffs and the stabilization of currencies. After flirting with the idea of currency stabilization, Roosevelt threw a bombshell into the conference by announcing that the United States would not return to the gold standard. Although he can justly be condemned for the supercilious and scolding tone of his statement, the economic nationalism behind his decision was, if wrong-headed, understandable enough in the depths of the depression. Like most other world leaders, Roosevelt placed revival of America's own limping economy ahead of general world recovery. Alas, aside from being shortsighted, his decision further increased international ill-feeling. The London Conference collapsed amid much anti-American recrimination. In every country, narrow-minded nationalists increased their strength. The German financier Hjalmar Schacht announced smugly that Roosevelt was adopting the maxim of the great *Führer*, Adolf Hitler: "Take your economic fate in your own hands."

American Isolationism

Against this background of depression and international tension, vital changes in American foreign policy took place. Unable to persuade the country that positive action against aggressors was necessary, internationalists like Secretary of State Stimson had begun, in 1931, to work for a *discretionary* arms embargo law, to be applied by the President in time of war against whichever side had broken the peace. As early as December 1931, while Japan was overrunning Manchuria, a resolution was introduced in Congress prohibiting the sale of arms to any nation violating the Kellogg-Briand Pact. By early 1933 Stimson had obtained Hoover's backing for an embargo bill, as well as the support of President-elect Roosevelt, who said: "I have long been in favor of the use of embargoes . . . against aggressor nations." The munitions interests managed to delay this bill; then the isolationists pounced upon it, and in the resulting debate it was amended to make the embargo apply impartially to *all* belligerents. While Roosevelt somewhat inexplicably accepted this change, the internationalists in Congress did not, and when they withdrew their support the measure died.

The amendment would have completely reversed the impact of any embargo. Instead of providing an effective, if essentially negative, weapon for influencing international affairs, a blanket embargo would only intensify America's ostrichlike isolationism. Stimson's original idea would have permitted arms shipments to China but not to Japan, which might have discouraged the Japanese from attacking. As amended, the embargo would have automatically applied to both sides, thus removing the United States as an influence in the conflict.

The attitude of the munitions-makers, who opposed both forms of the embargo, led to a series of studies of the industry. The most important of these was a Senate investigation (1934–36) headed by the isolationist Gerald P. Nye of North Dakota. Nye, a progressive of the La Follette type, was convinced that "the interests" had conspired to drag America into the Great War; his investigation was more an inquisition than an honest effort to discover what the bankers and munitions-makers had been doing between 1914 and 1918. His assistants, ferreting into subpoenaed records, uncovered some sensational facts about the lobbying activities and profits of various concerns. The Du Pont company's earnings, for example, had soared from $5 million in 1914 to $82 million in 1916. When one senator suggested to Irénée Du Pont that he was displaying a somewhat different attitude toward war than most citizens, Du Pont replied coolly: "Yes; perhaps. You were not in the game, or you might have a different viewpoint." The facts indicated that the munitions-makers had profited far more from neutrality than from participation in the war, but Nye, abetted by the press, exaggerated the significance of his findings. Millions of Americans became convinced that the House of Morgan and the "merchants of death" had tricked the country into war and that the "mistake" of 1917 must never be repeated.

While the Nye committee labored, Walter Millis published *The Road to War: America, 1914–1917* (1935). In this best seller, Millis advanced the thesis that British propaganda, the heavy purchases of American supplies by the

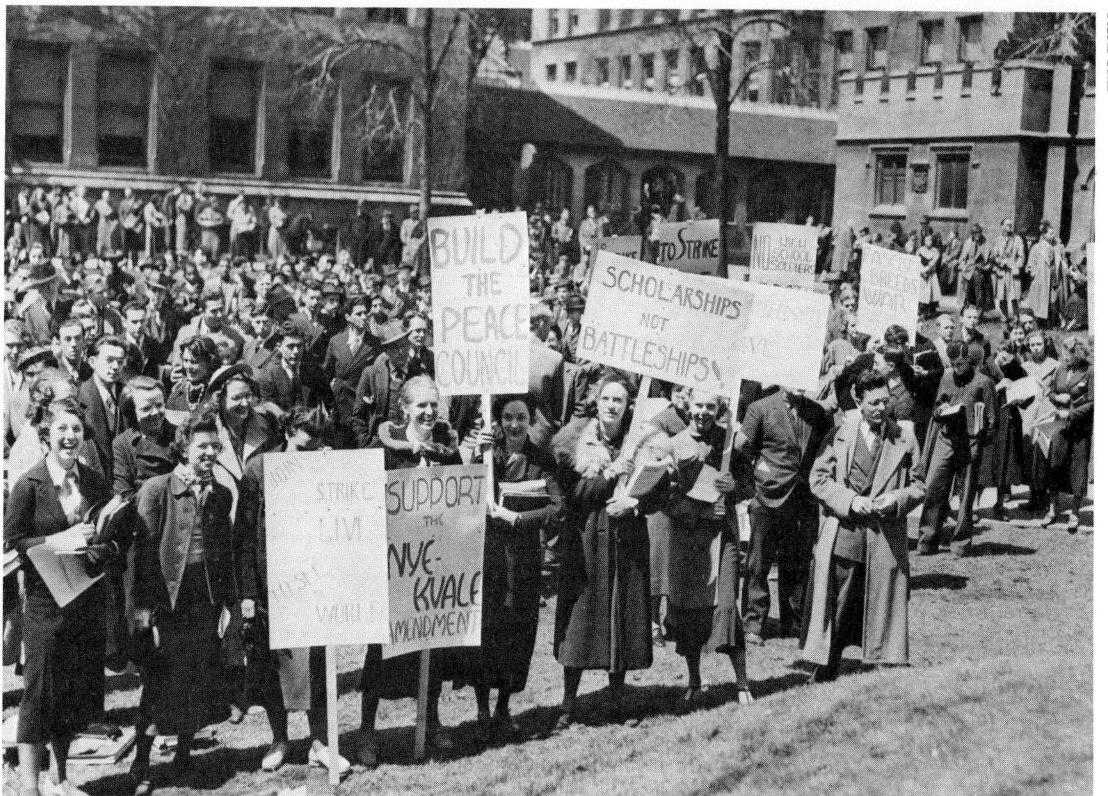

WIDE WORLD

University of Chicago undergraduates were photographed as they prepared to march in support of a nationwide antiwar demonstration in April 1937. During the spring of that year American isolationism reached its height.

Allies, and Wilson's differing reactions to violations of neutral rights by Germany and Great Britain had drawn the United States into a war it could and should have steered clear of. Thousands found Millis' logic convincing. International lawyers, most notably Charles Warren, a former assistant attorney general, were also beginning to argue at this time that modern warfare had made freedom of the seas for neutrals meaningless. The United States could stay out of future wars, Warren claimed, only by abandoning the seas, clamping an embargo on arms shipments, closing American ports to belligerent vessels, and placing quotas based on prewar sales upon the exportation of all contraband. "Under modern conditions there is no reason why the United States Government should run the risk of becoming involved in a war simply to preserve and protect . . . [the] excessive profits to be made out of war-trading by some of its citizens," Warren wrote.

All these developments led, in 1935, to what historian Robert A. Divine has called "the triumph of isolation." The danger of a general war mounted steadily as Germany, Italy, and Japan repeatedly resorted to force to achieve their expansionist aims. In March 1935 Hitler instituted universal military training and began to raise an army of half a million. In May Mussolini massed troops in Italian Somaliland, using a trivial border clash as the pretext for threatening the primitive kingdom of Ethiopia. Each aggression only drove the United States deeper into its shell; Congress responded by passing the Neutrality Act of 1935, which forbade the sale of munitions to *all* belligerents whenever the President should proclaim that a state of war existed. Americans who took passage on belligerent ships after such a proclamation had been issued would do so at their own risk. Roosevelt, reverting to his position at the time of his inauguration, fought hard for a discretionary embargo, but he dared not risk rousing the ire of the isolationists by vetoing the bill.

In October 1935 Italy invaded Ethiopia, and Roosevelt invoked the new neutrality law. Secretary of State Hull asked American exporters to support a "moral embargo" on the sale of oil and other products not covered by the act, but his plea was ignored. Oil shipments to Italy tripled between October and January. Italy quickly overran and annexed Ethiopia. In February 1936 Congress passed a second neutrality act forbidding all loans to belligerents.

Then, in the summer of 1936, civil war broke out in Spain, the rebels, led by the reactionary General Francisco Franco and strongly backed by Italy and Germany, seeking to overthrow the somewhat leftist Spanish Republic. Here, clearly, was a clash between democracy and the new fascism, and the neutrality laws did not apply to civil wars. Roosevelt, however, now became more fearful of involvement than some of the isolationists. (Senator Nye, for example, favored selling arms to the legitimate Spanish government.) The President evidently believed that American interference might cause the conflict in Spain to escalate into a global war, and he was also wary of antagonizing the pro-Franco element in the United States. At his urging, Congress soon passed another neutrality act broadening the arms embargo to cover civil wars.

Now isolationism reached its peak. A Gallup public-opinion poll revealed in March 1937 that 94 per cent of the people thought that American policy should be directed at keeping out of all foreign wars rather than trying to prevent the wars from breaking out. In April Congress passed still another neutrality law, which continued the embargo on munitions and loans, *forbade* Americans to travel on belligerent ships, and gave the President discretionary authority to place the sale of other goods to belligerents on a cash-and-carry basis. In theory, this would preserve the nation's profitable foreign trade without the risk of war, but in fact it played directly into the hands of the aggressors. While German planes and cannon were turning the tide in Spain, the United States was denying the hard-pressed Spanish loyalists even a case of cartridges. The blindness of this policy appalled those who recognized the fascist danger. "With every surrender the prospects of a European war grow darker," Claude G. Bowers, the American ambassador to Spain, warned. The internationalist-oriented New York *Herald Tribune* pointed out that the neutrality legislation was literally reactionary—designed to keep the United States out of the war of 1914–18, not the new conflict looming on the horizon. President Roosevelt, partly because of his own vacillation, seemed to have lost control over the formulation of American foreign policy. The American people, like wild creatures before a forest fire, were rushing in blind panic from the conflagration, they knew not where.

The Road to Pearl Harbor

Yet at the moment of its greatest success, isolationism began to crumble; there were limits beyond which Americans would not go merely to avoid the possibility of war. In July 1937 the Japanese again attacked China. Peiping quickly fell and the invaders pressed ahead on a broad front. Roosevelt felt that by invoking the neutrality law he would be helping the well-armed Japanese. Taking advantage of the fact that neither side had formally declared war, he pursued a waiting policy, allowing the shipment of arms and supplies to both sides. In the last half of 1937 Chinese munitions purchases exceeded $7 million; those of Japan were less than $2 million. The President tried to go still further. Speaking at Chicago in October, he proposed a "quarantine" of nations—he mentioned none by name—who were "creating a state of international anarchy and instability *from which there is no escape through mere isolation or neutrality*." However, this roused a windy burst of isolationist rhetoric which forced him to abandon the idea of a quarantine. "It's a terrible thing," he said, "to look over your shoulder when you are trying to lead—and to find no one there."

Roosevelt came only gradually to the conclusion that resisting aggression was more important than keeping out of war, and when he did, the need to keep the country united led him at times to be less than candid in his public statements. Hitler's annexation of Austria in March 1938 caused him deep concern. Then in September Hitler demanded that Czechoslovakia cede the

German-speaking Sudetenland region to the Reich. If the democracies had stood firm, as their treaties with Czechoslovakia required, the dictator might have backed down; instead, British Prime Minister Neville Chamberlain and French Premier Edouard Daladier, in a fateful conference with Hitler at Munich, yielded to Hitler's threats and promises and persuaded the Czechs to surrender the Sudetenland. Roosevelt, although he found this example of appeasement disturbing, did not speak out against the Munich pact. But when the Nazis seized the rest of Czechoslovakia in March 1939, no one could any longer question the aggressive purposes of Hitler's National Socialist (Nazi) movement. In a memorable address to Congress, Roosevelt said: "Acts of aggression against sister nations . . . automatically undermine all of us." He called for "methods short of war" to demonstrate America's determination to defend its institutions. "God-fearing democracies," he added, "cannot safely be indifferent to international lawlessness anywhere."

When the insatiable Hitler began to threaten Poland in the spring of 1939, demanding the free city of Danzig and the Polish Corridor separating East Prussia from the rest of Germany, and when Mussolini invaded Albania, Roosevelt sent both dictators urgent appeals to keep the peace, but he was no longer an appeaser. He urged Congress to repeal the 1937 Neutrality Act so that the United States could sell arms to Britain and France in the event of war.

Congress refused. "Captain," Vice President Garner told Roosevelt after counting noses in the Senate, "you haven't got the votes," and the President, perhaps unwisely, accepted this judgment and did not press the issue. However, the national mood was changing. In August 1939 Germany and Russia signed a "nonaggression" pact, prelude to their joint assault on Poland. On September 1 Hitler's troops invaded Poland, at last provoking Great Britain and France to declare war.

Roosevelt immediately summoned Congress into special session and again asked for repeal of the arms embargo. In November, in a vote that followed party lines closely, the Democratic majority pushed through a new neutrality law permitting the sale of arms and other contraband on a cash-and-carry basis. Short-term loans were also authorized, but American vessels were forbidden to carry *any* products to the belligerents. Since the Allies controlled the seas, cash-and-carry gave them a tremendous advantage—exactly what Roosevelt and the majority of the American people desired.

The German attack on Poland effected a basic change in American thinking. Keeping out of the war remained an almost universal hope, but preventing a Nazi victory became the ultimate, if not always conscious, wish of most citizens. In Roosevelt's case the wish was clearly conscious, although he dared not express it candidly because of continued isolationist strength in Congress and the country. He moved slowly, responding to developments overseas rather than directing the course of events. But his course was perfectly consistent.

Time quickly proved that cash-and-carry was not enough to stop the Nazis. Poland fell in less than a month; then, after a winter lull that cynics called the "phony war," Hitler loosed his armored divisions against the western powers. Between April 9 and June 22 he taught the world the awful meaning of *Blitzkrieg*—lightning war. Denmark, Norway, the Netherlands, Belgium, and France were successively battered into submission. The British army, pinned against the sea at Dunkirk, saved itself from annihilation only by fleeing across the English Channel. After the French submitted to his harsh terms on June 22 at Compiègne, outside Paris, Hitler controlled nearly all of western Europe.

Roosevelt responded to these disasters in a variety of ways. In the fall of 1939, reacting to warnings from Albert Einstein and other scientists that the Germans were seeking to develop an atomic bomb, he committed federal funds to a top-secret atomic energy program. Even while the British and French were falling back, he sold them, without legal authority, surplus government arms. When Italy entered the war against France while that nation was reeling before the force of Hitler's panzer divisions, the President cast aside all pretense of impartiality and characterized the invasion as a stab in the back. He also froze the

American assets of the conquered nations to keep them out of German hands and maintained diplomatic relations with the exiled governments of these countries. During the first five months of 1940 he asked Congress to appropriate over $4 billion for national defense. To strengthen national unity he named Henry L. Stimson secretary of war* and another Republican, Frank Knox, secretary of the navy. The United States, in short, had abandoned neutrality for nonbelligerency.

After the fall of France, Hitler attempted to bomb and starve the British into submission. The great air battles over England during the summer of 1940 ended in a decisive defeat for the Nazis, but the Royal Navy, which had only about 100 destroyers, could not control German submarine attacks on shipping. In this desperate hour, Prime Minister Winston Churchill, who had replaced the discredited Chamberlain in May 1940, asked Roosevelt for 50 old American destroyers to fill the gap. The ships were available; the navy had 240 destroyers in commission and more than 50 others on the way. But a direct loan or sale of these vessels would have violated both international and American laws. Any attempt to obtain new legislation would have meant long delay if not actual defeat. Roosevelt, therefore, arranged to "trade" the destroyers for six naval bases in the Caribbean. In addition, Great Britain leased bases in Bermuda and Newfoundland to the United States and Churchill also promised that even if the Germans invaded Great Britain, the British fleet would never be scuttled or surrendered.

This destroyers-for-bases deal was one of Roosevelt's most masterful achievements, both as a statesman and as a politician. It helped save Great Britain, which was the major objective at the moment. It also circumvented isolationist prejudices, because the President could present it as a shrewd bargain that bolstered America's defenses. A string of vital island bastions along the Atlantic frontier was surely more valuable to the country than 50 World War I destroyers.

Lines were hardening, all over the world. In September, despite bitter isolationist resistance, Congress enacted the first peacetime draft in American history. Some 1.2 million draftees were summoned for one year of service and 800,000 reservists were called to active duty. That same month, Japan signed a mutual-assistance pact with Germany and Italy directed primarily against the United States. This Rome-Berlin-Tokyo axis fused the conflicts in Europe and Asia, turning the struggle between fascism and democracy into a global war.

In the midst of these events the 1940 Presidential election took place. Why Roosevelt decided to run for a third term is a much-debated question. Partisanship had something to do with it, for no other Democrat seemed so likely to carry the country. Nor would the President have been human had he not been tempted to hold on to power, especially in such critical times. His conviction that his own brand of internationalism was necessary and that no one else could keep a rein on the isolationists was probably decisive. In any case, while outwardly reluctant to run again, he used his authority as party chief to control the Democratic convention and was overwhelmingly renominated. Vice President Garner, who had become disenchanted with Roosevelt and the New Deal, did not seek a third term; at Roosevelt's dictation, the party chose Secretary of Agriculture Henry A. Wallace for the second spot on the ticket.

The two leading Republican candidates were Senator Robert A. Taft of Ohio, son of the former President, and District Attorney Thomas E. Dewey of New York, who had won fame as a "racket buster" and political reformer. But Taft was too conservative and totally lacking in political glamour, while Dewey, barely 38, seemed too young and inexperienced. Instead, the Republicans nominated the darkest of dark horses, Wendell L. Willkie of Indiana, the utility magnate who had led the fight against TVA.

Despite his political inexperience and Wall Street connections, Willkie made an appealing candidate. He was an energetic, charming, openhearted man capable of inspiring deep loyalties. His roughhewn, rural manner (one Democrat called him "a simple, barefoot Wall Street law-

*Stimson had held this post from 1911 to 1913 in the Taft Cabinet!

FRANKLIN D. ROOSEVELT LIBRARY

A cartoon of August 1941 reflects the growing shift away from isolationism. Montana Senator Burton K. Wheeler and the famous aviator Charles A. Lindbergh join an America Firster in "Appeasing a Polecat."

yer") won him wide support in farm districts. He had difficulty, however, finding issues on which to oppose Roosevelt. Good times were at last returning. The basic New Deal reforms were both too popular and too much in line with his own thinking to invite attack. He believed as strongly as the President that America could no longer ignore the Nazi threat.

In the end Willkie focused his campaign on Roosevelt's conduct of foreign relations. A preponderance of the Democrats favored all-out aid to Britain, while most Republicans still wished to avoid foreign "entanglements." But the crisis was causing many persons to shift sides. Among interventionists, organizations like the Committee to Defend America by Aiding the Allies, headed by Republican William Allen White, and the small but influential Century Group contained important men of both parties. On the other side, the America First Committee, led by Robert E. Wood of Sears Roebuck, included Democrats as well as Republicans in its ranks. Unwilling to take an isolationist position, Willkie argued that Roosevelt intended to make the United States a direct participant in the war. "If you re-elect him," he told one audience, "you may expect war in April, 1941," to which Roosevelt retorted, disingenuously since he knew he was not a free agent in the situation, "I have said this before, but I shall say it again and again and again: Your boys are not going to be sent into any foreign wars." In November Roosevelt carried the country handily, although by a much smaller majority than in 1932 or 1936. The popular vote was 27 million to 22 million, the electoral count 449 to 82.

While the election by no means ended the debate over foreign policy, it indicated the direction in which the nation was moving and encouraged Roosevelt to act more boldly against the Axis powers. When Churchill informed him that the cash-and-carry system would no longer suffice because Great Britain was rapidly exhausting its financial resources, he decided at once to provide the British with whatever they needed. Instead of proposing to lend them money, a step sure to rouse memories of the vexatious war debt controversies of the twenties, he devised the "lend-lease" program, one of his most ingenious and imaginative creations.

First he spoke directly to the people in a "fireside chat," stressing the evil intentions of the Nazis and the dangers that their triumph would create for America. Aiding Britain should be looked at simply as part of the general defense effort. "As planes and ships and guns and shells are produced," he said, American defense experts would decide "how much shall be sent abroad and how much shall remain at home." When this talk provoked a favorable public response, Roosevelt went to Congress in January 1941 with a specific plan calling for the expenditure of $7 billion for war materials that the President could sell, lend, lease, exchange, or transfer to any country whose defense he deemed vital to that of the United States. After two months of spirited debate, Congress gave him what he had asked for. Thereafter, as Roosevelt put it, the United States became "the arsenal of democracy."

Although the wording of the Lend-Lease Act obscured its immediate purpose, the saving of Great Britain, the President was quite frank in explaining his plan to the public. He did not obscure the risks involved nor repeat his campaign promise not to send American boys into "foreign" wars. Yet his mastery of practical politics was never more clearly in evidence. To counter Irish-American prejudices against the English, he pointed out that the independent Irish Republic would surely fall under Nazi domination if Hitler won the war. He also coupled his demand for heavy military expenditures with his enunciation of the idealistic "Four Freedoms" –freedom of speech, freedom of religion, freedom from want, and freedom from fear–for which, he said, the war was being fought.

After the enactment of lend-lease, aid short of war was no longer seriously debated. The American navy rapidly expanded its activities in the North Atlantic, shadowing German submarines and radioing their locations to Allied warships and planes. In April 1941 United States forces occupied Greenland; in May the President declared a state of unlimited national emergency. When Hitler invaded the Soviet Union in June, Roosevelt moved slowly, for anti-Russian feeling in the United States was intense,* but it was obviously to the nation's advantage to help anyone who was resisting Hitler's armies. In November $1 billion in lend-lease was put at the disposal of the Russians.

Meanwhile, Iceland was occupied in July 1941, and the draft law was extended in August–by the margin of a single vote in the House of Representatives. In September the German submarine *U-652* attacked the destroyer *Greer* in the North Atlantic. The *Greer* had provoked the attack by tracking the *U-652* and flashing its position to a British plane, which had dropped depth charges in the area. However, Roosevelt (no action has provided more ammunition for his critics) announced that the *Greer* had been innocently "carrying mail to Iceland." He used the incident as an excuse to order the navy to "shoot on sight" any German craft in the waters south and west of Iceland and to convoy merchant vessels as far as that island. After the sinking of the destroyer *Reuben James* on October 30, Congress voted to allow the arming of American merchantmen and to permit them to carry cargoes to Allied ports.

By December 1941 the United States was actually at war, but it is hard to see how a formal declaration could have come about or how American soldiers could have been committed to the fray had it not been for Japan. Japanese-American relations had worsened steadily after Japan resumed its war against China in 1937. As they extended their control over ever larger areas of Chiang Kai-shek's domain, the invaders systematically froze out American and other foreign business interests, declaring that the Open Door policy was obsolete. Roosevelt, already shocked by Japan's cold-blooded expansionism, retaliated by lending money to Chiang's government and by asking American manufacturers not to sell airplanes to Japan. In July 1940, with Japanese troops threatening French Indochina, Congress placed exports of aviation gasoline and certain types of scrap iron to Japan under a licensing system; in September all sales of scrap were banned and loans to China increased. After the creation of the Rome-Berlin-Tokyo axis in September 1940, Roosevelt extended the embargo to include machine tools and several other items, but the Japanese, determined to create what they euphemistically called a Greater East Asia Co-Prosperity Sphere, pushed ahead relentlessly despite these economic pressures.

Neither the United States nor Japan wished to fight with the other. In the spring of 1941 Secretary of State Cordell Hull began a long series of talks in Washington with the Japanese ambassador, Kichisaburo Nomura, in an effort to resolve their differences. Hull's approach, while morally sound, showed little appreciation of the political and military situation in the Far East. He demanded that Japan withdraw from China and pledge itself not to attack the Dutch and French colonies in southeast Asia, ripe for the plucking after Hitler's victories in Europe. The Japanese had no moral right to their conquests, but how Hull expected to get them to give them up with-

*During the 1930's Russia took a far firmer stand against the fascists than any other power, but after joining Hitler in swallowing up Poland, it also attacked and defeated Finland during the winter of 1939–1940 and annexed the Baltic states. These cynical acts practically destroyed the small communist movement in the United States and caused much indignation in liberal as well as conservative circles.

out either making concessions or going to war is not clear. He refused to recognize that the old balance of power that had enabled the United States to attain its modest objectives in the Far East without the use of force had ceased to exist.

Fully aware of the potential strength of the United States, Japan might well have accepted a limited victory in the area in return for the removal of American trade restrictions, but Hull, confident of his moral position, insisted upon total withdrawal. He seemed bent on converting the Japanese to pacifism by exhortation. Even the moderates in Japan rejected this solution to the problem. When Hitler invaded the Soviet Union, thus removing the threat of Russian intervention in the Far East, Japan decided to occupy Indochina even at the risk of war with America. Roosevelt retaliated (July 1941) by freezing Japanese assets in the United States and clamping a total embargo on oil.

Now the war party in Japan assumed control. Nomura was instructed to tell Hull that his country would refrain from further expansion if the United States and Great Britain would cut off all aid to China and lift the economic blockade. Japan also promised to pull out of Indochina once "a just peace" had been established with China. When the United States rejected these demands and repeated (November 26) its insistence that Japan "withdraw all military, naval, air, and police forces" from China and Indochina, the Japanese prepared to assault the Dutch East Indies, British Malaya, and also the Philippines. To immobilize the United States Pacific Fleet, they planned a surprise aerial raid on the great Hawaiian naval base at Pearl Harbor.

An American cryptanalyst, Colonel William F. Friedman, had "cracked" the Japanese diplomatic code and the government therefore knew that war was imminent. As early as November 27 Hull warned an American general: "Those fellows mean to fight and you will have to watch

The American battleships at Pearl Harbor were sitting ducks for Japanese bombers on December 7. A picture taken three days later shows (from left) the damaged Maryland *inboard of the capsized* Oklahoma; *the* West Virginia, *hit by six torpedoes, awash next to the* Tennessee; *and the shattered* Arizona, *on which 1,100 seamen died.*

NAVY DEPARTMENT, NATIONAL ARCHIVES

out." The code-breakers had also made it possible to keep close tabs on the movements of Japanese navy units. But in the hectic rush of events both the military and civilian authorities failed to make effective use of the information collected. They expected the blow to fall somewhere in southeast Asia, possibly in the Philippines.

The garrison at Pearl Harbor was alerted against "a surprise aggressive move in any direction," but the commanders there, Admiral Husband E. Kimmel and General Walter C. Short, believed an attack impossible and took precautions only against Japanese sabotage. Thus when planes from Japanese aircraft carriers swooped down upon Pearl Harbor on the morning of December 7, they found easy targets. In less than two hours they reduced the Pacific Fleet to a flaming ruin: two battleships destroyed, six others heavily battered, nearly a dozen lesser vessels put out of action. More than 150 planes were wrecked, over 2,300 servicemen killed and 1,100 wounded. Never had American arms suffered a more devastating or shameful defeat, and seldom has an event roused so much controversy or produced such intensive historical study. The official blame was placed chiefly on Admiral Kimmel and General Short, but while they might well have been more alert, it is clear that responsibility for the disaster was widespread. Military and civilian officials in Washington failed to pass on all that they knew to Hawaii or even to each other. Moreover, the crucial intelligence that the code-breakers provided, easy to isolate in retrospect, was mixed in with huge masses of other information and thus extremely difficult to evaluate at the moment. Perhaps, instead of seeking to find a scapegoat, we should admit that the Japanese attack, while immoral, was both daring and brilliantly executed.

In any case, the next day Congress declared war on Japan. Formal war with Germany and Italy was still not inevitable, for isolationists were far more ready to resist the "yellow peril" in the Orient than to fight in Europe. The Axis powers, however, honored their treaty obligations to Japan and on December 11 declared war on the United States. America was now fully engaged in the great conflict.

Mobilizing the Home Front

Entry into the war put immense strains on the American economy and produced immense results. About 15 million men and women entered the armed services; they, and in part the millions more in Allied uniforms, had to be fed, clothed, housed, and supplied with equipment ranging from typewriters and paper clips to rifles and grenades, tanks and airplanes, and (eventually) atomic bombs. The task of organizing this massive effort centered in Washington and finally in the person of Franklin Roosevelt. As in every national crisis, Congress granted wide emergency powers to the President. It also, in this instance, refrained from excessive meddling in administrative problems and in military strategy. However, although the Democrats retained control of both houses throughout the war, their margins were relatively narrow. A coalition of conservatives in both parties frequently prevented the President from having his way and exercised close control over all government spending.

Roosevelt was an imaginative and inspiring war leader but not a very good administrator. Any honest account of the war on the home front must reveal glaring examples of confusion, inefficiency, and pointless bickering. The squabbling and waste characteristic of the early New Deal period made relatively little difference—what mattered then was raising the nation's spirits and keeping men occupied; efficiency was less than essential, however desirable. In wartime, however, men's very existence, perhaps that of the whole free world, depended on the volume of weapons and supplies actually delivered to the battle fronts.

Yet the confusion attending economic mobilization can easily be overstressed. Nearly all Roosevelt's basic decisions were wise and humane: to pay a large part of the cost of the war by collecting taxes rather than by borrowing and to base taxation on the individual citizen's ability to pay; to ration scarce raw materials and consumer goods; to regulate prices and wages; to treat minority groups and dissident elements fairly. If these decisions were not always translated into action with perfect effectiveness, they always operated in the direction of efficiency and the public

LIBRARY OF CONGRESS

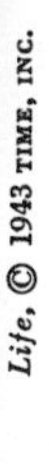

Posters like the one above sought to mobilize public opinion in support of the war effort. The women welders at right, photographed in 1943 by Margaret Bourke-White of Life, *work on an aircraft carrier.*

good. Furthermore, what happened in Washington, while important, had less to do with war production than what happened in the factories and in the fields. Roosevelt's greatest accomplishment was his inspiring of businessmen, workers, and farmers with a sense of national purpose. In this respect his function exactly duplicated his earlier role in fighting the depression, and he performed it with even greater success.

A sense of the tremendous economic expansion caused by the demands of war can most easily be captured by reference to official statistics of production. The gross national product of the United States in 1939 was valued at $91.3 billion. In 1945, after allowing for changes in the price level, it was $166.6 billion. More specifically, and using volume of production rather than value to avoid complicated adjustments to compensate for inflation, manufacturing output nearly doubled, agricultural rose 22 per cent. In 1939 the United States turned out fewer than 6,000 airplanes, in 1944 more than 96,000. Shipyards produced 237,000 tons of vessels in 1939, 10 million tons in 1943. The index of iron and steel production leaped from 87 in 1938 to 258 in 1944, of rubber goods from 113 to 238 in the same years. Raw materials were produced in equal profusion. Petroleum output rose from 1.2 billion barrels in 1939 to 1.7 billion in 1945; iron ore from 28 million tons in 1938 to 105 million in 1942; copper from 562,000 tons in 1938 to over 1 million in 1942; aluminum from 286 million pounds in 1938 to 1 billion in 1942 and 1.8 billion in 1943. The production of electric power expanded from 41 billion kilowatt-hours to 279 billion between 1938 and 1944.

These figures have been drawn almost at random from a record of expansion unparalleled in history. Wartime experience proved how shrewd had been the insights of the Keynesian economists, how vital the role of government spending in sparking economic growth. About 8.5 million men were unemployed in June 1940. After Pearl Harbor, unemployment practically disappeared, and by 1945 the *civilian* work force had increased by nearly 7 million more. Millions of women flocked into the new defense industries, a trend memorialized in the popular song, "Rosie the Riveter."

The task of mobilization had begun well before December 1941. At that time, 1.6 million men were already under arms. Economic mobilization got under way in August 1939, when the President created a War Resources Board with instructions to plan for possible conversion of industry to war production. After a number of essentially meaningless reorganizations, this board became the Office of Production Management (January 1941) under William S. Knudsen, president of General Motors. As early as June 1940 scientific research planning was put under the control of a National Defense Research Committee (later the Office of Scientific Research and Development) headed by Dr. Vannevar Bush of the Carnegie Institution. In April 1941 Roosevelt set up an Office of Price Administration (OPA), headed by the economist Leon Henderson, in an attempt to check profiteering and control consumer prices, and in August a Supplies Priorities and Allocation Board, directed by Donald M. Nelson of Sears Roebuck, to coordinate the requests for scarce materials of American and Allied military purchasers with those of industry.

With the exception of scientific planning, these prewar efforts worked poorly, mainly because the President refused to centralize authority and to accept the need for fundamental changes in the structure of the economy. The separation of responsibility for dispensing materials from the control of the prices paid for materials, for example, practically hamstrung both Nelson's and Henderson's organizations. Throughout this period, and for months after Pearl Harbor, these civilian boards had to battle constantly with the military over everything from the allocation of scarce raw materials to the technical specifications of weapons. Roosevelt refused to settle these conflicts as only he could have.

Yet long before the formal outbreak of hostilities the concept of economic planning and control had been firmly established, and by early 1943 the nation's economic machinery had been converted to a wartime footing and was functioning smoothly. Supreme Court Justice James F. Byrnes, who, as a former senator from South Carolina, had a thorough knowledge of the workings of politics, resigned from the Court to become a sort of "economic czar." His Office of War Mobilization had complete control over the issuance of priorities and also over prices. Strict regulation of rents, food prices, and wages had been put into effect, and items in short supply were being rationed to consumers. While wages and prices had soared during 1942, after April 1943 they leveled off. Thereafter the cost of living scarcely changed at all until controls were lifted after the war.

Expanded industrial production together with the military draft produced a labor shortage which greatly increased the bargaining power of workers. On the other hand, the national emergency required placing some limitation on the workers' right to exercise this power. As early as March 1941 Roosevelt appointed a National Defense Mediation Board to assist labor and management in avoiding work stoppages. After Pearl Harbor he created a National War Labor Board with power to arbitrate disputes and "stabilize" wage rates and banned all changes in wages without NWLB approval. In the "Little Steel" case (July 1942), the NWLB laid down the principle that wage increases should not normally exceed 15 per cent of the rates of January 1941, a figure roughly in line with the increase in the cost of living since that date.

Prosperity and stiffer government controls added significantly to the strength of organized labor. The last bastions of industrial resistance to collective bargaining crumbled, and as workers began to see the material benefits of union membership at every turn, they flocked into the organizations. Strikes declined sharply at first: 23 million man-hours had been lost in 1941 because of strikes; only 4.18 million were lost in 1942. However, some crippling work stoppages did occur. In May 1943 the government was forced to seize the coal mines when John L. Lewis' United Mine Workers walked out of the pits. This strike led Congress to pass, over Roosevelt's veto, the Smith-Connally War Labor Disputes Act (June 1943), which gave the President the power to take over any war plant threatened by a strike. The act also declared strikes against seized plants illegal and imposed stiff penalties on violators. Although strikes continued to occur —the man-hour loss zoomed to 38 million in 1945— when Roosevelt asked for a labor draft law, Congress refused to go along.

Generally speaking, however, labor-management relations during the war were harmonious, and wages and prices remained in fair balance. Overtime work fattened the pay checks of millions, and a new stress in labor contracts on "fringe benefits" such as paid vacations, premium pay for night work, and various forms of employer-subsidized health insurance added to the prosperity of labor. Between 1941 and 1945, worker income rose from $65 billion to $123 billion.

The war effort had almost no adverse effect on the standard of living of the average citizen, a vivid demonstration of the remarkable productivity of the American economy. The manufacture of automobiles ceased and extensive pleasure driving became next to impossible because of gasoline rationing, but most ordinary civilian activities went on much as they had before Pearl Harbor. Because of the need to conserve cloth, cuffs disappeared from men's trousers, and the vest passed out of style. Plastics replaced metals in toys, containers, and various other items. Although many items such as meat, sugar, and shoes were rationed, they were doled out in amounts perfectly adequate for the needs of most persons. Americans had both guns *and* butter; belt-tightening of the type experienced by all the other belligerents was unheard of.

The federal government spent twice as much money between 1941 and 1945 as in its entire previous history. This unprecedented expense made heavy borrowing necessary. The national debt, which stood at less than $49 billion in 1941, increased by more than that amount *each year* between 1942 and 1945 and totaled nearly $260 billion when the war ended. Roosevelt, however, insisted that as much of the cost as possible be paid for at the time: over 40 per cent of the total was met by taxation, a far larger proportion than in any earlier war. This policy helped to check inflation by siphoning off money that would otherwise have competed for scarce consumer goods. Heavy excise taxes on amusements and luxuries further discouraged spending, as did the government's war-bond campaigns, which persuaded patriotic citizens to lend part of their income to Uncle Sam. The tax program also helped to maintain public morale. High taxes on incomes (up to 94 per cent), on corporation profits (up to 40 per cent), and on excess profits (95 per cent) together with a limit of $25,000 a year after taxes on salaries convinced the people that no one was profiting inordinately from the war effort.

Furthermore, the income tax, which had never before touched the mass of white-collar and industrial workers, was extended downward to cover nearly everyone. To collect efficiently the relatively small sums paid by most persons, Congress adopted the payroll-deduction system proposed by Beardsley Ruml, chairman of the Federal Reserve Bank of New York, whereby employers "withheld" the taxes of wage earners and salaried personnel and paid them directly to the government.

The steeply graduated tax system combined with a general increase in the income of workers and farmers effected a major shift in the distribution of wealth in the United States. The poor got richer, while the rich, if not actually poorer, collected a smaller proportion of the national income. The wealthiest 1 per cent of the population had received 13.4 per cent of the national income in 1935 and 11.5 per cent as late as 1941. In 1944 this group received only 6.7 per cent.

Enormous social effects stemmed from this shift, but World War II altered the patterns of American life in so many ways that it would be wrong to ascribe the transformations to any single source. For one thing, it stimulated the already strong tendency of Americans to pull up stakes and move to greener pastures. Never was the population more fluid. The millions who put on uniforms found themselves transported first to training camps in every section of the country and then to battlefields scattered from Europe and Africa to the far reaches of the Pacific, even to China. More important, burgeoning new defense plants drew other millions to places like Hanford, Washington, and Oak Ridge, Tennessee, where great atomic energy installations were constructed, and to the aircraft factories of California and other states. As in earlier periods the trend was from east to west, from south to north, and from countryside to the cities. The population of California increased by more than 50 per cent in the forties, that of other far-western states almost as much. New England, the South (except for Florida and Texas), and the plains states either grew more slowly than the national average in these years or in some cases, such as Mississippi, Arkansas, and North Dakota, actually declined in population.

The war also affected the Negroes in many ways. Several factors operated to improve their lot. One was the reaction of Americans to the racial persecutions of the Nazis. Hitler's senseless murder of millions of Jews, an outgrowth of his doctrine of Aryan superiority, compelled many Americans to re-examine their own views about race and to strive to treat not only Jews but Negroes and other ethnic groups more decently: if the nation expected Negroes to risk their lives for the common good, how could it continue to treat them as second-class citizens? Black leaders did not hesitate to point out the inconsistency between fighting for democracy abroad while ignoring it at home. "We want democracy in Alabama," the NAACP announced, and this argument, too, had some effect on white thinking.

Negroes in the armed forces were treated somewhat better than in World War I. Although segregation in the military continued, blacks were enlisted for the first time in the air force and the marines, and permitted to hold more responsible positions in the army and navy. The army commissioned its first Negro general. Some 600 Negro pilots won their wings. Altogether about a million served, about half of these overseas, and the extensive and honorable performance of many of these Negro units could not be ignored by the white majority.

Economic realities operated even more importantly to the Negro's advantage. More Negroes had been unemployed in proportion to their numbers than any other group; now the manpower shortage brought employment for all. The CIO industrial unions continued to enroll blacks by the thousands.

War-related gains, however, failed to satisfy most Negro leaders. The NAACP, which increased its membership from 50,000 in 1940 to almost 405,000 in 1946, adopted a more militant stand than in World War I. Discrimination in defense plants seemed far less tolerable than it had in 1917–18. Even before Pearl Harbor, A. Philip Randolph, president of the Brotherhood of Sleeping Car Porters, set out to protest this discrimination. He organized a massive march of blacks on Washington to demand equal opportunity for black workers. To prevent this march from taking place at a time of national crisis, President Roosevelt agreed to issue an order prohibiting discrimination in plants with defense contracts, and he set up a Fair Employment Practices Committee to see that the order was carried out. Executive Order 8802 was not perfectly enforced, but it opened up better jobs to countless black workers and led many employers to change their hiring practices.

Prejudice and the mistreatment of Negroes did not cease. Race riots erupted in many cities during the war, black soldiers were often provided with inferior recreational facilities and otherwise discriminated against in and around army camps. Negro blood plasma was kept separate from white, even though the two "varieties" were indistinguishable and the process of storing plasma had been invented by a Negro, Dr. Charles Drew. Negroes, therefore, became increasingly embittered. Roy Wilkins, head of the NAACP, put it this way as early as 1942: "No Negro leader with a constituency can face his members today and ask full support for the war in the light of the atmosphere the government has created." Many Negro newspaper editors were so critical of the administration that conservatives began to demand that they be indicted for sedition.

Roosevelt would have none of this, but the militants annoyed him; he felt that they should hold their demands in abeyance until the war had been won. He apparently failed to realize the depth of black anger, and in this he was no different from the majority of whites. A revolution was in the making, yet in 1942 a poll revealed that six out of ten whites still believed that black Americans were "satisfied" with their place in society.

Although the great struggle affected the American people far more drastically than World War I, it produced much less intolerance and fewer examples of the repression of individual freedom of opinion. Perhaps this reflected the soberer, less emotional reaction of the nation to this war than to the war of 1914–18. Hitler represented a far more serious threat to democratic institutions than had the kaiser, yet the people seemed able to distinguish between the Nazis and Americans of German descent in a way that had escaped their fathers. The fact that nearly all German-Americans were vigorously anti-Nazi helps explain this, but the underlying public attitude was even more important. Men went to war in 1941 without illusions and without enthusiasm, determined to win but expecting only to preserve what they had. They therefore found it easier to tolerate dissent, to view the dangers they faced realistically, and to concentrate on the real foreign enemy without venting their feelings on domestic scapegoats. The nation's 100,000 conscientious objectors—a tiny fraction of the 37 million persons who registered for the draft—met with little hostility. The only flagrant example of intolerance was the deportation of the West Coast Japanese to internment camps in the interior of the country. About 110,000 Americans of Japanese ancestry were rounded up, simply because of a totally unjustified fear that they might be disloyal. The Supreme Court, generally in this century so vigilant in the protection of civil liberties, upheld this action in the case of *Korematsu v. U.S.* (1944). In *Ex parte Endo*, however, the Court forbade the internment of Japanese-American *citizens,* that is, of the *Nisei*, the second-generation Japanese who had been born in the United States.

Other social changes occurring during the war included a revival of interest in religion and a boom in movie attendance and in the sale of books. More significantly, a sharp increase in the marriage and birthrates occurred, a response both to the return of prosperity and to the natural desire of young men going off to risk death in distant lands to establish roots before departing. The population of the United States had increased by only 3 million during the depression decade of the thirties; during the next five years it rose by 6.5 million. However, large numbers of hasty marriages followed by long periods of separation also produced a great acceleration of the national divorce rate, from about 170 per thousand marriages in 1941 to 310 per thousand in 1945.

The War in Europe

Within days after Pearl Harbor, Prime Minister Churchill and his military chiefs were meeting in Washington with Roosevelt and his advisers to plan the strategy of the Grand Coalition against the Axis. In every quarter of the globe, disaster threatened. The Japanese were gobbling up the Far East for their Greater East Asia Co-Prosperity Sphere. The Philippines, Guam, Wake, Hong Kong, Malaya, Burma, the Dutch Indies, the Solomon Islands, and northern New Guinea were all in Japanese hands by April 1942. In Russia, Hitler's armies, checked outside Leningrad and Moscow, were preparing a massive attack in the south, directed at Stalingrad, on the Volga River. German divisions in Africa, under General Erwin Rommel, were beginning a drive toward the Suez Canal. U-boats were taking a heavy toll of Allied shipping in the North Atlantic. British and American leaders believed that eventually they could muster enough force to smash their enemies, but whether or not the troops already in action could hold out until this force arrived was an open question.

The basic decision of the Anglo-American strategists was to concentrate first against the Germans. Japan's conquests were in remote and, from the Allied point of view, relatively unimportant regions. Even the most pessimistic did not see Japan as a threat to any part of the Western Hemisphere or to Europe. On the other hand, if Russia surrendered or if Rommel cut the Suez life line, Hitler might well be able to invade Great Britain, thus making his position in Europe impregnable by depriving the United States of a base for any counterattack. But how to strike at Hitler? American leaders wanted to aim directly at establishing a second front in France, and the harried Russians backed them up. The British, however, felt that this would require more power than the Allies could presently command and advocated instead air bombardment of German industry combined with small-scale, peripheral attacks by land forces to harass the enemy while armies and supplies were being massed. Later events proved the soundness of the British position, for when the invasion of France did come against a greatly weakened Germany in 1944, the

U.S. AIR FORCE

German oil resources were a major target of Allied bombing. A daring American low-level attack on the Ploesti, Rumania, refineries in 1943 is shown here.

difficulties were still enormous. A major landing in 1942 would almost certainly have been repulsed.

During the summer of 1942 Allied planes began to hit at German cities. In a rising crescendo throughout 1943 and 1944, British and American bombers pulverized the centers of Nazi might. While air attacks did not destroy the German armies' capacity to fight, they hampered war production, tangled communications, and brought the war home to the German people in awesome fashion. Humanitarians deplored the heavy loss of life among the civilian population, but the response of the realists was unanswerable: Hitler had begun indiscriminate bombing, and Allied survival depended upon smashing the German war machine.

In November 1942 an Allied army commanded by General Dwight D. Eisenhower struck at French North Africa. After the fall of France, the Nazis had set up a puppet regime in those parts of France not occupied by their troops, headed by the octogenarian French World War I hero Marshal Henri-Philippe Pétain, with headquarters at Vichy. This collaborationist Vichy government controlled French North Africa. But the local commandant, Admiral Jean Darlan, promptly switched sides when Eisenhower's forces landed. After a brief show of resistance, the French surrendered. The Allies were willing to do business with Darlan despite his record as a collaborationist. This greatly angered General Charles de Gaulle, who had organized a government-in-exile immediately after the collapse of France and who considered himself the true representative of the French people. Many liberals in the United States agreed with De Gaulle and denounced the "deal" with Darlan. Darlan was assassinated in December, and eventually the Free French obtained control of North Africa, but the Allied attitude had much to do with De Gaulle's postwar suspicion of both Britain and the United States.

In 1942, however, the arrangement with Darlan paid large dividends. Eisenhower was able to press forward quickly against the Germans. The first major engagement of the campaign took place in February 1943 at Kasserine Pass in the desert south of Tunis, where American tanks met Rommel's *Afrika Korps.* This battle ended in a stand-off, but with British troops closing in from their Egyptian bases to the east, the Germans were soon trapped and crushed. In May, after Rommel had been recalled to Germany, his army surrendered. The Allies killed or captured some 350,000 men, and seized large quantities of military supplies.

In July 1943, while air attacks on Germany continued and the Russians slowly pushed the Germans back from the gates of Stalingrad, the Allies invaded Sicily from Africa. Then in September they advanced to the Italian mainland. Mussolini had already fallen from power (eight months later he was caught and killed by Italian partisans) and his successor, Marshal Pietro Badoglio, surrendered. However, the Germans seized control and threw up an almost impregnable defense across the rugged Italian peninsula. The Anglo-American army inched forward, paying heavily for every advance. Monte Cassino, halfway between Naples and Rome, did not fall until May 1944, the capital itself until June; months

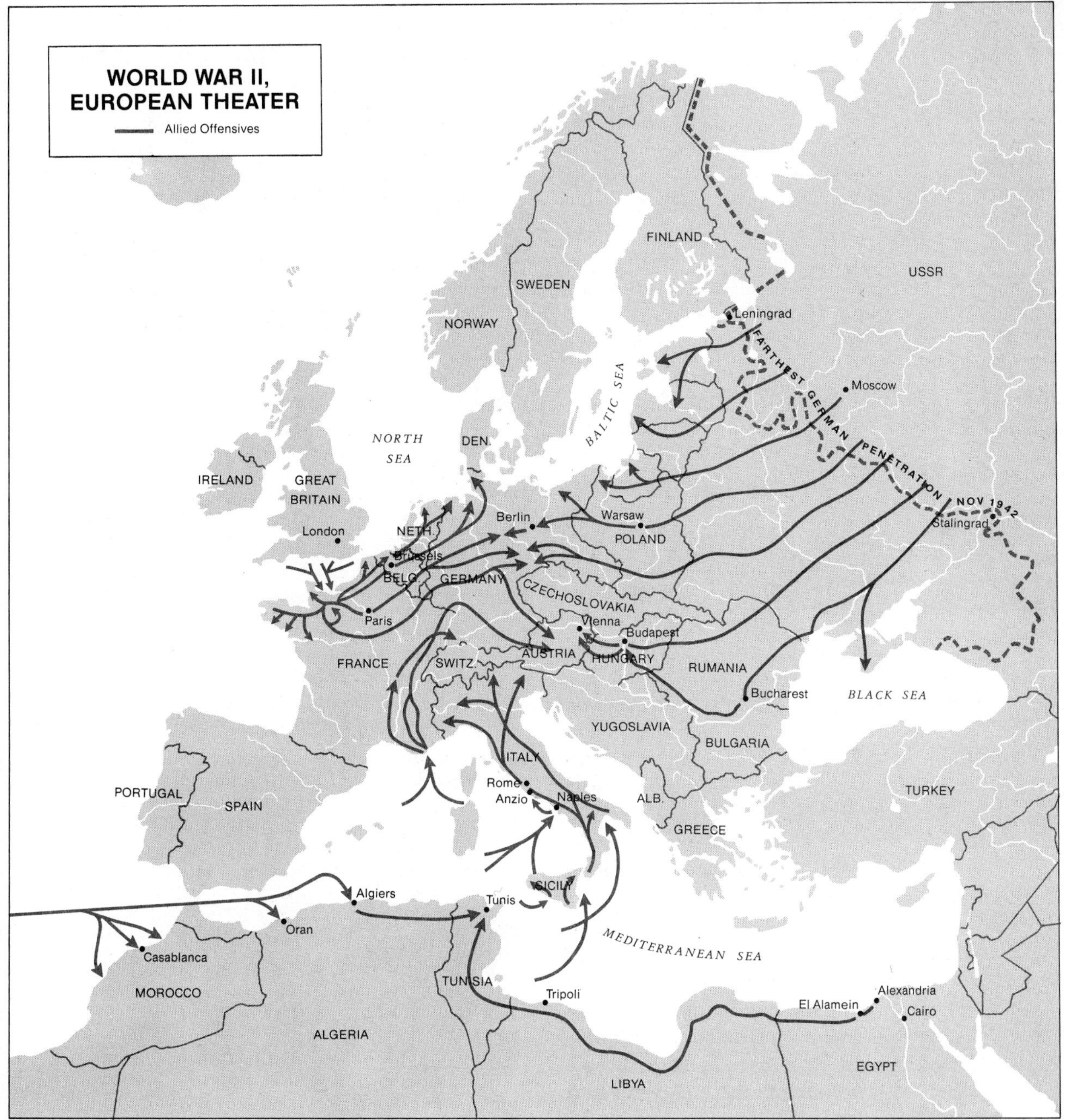

of bitter fighting still remained before the country was cleared of Germans. The Italian campaign was an Allied disappointment, although it did further weaken the enemy.

By the time the Allies had taken Rome, the mighty army needed to invade France had been collected in England under Eisenhower's command. On D-Day, June 6, supported by a great armada and thousands of planes and paratroops, the assault forces stormed ashore at five points (Utah, Omaha, Gold, Juno, and Sword beaches) along the coast of Normandy. Against fierce but ill-coordinated German resistance, they established a solid beachhead: within a few weeks a million Allied troops were on French soil. Thereafter, victory was certain, although nearly a year of hard fighting still lay ahead. In August the American Third Army under General George S. Patton, an eccentric, ruthless, but brilliant field commander, erupted southward into Brittany and then veered east toward Paris. Another Allied army invaded France from the Mediterranean in mid-August and drove rapidly north. Free French troops were given the honor of liberating Paris on August 25, Belgium was cleared by British and Canadian units a few days later, and by mid-September the Allies were fighting on the edge of Germany itself.

The front now stretched from the Netherlands along the borders of Belgium, Luxembourg, and France all the way to Switzerland. If the Allies had mounted a massive assault at any one point, as the British commander, Field Marshal Bernard Montgomery, urged, the struggle might have been brought to a quick conclusion. Although the two armies were roughly equal in size, the Allies had complete control of the air and 20 times as many tanks as the foe. The pressure of the advancing Russians on the eastern front made it very difficult for the Germans to reinforce their troops in the west. General Siegfried Westphal, chief of staff to the German commander in the west, later claimed that the Allies could have broken through at almost any point at this time. But General Eisenhower believed a concentrated attack too risky. His supply and communications problems were fantastically complex and the defenses of Hitler's Siegfried Line, in some regions three miles deep, presented a formidable obstacle. He prepared instead for a general advance.

While he was regrouping for the final assault, however, the Germans, on December 16, launched a heavy counterattack, planned by Hitler himself, against the Allied center in the Ardennes Forest. The Germans hoped to break through to the Belgian port of Antwerp, thus splitting the Allied armies in two. The plan was foolhardy, but therefore unexpected, and it almost succeeded. On December 20 the Germans surrounded the key communications center of Bastogne. When a party under a flag of truce demanded its surrender, the American commander, General Anthony C. McAuliffe, replied "Nuts!" The Germans expressed puzzlement over the meaning

BILL MAULDIN, *Up Front*, 1945

Bill Mauldin's long-suffering Willie and Joe (above) discover their enemies will stop at nothing: "Them rats! Them dirty, cold-blooded, sore-headed, stinkin' Huns! Them atrocity-committin' skunks!" Below, GI's counterattack during the Battle of the Bulge.

SIGNAL CORPS

of this cryptic colloquialism, so one of McAuliffe's aides added: "If you don't understand what 'Nuts!' means, in plain English it is the same as 'Go to hell!' "

The Germans pressed ahead without capturing Bastogne, extending their salient about 50 miles into Belgium, but once the element of surprise had been overcome, their hopes of breaking through to the sea were destroyed. Eisenhower concentrated first on preventing them from broadening the break in his lines and then on blunting the point of their advance. On Christmas Day the drive was stopped a few miles from the Meuse River near Dinant. By late January 1945 the old line had been re-established. This "Battle of the Bulge" cost the United States 77,000 casualties and delayed Eisenhower's planned offensive, but it also destroyed the Germans' last reserves.

Quickly the Allies then pressed forward to the Rhine, winning a bridgehead on the right bank of the river across from Remagen on March 7. Thereafter, some German city fell almost daily. With the Russians racing westward against crumbling resistance, the end could not be long delayed. In April American and Russian forces made contact at the Elbe River. A few days later, with Russian shells reducing his capital to rubble, Hitler, by then probably insane, took his own life in his luxurious Berlin air raid shelter. On May 8 Germany officially surrendered.

The War in the Pacific

Defeating Germany first had not meant abandoning the Pacific region entirely to the Japanese; while huge armies were being trained and masses of materiel accumulated for the attack on Hitler, much of the already available American strength was diverted to the task of maintaining vital communications in the Far East and checking further Japanese expansion. The navy's aircraft carriers had escaped destruction at Pearl Harbor, a stroke of immense good fortune, since events were soon to prove that the airplane had revolutionized naval warfare. Commanders discovered that because of their greater range and more concentrated fire power, carrier-based planes were far more effective against warships than the heaviest naval artillery. Battleships made excellent gun platforms from which to pound shore installations and support land operations, but against other vessels aircraft were of prime importance.

This truth was demonstrated in the Battle of the Coral Sea in May 1942. Repeated success had made the Japanese overconfident. Having captured an empire in a few months without the loss of any warship larger than a destroyer, they believed the war already won and suffered from what one of their admirals who knew better called the "victory disease." This led them to overextend themselves in seeking still greater conquests.

The Coral Sea, which the navy's historian, Admiral Samuel E. Morison, has called "one of the most beautiful bodies of water in the world," lies northeast of Australia and south of New Guinea and the Solomon Islands. Domination of these waters would cut Australia off from Hawaii, and thus from American aid. Japanese Admiral Isoroku Yamamoto, believing that he could range freely over all the waters west of Pearl Harbor, had dispatched a large fleet of transports, screened by many warships, to attack Port Moresby, on the southern New Guinea coast. On May 7-8 planes from the American carriers *Lexington* and *Yorktown* struck the convoy's screen, sinking a small carrier and damaging a large one. Superficially, the battle seemed a victory for the Japanese, for their planes mortally wounded the *Lexington* and destroyed two other ships, but the troop transports had been forced to turn back—Port Moresby was saved. Although large numbers of cruisers and destroyers took part in the action, none came within sight or gun range of an enemy ship. All the destruction was wrought by carrier aircraft.

Encouraged by this Coral Sea "victory," Admiral Yamamoto decided to force the American fleet into a showdown battle by assaulting Midway Island, west of Hawaii. His armada never reached the island. Between June 4 and 7 control of the Central Pacific was decided, entirely by air power. American dive bombers sent four large carriers to the bottom. About 300 Japanese planes were destroyed. The United States lost only the *Yorktown* and a destroyer, retaining the bulk of its planes. The powerful fleet of Japanese battleships played no role in the action and when deprived of air cover had to withdraw ignominiously. Thereafter, the initiative in the Pacific war shifted to the Americans.

Victory, however, came slowly and at painful cost. American land forces were under the command of Douglas MacArthur, a brilliant and dedicated but egocentric and rather vain general whose judgment was sometimes distorted by his intense concern for his own reputation. Son of General Arthur MacArthur, who had played a major role in the original conquest of the Philippines, MacArthur had been in command of American troops in the islands when the Japanese struck in December 1941. After his heroic but hopeless defense of Manila and the Bataan peninsula, President Roosevelt had him evacuated by PT boat to escape capture. Thereafter, MacArthur was obsessed with the idea of personally leading the American army back to the islands, although many strategists believed they should be by-passed in the drive on the Japanese homeland.

In the end he convinced the Joint Chiefs of Staff, who determined strategy. The Americans organized two separate drives, one from New Guinea toward the Philippines under MacArthur, the other through the Central Pacific toward Tokyo under Admiral Chester W. Nimitz. Before commencing this two-pronged advance, the Americans had to eject the Japanese from the Solomon Islands in order to protect Australia against a flank attack. Beginning in August 1942, a series of land-sea-air battles raged around Guadalcanal Island in this archipelago. Once again, American air power was decisive, although the bravery and skill of the ground forces that actually won the island must not be underemphasized. American pilots, better trained and with tougher planes, had a relatively easier task. They inflicted losses five to six times heavier on the enemy than they sustained themselves. Japanese air power disintegrated progressively during the long battle, and this in turn helped the fleet take a heavy toll of the Japanese navy. By February of 1943 Guadalcanal had been secured.

In the autumn of 1943 the American drives toward Japan and the Philippines got under way at last. In the Central Pacific campaign the Guadalcanal action was repeated on a smaller but equally bloody scale from Tarawa in the Gilbert Islands to Kwajalein and Eniwetok in the Marshalls, islets theretofore unknown to history. The Japanese soldiers fought like the Spartans at Thermopylae for every foot of ground. They had to be blasted and burned from countless tunnels and concrete pillboxes with hand grenades, flame throwers, and dynamite. They almost never surrendered. Although thousands found

In this sequence a blazing Japanese kamikaze *rams the flight deck of the carrier* Essex *off the Philippines in November 1944. In the Okinawa campaign in 1945* kamikaze *attacks killed over 4,000 U.S. seamen.*

heroes' graves, Admiral Nimitz' forces, supported by clouds of planes and the mighty rifles of the fleet, were in every case victorious. By midsummer of 1944 this arm of the American advance had taken Saipan and Guam in the Marianas, bringing land-based bombers within range of Tokyo.

Meanwhile, MacArthur was leapfrogging along the New Guinea coast toward the Philippines, and in October 1944 he made good his promise to return to the islands, landing on Leyte, south of Luzon. Two great naval clashes in Philippine waters, the Battle of the Philippine Sea (June 1944) and the Battle for Leyte Gulf (October 1944), completed the destruction of Japan's sea power and reduced its air force to a band of fanatical suicide pilots called *kamikazes,* who flew beyond range of return and tried to crash their bomb-laden planes against American warships and airstrips. The *kamikazes* caused much damage but could not turn the tide. In February 1945 MacArthur liberated Manila.

The end was now inevitable. B-29 Superfortress bombers from the Marianas were raining high explosives and fire bombs on the Japanese homeland. The islands of Iwo Jima and Okinawa, only a few hundred miles from Tokyo, fell to the Americans in March and June 1945. But such was the blind courage of the Japanese soldiers that military experts were predicting another year of fighting and a million additional American casualties before the main islands could be subdued.

At this point came the most controversial decision of the entire war, perhaps of all history, and it was made by a newcomer on the world scene. In November 1944 Roosevelt had been elected to a fourth term, easily defeating Thomas E. Dewey. But instead of renominating Henry A. Wallace for Vice President, the Democrats had picked Senator Harry S. Truman of Missouri, who had done an excellent job as head of a special Senate committee investigating military spending. The conservative Democratic politicos had considered Wallace too radical and too unstable, whereas Truman, although possessed of a good liberal record, was a regular party man well liked by the Democratic hierarchy. In April 1945, however, Roosevelt died of a cerebral hemorrhage. Thus it was Truman, a man painfully conscious of his inferiority to his great predecessor but equally aware of the power and responsibility of his office, who had to decide what to do when, in July 1945, American scientists placed in his hands a new and awful weapon, the atomic bomb.

After Roosevelt had responded to Albert Einstein's warning in 1939, government-sponsored atomic research had proceeded rapidly, especially after the establishment of the so-called Manhattan Project in May 1943. The manufacture of the artificial element plutonium at Hanford, Washington, and uranium 235 at Oak Ridge, Tennessee, went on side by side with the design and con-

ALL: NAVY DEPARTMENT, NATIONAL ARCHIVES

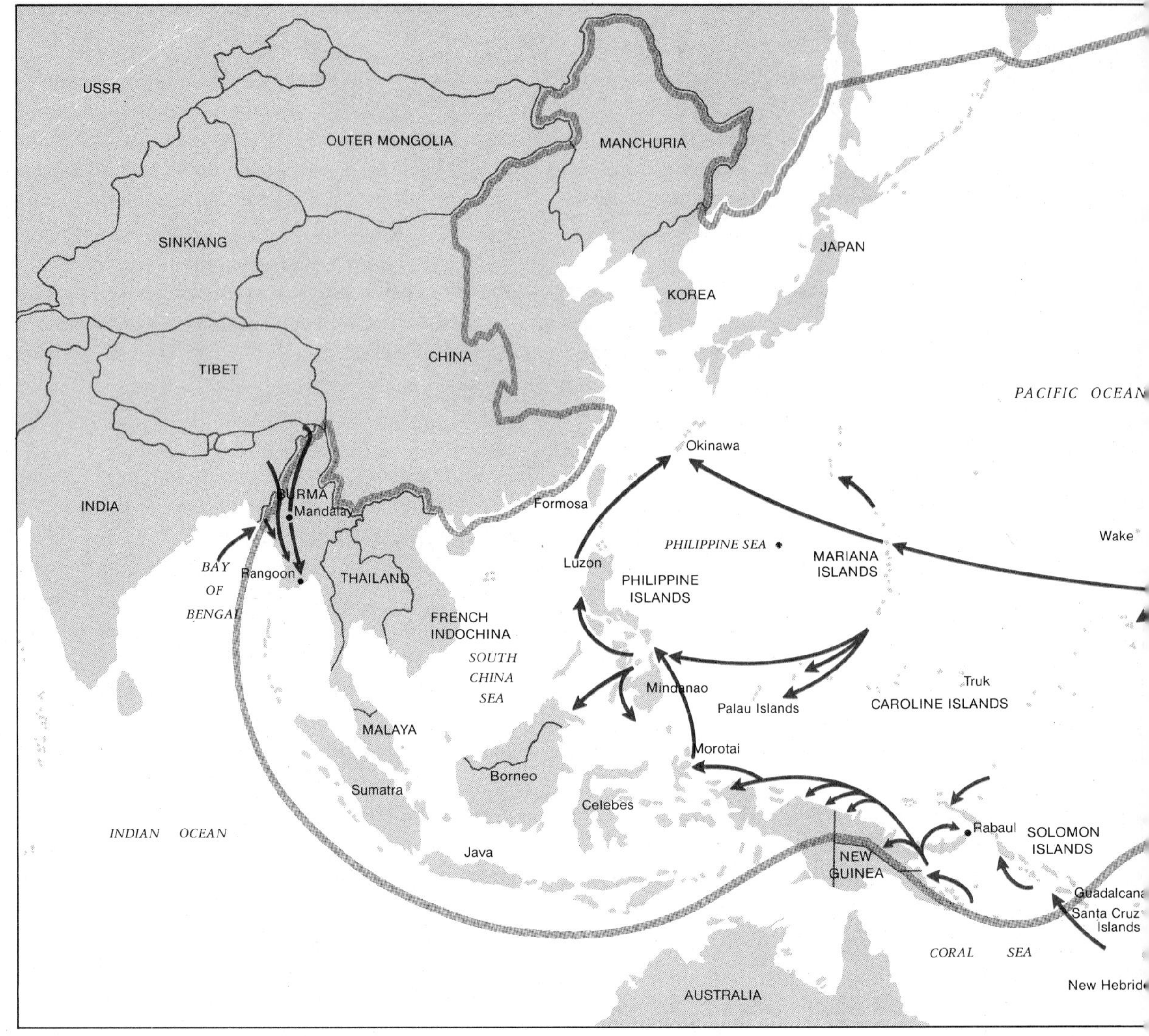

struction of a transportable atomic bomb at Los Alamos, New Mexico, under the direction of the physicist J. Robert Oppenheimer. Almost $2 billion was spent before a successful bomb was exploded at Alamogordo, in the New Mexican desert, on July 16.

Should a bomb with the destructive force of 20,000 *tons* of TNT be employed against Japan? By striking a major city, its dreadful power could be demonstrated convincingly, yet doing so would bring death to tens of thousands of Japanese civilians. Many of the scientists who had made the bomb now somewhat inconsistently argued against its use. To Truman, there really seemed no choice. Every past experience indicated that the Japanese army intended to fight to the last man,* but the bomb might cause a revolution in Japan, might lead the emperor to intervene, might even persuade the military fanatics to give up. Weighing American lives against Japanese, and also influenced by a desire to end the Pacific war before Russia could intervene effectively and thus claim a role in the peacemaking, the President chose to go ahead. On August 6 the Superfortress *Enola Gay* dropped an atom bomb on Hiroshima, killing about 75,000 persons and injuring nearly 100,000 more out of a population of 344,000. Over

*In recapturing Guam, for example, the Americans killed 17,238 Japanese but took only 438 prisoners.

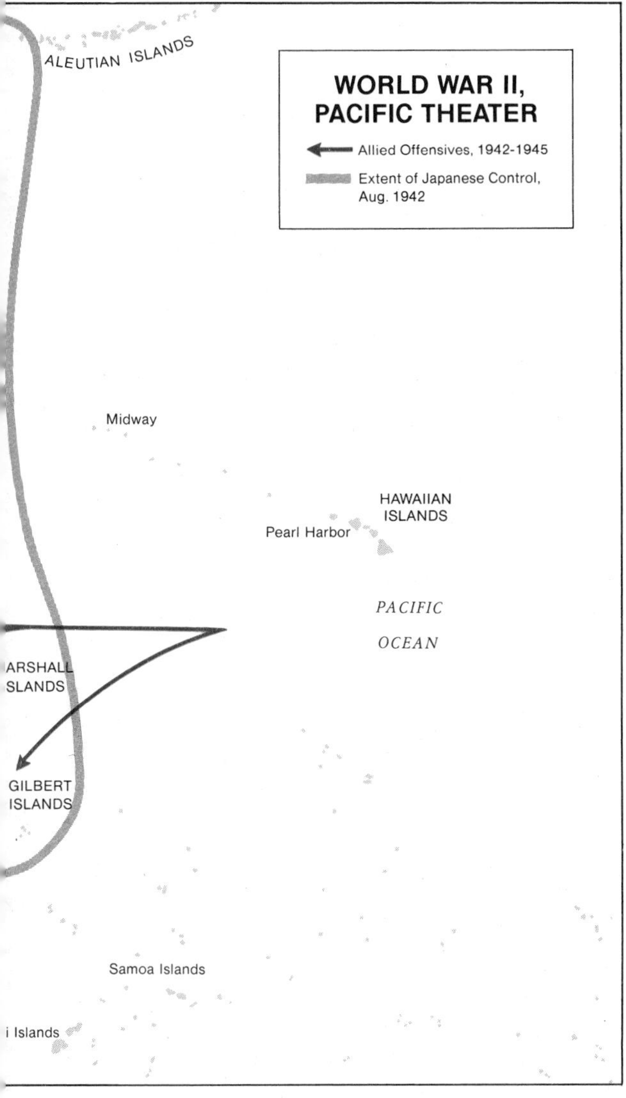

96 per cent of the buildings in the city were destroyed or damaged. Three days later, while the stunned Japanese still hesitated, a second bomb hit Nagasaki. This second drop was far less defensible morally, but it had the desired result. On August 15 Japan surrendered.

Thus ended the greatest war in history. Its cost had been beyond calculation; no accurate count could be made even of the dead, although the total came to somewhere in the neighborhood of 20 million. As in World War I, American casualties—291,000 battle deaths and 671,000 wounded—were relatively smaller than those of the other major belligerents. About 7.5 million Russians died in battle, 3.5 million Germans, 1.2 million Japanese, and 2.2 million Chinese; Britain and France, despite much smaller populations, suffered losses almost as large as America's. But far more than in World War I, American power, human and material, had made victory possible.

No one could account the war a benefit to mankind, but in the late summer of 1945 the future looked bright. Fascism was dead. Successful wartime diplomatic dealings between Roosevelt, Churchill, and Joseph Stalin, the Soviet dictator, encouraged many to hope that the communists were ready to abandon their implacable opposition to the capitalist way of life and cooperate in rebuilding Europe. In America isolationism had almost disappeared; the message of Wendell Willkie's best-selling *One World*, written after a globe-circling tour made by the 1940 Republican Presidential candidate at the behest of President Roosevelt in 1942, appeared to have been absorbed by the great majority of the people. Out of the death and destruction had also come technological advances that seemed to herald a better world as well as a peaceful one. Above all, there was the power of the atom. The force that seared Hiroshima and Nagasaki could be harnessed to serve peaceful needs, the scientists promised, with results that would free man forever from his heritage of poverty and toil. Great strides in transportation and communication lay ahead, products of wartime research in electronics, airplane design, and rocketry. The development of penicillin and other antibiotics, which had greatly reduced the death rate among troops, would assuredly increase man's normal span of life, perhaps banish all disease.

The period of reconstruction would be prolonged, but with all the great powers adhering to the new United Nations charter, drafted at San Francisco in June 1945, international cooperation could be counted upon to ease the burdens of the victims of war and help the poor and underdeveloped parts of the world toward economic and political independence. Above all, although in some respects a less powerful organization than the defunct League of Nations, the UN would stand guard over the peace of the world. Such at least was the hope of millions in the victorious summer of 1945.

SUPPLEMENTARY READING There are good summaries of diplomatic developments in Selig Adler, *The Uncertain Giant: American Foreign Policy Between the Wars* (1965), and F.R. Dulles, *America's Rise to World Power** (1955); see also J.D. Hicks, *Republican Ascendancy** (1960), and W.E. Leuchtenburg, *Franklin Roosevelt and the New Deal** (1963). J.C. Vinson, *The Parchment Peace* (1955), is the standard account of the Washington Armament Conference. R.H. Ferrell, *Peace in Their Time* (1952), is excellent on the Kellogg-Briand Pact. Other important works on the diplomacy of the twenties include M.J. Pusey, *Charles Evans Hughes* (1951), Dexter Perkins, *Charles Evans Hughes and American Democratic Statesmanship* (1956), A.W. Griswold, *The Far Eastern Policy of the United States** (1938), E.E. Morison, *Turmoil and Tradition: A Study of the Life and Times of Henry L. Stimson** (1960), and R.N. Current, *Secretary Stimson* (1954). R.H. Ferrell, *American Diplomacy and the Great Depression* (1957), and Alexander De Conde, *Herbert Hoover's Latin American Policy* (1951), are also useful.

On isolationism and the events leading to Pearl Harbor, see R.A. Divine, *The Reluctant Belligerent** (1965), brief but comprehensive, and *The Illusion of Neutrality** (1962), Donald Drummond, *The Passing of American Neutrality* (1955), two volumes by W.L. Langer and S.E. Gleason, *The Challenge to Isolation** (1952) and *The Undeclared War* (1953), Selig Adler, *The Isolationist Impulse** (1957), Manfred Jonas, *Isolationism in America** (1966), Dorothy Borg, *The United States and the Far Eastern Crisis* (1964), T.R. Fehrenbach, *F.D.R.'s Undeclared War* (1967), W.S. Cole, *Senator Gerald P. Nye and American Foreign Relations* (1962) and *America First* (1953), Herbert Feis, *The Road to Pearl Harbor** (1962), Basil Rauch, *Roosevelt from Munich to Pearl Harbor* (1950), Roberta Wohlstetter, *Pearl Harbor: Warning and Decision** (1962), and J.W. Pratt, *Cordell Hull* (1964). C.C. Tansill, *Back Door to War* (1952), C.A. Beard, *American Foreign Policy in the Making* (1946) and *President Roosevelt and the Coming of the War* (1948), are interesting interpretations by isolationists.

American mobilization is treated briefly in A.R. Buchanan, *The United States in World War II** (1964). Special aspects of the subject are covered in Bruce Catton, *War Lords of Washington* (1948), Eliot Janeway, *The Struggle for Survival* (1951), David Novik, *et al.*, *Wartime Production Controls* (1949), Joel Seidman, *American Labor from Defense to Reconversion* (1953), D.M. Nelson, *Arsenal of Democracy* (1946), W.W. Wilcox, *The Farmer in the Second World War* (1947), R.E. Paul, *Taxation for Prosperity* (1947), Roland Young, *Congressional Politics in the Second World War* (1956), and J.P. Baxter, *Scientists Against Time** (1946). Social trends are covered in Jack Goodman (ed.), *While You Were Gone* (1946). On the treatment of conscientious objectors, see P.E. Jacob and M.Q. Sibley, *Conscription of Conscience* (1952); on the relocation of the Japanese, see Morton Grodzins, *Americans Betrayed* (1949). The effect of the war on Negroes is discussed in Ulysses Lee, *The Employment of Negro Troops* (1966), and Herbert Garfinkel, *When Negroes March* (1959).

A.R. Buchanan, *The United States in World War II*, already mentioned, provides an excellent overall survey of the military side of the conflict. The role of the army is covered exhaustively in the Department of the Army's multivolume *The United States Army in World War II* (1947–) by various authors; that of the navy, in similar fashion, in S.E. Morison, *History of United States Naval Operations in World War II* (1947–1962), which Morison has condensed in *The Two-Ocean War* (1963). For the air force, see W.F. Craven, J.L. Cate, *et al.*, *The Army Air Forces in World War II* (1948–1958).

*Available in paperback.

28

Foreign Affairs: 1942–1964

On Christmas Eve 1943 Franklin D. Roosevelt reported to the nation on his first meeting with Soviet Premier Joseph Stalin at Teheran, in Iran. "I 'got along fine' with Marshal Stalin," he said, "and I believe that we are going to get along very well with him and the Russian people—very well indeed." A little over a year later, describing to Congress his second meeting with Stalin, at Yalta in the Crimea, the President stressed again the good feeling that existed between the two nations and their leaders. "We argued freely and frankly across the table," he explained. "But at the end, on every point, unanimous agreement was reached. I may say we achieved a unity of thought and a way of getting along together." Privately he characterized Stalin as "a very interesting man" whose rough exterior clothed an "old-fashioned elegant European manner." He referred to him almost affectionately as "that old buzzard," and on one occasion even called him "Uncle Joe" to his face. At Yalta Stalin gave Roosevelt a portrait photograph, with a long Cyrillic inscription in his small, tightly written hand.

By April 1945, however, Roosevelt was writing to Stalin of his "astonishment," "anxiety," and "bitter resentment" over the Soviet Union's "discouraging lack of application" of the agreements made at Yalta. "It would be one of the greatest tragedies in the history of the world," he warned, "if, in the very hour of victory—which is now in our grasp—suspicion and lack of faith should compromise the whole undertaking." A few days after dictating these words Roosevelt was dead. Before the end of the month, his successor, President Harry S. Truman, was complaining that "our agreements with the Soviet Union had so far been a one-way street" and telling Foreign Minister Vyacheslav M. Molotov with characteristic bluntness that Stalin must learn to keep his promises. "I have never been talked to like that in my life," said Molotov. "Carry out your agreements," Truman retorted, "and you won't get talked to like that!" Thus ended the brief period of amity born of the struggle against Hitler, an interlude in the conflict between capitalist democracy and Soviet communism which Hans J. Morgenthau has described as "an international civil war which began in 1917 and has continued to this day."

Wartime Diplomacy During the course of World War II every instrument of mass persuasion in the country was directed at convincing the people that the Russians were fighting America's battle as well as their own. Even before Pearl Harbor, former Ambassador Joseph E. Davies wrote in his best-selling *Mission to Moscow* (1941): "Russia is in the thick of this fight. . . . Hundreds of thousands of Russian men, women, and Soviet leaders . . . are now very gallantly fighting and dying for a cause which is vital to our security." According to Davies, the communist leaders were "a group of able, strong men" with "honest convictions and integrity of purposes" who were "devoted to the cause of peace for both ideological and practical reasons." Stalin possessed great dignity and charm, combined with much wisdom and strength of character, Davies said. "His brown eye is exceedingly kind and gentle. A child would like to sit in his lap and a dog would sidle up to him."

During the war American newspapers and magazines published many laudatory articles about Russia. *Life* praised Stalin's "magnetic personality," reported that Russians "think like Americans," and described the Russian secret police organization (the NKVD) as "similar to the FBI." A number of motion pictures also contributed to revising the attitude of the average American toward the USSR. *Song of Russia* described the heroic defense the Soviet people were throwing up against the Nazi hordes; *Mission to Moscow*, a whitewash of the dreadful Moscow treason trials of the thirties based on Ambassador Davies' book, portrayed Stalin as a wise, grandfatherly type, puffing comfortably on an old pipe. In a radio address early in 1942 President Roosevelt saluted "the superb Russian Army as it celebrates the twenty-fourth anniversary of its first assembly." A year later he gave Stalin personal credit "for the very wonderful detailed plan" that was enabling Russian troops to drive the Germans back from Stalingrad. In *One World* (1943) Wendell Willkie wrote glowingly of the Russian people, their "effective society," and their simple, warm-hearted leader. When he suggested jokingly to Stalin that if he continued to make

Courier MAGAZINE, 1943

Above: The close wartime cooperation between Roosevelt and Churchill is captured in this 1943 cartoon, from a London magazine. Below is a Persian print, done at the 1943 Teheran Conference, which depicts Churchill, Stalin, and Roosevelt tying up the Axis.

FRANKLIN D. ROOSEVELT LIBRARY

progress in improving the education of his people he might educate himself out of a job, the dictator "threw his head back and laughed and laughed," Willkie recorded. "Mr. Willkie, you know I grew up a Georgian peasant. I am unschooled in pretty talk. All I can say is I like you very much."

These views of the character of Joseph Stalin were naive, to say the least, but the identity of interest of the United States and the Soviet Union was very real during the war, and the two nations, realizing this fact, cooperated effectively. Russian military leaders conferred regularly with their British and American counterparts and fulfilled their obligations scrupulously. As early as October 1943 Foreign Minister Molotov committed his country to joining in the war against Japan as soon as the Germans were defeated, a promise confirmed the following month by Stalin at his meeting with Churchill and Roosevelt at Teheran.

The Soviets also repeatedly expressed a willingness to cooperate with the Allies in dealing with postwar problems. Russia was one of the 26 signers of the Declaration of the United Nations (January 1942), in which the Allies promised to eschew territorial aggrandizement after the war, respect the right of all peoples to determine their own form of government, work for freer trade and international economic cooperation, and force the disarmament of the aggressor nations.* In May 1943 Russia dissolved the Comintern, its official agency for the promulgation of world revolution. That October, during a conference in Moscow with Secretary of State Cordell Hull and British Foreign Minister Anthony Eden, Molotov joined in setting up a European Advisory Commission to divide Germany into occupation zones after the war and recognized "the necessity of establishing . . . a general international organization . . . for the maintenance of international peace and security." At the Teheran Conference Stalin willingly discussed plans for a new league of nations. When Roosevelt described specifically the kind of a world organization he envisaged, the Russian dictator offered a number of constructive suggestions.

Between August and October 1944, Allied representatives met at Dumbarton Oaks, outside Washington. The chief Russian delegate, Andrei A. Gromyko, adamantly opposed all suggestions for limiting the use of the veto by the great powers on the future UN Security Council, but he did not take a deliberately obstructionist position. At the Yalta Conference Stalin promised to permit "free and unfettered elections as soon as possible" in Poland and other eastern European countries under the control of the Red Army. He also joined in the call for a conference to be held in April 1945 at San Francisco to draft a charter for the United Nations, incidentally modifying the Russian position on the veto slightly by agreeing that no power might veto Security Council *discussion* of a controversy in which it had a stake.

Although the powers argued at length over the exact form of that charter at the 50-nation San Francisco Conference, they conducted the debates in an atmosphere of optimism and international amity. Each UN member received a seat in the General Assembly, a body designed for discussion rather than action. Since all nations great and small had one vote in the Assembly, it was not intended to legislate or to make significant decisions. The locus of authority in the new organization resided in the Security Council, "the castle of the great powers." This consisted of five permanent members (the United States, Russia, Great Britain, France, and China) and six others elected for two-year terms. The Council was charged with the responsibility for maintaining world peace. It could apply diplomatic, economic, or military sanctions against any nation threatening that peace. A majority of seven members was required to implement its decisions, but since the majority had to include the votes of the five permanent members, any great power could block UN action whenever it wished to do so. The United States insisted upon this veto power as strongly as the Soviet Union. In effect the charter paid lip service to the Wilsonian ideal of a powerful international police force, but to assure Senate ratification it incorporated the basic limitations

*These were the principles first laid down in the so-called Atlantic Charter, drafted by Roosevelt and Churchill at a dramatic meeting on the U.S.S. *Augusta* off Newfoundland in August 1941.

that Senator Lodge had proposed in his 1919 reservations. For example, the big-power veto represented Lodge's reservation to Article X of the League Covenant, which would have relieved the United States from the obligation of enforcing collective security without the approval of Congress.

The UN charter also provided for a Secretariat to handle routine administration, headed by a secretary general who was in addition the chief executive officer of the entire organization; a Trusteeship Council to supervise dependent areas much in the fashion of the mandate system of the League; and an International Court of Justice. An Economic and Social Council was created to supervise a host of agencies related to the UN such as the International Labor Organization, the International Bank for Reconstruction and Development, the International Monetary Fund, the World Health Organization, and the United Nations Educational, Scientific and Cultural Organization (UNESCO), which was assigned the task of "promoting collaboration among the nations through education, science, and culture."

Although Russia displayed less enthusiasm for the UN than most of the powers, it went along with the others, Molotov signing the charter on the flag-decked stage of the Veterans' War Memorial Building in San Francisco on June 26, 1945. Millions all over the globe hoped, as President Truman said in addressing the final plenary session of the conference, that "a solid structure upon which we can build a better world" had been established.

OSCAR BERGER, NEW YORK *Times*

Oscar Berger made this sketch during the UN Conference in San Francisco at a cocktail party given by Russian Foreign Minister Vyacheslav Molotov (right). Among the others are Michigan Senator Arthur H. Vandenberg, a one-time isolationist (2nd from left), Texas' Tom Connally, chairman of the Senate Foreign Relations Committee (3rd from left), and Secretary of State Edward R. Stettinius, Jr. (3rd from right).

Developing Conflicts

Yet long before the war in Europe ended, the Allied powers had clashed over important policy matters. Since present-day world tensions have developed from decisions made at this time, an understanding of these disagreements is essential for evaluating whole decades of history. Unfortunately, complete understanding is not yet possible, which explains why the subject remains hotly controversial. Much depends upon one's opinion of the Soviet system: if Russian communism is a threat to democracy and humane values the world over, or even if the Soviet government under Stalin was bent on world domination, events of the so-called Cold War fall readily into one pattern of interpretation. If Russia is seen as a nation that, having bravely and at enormous cost endured an unprovoked assault by the Nazis, was determined to protect itself against the possibility of another invasion, these events are best explained differently. In other words, the conflicts have had roots in ideological differences and in national rivalries. If the former are stressed, compromise solutions are harder to justify than if the latter are considered more important. The problem is made more difficult by the fact that relatively little is known of the motivations and inner workings of Soviet policy.

The Russians naturally resented the British-American delay in opening up a second front, for they were fighting for survival against the full power of the German armies and knew that any invasion, even an unsuccessful one, would relieve some of the pressure. Roosevelt and Churchill would not move until they were ready, and the Russians had to accept their decision. The Russians also objected strongly to the western nations' dealings with Vichy France, which they took as a sign of a willingness to compromise with fascism. On the other hand, the Russians never concealed their determination to protect themselves against future attacks by extending their western frontier after the war. In December 1941 Stalin had demanded that Great Britain recognize his right to a large section of eastern Poland. He warned the Allies repeatedly that he would not tolerate any anti-Soviet government along Russia's western frontier. Most Allied leaders, including Roosevelt, admitted privately during the war that the Soviet Union would annex territory and possess preponderant power in eastern Europe after the defeat of Germany, but they never said this publicly and appear to have hoped that Stalin could be persuaded to adhere to the democratic principles of the Atlantic Charter. Somehow, they believed free governments could be created in countries like Poland and Bulgaria that the Russians would trust enough to leave to their own devices. "The Poles," said Winston Churchill early in 1945, "will have their future in their own hands, with the single limitation that they must honestly follow . . . a policy friendly to Russia. This is surely reasonable."

At the Yalta Conference, Roosevelt and Churchill agreed to Russian annexation of large sections of eastern Poland. The Polish question was a terribly difficult one. The war, after all, had been triggered by the German attack on Poland; the British particularly felt a moral obligation to restore that nation to its prewar independence. During the war a Polish government-in-exile was set up in London, and its leaders were determined, especially after the murder of some 5,000 Polish officers in 1943 at Katyn, in Russia, presumably by the Soviet secret police, to make no concessions to Soviet territorial demands. Yet Russia's legitimate interests (to say nothing of its power in the area) could not be ignored. Stalin apparently could not understand why his allies were so concerned about the fate of a small country so remote from their strategic spheres; that they professed to be concerned seemed to him an indication that they had some secret, devious purpose. He could see no difference (and "revisionist" American historians agree with him) between the Soviet Union dominating Poland and maintaining a government there that did not reflect the wishes of a majority of the Polish people, and the United States dominating many Latin-American nations and supporting unpopular regimes within them.

Stalin did agree at Yalta, almost certainly without intending to keep his promise, to allow free elections in the reconstituted Polish republic. But the elections were never held, and Poland was run by a pro-Russian puppet regime. Thus, the West "lost" Poland, although how it might have "won" the country when it was already occupied by Russian armies has never been explained.

Alarmed by rapid Russian advances into central Europe in the closing days of the war, which he saw as a drastic disruption of the balance of power, Churchill urged Truman to order General Eisenhower to press forward as far as possible against the rapidly crumbling German armies in order to limit the area of Russian control. Had his advice been taken, Allied troops could probably have occupied most of Czechoslovakia and Germany as far east as Berlin. However, when Eisenhower pointed out the military disadvantage of such a headlong advance, Truman refused to overrule him.

After the surrender of Germany, Truman, Stalin, and Churchill met at Potsdam,* outside Berlin. They agreed to try the Nazi leaders as war criminals, made plans for exacting reparations from Germany, and confirmed the division of the country into four zones to be occupied separately by American, Russian, British, and French forces. Berlin itself, deep in the Soviet zone, had also been split into four sectors. Stalin rejected all arguments that he loosen his hold on eastern Europe, and Truman (who received news of the successful testing of the atom bomb while at Potsdam) took a much tougher stance in the negotiations. On both sides, suspicions were mounting, positions hardening.

At this point the United States stood, as Cassius said of Caesar, "bestride the narrow world like a Colossus." Besides its army, navy, and air force and its immense industrial potential, alone among the nations it possessed the atomic bomb. When Stalin's actions made it clear that he intended to control all eastern Europe and to exert an important influence elsewhere in the world, most Americans first reacted somewhat in the manner of a mastiff being worried by a yapping terrier: their resentment was tempered by amazement. Holding so much power and wanting nothing more but peace, they refused to believe that the Russians could honestly suspect their motives, and they viewed Stalin's obvious determination to control all the nations along Russia's western border with horror. They were slow to grasp the fundamental change that the war had produced in international politics. America might be the strongest country in the world, but all the western European nations, victors and vanquished alike, had been reduced to the status of second-class powers. Russia, however, had regained the influence it had held under the czars and lost as a result of World War I and its communist revolution.

American and Russian attitudes stood in sharp confrontation when the control of atomic energy came up for discussion in the UN. Everyone realized the threat to human survival posed by the atomic bomb. As early as November 1945, the United States suggested allowing the UN to supervise all nuclear energy production, and the General Assembly promptly created an Atomic Energy Commission to study the question. In June 1946 Commissioner Bernard Baruch offered a plan under which atomic weapons would be outlawed. UN inspectors would have the authority to operate without restriction anywhere in the world to make sure that no country was making bombs clandestinely. "There must be no veto to protect those who violate their solemn agreements not to develop or use atomic energy for destructive purposes," Baruch declared. When such a supranational system had been established, the United States would destroy its stockpile of bombs.

Most Americans thought the Baruch plan exceedingly magnanimous and some considered it positively foolhardy, but the Soviets rejected it. Displaying an almost paranoid fear of any invasion of their sovereign independence, they would neither permit UN inspectors into Russia nor surrender their veto power over Security Council actions dealing with atomic energy. At the same time they demanded that the United States destroy its bombs at once. Unwilling to trust the Russians not to produce bombs secretly under these conditions, the United States refused to agree. The result was a stalemate and increased international tension.

The Containment Policy

Postwar cooperation had failed. In a series of actions the Soviets were probing outward in every direction, seeking to expand their power and influence. By the end of 1945, besides dominating most of eastern Europe, they controlled Outer Mongolia, parts of Manchuria, and nothern Korea. They had annexed the Kurile Islands and regained from Japan the southern half of Sakhalin Island.* They were also fomenting trouble in Iran, where they hoped to take over the northern province of Azerbaijan and win important oil concessions,

*Clement R. Attlee replaced Churchill during the conference after his Labour party won the British elections.

*Roosevelt and Churchill had agreed to these Russian moves in the Far East as part of the Yalta settlement.

and soon they began to exert heavy pressure on Turkey and Greece in order to obtain access to the eastern Mediterranean.

The United States, on the other hand, had indulged the natural desire of its people to relax after the war, to demobilize the bulk of its armed forces, and reconvert the economy to peacetime production, thus reducing its ability to resist Soviet expansion. It reacted to Russia's moves first by direct diplomatic appeals and threats and then by strenuous objections in the UN, where American influence was great. In the cases of Iran and Turkey, these methods proved at least temporarily sufficient. The Greek problem, however, was more serious. Local communists, waging a guerrilla war against the pro-western monarchy, were receiving aid from the Russian-dominated "satellite" nations of Yugoslavia, Bulgaria, and Albania. Great Britain was assisting the monarchists. For more than a year an inconclusive civil war had been wracking the country. However, Britain, its economy shaken by World War II, could not long afford this drain on its resources. A postwar American loan of $4.4 billion was being rapidly exhausted. In February 1947 the British informed President Truman that they would have to cut off further aid to Greece.

Russia's "Iron Curtain" (a phrase popularized by Winston Churchill) seemed about to ring down on still another nation. The Greek government was conservative, even reactionary, but it was threatened by outside forces. As Truman later explained: "The ideals and traditions of our nation demanded that . . . we put the world on notice that it would be our policy to support the cause of freedom wherever it was threatened."

On March 12 the President went before a joint session of Congress and enunciated what became known as the Truman Doctrine. If Greece or Turkey fell to the communists, he said, all the Middle East might be lost. This, in turn, might shake the morale of anticommunist elements throughout western Europe. To prevent this "unspeakable tragedy," he asked Congress for $400 million in military and economic aid for Greece and Turkey. "It must be the policy of the United States to support free peoples who are resisting attempted subjugation by armed minorities or by outside pressures," he said. Isolationists raised a storm, and many liberals criticized Truman for by-passing the UN and supporting the reactionary Greek regime, but the overwhelming majority accepted the President's reasoning. Congress appropriated the necessary money by margins approaching three to one in both houses. No more convincing proof that Americans had assumed enormous new international responsibilities could be imagined.

Although the Truman Doctrine was a response to a specific crisis, it heralded the birth of a broad policy of resistance to Russian expansion everywhere. Some of the western European nations stood in danger of falling into the communist orbit. Neither the Red Army nor Soviet subversion had anything to do with this. The war had shattered their economies. The Continent, as Winston Churchill said, had become "a rubble-heap, a charnel house, a breeding-ground of pestilence and hate," and these conditions fostered the growth of communism. For ideological as well as humanitarian reasons the United States felt obliged to protect this vital area and provide the means of restoring its prosperity and social health.

But how to do so without appearing to be as imperialistic and expansionist as the Russians? For weeks in the spring of 1947, American foreign policy experts pondered this question. Many minds contributed to the solution, but the key ideas were provided by George F. Kennan, a scholarly Foreign Service officer with long practical experience in diplomacy. Kennan had served for five years in Russia and had studied its history carefully. He was particularly impressed by the "traditional and instinctive sense of insecurity" which he perceived in the attitude of Russians toward the capitalist world. Russian statesmen tended to see their country "as in a state of siege, with the enemy lowering beyond the walls," and their experiences in World War II had undoubtedly intensified this feeling. Ordinary diplomatic negotiations with the USSR were doomed to fail. Soviet leaders, Kennan implied, were afraid to compromise; "their whole training has taught them to mistrust and discount the glib persuasiveness of the outside world."

In an anonymous article in the July 1947 issue

of *Foreign Affairs,* "The Sources of Soviet Conduct," Kennan advocated a policy of "long-term, patient but firm and vigilant containment" based on the "application of counter-force" as the best means of dealing with Soviet pressures. The Cold War might be "a duel of infinite duration," Kennan admitted, but it could be won if, without bluster, America maintained its own strength and convinced the communists that it would resist aggression firmly in any quarter of the globe.

Although he was the chief architect of the containment policy, Kennan disagreed with the *psychology* of the Truman Doctrine, which seemed to him essentially defensive as well as open to criticism by anti-imperialists. He proposed, therefore, along with containment, a broad aid program, free of "ideological overtones," to be offered even to Russia, provided the Soviets would contribute some of their own resources to the cause of European economic recovery. The European nations themselves should work out the details, America providing only money, materials, and technical advice.

George C. Marshall, army chief of staff during World War II and now secretary of state, formally suggested this aid program, which became known as the Marshall Plan, in a Harvard commencement speech on June 5, 1947. The objective, he said, was to restore "the confidence of the European people in the economic future of their own countries." America intended to attack no nation or political system, only "hunger, poverty, desperation, and chaos," the real enemies of freedom and democracy. It would be "neither fitting nor efficacious" for the United States to impose such a plan on any country. "This is the business of the Europeans. . . . The program should be a joint one, agreed to by a number, if not all European nations."

The Marshall Plan and the policy of containment succeeded brilliantly. Led by Great Britain and France, the European powers seized avidly on Marshall's suggestion. Although the Soviet Union refused to participate, within six weeks of Marshall's speech 16 nations were setting up a Committee for European Economic Cooperation, which soon submitted plans calling for up to $22.4 billion in American aid. After protracted debate, much influenced by a communist coup in Czechoslovakia in February 1948 which drew still another country behind the Iron Curtain, Congress appropriated over $13 billion for the program. Results exceeded the expectations even of the optimists. By 1951 western Europe was booming and Communist parties in all the democracies were shrinking. Whether the policymakers realized it or not, containment and the Marshall Plan were America's response to the power vacuum created in Europe by the debilitating effects of the war, comparable to the Soviet Union's response. Just as Russia extended its influence over the eastern half of the Continent, the United States extended its influence in the west. But with this vital difference: in the east "influence" meant (and still means) almost total domination, in the west it meant what the dictionaries say it means—"power independent of force or authority."

Economic aid laid the basis for a broader European political cooperation, presaging a possible end to centuries of bitter national rivalries on the Continent. At Brussels, in March 1948, Great Britain, France, Belgium, the Netherlands, and Luxembourg signed an alliance aimed at social and cultural collaboration as well as economic. The western nations soon abandoned their understandable but self-defeating policy of crushing Germany economically. They instituted currency reforms in their zones and announced plans for creating a single West German Republic, with a large degree of autonomy.

These decisions caused the Russians to close off Allied surface access to Berlin in June 1948. For a time it seemed that the Allies must either fight their way into the city or abandon it to the communists. Unwilling to adopt either of these alternatives, Truman decided to fly supplies through the air corridors leading to the capital from Frankfurt, Hanover, and Hamburg. This "Berlin Airlift" put the Russians in an uncomfortable position; if they were really determined to keep supplies from West Berlin, they would have to begin the fighting. They were unprepared to do so. C-47 and C-54 transports shuttled back and forth in weather fair and foul, carrying the food, fuel, and other goods necessary to maintain more

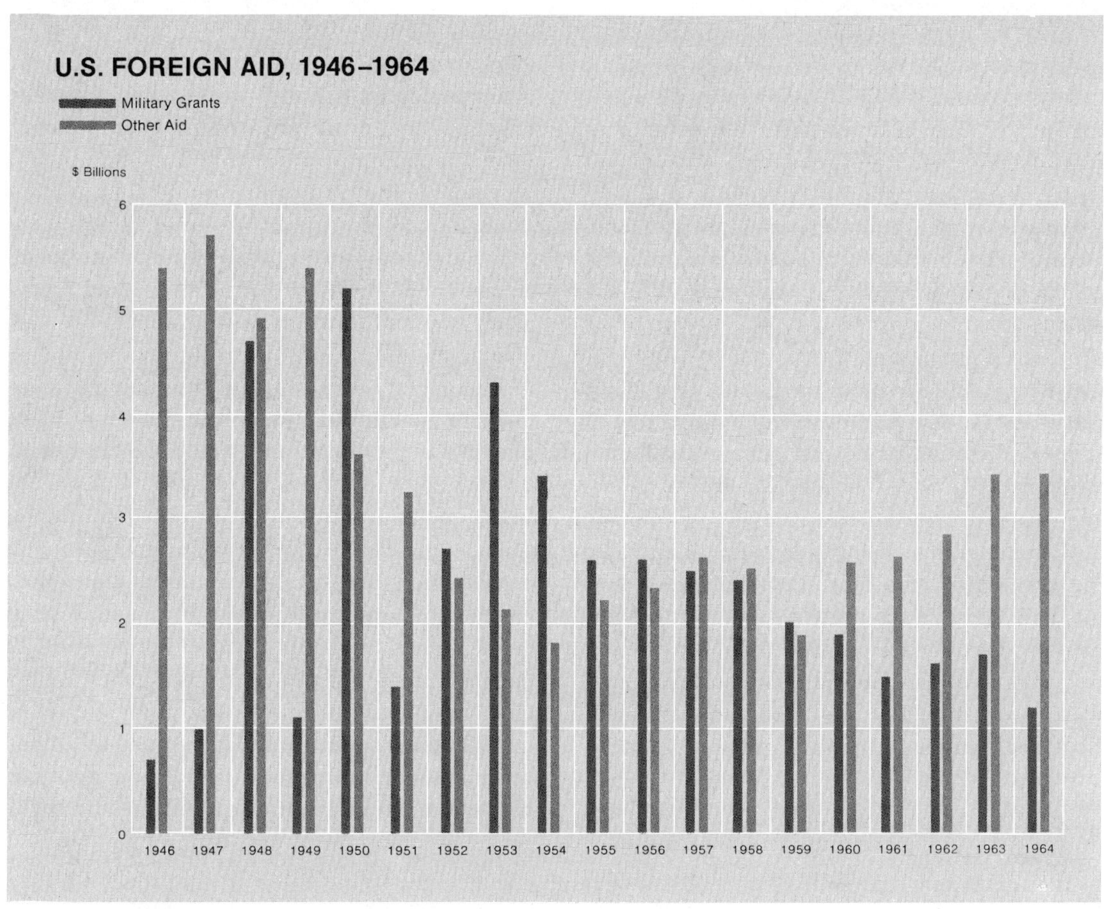

than 2 million West Berliners. By August 3,000 tons a day were reaching the city, by October nearly 5,000. Berlin was saved, and in May 1949 the Russians gave up the blockade. The success of the Berlin Airlift provided a powerful boost to European morale and solidly vindicated the containment policy.

Containment, however, also required the development of a powerful military force. In May 1948 Republican Senator Arthur H. Vandenberg of Michigan, a prewar leader of the isolationists who had been converted to internationalism largely by President Roosevelt's solicitous consideration of his views, introduced a resolution stating the "determination" of the United States "to exercise the right of individual *or collective* self-defense . . . should any armed attack occur affecting its national security." The Senate approved this resolution by a vote of 64 to 4, further proof that isolationism was no longer an effective force in American politics. Negotiations began promptly with the western powers, and in April 1949 the North Atlantic Treaty was signed in Washington. The United States, Great Britain, France, Italy, Belgium, the Netherlands, Luxembourg, Denmark, Norway, Portugal, Iceland, and Canada* agreed "that an armed attack against one or more of them in Europe or North America shall be considered an attack against them all," and that in the event of such an attack each would take "individually and in concert with the other Parties, such action as it deems necessary, including the use of armed force." No more entangling alliance could be imagined, yet the Senate ratified this treaty by a vote of 82 to 13.

Under this pact the North Atlantic Treaty Organization (NATO) was established. Further alarmed by the news, released in September 1949, that the Russians had produced an atomic bomb,

*In 1952 Greece and Turkey also joined the alliance, and in 1954 West Germany was admitted.

Congress appropriated $1.5 billion to arm NATO, and in 1951 General Eisenhower was recalled to active duty and placed in command of all NATO forces. This international army included four American divisions and even some newly created German units, although the powers were still unwilling to permit West Germany to organize and control an army of its own. NATO forces never approached the Soviet armies in size, but along with the nuclear power of the United States they persuaded the Russians to restrain themselves in Europe. Restraint, of course, did not mean passivity; every effort at containment evoked a Russian response. The Marshall Plan led to the seizure of Czechoslovakia, the buildup of Germany to the Berlin blockade, the creation of NATO to the multilateral military alliance known as the Warsaw Pact. Whatever the origins of the contest, both sides contributed by their actions and their continuing suspicions to the heightening of Cold War tensions.

Containing Communism in Asia

Containment worked well in Europe; in the Far East, where the virtues of the policy were less clear and where the United States lacked powerful and determined allies, it was both more expensive and less effective. V-J Day found the Far East a shambles. Much of Japan was a smoking ruin. In China, where poverty had been endemic to begin with, social chaos was complicated by a disorganized political situation, the nationalists under Chiang Kai-shek dominating the south, the communists under Mao Tse-tung controlling the northern countryside, and Japanese troops still holding most of the northern cities. Faced with tremendous problems in this whole region, President Truman acted decisively and effectively with regard to Japan, unsurely and with unfortunate results where China was concerned.

Even before the Japanese surrendered, Truman had decided not to allow the Soviet Union any significant role in the occupation of Japan. "I did not want to give the Russians any opportunity to behave as they had in Germany and Austria," he later explained. A four-power Allied Control Council was established, but American troops, commanded by General MacArthur, ran the country. MacArthur displayed exactly the proper combination of imperiousness, tact, and intelligence needed to accomplish his purposes, and the Japanese, revealing the same remarkable adaptability that had made possible their swift "westernization" in the latter half of the 19th century, placidly accepted a new political and social system that involved de-emphasizing the importance of the emperor, universal suffrage and parliamentary government, the encouragement of labor unions, and the breakup of both large estates and big industrial combines. Japan lost its far-flung island empire as well as all claim to Korea and the Chinese mainland. Efforts to restrict economic development, however, were soon abandoned, partly because of the high cost of the occupation to the United States but mainly in order to build up the country as a Far Eastern bastion against communism. In 1951 a peace treaty formally ended the occupation, although American troops remained in Japan under an agreement with the new government. Japan emerged from the occupation economically strong, politically stable, and firmly allied with the United States.

The difficulties in China were probably insurmountable. No one, not even Marshal Stalin, appreciated the latent power of the Chinese communists. When the war ended, the United States tried to install Chiang in control of all China, allowing the Japanese to hold key north Chinese sectors until Chiang could take them over and even sending 50,000 marines into the region, a step which infuriated Mao Tse-tung. At the same time, however, Truman made a sustained effort to bring Chiang's nationalists and Mao's communists together, for he realized that no strong Chinese government could exist without the support of both groups. On August 16, 1945, the day after V-J Day, Patrick J. Hurley, the United States ambassador to China, persuaded Chiang to invite Mao to a conference. When the two leaders failed to agree, Truman sent General Marshall, whom he considered "the greatest living American," to try to arrange a settlement. Marshall managed to bring Chiang and Mao together twice during the first half of 1946, but neither would make significant concessions. Mao was convinced

—rightly as time soon proved—that he could win all China by force, while Chiang, presiding over a corrupt, incredibly incompetent regime almost totally out of contact with the Chinese masses, grossly exaggerated his own strength. The kindly and hard-working Marshall finally gave up in disgust, having been "frustrated time and again," as he explained, "by extremist elements of both sides." In January 1947 Truman recalled him and named him secretary of state. Soon thereafter a full-scale civil war erupted in China.

This war resulted in the total defeat of the nationalists; by the end of 1949 Mao ruled all China and Chiang's shattered armies had fled to sanctuary on the island of Formosa, now called Taiwan. The loss of China to communism caused an outburst of indignation in the United States and deeply divided the American people. Critics claimed that Truman had not backed the nationalists strongly enough and that he had stupidly underestimated both Mao's power and his dedication to the cause of world revolution. Despite a superficial plausibility, neither of these charges made much sense. Saving China from communism would have been worth great sacrifices, but nothing short of massive American military aid, including the commitment of American troops, could have prevented the communist victory. This American opinion would not have supported. Furthermore, American intervention in the civil war would unquestionably have alienated the Chinese people, who were thoroughly and rightly fed up with foreign meddling in their affairs. That *any* action could have prevented the loss of China is unlikely, given the unpopularity of Chiang's government and the ruthless zeal of the Chinese communists. Probably the United States gave the nationalists too much aid rather than too little. A hands-off policy might have tempered Mao's resentment. Such a policy was also impracticable, considering the hostility of Americans to communism in the midst of the Cold War.

The attacks of his American critics roused Truman's combativeness and led him into serious miscalculations elsewhere in the Orient. After the war, the province of Korea was taken from Japan and divided along the 38th parallel, the Russians controlling the northern half of the country, the Americans the southern. In December 1945 the occupying powers agreed in principle to set up a unified and independent Korean republic at some future date, but in the angry atmosphere of the postwar years, they could not agree as to how this should be done. By September 1948 there were two "independent" governments in Korea, the Democratic People's Republic, backed by the Soviet Union, and the Republic of Korea headed by President Syngman Rhee, backed by the United States and the UN. Both the major powers withdrew their troops from the peninsula, but the Russians left behind a well-armed local force, whereas the Republic of Korea's army was weak and ill-trained.

American military strategists had decided as early as 1947 that Korea was not worth defending. Truman accepted this decision without facing its implications: by leaving Korea weak he was tempting the communists to take it over, despite the fact that it was nominally under the protection of the UN. In January 1950, defining the "defensive perimeter" of the United States in the Far East, Dean Acheson, who had succeeded Marshall as secretary of state, deliberately excluded Korea, saying that it was up to the local populace, backed by the UN, to protect the country against attack. Although Congress appropriated large sums for Korean economic rehabilitation, it did little for the Korean army. Thus, when North Korean armored divisions struck suddenly across the 38th parallel in June 1950, they quickly routed the defenders.

At this point, Truman exhibited his finest qualities: decisiveness and courage. Recalling the dire results that had followed when earlier acts of aggression—beginning with the Japanese assault on Manchuria and the Italian invasion of Ethiopia—had been allowed to pass unchecked, he decided to defend South Korea. "This was the test of all the talk of the last five years of collective security," he reasoned. With the backing of the UN Security Council,* he sent American planes

*Russia, which could have vetoed this action, was at the moment boycotting the Security Council because the UN had refused to give the Mao Tse-tung regime China's seat on that body.

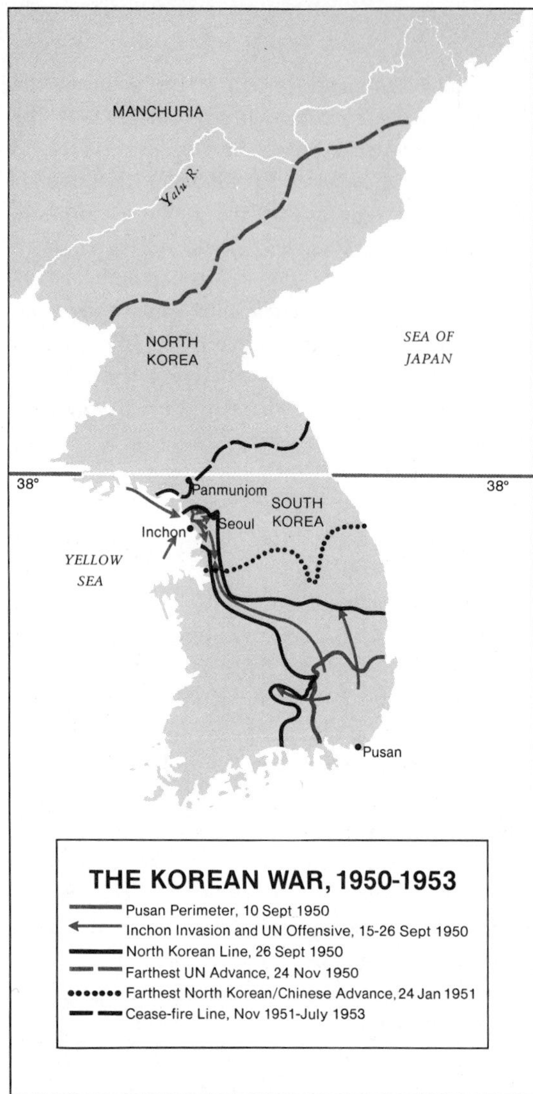

into battle. Ground troops soon followed.

Nominally, the Korean War was a struggle between the invaders and the United Nations. General MacArthur, placed in command, flew the blue UN flag over his headquarters and no less than 16 nations supplied troops for his army. However, more than 90 per cent of the forces employed were American. At first the North Koreans pushed them back rapidly, but by the beginning of September a front was stabilized around the port of Pusan, at the southern tip of Korea. Then General MacArthur executed a brilliant amphibious flanking maneuver, striking at the west coast city of Inchon, about 50 miles south of the 38th parallel. Outflanked, the North Koreans fled northward, losing thousands of men and much equipment. By October the battle front had moved *north* of the old boundary.

Despite an earlier statement that he sought only to restore the former frontier, Truman, with UN approval, now permitted MacArthur to drive toward the Yalu River, boundary between North Korea and Communist China. It was a momentous and unfortunate decision, an example of how power, once unleashed, so often gets out of hand. As the UN army advanced, ominous rumblings came from north of the Yalu, Foreign Minister Chou En-lai warning the world that the Chinese would not "supinely tolerate seeing their neighbors being savagely invaded by imperialists." Red Chinese "volunteers" began to turn up among the captives taken by UN units. Much alarmed, Truman flew to Wake Island, in the Pacific, to confer with MacArthur, but the general assured the President that the Chinese would not dare to intervene. If they did, he added, his army would crush them easily; the war would be over by Christmas.

Seldom has a general miscalculated so badly. On November 26, 33 Chinese divisions smashed suddenly through the center of MacArthur's line. Overnight a triumphant advance became a disorganized retreat. Amid incredible hardships, across broken country in subzero weather, the UN troops fled southward, suffering heavy casualties. MacArthur now spoke of the "bottomless well of Chinese manpower" and justified his earlier confidence by claiming, not without reason, that he was fighting "an entirely new war."

The UN army finally rallied south of the 38th parallel and even managed to battle its way back across that line in the eastern sector. By the spring of 1951 the front had been stabilized, although bitter fighting continued. MacArthur then urged that he be permitted to bomb Chinese installations north of the Yalu. He also suggested a naval blockade of the coast of China and the use of Chinese nationalist troops in Korea. When Truman rejected these proposals on the ground that they would lead to a third world war, MacArthur, who tended to ignore the larger political aspects of the conflict, attempted to rouse Congress and the public against the President by issuing public statements criticizing administration policy. Truman first ordered him to be silent, and when the general persisted, he removed him from command.

This unpopular but necessary step (a fundamental principle of democracy, civilian control over the military, was at stake) brought down a storm of abuse on the President. At first the Korean "police action" had been popular in the United States, but as the months passed and the casualties mounted, many citizens became disillusioned and angry. The war had brought into the open a basic political (or better, psychological) disadvantage of the containment policy: its object was not victory but balance; it involved apparently unending tension without the satisfying release of an action completed. To Americans accustomed to triumph and fond of oversimplifying complex questions, containment seemed, as time passed and its costs in blood and dollars mounted, a monumentally frustrating policy. MacArthur's simple if dangerous strategy offered at least the hope of victory; all the President seemed to offer was a further waste of American lives and money. MacArthur returned home to a series of triumphal receptions in cities from San Francisco to Washington, climaxed by a dramatic speech before a joint session of Congress on April 19. He then launched what he called a "crusade" to rally opinion to his cause.

Fortunately, the fundamental correctness of both Truman's policy and his decision to remove MacArthur eventually became apparent to the public. As he reminded the country, an all-out war with Communist China, besides costing thousands of lives, would alarm America's allies and weaken the nation while Russia watched from the sidelines unscathed. Military men backed the President almost unanimously, the highly respected General Omar N. Bradley, chairman of

Photographer David Douglas Duncan was with the 1st Marine Division in Korea when it was virtually isolated by the sudden Red Chinese offensive in November 1950. Conducting in frigid weather what the military historian S.L.A. Marshall called "the greatest fighting withdrawal of modern history," the marines broke out to safety.

© DAVID DOUGLAS DUNCAN, *Life*

the Joint Chiefs of Staff, declaring that a showdown with the Chinese "would involve us in the wrong war, at the wrong place, at the wrong time and with the wrong enemy." In June 1951 the communists agreed to negotiate an armistice in Korea, and although the talks dragged on, with interruptions, for two years while thousands more died along the static battle front, both MacArthur and talk of bombing China subsided.

The Communist Issue at Home: McCarthyism

The frustrating Korean War highlighted the paradox that at the very pinnacle of its power, America's influence in world affairs was declining. Its monopoly of nuclear weapons had been broken. China had passed into the communist orbit. Elsewhere in Asia and throughout Africa, new nations, formerly colonial possessions of the western powers, were adopting a "neutralist" position in the Cold War similar in purpose and method to the policy adopted by the United States after the Revolution, when it had steered a middle course in the struggle between Britain and France. Despite all the billions poured into armaments and foreign aid, the safety, even the survival of the country seemed far from assured.

Internal as well as external dangers appeared to threaten the nation. Alarming examples of communist espionage in Canada, Great Britain, and in America itself convinced many citizens that clever conspirators were everywhere at work undermining American security. In 1947, responding to these fears, Truman established a Loyalty Review Board to check up on government employees. Investigators found no significant trace of subversion, but apprehension remained in many hearts.

In 1948 Whittaker Chambers, an editor of *Time* who had formerly been a communist, charged that Alger Hiss, president of the Carnegie Endowment for International Peace and a former State Department official, had been a communist in the thirties. Hiss denied the charge and sued Chambers for libel. Chambers then produced microfilms purporting to show that Hiss had actually spied for Russia by making copies of classified documents for dispatch to Moscow. Hiss could not be indicted for espionage because of the statute of limitations; instead he was charged with perjury. His first trial resulted in a hung jury, his second, ending in January 1950, in conviction and a five-year jail term.

Although many thought Chambers a pathological liar and Hiss the innocent victim of anticommunist hysteria, the case fed the fears of those who believed in the existence of a powerful communist underground in the United States. The disclosure in February 1950 that a respected British scientist, Dr. Klaus Fuchs, had betrayed atomic secrets to the Russians heightened these fears, as did the arrest and conviction of his American associate, Harry Gold, and two other American traitors, Julius and Ethel Rosenberg, on the same charge.

Beyond doubt, information gathered by spies had greatly aided Russian scientists in their development of nuclear weapons. This fact encouraged some Republican leaders to make political capital of the communists-in-government issue. On February 9, 1950, an obscure senator, Joseph R. McCarthy of Wisconsin, casually introduced this theme in a speech before the Women's Republican Club of Wheeling, West Virginia. "The reason we find ourselves in a position of impotency," he argued, "is not because our only powerful potential enemy has sent men to invade our shores, but rather because of the traitorous actions of those who have been treated so well by this nation." The State Department, he added, was "infested" with communists. "I have here in my hand a list of 205*—a list of names that were known to the Secretary of State as being members of the Communist Party and who nevertheless are *still working and shaping . . . policy*."

McCarthy had no shred of evidence to back up these statements, and a Senate committee headed by the conservative Democrat Millard Tydings of Maryland soon exposed his mendacity. But thousands of persons were too eager to believe

*McCarthy was speaking from rough notes and no one made an accurate record of his words. The exact number mentioned has long been in dispute. On other occasions, he said there were 57 and 81 "card-carrying communists" in the State Department.

him to listen to reason. Within a few weeks of the Wheeling speech, he had become the most talked-of man in Congress. Inhibited neither by scruples nor logic, he lashed out in every direction, attacking international experts like Professors Owen Lattimore of Johns Hopkins ("the top Russian espionage agent" in America) and Philip C. Jessup of Columbia and professional diplomats such as John S. Service and John Carter Vincent, whose chief crime had been to point out the deficiencies of the Chiang Kai-shek regime during the Chinese civil war. When McCarthy's victims indignantly denied his charges, he distracted the public by striking out with still more sensational accusations directed at other innocents. Even General Marshall, a man of the highest character and patriotism, was subject to McCarthy's abuse. The general, he said, was "steeped in falsehood," part of a "conspiracy so immense and an infamy so black as to dwarf any previous venture in the history of man." The "big lie" was McCarthy's most effective weapon: the enormity of his charges and the status of his targets convinced thousands that there must be *some* truth to what he was saying.

Although McCarthy was at least potentially a fascist, he probably had no specific plan for seizing power. He was too disorganized, too muddle-headed to be a leader of any kind. Nevertheless, by the fall of 1950 he had become a major force, the word *McCarthyism* a part of the lexicon of politics.

In the 1950 election McCarthy "invaded" Maryland and contributed mightily to the defeat of Senator Tydings; two years later William Benton of Connecticut, who had introduced a resolution calling for his expulsion from the Senate, also failed of re-election when McCarthy campaigned against him. Thereafter, many congressmen who detested him dared not incur his wrath, and large numbers of Republicans found the temptation to take advantage of his voter-appeal irresistible. Even the Republican Senate leader, Robert A. Taft of Ohio, son of the former President and generally a man of the finest integrity, condoned McCarthy's methods. "Whether Senator McCarthy has legal evidence . . . is of lesser importance," Taft argued. "The question is whether Communist influence in the State Department still exists."

The frustrations attending the Korean War added to McCarthy's effectiveness. Naturally, he championed the cause of General MacArthur. In the 1952 Presidential campaign the Wisconsin senator led a merciless assault on Truman's handling of the conflict. The Republicans nominated General Eisenhower for President, the Democrats the articulate and witty Governor Adlai E. Stevenson of Illinois. Eisenhower's tremendous popularity probably assured his election in any case, but McCarthyism and the Korean War issue added to his strength. Many Democrats considered McCarthy a hero, others voted Republican because they thought the senator would restrain himself once his own party was in power. Dissatisfaction with the course of events in Korea was widespread. General Eisenhower aided his cause immeasurably by promising to go to Korea himself if elected to try to bring the long conflict to an end. The result was a Republican landslide: Eisenhower received almost 34 million votes to Stevenson's 27 million, and in the Electoral College his margin was 442 to 89.

After the election, President-elect Eisenhower kept his pledge to go to Korea. His trip produced no immediate results, but the truce talks, suspended before the election, were resumed. In July 1953, perhaps influenced by an American hint that it might use small "tactical" atomic bombs in Korea, the communists agreed to an armistice. Korea remained divided, its poverty-stricken people far worse off than when the fighting began. The United States had suffered over 135,000 casualties, including 33,000 dead. Yet aggression had been confronted and fought to a standstill. Containment had proved far more expensive than anyone anticipated, but it had worked.

John Foster Dulles

Troubled and uncertain, the American people were counting upon Eisenhower to find a way to employ the nation's immense strength constructively. The new President's experiences in World War II and later as commander of the NATO forces had convinced him that national survival depended upon collective security.

He had no intention of abandoning internationalism. Nevertheless, he shared the general feeling that a drastic change of tactics in foreign affairs was needed. Lacking political training and uninterested in the small details of complex operations, he counted upon Congress and his secretary of state to solve the practical problems.

Given this attitude, his choice of John Foster Dulles as secretary of state seemed inspired. Like Eisenhower, Dulles believed in change within the framework of internationalism. "What we need to do," he said, "is to recapture the kind of crusading spirit of the early days of the Republic." He saw himself as a man of high moral principle. "There is no way to solve the great perplexing international problems except by bringing to bear on them the force of Christianity," he insisted. Dulles also filled admirably Eisenhower's requirement that his secretary of state manage the details of foreign relations. Dulles' experience in diplomacy dated back to 1907, when he had served as secretary to the Chinese delegation at the Second Hague Conference.* Later he had a small place among the army of experts advising Wilson at Versailles. More recently he had been an adviser to the American delegation to the San Francisco Conference and a representative of the United States in the UN General Assembly. Since 1948 he had been recognized as one of the Republican party's chief foreign policy experts, by no one more unquestioningly than himself. "With my understanding of the intricate relationships between the peoples of the world and your sensitiveness to the political considerations involved, we will make the most successful team in history," he told Eisenhower.

As secretary, Dulles combined strong moral convictions with amazing energy. In seven years he traveled nearly half a million miles outside the United States, visiting some 46 nations. His objectives were magnificent, his strategy grandiose. Instead of waiting for the communists to attack and then "containing" them with expensive but inherently inadequate local countermeasures, the

*The delegation was headed by Dulles' grandfather John W. Foster, who had been secretary of state under Benjamin Harrison.

HERBERT BLOCK, *Herblock's Special For Today*, 1958

The Washington Post*'s Herblock was a sharp critic of the Eisenhower administration. Above, in a comment on John Foster Dulles' "brinkmanship" diplomacy, Dulles assures Uncle Sam, "Don't be afraid—I can always pull you back." McCarthy's "crusade" continued unabated under Republican rule; below, Eisenhower cautions the senator, "Have a care, sir."*

HERBERT BLOCK, *Herblock's Here and Now*, 1955

United States should warn the enemy that "massive retaliation," directed at Moscow or Peking rather than at the periphery of the red empire, would be the fate of all aggressors. With the communists held in check by this threat, positive measures aimed at "liberating" eastern Europe and "unleashing" Chiang Kai-shek against the Chinese mainland would follow. Dulles placed great faith in grand alliances in the image of NATO, forging the Southeast Asia Treaty Organization (SEATO) and the Central Treaty Organization (CENTO) in the Middle East, but he believed that if America's allies lacked the courage to follow its lead, the nation would have to undertake an "agonizing reappraisal" of its commitments to them.

In short, Dulles envisioned a policy at once internationalist and nationalistic, a policy broader, more idealistic, and more aggressive than Truman's. Not the least of its virtues, he claimed, was that it would save money; by concentrating on nuclear deterrents and avoiding "brushfire" wars in remote regions, the cost of defense could be dramatically reduced.

Despite his determination, energy, and high ideals, Dulles failed to make the United States a more effective force in world affairs. Time soon demonstrated the impracticality of his innovations. Massive retaliation made little sense when Russia possessed nuclear weapons as powerful as those of the United States. In November 1952 America had won the race to make a hydrogen bomb, but the Russians duplicated this feat the following August. Thereafter, the only threat behind massive retaliation was the threat of human extinction.

Most of Dulles' other schemes were equally unrealistic. "Unleashing" Chiang Kai-shek would have been like matching a Pekingese against a tiger. "Liberating" Russia's European satellites would of necessity have involved a third world war. "You can count on us," Dulles told the peoples of eastern Europe in a radio address in January 1953. But when East German workers rioted in June of that year and when the Hungarians revolted in 1956, no actual help was forthcoming from America. Although Dulles certainly did not err in refusing to prevent the Russians from crushing these rebellions, his earlier statements had roused hopes behind the Iron Curtain that now were shattered. "We can never believe the West again," one Hungarian refugee explained sadly after the failure of the 1956 uprising.

Furthermore, Dulles' saber-rattling tactics were badly timed. While he was planning to avert future Koreas, the Soviet Union was shifting its approach. Marshal Stalin died in March 1953, and after a period of internal conflict within the Kremlin, Nikita Khrushchev emerged as the new master of Russia. Khrushchev cleverly set out to obtain communist objectives by indirection rather than by arms. He appealed to the anti-western prejudices of the underdeveloped countries just emerging from under the yoke of colonialism, offering them economic aid and pointing to Russian achievements in science and technology, such as the launching of the first earth satellite (1957), as proof that communism would soon "bury" the capitalist system without troubling to destroy it by force. The Soviet Union was the friend of all peace-loving nations, the dictator insisted.

Of course Khrushchev was a master hypocrite, but he was a realist, too. Korea had proved that the United States would resist direct assaults on noncommunist nations, and the perfection of the hydrogen bomb made total war suicidal. While Dulles, product of a system that made a virtue of compromise and tolerance, insisted that the world must choose sides between American good and Russian evil, Khrushchev, trained to believe in the complete incompatibility of communism and capitalism, began to talk of "peaceful coexistence." The battle of words had relatively little impact on events or on world opinion, but what effect it did have generally favored the Russians.

Dulles also failed to win the confidence of America's allies and even of his own department. His sanctimonious manner and generous estimation of his own talents irritated western diplomats; some came to the conclusion that in spite of his stress on morality, his word could not be counted upon. His truckling to Senator McCarthy, who continued his pursuit of imaginary communists in the State Department even when his own party was in control, gravely weakened the morale of many career Foreign Service officers. He spent so much time traveling about the world that he neglected the proper administration of general State Department affairs.

The "New Look" in Asia

Thus, although Dulles and Eisenhower hoped to wrest the initiative in world affairs from the communists, they seldom succeeded in doing so. While the final truce talks were taking place in Korea, new trouble was erupting far to the south in French Indochina. Since December 1946 nationalist rebels led by the communist Ho Chi Minh had been harassing the French in Vietnam, one of three puppet kingdoms (the others were Laos and Cambodia) fashioned by France in Indochina after the defeat of the Japanese. When Communist China began supplying arms to the rebels, who were known as the Vietminh, the Truman administration, applying the containment policy, countered with economic and military assistance to the French. After Eisenhower succeeded to the Presidency, he continued and expanded this assistance.

Early in 1954 the situation became critical when Ho Chi Minh trapped the flower of the French army in the remote stronghold of Dien Bien Phu. Faced with the loss of 20,000 soldiers, France asked the United States to commit its air force to the battle. The logic of massive retaliation dictated a strike not at Dien Bien Phu but at Peking, yet Eisenhower, after long deliberation, decided against taking such a step. In May the garrison at Dien Bien Phu surrendered, and in July, while Dulles watched from the sidelines, France, Great Britain, Russia, and China signed an agreement at Geneva dividing Vietnam along the 17th parallel. France withdrew from the whole area. The northern sector became the Democratic Republic of Vietnam controlled by Ho Chi Minh; the southern remained in the hands of the emperor, Bao Dai. In 1955 Bao Dai was overthrown by Ngo Dinh Diem, who established an authoritarian but pro-western republic. The United States recognized Diem at once and supplied him liberally with aid.

Dulles responded to the diplomatic setback in Vietnam by establishing the Southeast Asia Treaty Organization (September 1954), but only three Asian nations—the Philippine Republic, Thailand, and Pakistan—joined this alliance.* At the same time, the unleashed Chiang Kai-shek was engaging in a meaningless artillery duel with the Chinese communists from the tiny, nationalist-held islands of Quemoy and Matsu, which lay in the shadow of the mainland. Eisenhower's decision to allow Chiang to take the offensive against Communist China was responsible for this fracas, but when it was suggested that the United States join in the fight, the President refused, on the ground, sensible but inconsistent with Dulles' rhetoric, that intervention might set off an atomic war. Thereafter, the administration devoted much energy to restraining the weak but ambitious Chiang. The United States would not protect the offshore islands, Dulles announced, but it would defend Taiwan at all costs.

Dulles and the Allies: Suez

In Europe the Eisenhower and Dulles policies differed little from those of Truman. In May 1952 the major European nations, including West Germany, signed a treaty creating a European Defense Community, closely allied to NATO, in order to set up a truly European army capable of checking any Russian attack. The cost of rearmament, however, proved staggering. Furthermore, when Eisenhower announced his plan to rely more heavily upon nuclear deterrents, the Europeans drew back in alarm, believing that in any atomic showdown the Continent was sure to be destroyed. In this atmosphere Khrushchev's talk of peaceful coexistence found many receptive ears, especially in France. This situation led to Dulles' threat to make an "agonizing reappraisal" of American policy if the EDC treaty was not ratified, implying that the United States might abandon Europe and rely upon its nuclear arsenal for its own defense. But when France refused to ratify the treaty and EDC collapsed, the United States did not withdraw from Europe. In October 1954 the

*The other signatories were Great Britain, France, the United States, Australia, and New Zealand.

powers finally created the Western European Union, a traditional military alliance, which also formally restored West Germany to the family of independent nations.

The Eisenhower administration even yielded to European pressures for a diplomatic "summit" conference with the Russians. In July 1955 Eisenhower, Prime Minister Anthony Eden of Great Britain, and French Premier Edgar Faure met at Geneva with Khrushchev and his then co-leader, Nikolai Bulganin, to discuss disarmament and the reunification of West and East Germany. The meeting produced no specific agreements, but with the Russians beaming cheerfully for the cameramen and talking of peaceful coexistence and with Eisenhower pouring martinis, sending a portable radio to the daughter of his former comrade-in-arms Marshal Georgi Zhukov, and projecting his famous charm, observers noted a softening of tensions which was promptly dubbed "the spirit of Geneva." What Dulles thought when the President said, "It is not always necessary that people should think alike and believe alike before they can work together," has not been recorded.

Actually, Geneva represented only a brief thaw in the Cold War; within a year the world teetered once again on the brink of a major conflict. This time trouble erupted in the Middle East. American policy in that region, aside from the ubiquitous question of restraining Russian expansion, was influenced by the huge oil resources of Iran, Iraq, Kuwait, and Saudi Arabia—about 60 per cent of the world's known reserves—and by the conflict between the new Jewish state of Israel and its Arab neighbors. Although he tried to woo the Arabs, President Truman had consistently placed support for Israel before other considerations in the Middle East. As early as 1945, he had urged the admission of large numbers of Jewish refugees into British-controlled Palestine, and when the new state of Israel formally declared its independence after the withdrawal of the British in 1948, he recognized it even more promptly than Theodore Roosevelt had recognized Panama after the Colombian revolution of 1903.

Alarmed by the creation of Israel, the surrounding Arab nations tried to smash the country by force of arms, but although badly outnumbered, the Israelis were better organized and better armed than their enemies and drove them off with relative ease. With them departed nearly a million Palestinian Arabs, creating a desperate refugee problem in nearby countries. Truman's support of Israel and the millions of dollars contributed to the new state by American Jews greatly increased Arab resentment of the United States.

Dulles and Eisenhower, worried by the growing influence of Russia in the Arab nations, tried to redress the balance by de-emphasizing American support of Israel. In 1952 a revolution in Egypt had overthrown the dissolute King Farouk. Colonel Gamal Abdel Nasser emerged as the strong man of Egypt and began to make his country the leader of the Arab states. Dulles promptly offered Nasser economic aid and tried to entice him into a broad Middle East security pact. Nasser, however, stayed clear of any commitment to the West. No one has accurately untangled his mental processes, but his main object was probably the destruction of Israel, partly because he genuinely hated the Jews and partly because the Israeli question had the same impact on Arab emotions that the "bloody shirt" had on Republicans after the Civil War. Dulles would not sell Egypt arms; the communists would. For this reason, while he accepted American economic assistance, Nasser drifted steadily toward the communist orbit.

In July 1956, when Dulles finally realized the futility of helping Nasser, he dramatically withdrew his offer of American financial support for the giant Aswan Dam project, the key element in an Egyptian irrigation program designed to expand agricultural production. Nasser responded a week later by nationalizing the Suez Canal. This precipitate action galvanized the British and French. Influenced by Dulles' argument that Egypt could be made an ally by cajolery, the British had acceded in 1954 to Nasser's demand that they evacuate their military base at Suez. Now what they considered Dulles' bad faith had left their traditional "life line" to the Orient at Nasser's mercy. In conjunction with the French, and without consulting the United States, the British decided to take the canal back by force. The Israelis, concerned by Nasser's mounting military strength and by repeated Arab hit-and-run raids along their borders, also decided to attack Egypt. Historians have not yet been able to discover if the British and French had a hand in this assault, but in any case, they seized upon it as a pretext for dispatching their own troops to "protect" the canal.

Events then moved swiftly. The Israelis crushed the Egyptian army in the Sinai Peninsula in a matter of days. France and Britain occupied Port Said, at the northern end of the canal. Nasser blocked the canal by sinking ships in the channel. In the UN both Russia and the United States introduced resolutions calling for a cease-fire. Both were vetoed by Britain and France. Then Khrushchev thundered a warning from Moscow that he might send "volunteers" to Egypt and launch atomic missiles against France and Great Britain if they did not withdraw. In Washington President Eisenhower also demanded that the invaders pull out of Egypt. In London angry crowds demonstrated against their own government. On November 6, only nine days after the first Israeli troops attacked Egypt, British Prime Minister Eden, haggard and shaken, announced a cease-fire. Israel also withdrew its troops. The crisis subsided as rapidly as it had arisen.

The United States had adhered to its principles, thus winning a measure of new respect in the Arab countries, but at great cost. Its major allies had been humiliated. Their ill-timed attack had enabled Russia to recover much of the prestige lost as a result of its brutal suppression of the Hungarian revolt which had broken out only a week before the Suez fiasco. Although no American action justified the Anglo-French assault, Eden and French Premier Guy Mollet could argue with considerable plausibility that Dulles' futile attempt to win Arab friendship without abandoning Israel had placed them in a dilemma and that the secretary had behaved dishonorably or at least disingenuously in handling the Egyptian problem.

Fortunately, the bad feeling within the western alliance soon passed away. When Russia seemed likely to profit from its "defense" of Egypt in the crisis, the United States adopted a more determined stance with the full support of its allies. In January 1957 the President announced the "Eisenhower Doctrine," declaring that the United States was "prepared to use armed force" anywhere in the Middle East against "aggression from any country controlled by international communism."

The doctrine represented, of course, a re-emphasis of the policy of containment. No sudden shift in the Middle Eastern balance of power resulted. Capitalizing on the Suez crisis, Nasser entered into a political union with Syria, creating the United Arab Republic. But his efforts to expand elsewhere in the area failed, in part because of the jealousies of other Arab leaders and in part because the United States and Britain responded to the requests of Lebanon and Jordan and sent troops into those countries when pro-Nasser elements threatened them in 1958.

The national mood in 1958 was one of sober, restrained determination; hopes of pushing back Russia with clever stratagems and moral fervor were fading. America's first successful earth satellite, launched in January 1958, brought cold comfort. It was so much smaller than the Russian "Sputniks" that many feared the Soviet Union had obtained an insurmountable lead in rocketry, which everyone acknowledged to be vital for national defense. At last the public was beginning to realize that no quick or cheap triumph over communism could be achieved.

The failure of Dulles' policies coincided with his physical decline. In 1957 he underwent surgery for an abdominal cancer. He returned courageously to his duties, but in April 1959 he had to resign. The next month he was dead. Christian A. Herter, a former congressman and governor of Massachusetts, became the new secretary of state. Although an experienced diplomat and totally free of his predecessor's unfortunate combination of sanctimoniousness and bombast, Herter did not make a particularly strong secretary. In the remaining months of the Eisenhower era the President took over personally much of the task of conducting foreign relations.

Actually, although he allowed Dulles to occupy center stage, Eisenhower never abdicated his responsibilities in the foreign policy area. The key to his policy was restraint. He did not abandon containment, but he exercised commendable caution in every crisis. Like U.S. Grant, whom he resembled in so many ways, he was a soldier who hated war. From Korea through the crises over Indochina, Hungary, and Suez, he held back from risky new commitments. His behavior, like his temperament, contrasted sharply with that of the aggressive, oratorically perfervid Dulles. The difference between the rhetoric of American foreign policy under Eisenhower and its underlying philosophy was, of course, confusing, and brought down upon the administration much unnecessary criticism.

The U-2 Affair

Amid the tension that followed the Suez crisis, the belief persisted in many quarters that the "spirit of Geneva" could be revived if only a new summit meeting could be arranged. World opinion was increasingly insistent that the great powers stop making and testing nuclear weapons, because every test explosion was contaminating the atmosphere with radioactive debris that threatened the future of all life on earth. Unresolved controversies, especially the argument over divided Germany, might erupt at any moment into a globe-shattering war.

Neither the United States nor the Soviet Union dared ignore these dangers; each, therefore, adopted a more accommodating attitude. In the summer of 1959 Vice President Richard M. Nixon visited the Soviet Union and his opposite number, Vice Premier Anastas I. Mikoyan, toured the United States. Although Nixon's visit was marred by a heated argument with Khrushchev, conducted before a gaping crowd in the kitchen of a model American home that had been set up at a Moscow fair, the results of these exchanges raised hopes that a summit conference would prove profitable. In September 1959 Khrushchev himself came to America. His cross-country tour had its full share of comic contretemps—when denied permission to visit Disneyland because authorities feared they could not protect him properly on the grounds, the heavy-handed Khrushchev accused the United States, only half humorously, of concealing rocket launching pads there. But the general effect of his visit was salutary. In talks with Eisenhower at the end of his stay, he and the President agreed to the summoning of a new four-power summit conference.

This meeting was scheduled for May 16, 1960, at Paris. It never took place. On May 1, high over Sverdlovsk, an industrial center deep in the Soviet Union, an American U-2 reconnaissance plane was shot down by antiaircraft fire. In announcing the event, the Russians merely stated that an American plane had been downed over their territory. Assuming that the pilot had died in the crash, officials in Washington foolishly claimed that a Turkish-based American weather plane had strayed accidentally across the frontier. "There has been absolutely no—N-O—no deliberate attempt to violate Soviet air space," a State Department spokesman announced.

Khrushchev then sprang his trap. The Americans lied, he said. The pilot of the plane, Francis Gary Powers, was alive, and he had confessed to being a spy. His cameras contained aerial photographs of military installations more than a thousand miles inside the Soviet Union. Eisenhower could still have avoided personal responsibility for Powers' flight; despite his show of righteous indignation, Khrushchev seemed willing to allow him to do so. But—perhaps goaded by criticisms that he habitually delegated too much authority to subordinates—the President assumed full responsibility. Such missions were "distasteful but vital," he said.

The statement left Khrushchev no choice but to demand an apology. Making full use of the impact of the U-2 affair on world opinion, he came to Paris in a rage, accusing the United States of "piratical" and "cowardly" acts of aggression and threatening to launch atomic missiles against American bases if such overflights were not stopped at once. Khrushchev's intemperance (and perhaps his own chagrin, for he must have realized that he had blundered) infuriated the usually amiable Eisenhower. He refused to apologize, although he did shortly announce that the U-2 flights would be stopped. The summit conference collapsed. The impact of the affair can be highlighted by comparing the almost hysterical welcome afforded Eisenhower on his good-will tour of India in December 1959 with the forced cancellation of his proposed visit to Japan in June 1960. Anti-American feeling was so high in Japan, the Tokyo government confessed, that it would be unwise for the President to go ahead with his tour.

Latin-American Problems

Meanwhile events in Latin America compounded Eisenhower's difficulties. During World War II the United States, needing Latin-American raw materials, had supplied its southern neighbors liberally with economic aid. In the period following victory an era of amity and prosperity seemed assured. A great hemispheric mutual-defense pact was signed at Rio de Janeiro in September 1947, and the following year the Organization of American States (OAS) came into being. The United States appeared to have committed itself to a policy of true cooperation with Latin America. In the OAS, for example, decisions were reached by a two-thirds vote; the United States had neither a veto nor any special position.

Unfortunately, however, the United States tended to neglect Latin America during the Cold War. Economic problems plagued the region, and in most nations reactionary governments did little to improve the lot of their peoples. Radical Latin Americans accused the United States of supporting cliques of wealthy tyrants, while conservatives tended to use the United States as a scapegoat, blaming lack of sufficient American economic aid for the desperate plight of the local masses. Neither charge was entirely fair, but under Truman the United States did appear to be more concerned with suppressing communism in Latin America than with improving economic conditions.

Eisenhower, aware of the resurgent Yankee-phobia south of the Rio Grande, appeared eager to redress the balance. He sent his brother Dr. Milton Eisenhower on a South American tour, and when Dr. Eisenhower recommended stepped-up economic assistance, the President concurred heartily. Nevertheless, he continued to give resistance to communism first priority. In 1954 the pro-red government of Jacobo Arbenz Guzmán in Guatemala began to import munitions from behind the Iron Curtain. The United States, much alarmed, promptly dispatched arms to the neighboring state of Honduras. Within a month, an army led by an exiled Guatemalan officer marched into the country from Honduras and overthrew Arbenz. Elsewhere in Latin America, Eisenhower, like Truman before him, continued to support unpopular conservative regimes, often kept in power only by the bayonets of the local military, simply because the alternative seemed communist revolution and social chaos.

The depth of Latin-American resentment of the United States became clear in the spring of 1958, when Vice President Nixon arrived at Montevideo, Uruguay, to open an eight-nation good-will tour. Everywhere he was met with hostility. In Lima, Peru, he was mobbed; in Caracas, Venezuela, radical students kicked his shiny Cadillac and pelted him with eggs and stones. He had to abandon the remainder of his trip. For the first time, the American people gained some inkling of Latin-American opinion and of the social and economic troubles behind this opinion.

There was no easy solution to Latin-American problems. This sad truth was made clear by the course of events in Cuba. During the late fifties a revolutionary movement headed by Dr. Fidel Castro, a colorful young lawyer, gradually undermined the government of Fulgencio Batista, one of the most noxious of the Latin-American dictators. In January 1959 Batista finally fled from Cuba, and Castro assumed power. Eisenhower recognized Castro at once, but the Cuban quickly demonstrated his fundamental anti-Americanism. He attacked the United States in interminable and highly colored speeches and seized American property in Cuba without adequate compensation. Eisenhower adopted a patient and tolerant attitude, leaning over backward to avoid being accused of meddling in Cuban affairs. This had no effect. Castro set up a communist-type government, entered into close relations with the Soviet Union, suppressed civil liberties, and drove

HERBERT BLOCK, *Straight Herblock*, 1964

In Herblock's cartoon, Russia's Khrushchev poses as James Monroe to announce "Another historic first!" to an aide, Anastas Mikoyan, and a Red Army general.

many of his original supporters into exile. After he negotiated a trade agreement with Russia in February 1960, which enabled the Russians to obtain Cuban sugar at bargain rates, the United States finally retaliated by prohibiting the importation of Cuban sugar into America. Further Cuban trade agreements followed with other communist countries, including China, and Premier Khrushchev announced that if the United States intervened in Cuba, he would defend the country with atomic weapons. "The Monroe Doctrine has outlived its time," Khrushchev warned. The worst aspect of the situation was that Castro's movement—called *Fidelismo*—was making inroads in many Latin-American countries. Finally, shortly before the end of his second term, Eisenhower broke off diplomatic relations with Cuba.

The new President, Democrat John F. Kennedy, had criticized Eisenhower's Latin-American policy as being unimaginative; his own policy, while certainly not unimaginative, was initially almost a disaster. Recognizing that American economic aid could accomplish little unless accompanied by internal reforms, he organized the Alliance for Progress, which committed the Latin-American nations to undertake land reform and economic development projects with the assistance of the United States. He also reversed the Truman-Eisenhower policy of backing reactionary regimes merely because they were anticommunist. In dealing with Cuba, however, Kennedy blundered badly. Anti-Castro exiles were eager to invade their homeland, reasoning that the Cuban masses would rise up against Castro as soon as "democratic" forces provided a standard they could rally to. Already the Central Intelligence Agency was training a group of some 2,000 of these men in Central America. The President, unwilling to use American troops and planes to drive Castro from Cuba, as might conceivably have been justified on the ground of the national interest, provided the guns and ships that enabled these exiles to attack.

They struck on April 17, 1961, landing at the Bay of Pigs, on Cuba's southern coast. The local populace, however, failed to flock to their lines, and the invaders were soon pinned down and forced to surrender. Since America's involvement could not be disguised, the affair exposed the country to all the criticisms that a straightforward assault would have produced without accomplishing the overthrow of Castro. Still worse, it made the new President appear indecisive as well as unprincipled, which was far from the truth.

Kennedy's mismanagement of the Bay of Pigs affair encouraged the communists to adopt a more aggressive stance in the Cold War. Castro soon openly admitted that he was a Marxist and further tightened his connections with the Soviet Union. In June Kennedy met with Khrushchev in Vienna. Their conference, marked, like the Eisenhower-Khrushchev meeting at Geneva, by much posing before the cameras and other superficial indications of good will, evidently failed to convince the Russian that the President would resist pressure with real determination. As soon as Khrushchev returned to Moscow, he threatened to turn over control of the West's access routes to West Berlin to his East German puppet. Since the western powers did not recognize East Germany, this would have precipitated another serious crisis. In August, alarmed by the continuing flow of dissident East Germans into the western sector of Berlin, Khrushchev suddenly closed the border between East and West Berlin and erected an ugly wall of concrete blocks and barbed wire across the city. When Kennedy did not order the wall destroyed by American forces in Berlin, the Russian leader found further reason to believe he could pursue aggressive tactics with impunity. Resuming the testing of nuclear weapons, he exploded a series of gigantic hydrogen bombs, one with a power 3,000 times that of the bomb which devastated Hiroshima.

Actually, nothing that Kennedy had done after the Bay of Pigs mistake had justified Khrushchev's assumptions. At Vienna the President had been firm, if polite. His failure to resist the construction of the Berlin wall was surely wise, since nothing short of all-out nuclear war could have prevented the Russians from swallowing up West Berlin if the West had chosen to fight on that isolated ground. When the Russians resumed nuclear testing, Kennedy ordered American tests as well, although he showed more concern for humanity than Khrushchev by confining the explosions to outer space and to underground sites in order to minimize the danger of polluting the atmosphere with radioactive fallout. Furthermore, he ordered an intensification of the American space program,* built up United States "conventional" armed strength, and called upon Congress for a large increase in the military budget. At the same time, he pressed forward along more constructive lines, pushing the Alliance for Progress, visiting Latin America in an effort to counteract the bad impression resulting from the Bay of Pigs incident, establishing an Agency for International Development to administer American economic aid throughout the world, and creating the Peace Corps, an organization that mobilized both American idealism and American technical skills to help underdeveloped nations. Peace Corps volunteers committed themselves to work for two years for a pittance as teachers and technicians in Africa, Asia, and South America. In all cases they were supervised by local authorities, and every effort was made to avoid the impression that they were acting to serve any direct American interest.

None of these examples of constructiveness and firmness had much effect on the Russians. Indeed, in 1962 Khrushchev devised the boldest and most reckless challenge of the Cold War, one that brought the world to the verge of nuclear disaster. During the summer months he began moving Russian military equipment and thousands of Soviet technicians into Cuba. Soon American intelligence reports revealed that, in addition to planes and conventional weapons, guided missiles were being imported and launching pads constructed on Cuban soil. Kennedy ordered U-2 reconnaissance planes to photograph these sites and by mid-October he had positive proof that intermediate-range missile sites capable of delivering hydrogen warheads to points as widely dispersed as Quebec, Minneapolis, Denver, and Lima, Peru, were rapidly being completed.

The President now faced a dreadful but unavoidable decision. To blast these sites before they became operational might result in a third world war. Yet to delay would be to expose the United States to tremendous danger and would certainly increase the Russians' ability to obtain their objectives elsewhere in the world by threats. In a meeting with Soviet Foreign Minister Andrei Gromyko, Kennedy, without revealing what he knew, asked for an explanation of Russian activity in Cuba. In a flat lie, Gromyko told him that only "defensive" (antiaircraft) missiles were being installed. This duplicity strengthened Kennedy's conviction that he must take strong action at once. On October 22 he went before the nation on television. Characterizing the Russian buildup as "a deliberately provocative and unjustified change in the status quo," he ordered the navy

*Russian superiority in this area was gradually reduced. In April 1961 the "cosmonaut" Yuri Gagarin orbited the earth; in August another Russian circled the globe 17 times. The first American to orbit the earth, John Glenn, did not make his voyage until February 1962, but by 1965 the United States had kept a two-man Gemini craft in orbit two weeks, effecting a rendezvous between it and a second Gemini.

The Toronto Star *comments on the Bay of Pigs affair. Wheeling his protégé Castro to safety, nursemaid Khrushchev snarls "Bully!" at President Kennedy. Khrushchev's bellicosity led to the subsequent Cuban missile crisis.*

to stop and search all vessels headed for Cuba and to turn back any containing "offensive" weapons. He called upon Khrushchev to dismantle the missile bases and remove from the island all weapons capable of striking the United States. Any Cuban-based nuclear attack would result, he warned, in "a full retaliatory response upon the Soviet Union." This was the Dulles concept of massive retaliation, but with the significant difference that Kennedy advanced it with every indication that he meant what he said.

For several days, while the whole world held its breath, work on the missile bases continued. Then Khrushchev backed down. He withdrew the missiles and cut back his military establishment in Cuba to modest proportions. Kennedy then lifted the blockade.

The President's firmness in the missile crisis, combined with a mature sense of his responsibility for the lives of hundreds of millions of people, repaired the damage done his reputation by the Bay of Pigs affair. It also led to a lessening of Soviet-American tensions. At last, it seemed, the Russians were beginning to realize what an all-out nuclear war would mean. Khrushchev agreed to the installation of a "hot line" telephone between the White House and the Kremlin so that in any future crisis leaders of the two nations could be in instant communication. In July 1963 all the powers except France and China signed a treaty banning the testing of nuclear weapons in the atmosphere, a small but significant step toward disarmament. Although many communists, following the lead of the Chinese, continued to advocate a war to the death with the free world, peaceful coexistence seemed more and more inevitable. Even the fall from power of Khrushchev in 1964 did not lead to an increase in Soviet pressure on the West. Russia, the United States, and all the major nations except China appeared to have learned from two decades of hostility and suspicion that no power can shape the earth in its own exclusive image, that the planet's teeming, diverse billions must live together in mutual tolerance if they would live at all.

SUPPLEMENTARY READING Among general surveys of the postwar years, the following contain useful treatments of diplomatic developments: E.F. Goldman, *The Crucial Decade—And After** (1961), Walter Johnson, *1600 Pennsylvania Avenue** (1960), and Herbert Agar, *The Price of Power** (1957). For wartime diplomacy, consult W.H. McNeill, *America, Britain and Russia: Their Cooperation and Conflict* (1953), W.L. Neumann, *After Victory: Churchill, Roosevelt, Stalin and the Making of the Peace** (1967), Gar Alperovitz, *Atomic Diplomacy** (1965), Gaddis Smith, *American Diplomacy During the Second World War** (1965), Herbert Feis, *Churchill, Roosevelt, Stalin** (1957) and *Between War and Peace: The Potsdam Conference** (1960), R.E. Sherwood, *Roosevelt and Hopkins** (1948), and Winston Churchill, *The Second World War** (1948–1953).

A good summary of the Cold War is J.M. Spanier, *American Foreign Policy Since World War II** (1962), but see also L.J. Halle, *The Cold War as History* (1967), and J.A. Lukacs, *A History of the Cold War** (1960). More critical of American policy are Gabriel Kolko, *The Politics of War* (1969), Walter La Feber, *America, Russia and the Cold War** (1968), and D.F. Fleming, *The Cold War and Its Origins* (1961). H.S. Truman's *Memoirs** (1955–56) contain much useful information, as does D.D. Eisenhower's *Mandate for Change** (1963). Among many analyses and evaluations of American foreign policy, the following are important: W.W. Rostow, *The United States in the World Arena** (1960), Norman Graebner, *New Isolationism* (1956), H.A. Kissinger, *Nuclear Weapons and Foreign Policy** (1957), G.F. Kennan, *Realities of American Foreign Policy** (1954) and *Russia and the West under Lenin and Stalin** (1961).

On the Truman Doctrine, see J.M. Jones, *The Fifteen Weeks** (1955); on the Marshall Plan, see H.B. Price, *The Marshall Plan and its Meaning* (1955). R.E. Osgood, *NATO: The Entangling Alliance* (1962), is excellent. For the rebuilding of West Germany, consult Harold Zink; *The United States in Germany* (1957), and Eugene Davidson, *The Death and Life of Germany* (1959).

American relations with China are covered in Herbert Feis, *The China Tangle** (1953), Tang Tsou, *America's Failure in China** (1963), and A.D. Barnett, *Communist China and Asia: Challenge to American Policy** (1960); for Japan, see E.O. Reischauer, *The United States and Japan** (1957). On the Korean War, consult David Rees, *Korea: The Limited War* (1964), and J.W. Spanier, *The Truman-MacArthur Controversy and the Korean War** (1959).

McCarthyism and the Hiss case are covered in Earl Latham, *The Communist Conspiracy in Washington* (1966), Alan Barth, *The Loyalty of Free Men* (1951), Alistair Cooke, *A Generation on Trial: USA v. Alger Hiss** (1950), Whittaker Chambers, *Witness** (1952), J.W. Caughey, *In Clear and Present Danger* (1958), and R.H. Rovere, *Senator Joe McCarthy** (1959).

John Foster Dulles' views are discussed in Richard Goold-Adams, *The Time of Power: A Reappraisal of John Foster Dulles* (1962), Roscoe Drummond and Gaston Coblenz, *Duel at the Brink* (1960), J.R. Beal, *John Foster Dulles* (1959), and in Dulles' own *War or Peace* (1950). For developments in the Far East, see R.H. Fifield, *The Diplomacy of Southeast Asia* (1958); for the Middle East, see J.C. Campbell, *Defense of the Middle East** (1960), and Herman Finer, *Dulles over Suez* (1964), which is extremely critical of the secretary. The diplomacy of the Eisenhower era is also discussed in R.J. Donovan, *Eisenhower: The Inside Story* (1956), Marquis Childs, *Eisenhower: Captive Hero* (1958), E.J. Hughes, *The Ordeal of Power** (1963), J.E. Smith, *The Defense of Berlin* (1963) and *The United States and Cuba** (1960).

On the Kennedy period, see A.M. Schlesinger, Jr., *A Thousand Days** (1965), T.C. Sorensen, *Kennedy** (1965), H.B. Johnson, *The Bay of Pigs* (1964), and Elie Abel, *The Missile Crisis* (1966).

*Available in paperback.

29

The Postwar Scene: 1945–1964

While foreign affairs dominated American political history after World War II, domestic events and conditions occupied the lion's share of the time and attention of most citizens. In one sense, the era was one of consolidation rather than of innovation. The social and economic changes wrought by the New Deal and confirmed through wartime experience were refined, sometimes by expanding or modifying existing laws, sometimes by executive act, sometimes by judicial decision. No major New Deal reform was done away with or even significantly reduced in scope. But the postwar decades were also a time of enormous development and change. American society evolved steadily and at an increasing pace, until by the mid-sixties it was an open question whether it was evolving or passing through a revolution.

The Political Climate

Superficially, the Democrats controlled the national government during most of the period. Only one Republican, Dwight D. Eisenhower, was elected President and he more in spite of being a Republican than because of it. In only two of the ten Congresses of these years did the GOP command majorities. Yet the Democrats seldom *really* dominated politics. In Congress particularly, southern Democrats tended to side with Republicans on key issues, forming a loose conservative coalition capable of thwarting legislation although not itself able to overturn established institutions or laws.

The times apparently favored moderation. On the one hand, society was becoming ever more homogeneous, in part because immigration had been reduced to a trickle by the restrictive legislation of the twenties, in part because improvements in transportation and communication were producing a more uniform national culture. Prosperity also fostered complacency. On the other hand, the rapidity of social change and the danger of nuclear annihilation frightened millions of Americans, leading them to adopt a cautious, conservative attitude that militated against drastic policies. Men either marveled at the wonders of their complex society or felt overwhelmed by it; in either case they tended to subordinate their individuality to its pervasive, inscrutable demands. The repeated glorification of democratic principles, especially the idea of majority rule, seemed at times to have made the United States a nation of what the sociologist David Riesman called "other directed" persons more concerned with conforming to established mores than with realizing themselves fully as individuals. From the failure of Henry A. Wallace's Progressive party to poll more than 1.2 million votes in 1948 to the overwhelming defeat of the Republican reactionary Barry Goldwater in 1964, the public usually rejected extremism, both of the left and of the right.

With politics stalled at dead center, the least partisan branch of the government, the Supreme Court, emerged as the most powerful instrument for change, not only in its decisions involving the rights of Negroes, but also in those requiring the redistricting of state legislatures, the great effect of which has scarcely begun to be felt.

Harry S. Truman

None of the postwar Presidents ranks with Lincoln or Franklin D. Roosevelt, nor was any a Buchanan, a Grant, or a Harding. Harry S. Truman was the most controversial. He was born in Missouri in 1884. After service with a World War I artillery unit, he opened a men's clothing store in Kansas City but failed in the postwar depression. Then he became a minor cog in the Missouri political machine of boss Tom Pendergast. In 1934 he was elected to the United States Senate, where he proved to be a loyal but obscure New Dealer. During World War II his "watchdog" committee on defense spending worked with admirable devotion and efficiency, saving the government immense sums. The 1944 Vice Presidential nomination marked for him the height of achievement; he seems never to have seriously considered the possibility that fate would place him in the White House itself.

When Roosevelt died in April 1945, Truman confessed frankly that he felt as though "the moon, the stars, and all the planets" had suddenly fallen upon him. Acutely conscious of his limitations, yet determined to live up to his new responsibilities, he sought to carry on in the Roosevelt tradition, and also to win a place in history in his own right. Curiously, he was both humble and cocky, idealistic and cold-bloodedly political. He had an immense fund of information about American history, but like most amateurs he lacked historical judgment and was prone to interpret past events in whatever manner best suited his current convenience. He read books but distrusted ideas, adopted liberal objectives only to pursue them sometimes by rash, even repressive, means. Admirable in stating his broad purposes, he often did not have the detailed grasp of problems and processes necessary to attain particular goals. He proposed a fine program of reform called the Fair Deal, but he failed to win congressional backing for the program.

Truman was his own worst enemy. Too often he insulted opponents instead of convincing or conciliating them. His hot temper frequently led him to act in ways strangely out of keeping with his liberal objectives. Complications tended to confuse him, in which case he dug in his heels or struck out blindly, usually with unfortunate results. Much of his energy was funneled into heated controversies with politicians and reporters; even a music critic who wrote slightingly of Truman's daughter Margaret's talents as a singer incurred the Presidential wrath. Although he appointed a number of first-rate men to high office, especially in the field of foreign affairs, he enjoyed the close company of small minds. Many of his advisers were men much like himself in background and training, some of them, alas, without his honesty and dedication to the public service.

Truman bungled the task of converting the economy back to peacetime conditions, angering both labor and capital by his efforts to control their activities, but failing to prevent a sharp rise in the cost of living. In rooting out "security risks" in the federal bureaucracy, he paid insufficient attention to fair judicial procedures and thus caused the discharge and disgrace of a number of innocent persons without uncovering more than a handful of real subversives. Yet he tried to dismiss the accusations against Alger Hiss as a "red herring" designed by the Republicans to discredit his administration.

Nevertheless, Truman was a strong and in many ways a successful Chief Executive. Like Jackson, Wilson, and the two Roosevelts, he effectively epitomized the national will and projected a sense of dedication and purposefulness in his management of national affairs. His greatest triumph came in the 1948 election. The international frustrations and domestic economic problems of the postwar period had enabled the Republicans to win the 1946 congressional elections handily, and the trend over the next two years seemed even more in their favor. The 1948 Republican candidate, Governor Thomas E. Dewey of New York, ran confidently, even complacently, sure that he would carry the country with ease.

Truman's position seemed hopeless because he had alienated both southern conservatives and northern liberals. The former were particularly distressed because the President had established a Committee on Civil Rights in 1946, headed by Charles E. Wilson, president of the General Electric Company, which had recommended antilynching and anti-poll tax legislation and the creation of a permanent Fair Employment Practices Commission. The southerners founded the States' Rights ("Dixiecrat") party and nominated J. Strom Thurmond of South Carolina for President. Among the liberals, a large faction simply considered Truman too small a man for the Presidency; a smaller group, led by former Vice President Henry A. Wallace, believed Truman's containment policy a threat to world peace and urged greater cooperation with the Soviet Union. The anticommunist liberals could find no one to compete with Truman for the Democratic nomination and went along with him, albeit reluctantly, but the others, calling themselves Progressives, nominated Wallace. With two minor candidates sure to cut into the Democratic vote, the President's chances seemed minuscule indeed. Public opinion polls showed Dewey far ahead.

Truman refused to believe the prognosticators. He launched an aggressive "whistle-stop" campaign, making hundreds of informal but hard-hitting speeches, most of them before small groups, in every section of the country. He excoriated the "do-nothing" Republican Congress, which had rejected his Fair Deal program and had passed a labor relations act that the unions considered reactionary, and he warned labor, farmers, and consumers that a Republican victory would undermine all the gains of the New Deal years.

Millions were moved by his arguments and by his courageous one-man fight against great odds. The Progressive party fell increasingly into the hands of communist sympathizers, driving away many liberals who might otherwise have supported Wallace. Dewey's smug, lackluster

UPI

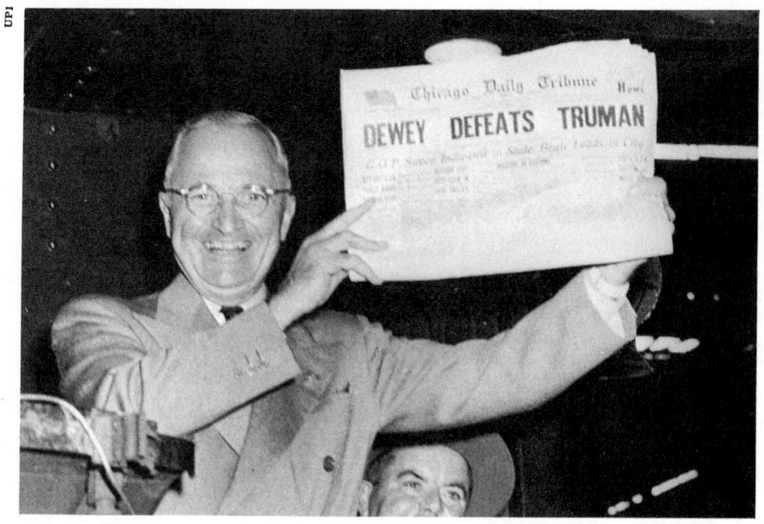

In 1948 the strongly Republican Chicago Daily Tribune *guessed disastrously wrong in headlining its post-election editions before all the returns were in. For Truman, it was the perfect climax to his hard-won victory.*

campaign failed to attract independents. The President, therefore, was able to reinvigorate the New Deal coalition and won an amazing upset victory on Election Day. He collected 24.1 million votes to Dewey's 21.9 million, the two minor candidates being held to about 2.3 million. In the Electoral College his margin was a thumping 303 to 189. Dewey's overconfidence contributed to the result, but Truman had shown that his understanding of the basic aspirations of the masses of the American people was sound. They had not forgotten the Great Depression and were still willing to believe the worst of the Republicans.

Dwight D. Eisenhower

This lesson was not lost on the Republicans. In 1952 they passed over the twice-defeated Dewey and their most prominent leader, Senator Robert A. Taft of Ohio, an outspoken conservative, and nominated General Dwight D. Eisenhower for the Presidency. Eisenhower's enormous popularity did not merely grow out of his achievements in World War II. Although a West Pointer (class of 1915), he struck most persons as anything but warlike. After Truman, his genial tolerance and evident desire to avoid controversy proved widely appealing. His reluctance to enter the political arena reminded the country of Washington, while his relative ignorance of current political issues was no more a handicap to his campaign than the similar ignorance of Jackson and Grant in their times. He defeated Adlai Stevenson decisively on Election Day.

In office, Eisenhower was the antithesis of Truman. Eschewing his predecessor's fondness for appealing to the masses against the "interests," he appointed a number of prominent businessmen to important Cabinet posts, including the banker George M. Humphrey, who became secretary of the treasury, and Charles E. Wilson, president of General Motors,* the secretary of defense. Eisenhower's prejudices were all against expanding the role of the national government in social and economic affairs. He spoke scornfully of "creeping socialism," called for more local control of governmental affairs, promised to reduce federal spending in order to balance the budget and cut taxes.

He believed that under Roosevelt and Truman the Presidency had lost much of its essential dignity. By battling with congressmen and pressure groups over the details of legislation, his immediate predecessors had sacrificed part of their status as chief representative of the American people. Instead, he proposed to concentrate on broad questions of policy, leaving to lesser functionaries the task of translating policy into action. Besides allowing John Foster Dulles to manage the details of foreign affairs, he granted his other advisers a remarkable degree of authority in their respective departments. When George Humphrey accepted the Treasury, he laid down one condition. "I want you," he told Eisenhower, "if anyone asks you about money, to tell them to go and see George." The President cheerfully accepted this extraordinary condition.

Eisenhower rarely found time for the newspapers and disliked reading long reports, preferring that any problem requiring his attention be summarized in a few paragraphs before being submitted to him. "If a proposition can't be stated in one page, it isn't worth saying," he claimed. He named former governor of New Hampshire Sherman Adams as his personal assistant and gave him almost unlimited control over the Presidential appointments calendar. Adams, in effect, determined whom the President saw and what he read; thus he came perilously close to determining his decisions as well.

The President almost never attempted personally to dragoon reluctant congressmen into supporting administration measures. "You do not *lead* by hitting people over the head," he was fond of saying. "I never thought that . . . appointments should be used for bringing pressure upon Congress." The conservative and McCarthyite elements in the Republican party repeatedly subjected him to abuse and harassment, but while he fumed in private, in public he bore their attacks patiently. When he nominated the career diplomat Charles E. Bohlen as ambassador to Russia, for example, the Republican right wing raised a storm, for Bohlen had been Roosevelt's

*Sometimes called "Engine Charlie" to distinguish him from "Electric Charlie" Wilson of General Electric.

UPI

With his wife at his side and flashing his famous grin, Eisenhower prepares to make his acceptance speech to the delegates at the 1952 Republican National Convention who nominated him on the first ballot.

adviser and interpreter at the now-notorious Yalta Conference. After Bohlen told the Senate Foreign Relations Committee that he did not consider Yalta "a sellout and a betrayal" of American interests, men like McCarthy denounced him as "worse than a security risk" and refused to vote for his confirmation as ambassador. Despite what Eisenhower called the "drive to get Bohlen's scalp," the nomination was finally confirmed, largely because Senator Taft, after making a personal study of FBI records, gave him a clean bill of health. Nevertheless, when Taft then irrationally demanded that there be "no more Bohlens," Eisenhower meekly agreed to avoid "controversial" appointments in the future.

However, Eisenhower was neither a reactionary nor a fool. The capitalism glorified by his businessmen-advisers was an enlightened variety. Liberal critics denounced the well-meaning but bumbling Charles E. Wilson for suggesting that whatever benefited General Motors (or, by implication, any great corporation) was likely to benefit the whole country. They also grumbled when the President allowed Congress to "give away" the national off-shore oil deposits to the states. But the administration made no effort to repeal existing social and economic legislation. Some economists believed that Eisenhower reacted too slowly in dealing with the several business recessions of his two terms and that he showed insufficient concern for speeding the rate of national economic growth, but he generally adopted a Rooseveltian, almost a Keynesian approach to these problems. In his memoir *Mandate for Change* (1963) he wrote of resorting to "preventative action to arrest the downturn [of 1954] before it might become severe" and of being ready to use "any and all weapons in the federal arsenal, including changes in monetary and credit policy, modification of the tax structure, and a speed-up in the construction of . . . public works" to accomplish this end.

The President also insisted repeatedly that the Republican party "yielded to no one in its concern for the human needs of human beings." He approved the extension of social security to an additional 10 million persons, created a new Department of Health, Education, and Welfare, and, in 1955, came out for federal support of school and highway construction. But his somewhat doctrinaire belief in decentralization and private enterprise reduced the effectiveness of his social welfare measures. His administration compiled a poor record in the area of conservation, for example, because of its tendency to turn control of natural resources over to state and private interests. When Dr. Jonas Salk's polio vaccine was introduced in 1955, Secretary of Health, Education, and Welfare Oveta Culp Hobby opposed its free distribution by the government as leading to socialized medicine "by the back door."

In general, political experience made Eisenhower less doctrinaire. His "conservatism" became first "dynamic conservatism" and then "progressive moderation." He summarized his new attitude by saying that he was liberal in dealing with individuals but conservative "when talking about . . . the individual's pocketbook," which led his Democratic rival, Adlai Stevenson, to retort: "I assume what [this] means is that you will strongly recommend the building of a great many new schools to accommodate the needs of our children, but not provide the money."

Americans loved Eisenhower because he epitomized what they wished the world was like. As James Reston of the New York *Times* put it, "he was a good man in a wicked time . . . a conservative in a radical age." This helps explain why, although devoted to the goal of permanently liberalizing the Republican party, Eisenhower never succeeded in forging an effective political coalition. The Republicans lost control of Congress as early as 1954 and did not regain it, even in 1956 when Eisenhower again defeated Stevenson decisively, although he had undergone a heart attack and a serious abdominal operation in the interval. It also explains why he could not transfer his popularity to a successor. In the 1960 election Vice President Richard M. Nixon ran with his full support but was narrowly defeated by Senator John F. Kennedy of Massachusetts.

John F. Kennedy

The new President was only 43, the youngest since Theodore Roosevelt and the youngest ever elected in his own right. He was born in Massachusetts in 1917, son of Joseph P. Kennedy, a wealthy financier and promoter, later ambassador to Great Britain under Franklin Roosevelt. After being graduated from Harvard, young Kennedy saw duty in the Pacific as a PT-boat commander in World War II and was severely injured in action. In 1946 he was elected to Congress.

Few men seemed so clearly destined for political success. Besides wealth, intelligence, good looks, and charm, he had the advantage of his war record and his Irish-Catholic ancestry, the latter a particularly valuable asset in Massachusetts. After three terms in the House, he moved on to the Senate in 1952 by defeating Henry Cabot Lodge, Jr., whose grandfather, Wilson's inveterate foe, had beaten Kennedy's grandfather for the Senate in 1916. However, Kennedy's religion seemed to limit his chances for national office. No Catholic had ever been elected President, and the defeat of Alfred E. Smith in 1928 had convinced most students of politics that none ever would be elected.

Nevertheless, Kennedy struck out boldly for the White House. As early as 1956 he made a strong bid for the Democratic Vice Presidential nomination. Four years later, after victories in the Wisconsin and West Virginia primaries had established him as an effective campaigner in non-Catholic regions, he was nominated for President by the Democratic convention on the first ballot, defeating the veteran Texas senator Lyndon B. Johnson.

During the campaign against Nixon, Kennedy stressed his youth and "vigor" (a favorite word), promising an imaginative, forward-looking administration. Nixon ran on the Eisenhower record, which he promised to extend in liberal directions. A series of television debates between the candidates, observed by some 70 million viewers, helped Kennedy greatly by enabling him to demonstrate his warmth, maturity, and mastery of the issues. Whereas Nixon appeared to lecture the huge unseen audience like an ill-at-ease schoolmaster, Kennedy seemed relaxed, thoughtful, and confident of his powers. Although both candidates laudably avoided it, the religious issue was important. His Catholicism helped Kennedy in eastern urban areas, but injured him in many farm districts and throughout the West. Kennedy's margin of victory, 303 to 219 in the Electoral College, was paper thin in the popular vote, 34,227,000 to 34,109,000.

Kennedy made a striking and popular President. Beginning with his brief, inspiring inaugural address, partly patterned after the first inaugurals of Lincoln and Franklin Roosevelt, he created an impression of originality and imaginativeness combined with moderation and good taste. He appointed two important Republicans to his Cabinet: Secretary of the Treasury C. Douglas Dillon, a Wall Street banker, and Secretary of Defense Robert S. McNamara, president of the Ford Motor Company. But he also named Arthur J. Goldberg, a liberal Jewish lawyer, as secretary of labor and flouted convention by making his younger brother Robert F. Kennedy attorney general. (When critics objected to this appointment, the President responded with a quip, saying that "he had always thought it was a good thing for a young attorney to get some government experience before going out into private practice.")

Notable among Kennedy's characteristics was his concern for culture and learning. He attracted a record number of intellectuals to Washington, but his personal behavior most clearly revealed this aspect of his nature. Already the author of two books, one of which, *Profiles in Courage* (1956), had won a Pulitzer prize, he astonished observers by continuing, despite the burdens of the Presidency, to devote much time to his own intellectual development. Unlike Eisenhower, he waded eagerly through long, tedious reports. He kept up with dozens of magazines and newspapers and consumed books of all sorts voraciously. He invited leading scientists, artists, writers, and musicians to the White House, along with a variety of other intellectuals. As Jefferson had sought to teach Americans to value the individual man regardless of status, Kennedy seemed intent on teaching the country to respect and understand its most talented minds.

He also seemed bent on being a strong President. He could act decisively upon occasion, as witnessed by his behavior in the Cuban missile crisis. In 1962, to cite another example, he brought the weight of his entire administration, even of the FBI, to bear upon the great steel corporations when they attempted to raise prices after having made what he considered a tacit promise not to do so in return for government help in persuading the steelworkers to forgo substantial wage increases. Faced with such a massive display of Presidential disapproval, including the threat of an antitrust suit, the steelmen backed down. Kennedy also lavished much energy upon Congress, showering the legislators with special messages and keeping himself closely informed about their doings, even to the extent of assigning to one of his aides the unenviable task of wading through the entire *Congressional Record* every day.

CECIL STOUGHTON, WHITE HOUSE PHOTO

President Kennedy offers congratulations to the virtuoso cellist Pablo Casals after his performance at a White House concert. At right is the First Lady.

But the President was no Wilson or Franklin Roosevelt when it came to bending Congress to his will. Perhaps he was too reasonable, too amiable, too diffident and conciliatory in his approach. The same coalition of Republicans and conservative southern Democrats that had plagued Truman resisted his plans for federal aid to education, for a new civil rights law, for medical care for the aged, even for reducing taxes without cutting federal expenditures in order to stimulate economic growth.

The President reacted mildly, almost ruefully, when partisan foes blocked proposals that in his view were both reasonable and moderate. He seemed to doubt, at times, that the cumbersome structure of the federal government could actually be made to work. He had been perhaps too much influenced by the penetrating study *Presidential Power*, written by one of his advisers, Professor Richard E. Neustadt of Columbia University. Drawing copiously upon the experience of recent Presidents, Neustadt argued that the full power of the White House could not be brought to bear upon every problem without quickly exhausting itself, that by calling up his reserves, a President incurred obligations that reduced his future influence and freedom of action. In any case, even to some of his warmest supporters, Kennedy sometimes appeared strangely paralyzed, unwilling either to exert strong pressure on congressmen or to appeal over their heads to their constituents. According to public opinion polls, the President was as popular as Eisenhower, but although unfettered by the ideological inhibitions that had kept Eisenhower from being a forceful leader, he seemed no more able than his predecessor to achieve his objectives. Some pundits began to talk of a permanent "deadlock of democracy," in which party discipline had crumbled and positive legislative action had become next to impossible.

On the other hand, Kennedy's very mildness and the reasonableness of his objectives might in time have broken the stalemate. In the fall of 1963 most observers believed he would easily win reelection. On November 22, however, while visiting Dallas, Texas, he was shot in the head by an assassin, Lee Harvey Oswald, and died almost instantly. This awful and senseless murder shocked the whole world and precipitated an extraordinary series of events. Oswald had fired upon the President with a rifle from the window of a distant warehouse. No one actually saw him pull the trigger. He was apprehended largely because, in his demented state, he killed a policeman later in the day in another part of the city. He denied his guilt, but a mass of evidence connected him with the crime. Yet before he could be brought to trial, he was himself murdered by one Jack Ruby, the owner of a small Dallas night club, while being transferred, in the full view of television cameras, from one place of detention to another.

This amazing incident, together with the fact that Oswald had defected to Russia in 1959 and then returned to the United States, convinced many persons, particularly those in foreign countries, that some nefarious conspiracy lay at the root of the tragedy. Oswald, the argument ran, was a pawn, his murder designed to keep him from exposing the masterminds who had engineered the assassination. No shred of evidence supported this theory, but even an investigation by a special commission headed by Chief Justice Earl Warren failed to allay the suspicions of some persons. Actually, the kind of madness exemplified by the assassination was only too common in America. Kennedy was the fourth President to die by an assassin's hand, and attempts had been made on many others. Even the killing of Oswald was not entirely without precedent. Garfield's assassin, Charles Guiteau, was twice fired upon by self-appointed avengers while awaiting trial, the second time receiving a slight wrist wound while being moved from one jail to another!

Lyndon B. Johnson

Kennedy's death made Lyndon B. Johnson President. A 55-year-old Texan, the first southerner to reach the White House since Woodrow Wilson, Johnson could draw upon a bottomless supply of political experience, having served in Congress almost continuously since 1937. A good New Deal liberal, he was also a practical man, a shrewd bargainer, a legislator who preferred to move with contemporary currents rather than to flail fruitlessly against them in search of perfection. Like General St. Pé in Jean Anouilh's play *The Waltz of the Toreadors*, he believed that the relentless pursuit of an ideal would cause more harm than good, to the pursuer and to innocent bystanders alike.* Johnson had little patience with intellectuals and their theories, little of Kennedy's eloquence and urbanity and

*The general says that the ideal is like a life buoy toward which all good swimmers head but never reach. "Fanatics who try a faster stroke to reach it at all costs, deluge everybody else and always finish up by drowning, generally dragging God knows how many poor devils under with them."

HANK WALKER, *Life*

After failing to gain the 1960 Democratic Presidential nomination, Johnson surprised most political observers when he accepted second spot on the ticket. Here, he is introduced by Kennedy at a press conference.

precision. He was a backslapper—or rather a lapel-grabber—who accomplished his purposes behind the scenes in Capitol cloakrooms, not on the rostrum or before the television cameras.

However, again like General St. Pé, Johnson was an idealist at heart, a compromiser where means were concerned but seldom of ultimate values. Reporter James Reston called him, despite his pragmatism, "an incorrigible believer." Early in his career he had not been an ardent supporter of civil rights—he voted against a federal antilynching bill in 1937 and in later years opposed bills outlawing state poll taxes and measures establishing a federal Fair Employment Practices Commission—but he was never a Negro-baiter, and after he became important in national affairs he consistently championed racial equality. During the Eisenhower era he refused to make party advantage the chief object of his policy; as Senate majority leader he cooperated with the administration better than most Republicans, placing political responsibility above partisan ambition.

Upon taking office, Johnson benefited from the sympathy of the world and from the shame felt by many of those who had opposed Kennedy's proposals for partisan or selfish reasons. Measures that had long been buried in committee suddenly moved through Congress and became law, most notably the tax reform bill and the new civil rights legislation. But Johnson could claim much personal credit for these accomplishments. No 20th-century President excelled him as a reconciler of executive-legislative conflicts. His prestige in Congress, where he had long been a major figure, enabled him to convert many whom Kennedy had failed to budge. His energy—*Time* magazine compared him to a "geyser at perpetual boil"—his persuasiveness, his flair for the dramatic—illustrated by his rushing about the White House at night turning off lights to call attention to his effort to cut the cost of government without reducing essential services—won him a series of victories on Capitol Hill. Remarkably adept at reconciling conflicting interests, he appeared to achieve what he called a "national consensus" without slipping into a series of meaningless compromises. As one political scientist said, he was "a Rooseveltian Eisenhower," adopting an "Eisenhower-like stance in the interest of rather Rooseveltian results."

Being what his biographer William S. White has called a "compulsive competitor," Johnson eagerly sought re-election in his own right in 1964. He achieved this ambition in unparalleled fashion. His championing of civil rights won him the almost unanimous support of Negroes; his economy drive attracted the well-to-do and the business interests; his "war on poverty" held the allegiance of labor and other elements traditionally Democratic. His southern antecedents counterbalanced his liberalism on the race question in the eyes of all but the most bigoted white southerners. The Republicans played into his hands by nominating an archconservative isolationist, Senator Barry M. Goldwater, who also proved to be an inept campaigner.

In November Johnson won the most sweeping victory in the history of the modern Presidency, collecting over 61 per cent of the popular vote and carrying all the country except Arizona and five states in the Deep South. Since the southern states would probably have gone to him if their Negroes had been able to vote freely, only Arizona, Goldwater's home state, really rejected him, and it by the narrowest of margins.

Other National Leaders

A number of other postwar political figures demand briefer consideration. During the Truman years Robert A. Taft was the outstanding leader of the opposition. "Mr. Republican," as his partisans fondly called him, was a man of keen intelligence and the finest character, conservative but open-minded enough to see the need for such things as federal aid to education, public housing, and civil rights legislation. Unpretentious but outspoken, he lacked only the common touch to become a great leader. He hated the ballyhoo and mindless, false friendliness of the campaign trail and could not conceal his discomfiture from the voters. When reporters, immediately after the war, asked him what people could do about the soaring price of meat, Taft responded coldly: "Eat less."

Taft's blind spot was foreign policy. Almost alone among the major statesmen of his generation, he never outgrew his prewar isolationism. He opposed the Truman Doctrine, the Marshall Plan, and the maintenance of an American army in Europe. He saw no danger to the United States in Soviet expansionism. "Keep America solvent and sensible," he said in 1947, "and she has nothing to fear from any foreign country." On the other hand, he believed the Democrats guilty of a "sympathetic acceptance of communism," which accounts for the major blot on his record, his willingness to tolerate the outrageous methods of Senator McCarthy.

As early as 1940, Taft was a prominent candidate for the Republican Presidential nomination, but, chiefly because of his colorlessness, he never attained it. After losing out to Eisenhower in 1952, he loyally supported the general. They became, in Eisenhower's words, "right good friends," and Taft was of inestimable help to the President until he died of cancer in July 1953.

During the Eisenhower era the outstanding Democratic leader was Adlai E. Stevenson. Stevenson emerged suddenly upon the national scene in 1952, when Truman decided that the 52-year-old governor of Illinois, whose grandfather had been Vice President under Cleveland, was Presidential timber. He had resisted Truman's suggestion that he run but was nominated nonetheless in one of the few genuine "drafts" in the history of American political conventions. Lucid, witty, urbane, his speeches capitivated intellectuals, who found Eisenhower's garbled syntax and cliché-ridden phraseology disconcerting. Stevenson's common sense and genuine humility won him the sympathy of millions.

In retrospect, it is clear that Stevenson had not the remotest chance of defeating the popular Eisenhower. Disillusionment with the Korean War and a general feeling that the Democrats had been too long in power were added handicaps. His foes turned his strongest assets against him, denouncing his humor as frivolity, characterizing his appreciation of the complexities of life as self-doubt, and tagging his intellectual followers as "eggheads," an appellation which caricatured the balding, slope-shouldered, endomorphic candidate effectively. "The eggheads are for Stevenson," one Republican pointed out, "but how many eggheads are there?" There were far too few to carry the country, as the election revealed.

For the next eight years, Stevenson functioned as a critic of the Eisenhower administration, calling the President to task for failing to denounce McCarthyism and shrewdly exposing the inconsistencies of his "middle-of-the-road" philosophy. In 1956 he ran for President again, only to be still more convincingly rejected by the voters. In truth, he made a less appealing candidate. He sought the office more eagerly and campaigned with somewhat less regard for his principles. In 1960 his undeclared but very real effort to win a third nomination led some observers to accuse him of hypocrisy. The victorious Kennedy, although obviously annoyed by Stevenson's tactics and less than enchanted by his equivocal attitude on many issues, named Stevenson ambassador to the UN, where his eloquence served the nation and his own reputation admirably until his death in July 1965.

In sharp contrast to Stevenson stood Republican Richard M. Nixon. One of the first to believe the worst of Alger Hiss, he had skyrocketed to national prominence by exploiting the public fear of communist subversion. "Traitors in the high councils of our government," he charged in 1950 without advancing a shred of proof, "have made sure that the deck is stacked on the Soviet side of the diplomatic tables." While insisting piously that "there is no difference between the loyalty of Democrats and Republicans," he denounced "misguided" Democratic officials who appeared "blind or indifferent" to the "repeated warnings" which he, the FBI, and other patriotic elements had given of the presence of subversives in the government. In 1947 he had been an obscure young congressman from California; in 1950 he won a seat in the Senate; two years later Eisenhower chose him as his running mate.

Whether Nixon actually believed what he said at this period of his career is not easily discovered; philosophically, he seemed wedded to the theory that statesmen should slavishly represent their constituent's opinions rather than hold to their own views. Frequently, he appeared to count noses before deciding what he thought. He projected an image of almost frantic earnestness, yet he pursued a flexible course more suggestive of calculation than sincerity. "He judged any declaration or speech not by its content but by its impact," one commentator noted. Reporters generally had a low opinion of Nixon and independent voters seldom found him attractive. He was always a sharply controversial character, distrusted by liberals even when he supported liberal measures. Following his loss to Kennedy in 1960, he sought to rebuild his fences by running for governor of California in 1962. His defeat, which he blamed on the newspapers, seemed to end his public career.

Another prominent figure of the Eisenhower years was Senator Joseph R. McCarthy. His rise we have already noted; his fall, inevitable result of his twisted psyche, came when the public finally tired of his endless unproved charges and deliberately obstructive tactics. McCarthy moderated his attacks on the State Department not a jot when it came under the control of his own party. In 1953 its overseas information program received his special attention. He denounced "Voice of America" broadcasters for quoting the works of "controversial" authors and sent Roy M. Cohn, youthful special counsel of his Committee on Governmental Operations, on a mission to Europe to ferret out subversives in the United States Information Service. Cohn, together with an unpaid protégé, G. David Schine, succeeded only in injuring the morale of the service (some terrified overseas librarians went so far as to burn books to please these investigators) and in arousing the contempt of America's allies.

Then, early in 1954, McCarthy turned his guns on the army. An obscure dentist, drafted during the Korean War, had been routinely promoted and later honorably discharged despite the fact that he had refused to testify on grounds of possible self-incrimination when quizzed about past radical connections by McCarthy's committee. Enraged, the senator had subjected the officer technically responsible for this action, Brigadier General Ralph Zwicker, to a merciless tongue-lashing, and when Secretary of the Army Robert T. Stevens defended General Zwicker, he accused Stevens of being a "dupe" of the communists.

At this point Cohn brought pressure on the

army to get special privileges for his friend Schine, who had been drafted in 1953. When army spokesmen publicized this, McCarthy accused them of trying to blackmail his committee and announced a broad investigation. The resulting Army-McCarthy Hearings, televised before the country, proved the senator's undoing. For weeks his dark scowl, his blind combativeness and disregard for every human value stood exposed for millions to see. When the hearings ended in June 1954 after some million words of testimony, his spell had been broken. The Senate moved at last to censure him in December of 1954, and this reproof completed the destruction of his influence. Although he continued to issue statements and wild charges,* the country no longer listened. In 1957 he died, victim of cirrhosis of the liver.

Regulating the Economy

In the years since 1945, every administration has accepted the necessity of employing federal authority to stabilize the economy and speed national development—the Great Depression taught this lesson to Democrats and Republicans alike. The Truman-sponsored Employment Act of 1946, which committed the government "to promote maximum employment, production and purchasing power" and created a Council of Economic Advisers to assist the President in deciding how these objectives could best be attained, highlighted this fact. Nevertheless, regulating the economy remained a source of political controversy, for the rejection of laissez faire did not mean that men would thereafter always agree as to what should actually be done.

When World War II ended, nearly everyone wanted to get back to normal as soon as possible, to demobilize the armed forces, remove wartime controls, resume production of civilian goods, and reduce taxes. Yet everyone also hoped to avoid a postwar depression, prevent any sudden economic dislocation, check inflation, and make sure that goods in short supply were fairly distributed. Neither the politicians nor the public were able to choose between these conflicting objectives. No group seemed willing to limit its own demands in the general interest. Labor wanted price controls retained but wage controls lifted; businessmen wished to raise prices but keep the lid on wages. As a result, confusion sometimes approaching chaos marked the immediate postwar period.

In this admittedly difficult situation, President Truman failed to provide effective leadership. He could not decide whether the threat of inflation or of unemployment and depression was the greater danger. Unlike Roosevelt in 1933, who had been equally in doubt as to how to proceed, Truman could not hold either the confidence of the people or the support of Congress.

This resulted partly from his asking for too much and demanding it too vociferously, and partly from the obviousness of his own uncertainty. On the one hand, he proposed, only four days after the Japanese surrendered, a tremendous program of new legislation, an "Economic Bill of Rights" he called it, including a federal public housing scheme, aid to education, medical insurance, civil rights guarantees, a higher minimum wage, broader social security coverage, new regional conservation and public power projects patterned after TVA, increased aid to agriculture, and the retention of many anti-inflationary controls. However desirable individually, so many new ventures proposed at a time when millions hoped to relax after the tensions of the war were sure to arouse strong resistance.

On the other hand, as historian Eric F. Goldman put it, Truman "began tossing out by the armloads rationing regulations and other controls affecting prices." In November 1945 he signed a bill cutting taxes by some $6 billion. He speeded the sale of government war plants and surplus goods to private interests. When Congress extended price controls in a watered-down form, he vetoed the measure, leaving the country temporarily with no controls at all. Whenever opposition to his plans developed, he vacillated between compromise and inflexibility.

Yet the country weathered the reconversion period with remarkable ease. The pent-up demand for housing, automobiles, clothing, washing machines, and countless other products, backed by

*During the censure debate, McCarthy announced that "the Communist party has now extended its tentacles to the United States Senate."

the war-enforced savings of millions, kept factories operating at capacity. The GI Bill of Rights, passed in 1944, which provided demobilized veterans with loans to start new businesses and subsidies to continue their education or acquire new skills, prevented unemployment from becoming a serious problem. However, the absence of uniform price and wage policies caused much resentment and frustration. Congress extended rent controls, although permitting a general 15 per cent increase. Attempts to hold the line on meat prices resulted in a "strike" by producers that left butcher shops bare until the government gave in and removed the controls. Automobile manufacturers, swamped with orders, were forced to base their prices on their production costs, which only enabled unscrupulous dealers and customers lucky enough to obtain cars to make large unearned profits by selling them in various underhand ways at black-market prices. Late in 1946 all price and wage controls, except those on rents, were abandoned.

BILL MAULDIN, *Back Home*, 1947

"Of course, the steering wheel costs $750, but we knock off fifty bucks for ex-soldiers. . . ." Bill Mauldin's Willie and Joe frequently found it difficult to adjust to the harsh realities of civilian life.

A period of rapid inflation followed. Food prices rose over 25 per cent between 1945 and 1947. Labor had already won large wage increases. These contributed to the rise of prices, which led to demands for still higher wages. Postwar strikes—nearly 5,000 in 1946 alone—delayed the satisfaction of consumer demands. Employers found it easier to raise prices than to engage in lengthy struggles with powerful unions. Between 1946 and 1948 three distinct "rounds" of wage and price increases took place.

The steel industry offers a typical example. Early in 1946 it granted steelworkers an 18.5-cent hourly wage increase, raising its prices $5 a ton. In the spring of 1947 it boosted wages another 15 cents an hour and the following year granted a similar raise, in each case elevating the price of steel in rough proportion. In 1948 the General Motors Corporation institutionalized the process of adjusting wages to prices by negotiating a contract with the United Automobile Workers containing an "escalator clause." Whenever the cost of living as defined by official Bureau of Labor Statistics figures rose or fell a stated amount, the wages of GM workers would be adjusted automatically to meet the change.

In the fall of 1948 the headlong advance of prices flattened out; the backlog of demand resulting from wartime shortages had finally been satisfied. In 1949 a business recession occurred and prices declined slightly. Fresh from his victory in the 1948 election, Truman used the downturn to flay the Republicans for their "do-nothing" attitude in 1947 and 1948 and to push a federal housing program and measures raising the minimum wage and increasing social security benefits through Congress. Although unemployment rose to 4.6 million in 1949, the economy rebounded quickly. Then, in 1950, the Korean War triggered another inflationary outburst, consumer prices jumping over eight per cent by the end of 1951.

This situation helps explain the almost obsessive concern of the Eisenhower administration for "preserving the value of the dollar," and its great but largely futile attempt to reduce government spending and balance the federal budget. Since defense and foreign aid outlays accounted for well over half the government's expenditures and since

Eisenhower was committed to maintaining these programs, he could not reverse the trend. Federal expenses, $65.4 billion in 1952, remained consistently above that figure, reaching $80.3 billion in 1959. The national debt—$260 billion when Eisenhower took office—increased steadily to $286 billion in 1960. Yet in part because of the President's efforts, the consumer price index rose only one per cent a year during his administration.

The trend of the Eisenhower years alarmed many economists. Although the gross national product jumped from less than $350 billion in 1952 to over $502 billion in 1960, America's economy was expanding at a much slower *rate* than those of Russia and the industrial nations of western Europe. Three distinct recessions occurred between 1953 and 1961, each marked by sharp increases in unemployment. During the decline of 1958 over 5.2 million were out of work, in January 1961 over 5.3 million. Observers noted a so-called "ratchet effect" during these periods. As Walter Heller, chairman of the Council of Economic Advisers, explained this phenomenon in his 1962 *Report*, "costs and prices have been relatively inflexible . . . in recessions but have been responsive to increases in demand during recoveries."

Each upward surge of prices both added to the cost of government, making it more difficult to reduce taxes and balance the budget, and stimulated labor to press for new wage increases, which handicapped American producers trying to compete in foreign markets. During each recession the Eisenhower administration reacted in what by the fifties had become the orthodox manner, cutting taxes, easing credit, and expanding public works programs. There could be no better proof that the principles of the Employment Act of 1946 had become gospel, that the welfare-state idea had been accepted by both parties. The administration's obsession with budget balancing, however, led critics to charge that these measures were not employed vigorously enough. Furthermore, many of Eisenhower's advisers resisted his growing willingness to increase federal expenditures. When he submitted a budget of nearly $72 billion in 1957, Secretary of the Treasury Humphrey astounded the country by saying: "There are a lot of places in this budget that can be cut," adding rather paradoxically that if taxes were not reduced, "I will predict that you will have a depression that will curl your hair." Still more astoundingly, Eisenhower then announced that Humphrey's statement "expresses my convictions very thoroughly," an open invitation to economy-minded congressmen to slash his requests. In the end they pared about $4 billion from the budget, surely a factor contributing to the 1957–58 recession.

President Kennedy had fewer inhibitions than his predecessor about federal spending. He was also deeply concerned about the lagging growth rate of the economy and the increasingly large percentage of the population that remained unemployed even in good times. He concentrated his efforts on projects aimed at social reform that would incidentally stimulate the economy: medical care for the aged, low-cost public housing, school construction, broader social security benefits, and an increase of the minimum wage to $1.25 an hour. Like Eisenhower, he was worried about the danger of inflation. Hoping to balance the budget, he rejected suggestions that taxes be cut. However, conservatives in Congress blocked most of his proposals. No noticeable improvement in the rate of economic growth occurred. Finally, in January 1963, he yielded to the pressure of some of his advisers, most notably economist Walter Heller, and came out for a large reduction in taxes.

Any considerable increase in federal spending, men like Heller argued, would either require higher taxes that would drain money out of the private sector of the economy and thus tend to be self-defeating, or spark a new inflationary explosion. But if taxes were lowered, the public would have more money to spend on consumer goods and corporations could invest in new facilities for producing these goods. Federal expenditures would not need to be cut because the increase in economic activity would raise private and corporate incomes so much that tax revenues would rise even though the tax rate had been lowered.

Although the prospect of lower taxes was tempting, Kennedy's call for reductions of $13.5 billion, combined with some redistribution of the tax burden and other reforms, ran into strong opposition. Both Republicans and many conservative Democrats thought the reasoning behind the scheme too complex and theoretical to be practicable. After Kennedy's assassination, however, President Johnson persuaded Congress to take the risk. Early in 1964 an $11.5 billion tax-cut bill was passed. By the end of the year the rate of economic growth had quickened markedly, the gross national product soaring to $628 billion, a rise of $39 billion over 1963.

The Workingman

The postwar decades were good ones, by and large, for American workers. War-time gains were consolidated and expanded. The civilian labor force grew from 53.8 million in 1945 to 71.6 million in 1963. The average weekly earnings of workers in manufacturing industries rose from about $44 to $97 in the same years, and when allowances are made for the inflation of the period, the increase still amounted to about 50 per cent. This improvement resulted, aside from the general prosperity, from a steady increase in industrial productivity and from the growth of the union movement. In 1940 fewer than 9 million workers belonged to unions; by 1955 nearly 17 million were members.

As workingmen grew more numerous and better organized their influence increased. Labor leaders tended to support the Democrats, for they remembered gratefully the Wagner Act and other help given them by the Roosevelt administration during the titanic labor-management struggles of the 1930's. In 1943 the CIO had created a Political Action Committee to mobilize the labor vote. Labor's political importance was highlighted at the Democratic National Convention of 1944, when Roosevelt, debating the question of a replacement for Vice President Henry Wallace, allegedly instructed his lieutenants to "clear it with Sidney," referring to Sidney Hillman of the Amalgamated Clothing Workers, a power in the PAC. The backing of Hillman and other labor leaders had much to do with the choice of Harry Truman by the convention.

The big industrial unions tried to keep their members informed about current political questions and to get across to them the importance of voting. Union leaders expended much energy in getting workers to the polls, maintained powerful lobbies in Congress and in state legislatures, and conducted extensive publicity campaigns to explain "the labor view" to the public at large. Since the united labor vote could often swing elections in major industrial states, the influence of the unions was especially great in Presidential contests. On the other hand, rank-and-file workers did not consistently follow their leaders' advice. Millions, for example, voted for Eisenhower. Furthermore, labor's political militancy drove many middle-class voters into the Republican camp.

Partly because the graduated income tax reduced the real value of every rise in wages, unions continued to stress "fringe benefits" such as pensions and health insurance when bargaining with employers. By 1962 about 90 per cent of all industrial workers were enjoying the protection of life insurance and hospitalization schemes at least partially financed by their employers. Nearly 65 per cent were covered by insurance against the loss of pay resulting from illness; nearly 70 per cent were participating in pension plans. Paid vacations had become almost universal by the sixties, extending in some industries to as long as four weeks for workers with 20 or 25 years' service. On the average, by 1961 fringe benefits were worth about 25 cents an hour to industrial workers. Unions also expanded their efforts to improve the lives of members. Union-financed housing, vacation resorts, and educational programs became more common. The growth of pension funds, which placed billions of dollars in their hands for investment, even made some union officials powers in the financial world.

The trend of the times also produced new problems for labor. Inflation constantly gnawed away at hard-won wage increases. The same expansion and integration of the economy that strengthened labor's bargaining power roused the public against its chief weapon, the strike, for a tie-up in a single vital field, such as steel or automobiles, quickly affected millions of innocent bystanders, leading to government intervention and threats of restrictive legislation. Large labor organizations were often undemocratic, ordinary members having little to say about who represented them or what policies these representatives adopted. In some cases, union officials paid themselves exorbitant salaries; in a few, they mismanaged pension funds and embezzled large sums from union treasuries.

Finally, workers faced new difficulties resulting from the very industrial advances that had elevated their living standards and working conditions. Rises in productivity grew out of the use of more complicated processes and automatic machinery. Manufacturers needed more technicians, engineers, and other specially trained hands, but far fewer unskilled laborers. While the total labor force increased, an ever larger percentage of American workers lacked the skills and intelligence necessary to fill modern job requirements. In coal mining, for example, new machines replaced thousands of pick-and-shovel miners; between 1947 and 1962 the number of man-hours needed to produce 1,000 tons of coal fell from 1,300 to 500, and employment in the industry dropped from over 400,000 to 123,000. But in the new electronics industry, dependent upon highly skilled operatives, employment soared to 788,000 by 1961.

The problem of technological unemployment was as old as the industrial revolution, but "automation," as the new trend was called, altered the size of the problem drastically, some said its very nature. As Commissioner of the Bureau of Labor Statistics Ewan Clague pointed out in 1964, the gross national product had expanded 40 per cent in the previous ten years, but employment had risen only 12 per cent. "The worker's greatest worry," A.H. Raskin, labor expert for the New York *Times*, reported, "is that he will be cast upon the slag heap by a robot." The ultimate solution lay perhaps in further reductions in the hours of labor and certainly in the expansion of educational opportunities. In any case, it would take time; meanwhile, America's unskilled workers faced a gloomy future.

From the perspective of the present, the history of labor-management relations after 1945 appears relatively untroubled. The labor disturbances of 1946, which led President Truman to seize the coal mines, threaten to draft railroad workers, and ask Congress for other special powers to prevent national tie-ups, subsided quickly after wage and price controls were lifted. The number of workers involved in strikes declined from 4.6 million in 1946 to 2.1 million in 1947, and the figure seldom exceeded 2.4 million after that date, despite the growth of the labor force. As an observer pointed out in 1963, "strikes are costing the country less productive time than coffee breaks."

However, when the Republicans won control of Congress in 1946, postwar disturbances were still very much in the air. In June 1947 Congress passed the Taft-Hartley Act, over the veto of President Truman. This measure outlawed the closed shop, a provision written into many labor contracts requiring new workers to join the union before they could be employed. The act also declared illegal certain "unfair labor practices" such as strikes called over jurisdictional disputes between unions, secondary boycotts, and union contributions to political campaigns. It compelled unions to register and file financial reports with the secretary of labor, and, unlike the Wagner Act, it allowed employers to present their side in labor disputes, provided they used no "threat of reprisal or force or promise of benefit" in so doing. Most important of all, the act authorized the President to seek court injunctions preventing strikes that endangered the national interest. These injunctions would hold for 80 days—a "cooling off" period during which a Presidential fact-finding board could investigate and make recommendations.* This procedure was employed no less than 17 times by Presidents Truman and Eisenhower.

The Taft-Hartley Act—which they called a "slave labor law" because the 80-day injunction provision forced men to work against their will—greatly alarmed labor leaders. The AF of L alone spent over $850,000 trying to rouse the public to prevent its passage. Union men resented especially the provision of the act that made union officers state under oath that they were not communists, a gratuitously insulting and largely ineffective requirement. The law made the task of unionizing unorganized industries more difficult, but it did not hamper existing unions seriously. Although it

*If the dispute were still unsettled, the President was to recommend "appropriate action" to Congress.

WASHINGTON *Evening Star*

Cartoonist Jim Berryman of the Washington Evening Star *drew President Truman in a classic doomed pose fighting the passage of the Taft-Hartley labor act.*

outlawed the closed shop, Section 14b permitted union-shop contracts, which forced new workers to join the union *after* accepting employment. The provision requiring unions to file financial statements and others aimed at protecting individual members against union officials had only salutary effects. Neither the unions nor the conditions of labor declined after the law was passed.

Indeed, by rousing labor's fears, the Taft-Hartley Act tended to unify and thus strengthen the labor movement. Truman's re-election in 1948 was one result of this, but the President's continued demands that Congress repeal or modify the law went unheeded.

During the Eisenhower years, a period of relative labor peace, the argument that the "Republican" Taft-Hartley Act was injuring them made little sense to many workers. Labor unity, on the other hand, was a much-desired goal. From a low point of 2.8 million in 1937, the AF of L grew steadily until in 1950 it had 7.1 million members. The CIO, after its original spectacular gains, leveled off by 1950 at about 5 million. As early as 1942, John L. Lewis, leading founder of the CIO, was claiming that the "accouplement" of the AF of L and the CIO would benefit workers, the government, and the public at large, but jurisdictional conflicts, as well as philosophical differences and personal jealousies, kept the two organizations apart.

Common dislike of the Taft-Hartley Act, however, together with the development of industrial unions within the AF of L and fear of what Philip Murray, president of the CIO, called "reactionary forces," gradually drew them together. In 1953, after George Meany of the plumbers' union succeeded William Green as president of the AF of L and Walter P. Reuther of the automobile workers took over the CIO, new merger negotiations began. Studies proving that the attempts of both organizations to invade the other's domain had been almost totally unsuccessful led to the signing of a "no-raiding" agreement, and in December 1955 a formal merger took place which recognized the need for both craft and industrial unions. Meany became president of the new AFL-CIO, which boasted over 16 million members.

Scandals exposed by Senate investigations of crime and labor racketeering, conducted in the fifties by Estes Kefauver of Tennessee and John McClellan of Arkansas, darkened the public's image of organized labor—somewhat unfairly, since most union officials were honest and dedicated men. As unions grew larger, however, they became less responsive to rank-and-file opinion; that more restraints should be imposed on the power of labor leaders became steadily more apparent. The Landrum-Griffin Act of 1959 sought to correct these ills. In effect, it made unions quasi-public organizations, requiring that their officials be chosen by secret ballot and that disciplinary actions taken by unions against individual members be conducted fairly and in public. Control over the management of the financial resources of unions was also tightened, and the law further strengthened some of the restraints imposed by the Taft-Hartley Act on union tactics vis-à-vis employers.

Nevertheless, in the sixties no significant force challenged the existence of American unions or sought to destroy their basic position in society. Except in agricultural regions, attempts to pass state "right to work" laws making union-shop contracts illegal almost uniformly met with defeat. It is revealing that in recent years the sharpest criticisms of organized labor have come from the left rather than from the right.

As unions grew wealthier (the net worth of the AFL-CIO exceeds $1 billion), they became more conservative and materialistic. In 1956 sociologist C. Wright Mills classified union officials among the "power elite"; their views, he argued, were not very different from those of corporation executives. In 1964 a former union organizer, B.J. Widick, charged that "labor leaders have adopted the standards and values of success which are acceptable to the business world with its middle-class ideology." Other critics scored unions for spending large sums on imposing headquarters buildings, for failing to accept Negro workers freely, and for paying insufficient attention to the problem of automation. They expressed much alarm over the fact that unions were no longer expanding, that they were failing to attract many of the new, highly skilled white-collar employees who represent an ever larger proportion of the work force.

The Farm Problem After the War

One of the most notable and uninterrupted trends in the history of the United States has been the movement of the population from rural areas to the cities. In the middle of the 18th century over 90 per cent of the American people earned their living in agriculture and related activities like fishing and lumbering. In the middle of the 20th century nearly 90 per cent did not. By the mid-sixties there were fewer than 3.5 million farms in the entire country, over half of these so small as to yield crops worth less than $2,000 a year. Between 1950 and 1959 alone, farm employment fell from 9.9 million to 7.4 million, although the population of the United States increased by over 25 million in that decade.

Despite this decline in numbers, agricultural production expanded enormously after World War II, mainly because a veritable technological revolution swept across the farm country. Besides using more machines, farmers stepped up their consumption of fertilizers by half during the 1950's alone. At the same time, new chemicals reduced the ravages of weeds, insect pests, and plant diseases. Better feeds made for meatier cattle and hogs; new antibiotics checked animal diseases. The vaunted efficiency of American manufacturing enabled industrial workers to increase their man-hour output from an index of 100 in 1947 to 135.7 in 1960, but in the same period agricultural output per man-hour jumped from 100 to 195.8.

Efficiency and expansion, however, did not bring prosperity to most farmers. Conditions roughly resembled those after the Civil War and after World War I; once again, overproduction and declining foreign markets caught the agriculturalist in a price squeeze. His relative share of the national income declined sharply. This situation made the farm problem an important political issue after 1945.

No significant group suggested abandoning the New Deal policy of subsidizing agriculture. The controversy concerned how much aid and what kind, not the idea of aid itself. The New Deal system of maintaining the price of staple crops like wheat and cotton at or near "parity" with the prices paid by farmers for manufactured goods, while reasonable in theory, left much to be desired in practice. The country paid a high price for the benefits obtained by its farmers. For one thing, declining farm income did not mean cheaper food for consumers; prices in groceries and butcher shops kept pace with those of other goods, for the cost of distributing and processing food rose rapidly. By boosting food prices still higher, the support program aggravated the problem of the rising cost of living. Secondly, acreage controls proved an ineffective means of curtailing production. When farmers withdrew land from cultivation, they plowed more fertilizer into their remaining acres and continued to increase output. Also, Henry Wallace's ever-normal-granary concept resulted in the piling up of huge reserves in government elevators and warehouses at great expense to the public. Finally, the system had never been helpful to small farmers, nor had it aided those who raised perishable commodities. Many critics argued that the program was accelerating the trend toward large-scale agriculture, thus stimulating the movement of people from farm to city. As the Council of Economic Advisers reported in 1959:

The majority of farm people derive little or no benefit from our agricultural price support legislation. Cattle ranchers, producers of poultry and eggs, and growers of fruits and vegetables operate their farms today practically without price supports. Only some 1.5 million of our commercial farmers are the recipients of price support outlays in any material amounts, and, within this group, those with the higher incomes are the main beneficiaries.

Despite the flaws in the New Deal system, it had won over many traditionally Republican farmers to the Democrats. As late as 1948, thousands of rural voters supported Truman largely because he convinced them that a return to Republican rule would mean scrapping the price-support program.* However, Truman was anything but satisfied with the price-support system. In 1949 his secretary of agriculture, Charles Brannan, drafted a new approach to the problem. While continuing to support the prices of storable crops, the government, he suggested, should guarantee fixed minimum incomes to farmers raising perishable crops. These products could then seek their own levels in the marketplace. Consumers would therefore benefit, but not at the expense of farmers.

This scheme ran into a wall of resistance, especially from large-scale farmers, who objected to its $20,000 upper limit of guaranteed income. Conservatives charged also that the Brannan plan was socialistic, but their real objection was to the method to be used in paying for the program. Since the price-support system was financed by processing taxes, consumers paid the bills. Under Brannan's proposal, payments would be made directly from the federal treasury, which would mean that the income tax payer would contribute most of the money. In any case, Congress rejected the plan along with most of Truman's other suggestions and continued to support many items, including butter, wool, sugar, and tobacco as well as cotton and cereal grains, at 90 per cent of parity.

*The 80th Congress had failed to pass a bill providing for adequate crop-storage facilities. Truman made devastating use of this fact while campaigning in states like Iowa, which he carried, and Kansas, which he lost by a narrow margin.

The Korean War eased the situation for farmers temporarily, but after it ended, surplus crops began to pile up alarmingly. Soon the government was even storing grain in the holds of idle merchant ships. In June 1952 there were $1.4 billion worth of crops in storage; by June 1956 this figure had risen to $8.3 billion. Yet food prices had gone up relentlessly during the period.

The Eisenhower administration tried to deal with this problem by adopting a system of flexible price supports, dropping the levels to as little as 75 per cent of parity, and by setting up in 1956 a "soil bank" plan, under which farmers were paid to divert land from commercial production to various conservation purposes. By 1960 some 28.7 million acres had been placed in the soil bank. However, the basic difficulties—high food prices, expensive support programs, and chronic poverty for tens of thousands of small farmers—remained when Eisenhower left office. In 1965 the net income of all American farmers was less than $15.2 billion, $2.5 billion of this represented by federal grants.

The Politics of Civil Rights

As we have seen, the World War II record of the federal government on civil rights was mixed. Except for the Japanese in California, there was no hysterical pursuit of imaginary spies and subversives. A beginning was made at increasing opportunities for Negroes in the armed forces, and because of the labor shortage, black workers improved their economic position considerably. After the war, the ideological conflict with the communists provided an additional reason for concern about racial intolerance. In Asia and Africa particularly, news of the mistreatment of Negroes or other signs of color prejudice in the United States always damaged the nation's reputation. Secretary of State Dean Acheson's argument that "the existence of discrimination against minority groups in this country has an adverse effect upon our relations with other countries" made obvious sense to most thoughtful persons.

Nevertheless, civil rights became the most controversial political and social problem in the United States after 1945, for two quite separate reasons. Fear of communist subversion led to repressions, culminating in the excesses of McCarthyism, that alarmed liberals without quieting the fears of conservatives. And the rising aspirations of American Negroes, highlighted by their awareness that as the centennial of the Emancipation Proclamation approached they were still second-class citizens, produced an increasing militancy among members of the race that shook the political structure of the country.

As early as 1940, in the Smith Act, Congress made it illegal to advocate or teach the overthrow of the government by force, or even to be a member of an organization with this objective. A dead letter during the era of Soviet-American cooperation, this law was used in the Truman era to jail the leaders of the American Communist party. The Supreme Court upheld its constitutionality in *Dennis et al. v. U.S.* (1951), in effect modifying the "clear and present danger" test established in the Schenck case of 1919. In 1950 Congress passed the McCarran Internal Security Act, restricting the civil rights of communists still further. Besides making it unlawful "to combine, conspire or agree with any other person to perform any act that would substantially contribute to the establishment . . . of a totalitarian dictatorship," this measure required every "Communist-front organization" to register with the attorney general. Members of front organizations were barred from defense work and from traveling abroad, while aliens who had ever been members of any "totalitarian party" were denied admission to the United States. This foolish provision prevented many anticommunists behind the Iron Curtain from fleeing to America; even a person who had belonged to a communist youth organization was kept out by its terms.

Although his own loyalty program was not always administered with sufficient regard for individual rights and proper judicial procedures, President Truman deplored these harsh new measures. He vetoed the McCarran Act, saying that it would "put the Government into the business of thought control." He warned the Congress: "Any governmental stifling of free expression of opinion is a long step toward totalitarianism." However, Congress overrode the veto by a voice vote. Truman also tried harder than any previous President to improve the lot of the Negro. As we have seen, he created a Committee on Civil Rights, and he pressed for the desegregation of the armed forces. But his efforts to obtain federal anti-poll tax and anti-lynching legislation were filibustered to death in the Senate, and Congress also refused his request for a permanent Fair Employment Practices Commission.

Under Eisenhower, while the McCarthy hysteria reached its peak and declined, the government compiled a spotty record on civil rights. The search for subversive federal employees continued. Although only a handful were charged with disloyalty, nearly 7,000 were declared "security risks" and fired. The refusal to grant security clearance to J. Robert Oppenheimer, one of the fathers of the atomic bomb, on the ground that he had associated with certain communists and communist sympathizers, was the most ill-advised instance of the administration's catering to anticommunist extremists, for it was based on the supposition that Oppenheimer could be denied access to his own discoveries.

As for the Negro, Eisenhower completed the formal integration of the armed forces, desegregated schools on military posts, appointed a Civil Rights Commission, and took other steps toward racial equality, but he was temperamentally incapable of making the kind of frontal assault on the racial problem that was necessary to stir the country to action. All in all, civil libertarians had little to cheer about as the nation passed mid-century.

At this point, the Supreme Court interjected itself into the civil rights controversy in dramatic fashion. Under pressure of litigation sponsored by the National Association for the Advancement of Colored People, the Court had been gradually undermining the "separate but equal" principle laid down in *Plessy v. Ferguson* (1896). Attention focused on the segregated public schools of the South. First the Court insisted that in graduate education segregated facilities be truly equal. In 1938 it ordered a Negro admitted to the University of Missouri law school because no Negro law school existed in the state. This decision gradually forced some southern states to admit Negroes to advanced programs. "You can't build a cyclotron for one student," the president of the University of Oklahoma confessed when the Court, in 1948, ordered Oklahoma to provide equal facilities for a petitioning Negro. Two years later, when Texas actually attempted to fit out a separate law school for a single Negro applicant, the Court ruled that truly equal education could not be provided under such circumstances. It also decided that state law schools could not segregate Negroes within classes, since this practice restricted their "ability to study, to engage in discussions, and exchange views with other students."

Then, in 1953, President Eisenhower appointed California's Governor Earl Warren as chief justice. Warren was a Republican moderate, a man of great dignity, good sense, and courage. Convinced that the Court must take the offensive in the cause of civil rights, he succeeded in welding his associates into a unit on the question. In 1954 an NAACP-sponsored case, *Brown v. Board of Education of Topeka,* came up for decision. In this case, Thurgood Marshall, leader of the NAACP campaign, directly challenged the "separate but equal" doctrine even at the elementary school level, submitting a mass of sociological evidence to show that the mere fact of segregation made equal education impossible and did serious psychological damage to both Negro children and white. Speaking for a unanimous Court, Warren accepted Marshall's reasoning and specifically reversed the Plessy decision. "In the field of public education, the doctrine of 'separate but equal' has no place," Warren declared. "Separate educational facilities are inherently unequal." Recognizing the problems posed by this edict, the Court, in 1955, ordered the states to proceed "with all deliberate speed" in integrating their schools.

In addition to backing up this decision by rejecting every southern attempt to avoid compliance, the Warren Court also handed down a series of rulings protecting the civil rights of radicals and persons accused of disloyalty. In *Yates v. U.S.* (1957) it modified the Dennis decision by holding that mere advocacy of revolution was not a crime, and in other cases it ruled that the State Department could not refuse passports to communists arbitrarily. The powers of congressional and state legislative investigators to compel witnesses to testify were also subjected to reasonable restraints by the Court in this period.

Such actions led conservatives to denounce the Court, but the justices held their ground firmly. In 1962 and 1964 they moved in still another direction, requiring that both state legislative and federal congressional districts be apportioned strictly in terms of population, in accordance with the principle of "one man, one vote." In nearly all the states rural areas were heavily overrepresented, chiefly because as the trend of population toward the cities proceeded, legislators had refused to reapportion election districts. Since this resulted in the votes of some citizens having less weight than others, the Court held that their right to equal protection of the law was being violated. It applied this rule even to the upper houses of state legislatures, some of which, in imitation of the United States Senate, were organized on a purely geographical basis. In *Lucas v. Colorado* (1964) the justices rejected this "federal analogy" even when the voters, in a referendum, had specifically approved the system. "A citizen's constitutional rights can hardly be infringed simply because a majority of the people choose to do so," they declared.

In the long run, these reapportionment decisions might become the most significant in the Court's history; the most immediately important, however, was the school desegregation case. Despite the Brown decision, few districts in the 17 southern and border states seriously tried to integrate their schools. Within two months after the ruling, White Citizens Councils dedicated to all-out opposition were springing up all over the South. In March 1956, 81 southern congressmen and 19 senators signed a "manifesto" approving the segregationists' efforts "to resist forced integration by all lawful means."

Unfortunately, not all such efforts were lawful. Some southern employers took reprisals against Negro jobholders who tried to enroll their children in white schools and some landlords evicted their tenants. When the school board of Clinton, Tennessee, integrated the local

BURT GLINN, MAGNUM

School desegregation comes to Arkansas, 1957. Acting on President Eisenhower's orders, 101st Airborne Division paratroopers escort black students (there were nine in all) into Central High School in Little Rock.

high school in September 1956, a mob roused by a northern fanatic rioted in protest, shouting "Kill the niggers!" and destroying Negro property. The school was kept open with the help of the National Guard, but the next year segregationists blew up the building with dynamite. In Virginia the governor announced a plan for "massive resistance" to integration which even denied state aid to local school systems willing to desegregate on an experimental basis. When the University of Alabama admitted a single Negro girl in 1956, riots broke out and university officials first forced her to withdraw and then expelled her when she complained more forcefully than they deemed proper.

President Eisenhower hoped to avoid federal involvement in these conflicts. Personally, he thought real equality for Negroes could not be obtained by government edict. "I am convinced that the Supreme Court decision *set back* progress in the South *at least fifteen years,*" he remarked to one of his advisers. "The fellow who tries to tell me you can do these things by *force* is just plain *nuts.*" But in 1957 events compelled him to act. That September the school board of Little Rock, Arkansas, opened Central High School to a handful of carefully picked Negro children. However, the governor of the state, Orval M. Faubus, called out the National Guard to prevent the Negroes from attending. Egged on by the governor, mobs formed to taunt the children and their parents. Eisenhower could not ignore this direct flouting of federal authority. He dispatched a thousand paratroopers to Little Rock and summoned 10,000 National Guardsmen to federal duty. The black children then began to attend classes, but it was necessary to maintain a token force of soldiers at Central High for the entire school year to protect them.

Such extremist resistance strengthened the determination both of Negroes and of many northern whites to make the South comply with the desegregation decision. Besides pressing a variety of cases in the federal courts, leaders of the movement sought to bring internal pressure on the southern states by conducting a drive to win political power for southern blacks, long systematically excluded from the polls. After protracted debate, in September 1957 Congress established a Civil Rights Commission with broad investigatory powers and a new Civil Rights Division in the Department of Justice. This law also authorized the attorney general to obtain injunctions to stop southern registrars and election officials from interfering with Negroes seeking to register and vote. However, progress was slow, partly because of the tremendous pressures exerted by the dominant whites on prospective black voters.

President Kennedy's original approach to the civil rights problem was to make full use of existing laws rather than to seek new legislation. Under the vigorous direction of his brother Robert, the Justice Department acted to force the desegregation of interstate transportation facilities in the South, to compel southern election officials to obey civil rights legislation, and to override resistance to school integration. In 1962, when Mississippi authorities, led by Governor Ross Barnett himself, blocked the admission of a Negro student, James H. Meredith, to the University of Mississippi, President Kennedy called the Mississippi National Guard to federal duty and, despite bloody riots, made the university accept the student.

Despite these federal efforts, progress remained painfully slow. The new aggressiveness of Negroes caused alarm in some quarters in the North and there was ominous talk of a "white backlash." Nevertheless, the belief that all citizens should be guaranteed the basic civil rights was growing steadily stronger. In 1961 the Twenty-third Amendment to the Constitution was ratified, giving residents of the District of Columbia the suffrage in Presidential elections. Three years later the Twenty-fourth Amendment outlawed state poll taxes in federal elections, a device traditionally employed to keep poor Negroes from voting in the South.

Responding to many pressures, in 1963 Kennedy called upon Congress to enact still another civil rights bill. As finally passed after his assassination, the Civil Rights Act of 1964 outlawed discrimination in all places of public accommodation, such as hotels, restaurants, and theaters. It also empowered the attorney general to bring suits on behalf of individuals to speed school desegregation and strengthened his hand still further in the campaign to register Negro voters. Racial discrimination by both employers and unions was also declared illegal, and federal agencies were authorized to withhold funds from state-administered programs that failed to treat Negroes and whites equally. As Burke Marshall, head of the Civil Rights Division of the Department of Justice, explained: "The thing that the act reaches is the official caste system in this country. . . . We are going to get rid of it."

The Supreme Court promptly upheld the constitutionality of this far-reaching law and the southern reaction, while anything but enthusiastic, was much less violent than many observers had feared. By the end of 1964 the public accommodations section was being enforced in such key southern cities as Jackson, Natchez, Baton Rouge, Montgomery, and Savannah. The pace of school desegregation, however, was painfully slow. At the end of the 1963–64 school year, only half the Negro children in the border states and barely one per cent of the 2.84 million in the states of the old Confederacy were attending white schools. Local customs died hard. In many communities, for example, traveling Negroes mixed with whites in restaurants and bus terminals, but local Negroes kept to themselves, partly out of fear, partly out of lack of money, partly through choice. Fear also kept many Negroes from appearing before the new federal registrars. "Too many Negroes are not desegregated mentally yet," one Nashville clergyman explained. Much, indeed, remained to be done before true racial equality could be achieved in the United States.

American Society in Flux

The postwar years saw enormous social changes in addition to those especially affecting black Americans. The population expanded rapidly and also became even more mobile than in earlier generations. During the depressed thirties the population had increased by only 9 million. In the fifties it rose by more than 28 million, and by the mid-sixties it had reached 195 million. Over 4 million babies were being born every year, and there were 60 million children under 15 in the United States, more than the total population in 1880.

Population experts also observed some startling internal shifts within the country. The historic westward movement by no means ended with the closing of the frontier in the 1890's. One obvious indication of this was the admission of Hawaii and Alaska to the Union in 1959; between 1940 and 1960 the population of Alaska more than tripled, that of Hawaii grew by 50 per cent. More significant, however, was the enormous growth of California and the Southwest. California added over 5 million to its numbers between 1950 and 1960. In 1963 it passed New York to become the most populous state in the Union, with over 17 million inhabitants, and it was growing at a rate of 1,600 persons per day. Nevada and Arizona were expanding at an even greater rate.

Close study of the Southwest and especially of California throws much light on many of the changes taking place in the United States. The climate of the area was particularly attractive to older people, and the enormous growth reflected the prosperity of the times, which enabled pensioners and other retired persons to settle there.* On the other hand, the area attracted millions of young workers, for it became the center of the aircraft and electronics industries and of the federal government's atomic energy and space programs. In the Los Angeles area alone over 150,000 persons were employed by 1962 in the manufacture of electronic equipment, a slightly smaller number in aircraft factories. Such industries displayed the best side of modern capitalism: high wages, comfortable working conditions, complex, highly efficient machinery, and the marriage of scientific technology and commercial utility.

Because these fields required so much skilled labor, the distinction between hired hand and executive became blurred and employers offered fantastic inducements to attract good workers. The General Dynamics plant in San Diego, for example, provided assembly-line workers with a swimming pool and tennis courts because, as one official explained, good recreational facilities were essential if his company was to compete with other manufacturers for labor. When Soviet Premier Khrushchev visited an International Business Machines plant in San Jose during his 1959 tour, he was visibly impressed by the wide green lawns, the gleaming glass, the pastel-tinted walls, and the similarity between the working conditions of assembly-line workers and the clerical force.

These modern industries employed increasing numbers of women, for much of the work, such as the assembly of small but complicated electronic devices, demanded manual dexterity rather than strength. This reflected another national trend. In 1940 male workers outnumbered female by nearly three to one, in 1966 by under two to one. Yet being gainfully employed did not seem to discourage women from marrying and having children: in 1940 about 15 per cent of American women in their early thirties were unmarried, in 1965 only 5 per cent.

*Florida experienced a similar boom; its population more than doubled between 1950 and 1965. The growth of the subtropical sections of the country was much stimulated by the perfection of cheap, mass-produced air conditioners.

J. R. EYERMAN, *Life* © TIME INC.

A picture taken in 1953 showing moving-in day in a Los Angeles suburban housing development is testimony to southern California's huge population gains.

Social mobility was greatly stimulated by improvements in transportation and communication. Although air travel had developed rapidly in the thirties and had profited enormously from wartime technical advances in military aircraft, it really came of age when the first jetliner—the Boeing 707, built in Seattle, Washington—went into service in 1958. Almost immediately, jets came to dominate long-distance travel, while railroad passenger service and transatlantic liners declined steadily in importance. In 1964 jets carried 4.2 million passengers across the Atlantic and flew 49.5 billion passenger miles in the United States itself. Liners carried only 714,000 passengers in that year, and the railroads totaled only 18 billion passenger miles. Meanwhile, developments in rocketry stimulated by competition to "beat the Russians in space" produced as by-products significant improvements in communication. By the early sixties the National Aeronautics and Space Agency (NASA) had launched a number of satellites capable of transmitting television pictures back to earth and collecting masses of meteorological data. Furthermore, the American Telephone and Telegraph Company had a private commercial satellite in orbit that could relay television programs between America and Europe.

The era saw also a marked broadening of the American middle class and a greater emphasis on leisure, entertainment, and cultural activities. In 1947 only 5.7 million American families had annual incomes equivalent to over $7,500 in 1959 dollars, but by the latter year 12.3 million families had such incomes. As they prospered, middle-class Americans became both more culturally homogeneous and broader-gauged in their interests.

The percentage of immigrants in the population declined steadily; by the mid-sixties over 95 per cent of all Americans were native-born. This trend made for social and cultural uniformity. So did the elevation of the incomes of industrial workers and the changing character of their labor. Blue-collar workers invaded the middle class by the tens of thousands; they populated suburbs previously reserved for junior executives, shopkeepers, and the like; they shed their work clothes for business suits; they took up golf and adopted values and attitudes commensurate with their new status. A study of one Philadelphia suburb in the late fifties revealed that about half of some 12,500 homes in the $10,000–$12,000 category were occupied by production workers and other persons who in a previous generation would have been classified as members of the proletariat. "During the war," a Detroit sociologist noticed in 1959, "you could sit on a streetcar and tell at a glance who were the defense workers and who were the white collars. . . . Today you just can't tell who's who."

Many social scientists found in this expansion of the middle class an explanation of the tendency of the country to glorify the conformist. They attributed to it the blurring of party lines in politics, the national obsession with "moderation" and "consensus," the complacency of so many Americans, their tendency, for example, to be at once more interested in churchgoing and less concerned with the philosophic aspects of religion than their forebears. One prominent divine complained of "the drive toward a shallow and implicitly compulsory common creed," a "religion-in-general, superficial and syncretistic, destructive of the profounder elements of faith." But no one could deny that the new middle class had more creature comforts (automobiles, household appliances—even swimming pools), more leisure, and wider cultural interests (as witnessed by a phenomenal increase in the sale of books, recorded classical music, and art reproductions) than any earlier generation. What *Fortune* magazine dubbed the "fun market" absorbed $41 billion of consumer income in 1959. The most encouraging aspect of this development was a certain shift in emphasis. People were spending relatively more on vacations and travel, relatively less on alcohol; engaging more in active sports like fishing, boating, golf, and bowling, and less in spectator sports. Hobbyists proliferated.

More debatable was the impact of the expansion of the middle class on national standards of taste, but these, too, seemed on the rise. Sales of tickets to concerts zoomed. There was a trend toward automobiles with cleaner lines and less useless chromium decoration; people turned more and more to well-designed furniture, took the best modern architecture to their hearts, increased their consumption of vintage wines and exotic foods.

"You can no longer design a thing so 'bad' it will sell or so 'good' it won't sell," an appliance manufacturer explained in the late fifties, and an advertising executive said: "It pays to give a product a high-class image. . . . You can get more for it." Businessmen made increasing use of works of art, traditional and modern, in their advertisements. The concept of the avant-garde as a revolt of creative minds against the philistinism of the middle class was rapidly crumbling, as witnessed by the quick acceptance of "pop" art and "action" painting, of "beatnik" literature, of "the theater of the absurd," and of the most difficult atonal music. Many critics found cause for alarm in this new popular enthusiasm for culture, arguing that the nation's really high culture was being engulfed by "status seekers" aping upper-class standards in their frenetic rush to conform, but in the long run the result would surely be a general improvement of taste.

Literature and Art

In the world of books and periodical literature, 20th-century Americans merely continued and expanded trends begun in the 19th. There were fewer newspapers, but they had larger circulations. Magazine sales soared. The success of tabloid newspapers like the New York *Daily News* and of magazines like *Reader's Digest*, founded in 1922, showed how the hectic pace of modern civilization was discouraging people from reading long articles. Illustrations occupied more and more space in newspapers, magazines—and textbooks. The public's desire for up-to-the-minute news and commentary found satisfaction in weeklies like *Time* (1923), *Newsweek* (1933), and the picture magazine *Life* (1936).

The most important new development in book publishing was the sudden flourishing of the paperback. European publishers had traditionally put out most of their wares in paper covers, but in the United States only the cheapest kind of fiction appeared in this format until 1939, when a new company, Pocket Books, began to publish respectable modern fiction and many of the classics in editions selling for 25 or 35 cents. After World War II, others began to experiment with cheap paper reprints of popular works of nonfiction. Sales reached enormous proportions but the real revolution came in 1953, when the firm of Doubleday started its Anchor series. Anchor Books sold for about a dollar. The paper and binding were of good quality and the type of book first-class. Their immediate success brought every major publisher into the paperback field; by 1965 about 25,000 titles were in print and sales were approaching 1 million copies *a day*.

Cheapness and portability only partly explained the popularity of paperbacks. Readers could purchase them in thousands of drugstores, bus terminals, and supermarkets, as well as in the bookstores. Teachers, delighted to find out-of-print volumes easily available, assigned hundreds of them in their classes. There was also a psychological factor at work: the paperback became fashionable. Persons who rarely bought hard-cover books cheerfully purchased by the tens of thousands weighty volumes of literary criticism, translations of the works of obscure foreign novelists, specialized historical monographs, and difficult philosophical treatises. A considerable "feedback" stimulated the hard-cover book market. Year after year, the sales of books increased, despite all the talk about how television and other diversions were undermining the public's interest in reading. In 1964 the industry grossed about $1.8 billion.

This flourishing of the book business heartened everyone concerned with improving American civilization and provided a powerful answer to those who claimed that Americans lacked intellectual interests.

It is difficult to generalize about the effect of modern conditions on American writers and artists. The expansion of the book market, for example, brought prosperity to many novelists, but not always to the best, and it remained hard for unknown writers of fiction to earn a decent living. At the same time, the temptations involved in book club contracts and movie rights undoubtedly diverted some authors from making the best use of their talents. The enthusiasm of an ever broader segment of the public for modern paintings and the quick acceptance of every new style placed a premium on innovation and broke down the traditional isolation of the artist, bringing within his ken the advertiser and the public relations expert. Under such circumstances, it remained an open question whether modern civilization was helping or hindering the full development of its most creative individuals.

In the thirties the Great Depression and the rise of fascism in Europe had stirred the social consciences of many writers and restored their faith in the positive values of their heritage. Although Ernest Hemingway wrote a gripping if overly romantic novel about the Spanish Civil War, *For Whom the Bell Tolls* (1940), most of the big figures of the twenties had relatively little to say in the following decade. Shaken by the economic collapse, some writers found Soviet communism attractive and wrote "proletarian" novels. Most of these were dull and of little artistic merit. More interesting were the works of men like John Dos Passos, James T. Farrell, and John Steinbeck, who, while critical of many aspects of American life, avoided the party line. Dos Passos had been a minor figure during the twenties. Born into a well-to-do family of Portuguese descent, he was educated at Harvard, drove an ambulance during the Great War, wrote an antiwar novel, *Three Soldiers* (1921), and a number of other books, but it was his trilogy *U.S.A.* (1930–36) that established his reputation. This massive work, rich in detail, intricately constructed, advanced a fundamentally anticapitalist and deeply pessimistic point of view. It portrayed American society between 1900 and 1930 in the broadest perspective, interweaving the stories of five major characters and a galaxy of lesser figures. Throughout the narrative, Dos Passos scattered graphic capsule sketches of famous men of the era, ranging from Andrew Carnegie and William Jennings Bryan to the movie idol Rudolph Valentino and the architect Frank Lloyd Wright. He also included "newsreel" sections recounting the actual events of the period and "camera eye" sections in which he revealed his personal reactions to the passing parade.

Dos Passos' method was relentless, cold, methodical—utterly realistic. He displayed immense craftsmanship, but no human sympathy for his characters or their world. His style was impressionistic yet concrete, experimental yet tightly controlled, his book a true epic, a monument to the despair and anger of liberals confronted with the Great Depression. However, *U.S.A.* seemed to exhaust his creativity. After World War II broke out, he rapidly abandoned his radical views and by the fifties had located himself far to the right, a caustic critic of the welfare state.

James T. Farrell was less talented than Dos Passos, a clumsy novelist in the naturalist tradition established by Theodore Dreiser around the turn of the century. He, too, wrote a trilogy in the thirties, the saga of *Studs Lonigan* (1932–35), which described the squalid life of Chicago's Irish slums. Farrell's realism was overly literal, but full of the man's anger and conviction, and therefore powerful. Unlike Dos Passos, Farrell held to his radical views in later, more prosperous times.

Probably the novel that portrayed the desperate plight of the millions impoverished by the depression best was John Steinbeck's *The Grapes of Wrath* (1939), which described the fate of the Joads, an Oklahoma family driven by drought and bad times to abandon their land and become migratory laborers in California. Steinbeck captured the patient bewilderment of the downtrodden, the callous brutality bred of fear that characterized their exploiters, and the furious resentments of the radicals of the thirties. He depicted the parching blackness of the Oklahoma dust bowl, the grandeur of California, the backbreaking toil of the migrant fruit pickers, and the ultimate indignation of a people repeatedly degraded. "In the eyes of the hungry there is a growing wrath. In the souls of the people the grapes of wrath are filling and growing heavy, growing heavy for the vintage." Like so many other writers of the thirties, Steinbeck was an angry man. "There is a crime here that goes beyond denunciation," he wrote. But he had a tenderness, a compassion, that men like Dos Passos and Farrell lacked, and this quality raised *The Grapes of Wrath* to the level of great tragedy. In other works, such as *Tortilla Flat* (1935)

ERICH HARTMANN, MAGNUM

BERN KEATING, BLACK STAR

"I am completely partisan," Steinbeck (left) wrote. "Every effort I can bring to bear is . . . at the call of the common working-people." Accepting the Nobel literature prize, Faulkner (above) spoke of a life-long attempt "to create out of the materials of the human spirit something which did not exist before."

and *The Long Valley* (1938), he described the life of California cannery workers and ranchers with moving warmth, yet without becoming overly sentimental.

Although too much wrapped up in himself to produce the kind of systematic analysis of America achieved by Dos Passos or the humane studies of Steinbeck, Thomas Wolfe also stands as a major interpreter of his times. Wolfe was born in Asheville, North Carolina, in 1900 and was educated at the state university and at Harvard. A passionate, intensely troubled young man of vast but undisciplined talents, he sought to describe in a series of novels the kaleidoscopic character of American life, the limitless variety of the nation. "I will know this country when I am through as I know the palm of my hand, and I will put it on paper and make it true and beautiful," he boasted. During the last ten years of his short life (he died in 1938), he wrote four major novels: *Look Homeward Angel* (1929), *Of Time and the River* (1935), and two published posthumously, *The Web and the Rock* (1939) and *You Can't Go Home Again* (1940). All were autobiographical and to some extent repetitious, for Wolfe was an unabashed egoist. Nevertheless, he was a superb interpreter of contemporary society. He crammed his pages with unforgettable vignettes—a train hurtling across the Jersey meadows in the dark, a young girl clutching her skirts on a windswept corner, a group of derelicts huddled for shelter in a public toilet on a frigid night. And no writer caught more clearly the frantic pace and confusion of the great cities, the despair of the depression, the divided nature of man, his fears, his hopes, his undirected, uncontrollable energy.

Probably the finest talent among modern American novelists was William Faulkner. Although born in 1897, within a year of both Fitzgerald and Hemingway, like Wolfe he attained literary maturity only in the thirties. After service in the Canadian air force in World War I, he returned to his native Mississippi, working at a series of odd jobs and publishing relatively inconsequential poetry and fiction. Suddenly, between 1929 and 1932, he burst into prominence with four major novels, *The Sound and the Fury, As I Lay Dying, Sanctuary,* and *Light in August.*

In one sense Faulkner was a regional novelist. He created a local world, Yoknapatawpha County, and peopled it with some of the most remarkable characters in American fiction—the Sartoris family, typical of the old southern aristocracy worn down at the heels, the Snopes clan, shrewd, unscrupulous, boorish representatives of the new day, and many others. He pictured vividly the South's poverty and its pride, its dreadful racial problem, the guilt and obscure passions plaguing white and black man alike. He also dealt effectively with the clash of urban and rural values. But Faulkner was more by far than a local colorist. No contemporary excelled him as a commentator on the multiple dilemmas of modern life. His characters are men possessed, driven to pursue high ideals yet weighted down with their awareness of their inadequacies and sinfulness. They are imprisoned in their surroundings however they may strive to escape them.

Although capable of genuine humor, full of the joy of life, Faulkner was essentially a pessimist. His weakness as a writer, aside from a sometimes exasperating obscurity and verbosity, resulted from his somewhat confused view of himself and of the world he described. Much of his work was passion frozen into words without discernible meaning; his characters continually experienced emotions too intense to be bearable, often too profound and too subtle for the natures he had given them. Nevertheless, his great stature was beyond question, and unlike so many other novelists of the period he maintained a high level in his later years, with works like *The Hamlet* (1940), *Intruder in the Dust* (1948), *A Fable* (1954), and *The Reivers* (1962). He was awarded the 1949 Nobel prize for literature and a Pulitzer prize in 1955.

For a time after World War II, the nation seemed on the verge of a literary outburst comparable to that which followed the First World War. A number of excellent novels based on the military experiences of young writers appeared, the most notable being Norman Mailer's *The Naked and the Dead* (1948) and James Jones's *From Here to Eternity* (1951). However, the new renaissance did not develop. It is, of course, impossible to estimate the eventual reputation of contemporary authors with assurance, but the majority of the most talented seemed lacking in conviction and obsessed more with themselves than with their surroundings. The generation of the twenties saw itself as "lost," that of the forties and fifties as alienated, or "beat." It preferred to bewail its fate rather than to rebel against it; it demanded admiration while deliberately insulting, even assaulting, its audience. A founder of the "beatnik school," Jack Kerouac, reveled in the chaotic description of violence, perversion, and madness, ignoring the writer's obligation to be a craftsman. At the other extreme, J.D. Salinger, perhaps the most popular postwar writer and the particular favorite of college students (*The Catcher in the Rye* sold nearly 2 million copies in hard-cover and paperback editions), was an impeccable stylist, witty, contemptuous of all pretense; but he also wrote about people entirely wrapped up in themselves.

A few novelists seriously attempted to deal with individuals interacting with one another in social situations. In works like *The Just and the Unjust*, *Guard of Honor*, and *By Love Possessed* James Gould Cozzens fashioned a gallery of interesting, "normal" people making the inevitable compromises that civilized persons must if they are to be productive human beings. In *Catch-22*, which replaced *Catcher in the Rye* in the hearts of college students, Joseph Heller produced a war novel at once farcical and an indignant denunciation of the stupidity and waste of warfare. Saul Bellow's *Adventures of Augie March* portrayed much of the confusion and sordidness of modern urban society without descending to mere sensationalism. Bellow exposed the weaknesses of men, but did not condemn mankind or lose sight of the positive values of modern existence. It was heartening also that talented Negro writers, such as Ralph Ellison and James Baldwin, and Jewish authors, such as Bellow and Bernard Malamud, were able, without ignoring their heritages or neglecting the social issuess that most directly concerned their peoples, to transcend parochial concerns of interest chiefly to Negroes and Jews and write books that were read eagerly by a general audience.

Such works were all too few considering the large number of novelists of real ability—older men like Steinbeck and Paul Bowles and younger ones like Mailer and Truman Capote—who were writing and being read by large numbers of educated persons. Nevertheless, there was reason to hope for better things. Several authors, still in their thirties, were producing works of promise.

In *The Centaur* John Updike, a writer of enormous sensitivity and skill, presented a remarkable portrait of a schoolteacher written in a daringly unconventional form. In plays like *The Zoo Story, Who's Afraid of Virginia Woolf?,* and *Tiny Alice,* Edward Albee offered dramas that were interesting, if not entirely understandable, to thousands. Such men were not mere exhibitionists or deliberately obscure nihilists, whatever their eventual place in the history of letters. American literature in the sixties was anything but moribund.

American painting, historically an appendage of European, achieved independence explosively after World War II. By the twenties some American painters had begun to absorb the new cubist abstractionism first introduced in the Armory Show in 1913, although they tended to maintain a closer contact with real forms than the European cubist masters. The geometric flowers of Georgia O'Keeffe, Joseph Stella's brilliant studies of the Brooklyn Bridge, the poster-like work of Stuart Davis, and John Marin's wild glimpses of Maine landscapes stand among the finest achievements of the decade. Cubist influences could also be seen in Charles Sheeler's starkly oversimplified studies of buildings and machinery. During the Great Depression, while such painters continued to flourish, others turned to a kind of regionalism, more conservative in technique, as illustrated by the work of Thomas Hart Benton, John Steuart Curry, and Grant Wood. Social critics roused by depression problems, such as William Gropper, Jack Levine, and Ben Shahn, spiritual descendants of the ashcan school, also did important work, and there was a new appreciation of American folk artists, both those of earlier periods and of modern primitives like John Kane and that amazing septuagenarian, "Grandma" Moses.

But in the forties and fifties, with the development of the abstract expressionism ("action" painting) of the "New York school," American artists placed themselves for the first time in the vanguard of the modern movement in art. Led by Jackson Pollock (1912–56), who composed huge abstract designs by laying his canvas on the floor of his studio and squeezing paint on it directly from the tube in a wild tangle of color, these men were utterly subjective in their approach to art. "The source of my painting is the Unconscious," Pollock explained. "I am not much aware of what is taking place; it is only after that I see what I have done." He tried to produce not the representation of a landscape, but, as the critic Harold Rosenberg put it, "an inner landscape that is part of himself."

Untutored critics found the abstract expressionists crude, chaotic, devoid of interest. The swirling, dripping chaos of the followers of Pollock, the vaguely defined planes of color favored by Mark Rothko and his disciples, and the sharp spacial confrontations composed by men like Franz Kline, Robert Motherwell, and Adolph Gottlieb required too much verbal explanation to communicate their meaning to the average observer. On the other hand, the school was a perfectly logical outgrowth of the modern movement. Surrealism, with its dreamlike ventures into the unconscious, the iconoclasm of the dadaists, and the angular abstractions of the cubists all contributed to the new form. Viewed in its social context, abstract expressionism reflected, like so much of modern literature, the estrangement of the artist from the world of the atomic bomb and the computer, his revolt against contemporary mass culture, with its unthinking acceptance of novelty for its own sake.

The experimental spirit released by the abstract expressionists led on to "op" art, which employed the physical impact of pure complimentary colors to produce dynamic optical effects. Even within the rigid limitations of severely formal designs composed of concentric circles, stripes, squares, and rectangles, such paintings appeared constantly in motion, almost alive. "Op" was devoid of social connotations, but another variant, "pop" art, playfully but often with acid incisiveness, satirized many aspects of American culture: its vapidity, its crudeness, its violence. Painters like Andy Warhol created huge portraits of mundane objects such as soup cans and packing cases. "Op" and "pop" art grew out of the mechanized aspects of life; these painters made use of modern technology in their work, enhancing the shock of vibrating complimentary colors with new fluorescent paints. Pop artists imitated newspaper-photograph techniques by fashioning their images of sharply defined dots of color; both borrowed from contemporary commercial art, employing spray guns, stencils, and masking tape to produce flat, "hard-edge" effects. The line between "op" and "pop" was frequently crossed, as, for example, in Robert Indiana's *Love,* which was reproduced and imitated on posters, Christmas cards, book jackets, buttons, rings, and in countless other forms.

Color and shape as ends in themselves, stark and on a heroic scale, typified the styles of the sixties. Color-field painters covered vast planes with flat, sometimes subtly shaded hues. Frank Stella, one of the most universally admired of the younger artists, composed complicated bands and curves of color on enormous, eccentrically shaped canvases. To an unprecedented degree, the artist's hand, the combination of patience and skill that had characterized traditional art, was removed from painting.

The pace of change in artistic fashion was dizzying and exciting. Although some believed it put too high a premium on mere novelty, it gave to both artists and art lovers a sense of participating in events of historic importance. Successful artists, like the most popular writers, film directors, and other creative people, became national personalities, a few of them enormously rich. For these, each new work was exposed to the glare of publicity and subject to minute critical analysis, sometimes with unfortunate results. Too much attention, like too much money, could be distracting, even corrupting, especially for young artists, who needed time and obscurity to develop their talents. Whether the conditions of modern life really were suitable for creative development, whether the new art *was* historically important, remained for future critics to determine.

DAYTON'S GALLERY 12

Robert Indiana's versions of Love *(this is a 1966 oil) include an aluminum sculpture.*

SUPPLEMENTARY READING Postwar domestic politics is treated briefly in E.F. Goldman, *The Crucial Decade—And After** (1961), Walter Johnson, *1600 Pennsylvania Avenue** (1960), Herbert Agar, *The Price of Power** (1957), and G.E. Mowry, *The Urban Nation** (1965). For more detail, consult Congressional Quarterly Service, (ed.), *Congress and the Nation: 1945–1964* (1965), an indispensable reference work. Interpretive works useful for understanding the period include Samuel Lubell, *The Future of American Politics** (1952) and *Revolt of the Moderates* (1956), A.M. Schlesinger, Jr., *The Vital Center** (1949), R.E. Neustadt, *Presidential Power** (1960), J.M. Burns, *The Deadlock of Democracy** (1963), Daniel Bell, *The End of Ideology** (1959), C. Wright Mills, *The Power Elite** (1962), and R.H. Rovere, *The American Establishment** (1962).

Biographical material on postwar political leaders is voluminous but seldom satisfactory from the scholarly point of view. On Truman, see H.S. Truman, *Memoirs** 1955–56) and *Mr. Citizen** (1960), and C.B. Phillips, *The Truman Presidency* (1966). Eisenhower's own view of his two terms can be found in D.D. Eisenhower, *Mandate for Change** (1963) and *Waging Peace* (1965). Of the biographies, R.J. Donovan, *Eisenhower: The Inside Story* (1956), and M.J. Pusey, *Eisenhower: The President* (1956), are favorable, while Marquis Childs, *Eisenhower: Captive Hero* (1958), is critical. See also Dean Albertson (ed.), *Eisenhower as President** (1963). Sherman Adams, *Firsthand Report** (1961), is a pro-Eisenhower memoir, E.J. Hughes, *The Ordeal of Power** (1963), an anti-Eisenhower one. For Kennedy, consult J.M. Burns, *John Kennedy: A Political Profile** (1960), which covers his pre-Presidential career, Theodore Sorenson, *Kennedy** (1965), and A.M. Schlesinger, Jr., *A Thousand Days** (1965). The best biography of Johnson is Rowland Evans and Robert Novak, *Lyndon B. Johnson: The Exercise of Power** (1966). W.S. White, *The Professional: Lyndon B. Johnson** (1964), is an uncritical biography of Johnson; Jack Bell, *The Johnson Treatment* (1965), is a good account of Johnson's political philosophy and method of operations. See also Tom Wicker, *JFK and LBJ* (1968), and E.F. Goldman, *The Tragedy of Lyndon Johnson* (1969). The Presidential elections of 1960 and 1964 are described in two books by T.H. White, each called *The Making of the President** (1961, 1965).

On the lesser figures, see W.S. White, *The Taft Story* (1954), N.F. Busch, *Adlai Stevenson of Illinois* (1952), R.M. Nixon, *Six Crises** (1962), William Costello, *The Facts About Nixon* (1960), and R.H. Rovere, *Senator Joe McCarthy** (1959).

Economic trends are considered in the annual *Economic Reports of the President* (1947–   ), and in A.A. Berle, *The 20th Century Capitalist Revolution** (1954) and *Power Without Property** (1959), J.K. Galbraith, *American Capitalism** (1952) and *The Affluent Society** (1958), Walter Heller, *New Dimensions of Political Economy** (1966), S.E. Harris, *Economics of the Kennedy Years** (1964), The Editors of *Fortune, America in the Sixties: The Economy and the Society** (1960), and Walter Adams and H.M. Gray, *Monopoly in America* (1955).

On labor, consult Philip Taft, *Organized Labor in American History* (1964), Joel Seidman, *American Labor from Defense to Reconversion* (1953), H.A. Millis and E.C. Brown, *From the Wagner Act to Taft-Hartley* (1950), B.J. Widick, *Labor Today* (1964), E.L. Dayton, *Walter Reuther* (1958), W.M. Leiserson, *American Trade Union Democracy* (1959), F.C. Mann and L.R. Hoffman, *Automation and the Worker* (1960), and P.A. Brinker, *The Taft-Hartley Act After Ten Years* (1958). On agriculture, see Theodore Schultz, *Agriculture in an Unstable Economy* (1945), M.R. Benedict and O.C. Stine, *The Agricultural Commodity Programs* (1956), and Lauren Soth, *Farm Trouble in an Age of Plenty* (1957).

The civil liberties issue is discussed in Alan Barth, *The Loyalty of Free Men* (1951), Rovere's above-mentioned life of McCarthy, R.S. Brown, Jr., *Loyalty and Security* (1958), and C.P. Curtis, *The Oppenheimer Case* (1955). On Negro rights, see B.M. Ziegler, *Desegregation and the Supreme Court** (1958), Anthony Lewis *et al.*, *Portrait of a Decade* (1964), C.V. Woodward, *The Strange Career of Jim Crow** (1955), and J.A. Garraty (ed.), *Quarrels That Have Shaped the Constitution** (1964).

Population trends are described in C. and I.B. Taeuber, *The Changing Population of the United States* (1958), the movement to the suburbs in R.C. Wood, *Suburbia** (1959). For critical analyses of modern American novelists, consult Alfred Kazin, *On Native Grounds** (1942) and *Contemporaries** (1962), Malcolm Cowley, *The Literary Situation** (1954), Robert Bone, *The Negro Novel in America* (1965), and Edmund Wilson, *The Shock of Recognition** (1955). Modern American art is discussed in J.I. Baur, *Revolution and Tradition in Modern American Art* (1951), O.W. Larkin, *Art and Life in America* (1949), Samuel Hunter, *Modern American Painting and Sculpture** (1959), and Barbara Rose, *American Art Since 1900** (1967).

*Available in paperback.

METROPOLITAN MUSEUM OF ART, GEORGE A. HEARN FUND

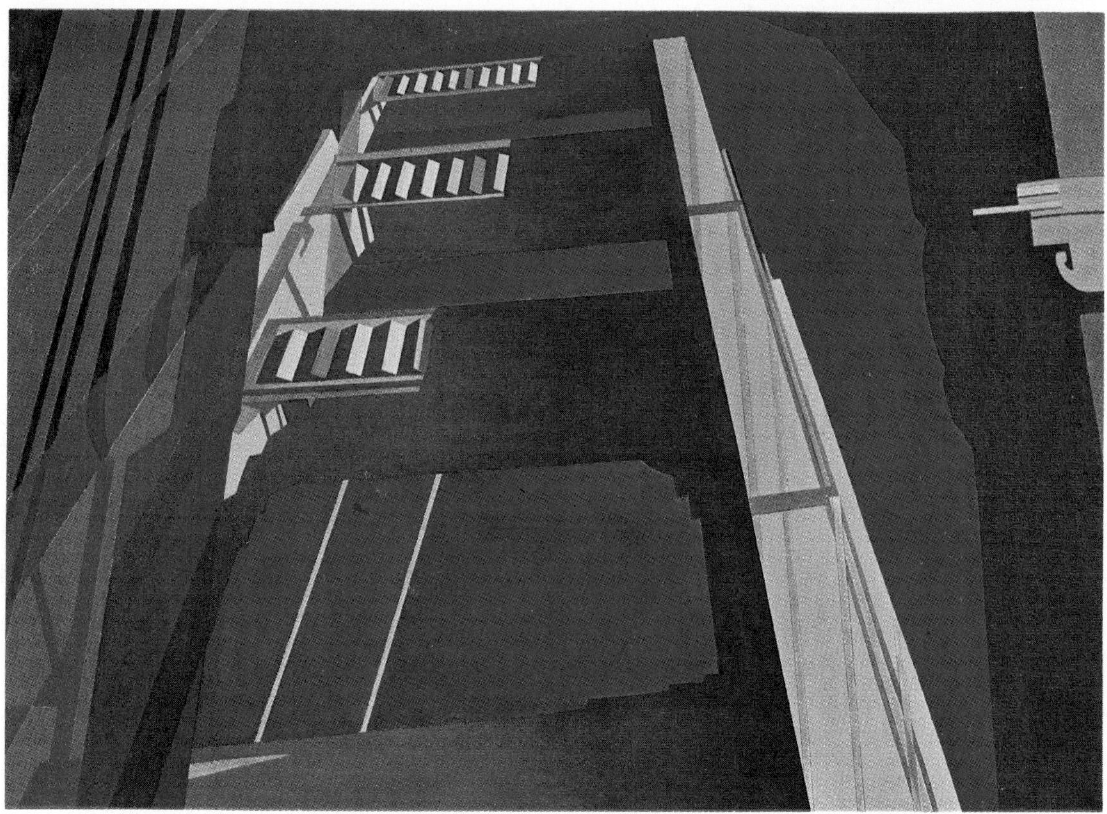

PORTFOLIO

VI *20th-Century American Painting*

American painting in the 20th century has been called everything from "psychological balderdash" to "anti-art." But by the seventies it seemed more likely that history would judge the best American painting of this century, as represented in the nation's 700 galleries, 500 museums, and 200 corporate art collections, to be a fitting, modern expression of Aristotle's classic definition: "In part art completes what nature cannot elaborate; and in part it imitates nature." The startling modernity of some of these canvases is, as one American painter has suggested, a reflection of 20th-century man's "fresh relationship to the courses of the sun and to the living swing of the earth."

Revolutionary times have called forth a procession of stylistic revolutions, yet transcending the diversity is a much older American quality, the pioneer's love of adventure and space. Charles Sheeler would not, for example, add *Bridge* to the title of his 1955 painting *Golden Gate* (above). "Then it would be limited to be the connecting link between two dots on the map," Sheeler said. "It is an opening, . . . a gateway, a beckoning into the new."

METROPOLITAN MUSEUM OF ART, ARTHUR H. HEARN FUND

METROPOLITAN MUSEUM OF ART, GIFT OF FRIENDS OF JOHN SLOAN

The Ashcan School

"Apostles of Ugliness," "The Revolutionary Blackgang," screamed the academicians. "To hell with artistic values," replied Robert Henri, teacher and leader of a group of eight pioneers determined to paint whatever they saw around them and not merely what others considered "proper" subjects. Today much of the painting of the ashcan school seems like the pleasant effulgence of French impressionism set in New York rather than in Paris. But in 1908, when The Eight (as the school was then called) held an independent showing in defiance of the National Academy of Design, their work "stabbed" the public right "in the optic nerve." An appreciative critic pointed out that the ashcan painters had offended by calling attention to what no one wanted to see—"our crude, vibrating, nervous, uncertain civilization."

As Everett Shinn, one of the original eight, later wrote, in the early 1900's "art in America . . . was merely an adjunct of plush and cut glass. . . . Its heart pumped only anemia." By daring, as John Sloan advocated, to paint the city in all its "drab, shabby, happy, sad, and human moods," these artists rescued American painting from being largely parlor ornamentation and an object of conspicuous consumption. Art should depict the life (in Aristotelian terms, the nature) of its times, pleasant or grim, they said. Secondly, and of equal importance, the ashcan artists adopted a highly personal approach toward painting. "Art . . . is an individual thing, the question of one man facing certain facts and telling his relations to them," Robert Henri never tired of reminding his students. For more than half a century Henri's dictum has been the watchword of American painters—as it has been the watchword of great artists in every age.

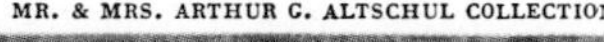

MR. & MRS. ARTHUR G. ALTSCHUL COLLECTION

H. V. ALLISON & CO.

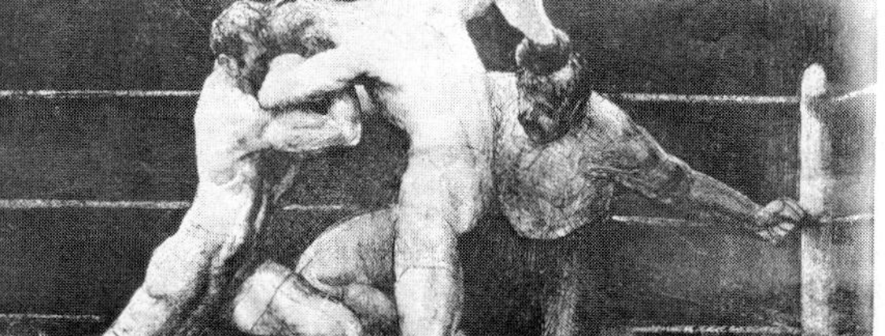

Upper left: William Glackens painted The Green Car *in 1910 using the bright palette and feathery strokes of the French impressionists to depict New York City in winter.*

Far left: John Sloan's The Lafayette, *1928. Believing cameras "mentally blind," Sloan thought painting should portray "the things that a blind man knows about the world."*

Left: Because of subject matter, Everett Shinn's warmly colored pastel, The Laundress, *was called "vulgar" by critics who objected to artists painting the life of the poor.*

Above: "Brutal" George Bellows' 1917 lithograph of his famous Stag at Sharkey's *is an example of the kind of realism that made the ashcan school an object of outrage.*

WHITNEY MUSEUM OF AMERICAN ART, MR. & MRS. ROY R. NEUBERGER GIFT

Arthur Dove, Ferry Boat Wreck, *1931.*

WHITNEY MUSEUM OF AMERICAN ART

Max Weber, Chinese Restaurant, *1915.*

Pioneers of Modernism

Between 1880 and about 1920 such European artists as Cézanne, Matisse, Kandinsky, and Picasso led a series of artistic revolutions and laid the foundations for modern art. They abandoned the rendering of three-dimensional space by means of linear perspective in favor of new visual orientations: cubism, which dissected, selected, and reassembled forms in terms of shifting planes and geometric shapes; abstraction, which cast aside the representations of visual reality in favor of the artist's personal conceptions of beauty, shape, and design; and expressionism, which concentrated on portraying the feeling a subject inspired rather than on its outward appearance. In the realm of color the Fauves, or "Wild Beasts," used unmixed pigments to record the artist's (and reject the camera's) vision.

Followers of no one school, American painters adapted all these innovations to their own individual and generally expressionistic purposes. Arthur Dove's *Ferry Boat Wreck,* for instance, combines realistic and abstract elements to express a sense of tragedy which goes beyond the single incident. The ocean is recognizable; the ferry is not, but its demise is clearly suggested by the semiabstract, loglike shapes in the foreground. Max Weber's *Chinese Restaurant* borrows the cubist technique of shattering and reassembling shapes to create the artist's own personal fantasy. In explaining his use of cubism, Weber wrote, "On entering a Chinese restaurant from the darkness of the night outside, a maze and blaze of light seemed to split into fragments the interior and its contents. . . . The light so piercing and so luminous, the color so liquid and the life and movement so enchanting! To express this, a kaleidoscopic means had to be chosen." Charles Burchfield's specter-ridden water color, *Church Bells Ringing,* however, owes its effect more to Burchfield's exploration of "a completely personal mood" than to any other influence. John Marin was another pioneer of American modernism whose style was largely of his own devising. Using brilliant colors and simplified shapes in cityscapes and seascapes, such as *Sun Spots,* Marin painted nature's "warring, pushing, pulling" forces which, he said, made "the whole human critter expand nigh to the bustin' point."

CLEVELAND MUSEUM OF ART, MRS. LOUISE M. DUNN GIFT

Charles Burchfield, Church Bells Ringing . . . , *1917.*

METROPOLITAN MUSEUM OF ART, ALFRED STIEGLITZ COLLECTION

John Marin, Sun Spots, *1920.*

METROPOLITAN MUSEUM OF ART, WHITTELSEY FUND

METROPOLITAN MUSEUM OF ART, GEORGE A. HEARN FUND

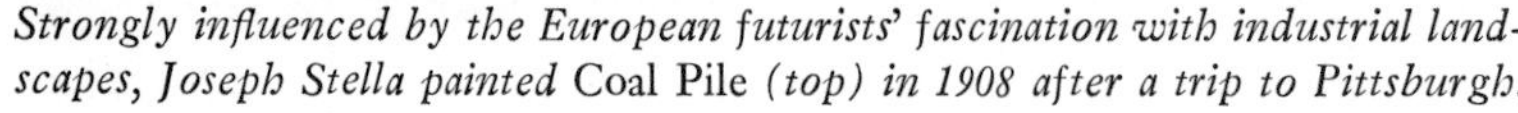

Strongly influenced by the European futurists' fascination with industrial landscapes, Joseph Stella painted Coal Pile *(top) in 1908 after a trip to Pittsburgh.*

Above: To explain how South of Scranton *(1931) developed into a surrealist fantasy, Peter Blume wrote, "As I tried to weld my impressions into the picture they lost all their logical connections. I moved Scranton into Charleston, and Bethlehem into Scranton, as people do in a dream. The German sailors appeared to lose the purpose of exercising and became . . . like birds soaring through space."*

At right is Edward Hopper's Early Sunday Morning *(1930). Hopper's aim was to paint "the most exact transcription" of his "most intimate impressions."*

Visions of Reality

In "The Man with the Blue Guitar" Wallace Stevens wrote, "They said, 'You have a blue guitar,/ You do not play things as they are.'/ The man replied, 'Things as they are/ Are changed upon the blue guitar.'" The artist's imagination is his blue guitar. The individualism that Henri encouraged, combined with the moderns' technical innovations, enormously widened the imaginative scope of 20th-century American painting. These canvases by Joseph Stella, Edward Hopper, and Peter Blume represent dramatically varied interpretations of typical American landscapes. Stella, an Italian immigrant, was thrilled to find that in America "Steel and electricity had created a new world. . . . A new polyphony was ringing all around with the scintillating, highly-colored lights. . . . A new architecture was created, a new perspective." This insight permeated industrial landscapes such as *Coal Pile* and his many renderings of the Brooklyn Bridge in which he sought to "exalt the joyful, daring endeavor of the American civilization." Edward Hopper responded very differently. Like Stella, he filled his canvases with light, but of a cruel and penetrating kind. In paintings such as *Early Sunday Morning* he used it to describe the "fear and anxiety" which he felt America's urban civilization inspired. Where Stella was dazzled by modern America and Hopper probed its loneliness, Blume translated its diversity into surrealist fantasies. *South of Scranton* recreates a trip through Pennsylvania steel and mining towns to Charleston, South Carolina, where the artist watched sailors doing calisthenics on the deck of a visiting German cruiser.

WHITNEY MUSEUM OF AMERICAN ART

America, America

In painting as in life, every innovation produces a complex variety of reactions. By the mid-1920's many painters felt that the "modern" artist had become too dependent upon European techniques and had lost his grip on reality—specifically, American reality. Generally speaking, these painters divided into two groups, rural and urban regionalists.

The rural regionalists set out to portray the virtues of America's farmlands. Their most vocal representative, Thomas Hart Benton, proclaimed in 1932, "no American art can come to those who do not live an American life, who do not have an American psychology, and who cannot find in America justification for their lives." Benton denounced the whole modern movement as "dirt."

Urban regionalists, largely centered in New York, were not so much concerned about painting "American" as they were about catching the many-sided and often vulgar life of America's most dynamic, polyglot metropolis. "Well-bred people are no fun to paint," Reginald Marsh said. The urban regionalists had no single artistic credo. Rather they sought, as the ashcan painters had before them, to let the city and all its complexities be their guide. "It offers itself," as Marsh put it.

FRANK REHN GALLERY, NEW YORK

WHITNEY MUSEUM OF AMERICAN ART

METROPOLITAN MUSEUM OF ART, GEORGE A. HEARN FUND

Regionalists paintings show a broad range of interests, from Reginald Marsh's 1930 canvas Subway, 14th Street *(above left) with its concentration on New York's energy, through Louis Bouché's quiet ferryboat scene,* Ten Cents a Ride *(above right), done in 1942, to Grant Wood's 1933 pencil sketches (below) for* Dinner for Threshers, *with their loving description of rural life.*

The Social Realists

On February 14, 1936, the first Artists' Congress ever held in America opened with a speech by the social historian Lewis Mumford. It was a grim era. The Great Depression gripped the United States, fascism was riding high in Germany and Italy, and there were portents of another world war. "The time has come," Mumford said, ". . . to be ready to protect, and guard, and if necessary, fight for the human heritage which we, as artists, embody." A number of American painters, now known as the social realists, were already using their work as just such a weapon. Their painting was social in its direct concern for American problems and, by appealing to emotions, dramatically realistic in technique.

The distinction of the social realists is largely attributable to three artists whose skill matched their concern for their fellow men—Philip Evergood, Ben Shahn, and Jack Levine. Shahn expressed their credo when he said, "I hate injustice. I guess that's about the only thing I really do hate . . . and I hope to go on hating it all my life." The social realists were also angered by the lack of commitment on the part of their "modern" colleagues. "Is all our pity and anger to be reduced to a few tastefully arranged straight lines or petulant squirts from a tube held over a canvas?" Shahn asked. Their anger was tempered by an awareness that mankind could never be wholly condemned. "On one hand we see gluttony and self-aggrandizement," Evergood pointed out, "and on the other self-abnegation, sacrifice, generosity, and heroism, in different members of the same human race."

MUSEUM OF MODERN ART, LINCOLN KIRSTEIN GIFT

MUSEUM OF MODERN ART, WPA ART PROGRAM LOAN

ARMAND G. ERPF COLLECTION

"You distort for editorial reasons," is Jack Levine's succinct artistic canon. In The Feast of Pure Reason *(above), painted in 1937, Levine used distortion and a startling, unnatural light to explore the faces of the three cronies. In* Willis Avenue Bridge *(1940) on the opposite page, Ben Shahn stunted and shriveled the old ladies to make them at once grotesque and pathetic, while Philip Evergood's* American Tragedy *(left), painted to commemorate a bloody labor clash in Chicago in 1937, is a compilation of dramatic distortion.*

The Federal Art Project

The year 1933 inaugurated a New Deal in art as well as in politics. The Roosevelt administration decided that artists, along with the other millions of unemployed, were a national resource and deserved federal assistance. The largest such effort was the Federal Art Project, begun in 1935 as a division of the Works Progress Administration. A truly gargantuan undertaking, the project employed over 5,000 persons in mural and easel painting, sculpture, crafts, photography, art instruction, the planning and creation of new museums, and other related ventures.

In statistical terms alone the project achieved immense results. It placed over a million pieces of art in the nation's galleries and museums, commissioned hundreds of murals for post offices, schools, and other public buildings, and started scores of new museums in rural areas.

Although project director Holger Cahill insisted that "We shall not tell painters what to paint or how to paint it," he believed that much of modern painting had become too obscure, and consequently he encouraged what he called "imaginative realism." At its best, imaginative realism combined the strengths of regional and social realist painting with an imaginative flair for interpreting American culture; at its worst, it degenerated into chauvinistic illustration.

In 1939 Congress terminated the Federal Art Project amid accusations that it had been a frivolous expense. Today it is clear that the contribution of the project to American culture was large, if difficult to pinpoint. Millions of Americans had their artistic horizons broadened. For the artists it provided not only a shelter in the storm—"a moment of peace," as one artist expressed it—but also the exhilarating experience of helping their country in a time of crisis.

In 1964 Ben Shahn, recalling his days with the project, said, "I felt in complete harmony with the times. I don't think I've ever felt that way before or since." Finally, the project produced for the public a number of 20th-century classics at bargain rates. For example, in 1965 a WPA mural, discovered in a New York City radio station, was valued by appraisers at between $60,000 and $100,000. It was the work of Stuart Davis, who was paid $24.50 a week in 1939 for the ten weeks it took him to paint it.

METROPOLITAN MUSEUM OF ART, NEW YORK CITY WPA GIFT

Jacob Lawrence, Blind Beggars, *1938.*

MUSEUM OF MODERN ART, WPA ART PROJECT LOAN

L. Guglielmi, Wedding in South Street, *1936.*

KING'S HIGHWAY ELEMENTARY SCHOOL, WESTPORT, CONN.

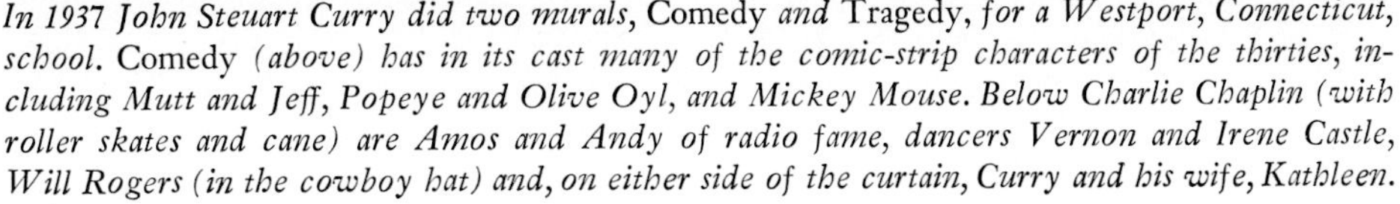

In 1937 John Steuart Curry did two murals, Comedy *and* Tragedy, *for a Westport, Connecticut, school.* Comedy *(above) has in its cast many of the comic-strip characters of the thirties, including Mutt and Jeff, Popeye and Olive Oyl, and Mickey Mouse. Below Charlie Chaplin (with roller skates and cane) are Amos and Andy of radio fame, dancers Vernon and Irene Castle, Will Rogers (in the cowboy hat) and, on either side of the curtain, Curry and his wife, Kathleen.*

ALFRED STIEGLITZ COLLECTION, FISK UNIVERSITY

The Precisionists

While the regionalists, the social realists, and the imaginative realists were rejecting the more daring visual perspectives of modern art, another group of painters in the twenties and thirties embraced them as a means of portraying the shape and feel of a machine-created civilization. Although the precisionists (sometimes called the "immaculates") were not a school and had no one artistic credo, they did share a common attitude toward reality. Unconcerned about the state of society, they painted, like the later "hard edge" artists, with the cool detachment of a scientific observer. This effect of emotional distance was achieved by a precision of style that has given them their name. "I favor the picture which arrives at its destination without the evidence of a trying journey rather than the one which shows the marks of battle. An efficient army buries its dead," Charles Sheeler once said. Another precisionist, Charles Demuth, who put perspective to often-dramatic uses, commented that he had drawn out his inspiration "with a teaspoon, but I never spilled a drop."

The immaculate surfaces and the careful geometric arrangement of forms give precisionist paintings their apparent impersonality, yet from this meticulousness emerges a pervasive, if understated, feeling of awe and excitement at the order, beauty, and power of industrial America. "Our factories," Sheeler said, "are our substitute for religious experience." The paintings of Stuart Davis illustrate another and far more lighthearted dimension of the precisionists' work. In brilliantly colored, collage-like canvases Davis combined ideas, symbols, and objects to express the jazzy tempo of 20th-century America. The components of his vision, which Davis called EYDEAS, included "the brilliant colors on gasoline stations, chain store fronts, and taxicabs . . . fast travel by train, auto, and airplane, which brought new and multiple perspectives; electric signs; the landscape and boats of Gloucester, Massachusetts; five-and-ten-cent-store kitchen utensils, movies and radio; Earl Hines's piano."

METROPOLITAN MUSEUM OF ART, ALFRED STIEGLITZ COLLECTION, 1949

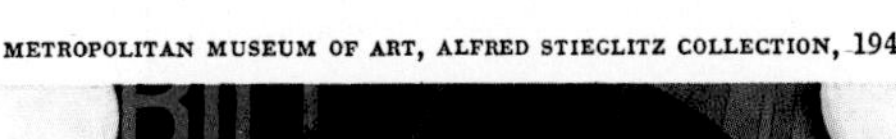

WHITNEY MUSEUM OF AMERICAN ART

In Georgia O'Keeffe's American Radiator Building *(left), telescopic clarity dramatizes the size and power of the skyscraper. The receding perspective in Charles Demuth's* I Saw the Figure 5 in Gold *(1928) was inspired by his friend William Carlos Williams' poem "The Great Figure": Among the rain/and lights/I saw the figure 5/in gold/ on a red / firetruck / moving /tense / unheeded / to gong clangs / siren howls/and wheels rumbling/through the dark city."* House and Street *(1931) by Stuart Davis revels in its childlike perspective.*

MR. & MRS. BEN HELLER COLLECTION

MUSEUM OF MODERN ART, A. CONGER GOODYEAR FUND

SAM KOOTZ GALLERY, NEW YORK

Above: Hans Hofmann, Fantasia, *1943.*

Left: Arshile Gorky, Agony, *1947.*

Below: Jackson Pollock, One, *1950.*

Abstract Expressionism

In 1946 the public got its first view of abstract expressionism; two decades later the shock waves were still reverberating. Neither abstraction nor expressionism were new to 20th-century painting, but combining them was not only new but revolutionary. Almost overnight New York replaced Paris as the world capital of avant-garde art. The abstract expressionists abandoned linear perspective, avoided all objects except those that symbolized the primary forces of life, and worked seemingly without plan or precision. But what they left out was far less shocking than what they often literally threw in—great splashes of color, tangles of paint, rude shapes in dramatic opposition, which combined to express powerful emotions devoid of specific allusion.

Conservatives cried "fraud," but these pioneering artists insisted that only revolutionary painting could express revolutionary times. In 1950 Jackson Pollock said, "The modern painter cannot express this age, the airplane, the atom bomb, the radio, in the old forms of the renaissance or any other past culture." A year later Robert Motherwell added, "The need is for felt experience—intense, immoderate, direct, subtle, unified, warm, vivid, rhythmic." Hans Hofmann, the movement's foremost teacher and theoretician, explained that abstract expressionism sought to "present" the inner and often subconscious world of the artist's mind rather than to "represent" the outer world of known objects. Thus Arshile Gorky's *Agony* is not a representation of a man in pain, but a presentation of pain itself. Pollock's *One* and Mark Rothko's *Number 10* carry this introspective bent to another conclusion. Neither painting is "of" anything; each is its own subject.

In order to tap the resources of the subconscious, the abstract expressionists painted as freely and as intuitively as their materials permitted. Pollock, the creator of "action painting," put his huge canvases on the floor, where he felt "nearer, more a part of the painting, since this way I can walk around it, work from the four sides, and literally be in the painting." Abstract expressionists held that spontaneity turned art into exploration, "an unknown adventure into an unknown space."

MUSEUM OF MODERN ART

Robert Motherwell, Elegy to the Spanish Republic, *1954.*

MUSEUM OF MODERN ART, PHILIP C. JOHNSON FUND

Adolph Gottlieb, Blast I, *1957.*

MUSEUM OF MODERN ART, PHILIP C. JOHNSON GIFT

Mark Rothko, Number 10, *1950.*

S.C. JOHNSON & SON, INC.

Willem de Kooning, Woman VIII, *1961.*

WHITNEY MUSEUM OF AMERICAN ART, FRIENDS OF THE WHITNEY MUSEUM GIFT

Theodoros Stamos, High Snow-Low Sun, II, *1957.*

MARTHA JACKSON GALLERY, NEW YORK

The Figure

"Today, the figure is the hardest thing in the world to do. If it doesn't turn into some sort of cornball realism, it becomes anecdotal." These words of artist Larry Rivers express a dilemma which has both plagued and stimulated figurative painters since the postwar move toward abstract expressionism. Paintings, the new figurative artists argue, need to have real subjects, but they insist that their works must speak a far more general language than what realistic portraiture or photographic realism allow.

Of the three artists represented here, Andrew Wyeth is the most realistically oriented, yet he says, "I honestly consider myself an abstractionist," and is concerned lest his superbly crafted paintings become "overfed and the objects over-expressed." He wants his subjects to transcend their individuality and become symbols of man's precious mortality.

Richard Diebenkorn, who left abstract expressionism because he came to distrust his desire "to explode the picture," considers figurative painting "a fantastic clutter of possibilities filled with booby traps and corn fields"—that is, the trite and the sentimental. As one critic has said, his canvases provide "the actual forms: figure, landscape, indication of action. . . . Now the viewer must project self into the mood, character, inner contemplation of human space within."

Larry Rivers, perhaps the most enigmatic of the three, says, "I can't put down on canvas what I can't see. I think of a picture as a smorgasbord of the recognizable." He is so deeply distrustful of "cornball realism" that he insists, "I can't express pity, hatred, joy, anxiety; I have to work on it until the expression or the look is something that you can't give a name to."

MR. & MRS. GUY A. WEILL COLLECTION

NATIONAL GALLERY, OSLO

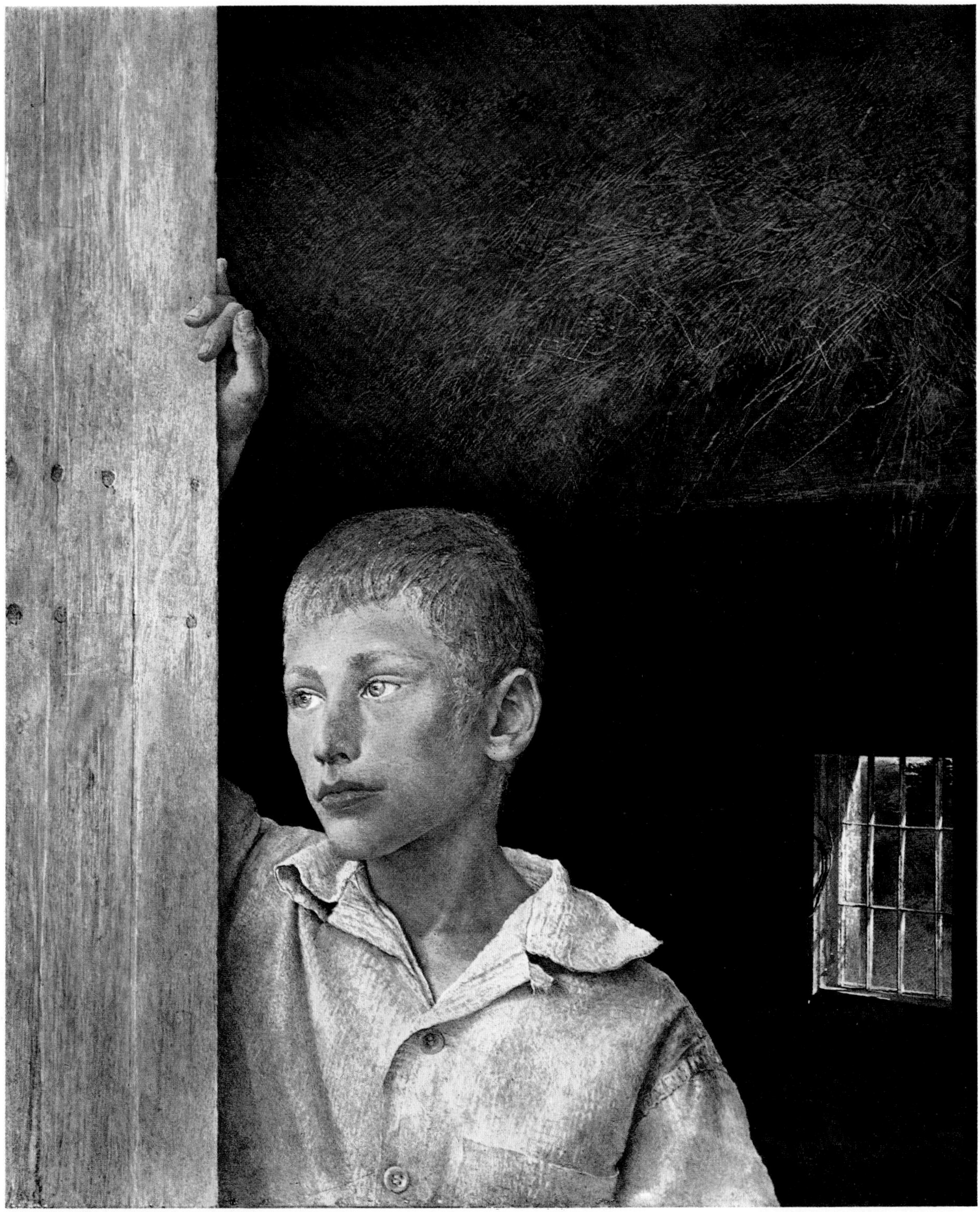

The figurative works reproduced here are attempts to go beyond the limits of realistic portraiture and, as Andrew Wyeth has advocated, show "Americans what America is like." Wyeth detests "the sweetness" of much current figurative painting and hopes that his studies of small-town, rural Americans, such as Albert's Son *(above), painted in Maine in 1959, will reveal the "real American personality." Richard Diebenkorn's* July *(upper left), painted in California in 1957, welds figure, landscape, and symbol together to create an American "rough-hewn, frontier quality." Larry Rivers' featureless* The Next to Last Confederate Soldier *(1959), left, uses a similar juxtaposition to satirize the romanticized myth of the Civil War.*

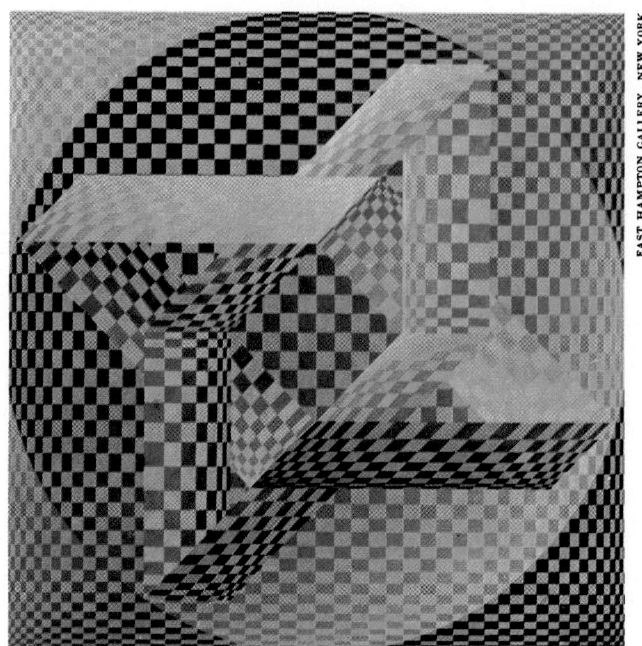

EAST HAMPTON GALLERY, NEW YORK

Benjamin Cunningham, Equivocation, *1964.*

ANDRE EMMERICH GALLERY, NEW YORK

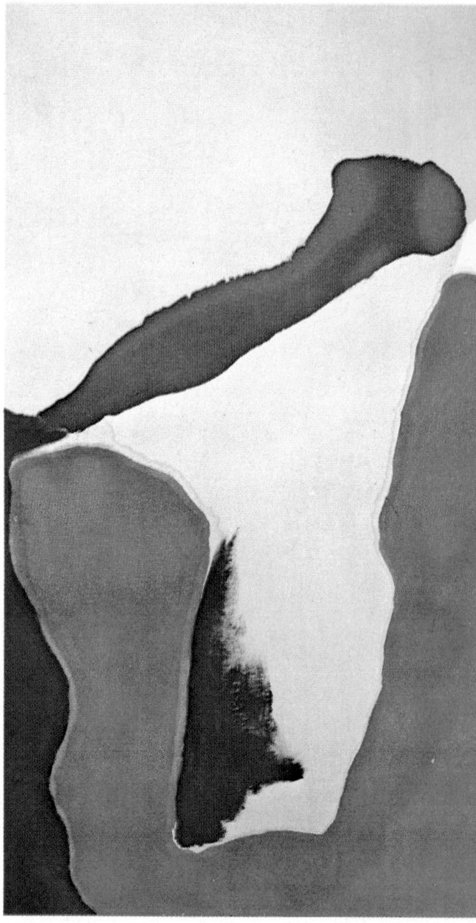

Helen Frankenthaler, Good Luck Orange, *1969.*

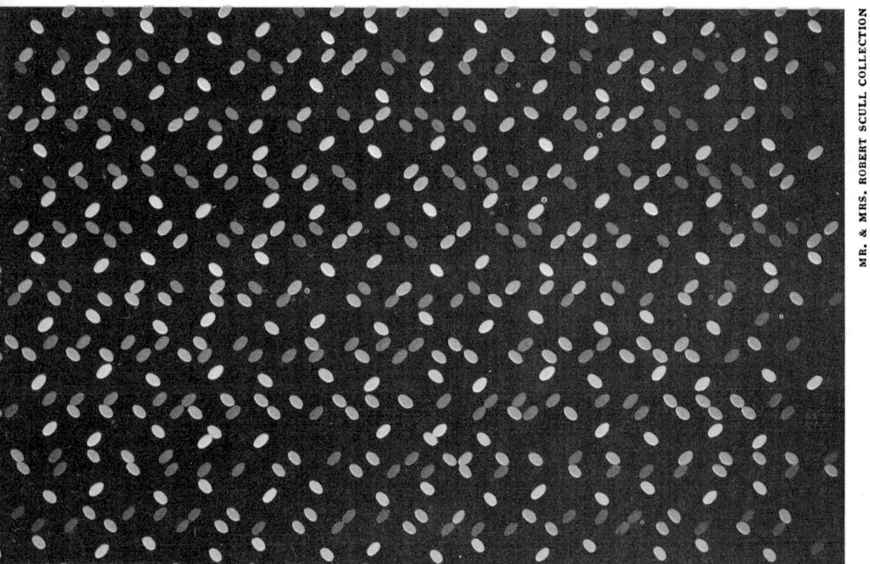

MR. & MRS. ROBERT SCULL COLLECTION

Larry Poon, Nixe's Mate, *1964.*

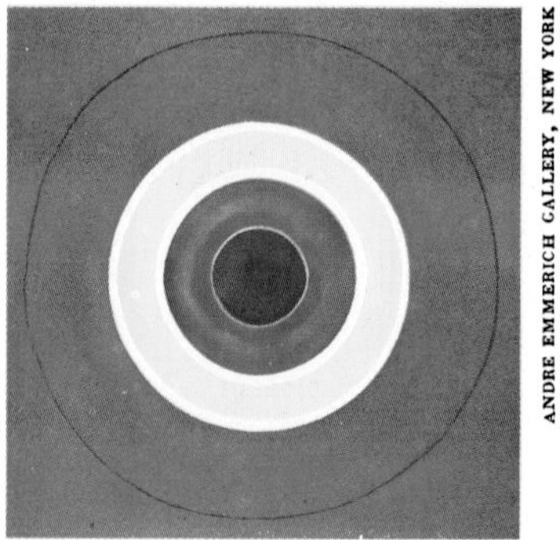

ANDRE EMMERICH GALLERY, NEW YORK

Kenneth Noland, Noon, Afloat, *1962.*

DAVID WHITNEY COLLECTION

M. KNOEDLER & CO. INC.

Barnett Newman, Who's Afraid of Red, Yellow, and Blue III, *1966–67.*

Frank Stella, Sabra II, *1967.*

New Visions of Vision

In the sixties American painters continued to explore new modes of perception. Defining their work, as one did, as the "programming of information permitting a confrontation with visual situations," these artists abandoned what they called the "easel-weasel" in order to probe the process of vision itself.

Using the science of modern optics, "op" artists—in such works as Larry Poon's *Nixe's Mate* or Ben Cunningham's *Equivocation* —investigated how the eye and the psyche respond to highly calculated arrangements of line, shape, color, density, and mass. While such paintings create remarkable visual effects in which stationary dots appear to move and flat surfaces to have infinite depth, the meaning of "op," according to its proponents, lies primarily not in such illusions but in the intellectual and emotional experiences it generates.

Insisting that paintings are not "space boxes" for creating an illusory "window on the world," artists such as Kenneth Noland and Frank Stella explore the potential of canvases shaped and designed in geometrical color patterns. Helen Frankenthaler employs non-geometric shapes and "expressionistic" colors to probe the psyche. Whatever the method, such painters find their work enormously challenging. As Barnett Newman, who spent a lifetime experimenting with monumental works (*Who's Afraid of Red, Yellow, and Blue III,* above, is 8 feet by 18 feet), put it: "I always want to do something I can't do. . . . Risk is the high road to glory."

ALL: LEO CASTELLI GALLERY, NEW YORK

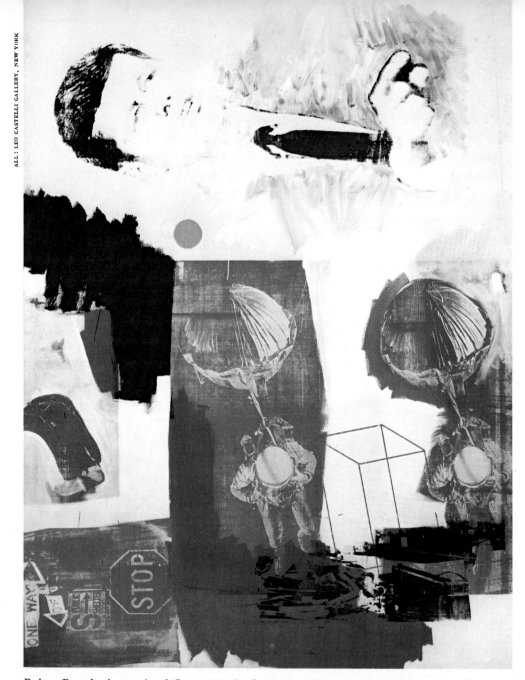

Robert Rauschenberg painted Quote *(1964), above, after years of experimenting with collages and "combines" to find a medium that would "affect a sense of non-selectivity." Andy Warhol's* Marilyn Monroe *(1967), below, is a detail from one of his many multiple-imaged renderings of the actress. Roy Lichtenstein's* Varoom *(1967), opposite, employs magnification to gain the texture of newsprint.*

The Processed Idiom

While some American painters were exploring the potential of new kinds of visual confrontation, others chose to confront the nation with itself. By transferring (sometimes directly) to the canvas the multiple images of a consumer-oriented, advertising-hounded, mass-media society, "pop" artists, the painters of the popular and commercial image, presented a satirical reflection of contemporary America. As one pop artist said, "When the remains of our civilization are dug up in a thousand years, it will be our washing machines more than the contents of our museums that will define our culture." Pop's cataloguing of American banalities made it heir to the tradition of social realism begun by the ashcan artists.

Although the techniques of pop painters differ, they share an urge to present images that go to the heart of contemporary experience by ingeniously displaying "processed idioms to express the quality of a way of life that is increasingly processed." For example, Andy Warhol's multi-imaged *Marilyn Monroe* employs a grotesque frame-by-frame mimicry of the movie idiom itself to produce a visual mime of the tortured and tragic career of a cinematic sex goddess. In a lighter vein Roy Lichtenstein's *Varoom* holds up a mirror to the tragicomic American admiration for the comic-strip world of action and romance.

On the other hand, the work of Robert Rauschenberg goes beyond the exhibiting of a microcosm of mass culture. Its processed idioms create a new kind of American landscape. By combining silk-screen reproductions of photographs with rich swatches of color, Rauschenberg attempts to retain the high tensions of abstract expressionism within a landscape "peopled" by "real" images drawn from the mass media. Painted a year after President Kennedy's assassination, but without deliberately exploiting the emotionalism of that event, Rauschenberg's *Quote* (opposite) creates an impression of the dynamic excitement and dramatic turbulence of the Kennedy years and their traumatic climax.

It is impossible to predict what directions American painting will take in the future. One thing does seem likely, however: American painters will continue the 20th-century tradition of employing their art to explore both the inner and the outer landscapes of American civilization.

30

Modern American Society

On March 4, 1929, Herbert Hoover, fresh from his overwhelming victory over Alfred E. Smith, delivered his inaugural address as President of the United States. The country was riding a wave of prosperity; everywhere pundits spoke of a new era of unlimited social and economic achievement. "In no nation are the institutions of progress more advanced," Hoover said. "In a large view we have reached a higher degree of comfort and security than ever existed before in the world. . . . I have no fears for the future." This prediction proved monumentally incorrect; within a year the nation was mired in the Great Depression.

On January 20, 1965, after a still more one-sided electoral triumph, Lyndon B. Johnson took the Presidential oath. The United States was even more prosperous than in 1929. Like Hoover, President Johnson extolled the virtues and achievements of the United States. "We have become a nation; prosperous, great and mighty," he said. But his view of the future, while hopeful, was far less complacent than Hoover's had been. "We have no promise from God that our greatness will endure," he warned. And he spoke of "this fragile existence," reminding the people that they lived "in a world where change and growth seem to tower beyond the control, and even the judgment, of men." His message, essentially, was a call for the preservation of traditional values and current accomplishments in a fantastically dynamic age, and he was acutely conscious of how difficult that task would be. The difference in mood between these two speeches tells us much about modern America. Change was the central theme of Johnson's inaugural; he mentioned the word over and over in his brief address. "The next man to stand here will look out on a scene that is different," he said. That society was in a state of flux, pulled in a dozen directions, no rational observer could deny.

Two Dilemmas

The central dilemmas seemed to be two. First of all, progress was often self-defeating. Reforms and innovations instituted with the highest of motives often made things worse rather than better. Illustrations of this dilemma, large and small, are so numerous as to defy summary. A powerful chemical, DDT, developed to

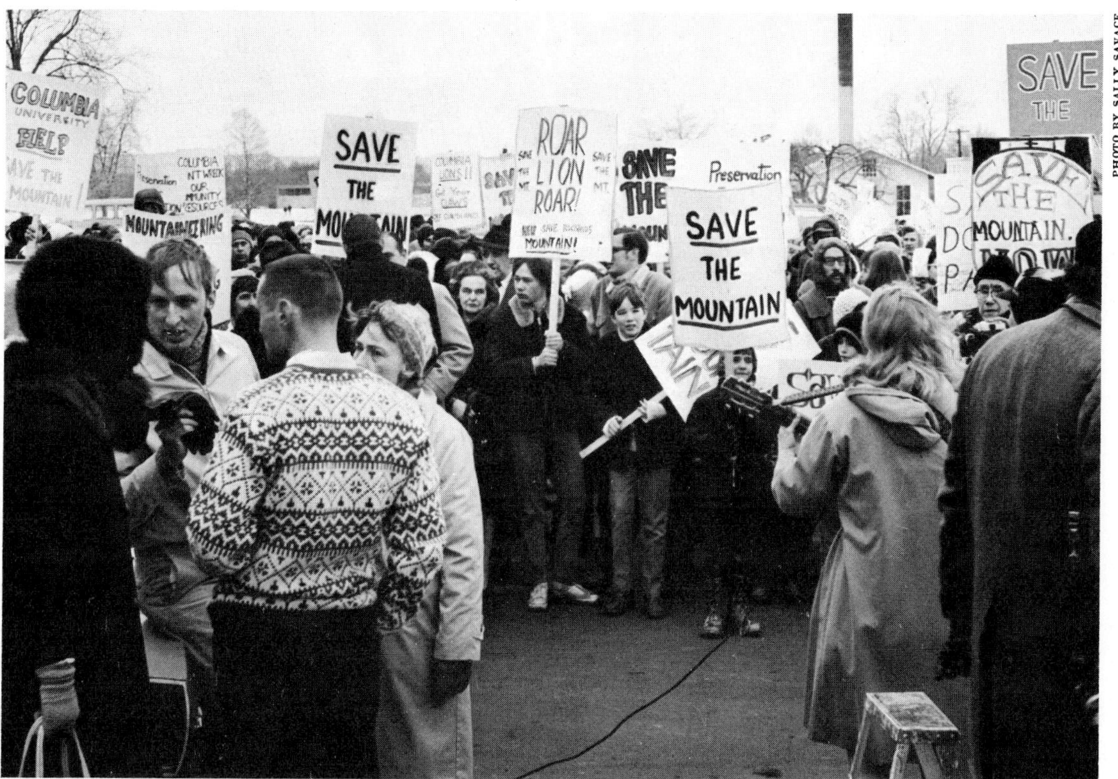

PHOTO BY SALLY SAVAGE

The persistent conflict between the needs of an expanding population and the urge to preserve the environment from encroachment may be seen in microcosm in a 1969 campaign to rescue an unspoiled area along New York's Hudson River from a housing development. Demonstrations like this have helped to save the mountain—so far.

kill insects that were spreading disease and destroying valuable food crops, proved to have lethal effects on birds, fish, and perhaps indirectly on human beings. Goods manufactured to make life fuller and happier (automobiles, detergents, electric power) produced waste products that disfigured the land and polluted air and water. Cities built to bring culture and wealth to millions became pestholes of poverty and depravity.

Moreover, change was occurring so fast that experience (the recollection of how things had been) tended to become less useful, and sometimes even counterproductive as a guide for dealing with current problems. Foreign policies designed to prevent wars, devised on the basis of knowledge of the causes of past wars, led, because the circumstances were different, to new wars. Parents who sought to transmit to their children the accumulated wisdom of their years found their advice rejected out of hand, and often with good reason, since that "wisdom" had little application to the problems their children had to face.

The second dilemma was that modern industrial society put an enormous premium on social cooperation, but at the same time undermined the individual citizen's sense of being essential to the proper functioning of society. The economy was as complicated as a fine watch; a breakdown in any sector had ramifications that spread swiftly to other sectors. Yet specialization had progressed so far that individual workers had little sense of the importance of their personal contributions and thus felt little responsibility for the smooth functioning of the whole. Mere numbers exaggerated this problem in every aspect of life. Effective democratic government required that all voters be knowledgeable and concerned, but few could feel that their individual voices had any effect on elections or public policies. The exhaust fumes of millions of automobiles were poisoning the air, but it was difficult to expect the single motorist to inconvenience himself by leaving his car in the garage when his restraint would have no measurable effect on the total pollution.*

Men tried to deal with this dilemma by joining groups, but the groups became so large that members felt as incapable of influencing them as they did of the larger society. Furthermore, the groups were so numerous and had so many conflicting objectives that instead of making citizens more socially minded they often made them more self-centered. The organization—union, club, party, pressure group—was a potent force in society, but few organizations were really concerned with the common interest, although logic required that the common interest be regarded if individuals or groups were to achieve their special interests.

These dilemmas produced a paradox. The United States was the most powerful nation in the world, its people the best educated, richest, and probably the most energetic. American society was technologically advanced and dynamic, American traditional values idealistic, humane, democratic. Yet increasingly by the late 1960's, the nation seemed incapable of mobilizing its resources intelligently to confront the most obvious challenges, citizens of achieving personal happiness or identification with their fellows, the society of living up to its most universally accepted ideals. President Johnson recognized this problem when he talked of establishing a "consensus" and of building a Great Society, but despite the achievements of his second term—Medicare, civil rights legislation, federal aid to education, tax reform—no real consensus emerged, and American society remained fragmented, its members divided against themselves and often within themselves.

*Shortly after writing these lines, I received a letter from my teen-age daughter: "It is frustrating because one person just can't feel that she's doing anything. I can use soap instead of detergents and no paper bags, but what good do I feel I'm doing when there are people next door having a party with plastic spoons and paper plates?"

Mixed Blessings

The vexing character of modern conditions could be seen in every aspect of life. The economy, after decades of rapid growth, speeded ahead even faster in the late sixties. The gross national product exceeded $900 billion in 1969. But inflation became increasingly serious. Prices rose faster than wages, so that workingmen were under constant pressure to demand raises, which only served to drive prices still higher. Average hourly wage rates in industry rose from $2.50 in 1966 to nearly $3 in 1970, but because of higher taxes and insurance costs, spendable income remained steady, thus real wages, eroded by inflation, declined. The effect was socially devastating, especially where workers in the service industries (and they made up a steadily increasing percentage of the labor force) were concerned. Their productivity often did not rise very rapidly, yet their need for more money could not be denied. It became impossible to expect workingmen to see inflation as a social problem and to restrain their personal demands. They put their individual interests before those of the whole and were prepared to disrupt the economy whatever the social cost. Public employees—teachers, garbage collectors, even policemen and firemen—traditionally committed to a no-strike policy because they worked for the whole community, succumbed to this selfish if understandable way of looking at life. In 1970 postal workers struck against the federal government, an unprecedented act, although its near-revolutionary character was less alarming because the justice of their demand for pay increases was universally conceded.

Economic expansion resulted in large measure from technological advances, but these, too, proved to be mixed blessings. As we have seen, World War II needs stimulated the development of plastics like nylon, of synthetic rubber, of radar, television, and other electronic devices. After the war, such products really came into their own. Plastics invaded field after field—automobile parts, building materials, adhesives, shoe "leather," packaging materials. By 1964 the annual consumption of plastic products had reached 9.75 billion pounds. To cite another example, television sets, produced only experimentally before the war, swept the country after 1946.

In 1951 scientists began to manufacture electricity from controlled nuclear energy; in 1954 the first atomic-powered ship, the submarine *Nautilus*, was launched. Although the peaceful use of atomic energy remained small compared to other sources of power, its implications were immense. Equally significant was the perfection of the electronic computer. These "mechanical brains" revolutionized the collection and storage of records, solved mathematical problems beyond the scope of the most brilliant human minds, speeded up and made incomparably more efficient the work of bank tellers, librarians, billing clerks, statisticians—and income-tax collectors. Computers also lay at the heart of industrial automation, for they could control the integration and adjustment of the most complex machinery. In automobile factories they made it possible to machine entire engine blocks automatically. In steel mills molten metal could be poured into molds, cooled, rolled, and cut into slabs without the intervention of a human hand, the computers locating defects and adjusting the machinery to correct them far more accurately than the most skilled steelworker, and in a matter of seconds. Taken in conjunction with a new oxygen smelting process some six or eight times faster than the open-hearth method, computer-controlled continuous casting promised to have an impact on steelmaking as great as that of the Bessemer process in the 1870's.

But the material benefits of technology had counterbalancing effects. The consumption of coal and oil necessary to produce power soared. The burning of these fuels released unmeasurable tons of smoke and other polluting gases into the atmosphere, endangering the health of millions and, some alarmists warned, threatening to alter the climate of the world drastically, even to make the globe incapable of supporting life. The vast outpouring of flimsy plastic products and the increased use of paper, metal foil, and other "disposable" packaging materials seemed about to bury the country beneath mountains of trash. The commercial use of nuclear energy also caused problems. Scientists insisted that the danger from radiation was nonexistent, but the possibility of accidents could not be eliminated entirely, and the safe disposal of radioactive wastes grew steadily more difficult.

Even an apparently ideal form of scientific advance, the use of commercial fertilizers to boost food output, had unfortunate side effects: phosphates washed from farmlands into streams sometimes upset the ecological balance and turned the streams into malodorous death traps for all aquatic life. Above all, technology increased the capacity of the earth to support people—temporarily. As population increased, production and consumption increased, speeding the pollution of the air and water supplies. And where would the process end? When viewed from a world perspective, it was obvious that the population explosion must be checked, or it would check itself by pestilence, war, starvation, or some combination of these scourges. Yet how to check it?

Technology also influenced American culture, and again the results were mixed. This trend, of course, was far from new; we have seen how machinery affected publishing and the arts in the late 19th century. In the 20th century, however, the impact of mechanization was both more profound and more pervasive. Around 1900 the motion picture made its appearance. The first films, such as the eight-minute epic *The Great Train Robbery* (1903), were brief, crude, and unpretentious, but they succeeded instantaneously. By 1908 the nation had between 8,000 and 10,000 nickelodeons, as the primitive exhibition halls were called, usually seating fewer than 100 persons each. However, the length and complexity of movies expanded rapidly, especially after David W. Griffith released his 12-reel *Birth of a Nation* in 1915, and by the mid-twenties the industry, centered in Hollywood, was the fourth largest in the nation in capital investment. Immense movie "palaces," each seating several thousand persons, sprang up in all the major cities. They counted their yearly audiences in the tens of millions. With the introduction of talking movies, beginning with *The Jazz Singer* (1927), and of color films a few years later, the motion picture reached technological maturity. Costs and profits mounted to enormous heights: by the thirties million-dollar productions were common;

Man against machine: Charlie Chaplin duels a folding Murphy bed in the film One A.M. The Great Dictator *(1940), one of Chaplin's most famous satires, flailed Hitler with deadly aim.*

by the fifties films grossing over $10 million were not unusual and average weekly attendance figures ran in the neighborhood of 55 million.

Most movies were tasteless, gaudy, mindless trash, aimed at titillating the senses and catering to the prejudices of the multitude. Sex, crime, romantic adventure, broad comedy, and luxurious living were their main themes, endlessly repeated in predictable patterns. Most popular actors were handsome, talentless sticks, type-cast over and over again as heroes, villains, comedians; yet they attracted armies of adoring fans and received thousands of dollars a week for their services. Critics charged that the movies were destroying the legitimate stage (which indeed underwent a sharp decline in the 20th century), corrupting the morals of youth, glorifying the materialistic aspects of life, and blackening the image of America abroad with their distorted images of American civilization.

Nevertheless, the motion picture made positive contributions to American culture as well, aside from its value as pure entertainment. Beginning with the work of Griffith, film-makers created an entirely new theatrical art, using close-ups to portray character and heighten tension, broad panoramic shots to transcend the limits of the stage. They employed special lighting effects, the fade-out, and other techniques impossible in the live theater with remarkable results. Movies also enabled dozens of established actors to reach wider audiences and developed many first-rate new ones. In Charlie Chaplin, whose characterization of the sad little tramp, with his cane, tight frock coat, and baggy trousers became famous all over the world, the new form found perhaps the supreme comic artist of all time. The animated cartoon, perfected by Walt Disney, was a lesser, but still significant achievement, giving endless delight to millions of children.

As the medium matured, it produced many works of the highest artistic quality; at its best it offered a breadth and power of impact superior to anything on the traditional stage. By its nature, the motion picture was international in scope. After World War II the finest films of every nation could be seen, either with dubbed-in dialogue or with translated subtitles, in every major city: by the sixties New York City had at least two dozen houses specializing in foreign productions. The motion picture, although made possible by modern technology, was a medium of astonishing variety and versatility. Millions still flocked to the great, empty spectacles, to the inane comedies and brutal "horse operas," and to the sordid and sexy potboilers, but films of subtle dramatic power, often dealing with serious social problems, also attracted large audiences, especially among intellectuals and students.

Even more pervasive was the impact of radio. Wireless transmission of sound was first developed in the late 19th century by many individual scientists in Europe and the United States, but an American, Lee De Forest, working in the decade before World War I, devised the key improvements that made long-distance broadcasting possible. During the war, radio was put to important military uses and was strictly controlled, but although the European nations maintained their government monopolies, in the United States the air waves were thrown open to everyone in 1919. Radio remained briefly the domain of hobbyists, thousands of "hams" chatting back and forth in indiscriminate fashion. Even under these conditions, the manufacture of radio equipment quickly became a big business; sales amounted to $18 million as early as 1920. In that year the first commercial station (KDKA in Pittsburgh) began broadcasting. It succeeded at once, and by the end of 1922 over 500 stations were in operation. Radio became a giant industry almost overnight. By 1930, 12 million families owned sets, by 1938, 40 million—soon the United States had far more radios than families.

It took little time for broadcasters to discover the power of the new medium. When one pioneer interrupted a music program to ask listeners to phone in requests, the station received 3,000 calls in an hour. The immediacy of radio explained its tremendous impact. As a means of communicating the latest news, it had no peer. Beginning with the broadcast of the 1924 Presidential nominating conventions, all major public events were covered "live," and alert reporters brought unforgettable moments of drama into millions of homes, most spectacularly, perhaps, when the German dirigible *Hindenburg* exploded while attempting to land at Lakehurst, New Jersey, after a transatlantic flight in 1937.

Franklin Roosevelt was the first political leader to master the use of radio as an instrument of mass persuasion. During World War II listeners heard the rantings of Hitler and Winston Churchill's deathless periods as they were actually delivered, and kept up with every aspect of the global war through the reports of dozens of on-the-spot correspondents and commentators. But the most convincing example of radio's power was provided accidentally in 1938, when Orson Welles presented a dramatization of H.G. Wells's novel *The War of the Worlds,* which described an invasion of the earth by Martians. Welles imitated radio techniques of news coverage so effectively that thousands of set owners, tuning in while the program was under way, believed an invasion was actually taking place and fled their homes in panic.

Advertisers seized upon radio at once, for it was as useful a device for selling soap and automobiles as for transmitting news. When the Pepsodent toothpaste company sponsored the popular comedy team of Amos and Andy, its sales increased 300 per cent. As early as 1929, the Ford Motor Company was paying $1,000 a minute to promote its cars over a national network. Advertising had mixed effects on broadcasting. The huge sums paid by businesses for air time made possible elaborate entertainments performed by the finest actors and musicians, and without cost to listeners, but advertisers hungered for mass markets and generally insisted on programs of little intellectual content, aimed at the lowest tastes and utterly uncontroversial. "Soap operas"—turgid, sentimental serial stories of domestic life—so dominated daytime programming in the 1930's that an investigator reported listening to 15 in a single day on one network and counting 35 others that he could have heard on other national hookups. Programs good and bad alike were constantly interrupted by irritating pronouncements extolling the supposed virtues of one product or another. However, advertising had no noticeable influence upon news broadcasting, which remained, by and large, free of prejudice and far more objective than most newspapers.

In 1927 Congress undertook to regulate the industry, limiting the number of stations and parceling out wavelengths to prevent interference. Further legislation in 1934 established the Federal Communications Commission with power to revoke the licenses of stations failing to operate in the public interest, but the FCC placed no really effective controls either on programming or on advertising practices. The general level remained lamentably inferior to that of government-owned European systems. While one could hear fine music, interesting discussion programs, and some first-rate drama on radio, critics agreed that far too little was available and that the networks were not doing enough in the way of educational broadcasting.

After World War II television became commercially feasible. Since it combined the immediacy of radio with the visual impact of the motion picture, it quickly replaced radio as a major means of entertainment and communication. Throughout the 1950's the public bought sets at the rate of 6 or 7 million annually, and by 1961 there were 55 million in operation, receiving the transmissions of 530 stations.

Television displayed most of radio's strengths and weaknesses in exaggerated form. It became indispensable to the political system, both in its coverage of public events and as a vehicle for political advertising. Television's handling of the events following President Kennedy's assassination, of national conventions and inaugurations, of the landing of American astronauts on the moon in 1969, and other news developments made history come alive for tens of millions. It brought sports events before the viewer so vividly that promoters often had to black out regions where games took place to avoid playing them in empty stadiums. Some excellent drama was presented on television, along with many filmed documentaries dealing with contemporary issues. By capturing so much of the mass audience, the medium indirectly improved the level of radio broadcasting. Much more radio time was devoted to high-quality discussion programs and to classical music, especially after the introduction of static-free frequency modulation (FM) transmission.

On the other hand, the entertainment offered on television was generally abominable. Uninspired and vulgar plays, routine variety shows, reruns of third-rate movies, giveaway programs, and quiz programs apparently designed to reveal the ignorance of the average citizen consumed the lion's share of TV time. Most sets had poor acoustical qualities, making them very inferior instruments for listening to good music. Educational programs were too often relegated to inconvenient periods, and there were not enough of them. Yet children found television especially fascinating, remaining transfixed before the TV screen when—their elders said—they should have been out of doors or curled up with a book.

Another defect of television's virtues was its capacity for influencing the opinions and feelings of viewers. Its commercial possibilities quickly displayed themselves, with the result that the insistent and strident claims of advertisers punctuated every program with monotonous regularity. Then politicians discovered that no other device or method approached television as a means of reaching large numbers of voters with an illusion of intimacy. But television time was extremely expensive; only candidates who possessed or had access to huge sums could afford to use the medium, obviously a dangerous state of affairs in a democracy. In addition, television put a premium on appearances, real and contrived. The sudden tendency of movie actors to seek political office (Governor Ronald Reagan and Senator George Murphy of California being pioneer examples) was undoubtedly a by-product of the use of television in politics.

Poverty Amid Plenty

In spite of the nation's prosperity and the vitality of its society, a major problem was the persistence of poverty. During the New Deal, Franklin Roosevelt had shocked the country by claiming that one-third of the nation was "ill-housed, ill-clad, ill-nourished." Actually, Roosevelt had underestimated the extent of American poverty. If it is fair to assume that a family of four with an annual income of less than $4,000 in current dollars is poor, then two-thirds of the population fell into that category in 1937. Nor did the New Deal produce any dramatic change in this situation; it was World War II that caused the really significant reduction of American poverty. Nevertheless, 37 per cent of the population still fell below the level of income necessary for a decent existence in 1947. During the prosperous postwar years this percentage shrank still further. In 1960, however, between one-fifth and one-fourth of all American families (perhaps 40 million persons) were still living on less than $4,000 a year. During the sixties, more rapid progress in the "war" on poverty was made, and by the end of the decade only about 11 per cent of the populace was poor. Yet over 20 million people remained in that category.

That so many could be poor in an "affluent" society was deplorable, but not difficult to explain. In any community a certain number of persons cannot support themselves because of physical incapacity, low intelligence, or psychological difficulties. There were also in the United States whole regions, the best-known being the Appalachian area, which had been by-passed by economic development and no longer provided their inhabitants with adequate economic opportunities. As we have seen, the increasingly rigorous demands of American industry for skills and the revolution in agriculture aggravated the poverty problem.

In addition, certain less obvious influences were at work. Poverty is naturally more prevalent among the old and the young than among those in the prime of life: in the postwar decades these two groups were growing more rapidly than any other. Social security payments amounted to far less than an elderly person needed to maintain himself decently, and some of the poorest workers, such as agricultural laborers, were not covered by the system to begin with. Unemployment was about twice as prevalent among youths in their late teens as in the nation as a whole. With the movement of the middle class to the suburbs, poverty became, in the words of Michael Harrington, whose book *The Other America* (1962) did much to call attention to the problem, "less visible" to those well-meaning citizens whose energies had to be mobilized if it was to be eradicated. Furthermore, the poor were becoming alienated from society, less hopeful, more resigned to their fate. In earlier times most of the poor were recent immigrants, believers in the American dream of rags-to-riches, strivers who

DORRENCE HOWELL AND HARYOU-ACT

Bar, with Pusher and Addict, *painted in 1968 by 18-year-old Dorrence Howell, is an interpretation of Harlem, New York's black ghetto, as viewed by one of its residents. Howell was enrolled in a commercial art workshop that was established in Harlem in 1964 under the auspices of the federal government's anti-poverty program.*

accepted their low status as temporary. The modern poor, many studies indicated, tended to lack motivation; they felt trapped by their condition and gave up. In the slums, sociologist Christopher Jencks has written, "young people are not seizing the opportunities. . . . Too many are dropping out of school before graduation (more than half in many slums)."

Poverty exacted a heavy price, both from its victims and from society. Statistics indicated the relationship between low income and bad health. Only about 4 per cent of persons from families with over $8,000 a year (the median for the nation) were chronically ill, whereas 8 per cent of those in the $2–4,000 bracket and 16.5 per cent of those with less than $2,000 were so afflicted. Mental illness also varied inversely with income, as did alcoholism and drug addiction. A study by a team of psychiatrists revealed that the poor "[are] rigid, suspicious . . . prone to depression, have feelings of futility, lack of belongingness . . . and a lack of trust in others." Crime was also connected with poverty. Thus, aside from the cost of direct relief, the well-to-do majority suffered in a variety of ways because of the poor, to say nothing of the general national waste of human potential involved.

The major federal effort to eradicate poverty was the Economic Opportunity Act of 1964, which set up a mélange of programs, including a Job Corps similar to the New Deal Civilian Conservation Corps, a community action program to finance local efforts, an educational program for small children (Project Head Start), and a system for training the unskilled unemployed and for lending money to small businessmen in poor areas. Steadily increasing sums—as much as $2 billion a year—were spent under this act, with mixed results: much of the money was wasted, some even stolen, but many poor people were benefited. Medicare and increases in social security payments also helped many of the aged poor.

Race Relations

Poverty was intimately related to the vexing problem of race relations. In 1960 a quarter of the poor were nonwhite, although nonwhites comprised only 11 per cent of the population.

TOM HOLLYMAN, PHOTO RESEARCHERS

"From my Christian background I gained my ideals," Martin Luther King, Jr., said, "and from Gandhi my operational technique." At right is a civil rights demonstration photographed in Birmingham, Alabama.

The average Negro earned only slightly more than half of what the average white earned; twice as large a percentage were unemployed. Half of New York City's million Negroes lived below the minimum subsistence level. Between 1960 and 1968, 17 million white Americans escaped from poverty as officially defined; only 3 million blacks did so. Yet, obviously, the racial problem was not solely an economic one. Deep-seated prejudices blighted the lives of even those Negroes who were relatively well off.

During the fifties and sixties the pent-up resentments of Negroes against this prejudice burst forth in a grass-roots drive for civil rights. The legal assault on school desegregation had been carefully planned by the NAACP, but the hopes roused by *Brown v. Board of Education of Topeka* inspired a few Negroes to act spontaneously against the system and when they did, thousands of others rushed to join them. This phenomenon first occurred in the tightly segregated city of Montgomery, Alabama. On the evening of December 1, 1955, Mrs. Rosa Parks boarded a Montgomery bus on her way home from work. She dutifully took a seat toward the rear as law and custom required, but after white workers and shoppers had filled the forward sec-

CHARLES MOORE, BLACK STAR

tion of the bus the driver ordered her to give up her place. She refused, having suddenly made up her mind, she later recalled, "never to move again."

Mrs. Parks was arrested. The Negroes of Montgomery, led by a young Baptist clergyman, Martin Luther King, Jr., promptly organized a boycott of the buses. For a full year they refused to ride and finally, after a Supreme Court ruling in their favor, Montgomery desegregated its public transportation system. This success encouraged blacks elsewhere in the South to band together against the caste system. It also made King, who preached civil disobedience as the best way to destroy segregation, a national figure. His organization, the Southern Christian Leadership Conference, moved into the forefront of the civil rights movement, and in 1964 his work won him the Nobel peace prize.

Other new organizations also joined in the struggle, most notably the Congress of Racial Equality (CORE) and the Student Nonviolent Coordinating Committee (SNCC). However, the most significant developments resulted from the actions of ordinary individuals, chiefly students. In February 1960 four black students in Greensboro, North Carolina, sat down at a segregated lunch counter in a local five-and-ten and refused to leave when they were denied service. Their "sit-in," a tiny defiance in itself, sparked a national movement. CORE rushed field workers to Greensboro, students in dozens of other southern towns and cities copied their example, until, by late 1961, over 70,000 persons had participated in sit-ins and over a hundred lunch counters had been desegregated.

In May 1961 another group of Negro and white foes of segregation organized a "freedom ride" to test the effectiveness of federal regulations prohibiting discrimination in interstate transportation. Boarding buses in Washington, they traveled across the South, heading for New Orleans. In Alabama they ran into trouble: at Anniston racists set fire to their bus, in Birmingham they were assaulted by a mob. Quickly other groups of freedom riders descended on the South, many deliberately seeking imprisonment in order to test local segregation ordinances in the courts. Repeatedly, these actions resulted in the breaking down of legal racial barriers.

The civil rights crusade soon spread to the North. Negroes, often joined by sympathetic whites, boycotted stores that refused to hire members of their race and picketed construction sites where black workers were not employed. In New York City some militants organized "rent strikes" to call attention to the noxious condition of Harlem tenements and school boycotts to protest against the de facto segregation that existed in predominantly black neighborhoods. The nationwide impact of the "Freedom Now" crusade was highlighted in August 1963 when 200,000 persons participated in an impressive "March on Washington" to demand racial equality. The orderly nature of the immense throng that gathered before the Lincoln Memorial and the evident sincerity of all concerned had a considerable impact upon public opinion.

The passage of the Civil Rights Act of 1964 after President Kennedy's assassination seemed like a major step forward, but the forces resisting change remained formidable. In the spring of 1965 peaceful Negro demonstrators in Selma, Alabama, were brutally assaulted by state policemen wielding clubs and tossing canisters of tear gas into their ranks. Liberal opinion was shocked as never before; thousands descended upon Selma from all over the nation to demonstrate their sympathy and support for American blacks. Congress passed still another civil rights act, giving the federal government power to send officials into the South to register black voters. Another law, passed in 1968, took important steps in the direction of outlawing discrimination in the sale and rental of housing, and imposed stiff criminal penalties on persons found guilty of interfering with anyone's civil rights.

Yet in spite of and to an extent because of civil rights legislation, racial conflict remained America's most serious domestic problem. As in so many other aspects of modern life, progress itself caused new difficulties to arise. Official recognition of past injustices made Negroes more insistent that all discrimination be ended, and the very process of righting past wrongs gave them the strength to carry on their fight more vigorously.

Black militancy, building steadily during the war and postwar years, had long been ignored by the white majority, but in the middle sixties it burst forth so powerfully that the most smug and obtuse white citizens had to accept its existence. Negro involvement in black nationalist movements was as old as the Republic. From the early black supporters of African colonization schemes through the late-19th-century efforts of men like Bishop Henry Turner and the 20th-century movement of Marcus Garvey, Negroes proud of their race and culture and contemptuous of white prejudices had urged their fellows to reject "American" society and all it stood for. In the 1950's and 1960's, however, black nationalism became a far more potent force than ever before. The followers of Elijah Muhammad, leader of the Black Muslim movement, disliked the dominant white majority so intensely that they favored racial separation, demanding that a part of the United States be set aside for the exclusive use of Negroes. These men rejected Christianity as "a white man's religion." They urged their followers to be industrious, thrifty, and abstemious, but they also urged them to view all white men with suspicion and hatred. "This white government has ruled us and given us plenty hell, but the time has arrived that you taste a little of your own hell," Elijah Muhammad said. "There are many of my poor black ignorant brothers . . . preaching the ignorant and lying stuff that you should love your enemy. What fool can love his enemy?"

Out of the Black Muslim movement came one of the most remarkable Americans of the 20th century, Malcolm X. Born Malcolm Little in 1925, son of a Baptist minister who was an organizer for Marcus Garvey's Universal Negro Improvement Association, he grew up in poverty in Michigan. At 15 he moved to Boston, then to New York's Harlem. For several years he lived on the edge of the underworld, taking and selling narcotics, working in the numbers racket, acting as a procurer for prostitutes. Soon he was carrying a gun. He became, as he later explained, "a true hustler—uneducated, unskilled at anything honorable . . . exploiting any prey that presented itself." At the age of 21 he was convicted of stealing a watch and sentenced to ten years in jail.

While in prison he was converted to the Black Muslim faith. He cast off his dissolute ways, and after being paroled in 1952, he rose rapidly in the

BERT SHAVITZ, PIX

Calling for black separatism, Malcolm X told an interviewer in 1964, "The Negro [must] develop his character and his culture in accord with his own nature."

Muslim hierarchy. A brilliant speaker and organizer, he preached the standard Muslim doctrine, a combination of idealism and hate. "Let us rid ourselves of immoral habits and God will be with us to protect and guide us," he told a Harlem audience in 1960. But he also said: "For the white man to ask the black man if he hates him is just like the rapist asking the *raped*, or the wolf asking the *sheep*, 'Do you hate me?' "

Gradually, however, Malcolm became disillusioned with Elijah Muhammad, especially after the 67-year-old Muslim leader was accused by two of his former secretaries of fathering their four illegitimate children. The militant black comedian, Dick Gregory, among others, told Malcolm that Muhammad was unworthy of his support and urged him to break with the Black Muslims. A trip through the Arab world served further to broaden his horizons, and in 1964 he left the Muslims and founded his own Organization of Afro-American Unity. While continuing to stress black self-help and the militant defense of black rights, he now saw the crusade as part of a larger struggle for all human rights. "What we do . . . helps all people everywhere who are fighting against oppression," he said. In February 1965, however, Malcolm was assassinated by Black Muslim gunmen. His posthumously published *Autobiography*, which tells his story vividly, has already become a classic.

Soon after the death of Malcolm X, Negro militants found a slogan: "Black Power." The term was given national currency by Stokely Carmichael, chairman of SNCC, in 1966. The time for white involvement in the fight for Negro rights has ended, Carmichael announced. "If we are to proceed toward true liberation, we must set ourselves off from white people." Since whites "cannot relate to the black experience," the movement "should be black-staffed, black-controlled, and black-financed." Black Power caught on swiftly among militant Negroes; the next year, at Newark, New Jersey, a national Black Power conference brought together some 400 leaders committed to the concept. The movement, however, deeply troubled white liberals because of its "refusal to discriminate between degrees of inequity" among whites and because the liberals feared that it would needlessly antagonize white conservatives. Since Negroes made up only slightly more than ten per cent of the population, liberals argued that any attempt to obtain racial justice through the use of naked power was sure to fail.

Meanwhile, black anger erupted in a series of destructive urban riots. The most important of these occurred in Watts, the black ghetto of Los Angeles, in August 1965. A trivial incident—policemen halted a Negro motorist who seemed to be drunk and attempted to give him a sobriety test—brought thousands of protesting blacks into the streets. The neighborhood almost literally exploded, and for six days Watts was swept by fire, looting, and bloody fighting between local residents and 15,000 National Guardsmen, called up to assist the police. Order was restored only after 34 persons had been killed, over 850 wounded, 3,100 arrested. Property damage in Watts was staggering, amounting to nearly $200 million.

The following summer saw similar outbursts in New York, Chicago, and other cities. In 1967, during another "long, hot summer," still more riots broke out, the most serious in Newark, where 25 were killed, and Detroit, where the death toll came to 43 and where looting and arson assumed monstrous proportions.

Then, in April 1968, the revered Negro leader, Martin Luther King, apostle of nonviolence, was murdered in Memphis, Tennessee, by a white man, James Earl Ray.* Blacks in more than 100 cities swiftly unleashed their righteous anger in paroxysms of burning and looting. The whole nation was shocked and profoundly depressed: the Negroes' anger was understandable even to those who would not condone their actions, and the death of King appeared to destroy the hope that his doctrine of pacific appeal to reason and right could solve the racial problem.

Public fear and puzzlement led to many investigations of the causes of these riots, the most important being that of the commission headed by Governor Otto Kerner of Illinois, which President Johnson appointed after the murder of Dr. King. The conclusions of most of these studies were complex but fairly clear. Race riots had a long history in the United States, but the outbursts of the 1960's were without precedent. Earlier troubles usually began with attacks by whites, which naturally led to black counterattacks. Riots of the Watts type were begun by blacks, and the fighting was mostly between blacks and law enforcement officers trying to control them; white citizens tended to avoid the centers of trouble, and blacks seldom ranged outside their own neighborhoods.

The rioters, in general, were expressing frustration and despair; their resentment was directed more at the social system than at individuals. As the Kerner commission put it, the basic cause was an attitude of mind, the "white racism" which deprived blacks of access to good jobs, crowded them into terrible slums, and, especially for the young, eroded all hope of escape from such misery. Ghettos bred crime and depravity—as slums always have—but the passive, complacent refusal of the white majority adequately to invest its wealth and energy in helping ghetto residents, or even truly to admit that the black poor deserved help, made the modern Negro slum unbearable. While the ghettos expanded, the white middle classes in the great cities tended more and more to "flee" to the suburbs or to call upon the police "to maintain law and order," a euphemism for cracking down mercilessly on every form of deviant black behavior no matter how obvious the connection between that behavior and the slum environment.

The victims of this racism employed violence not so much to force change as to obtain release; it was a way of destroying what they could not stomach. Thus the concentration of the riots in the ghettos themselves, the smashing, Sampson-like, of the source of degradation even when this meant self-destruction. When fires broke out in black districts, the very firemen who tried to extinguish them were often showered with bottles and bricks, even shot at, while above the roar of the flames and the hiss of steam rose the apocalyptic chant: "*Burn, baby, burn!*"

The most frightening aspect of these developments was their tendency to polarize society still more sharply on racial lines. Advocates of Black Power became more determined than ever to separate themselves from white influence. They exasperated white supporters of school desegregation by demanding schools of their own. Extremists formed the Black Panther party, collected weapons to resist the police. "Shoot, don't loot," the radical H. Rap Brown advised all who would listen. The Panthers demanded public compensation for injustices done to Negroes in the past, pointing out that after World War II, West Germany had made such payments to Jews to make up for Hitler's persecutions, and in 1968, they nominated Eldridge Cleaver, a convict on parole, for President. Although Cleaver was an articulate and intelligent man, whose autobiographical *Soul on Ice,* written while in prison, had attracted much praise, his nomination for the Presidency widened the racial breach still further.

*Ray fled to England, but he was eventually apprehended, extradited, convicted, and sentenced to 99 years in prison.

On the other hand, both black violence and black separatism hardened the resistance of many whites against further efforts to aid Negroes. Middle-class city residents often resented what seemed the "favoritism" of the federal government and of many state and local administrations, which sought to provide blacks with new economic opportunities and social benefits. Efforts to desegregate ghetto schools, involving the transportation of black children, and white ones too, out of their local neighborhoods, was a particularly bitter cause of conflict. Such persons, already subjected to the pressures caused by inflation, specialization, and rapid change that were undermining social solidarity, and worried by the sharp rise in urban crime rates and in welfare costs, found black radicalism infuriating. In the face of the greatest national effort in history to aid Negroes, the Negroes (they said) were displaying not merely ingratitude but contempt. In some instances, local police forces searched out and shot down Panthers without real provocation, which further embittered black militants and caused moderates of both races to fear that an organized campaign against black radicals was in progress.

Yet it was impossible to predict what the future would bring. Racial controversies were as heated as ever, but American Negroes had achieved by 1970 gains that would have seemed inconceivable a generation earlier. President Johnson had placed a Negro on the Supreme Court (Thurgood Marshall, tactician of the NAACP's legal fight for school desegregation), and another in his Cabinet (Robert Weaver, Secretary of Housing and Urban Development). The first Negro since Reconstruction (Edward W. Brooke of Massachusetts) had been elected to the U.S. Senate. More than 518,000 black children were attending schools with whites in the southern states by 1968, and more than 3.1 million adult southern blacks (62 per cent of the black voting-age population) were registered to vote. Above all, American Negroes had achieved real self-awareness. They continued to differ among themselves in style and tactics, as all men do. Some still sought accommodation; others favored confrontation; others outright revolution. But the attitude of mind that ran from the lonely Denmark Vesey, to Frederick Douglass, to W.E.B. Du Bois had become the black consensus. The old complacency of blacks as well as whites was dead. Vast philosophical differences separated modern Negroes, just as they separated modern whites, but black Americans had become a formidable force in society and they were determined to exercise that force like any other group.

Education: Youth in Revolt

Young people, particularly shaken by the dilemmas and conflicts of the times, frequently complained that the educational system poorly suited many of their needs. This was still another paradox of modern life, for in many respects the American educational system was the best (it was certainly the most comprehensive) in the world. By 1970 nearly 59 million students were attending American schools, and public expenditures for education exceeded $35 billion. Approximately three of every four American youths were completing high school, and the annual number earning college and university degrees had approached 1 million. Teachers' salaries were rising; countless interesting educational experiments were in progress. Yet dissatisfaction reigned.

After World War I, under the impact of Freudian psychology, the emphasis in elementary education shifted from using the schools as instruments of social change, as John Dewey had recommended, to using them to promote the emotional development of the students. "Child-centered" educators played down academic achievement in favor of "adjustment." The training they offered probably stimulated the students' imaginations and may possibly have improved their psychological well-being, but observers soon noted that poor work habits, fuzzy thinking, and plain ignorance inevitably resulted. The "educationists" insisted that they were not abandoning traditional academic subjects, yet they certainly de-emphasized them. "We've built a sort of halo around reading, writing, and arithmetic," one school principal explained. To say that "every student must know the multiplication tables before graduation," he added, "attaches more importance to those tables than I'm willing to accord them."

The demands of society for rigorous intellectual achievement made this distortion of progressive education increasingly less satisfactory in the modern world. After World War II, critics like the historian Arthur E. Bestor of the University of Illinois began a concerted assault on the system. With books like *Educational Wastelands* (1953) and *The Restoration of Learning* (1955), Bestor caused a powerful stir in educational circles. More important in reaching the general public was James B. Conant, former president of Harvard. His book *The American High School Today* (1959) sold nearly half a million copies and his later studies of teacher education and the special problems of urban schools attracted wide attention. Conant flayed the schools for their failure to teach English grammar and composition effectively, for neglecting foreign languages, and for ignoring the needs of both the brightest and the slowest of their students. He insisted that teachers' colleges should place subject matter above educational methodology in their curricula.

The success of the Russians in launching their first "Sputnik" in 1957 greatly increased the influence of men like Bestor and Conant. To match this achievement, the United States needed thousands of engineers and scientists, but the schools were not turning out enough graduates prepared to study science and engineering at the college level. Suddenly the schools were under enormous pressure, for with more and more young people desiring to go to college, the colleges were raising their admission standards. As a result, the "traditionalists" gained the initiative, academic subjects a revived prestige. The National Defense Education Act of 1958 supplied a powerful stimulus by allocating funds for upgrading work in the sciences, foreign languages, and other subjects, and for expanding guidance services and experimenting with television and other new teaching devices.

However, other developments, most notably concern for improving the training of the children of disadvantaged minority groups (Mexican-Americans, Puerto Ricans, and Indians, as well as blacks), pulled the system in a different direction. Many of these children lived in horrible slums, often in broken homes. They lacked the incentives and training that most white middle-class children received in the family. Many of them did poorly in school, partly because they were poorly motivated, partly because the system was poorly adapted to their needs. The Elementary and Secondary Education Act of 1965, the first general federal-aid-to-education law in history, concentrated large sums on upgrading the training of students in urban slums and in impoverished rural areas in an effort to deal with this problem. But catering to the requirements of such children threatened to undermine the high standards being set for other children. Especially in the great cities, where the blacks and other minorities were becoming steadily more numerous, many schools failed to serve adequately either the disadvantaged or those fairly well off. Added to the strains imposed by racial conflicts, the effect was to create the most serious crisis American public education had ever faced.

The post-Sputnik stress on academic achievement also profoundly affected higher education. "Prestige" institutions like Harvard, Yale, Columbia, Stanford, Swarthmore, and a dozen other colleges, inundated by floods of first-rate applicants, ceased to be superior finishing schools for scions of rich and socially prominent families and became training centers for the nation's intellectual elite. The federal and state governments, together with private philanthropic institutions such as the Carnegie Corporation and the Ford Foundation, poured millions into dormitory and classroom construction, teacher education, and scholarship funds. At the graduate level, the federal government's post-Sputnik research and development program, administered by the National Science Foundation, established in 1950, provided billions of dollars for laboratories, equipment, professors' salaries, and student scholarships. In 1957 the United States spent $3.4 billion on research and development, in 1964 $15.2 billion. Of these sums, universities received about 13 per cent.

Directly or indirectly, such infusions affected every department of the great universities. Expansion created a grave shortage of professors, leading to higher professorial salaries. Competition for talent developed on an international scale. In Great Britain, for example, alarmists warned of a "brain drain" caused by the migration of top-flight British professors to American institutions.

At the same time, population growth and the demands of society for specialized intellectual skills were causing American colleges to burst at the seams. In 1870 only 1.7 per cent of those in the 17–21 year age group were in college, in 1970 about 40 per cent. To bridge the gap between high school and college, the two-year junior college proliferated. Almost unknown before 1920, there were 600-odd junior colleges by the late sixties. They were the most rapidly growing educational institutions in the country, their enrollment leaping from about 300,000 in 1955 to over 840,000 in 1965.

For a time after the war, the expansion of higher education took place with remarkable smoothness. Thousands of veterans took advantage of the G.I. bill to earn college degrees, and more thousands of young men and women whose parents had not gone to college seized the new opportunity eagerly. During the 1950's the general mood among students was complacency. But in the 1960's the mood changed. For one thing, a college degree was ceasing to seem like a privilege or opportunity and becoming a necessity. Few interesting or remunerative careers were open to those who did not have one; thus many students began to look upon higher education as a chore, still another academic hurdle to be surmounted, a restriction on freedom of choice more than the gateway to a freer, more fruitful existence.

Moreover, many of the universities, each with its tens of thousands of students, were in danger of becoming soulless educational factories. Especially for undergraduates (who needed it most), the close contact between professor and student tended to disappear in these institutions. Student dissatisfaction increased rapidly under such conditions and often led to protests, riots, and other troubles. The first great outburst of unrest convulsed the University of California at Berkeley in the fall of 1964. Angry students staged sit-down strikes in university buildings, organized a "filthy speech" campaign, and generally disorganized the institution over a period of weeks. Hundreds were arrested; conservatives in the state legislature threatened reprisals; the faculty became involved in the controversy; and the crisis led eventually to the resignation of the president of the University of California, Clark Kerr.

Still more significant in altering the student mood was the frustration that so many of them felt with the colleges and with the larger society. Rapid change was making numerous traditional aspects of college life outmoded, yet like all institutions the colleges adapted only slowly to new conditions. The so-called "now" generation swiftly lost patience with the glacial pace of campus adjustment. Regulations that students had formerly merely grumbled about now evoked determined, even violent opposition. Dissidents denounced parietal rules that restricted their personal lives, such as prohibitions on the use of alcohol and the banning of members of the opposite sex from dormitories. They complained that required courses inhibited their intellectual development. They demanded a share in the government of their institutions, long the private preserve of administrators and professors.

Beyond their specific dissatisfactions, they developed an almost total refusal to endure anything they considered wrong. The knotty social problems which made their elders gravitate toward moderation led these students to become intransigent absolutists. The line between right and wrong became for radicals as sharply defined as the edge of a ruler. Racial prejudice was evil: it must be totally eradicated. War in a nuclear age was insane: armies must be disbanded. Poverty amid plenty was an abomination: eliminate poverty *now*. To the counsel that evil can only be eliminated gradually, that misguided persons must be persuaded to mend their ways, that compromise was the path to true progress, they responded with scorn. Extremists among them, observing the weaknesses of American civilization, adopted a nihilistic position–the only way to deal with a "rotten" society was to destroy it; reform was impossible; constructive compromise corrupting.

Critics found the radical students infantile, old-fashioned, and authoritarian: infantile because

UPI

Prelude to violence: Behind a barrage of tear gas, National Guardsmen move against antiwar demonstrators on the campus of Ohio's Kent State University in May 1970. A few minutes after this picture was taken, the Guardsmen, later claiming their lives were endangered by the demonstrators, opened fire, killing four and wounding nine.

they could not tolerate frustration or delay, old-fashioned because their absolutist ideas had been exploded by several generations of philosophers and scientists, authoritarian because they rejected majority rule, believed that the end justified the means, and would not tolerate views in disagreement with their own. The radicals were seldom very numerous in any college, but they were tightly knit (in organizations such as the Students for a Democratic Society) and totally committed. On campus after campus in the late sixties, they roused large numbers of their less extreme fellows to take part in "sit-ins" and other disruptive tactics. Frequently, faculties and administrators played into their hands, being so offended by their methods and manners that they refused to recognize the legitimacy of some of their demands. At Columbia, in 1968, SDS and black students—the latter sharply disassociating themselves from the former—occupied university buildings and refused to leave unless a series of "non-negotiable" demands (including such matters as the university's involvement in secret military research and its relations with minority groups living in the Columbia neighborhood) were granted. When, after long delays, President Grayson Kirk called in the police to clear the buildings, a riot broke out in which dozens of bystanders were clubbed and beaten. General student revulsion against the use of the police led to the resignation of Kirk and to many university reforms. A similar incident convulsed Harvard in 1969; indeed literally hundreds of colleges were shaken by riots and lesser disturbances. In May 1970 four demonstrating students at Kent State University in Ohio were killed by National Guardsmen, and two black students were shot down by Mississippi state police at Jackson State.*

The turmoil seemed endless. Extremist groups were torn by factionalism and found it increasingly difficult to mobilize mass campus support, but—it was the bane of modern society—the ability of small groups to disrupt did not diminish.

One heartening aspect of the situation was the great increase of black students in the colleges and their generally responsible, if radical, way of handling themselves. Almost without exception, the colleges tried to increase the number of blacks enrolled, even when it meant allocating large percentages of their scholarship funds and lowering academic requirements to compensate for the poor preparation many of these students had received in the schools. Between 1964 and 1968 Negro enrollments increased by 85 per cent, to 434,000. In 1969 the eight Ivy League colleges, leaders in the movement, accepted over 1,100 black applicants in a combined freshman class of only 8,080.

Black college students tended to keep to themselves, and they wanted more control over all aspects of their education than did the typical white. Intent on learning about the Negro past and on instilling pride in this heritage among all of their race, they called for the creation of Black Studies programs, taught and administered by blacks, and often under student control. Achievement of these goals was difficult, both because of the shortage of Negro teachers and because professors—even some Negro professors—considered student control of appointments and curricula unwise and in violation of the principles of academic freedom. Nevertheless, the general academic response to black demands was accommodating; "confrontations" occurred frequently but were usually resolved by negotiation. Unlike white radical students, the blacks tended to confine their demands to matters directly related to local conditions. Generalization is difficult at such short range, but probably the majority of academics drew a distinction between black radicals, whose actions they found understandable even when they could not in conscience approve of them, and white radicals, most of whom they thought self-indulgent, overly pampered, or emotionally disturbed.

*In each of these incidents a number of other students were wounded. The Kent State tragedy was caused by inexperienced Guardsmen losing their heads when provoked by rock-throwers, but the Jackson State killings were carried out in cold blood, apparently because the students were black rather than because of their disruptive activities.

The War in Vietnam

All the problems confronting Americans in the 1960's were inextricably entangled with the war in South Vietnam. When Vietnam was divided after the defeat of the French in 1954 and the United States began supplying aid to Bao Dai's anticommunist regime, a handful of American military "advisers" were sent in to train a South Vietnamese army. After Bao Dai was deposed, American aid and "advice" were increased, but President Ngo Dinh Diem was unable to establish a stable government. Rebel forces, called Vietcong, soon controlled large sections of the country; in 1956 Diem refused to permit the Vietnam-wide elections called for by the international settlement of 1954, which he felt he could not win. Gradually, the Vietcong, drawing supplies from North Vietnam and indirectly from China and the Soviet Union, increased in strength. As they did, more American money and more military advisers were sent to bolster Diem's regime.

President Kennedy continued this policy and by the end of 1961 there were 3,200 American military men in the country. Kennedy insisted that the South Vietnamese themselves must win what he called "their war," but by the time of his assassination, the American military presence had risen to over 16,000. No combat troops were involved, however, and only 120 Americans had so far been killed.

At first President Johnson did not change Kennedy's tactics significantly. But in August 1964, after some North Vietnamese gunboats had fired on American destroyers in the Gulf of Tonkin, he demanded, and in an air of crisis obtained, an authorization from Congress to "repel any armed attack against the forces of the United States and to prevent further aggression." With this blank check and buttressed by his sweeping defeat of Goldwater in the 1964 Presidential election, Johnson took a fateful step. Shortly after his inauguration he began to send *combat* troops to South Vietnam and to unleash air attacks against targets in both South and North Vietnam. His "escalation" of the American commitment occurred piecemeal and apparently without plan. By the end of 1964, 184,000 Americans were in the field; a year later, 385,000; after another year, 485,000; and by the middle of 1968, the number exceeded 538,000. Each increase was met by corresponding increases from the other side. Russia and China stepped up their aid, and thousands of North Vietnamese regulars filtered across the 17th parallel to join the Vietcong insurgents. The United States was engaged in a full-scale war, yet war was never declared: Johnson based his decisions on the highly controversial Gulf of Tonkin resolution.

From the beginning, the war bitterly divided the American people. Defenders of the President's policy emphasized the nation's moral responsibility to resist aggression, its supposed treaty obligations under the SEATO pact, and what President Eisenhower had called the "domino" theory (based on an analogy with the western powers' failure to resist Hitler before 1939), which hy-

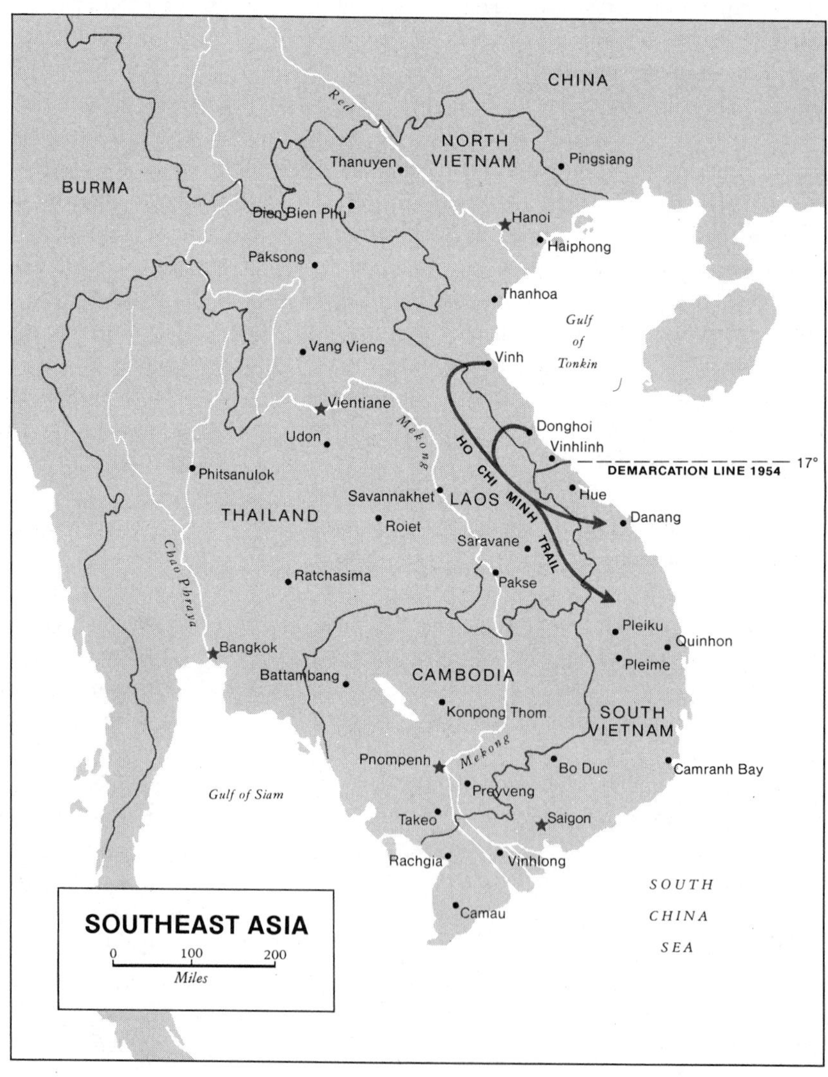

The London Observer *suggested that President Johnson was playing with fire in Asia: "All I'm trying to do is to limit our conflict to this small area."*

ABU ABRAHAM, *The Observer*

pothesized that if the communists were allowed to "take over" one country, they would soon take its neighbors, then *their* neighbors, and so on until the whole world had been conquered. They insisted that the United States was not an aggressor in Vietnam, stressing Johnson's oft-expressed willingness to negotiate a general withdrawal of "foreign" forces from the country, which the communists repeatedly rejected.

Johnson's critics, popularly called "doves,"* argued that the struggle between the South Vietnamese government and the Vietcong was a civil war in which Americans should not meddle. They stressed the repressive, reactionary character of the Diem government and of those which followed it after Diem was assassinated in 1963 as proof that the war was not a contest between democracy and communism. They objected to the massive aerial bombings (more explosives were dropped on Vietnam between 1964 and 1968 than on Germany and Japan combined in World War II), to the use of napalm and of other chemical weapons such as the defoliants that were sprayed on forests and crops, wreaking havoc among noncombatants, and to the direct killing of civilians by American troops. They discounted the domino theory, pointing both to the growing communist split into Chinese and Russian camps, and to the traditional hostility of all Vietnamese to the Chinese, which they claimed made Chinese expansion into Southeast Asia unlikely. And they deplored both the heavy loss of American life—over 40,000 dead by 1970—and also the enormous cost in money, which came to exceed $20 billion a year. Besides being a major cause of the inflation of the 1960's, the war was diverting public funds from domestic programs aimed at solving the problems of poverty and race relations, at reducing pollution, at improving education and urban life.

Although President Johnson sometimes acted so deviously as to lead observers to talk of a "credibility gap" in his administration, there is little reason to doubt that he and his advisers, especially Secretary of State Dean Rusk, sincerely believed they were fighting in defense of freedom and democracy. There were, in short, moral arguments on both sides of the issue. What became increasingly clear as time passed and the costs mounted, was that an American military victory was impossible. Yet American military leaders were extraordinarily slow to grasp this fact. Repeatedly they advised the President that one more escalation (so many more soldiers, so many more air raids) would break the enemy's will to resist. Like the proverbial donkey plodding after the carrot on the stick, Johnson repeatedly followed their advice. And for a long time, as the polls demonstrated, a majority of the American people believed he was correct. All the forces of patriotism and pride, along with the hard-won "lessons" of 1931–39 and their stubborn refusal to admit that a mistake had been made, held them to this course.

*Supporters of the war were dubbed "hawks," but some of these also disapproved of the Johnson policy. Extremists wanted to extend ground action into North Vietnam, use nuclear weapons if necessary, and convert the conflict into a general war against China, perhaps even against Russia.

Election of 1968

Gradually, however, the doves increased in number. Students, for idealistic reasons and because they resented being drafted to fight in Vietnam; businessmen, alarmed by the effects of the war on the economy; and others for different reasons became increasingly dissatisfied with the President's policy. But as late as the fall of 1967 outspoken opposition to the war, in Congress and elsewhere, remained small. Then, in November 1967, Senator Eugene McCarthy of Wisconsin, a low-keyed, rather introspective man, never a leading figure in the Upper House, announced that he was a candidate for the 1968 Democratic Presidential nomination against Johnson, making opposition to the war his issue.

McCarthy had no real organization and few of the traditional political skills, nor did he seriously think he could be nominated. But he felt that someone must step forward to put the war issue before the voters. He prepared to campaign in the primaries. Suddenly, early in 1968, immediately on the heels of the latest announcement by the American military that the communists were about to crack, North Vietnam and Vietcong forces launched a general offensive against South Vietnamese cities to correspond with their Lunar New Year (Tet). Striking everywhere at once, they managed to hold parts of Saigon, the capital, for days; other cities fell entirely into their hands.

This Tet offensive was eventually thrown back, but it thoroughly discredited the American military. When General William C. Westmoreland described the Tet offensive as a communist defeat and asked for an additional 206,000 troops to follow up his "victory," American public opinion rebelled. McCarthy, who was campaigning in New Hampshire, at once became a formidable figure. Hundreds of students and other volunteers flocked to the state to ring doorbells and distribute leaflets in his behalf. When he polled an astounding 42 per cent of the vote in the Democratic primary and then went on to win the Wisconsin primary, President Johnson, acknowledging that he could no longer "unify" the country, withdrew as a candidate for re-election.

The political situation was monumentally confused. Before the New Hampshire primary, former Attorney General Robert F. Kennedy, brother of the slain President, had refused either to seek the Democratic nomination or support McCarthy, although he was opposed to the Johnson policy in Vietnam. After McCarthy's strong showing, Kennedy reversed himself and entered the race. Had he done so earlier, McCarthy might have withdrawn in his favor, for Kennedy had powerful political and popular support, but after New Hampshire, McCarthy quite naturally decided to remain in the contest. Vice President Hubert Humphrey, backed by Johnson, also announced his candidacy, although not until it was too late for him to run in the primaries.

Kennedy carried the primaries in Indiana and Nebraska, but McCarthy defeated him in Oregon. In the climactic contest in California, Kennedy won by a small margin. However, immediately after his victory speech in a Los Angeles hotel, he was assassinated by Sirhan Sirhan, a young Arab nationalist who had been incensed by Kennedy's support of Israel. In effect, Kennedy's death assured the nomination of Humphrey; most of the professional politicians distrusted McCarthy, who was indeed rather diffident and aloof for a politician, unwilling or unable to organize an effective campaign despite his articulateness, intelligence, and evident sincerity.

The contest for the Republican nomination was far less dramatic, although its outcome, the nomination of Richard M. Nixon, would have been hard to predict a few years earlier. After his defeat in the California gubernatorial election of 1962, Nixon appeared to have lost all chance of achieving his Presidential ambitions. He moved to New York City and joined a prominent law firm. However, he remained active in Republican affairs, making countless speeches and attending political meetings all over the country. In 1967 Governor George Romney of Michigan seemed the likely Republican nominee, but he failed to develop extensive support. Although Governor Nelson Rockefeller of New York was also widely mentioned, conservative Republicans would not forgive his refusal to help Goldwater in 1964, and he decided not to enter the race. Nixon announced his candidacy in February 1968, and after Romney withdrew in the midst of the New

UPI

Candidate Nixon at a press conference in 1968. Previously unskilled at press relations, Nixon sought to establish rapport with reporters in the campaign.

Hampshire contest, he swept the Republican primaries. Rockefeller belatedly declared himself a candidate, but by the time of the Republican National Convention in August, Nixon had a large majority of the delegates in his pocket and won an easy first-ballot victory.

He then astounded the country and dismayed liberals by choosing Governor Spiro T. Agnew of Maryland as his running mate. Aside from the fact that he had little national reputation ("Spiro who?" jokesters asked) Agnew had taken a tough, almost brutal stand on such matters as racial disturbances, urban crime, and other social problems. Nixon chose him primarily to attract southern votes; it was even said that right-wing southern leaders like Strom Thurmond of South Carolina had "dictated" Agnew's selection. Placating such men seemed necessary because Governor George C. Wallace of Alabama was making a determined bid to win enough electoral votes for his American Independent party to prevent either major party from obtaining a majority. Wallace was flagrantly anti-Negro and sure to attract wide southern and conservative support. His meetings drew large crowds all over the nation, and he was frequently cheered to the rafters when he denounced federal "meddling," the "coddling" of criminals, and the forced desegregation of schools. Wallace ridiculed intellectuals, planners, and any form of professional ability or mental distinction. Nixon's choice of Agnew seemed an effort to appeal to the very groups that Wallace was attracting—bigots, lower-middle-class white city dwellers, suburbanites, and the residents of small towns. This Republican strategy gravely disturbed liberals, and heightened the tension surrounding the Democratic convention, which met in Chicago in late August.

Humphrey-Johnson delegates controlled the convention. The Vice President had a solid liberal record on domestic issues, but he had supported Johnson's Vietnam policy with equal solidity. Those who could not stomach the Nixon-Agnew ticket but who opposed the war faced a difficult choice. Hordes of radicals and young activists descended upon Chicago to put pressure on the delegates to repudiate the Johnson Vietnam policy. In the tense and bitter atmosphere that resulted, the party hierarchy overreacted. The city government was dominated by Mayor Richard J. Daley, an old-fashioned political boss. He ringed the convention with barricades and policemen to protect it from disruption, a policy that was reasonable in purpose but which he carried out with foolish bravado and display. Inside the building, administration forces easily pushed through Humphrey and a war plank satisfactory to Johnson. Outside, the police, provoked it is true by the abusive language and violent behavior of radical demonstrators, tore into the crowds of

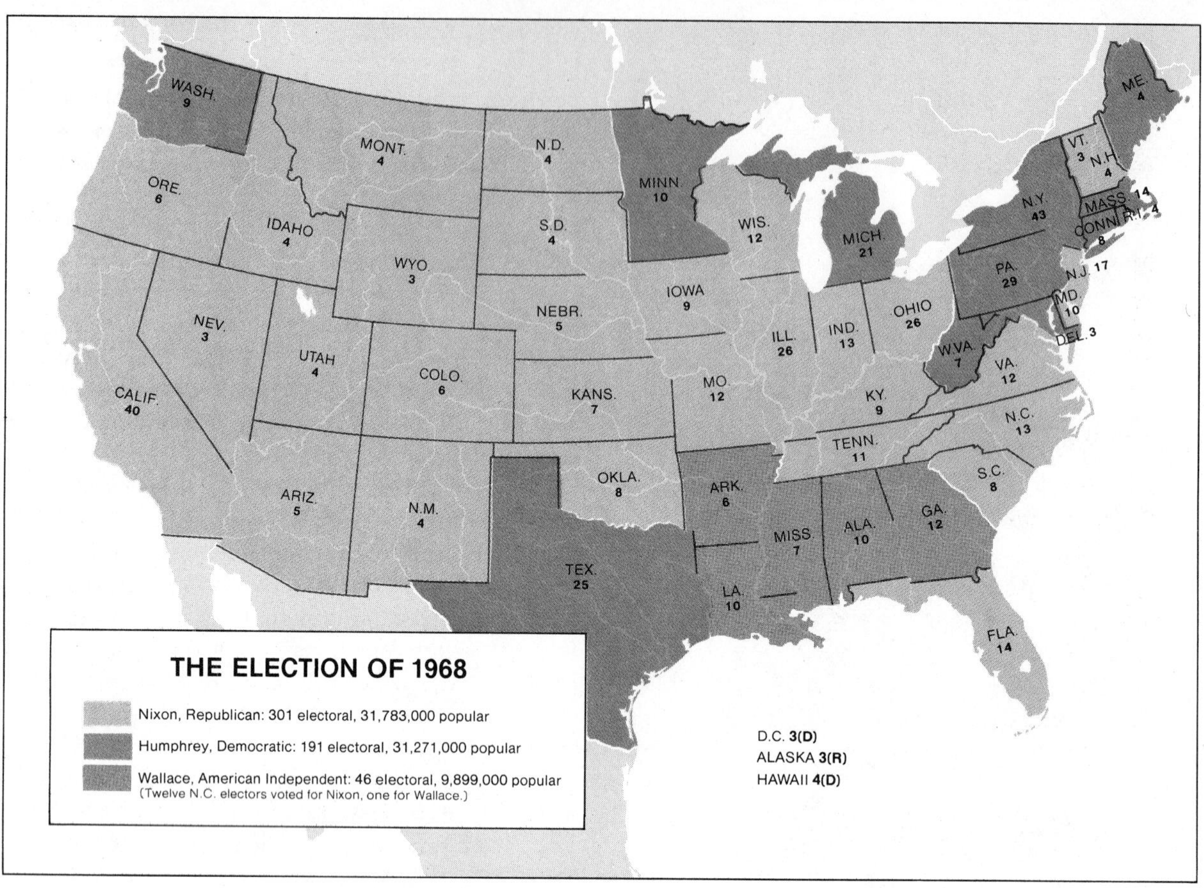

protestors, brutally beating dozens of them while millions watched in fascinated horror on television.

At first these dreadful developments seemed to benefit Nixon. The violence at Chicago strengthened the convictions of many persons that the tougher treatment of criminals and dissenters that he and Agnew were calling for was necessary, and those who were offended by the actions of the police tended to blame Humphrey. Nixon campaigned at a deliberate, dignified pace, stressing moderation, firm enforcement of the law, and his desire "to bring us together." Agnew, in a series of blunt, coarse speeches—critics, remembering Nixon's own political style in the era of Joseph McCarthy, called Agnew "Nixon's Nixon"—assaulted Humphrey, the Democrats, and left-wing dissident groups.

Humphrey's campaign was badly organized, the candidate subject to merciless heckling from antiwar audiences. But he endured this ordeal without losing his temper, and he displayed boundless, almost frantic (some said mindless) energy. He seemed far behind in the early stages, but gradually gained ground. Shortly before Election Day, President Johnson helped him greatly by suspending air attacks on North Vietnam, and in the long run the Republican strategy helped him too. Black voters and the urban poor had no practical choice but to vote Democratic. As a result, the popular vote was close. Nixon received slightly less than 31.8 million votes, Humphrey nearly 31.3 million. Nixon's Electoral College margin was, however, substantial—301 to 191. The remaining 46 went to Wallace, whose 9.9 million votes came to 13.5 per cent of the total. Despite Nixon's triumph, the Democrats retained control of both houses of Congress.

Nixon as President

When he took office in January 1969, Nixon projected an image of calm and deliberate statesmanship; he introduced no startling changes, demanded no important new legislation, and focused on reordering the cumbersome machinery of the federal bureaucracy. The major economic problem facing him, inflation, was primarily a result of the heavy military expenditures and "easy money" policies of the Johnson administration. Nixon cut federal spending and balanced the budget, while the Federal Reserve Board forced up interest rates in order to slow the expansion of the money supply. The aim of this strategy was to reduce the rate of economic growth without causing heavy unemployment or precipitating a recession (the word *depression* had apparently passed out of the vocabulary of economists). Even its supporters admitted that this policy would check inflation only slowly, and when prices continued to go up, there was mounting uneasiness and a continuation of labor's demands for wage increases. Nixon, however, displayed great firmness, and the weight of economic opinion supported his actions.

In handling other domestic issues, the President was less firm, sometimes appearing confused and ambivalent. In matters concerning poverty and race, for example, he advocated a bold plan for shifting the burden of welfare payments to the federal government and equalizing such payments in all the states. He even came out for a "minimum income" for poor families, which alarmed his conservative supporters. But he and his attorney general, John N. Mitchell, were so openly resistant to further federal efforts to force school desegregation upon reluctant local districts as to dismay southern moderates and northern liberals. And in his eagerness to add what he called "strict constructionists" to the Supreme Court, which he believed had swung too far to the left in such areas as race relations and the rights of persons accused of committing crimes, Nixon allowed himself to be drawn into two foolish confrontations with the Senate.

When Chief Justice Earl Warren retired from the Court in June 1969, Nixon named a respected conservative, Warren E. Burger, as the new Chief Justice, which caused no difficulties. But when he sought to fill the seat of Justice Abe Fortas, who had resigned under fire after it was learned that he had accepted fees from questionable sources while on the bench, he blundered. He first selected Judge Clement F. Haynesworth, Jr., of South Carolina, whom the Senate rejected because of his having failed to disqualify himself when cases involving corporations in which he had invested came before his court, and then Judge G. Harrold Carswell of Florida, who was turned down because of his alleged racist attitudes and because of his generally mediocre record. In the face of a mass of evidence, Nixon refused to believe that these nominations were rejected for the reasons stated; he declared that "no southern conservative" could run the "liberal" Senate gauntlet successfully, and to prevent the Senate from proving him wrong he nominated Harry A. Blackmun of Minnesota. Blackmun won the unanimous approval of the Senate, but Nixon's analysis was as incorrect as his political tactics were ineffective, and his prestige suffered accordingly.

Whatever his difficulties on the domestic front, Nixon considered foreign relations his major concern, the solution of the Vietnam problem his chief task. When the war in Southeast Asia first burst upon American consciousness in 1954, he had favored military intervention in keeping with the containment policy, but he went along with Eisenhower's decision merely to send in aid and advisers. As controversy over American policy developed, Nixon generally supported the actions of Presidents Kennedy and Johnson. During the 1968 campaign, he played down the Vietnam issue on the ground that he did not want to risk upsetting negotiations between the United States and North Vietnam, which had been going on in Paris, albeit without significant results, since May 1968. Basically he suggested nothing very different from what Johnson was doing, although he insisted he would end the war on "honorable" terms if elected.

In office, Nixon strove to make good on this promise. When the Paris negotiations, now expanded to include representatives of South Vietnam and the Vietcong, continued to show no progress, he offered a plan for a phased withdrawal of all non-South Vietnamese troops and for an internationally supervised election in South Vietnam. The North Vietnamese rejected this scheme, however, insisting that the United States withdraw all its forces unconditionally.

Their intransigence left the President in a difficult position. Probably the majority of Americans considered his proposal eminently fair, but with equal certainty a majority was unwilling to increase the scale of the fighting to compel the communists to accept it, and as the war dragged on, costs in men and money rising, the desire to extricate American troops from the conflict became more intense. However, large numbers would not face up to the consequences of gratifying this desire: ending the war on the communists' terms. Nixon could not compel the foe to negotiate meaningfully, yet every passing day added to the strength of antiwar sentiment, which, as it expressed itself in ever more emphatic terms, in turn led to deeper divisions in the country.

The President responded to this dilemma by trying to build up the South Vietnamese army so that American troops could withdraw without allowing the communists to overrun South Vietnam. The trouble with this strategy (called Vietnamization) was that the United States had been employing it without success for 15 years. For complicated reasons–the incompetence, corruption, and reactionary character of the South Vietnamese government being probably the most important–South Vietnamese troops had seldom displayed much enthusiasm for the kind of tough jungle fighting at which the North Vietnamese and the Vietcong excelled. Nevertheless, efforts at Vietnamization were stepped up and in June 1969, after a meeting with President Nguyen Van Thieu of South Vietnam at Midway Island, Nixon announced that he would soon reduce the number of American soldiers in Vietnam by 25,000. In September he promised that an additional 35,000 men would be withdrawn by mid-December.

These steps did not quiet the protesters. On October 15 a nationwide antiwar demonstration, Vietnam Moratorium Day, organized by students, produced an unprecedented outpouring all over the country. Millions of persons from every walk of life joined in meetings, processions, and other peaceful demonstrations against the war. This massive display produced one of Vice President Agnew's most notorious blasts of adjectival invective: he said that the moratorium was an example of "national masochism," led by "an effete corps of impudent snobs who characterize themselves as intellectuals."*

A month later, a second Moratorium Day brought a crowd estimated at 250,000 to Washington to march past the White House. The President was unmoved. He would not be influenced by protests, he insisted, and indeed, during one of the Washington demonstrations he passed the time watching a football game on television. Then, on November 3, he defended his policy in a televised speech. He stressed the sincerity of his peace efforts, the unreasonableness of the communists, the responsibility of the United States to protect the South Vietnamese people from communist reprisals and to honor its international commitments. He also announced that he planned to remove all American ground forces from Vietnam, although he did not specify the details of the withdrawal. The next day, reporting a flood of telegrams and calls supporting his position, he declared that a "silent majority" of the American people approved his course.

For a season, events appeared to vindicate Nixon's position. A gradual reduction of military activity in Vietnam had lowered American casualties to what those who did not find the war morally unbearable considered "tolerable" levels. Troop withdrawals continued in an orderly fashion, 150,000 by the spring of 1970. A new lottery system for drafting men for military duty eliminated some of the inequities in the selective service law. These developments reduced the level of protest.

But the war continued. Early in 1970 reports that in 1968 an American unit had brutally massacred civilians, including dozens of women and children, in a Vietnamese hamlet known as Mylai 4, revived the controversy about the purposes of the war and its corrosive effects on those who were fighting it. After the massacre was brought to public attention, the army moved to punish

*A few days later he called upon the country to "separate" radical students from society "with no more regret than we should feel over discarding rotten apples from a barrel," which at least had a quality of terseness that most of Agnew's pronouncements lacked.

both the soldiers who had done the killing and the high officers who had tried to cover it up, but such incidents were difficult to prevent in the kind of conflict that was going on in Vietnam.

The American people, it seemed, were being torn apart by the war: one from another according to each's interpretation of events, many within themselves as they tried to balance the war's hopeless horrors against their pride, their detestation of communism, and their unwillingness to turn their backs on their elected leader. That leader—the time for judgment is not now—was probably as torn as any of his fellow citizens. It is true that he had often been accused of lacking deep convictions, that despite his penchant for moralizing, his record did not suggest a man prepared to sacrifice personal advantage for an end beyond himself. But his most bitter enemy could find no reason to think he wished the war to go on. Its human, economic, and social costs could only vex his days and threaten his future reputation. When he reduced the level of the fighting, the communists merely waited for further reductions. When he raised it, many of his own people denounced him. If he pulled out of Vietnam entirely, other Americans would be outraged.

Perhaps his error lay in his unwillingness to admit his own uncertainty, something the greatest Presidents—one thinks immediately of Lincoln and Franklin Roosevelt—were never afraid to do. Facing a dilemma, he tried to convince the whole world that he was firmly in control of events, with the result that at times he seemed more like a high school valedictorian declaiming sententiously about the meaning of life than the mature statesman he so desperately wished to be. Thus he heightened the tensions he sought to relax—in America, in Vietnam, elsewhere too.

Late in April 1970 Nixon confidently announced that Vietnamization was proceeding more rapidly than he had hoped, that communist power was weakening, that within a year another 150,000 American soldiers would be extracted from Vietnam. Then a week later he announced that military intelligence had indicated that the enemy was consolidating its "sanctuaries" in neutral Cambodia and that he was therefore dispatching thousands of American troops to destroy these bases. In other words he was escalating (dread word) the war; indeed, he even resumed the bombing of targets in North Vietnam.

To foes of the war, Nixon's decision seemed so appallingly unwise that a few of them began to fear that he had become mentally unbalanced. The contradictions between his confident statements about Vietnamization and his alarmist description of powerful enemy forces poised like a dagger 30-odd miles from Saigon, and the fact that he made the decision to invade Cambodia in the face of the furor it was bound to trigger, did not seem the product of a reasoning mind. His failure to consult congressional leaders or many of his personal advisers before drastically altering his policy, the critics claimed, was both unconstitutional and irresponsible. His insensitive response to the avalanche of criticism that descended upon him from the universities, from Congress, and from other quarters further disturbed observers.

Students took the lead in opposing the invasion of Cambodia. The coincidental killing of the Kent State demonstrators by panicky National Guardsmen (which the President reacted to with one of his homilies about violence begetting violence) added to their indignation. A wave of student strikes closed down hundreds of colleges, including many that had seen no previous unrest, as moderate students by the tens of thousands joined with the radicals.

The almost universal condemnation of the invasion and of the way it had been planned and announced to the country shook Nixon hard. He backtracked, pulling American ground troops out of Cambodia quickly. The ultimate effect of the venture was hard to gauge, but aside from its domestic repercussions it considerably extended the area of fighting in Southeast Asia.

The war in Vietnam was not, of course, the only international problem confronting the United States in 1970; indeed, opposition to the war was so strong in part because of its effect on the reputation of the nation abroad, and thus on the success of other American policies. Anti-Americanism remained endemic in Latin America. Castro still reigned in Cuba. In the Middle East, a third Arab-Israeli war in 1967 had produced a

Astronaut Edwin Aldrin on the moon, July 1969. Reflected in his helmet visor are flight commander Neil Armstrong, who took this picture, and a part of their spacecraft. Television enabled some 600 million people to witness the historic event.

swift, overwhelming victory for Israel, but the Arab nations remained unreconciled to the existence of the Jewish state and the Soviet Union bolstered their depleted military resources, even sending Russian pilots to aid Egypt. A new outbreak in that region could occur at any moment and might easily result in a major confrontation between Russia and the United States. The nuclear arms race continued, despite a growing awareness that since the United States and the Soviet Union each already had more than enough power in their arsenals to destroy the entire world, further escalation was a waste of resources and a source of still more anxiety for the whole human race.

The conflict between communism in its Russian, Chinese, and other varieties and the western democracies (whose societies also differed from one another in many ways) was fundamentally one of human rights, not of economic systems. The United States did not provide full equality for all its citizens, but the most deprived of them were far freer than the citizens of communist nations. American interference in the affairs of foreign countries never took the brutal form employed by the Soviet Union in smashing the Czechoslovakian experiment in "liberal communism" in 1968. This conflict about human rights did not appear amenable to honorable compromise, and the best hope for a true settlement lay in the possibility that the communists would gradually modify their repressive system.

But all the nations, the United States as much as any other, needed to re-examine their basically parochial, highly emotional commitment to nationalism, to learn that pride in one's heritage did not entail hostility or contempt for others. The world's problems—the danger of nuclear war, overpopulation, pollution—increasingly transcended national boundaries. So, fortunately, did men's capacity for solving them. Modern history repeatedly demonstrated that people everywhere responded to changing conditions in similar ways. Student unrest and the larger problem of the "generation gap," for example, existed in Latin America, in Asia, in western Europe, even in Russia, and rose in each region from the same causes. Furthermore, dramatic events could make people aware of their common interests. When the first American astronauts landed on the moon in July 1969, they were watched on television by hundreds of millions, and they, and their country, were warmly congratulated in a hundred tongues. Perhaps even more revealing was the equally profound concern expressed all over the world when the second moon expedition, Apollo 13, suffered a serious accident in mid-course, and the relief that was felt when the three astronauts managed to repair their ship sufficiently to return safely to earth. These two adventures offer simple lessons: mankind possesses the technology and wealth to achieve wonders, and in a world growing steadily smaller, men can recognize their common humanity without surrendering the rich local cultural differences that result from their individual differences.

A Search for Meaning

As long as Americans have been conscious of their existence as a nation, their historians have tried to find some special significance in the course of national development and to understand the unique qualities that distinguish Americans from other peoples. Nearly all have concluded that the country's democratic institutions were of special importance in shaping both American civilization and the national character. In the Age of Jackson, George Bancroft saw American history as the working out of a divine plan. "A favoring Providence, calling our institutions into being, has conducted the country to its present happiness and glory," he wrote in 1834. In essence, God's plan called for "the diffusion of intelligence among the masses" and the triumph of democracy.

Thousands of Americans still accept this analysis, but over the years many historians have subjected Bancroft's faith to sharp re-examination. In the 1890's Frederick Jackson Turner attempted to explain American history in terms of the frontier, which, he said, had branded the whole country with particular characteristics. While he believed that the frontier had been a democratizing influence, Turner also stressed the internal conflicts in the American experience. In the next generation, Charles A. Beard expanded upon this aspect of the Turnerian interpretation, arguing that the history of democracy in the United States was the sum of a series of clashes between rival social and economic interests: the Constitution between owners of land and owners of government securities, the Civil War between southern agriculture and northern industry, and so on.

Still later, the historian David M. Potter found the unique quality of American life in the material abundance which the rich continent bestowed upon the people. Out of this abundance, he wrote, has come a relatively classless, mobile, democratic society, America's sense of mission, a fundamental optimism. Other modern historians emphasized the absence of basic conflicts among Americans. Historians like Turner and Beard, they reasoned, had unintentionally exaggerated the conflicts, either in order to make their narratives more dramatic or because they were misled by the rhetoric of politicians, the enthusiasms of reformers, or the ravings of fanatics. What was most significant about the United States, these writers claimed, was the remarkable degree of "consensus" that had always existed among its people, the sameness of their chief assumptions and objectives, which made the democratic system work. On the other hand, "New Left" historians, pointing to the mistreatment of blacks and other minorities and to the extremes of wealth and poverty that have existed in the United States, insisted that America had always been riven by conflicts and that its government had never been truly democratic.

In one sense, none of the later historians escaped entirely from George Bancroft's naive assumption that he was telling the story of God's American Israel. For Americans have always assumed, and not entirely without reason, that their society represented man's best hope, if not necessarily the Creator's. The pride of the Puritans in their wilderness Zion, the Jeffersonians' fondness for contrasting American democracy with European tyranny, what Tocqueville called the "garrulous patriotism" of the Jacksonians, even the paranoid rantings of the latter-day isolationists all reflected this underlying faith. Historians, immersed in the records of this belief, have inevitably been affected by it. Their doubts have risen from what the theologian Reinhold Niebuhr has dubbed "the irony of American history": the people of the United States have been beguiled by their real achievements and the relative superiority of their institutions into assuming that they are better than they are.

Recent history, however, has shaken, if it has not shattered, their illusions. Ironically, the possession of world power has made Americans aware of their human weaknesses, of what President Johnson referred to as their "fragile existence" in his inaugural. "The so-called free world," Niebuhr reminds us, "must cover itself with guilt in order to ward off the perils of communism." The struggle against Marxian materialism has exposed the preoccupation of Americans with the things of this world; the by-product of technological advance has been the humbling of Americans' pride in their individualism and self-reliance.

What effect this awareness will have on the American character (and on American actions) remains for time to reveal, and prediction is not the task of the historian. However, one may fairly ask two questions about the future of the United States, actually of all nations. First: *Has modern technology outstripped human intelligence?* This is not the question, often asked by writers of science fiction, of thinking machines dominating their human creators. But does modern society require more brains than its members collectively possess? We rightly seek to improve each individual's education, and many talents are presently undeveloped, but is there enough *potential* intelligence to satisfy the demands of society for technicians, professionals, and other trained minds? Once more than half of any generation is sent to college, the colleges will be attempting, by definition, to give "higher" education to those of literally below average intelligence.

Second: *Has man's social development outstripped his emotional development?* Men must live at peace or face annihilation. They must control their propensity to reproduce now that they have eliminated so many of the causes of premature death, or overwhelm the world's resources and die of starvation. One of the paradoxes of modern life is that to effect change through constructive action is difficult, to do so by destructive behavior easy. This explains much of the violence in the world today. (Martin Luther King and a host of other Americans failed to eliminate race prejudice, but a sordid drifter, shooting King down from ambush, could cause a dozen cities to burn.) Men must find new ways to express their individuality in a world of enormous, ego-stifling institutions, to gain some sense of personal achievement through socially constructive activity. Is the human organism temperamentally capable of such adjustments?

No one can currently answer these questions. Nevertheless, we may surely hope that with their growing maturity, their awareness of their own limitations as a political entity, the American people will grapple with them realistically yet with all their customary imagination and energy.

SUPPLEMENTARY READING There are a great many interesting volumes that attempt to describe and explain various aspects of modern American society. It is difficult to evaluate or even to categorize these books—time must pass before we can know which are the most insightful. For the present, each reader must test these works against his own experience and knowledge in determining their worth. Among those dealing most comprehensively with American life, Max Lerner, *America as a Civilization** (1957), is probably the most ambitious. Others include F.L. Allen, *The Big Change** (1952), R.E. Spiller and Eric Larrabee (eds.), *American Perspectives* (1961), Bernard Rosenberg and D.M. White (eds.), *Mass Culture** (1957), Philip Olson (ed.), *America as a Mass Society* (1963), Jacques Barzun, *God's Country and Mine** (1954), David Riesman, *Individualism Reconsidered** (1954), and J.W. Gardner, *The Recovery of Confidence* (1970). Marshall McLuhan, *Understanding Media** (1964), an attempt to explain contemporary trends chiefly in terms of the impact of television and other electronic means of communication, caused a great stir, but is generally considered an exaggerated and somewhat frivolous analysis.

Books attempting to analyze economic trends include Peter Drucker, *The New Society** (1950), J.K. Galbraith, *The Affluent Society** (1958) and *The New Industrial State** (1967), the Editors of *Fortune*, *America in the Sixties: The Economy and the Society** (1960), T.C. Cochran, *The American Business System** (1957), and A.A. Berle, *Power Without Property** (1959).

Students of the contemporary American character should begin with David Riesman *et al.*, *The Lonely Crowd** (1950), and continue with two works by C. Wright Mills, *White Collar** (1951) and *The Power Elite** (1956). Other interesting volumes include W.H. Whyte, Jr., *The Organization Man** (1956), Paul Goodman, *Growing Up Absurd** (1960), Kenneth Kenniston, *The Uncommitted* (1965), and C.A. Reich, *The Greening of America* (1970).

Educational trends are discussed in Richard Hofstadter and C.D. Hardy, *The Development and Scope of Higher Education in the United States* (1952), Jacques Barzun, *The House of Intellect** (1959), R.N. Sanford (ed.), *The American College* (1962), R.O. Bower (ed.), *The New Professors* (1960), Martin Mayer, *The Schools** (1961), A.E. Bestor, *The Restoration of Learning* (1955), J.B. Conant, *The American High School Today** (1959) and *Slums and Suburbs** (1964), and Robert Coles, *Children of Crisis** (1967). On militancy among college students, see S.M. Lipset and P.G. Altbach (eds.), *Students in Revolt* (1969), and Roger Kahn, *The Battle of Morningside Heights* (1970).

On mass tastes, see, in addition to many of the volumes mentioned above, Russell Lynes, *The Tastemakers** (1954), Gilbert Seldes, *The Great Audience* (1950) and *The Public Arts** (1957). Lewis Jacobs, *The Rise of the American Film** (1939), Hortense Powdermaker, *Hollywood** (1950), Nathan Leites and Martha Wolfenstein, *Movies* (1950), Llewellyn White, *The American Radio* (1947), G.A. Steiner, *The People Look at Television* (1963), F.L. Mott, *American Journalism* (1962), and B.A. Weisberger, *The American Newspaperman* (1961), treat the changing communications and amusement industries.

On contemporary poverty and urban problems, see Michael Harrington, *The Other America** (1962), J.C. Donovan, *The Politics of Poverty** (1967), Oscar Lewis, *La Vida: A Puerto Rican Family in the Culture of Poverty** (1966), Mitchell Gordon, *Sick Cities: Psychology and Pathology of American Urban Life** (1963), R.C. Weaver, *The Urban Complex** (1964), and Jane Jacobs, *The Death and Life of Great American Cities** (1962).

Students of contemporary race relations should begin with a number of brilliant, highly personal books by black Americans. James Baldwin, *The Fire Next Time** (1963), first called the new black anger to white attention, but see also M.L. King, Jr., *Stride Toward Freedom** (1958), Malcolm X, *Autobiography** (1966), Stokely Carmichael and C.V. Hamilton, *Black Power: The Politics of Liberation in America** (1967), and Eldridge Cleaver, *Soul on Ice** (1967). Other important books on race relations include C.E. Silberman, *Crisis in Black and White** (1964), K.B. Clark, *Youth in the Ghetto* (1964), and L.E. Lomax, *The Negro Revolt** (1963). The *Report** of the National Advisory (Kerner) Commission on Civil Disorders (1968) is full of interesting material.

On political developments, not only for the details of legislation but also for useful summaries of many aspects of recent history, see Congressional Quarterly Service, *Congress and the Nation: 1965–1968* (1969). On the election of 1968, the most recent of T.H. White's series, *The Making of the President, 1968** (1969), is lively and entertaining, while J. McGinniss, *The Selling of the President, 1968* (1969), is bitterly anti-Nixon. We have as yet no adequate biography of Nixon, but his own *Six Crises** (1962) offers some insights into his character and view of political life. The literature on the war in Vietnam is, of course, already enormous. The following are only a few of the most important studies: B.B. Fall, *Viet-Nam Witness* (1966), A.M. Schlesinger, Jr., *Bitter Heritage: Vietnam and American Democracy** (1967), Robert Shaplen, *The Lost Revolution** (1965), and R.N. Goodwin, *Triumph or Tragedy: Reflections on Vietnam** (1966).

*Available in paperback.

The Declaration of Independence

When in the Course of human events, it becomes necessary for one people to dissolve the political bands which have connected them with another, and to assume among the Powers of the earth, the separate and equal station to which the Laws of Nature and of Nature's God entitle them, a decent respect to the opinions of mankind requires that they should declare the causes which impel them to the separation.

We hold these truths to be self-evident, that all men are created equal, that they are endowed by their Creator with certain unalienable Rights, that among these are Life, Liberty and the pursuit of Happiness. That to secure these rights, Governments are instituted among Men, deriving their just powers from the consent of the governed, That whenever any Form of Government becomes destructive of these ends, it is the Right of the People to alter or to abolish it, and to institute new Government, laying its foundation on such principles and organizing its powers in such form, as to them shall seem most likely to effect their Safety and Happiness. Prudence, indeed, will dictate that Governments long established should not be changed for light and transient causes; and accordingly all experience hath shown, that mankind are more disposed to suffer, while evils are sufferable, than to right themselves by abolishing the forms to which they are accustomed. But when a long train of abuses and usurpations, pursuing invariably the same Object evinces a design to reduce them under absolute Despotism, it is their right, it is their duty, to throw off such Government, and to provide new Guards for their future security.—Such has been the patient sufferance of these Colonies; and such is now the necessity which constrains them to alter their former Systems of Government. The history of the present King of Great Britain is a history of repeated injuries and usurpations, all having in direct object the establishment of an absolute Tyranny over these States. To prove this, let Facts be submitted to a candid world.

He has refused his Assent to Laws, the most wholesome and necessary for the public good.

He has forbidden his Governors to pass Laws of immediate and pressing importance, unless suspended in their operation till his Assent should be obtained; and when so suspended, he has utterly neglected to attend to them.

He has refused to pass other Laws for the accommodation of large districts of people, unless those people would relinquish the right of Representation in the Legislature, a right inestimable to them and formidable to tyrants only.

He has called together legislative bodies at places unusual, uncomfortable, and distant from the depository of their Public Records, for the sole purpose of fatiguing them into compliance with his measures.

He has dissolved Representative Houses repeatedly, for opposing with manly firmness his invasions on the rights of the people.

He has refused for a long time, after such dissolutions, to cause others to be elected; whereby the Legislative Powers, incapable of Annihilation, have returned to the People at large for their exercise; the State remaining in the mean time exposed to all the dangers of invasion from without, and convulsions within.

He has endeavoured to prevent the population of these States; for that purpose obstructing the Laws of Naturalization of Foreigners; refusing to pass others to encourage their migration hither, and raising the conditions of new Appropriations of Lands.

He has obstructed the Administration of Justice, by refusing his Assent to Laws for establishing Judiciary Powers.

He has made Judges dependent on his Will alone, for the tenure of their offices, and the amount and payment of their salaries.

He has erected a multitude of New Offices, and sent hither swarms of Officers to harass our People, and eat out their substance.

He has kept among us, in times of peace, Standing Armies without the Consent of our legislature.

He has affected to render the Military independent of and superior to the Civil Power.

He has combined with others to subject us to a jurisdiction foreign to our constitution, and unacknowledged by our laws; giving his Assent to their acts of pretended legislation:

For quartering large bodies of armed troops among us:

For protecting them, by a mock Trial, from Punishment for any Murders which they should commit on the Inhabitants of these States:

For cutting off our Trade with all parts of the world:

For imposing taxes on us without our Consent:

For depriving us in many cases, of the benefits of Trial by Jury:

For transporting us beyond Seas to be tried for pretended offences:

For abolishing the free System of English Laws in a neighbouring Province, establishing therein an Arbitrary government, and enlarging its Boundaries so as to render it at once an example and fit instrument for introducing the same absolute rule into these Colonies:

For taking away our Charters, abolishing our most

valuable Laws, and altering fundamentally the Forms of our Governments:

For suspending our own Legislature, and declaring themselves invested with Power to legislate for us in all cases whatsoever.

He has abdicated Government here, by declaring us out of his Protection and waging War against us.

He has plundered our seas, ravaged our Coasts, burnt our towns, and destroyed the lives of our people.

He is at this time transporting large armies of foreign mercenaries to compleat the works of death, desolation and tyranny, already begun with circumstances of Cruelty & perfidy scarcely paralleled in the most barbarous ages, and totally unworthy the Head of a civilized nation.

He has constrained our fellow Citizens taken Captive on the high Seas to bear Arms against their Country, to become the executioners of their friends and Brethren, or to fall themselves by their Hands.

He has excited domestic insurrections amongst us, and has endeavoured to bring on the inhabitants of our frontiers, the merciless Indian Savages, whose known rule of warfare, is an undistinguished destruction of all ages, sexes and conditions.

In every stage of these Oppressions We have Petitioned for Redress in the most humble terms: Our repeated Petitions have been answered only by repeated injury. A Prince, whose character is thus marked by every act which may define a Tyrant, is unfit to be the ruler of a free People.

Nor have We been wanting in attention to our British brethren. We have warned them from time to time of attempts by their legislature to extend an unwarrantable jurisdiction over us. We have reminded them of the circumstances of our emigration and settlement here. We have appealed to their native justice and magnanimity, and we have conjured them by the ties of our common kindred to disavow these usurpations, which, would inevitably interrupt our connections and correspondence. They too have been deaf to the voice of justice and of consanguinity. We must, therefore, acquiesce in the necessity, which denounces our Separation, and hold them, as we hold the rest of mankind, Enemies in War, in Peace Friends.

We, therefore, the Representatives of the united States of America, in General Congress, Assembled, appealing to the Supreme Judge of the world for the rectitude of our intentions, do, in the Name, and by Authority of the good People of these Colonies, solemnly publish and declare, That these United Colonies are, and of Right ought to be Free and Independent States; that they are Absolved from all Allegiance to the British Crown, and that all political connection between them and the State of Great Britain, is and ought to be totally dissolved; and that as Free and Independent States, they have full Power to levy War, conclude Peace, contract Alliances, establish Commerce, and to do all other Acts and Things which Independent States may of right do. And for the support of this Declaration, with a firm reliance on the Protection of Divine Providence, we mutually pledge to each other our Lives, our Fortunes and our sacred Honor.

The Constitution of the United States

We the people of the United States, in Order to form a more perfect Union, establish Justice, insure domestic Tranquility, provide for the common defence, promote the general Welfare, and secure the Blessings of Liberty to ourselves and our Posterity, do ordain and establish this CONSTITUTION for the United States of America.

ARTICLE I

Section 1. All legislative Powers herein granted shall be vested in a Congress of the United States, which shall consist of a Senate and House of Representatives.

Section 2. The House of Representatives shall be composed of Members chosen every second Year by the People of the several States, and the Electors in each State shall have the Qualifications requisite for Electors of the most numerous Branch of the State Legislature.

No Person shall be a Representative who shall not have attained to the Age of twenty-five Years, and been seven Years a Citizen of the United States, and who shall not, when elected, be an Inhabitant of that State in which he shall be chosen.

Representatives and direct Taxes shall be apportioned among the several States which may be included within this Union, according to their respective Numbers, which shall be determined by adding to the whole Number of free Persons, including those bound to Service for a Term of Years, and excluding Indians not taxed, three fifths of all other Persons. The actual Enumeration shall be made within three Years after the first Meeting of the Congress of the

United States, and within every subsequent Term of ten Years, in such Manner as they shall by Law direct. The Number of Representatives shall not exceed one for every thirty Thousand, but each State shall have at Least one Representative; and until such enumeration shall be made, the State of New Hampshire shall be entitled to chuse three, Massachusetts eight, Rhode-Island and Providence Plantations one, Connecticut five, New-York six, New Jersey four, Pennsylvania eight, Delaware one, Maryland six, Virginia ten, North Carolina five, South Carolina five, and Georgia three.

When vacancies happen in the Representation from any State, the Executive Authority thereof shall issue Writs of Election to fill such Vacancies.

The House of Representatives shall chuse their Speaker and other Officers; and shall have the sole Power of Impeachment.

Section 3. The Senate of the United States shall be composed of two Senators from each State, chosen by the Legislature thereof, for six Years; and each Senator shall have one Vote.

Immediately after they shall be assembled in Consequence of the first Election, they shall be divided as equally as may be into three Classes. The Seats of the Senators of the first Class shall be vacated at the Expiration of the second Year, of the second Class at the Expiration of the fourth Year, and of the third Class at the Expiration of the sixth Year, so that one-third may be chosen every second Year; and if Vacancies happen by Resignation, or otherwise, during the Recess of the Legislature of any State, the Executive thereof may make temporary Appointments until the next Meeting of the Legislature, which shall then fill such Vacancies.

No Person shall be a Senator who shall not have attained to the Age of thirty Years, and been nine Years a Citizen of the United States, and who shall not, when elected, be an Inhabitant of that State in which he shall be chosen.

The Vice President of the United States shall be President of the Senate, but shall have no vote, unless they be equally divided.

The Senate shall chuse their other Officers, and also a President pro tempore, in the absence of the Vice President, or when he shall exercise the Office of the President of the United States.

The Senate shall have the sole Power to try all Impeachments. When sitting for that purpose, they shall be on Oath or Affirmation. When the President of the United States is tried, the Chief Justice shall preside: And no person shall be convicted without the Concurrence of two thirds of the Members present.

Judgment in Cases of Impeachment shall not extend further than to removal from Office, and disqualification to hold and enjoy any Office of honor, Trust, or Profit under the United States: but the Party convicted shall nevertheless be liable and subject to Indictment, Trial, Judgment, and Punishment, according to Law.

Section 4. The Times, Places and Manner of holding Elections for Senators and Representatives, shall be prescribed in each state by the Legislature thereof; but the Congress may at any time by Law make or alter such Regulations, except as to the Places of Chusing Senators.

The Congress shall assemble at least once in every Year, and such Meeting shall be on the first Monday in December, unless they shall by Law appoint a different Day.

Section 5. Each House shall be the Judge of the Elections, Returns and Qualifications of its own Members, and a Majority of each shall constitute a Quorum to do Business; but a smaller number may adjourn from day to day, and may be authorized to compel the Attendance of absent Members, in such Manner, and under such Penalties, as each House may provide.

Each House may determine the Rules of its Proceedings, punish its Members for disorderly Behavior, and, with the Concurrence of two thirds, expel a Member.

Each House shall keep a Journal of its Proceedings, and from time to time publish the same, excepting such Parts as may in their Judgment require Secrecy; and the Yeas and Nays of the Members of either House on any question shall, at the Desire of one fifth of those Present, be entered on the Journal

Neither House, during the Session of Congress, shall, without the Consent of the other, adjourn for more than three days, nor to any other Place than that in which the two Houses shall be sitting.

Section 6. The Senators and Representatives shall receive a Compensation for their Services, to be ascertained by Law, and paid out of the Treasury of the United States. They shall in all Cases, except Treason, Felony, and Breach of the Peace, be privileged from Arrest during their Attendance at the Session of their respective Houses, and in going to and returning from the same; and for any Speech or Debate in either House, they shall not be questioned in any other Place.

No Senator or Representative shall, during the Time for which he was elected, be appointed to any civil Office under the Authority of the United States, which shall have been created, or the Emoluments whereof shall have been increased, during such time; and no Person holding any Office under the United States shall be a Member of either House during his continuance in Office.

Section 7. All Bills for raising Revenue shall originate in the House of Representatives; but the Senate may propose or concur with Amendments as on other bills.

Every Bill which shall have passed the House of Representatives and the Senate, shall, before it become a Law, be presented to the President of the United States; If he approve he shall sign it, but if not he shall return it, with his Objections, to that House in which it shall have originated, who shall enter the Objections at large on their Journal, and proceed to reconsider it. If after such Reconsideration two thirds of that House shall agree to pass the bill, it shall be sent, together with the objections, to the other House, by which it shall likewise be reconsidered, and if approved by two thirds of that House, it shall become a Law. But in all such Cases the Votes of both Houses shall be determined by Yeas and Nays, and the Names of the Persons voting for and against the Bill shall be entered on the Journal of each House respectively. If any Bill shall not be returned by the President within ten Days (Sundays excepted) after it shall have been presented to him, the Same shall be a Law, in like Manner as if he had signed it, unless the Congress by their Adjournment prevent its Return, in which Case it shall not be a Law.

Every Order, Resolution, or Vote to which the Concurrence of the Senate and House of Representatives may be necessary (except on a question of Adjournment) shall be presented to the President of the United States; and before the Same shall take Effect, shall be approved by him, or being disapproved by him, shall be repassed by two thirds of the Senate and House of Representatives, according to the Rules and Limitations prescribed in the Case of a Bill.

Section 8. The Congress shall have Power To lay and collect Taxes, Duties, Imposts and Excises, to pay the Debts and provide for the common Defence and general Welfare of the United States; but all Duties, Imposts and Excises shall be uniform throughout the United States;

To borrow money on the credit of the United States;

To regulate Commerce with foreign Nations, and among the several States, and with the Indian Tribes;

To establish an uniform Rule of Naturalization, and uniform Laws on the subject of Bankruptcies throughout the United States;

To coin Money, regulate the Value thereof, and of foreign Coin, and fix the Standard of Weights and Measures;

To provide for the Punishment of counterfeiting the Securities and current Coin of the United States;

To establish Post Offices and post Roads;

To promote the Progress of Science and useful Arts, by securing for limited Times to Authors and Inventors the exclusive Right to their respective Writings and Discoveries;

To constitute Tribunals inferior to the Supreme Court;

To define and punish Piracies and Felonies committed on the high Seas, and Offences against the Law of Nations;

To declare War, grant Letters of Marque and Reprisal, and make Rules concerning Captures on Land and Water;

To raise and support Armies, but no Appropriation of Money to that Use shall be for a longer Term than two Years;

To provide and maintain a Navy;

To make Rules for the Government and Regulation of the land and naval forces;

To provide for calling forth the Militia to execute the Laws of the Union, suppress Insurrections and repel Invasions;

To provide for organizing, arming, and disciplining the Militia, and for governing such Part of them as may be employed in the Service of the United States, reserving to the States respectively, the Appointment of the Officers, and the Authority of training the Militia according to the discipline prescribed by Congress;

To exercise exclusive Legislation in all Cases whatsoever, over such District (not exceeding ten Miles square) as may, by Cession of particular States, and the acceptance of Congress, become the Seat of Government of the United States, and to exercise like Authority over all Places purchased by the Consent of the Legislature of the State in which the Same shall be, for the Erection of Forts, Magazines, Arsenals, dock-Yards, and other needful Buildings;—And

To make all Laws which shall be necessary and proper for carrying into Execution the foregoing Powers, and all other Powers vested by this Constitution in the Government of the United States, or in any Department or Officer thereof.

Section 9. The Migration or Importation of such Persons as any of the States now existing shall think proper to admit, shall not be prohibited by the Congress prior to the Year one thousand eight hundred and eight, but a tax or duty may be imposed on such Importation, not exceeding ten dollars for each Person.

The privilege of the Writ of Habeas Corpus shall not be suspended, unless when in Cases of Rebellion or Invasion the public Safety may require it.

No Bill of Attainder or ex post facto Law shall be passed.

No capitation, or other direct, Tax shall be laid unless in Proportion to the Census or Enumeration herein before directed to be taken.

No Tax or Duty shall be laid on Articles exported from any State.

No Preference shall be given by any Regulation of Revenue to the Ports of one State over those of another: nor shall Vessels bound to, or from, one State, be obliged to enter, clear, or pay Duties in another.

No Money shall be drawn from the Treasury, but in Consequence of Appropriations made by Law; and a regular Statement and Account of the Receipts and Expenditures of all public Money shall be published from time to time.

No Title of Nobility shall be granted by the United States: And no Person holding any Office of Profit or Trust under them, shall, without the Consent of the Congress, accept of any present, Emolument, Office, or Title, of any kind whatever, from any King, Prince, or foreign State.

Section 10. No State shall enter into any Treaty, Alliance, or Confederation; grant Letters of Marque and Reprisal; coin Money; emit Bills of Credit; make any Thing but gold and silver Coin a Tender in Payment of Debts; pass any Bill of Attainder, ex post facto Law, or Law impairing the Obligation of Contracts, or grant any Title of Nobility.

No State shall, without the Consent of the Congress, lay any Imposts or Duties on Imports or Exports, except what may be absolutely necessary for executing its inspection Laws: and the net Produce of all Duties and Imposts, laid by any State on Imports or Exports, shall be for the Use of the Treasury of the United States; and all such Laws shall be subject to the Revision and Control of the Congress.

No State shall, without the Consent of Congress, lay any duty of Tonnage, keep Troops, or Ships of War in time of Peace, enter into any Agreement or Compact with another State, or with a foreign Power, or engage in War, unless actually invaded, or in such imminent Danger as will not admit of delay.

ARTICLE II

Section 1. The executive Power shall be vested in a President of the United States of America. He shall hold his Office during the Term of four years, and, together with the Vice-President, chosen for the same Term, be elected, as follows:

Each State shall appoint, in such Manner as the Legislature thereof may direct, a Number of Electors, equal to the whole Number of Senators and Representatives to which the State may be entitled in the Congress; but no Senator or Representative, or Person holding an Office of Trust or Profit under the United States, shall be appointed an Elector.

The Electors shall meet in their respective States, and vote by Ballot for two persons, of whom one at least shall not be an Inhabitant of the same State with themselves. And they shall make a List of all the Persons voted for, and of the Number of Votes for each; which List they shall sign and certify, and transmit sealed to the Seat of the Government of the United States, directed to the President of the Senate. The President of the Senate shall, in the Presence of the Senate and House of Representatives, open all the Certificates, and the Votes shall then be counted. The Person having the greatest Number of Votes shall be the President, if such Number be a Majority of the whole Number of Electors appointed; and if there be more than one who have such Majority, and have an equal Number of Votes, then the House of Representatives shall immediately chuse by Ballot one of them for President; and if no Person have a Majority, then from the five highest on the List the said House shall in like Manner chuse the President. But in chusing the President, the Votes shall be taken by States, the Representation from each State having one Vote; a quorum for this Purpose shall consist of a Member or Members from two-thirds of the States, and a Majority of all the States shall be necessary to a Choice. In every Case, after the Choice of the President, the Person having the greatest Number of Votes of the Electors shall be the Vice President. But if there should remain two or more who have equal votes, the Senate shall chuse from them by Ballot the Vice-President.

The Congress may determine the Time of chusing the Electors, and the Day on which they shall give their Votes; which Day shall be the same throughout the United States.

No person except a natural-born Citizen, or a Citizen of the United States, at the time of the Adoption of this Constitution, shall be eligible to the Office of President; neither shall any Person be eligible to that Office who shall not have attained to the Age of thirty-five years, and been fourteen Years a Resident within the United States.

In Case of the Removal of the President from Office, or of his Death, Resignation, or Inability to discharge the Powers and Duties of the said Office, the same shall devolve on the Vice President, and the Congress may by Law provide for the Case of Removal, Death, Resignation, or Inability, both of the President and Vice President, declaring what Officer shall then act as President, and such Officer shall act accordingly, until the disability be removed, or a President shall be elected.

The President shall, at stated Times, receive for his Services a Compensation, which shall neither be increased nor diminished during the Period for which he shall have been elected, and he shall not receive within that Period any other Emolument from the United States, or any of them.

Before he enter on the execution of his Office, he shall take the following Oath or Affirmation:— "I do solemnly swear (or affirm) that I will faithfully execute the Office of President of the United States, and will, to the best of my Ability, preserve, protect, and defend the Constitution of the United States."

Section 2. The President shall be Commander in Chief of the Army and Navy of the United States, and of the Militia of the several States, when called into the actual Service of the United States; he may require the Opinion, in writing, of the principal Officer in each of the executive Departments, upon any subject relating to the Duties of their respective Offices, and he shall have Power to Grant Reprieves and Pardons for Offences against the United States, except in Cases of Impeachment.

He shall have Power, by and with the Advice and

Consent of the Senate, to make Treaties, provided two thirds of the Senators present concur; and he shall nominate, and by and with the Advice and Consent of the Senate, shall appoint Ambassadors, other public Ministers and Consuls, Judges of the supreme Court, and all other Officers of the United States, whose Appointments are not herein otherwise provided for, and which shall be established by Law: but the Congress may by Law vest the Appointment of such inferior Officers, as they think proper, in the President alone, in the Courts of Law, or in the Heads of Departments.

The President shall have Power to fill up all Vacancies that may happen during the Recess of the Senate, by granting Commissions which shall expire at the End of their next Session.

Section 3. He shall from time to time give to the Congress Information of the State of the Union, and recommend to their Consideration such Measures as he shall judge necessary and expedient; he may, on extraordinary occasions, convene both Houses, or either of them, and in Case of Disagreement between them, with respect to the Time of Adjournment, he may adjourn them to such Time as he shall think proper; he shall receive Ambassadors and other public Ministers; he shall take Care that the Laws be faithfully executed, and shall Commission all the Officers of the United States.

Section 4. The President, Vice President and all civil Officers of the United States, shall be removed from Office on Impeachment for, and Conviction of, Treason, Bribery, or other high Crimes and Misdemeanors.

ARTICLE III

Section 1. The judicial Power of the United States, shall be vested in one supreme Court, and in such inferior Courts as the Congress may from time to time ordain and establish. The Judges, both of the supreme and inferior Courts, shall hold their Offices during good Behaviour, and shall, at stated Times, receive for their Services, a Compensation, which shall not be diminished during their Continuance in Office.

Section 2. The judicial Power shall extend to all Cases, in Law and Equity, arising under this Constitution, the Laws of the United States, and treaties made, or which shall be made, under their Authority;—to all Cases affecting ambassadors, other public ministers and consuls;—to all cases of admiralty and maritime Jurisdiction;—to Controversies to which the United States shall be a Party;—to Controversies between two or more States;—between a State and Citizens of another State;—between Citizens of different States,—between Citizens of the same State claiming Lands under Grants of different States, and between a State, or the Citizens thereof, and foreign States, Citizens or Subjects.

In all Cases affecting Ambassadors, other public Ministers and Consuls, and those in which a State shall be Party, the supreme Court shall have original Jurisdiction. In all the other Cases before mentioned, the supreme Court shall have appellate Jurisdiction, both as to Law and Fact, with such Exceptions, and under such Regulations as the Congress shall make.

The trial of all Crimes, except in Cases of Impeachment, shall be by Jury; and such Trial shall be held in the State where the said Crimes shall have been committed; but when not committed within any State, the Trial shall be at such Place or Places as the Congress may by Law have directed.

Section 3. Treason against the United States, shall consist only in levying War against them, or in adhering to their Enemies, giving them Aid and Comfort. No Person shall be convicted of Treason unless on the Testimony of two Witnesses to the same overt Act, or on Confession in open Court.

The Congress shall have power to declare the Punishment of Treason, but no Attainder of Treason shall work Corruption of Blood, or Forfeiture except during the Life of the Person attainted.

ARTICLE IV

Section 1. Full Faith and Credit shall be given in each State to the public Acts, Records, and judicial Proceedings of every other State. And the Congress may by general Laws prescribe the Manner in which such Acts, Records and Proceedings shall be proved, and the Effect thereof.

Section 2. The Citizens of each State shall be entitled to all Privileges and Immunities of Citizens in the several States.

A Person charged in any State with Treason, Felony, or other Crime, who shall flee from Justice, and be found in another State, shall on demand of the executive Authority of the State from which he fled, be delivered up, to be removed to the State having Jurisdiction of the crime.

No Person held to Service or Labour in one State, under the Laws thereof, escaping into another, shall, in Consequence of any Law or Regulation therein, be discharged from such Service or Labour, but shall be delivered up on Claim of the Party to whom such Service or Labour may be due.

Section 3. New States may be admitted by the Congress into this Union; but no new State shall be formed or erected within the Jurisdiction of any other State; nor any State be formed by the Junction of two or more States, or parts of States, without the Consent of the Legislatures of the States concerned as well as of the Congress.

The Congress shall have Power to dispose of and make all needful Rules and Regulations respecting the Territory or other Property belonging to the United States; and nothing in this Constitution shall be so construed as to Prejudice any Claims of the United

States, or of any particular State.

Section 4. The United States shall guarantee to every State in this Union a Republican Form of Government, and shall protect each of them against Invasion; and on Application of the Legislature, or of the Executive (when the Legislature cannot be convened) against domestic Violence.

ARTICLE V

The Congress, whenever two-thirds of both Houses shall deem it necessary, shall propose Amendments to this Constitution, or, on the Application of the Legislatures of two-thirds of the several States, shall call a Convention for proposing Amendments, which, in either Case, shall be valid to all Intents and Purposes, as part of this Constitution, when ratified by the Legislatures of three-fourths of the several States, or by Conventions in three-fourths thereof, as the one or the other Mode of Ratification may be proposed by the Congress; Provided that no Amendment which may be made prior to the Year One thousand eight hundred and eight shall in any Manner affect the first and fourth Clauses in the Ninth Section of the first Article; and that no State, without its Consent, shall be deprived of its equal Suffrage in the Senate.

ARTICLE VI

All Debts contracted and Engagements entered into, before the Adoption of this Constitution, shall be as valid against the United States under this Constitution, as under the Confederation.

This Constitution, and the Laws of the United States which shall be made in Pursuance thereof; and all Treaties made, or which shall be made, under the Authority of the United States, shall be the supreme Law of the Land; and the Judges in every State shall be bound thereby, any Thing in the Constitution or Laws of any State to the Contrary notwithstanding.

The Senators and Representatives before mentioned, and the Members of the several State Legislatures, and all executive and judicial Officers, both of the United States and of the several States, shall be bound by Oath or Affirmation to support this Constitution; but no religious Test shall ever be required as a qualification to any Office or public Trust under the United States.

ARTICLE VII

The Ratification of the Conventions of nine States shall be sufficient for the Establishment of this Constitution between the States so ratifying the same.

Done in Convention by the Unanimous Consent of the States present the Seventeenth Day of September in the Year of our Lord one thousand seven hundred and Eighty seven, and of the Independence of the United States of America the Twelfth. In Witness whereof We have hereunto subscribed our Names.

Articles in Addition to, and Amendment of, the Constitution of the United States of America, Proposed by Congress, and Ratified by the Legislatures of the Several States, Pursuant to the Fifth Article of the Original Constitution.

AMENDMENT I [1791]

Congress shall make no law respecting an establishment of religion, or prohibiting the free exercise thereof; or abridging the freedom of speech, or of the press; or the right of the people peaceably to assemble, and to petition the Government for a redress of grievances.

AMENDMENT II [1791]

A well regulated Militia, being necessary to the security of a free State, the right of the people to keep and bear Arms shall not be infringed.

AMENDMENT III [1791]

No Soldier shall, in time of peace, be quartered in any house, without the consent of the Owner, nor in time of war, but in a manner to be prescribed by law.

AMENDMENT IV [1791]

The right of the people to be secure in their persons, houses, papers, and effects, against unreasonable searches and seizures, shall not be violated, and no Warrants shall issue, but upon probable cause, supported by Oath or affirmation, and particularly describing the place to be searched, and the persons or things to be seized.

AMENDMENT V [1791]

No person shall be held to answer for a capital or otherwise infamous crime, unless on a presentment or indictment of a Grand Jury, except in cases arising in the land or naval forces, or in the Militia, when in actual service in time of War or public danger; nor shall any person be subject for the same offence to be twice put in jeopardy of life or limb; nor shall be compelled in any criminal case to be a witness against himself, nor be deprived of life, liberty, or property, without due process of law; nor shall private property be taken for public use, without just compensation.

AMENDMENT VI [1791]

In all criminal prosecutions, the accused shall enjoy the right to a speedy and public trial, by an impartial jury of the State and district wherein the crime shall have been committed, which district shall have been previously ascertained by law, and to be informed of the nature and cause of the accusation; to be confronted with the witnesses against him; to have compulsory process for obtaining witnesses in his favor, and to have the Assistance of Counsel for his defence.

AMENDMENT VII [1791]

In suits at common law, where the value in controversy shall exceed twenty dollars, the right of trial by jury shall be preserved, and no fact tried by a jury, shall be otherwise reexamined in any Court of the United States, than according to the rules of the common law.

AMENDMENT VIII [1791]

Excessive bail shall not be required, nor excessive fines imposed, nor cruel and unusual punishments inflicted.

AMENDMENT IX [1791]

The enumeration in the Constitution, of certain rights, shall not be construed to deny or disparage others retained by the people.

AMENDMENT X [1791]

The powers not delegated to the United States by the Constitution, nor prohibited by it to the States, are reserved to the States respectively, or to the people.

AMENDMENT XI [1798]

The Judicial power of the United States shall not be construed to extend to any suit in law or equity, commenced or prosecuted against one of the United States by Citizens of another State, or by Citizens or Subjects of any Foreign State.

AMENDMENT XI [1798]

The Electors shall meet in their respective States and vote by ballot for President and Vice-President, one of whom, at least, shall not be an inhabitant of the same State with themselves; they shall name in their ballots the person voted for as President, and in distinct ballots the person voted for as Vice-President, and they shall make distinct lists of all persons voted for as President, and of all persons voted for as Vice-President, and of the number of votes for each, which lists they shall sign and certify, and transmit sealed to the seat of the government of the United States, directed to the President of the Senate;—The President of the Senate shall, in the presence of the Senate and House of Representatives, open all the certificates and the votes shall then be counted;—The person having the greatest number of votes for President, shall be the President, if such number be a majority of the whole number of Electors appointed; and if no person have such majority, then from the persons having the highest numbers not exceeding three on the list of those voted for as President, the House of Representatives shall choose immediately, by ballot, the President. But in choosing the President, the votes shall be taken by states, the representation from each state having one vote; a quorum for this purpose shall consist of a member or members from two-thirds of the states, and a majority of all the states shall be necessary to a choice. And if the House of Representatives shall not choose a President whenever the right of choice shall devolve upon them, before the fourth day of March next following, then the Vice-President shall act as President, as in the case of the death or other constitutional disability of the President.—The person having the greatest number of votes as Vice-President, shall be the Vice-President, if such number be a majority of the whole number of Electors appointed, and if no person have a majority, then from the two highest numbers on the list, the Senate shall choose the Vice-President; a quorum for the purpose shall consist of two-thirds of the whole number of Senators, and a majority of the whole number shall be necessary to a choice. But no person constitutionally ineligible to the office of President shall be eligible to that of Vice-President of the United States.

AMENDMENT XIII [1865]

Section 1. Neither slavery nor involuntary servitude, except as a punishment for crime whereof the party shall have been duly convicted, shall exist within the United States, or any place subject to their jurisdiction.

Section 2. Congress shall have power to enforce this article by appropriate legislation.

AMENDMENT XIV [1868]

Section 1. All persons born or naturalized in the United States, and subject to the jurisdiction thereof, are citizens of the United States and of the State wherein they reside. No State shall make or enforce any law which shall abridge the privileges or immunities of citizens of the United States; nor shall any State deprive any person of life, liberty, or property, without due process of law; nor deny to any person within its jurisdiction the equal protection of the laws.

Section 2. Representatives shall be apportioned among the several States according to their respective numbers, counting the whole number of persons in each State, excluding Indians not taxed. But when the right to vote at any election for the choice of electors for President and Vice-President of the United States, Representatives in Congress, the Executive and Judicial officers of a State, or the members of the Legislature thereof, is denied to any of the male inhabitants of such State, being twenty-one years of age, and citizens of the United States, or in any way abridged, except for participation in rebellion, or other crime, the basis of representation therein shall be reduced in the proportion which the number of such male citizens shall bear to the whole number of male citizens twenty-one years of age in such State.

Section 3. No person shall be a Senator or Representative in Congress, or elector of President and

Vice-President, or hold any office, civil or military, under the United States, or under any State, who, having previously taken an oath, as a member of Congress, or as an officer of the United States, or as a member of any State legislature, or as an executive or judicial officer of any State, to support the Constitution of the United States, shall have engaged in insurrection or rebellion against the same, or given aid or comfort to the enemies thereof. But Congress may by a vote of two-thirds of each House, remove such disability.

Section 4. The validity of the public debt of the United States, authorized by law, including debts incurred for payment of pensions and bounties for services in suppressing insurrection or rebellion, shall not be questioned. But neither the United States nor any State shall assume or pay any debt or obligation incurred in aid of insurrection or rebellion against the United States, or any claim for the loss or emancipation of any slave; but all such debts, obligations, and claims shall be held illegal and void.

Section 5. The Congress shall have the power to enforce, by appropriate legislation, the provisions of this article.

AMENDMENT XV [1870]

Section 1. The right of citizens of the United States to vote shall not be denied or abridged by the United States or by any State on account of race, color, or previous condition of servitude—

Section 2. The Congress shall have power to enforce this article by appropriate legislation.

AMENDMENT XVI [1913]

The Congress shall have power to lay and collect taxes on incomes, from whatever source derived, without apportionment among the several States, and without regard to any census or enumeration.

AMENDMENT XVII [1913]

The Senate of the United States shall be composed of two Senators from each State, elected by the people thereof, for six years; and each Senator shall have one vote. The electors in each State shall have the qualifications requisite for electors of the most numerous branch of the State legislatures.

When vacancies happen in the representation of any State in the Senate, the executive authority of such State shall issue writs of election to fill such vacancies: *Provided,* That the legislature of any State may empower the executive thereof to make temporary appointments until the people fill the vacancies by election as the legislature may direct.

This amendment shall not be so construed as to affect the election or term of any Senator chosen before it becomes valid as part of the Constitution.

AMENDMENT XVIII [1919]

Section 1. After one year from the ratification of this article the manufacture, sale, or transportation of intoxicating liquors within, the importation thereof into, or the exportation thereof from the United States and all territory subject to the jurisdiction thereof for beverage purposes is hereby prohibited.

Section 2. The Congress and the several States shall have concurrent power to enforce this article by appropriate legislation.

Section 3. This article shall be inoperative unless it shall have been ratified as an amendment to the Constitution by the legislatures of the several States, as provided in the Constitution, within seven years from the date of the submission hereof to the States by the Congress.

AMENDMENT XIX [1920]

The right of citizens of the United States to vote shall not be denied or abridged by the United States or by any State on account of sex.

Congress shall have power to enforce this article by appropriate legislation.

AMENDMENT XX [1933]

Section 1. The terms of the President and Vice-President shall end at noon on the 20th day of January, and the terms of Senators and Representatives at noon on the 3d day of January, of the years in which such terms would have ended if this article had not been ratified; and the terms of their successors shall then begin.

Section 2. The Congress shall assemble at least once in every year, and such meeting shall begin at noon on the 3d day of January, unless they shall by law appoint a different day.

Section 3. If, at the time fixed for the beginning of the term of the President, the President elect shall have died, the Vice-President elect shall become President. If a President shall not have been chosen before the time fixed for the beginning of his term, or if the President elect shall have failed to qualify, then the Vice-President elect shall act as President until a President shall have qualified; and the Congress may by law provide for the case wherein neither a President elect nor a Vice-President elect shall have qualified, declaring who shall then act as President, or the manner in which one who is to act shall be selected, and such person shall act accordingly until a President or Vice-President shall have qualified.

Section 4. The Congress may by law provide for the case of the death of any of the persons from whom the House of Representatives may choose a President whenever the right of choice shall have devolved upon them, and for the case of the death of any of the persons from whom the Senate may choose a Vice-President whenever the right of choice shall have devolved upon them.

Section 5. Sections 1 and 2 shall take effect on the 15th day of October following the ratification of this article.

Section 6. This article shall be inoperative unless it shall have been ratified as an amendment to the Constitution by the legislatures of three-fourths of the several States within seven years from the date of its submission.

AMENDMENT XXI [1933]

Section 1. The eighteenth article of amendment to the Constitution of the United States is hereby repealed.

Section 2. The transportation or importation into any State, Territory, or possession of the United States for delivery or use therein of intoxicating liquors, in violation of the laws thereof, is hereby prohibited.

Section 3. This article shall be inoperative unless it shall have been ratified as an amendment to the Constitution by conventions in the several States, as provided in the Constitution, within seven years from the date of the submission hereof to the States by the Congress.

AMENDMENT XXII [1951]

No person shall be elected to the office of the President more than twice, and no person who has held the office of President, or acted as President, for more than two years of a term to which some other person was elected President shall be elected to the office of the President more than once.

But this Article shall not apply to any person holding the office of President when this Article was proposed by the Congress, and shall not prevent any person who may be holding the office of President, or acting as President, during the term within which this Article becomes operative from holding the office of President or acting as President during the remainder of such term.

AMENDMENT XXIII [1961]

Section 1. The District constituting the seat of Government of the United States shall appoint in such manner as the Congress may direct:

A number of electors of President and Vice President equal to the whole number of Senators and Representatives in Congress to which the District would be entitled if it were a State, but in no event more than the least populous State; they shall be in addition to those appointed by the States, but they shall be considered, for the purposes of the election of President and Vice President, to be electors appointed by a State; and they shall meet in the District and perform such duties as provided by the twelfth article of amendment.

Section 2. The Congress shall have power to enforce this article by appropriate legislation.

AMENDMENT XXIV [1964]

Section 1. The right of citizens of the United States to vote in any primary or other election for President or Vice President, for electors for President or Vice President, or for Senator or Representative in Congress, shall not be denied or abridged by the United States or any State by reason of failure to pay any poll tax or other tax.

Section 2. The Congress shall have the power to enforce this article by appropriate legislation.

AMENDMENT XXV [1967]

Section 1. In case of the removal of the President from office or his death or resignation, the Vice President shall become President.

Section 2. Whenever there is a vacancy in the office of the Vice President, the President shall nominate a Vice President who shall take the office upon confirmation by a majority vote of both houses of Congress.

Section 3. Whenever the President transmits to the President pro tempore of the Senate and the Speaker of the House of Representatives his written declaration that he is unable to discharge the powers and duties of his office, and until he transmits to them a written declaration to the contrary, such powers and duties shall be discharged by the Vice President as Acting President.

Section 4. Whenever the Vice President and a majority of either the principal officers of the executive departments, or of such other body as Congress may by law provide, transmit to the President pro tempore of the Senate and the Speaker of the House of Representatives their written declaration that the President is unable to discharge the powers and duties of his office, the Vice President shall immediately assume the powers and duties of the office as Acting President.

Thereafter, when the President transmits to the President pro tempore of the Senate and the Speaker of the House of Representatives his written declaration that no inability exists, he shall resume the powers and duties of his office unless the Vice President and a majority of either the principal officers of the executive departments, or of such other body as Congress may by law provide, transmit within four days to the President pro tempore of the Senate and the Speaker of the House of Representatives their written declaration that the President is unable to discharge the powers and duties of his office. Thereupon Congress shall decide the issue, assembling within 48 hours for that purpose if not in session. If the Congress, within 21 days after receipt of the latter written declaration, or, if Congress is not in session, within 21 days after Congress is required to assemble, determines by two-thirds vote of both houses that the President is unable to discharge the powers and duties of his office, the Vice President shall continue to discharge the same as Acting President; otherwise, the President shall resume the powers and duties of his office.

Presidential Elections, 1789–1968

Year	Candidates	Party	Popular Vote	Electoral Vote
1789	**George Washington**			69
	John Adams			34
	Others			35
1792	**George Washington**			132
	John Adams			77
	George Clinton			50
	Others			5
1796	**John Adams**	Federalist		71
	Thomas Jefferson	Democratic-Republican		68
	Thomas Pinckney	Federalist		59
	Aaron Burr	Democratic-Republican		30
	Others			48
1800	**Thomas Jefferson**	Democratic-Republican		73
	Aaron Burr	Democratic-Republican		73
	John Adams	Federalist		65
	Charles C. Pinckney	Federalist		64
1804	**Thomas Jefferson**	Democratic-Republican		162
	Charles C. Pinckney	Federalist		14
1808	**James Madison**	Democratic-Republican		122
	Charles C. Pinckney	Federalist		47
	George Clinton	Independent-Republican		6
1812	**James Madison**	Democratic-Republican		128
	DeWitt Clinton	Federalist		89
1816	**James Monroe**	Democratic-Republican		183
	Rufus King	Federalist		34
1820	**James Monroe**	Democratic-Republican		231
	John Quincy Adams	Independent-Republican		1
1824	**John Quincy Adams**	Democratic-Republican	108,740 (30.5%)	84
	Andrew Jackson	Democratic-Republican	153,544 (43.1%)	99
	Henry Clay	Democratic-Republican	47,136 (13.2%)	37
	William H. Crawford	Democratic-Republican	46,618 (13.1%)	41
1828	**Andrew Jackson**	Democratic	647,231 (56.0%)	178
	John Quincy Adams	National-Republican	509,097 (44.0%)	83
1832	**Andrew Jackson**	Democratic	687,502 (55.0%)	219
	Henry Clay	National Republican	530,189 (42.4%)	49
	William Wirt	Anti-Masonic	33,108 (2.6%)	7
	John Floyd	National Republican		11
1836	**Martin Van Buren**	Democratic	761,549 (50.9%)	170
	William H. Harrison	Whig	549,567 (36.7%)	73
	Hugh L. White	Whig	145,396 (9.7%)	26
	Daniel Webster	Whig	41,287 (2.7%)	14
1840	**William H. Harrison**	Whig	1,275,017 (53.1%)	234
	(**John Tyler**, 1841)			
	Martin Van Buren	Democratic	1,128,702 (46.9%)	60
1844	**James K. Polk**	Democratic	1,337,243 (49.6%)	170
	Henry Clay	Whig	1,299,068 (48.1%)	105
	James G. Birney	Liberty	62,300 (2.3%)	
1848	**Zachary Taylor**	Whig	1,360,101 (47.4%)	163
	(**Millard Fillmore**, 1850)			
	Lewis Cass	Democratic	1,220,544 (42.5%)	127
	Martin Van Buren	Free Soil	291,263 (10.1%)	

Year	Candidates	Party	Popular Vote	Electoral Vote
1852	**Franklin Pierce**	Democratic	1,601,474 (50.9%)	254
	Winfield Scott	Whig	1,386,578 (44.1%)	42
1856	**James Buchanan**	Democratic	1,838,169 (45.4%)	174
	John C. Frémont	Republican	1,335,264 (33.0%)	114
	Millard Fillmore	American	874,534 (21.6%)	8
1860	**Abraham Lincoln**	Republican	1,865,593 (39.8%)	180
	Stephen A. Douglas	Democratic	1,382,713 (29.5%)	12
	John C. Breckinridge	Democratic	848,356 (18.1%)	72
	John Bell	Constitutional Union	592,906 (12.6%)	39
1864	**Abraham Lincoln** (**Andrew Johnson**, 1865)	Republican	2,206,938 (55.0%)	212
	George B. McClellan	Democratic	1,803,787 (45.0%)	21
1868	**Ulysses S. Grant**	Republican	3,013,421 (52.7%)	214
	Horatio Seymour	Democratic	2,706,829 (47.3%)	80
1872	**Ulysses S. Grant**	Republican	3,596,745 (55.6%)	286
	Horace Greeley	Democratic	2,843,446 (43.9%)	66
1876	**Rutherford B. Hayes**	Republican	4,036,572 (48.0%)	185
	Samuel J. Tilden	Democratic	4,284,020 (51.0%)	184
1880	**James A. Garfield** (**Chester A. Arthur**, 1881)	Republican	4,449,053 (48.3%)	214
	Winfield S. Hancock	Democratic	4,442,035 (48.2%)	155
	James B. Weaver	Greenback-Labor	308,578 (3.4%)	
1884	**Grover Cleveland**	Democratic	4,874,986 (48.5%)	219
	James G. Blaine	Republican	4,851,981 (48.2%)	182
	Benjamin F. Butler	Greenback-Labor	175,370 (1.8%)	
1888	**Benjamin Harrison**	Republican	5,444,337, (47.8%)	233
	Grover Cleveland	Democratic	5,540,050 (48.6%)	168
1892	**Grover Cleveland**	Democratic	5,554,414 (46.0%)	277
	Benjamin Harrison	Republican	5,190,802 (43.0%)	145
	James B. Weaver	People's	1,027,329 (8.5%)	22
1896	**William McKinley**	Republican	7,035,638 (50.8%)	271
	William J. Bryan	Democratic; Populist	6,467,946 (46.7%)	176
1900	**William McKinley** (**Theodore Roosevelt**, 1901)	Republican	7,219,530 (51.7%)	292
	William J. Bryan	Democratic; Populist	6,356,734 (45.5%)	155
1904	**Theodore Roosevelt**	Republican	7,628,834 (56.4%)	336
	Alton B. Parker	Democratic	5,084,401 (37.6%)	140
	Eugene V. Debs	Socialist	402,460 (3.0%)	
1908	**William H. Taft**	Republican	7,679,006 (51.6%)	321
	William J. Bryan	Democratic	6,409,106 (43.1%)	162
	Eugene V. Debs	Socialist	420,820 (2.8%)	
1912	**Woodrow Wilson**	Democratic	6,286,820 (41.8%)	435
	Theodore Roosevelt	Progressive	4,126,020 (27.4%)	88
	William H. Taft	Republican	3,483,922 (23.2%)	8
	Eugene V. Debs	Socialist	897,011 (6.0%)	
1916	**Woodrow Wilson**	Democratic	9,129,606 (49.3%)	277
	Charles E. Hughes	Republican	8,538,221 (46.1%)	254

Presidential Elections, 1789–1968

Year	Candidates	Party	Popular Vote	Electoral Vote
1920	**Warren G. Harding**	Republican	16,152,200 (61.0%)	404
	(**Calvin Coolidge**, 1923)			
	James M. Cox	Democratic	9,147,353 (34.6%)	127
	Eugene V. Debs	Socialist	919,799 (3.5%)	
1924	**Calvin Coolidge**	Republican	15,725,016 (54.1%)	382
	John W. Davis	Democratic	8,385,586 (28.8%)	136
	Robert M. La Follette	Progressive	4,822,856 (16.6%)	13
1928	**Herbert C. Hoover**	Republican	21,392,190 (58.2%)	444
	Alfred E. Smith	Democratic	15,016,443 (40.8%)	87
1932	**Franklin D. Roosevelt**	Democratic	22,809,638 (57.3%)	472
	Herbert C. Hoover	Republican	15,758,901 (39.6%)	59
	Norman Thomas	Socialist	881,951 (2.2%)	
1936	**Franklin D. Roosevelt**	Democratic	27,751,612 (60.7%)	523
	Alfred M. Landon	Republican	16,681,913 (36.4%)	8
	William Lemke	Union	891,858 (1.9%)	
1940	**Franklin D. Roosevelt**	Democratic	27,243,466 (54.7%)	449
	Wendell L. Willkie	Republican	22,304,755 (44.8%)	82
1944	**Franklin D. Roosevelt**	Democratic	25,602,505 (52.8%)	432
	(**Harry S. Truman**, 1945)			
	Thomas E. Dewey	Republican	22,006,278 (44.5%)	99
1948	**Harry S. Truman**	Democratic	24,105,812 (49.5%)	303
	Thomas E. Dewey	Republican	21,970,065 (45.1%)	189
	J. Strom Thurmond	States' Rights	1,169,063 (2.4%)	39
	Henry A. Wallace	Progressive	1,157,172 (2.4%)	
1952	**Dwight D. Eisenhower**	Republican	33,936,234 (55.2%)	442
	Adlai E. Stevenson	Democratic	27,314,992 (44.5%)	89
1956	**Dwight D. Eisenhower**	Republican	35,590,472 (57.4%)	457
	Adlai E. Stevenson	Democratic	26,022,752 (42.0%)	73
1960	**John F. Kennedy**	Democratic	34,227,096 (49.9%)	303
	(**Lyndon B. Johnson**, 1963)			
	Richard M. Nixon	Republican	34,108,546 (49.6%)	219
1964	**Lyndon B. Johnson**	Democratic	43,126,233 (61.1%)	486
	Barry M. Goldwater	Republican	27,174,989 (38.5%)	52
1968	**Richard M. Nixon**	Republican	31,783,783 (43.4%)	301
	Hubert H. Humphrey	Democratic	31,271,839 (42.7%)	191
	George C. Wallace	Amer. Independent	9,899,557 (13.5%)	46

Because only the leading candidates are listed, popular vote percentages do not always total 100. The elections of 1800 and 1824, in which no candidate received an electoral-vote majority, were decided in the House of Representatives.

The Vice Presidency and the Cabinet, 1789–1970

Vice President

John Adams	1789–97
Thomas Jefferson	1797–1801
Aaron Burr	1801–05
George Clinton	1805–13
Elbridge Gerry	1813–17
Daniel D. Tompkins	1817–25
John C. Calhoun	1825–33
Martin Van Buren	1833–37
Richard M. Johnson	1837–41
John Tyler	1841
George M. Dallas	1845–49
Millard Fillmore	1849–50
William R. King	1853–57
John C. Breckinridge	1857–61
Hannibal Hamlin	1861–65
Andrew Johnson	1865
Schuyler Colfax	1869–73
Henry Wilson	1873–77
William A. Wheeler	1877–81
Chester A. Arthur	1881
Thomas A. Hendricks	1885–89
Levi P. Morton	1889–93
Adlai E. Stevenson	1893–97
Garret A. Hobart	1897–1901
Theodore Roosevelt	1901
Charles W. Fairbanks	1905–09
James S. Sherman	1909–13
Thomas R. Marshall	1913–21
Calvin Coolidge	1921–23
Charles G. Dawes	1925–29
Charles Curtis	1929–33
John Nance Garner	1933–41
Henry A. Wallace	1941–45
Harry S. Truman	1945
Alben W. Barkley	1949–53
Richard M. Nixon	1953–61
Lyndon B. Johnson	1961–63
Hubert H. Humphrey	1965–69
Spiro T. Agnew	1969–

Secretary of State (1789–)

Thomas Jefferson	1789
Edmund Randolph	1794
Timothy Pickering	1795
John Marshall	1800
James Madison	1801
Robert Smith	1809
James Monroe	1811
John Q. Adams	1817
Henry Clay	1825
Martin Van Buren	1829
Edward Livingston	1831
Louis McLane	1833
John Forsyth	1834
Daniel Webster	1841
Hugh S. Legaré	1843
Abel P. Upshur	1843
John C. Calhoun	1844
James Buchanan	1845
John M. Clayton	1849
Daniel Webster	1850
Edward Everett	1852
William L. Marcy	1853
Lewis Cass	1857
Jeremiah S. Black	1860
William H. Seward	1861
E.B. Washburne	1869
Hamilton Fish	1869
William M. Evarts	1877
James G. Blaine	1881
F.T. Frelinghuysen	1881
Thomas F. Bayard	1885
James G. Blaine	1889
John W. Foster	1892
Walter Q. Gresham	1893
Richard Olney	1895
John Sherman	1897
William R. Day	1897
John Hay	1898
Elihu Root	1905
Robert Bacon	1909
Philander C. Knox	1909
William J. Bryan	1913
Robert Lansing	1915
Bainbridge Colby	1920
Charles E. Hughes	1921
Frank B. Kellogg	1925
Henry L. Stimson	1929
Cordell Hull	1933
E.R. Stettinius, Jr.	1944
James F. Byrnes	1945
George C. Marshall	1947
Dean Acheson	1949
John Foster Dulles	1953
Christian A. Herter	1959
Dean Rusk	1961
William P. Rogers	1969

Secretary of the Treasury (1789–)

Alexander Hamilton	1789
Oliver Wolcott	1795
Samuel Dexter	1801
Albert Gallatin	1801
G.W. Campbell	1814
A.J. Dallas	1814
William H. Crawford	1816
Richard Rush	1825
Samuel D. Ingham	1829
Louis McLane	1831
William J. Duane	1833
Roger B. Taney	1833
Levi Woodbury	1834
Thomas Ewing	1841
Walter Forward	1841
John C. Spencer	1843
George M. Bibb	1844
Robert J. Walker	1845
William M. Meredith	1849
Thomas Corwin	1850
James Guthrie	1853
Howell Cobb	1857
Philip F. Thomas	1860
John A. Dix	1861
Salmon P. Chase	1861
Wm. P. Fessenden	1864
Hugh McCulloch	1865
George S. Boutwell	1869
William A. Richardson	1873
Benjamin H. Bristow	1874
Lot M. Morrill	1876
John Sherman	1877
William Windom	1881
Charles J. Folger	1881
Walter Q. Gresham	1884
Hugh McCulloch	1884
Daniel Manning	1885
Charles S. Fairchild	1887
William Windom	1889
Charles Foster	1891
John G. Carlisle	1893
Lyman J. Gage	1897
Leslie M. Shaw	1902
George B. Cortelyou	1907
Franklin MacVeagh	1909
William G. McAdoo	1913
Carter Glass	1919
David F. Houston	1919
Andrew W. Mellon	1921
Ogden L. Mills	1932
William H. Woodin	1933
Henry Morgenthau, Jr.	1934
Fred M. Vinson	1945
John W. Snyder	1946
George M. Humphrey	1953
Robert B. Anderson	1957
C. Douglas Dillon	1961
Henry H. Fowler	1965
David M. Kennedy	1969

Secretary of War (1789–1947)

Henry Knox	1789
Timothy Pickering	1795
James McHenry	1796
John Marshall	1800
Samuel Dexter	1800
Roger Griswold	1801
Henry Dearborn	1801
William Eustis	1809
John Armstrong	1813
James Monroe	1814
William H. Crawford	1815
Isaac Shelby	1817
George Graham	1817
John C. Calhoun	1817
James Barbour	1825
Peter B. Porter	1828
John H. Eaton	1829
Lewis Cass	1831
Benjamin F. Butler	1837
Joel R. Poinsett	1837
John Bell	1841
John McLean	1841
John C. Spencer	1841
James M. Porter	1843
William Wilkins	1844
William L. Marcy	1845
George W. Crawford	1849
Charles M. Conrad	1850
Jefferson Davis	1853
John B. Floyd	1857
Joseph Holt	1861
Simon Cameron	1861
Edwin M. Stanton	1862
Ulysses S. Grant	1867
Lorenzo Thomas	1868
John M. Schofield	1868
John A. Rawlins	1869
William T. Sherman	1869
William W. Belknap	1869
Alphonso Taft	1876
James D. Cameron	1876
George W. McCrary	1877
Alexander Ramsey	1879
Robert T. Lincoln	1881
William C. Endicott	1885
Redfield Proctor	1889
Stephen B. Elkins	1891
Daniel S. Lamont	1893
Russell A. Alger	1897
Elihu Root	1899
William H. Taft	1904
Luke E. Wright	1908
J.M. Dickinson	1909
Henry L. Stimson	1911
L.M. Garrison	1913
Newton D. Baker	1916
John W. Weeks	1921
Dwight F. Davis	1925
James W. Good	1929
Patrick J. Hurley	1929
George H. Dern	1933
H.A. Woodring	1936
Henry L. Stimson	1940
Robert P. Patterson	1945
Kenneth C. Royall	1947

Secretary of the Navy (1798–1947)

Benjamin Stoddert	1798
Robert Smith	1801
Paul Hamilton	1809
William Jones	1813
B.W. Crowninshield	1814
Smith Thompson	1818
S.L. Southard	1823
John Branch	1829
Levi Woodbury	1831
Mahlon Dickerson	1834
James K. Paulding	1838
George E. Badger	1841
Abel P. Upshur	1841
David Henshaw	1843
Thomas W. Gilmer	1844
John Y. Mason	1844
George Bancroft	1845
John Y. Mason	1846
William B. Preston	1849
William A. Graham	1850
John P. Kennedy	1852
James C. Dobbin	1853
Isaac Toucey	1857
Gideon Welles	1861
Adolph E. Borie	1869
George M. Robeson	1869
R.W. Thompson	1877
Nathan Goff, Jr.	1881
William H. Hunt	1881
William E. Chandler	1881
William C. Whitney	1885
Benjamin F. Tracy	1889
Hilary A. Herbert	1893
John D. Long	1897
William H. Moody	1902
Paul Morton	1904
Charles J. Bonaparte	1905
Victor H. Metcalf	1907
T.H. Newberry	1908
George von L. Meyer	1909
Josephus Daniels	1913
Edwin Denby	1921
Curtis D. Wilbur	1924
Charles F. Adams	1929
Claude A. Swanson	1933
Charles Edison	1940
Frank Knox	1940
James V. Forrestal	1945

The Vice Presidency and the Cabinet, 1789–1970

Secretary of Defense (1947–)

James V. Forrestal	1947
Louis A. Johnson	1949
George C. Marshall	1950
Robert A. Lovett	1951
Charles E. Wilson	1953
Neil H. McElroy	1957
Thomas S. Gates, Jr.	1959
Robert S. McNamara	1961
Clark M. Clifford	1968
Melvin R. Laird	1969

Postmaster General (1789–)

Samuel Osgood	1789
Timothy Pickering	1791
Joseph Habersham	1795
Gideon Granger	1801
Return J. Meigs, Jr.	1814
John McLean	1823
William T. Barry	1829
Amos Kendall	1835
John M. Niles	1840
Francis Granger	1841
Charles A. Wickliffe	1841
Cave Johnson	1845
Jacob Collamer	1849
Nathan K. Hall	1850
Samuel D. Hubbard	1852
James Campbell	1853
Aaron V. Brown	1857
Joseph Holt	1859
Horatio King	1861
Montgomery Blair	1861
William Dennison	1864
Alexander W. Randall	1866
John A.J. Creswell	1869
James W. Marshall	1874
Marshall Jewell	1874
James N. Tyner	1876
David M. Key	1877
Horace Maynard	1880
Thomas L. James	1881
Timothy O. Howe	1881
Walter Q. Gresham	1883
Frank Hatton	1884
William F. Vilas	1885
Don M. Dickinson	1888
John Wanamaker	1889
Wilson S. Bissel	1893
William L. Wilson	1895
James A. Gary	1897
Charles E. Smith	1898
Henry C. Payne	1902
Robert J. Wynne	1904
George B. Cortelyou	1905
George von L. Meyer	1907
F.H. Hitchcock	1909
Albert S. Burleson	1913
Will H. Hays	1921
Hubert Work	1922
Harry S. New	1923
Walter F. Brown	1929
James A. Farley	1933
Frank C. Walker	1940
Robert E. Hannegan	1945
J.M. Donaldson	1947
A.E. Summerfield	1953
J. Edward Day	1961
John A. Gronouski	1963
Lawrence F. O'Brien	1965
W. Marvin Watson	1968
Winton M. Blount	1969

Attorney General (1789–)

Edmund Randolph	1789
William Bradford	1794
Charles Lee	1795
Theophilus Parsons	1801
Levi Lincoln	1801
Robert Smith	1805
John Breckinridge	1805
Caesar A. Rodney	1807
William Pinkney	1811
Richard Rush	1814
William Wirt	1817
John M. Berrien	1829
Roger B. Taney	1831
Benjamin F. Butler	1833
Felix Grundy	1838
Henry D. Gilpin	1840
John J. Crittenden	1841
Hugh S. Legaré	1841
John Nelson	1843
John Y. Mason	1845
Nathan Clifford	1846
Isaac Toucey	1848
Reverdy Johnson	1849
John J. Crittenden	1850
Caleb Cushing	1853
Jeremiah S. Black	1857
Edwin M. Stanton	1860
Edward Bates	1861
Titian J. Coffey	1863
James Speed	1864
Henry Stanbery	1866
William M. Evarts	1868
Ebenezer R. Hoar	1869
Amos T. Ackerman	1870
George H. Williams	1871
Edward Pierrepont	1875
Alphonso Taft	1876
Charles Devens	1877
Wayne MacVeagh	1881
Benjamin H. Brewster	1881
A.H. Garland	1885
William H.H. Miller	1889
Richard Olney	1893
Judson Harmon	1895
Joseph McKenna	1897
John W. Griggs	1897
Philander C. Knox	1901
William H. Moody	1904
Charles J. Bonaparte	1907
G.W. Wickersham	1909
J.C. McReynolds	1913
Thomas W. Gregory	1914
A. Mitchell Palmer	1919
H.M. Daugherty	1921
Harlan F. Stone	1924
John G. Sargent	1925
William D. Mitchell	1929
H.S. Cummings	1933
Frank Murphy	1939
Robert H. Jackson	1940
Francis Biddle	1941
Tom C. Clark	1945
J.H. McGrath	1949
J.P. McGranery	1952
H. Brownell, Jr.	1953
William P. Rogers	1957
Robert F. Kennedy	1961
Nicholas Katzenbach	1964
Ramsey Clark	1967
John N. Mitchell	1969

Secretary of the Interior (1849–)

Thomas Ewing	1849
T.M.T. McKennan	1850
Alexander H.H. Stuart	1850
Robert McClelland	1853
Jacob Thompson	1857
Caleb B. Smith	1861
John P. Usher	1863
James Harlan	1865
O.H. Browning	1866
Jacob D. Cox	1869
Columbus Delano	1870
Zachariah Chandler	1875
Carl Schurz	1877
Samuel J. Kirkwood	1881
Henry M. Teller	1881
L.Q.C. Lamar	1885
William F. Vilas	1888
John W. Noble	1889
Hoke Smith	1893
David R. Francis	1896
Cornelius N. Bliss	1897
E.A. Hitchcock	1899
James R. Garfield	1907
R.A. Ballinger	1909
Walter L. Fisher	1911
Franklin K. Lane	1913
John B. Payne	1920
Albert B. Fall	1921
Hubert Work	1923
Roy O. West	1928
Ray L. Wilbur	1929
Harold L. Ickes	1933
Julius A. Krug	1946
Oscar L. Chapman	1949
Douglas McKay	1953
Fred A. Seaton	1956
Stewart L. Udall	1961
Walter J. Hickel	1969

Secretary of Agriculture (1889–)

Norman J. Colman	1889
Jeremiah M. Rusk	1889
J. Sterling Morton	1893
James Wilson	1897
David F. Houston	1913
Edward T. Meredith	1920
Henry C. Wallace	1921
Howard M. Gore	1924
William M. Jardine	1925
Arthur M. Hyde	1929
Henry A. Wallace	1933
Claude R. Wickard	1940
Clinton P. Anderson	1945
Charles F. Brannan	1948
Ezra Taft Benson	1953
Orville L. Freeman	1961
Clifford M. Hardin	1969

Secretary of Commerce and Labor (1903–1913)

George B. Cortelyou	1903
Victor H. Metcalf	1904
Oscar S. Straus	1906
Charles Nagel	1909

Secretary of Commerce (1913–)

William C. Redfield	1913
Joshua W. Alexander	1919
Herbert Hoover	1921
William F. Whiting	1928
Robert P. Lamont	1929
Roy D. Chapin	1932
Daniel C. Roper	1933
Harry L. Hopkins	1939
Jesse Jones	1940
Henry A. Wallace	1945
W.A. Harriman	1946
Charles Sawyer	1948
Sinclair Weeks	1953
Lewis L. Strauss	1958
F.H. Mueller	1959
Luther Hodges	1961
John T. Connor	1965
A.B. Trowbridge	1967
C.R. Smith	1968
Maurice H. Stans	1969

Secretary of Labor (1913–)

William B. Wilson	1913
James J. Davis	1921
William N. Doak	1930
Frances Perkins	1933
L.B. Schwellenbach	1945
Maurice J. Tobin	1948
Martin P. Durkin	1953
James P. Mitchell	1953
Arthur J. Goldberg	1961
W. Willard Wirtz	1962
George P. Shultz	1969
James D. Hodgson	1970

Secretary of Health, Education, and Welfare (1953–)

Oveta Culp Hobby	1953
Marion B. Folsom	1955
Arthur S. Flemming	1958
Abraham A. Ribicoff	1961
Anthony J. Celebrezze	1962
John W. Gardner	1965
Wilbur J. Cohen	1968
Robert H. Finch	1969
Elliot L. Richardson	1970

Secretary of Housing and Urban Development (1966–)

Robert C. Weaver	1966
George W. Romney	1969

Secretary of Transportation (1967–)

Alan S. Boyd	1967
John A. Volpe	1969

The States

	State	Date
1.	Delaware	Dec. 7, 1787
2.	Pennsylvania	Dec. 12, 1787
3.	New Jersey	Dec. 18, 1787
4.	Georgia	Jan. 2, 1788
5.	Connecticut	Jan. 9, 1788
6.	Massachusetts	Feb. 6, 1788
7.	Maryland	Apr. 28, 1788
8.	South Carolina	May 23, 1788
9.	New Hampshire	June 21, 1788
10.	Virginia	June 25, 1788
11.	New York	July 26, 1788
12.	North Carolina	Nov. 21, 1789
13.	Rhode Island	May 29, 1790
14.	Vermont	Mar. 4, 1791
15.	Kentucky	June 1, 1792
16.	Tennessee	June 1, 1796
17.	Ohio	Mar. 1, 1803
18.	Louisiana	Apr. 30, 1812
19.	Indiana	Dec. 11, 1816
20.	Mississippi	Dec. 10, 1817
21.	Illinois	Dec. 3, 1818
22.	Alabama	Dec. 14, 1819
23.	Maine	Mar. 15, 1820
24.	Missouri	Aug. 10, 1821
25.	Arkansas	June 15, 1836
26.	Michigan	Jan. 26, 1837
27.	Florida	Mar. 3, 1845
28.	Texas	Dec. 29, 1845
29.	Iowa	Dec. 28, 1846
30.	Wisconsin	May 29, 1848
31.	California	Sept. 9, 1850
32.	Minnesota	May 11, 1858
33.	Oregon	Feb. 14, 1859
34.	Kansas	Jan. 29, 1861
35.	West Virginia	June 20, 1863
36.	Nevada	Oct. 31, 1864
37.	Nebraska	Mar. 1, 1867
38.	Colorado	Aug. 1, 1876
39.	North Dakota	Nov. 2, 1889
40.	South Dakota	Nov. 2, 1889
41.	Montana	Nov. 8, 1889
42.	Washington	Nov. 11, 1889
43.	Idaho	July 3, 1890
44.	Wyoming	July 10, 1890
45.	Utah	Jan. 4, 1896
46.	Oklahoma	Nov. 16, 1907
47.	New Mexico	Jan. 6, 1912
48.	Arizona	Feb. 14, 1912
49.	Alaska	Jan. 3, 1959
50.	Hawaii	Aug. 21, 1959

Territorial Expansion

Louisiana Purchase	1803
Florida	1819
Texas	1845
Oregon	1846
Mexican Cession	1848
Gadsden Purchase	1853
Alaska	1867
Hawaii	1898
The Philippines	1898–1946
Puerto Rico	1899
Guam	1899
Amer. Samoa	1900
Canal Zone	1904
U.S. Virgin Islands	1917
Pacific Islands Trust Terr.	1947

Population, 1790–1970

1790	3,929,214
1800	5,308,483
1810	7,239,881
1820	9,638,453
1830	12,866,020
1840	17,069,453
1850	23,191,876
1860	31,443,321
1870	39,818,449
1880	50,155,783
1890	62,947,714
1900	75,994,575
1910	91,972,266
1920	105,710,620
1930	122,775,046
1940	131,669,275
1950	151,325,798
1960	179,323,175
1970	204,765,770

Index

A

B

C

D

E

F

G

H

I

J

K

L

M

O

P

Q

R

S

T

U

V

W

X

Y

Z

1 2 3 4 5 6 7 76 75 74 73 72 71

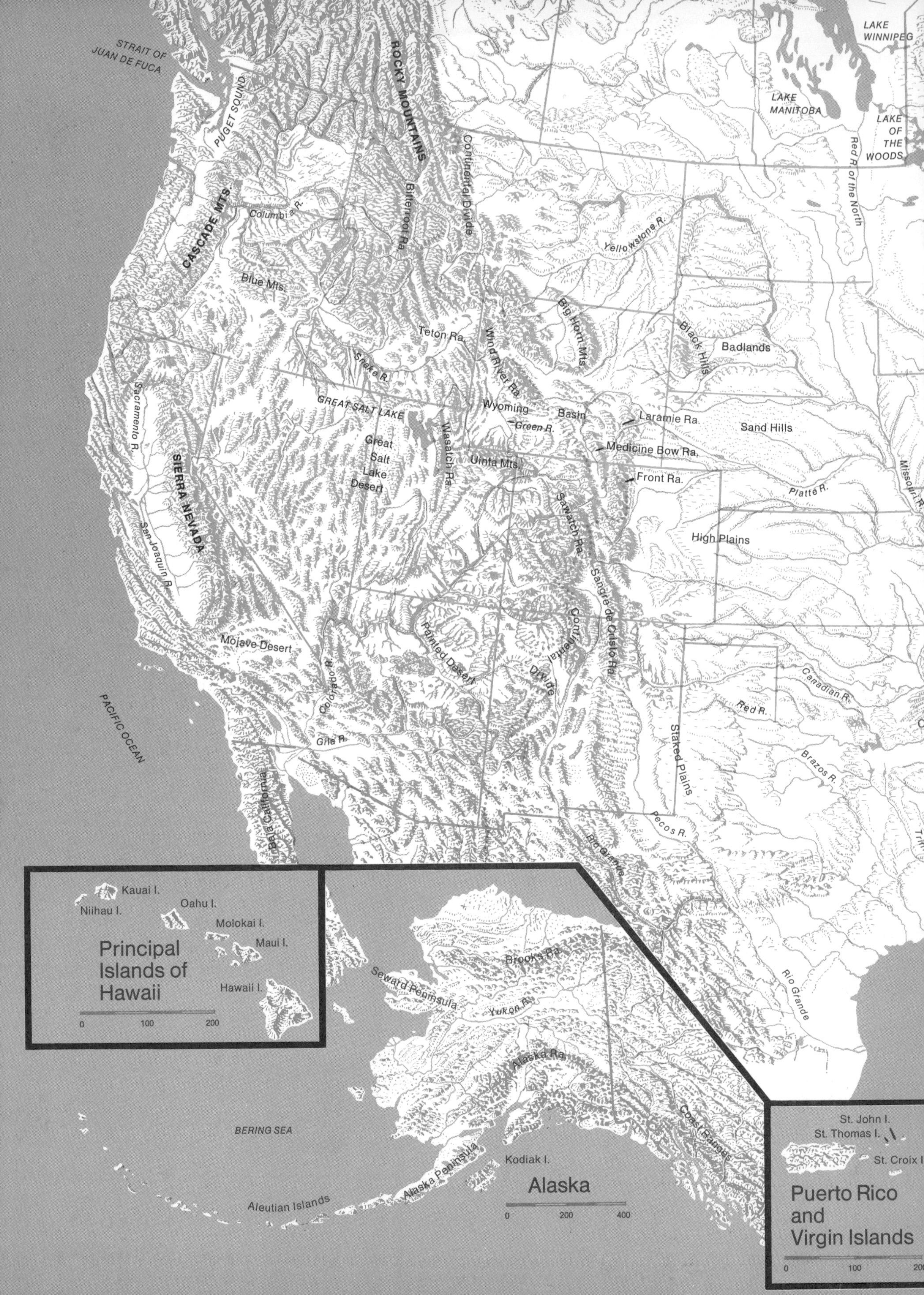

STRAIT OF JUAN DE FUCA
PUGET SOUND
ROCKY MOUNTAINS
CASCADE MTS.
Columbia R.
Bitterroot Ra.
Continental Divide
LAKE WINNIPEG
LAKE MANITOBA
LAKE OF THE WOODS
Red R. of the North
Yellowstone R.
Blue Mts.
Big Horn Mts.
Black Hills
Badlands
Teton Ra.
Wind River Ra.
Snake R.
Sacramento R.
GREAT SALT LAKE
Wyoming
Basin
Green R.
Laramie Ra.
Sand Hills
Great Salt Lake Desert
Wasatch Ra.
Uinta Mts.
Medicine Bow Ra.
Front Ra.
Missouri R.
Platte R.
SIERRA NEVADA
Sawatch Ra.
High Plains
San Joaquin R.
Sangre de Cristo Ra.
Continental Divide
Painted Desert
Mojave Desert
Colorado R.
Canadian R.
Red R.
PACIFIC OCEAN
Staked Plains
Brazos R.
Gila R.
Baja California
Pecos R.
Rio Grande
Kauai I.
Niihau I.
Oahu I.
Molokai I.
Maui I.
Principal Islands of Hawaii
Hawaii I.
0
100
200
Brooks Ra.
Seward Peninsula
Yukon R.
Alaska Ra.
Coast Ranges
BERING SEA
Alaska Peninsula
Kodiak I.
Alaska
Aleutian Islands
0
200
400
St. John I.
St. Thomas I.
St. Croix I.
Puerto Rico and Virgin Islands
0
100
200